PENNSYLVANIA CHILD CUSTODY

LAW, PRACTICE AND PROCEDURE

2021 EDITION

Michael E. Bertin, Esquire

and

The Honorable Emanuel A. Bertin

GEORGE T. BISEL COMPANY, INC.

710 S. WASHINGTON SQUARE

PHILADELPHIA PENNSYLVANIA

www.bisel.com

Pennsylvania child custody

HOW TO USE

First refer to main text, then check any supplement, using the same reference numbers. Sections added subsequent to publication of the main text, if any, will be included in a supplemental table of contents.

ALWAYS VERIFY CITATIONS BY CONSULTING THE OFFICIAL COURT DECISIONS, RULES, REGULATIONS AND STATUTES.

If you have any questions, please call us at 800-247-3526. Contact the Bisel Editorial Department directly with your questions and suggestions at tonyd@bisel.com.

DEDICATION

Dedicated to my wife, Sarah, for her love and support.

Michael E. Bertin, Esquire
Fall, 2021

Dedicated to my wife, Roz, for our wonderful 53 years of marriage and looking forward to many more years together.

Honorable Emanuel A. Bertin
Fall, 2021

ACKNOWLEDGMENT

The authors acknowledge, with deep appreciation, Arthur S. Zanan, Esquire, Director Emeritus of the Law Library of Montgomery County, Pennsylvania, for his tremendous input in developing and writing the supplements to the original book and formulation of this present book.

Michael E. Bertin, Esquire
Honorable Emanuel A. Bertin
Fall, 2021

ABOUT THE AUTHOR

MICHAEL E. BERTIN, ESQUIRE

Mr. Bertin is a partner at the Philadelphia law firm of Obermayer Rebmann Maxwell & Hippel LLP, where he concentrates his practice in the area of family law. Mr. Bertin is a member of the Pennsylvania Joint State Government Commission Domestic Relations Advisory Committee. Mr. Bertin is a Fellow of the American Academy of Matrimonial Lawyers (AAML). He is a former member of the Board of Governors of the Pennsylvania Chapter of the AAML. Mr. Bertin is the Immediate Past Chair of the Family Law Section of the Pennsylvania Bar Association, is a former Chair-Elect, Vice-Chair, Secretary, and Treasurer of the Section, a current member of the Executive Committee and Council (the governing bodies of the Section), and former chair and member of that Section's Rules Committee, Legislative Committee, and Program Committee. Mr. Bertin is a former Chair, Chair-Elect, Treasurer, and Secretary of the Family Law Section of the Philadelphia Bar Association. Mr. Bertin is also co-chair of the Custody Committee and a member of the Executive Committee of the Family Law Section of the Philadelphia Bar Association. Mr. Bertin is a former member of the Board of Governors of the Philadelphia Bar Association. Mr. Bertin is also a Zone One Delegate of the Pennsylvania Bar Association House of Delegates.

Mr. Bertin is listed in the Best Lawyers In America. Mr. Bertin was named the 2021 Lawyer of the Year for Family Law in Philadelphia and the eastern counties of the Commonwealth of Pennsylvania by the Best Lawyers In America. Mr. Bertin has also been named to the Pennsylvania Super Lawyers® list as seen in both Philadelphia Magazine and Pennsylvania Super Lawyers magazine, and also received an AV ® preeminent rating from Martindale-Hubbell, indicating his preeminent legal ability and very high ethical standards. Mr. Bertin was listed in Philadelphia Magazine's 2018 Makers of the Main Line, and Philadelphia Magazine's annual feature on the influential leaders who are making their mark on the Main Line. Mr. Bertin is also listed as one of the Greater Philadelphia Region's Ten Leaders in Divorce Law, Age 45 & Under, by the Ten

ABOUT THE AUTHOR

Leaders Cooperative. Mr. Bertin was also one of 35 Pennsylvania attorneys selected by The Legal Intelligencer and Pennsylvania Law Weekly as a "2007 Lawyer on the Fast Track," an honor recognizing the future leaders of Pennsylvania's legal community. Mr. Bertin received a 2011 Pennsylvania Bar Association Special Achievement Award for his contributions and work with the Pennsylvania Bar Association Family Law Section to enact new custody legislation.

Mr. Bertin is a frequent lecturer, moderator, and author on family law topics. He has written over 100 legal articles. He is the Family Law Columnist for The Legal Intelligencer and was on the Editorial Board of The Pennsylvania Family Lawyer. His articles have also appeared in *The Pennsylvania Lawyer;* The Philadelphia Lawyer; Family Lawyer Magazine; Pennsylvania Family Lawyer; and Pennsylvania Bar Institute and American Academy of Matrimonial Lawyers course materials. Mr. Bertin is the course planner and moderator of the recurring Pennsylvania Bar Institute program: Family Law in Bucks, Chester, Delaware, & Montgomery Counties. Mr. Bertin is a member of the Family Law Advisory Council for the Volunteers for Indigent Program and Philadelphia Law Works, the Doris Jonas Freed American Inn of Court, and the Family Law Section of the Montgomery Bar Association, and former member of the Nicholas J. Cipriani Family Law American Inn of Court. He received his B.A. cum laude from the University of Pittsburgh and his J.D. from Temple University School of Law, where he was the recipient of the American Academy of Matrimonial Lawyer's Eric D. Turner Award.

ABOUT THE AUTHOR

HONORABLE EMANUEL A. BERTIN

Judge Bertin assumed his judicial duties on the Court of Common Pleas of Montgomery County on January 1, 1996 and retired on December 31, 2014. Judge Bertin is now a Senior Judge. In addition to serving in the Civil and Family Divisions, he has served as Administrative Judge of Family Court. Judge Bertin has regularly served as a lecturer in Family Law at the Pennsylvania Judges School for newly elected judges and has lectured on Family Law to judges at the Pennsylvania Conference of State Trial Judges. He also lectures and authors articles for the legal profession on behalf of the Pennsylvania Bar Institute and the Pennsylvania Bar Association.

Judge Bertin has received statewide appointments as Chairman of the Pennsylvania Joint State Government Commission Domestic Relations Advisory Committee and to the Commission for Justice Initiatives in Pennsylvania, Changing the Culture of Custody Committee. Before becoming a judge he was listed in all editions of THE BEST LAWYERS IN AMERICA; served as President of the American Academy of Matrimonial Lawyers, Pennsylvania Chapter; Chairman of the Pennsylvania Bar Association, Family Law Section; Chairman of the Montgomery Bar Association, Family Law Committee; Editor-in-Chief of the Pennsylvania Family Lawyer; author of the original law book titled PENNSYLVANIA CHILD CUSTODY LAW, PRACTICE, AND PROCEDURE (1983); was a three-time recipient of the Pennsylvania State Bar Special Achievement Award (most recently in 2011 for his contributions and work to enact new custody legislation); Legal Counsel, International Academy of Matrimonial Lawyers, U.S.A. Chapter; and Diplomate, The American College of Family Trial Lawyers. Judge Bertin was the 2011 recipient of the Eric D. Turner Award given by the Pennsylvania Bar Association, Family Law Section, for recognition of his service to the family law practitioners of Pennsylvania as mentor and friend. Judge Bertin received his B.A. from Moravian College in 1966 and his Juris Doctor from the University of Richmond Law School in 1969.

PREFACE

In 1983, when Michael E. Bertin was 10 years old, PENNSYLVANIA CHILD CUSTODY LAW, PRACTICE, AND PROCEDURE, authored by his father, attorney Emanuel A. Bertin, then 38 years old, was published. That book was the first treatise on child custody law in Pennsylvania and was well received by the bench and bar.

In 2011, 28 years later, Michael E. Bertin, Esquire, then age 38 (coincidentally the same age as his father was when his father wrote the first book), a family law practitioner and partner in the law firm of Obermayer Rebmann Maxwell & Hippel LLP, took the laboring oar in writing the major revision of the first book with his father, the now Honorable Emanuel A. Bertin.

Over those 28 years, custody law in Pennsylvania has developed dramatically and has expanded into new areas. The cases that were decided over that period of time, both appellate court and lower court, were extensive and the revision of this book encompasses the same. Likewise, statutory law progressed over the years, culminating in the most recent revamp of child custody law, Act No. 112 of 2010 (23 Pa.C.S. § 5321 *et seq.*), which has been covered carefully in this book. This statute had its genesis from the work product of the Pennsylvania Joint State Government Commission Domestic Relations Advisory Committee, chaired by Judge Bertin, with final input from the Legislative Committee of the Family Law Section of the Pennsylvania Bar Association with substantial contribution thereto from Michael E. Bertin, Esquire. For this participation, by both Michael E. Bertin and Emanuel A. Bertin, each received from the Pennsylvania Bar Association a Special Achievement Award at the House of Delegates meeting in Philadelphia, Pennsylvania, in 2011.

The goal of the authors in creating this book was to have a product of carefully condensed law (together with cases, statutes, rules, and forms) at the fingertips of the practitioner whether in the office, at home, or in the courtroom. In reaching this goal, the authors drew from the original book, the supplements, recent case law, statutes, and other source materials. The authors felt that, above all, the book had to be tight and cohesive for easy access to busy lawyers dealing with a custody issue. For the future, the authors intend to have a new edition of the book published

PREFACE

annually to keep the bench and bar updated on all new developments in Pennsylvania child custody law.

Judge Bertin gives his heartfelt thanks to his wife Roz, son Michael and his wife Sarah and children, Julia and Jake, daughter Beverly, her husband Lee and their triplet daughters, Alexis, Amanda, and Ashley, and to his mother Ruth, and sister Diane, and to the memory of his father Bob, and grandmother Sarah (to whom the first book was dedicated).

Michael would like to thank his wife Sarah, and his children, Julia and Jake, in addition to his mother and father, and sister and her family.

Michael would also like to thank the Family Law Group at Obermayer (Robert I. Whitelaw, Esquire, Ann G. Verber, Esquire, Maris J. Weiner, Esquire, and Shari B. Veisblatt, Esquire) for their support in the practice of family law.

Lastly, Michael would like to extend his appreciation to all of the educators and professionals who have been instrumental in his life.

This book would not be possible without the assistance and guidance of Anthony J. DiGioia, Editor in Chief, George T. Bisel Company, Inc.

Michael E. Bertin, Esquire

Honorable Emanuel A. Bertin

Fall, 2011

TABLE OF CONTENTS
CONDENSED

TABLE OF CONTENTS

TABLE OF CONTENTS
DETAILED

TABLE OF CONTENTS

Chapter 4
STANDING

Chapter 5
GRANDPARENTS

Chapter 6
THIRD PARTIES

TABLE OF CONTENTS

Chapter 7
BURDEN OF PROOF

Chapter 8
RELOCATION

Chapter 9
CHILD PREFERENCE/CHILD TESTIMONY/
IN CAMERA INTERVIEW OF CHILD

Chapter 10
EVIDENCE

TABLE OF CONTENTS

Chapter 11
EXPERTS

Chapter 12
COURT-ORDERED COUNSELING

Chapter 13
COUNSEL FOR CHILD/GUARDIAN *AD LITEM*

Chapter 14
ENFORCEMENT

Chapter 15
MODIFICATION OF COURT ORDER

Chapter 16
JURISDICTION

TABLE OF CONTENTS

Chapter 17

APPEALS

Chapter 18

TERMINATION OF PARENTAL RIGHTS

Chapter 19

PARENTING COORDINATION

Chapter 20

DISCOVERY

Appendices

TABLE OF CONTENTS

Chapter 1

CHILD CUSTODY GENERALLY

§ 1.1. BEST INTEREST OF THE CHILD

The polestar followed by Pennsylvania in deciding child custody cases is, as it is in most jurisdictions, the best interests and permanent welfare of the child.[1] The best interest includes consideration of the child's physical, intellectual, moral, and spiritual wellbeing, as well as the factors enumerated in 23 Pa.C.S. § 5328.[2] So singular is the state's

---

[1] See 23 Pa.C.S. §§ 5323 & 5328. Commonwealth ex rel. Parikh v. Parikh, 449 Pa. 105, 296 A.2d 625 (1972); Fisher v. Fisher, 370 Pa. Super. 87, 535 A.2d 1163 (1988) (Paramount concern of court deciding custody or visitation matter is best interest of child.); see also Cardamone v. Elshoff, 442 Pa. Super. 263, 659 A.2d 575 (1995); Hockenberry v. Thompson, 428 Pa. Super. 403, 631 A.2d 204 (1993); Baines v. Williams, 431 Pa. Super. 72, 635 A.2d 1077 (1993); Wiskoski v. Wiskoski, 427 Pa. Super. 531, 629 A.2d 996 (1993); Nonnenman v. Elshimy, 419 Pa. Super. 597, 615 A.2d 799 (1992); Norris v. Tearney, 422 Pa. Super. 246, 619 A.2d 339 (1992); Harashack v. Haraschak, 268 Pa. Super. 173, 407 A.2d 886 (1979).

[2] See 23 Pa.C.S. §§ 5323 & 5328. See generally McMillen v. McMillen, 529 Pa. 198, 602 A.2d 845 (1992); In Re: Davis, 502 Pa. 110, 465 A.2d 614 (1983); Commonwealth ex rel. Parikh v. Parikh, 449 Pa. 105, 296 A.2d 625 (1972); Commonwealth ex rel. Holschuh v. Holland-Moritz, 448 Pa. 437, 292 A.2d 380 (1972); Dorsey v. Freeman, 438 Pa. Super. 236, 652 A.2d 352 (1994); In re Donna H., a Minor: The Appeal of Donna H., 412 Pa. Super. 205, 602 A.2d 1382 (1992); Warren v. Rickabaugh, 410 Pa.

interest in assuring that the child's welfare be the paramount concern, that all other interests, including the rights of the contending parties[3] or principles of justice as between them,[4] are invariably deemed subordinate.[5]

Although repetition of the best interests doctrine is reflex in every child custody action, the concept is admittedly "a nebular term, rendering itself amenable to neither simple definition nor application."[6]

While any fact relevant to the care and nurture of the child will be considered by the courts,[7] prior to the enactment of Act No. 112 of 2010 (23 Pa.C.S. § 5321 *et seq.*), the factors most frequently presented for analysis include the character and fitness of the parties seeking custody, the nature of the proposed custodial homes, the child's preference, the parenting abilities and inclinations of the contestants, and the ability of each party to provide financially for the child.[8] Since the enactment of 23 Pa.C.S. §§ 5323 & 5328, there are now enumerated factors that the court

---

Super. 431, 600 A.2d 218 (1991); Andrews v. Andrews, 411 Pa. Super. 286, 601 A.2d 352 (1991*)*; Gerber v. Gerber, 337 Pa. Super. 580, 487 A.2d 413 (1985); Morris v. Morris, 271 Pa. Super. 19, 412 A.2d 139 (1979); Trefsgar v. Trefsgar, 261 Pa. Super. 1, 395 A.2d 273 (1978); In re Custody of Hernandez, 249 Pa. Super. 274, 376 A.2d 648 (1977).

[3] Commonwealth ex rel. Staunton v. Austin, 209 Pa. Super. 187, 233 A.2d 892 (1966).

[4] *See* English v. English, 322 Pa. Super. 234, 469 A.2d 230 (1983) (categorically states that the purpose of a child custody decree is to help the child, not to punish a parent); G.J.F. v. K.B.F., 284 Pa. Super. 139, 425 A.2d 461 (1981); Commonwealth ex rel. Bordlemay v. Bordlemay, 201 Pa. Super. 435, 193 A.2d 845 (1963).

[5] Prior to the existence of the custody order, parents stand on equal footing and their burden is to establish what is in the best interest and welfare of the child. All other considerations are deemed subordinate to the child's physical, intellectual, moral, and spiritual well-being. *See* Michael T.L. v. Marilyn J.L., 363 Pa. Super. 42, 525 A.2d 414 (1987); Beers v. Beers, 363 Pa. Super. 465, 493 A.2d 116 (1985); Kessler v. Gregory, 271 Pa. Super. 121, 412 A.2d 605 (1979); Garrity v. Garrity, 268 Pa. Super. 217, 407 A.2d 1323 (1979).

[6] Morris v. Morris, 271 Pa. Super. 19, 412 A.2d 139, 141–42 (1979). However, *see* 23 Pa.C.S. § 5328 for the enumeration of certain factors that the court shall consider in determining the best interest of the child.

[7] Shoemaker Appeal, 336 Pa. 378, 152 A.2d 666 (1959); Commonwealth ex rel. J.J.B. v. R.A.McG., 283 Pa. Super. 185, 423 A.2d 1050 (1980).

[8] Gerald G. v. Theresa G., 284 Pa. Super. 498, 426 A.2d 157 (1981); *id.*; Kessler v. Gregory, 271 Pa. Super. 121, 412 A.2d 605 (1979).

shall consider in addition to all other relevant factors in determining the best interest of the child.[9]

The duty to evaluate the relevant criteria and produce a reasoned resolution lies almost entirely within the sound discretion of the trial judge[10] acting upon the mandate to "abjure the simple solution of Solomon's Sword in favor of a dispassionate and comprehensive analysis of all alternatives to find what solution is indeed in the best interests of the child!"[11]

Upon the enactment of 23 Pa.C.S. § 5321 *et seq.*, debate arose as to the application of the new statute on cases already pending before the trial courts at that time. The Act provides: "A proceeding under the former provisions of 23 Pa.C.S. Ch. 53 which was commenced before the effective date of this section shall be governed by the law in effect at the time the proceeding was initiated."[12] The Pennsylvania Superior Court has since held that "if the evidentiary proceeding commences on or after the effective date of the Act, the provisions of the Act apply even if the request or petition for relief was filed prior to the effective date. Under this scenario, it is the date of the commencement of the hearing that determines whether the Act applies, not the date the petition or complaint was filed."[13]

Custody cases have not been extended to custody disputes over household pets. In *DeSanctis v. Prichard*, 803 A.2d 230 (Pa. Super. 2002), the

---

[9] *See* 23 Pa.C.S. § 5328. *See* J.R.M. v. J.E.A., 33 A.3d 647 (Pa. Super. 2011) (Superior Court held that trial court erred as a matter of law in failing to properly consider all of the enumerated factors under Section 5328(a)); E.D. v. M.P., 33 A.3d 73 (Pa. Super. 2011) (the trial court must perform a "best interest of the child" analysis considering all of the Section 5328(a) factors).

[10] Commonwealth ex rel. Spriggs v. Carson, 470 Pa. 290, 368 A.2d 635 (1977); Commonwealth ex rel. E.H.T. v. R.E.T., 285 Pa. Super. 444, 427 A.2d 1370 (1981); *but see* W.C.F. v. M.G., 115 A.3d 323 (Pa. Super. 2015) (When reasoning by trial court and its analysis of the custody factors are inconsistent with the ruling/custody decision, Superior Court vacated order and remanded case).

[11] Morris v. Morris, 271 Pa. Super. 19, 412 A.2d 139, 141–42 (1979), *quoting* Grillo v. Shuster, 226 Pa. Super. 228, 312 A.2d 58, 61 (1973).

[12] *See* 2010 Pa. Legis. Serv. Act 2010-112 (H.B. 1639).

[13] *See* C.R.F. v. S.E.F., 45 A.3d 441 (Pa. Super. 2012).

Superior Court found that the trial court properly dismissed plaintiff-husband's complaint in equity for "shared custody" of a dog that wife purchased during the marriage because the dog was wife's personal property pursuant to the parties' property settlement agreement. The court noted that dogs are personal property under Pennsylvania law. Therefore, 23 Pa.C.S. §§ 3503 and 3504, which pertain to the effect of divorce on property rights and to the disposition of property after a divorce, controlled. Because the parties' agreement explicitly awarded the dog to wife, the court ruled that the dog and his social schedule belonged exclusively to wife. "In seeking 'shared custody' and a 'visitation' arrangement, appellant appears to treat Barney, a dog, as a child. Despite the status owners bestow on their pets, Pennsylvania law considers dogs to be personal property."

In some child custody cases, the trial court may enter an order precluding the parties and attorneys from discussing the case with the media and publishing facts about the case.[14]

LOWER COURT CASES

Clearfield County

Huber v. Smith, C.P. Clearfield County, No. 16-235-CD (C.C.P. June 26, 2017), *aff'd*, Memorandum Decision, No. 536 WDA 2017 (Pa. Super. November 13, 2017) (Trial court awarded ownership of the parties' dog to appellee, as he cared for, licensed, and financially supported the dog).

Delaware County

Jillson v. Costello, C.P. Delaware County, No. 10-8523 (C.C.P. 2011) (In a property dispute to determine custody of a dog, the trial court awarded the dog to defendant, plaintiff's former boyfriend, despite plaintiff's claim of ownership interest following the dissolution of their live-in relationship. Plaintiff claimed that she was entitled to

---

[14] S.B. v. S.S., 201 A.3d 774 (Pa. Super. 2018) (where mother alleged during custody case that father had sexually abused their child, trial court did not violate her free speech rights by proscribing her and her attorneys from discussing the facts of case with members of the news media; as order proscribed only information that would tend to identify child, it was content-neutral, and it was narrowly tailored to serve a significant governmental interest in safeguarding children from physical and emotional harm and promoting their wellbeing).

custody of a Bichon dog after she broke up with the defendant, her former boyfriend, and they no longer lived together. Evidence showed that defendant's mother purchased the Bichon while plaintiff and defendant lived together. Plaintiff claimed that, when the mother was repaid for the cost of the dog by the parties, plaintiff contributed approximately one-quarter of the purchase price of the dog because defendant did not have enough money in his checkbook to cover the cost. Plaintiff also alleged that she cared for the dog, took it to the groomer and expended money for its maintenance and well-being. Defendant's mother testified that she bought the dog for her son. Defendant contended that plaintiff did not want a dog and so he asked his mother to purchase the animal for him without telling plaintiff. Defendant also testified that plaintiff paid bills and kept his checkbooks and that there was sufficient money in his account to repay his mother for the dog, so that plaintiff was not required to contribute to its cost. The case was tried as a bench trial, and Judge Chadd F. Kenny awarded custody of the dog to defendant boyfriend).

§ 1.2. DEFINITIONS

The perennial laxity in the use of the various terms employed to describe custodial arrangements has, over the years, led to a somewhat garbled custody jargon. As noted by Judge Spaeth in a concurring opinion, the importance of consistently using and defining custody terms lies in the fact that when a precisely defined term is used, the applicable legal standard will be immediately evident.[15] With the enactment of 23 Pa.C.S. § 5322, and the amendment to Pa.R.C.P. 1915.1 many of the terms used in child custody law have been defined which will hopefully create consistency. Under Section 5322 and Rule 1915.1, the term "visitation" has been removed.[16] Therefore, there no longer is a legal meaning for the term "visitation." In the past, many litigants and even court opinions incorrectly referred to the term "visitation." Section 5322 and Rule 1915.1 now alleviate this issue.

The following are the definitions provided under Section 5322:

"**Abuse**." As defined in section 6102 (relating to definitions).

---

[15] Scott v. Scott, 240 Pa. Super. 65, 368 A.2d 288 (1976) (Spaeth, J., concurring).

[16] "Visitation" was previously defined under the now repealed Section 5302 as "the right to visit a child. The term does not include the right to remove a child from the custodial parent's control."

"**Adult**." An individual 18 years of age or older.

"**Agency**." Any organization, society, institution, court facility or other entity which provides for the care of a child. The term does not include a county children and youth social service agency.

"**Child**." An unemancipated individual under 18 years of age.

"**Legal custody**." The right to make major decisions on behalf of the child, including, but not limited to, medical, religious and educational decisions.

"**Parental duties**." Includes meeting the physical, emotional and social needs of the child.

"**Partial physical custody**." The right to assume physical custody of the child for less than a majority of the time.

"**Physical custody**." The actual physical possession and control of a child.

"**Primary physical custody**." The right to assume physical custody of the child for the majority of time.

"**Relocation**." A change in a residence of the child which significantly impairs the ability of a nonrelocating party to exercise custodial rights.

"**Shared legal custody**." The right of more than one individual to legal custody of the child.

"**Shared physical custody**." The right of more than one individual to assume physical custody of the child, each having significant periods of physical custodial time with the child.

"**Sole legal custody**." The right of one individual to exclusive legal custody of the child.

"**Sole physical custody**." The right of one individual to exclusive physical custody of the child.

"**Supervised physical custody**." Custodial time during which an agency or an adult designated by the court or agreed upon by the parties monitors the interaction between the child and the individual with those rights.

Rule 1915.1 has now been amended so as to be consistent with 5322.

The foregoing applies only to unemancipated children under the age of 18, and it has been held that a 19-year-old, who was found to have reached adulthood for most legal purposes, could not be compelled to have contacts with the non-custodial parent.[17] A twenty-six-year-old woman with a mental capacity between the ages of four and eight years, who received support payments from a parent, could not be ordered to visit with that parent.[18]

LOWER COURT CASES

Berks County

Buck v. Buck, C. P. Berks County, No. 06-6090 (C.C.P. 2008) (Granting primary custody to father would best serve the child's interests where father provided a better emotional and intellectual environment for the child than did mother. Mother had a history of mental illness during multiple suicide attempts. Mother also had a difficult time focusing on the child's needs. Father, on the other hand, focused on the child's needs and provided her with stable, consistent care. "A parent acting reliably and consistently as a parent, not a friend, is an important trait for a primary caregiver. *King v. King*, 889 A.2d 630, 635 (Pa. Super. 2005)." Father also was more involved in the child's schoolwork and, unlike mother, took the child to religious services. With regard to the child's preference, the court noted that the child preferred the custody schedule to remain the same. "However, the child is only seven years old, and she did not articulate logical reasons for her preference. Some of her testimony revealed facts why maintaining the status quo would not be in her best interest. For all of these reasons, the child's preference is only a minor factor in favor of maintaining the equal physical custody division.").

---

[17] Fernald v. Fernald, 224 Pa. Super. 93, 302 A.2d 470 (1973).

[18] Schmidt v. Schmidt, 313 Pa. Super. 83, 459 A.2d 421 (1983); *see also* Walker v. Walker, 362 Pa. Super. 75, 523 A.2d 782 (1987) (trial court, in custody proceeding, lacked subject matter jurisdiction to compel an 18-year-old daughter to visit her mother, even though the daughter functioned at a moderate level of retardation)); M.B.S. v. W.E., 232 A.3d 922 (Pa. Super. 2020) (Superior Court ruled that since the child at issue would turn 18 prior to any potential remand, and the Child Custody Act did not provide an exception for a child who was 18 and still in high school, the court had no jurisdiction and mother's claims challenging the trial court's grant of legal custody to father were moot).

Salazar v. Gabriel, C. P. Berks County, No. 03-6532 (C.C.P. 2003) (Trial court refused to stay father's custody proceedings under the Soldiers' and Sailors' Civil Relief Act of 1940. Aunt's motion for a stay of proceedings was denied, and court directed that counsel be appointed to protect mother's interest while serving in the military. "Clearly, given the absence of Mother while she is serving our nation in the Armed Forces stationed in Iraq, and the fact that the children have not been with a parent since January 2003, an inquiry into the status of the children, their safety, and what temporary custodial arrangement would be in their best interest is required.").

Miltenberger v. Miltenberger, C.P. Berks Co., No. 2060-95 A.D. (C.C.P. 1997) (The best interests of the children would be served by leaving them in the custody of their grandmother rather than returning them to their mother. Held that it would be in the best interests of the children to continue living with their grandmother, because she has been a more positive influence on them than their mother. The only time when these children have known continuity and stability is during the period grandmother has had custody of them. Under her care the children have healed and begun flourishing. The court specified that mother, although allowed virtually unlimited visitation while children are at their grandmother's home, must obtain counseling to improve her parenting skills, with reports of such counseling provided to the court. Grandmother was ordered to encourage regular phone contact with mother, to send videos of important events to mother, and to keep mother informed about the children's health and progress in school).

Myers v. Myers, 85 Berks L. J. 27 (C.C.P. 1992) (The polestar followed by Pennsylvania in deciding child custody cases is, as it is in most jurisdictions, the best interests and permanent welfare of the child).

Centre County

Noss v. Merrill, C.P. Centre County, No. 2015-4607 (C.C.P. 2016) (Trial court found that the factors for relocation did not outweigh the disruption it would cause the children, and mother's petition for relocation was denied and the established custody schedule and parenting plan remained in effect. The court found that the best interests of the children were served by remaining in Centre County, Pennsylvania with father during the school year).

Chester County

S.A. v. K.A., C.P. Chester County, No. 2013-12558-CU, *aff'd*, Memorandum Decision, No. 1833 EDA 2018 (Pa. Super. November 21, 2018) (Father's petition seeking shared physical custody was motivated by his desire to reduce his child support obligation; this was evidenced by several text messages written by father, where he referred to child support payments. Father responded with "waive my child support payments" when contacted by mother. The court noted that father did not understand that his relationship with his son was not dependent on how much child support he paid. Applying the sixteen factors listed in 23 Pa.C.S. § 5328(a), and considering the totality of the circumstances, the court found that it was clear that it was not in the child's best interests for the parties to have shared physical custody. To the contrary, it was in the child's best interest for mother to have primary physical custody of the child).

Delaware County

Lopez v. Vasquez, C.P. Delaware County, No. 2014-009787 (C.C.P. 2015) (The trial court rejected mother's argument that because the child remained enrolled in and was attending high school, she was jurisdictionally a "minor child" over whom the court retained jurisdiction for purposes of determining custody and allowing a parent to maintain custodial rights over the child. Mother analogized that for the purpose of support, the support statutes permit the court to retain jurisdiction and enforcement purposes require a parent to continue to support a "child" who was no longer under the age of 18 as long as that "child" remains enrolled in high school. The trial court disagreed, noting that a review of the relevant Pennsylvania statutes, Rules of Civil Procedure and case law was not in agreement with mother's position. "There is no analogous statute or rule of law or case law in the Commonwealth of Pennsylvania that provides that a parent maintains custodial rights over their child or any child for which there was a prior custody order, after the child reaches the age of majority in the United States, that being eighteen." The court also noted that 23 Pa.C.S. § 5322(a) contained the definitions for Chapter 53: Child Custody, and defined "adult" as "any individual 18 years of age or older" and "child" as "an unemancipated individual under 18 years of age." The court noted that there was no statute or commentary in 23 Pa.C.S. Chapter 53, which provides that an individual who has reached the age of majority, 18 years of age, must remain in the physical custody of a legal parent or guardian as long as that person remains enrolled in a high school. Similarly, the court explained, the UCCJEA defined "child" as "an individual who has not attained 18 years of age.").

Dauphin County

Wingate v. Wingate, 112 Dauph. 62 (C.C.P. 1992) (The paramount concern in child custody cases is the best interests and welfare of the children; all other considerations are deemed subordinate to the child's physical, intellectual, moral, and spiritual well-being).

Montgomery County

Schulman v. Schulman, 129 Montg. Co. L.R. 370 (C.C.P. 1993) (The polestar followed by Pennsylvania in deciding child custody cases is, as it is in most jurisdictions, the best interests and permanent welfare of the child).

Crouse, Jr. v. Thompson, 117 Montg. Co. L.R. 291 (C.C.P. 1986) (The paramount concern in child custody cases is the best interests and welfare of the children; all other considerations are deemed subordinate to the child's physical, intellectual, moral, and spiritual well-being).

Philadelphia County

C.C.L. v. G.S.L., C.P. Philadelphia County, No. OC 1213057, *aff'd*, Memorandum Decision, No. 2733 EDA 2018 (Pa. Super. March 22, 2019) (Trial court entered a final custody order providing that the parties continue equally shared physical custody and shared legal custody of the child pursuant to their agreement. The trial court did not restrict father's travel with the child, and specifically determined that it did not consider father a flight risk given his extensive ties to Philadelphia and that both mother and father believed travel to be beneficial to the child. The trial court's order provided that the "party traveling overnight with child shall provide the other party with the telephone number and address where the child will be staying, as well as a travel itinerary (including flight numbers) no less than 24 hours in advance of any scheduled travel.").

Somerset County

Peterman v. Wellington, 52 Somerset Leg. J. 62 (C.C.P. 1993) (It is an established axiom that the best interests of the child govern custody and visitation determinations; factors to be considered in determining the child's best interests include the child's physical, intellectual, emotional, and spiritual well-being).

Volchko v. Volchko, 59 Somerset Leg. J. 120 (C.C.P. 1991) (In child custody cases, the rights of the parents must be deemed subordinate to the child's physical, intellectual, emotional, moral, and spiritual well-being).

Perry County

M.L.G. v. L.M.G, C.P. Perry County, No. FC-2017-144, *aff'd* Memorandum Decision, No. 335 MDA 2018 (Pa. Super. January 4, 2019) (A trial court possesses the broad authority, pursuant to Pa.R.Civ.P. 1915.8, to order a party to undergo any mental and physical examinations it deems fit in actions for custody or visitation, and such examinations do not violate the Fourth Amendment, citing *Luminella v. Marcocci,* 814 A.2d 711 (Pa. Super. 2002) (holding that, a provision in child custody order requiring mother to undergo random drug testing did not violate reasonableness requirement of Fourth Amendment. The court reiterated its concerns that father had repeatedly disregarded its prior orders directing him to submit to hair follicle drug testing, and ordered father, once again, to submit to the hair follicle test and to have the results forwarded to the court or the court would stop father's visitation with the minor child and said visitation would be resumed only upon a receipt from the testing facility that father had passed said test).

Wayne County

K.D. v. E.D., C.P. Wayne County, No. 336-2015 DR, *aff'd* Memorandum Decision, No. 485 EDA 2018 (Pa. Super. August 23, 2018) (Clinically supervised visitation with father, who had exhibited behavior of such severe mental or moral deficiency, would constitute a grave threat to the children's welfare; therefore, the Master erred as a matter of law and abused his discretion in recommending that the children have supervised visitation with father. Citing *Moran v. Moran*, 839 A.2d 1091, 1093 (Pa. Super. 2003), the court recognized that the Report and Recommendation from a Master is only advisory).

York County

In the Interest of: J.P., a Minor, C.P. York County, No. CP-67-DP-000-0561-2006, *aff'd* Memorandum Decision, No. 255 MDA 2018 (Pa. Super. August 3, 2018) (Trial court decided to suspend father's unsupervised visits with the child. The court noted that father's actions at the unsupervised visits with the child caused depression and extreme anxiety, and were counterproductive to reunification).

§ 1.3. PATERNITY BY ESTOPPEL

The doctrine of Paternity by Estoppel is most often applied in support cases. However, the doctrine may be applied in custody cases.[19] The doctrine can be summed up as follows: "those who mislead a child as to the identity of his or her natural father, cannot then turn around and disprove their own fiction to the detriment of the child."[20] Paternity by Estoppel will apply only where it can be shown that it is in the best interest of the child.[21]

Paternity by Estoppel can also be applied to preclude a biological father from asserting his parental rights.[22]

Where, after the birth of the child, a biological father immediately asserted that he was the father of the child and attempted to be part of the child's life both through the mother's consent and then by taking legal action, but was blocked by the mother and her then husband, the biological father was not equitably estopped and permitted to intervene in a custody action between the mother and mother's then husband when the child was born during the marriage of the mother and mother's then

---

[19] *See* C.A.B. v. P.D.K. (In re T.E.B.), 74 A.3d 170 (Pa. Super. 2013).
[20] *See* Bahl v. Lambert Farms, Inc., 819 A.2d 534 (Pa. 2003); *see also* Fish v. Behers, 741 A.2d 721 (Pa. 1999); J.C. v. J.S., 826 A.2d 1 (Pa. Super. 2003).
[21] *See* K.E.M. v. P.C.S., 38 A.3d 798 (Pa. 2012).
[22] *See* C.T.D. v. N.E.E., 653 A.2d 28 (Pa. Super. 1995).

husband.[23] In the C.A.B. case, the court awarded shared legal custody to mother, mother's now ex-husband, and father, and father was permitted to share custodial time of the child with mother's ex-husband and the mother who he was now engaged to marry.

§ 1.4. PROMPT DISPOSITION OF CUSTODY CASES

Pennsylvania Rule of Civil Procedure 1915.4 provides time deadlines to keep custody actions moving swiftly through the court system. Rule 1915.4(a) pertains to the parties' initial in-person contact with the court. The requirement under subsection (a) is 45 days from the filing of the complaint or petition.

Rule 1915.4(b) has been the focus of 2 recent cases: *Dietrich v. Dietrich*,[24] and *Harrell v. Pecynski*.[25] Rule 1915.4(b), provides, in part: "within 180 days of the filing of the complaint either the court shall automatically enter an order scheduling a trial before a judge or a party shall file a praecipe, motion or request for trial," unless the moving party obtains an extension of no more than 60 days. The Superior Court held in *Dietrich* and later followed in *Harrell* that Rule 1915.4(b) requires, in essence, that if a custody action does not come to trial within 180 days of the filing of the complaint and no extension has been granted, the matter shall be dismissed either by motion of a party or by the court *sua sponte*.[26] Rule 1915.4(b) has since be amended to provide the court with discretion as to whether to dismiss an action pursuant to the rule "so that the fundamental concern for the best interests of the child [can] be considered."[27] Another amendment to Rule 1915.4(b) enables the court to grant an extension to the deadline for good cause shown or if the court "finds that dismissal is not in the best interests of the child." Pursuant to the rule, the extension shall not exceed 60 days beyond the 180 day limit, though "[a] further reasonable extension may be granted by the court

---

[23] *See* C.A.B. v. P.D.K. (In re T.E.B.), 74 A.3d 170 (Pa. Super. 2013).

[24] Dietrich v. Dietrich, 923 A.2d 461 (Pa. Super. 2007).

[25] Harrell v. Pecynski, 11 A.3d 1000 (Pa. Super. 2011).

[26] *But see* Pa.R.C.P. 1915.4(c) (requiring the commencement of the trial within 90 days of the date the scheduling order is entered).

[27] Harrell v. Pecynski, 11 A.3d 1000 (Pa. Super. 2011).

upon agreement of the parties or when the court finds, on the record, compelling circumstances for a further reasonable extension." However, effective June 25, 2013, the Rule has been amended again, providing that if an extension is granted and neither party files to request a trial within the extended time period, "the court shall, *sua sponte*, or on the motion of a party, dismiss the matter unless the court finds that dismissal is not in the best interest of the child."[28] The parties have 20 days to object to a dismissal of the action. If no objection is filed, the matter shall be dismissed by the court.[29]

Subsections (c) & (d) of Rule 1915.4 provide further time restrictions regarding commencement of trials and the entry of decisions.

Effective June 25, 2013, Rule 1915.3-1 was promulgated which provides restrictions for withdrawing a pleading or discontinuing an action. Pursuant to Rule 1915.3-1(a), "a custody pleading cannot be withdrawn after the issuance of a scheduling order or notice of conference regarding claims made in the pleading except (1) by leave of court after notice to the non-moving party, or (2) by written agreement of the parties."[30] Further, pursuant to Rule 1915.3-1(b): "a custody action may be discontinued by praecipe only upon a verified statement by the moving party that the complaint has not been served." Also, "a custody action cannot be discontinued after the complaint has been served except (A) by leave of court after notice to the non-moving party, or (B) by written agreement of the parties."[31]

LOWER COURT CASES

Cumberland County

R.A.G. v. A.L.R., 61 Cumberland L. J. 201 (C.C.P. 2012) (The trial court, citing *Wiseman v. Wall,* 718 A.2d 844, 851 (Pa. Super. 1998), held that while a parent's work schedule may not deprive the parent of custody, a parent's availability should be considered when determining a custody schedule that will serve the best interest of the

---

[28] *See* Pa.R.C.P. 1915.4(b).
[29] *Id.*
[30] Pa.R.C.P. 1915.3-1(a).
[31] Pa.R.C.P. 1915.3-1(b).

child. The court also held that although Pa.R.Civ.P. 1915.4 states that custody cases are to be disposed of promptly, this rule is explicitly subject to the local rules of the judicial district and the rule cannot be viewed and interpreted in a vacuum, but must be construed *in pari materia* with the other rules relating to the same class of proceedings. The court also held that where the record included (a) numerous conciliation hearings, (b) an agreement of the parties, (c) opinion and position of the conciliator, (d) drug/alcohol evaluation ordered and completed, and (e) co-parenting counseling sessions attended, it was clear that sufficient good cause to extend the 180-day deadline was evidenced in the record).

Northampton County

Bakos v. Bakos, 56 Northampton Co. Rep. 798 (C.C.P. 2011) (Defendant-wife's petition to dismiss a pending custody proceeding was granted where the trial was not scheduled within 180 days of filing, as required by Pa.R.Civ.P. 1915.4(b). On March 14, 2008, the parties entered into a custody agreement regarding their minor child. Thereafter, on August 29, 2008, father filed a Petition to Modify Custody. Father filed an amended petition on August 21, 2009. This matter was first listed for trial on the March 2011 Non-Jury List by praecipe dated February 2, 2011. Wife filed a Petition to Dismiss Pending Custody Proceedings Pursuant to Pa.R.Civ.P. 1915.4(b). The trial court granted defendant's petition to dismiss, holding that it was clear that trial was not scheduled within 180 days, as required by Pa.R.Civ.P. 1915.4(b). No extension was sought or granted by the court. The matter was pending in excess of 30 months since the filing of father's original petition, and in excess of 18 months since father's amended petition. The court ruled that dismissal of the outstanding custody pleadings was mandatory and outside the discretion of the court where a trial had not been scheduled within 180 days of filing and an extension had not been granted, citing *Dietrich v. Dietrich*, 923 A.2d 461, 464–465 (Pa. Super. 2007)).

§ 1.5.   QUASI-JUDICIAL IMMUNITY

In *Galvani v. Commonwealth of Pennsylvania, et al.*, 329 Fed.Appx. 344 (3rd Cir. 2009), the Third Circuit held that a custody conciliator working for the District Court administration was a court-appointed officer and, thus, entitled to quasi-judicial immunity from a civil rights action brought by mother who alleged that her children were unlawfully seized at a custody conciliation conference. Mother alleged that her children were unlawfully seized at a custody conciliation conference, and filed an action against the Commonwealth of Pennsylvania, the District Court administration, a custody conciliator, and others for violation of the Fourth and Fourteenth Amendments of the Federal Constitution, the

Pennsylvania Constitution and Pennsylvania tort law. Mother alleged that defendant Carr was an attorney and custody conciliator working for the District Court Administration of York County.

The Third Circuit Court of Appeals held that the Commonwealth and District Court administration were entitled to Eleventh Amendment immunity; the custody conciliator was entitled to quasi-judicial immunity, an attorney and grandparents were not "persons acting under the color of state law" under § 1983, and that the District Court did not abuse its discretion in refusing to exercise supplemental jurisdiction over state law claims. The court noted that, under the York County Rules of Civil Procedure, a custody conciliator assists the family court in conducting a conciliation conference shortly after a complaint is filed. The conciliator has authority to address interim orders, the appointment of counsel for the child, the allocation of costs, and any issues approved by the court. As court-appointed officers, custody conciliators perform quasi-judicial functions and exercise the kind of discretion protected by judicial immunity. Therefore, mother's claims against defendant custody conciliator were properly dismissed.

§ 1.6.   PRETRIAL PROCEDURE

Effective June 25, 2013, Rule 1915.4-4 was promulgated which provides pretrial procedures in custody actions. A complete copy of Rule 1915.4-4, including the form Praecipe for a Pre-Trial Conference, is located in Appendix C of this book.

§ 1.7   WRITTEN AGREEMENTS

It is clear that children may not be contractually dealt with as parental property, all right and title inuring to the owner.[32] As such, agreements

---

[32] Commonwealth ex rel. Children's Aid Society v. Gard, 362 Pa. 85, 66 A.2d 300 (1949); Commonwealth ex rel. Veihdeffer v. Veihdeffer, 235 Pa. Super. 447, 344 A.2d 613 (1975); Commonwealth ex rel. Robinson v. Ziegler, 205 Pa. Super. 29, 206 A.2d 324 (1965); Mallinger v. Mallinger, 197 Pa. Super. 34, 195 A.2d 890 (1961).

with respect to the custody of children are not binding on the courts,[33] cannot oust the jurisdiction of a tribunal,[34] and will always yield to the best interests of the child.[35]

Although voidable, such agreements are not irrelevant since the surrender of custody may implicate the party's unwillingness to care for the child and consequently his or her overall parental fitness.[36] Where, however, the agreement has been incorporated into a court order, the order binds the parties in the same manner as any other order issued by the

---

[33] Parks v. Parks, 284 Pa. Super. 400, 426 A.2d 108 (1981); In re Custody of Neal, 260 Pa. Super. 151, 393 A.2d 1057 (1978); Commonwealth ex rel. Veihdeffer v. Veihdeffer, 235 Pa. Super. 447, 344 A.2d 613 (1975).

[34] Miller v. Miller, 423 Pa. Super. 162, 620 A.2d 1161 (1993) (Child custody agreements by parents, while encouraged, will always be subject to close scrutiny by court and are subject to being set aside, as courts will not be bound by such agreements. Therefore, while arbitration proceedings in custody disputes are not void as against public policy, the question of the enforceability of arbitration awards in this context is a very different matter. Thus while agreements entered into between the parties are binding as between the parties, they may not bind the court once its jurisdiction is invoked. It follows necessarily that an award rendered by an arbitration panel would be subject to the supervisory power of the court in its parens patriae capacity in a proceeding to determine the best interests of the child. It has long been recognized by the courts that it is the Commonwealth who is charged with the duty of protecting the rights and interests of children); Commonwealth ex rel. Scholtes v. Scholtes, 187 Pa. Super. 22, 142 A.2d 345 (1958).

[35] Williams v. Williams, 223 Pa. Super. 29, 296 A.2d 870 (1972); Miller v. Miller, 423 Pa. Super. 162, 620 A.2d 1161 (1993) (An arbitration award on the issue of custody is subject to review by a court of competent jurisdiction based upon its responsibility to look to the best interests of the child. The trial court must view the decision of the arbitrators in light of the best interests of the child. However, if the court following its review finds that the arbitrators' award is in the best interests of the child, the court may adopt the decision as its own); Dolan v. Dolan, 378 Pa. Super. 321, 548 A.2d 632 (1988) (trial court has the power to modify parties' marriage settlement agreement in order to protect the best interests of the child when making custody order); Walker v. Walker, 308 Pa. Super. 280, 454 A.2d 130 (1982).

[36] Commonwealth ex rel. Foster v. Foster, 225 Pa. Super. 436, 311 A.2d 663 (1973); Commonwealth ex rel. Traeger v. Ritting, 206 Pa. Super. 446, 213 A.2d 681 (1965); Commonwealth ex rel. Bordlemay v. Bordlemay, 201 Pa. Super. 435, 193 A.2d 845 (1963).

court.[37] If the parties have an agreement regarding custody and request that the court enter a consent order incorporating the agreement's terms, (a) the parties shall submit to the court a proposed custody order bearing the parties' written consent; or (b) the parties may state the agreement on the record, provided that: (1) within ten days of placing the agreement on the record, the parties submit to the court a proposed custody order bearing the parties' written consent; or (2) the court memorializes the oral agreement from the record into a written custody order.[38]

A custody order "temporarily" awarding primary physical custody of child to father pursuant to a separation agreement incorporated in the decree, which provided for a change in custody if mother could not provide a "home environment" that was in the best interest of the child, was not abuse of discretion, notwithstanding the use of the word "temporary"; the trial court could reinstate the original custody agreement if, after full consideration of the mother's petition for further custody modification, it determined that the child's best interest would be served with her mother.[39]

The custody claim of a party surrendering custody, pursuant to a written agreement, in order to promote the welfare of the child will be unaffected by the agreement if the conditions spawning the agreement have abated, whereas a party who does so to avoid parental responsibility or to pursue amorous inclinations will seriously jeopardize his or her chances of gaining custody.[40]

Interestingly, the Superior Court *en banc* ruled that the trial court erred in ruling that a clause in an agreement between the parents of a child which provided that father would pay $10,000 if he challenged in court the custody provisions in the agreement was void and unenforceable as

---

[37] Daniel K.D. v. Jan M.H., 301 Pa. Super. 36, 446 A.2d 1323 (1982); Smith v. Smith, 307 Pa. Super. 554, 453 A.2d 1020 (1982); *but see* Yates v. Yates, 936 A.2d 1191 (Pa. Super. 2007) (improper for parties to agree to be bound by whatever terms the court eventually orders to "short-cut" the judicial process).

[38] *See* Pa.R.C.P. 1915.7.

[39] Belan v. Belan, 399 Pa. Super. 458, 582 A.2d 684 (1990).

[40] Commonwealth ex rel. Bordlemay v. Bordlemay, 201 Pa. Super. 435, 193 A.2d 845 (1963).

against public policy.[41] In the *Huss* case, the trial court relied heavily on the public policy argument that parents have no power to "bargain away the rights of their children" with regard to parents' being precluded from agreeing to child support "less than required or less than can be given." Though parents cannot bargain away the rights of children with regard to child support, the Superior Court iterated that "no similar appellate authority exists with respect to agreements between parents regarding custody and visitation." The reason for the difference between child support and custody as to the public policy argument is that the right to child support belongs to the child, and the rights to custody belong to parents or guardians.[42]

Where the facts indicate that the document was executed under circumstances showing that relinquishment of the child was less than voluntary, the court may minimize the adverse impact of the agreement.[43] In addition, a court may accord little weight to a custody agreement where it finds that despite the terms of the agreement, the child or children actually spend large portions of their time in the care of the non-custodian.[44]

It should also be noted that informal unwritten agreements when supported by practice in accordance with the agreement may be accorded substantial weight if the bargaining power of the parties is roughly equal and circumstances have not changed since the time of entry into the agreement.[45]

LOWER COURT CASES

Berks County

Morganti v. Morganti, 104 Berks Co. L. J. 40 (C.C.P. 2011) (Trial court refused to strike a custody agreement based on the maternal grandparents' allegations of duress and emotional distress, where the agreement was entered into an open court, the

---

[41] *See* Huss v. Weaver, 134 A.3d 449 (Pa. Super. 2016).
[42] *Id.*
[43] *See* Parks v. Parks, 284 Pa. Super. 400, 426 A.2d 108 (1981).
[44] *See* Commonwealth ex rel. Grimes v. Grimes, 281 Pa. Super. 484, 422 A.2d 572 (1980).
[45] Witmayer v. Witmayer, 320 Pa. Super. 372, 467 A.2d 371 (1983).

grandparents were represented by counsel and no duress was alleged at the time of the agreement. Any objection to the custody agreement was waived. In 2006, maternal grandparents filed a custody complaint against their daughter (mother) and her paramour (father), seeking custody of their minor child. Maternal grandparents were awarded temporary legal and physical custody of the child, while mother and father were granted visitation. The trial court subsequently entered a final custody order which granted maternal grandparents primary physical custody with visitation awarded to parents. Father died in a vehicle accident in 2009, and mother subsequently sought custody of her child. In 2011, the parties entered into an oral custody agreement in open court and with the benefit of counsel. The agreement essentially granted mother primary custody of the child. The court accepted the agreement as presented by the parties and signed the agreement into a court order. Four days later, maternal grandparents filed a petition to recant the oral agreement, alleging that at the time they consented to the agreement, they did so in "an unfit state of mind," that they were "blindsided" by the information contained in mother's pretrial memorandum and that they "panicked." Maternal grandparents argued that they felt pressured to enter into the agreement and that they were denied the opportunity to present evidence. Further, maternal grandparents alleged that the trial court had coerced them into an agreement by intimating that mother would prevail in her request for custody. The trial court ruled that since maternal grandparents had not raised any legal grounds as to why the agreement should be stricken, their petition to strike was denied. The court noted that maternal grandparents were at all times represented by counsel throughout the proceedings and there was no evidence that they were unduly pressured into entering the agreement. Rather, the record demonstrated that the parties were heard in open court, were represented by counsel and that each confirmed their consent to the agreement under oath. Moreover, maternal grandparents failed to show how refusing to grant their petition to recant or to vacate the order by agreement would be contrary to the best interests of the child).

Montgomery County

R.M. v. S.B., 150 Montgomery Co. L. Rep. 429 (C.C.P. 2013) (Trial court held that when a custodial parent so obstructs the visits between the child and the non-custodial parent that the best interests of the child are no longer being served, a change of custody is warranted. An essential parental duty is encouraging the child to have an independent and meaningful relationship with the non-custodial parent. An agreement was reached wherein the child was to stay with mother the majority of the year, traveling to stay with father in France over an extended period during the summer, staying with father in Pennsylvania for some additional periods, and was to regularly communicate with father via video. The custody agreement was broken by mother's failure to maintain the child's passport and failure to make the child available for the scheduled video communication with father. The trial court determined that due to its chronic and contemptuous nature, mother's breach of the agreement justified transfer of primary physical custody to father as well as an award of attorney's fees to father. Based on the custody factors set forth in 23 Pa.C.S. § 5328(a), modification of the parties' custody agreement was in the best interests of the child when mother incessantly violated the agreement and interfered with father's visitations and communications with the child. Thus, the court properly determined that the best interest of the child would be served in father's primary physical custody in France. The court considered at length one particular custody factor—which party was more likely to encourage and permit frequent and continuing contact between the child and another party. The court noted that it has long been against public policy to limit or destroy the relationship between parent and child, citing *Pamela J.K. v. Roger D.J.,* 419 A.2d 1301, 1309 (Pa. Super. 1980). "When a custodial parent so obstructs the visits between the child and the non-custodial parent that the best interests of the child are no longer served, a change of custody is warranted.").

York County

Strine v. Strine, 113 York Leg. J. 27 (C.C.P. 1999) (Trial court refused to enforce a provision of the parties' custody agreement which called for return of the children to mother if father resumed living with his second wife, since the agreement contravened the public policy of the Divorce Code strongly favoring reconciliation. The court noted that agreements concerning custody of children are subject to the limitations placed on them by public policy. The court cited the strong policy statement found in the Divorce Code favoring reconciliation and held that the agreement was in contravention of that policy).

§ 1.8   DUTY TO DEVELOP A FULL, COMPLETE, AND CURRENT CUSTODY TRIAL RECORD

In child custody cases, due to, *inter alia*, the processing of the case, and procedural events, time passes from when the matter is initially filed to when the hearing occurs. In some instances, a matter is relisted due to an unforeseen circumstance or a scheduling issue. In other instances, a matter does not conclude on the date of the initial hearing and the parties and counsel have to return to court on a future date or dates many months later. In such situations, the court strives to avoid stale facts and evidence by having reports and evaluations updated so that the court may hear the current circumstances and situations.

A "unique obligation" has been placed upon a trial judge in child custody cases by the appellate courts (there is no such obligation in any other form of civil litigation) to have an affirmative duty to create as full and complete of a record as possible.[46] In *Moore v. Moore*, the Pennsylvania Supreme Court warned trial courts, with respect to that unique obligation, as follows:

> In the context of a custody case a trial court must ensure that as full and complete a record as possible is created when a decision as important as the welfare of a child is at issue. In *Tettis v. Boyum, 317 Pa. Super. 8, 463 A.2d 1056 (1983)* the Superior Court reversed and remanded a custody case to the trial court for failure to create a complete record.
>
> As we have cautioned the lower courts time and again, in order to assess the best interests and general welfare of the child or children, it is the duty of the trial judge to make the fullest possible inquiry in custody actions. *Commonwealth ex rel. Cox v. Cox, 255 Pa. Super. 508, 388 A.2d 1082 (1978)*; *Commonwealth ex rel. Ashfield v. Cortes, 210 Pa. Super 515, 234 A.2d 47 (1967)*. All pertinent facts and circumstances surrounding the contesting parties must be fully explored and developed. *Sipe v. Shaffer, 263 Pa. Super. 27, 396 A.2d 1359 (1979)*. The hearing judge should consider the character and fitness of the respective parties, the type of home they can offer, their ability to financially provide for the child. *Gerald G. v. Theresa G., 284 Pa. Super. 498, 502, 426 A.2d 157, 159 (1981)*, quoting *Commonwealth ex rel. Leighann A. v. Leon A., 280 Pa. Super. 249, 252, 421 A.2d 706, 708 (1980)*.
>
> *Tettis at 23, 463 A.2d at 1064.*
>
> In light of the unique obligation placed upon the trial court in a custody case, to consider all pertinent information regarding the issue of what is in the best interest of the child, we can find no abuse of discretion by the trial court herein, in holding the supplemental hearing.[47]

---

[46] *See* Moore v. Moore, 634 A.2d 163 (Pa. 1993).
[47] *Id.* (emphasis added).

In custody cases, old evidence may be relevant, but new and current evidence is always relevant. Pennsylvania child custody law requires the court to develop a complete record.[48]

In *Artzt v. Artzt*, because of procedural issues, among other things, the record became 2½ years old when the parties went before the appellate court. The Pennsylvania Superior Court remanded the case for a hearing to reconsider the merits of the previous order, since the circumstances had changed since the entry of the custody order that was on appeal.[49] In *Kozlowski v. Kozlowski*, where the record was 2 years old, the Superior Court held: "[b]ecause our decision, as well as that of the trial court, rests upon what is *currently* in the children's best interest, it must be based upon an up-to-date record."[50] Similarly, in *Tracey L. v. Mattye F.*, a caretaker was permitted to testify at a prior custody matter but precluded at a hearing approximately 10 months later. In reversing the trial court order and remanding the matter, the Superior Court held: "We realize that a significant amount of time has passed since the September 26, 1994 hearing. Therefore, the trial court should also entertain testimony from appellee and her witnesses, as circumstances may have changed, before entering a custody order."[51]

§ 1.9 THE 16 STATUTORY CUSTODY FACTORS

In Pennsylvania, when entering a custody order, in determining the best interest of the child, the court must consider the factors enumerated in 23 Pa.C.S. § 5328(a).[52] However, a court need not address all 16

---

[48] *Id.*

[49] Artzt v. Artzt, 556 A.2d 409 (Pa. Super. 1989).

[50] Kozlowski v. Kozlowski, 524 A. 2d 995 (Pa. Super. 1987).

[51] Tracey L. v. Mattye F., 666 A.2d 734 (Pa. Super. 1995) (citing Artzt, 556 A.2d 409 (Pa. Super. 1989)).

[52] *See also* C.M. v. M.M., 215 A.3d 588 (Pa. Super. 2019) (Superior Court held that the trial court erred in failing to consider the best interest factors set forth in 23 Pa.C.S. § 5328(a), where mother's custody petition specifically requested a change in custody of the parties' minor child. The court noted that the record revealed that the trial court did not consider any of the custody factors from § 5328(a) on the record in open court or in a written opinion or order. The court held that even in cases where the trial court

factors under § 5328 when deciding discrete and narrow issues ancillary to a materially unchallenged custody arrangement.[53]

23 Pa.C.S. § 5328(a) provides:

(a) Factors.—In ordering any form of custody, the court shall determine the best interest of the child by considering all relevant factors, giving weighted consideration to those factors which affect the safety of the child, including the following:

(1) Which party is more likely to encourage and permit frequent and continuing contact between the child and another party.

(2) The present and past abuse committed by a party or member of the party's household, whether there is a continued risk of harm to the child or an abused party and which party can better provide adequate physical safeguards and supervision of the child.

(2.1) The information set forth in section 5329.1(a) (relating to consideration of child abuse and involvement with protective services).

(3) The parental duties performed by each party on behalf of the child.

(4) The need for stability and continuity in the child's education, family life and community life.

(5) The availability of extended family.

---

merely reaffirms its prior custody order, it is nevertheless making a ruling on a request to change the form of physical custody. The subject order modified the existing order by awarding father "partial physical custody," rather than "supervised physical custody."); A court need not address all 16 factors under § 5328 when deciding discrete and narrow issues ancillary to a materially unchallenged custody arrangement.

[53] (See M.O. v. J.T.R., 85 A.3d 1058 (Pa. Super. 2014); see also S.W.D. v S.A.R., 96 A.3d 396 (Pa. Super. 2014) (deciding a legal custody dispute such as the selection of a school that does not affect the form of the custody arrangement does not require an analysis of all of the 16 custody factors under Section 5328(a) as it is considered an ancillary issue, but the court must analyze all of the 16 custody factors when changing the form of custody such as the amount of time a parent has custody of the child).

(6) The child's sibling relationships.

(7) The well-reasoned preference of the child, based on the child's maturity and judgment.

(8) The attempts of a parent to turn the child against the other parent, except in cases of domestic violence where reasonable safety measures are necessary to protect the child from harm.

(9) Which party is more likely to maintain a loving, stable, consistent and nurturing relationship with the child adequate for the child's emotional needs.

(10) Which party is more likely to attend to the daily physical, emotional, developmental, educational and special needs of the child.

(11) The proximity of the residences of the parties.

(12) Each party's availability to care for the child or ability to make appropriate child-care arrangements.

(13) The level of conflict between the parties and the willingness and ability of the parties to cooperate with one another. A party's effort to protect a child from abuse by another party is not evidence of unwillingness or inability to cooperate with that party.

(14) The history of drug or alcohol abuse of a party or member of a party's household.

(15) The mental and physical condition of a party or member of a party's household.

(16) Any other relevant factor.

See Chapter 3 for a more detailed discussion of the cases addressing the statutory factors pertaining to physical custody and Chapter 2 pertaining to legal custody. Cases involving the statutory factors are also addressed throughout this treatise.

Chapter 2

LEGAL CUSTODY

§ 2.1. LEGAL CUSTODY AND SHARED LEGAL CUSTODY

"Legal Custody" is defined as: "The right to make major decisions on behalf of the child, including, but not limited to, medical[1], religious and educational decisions."[2]

---

[1] The issue of immunization of children is a legal custody decision. *See* H.C. v. J.C., 60 A.3d 863 (Pa. Super. 2012) (The Superior Court affirmed the Lehigh County trial court giving father authority to obtain human papillomavirus vaccinations for the parties' twin teenage daughters over mother's objections. The lower court held that the health benefits to be gained by the administration of the vaccine pursuant to established medical guidelines outweighed Mother's beliefs as to why the vaccine should not be administered); Schoen v. Schoen, 48 A.3d 490 (Pa. Super. 2012) (the Superior Court affirmed the lower court's decision to grant father authority to have the parties' children immunized over mother's objections. The lower court was within its discretion to grant father the right to have the children vaccinated where there was competent, expert medical testimony that having the children vaccinated was in their best interests and where mother proffered no evidence whatsoever that the vaccinations would be harmful to the children even where mother framed her objection on religious principles).

[2] 23 Pa.C.S. § 5322; Pa.R.C.P. 1915.1(b); *see also* Staub v. Staub, 960 A.2d 848 (Pa. Super. 2008) (deciding between public and home schooling); Fox v. Garzilli, 875 A.2d 1104 (Pa. Super. 2005) (ordering that the children attend school in the mother's school district); Dolan v. Dolan, 548 A.2d 632 (Pa. Super. 1988) (deciding between public and private school).

The statutory definition of "shared legal custody" is as follows: "The right of more than one individual to legal custody of the child."[3]

Historically, the seminal cases regarding the court awarding shared legal and/or physical custody were *In re Wesley J. K.*, 445 A.2d 1243 (Pa. Super. 1982) and *Wiseman v. Wall*, 718 A.2d 844 (Pa. Super. 1998). In *Wesley* and *Wiseman*, four factors are enumerated which must be considered when awarding shared custody. The four factors are as follows: (1) Both parents must be fit, capable of making reasonable childrearing decisions and willing and able to provide love and care for their children; (2) Both parents must evidence a continuing desire for active involvement in the child's life; (3) Both parents must be recognized by the child as a source of security and love; and (4) A minimal degree of cooperation between the parents must be possible. In *Wesley*, the Superior Court stressed that the minimal degree of cooperation "does not translate into a requirement that the parents have an amicable relationship."[4] However, in the case of P.J.P. v. M.M., 185 A.3d 413 (Pa. Super. 2018), the Superior Court held that trial courts "need no longer engage in the Wiseman analysis when determining whether shared custody is appropriate . . ." The Superior Court found that the four *Wiseman* factors are assimilated into the 16 enumerated custody factors of 23 Pa.C.S. § 5328(a). According to the Superior Court: "Section 5328(a), unlike Wiseman, does not require certain findings before a court may award shared custody. Under the current statute, courts must now consider all relevant factors, including the 'the ability of the parties to cooperate,' when making an award of any form of custody, and poor cooperation need not be dispositive."[5]

It has been held that shared legal custody cannot have a provision that one parent has final authority in the event of a dispute between the parties regarding a legal custody issue.[6] Likewise, in the converse, if a parent has sole legal custody, the court cannot prohibit a legal custody

---

[3] *Id.*; *see also,* Pa.R.C.P. 1915.1(b).

[4] In re Wesley J. K., 445 A.2d 1243 (Pa. Super. 1982).

[5] P.J.P. v. M.M., 185 A.3d 413 (Pa. Super. 2018).

[6] *See* Hill v. Hill, 619 A.2d 1086 (Pa. Super. 1993).

decision of that parent because the parent without legal custody objects to same.[7]

In some instances, sole legal custody may be appropriate.[8] The statutory definition of sole legal custody is defined as follows: "The right of one individual to exclusive legal custody of the child."[9]

Citizenship and the issuance of passports is a legal custody issue. The trial court has the authority to order parties to obtain passports and dual citizenship for the parties' children if it is in the children's best interest.[10]

LOWER COURT CASES

Allegheny County

J.L. v. A.N., C.P. Allegheny County, No. FD-09-009023-005 (C.C.P. August 18, 2016), *aff'd*, Memorandum Decision, No. 1393 WDA 2016 (Pa. Super. June 5, 2017) (Child's best interest was served by awarding legal custody with respect to education decisions to mother, as her testimony revealed that she conducted thorough research into which school district would provide the child with the best opportunity for academic success, and that she was committed to providing the child with a quality education. The court further emphasized that father showed less interest in the child's education, and apparently made little effort to conduct similar research).

Armstrong County

Fickes v. Pinkerton, C. P. Armstrong County, No. 2007-1909-Civil (C.C.P. 2009) (The parties met the four-part test for shared custody as set forth in *Johnson v. Lewis*, 870 A.2d 368 (Pa. Super. 2005). A consent order of January 18, 2008 gave the parties shared legal and physical custody. Father then petitioned to modify custody in October 2008. Mother also petitioned for modification of custody. The trial court concluded that

---

[7] M.P. v. M.P., 54 A.3d 950 (Pa. Super. 2012) (trial court order denying mother with sole legal custody permission to travel to Ecuador with child reversed by Superior Court).

[8] Barron v. Barron, 406 Pa. Super. 401, 594 A.2d 682 (1991) (holding that the trial court erred by granting joint legal custody while failing to address the father's excessive drinking habits). *See also* Fisher v. Fisher, 535 A.2d 1163 (Pa. Super. 1988); Mumma v. Mumma, 550 A.2d 1341 (Pa. Super. 1988); In re Wesley J. K., 445 A.2d 1243 (Pa. Super. 1982).

[9] 23 Pa.C.S. § 5322.

[10] *See* Nagle v. Nagle, 871 A.2d 832 (Pa. Super. 2005).

it was in the child's best interest that the parties continue to have shared legal and physical custody. The court noted that it was required to make four findings before it could order shared custody).

Berks County

Tanhouser v. Tanhouser, C.P. Berks County, No. 10-10487 (C.C.P. 2012) (The trial court awarded shared primary physical custody to each parent where each was equally capable of providing care and a stable environment for the children, even though both parents' parenting behavior was not ideal. The court acknowledged that the children lacked stability since the parties separated. They moved back-and-forth between households, but each parent ran his or her household with a different level of discipline. Nevertheless, the children were able to maintain stable grades and friendships. The children had adjusted well to the blended families in each household. The court found that sharing physical custody on a 50/50 basis was the most appropriate option. "It is true that a 50/50 arrangement is likewise not optimal, considering the animosity between the parties and the divergent philosophies of the two households on structure and discipline. That being said, these issues could surface under any form of schedule.").

Centre County

P.M. v. L.M., C.P. Centre County, No. 2017-2654 (C.C.P. September 6, 2019), *aff'd*, Memorandum Decision, No. 1637 MDA 2019 (Pa. Super. March 20, 2020) (Trial court ordered that the parties' children, ages 12 and 6, did not need to be vaccinated. Pennsylvania law allows parents to choose not to vaccinate their children. The court acknowledged that pursuant to the Pennsylvania Administrative Code, children who would otherwise be required to be immunized need not be immunized if the parent "objects in writing to the immunization on religious grounds or on the basis of a strong moral or ethical conviction similar to a religious belief," citing 28 Pa. Code §23.84. The trial court left open the option to order vaccination in the future).

Cumberland County

Layton v. Layton, C. P. Cumberland County, No. 04-4217 (C.C.P. 2009) (Trial court held that a child's transfer to a new school based on mother's move to a new school district was not a basis to modify custody. Transfer to a new school district was not viewed as a change in circumstances sufficient to warrant modification of a custody order. An existing trial court order had granted mother primary physical custody but gave father partial physical custody six out of every 14 days. When mother remarried, she moved approximately 6 miles away from the child's current school district. Father filed a petition seeking equal shared custody so that the child could maintain enrollment in her current school. Father did not want the child to change from her previous elementary school where she had done well, was involved in numerous activities, and where she had a lot of friends. The trial court denied father's petition and amended the parties' custody order to grant mother's request to allow the parties' daughter to change schools).

Lawrence County

Ciafre v. Ciafre, C.P. Lawrence County, No. 10065 of 2000, C.A. (C.C.P. 2010) (Trial court held that shared legal custody is the right to make major decisions affecting the best interests of a child. Except in the case of medical emergencies, the custodial parent shall consult with the non-custodial parent. Shared legal custody does not give one parent final authority in the event of a dispute).

Lebanon County

Cruz v. Melendez, C.P. Lebanon County, No. 2016-20597 (C.C.P. June 25, 2018) (The trial court imposed a parallel parenting program for the shared custody of the parties' minor child where the parties had a history of conflict, and set forth detailed parameters for the custody relationship. The court's plan provided that the parties would each have the child during alternate weeks. The plan was structured so that the parties had as little communication with one another as possible in an attempt to eliminate ongoing conflict. Each party had responsibility for certain of the child's healthcare needs. To assist with the implementation of the parallel parenting plan, the court included the guardian *ad litem* in the process. The court directed that any difficulties between the parents were to be addressed to the guardian *ad litem* in an attempt to attain resolution prior to filing future court proceedings. The court further explained that parallel parenting is not without its detractors. Almost all psychologists who have studied the concept agree that collaborative parenting is better than disengaged parenting. Moreover, the court noted, there is a dearth of research to assess the long-term impact of parallel parenting. Given these realities, the court stated that almost every expert agrees that parallel parenting should be reserved only for cases of "extreme conflict.").

Montgomery County

J.P.H. v. S.M.R.H., No. 2013-07094 (C.C.P. June 3, 2016), *aff'd*, Memorandum Decision, No. 2067 EDA 2016 (Pa. Super. March 31, 2017) (Pursuant to an agreed order, the parties shared legal custody of their children. They shared physical custody of their two sons, and mother had primary physical custody of the parties' daughter. Father subsequently filed a petition for contempt, alleging that mother had unilaterally enrolled their daughter at South Elementary in the Perkiomen Valley School District, a different school, in violation of the parties' agreement. The court held a hearing on the contempt petition, noting that since the parents shared legal custody of the children, neither parent could change their schooling unilaterally. The trial court did not hold that the parents could not change the children's schools, but that they could not do so *unilaterally*, stating that the children would remain in their current schools absent written agreement signed by both parties that was specific that they attend another school. The trial court directed mother to pay father's attorney's fees in the amount of $7,171.25).

Bach v. Bach, Jr., 134 Montg. Co. L.R. 56 (C.C.P. 1996) (Trial court held that despite the existence of an agreed-upon custody order providing the parents with shared legal custody, mother, as primary physical custodian, can unilaterally enroll the child in the school district where she resides. Under the Public School Code, a child is a resident of the school district in which his parent resides. A child whose parents are separated and residing in different school districts is not a resident of both districts).

§ 2.2.   NAME CHANGE OF CHILD

§ 2.2.1. Generally

The choice of a child's surname is a legal custody issue.[11] Section 1.7(b) of the Pennsylvania Code provides that if the parties are separated at the time of a child's birth "the choice of surname rests with the parent who has custody of the newborn child."[12] However, "custody" under Section 1.7 has been considered legal custody, not physical custody.[13] The best interests of the child controls in a proceeding to change a minor child's surname.[14]

§ 2.2.2. Contested Name Change of a Minor Child

Contested name changes of a minor child (change of surname) are in reality mini-child custody cases.

Ordinarily, name change procedures for adults are rather perfunctory. Those petitions set forth the reason for the name change (hard to spell or pronounce last name, desire to resume maiden name or sentimental family name, to "Americanize" the last name, for transgender changes, and the like). There are required proofs of publication in two newspapers, judgment searches, and criminal background searches.

---

[11] *See* 28 Pa. Code § 1.7(b); In Re Schidlmeier, 496 A.2d 1249 (Pa. Super. 1985).
[12] 28 Pa. Code § 1.7(b).
[13] In Re Schidlmeier, 496 A.2d 1249, 1252–53 (Pa. Super. 1985).
[14] *Id.*

With minors, the procedure goes smoothly when there is no contest and all consent.

However, when there is a contest, the hearing is detailed and every bit as contentious as a contested child custody case. First, procedurally, the statute requires, in addition to notice by publication in two newspapers, individual notice to the non-petitioning parent.[15]

In the great majority of reported cases, the non-petitioning parent is the father, whose last name the child bears, as a result of mother putting it on the child's birth certificate upon the birth of the child.

However, now, mother, petitioning on behalf of the minor child, requests that the court change the child's last name (that of the father's) to some other name, usually her maiden name or her new husband's name, or live-in boyfriend's name, who has acted as a step-father to the child.

In most contested cases, there is great animosity between father and mother. As reflected in the reported cases, the age of the minor child is very important. If the child is two years of age, and it is impossible for him or her to testify and render a reasoned preference as to the change of his or her last name, an important ingredient is missing for the judge from the case. On the other hand, if the child is a mature sixteen-year-old and has a reasoned preference as to the change of his or her last name, an important ingredient in the case is present for the judge.

The case of *Appeal of David Grimes,* a Pennsylvania Supreme Court case of first impression, established the legal standard in Pennsylvania for trial judges to use in hearings to decide contested and non-contested cases for the change of a surname of a minor child. That standard, it turns out, is Pennsylvania's child custody standard in deciding child custody cases generally: what is in the best interest and welfare of the minor child.[16]

In *Grimes*, the Supreme Court stated: "we further hold that a petitioner in such instance must bear the burden of establishing that a change would be in the best interest of said child."[17]

---

[15] *See* 54 Pa.C.S. § 701 et seq.
[16] Appeal of David Grimes, 609 A.2d 158, 161 (Pa. 1992).
[17] *Id.*

The *Grimes* case stated:

Specific guidelines are difficult to establish, for the circumstances in each case will be unique, as each child has individual physical, intellectual, moral, social and spiritual needs. See generally *In re: Davis,* 502 Pa. 110, 465 A.2d 614 (1983). However general consideration should include the natural bonds between the parent and the child, the social stigma or respect afforded a particular name within the community and where the child is of sufficient age, whether the child intellectually and rationally understands the significance of changing his or her name.[18]

Many of these contested minor name change cases have long and bitter histories between father and mother. It is not unusual for father to take the position that mother's petition represents her final act in putting the last nail in father's coffin with respect to father's relationship with the child, contending that mother has for years poisoned the child against the father and blocked father's attempts at partial custody with the child on weekends, vacations, and summers. While the judge does not want to go through the prior custody proceedings between the parties, the judge will be sure to hear about them. Mother, on the other hand, will present what she perceives as father's lack of interest in the child for partial custody and his lack of sending to the child holiday and birthday cards. Surely, the issue of payment or non-payment of child support, whether by court order or otherwise, and any child support contempt proceedings, will be covered.

As with child custody litigation, the preference of the child on the issue of name change is important. The general considerations to be weighed for child preferences, as set forth in this book for custody cases, is applicable in contested name change cases. The chronological age of the child is important. However, the emotional and mental age of the child is important as well. The judge may be faced with a mature seven-year-old or an immature twelve-year-old.

Because child preference in name change cases seems to be so important, there appears to be a reluctance on the part of trial judges in a great number of cases to grant name changes with young children, suggesting

---

[18] *Id.*

that mother can re-apply at a later time when the child is mature and can provide the court with a reasoned preference on the issue.[19]

Following the rationale of the cases provided in the preceding foot-note, and expanding on that rationale, two recently reported trial court cases, both from the same county, denied mothers' petitions, in separate contested cases, to change the surnames of the minor children, who were too young to express a reasoned preference. The opinions therein made clear that the denials of mothers' petitions were without prejudice to the mothers to re-apply at a later time when the children were mature enough to provide the court with a reasoned preference on the issue of name change.[20]

§ 2.3. CITIZENSHIP AND PASSPORTS

Citizenship and the issuance of passports is a legal custody issue. The trial court has the authority to order parties to obtain passports and dual citizenship for the parties' children if it is in the children's best interest.[21]

---

[19] *See* Petition of Falcucci, 50 A.2d 200 (Pa. 1947); Rounick's Petition, 47 Pa. D.&C. 2d 71 (Philadelphia Cty., 1942); Pollock Petition, 31 Pa. D.&C. 2d 514 (Westmoreland Cty., 1963); In re Lavin Name Change Petition, 4 Pa. D.&C. 4th 1 (Dauphin Cty., 1989); In re Niedbabla a/k/a Hickey, 36 Pa. D.&C. 3rd 397 (Allegheny 1985); In re Petition of Stoves, 35 Pa. D.&C. 3d 40 (Westmoreland Cty., 1985); Browne v. Burnett, 28 Pa. D.&C. 3d 533 (Dauphin Cty., 1984); In re Fink, 75 Pa. D.&C. 2d 234; 13 Lycoming 216 (1976); DeVane Petition, 3 Pa. D.&C. 3d 515 (Chester Cty., 1977); In re Bennetch, 13 Pa. D.&C. 2d 308; 50 Berks 70 (1957); In re Bilske, 75 Pa. D.&C. 288, 31 Wash. Co. 102 (1951).

[20] *See* In re: Change of Name of O.J.E., 156 Montg. Co. L. Rep. 229 (2019); In re: Change of Name of L.S., 156 Montg. Co. L. Rep. 415 (2019).

[21] *See* Nagle v. Nagle, 871 A.2d 832 (Pa. Super. 2005); *see also* O.G. v. A.B., 234 A.3d 766 (Pa. Super. 2020) (Superior Court remanded and directed the trial court to determine whether its restriction on the renewal of the children's Russian passports would affect the children's status as dual citizens of the United States and Russia. If such restriction would cause a loss of the children's dual citizenship, the trial court was directed to allow the renewal of the children's Russian passports while requiring additional safeguards to prohibit those passports from being used without prior court approval).

Chapter 3

PHYSICAL CUSTODY

---

§ 3.1. GENERALLY

"**Physical Custody**" is defined as: "The actual physical possession and control of a child."[1]

"**Partial physical custody**" is defined as "The right to assume physical custody of the child for less than a majority of the time."[2]

"**Primary physical custody**" is defined as "The right to assume physical custody of the child for the majority of time."[3]

"**Sole physical custody**" is defined as "The right of one individual to exclusive physical custody of the child."[4]

"**Supervised physical custody**" is defined as "Custodial time during which an agency or an adult designated by the court or agreed upon by the parties monitors the interaction between the child and the individual with those rights."[5]

When entering a custody order, in determining the best interest of the child, the court must consider the factors enumerated in 23 Pa.C.S. § 5328.[6]

---

[1] 23 Pa.C.S. § 5322; *see also*, Pa.R.C.P. 1915.1(b).

[2] *Id.*; *see also*, Pa.R.C.P. 1915.1(b).

[3] *Id.*; *see also*, Pa.R.C.P. 1915.1(b).

[4] *Id.*; *see also*, Pa.R.C.P. 1915.1(b).

[5] *Id.*; *see also*, Pa.R.C.P. 1915.1(b).

[6] *See also* C.B. v. J.B. and M.B. and T.B., 65 A.3d 946 (Pa. Super. 2013) (New custody Act requires that the trial court address each factor in Section § 5328 before deadline by which litigant must file notice of appeal and preferably by time custody order issued or shortly thereafter); A.M.S. v. M.R.C., 70 A.3d 830 (Pa. Super. 2013) (Reasoning in C.B. v. J.B. and M.B. and T.B., 65 A.3d 946 (Pa. Super. 2013) applies to relocation decisions as well); C.M. v. M.M., 215 A.3d 588 (Pa. Super. 2019) (Superior Court held that the trial court erred in failing to consider the best interest factors set forth in 23 Pa.C.S. § 5328(a), where mother's custody petition specifically requested a change in custody of the parties' minor child. The court noted that the record revealed that the trial court did not consider any of the custody factors from § 5328(a) on the record in open court or in a written opinion or order. The court held that even in cases where the trial court merely reaffirms its prior custody order, it is nevertheless making a ruling on a request to change the form of physical custody. The subject order modified the existing order by awarding father "partial physical custody," rather than "supervised physical custody."); M.J.N. v. J.K., 169 A.3d 108 (Pa. Super. 2017) (Superior Court reversed trial court's order modifying equal custody to primary custody to mother, finding that several of the trial court's conclusions regarding the weight of the

However, a court need not address all 16 factors under 5328 when deciding discrete and narrow issues ancillary to a materially unchallenged custody arrangement.[7] Further, under Section 5323(h), parties living separate and apart in the same home may seek a custody order, but the custody order shall be effective only upon either one party physically vacating the residence, or one party being awarded exclusive possession of the home.[8]

With regard to petitions for primary physical custody, the Pennsylvania Supreme Court, in *Van Dine v. Gyuriska*,[9] held that the trial court erred when it appointed a master to conduct a hearing on father's petition for primary physical custody of his three minor children, because the Rules of Civil Procedure entitled father to a *de novo* hearing before a trial judge and pursuant to Pa.R.C.P. 1920.51 a master is only permitted to hear partial custody matters. The trial court abused its discretion when it failed to give father his right to a *de novo* review.[10]

---

certain factors were unreasonable under the circumstances of the case); W.C.F. v. M.G., 115 A.3d 323 (Pa. Super. 2015) (When reasoning by trial court and its analysis of the custody factors are inconsistent with the ruling/custody decision, Superior Court vacated order and remanded case); R.S. v. T.T., 113 A.3d 1254 (Pa. Super. 2015) (Superior Court reversed trial court's order modifying equal custody to primary custody to mother finding that several of the trial court's conclusions were unreasonable under the circumstances of the case); M.E.V. v. F.P.W., 100 A.3d 670 (Pa. Super. 2014) (court cannot incorporate by reference a prior analysis of § 5328 factors, as circumstances may have changed since the prior findings of fact)..

[7] *See* M.O. v. J.T.R., 85 A.3d 1058 (Pa. Super. 2014); *see also* S.W.D. v S.A.R., 96 A.3d 396 (Pa. Super. 2014) (deciding a legal custody dispute such as the selection of a school that does not affect the form of the custody arrangement does not require an analysis of all of the 16 custody factors under Section 5328(a) as it is considered an ancillary issue, but the court must analyze all of the 16 custody factors when changing the form of custody such as the amount of time a parent has custody of the child. A portion of the trial court's order was vacated in this case because of this).

[8] 23 Pa.C.S. § 5323(h).

[9] Van Dine v. Gyuriska, 552 Pa. 122, 713 A.2d 1104 (1998).

[10] *See also* Littman v. Van Hoek, 789 A.2d 280 (Pa. Super. 2001) (the Superior Court held that a custody order awarding primary physical custody to father based on a report and recommendation of a Master was improper, where no statutory authority existed for the Master to hear a case of primary custody. The court declared that the Master did not have the necessary statutory authority to conduct a hearing and make recommendations with respect to father's petition seeking primary physical custody of his son).

LOWER COURT CASES

Lackawanna County

M.S. v. D.R., C.P. Lackawanna County, No. 2014-FC-40889, *aff'd*, Memorandum Decision, No. 1819 MDA 2019 (Pa. Super. April 22, 2020) (The trial court issued an Order and Opinion, which ordered the child to attend school in a particular school district beginning in the 2020-2021 school year. The court cited *S.W.D. v. S.A.R.*, 96 A.3d 396, 400 (Pa. Super. 2014) (a trial court was not required to consider and apply the § 5328(a) custody factors when the court decided where a child should attend school, without changing the form of legal custody). The *S.W.D.* court reasoned that while the choice of where a child will attend school is not trivial and certainly is a major life decision, the court's decision here merely resolved an impasse between the parties who shared the legal right to make this decision. Stated another way, the trial court merely arbitrated a dispute between mother and father regarding schooling, instead of granting one of them the right to make that decision).

§ 3.2. SHARED PHYSICAL CUSTODY

The statutory definition of "shared custody" is as follows: "The right of more than one individual to assume physical custody of the child, each having significant periods of physical custodial time with the child."[11]

The Superior Court has ruled that an award of shared physical custody does not require the equal division of the child's time between both parents.[12]

Historically, the seminal cases regarding shared physical and/or legal custody are *In re Wesley J. K.*, 445 A.2d 1243 (Pa. Super. 1982) and *Wiseman v. Wall*, 718 A.2d 844 (Pa. Super. 1998). In *Wesley* and *Wiseman*, four factors are enumerated which must be considered when awarding shared custody. The four factors are as follows: (1) Both parents must be fit, capable of making reasonable childrearing decisions and willing and able to provide love and care for their children; (2) Both parents must evidence a continuing desire for active involvement in the child's life; (3) Both parents must be recognized by the child as a source of security and love; and (4) A minimal degree of cooperation between the parents must be possible. In *Wesley*, the Superior Court stressed that the minimal degree of cooperation

---

[11] 23 Pa.C.S. § 5322.

[12] Jackson v. Beck, 858 A.2d 1250 (Pa. Super. 2004).

"does not translate into a requirement that the parents have an amicable relationship." In that regard, an award of shared custody has been upheld even though an amicable relationship did not exist between the parents.[13] Also, divorced parents who had the ability to cooperate and isolate their personal conflicts from their roles as parents were awarded shared legal and physical custody.[14] However, in the case of P.J.P. v. M.M., 185 A.3d 413 (Pa. Super. 2018), the Superior Court held that trial courts "need no longer engage in the Wiseman analysis when de-termining whether shared custody is appropriate . . . ." The Superior Court found that the four Wiseman factors are assimilated into the 16 enumerated custody factors of 23 Pa.C.S. § 5328(a). According to the Superior Court: "Section 5328(a), unlike Wiseman, does not require certain findings before a court may award shared custody. Under the current statute, courts must now consider all relevant factors, including the 'the ability of the parties to cooperate,' when making an award of any form of custody, and poor cooperation need not be dispositive." [15]

It has been found that a weekly-rotating shared custody arrangement is not inherently damaging to an infant child, and a shared physical custody schedule was appropriate despite mother having been the primary caretaker.[16] Shared physical custody has been ordered even though the parties lived 120 miles apart.[17] However, the Pennsylvania Superior Court vacated a trial court's order awarding shared physical custody on an alternating week basis where mother resides in North Carolina and father resides in Pennsylvania.[18] Further, where father lived in Philadelphia and mother in St. Louis, annual shifts in physical custody was disapproved by the

---

[13] Murphey v. Hatala, 350 Pa. Super. 433, 504 A.2d 917 (1986).

[14] Brown v. Eastburn, 351 Pa. Super. 479, 506 A.2d 449 (1986).

[15] P.J.P. v. M.M., 185 A.3d 413 (Pa. Super. 2018).

[16] Johnson v. Lewis, 870 A.2d 368 (Pa. Super. 2005) (The court noted that although a "broad reading" of Wiseman v. Wall may suggest such an arrangement is never appropriate because of negative psycholog-ical impact on a young child, the specific facts of each case must always be considered, including evidence of some basic cooperation).

[17] Smith v. Smith, 307 Pa. Super. 544, 453 A.2d 1020 (1982). But see Johnson v. Diesinger, 404 Pa. Super. 41, 589 A.2d 1160 (1990) (court found that the frequency of visits ordered by the trial court, given the long distance appellee had to travel with the children, four to five hours each way over a forty-eight hour period, to be unreasonable).

[18] Durning v. Balent/Kurdilla, 19 A.3d 1125 (Pa. Super. 2011).

Pennsylvania Superior Court, though the parties could retain shared legal custody.[19]

Shared custody does not work in every case and the court should consider all circumstances.[20]

A trial court's modification from shared physical custody to primary physical custody to mother was upheld because though the prior arrangement had in the past inured to the child's benefit, his needs as he grew older and began more involvement in school and other activities, had already, and would continue to, change in ways that would render the constant shifting called for by the schedule no longer workable.[21] However, where a trial court modified father's shared physical custody to partial physical custody due to his making unilateral decisions regarding the child, the Superior Court reversed the trial court and reinstated the shared physical custody order.[22] In some instances, dividing school-year vacations serves the child's best interest.[23]

---

[19] Fisher v. Fisher, 370 Pa. Super. 87, 535 A.2d 1163 (1988).

[20] *See* P.J.P. v. M.M., 185 A.3d 413 (Pa. Super. 2018); Wiseman v. Wall, 718 A.2d 844 (Pa. Super. 1998) (court explained, among other things, that a shared custody arrangement requires communication and a minimal degree of cooperation between the parties); R.S. v. T.T., 113 A.3d 1254 (Pa. Super. 2015) (the Wesley factors should be met for shared custody); Schwarcz v. Schwarcz, 378 Pa. Super. 170, 548 A.2d 556 (1988) (evidence was sufficient to support finding that father was not fit to have physical and legal custody of children and that parties do not demonstrate minimal level of parental cooperation that would support award of shared custody); Mumma v. Mumma, 380 Pa. Super. 18, 550 A.2d 1341 (1988) (Property Settlement Agreement provided for shared custody of son who moved from parent to parent on a weekly basis. However, the weekly transfer of custody became unworkable because of the hostility and lack of cooperation of the parties); In re Wesley J.K., 299 Pa. Super. 504, 445 A.2d 1243 (1982).

[21] Altus-Baumhor v. Baumhor, 407 Pa. Super. 276, 595 A.2d 1147 (1991).; *but see*, R.S. v. T.T., 113 A.3d 1254 (Pa. Super. 2015) (Child's entrance into full-day schooling does not require that one parent must have primary physical custody so that the child may establish routine. Superior Court reversed trial court's decision to modify equal custody order to mother having primary custody during school year).

[22] Andrews v. Andrews, 411 Pa. Super. 286, 601 A.2d 352 (1991).

[23] Smith v. Smith, 337 Pa. Super. 9, 486 A.2d 453 (1984).

In addressing whether to order shared physical custody or primary/ partial physical custody, the lower court is not to base its decision on local customs and practices.[24] It is important to note that there is no presumption either for or against shared custody.[25]

In cases where the parties have equally shared physical custody of the children, the parties may not live in the same school district. When parties cannot resolve a dispute over which school to send their children, the court may decide based on the best interests of the children.[26] "If the court is addressing a request to modify custody in conjunction with the choice of school, the court's choice of school may factor into the court's custody decision. . . . The court's choice of school may in fact require it to modify the parties' physical custody award, in particular "when the parties live far apart, making it impractical for one parent to transport the child to school."[27] "Continuity in an educational environment is an important, but not controlling, factor to be considered by the court in making a school or custody decision, and over-emphasis on this factor may constitute an abuse of discretion."[28]

In the case of *S.S. v. K.F.*, 189 A.3d 1093 (Pa. Super. 2018), a mother requested to relocate to Chester County, Pennsylvania from Bucks County, Pennsylvania. The trial court allowed mother to move to Chester County, but ordered that the children remain in the Pennsbury School District in Bucks County where the mother previously lived but where neither party lived at the time of the trial. As stated by the Superior Court: "[t]he [trial] court therefore allowed Mother to move to Chester County, while purportedly denying a 'relocation,' as the Child Custody Act defines that term."[29] This created a financial burden on the parties who would have to pay

---

[24] B.C.S. v. J.A.S., 994 A.2d 600 (Pa. Super. 2010).
[25] Schwarcz v. Schwarcz, 378 Pa. Super. 170, 548 A.2d 556 (1988) (although under the Custody Act shared custody in appropriate circumstances is desired, there is no presumption favoring shared custody. A trial court has broad discretion in awarding shared custody); In re Wesley, J. K., 299 Pa. Super. 504, 445 A.2d 1243 (1982).
[26] *See* S.W.D. v. S.A.R., 96 A.3d 396, 403-04 (Pa. Super. 2014).
[27] S.S. v. K.F., 189 A.3d 1093 (Pa. Super. 2018) (citing S.W.D. v. S.A.R., 96 A.3d 396, 403-04 (Pa. Super. 2014)).
[28] Id. (citing Fox v. Garzilli, 875 A.2d 1104, 1110 (Pa. Super. 2005)).
[29] S.S. v. K.F., 189 A.3d 1093 (Pa. Super. 2018).

tuition to send their children to the Pennsbury School District. Because neither party requested such relief, and the trial court considered school choice as a custody issue only and made scarce inquiry into the parties' financial situations, the trial court's decision was reversed by the Superior Court. The case was remanded. The Superior Court held: "[o]n remand, unless the parties request otherwise, the court must choose a school that does not financially burden the parties, and it must make its decision by considering both the relocation and custody factors."[30]

The question then arises as to the transportation of the children by the school district. In *Wyland v. West Shore School District*,[31] Mr. Wyland and his ex-wife initially both lived in the same school district and the school district provided transportation for the children from both parties' residences to the private school that they attended. When mother moved out of the school district and the new school district began providing transportation for the children from her home to attend the private school, the school district where father resided discontinued providing transportation from his residence on the mornings that he had custody of the children. Father filed a complaint against his school district seeking injunctive relief, arguing that he was a custodial parent and his children resided in the district under the shared custody arrangement. Father argued that under § 1361 of the Public School Code, the district was obligated to continue transporting his children from his home to the private elementary school. The district contended that it had no duty to bus the children because another school district provided transportation to and from mother's residence, which was located in a different school district. The district argued that the district where mother resided was the district of primary residence and had the sole obligation to provide transportation and only one school district was required to provide transportation under the School Code. The district claimed that the Pennsylvania Department of Education (PDE) applied a "single residency rule" for both enrollment and transportation purposes and that children could not have dual residency. The district claimed that PDE's policy was to provide transportation reimbursement to only one school district. When students of separated parents lived in two different school districts, PDE designates a district as the district of residence and

---

[30] *Id.*
[31] Wyland v. West Shore School District, 52 A.3d 572 (Pa. Cmwlth. 2012).

provides transportation reimbursement to the district in which the child resides. Here, PDE designated mother's district as the district of residence. The trial court granted the preliminary injunction and ordered the district where father resided to resume transportation of the children from father's residence. The district appealed and the Commonwealth Court affirmed the trial court, finding that since the parents had joint and equal custody, the children resided in two different school districts, and the designation of a single school district was not required. Section 1361 of the School Code ensures that if transportation is provided, it is provided to both public and private school students. The court determined that any rule PDE applied to restrict § 1361 was unauthorized.[32]

LOWER COURT CASES

Allegheny County

E.W.H. v. S.M. and M.C., Jr., C.P. Allegheny County, No. FD 17-3448-010 (C.C.P. April 18, 2019), *aff'd* Memorandum Decision, No. 794 WDA 2019 (Pa. Super. October 16, 2019) (Where mother and father were incarcerated and were unable to provide daily care for their child and could not have primary physical custody of the child, it was in the best interests of the child that they did not have shared legal custody of the child. The trial court entered a modified custody order granting paternal grandmother primary physical custody and sole legal custody of the child. Mother and father did not know the child's day-to-day needs well enough to make major decisions on behalf of the child, including, but not limited to, medical, religious and educational decisions. Therefore, it was in the best interest of the child that they do not have shared legal custody of the child).

M.J.R. v. K.S.U., C.P. Allegheny County, No. FD-12-08295-008 (C.C.P. August 21, 2017), *aff'd*, Memo-randum Decision, No. 1333 WDA 2017 (Pa. Super. March 1, 2018) (Trial court recognized that a shared custody award in this circumstance could not be supported by the evidence. The court determined, that because the parties lived approximately 50 minutes from each other, that distance was simply unworka-ble for

---

[32] *See also* Watts v. Manheim Township School District, 84 A.3d 378 (Pa. Cmwlth. 2014) (school districts to provide transportation to both parent's homes in the district); *see also* S.W.D. v. S.A.R., 96 A.3d 396 (Pa. Super. 2014) (deciding a legal custody dispute such as the selection of a school that does not affect the form of the custody arrangement does not require an analysis of all of the 16 custody factors under Section 5328(a) as it is considered an ancillary issue).

shared physical custody during the school year. The court awarded mother primary physical and primary legal custody of the parties' seven-year-old son).

Livingston v. Livingston, 32 D.&C. 4th 182 (Allegheny Co. 1996) (Father, who shared legal custody with the mother, petitioned the court to determine where their children should go to church, attend school and participate in sports. The trial judge ruled that courts cannot assume the responsibility to decide everyday parenting decisions. Citing 23 Pa.C.S. § 5302, the court noted that legal custody is defined as: "The legal right to make major decisions affecting the best interest of a minor child." The court noted that there was not a "major decision" in this case. The dispute was not a concern over what was best for the children, but rather concern over drive-time and the convenience of the adults. The court stated that the underlying reason the father had petitioned the court was not where the children should attend certain functions, but which parent had to drive longer to get them there. The trial judge stated that courts cannot decide whether children should take aspirin or Tylenol® or what type of sunscreen they should wear, or whether to wear a raincoat or a heavy coat on a chilly-drizzly day. The school choice issue, on the other hand, was clearly appropriate for intervention by the court because it constituted a major decision).

Chiarulli v. Hart, 143 P.L.J. 148 (1994) (The parties' significant discord precluded shared legal custody; however, minimal cooperation to implement legal custodial decisions justified an award of shared physical custody. The court remarked that while shared physical custody required minimal cooperation on day-to-day issues, legal custody required that parties reach a consensus on life's potentially crucial and far-reaching decisions. These parties had been singularly unable to accomplish this task for their children. Accordingly, an order of sole legal custody in father and shared physical custody in both parents was entered).

D'Ippolito v. D'Ippolito, C.P. Allegheny Co, No. FD82-11532 (C.C.P. 1990) (Week-to-week shared physical/legal custody granted to mother for educational and medical issues; trial court would not disturb the 6 years of week-to-week shared physical custody; the parties had numerous conflicts regarding schooling, tutoring, religious training, and extracurricular activities. There was a pattern of lack of cooperation and communication between the parents. Judge Strassburger modified the existing legal custody to grant to mother the sole decision-making responsibility for the medical and educational areas while the remaining legal decisions were not removed from the joint domain of the parents. Week-to-week shared physical custody remained unchanged, thus providing the children with the continued stability that they had known for nearly half of their lives).

M.M. v. D.M., C.P. Allegheny Co., No. FD87-08034 (C.C.P. 1989) (Judge Strassburger entered an order for shared legal and physical custody of 4-year-old son upon mother's complaint for custody and father's cross-claim for shared custody. Fourteen-month period of custody, from separation to trial, during which the minor resided primarily with mother, was not controlling. "Mother places great emphasis on the *pendente lite* period. While the status quo certainly cannot be ignored, even a status quo created by the litigation process itself, surely such a status quo does not carry weight of one explicitly or even tacitly agreed to by the parties. Were it otherwise, the courts would be signaling separating parents to grab the child and hold on. . . . To give undue weight to the fourteen month period between separation and trial would be to sanction similar actions rather than the reasoned accommodations parties should be seeking in the best interests of the children").

Berks County

Gentry v. Gentry, C.P. Berks County, No. 12-6715 (C.C.P. 2014) (Trial court denied plaintiff's petition to modify the shared custody arrangement to give her primary physical custody, where the existing shared physical 50/50 custody arrangement was in the best interest of the children and both parents wanted to be immersed in their children's lives. As part of their divorce action, the parties agreed to shared legal custody and shared physical custody on a 50/50 basis. Mother filed a petition to modify custody to give her primary physical custody. She argued that husband did not make himself as available as he should and that as a "stay-at-home" mom, she was more available. The trial court concluded that a shared 50/50 arrangement was in the best interests of the children and denied plaintiff's motion for modification. The court found that both parties were very active with the day-to-day care of the children. Both parents were involved with the children's daily physical, emotional, developmental and educational development. Moreover, the proximity of the parties' residences permitted a liberal interaction between them and the children. The court believed that continuing the liberal interaction with both parents was very beneficial to the well-being of the minor children).

Bryan v. Hunt, C.P. Berks County, No. 09-12004 (C.C.P. 2011) (Trial court held that the parties shall equally share physical custody of their child on a alternating week scheduled where the child had grown accustomed to living in two separate households and both parents were willing and able to properly care for the child. The court noted that after determining that the paramount issue in any custody proceeding is the best interest of the child, the court must also consider numerous factors set forth in the new custody statute, 23 Pa.C.S. § 5328. After evaluating each of the factors, the court concluded that both parents were able and willing to provide day-to-day care for the child and both had flexible work schedules and both wanted to spend as much time with the child as possible. The court noted: "On balance, the overriding factor, the factor that is prevailing throughout the course of the proceedings, is the tremendous attachment this minor child has for each of his parents. This minor child needs to spend as much time with each parent as possible. To restrict access through a partial custody arrangement would result in unnecessary deprivation.").

Berryman v. Berryman, C.P. Berks County, No. 10-14880 (C.C.P. 2011) (Trial court entered a shared custody order in which father was awarded primary physical custody during the school year, where his residence (the former marital residence) in the children's school district would provide a better level of stability and continuity for the children, and mother was awarded primary custody during the summer months, and the noncustodial parent would have three weekends per month and one weeknight. Mother and father had two children during their relationship. When the parties separated, mother moved in with her paramour and his daughter and grandmother while father resided with the children in the family home. Both parties sought primary custody. The court noted that both parties appeared to have a strong bond with the children, were capable parents and had the children's best interest at heart. However, father was best able to provide continuity and stability for the children, as the children could continue in their current school district where they were doing well and the children would live in the same house and maintain the same general lifestyle. The court also questioned the level of stability in mother's household and in her relationship with her paramour.).

Sharp v. Sharp, C.P. Berks County, No. 07-12866 (C.C.P. 2010) (Trial court found that in this case, where both parties sought primary custody, shared physical custody appeared to be appropriate. Both parties sought primary custody of their two minor children. Father argued that mother was not currently capable of adequately performing her duties as a parent, and cited several examples as evidence of mother's inattentiveness. Mother argued that father has made the parties' interaction more difficult, alleging that father often hides information from mother and that father has violent tendencies. The court observed that both parents loved their minor children and had established a strong bond with them. Both appeared to want what was best for the minor children. Both were invested in the minor children's medical and educational needs. Additionally, the parties resided in close proximity and were previously able to informally work out a shared custody agreement. These qualities supported continuing a shared physical custody arrangement).

Seidel v. Feltenberger, 38 D.&C. 4th 520 (Berks Co. 1998) (Trial court ruled that mother and father should have joint legal custody and shared physical custody of their minor daughter, where both parents demonstrated fitness as parents and a willingness to assume parental responsibility for the child. In order to keep the bond with her grandmother and create a stronger one with her father, the court explained, it would be in the child's best interests if the parents had joint custody).

West v. West, 27 D.&C. 4th 9 (Berks Co. 1995) (Where the parties cannot get along, and may never get along, it was proper for the court to refuse father's request for primary or shared custody. *Citing Fisher v. Fisher*, 535 A.2d 1163 (Pa. Super. 1988), the court held that where the natural parents are both fit, the hearing judge must give positive consideration to the parent who had been the primary caretaker).

Reed v. Gerber, 81 Berks L. J. 122 (1988) (Continued joint custody was ordered where the child was accustomed to this arrangement and both parents possessed good nurturing skills. One parent's former addiction to drugs and alcohol had little relevancy in this custody proceeding).

Noecker v. Noecker, 79 Berks L. J. 39 (1986) (Shared custody is appropriate when both parents are 1) capable of making mature childrearing decisions and are willing to provide care and love to the child; 2) desirous of continued active involvement in the child's life; 3) recognized by the child as sources of love and security; and 4) exhibiting a minimal degree of cooperation between themselves. Shared custody does not mean equal time. Instead, it reflects an assurance that the child will have frequent and continued contact with both parents. The onset of school age usually makes equal time impossible. Thus, once a child reaches school age it is usually impossible under shared custody to arrange an equal number of custodial days between the parties).

Bucks County

R.B.H. v. J.R.H., C.P. Bucks County, No. 2017-61201-C (C.C.P. April 15, 2019), *aff'd*, Memorandum Decision, No. 1413 EDA 2019 (Pa. Super. November 12, 2019) (Trial court awarded primary physical custody of the parties' child to mother. The court noted that equally shared physical custody, at a minimum, requires a high degree of collaboration, cooperation, and often compromise, and that was not present in this case. The child was flourishing under the current physical custody schedule and the trial court agreed that the agreed temporary physical custody schedule should be the final order of court).

Warren v. McGrory, 84 Bucks Co. L. Rep. 238 (C.C.P. 2010) (Trial court granted father's petition for shared custody of the parties' 13-year-old son, where father agreed to drop off and pick up the child at school near the home of mother to accommodate additional custody time, a strong bond existed between father and the child, and the child himself indicated a desire for more time with father. Mother objected to shared custody citing the long-standing current arrangement, the negative effect on her other children of less time with the child, and the additional driving time the child would be subjected to. Mother was concerned that the increased time that the child would spend with father would detract from the time he spent with his siblings. In granting father's petition, the trial court noted that in deciding custody, the policy against separation of siblings known as the whole family or family unity doctrine is only one factor, and it is not a controlling factor. The doctrine is more likely to prevail where the children have been reared together prior to separation or divorce of the parents. The court cited with approval *Johns v. Cioci*, 865 A.2d 931, 943 (Pa. Super. 2004) The court also found that mother and father were able to demonstrate sufficient cooperation with each other to allow for a successful shared custody schedule).

Centre County

Wagner v. Wagner, C.P. Centre County, No. 2005-3366 (C.C.P. 2011) (Trial court expanded father's custody to equal shared physical custody based on the stated preferences of the children as well as a means to end father's repeated litigation of the matter.

Mother had primary custody of the parties' three children. Father lived with his wife and her son. Both parents were involved in the children's medical care, education and extracurricular activities. Extensive custody litigation had taken place, most of which had been initiated by father. Two of the children expressed a strong preference to live with father, stating that mother made many negative comments about father and displayed much animosity when it came to matters involving their father. The children also said they would prefer to spend equal time with each parent. Additionally, mother presented over 50 letters father had sent her on custody issues. Father filed a Petition to Modify Custody. The trial court, after considering 23 Pa.C.S. § 5328(a), granted father's petition to modify custody in part and granted him equal shared custody with mother. The court observed that pursuant to 23 Pa.C.S. § 5328(b), in making a custody determination, no party shall receive preference based upon gender in any award granted under the custody statute. The court noted that while the children had thrived socially, emotionally and academically, and that both parents adequately performed their parental duties, it was clear that the prolonged animosity that existed between the parties was not in the children's best interest. While mother expressed her frustration in front of the children in an inappropriate manner, the court noted that father's "litigious, inflexible approach to custody" undoubtedly fueled mother's behavior. The court was convinced that if mother continued as the primary custodian, father would continue litigating this matter, and the children would be stuck in the middle of the dispute. Rather than attempt to control father's behavior, and based on the unambiguous wishes expressed by the children to spend more time with father, the court granted father extended custody to the extent that the children were to alternate weekly between their parents' houses, a 50/50 custody arrangement. The court also noted that this was the recommendation of the guardian *ad litem*).

Strauss v. Strauss, C.P. Centre County, No. 2009-1567 (C.C.P. 2010) (Trial court ruled that the parties should continue to equally share custody of their two children where the children have adapted well to the arrangement and the parties have demonstrated an ability to cooperate regarding the care and scheduling of the children. The trial court declined to change a shared custody arrangement, despite petitions from both parents for primary custody, where the children had been doing well in such an arrangement. Where the children saw both parents as sources of security and love, there was no reason to change an existing shared custody arrangement).

Cumberland County

Seeger v. Seeger, 58 Cumberland L. J. 256 (C.C.P. 2009) (Trial court held that where the evidence produced showed that plaintiff-wife had been the primary caretaker of the child since birth and where defendant's history of involvement in the child's upbringing had been minimal and where defendant had failed to utilize custodial periods available to him, the court correctly declined to impose the 50/50 shared custodial arrangement requested by defendant).

Dauphin County

S.L. v. J.W., 107 Dauph. 85 (C.C.P. 1986) (Trial court held that notwithstanding a distance of 300 miles between the parties, shared legal and physical custody of their child is appropriate where the parties are equally fit as parents).

Greene County

Hillberry v. Eddy, 30 Greene Reports 8 (C.C.P. 2012) (Trial court ruled that in a shared custody arrangement, it was perfectly acceptable for the four-year-old child to attend two pre-school programs and therefore divide his time between both parents. The parties entered a consent order which provided for an equal custody arrangement on a week-on, week-off basis. Travel time between the two locations was approximately one hour, too far for the child to attend the same pre-school. Instead, he spent alternating weeks at each of two different facilities. There was no evidence to suggest that this variety of experience was harmful to him. Father believed the child was doing well under the current arrangement and therefore preferred to maintain the status quo. The trial court agreed with father. The court held that if the choice for a four-year-old child is whether it is more important for him to be in one pre-school program and therefore live with one parent, or be in two pre-school programs and therefore divide his time between two parents, the answer was an easy one. The court believed it was more important that the child spend the maximum amount of time possible with both parents. The court acknowledged that a time will come when the child will have to attend a school full time, but it would address that issue at that time).

Lawrence County

Nero v. Nero, C.P. Lawrence County, No. 11965 of 2007, C.A. (C.C.P. 2011) (Trial court modified the parties' prior custody arrangement to grant father equally shared custody during the summer months but not during the school year. The child required time to adjust to a new environment and school before experiencing a major custody adjustment. After considering the factors set forth in § 5327(b), the court concluded that both parties encouraged frequent and continuing contact between the child and the other parent, were fully capable of caring for the child and were equally likely to maintain a loving and stable relationship with the child. The court did note, however, that there was a high degree of conflict between the parties and ordered the parties to attend co-parenting classes. The court found it difficult to come up with an alternative custody arrangement that would not adversely affect the child's school schedule. The child had just recently enrolled in school and was still adjusting to her school and new environment. The court wanted to give the child more time to adjust before making any more drastic changes to her current schedule).

Buckley v. Feil, C.P. Lawrence County, No. 10797 of 2004, C.A. (C.C.P. 2010) (Trial court found that a continued shared physical and legal custody arrangement was in the best interest of the children despite mother's attempted suicide in 2006. Father argued that mother attempted suicide in November 2006. However, the trial court believed that mother had put those actions in her past and "redirected her focus towards a healthier lifestyle for herself and towards caring for and providing for her children." The court ruled that the best interest of the children would be served by continuing with the existing shared custody arrangements. The court ordered the parties to share primary physical custody on alternating weeks with exchanges taking place on Sunday evenings. The parties shared legal custody and were extended that privilege, and, upon mutual agreement, to modify the terms of the Order in the best interest of the children).

Lebanon County

Kreiser v. Savich, 34 Lebanon Co. Leg. J. 91 (C.C.P. 1996) (Trial court ordered that mother have primary physical custody rather than continuing shared physical custody, because the court firmly believed it was in the child's best interest to establish one parent as having primary physical custody in order to create stability in the child's life which had been missing. In reaching this decision, the court observed that it did not think it was beneficial for a child to be moving back and forth as frequently as this child had, since a child needs a "sense of place and a sense of home.").

L.R.W. v. K.J.W., C.P. Lebanon County, No. 2013-20723, *aff'd*, Memorandum Decision, No. 146 MDA 2018 (Pa. Super. August 3, 2018) (Mother's contention that the trial court should have based its decision on her conduct at the time of the hearing and not what occurred in the past is no longer viable; rather, 23 Pa.C.S. § 5328(a) factors are what controls. Mother argued that the trial court focused on her past behavior and overlooked her testimony about her completion of an inpatient drug and alcohol treatment program, and that she was attending classes at a community college. Mother relied on *Wiseman v. Wall*, 718 A.2d 844, 847 (Pa. Super. 1998), for the proposition that "a parent's ability to care for a child must be determined as of the time of the custody hearing, not as of an earlier time." The *Wiseman* analysis, relied on by mother, was obsolete, citing *P.J.P. v. M.M.*, No. 1586 MDA 2017 (Pa. Super. April 27, 2018).

Lehigh County

Bargher v. Saluta, C.P. Lehigh County, No. 2010-FC-0434 (C.C.P. 2011) (Trial court ruled in favor of equal shared physical custody of the parties' minor child, where the parties had a strong ability to communicate effectively regarding the child's needs, lived very close to each other and were significantly involved in the child's life. Mother petitioned to modify the custody order, seeking a shared physical custody arrangement. The trial court granted mother's petition and found, after considering the applicable factors set forth in 23 Pa.C.S. § 5328(a) in determining the child's best interest, that the parties should equally share physical custody of the child. The court noted that the parties lived only 14 blocks away from each other and both had extended family that lived in the area. Mother also participated in activities with the child and changed her work schedule so that she could be at home with him when she had physical custody. Father was also able to spend significant time with the child during his periods of physical custody and arranged his work schedule to maximize this time. The court observed that, since their separation, the parties had more equally shared physical custody and that the arrangement had worked well for the child. The court found it significant that the parties regularly communicated with each other regarding matters that affected the child. "This case is a breath of fresh air in terms of the co-parenting that is done.").

Hayes v. Hayes, 41 Leh. L. J. 172 (C.C.P. 1984) (Trial court found that a transfer of the pre-school child every four months was in the child's best interests. The matter was also listed for review prior to the time the child would enter the first grade).

Luzerne County

Rodino v. Rodino, 77 Luzerne Leg. Rep. 134 (C.C.P. 1986) (A shared custody arrangement is modified and primary physical custody is given to the mother where the child is about to start first grade and where the mother is at home all day, thus avoiding the need for babysitters during vacations and after school. Although Pennsylvania courts are afforded the option of awarding "shared custody," the settled case law indicates that these arrangements are beneficial in very limited circumstances. Inherent in every shared custody arrangement is a degree of disruption and inconsistency. The court must ask the question as to what is best for the child, not what is best for the parent).

Lycoming County

Shnyder v. Shnyder, C. P. Lycoming County, No. 03-20, 677 (C.C.P. 2006) (Trial court held that even though father may have spent a few extra days with the children over and above the 50% share he had been given, the time spent was so small that it could not serve to decrease his support obligation. Father alleged that the hearing officer erred in failing to rely on evidence presented that the children spent between 50%–65% of their time with father, thus negating his obligation to pay support. "The Master did not err when she failed to consider the Respondent/Defendant's evidence regarding the time the parties' children spent with him above and beyond the court-ordered 50/50 split. Although, pursuant to Pa.R.Civ.P. 1910.16-4(c)(1) the Respondent/Defendant is entitled to a reduction of his basic support obligations to reflect the actual time spent with his children, herein the Master correctly noted, that if she were to allow the Respondent/Defendant, in this situation, to receive credit for less than one week's worth of extra time spent with his children, she would be opening the doors to a flood of litigation seeking credit for the most minuscule amounts of extra time. Moreover, the Master intuitively states that allowing the obligor parent to receive credit for a few extra days would likely deter the obligee/custodial parent to refuse to allow the obligor/non-custodial parent to spend this extra time with the children.").

Montgomery County

J.C. v. J.W., C.P. Montgomery County, No. 2014-00458 (C.C.P. March 23, 2017), *aff'd* Memorandum Decision, No. 1104 EDA 2017 (Pa. Super. October 30, 2017) (The rule in *Wiseman v. Wall*, that parents must have a minimal degree of cooperation in order for a court to award shared custody, contradicts the plain language of the current custody statute, as well as Pennsylvania precedent interpreting that language, which makes clear that courts must merely consider the parties' level of cooperation when making an award of custody, and that poor cooperation need not be dispositive. Upon completing its analysis of the § 5328(a) factors, the court concluded that the child's best interest would be served by maintaining the current shared custody schedule. Trial court explained that it found mother and father did have the minimal degree of cooperation necessary to share custody of their child).

Philadelphia County

Vandegrift v. Martinelli, 28 Phila. 578 (C.C.P. 1994) (Since it is the public policy of the Commonwealth to assure reasonable and continuing contact between the child and both parents after separation, and to ensure that both parents share the rights and responsibilities of child rearing, a shared custody arrangement would be more appropriate. This arrangement would offer the child more time to bond with the father, who clearly demonstrated a willingness to meet his parental responsibilities).

Saplansky v. Saplansky, 19 Phila. 29 (C.C.P. 1989) (Shared custody does not require equal time; frequent and continuing contact may be assured by many custody arrangements other than that which gives each parent an equal number of days or hours with the child; shared custody need not encompass shared physical custody; it may constitute merely shared legal custody that entails joint input in major decisions affecting the child).

Putter v. Newlin, C.P. Philadelphia County (C.C.P. 1986) (Both mother and father were considered fit parents. They were granted shared physical custody, while mother was granted sole legal custody as a result of the parties' inability to communicate with each other).

Collier v. Collier, 14 Phila. 129 (C.C.P. 1985) (Trial courts may fear that shared custody will impose additional burdens on them because they will be drawn into conflicts between parents when they disagree on decisions affecting the child. While theoretically this may be, we trust this will happen only rarely. Giving both parents legal and physical responsibility for the child should attenuate the animosity and the "have not" feeling that so often existed in the non-custodial parent that caused the non-custodial parent to petition regularly for custody).

§ 3.3. CONDITIONS/RESTRICTIONS ON PHYSICAL CUSTODY

In setting forth an order granting partial custody to a non-custodian, the court may, in its discretion, make the continued exercise of the privileges contingent upon compliance with certain conditions as dictated by the best interests of the child. Such conditions must, however, be reasonable and related to the welfare of the child.[33] A restriction will also be imposed if the parties have agreed to a restriction or if a party requesting a restriction shows that without it, partial physical custody will have a detrimental effect on the child.[34] Section 5323(e) provides: "Safety conditions.—After considering the factors under section 5328(a)(2), if the court finds that there is an ongoing risk of harm to the child or an abused party and awards any form of custody to a party who committed the abuse or who has a household member who committed the abuse, the court shall include in the custody order safety conditions designed to protect the child or the abused party."[35]

Conditions may include partial custody away from the custodial domicile;[36] transfer of the child in the absence of specified individuals;[37] or transfer of the child by a neutral third party, telephone or computer-facilitated contact with the child.[38] Where a fear exists that custodial time with the non-custodial parent may in some way result in physical or emotional injury to the child, the court may, before rescinding all privileges, order

---

[33] Dile v. Dile, 284 Pa. Super. 459, 426 A.2d 137 (1981).

[34] See Fatemi v. Fatemi, 489 A.2d 798 (Pa. Super. 1985).

[35] 23 Pa.C.S. § 5323(e); Pa.R.C.P 1915.10(b).

[36] Dena Lynn F. v. Harvey H.F., 278 Pa. Super. 95, 419 A.2d 1374 (1980); Commonwealth ex rel. Ermel v. Ermel, 259 Pa. Super. 219, 393 A.2d 796 (1978); Commonwealth ex rel. Peterson v. Hayes, 252 Pa. Super. 487, 381 A.2d 1311 (1977).

[37] See Dena Lynn F. v. Harvey H.F., 278 Pa. Super. 95, 419 A.2d 1374 (1980).

[38] Steele v. Steele, 376 Pa. Super. 174, 545 A.2d 376 (1988) (to protect child during visitation, visits supervised by Children and Youth Services, and parents directed to attend parenting classes with Children and Youth Services); Scott v. Scott, 240 Pa. Super. 65, 368 A.2d 288 (1976); see also, Pa.R.C.P. 1915.10 Explanatory Comment—2013.

supervised physical custody.[39] If the court does not make a finding that the parent with partial physical custody is unfit or unable to care for the child on his/her own or that the parent posed any threat to the child if left entirely unattended, a restriction of supervised custody may be inappropriate.[40] Without a finding that a parent's home is not equipped to have a child overnight, a restriction against overnight custody may be inappropriate.[41]

In *Luminella v. Marcocci*,[42] the Superior Court ruled that the trial court's order pursuant to Pa.R.Civ.P. 1915.8 requiring mother to submit to random drug testing as a condition of maintaining primary custody did not violate the Fourth Amendment to the United States Constitution. The court noted that the trial court possessed the authority to order drug testing pursuant to Pa.R.Civ.P. 1915.8, which provides for court-ordered physical and mental examinations of children or parties in actions for custody or visitation. The court observed that Pa.R.Civ.P. 1915.8 does not explicitly require that the court articulate a basis of reasonable suspicion—based on evidence presented by the parties—to support an order issued pursuant to its provisions. "In light of mother's minimal reasonable expectation of privacy, the unobtrusiveness of conventional drug testing, and the compelling nature of the state's interest in the protection of children, we find that compelling mother to undergo drug testing is reasonable under the Fourth Amendment, if it applies."

A trial court had authority under the Custody Act to require father to undergo psychotherapy for the purpose of advising the trial court as to whether overnight visitation with the children and father was appropriate.[43]

---

[39] *Id.*; In re Rhine, 310 Pa. Super. 275, 456 A.2d 608 (1983); S.H. v. B.L.H., 392 Pa. Super. 137, 572 A.2d 730 (1990) (the natural father's visitation rights are properly modified to require supervised visits with no provisions for overnight visits, where evidence indicates that the father sexually abused his daughter and that unsupervised and/or overnight visits will have a detrimental effect on the child and previous sexual abuse occurred during overnight visits at home of father's family); Commonwealth ex rel. Ermel v. Ermel, 259 Pa. Super. 219, 393 A.2d 796 (1978); *see also* 23 Pa.C.S. §§ 5328(a)(2) & 5322.

[40] *See* J.R.M. v. J.E.A., 33 A.3d 647 (Pa. Super. 2011).

[41] *Id.*

[42] Luminella v. Marcocci, 814 A.2d 711 (Pa. Super. 2002).

[43] Schwarcz v. Schwarcz, 378 Pa. Super. 170, 548 A.2d 556 (1988).

In *Siliquini v. Kegel-Siliquini*, 786 A.2d 275 (Pa. Super. 2001), the Superior Court denied father permission to pilot his four-year-old daughter to and from visitations in a rented airplane. The court found that the trial court failed to consider all of the factors affecting the child's physical wellbeing. The court noted that father would be renting the planes in which he would be transporting his daughter and thus would not be responsible for the planes' maintenance and upkeep. In addition, because the planes are rentals, father would likely not become intimately familiar with any of the planes in which he would be transporting his daughter.

In situations in which the question of the adverse effects of a meretricious relationship, either heterosexual or homosexual, is presented, the court may mandate that partial custody privileges be exercised out of the presence of the paramour.[44] Such orders specifically name the individuals whose presence the court considers detrimental. An order restricting a mother from exercising partial custody in the presence of any adult male not related to the mother by blood or marriage has been overturned as being unnecessarily broad.[45]

Where a fear arises that the non-custodial party may refuse to return the child in the future, after removing the child from the jurisdiction during a partial custody period in the past, the court may order the non-custodian to post a bond.[46] The amount of the bond will vary in each case but will be of such sum which, in the eyes of the court, is sufficient to assure the return of the child.[47] A bond may likewise be required of a

---

[44] Somers v. Somers, 326 Pa. Super. 556, 474 A.2d 630 (1984) (court found restriction that father's girlfriend not be present during visitations from the hours of 9:30 p.m. to 9:00 a.m. to be reasonable); Pascarella v. Pascarella, 355 Pa. Super. 5, 512 A.2d 715 (1986); Dile v. Dile, 284 Pa. Super. 459, 426 A.2d 137 (1981); Commonwealth ex rel. Drum v. Drum, 263 Pa. Super. 248, 397 A.2d 1192 (1979); Scarlett v. Scarlett, 257 Pa. Super. 468, 390 A.2d 1331 (1978).

[45] Somers v. Somers, 326 Pa. Super. 556, 474 A.2d 630 (1984); *see also* Fatemi v. Fatemi, 339 Pa. Super. 590, 489 A.2d 798 (1985) (restriction prohibiting partial custody in the presence of any male was reformed to only prohibit presence of mother's boyfriend); Dile v. Dile, 284 Pa. Super. 459, 426 A.2d 137 (1981).

[46] Commonwealth ex rel. Logan v. Toomey, 241 Pa. Super. 80, 359 A.2d 468 (1976); deNunez v. Nunez, 220 Pa. Super. 77, 283 A.2d 730 (1971).

[47] deNunez v. Nunez, 220 Pa. Super. 77, 283 A.2d 730 (1971).

non-resident custodian to ensure that the child will be delivered to the non-custodian at the appointed hour.[48] As an alternative to demanding a bond from the non-custodian, the court may require that the visitation take place at a supervised location to prevent the party from absconding with the child. Similarly, a supervised location may be utilized wherever the possibility of physical or emotional harm to the child exists.[49]

In *Ferencak v. Moore*, 300 Pa. Super. 28, 445 A.2d 1282 (1982) the trial court awarded custody of a child to the mother on condition that she not remove the child from the jurisdiction, that the grandparents be allowed visitation, and that she continue to reside with the grandparents.[50]

A conditional custody arrangement whereby the primary custody is given to the mother unless she moves out of Pennsylvania and to the father if she does was found proper where the child's ties are in Pennsylvania;

---

[48] Commonwealth ex rel. Balla v. Wreski, 165 Pa. Super. 6, 67 A.2d 595 (1949); Commonwealth ex rel. Keller v. Keller, 90 Pa. Super. 357 (1927).

[49] *See* S.H. v. B.L.H., 392 Pa. Super. 137, 572 A.2d 730 (1990) (the natural father's visitation rights are properly modified to require supervised visits with no provisions for overnight visits where evidence indicates that the father sexually abused his daughter and that unsupervised and/or overnight visits will have a detrimental effect on the child); M.C. v. R.W., 398 Pa. Super. 183, 580 A.2d 1124 (1990) (the trial court did not abuse its discretion and did not endanger the child by denying one parent's petition to suspend the other parent's unsupervised visitation where it is determined that the parent's allegations of sexual abuse of the child were fabricated; after several restrictive custody orders were awarded and subsequently vacated when the charges of sexual abuse were determined to be unfounded, mother again petitioned the court; after finding the mother's testimony and evidence incredible and "consistently fabricated," the trial court again restored father's partial, unsupervised custody; it also awarded $2,000 in counsel fees to father; the Superior Court affirmed the trial court in all respects and noted that counsel fees can be assessed in cases where a party's actions in conducting litigation are arbitrary, vexatious or in bad faith); In re: Constance W., Appeal of Hoover, 351 Pa. Super. 393, 506 A.2d 405 (1986) (termination of natural father's visitation rights for one year was improper when it was in the best interest of the child to see the father under supervised conditions); Commonwealth ex rel. Williams v. Miller, 254 Pa. Super. 227, 385 A.2d 992 (1978).

[50] *See also* Pappert v. Pappert, 137 P.L.J. 201 (1989); O.G. v. A.B., 234 A.3d 766 (Pa. Super. 2020) (the court found that it was within the trial court's discretion to include the *ne exeat* clause to instruct both parents not to take the children out of the United States without consent of the other parent).

Mother was given 30 days to decide whether she would live in Pennsylvania or out-of-state.[51]

The court held that the father, a Jehovah's Witness, could be barred from forcing his daughter to accompany him on the door-to-door missionary visits attendant to the practice of that faith.[52] While the court did not forbid the father from discussing his beliefs with the child, the court found that the draping of the whole of his beliefs over the child would directly conflict with the custodial mother's Catholic teachings and would produce a sufficient danger of mental disorientation to justify the restrictive order.[53]

The fact that a child is being breast-fed does not automatically preclude unsupervised custody of the father.[54]

LOWER COURT CASES

Allegheny County

Donna S. v. Bernard S., 138 P.L.J. 86 (C.C.P. 1989) (Trial court can bar supervised visitation only if the evidence clearly and convincingly establishes that such visitation would be contrary to the child's welfare. Where previous court proceedings established that a father has sexually abused his daughter but testimony by father's psychologist indicates that his attitude has changed and expert testimony fails to establish by clear and convincing evidence that visitation will gravely threaten the daughter, strictly supervised visitation by father will be permitted. The court allowed supervised visitation under strict guidelines for the purpose of determining whether a relationship between the father and the child could be established).

Clarke v. Clarke, C.P. Allegheny County (C.C.P. 1983) (Trial court declined to require the father to accompany the children on a flight from Pittsburgh to Los Angeles for summer vacation as they were only five years of age and the airline had adequate services for the supervision of unaccompanied minors).

---

[51] Lozinak v. Lozinak, 390 Pa. Super. 597, 569 A.2d 353 (1990).
[52] Morris v. Morris, 271 Pa. Super. 19, 412 A.2d 139 (1980).
[53] *Id.*
[54] *See* J.R.M. v. J.E.A., 33 A.3d 647 (Pa. Super. 2011).

Berks County

Hallock v. Fatzinger, C.P. Berks County, No. 07-13733 (C.C.P. 2011) (Trial court entered a custody order restricting father from leaving Pennsylvania with the parties' minor child without mother's agreement or further court order. Mother expressed concern that father would take the minor child and move to some undisclosed location, and that father did not have the capacity to properly care for the child. Father acknowledged some of mother's concerns, but also stated that he had completed anger management counseling and had made strides to change his behavior. Father argued that he should not be required to have his visits with the minor child supervised. The trial court acknowledged that an award of partial custody/visitation should generally not contain any restrictions. "However, restrictions may be imposed when the party requesting the restrictions shows that without it, partial custody will have a detrimental impact on the child. Even so, restrictions must be phrased in the least intrusive language reasonably needed to safeguard the child." The court noted that while father exhibited a lack of discipline, the evidence did not support the conclusion that father would cause any harm to the child. It was also unlikely that he would relocate from the jurisdiction).

Valeriano v. Krasowski-Gegenheimer, C.P. Berks County, No. 04-1791 (C.C.P. 2010) (The sole issue at trial was whether the trial court should impose a supervised-only restriction on the child's partial custody time with father, as mother requested. Mother argued that the overwhelming testimony and expert testimony demonstrated that father had significant psychological problems and therefore should be placed under supervised visitation with his son. Trial court refused to impose such a restriction, as it was not in the child's best interest. The court found that mother's request that the child be allowed to spend time with his father under supervised visitation conditions was not supported by the expert's report and testimony. The court noted that with regard to restrictions such as supervised visits, the Superior Court stated in *Fatemi v. Fatemi*, 489 A.2d 798 (Pa. Super. 1985) that "a restriction will be imposed if the parties have agreed to a restriction or if the party requesting a restriction shows that without it, partial custody will have a detrimental impact on the child." The court found that in this case, the evidence established that father's personality included some "major character flaws" and a crude sense of humor. However, the court found that despite the specific incidents cited by mother, it was not shown at the time of the custody trial that father posed any danger to the child's safety or that having partial custody time with father was detrimental to the child).

Aldana v. Miller, C. P. Berks County, No. 07-5851 (C.C.P. 2009) (Trial court determined that father should no longer be subject to supervised visitation and that father should have partial physical custody of the parties' child. Mother alleged that father could not properly care for the child, that he did not have genuine concern for the child, and that he sought expanded custody only to antagonize mother. Father had visitation sporadically, with all visitation supervised by mother or someone on her behalf, or at father's home through Kids First Agency. Father believed that he was capable of being a responsible parent and denied threatening mother. His fiancée testified that while she was at work and her children were not in school, father looked after the children responsibly. At issue was whether father should be permitted partial custody and whether his visits should continue to be supervised).

Frankenberg v. Frankenberg, 83 Berks L. J. 95 (C.C.P. 1990) (In order to protect the children, the court prohibited the father from using drugs and alcohol during his periods of partial custody. This restriction was based on the father's past substance abuse; if father were to drink or use drugs during the specified period in the order which prohibits such conduct, then the court would find that a serious violation of the order had occurred and would proceed accordingly).

Brown v. Brown, 83 Berks L. J. 35 (C.C.P. 1990) (A petition to modify a custody order to require child to fly to father's home in Illinois, instead of father being required to drive the child there and back, is granted; however, the father must accompany the child on all flights).

Bucks County

Orozco v. Wilson, C.P. Bucks County, No. A06-07-61401-C (C.C.P. 2011) (Trial court reduced father's custody rights to limited periods of supervised visitation where he made allegations of child abuse against mother that were intended to terminate her relationship with the child and were detrimental to the child. The issue before the court was whether the child was being physically, psychologically or emotionally abused by mother, mother's boyfriend or any other person or whether these accusations were false. The trial court found that the child was not being abused and that father was merely attempting to terminate the child's relationship with mother. Accordingly, the court granted mother's petition for sole legal and physical custody, and granted father limited supervised visitation. The court determined that the three expert witnesses father presented to substantiate his allegations of abuse were not credible. Each expert's testimony was contradicted by other evidence. Each expert witness demonstrated clear bias in favor of father and against mother. The court also found that the factual evidence offered by father did not support his allegations).

Stephon v. Malmad, 68 Bucks Co. L. Rep. 132 (C.C.P. 1996) (A trial court refused to limit a non-custodial father's visitation rights to accommodate the mother's wish to breast-feed her child until age three. While acknowledging the benefits from breast feeding, the court noted the policy favoring the non-custodial parent's right to a meaningful relationship with a child and the recognized benefits that flow from frequent contact with both parents. The trial judge found that the mother's request was an unwarranted limitation in the face of the father's justifiable request for a reasonable order assuring extensive unsupervised contact with his daughter. In weighing the benefits of nursing the child against the custodial rights of father, the court found no evidence that would suggest harm to the child from modestly limited access to breastfeeding. Further, the court strongly considered the benefit to the child of bonding with her father during her early life, which the court determined could not occur while visitation took place in mother's home or office).

Carbon County

Kuzo v. Kuzo, 15 Carbon Co. L. J. 35, No. 97-0640 (C.C.P. 1998) (Trial court refused father immediate partial physical custody of his eleven-year-old daughter because father had no contact with her for over eight years and daughter preferred not to see father. The court determined that daughter's best interest was best served by having father come back into daughter's life in a gradual, non-physical way over a period of time. The court ordered father's contacts be limited to telephone communication, letters, and cards until daughter receives psychological counseling and an appropriate phased-in visitation schedule is established).

Delaware County

Heron v. Rosso, 33 D.&C. 4th 179 (Del. Co. 1996) (Trial court ruled that a change in a father's visitation from all day Saturday to a period from Saturday evening through Sunday evening did not violate First Amendment rights, although part of the court's purpose was to prevent the visitation from being dominated by attendance at religious Seventh Day Adventist services. The court cited the child's best interests as the justification for the change. The court explained that father's time with his daughter during his one-day-per-week visitation was dominated by his religious pursuits. As a result, the child's best interests were not being served and the child was deprived of the opportunity to build a relationship with father. In this case, the court noted, although the temporary order effectively prevented father from taking the child to Saturday morning services, it was not designed to frustrate father's religious beliefs nor did it place any restrictions upon father's desire to expose his child to his religion. At no time did the court pass any judgment as to the type of religion to which the child was exposed or otherwise favor either parent's religion. Further, the court never placed any restrictions upon either parent taking the child to services or discussing religious beliefs. Instead, the court held, the custody schedule provided father with an opportunity to build a broader relationship with his daughter that was not centered exclusively upon religious beliefs).

Fayette County

Lucas v. Lucas, 54 Fayette Leg. J. 11 (C.C.P. 1990) (Where a custodial parent believes that the non-custodial parent is sexually abusing their children and obtains supporting examinations by medical professionals, a refusal to allow continued visitation does not constitute contempt of a custody order. The non-custodial parent will be limited to supervised visits and will be required to undergo psychiatric counseling for treatment of sexual aggression).

Lancaster County

Ziegler v. Ziegler, C.P. Lancaster County, No. CI-04-08530 (C.C.P. 2011) (Father failed to present any evidence to show that his behavior had improved from the time the court initially required supervised visitation. Supervision will be removed from the visitation arrangement only if the conditions that led to supervision are remedied and the best interests of the child can be served by removing supervision. Mother filed a petition for contempt requesting that father be awarded only supervised visitation. A custody evaluator advised a therapeutic supervised visitation program and both parties agreed to participate. Father subsequently filed for modification, seeking removal of supervised visitation. The trial court denied father's petition for modification and ruled that father continued to require supervised visitation. The court noted that when he had supervised visitation, father consistently violated the rules in the agreement he had signed. He engaged in physical contact with the child and discussed mother's activities with the child. The court found it apparent that father's conduct had not improved and that supervised visitation was still necessary. Although recognizing that the child loved and missed her father, the court believed that father's need for professional help was such that the child must be protected from him).

Hashem v. Hashem, 72 Lanc. L. Rev. 29 (C.C.P. 1989) (During periods of father's custody, he is ordered to surrender his passports as a safeguard against his absconding with the child to Jordan, a country not signatory to the Hague Convention, and where mother would be powerless to enforce the court order; court further ordered that father provide certification that no duplicate passport has been issued and that the custody order must be recorded with the United States Department of State to assure that no passport shall be issued to the child without permission of the court).

Lehigh County

Yampol v. Andrini, C.P. Lehigh County, No. 2007-FC-0884 (C.C.P. February 29, 2012) (Trial court granted father's petition to modify custody and awarded primary physical custody of the parties' child to father due to mother's husband's alcoholism. When determining primary custody of a child, the safety of the child's environment is of prime importance. Mother's husband suffered from alcoholism and appeared to be under the influence of alcohol when he testified at trial. Husband had several alcohol-related convictions that triggered application of 23 Pa.C.S. § 5329 of the new Custody Act. Here, mother's husband was a member of the same household as mother. His DUI was one of the enumerated offenses listed in § 5329. Based on this and other alcohol-related offenses, mother's husband's appearance on the witness stand and the testimony about his frequent intoxication, the court concluded that mother's husband had a serious, active alcohol problem which had a direct adverse impact on the child at issue, particularly since he had driven him in a car on occasions. The court found that under 23 Pa.C.S. § 5329(c), mother's husband, as a household member, must undergo a drug and alcohol evaluation and then proceed with counseling which is deemed to be necessary. Until that happened or mother changed residences, appropriate restrictions were placed on mother's custody to protect the child. Accordingly, primary physical custody was awarded to father, but the court left the door open for the child's return to mother if she were to change her living circumstances).

Montgomery County

Tague v. Edens, C.P. Montgomery County, No. 91-00166 (C.C.P. 1998) (Trial court denied defendant's Petition for Modification of a Custody Order and held that supervised visitation shall continue until defendant undergoes further psychiatric evaluation and a doctor suggests unsupervised visitation is warranted).

Rebert v. Manildo, C.P. Montgomery County, No. 95-12474 (C.C.P. 1996) (Trial court held that where father made serious threats that he possessed a gun and would kill child and himself as well as threats that he would remove the child from mother and secret the child in a foreign country, and where father was subject to impending federal deportation proceedings and criminal proceedings, the court did not commit a gross abuse of discretion when it granted father supervised visitation of the child. The court concluded that mother appropriately and wisely protected the child by providing supervised visitation for father in grandmother's home. The court reviewed supervised visitation as the only prudent way to protect the best interests of the child, which override the interest of either parent. The court was satisfied that a healthy, safe, secure, and overall appropriate environment existed in grandmother's home for supervised visits and was preferred, in the child's interests, to the sterile environment of a governmental agency).

York County

D.E.M. v. T.A.M., 111 York Co. L. Rep. 90 (C.C.P. 1997) (Trial court ruled that mother have only supervised visitation with the children provided that her therapist and the children's therapist agree after mother progresses to a level that is appropriate. After a lengthy hearing, the court confirmed custody in father, finding credible the evidence of sexual abuse while children were with mother).

§ 3.4. ASPECTS OF PHYSICAL CUSTODY

§ 3.4.1. Generally

In approaching a child custody case, there are several general principles which are part of the best interest of the child analysis.

Initially, the fact-finder must focus on the particular facts of each case as they exist at the time of the hearing on a case-by-case basis.[55] Evidence

---

[55] B.C.S. v. J.A.S., 994 A.2d 600 (Pa. Super. 2010); M.A.T. v. G.S.T., 989 A.2d 11 (Pa. Super. 2010); Parks v. Parks, 284 Pa. Super. 400, 426 A.2d 108 (1981); Appeal of Dona Schidlmeier, 344 Pa. Super. 862, 496 A.2d 1249 (1985) (The court held that the child's best interest must control in a proceeding to change a minor's surname); In re Leskovich, 253 Pa. Super. 349, 385 A.2d 373 (1978).

of past actions or characteristics are relevant only insofar as they affect the current welfare of the child or provide the court with a pattern of conduct likely to extend into the future.[56] The court's personal opinions and/ or local norms or practices should not be applied in deciding the case.[57]

In terms of the type of evidence which will be considered by the court, it may be safely said that in addition to the factors enumerated under 23 Pa.C.S. § 5328(a), a court will take into account any factor which can be shown to have an effect on the welfare of the child.[58] Also, while the reasoning processes used to siphon through the testimony are unique to each judge, the seriousness involved in deciding most custody cases is shared by all. As one commentator noted:

"[A] Judge agonizes more about reaching the right result in a contested custody than any other type of decision he renders.

The lives and personalities of at least two adults and one child are telescoped and presented to him in a few hours. From this capsule presentation he must decide where lie the best interests of the child, or, very often, which parent will harm the child least. The judge's verdict is distilled from the hardest kind of fact-finding. From sharply disputed

---

[56] Commonwealth ex rel. Meyers v. Meyers, 468 Pa. 134, 360 A.2d 587 (1976); Snarski v. Krincek, 372 Pa. Super. 58, 538 A.2d 1348 (1988) (where the parent's past reveals character traits that undermine the ability or willingness of that parent to provide for his child, the court can rightfully conclude that the risk that the past will be repeated justifies an award of custody to a third party if there is no evidence that the parent's past traits have somehow changed so as to produce new parenting abilities and concerns; *Accord* Michael T.L. v. Marilyn J.L., 525 Pa. Super. 42, 525 A.2d 414, 418 (1987) (the unsettled past of the custodian parent's life should be emphasized only where that instability has had an ongoing negative effect on the child); Commonwealth ex rel. Gorto v. Gorto, 298 Pa. Super. 509, 444 A.2d 1299, 1301 (1982) (the primary concern in custody matters lies not with the past but with the present and future. Facts as of time of hearing are the foundation for determination of the court. Past conduct is not relevant unless it will produce an ongoing, negative effect upon the child's welfare).

[57] B.C.S. v. J.A.S., 994 A.2d 600 (Pa. Super. 2010); M.A.T. v. G.S.T., 989 A.2d 11 (Pa. Super. 2010).

[58] In re Lewis, 396 Pa. 378, 152 A.2d 666 (1959); *see also* 23 Pa.C.S. § 5328.

evidence, he must predict the future conduct of the parents on his appraisal of their past conduct."[59]

A major factor to be considered in the best interests determination is an examination of the individuals who will be responsible for the care of the child at each of the proposed custodial settings. Immediately coming to mind is the threshold determination of each party's parental fitness.

In assessing a party's fitness, all relevant aspects of the litigant's personal history will be evaluated by the trial court and a determination made. Assuming both parties to be fit, the evidence utilized to make that determination will be factored in with the various other elements and the best interests of the child will be established.

In analyzing parenting capabilities of the parties, the court must focus on conditions as they exist at the time of the hearing.[60] Past actions are not, however, entirely overlooked and may have a major role as indicators of possible future conduct.[61]

In addition to timeliness, any conduct or trait which is to have relevance to the determination must be shown to have an effect on the best interests or welfare of the child.[62]

It should also be noted that the factors discussed in this section are not exclusive but merely represent those issues most frequently litigated. In

---

[59] Botein, *Trial Judge* 273 (1952).

[60] Nancy E.M. v. Kenneth D.M., 316 Pa. Super. 351, 462 A.2d 1386 (1983); McAnallen v. McAnallen, 300 Pa. Super. 406, 446 A.2d 918 (1982) (court placed emphasis on development from teenaged mother, who made a lot of mistakes, to well-organized, competent, 22-year-old mother). Parks v. Parks, 284 Pa. Super. 400, 426 A.2d 108 (1981); In re Leskovich, 253 Pa. Super. 349, 385 A.2d 373 (1978); Augustine v. Augustine, 228 Pa. Super. 312, 324 A.2d 477 (1974). *See also* In re Adoption of Michael J.C., 326 Pa. Super. 143, 473 A.2d 1021 (1984) (past misconduct insufficient ground for termination of parental right where parent is presently fit).

[61] Snarski v. Snarski, 538 A.2d 1348 (Pa. Super. 1988); Commonwealth ex rel. Bendrick v. White, 403 Pa. 55, 169 A.2d 69 (1961); *see* Commonwealth ex rel. Murphy v. Walters, 258 Pa. Super. 418, 392 A.2d 863 (1978); Commonwealth ex rel. Burke v. Birch, 169 Pa. Super. 537, 83 A.2d 426 (1951).

[62] Commonwealth ex rel. Myers v. Myers, 468 Pa. 134, 360 A.2d 587 (1976); Commonwealth ex rel. Steiner v. Steiner, 257 Pa. Super. 457, 390 A.2d 1226 (1978).

general, any factor which impacts the best interest of the child and/or bears either favorably or unfavorably on the parental fitness of a contestant will be received by the court.[63]

LOWER COURT CASES
Berks County

Andrzjewski v. Andrzjewski, 91 Berks Co. Leg. J. 61 (C.C.P. 1998) (Trial court ruled that one of the factors which a court must consider in forming a custody order is the willingness of the parties to encourage frequent and continuous contact between both parents and the rest of the immediate family, citing *Robinson v. Robinson*, 538 Pa. 52, 645 A.2d 836 (1994).

Delaware County

Serody v. Maine, 80 Del. Co. Rep. 153 (C.C.P. 1993) (Custody cases are to be decided on the basis of the best interest of the child, on a case-by-case basis, considering all factors that legitimately have an effect on the child's physical, intellectual, moral, and spiritual well-being).

Lehigh County

T.H. v. T.H. N/K/A T.D. No. 2015-FC-0976 (C.C.P. July 14, 2017), *aff'd*, Memorandum Decision, No. 2620 EDA 2017 (Pa. Super. April 10, 2018) (Mother resided with stepfather in El Paso, Texas. Father lived near Allentown, Pennsylvania. The trial court awarded father primary physical custody of the child, gave mother partial physical custody during the child's summer and spring breaks, and half of each winter vacation, and awarded shared legal custody. The court explained that it found that father was more likely to encourage contact between mother and child, and that mother had violated the parties' custody schedule on several occasions. The court also found that father offered the child a more stable life than mother. The court emphasized that it had designed its custody order, in part, to reduce the amount of travel that the child would face, and to provide primary custody to father, as it found these to be in the child's best interest).

---

[63] 23 Pa.C.S. § 5328; In re Lewis, 396 Pa. 378, 152 A.2d 666 (1959); *see also* MOMJIAN & PERLBERGER, PENNSYLVANIA FAMILY LAW, § 5.1.3(a) (1978).

Somerset County

Gramann v. Cole, 51 Somerset Leg. J. 213 (C.C.P. 1992) (Best interests standard is an indefinite one, and the court must avoid mechanical determinations by analyzing the particular facts and circumstances of each case).

Peterman v. Wellington, 52 Somerset Leg. J. 62 (C.C.P. 1993) (A child's best interest lies in preserving and nurturing those relationships which are meaningful, while avoiding situations which might prove harmful).

§ 3.4.2. Religion and Religious Training

The courts of the Commonwealth have long held that, although not controlling, the religious training of a child is a matter of serious concern and should be considered in rendering a custody order.[64] In keeping with the dictates of the First Amendment to the United States Constitution, courts have refrained from basing custody decisions on the merits of one faith over those of another.[65] Thus, where both contestants have demonstrated their desire to promote the religious education of the child, each in his or her own faith, courts will assume a neutral stance as to this issue and will permit religious training to follow custody.[66]

---

[64] Commonwealth ex rel. Bendrick v. White, 403 Pa. 55, 169 A.2d 69 (1961); Egelkamp v. Egelkamp, 362 Pa. Super. 269, 524 A.2d 501 (1987) (although courts may not render value judgments on the merits of a particular religious view or belief, they may properly examine the effect that those views or beliefs have on the development of a child involved in a custody dispute); K.L.H. v. G.D.H., 318 Pa. Super. 330, 464 A.2d 1368 (1983); Morris v. Morris, 271 Pa. Super. 19, 412 A.2d 139 (1979); Commonwealth ex rel. Bordlemay v. Bordlemay, 201 Pa. Super. 435, 193 A.2d 848 (1963); Commonwealth ex rel. Shamenek v. Allen, 179 Pa. Super. 169, 116 A.2d 336 (1955).

[65] Morris v. Morris, 271 Pa. Super. 19, 412 A.2d 139 (1979); Commonwealth ex rel. Ackerman v. Ackerman, 204 Pa. Super. 403, 205 A.2d 49 (1965); Commonwealth ex rel. Sabath v. Mendelson, 187 Pa. Super. 73, 143 A.2d 665 (1958).

[66] Rinehimer v. Rinehimer, 336 Pa. Super. 446, 485 A.2d 1166 (1984) (court's visitation schedule, which did not provide for partial custody by father on Sunday mornings and thus effectively precluded him from taking the boys to Lutheran services, was not error. In this case, mother took the boys to Catholic services, father had no objection to the boys being raised in the Catholic faith, and father was in no other way prevented from exposing them to the tenets of his faith); Commonwealth ex rel. Ackerman v. Ackerman, 204 Pa. Super. 403, 205 A.2d 49 (1965);

In *Zummo v. Zummo*,[67] the Superior Court provided an excellent and detailed historical review and analysis of religious issues related to custody and the impact of a dispute over religious upbringing on the issues of custody and visitation.

Zummo involved a controversy between a mother who was a devout and observant Jew and a father who was Catholic in upbringing but was not particularly devout or practicing. The trial court found that the parties had orally agreed to raise their children in the Jewish faith and that in fact the children had been so raised, actively participating and observing their mother's faith. The parties stipulated that primary physical custody was in the mother, with shared legal custody. The only issues in the case were whether father could be prohibited from attending Catholic services with the children during his periods of visitation and whether father could be compelled to arrange for the children's attendance at Sunday School at the synagogue during those weekends when they were with him. The trial court ordered father to refrain from taking the children to any services "contrary to the Jewish faith" and ordered him in addition to arrange for their Sunday School attendance. The Superior Court, per Judge Kelly, reversed the first part of the order and affirmed the second part.

In reversing the order prohibiting father from attending Catholic services with the children, Judge Kelly found (1) the oral prenuptial agreement was unenforceable (too vague) over the objection of either party; (2) during periods of visitation, the non-custodial parent has parental authority which must not be unduly restricted; (3) this parental authority is augmented by rights established in the First Amendment regarding religious freedoms; (4) only when the objecting parent can show a "substantial threat" of "physical or mental harm to the child" can restrictions on this freedom be imposed; (5) it was constitutionally impermissible for a court to consider the presumed interests of the children in "spiritual stability" or to assess the parents' relative devoutness; (6) it was further constitutionally impermissible to determine whether Judaism and Christianity constituted "contrary" beliefs; (7) speculation by a parent or experts regarding potential emotional harm from exposure

---

[67] Zummo v. Zummo, 394 Pa. Super. 30, 574 A.2d 1130 (1990).

to two religions will not support restricting the non-custodial parent's parental authority and free exercise rights.

In affirming the trial court's order directing father to present the children at synagogue for Sunday School, Judge Kelly noted that both parents have the right to inculcate religious beliefs and found that father's visitation rights were not interfered with given the narrowly drawn order and the fact that mother was willing to have father "make up" any lost custody time that might occur as a result of the order. The court rejected the dicta in *Morris v. Morris*, 271 Pa. Super. 19, 412 A.2d 139 (1979) and ruled that a parent who objects to the course of religious indoctrination pursued by the other parent after a divorce and who seeks a restriction must:

" . . . demonstrate by competent evidence that the belief or practice of the party to be restricted actually presents a substantial threat of present or future physical or emotional harm to the particular child or children involved in absence of the proposed restriction, and that the restriction is the least restrictive means adequate to prevent the specified harm."

Under *Zummo*, the standard requires proof of a "substantial threat," and not speculation by parents and experts as to potential harm. While the substantial threat may be in the future, "mere disquietude, disorientation, or confusion arising from exposure to 'contradictory' religions would be patently insufficient" to justify the restriction. The court concluded that stress upon a child is not always harmful, nor is it always to be avoided and protected against. If stress is presented to a trial court, the court must address the question of the causation of stress. It must result from the religious upbringing dispute. If the stress is traceable to numerous other factors inherent in the divorce/custody process, it is not the kind of stress that will support restrictions.

Consequently, each parent has the lawful authority to pursue whatever course of religious indoctrination that the parent deems appropriate during the period of lawful custody or visitation. While a parent's religious freedom may yield to other compelling interests, it may not be bargained away. A child's best interests with regard to the spiritual aspect of religion cannot be determined by any government authority. The government is inherently and constitutionally incompetent to determine whether stability or instability in religious beliefs would be in the best interest of the child. Courts constitutionally cannot have any interest in the stability of a child's religious beliefs. Neither a determination of, nor consideration of, a parent's relative devoutness or involvement with religious activities can have any place in a custody determination nor may be considered in awarding primary physical custody. The appellate court in *Zummo* found a material and controlling distinction between prohibiting the father's affirmative act of taking his children to Catholic services and the direction that the father present the children at synagogue for Sunday School during his periods of partial custody. The Superior Court stated that both parents have the right to inculcate religious beliefs in their children and the court may accommodate one parent's rights with a directive such as exists in this case. For an analysis of the *Zummo* decision, *see* Bertin, Emanuel A., "Religious Restriction in Custody Order Struck Down," 11 *Pennsylvania Family Lawyer* 143 (June, 1990); Ladov, David L., "Parents Have a Constitutional Right to Inculcate Their Religious Beliefs Upon Their Children," 11 *Pennsylvania Family Lawyer* 167 (August 1990).

In *Boylan v. Boylan*,[68] the Superior Court held that religion, while a consideration in custody cases, is not a determinative factor in awarding custody of children. Here, the father appealed the trial court's order, which awarded primary physical custody to mother, arguing in part that the trial court failed to give requisite consideration to the religious upbringing and training of the children. The father was Catholic and the children had been baptized Catholic, attended Catholic schools, and attended Catholic services regularly. After separation, mother began to take children to a Methodist church and failed to continue the children's Catholic training. A Catholic priest testified regarding the potential for confusion for the children. The trial court stated that although religion appeared to have significant importance to the children, nevertheless primary physical custody should remain in the mother. The trial court considered the children's religious background, but refused to make this one factor alter its determination of what it considered to be in the best interest of the children. The trial court properly considered a stable home

---

[68] Boylan v. Boylan, 395 Pa. Super. 280, 577 A.2d 218 (1990).

environment, the primary caretaker role of the mother, and preference of the children in its custody decision. The Superior Court affirmed. The court noted that religion is "important" but "not determinative." It is only one factor in assessing the overall best interests of the child. The Superior Court cited established case law in this area, which suggested that where both parties demonstrate a desire to promote the religious upbringing of the child, each in his or her own faith, the courts must adopt a neutral stance. Thus, the father was not entitled to primary custody based on the similarity of his religious faith to that of the children. The court's inquiry is limited to whether the religious practice has any detrimental effect on the development of the children. For an analysis of the *Boylan* decision, *see* Bertin, Emanuel A., "Custody–Importance of Religious Training Revisited," 11 *Pennsylvania Family Lawyer* 178 (October, 1990). A slight preference has, however, been expressed to the effect that, where possible, a child's religious instruction should continue in the faith in which the child received early training.[69]

Similarly, in *Stolarik v. Stolarik*,[70] the Superior Court held that, while religion is an important matter and should be given consideration in child custody matters, it is not determinative. In *Stolarik*, father appealed a trial court's order awarding custody to mother on the basis of the court's disapproval of father's fundamentalist Christian beliefs and enrollment of the children in a Christian school. The Superior Court reversed. Again, the Court discussed the importance of religion in custody matters but noted that it is not determinative. The Superior Court stressed the impropriety and indeed the impossibility of a court rendering value judgments on the relative worth of varying religious beliefs. The inquiry for the court, therefore, is confined to assessing whether the child's best interests are detrimentally affected. In stating this standard, *Stolarik* cites *Morris v. Morris*, 271 Pa. Super. 19, 412 A.2d 139 (1979), the seminal case in this area prior to *Zummo*. Here, the Superior Court found that the trial court had impermissibly interposed its own value judgments regarding the detrimental impact of religion on the children and that these judgments were unsupported by the record. The appellate court found no

---

[69] Commonwealth ex rel. Bendrick v. White, 403 Pa. 55, 169 A.2d 69 (1961).
[70] Stolarik v. Stolarik, 401 Pa. Super. 171, 584 A.2d 1034 (1991).

evidence that father practiced his beliefs at the expense of his children or that their education or upbringing was in any way deficient or detrimental. Therefore, the trial court abused its discretion in taking the children from the father's home and awarding custody to mother on basis of the court's disapproval of father's fundamentalist Christian beliefs and his enrollment of the children in a Christian school; the children lived with father for approximately five years after mother left home, father was an exemplary parent, and there was no evidence to support trial court's belief that children were deprived of social and educational opportunities or restricted in artistic expression or individual development of logic because of their attending the religious school.

In *Luminella v. Marcocci,* 814 A.2d 711 (Pa. Super. 2002), the Superior Court held that father's religious beliefs did not affect the custody determination where no showing was made that the beliefs had a negative impact on the children. The court noted that unless it can be shown that a parent's conduct has had harmful effects on a child, it should have little weight in making a custody decision. "Mother's exhortations that the children did not like their father's practice of Neo-paganism do not lead inevitably to the conclusion that father's religious practices were harming the children."

In *Frank v. Frank,* 833 A.2d 194 (Pa. Super. 2003), the Superior Court ruled that a court may interfere with a parent's installation of religious beliefs only when it poses a threat of physical or emotional harm to the child, citing *Zummo v. Zummo,* 574 A.2d 1130 (Pa. Super. 1990). "Here, there is no threat of present or future physical or emotional harm from the practice of two traditional religions, Judaism or Christianity. For children of divorce, exposure to parents' conflicting values, lifestyles, and religious beliefs may indeed cause doubts and stress. Stress, however, is not always harmful nor is it always to be avoided and protected against. Restrictions must be imposed sparingly. Therefore, we find no error or abuse of discretion on the part of the trial court when it urged tolerance of each parent's religious faith."

In *Shepp v. Shepp,* 588 Pa. 691, 906 A.2d 1165 (2006), the Pennsylvania Supreme Court ruled that a fundamentalist Mormon father was not prohibited from discussing his belief in polygamy with his minor daughter, against mother's wishes, because there was no evidence that such discussions would jeopardize the health or safety of the child. A court may prohibit a parent from advocating to his or her child religious beliefs that would constitute a crime if acted upon only where it is established that such advocation would jeopardize the child's health or safety, or have a potential for significant social burdens as per the United States Supreme Court case of *Wisconsin v. Yoder*.[71] Finding that no such harm was established in the case before it, the court held that a divorced father who believes in polygamy should not have been prohibited from telling his daughter about such belief. The majority concluded: "Based on the record before us, it is clear that the Commonwealth's interest in promoting compliance with the statute criminalizing bigamy is not an interest of the 'highest order' that would supersede the interest of a parent in speaking to a child about a deeply held aspect of his faith." However, this conclusion did not end the inquiry. *Yoder* also requires a determination that parental decisions will not jeopardize the health or safety of the child or have a potential for significant social burdens. The majority pointed out that the trial court here did not find that the teaching of plural marriage constituted "a grave threat." The court further stated: "Where, as in the instant matter, there is no finding that discussing such matters constitutes a grave threat of harm to the child, there is insufficient basis for the court to infringe on a parent's constitutionally protected right to speak to a child about religion as he or she sees fit."

In *Hicks v. Hicks,* 868 A.2d 1245 (Pa. Super. 2005), the Superior Court permitted a daughter's baptism against father's wishes because father failed to demonstrate a substantial threat of present or future harm to the child undergoing the ritual. Mother proposed having daughter baptized in the Russian Orthodox Church. Father filed a motion for special relief to enjoin the ceremony. Father testified that he believed that daughter would be confused by the baptism, since this was the third religion to which she had been exposed. Mother testified that child was excited at the prospect of her baptism in the Russian Orthodox Church. The Superior

---

[71] Wisconsin v. Yoder, 406 U.S. 205 (1972) (only those interests of the highest order and those not otherwise served can overbalance legitimate claims to the free exercise of religion).

Court concluded that father had not proven that a Russian Orthodox baptism would cause his nine-year-old daughter substantial harm.

In spite of the court's desire to remain neutral on religious matters, a decided preference exists for religious training in any faith when the proposed alternative provides for no religious inculcation whatsoever.[72] Where it appears that the religious instruction of the child will cease upon placement in a given custodial setting, courts will lean in favor of the religious-minded contestants.[73]

Finally, as with any other factor, any consideration, positive or negative, given to religious practices, must be based on the demonstrated effect on the child.[74]

LOWER COURT CASES

Berks County

Fritzinger v. Fritzinger, 96 Berks County L. J. 383 (C.C.P. 2004) (Trial court awarded mother primary custody of her 15-year-old daughter because the daughter would be able to practice her religious beliefs with mother and because daughter was uncomfortable in father's all-male household. Mother was the best parent to help the child further her educational and spiritual development, and there was a strong mother–daughter bond in practicing their religion. Although the court found father fit and commended him on the upbringing of his children, it concluded that it was in daughter's best interests to reside with mother. In its findings of fact, the court noted: "Religion is an important issue in this case, and the parents of the minor child do not share the same religious convictions." The court observed that without taking a stance on the

---

[72] Commonwealth ex rel. Stipe v. Anderson, 205 Pa. Super. 34, 206 A.2d 335 (1965); Commonwealth ex rel. Bordlemay v. Bordlemay, 201 Pa. Super. 435, 193 A.2d 845 (1963); Commonwealth ex rel. Mendelson v. Mendelson, 187 Pa. Super. 73, 143 A.2d 665 (1958); Commonwealth ex rel. McDonald v. McDonald, 183 Pa. Super. 411, 132 A.2d 710 (1957).

[73] Commonwealth ex rel. McDonald v. McDonald, 183 Pa. Super. 411, 132 A.2d 710 (1957); Commonwealth ex rel. Sheftie v. Sheftie, 17 Som. 73 (1954), *aff'd*, 178 Pa. Super. 649, 115 A.2d 861 (1955).

[74] In re Custody of Pearce, 310 Pa. Super. 254, 456 A.2d 597 (1983); *see also* Commonwealth of Pennsylvania v. Barnhart, 345 Pa. Super. 10, 497 A.2d 616 (1985) (Parents may be held criminally liable when the exercise of his or her religion results in the child's death).

specific religious beliefs of the parties, it may consider the parties' respective religious practices and how those practices will affect the child. "It is legitimate for a court to examine the impact of the parents' religious beliefs on the child. In fact, since the religious practices of the parties will have an impact on the child, and the Court *should* examine them as it would any other factor.").

Centre County

P.M. v. L.M., C.P. Centre County, No. 2017-2654 (C.C.P. September 6, 2019), *aff'd*, Memorandum Decision, No. 1637 MDA 2019 (Pa. Super. March 20, 2020) (Trial court ordered that the parties' children, ages 12 and 6, did not need to be vaccinated. Pennsylvania law allows parents to choose not to vaccinate their children. The court acknowledged that pursuant to the Pennsylvania Administrative Code, children who would otherwise be required to be immunized need not be immunized if the parent "objects in writing to the immunization on religious grounds or on the basis of a strong moral or ethical conviction similar to a religious belief," citing 28 Pa. Code § 23.84. The trial court left open the option to order vaccination in the future).

Chester County

Aspito v. Aspito, 54 Chester Co. Rep. 323 (C.C.P. 2006) (The United States Supreme Court has specifically held that parental authority in matters of religious upbringing may be encroached upon only upon a showing of a substantial threat of physical or mental harm to the child, or to the public safety, peace, order or welfare. The burden of proof is on the objecting parent to establish a substantial risk of harm in the absence of the restriction proposed. Held, that defendant-mother's fears did not rise to the standard of "substantial threat." The court noted that, regardless of mother's fears, there was no evidence supporting her concerns. Only if a "substantial threat" of "physical or mental harm to the child" is established, can the court place restrictions on a parent's postdivorce parental rights regarding the religious upbringing of his or her children. Permitting father to take the children to his religious services would not change the amount or quality of access that father has had to the children under the present Custody Order, and father had a history of returning the children to mother after his custodial weekends. Mother's evidence did not rise to the level needed to prove that there was a substantial threat of harm to the physical or mental well-being of the children if they were permitted to participate in religious services and activities with father).

Cumberland County

D.M.S. v. M.K.R., C.P. Cumberland County, No. 19-6199 (C.C.P. December 18, 2019) (Father's request to restrict a baptism of a young child was denied since there was no evidence indicating baptism was a substantial threat to the child, particularly when the other children of the parents were baptized and father did not object to the child attending religious services. The court noted that the seminal Pennsylvania decision regarding religious freedom within the context of custody disputes is *Zummo v. Zummo*, 574 A.2d 1130 (Pa. Super. 1990) (It is the parent's right to choose religious avenues for their children, and there must be a "substantial threat" of physical or emotional harm to impair that choice). The court also noted that in *Hicks* v. *Hicks*, 868 A.2d 1245 (Pa. Super. 2005), the court allowed a baptism, noting that there was no competent evidence offered by appellee that there was a threat of present or future physical or emotional harm to the child should be baptismal ceremony be performed, finding instead that appellee's fear of confusion for his child was speculative, and more of a perceived harm. Similarly, the court held, here there was no evidence or argument presented that would rise to the level of "substantial threat" to the child that mother sought to have baptized. The court noted that all of father's other children had been baptized into the Catholic faith. Furthermore, as in *Hicks*, father did not object to the child attending mother's Catholic Church services. Accordingly, father's request to restrict mother from baptizing their minor child was denied, as his objection was not supported by evidence of any threat, either physical or emotional, much less a substantial threat).

Delaware County

Heron v. Rosso, 33 D.&C. 4th 179 (Del. Co. 1996) (Trial court ruled that a change in a father's visitation from all day Saturday to a period from Saturday evening through Sunday evening did not violate First Amendment rights, although part of the court's purpose was to prevent the visitation from being dominated by attendance at religious Seventh Day Adventist services. The court cited the child's best interests as the justification for the change. The court explained that father's time with his daughter during his one-day–per-week visitation was dominated by his religious pursuits. As a result, the child's best interests were not being served and the child was deprived of the opportunity to build a relationship with father. In this case, although the temporary order effectively prevented father from taking the child to Saturday morning services, it was not designed to frustrate father's religious beliefs nor did it place any restrictions upon father's desire to expose his child to his religion. At no time did the court pass any judgment as to the type of religion to which the child was exposed or otherwise favor either parent's religion. Further, the court never placed any restrictions upon either parent taking the child to services or discussing religious beliefs. Instead, the court held, the custody schedule provided father with an opportunity to build a broader relationship with his daughter that was not centered exclusively upon religious beliefs).

Erie County

Kuntz v. Kuntz, 90 Erie Co. Leg. J. 222 (C.C.P. 2007) (While religion merits consideration in child custody cases, it has little weight in making a custody decision unless it can be shown to have harmful effects on the child. A court may prohibit a parent from advocating religious beliefs, which, if acted upon, would constitute a crime; however, the court may not infringe on a parent's constitutional right to speak to a child about religion as he/she sees fit. Further, a court may not bar a parent from taking a child to religious activities simply because the other parent disagrees with them. A custodial parent may direct the children's religious training. "Hence, the Court is not persuaded that Defendant's religion presents any harm to the children, nor that Plaintiff's disputes with the Church and homeschooling have interfered with Defendant's fundamental rights.").

Fayette County

Livingston v. Thorpe, 64 Fayette Leg. J. 167 (C.C.P. 2001) (Father argued that he regularly attends church and that mother and their son do not regularly attend church, and that this should be a determining factor in their custody action. Trial court held that religion is an important matter and should be given some consideration, but is not determinative of child custody).

Lehigh County

Abeln v. Abeln, C.P. Lehigh County, No. 2007-FC-0427 (C.C.P. 2011) (Trial court found that both mother and father should be on an equal footing in providing religious instruction for their child, and therefore the child should be placed in a public school rather than in a Catholic curriculum. Father filed a petition to enroll the parties' son in kindergarten at a Catholic school. Mother wanted the child to enroll in the local public school. Father was raised Roman Catholic, while mother was raised Lutheran. Mother made it clear that she wanted to be part of any decision regarding her son's religious faith and baptism. However, father scheduled and proceeded with the child's baptism without mother's consent or knowledge, even though she shared legal custody of the child at the time. The trial court entered an Order directing that the child be enrolled for kindergarten in the public school. The court explained that a factor in its decision on father's petition was the way father went about the baptism of the child at the parish church which created a taint for mother in educating her son there. The court noted that a second reason for directing that the child be enrolled in public school rather than Catholic school was the fashion in which the parents addressed religion with their son. Both parents tried to teach their respective religious beliefs to their son. Mother was concerned that placing her son in a Catholic school would undermine her attempts to instill her religious values in the child. The court found that mother's concerns were not groundless, and declared "under the circumstances of this case, for each parent to be on an equal footing in providing religious instruction for the child, the child should not be placed in a Catholic curriculum particularly at this parish where the baptism incident took place." Finally, the court found that there was insufficient basis to find that one school was superior to the other. Both schools were academically excellent, and both would provide wonderful educational opportunities for the child. The court concluded that the placement of the child in the public school would serve the child's best interest).

Lycoming County

KW v. KH, C.P. Lycoming County, No. 12-20, 266 (C.C.P. 2013) (The parties five-year-old daughter's interests were best served by enrolling the child in a local private Catholic school rather than a public school, where the daughter had attended the Catholic Church regularly for the past three years. While father had no objection to public schools, he believed that the child would benefit from a Catholic school education. Mother believed that public school offered more than private school and that the child would receive broader socialization by attending school in the public school setting. Mother believed it was important for the child to be introduced to how the real world is and to be exposed to different people. Mother believed that the public school setting could offer this opportunity better than the Catholic school setting. The trial court ruled that while it could not determine if one school was better than the other, it did find that the child's best interests would be best served if she was able to attend the Catholic school. The court was convinced that there was a substantial amount of information available that would support both Catholic schools over public schools, as well as a substantial amount of documentation that would support public schools over Catholic schools. Based upon the testimony presented, there was no reason for the court to believe that the child's educational needs could not be made in either the public school setting or the Catholic school setting. However, it was clear that father's desire was that his daughter be raised in a Catholic school setting as he was so raised. Father, his wife, and child all attended church on a regular basis at the church which was affiliated with the Catholic school which the child would be attending. The child would have classmates who would also attend both her church and her school. It was clear that the Catholic school would address the child's educational needs).

Northampton County

McCloskey v. McCloskey, C. P. Northampton County, No. 1994-7159 (C.C.P. 2005) (Trial court held that father was not permitted to take the parties' child to religious services during weekends on which mother has custody because that practice could adversely affect the child's relationship with mother. The trial court denied father's petition for modification. Citing *Zummo v. Zummo,* 574 A.2d 1130 (Pa. Super. 1990), the court noted that each parent has a right to maintain a meaningful parental relationship with the child. Even "the full benefits of a desired program of religious indoctrination" must yield to that interest, the court explained. Thus, the court held that under Pennsylvania law, if the court must choose between meaningful visitation and the full benefits of a desired program of religious indoctrination, the religious indoctrination must yield to the greater interest in preserving the parent–child relationship. The court found that father's desire to have the child raised in the Roman Catholic faith was being amply met, while the requested modification would impact adversely because the child could not be included in mother's family activities. The court found that this case differed from the facts in *Zummo,* where the father was required to take the child to religious services of the mother's faith during his period of custody. In that case, there was no showing that requiring the father to do so would materially impact his relationship with the child. The father's request to interrupt the time that the boy spends with the mother and her family would significantly interrupt the mother's custody and interfere with the establishment of a strong family bond).

Philadelphia County

Sauer v. Sauer, 14 Phila. Rep. 335 (C.C.P. 1986) (While religion is an important matter and should be given some consideration in child custody disputes, it is not determinative. Where both parents demonstrate their desire to promote the religious education of the child, each in his or her own faith, the court shall assume a neutral stance as to the issue).

Saplansky v. Saplansky, 19 Phila. 29 (1989) (Religion, while a consideration in custody cases, is not a determining factor).

York County

Humphrey v. Humphrey, 117 York Leg. Rec. 17 (C.C.P. 2006) (Trial court, following *Zummo v. Zummo*, 574 A.2d 1130 (Pa. Super. 1990), held that religious agreements between parents may not be legally enforceable and noted several persuasive grounds upon which to deny them legal effect. Mother filed a petition for contempt alleging that father violated the stipulated custody order in which he had agreed that the children should be "raised Catholic," by failing to take them to Mass. The court denied the petition, finding that the provision was vague and did not provide an objective basis for enforcement and further would interfere with father's right to choose what religion he practices without showing that such practices constitute a grave threat to the health, safety or welfare of the children. The court declared that such agreements are generally too vague to demonstrate a meeting of minds, or to provide an adequate basis for objective enforcement. Enforcement of such an agreement would promote a particular religion, serve little or no secular purpose, and would excessively entangle the courts in religious matters. Enforcement would be contrary to the public policy embodied in the First Amendment, as well as state equivalents, that parents be free to doubt, question and change their beliefs, and that they be free to instruct their children in accordance with those beliefs).

§ 3.4.3 Sexual Preference

In *M.A.T. v. G.S.T.*, 989 A.2d 11 (Pa. Super. 2010), a majority of the Superior Court held that there is no longer an evidentiary presumption against a homosexual parent in a custody dispute, overruling *Constant A. v. Paul C.A.*, 496 A.2d 1 (Pa. Super. 1985), which held that a mother's lesbian relationship showed "moral deficiency" and was grounds to limit custody. A trial court may not presume that a parent's same-sex relationship will have an adverse impact on the child. The trial court is not free to substitute its unsubstantiated personal opinion for uncontroverted expert testimony.

Because of the significance of *M.A.T.*, the following is a summary of the facts of the case. Mother and father adopted a daughter, born in 2004, as an infant. Two years later, mother and father divorced as mother had become involved in a same-sex relationship. Father sought primary physical custody. A jointly retained custody evaluator provided a custody evaluation and recommended a shared custody arrangement where the parties would alternate custody every two or three days. The trial court initially approved the arrangement for an 18-month period of transition. However, the court then awarded father primary physical custody to follow that transition period. Mother later sought to modify the order. The custody evaluator testified that a continuation of that arrangement was in the best interest of the child.

The trial court denied mother's petition and stated its personal opinion that shared custody was not in the best interests of the child. The trial court further held that it was in the child's best interest to be placed in a "traditional heterosexual environment." The trial court found that both parents were loving and caring parents quite capable of assuming the role of primary physical custodian, but stated that mother had failed to meet the burden imposed on a parent in a same-sex relationship by *Constant A.* and *Barron v. Barron*, 594 A.2d 682 (Pa. Super. 1991), which held that in custody determinations, "the burden is on the parent who is involved in a gay relationship to prove that there will be no adverse effect on the child exposed to the relationship." The court also disregarded the expert's recommendation that an alternating relationship would be in the best interest of the child, instead opining without citing any evidence that such an arrangement would be detrimental for the child once she was enrolled in a school.

The Superior Court, sitting *en banc*, vacated the trial court's order and granted mother's petition for modification of the custody order. The court overruled *Constant A.* and its progeny, and found that no evidentiary presumption against a parent in a homosexual relationship should exist in a child custody case. That presumption was based on unsupported preconceptions and prejudices. "Such preconceptions and prejudices have no proper place in child custody cases, where the decision should be based exclusively upon a determination of the best interest of the child given the evidence presented to the trial court." Judge Donohue wrote that such a rule was "fundamentally contrary to our Supreme Court's admonition that presumptions should not be relied upon when deciding child custody cases between parents." The Superior Court further stressed that the Supreme Court has espoused that neither parent should have a burden of proof in custody matters.

With regard to the trial court's decision that an alternating schedule was not in the child's best interest, the Superior Court found that it was an abuse of discretion to discount totally uncontradicted expert testimony. While a trial court is not required to accept the conclusion of the expert, it cannot ignore them, and it must support a decision to not accept those conclusions with evidence of record, not the trial court's own preconceptions. The trial court may not ignore uncontroverted expert testimony unless the decision to do so is supported by competent evidence. Here, the trial court's decision was based on the trial judge's personal experience and beliefs.

§ 3.4.4. Meretricious Relationships

The mere existence of a meretricious or non-marital relationship is insufficient to support a denial of custody.[75] While courts may frown on such activity, it is clear that a child custody action is not the proper forum in which to punish an individual for conduct viewed as morally deficient.[76] Any allegations of non-marital relationships must, therefore, be accompanied by a finding that the conduct has an adverse effect on the child if they are to have any significant impact on the outcome.[77]

---

[75] Commonwealth ex rel. Myers v. Myers, 468 Pa. 134, 360 A.2d 587 (1976); *see also* Karis v. Karis, 353 Pa. Super. 561, 510 A.2d 804 (1986); Commonwealth ex rel. Grimes v. Grimes, 281 Pa. Super. 484, 422 A.2d 572 (1980); Gunter v. Gunter, 240 Pa. Super. 382, 361 A.2d 307 (1976).

[76] Commonwealth ex rel. Grimes v. Grimes, 281 Pa. Super. 484, 422 A.2d 572 (1980).

[77] Commonwealth ex rel. Myers v. Myers, 468 Pa. 134, 360 A.2d 587 (1976); Michael T.L. v. Marilyn J.L., 363 Pa. Super. 42, 525 A.2d 414 (1987) (without evidence of a

Consequently, non-marital relationships conducted out of the presence of the child or at a time when the child was too young to appreciate the implications will not substantially damage a contestant's claim.[78]

Even where no detrimental effects are shown, the court may nonetheless consider the relationship in its assessment of the party's overall parental fitness.[79] A litigant's past moral lapse may, however, be for-

---

harmful effect on the child, a parent's past conduct should have little weight on the court's custody decision—trial court abused its discretion in awarding custody to the child's father based on the mother's alleged "immoral conduct," where the mother was primary caretaker for the child and where there was no evidence that mother's active sex life had any adverse effect on child's welfare); Haag v. Haag, 336 Pa. Super. 491, 485 A.2d 1189 (1984) (adverse effect found in case where child saw mother and paramour "naughty in the bedroom," where they slept in the same bedroom and walked around the house without clothing in front of child); Witmayer v. Witmayer, 320 Pa. Super. 372, 467 A.2d 371 (1983) (no adverse effect established); Hall v. Mason, 316 Pa. Super. 160, 462 A.2d 847 (1983); Smith v. Smith, 307 Pa. Super. 544, 453 A.2d 1020 (1982); McAnallen v. McAnallen, 300 Pa. Super. 406, 446 A.2d 918 (1982); Robert H.H. v. May L.H., 293 Pa. Super. 431, 439 A.2d 187 (1982); G.J.F. v. K.B.F., 284 Pa. Super. 139, 425 A.2d 459 (1981); Commonwealth ex rel. Michael R. v. Robert R.R., 293 Pa. Super. 18, 437 A.2d 969 (1981) (remand for trial court's failure to analyze effect of non-marital relationship); Commonwealth ex rel. Grimes v. Grimes, 281 Pa. Super. 484, 422 A.2d 572 (1980); Commonwealth ex rel. Steiner v. Steiner, 257 Pa. Super. 457, 390 A.2d 1326 (1978); Gunter v. Gunter, 240 Pa. Super. 382, 361 A.2d 307 (1976); Crouse, Jr. v. Thompson, 117 Montg. Co. L. Rep. 291 (1986); *but see* Constant A. v. Paul C.A., 344 Pa. Super. 49, 496 A.2d 1 (1985); Britton v. Britton, 8 Mifflin Co. L. J. 131 (1990) (finding the mother's extramarital relationship detrimental to the child's best interest because she was financially dependent on her boyfriend while no legal commitment between them existed).

[78] Commonwealth ex rel. Holschuh v. Holland-Moritz, 448 Pa. 437, 292 A.2d 380 (1972).

[79] Haller v. Haller, 377 Pa. Super. 330, 547 A.2d 393 (1988) (where the custodial parent would be living in a meretricious relationship with another person, or a person will exert a substantial influence over the child, it requires that that person be viewed by the court and subjected to cross-examination as to his supervision, values, and relationship with the children. Trial court in custody matter should have inquired about mother's boyfriend and required testimony from him in light of frequent contacts with children by boyfriend, his disciplining of them, being with them and mother on camping trips, and in general his acting in a quasi-parental role, and failure to do so required remand); *see also* Andrews v. Andrews, 411 Pa. Super. 286, 601 A.2d 352 (1991) (holding that the trial court erred by refusing to address the character and habits of the mother's paramour, and in finding information regarding mother's paramour to be

given, particularly where an isolated incident not of recent vintage was involved.[80]

As the aim of custody decisions is to determine which custodian will provide a stable, healthy environment in which to raise the child, evidence indicating a recent series of fleeting affairs will be viewed in an unfavorable light.[81] Conversely, where a party can demonstrate that a long-standing relationship is of "durable, de facto" status, his or her probabilities of a favorable custody order are enhanced.[82] Furthermore, if the partner to the relationship is of good character, exhibits a rapport with the child, and is willing to accept and care for the child, the meretricious relationship standing alone will not bar an award.[83] Where, however, the partner possesses character traits which may have an adverse effect on the child, the combination of this fact and the meretricious relationship may injure the contestant's claim for custody.[84]

The fact that the extramarital activity of one of the parties "caused" the failure of the marriage is not relevant as an independent element, but

---

irrelevant and a psychological evaluation unnecessary); Brooks v. Brooks, 319 Pa. Super. 268, 466 A.2d 152 (1982); L.D. v. B.D., 291 Pa. Super. 589, 436 A.2d 657 (1981) (thirty-year-old mother's affair with fifteen-year-old boy is cause to question emotional stability and maturity); McCann v. McCann, 270 Pa. Super. 171, 411 A.2d 234 (1979).

[80] Commonwealth ex rel. Stevens v. Stevens, 62 Luz. 87 (1972); Commonwealth ex rel. Shamon v. Shamon, 12 Bucks 586 (1962).

[81] McCann v. McCann, 270 Pa. Super. 171, 41 1 A.2d 234 (1979); Commonwealth ex rel. Kraus v. Kraus, 185 Pa. Super. 167, 138 A.2d 225 (1958). It is interesting to note that some behavioral experts have pointed out that the need to experiment sexually through a series of fleeting affairs may be of vital importance to the restructuring of the divorced individual's identity. Wiseman, *Crisis Theory and the Process of Divorce*, 56 Soc. Casework 205 (1975) *cited in* Kaslow, *Stages of Divorce: A Psychological Perspective, Symposium: Recent Developments in Pennsylvania Family Law*, 25 Vill. L. Rev. 718, 747 (1980).

[82] Gunter v. Gunter, 240 Pa. Super. 382, 361 A.2d 307 (1976); Commonwealth ex rel. Staunton v. Austin, 209 Pa. Super. 187, 223 A.2d 892 (1966).

[83] Gunter v. Gunter, 240 Pa. Super. 382, 361 A.2d 307 (1976); Commonwealth ex rel. Gervasio v. Gervasio, 188 Pa. Super. 95, 145 A.2d 732 (1958).

[84] Dile v. Dile, 284 Pa. Super. 459, 426 A.2d 137 (1981).

only insofar as the adverse effect on the child, or the party's overall fitness as a parent will dictate.[85]

Likewise, in the area of partial custody, the fact that a party is conducting a non-marital relationship is, by itself, insufficient to support a denial of partial custody.[86] In order to have such evidence considered, the custodian must demonstrate that the relationship has an adverse effect on the child.[87] Even where a harmful effect is established, before denying partial custody, the court may dictate that any contact the non-custodian has with the child must occur out of the presence of the paramour.[88] Where, however, the relationship may be characterized as a durable one, built around the cohesive force of a family unit, the court may forego such a restriction, seeing no danger of adverse effects from such an atmosphere.[89]

LOWER COURT CASES

Berks County

Woods v. Woods, 91 Berks Co. Leg. J. 265 (C.C.P. 1999) (Father's superior parental skills are greatly outweighed by the unacceptable possibility of placing the children in the care of an abusive paramour. While father was found to be better equipped to raise the children, his lack of nurturing ability, the presence of his paramour (mother's former best friend) in his home, and the strong bond between mother and children militated in her favor. The court did go on at length regarding its belief that the paramour posed a threat to the children and noted that custody of her own children had been awarded to their father due to her overuse of physical discipline).

---

[85] Brooks v. Brooks, 319 Pa. Super. 268, 466 A.2d 152 (1983); G.J.F. v. K.B.F., 284 Pa. Super. 139, 425 A.2d 459 (1981); Commonwealth ex rel. George v. George, 167 Pa. Super. 563, 76 A.2d 459 (1950); Commonwealth ex rel. Gates v. Gates, 161 Pa. Super. 423, 55 A.2d 562 (1947).

[86] Commonwealth ex rel. Sorace v. Sorace, 236 Pa. Super. 42, 344 A.2d 553 (1975).

[87] Commonwealth ex rel. Drum v. Drum, 263 Pa. Super. 248, 397 A.2d 1192 (1979); Commonwealth ex rel. Sorace v. Sorace, 236 Pa. Super. 42, 344 A.2d 553 (1975).

[88] Dile v. Dile, 284 Pa. Super. 459, 426 A.2d 137 (1981); Commonwealth ex rel. Drum v. Drum, 263 Pa. Super. 248, 397 A.2d 1192 (1979); Scarlett v. Scarlett, 257 Pa. Super. 468, 390 A.2d 1331 (1978).

[89] Commonwealth ex rel. Sorace v. Sorace, 236 Pa. Super. 42, 344 A.2d 553 (1975).

§ 3.4.5. Morality and Character

It is clear that the introduction of evidence of unchaste conduct or loose morals, without more, will not be sufficient to support a determination of unfitness and consequently a denial of custody.[90] Moral lapses or non-marital relationships occurring in the past may be forgiven[91] and it is only conduct which is "persistent and flagrant" which will not be excused by the courts.[92] Also, evidence of past misconduct of an extended nature will have an influence on present fitness, particularly where the litigant has demonstrated or expressed little propensity toward permanent reform.[93]

---

[90] Commonwealth ex rel. Myers v. Myers, 468 Pa. 134, 360 A.2d 587 (1976); Gunter v. Gunter, 240 Pa. Super. 382, 361 A.2d 307 (1976).

[91] Vicki N. v. Josephine N., 437 Pa. Super. 166, 649 A.2d 709 (1994) (Past conduct was not relevant in child custody proceeding in which child's maternal aunt sought custody of child, unless it would produce an ongoing negative effect on child's welfare); Commonwealth ex rel. Grillo v. Shuster, 226 Pa. Super. 229, 312 A.2d 58 (1973).

[92] Michael T.L. v. Marilyn J.L., 363 Pa. Super. 42, 525 A.2d 414 (1987) (in making its decision, the trial court must not dwell on matters buried in the past, but must concentrate only on those matters that affect the present and future of the child); Bresnock v. Bresnock, 346 Pa. Super. 563, 500 A.2d 91 (1985) (a parent's ability to care for her child must be determined as of the time of the custody hearing, not as of an earlier time. Thus, custody cannot reasonably be granted on the basis of a parent's unsettled past unless the past behavior has an ongoing negative effect on the child's welfare); In re Snellgrose, 432 Pa. 158, 247 A.2d 596 (1968); Commonwealth ex rel. Likovich v. Likovich, 220 Pa. Super. 202, 287 A.2d 156 (1971); Shipp v. Shipp, 209 Pa. Super. 58, 223 A.2d 906 (1966);

[93] Cardamone v. Elshoff, 442 Pa. Super. 263, 659 A.2d 575 (1995) (trial court's consideration of mother's past conduct including prior homelessness, drug addiction, and alcoholism, in fashioning custody order was not error as this was but one factor in ascertaining best interests of child. "While we applaud Mother's accomplishments to date, we can not find that the trial court erred in considering some of her past conduct in fashioning the custody order. The prevailing issue must remain the best interests of daughter, and, in determining what those best interests are, the court must sometimes delve into the tarnished past of one or both of the parents or parties"); Commonwealth ex rel. Likovich v. Likovich, 220 Pa. Super. 202, 287 A.2d 156 (1971); Commonwealth ex rel. Holschuh v. Holland-Moritz, 219 Pa. Super. 402, 281 A.2d 729 (1971), *remanded for additional hearing*, 448 Pa. 437, 292 A.2d 380 (1972); Commonwealth ex rel. Shaak v. Shaak, 171 Pa. Super. 122, 90 A.2d 270 (1952).

In addition to a showing that the circumstances constituting the immoral conduct have not been remedied, there must also be a demonstration of a material detrimental effect on the best interests of the child.[94]

In *E.A.L. v. L.J.W.*,[95] the Superior Court ruled that in awarding primary custody of minor children to mother after children were raised by the grandparents, the trial court improperly failed to consider the rational preferences of the children, ages 12 and 10 at the time of hearing, to stay with grandparents. In mother's home, there were dirty movies, foul language, yelling, sexual activity by parents within children's hearing, smoking, and a stepfather who may have raped his stepdaughter, who drank regularly and to excess, and who may have obstructed contact with grandparents. The children expressed a preference for their grandparent's home, based on the more wholesome atmosphere of their grandparents' home. The children were 12 and 10 at the time of the hearing, old enough for the court to give significant weight to their preference.

Where the misconduct has occurred out of sight and sound of the child, the gravity of the lapse will diminish.[96] Similarly, where the conduct is not compounded by other types of behavior indicating a lack of concern for the proper upbringing of the child, courts will give less weight to the transgression.[97]

Appellate courts have emphasized, on several occasions, the requirement of a nexus between the misconduct and the best interests of the child, pointing out that courts must not attempt to impose their personal codes of conduct on the parties but rather must examine any misconduct for its deleterious effects on the child.[98]

---

[94] Commonwealth ex rel. Myers v. Myers, 468 Pa. 134, 360 A.2d 587 (1976); Commonwealth ex rel. Cutler v. Cutler, 246 Pa. Super. 82, 369 A.2d 821 (1977); Gunter v. Gunter, 240 Pa. Super. 382, 361 A.2d 307 (1976); Augustine v. Augustine, 228 Pa. Super. 312, 324 A.2d 477 (1974).

[95] E.A.L v. L.J.W., 443 Pa. Super. 573, 662 A.2d 1109 (1995).

[96] Commonwealth ex rel. Holschuh v. Holland-Moritz, 448 Pa. 437, 292 A.2d 380 (1972); *compare* Tavoletti v. Tavoletti, 203 Pa. Super. 4, 198 A.2d 427 (1964).

[97] *E.g.,* Commonwealth ex rel. Myers v. Myers, 468 Pa. 134, 360 A.2d 587 (1976).

[98] McAnallen v. McAnallen, 300 Pa. Super. 406, 446 A.2d 918 (1982); Robert H.H. v. May L.H., 293 Pa. Super. 431, 439 A.2d 187 (1981).

Evidence of good moral conduct or reform in the face of former lapses will be received by the court positively. Testimony to the effect that an individual enjoys a reputation in the community for good character may, however, run into evidentiary problems.[99]

In addition to conduct which falls within the non-marital relationship category, certain types of behavior have been designated by the courts as bearing unfavorably on the character and fitness of a contestant. Obtaining physical custody of a child through self-help remedies, and in violation of a court order, is not viewed favorably by the courts since such actions are generally seen as being directly pertinent to the actor's bad faith, lack of respect for the legal system, and consequently his or her questionable parental fitness.[100] Where both parties are guilty of "child-snatching," courts have found the conduct to cancel out and have looked to other factors.[101]

In *Wheeler v. Mazur*,[102] the Superior Court found that a parent's ability to care for a child must be determined as of the time of the custody hearing, not as of an earlier time, citing *Wiseman v. Wall*, 718 A.2d 844 (Pa. Super. 1998). Moreover, the court found, unless it can be shown that the parents' conduct has had a harmful effect on the child, it should have little weight when making the custody determination. "Stated differently, custody cannot reasonably be granted on the basis of a parent's unsettled past unless the past behavior has an ongoing negative effect on the child's welfare."

Prior to the enactment of 23 Pa.C.S. § 5328, the frequent use of alcohol has been held, standing alone, to be insufficient to constitute parental unfitness.[103] Similarly, prior to the enactment of Section 5328, a mother's

---

[99] Commonwealth ex rel. Grimes v. Grimes, 281 Pa. Super. 484, 422 A.2d 572 (1980).

[100] Commonwealth ex rel. Rogers v. Daven, 298 Pa. 416, 148 A.2d 524 (1930); In re Leskovich, 253 Pa. Super. 345, 385 A.2d 373 (1978); Trefsgar v. Trefsgar, 261 Pa. Super. 1, 395 A.2d 273 (1978); In re Irizarry, 195 Pa. Super. 104, 169 A.2d 307 (1961).

[101] Kriss v. Kriss, 272 Pa. Super. 383, 416 A.2d 92 (1979).

[102] Wheeler v. Mazur, 793 A.2d 929 (Pa. Super. 2002).

[103] Commonwealth ex rel. Hough v. Hough, 177 Pa. Super. 530, 110 A.2d 853 (1955); *but see* Barron v. Barron, 406 Pa. Super. 401, 594 A.2d 682 (1991) (holding that the trial court erred by granting joint legal custody while failing to address the father's excessive

open admission that she regularly used marijuana as a substitute for alcohol, contending that it was socially acceptable, did not render her unfit for custody.[104] Further, also prior to the enactment of Section 5328, a party's conduct during her former drug addiction has been held to be properly excluded from the record.[105] However, the history of drug or alcohol abuse of a party or member of the party's household is now an enumerated factor for the court to consider in determining the best interest of the child in custody actions.[106]

Evidence that a party has been convicted of a crime has produced varying results with one court finding that such evidence rendered the party unfit for custody.[107] In another instance, however, a court found

---

drinking habits. Although the father had not missed work and had never been cited for DWI, more investigation is necessary to determine if his behavior is detrimental to the child's best interest; although several witnesses testified as to father's drinking habits and tendencies to violence when under the influence, the lower court failed to make any specific findings regarding father's drinking habits, his attitude, and the resultant danger to the child, and to order appropriate intervention; the case was remanded for the lower court to make findings and to re-evaluate its order in view of such findings).

[104] Commonwealth ex rel. Holschuh v. Holland-Moritz, 448 Pa. 437, 292 A.2d 380 (1972).

[105] Commonwealth ex rel. Jacobson v. Jacobson, 181 Pa. Super. 369, 124 A.2d 462 (1956).

[106] 23 Pa.C.S. § 5328(a)(14); see also H.R. v. C.P., 224 A.3d 729 (Pa. Super. 2019) (This case reiterates that because a parent has a medical marijuana card, that alone does not preclude the trial court from reviewing and analyzing the impact and history of that parent's drug use and the ailments that necessitate the need for prescribed medical marijuana. In this case, the certified record established that Father abused marijuana and was unsafe around his child. Because of such history, it was not in the child's best interest to remove the conditions on Father's supervised physical custody, including a drug screening regimen. Further, the Medical Marijuana Act does not preclude the trial court from doing its full historic analysis and consideration of all the custody factors in the case).

[107] DeNillo v. DeNillo, 369 Pa. Super. 363, 535 A.2d 200 (1987) (parent's arrest for charges of indecent exposure and participation in accelerated rehabilitation program were proper considerations for court in determining child's best interests in custody dispute); see also Williams v. Thornton, 395 Pa. Super. 276, 577 A.2d 215 (1990) (trial court's *sua sponte*, temporary termination of father's partial custody rights, without taking testimony or developing factual record of any kind, pending full custody hearing on father's petition seeking custody of children from sister of children's mother, was justified, given father's

that a convicted felon was parentally fit and that under the circumstances, the interests of the children were best served through custody in that party.[108] Under 23 Pa.C.S. § 5329, the court shall consider whether a party's criminal conviction or a member of his/her household's criminal conviction poses a threat of harm to the child before making any order of custody.[109] There are also evaluation requirements contained in that Section as well.[110] Section 3.4.23 of this book discusses the effect of criminal convictions on custody actions in more detail.

Interestingly, it has been held that a non-custodial parent cannot be held liable for failing to supervise a child regarding the poor conduct of a child. In *K.H. and D.A.H. v. J.R. and N.R.*, 826 A.2d 863 (Pa. 2003), the Pennsylvania Supreme Court ruled that a father with shared legal custody who gave his son a BB gun as a Christmas present could not be held liable for the child's shooting of a neighbor with the gun, because the child was in the physical custody of his mother at the time of the accident. A non-custodial parent could not be held liable for failing to supervise a child based solely on the fact that the parents shared legal custody of the child. The court adopted the reasoning of *J. H. ex rel. Hoffman v. Pellak*, 764 A.2d 64 (Pa. Super. 2000), where the Superior Court held that mother could not be held liable after her son shot another child with an air pistol, despite the fact that mother and father had a shared custody arrangement, because the shooting occurred while the

---

prior actions and history of violence; record showed that father violated custody order by taking children for two weeks and refusing to return them to mother's sister, that mother's sister was able to regain custody only through police intervention, and that father had a criminal record); In Interest of C.S., 397 Pa. Super. 519, 580 A.2d 418 (1990) (a child is properly declared dependent and placed in foster care custody with the county children and youth social services agency where the mother suffers from mental health problems and the father suffers from an alcohol and substance abuse problem and is presently incarcerated for alcohol and drug-related offenses and where a danger would be presented in placing the child in the care of certain family members).

[108] Commonwealth ex rel. Gorto v. Gorto, 298 Pa. Super. 509, 444 A.2d 1299 (1982) (mother who had been convicted of theft, served probation, and had no other record, awarded custody); Commonwealth ex rel. Witherspoon v. Witherspoon, 252 Pa. Super. 589, 384 A.2d 936 (1978).

[109] 23 Pa.C.S. § 5329.

[110] *Id.*

child was in father's physical custody, and mother was unaware of the air pistol's existence.

LOWER COURT CASES
Adams County

Smith et ux. v. Moore, 33 Adams Leg. J. 83 (C.C.P. 1990) (Past behavior cannot be the basis for denying custody unless that past behavior will have a continuing harmful effect on the child's well-being; the parents' ability to care for child must be determined at the time of the hearing).

Lefevre v. Null, 28 Adams Leg. J. 17 (C.C.P. 1986) (Custody cannot be determined on the basis of a parent's unsettled past unless the past behavior has an ongoing negative effect on the child's welfare).

Berks County

Pietrusewicz v. Pietrusewicz, C.P. Berks County, No. 05-2213 (C.C.P. 2014) (The trial court awarded sole legal custody and primary physical custody of the minor children to father, where mother's lack of credibility had compromised the minor children's ability to trust her. Father focused on complaints against mother, including spying on the minor children and on father when he resided in the home, calling the police to attempt to control the minor children's behavior, videotaping the minor children's actions while following them, searching their belongings, and having their lockers searched at school. The court explained that one of the stronger factors in support of its decision was mother's improper behaviors, and the resulting loss of credibility with the children. While she pointed to father pulling the children from her, in fact, it was she that drove them away. The children's preference to reside with father also weighed in favor of granting him sole legal and primary physical custody).

Guiracocha v. Ramirez, C.P. Berks County, No. 13-3975 (C.C.P. 2013) (Trial court granted father primary custody of the parties' minor children during the school year, but warned father to abstain from alcohol when he had custody of the child. Father had an active relationship with the child, provided a stable household for the child and his half-sibling, and had chosen a school district which met his expectations. On the other hand, mother did not appear to have the same commitment to the child's education. In addition, she had difficulty maintaining a household, having moved on several occasions. Mother alleged, and father admitted, that he sometimes consumed alcohol. Mother stated that father consumed alcohol at least twice a week. Father downplayed the frequency of his drinking, and denied that he became intoxicated. However, father had been charged with driving under the influence. The trial court granted father primary custody during the school year, with certain cautionary directives, which if violated, could result in a change of custody. The court considered the "history of drug or alcohol abuse of a party or a member of a party's household," and cautioned father to abstain from alcohol when he had custody of the child).

Caraballo v. Mercado, C.P. Berks County, No. 06-7816 (C.C.P. 2007) (Father's more stable home and his role as a primary caretaker supported an award of primary custody to him, despite his criminal background and past drug use. The best interest of the child dictated that he live with father who had been the primary custodian during his young life, despite father's past criminal behavior. The court noted father's role as a primary caretaker of the child, and found that the continued stability and care that the child had found in father's household was in his best interests. "Father has had more serious trouble in his past than Mother. However, Father appears to have straightened out his life; Father has been stable and settled for at least the past year. Mother has had trouble within the last year and appears to have current struggles and ongoing challenges.").

Metz v. Wisniewski, 94 Berks Co. L. J. 237 (C.C.P. 2002) (Biological father was entitled to primary custody of his child, despite the fact that the child was living with mother and stepfather when mother suddenly died, because father had made extensive efforts to recover from drug and alcohol problems and because his wife created a stable home environment for the child and his stepbrother. The court acknowledged that father had problems with drug and alcohol abuse and a history of arrests and criminal convictions. However, the court noted the extensive efforts by father to rehabilitate himself as well as the stable home environment created by father's wife for their son and his stepbrother. The court declared: "It is the ability of the caretaker to care for the child as of the time of the custody hearing, not as of an earlier time, which is determinative.").

Woods v. Woods, 91 Berks Co. Leg. J. 265 (C.C.P. 1999) (Father's accusation of mother's poor housekeeping was discounted in a custody action, where the accusation was based on a video taken three years previous and no negative impact on the children had been shown; mother previously was unable to keep up with household cleaning at the time of the parties' separation, but was better able to maintain the home at time of trial. Further, no negative impact on the children was shown).

Carbon County

Boyle v. Ramirez, 17 Carbon Co. L. J. 79 (C.C.P. 2005) (Trial court granted custody of a seven-year-old girl to the biological mother, despite allegations of sexual abuse and past misconduct by the mother. The court found that no sexual abuse occurred, that the mother should not be punished for her previous lifestyle choices as her current disposition indicates that she is capable of caring for the child, and that it was in the best interests of the child that she be placed with her mother).

Clearfield County

Krepps v. Krepps, C.P. Clearfield County, No. 01-891-CD (C.C.P. 2006) (Mother's retention of custody was not in the best interests of her two children because her past actions put the stability of their home environment in jeopardy. The court acknowledged that the role of the primary caretaker is a substantial factor to be considered, but is not absolute in a custody decision. The court found that mother's past judgment was guided by her own needs and relationships, jeopardizing the stability of the children's home environment: for example, mother's decision to ignore father's ongoing request to limit the children's relationship with mother's male friend, and a loud, profanity-laced altercation outside mother's house that attracted a neighbor's attention one night. The court also questioned mother's credibility, noting, among other things, that mother pleaded guilty to welfare fraud and making false statements/failure to disclose).

Dauphin County

Bello v. Bello, 110 Dauphin Rep. 169 (C.C.P. 1990) (Father had problems with drugs and violent behavior in the past, however, several witnesses and father himself testified that this behavior was behind him, and there was no testimony that any of the past problems had a negative impact on the child. Placing custody of the child with the father would give her a stable and loving environment, physically, and emotionally).

Groff v. Groff, 108 Dauphin Rep. 86 (C.C.P. 1987) (Where the mother is given to immature and occasionally life-threatening fits of rage, and has long-standing emotional problems originating in her inability to adapt or to cope with her husband's children by his first marriage, custody of the parties' three sons is awarded to the father).

Delaware County

Grambo v. Hood, 44 Del. L. J. 63 (C.C.P. 1992) (Where a parent's past reveals character traits that undermine the ability or the willingness of a parent to provide for his or her child and in the absence of evidence that those traits have somehow changed, so as to produce new parenting abilities and concerns, the court can rightfully conclude that the risk that the past will be repeated in the future justifies a change in the award of custody).

Fayette County

Badger v. West, 68 Fayette Leg. J. 58 (C.C.P. 2005) (It was in the best interests of the child to grant full custody to her biological mother, despite the mother's prior inability to provide a stable environment for her and her child. A parent's ability to care for a child must be determined at the time of the custody hearing, not as of an earlier time. Although the child stated she wished to stay with her grandmother, the court felt she lacked the maturity, at age seven, to make such a decision. While there is no presumption that the parent is the best guardian, parenthood "will always be a factor of significant weight." *Rowles v. Rowles*, 542 Pa. 443, 448. The parent–child relationship is important, but must serve the best interests of the child. Although the child was doing well with grandmother, a parent's ability to care for a child must be determined at the time of the custody hearing, not as of an earlier time. *Wiseman v. Wall*, 718 A.2d 844, 847 (Pa. Super. 1998). While the court recognized that grandmother has provided her granddaughter with a loving, stable environment, it felt that mother was capable of doing the same. Therefore, primary custody was awarded to mother, and grandmother was granted partial custody so that her relationship with her granddaughter was not negatively impacted by the new arrangements).

Lebanon County

L.R.W. v. K.J.W., C.P. Lebanon County, No. 2013-20723 (C.C.P. December 21, 2017), *aff'd*, Memorandum Decision, No. 146 MDA 2018 (Pa. Super. August 3, 2018) (Mother argued that the trial court fo-cused on her past behavior and overlooked her testimony about her completion of an inpatient drug and alcohol treatment program, and that she was attending classes at a community college. Mother relied on *Wiseman v. Wall*, 718 A.2d 844, 847 (Pa. Super. 1998), for the proposition that "a parent's ability to care for a child must be determined as of the time of the custody hearing, not as of an earlier time." Court noted that the *Wiseman* analysis, relied on by mother, was obsolete, citing *P.J.P. v. M.M.*, No. 1586 MDA 2017 (Pa. Super. April 27, 2018). The court found that mother's contention that the trial court should have based its decision on her actions at the time of the hearing and not what occurred in the past, was no longer viable. Rather, 23 Pa.C.S. § 5328(a) factors are what controls).

Lehigh County

T.L.C. v. J.W.K., C.P. Lehigh County, No. 2011-FC-1433 (C.C.P. January 13, 2020), *aff'd*, Memorandum Decision, No. 585 EDA 2020 (Pa. Super. August 14, 2020) (23 Pa.C.S. §5328(a)(8) was determinative in a custody action—the attempts of the parent to turn the child against the other parent. Father had effectively turned the two oldest children against mother for no apparent rea-son other than being vindictive because of the breakup of the marriage and a resultant obligation to pay child support. The trial court placed weight on father's hostility towards mother and its damaging effect on the children, which the appellate court found it may not disturb).

Muffley v. Muffley, C.P. Lehigh County, No. 2008-FC-0713 (C.C.P. 2010) (Trial court found that father's failure to include mother in any aspect of the child's life, and his constant interference with mother's partial custody, was not in the child's best interests and supported a change of primary custody from father to mother. The trial court modified its previous shared custody order and awarded mother primary physical custody. The court found that father was dictatorial, rude, and demeaning to mother. Despite this, mother had not resorted to self-help and had abided by the court's orders, including the payment of support despite her part-time income. Father was unapologetic about his treatment of mother and his interference with her attempts to be a good parent. Father saw nothing wrong with the way he treated mother and excluded her from the child's life).

Wheatley v. Wheatley, 49 Lehigh L. J. 36 (C.C.P. 2000) (A court order granting mother primary physical custody of the parties' children was warranted where mother had recovered from a drug addiction and remained drug-free, while father continued to demonstrate problems with violence and aggression and continued to discipline the children by means of corporal punishment. The court declared: "If the best interests of the children were originally served by primary physical custody in a healthy, drug-free mother, and the best interests of the children were served by the transfer of custody because of mother's addiction, then presumably the best interests of the children would be served in the future by returning primary physical custody to the mother when she has successfully stayed free of drug use for a period that is more than three years.").

Lycoming County

T.H. v. I.M., C.P. Lycoming County, No. 02-20, 271 (C.C.P. 2007) (The court awarded primary custody to father even though the child had lived with mother more than 11 years, due to mother's history of drug abuse and mental illness. Father's home provided more stability and served the child's best interests, even though mother had been the primary caretaker for most of the child's life. The court found that father's home environment was deemed to more likely promote the child's best interest, and therefore awarded primary physical custody to father. While the child told the court that he preferred living with mother, the court did not find that he had a mature basis for his opinion. Based on the environment in father's home and the difficulty mother had had over the years, the court was reluctant to jeopardize the child's stability by returning him to mother. Although mother's health had improved, the court placed a greater weight on the stability and predictability of father's home. The court found that mother's role as the child's former primary caretaker was greatly outweighed by the advantages of living with his father, who had a stable home, steady employment, and no history of mental illness. The court rejected mother's argument that father had abdicated his child-rearing responsibilities to his wife. While the child's stepmother was a stabilizing influence, the court found that the father had fully participated in the child's life).

Northampton County

M.A.C. v. B.J.B., C.P. Northampton County, C.P. No. C0048CV2016-11301 (C.C.P. September 20, 2017), *aff'd*, Memorandum Decision, No. 3293 EDA 2017 (Pa. Super. March 29, 2018) (Mother acknowledged a history of alcohol abuse. The trial court granted mother's Petition for Custody. The trial court found mother's testimony regarding her efforts to maintain sobriety to be credible and opined that, while father may have placed greater weight on mother's past substance abuse and psychological history than did the trial court, that did not negate the fact that the court clearly considered those issues. The trial court found that it was clear that mother had maintained her sobriety for many months, and that she was actively working to better herself to be the best possible mother to the child. Insofar as mother was clearly now on the right path in her own life and had an excellent support system in her home, the trial court appropriately placed less weight on her past behavior than it placed on the child's need for stability and consistency and what was clearly a healthy, stable, and loving home with mother. The court referred to 23 Pa.C.S. § 5328(a)(2), regarding the "present and past abuse committed by a party or member of a party household.").

Montgomery County

Pearson v. Copeland, C.P. Montgomery Co., No. 97-16199 (C.C.P. 1999) (Where the record demonstrates that Mother admitted to previously abusing alcohol and continues to imbibe, the best interests of child favor a custody award to Father; where Mother's alcohol abuse has been detrimental to the child, this is a significant factor in the custody determination. "Although this court is cognizant of the line of cases which hold that a parent's past conduct alone is not relevant to a custody determination, we find Mother's history of alcohol abuse highly relevant here. On this issue we are guided by the Superior Court's decision in *Barron v. Barron*, 406 Pa. Super. 401, 594 A.2d 682 (1991)."

Crouse, Jr. v. Thompson, 117 Montg. Co. L. Rep. 291 (C.C.P. 1986) (Custody of two minor children is awarded to the father where the mother has a drug and alcohol problem that prevents her from properly caring for the children).

Northumberland County

Campbell v. Broschart, 68 Northumberland Leg. J. 107 (C.C.P. 1996) (Mother had overcome the past problems that caused her to relinquish custody to the maternal grandparents more than four years ago and was now capable of raising her daughter. Citing *Michael T.L. v. Marilyn J.L.*, 525 A.2d 414 (Pa. Super. 1987), the court held that a custody determination is to be made at the time of the hearing and past conduct is important only as it is likely to impact the present and future interests of the child).

Philadelphia County

T.D. v. A.H., C.P. Philadelphia County, No. OC1007233 (C.C.P. September 20, 2017), *aff'd*, Memorandum Decision, No. 3421 EDA 2017 (Pa. Super. July 12, 2018) (Custody cases should not be heard and reviewed in a vacuum, and the history and past conduct of a party, especially if the behaviors or issues continue to process, is important and necessary to consider when potentially modifying custody, citing *R.M.G. v. F.M.G.*, 986 A.2d 1234, 1239 (Pa. Super. 2009) ("Best interest cannot be considered in a vacuum, and where the circumstances are unchanged from those that resulted in the initial custody arrangement, it must be presumed that what was in the child's best interest continues."). Unless and until mother's pattern of conduct and attitude changed, shared physical and shared legal custody were not in the child's best interest).

Pike County

A.M.M. v. G.J.M., C.P. Pike County, No. 2011-2008-CV, *aff'd,* Memorandum Decision, No. 569 EDA 2018 (Pa. Super. August 8, 2018) (In a custody conflict, it is within the trial court's purview as the finder of fact to determine which factors are most salient and critical in each particular case. While the primary caretaker doctrine is no longer viable, a court may still consider a parent's role as primary caretaker in its consideration of the custody factors. No evidence presented of any past or present alcohol or drug abuse by any household member of the parties. Mother's fiancé testified that, while mother drinks alcohol and consumes one drink of alcohol when they go out socially, he had never seen her intoxicated. The court noted that although a court is required to give "weighted consideration to those factors which affect the safety of the child," pursuant to 23 Pa.C.S. § 5328(a), courts have acknowledged that the amount of weight a court gives any one factor is almost entirely discretionary, citing *M.J.M. v. M.L.G.,* 63 A.3d 331, 339 (Pa. Super. 2013).

York County

Blymire v. Crone, 116 York Leg. Rec. 9 (C.C.P. 2002) (Trial court required mother, who had been convicted of recklessly endangering one of her children, to make a showing of suitability of her contact with the children, before the court would appoint a qualified professional, as required by 23 Pa.C.S. § 5303(c), to counsel mother and report on her ability to have contact with the children. The court noted that § 5303(c) required that the court appoint a qualified professional to provide counseling to mother and to recommend to the court mother's suitability for contact with the children. The court interpreted the statute to require an evaluation by a qualified professional only after the court determines that she is no longer precluded from contact with the child. The court therefore directed mother to present evidence to rebut the presumption that she is no longer a grave threat of harm to the child and it will then determine what evaluation is appropriate and who should bear the cost).

Emig v. Emig, 100 York Leg. Rec. 18 (C.C.P. 1986) (Although the evidence showed that both parents had used drugs and alcohol, custody will be awarded to the mother since her use had stopped, while there was evidence that the father's use continued. Although the court did not approve of the mother's previous use of marijuana, on comparing the parents' uses of drugs and alcohol, it was obvious that the mother had stopped using marijuana, whereas the father still continued to use marijuana, cocaine, and alcohol, and currently had his drivers' license suspended, having been convicted of driving under the influence).

§ 3.4.6. Mental, Emotional, and Physical Health

As is true with most custody considerations, the mental, emotional, and physical health of a custody contestant will be subject to scrutiny in terms of its present potential of having a negative impact on the well-being of the child.[111] Thus, the mere fact that a party is mentally ill or is undergoing psychiatric treatment does not exclude that party from consideration as a custodian unless the deleterious effects on the child are also established,[112] with the burden of proof lying with the party asserting the mental illness. Evidence of past mental or emotional illness alone is generally accorded little weight since courts, focusing on the present fitness of the litigant, will require a showing of present adverse impact on the child before the condition will be weighed against the party.[113] Once the asserting party has demonstrated the adverse effects on the child, it becomes necessary for the party whose health has been placed at issue to refute that evidence. However, while psychiatric testimony giving assurances as to the party's future good health would undoubtedly support that party's position, such evidence is not a prerequisite to custody. As one court noted:

"If this Court waits until a reputable physician categorically certifies that (a party) will never experience a recurrence of (the) ailment, it will wait forever and a day."[114]

In examining the mental or emotional illness and subsequent restoration, courts will pay close attention to the length of the period which

---

[111] 23 Pa.C.S. § 5328(a)(15).

[112] Commonwealth ex rel. Beishline v. Beishline, 176 Pa. Super. 231, 107 A.2d 580 (1954).

[113] Edinger v. Edinger, 374 Pa. 586, 98 A.2d 172 (1953); Hall v. Mason, 316 Pa. Super. 160, 462 A.2d 847 (1983) (mother's emotional instability as evidenced by suicide attempts and vilification of father to child, supported award of custody to father); Brooks v. Brooks, 319 Pa. Super. 268, 460 A.2d 152 (1983) (trial court did not place great weight on them); McGowan v. McGowan, 248 Pa. Super. 41, 374 A.2d 1306 (1977).

[114] *E.g.,* Commonwealth ex rel. Gorto v. Gorto, 298 Pa. Super. 509, 444 A.2d 1299 (1982) (mother's psychiatric prognosis "guarded" but emotional state had stabilized—award of custody to mother affirmed); Commonwealth ex rel. Edinger v. Edinger, 172 Pa. Super. 93, 98, 92 A.2d 230, 232 (1952) (Reno, J. dissenting), *reversed,* 374 Pa. 586, 98 A.2d 172 (1953).

has elapsed since the party's last treatment or relapse in order to attempt to discern the permanence of the rehabilitation.[115] Likewise, courts will scrutinize psychiatric evidence as to the cause of the illness. Where the illness follows a recurring pattern which is stress related, courts are quick to realize that the rearing of children is an inherently stressful experience and may regard this as a weighty element leaning toward denial of custody to an individual.[116]

In *In Re: Morgan L.*,[117] the Superior Court ruled that a change of custody was warranted where mother, who suffered from factitious disorder by proxy, repeatedly subjected the child to physical and mental examinations due to her suspicion that father was abusing the child, thereby placing the child in imminent risk of emotional and physical harm. "We conclude that the trial court did not err in determining that Mother was unable to provide the proper parental care and control necessary for Morgan's physical, mental, or emotional health. Moreover, we believe the trial court correctly determined that Morgan is in imminent risk of harm due to the behavior and mental illness of Mother."

If a parent's physical health prevents him or her from caring for the child, a change in custody may be warranted.[118]

LOWER COURT CASES

Berks County

Orlando v. Orlando, C.P. Berks Co., No. 97-6873 (C.C.P. 1998) (Trial court held that father was entitled to retain primary physical custody of his minor children where the evidence established that mother suffered from both physical and mental problems and that she had failed to address her problems in a coordinated and consistent fashion.

---

[115] In re Custody of JZC, 28 Som. 94 (1972); Commonwealth ex rel. Pfennig v. Pfennig, 65 Berks 118 (1972).

[116] Commonwealth ex rel. Cutler v. Cutler, 246 Pa. Super. 82, 369 A.2d 821 (1977); In re Clouse, 244 Pa. Super. 404, 368 A.2d 780 (1976).

[117] In Re: Morgan L., 716 A.2d 658 (Pa. Super. 1998).

[118] Vicki N. v. Josephine N., 437 Pa. Super. 166, 649 A.2d 709 (1994) (Trial court did not abuse its discretion in child custody proceeding in awarding custody of child to child's maternal aunt where mother's health was declining and she was unable to care for child due to cancer and the treatment thereof).

Because the physical, intellectual, and emotional environment provided by father's residence was more stable than at mother's home, father was entitled to retain primary physical custody of the children).

Bucks County

Burchell v. Hunsberger, C.P. Bucks County, No. A06-02-63269-C (C.C.P. 2013) (The trial court issued a temporary order suspending father's partial custody and modified his visitation until father entered into an alcohol evaluation program at a professional treatment center. The court concluded that father was in denial about the severity of his alcohol abuse and ruled that it was in the children's best interests to suspend father's custody and visitation rights. The court suggested, but did not order, that father participate in an inpatient alcohol treatment program. Mother cited specific incidences of father's unsafe conduct with the children. As a result of his alcoholism, the children were very anxious around father. Mother argued that father's visitation with the children should be continued only upon father's participation in an alcohol treatment program and anger management counseling. The court explained that although the matter before it was father's petition to modify custody, it acted within its discretion to grant special relief on his own accord, and the weight of the evidence supported its decision to temporarily suspend father's visitation rights and grant sole physical custody to mother. The court noted that father's alcohol abuse had a toxic impact on the children such that their best interests could be served only by suspending contact with father until he addressed his problem).

Cumberland County

D.J. v. H M., C.P. Cumberland County, No. 2016-00803 (C.C.P. May 27, 2016), *aff'd*, Memorandum Decision, No. 1033 MDA 2016 (Pa. Super. January 11, 2017) (Where father failed to provide any specific basis for requesting that mother submit to a psychological evaluation, the trial court denied father's Motion for Mental Examination Pursuant to Pa.R.Civ.P. 1915.8. The court held that Pa.R.Civ.P. 1915.8 is permissive, not mandatory, and the motion, on its facts, provided no valid reason for such relief. Further, mother's only known health issue was fibromyalgia. As father failed to provide any specific basis for requesting that mother submit to a psychological evaluation, the trial court did not abuse its discretion when it denied the motion).

Delaware County

Commonwealth ex rel. Richards v. Richards, 57 Del. 164 (C.C.P. 1969) (Where the illness follows a recurring pattern which is stress related, courts are quick to realize that the rearing of children is an inherently stressful experience and may regard this as a weighty element leaning toward denial of custody to an individual).

Luzerne County

Commonwealth ex rel. Stevens v. Stevens, 62 Luz. 87 (C.C.P. 1972) (Psychiatric testimony giving assurances as to the party's future good health would undoubtedly support that party's position).

Somerset County

In *Stapleton v. Strong*, 57 Somerset Leg. J. 182 (C.C.P. 2000) (trial court held that Rule 1915.8 outlines a court's power in ordering physical and mental examinations of persons during discovery in custody actions; the rule provides that the court may order the child or a party to submit to an evaluation by an appropriate expert or experts upon its own motion or on motion of a party. The court declared: "Assuming that a court determines that discovery is warranted, Rule 1915.8 outlines a court's power in ordering physical and mental examinations of persons during discovery in custody actions).

Washington County

R.M. v. D.J.M., 75 Washington Co. Rep. 103 (C.C.P. 1995) (Primary physical custody in the father was in the best interests of the children where the mother was psychologically unstable and the children improved while in father's custody. Evidence showed that the children's scholastic performance improved while they were with their father, and the oldest son's psychological problems were slowly improving. Father provided treatment for the children's mental and physical problems, while mother did not.)

§ 3.4.7. Proposed Custodial Home and Inhabitants

Since the custody decision is centered on the determination of which party is better able to promote the best interests of the child, the physical aspects of the custodial residences are generally of minor significance.[119] However, in cases where there is a great disparity between the proposed settings, courts will consider the differences as they relate to the welfare of the child.[120] In instances where the quality of the living arrangements does become a factor, considerations include the physical facilities

---

[119] Commonwealth ex rel. Jordan v. Jordan, 302 Pa. Super. 421, 448 A.2d 1113 (1982).

[120] Mahoney v. Mahoney, 354 Pa. Super. 585, 512 A.2d 694 (1986) (the trial court found that the child's greater attachment to the father which provided a stronger and more stable relationship is a relevant factor when determining with whom the child should live); Commonwealth ex rel. Stipe v. Anderson, 205 Pa. Super. 34, 206 A.2d 335 (1965).

proposed, the character of the neighborhoods, and access to schools, playmates and safe play areas. In *Commonwealth ex rel. Davenport v. Montgomery County Children and Youth Services*,[121] the court analyzed a number of these factors and found them, among others, to support an order of custody favoring grandparents over the natural father.

In *E.A.L. v. L.J.W.*,[122] the Superior Court vacated a trial court order granting custody to the mother rather than the grandparents and remanded the matter for further proceedings. The court emphasized the importance of a stable and familiar family environment, noting that the children had lived with the grandparents for a substantial number of years and were happy with the arrangement.

Similarly, courts have long held that the relative wealth of the parties is not relevant unless it is evident that one party is unable to adequately provide for the child.[123]

In *Roadcap v. Roadcap,* 778 A.2d 687 (Pa. Super. 2001), the Superior Court held that the trial court erred when it found mother to be the more available parent and the one who was more likely to foster a relationship with the non-custodial parent, but awarded custody of the children to father because his financial superiority could provide more advantages for the children. Citing *Commonwealth ex rel. Holschuh v. Holland-Moritz,* 292 A.2d 380 (Pa. 1972), the court declared: "The law in Pennsylvania has long been that custody is not to be awarded merely on the basis that a better home in physical aspects, or a higher standard of living can be provided elsewhere." The court noted that the sole permissible inquiry into the relative wealth of the parties in a custody case is whether either party is

---

[121] 501 Pa. 472, 462 A.2d 221 (1983).

[122] 443 Pa. Super. 573, 662 A.2d 1109 (1995).

[123] Commonwealth ex rel. Holschuh v. Holland-Moritz, 448 Pa. 437, 292 A.2d 380 (1972); In re Neff, 394 Pa. 162, 145 A.2d 857 (1958); Gerber v. Gerber, 337 Pa. Super. 580, 487 A.2d 413 (1985); Brooks v. Brooks, 319 Pa. Super. 268, 466 A.2d 152 (1983); In re Custody of Pearce, 310 Pa. Super. 254, 456 A.2d 597 (1983); G.J.G. v. K.B.F., 284 Pa. Super. 139, 425 A.2d 459 (1981); Commonwealth ex rel. Cutler v. Cutler, 246 Pa. Super. 82, 369 A.2d 821 (1977); Commonwealth ex rel. Grillo v. Shuster, 226 Pa. Super. 229, 312 A.2d 58 (1973); Commonwealth ex rel. Shipp v. Shipp, 209 Pa. Super. 58, 223 A.2d 906 (1966).

unable to provide adequately for the child. Unless the income of one party is so inadequate as to preclude raising the children in a decent manner, the matter of relative income is irrelevant, the court declared, *citing Brooks v. Brooks,* 319 Pa. Super. 268, 466 A.2d 152 (1983).

Moreover, it has been held that the fact that a mother relied on public assistance to support her child was not a compelling reason to deny custody.[124]

It is evident that the character and conduct of the parties to the action merit the closest form of scrutiny. Considering the newly enacted enumerated factors contained in 23 Pa.C.S. § 5328, this appears to be more evident than ever. It is equally true, however, that the behavior of all persons who will either reside in the proposed home or will exert a substantial influence over the child falls within the purview of the court.[125] Thus, in virtually every custody action, friends, parents, relatives or any individuals who will be partially responsible for the care of the child, should be brought forth to testify. Such evidence becomes particularly vital where the contestant resides in the home of relatives, friends, or paramours, since courts are greatly concerned with the character of such individuals as well as the reception which the child will receive in the proposed home, along with the fact that the courts must now consider the mental and physical condition of members of a party's household under Section 5328(a)(15) when deciding the child's best interest.[126]

---

[124] In re Custody of Pearce, 310 Pa. Super. 254, 456 A.2d 597 (1983); Jones v. Kniess, 249 Pa. Super. 134, 375 A.2d 795 (1977); In re Custody of Myers, 242 Pa. Super. 225, 363 A.2d 1242 (1976); Commonwealth ex rel. Gifford v. Miller, 213 Pa. Super. 269, 248 A.2d 63 (1968).

[125] *See* 23 Pa.C.S. § 5328(a)(15); Commonwealth ex rel. Bordlemay v. Bordlemay, 201 Pa. Super. 435, 193 A.2d 845 (1963).

[126] Tracey L. v. Mattye F., 446 Pa. Super. 281, 666 A.2d 734, (1995) (custody order reversed and remanded for further proceedings where the trial court did not allow the party with custody to testify or to call witnesses. The court explained that a trial court has a duty to make the fullest possible inquiry in custody actions. Trial court had obligation to hear all evidence relevant to child's best interests, including testimony of child's primary caretaker, whose testimony was over nine months old at time of hearing.); Dile v. Dile, 284 Pa. Super. 459, 426 A.2d 137 (1981); J.F.G. v. K.A.G., 278 Pa. Super. 25, 419 A.2d 1337 (1979); Lewis v. Lewis, 267 Pa. Super. 235, 406 A.2d 781 (1979);

The failure of a party to present such evidence is not, however, dispositive of the child's best interests, since it is the duty of the trial court to take action which will remedy the failure.[127] Where a record is presented on appeal with such evidence absent, a remand with orders for further testimony on the character and abilities of the inhabitants is likely.[128]

Where a party has remarried, testimony by and about the newly acquired spouse is indispensable and courts are quick to note the absence of such evidence when handing down a decision adverse to that party or remanding for further development of the record.[129]

In cases where a party cohabits with another, the character of the cohabitant as well as the nature, duration, and stability of the relationship will be reviewed by the court.[130] Several custody decisions have, however, favored cohabitants who satisfied the court that the home provides a stable, loving, environment for the child and that the relationship is not a trifling one, but rather is a durable "de facto" relationship.[131]

The character and conduct of the non-party inhabitants are weighed on the same scale used to judge the principals to the action with the emphasis placed on present circumstances and the effect certain behavior will have on the child rather than its mere existence. Evidence to the effect that an inhabitant of the home enjoys a good relationship with the child and is willing to accept and care for the child as if it were his or her

---

Commonwealth ex rel. Steiner v. Steiner, 257 Pa. Super. 457, 390 A.2d 1326 (1978); Commonwealth ex rel. Schwarz v. Schwarz, 252 Pa. Super. 95, 380 A.2d 1299 (1977).

[127] Parks v. Parks, 284 Pa. Super. 400, 426 A.2d 108 (1981); Lewis v. Lewis, 267 Pa. Super. 235, 406 A.2d 781 (1979); Commonwealth ex rel. Cox v. Cox, 255 Pa. Super. 508, 388 A.2d 1082 (1978).

[128] J.F.G. v. K.A.G., 278 Pa. Super. 25, 419 A.2d 1337 (1980); Lewis v. Lewis, 267 Pa. Super. 235, 406 A.2d 781 (1979).

[129] J.F.G. v. K.A.G., 278 Pa. Super. 25, 419 A.2d 1337 (1980); Summers v. Summers, 273 Pa. Super. 285, 417 A.2d 651 (1979).

[130] 23 Pa.C.S. § 5328(a)(15).

[131] Gunter v. Gunter, 240 Pa. Super. 382, 361 A.2d 307 (1976); Commonwealth ex rel. Staunton v. Austin, 209 Pa. Super. 187, 223 A.2d 892 (1966). *Compare* Rupp v. Rupp, 268 Pa. Super. 467, 408 A.2d 883 (1979).

own will invariably strengthen a contestant's case,[132] whereas instances of mistreatment or abuse of the child by an inhabitant will be weighed heavily against the contestant associated with that individual.[133] Similarly, the presence of individuals of poor character in the custodial home will undoubtedly lessen the litigant's chances of receiving a favorable custody order.[134]

In accordance with the separation of siblings policy, the fact that brothers and sisters of the subject child live in a proposed home will warrant a placement of the child in that home in the absence of countervailing considerations.[135] However, it is important to note that an argument can be made that the separation of siblings policy is now watered down since the ruling in *M.J.M. v. M.L.G.*, 63 A.3d 331 (Pa. Super. 2013), held that the primary care doctrine is now woven into the factors of Section 5328(a) and there is no longer a positive emphasis to be given on the primary caretaker's status.

---

[132] Commonwealth ex rel. Cutler v. Cutler, 246 Pa. Super. 82, 369 A.2d 821 (1977); Gunter v. Gunter, 240 Pa. Super. 382, 361 A.2d 307 (1976); Commonwealth ex rel. Gervasio v. Gervasio, 188 Pa. Super. 95, 145 A.2d 732 (1958).

[133] 23 Pa.C.S. § 5328(a)(2); Davis v. Davis, 237 Pa. Super. 516, 352 A.2d 78 (1975); Commonwealth ex rel. Stipe v. Anderson, 205 Pa. Super. 34, 206 A.2d 335 (1965).

[134] 23 Pa.C.S. § 5328(a)(15); Dile v. Dile, 284 Pa. Super 459, 426 A.2d 137 (1981); *see also* O.G. v. A.B., 234 A.3d 766 (Pa. Super. 2020) (trial court abused its discretion in entering its custody order without an adequate review of father's tenant. When awarding custody, § 5328(a) provides that a court must place weighted consideration on those factors affecting the safety of the child or children. Here, the trial court heard undisputed testimony that father's tenant had a history of criminal charges, and a PFA order entered against him, which indicated that he may pose a risk of harm to the children. There was no detail as to the extent of father's investigation into his tenant's background. Accordingly, the Superior Court directed the trial court to make a more detailed inquiry and findings concerning any risk of harm to the children. The trial court was also directed that its order must include a provision directing that father must conduct a thorough background investigation of any potential tenant before allowing any tenant into his home and timely provide mother with the results of such investigation).

[135] 23 Pa.C.S. § 5328(a)(6); Beers v. Beers, 342 Pa. Super. 465, 493 A.2d 116 (1985) (the trial court's award of custody of daughter to mother instead of father during the academic year was justified on the basis of mother's prior role as caretaker and presence of child half-brother in mother's home). *See also* § 3.4.16 of this book.

LOWER COURT CASES
Beaver County

Metz v. Metz, C.P. Beaver County, No. 20337 of 2004 (C.C.P. 2007) (Mother was entitled to primary custody of the parties' child since the child had made progress in his new school, mother had been the child's primary caretaker, and father had a negative view of mother and a history of domestic violence against her. The child had adjusted well to his new school and to uproot him now to reside with father and return to his prior school would disrupt his life and would not be in his best interests. The court also observed that mother had been the child's primary caretaker. She did not work outside the home and had been primarily responsible for the child's daily necessities. Father worked full-time and was vague in describing how the child would be cared for while he was working. The primary caretaker doctrine requires the court to give positive consideration to the parent who has been the primary caretaker of the child in order to determine what is in the child's best interest. The court concluded that mother was more willing than father to encourage a relationship between the child and the other parent, even though father had disparaged mother in vulgar terms. Because father also had a history of domestic violence against mother, an award of primary custody to him would not be in the child's best interest).

Berks County

Bechtel v. Bechtel, C.P. Berks County, No. 11-15506 (C.C.P. 2014) (Trial court granted father primary custody of the parties' two minor children after considering all of the statutory factors, noting the significance of stability and concluding that the children here would benefit from residing with father as well as their paternal grandparents. Father argued that he should be granted primary custody of the children because he was able to provide a stable, supportive, multigenerational environment in which to raise the children. Emphasizing a significant role of the paternal grandparents in the children's lives, the court held that to grant mother primary custody in this case would be destructive to the extended family structure. Accordingly, the trial court granted father primary custody of the children since the children would benefit immensely from being raised in father's household).

Gilmour v. Churico, C. P. Berks County, No. 00-9384 (C.C.P. 2008) (Father's motion for primary physical custody of the parties' minor daughter granted, where his home, which he shared with the child's stepmother and stepsiblings, provided a more stable and secure environment for the child than mother's home. Mother was unable to provide a stable, safe environment for the child due to her financial and emotional difficulties. The court's custody evaluator noted that mother had moved four times in six years and her instability affected her ability to provide a safe environment for the child. The court also had concerns that mother's brother, who had a criminal history, would not be a good role model for the child. "Character development is very important for this child and mother's household does not offer healthy examples for this child. It will be important for the child to stay connected to her mother and we will provide ample visitation. But we are also of the opinion that it is crucial for this child to have a stable home base." The court ruled that father was able to provide the more stable and secure home for the child at this point in her life, while mother's home did not have any of the same stability).

Levan v. Griffith, C. P. Berks County, No. 99-8043 (C.C.P. 2006) (Trial court entered an order in which mother retained primary physical custody of the parties' child. However, the court reserved the right to take immediate action, including transfer of custody to father, if mother did not conform to certain conditions, including refraining from comments intended to alienate the child from father. The court placed several conditions on mother's custody award. The court expressed concern about mother's attempt to alienate father from the child's life, declaring that it would monitor mother's behavior. The court instructed mother not to allow the child to call her current husband "Dad", and not to hyphenate the child's last name, which is father's last name. Based on the child's special education needs and mother's history of failing to attend special education counseling and medical appointments, the court also allowed father to bring such failure to the court's attention, without petition, for an immediate hearing with a strong consideration to be given to transfer of custody to father).

Armistead v. Sewell, C. P. Berks Co., No. 97-7837 (C.C.P. 2005) (Because the evidence indicated that father was able to provide a more stable environment, he was entitled to primary physical custody of the child. According to the evidence, father lived with the child, his girlfriend, her son, their daughter and father's two other children. Father had regular contact with child's teachers. Father testified that he wanted to retain primary physical custody of child because he was concerned that mother's husband was an alcoholic and that there was frequent yelling and verbal abuse in mother's household. The court noted that although mother had partial custody of child, she did not always exercise her custodial rights. She either did not show up or called just 15 to 20 minutes before her scheduled custodial period to say that she was not coming. Mother also found child difficult to manage without behavioral medication. Since child began living with father, she had not taken medications to control her behavior. The *guardian ad litem* opined that father offered a more stable environment for child. The court explained that the paramount concern in a custody dispute is the best interest of the child. The court agreed with the *guardian ad litem* that father's household offered a much more stable environment than mother's residence).

Graff v. Graff, 95 Berks Co. L. J. 145 (C.C.P. 2002), *aff'd*, 817 A.2d 1188 (Pa. Super. 2002) (Held, that a trial court, while not judging the moral implications of meretricious relationships, does have a responsibility to consider whether the relationship has an adverse effect on the child, citing *Dile v. Dile*, 426 A.2d 137 (Pa. Super. 1981).

Bucks County

Smith v. McCollum, C. P. Bucks County, No. A06-02-61560-C- 31 (C.C.P. 2005) (Trial court found both parents to be caring and fit, but determined that it was in the child's best interest to allow mother to retain primary custody. The court acknowledged that during the first two years of the child's life, mother's living situation was not ideal but found that she managed to protect and nurture the child nonetheless. "[Mother] maintained a stable, safe and nurturing home living environment for the child despite all of the adversities thrown into her path. Remarkably, she provided adequate physical, emotional and developmental support for the child. . . . [Mother] was doing the best she could with what she had available to her; and at all times, she demonstrated extraordinary commitment to the child in the face of daunting odds." Mother had since moved into a larger home with better living conditions. The court looked to the fact that father did nothing to help or accommodate mother in the face of these struggles and was often critical and accusatory of her. The court also determined that mother was more likely to accommodate father and keep him informed of issues concerning the child than father was likely to do the same with mother).

Carbon County

Char-Ann C.B. v. Keith A.B., 13 Carbon L. J. 23 (C.C.P. 1991) (Where both parents are equally fit, court will continue placement with father because he maintains stability in child's life and home environment and actively fosters her spiritual development).

Clearfield County

Abernethy v. Abernethy, C.P. Clearfield County, No. 2009-1692-CD (C.C.P. 2012) (Trial court granted primary custody of the parties' son to father, where father lived much closer to the child's school and father's retirement allowed him to be more available to the child and was in the child's best interest. In addition, the child's school was located near to father's home. Father lived only a few miles from the child's school and could get the child to and from school with little difficulty or inconvenience. He would also be available in events such as sickness during school, school delays, snow days, early dismissals, and any other emergencies. Primary custody with mother would mean that the child would have a 50 mile commute to school. The child's day-to-day life would be more stable in father's care based on his proximity to the child's school and his accessibility. "Simply put, father is available during the week, where mother is not. Further, the child's proximity to his school, school friends, school activities, and other extra-curricular activities will only continue to be more paramount as the child grows older.").

Mort v. Butler, C.P. Clearfield County, No. 91-956-CD (C.C.P. 1998) (Trial court awarded father primary physical custody of his minor son where the court determined that the home life provided by mother was unstable and therefore that the best interests of the child would be served by awarding father custody. The court determined that the home life maintained by mother, as demonstrated by her lack of supervision and discipline, was too unstable to provide a proper home environment. Stability in remaining with the primary custodial parent is also considered, but, "stability is not to be preserved when there are other reasons why the environment in which the child is living under the present custody order is no longer the one that will overall serve the child's best interests.").

Dauphin County

Ramer v. Ramer, 123 Dauphin Co. Rep. 21 (C.C.P. 2006) (Trial court held that in a custody proceeding, the sole permissible inquiry into the relative wealth of the parties is whether either party is unable to provide adequately for the child. Unless the income of one party is so inadequate as to preclude raising the children in a decent manner, the matter of relative income is irrelevant, citing *Roadcap v. Roadcap*, 778 A.2d 687 (Pa. Super. 2001). "Neither parent presented themselves as wealthy. The award of physical custody to father was not based upon the fact that mother appears to have less wealth than father. This court's custody determination was based upon numerous factors unrelated to mother's relative wealth, including her choice to live with her children on a dangerous property, her inability to perceive these dangers, her inability to at times supervise the children on the property and her inability to acknowledge and address her depression.").

Erie County

Flynn v. Bimber, 88 Erie Co. Leg. J. 8 (C.C.P. 2005) ("While a court may take into account the economic status of a party, it cannot ignore all other aspects of the child's well-being and best interests. A court is not obligated to award custody of a child to one party over another based solely on a bigger house or a better standard of living either. . . . This Court does not dispute that Plaintiff and his paramour have more than enough financial resources and space in their home to provide for the children. But, . . . the Court cannot ignore other factors affecting their welfare. Defendant is better able, at this time, to provide daily, hands-on care for the children. Plaintiff has shown that he is not. He has not altered his work schedule to make himself available to care for the children. . . . Plaintiff, his paramour, and her family seem more concerned with their relative wealth and upscale community than the welfare of the children. Right now, the triplets are not old enough to appreciate how big their house is or how much money their parents make or where they will go to school. They are only aware of who cares for them, feeds them, bathes them, clothes them, changes their diapers, etc. The party that is better able to provide that kind of care should be the primary custodian of the children.").

Greene County

C.A.B. v. P.S., 29 The Greene Reports 10 (C.C.P. April 7, 2011) (Trial court reiterated that the relative economic resources of a parent should play no part in a determination of custody. In this custody action, mother argued that the trial court limited her inquiry into father's finances during the parties' custody hearing. Citing *Roadcap v. Roadcap*, 778 A.2d 687 (Pa. Super. 2001), the trial court emphasized that the economic resources of a parent has no place in a determination of custody. The court noted that there was nothing in the record to suggest that the child lacked for any necessity while he was staying with father).

Indiana County

C.D. v. T.M., C.P. Indiana County, No. 11074 C.D. 2014 (C.C.P. October 24, 2018), *aff'd*, Memorandum Decision, No. 1655 WDA 2018 (Pa. Super. July 26, 2019) (Factor fourteen under 23 Pa.C.S. § 5328(a) requires the trial court to consider "the history of drug or alcohol abuse of a party or member of a party's household. That factor does not apply when the individual is not a member of the party's household. Here, mother clearly testified that her paramour does not reside in her house with herself and the children. There was no other testimony or evidence presented that indicated that mother's paramour was a member of her household).

Lawrence County

Blackshear v. Blackshear, C.P. Lawrence County, No. 10999-2013, C.A., (C.C.P. 2015) (The trial court modified the consent order between the parties and awarded primary physical custody to father, where the parties' child was enjoying a positive lifestyle with her father and siblings and doing well in school. Mother and father entered into a Custody Agreement whereby mother would have primary physical custody of the child and father would have partial custody every other weekend. Father retained primary custody of the other two minor children. The parties' agreement permitted all of the minor children to be together with the custodial parent every weekend. Mother subsequently refused to return the child to father's custody. Father filed a petition for special relief and modification of the custody order, requesting that the court modify the consent custody order to reflect the current agreement entered into by the parties whereby father maintained primary custody of the child. The court found that it was crucial for the child to continue to attend school in the New Castle Area School District because she was flourishing academically there. The court declined to disrupt the child's positive and stable lifestyle).

Matthews v. Fitzpatrick, C.P. Lawrence County, No. 10272 of 2014, C.A. (C.C.P. October 29, 2014) (The trial court denied mother's request for primary custody and issued an order providing for shared legal custody, with primary physical custody to father and partial custody to mother on weekends during the academic year, and primary custody to mother during the summer months, with father having partial custody on weekends. The children had consistently lived in the residence occupied by father. They attended the local school and had strong connections to the community. Mother's request for primary custody would remove the children and place them in an unfamiliar school district and they would not have the benefit of their paternal family with whom they were accustomed to spending time. Also, if mother's motion were granted, she would have to place the children in day care while she worked).

Giammatteo v. York, C.P. Lawrence County, No. 11377 of 2011, C.A. (C.C.P. 2013) (Trial court transferred primary custody of the parties' children from father, who had relocated to Warren, Ohio, to mother, who continued to reside in Lawrence County, Pennsylvania, because of father's lack of a nearby support system and his "aggressive work schedule" in Ohio. Subsequently, after examining the best interest factors set forth at 23 Pa.C.S. § 5328(a), the trial court concluded that the children's best interest would be served if mother had primary custody. The court observed that since the parties' separation, mother made efforts to create a stable environment for the children, maintained a steady job, and purchased a suitable home close to maternal grandparents. Although father played the role of primary custodian since the parties' separation, the court found that his current lack of a support system, along with his "aggressive" work schedule, which included three different shifts during each week, did not put him in the best position to fully adhere to the best interests of the children).

Berresford v. Welsh, C.P. Lawrence County, No. 10560 of 2003, C.A. (C.C.P. 2012) (The trial court granted father primary custody of the parties' child during the school year where father was in a better position to provide a stable environment for the child than mother, and where the child preferred to go to the school in father's school district. Father was remarried with children, and his wife maintained a structured schedule that accommodated the children's daily activities while providing sufficient amount of available family time. The child also testified that he wished to attend the school district in father's district because he had friends there and his stepsiblings attended school there. On the other hand, mother had moved several times with the child since the parties' separation, requiring the child to change school districts twice).

Lehigh County

Yampol v. Andrini, C.P. Lehigh County, No. 2007-FC-0884 (C.C.P. February 29, 2012) (Trial court granted father's petition to modify custody and awarded primary physical custody of the parties' child to father due to mother's husband's alcoholism. When determining primary custody of a child, the safety of the child's environment is of prime importance. Mother's husband suffered from alcoholism and appeared to be under the influence of alcohol when he testified at trial. Husband had several alcohol-related convictions that triggered application of 23 Pa.C.S. § 5329 of the new Custody Act. Here, mother's husband was a member of the same household as mother. His DUI was one of the enumerated offenses listed in § 5329. Based on this and other alcohol-related offenses, mother's husband's appearance on the witness stand and the testimony about his frequent intoxication, the court concluded that mother's husband had a serious, active alcohol problem which had a direct adverse impact on the child at issue, particularly since he had driven him in a car on occasions. The court found that under 23 Pa.C.S. § 5329(c), mother's husband, as a household member, must undergo a drug and alcohol evaluation and then proceed with counseling which is deemed to be necessary. Until that happened or mother changed residences, appropriate restrictions were placed on mother's custody to protect the child. Accordingly, primary physical custody was awarded to father, but the court left the door open for the child's return to mother if she were to change her living circumstances).

Imlay v. Miller, C.P. Lehigh County, No. 2004-FC-0713 (C.C.P. 2011) (Trial court denied father's petition to modify the existing custody order for the parties' children where father's chief motivation seemed to be reduction of his support obligation. Father requested both modification of the custody order and contempt by mother based on the conduct of the parties' 13-year-old daughter in caring for her younger siblings before mother returned home from work and mother's alleged improper monitoring of that conduct. Father alleged that the daughter's behavior corrupted the younger children. Father cited the atmosphere in mother's residence, as well as the children's difficulties in school as reasons for transferring custody of the younger children to him during the school year. The court noted that father lived in a motor home which was insufficient as a residence for the children. Furthermore, father's proposal was not acceptable because it would separate the younger children from their older sister. Finally, the court discussed father's continuing emphasis on the support order he paid for the children and concluded that his primary motivation in requesting a custody modification was so that he could reduce the amount of his court-ordered support).

Altenbach v. Altenbach, 52 Lehigh L. J. 210 (C.C.P. 2006) (Trial court held that, while all factors legitimately having an effect on the children's physical, intellectual, moral and spiritual well-being must be considered by the trial court, the court, in determining a proper custodial arrangement for the children, has the obligation to perform an analysis and determine, along with all other factors, which parent is more likely to encourage, permit and allow frequent and continuing contact and physical access between the non-custodial parent and the child. "Mother demonstrated her flexibility and willingness to cooperate. She has participated with Children in all Court ordered counseling. She keeps Father informed about Children's education and social activities and encourages them to talk to Father on the telephone. Although she did not favor their involvement in sports activities, she was there for them in providing support and transportation. Father, on the other hand, shows virtually no flexibility in dealing with the parenting issues faced by this couple. He seems bent on undermining the authority of Mother with a 'my way or the highway' attitude that I can only characterize as worrisome. The foregoing factors convinced me that Mother should be the primary physical custodian during the academic year and the parties should share physical custody during the summer months.").

Luzerne County

Laiuvara v. Thiede, 94 Luzerne Leg. Reg. 137 (C.C.P. 2002) (In a custody dispute, the parents begin on equal footing. They appear before the court absolutely equal in standing and neither is granted the benefit of any presumption due to any pre-existing factual circumstances. The fact that a parent has a more expensive home or a higher income than the other so that he or she could provide for the children's financial well-being is irrelevant unless a parent's financial ability is so inadequate as to preclude raising the child in a decent manner. The court further declared: "Parents' employment and consequent absence from the house cannot be a factor weighed against a parent if he or she provides adequate child care in his or her absence. *Murphey v. Hatala*, 350 Pa. Super. 433, 504 A.2d 917 (1986).").

Lycoming County

AW v. CW, C.P. Lycoming County, No. 12-21, 698 (C.C.P. 2015) (Trial court ruled that the children should continue to attend school in the school district in which defendant father resided because of the need for stability and continuity. Father resided in the former marital residence in Williamsport. The parties' son attended first grade in the Williamsport Area School District, and their daughter was eligible to attend kindergarten during the 2015–2016 academic year. Mother filed a petition for special relief, seeking to have both children attend school in the Loyalsock Township School District. Mother believed that the Loyalsock school district was in the children's best interest because it would not be necessary for the children to attend before-school care due to the start time of the school. The court found that the children's need for stability and continuity would be best met by remaining in the Williamsport school district).

JM v. MH, C.P. Lycoming County, No. 08-21, 702 (C.C.P. 2013) (The child's best interests would be served by her attending kindergarten in the father's school district, as father's stability and likelihood remaining in his school district was stronger than mother remaining in her school district. Mother desired the child to attend kindergarten in her school district. Mother resided with her fiancé and his children. Mother testified that the child at issue enjoyed a good relationship with her future step-brothers, and that it was important to her to attend the same school that they attended. Mother was renting her current home, and her employment required that she travel, with much of the travel going through father's school district. If the child were to go to school in mother's school district, she would require daycare for two hours after school. The trial court ruled that while it could not determine that one school district was better than the other, it appeared that the child's needs were best served by enrollment in the school district of father's home. Father owned his home in that school district for the past four years, so his likelihood of remaining in that school district was greater. Mother had been renting her residence for only a few months, and there was no indication that she would stay there long-term. Moreover, the only activity that the child was currently involved with, gymnastics, took place in father's school district).

AC v. SC, C.P. Lycoming County, No. 11-20, 887 (C.C.P. 2012) (Trial court declared that while it could not determine that one school district was better than the other school district, the child's best interests would be served by attending the school in the Montoursville Area School District. Father argued that there was a family tradition of his family attending the Montoursville Area School District. Father also argued that the child would know at least two children in his elementary school as his cousins would be attending that school. Three of the child's cousins would ride the school bus with him

111

and father believed that there was an important support network for the child in the Montoursville Area School District. The trial court agreed with father that providing an important support network for the child that was already established in the Montoursville Area School District would be in the child's best interests. The court noted that neither parent presented any testimony from the respective school districts or provided any information as to the curriculum offered by the school, class-size, school ranking, or special programs offered by either school. There was no reason for the court to believe that either school district would not meet the child's educational needs. The deciding factor for the court was that in father's school district, the child would have the benefit of attending school with cousins whom he had weekly contact and whom he had a good relationship. He would also ride the bus to and from school with three of his cousins).

Mifflin County

Britton v. Britton, 8 Mifflin Leg. J. 131 (C.C.P. 1990) (Trial court held it was in the best interest of the child to award primary custody to the father, for he is best able to provide a stable environment. The court based its decision on the fact that the father was moving back to Michigan, closer to the child's parental and maternal relatives—an apartment house also occupied by his parents, aunt and uncle and several cousins—and thus a more supportive living environment. The court also found that the mother could not foster the appropriate living environment for the child—she had no current means of support, and was living in Pennsylvania, separated from both sides of the child's extended family, with her new boyfriend. Such an unstable arrangement would be detrimental to the child's well-being).

Monroe County

Goode v. Orozco, C.P. Monroe County, No. 7893 CV 2012 (C.C.P. 2013) (Trial court granted primary physical custody of the children to father, where the factors for safety and continuity of routine favored father, who was retired from employment and provided a more beneficial home environment for the children. The trial court found that based on all the relevant factors, it was in the children's best interests for father to have primary physical custody. The court noted that father was more likely to encourage and allow frequent and continuing contact between the children and mother. Both parents were found equally capable of parenting the children. Although both parents adequately performed their parental duties, father was favored because of his retirement status and mother's varying shift schedules at work. The court noted the neighborhood's stability and safety and the nearby location of the elementary school as important considerations. On the other hand, mother's neighborhood had more incidents of crime and mother was assaulted while in the company of her children, which the court noted as particularly disturbing. Mother conceded that father's residence was safer for the children).

Grabko v. Grabko, C. P. Monroe County, No. 758 DR 1993 (C.C.P. 2004) (Trial court granted father's petition for primary physical custody of the parties' child, finding that in light of the child's poor academic performance and excessive absences from school, and considering the child's physical and emotional well-being, it would be in the child's best interests for father to have primary custody. Father awarded primary physical custody, where, the court determined, he could provide more discipline and structure to help the child with his academic problems. The court was concerned that mother did not believe that any actions she could take would improve the child's academic performance. The court concluded that when a child was equally bonded to both parents, and their physical accommodations were equivalent, father's ability to provide more structure and discipline for the child was a basis to award primary custody to him).

Adams v. Harper, 33 D.&C. 4th 460 (Monroe Co. 1996) (Where mother was unable to provide a safe and stable environment for the parties' two minor children, it was in the best interests of the children for father to have primary physical custody. The court also concluded, upon review of the juvenile records of the other children living in the home, that mother could not provide a safe, stable environment for the children, despite her love for them. However, the court determined father to be a stable and caring parent capable of providing his children with the care and guidance necessary for them to grow. Accordingly, the court determined that it was in the best interests of the children for father to have primary custody, but to allow both parents to share legal custody).

Montgomery County

A.D. a/k/a/ A.A. v. A.B., C.P. Montgomery County, No. 2012-20761 (C.C.P. Feb. 1, 2017), *aff'd,* Memorandum Decision, No. 747 EDA 2017 (Pa. Super. October 3, 2017) (Trial court held that the child had resided in five differ-ent residences with mother, which was disruptive of the child's stability and continuity. In contrast, the court found that father had resided in the same residence for nearly 4 years and the child was clearly completely enmeshed in his life in father's household. The trial court stated that it weighed heavily the need for stability and continuity in the child's education, family life and community life. The court granted father primary physical custody during the school year, when the child would be in first grade).

§ 3.4.8. Full Time Employment and Child Care Providers

It is well settled that the fact that a party must work for a living is not sufficient justification for a denial of custody.[136] The employed party must, however, demonstrate that the child will be adequately cared for

---

[136] Witmayer v. Witmayer, 320 Pa. Super. 372, 467 A.2d 371 (1983); K.L.H. v. G.D.H., 318 Pa. Super. 330, 464 A.2d 1368 (1983); Commonwealth ex rel. Holschuh v. Holland-Moritz, 448 Pa. 437, 292 A.2d 380 (1972); Hooks v. Ellerbe, 257 Pa. Super. 219, 390 A.2d 791 (1978), *reversed on other grounds,* Ellerbe v. Hooks, 490 Pa. 363, A.2d 512 (1980); Commonwealth ex rel. Lettie H.W. v. Paul T.W., 281 Pa. Super. 262, 422 A.2d 159 (1980);

during work hours and that this environment will be characterized by stability and genuine concern for the child's well-being.[137]

In balancing the best interests scales, courts cast a discerning eye on the nature and quality of the proposed care. In spite of the adequacy of the childcare arrangements, however, where both parties are fit but only one must work, the non-working parent may argue that he/she is able to stay home and care for the child.[138] Where both parents must work, the court will compare the daily care arrangements proposed by each party.[139] At this stage, it is the character and abilities of the childcare providers that become relevant,[140] although it has been stated that this factor is not controlling.[141] The existence of prior experience and familiarity with the children by the childcare provider/s will be considered.[142]

---

[137] 23 Pa.C.S. § 5328(a)(12); Johnson v. Lewis, 870 A.2d 368 (Pa. Super. 2005); Commonwealth ex rel. Cutler v. Cutler, 246 Pa. Super. 82, 369 A.2d 821 (1977); Gerber v. Gerber, 337 Pa. Super. 580, 487 A.2d 413 (1985); Witmayer v. Witmayer, 320 Pa. Super. 372, 467 A.2d 371 (1983) (mother demonstrated adequate care for child during work hours and evening social activities, court also noted lack of evidence of deleterious effects on child); K.L.H. v. G.D.H., 318 Pa. Super. 330, 464 A.2d 1368 (1983); *but see* Wiseman v. Wall, 718 A.2d 844 (Pa. Super. 1998).

[138] Commonwealth ex rel. Baisden v. DeMarco, 215 Pa. Super. 38, 257 A.2d 365 (1969); *see also* McCourt v. Meyers, 268 Pa. Super. 152, 407 A.2d 875 (1979).

[139] Wiseman v. Wall, 718 A.2d 844 (Pa. Super. 1998) (primary physical custody in mother was preferred over shared physical custody when mother worked the night shift and was available for more of child's "waking hours").

[140] In re Custody of Neal, 260 Pa. Super. 151, 393 A.2d 1057 (1978); Augustine v. Augustine, 228 Pa. Super. 312, 324 A.2d 477 (1974).

[141] Robinson v. Robinson, 538 Pa. 52, 645 A.2d 836 (1994) (Trial court did not commit gross abuse of discretion in awarding primary custody to father, even though mother's unemployed status would allegedly have allowed her to be available to care for child all day; trial court considered child's best interest in forming custody order and considered various factors, including child's affection for both parents and both sets of grandparents, evidence that father would be more willing than mother to encourage frequent and continuing contact between both parents and rest of immediate family, and willingness and availability of father's family to care for child while he worked); Murphey v. Hatala, 350 Pa. Super. 433, 504 A.2d 917 (1986) (a parent's employment and consequent absence from the house cannot be a factor weighed against the parent if he or she provides adequate child care in his or her absence).

[142] Commonwealth ex rel. Debeary v. Debeary, 310 Pa. Super. 137, 456 A.2d 221 (1983) (grandmother and neighbor more familiar to children than father's girlfriend). In re Custody of Neal, 260 Pa. Super. 151, 393 A.2d 1057 (1978).

The hours each parent must work will also be considered as a reflection on the amount of time each has available to spend with the child.[143] However, while it is generally considered best to maximize the parent–child contact, it has been stated that the serving of the best interests of the child is not necessarily directly proportional to the number of hours spent in the company of the child.[144]

LOWER COURT CASES

Adams County

Lefevre v. Null, 28 Adams. Leg. J. 17 (C.C.P. 1986) (A one-parent household may not be presumed as a matter of law to be inferior to a two-parent household in the determination of child custody issues. The mere fact that a parent is employed full-time is not sufficient to deny custody if appropriate arrangements are made for the child's care while the parent is away, especially where the child is involved in a stable family environment).

Allegheny County

S.B. v. B.P., 160 P.L.J. 337 (Allegheny County, 2012) (Despite the roadblocks mother threw in his way in attempting to obstruct contact between the child and father, father had evidenced a determination to have a relationship with his daughter and to be a continuing presence in her life. It was the court's judgment that by establishing a schedule of shared custody, the daughter would be better able to enjoy meaningful time with her father. Mother had historically refused to produce the child for custody exchanges, changed her cellphone number without informing father, and enrolled the child in a different school without telling father and without informing father as to where the child was attending school. The trial court determined that despite mother's lack of cooperation, father evidenced a determination to have a meaningful relationship with his daughter. Mother's complaint that father worked overnight was not a roadblock to father's having overnight custody, as his mother was available to provide for the child's

---

[143] Johnson v. Lewis, 870 A.2d 368 (Pa. Super. 2005); Wiseman v. Wall, 718 A.2d 844 (Pa. Super. 1998); In re Custody of Neal, 260 Pa. Super. 151, 393 A.2d 1057 (1978).

[144] Hartman v. Hartman, 328 Pa. Super. 154, 476 A.2d 938 (1984) (trial court's decision reversed based partly on erroneous emphasis on parties' work schedules); *see also* W.C.F. v. M.G., 115 A.3d 323 (Pa. Super. 2015) (In some instances it may be beneficial for a child to spend some periods of time in childcare as opposed to with a parent or family members); Johnson v. Lewis, 870 A.2d 368 (Pa. Super. 2005); *but see* Wiseman v. Wall, 718 A.2d 844 (Pa. Super. 1998); Garrity v. Garrity, 268 Pa. Super. 217, 407 A.2d 1323 (1979).

care overnight when father would be working. The court did not perceive that father's work schedule would leave the child unsupervised or interfere with his ability to raise his daughter).

Berks County

Feight v. Labruno, C.P. Berks County, No. 14-2193 (C.C.P. August 22, 2017) (Where the parents had a history of poor communication, primary physical custody of the child during the school year was award-ed to mother, who had a more flexible schedule. Mother's work schedule was flexible, so she scheduled her hours at times when the child was with father. The parties wanted the court to determine the custodial schedule during weekdays during the school year, and to choose the school district. The trial court con-sidered the factors in 23 Pa.C.S. § 5328(a) to determine the best interests of the child. The court noted that mother was more available to care for the child's daily needs due to her flexible work schedule, so the court decided that factor in her favor. The court explained that when a parent is willing and able to care for a child, and when the other parent is unavailable, the parent should be permitted to care for the child, superseding any arrangement involving a grandmother or other third party).

Brownlee v. Fenical-Brownlee, C. P. Berks County, No. 00-12703 (C.C.P. 2004) (Trial court refused to modify the parties' custodial arrangement on the basis of moth-er's allegation that during periods in which father had custody of the parties' child, he focused more on his work than on his relationship with the child. Mother requested that father's time be limited to alternate weekends and that his weekly schedule be elimi-nated. The court found that mother doted over the child and spent a great deal of time with him, while father's work schedule prevented him from doing the same. The court commented that a parent should not be deprived of custody if he or she must work. "The law is clear that the fact that a parent must work may not deprive a parent of cus-tody if suitable arrangements are made for the child's care in his or her absence. . . . While Father's involvement with the minor child is certainly not as extensive as Moth-er's, it does appear appropriate and adequate.").

Adam v. Klinger, 82 Berks L. J. 153 (C.C.P. 1989) (A mother will retain primary physical custody of the children where they have lived with her for more than seven years, where the children want to remain with their mother, and where the mother has adequate day care for periods when she is working; when a working parent provides good care for the children in question in the parent's absence, the parent's employment cannot be a factor weighed against the parent by the court).

Carbon County

Stephanie R.W. v. Ronald L.W., 14 Carbon Co. L. J. 146 (C.C.P. 1995) (Father's work schedule should not be viewed as a detriment to his ability to parent his child when he has made adequate day-care arrangements with grandparents; court stated that "a parent's work schedule will not be considered detrimental to his or her ability to provide for a child when proper measures have been arranged for child care during working hours").

Centre County

T.C.T. v. J.E.T., C.P. Centre County, No. 2018-4509 (C.C.P. May 7, 2019), *aff'd*, Memorandum Decision, No. 918 MDA 2019 (Pa. Super. February 21, 2020) (Trial court used father's work schedule as the determining factor in not awarding father shared physical custody. Mother was willing and able to transport the children on weekdays, whereas father was unable to do so, without significant, ongoing assistance from third parties. Father relied upon the Superior Court's decisions in *Witmayer v. Witmayer*, 467 A.2d 371 (Pa. Super. 1983) ("the fact that a parent must work is certainly not a factor that may be used to deprive the parent of custody where adequate arrangements have been made for the child's care in the parent's absence."), and *Johnson v. Lewis*, 870 A.2d 368 (Pa. Super. 2005) ("where, as here, other factors favor awarding custody to a parent, his work schedule may not deprive that parent of custody if suitable arrangements are made for the child's care in his absence."), to support his claims. The court noted that *Witmayer* and *Johnson* were distinguishable from the instant situation. In *Witmayer*, the father stayed at home full-time, and the mother went to work outside of her home. Here, both parents worked outside of the home. The trial court determined that it was in the best interest of the children to be in the overnight physical custody of mother during the school year because father's early start to his work day did not allow him to take the children to school/daycare, both of which were a significant distance from father and mother's respective residences. The trial court felt that it was best for the children to be transported to school and day-care by a parent).

Jordan v. Jordan, C. P. Centre County, No. 2005-2145 (C.C.P. 2007) (Father awarded primary physical custody where his employment history and available child-care options were more stable than those of mother, and where mother had recently been arrested for drunk driving. The court determined both parents to be loving and capable, but found that father's work schedule—which was more stable and flexible—more conducive to primary custody. Father's position was administrative, with flexible hours allowing him to set his own schedule. Father's supervisor testified that father's employment was stable. Mother had an unstable employment history, with frequent job changes, travel commitments, and a relocation change that required her to move to a new city. Mother testified she had suitable childcare available, citing multiple available providers, but the court determined it was preferable for the child to be cared for by a parent. The court also determined that father had better childcare available, noting that he employed a single provider to baby-sit the child whenever necessary. "This court determines it is not in [the child's] best interests to have multiple care providers while in the custody of one parent, as such circumstances cause more uncertainty and instability in the child's life.").

Cumberland County

R.A.G. v. A.L.R., 61 Cumberland L. J. 201 (C.C.P. 2012) (The trial court, citing *Wiseman v. Wall*, 718 A.2d 844, 851 (Pa. Super. 1998), held that while a parent's work schedule may not deprive the parent of custody, a parent's availability should be considered when determining a custody schedule that will serve the best interest of the child. The court also held that although Pa.R.Civ.P. 1915.4 states that custody cases are to be disposed of promptly, this rule is explicitly subject to the local rules of the judicial district and the rule cannot be viewed and interpreted in a vacuum, but must be construed *in pari materia* with the other rules relating to the same class of proceedings. The court also held that where the record included (a) numerous conciliation hearings, (b) an agreement of the parties, (c) opinion and position of the conciliator, (d) drug/alcohol evaluation ordered and completed, and (e) co-parenting counseling sessions attended, it was clear that sufficient good cause to extend the 180-day deadline was evidenced in the record).

Lawrence County

Matthews v. Fitzpatrick, C.P. Lawrence County, No. 10272 of 2014, C.A. (C.C.P. October 29, 2014) (Trial court denied mother's request for primary custody and issued an order providing for shared legal custody, with primary physical custody to father and partial custody to mother on weekends during the academic year, and primary custody to mother during the summer months, with father having partial custody on weekends. The children had consistently lived in the residence occupied by father. They attended the local school and had strong connections to the community. Mother's request for primary custody would remove the children and place them in an unfamiliar school district and they would not have the benefit of their paternal family with whom they were accustomed to spending time. Also, if mother's motion were granted, she would have to place the children in day care while she worked. It was in the children's best interests to maximize the time spent with parents and family as opposed to day care. The court concluded that the current custody arrangement, where father served as the primary caregiver, promoted the most stable lifestyle for the children).

Ritter v. Pagnotta, C.P. Lawrence County, No. 11279 of 2003, C. A. (C.C.P. 2006) (Mother was entitled to primary custody of the parties' two minor children because father's work schedule would prevent him from having as much quality time with the children as mother. With both parents being on equal footing, mother had the ability to spend more quality time with the children. Father testified that most working days he only has one hour in the evening to spend with the children. The court concluded that it was in the best interest of the children to spend time with father, but mother had more time day-to-day to spend with their children. "The factual record developed leads the Court to believe that Mother has more quality time available to spend directly, or hands-on, with the minor children then Father does. Father's hands-on time with the two children is very limited, based upon his work schedule. In fact, while in Father's custody, most of the caretaking for the children, albeit appropriately arranged by Father, is actually provided by individuals other than himself.").

Lebanon County

Miller v. Miller, 32 Lebanon Co. Leg. J. 184 (C.C.P. 1995) (The best interests of the children would be served by granting custody to the mother. The court was also concerned that father did not spend enough time with the children, and often chose to work instead of spending time with the children.)

Lehigh County

Marks v. Brown, C.P. Lehigh County, No. 2012-FC-0579 (C.C.P. 2012) (The trial court awarded primary custody of the parties' child to father where the evidence showed that father's family would care for the child during father's absence, and mother had no familial assistance. Mother's job required her to work long hours, during which time the 18-month-old child at issue and his three siblings were cared for at a 24-hour daycare. Father lived with his mother and had a full-time and part-time job. Father's mother took care of the child while father was at work. The trial court found that father was more capable of providing stability and continuity for the child. While both parents had non-conventional work schedules, there was testimony from the child's paternal grandmother that she would continue to care for the child during the hours that father worked. On the other hand, the court found that mother's arrangements for the child's care were tenuous. The court examined the statutory custody factors set forth at 23 Pa.C.S. § 5328(a), and found that the factor of availability of extended family weighed heavily in father's favor. Father maintained strong ties with his siblings and their families and had a good relationship with the mother of his daughter. Father's mother was available and willing to care for the child. There was no evidence presented that mother had similar relationships, as most of mother's family members resided in New York. The court's decision was based on 23 Pa.C.S. § 5328(a)(12), which is "each party's availability to care for the child or ability to make appropriate child-care arrangements." The court noted that father had a better plan on this important subject than did mother).

Luzerne County

Laiuvara v. Thiede, 94 Luzerne Leg. Reg. 137 (C.C.P. 2002) (In a custody dispute, the parents begin on equal footing. They appear before the court absolutely equal in standing and neither is granted the benefit of any presumption due to any pre-existing factual circumstances. The fact that a parent has a more expensive home or a higher income than the other so that he or she could provide for the children's financial well-being is irrelevant unless a parent's financial ability is so inadequate as to preclude raising the child in a decent manner. The court further declared: "Parents' employment and consequent absence from the house cannot be a factor weighed against a parent if he or she provides adequate child care in his or her absence. *Murphey v. Hatala*, 350 Pa. Super. 433, 504 A.2d 917 (1986).").

Monroe County

Szpara v. Collazo, C.P. Monroe Co., No. 168 D.R. 1997 (C.C.P. 1999) (Father was awarded primary physical custody despite the fact that mother was able to stay at home to care for their son, because father was able to provide adequate care through sitters or day care and therefore work was not a factor in deciding custody. The court noted that under *Wittmayer v. Wittmayer*, 467 A.2d 371 (Pa. Super. 1983), the fact that a parent that must work cannot be used to deprive a parent of custody where adequate care arrangements can be made. Father presented evidence that he did have adequate care available).

Philadelphia County

Vandegrift v. Martinelli, 28 Phila. 578 (C.C.P. 1994) (It is the public policy of the Commonwealth to assure reasonable and continuing contact between the child and both parents after separation, and to ensure that both parents share the rights and responsibilities of childrearing. The court declared that rather than have extended family members care for the child while the mother worked, a shared custody arrangement would be more appropriate. This arrangement would offer the child more time to bond with the father, who clearly demonstrated a willingness to meet his parental responsibilities. The court reasoned that the father was the more appropriate caretaker because of his desire to spend more time with the child, which would result in a strengthening of the parent–child bond).

§ 3.4.9. Primary Caretaker / Caregiver Doctrine

The fact that a child is or has been residing with one of the parties to a custody dispute is always relevant and may, in some cases, be controlling.[145] 23 Pa.C.S. § 5328 lists "the parental duties performed by

---

[145] Children's Aid Society v. Gard, 362 Pa. 85, 66 A.2d 300 (1949); Wiskoski v. Wiskoski, 427 Pa. Super. 531, 629 A.2d 996 (1993) (Where both parents are otherwise fit, one parent's role as child's primary caretaker may be given weight as determining factor in custody determination); Gerber v. Gerber, 337 Pa. Super. 580, 487 A.2d 413 (1985) (court placed substantial weight on fact that 5-year-old child had been with mother since birth); Gonzalez v. Gonzalez, 337 Pa. Super. 1, 486 A.2d 449 (1984); Hartman v. Hartman, 328 Pa. Super. 154, 476 A.2d 938 (1984); Commonwealth ex rel. Debeary v. Debeary, 310 Pa. Super. 137, 456 A.2d 221 (1983); K.L.H. v. G.D.H., 318 Pa. Super. 330, 464 A.2d 1368 (1983); In re Custody of Pearce, 310 Pa. Super. 254, 456 A.2d 597 (1983); Boland v. Leska, 308 Pa. Super. 169, 454 A.2d 75 (1982);

each party on behalf of the child" as an enumerated factor to consider in deciding a child's best interest.[146] Traditionally, the weight to be attached to this factor varied according to the duration of the child's residence with a party, the age of the child, the emotional ties which have developed between the child and the custodian and the circumstances under which the custody arrangement was initiated and retained.[147] This leads us to what is commonly referred to as the Primary Caretaker Doctrine. Prior editions of this book raised the question as to whether the Primary Caretaker Doctrine should be given less weight, as "the parental duties performed by each party on behalf of the child" is but one of the sixteen factors enumerated under Section 5328 which is part of the Custody Act enacted in 2011. In 2013, the Pennsylvania Superior Court answered the question in the case of *M.J.M. v. M.L.G.*[148] The superior court held that the language in the statute is clear, "and we cannot expand it to provide that a trial court must also give weighted consideration to a party's role as primary caretaker. We simply cannot graft the judicially-created primary caretaker doctrine onto the inquiry that the Legislature has established, and so we conclude that the primary caretaker doctrine, insofar as it requires positive emphasis on the primary caretaker's status, is no longer viable."[149] However, the superior court also indicated that its conclusion does not mean the trial court cannot consider "a parent's role as the

---

Commonwealth ex rel. Montgomery v. Montgomery, 296 Pa. Super. 325, 442 A.2d 791 (1982); Commonwealth ex rel. Parks v. Parks, 284 Pa. Super. 400, 426 A.2d 108 (1981); Commonwealth ex rel. Oxenreider v. Oxenreider, 290 Pa. Super. 63, 434 A.2d 130 (1981) (reversal of lower court award to mother based largely on continued residence of child with father and new family by remarriage); Pamela J.K. v. Roger D.J., 277 Pa. Super. 579, 419 A.2d 1301 (1980); Commonwealth ex rel. Cutler v. Cutler, 246 Pa. Super. 82, 369 A.2d 821 (1977); *but see* W.C.F. v. M.G., 115 A.3d 323 (Pa. Super. 2015) (the trial court's finding that a change in custody to father would be disruptive to child because father had not primarily cared for child was deemed by the Superior Court, in part, not a basis for denying father primary custody, since mother took child from the house creating a status quo where father was not primarily caring for child and all factors pointed in favor of father's having custody).

[146] 23 Pa.C.S. § 5328(a)(3).

[147] *See* footnote 145, above.

[148] *See* M.J.M. v. M.L.G., 63 A.3d 331 (Pa. Super. 2013); *see also* W.C.F. v. M.G., 115 A.3d 323 (Pa. Super. 2015).

[149] *Id.*

primary caretaker when engaging in the statutorily-guided inquiry" and that when necessary the trial court may "explicitly consider" one's role as the primary caretaker.[150]

Therefore, the question has been answered and a party's role as the primary caretaker will no longer be given weighted consideration over the other factors enumerated under Section 5328.

It appears that the M.J.M. case also answers the question pertaining to the weight of other doctrines and policies such as the separation of siblings policy. However, at this time, no cases take on those doctrines and policies head-on.

The genesis of the Primary Caretaker Doctrine is the case of *Commonwealth ex rel. Jordan v. Jordan*.[151] As stated in *Commonwealth ex rel. Jordan*: "the continued presence of a fit parent who through daily affection, guidance, companionship and discipline fulfills the child's psychological and physical needs is crucial to a child's well-being." The court further stated that the identification of the primary caretaker by the court serves a useful, productive purpose as evidence of continued caring and commitment in the past can be extrapolated into the future. The court went on to cite ten factors which could be weighed in making this determination. Although the court stated that where two natural parents are both fit, and the child is of tender years, the trial court must give positive consideration to the parent who has been the primary caretaker, this statement is tempered by the fact that "where the court awards shared custody, the considerations of the primary caretaker . . . are not applicable," and "where the child is of an age and/or maturity such that his or her preference should be given weight, a court might justifiably attach less importance to who had been the primary caretaker."[152]

Although evidence of the party's desire to raise the child will be considered, it must be noted that it is the child's affection for the parent which primarily concerns the court rather than the strength of a litigant's

---

[150] *Id.*
[151] Jordan v. Jordan, 302 Pa. Super. 421, 488 A.2d 1113 (1982).
[152] *Id.*

attachment to the child.[153] The strength of the child–parent bond and the probable trauma resulting from severance is usually ascertainable through the expression of the child's preference, as well as through psychological examination of the child.[154]

It is an abuse of discretion to award primary physical custody to mother when father has been the primary caretaker for quite some time and where no evidence whatsoever is introduced proving father is unfit to continue as primary caretaker.[155] In *Moore v. Moore*,[156] mother and father had shared custody of the 4½ year old child until mother decided to move to Florida to attend college. During her absence, father had primary custody and was a fit primary caretaker. Also during that time mother flew back to Pennsylvania once a month to see child. Mother then sought primary custody of child to take him to Florida with her. At first, the trial court awarded primary custody to father. Mother petitioned for rehearing, which the court granted. After hearing expert testimony at the second hearing primarily regarding mother's flexibility and willingness to encourage expanded relationship between child and father and extended family, the trial court changed its mind and awarded custody to mother. Superior Court reversed. The appellate court found that there was not sufficient reason to remove the child from an established, wholesome environment and place him in a wholly new and uninvestigated one. The court cautioned that the now repealed 23 Pa.C.S. § 5303, regarding encouragement of continuing contacts, is only one factor to be considered in determining the child's best interests. The Superior Court found father to be the primary custodian, and as such, mother's flexibility regarding the custody arrangement was not sufficient evidence to change the status quo since there was no suggestion that father was unfit. The Superior Court reinstated the original custody order.

---

[153] In re Davis, 502 Pa. 110, 465 A.2d 614 (1983) (psychological bonding is only one of the many factors to be considered and, although an important factor, may be outweighed by countervailing factors); Commonwealth ex rel. Staunton v. Austin, 209 Pa. Super. 187, 223 A.2d 892 (1966).
[154] English v. English, 322 Pa. Super. 234, 469 A.2d 270 (1983) (remand for trial court's failure to assess effect of transfer of custody on child); Commonwealth ex rel. Strunk v. Cummins, 258 Pa. Super. 326, 392 A.2d 817 (1978).
[155] Moore v. Moore, 393 Pa. Super. 256, 574 A.2d 105 (1990).
[156] *Id.*

A trial court was found to have abused its discretion in failing to maintain primary physical custody of a child with the mother based on the mother's historical role as the primary caregiver and the potential dangers of disruption of established patterns.[157]

In *Wheeler v. Mazur*, 793 A.2d 929 (Pa. Super. 2002), the Superior Court ruled that the trial court erred in granting primary physical custody of the parties' two children to father where the court gave little consideration to mother's role as primary caretaker and significant weight to testimony regarding past observations of mother rather than her present ability to care for the children. "This Court has consistently held that, 'where the child's parents are equally fit, or nearly so, . . . the fact that a stable, long-continued and happy relationship has developed between the child and one of the parents may be of critical importance to the formulation of an appropriate custody decree," citing *Pamela J. K. v. Roger D. J.*, 419 A.2d 1301 (Pa. Super. 1980). The court noted that when both parents are otherwise fit, one parent's role as the primary caretaker may be given weight as the determining factor in a custody determination.[158] However, in light of the recent decision in the case of *M.J.M. v. M.L.G.*, 63 A.3d 331 (Pa. Super. 2013), this would appear to be most applicable when all other factors are equal.

In terms of the length of the custodial arrangement, it is clear that the longer the period of continuous care, the more enhanced are the custodian's chances for a custody award, assuming that the custodian has provided the child with a stable, healthy environment.[159] Although there are no specific guidelines correlating the length of a child's stay with the weight to be accorded, it is evident that in contests between fit parents, relatively short periods, in several cases as little as one year, may shift the balance substantially in that party's favor.[160] This is particularly true

---

[157] Durning v. Balent/Kurdilla, 19 A.3d 1125 (Pa. Super. 2011).

[158] *See also* Wiseman v. Wall, 718 A.2d 844 (Pa. Super. 1998).

[159] *See* Ellerbe v. Hooks, 490 Pa. 363, 416 A.2d 512 (1980); Commonwealth ex rel. McKee v. Reitz, 193 Pa. Super. 125, 163 A.2d 908 (1960).

[160] Haraschak v. Haraschak, 268 Pa. Super. 173, 407 A.2d 886 (1979); Commonwealth ex rel. Cutler v. Cutler, 246 Pa. Super. 82, 369 A.2d 821 (1977); B. v. B., 27 Som. 213 (1969). *But see* Commonwealth ex rel. Grimes v. Grimes, 281 Pa. Super. 484, 422 A.2d 572 (1980).

where the child has adjusted well to the present environment and it is a stable one.[161]

It must also be stressed that although the period of time in which the child has been in the custody of a party will be assessed favorably toward that party, when a party acts to hamper the contacts or relationship between the child and a parent, those actions will weigh heavily against them in a custody dispute. In fact, it has been held that such obstructive conduct may warrant a change of custody.[162]

In cases where a non-parent is seeking custody and argues that he or she has cared for the child for a stated period, the duration of the custodial arrangement must be substantially greater if the third party is to prevail over the parent's prima facie right to custody.[163]

In *E.A.L. v. L.J.W.*,[164] the Superior Court vacated a trial court order granting custody to the mother rather than the grandparents and remanded the matter for further proceedings. The court emphasized the importance of a stable and familiar family environment, noting that the children had lived with grandparents for a substantial number of years and were happy with the arrangement.

It must also be noted that when a third party asserts that an extended period of custodial care and the consequent stability for the child should be weighted in his or her favor, evidence must also be presented as to the reasons why the child has stayed so long with the third party.[165] The rationale in this regard is that to hold otherwise would enable a third party to defeat the child's parent by refusing to return the child and prolonging

---

[161] Haraschak v. Haraschak, 268 Pa. Super. 173, 407 A.2d 886 (1979); Commonwealth ex rel. Cutler v. Cutler, 246 Pa. Super. 82, 369 A.2d 821 (1977).

[162] Pamela J.K. v. Roger D.J., 227 Pa. Super. 579, 419 A.2d 1301 (1980).

[163] Ellerbe v. Hooks, 490 Pa. 363, 416 A.2d 512 (1980); Commonwealth ex rel. Children's Aid Society v. Gard, 362 Pa. 85, 66 A.2d 300 (1949); Miller v. Miller, 327 Pa. Super. 45, 474 A.2d 1165 (1984); English v. English, 322 Pa. Super. 234, 469 A.2d 270 (1983) (remand for trial court's failure to assess effect of transfer of custody on child); Commonwealth ex rel. Strunk v. Cummins, 258 Pa. Super. 326, 392 A.2d 817 (1978); In re Minor Children of George Brody, 62 Luz. 91 (1972).

[164] 443 Pa. Super. 573, 662 A.2d 1109 (1995).

[165] In re James John M., 333 Pa. Super. 417, 482 A.2d 637 (1984).

possession by litigation.[166] Similarly, where a parent absconds with a child and upon return seeks to assert the importance of the element of stability, not only will the weight attached to the length of the custodial period dwindle, but the parent's asserted promotion of the best interests of the child will be seriously in question as a result of the parent's estrangement of the child from the other parent.[167]

An interesting situation occurs when the breakup of the household is recent and the primary caretaker has or will soon be entering the working world and will consequently be unable to devote the whole day to the child, as the best interests of the child must be considered as of the time of the hearing.[168]

In *Stolarick v. Novak*,[169] it was held that where both parents are determined to be equally fit, the fact that a stable, long-continued, and happy relationship has developed between the child and one parent may be of critical importance to the formulation of a custody decree. In *Stolarick*, the Superior Court reversed a trial court that had transferred custody from the father to the mother. The trial court had transferred custody despite its finding that the father had been an exemplary parent, because the court disapproved of the father's fundamentalist Christian beliefs, holding them to be restricted, sterile, and doctrinaire. In reversing the trial court, the Superior Court emphasized the loving, stable, and devoted parenting that father had indisputably provided for the children during the five years since separation. Where both parents are fit, the importance of the bonds established with the primary caretaker and the negative impact of disrupting those ties were determinative factors for the court.

In another case, the Superior Court acknowledged the importance of stability in the home environment as a factor in a custody decision. However, the court gave primacy instead to the continuity of the custodial relationship the children had developed with their "primary caretaker."

---

[166] *Id.* at 424, 482 A.2d at 640.

[167] Commonwealth ex rel. Newcomer v. King, 301 Pa. Super. 239, 447 A.2d 630 (1982).

[168] Brooks v. Brooks, 319 Pa. Super. 268, 466 A.2d 152 (1983).

[169] Stolarack v. Novak, 401 Pa. Super. 171, 584 A.2d 1034 (1991); *see also* Nancy E.M. v. Kenneth D.M., 316 Pa. Super. 351, 462 A.2d 1386 (1983).

The court placed great weight on the emotional ties formed with the parent who continually served their emotional needs despite the fact that the parent and children had moved frequently and had finally settled in a small home a considerable distance from the former marital home where the children once lived. Thus, the father was not entitled to primary physical custody of the children on the grounds that mother had moved three times and was not providing as desirable living quarters for children as was father; one of the moves was more in the nature of a visit to an aunt, the second was required because their existing house was sold, and although the present residence was not as "sumptuous" as the father's, it was "more than adequate" for the needs of the children.[170]

In *Johns v. Cioci*, 865 A.2d 931 (Pa. Super. 2004) the Superior Court ruled that the trial court abused its discretion by transferring primary custody to father because the court did not give sufficient consideration to issues of stability and potential harm to the child, or to the child's preference. Mother argued that the trial court abused its discretion in transferring primary physical custody to father, apparently disregarding the fact that mother had been the primary caregiver for almost all of the child's life; in not ordering a full custody evaluation; in not directly inquiring as to the child's preference during the court's first interview with the child; and in not affording significant weight to the preference stated by the child in the court's second interview with her. The Superior Court agreed, and held that the trial court had abused its discretion in transferring primary physical custody to father "without directly assessing the benefits of stability in custody arrangements and the potential harm to the child from disruption of her long-standing patterns of care." The trial court failed to give adequate consideration to the fact that mother had been the child's primary caretaker since the parents divorced when the child was two years old. "When both parents are otherwise fit, one parent's role as the primary caretaker may be given weight as the determining factor in a custody determination. . . . The court must give attention to the benefits of continuity and stability in custody arrangements and to the possibility of harm arising from disruption of long-standing patterns of care. . . . However compelling Father's case for modification may be, any benefits

---

[170] Boylan v. Boylan, 395 Pa. Super. 280, 577 A.2d 218 (1990).

of a change in custody must be weighed against the benefits of stability and the potential harm of an abrupt switch in primary caregiver. The trial court abused its discretion by giving virtually no consideration to Mother's historical role as caregiver."

In *Swope v. Swope*,[171] the court rejected father's claim that awarding mother custody would disrupt the children's lives because they would have to change school districts. While continuing in school is an important factor and must be considered, it, like any other single factor, is not controlling. Here, the trial court clearly considered the disruption that attending a new school would occasion for the children, but concluded that it was necessary in order for their best interests to be achieved.

The Primary Caretaker Doctrine had a predecessor in child custody law known as the Roots of The Tree Policy. The Roots of The Tree Policy had its origin in a 1949 Pennsylvania Supreme Court opinion in which Chief Justice Maxey analogized the nurturing of a child to the growth of a young tree.[172] Before the age of two, the opinion noted, the "roots have not yet taken deep hold in the nourishing earth."[173] After that time, however, the child becomes strongly attached to those standing in a parental relationship.[174] Therefore, to uproot the child at any point beyond the very early years could result in severe unhappiness or even physical harm to the child.[175] A Superior Court decision abrogated the Roots of The Tree Policy stating that "(w)e no longer so lightly assume that very young children will weather drastic changes in environment without psychological damage."[176] One year after this decision, the case of *Commonwealth ex rel. Jordan v. Jordan* was decided, which no longer

---

[171] Swope v. Swope, 455 Pa. Super. 587, 689 A.2d 264 (1997).

[172] Commonwealth ex rel. Children's Aid Society v. Gard, 362 Pa. 85, 66 A.2d 300 (1949).

[173] *Id.* at 97, 66 A.2d 306. *See Psychological Parents v. Biological Parents: The Courts' Response to New Directions in Child Custody Dispute Resolution,* 17 J. Fam. L. 545, 546 (1979).

[174] Commonwealth ex rel. Children's Aid Society v. Gard, 362 Pa. 85, 66 A.2d 300 (1949).

[175] *Id.*; Commonwealth ex rel. Kraus v. Kraus, 185 Pa. Super. 167, 138 A.2d 225 (1958).

[176] In re Tremayne Quame Indress R., 286 Pa. Super. 480, 429 A.2d 40 (1981).

retains a distinction between children up to age two and after. The Primary Caretaker Doctrine was applicable to children of all ages and mandated application of the policy on a case-by-case basis. However, a parent's role as the primary caretaker is now one of sixteen factors as directed by the superior court in the case of *M.J.M. v. M.L.G.*, 63 A.3d 331 (Pa. Super. 2013).

LOWER COURT CASES

Adams County

Smith et ux. v. Moore, 33 Adams Leg. J. 83 (C.C.P. 1990) ("The fact that a child has not lived with a parent for a considerable time will not alone defeat a parent's right to custody").

Beaver County

Metz v. Metz, C.P. Beaver County, No. 20337 of 2004 (C.C.P. 2007) (Mother was entitled to primary custody of the parties' child since the child had made progress in his new school, mother had been the child's primary caretaker, and father had a negative view of mother and a history of domestic violence against her. The child had adjusted well to his new school and to uproot him now to reside with father and return to his prior school would disrupt his life and would not be in his best interests. The court noted that the argument made by father, that continuing primary custody with the mother would disrupt the child's life, primarily because he must change school districts, was made in the case of *Swope v. Swope*, 689 A.2d 264 (Pa. Super. 1999). There, the Superior Court declared that, while continuity in school is an important factor and must be considered, it, like any other single factor, is not controlling. The court also observed that mother had been the child's primary caretaker. She did not work outside the home and had been primarily responsible for the child's daily necessities. Father worked full-time and was vague in describing how the child would be cared for while he was working. The primary caretaker doctrine requires the court to give positive consideration to the parent who has been the primary caretaker of the child in order to determine what is in the child's best interest. The court concluded that mother was more willing than father to encourage a relationship between the child and the other parent, even though father had disparaged mother in vulgar terms. Because father also had a history of domestic violence against mother, an award of primary custody to him would not be in the child's best interest).

Berks County

Heidel v. Eck, C.P. Berks County, No. 13-5091 (C.C.P. 2013) (Trial court denied father's petition for equal physical custody when it concluded that mother was more likely to encourage continuing contact with the other parent and that she had been the more stable force in the children's lives since the parties' separation. Father, who lived with his paramour and his paramour's two children, sought to have custody of his children when his paramour had custody of her children. The court found that mother was better able to provide the stability the children needed in their education, family and community because father relocated frequently while mother had been the more stable force in the children's lives since the parties' separation, that she appeared to be the "better nurturer" and that she was more focused on completion of the children's homework then father).

Herndon v. Lopez, C.P. Berks County, No. 07-9532 (C.C.P. 2011) (Trial court awarded primary physical custody of the school-age child to father since father had provided the child with a consistent, stable home, and mother's finances did not allow her to provide a regular residence. The best interest of the child is served by being able to be raised in a consistent residence and stable environment. The trial court granted father's petition and awarded him primary physical custody during the school year. The court acknowledged that both parents loved their daughter, but ruled that father was more capable of providing the stability that best served the child's needs. The court considered the factors set forth in 23 Pa.C.S. § 5328. The court held that the deciding factor in this case was the need for stability and continuity in the child's life, which father could provide. "It is apparent that father has provided stability and continuity and has a greater capacity to continue to so provide. Mother does not have the same track record.").

Strausser v. Strausser, C.P. Berks County, No. 04-239 (C.C.P. 2011) (Father should retain primary physical custody of the parties' child where the child would suffer adverse effects from changing homes and school districts. Father was awarded primary custody and mother had visitation rights of their only child, a 15-year-old daughter. Mother later petitioned to modify custody seeking primary custody. Mother was concerned that there was dissension between father's fiancé and the child, causing the child's schoolwork to suffer. While father acknowledged that he and his fiancée had separated briefly on two occasions, he noted that some of the problems between himself and his fiancée arose from the behavioral difficulties created by the child. Father also testified to his belief that mother was coercing the child to disrupt father's home and testify against him in court. The court determined that father should retain primary custody and denied mother's petition to modify custody. The court concluded that remaining with father would provide stability and continuity for the child because there would be no disruption to the child's lifestyle. The court also relied on expert testimony that a change in residence and school districts would be adverse to the child's needs. The court was reluctant to transfer custody of the child when the primary custodian was satisfactorily serving the child's best interest, citing *Wiseman v. Wall*, 718 A.2d 844, 846 (Pa. Super. 1998).

Ulshafer v. Ulshafer, C. P. Berks County, No. 00-705 (C.C.P. 2006) (Trial court declined to modify a custody order to grant father shared physical custody, where mother was more actively involved in the child's life, and where father could not prove that mother limited his visitation with the child because of father's homosexuality. The court noted that it was satisfied that the evidence strongly favored continuing mother as the primary custodian, particularly during the school year. Despite the fact that mother worked many long hours at various jobs, she always had time for her child, even to the point of appearing in school. "In this manner, the continuity and stability established by Mother in the Minor Child's life will be continued. As a general rule, a continuing and stable custodial relationship with a parent that satisfactorily serves the child's needs should not be disturbed. *Harner v. Harner*, 479 A.2d 583 (Pa. Super. 1984)." The court focused on mother's high level of involvement in the child's life and her unconditional commitment to the child. The court found that the child's stability with mother should not be disrupted).

Norris v. Dussinger, C. P. Berks County, No. 04-7530 (C.C.P. 2006) (Trial court awarded custody of the parties' daughter to father, where the child currently lived and had prospered, and who was better at facilitating communication. Maintenance of the status quo will control the custody of a child, where the child has prospered and the non-custodial parent does not present sufficient evidence to support uprooting the child. The fact that the child had prospered in her present environment made father's residence the more viable option. The court noted that mother did not avail herself of the weekly visitation that had been ordered, thus calling into question her desire to have the child on a primary basis. "Courts are reluctant to disturb existing custody arrangements which have satisfactorily served the best interests of the child. *Wiseman v. Wall*, 718 A.2d 844, 846 (Pa. Super. 1998)."

Matos v. Matos, 96 Berks Co. L. Rep. 347 (C.C.P. 2004) (Courts are reluctant to disturb existing custody arrangements that have satisfactorily served the best interest of the child. The removal of a young child from an established home with one parent has long been recognized as a factor which bears upon his emotional well-being. Where two natural parents are fit and the child is of tender years, the court must give positive consideration to the parent who has been the primary caretaker. "Not to do so ignores the benefits likely to flow to the child from maintaining day-to-day contact with the parent on whom the child has depended for satisfying his basic physical and psychological needs. . . . The Court is cautiously ordering primary custody remain with Mother, despite what appears from all accounts to be her poor choice in boyfriends.").

Cichocki v. Mazurek-Smith, 97 Berks Co. L. J. 137 (C.C.P. 2004) (Continuing in the same school system can be a factor in a custody decision. "Bradley is comfortable with his school and his teachers are addressing his problems. If Bradley were to live with Father primarily during the school year, he would have to make new friends and adjust to new routines. That would not be in the child's best interest." Citing *Fisher v. Fisher*, 535 A.2d 1163 (Pa. Super. 1988), the court held that continuing in the same school system can be a factor in a custody decision).

Morales v. Morales, 95 Berks Co. 357 (C.C.P. 2003) (If in the past, the primary caretaker has tended to the children's physical needs and has exhibited love, affection, concern, tolerance, discipline, and a willingness to sacrifice, the trial judge may predict that those qualities will continue, citing *Stolarick v. Novak*, 401 Pa. Super. 171, 584 A.2d 1034 (1991). The court found that mother would continue to devote herself to the children's care and needs).

Delancey. v. Hoover, 95 Berks Co. L. J. 257 (C.C.P. 2003) (Trial court held that if, in the past, the primary caretaker has tended to the child's physical needs and has exhibited love, affection, concern, tolerance, discipline, and a willingness to sacrifice, the trial judge may predict that those qualities will continue. "Father has done a wonderful job of learning to parent Michael. He provides Michael with fun times in social activities. The court does not denigrate his involvement in the child's life. However, without Mother attending to the 'details', Michael would be missing essential ingredients to a successful life. A parent must be more than a buddy or playmate.").

Baker v. Montonya, 95 Berks Co. L. J. 269 (C.C.P. 2003) (Trial court noted that where two natural parents are fit and the child is of tender years, the court must give positive consideration to the parent who has been the primary caretaker. "Not to do so ignores the benefits likely to flow to the child from maintaining day-to-day contact with the parent on whom the child has depended for satisfying his basic physical and psychological needs." The court also noted that while it is important that in a custody situation each party's history is examined, it is the ability of the caretaker to care for the child as of the time of the custody hearing, not as of an earlier time, which is determinative, citing *Wiseman v. Wall*, 718 A.2d 844, 848 (Pa. Super. 1998).

Templin v. Templin, 94 Berks Co. L. J. 333 (C.C.P. 2002) (Where a child's parents are equally fit, or nearly so, the fact that a stable, long-continued and happy relationship has developed between the children and one of the parents may be of critical importance to the formulation of an appropriate custody decree. "Both children want to remain in their current schools. They have friends in their schools. They participate in sports related activities in their schools. They have no guarantee that they would be able to participate in these activities in Father's school district which is larger than mother's district. For these reasons, the court finds that continuing in the same school system is a factor in the case").

Boyer v. Stitt, 92 Berks Co. Leg, J. 275 (C.C.P. 2000) ("Continuing in the same school system is a factor in custody decisions. *Fisher v. Fisher*, 570 Pa. Super. 87, 535 A.2d 1163 (1988). In the case sub judice the court finds that this is a significant factor. The children like their school and are doing well there. This is the one area of their lives, which has given them the most stability").

Jacobs v. Jacobs, 92 Berks Co. Leg. J. 327 (C.C.P. 2000) (Trial court held that continuing in the same school system is a factor in custody decisions, citing *Fisher v. Fisher*, 370 Pa. Super. 87, 535 A.2d 1163 (1988).)

Klein v. Klein, 92 Berks Co. Leg. J. 89 (C.C.P. 1999) (A parent's ability to care for his children must be determined as of the time of the custody hearing, not as of an earlier time; unless it can be shown that the parent's past conduct has had a harmful effect on the child, it should have little weight in making a custody decision. The court noted that insofar as a parent's past performance is likely to be predictive, a judicial inquiry to determine the identity of the primary caretaker will yield evidence concerning the future commitment of a parent. If in the past, the primary caretaker has tended to the child's physical needs and has exhibited love, affection, concern, tolerance, discipline, and a willingness to sacrifice, the trial judge may predict that those qualities will continue. Here, father has been the custodial parent since January 1999. "He has shown the children love, affection, concern, tolerance, and discipline. He has moved to a larger residence to be able to accommodate the children. In order to be available for the children he has worked less hours. Thus, the court predicts that Father will continue to parent these children effectively if they remain in his custody." *See also Boyer v. Stitt*, 92 Berks Co. Leg. J. 275 (C.C.P. 2000).

Boyer v. Churico, 91 Berks Co. Leg. J. 377, No. 975904 (C.C.P. 1999) (Courts are reluctant to disturb existing custody arrangements that have satisfactorily served the best interests of the child; where both parents are fit and the child is of tender years, the court must give positive consideration to the parent who has been the primary caregiver. "[C]ourts are reluctant to disturb existing custody arrangements which have satisfactorily served the best interests of the child. *Wiseman v. Wall*, 718 A.2d 844, 846 (Pa. Super. 1998). The removal of a young child from an established home with one parent is a factor that should be considered in resolving a custody issue because it bears upon a child's emotional well-being.").

Geiger v. Morrison, 92 Berks Co. Leg. J. 69 (C.C.P. 1999) (Where both parents are fit and a child is of tender years, the court must give positive consideration to the parent who has been the primary caregiver; this consideration is given to recognize the benefits that are likely to flow to the child from maintaining day-to-day contact with the parent on whom the child has depended for basic physical and psychological needs. "Because mother has been the primary caregiver and Father has had little caregiving experience with Richard, transferring custody of the child from Mother to Father could have a devastating effect on the basic physical, psychological, and emotional benefits which have been flowing to the child for his entire life").

Lessig v. Lessig, 92 Berks Co. Leg. J. 49 (C.C.P. 1999) (Continuing in the same school system can be a factor in custody cases).

Klahold v. Klahold, 36 D.&C. 4th 469 (Berks Co. 1996) (Trial court held that no change of primary physical custody was warranted where mother had always been the primary caretaker and had done a good job, where the child had a strong preference for remaining with mother, and where the recommendation of the custody evaluation was not to change primary custody. While acknowledging that a child's wishes are not controlling, the court emphasized that it had to consider these wishes as an important factor in determining the child's best interests, citing *In Re Custody of Pearce*, 456 A.2d 597 (Pa. Super. 1983). Here, the child told the court that she wanted to live with mother and visit father less often. Citing the child's best interests as the prevailing standard in all custody disputes, the court accorded great weight to the findings and recommendations of the psychologist who had performed the custody evaluation. A hearing judge must consider uncontradicted expert testimony, the court stated, referring to *Murphy v. Hatala*, 504 A.2d 917 (Pa. Super. 1986). The recommendation that there be no change in primary physical custody was consistent with both the child's stated preference and the court's independent assessment that there was no basis for such a change).

In Re: Guardianship of Zachary M. Althouse, 88 Berks Co. Leg. J. 10 (C.C.P. 1996) (Trial court found that continuity and stability are important elements in a young child's emotional development, and the continuous residence of children with one parent may be the controlling factor in custody decisions. The court awarded guardianship to Jennifer and Jeffrey Roe, finding that this was in Zachary's best interests. The court initially noted that pursuant to *Rowles v. Rowles*, 668 A.2d 126 (Pa. 1995), the presumption that a parent has a prima facie right to custody as against third parties has been abolished. Custody must now be determined by a preponderance of the evidence, weighing parenthood as a strong factor for consideration in the determination of what affiliation will best serve the child's interests, including physical, emotional, intellectual, moral, and spiritual well-being. The court held that the continuous residence of children with one parent may be the controlling factor in a custody dispute, citing *Egelkamp v. Egelkamp*, 524 A.2d 501 (Pa. Super. 1987). The court found that the fact that Zachary had never lived alone with father and is familiar and comfortable with the environment provided by the Roes is controlling. Moreover, Jennifer has helped care for Zachary since his birth, and she and her husband have provided the daily parental duties for Zachary since his mother died. The court acknowledged that father is a good man who loves his child, but that love does not conquer everything and a parent does not own a child just because they share a blood relationship).

Carbon County

E.M. v. M.M., 15 Carbon Co. L. J. 327 (C.C.P. 2000) (Trial court held that in a contested custody case where parents were equally fit, the custodial scales tipped in favor of mother, where she had been the children's primary caregiver since birth, would ensure continuity and stability in the children's lives, and had displayed more flexibility than father in ensuring that both parents would continue to play a maximum role in the children's lives. "It is clear that when a child receives love, guidance, companionship and direction from a parent on a consistent basis, a firm foundation is being laid for the child's future healthy development. The need for continuity can be a controlling factor in the custodial decision, and we must give positive weight to the parent who has been the child's primary caregiver. . . . In this case, it was clear that the children's principal caregiver since their birth has been, and continues today, their Mother. She was the hub around which this household revolved. She managed the finances and orchestrated the care and activities of the girls. She is the one to whom the children's look for guidance and for their basic physical and emotional needs, and she serves as their role model. . . . Our courts have long recognized the importance of a continuing and stable custodial relationship with a parent which satisfactorily serves the child's needs. . . . Continuity and stability are important elements in a child's emotional development.)".

Sander v. Sander, 15 Carbon Co. L. J. 1 (C.C.P. 1997) (Trial court refused father shared equal custody where the children were thriving under the mother's primary physical custody. "Courts have long recognized the importance of a continuing and stable custodial relationship with a parent which satisfactorily serves the child's needs. Continuity and stability are important elements in the child's emotional development. . . . The custodial environment in which a child has done well should not be disrupted unless the weight of countervailing factors indicates that a different setting would better serve the children's best interest. Applying these legal guidelines to the facts in this case, it is clear to the Court that it would be in children's best interest that they continue, for the most part, in the custodial arrangement that has been in existence for three (3) years and presently exists between the parties.").

Stephanie R.W. v. Ronald L.W., 14 Carbon Co. L. J. 146 (C.C.P. 1995)(Trial court held that a child's long-term custody with father in which he is flourishing should not be disrupted without compelling reasons. The court noted that a custodial environment in which the child has been thriving should not be disrupted unless the weight of countervailing factors indicates that a different setting would better serve the child's best interests. The court observed that Pennsylvania case law cautions that when a child has lived a considerable amount of time with one party, the court must weigh the advantages and risks that may result from a change in custody).

Centre County

Emminger v. Burgos, C.P. Centre County, No. 2004-2845 (C.C.P. 2014) (Trial court ruled that father's continued failure to cooperate was the basis for denial of his petition to increase his custody. Failure to foster communication with the other parent may support a limitation of a parent's custody/visitation. The trial court noted that both parties were actively involved in the child's life, but in different ways. While the court was concerned that mother's changing romantic life jeopardized the stability of her home, it gave her a preference as the parent who had provided the consistent, nurturing care for the child since birth. Even though the court sought to expand the child's time spent with father, his repeated efforts to sabotage mother's custody time with the child, as well as his actions in videotaping custody exchanges made expanding his time untenable).

Davis v. Shawley, C.P. Centre County, No. 2004-2382 (C.C.P. 2005) (It was in the child's best interests to award father primary physical custody where the child had a good relationship with father's family and experienced anxiety while residing with mother. The court granted father's petition for primary physical custody, determining that the present custody arrangement did not promote the child's best interests. The court explained that in *In the Interest of Coast*, 561 A.2d 762 (Pa. Super. 1989), the Superior Court held that the best interests of the child controls a custody determination where neither parent has been found unfit. "Before this court, therefore, Father and

Mother are viewed as equally suitable to be the primary custodian of the child. This court must then look to which environment provided by each parent would serve the best interests of the child." The court cited a number of factors, including the facts that father lived with his mother and sister, both of whom had acted as long-term, positive influences in the child's life, and that the child had experienced anxiety and physical distress over the existing custody arrangement. The court further determined that the "custody scale" did not tip in mother's favor merely because the child's half-sister resided with mother. "The presence of a sibling in mother's home is just one factor that must be considered in conjunction with the remaining factors.").

Clearfield County

Mort v. Butler, C.P. Clearfield County, No. 91-956-CD (C.C.P. 1998) (Trial court awarded father primary physical custody of his minor son where the court determined that the home life provided by mother was unstable and therefore that the best interests of the child would be served by awarding father custody. The court determined that the home life maintained by mother, as demonstrated by her lack of supervision and discipline, was too unstable to provide a proper home environment. Stability in remaining with the primary custodial parent is also considered, but, "stability is not to be preserved when there are other reasons why the environment in which the child is living under the present custody order is no longer the one that will overall serve the child's best interests.").

Clinton County

Wadsworth v. Wadsworth, C.P. Clinton County, No. 1220-95 (C.C.P. 1996) (Where the grandmother had been the child's primary caretaker since infancy with only minimal contact with his natural mother, it would not be in the child's best interest to award primary custody to the child's mother. The court explained that pursuant to *Rowles v. Rowles*, 668 A.2d 126 (Pa. 1995), parents no longer enjoy a prima facie right to custody as against third parties. Rather, courts must now focus on the best interests of the child in deciding custody disputes between parents and third parties. In making this determination, the court must weigh "parenthood as a strong factor for consideration;" however, the ultimate concern of the court should be what affiliation will best serve the child's best interests, including physical, emotional, intellectual, moral, and spiritual well-being. The court determined that the child's best interests would be served by awarding physical and legal custody to the grandmother. The court held that mother was not yet ready to resume the full-time parenting of the child that she previously gave up many years ago).

Delaware County

Sternlieb v. Bilker, 74 Del. Rep. 160 (C.C.P. 1986) (Trial court may, where it finds the parties equally fit to provide for the best interests of the child, consider the desirability of maintaining a continued residence between parent and child as a factor in making its custody determination).

Erie County

Kuntz v. Kuntz, 90 Erie Co. Leg. J. 222 (C.C.P. 2007) (While there is a dearth of homeschooling/child custody cases in Pennsylvania, the homeschooling program provided by mother for the parties' two children complied with the Compulsory School Law and the Pennsylvania Homeschooling Act, and mother could continue homeschooling the parties' minor children. The trial court rejected husband's arguments against homeschooling and noted: "Defendant [mother] presented undisputed testimony that the children are involved in sports and other activities not affiliated with the Church, that they are outgoing, enthusiastic, and sociable. Neither their faith nor their homeschooling appears to have limited their progression." No evidence was presented that the children were failing or not making progress in their studies).

Indiana County

S.W. v. C.W., C. P. Indiana County, No. 11665 CD 1999 (C.C.P. 2007) (Trial court allowed father to retain primary physical custody of the child where father had functioned as the child's primary caretaker for two years, thus creating a stable environment for the child. Quoting *Wheeler v. Mazur*, 793 A.2d 929 (Pa. Super. 2002), which in turn cited *Wiseman v. Wall*, 718 A.2d 844 (Pa. Super. 1998), the court observed, "The Pennsylvania Superior Court has held that '[w]hen both parents are otherwise fit, one parent's role as the primary caretaker may be given weight as the determining factor in a custody determination." The court noted that although *Wheeler* and *Wiseman* dealt with primary caregivers who have been caring for children since birth, this authority provided an appropriate analogy here. In *Wheeler* and *Wiseman*, both parents were equally fit, so the status of primary caregiver was the determining factor, the court noted. Here, both parents concerned the court equally, and the court reasoned, "It seems that the most recent primary caregiver should be the determining factor." The court considered the issue of stability and noted that at the time of the hearing, the child had been living with father for two years and had settled into a routine. Moreover, after an *in camera* interview with the child, the court concluded that she was well adjusted, a good student, and responsible for her age. "The Superior Court has stated, a child's sense of stability involves more than just physical structures and location; stability with regard to caregiver and patterns of care must also be considered. In the present case, the child had been living with Father for two years at the time of the hearing. She has settled into a routine with regard to the custody plan, her education, and family and community relationships.").

Lawrence County

Thomas v. Thomas, C.P. Lawrence County, No. 11297 of 2006, C.A. (C.C.P. 2013) (Trial court granted sole legal custody and primary physical custody to mother despite the child's strong preference to reside with father; the court found that father was unlikely to foster and encourage a relationship between the child and mother. Failure to facilitate a child's relationship with the other parent may support an award of sole legal custody to the other parent. The child provided testimony which clearly demonstrated a preference to be with father. Mother testified that father had acted to alienate the child, and the child could not give a specific reason for wanting to live with father. The court found that mother was the parent who facilitated contact between the two, and that father's actions were largely controlling of the child, in an attempt to control the entire custody dispute. The court believed that father's actions caused mother's relationship with the child to suffer. The court was concerned that if the child went to live with father, his relationship with mother would be damaged beyond repair).

Lebanon County

Roof v. Roof, 35 Lebanon Co. Leg. J. 876 (C.C.P. 1997) (Trial court dismissed mother's complaint for custody, since the parties still lived with the children in the same house. In dismissing the complaint, the court found the issue was not yet ripe for judicial determination, since implicit in a custody award is the fact that the parties live apart. The court could not contemplate how such an order could be fashioned without creating a chaotic situation for the children in their home).

Lehigh County

Clark v. Clark, C.P. Lehigh County, No. 2011-FC-0827 (C.C.P. 2011) (Trial court granted mother primary physical custody of the parties' youngest child where mother already had primary physical custody of the child's older siblings. Father filed a complaint seeking sole legal and physical custody of the parties' youngest child. Father had only sporadic contact with the children and acknowledged that mother was competent and caring as a parent. The trial court denied father's complaint for primary custody and directed that mother be awarded primary physical custodianship. The court noted that a court-ordered custody arrangement must promote a child's relationship with his siblings. Citing *Johns v. Cioci*, 865 A.2d 931 (Pa. Super. 2004), the court declared: "This worthwhile objective of the law is better achieved by [the child's] primary residence with mother who has a healthy relationship with each child as opposed to primary residence with father who is estranged from two of [the child's] siblings.").

Hardner v. Hardner, C.P. Lehigh County, No. 2011-FC-0079 (C.C.P. 2011) (Trial court awarded father primary physical custody of the parties' child where he was better able to provide for the child's needs than mother and created a lifestyle that offers stability and continuity for the child. After the parties separated, mother moved from the marital home in Lehigh County to her parents' home in Northumberland County, a distance of approximately 80 miles. Mother and father both petitioned for custody of the child. Mother also petitioned to relocate with the child to Northumberland County. The court granted father's petition for primary physical custody and granted both parties shared legal custody. After considering the factors set forth in 23 Pa.C.S. § 5328(a), the court determined that the most significant factors in the case were the parental duties performed by the parties, the need for stability and continuity in the child's life, the party that was best able to meet the child's emotional needs and the party that was better able to attend to the special needs of the child. The court noted that the child needed extra supervision during the school year as a result of his attention deficit hyperactivity disorder. The court concluded that father had "competently and constantly" handled the child's school requirements and professional care needs throughout his education. Mother, on the other hand, had not shown that she could be as proficient a caregiver as father. Because of mother's disabilities and being periodically bed-ridden and unable to perform any of the activities of daily living since December 2006, father became the parent who primarily cared for the child. Mother participated to the extent that she could, but it was a limited participation. The court also found that it would be harmful to the child to grant mother's request to allow him to relocate with her, because his educational, moral, social and emotional needs were being met through his lifestyle in Lehigh County. The court found that mother also failed to show how relocation would improve the child's quality of life, after considering the provisions of the relocation statute act 23 Pa.C.S. § 5337(h).).

Lycoming County

Hull v. Hull, 20 Lycoming Rep. 124 (C.C.P. 1996) (Trial court held that although the court is to give consideration to the parent who has been the primary caregiver of the children, where both parents have proved themselves to be adequate, caring and loving parents, where father is more likely to see that a strong, loving relationship is allowed to develop and continue with both parents and where father is more likely to seek proper medical care for the children when they are sick, the father is entitled to primary physical custody of the children. Even though mother had been the primary caretaker prior to separation and held the more stable job and the children were closer to mother's family, mother had no greater advantage in parenting the children. Trial court determined that father was more likely to foster children's relationship with mother and therefore awarded him custody).

Montgomery County

Merryman, Jr. v. Larkin, 141 Montg. Co. L. Rep. 189 (C.C.P. 2003) (Trial court ruled that when both parents are otherwise fit, one's parent's role as the primary caretaker may be given weight as the determining factor in a custody determination. Custody cannot reasonably be granted on the basis of a parent's unsettled past unless the past behavior has an ongoing negative effect on the child's welfare. "It is clear to this Court that it is not in the best interest of the child to uproot her from her home, which she has lived in for over two years and from the parent who has been her primary caretaker for the child's entire life based on Appellant's notion that a normal family consists of two adults and not a single parent.").

Schulman v. Schulman, 129 Montg. Co. L.Rep. 370 (C.C.P. 1993) (Continuity and stability are important elements in a young child's emotional development).

Monroe County

Goode v. Orozco, C.P. Monroe County, No. 7893 CV 2012 (C.C.P. 2013) (Trial court granted primary physical custody of the children to father, where the factors for safety and continuity of routine favored father, who was retired from employment and provided a more beneficial home environment for the children. The court noted that father was more likely to encourage and allow frequent and continuing contact between the children and mother. Both parents were found equally capable of parenting the children. Although both parents adequately performed their parental duties, father was favored because of his retirement status and mother's varying shift schedules at work. Due to the young age of the children, the court specifically cited the need for continuity and minimal disruption in their routines. The children resided with their father for two years).

Crowell v. Lasker, C. P. Monroe County, No. 1135 DR 2002 (C.C.P. 2006) (Trial court held that even though father was better able to care for the child financially and offered the child a two-parent household, mother was entitled to primary physical custody of the child because she had cared for the child since birth. The court concluded that the best interests of the child favored placing primary custody with mother. Father was better able to support the child financially and could offer the child a two-parent home, since father had married. However, mother had raised the child since birth and had made significant sacrifices in order to move away from public assistance and become self-sufficient in order to care for the child. "Pennsylvania courts are reluctant to disturb existing custody arrangements which have satisfactorily served the best interest of the child. Under the primary caretaker doctrine, the trial court is required to give positive consideration to the parent who has been the primary caretaker and a child should not be lightly removed from a parent with whom the child has lived since birth. When both parents are otherwise fit, one parent's role as the child's primary caretaker may be given weight as a determining factor in a custody determination.").

Northumberland County

Dreese v. Dreese, 70 Northumb. Leg. J. 99 (C.C.P. 1998) (The length of time that a child has resided in his present home, although important, is not determinative. "The fact that a child has not lived with a parent for a considerable length of time will not alone defeat that parent's right to custody.").

Heimann v. Tomedi, 60 Northumb. Leg. J. 67 (C.C.P. 1987) (Where the children have prospered, primary custody will remain with the father. Where the children have lived with their father for four years and one of the children expresses a desire to continue this relationship and the other child is neutral and the children's physical, intellectual, emotional, and spiritual well-being has been maintained, primary physical custody will be awarded to the father).

Philadelphia County

Smith v. Phillips, 20 Phila. 255 (C.C.P. 1990) (Pennsylvania courts have repeatedly emphasized the importance of continuity in a child's life, and that, in custody disputes, the continued residence of the child with one party may be controlling; stability is not the sole criterion in a custody action; the fact that a child has not lived with a parent for a considerable length of time will not alone defeat his or her right to custody; stability is not to be preserved when there are other reasons why the environment in which the child is living under the present custody order is no longer the one that will serve his/her overall best interest).

Pike County

A.M.M. v. G.J.M., C.P. Pike County, No. 2011-2008-CV, *aff'd*, Memorandum Decision, No. 569 EDA 2018 (Pa. Super. August 8, 2018) (In a custody conflict, it is within the trial court's purview as the finder of fact to determine which factors are most salient and critical in each particular case. While the primary caretaker doctrine is no longer viable, a court may still consider a parent's role as primary caretaker in its consideration of the custody factors. No evidence presented of any past or present alcohol or drug abuse by any household member of the parties. Mother's fiancé testified that, while mother drinks alcohol and consumes one drink of alcohol when they go out socially, he had never seen her intoxicated. The court noted that although a court is required to give "weighted consideration to those factors which affect the safety of the child," pursuant to 23 Pa.C.S. § 5328(a), courts have acknowledged that the amount of weight a court gives any one factor is almost entirely discretionary, citing *M.J.M. v. M.L.G.*, 63 A.3d 331, 339 (Pa. Super. 2013).

Somerset County

Gramann v. Cole, 51 Somerset Leg. J. 213 (C.C.P. 1992) ("Influencing our decision is the fact that father has provided a stable environment for the children since March 1990, while mother has moved frequently since separation, and has only recently established what could be termed a home. Stability is an important factor in determining a child's best interests. A child's need for an established parental figure, a known physical environment, and continued residence with one parent are important factors in determining custody issues.").

Susquehanna County

M.W. v. A.R., C.P. Susquehanna County, No. 2017-979, *aff'd*, Memorandum Decision, No. 22 MDA 2018 (Pa. Super. November 9, 2018) (Relocation case where trial court denied Mother's petition to relocate and court ruled against Mother's argument based on the primary caretaker doctrine, as the law no longer requires the trial court to give emphasis to a parent's status as the primary caregiver. *See M.J.M. v. M.L.G.*, 63

A.3d 331 (Pa. Super. 2013) (the primary caretaker doctrine, insofar as it required positive emphasis on the primary caretaker's status, is no longer viable)).

York County

K.H. v. J.D.-T., C.P. York County, No, 2015-FC-001816-03 (C.C.P. June 27, 2017), *aff'd*, Memorandum Decision, No. 1178 MDA 2017 (Pa. Super. January 22, 2018) (While the primary caretaker doctrine is no longer viable, a trial court may still consider a parent's role as primary caretaker in its consideration of the custody factors. The court cited with approval *M.J.M. v. M.L.G.*, 63 A.3d 331, 339 (Pa. Super. 2013), where the court held that a trial court may consider a parent's role as the primary caretaker when engaging in the statutorily guided inquiry. A trial court will necessarily consider a parent's status as a primary caretaker implicitly as it considers the § 5328(a) factors, and to the extent the trial court finds it necessary to explicitly consider one parent's role as the primary caretaker, it is free to do so under subsection (a)(16).).

§ 3.4.10. Present and/or Past Improper Treatment of the Child

The treatment of children in periods of possession prior to the present proceeding often provides the court with one of the most pointed predictors of potentially prevalent parental patterns. In cases where children are treated "like dirt,"[177] provided with inadequate food or health care,[178] subjected to verbal or physical abuse,[179] or generally neglected by a custodian,[180] courts have denied custody to the offending party.

---

[177] Commonwealth ex rel. Husack v. Husack, 273 Pa. Super. 192, 196, 417 A.2d 233, 235 (1979).

[178] Commonwealth ex rel. Murphy v. Walters, 258 Pa. Super. 418, 392 A.2d 863 (1978).

[179] 23 Pa.C.S. § 5328(2); In re Davis, 237 Pa. Super. 516, 352 A.2d 78 (1975); Commonwealth ex rel. Stipe v. Anderson, 205 Pa. Super. 34, 206 A.2d 335 (1965); *see also* N.B. v. Comm. Department of Public Welfare, 107 Pa. Commonwealth Ct. 26, 527 A.2d 623 (1987) (absent a substantial risk of death, disfigurement, serious bodily injury, gross degradation, extreme pain, or mental distress, Pennsylvania accepts corporal punishment as a permissible means of child discipline, provided, of course, that the parent does not act with malicious intent in punishing the child.); Boland v. Leska, 308 Pa. Super. 169, 454 A.2d 75 (1982) (court distinguished between permissible corporal punishment and malicious abuse);

[180] Commonwealth ex rel. Murphy v. Walters, 258 Pa. Super. 418, 392 A.2d 863 (1978); Commonwealth ex rel. Likovich v. Likovich, 220 Pa. Super. 202, 287 A.2d 156 (1972). A parent has the right to raise his child as he sees fit within bounds of decency

Evidence that a party has lovingly cared for a child will, on the other hand, be considered most favorably by the court.[181]

In *R.A.R. v. T.M.*,[182] the court held that compelling circumstances required that maternal grandfather, rather than natural mother, have primary physical custody of child in light of mother's unwillingness and inability to care for child in his early years and time child spent in grandfather's custody. Specifically, the court found that mother had been unwilling and unable to care for the child in his early years, and that it would be destructive to remove him from a stable environment where Grandfather has provided him with constant, consistent care.

LOWER COURT CASES

Berks County

Moyer v. Moyer, C.P. Berks County, No. 08-11837 (C.C.P. 2013) (Trial court granted father's request for primary custody where mother's recent history appeared to be one of allowing family to care for the children while mother spent time with her paramour. Mother had been the primary custodian of the parties' children since 2008. Father filed a petition to modify custody stating that he was concerned that mother's current lifestyle left the children on their own too much and caused her to neglect their care. Mother began a pattern of leaving the children with family while engaging in social activities without them. The trial court determined that father was the more stable parent, and that, even though an award of custody to him would require a change in schools for the children, father's involvement with them on a day-to-day basis would be a benefit. The court emphasized that father had the means and ability not only to meet the children's needs to broaden their horizons but to also get them involved in more activities. Father also appeared to be able to maintain a sense of consistency in caring for the children, whereas mother had been preoccupied with her new romantic relationship).

Shepard v. Shepard, 83 Berks L. J. 25 (C.C.P. 1991) (Holding that although the mother had provided the children stability in the past, the father is best able to do so now. The court focused on the current facts and not the previous conduct by the parties

---

and reason, but he does not have license to abuse and neglect his helpless dependent. In re Adoption of J.J., 366 Pa. Super. 94, 530 A.2d 908 (1987).

[181] Ellerbe v. Hooks, 470 Pa. 363, 416 A.2d 512 (1980); Parks v. Parks, 284 Pa. Super. 400, 426 A.2d 108 (1981); *see also* 23 Pa.C.S. § 5328(9).

[182] R.A.R. v. T.M., 434 Pa. Super. 592, 644 A.2d 767 (1994).

and noted that a custody decision must be based on current facts rather than the parties' past conduct).

Cumberland County

A.J.S. v. M.L.S., C.P. Cumberland County, No. 2010-2689 Civil (C.C.P. 2016) (Trial court held that the attempts of a parent to turn the children against the other parent weighed in favor of awarding father primary physical custody, as the court must consider that issue under 23 Pa.C.S. § 5328(a)(8)).

Dauphin County

In The Interest of D.T., 116 Dauph. Co. L. Rep. 423 (C.C.P. 1996) (That the former foster parents of a child mildly spanked him four times over a four and one-half year period did not preclude the court from allowing the child to visit his former foster parents. The court held that mild spanking does not equate with child abuse under the law. By the child's own testimony, the court determined that the spankings were mild. Stating that it was not bound by DPW regulations, the court looked instead to the Crimes Code, the Child Protective Services Law and the Protection from Abuse Act, and concluded that under none of those laws did mild spankings constitute a crime or abuse. The court observed that although most parenting professionals do not recommend spanking, the Superior Court has held in *Commonwealth v. Ogin,* 540 A.2d 549 (Pa. Super. 1988), that it is not a crime for biological parents to mildly spank their child).

Delaware County

McShane v. McShane, C.P. Delaware County, No. C.P.-23-CV-014826-2000 (C.C.P. 2015) (Trial court held that the estrangement of the minor child from father, as a direct result of mother's actions in repeatedly excluding father from all major decisions affecting the child despite their joint legal custody, had undoubtedly harmed the minor child, father and the minor child's relationship, and their ability to communicate. The trial court granted father primary physical custody in California and mother partial physical custody).

Lawrence County

Waddington v. Waddington-Silvestre, C. P. Lawrence County, No. 10301 of 2004 (C.C.P. 2006) (Where the child's grandparents had provided a loving and stable home for the child while mother appeared unable to act in accordance with the child's best interest, primary physical custody would remain with the child's paternal grandparents rather than with mother. The court explained that a custody determination ultimately rests on the best interest of the child. The court noted that mother had made steps toward creating a stable household, that she loved the child and had grown increasingly more responsible regarding his care. However, the court believed that mother had approached this custody action with the belief that she was entitled to full custody simply because the child was her son, and expressed concern that mother was not sensitive to the child's wishes or to the lifestyle he had grown accustomed to under grandparents' care. The court observed that the grandparents had done a "remarkable job" in raising the child. They had provided him with stability and allowed him significant opportunities to learn and grow outside of school. The court noted that it is paramount for a minor child to have a certain measure of stability in his life, and also noted that the child indicated a preference to remain with grandparents. Consequently, the court determined that it was in the child's best interests to remain in the primary physical custody of grandparents).

Lebanon County

L.R.W. v. K.J.W., C.P. Lebanon County, No. 2013-20723, *aff'd*, Memorandum Decision, No. 146 MDA 2018 (Pa. Super. August 3, 2018) (Mother's contention that the trial court should have based its decision on her conduct at the time of the hearing and not what occurred in the past is no longer viable; rather, 23 Pa.C.S. § 5328(a) factors are what controls. Mother argued that the trial court focused on her past behavior and overlooked her testimony about her completion of an inpatient drug and alcohol treatment program, and that she was attending classes at a community college. Mother relied on *Wiseman v. Wall*, 718 A.2d 844, 847 (Pa. Super. 1998), for the proposition that "a parent's ability to care for a child must be determined as of the time of the custody hearing, not as of an earlier time." The *Wiseman* analysis, relied on by mother, was obsolete, citing *P.J.P. v. M.M.*, No. 1586 MDA 2017 (Pa. Super. April 27, 2018).

Lehigh County

Edwards v. Rahab, C.P. Lehigh County, No. 2007-FC-1172 (C.C.P. 2011) (Trial court ruled that mother should have sole legal custody of the parties' daughter and to make all significant decisions in the child's life where father did not desire a relationship with his daughter and failed to exercise his court-ordered custody rights. The court noted that the child looked forward to her custody times with father, but she was disappointed and upset on the occasions that she knew father was supposed to have custody with her and father did not exercise custody rights. The court noted that providing specified periods for father's exercise of partial physical custody would be a wasted effort because father did not spend the court-ordered time already granted to spend with his daughter. The court declared that mother should no longer be burdened with having to deal with court-ordered custody times for father, which he did not follow. The court noted that father could still have contact with his daughter, but emphasized that the onus was on father to contact mother and agree on visitation. Mother was not obligated to agree to any custodial times for father unless she was satisfied that father would abide by agreements that they reached).

Dieterly v. Muffley, C.P. Lehigh County, No. 2008-FC-0713 (C.C.P. March 15, 2012) (Trial court ruled that father should continue to have primary custody of the child based on his ability to provide stability/continuity in the child's life, despite his contempt of the court's custody order shown by obstructing mother's relationship with the child. The trial court granted the contempt petition against father, finding that father had violated the custody order by failing to cooperate with mother. Father had obstructed mother's custody rights by placing restrictions on her periods of custody, denigrating mother and her new husband in front of the child and failing to follow the court's instructions regarding telephone contact between mother and the child. However, the court refused mother's request to award her primary custody of the child. The court examined in detail the factors for determining custody set forth in 23 Pa.C.S. § 5328(a) and concluded that the child should remain with father. The court noted that both parents loved and took care of the child, were involved in her education and lived close enough to each other to allow for easy visitation. In making its decision, the court found persuasive the need for the child to remain at the same school in order to provide continuity and stability in her life. Moreover, the child expressed a preference for living with father and cited her strong bond with her paternal grandmother as one reason for that preference).

Monroe County

Minter v. Delgado, C.P. Monroe County, No. 6599 CV 2012 (C.C.P. 2013) (Trial court awarded mother primary physical custody of the parties' daughter and awarded father partial physical custody, despite father's history of abuse, where father's abuse was directed toward mother rather than the child. One of the primary factors in dispute was whether there was a risk of harm to the child. Mother alleged physical abuse by father against her. Father agreed to the PFA order she requested, without admission. Father also admitted to violation of the PFA on one occasion and was held in contempt as a result. However, the court found the matters involving the PFA did not indicate there was a likelihood of harm to the child. The court noted that father had completed anger management counseling and that he was open and forthright in counseling. Father had completed all requirements of the PFA orders and prior custody orders. Moreover, mother's fears were contradicted by father, father's step-father, and counseling and childcare providers who were involved with the child. The court noted that mother acknowledged that the matters involving the PFA did not give rise to a likelihood of harm to the child. While mother may have had concerns that father would hurt the child, they were not founded upon evidence presented of father's behavior toward the child).

Adams v. Harper, 33 D.&C. 4th 460 (Monroe Co. 1996) (Where mother was unable to provide a safe and stable environment for the parties' two minor children, it was in the best interests of the children for father to have primary physical custody. The Court also concluded, upon review of the juvenile records of the other children living in the home, that mother could not provide a safe, stable environment for the children, despite her love for them; court determined father to be a stable and caring parent capable of providing his children with the care and guidance necessary for them to grow; court determined that it was in the best interests of the children for father to have primary custody, but to allow both parents to share legal custody).

§ 3.4.11. Remarriage and Newly Acquired Families

The optimum environment in which to raise a child is concededly the home with two competent, loving, natural parents.[183] With that alternative eliminated by the separation of the parties and/or dissolution of the marriage, courts are forced to choose the setting which most nearly approximates the ideal. When a parent remarries and presents a durable relationship with a spouse of good character, the court, seeing a stable environment for a child who has already experienced the dissolution of one family, may consider this and compare the same with the circumstances of the unmarried party.[184] A party who remains single and provides a "stable family environment" will, however, suffer no detriment due to the failure to remarry.[185] Conversely, a party who has been through a number of partners subsequent to the divorce,[186] or who introduces a spouse of poor character or weak parental inclinations,[187] will have to present strong countervailing considerations, since such unstable conditions may negatively impact the best interests of the child.

The fact that a newly acquired spouse has children from another marriage or is about to have a first child from the present marriage will be considered, as a court may be concerned that the spouse will favor his or her progeny over the subject child.[188] Therefore, evidence to the

---

[183] See In re LaRue, 244 Pa. Super. 218, 366 A.2d 1271 (1976); but see M.E.V. v. F.P.W., 100 A.3d 670 (Pa. Super. 2014) (no presumption in Pennsylvania child custody law favoring two-parent families).

[184] See Sipe v. Shaffer, 263 Pa. Super. 27, 396 A.2d 1359 (1979); Tobias v. Tobias, 248 Pa. Super. 196, 374 A.2d 1372 (1977); Commonwealth ex rel. Cutler v. Cutler, 246 Pa. Super. 82, 369 A.2d 821 (1977); Carlisle Appeal, 225 Pa. Super. 18 1, 310 A.2d 280 (1973). But see Commonwealth ex rel. Jordan v. Jordan, 302 Pa. Super. 421, 448 A.2d 1113 (1982) (states emphatically that two-parent families may not be presumed to provide a better child rearing setting and that court must analyze effect of presence of step-parent on a case-by-case basis).

[185] Commonwealth ex rel. Jordan v. Jordan, 302 Pa. Super. 421, 448 A.2d 1113 (1982); Jon M.W. v. Brenda K., 279 Pa. Super. 50, 420 A.2d 738, 740–41 (1980).

[186] See Commonwealth ex rel. Kraus v. Kraus, 185 Pa. Super. 167, 138 A.2d 225 (1958).

[187] See Commonwealth ex rel. Doberstein v. Doberstein, 201 Pa. Super. 102, 192 A.2d 154 (1963).

[188] Commonwealth ex rel. Cutler v. Cutler, 246 Pa. Super. 82, 369 A.2d 821 (1977); Commonwealth ex rel. Grillo v. Shuster, 226 Pa. Super. 229, 312 A.2d 58 (1973).

effect that the child has adjusted well to a new spouse and any children of that spouse will be favorably received and tend to negate the court's fear of favoritism.[189] In fact, when it is demonstrated that the child has developed strong bonds to the newly acquired family, courts have viewed the continuation of such relationship as a weighty factor in refusing to transfer custody.[190] Furthermore, testimony by the new spouse as to his or her willingness to accept the child and care for it as one of his or her own is generally vital to a custody award and courts have remanded on numerous occasions citing the absence of such testimony as a cause.[191] A step-parent should, however, be cautious with regard to usurpation of the natural parent's role or involvement in the child's life as such conduct may create a negative inference if it is found to be harmful to the child.[192]

§ 3.4.12. Relinquishment or Transfer of Custody

The release of a child into the custody of another is ordinarily viewed as an indicator of that party's willingness not to raise the child and is thus relevant to the custody determination.[193] The mere fact that a child has been separated from a parent for an extended period of time will

---

[189] Commonwealth ex rel. Cutler v. Cutler, 246 Pa. Super. 82, 369 A.2d 821 (1977); Tobias v. Tobias, 248 Pa. Super. 168, 374 A.2d 1372 (1977).

[190] Commonwealth ex rel. Oxenreider v. Oxenreider, 290 Pa. Super. 63, 434 A.2d 130 (1981); Commonwealth ex rel. Montgomery v. Montgomery, 296 Pa. Super. 325, 442 A.2d 791 (1982).

[191] J.F.G. v. K.A.G., 278 Pa. Super. 25, 419 A.2d 1337 (1980); Summers v. Summers, 273 Pa. Super. 285, 417 A.2d 651 (1979); Gunter v. Gunter, 240 Pa. Super. 382, 361 A.2d 307 (1976); Commonwealth ex rel. Kraus v. Kraus, 185 Pa. Super. 167, 138 A.2d 225 (1958).

[192] Commonwealth ex rel. Oxenreider v. Oxenreider, 290 Pa. Super. 63, 434 A.2d 130 (1981).

[193] Commonwealth ex rel. Ruczynski v. Powers, 421 Pa. 2, 219 A.2d 460 (1966); Commonwealth ex rel. Bordlemay v. Bordlemay, 201 Pa. Super. 435, 193 A.2d 845 (1963).

not, of itself, cause a forfeiture of the parental right to custody.[194] Rather, account must be taken of the motivation underlying the separation.[195]

A party who has placed the child with others while attempting to secure the means to support the child,[196] or to complete an education,[197] will not be penalized since the party's action was, at that time, consistent with the child's best interests.[198] Likewise, a party who was mentally or physically ill will be excused for relinquishing custody where the illness interfered with or precluded proper care of the child.[199] However, where a party surrenders custody and offers no explanation, courts will readily refuse to grant custody.[200] Moreover, a party who has relinquished custody in order to pursue a non-marital relationship has disadvantaged his or her case.[201] Evidence which indicates that the releasing party

---

[194] In re: Adoption of Farabelli, 460 Pa. 423, 333 A.2d 846 (1975); Auman v. Eash, 228 Pa. Super. 242, 323 A.2d 94 (1974).

[195] In Interest of Garthwaite, 422 Pa. Super. 280, 619 A.2d 356 (1993) (When proper care and control of child is lacking, child may be removed from parent, guardian, or custodian); In the Interest of Anita H., 351 Pa. Super. 342, 505 A.2d 1014 (1986) (children were improperly adjudicated dependent when mother was incarcerated for not providing proper parental care. The court could not adequately rule upon whether proper parental care was immediately available when it refused to hear testimony of children's father as to their parental fitness); In re James John M., 333 Pa. Super. 417, 482 A.2d 637 (1984) (father placed child with maternal grandparents for a short period following death of the mother and attempted to regain custody consistently thereafter); In re Custody of Hernandez, 249 Pa. Super. 274, 376 A.2d 648 (1977).

[196] In re Custody of Hernandez, 249 Pa. Super. 274, 376 A.2d 648 (1977).

[197] Mooreman v. Tingle, 320 Pa. Super. 348, 467 A.2d 359 (1983); Commonwealth ex rel. Holschuh v. Holland-Moritz, 448 Pa. 437, 292 A.2d 380 (1972); Johnson v. Pinder, 217 Pa. Super. 180, 269 A.2d 511 (1970); *but see* Moore v. Moore, 574 A.2d 105 (Pa. Super. 1990).

[198] In re Wesley J.K., 299 Pa. Super. 504, 445 A.2d 1243 (1982).

[199] Commonwealth ex rel. Gorto v. Gorto, 298 Pa. Super. 509, 444 A.2d 1299 (1982); Commonwealth ex rel. Strunk v. Cummins, 258 Pa. Super. 326, 392 A.2d 817 (1978); Commonwealth ex rel. Staunton v. Austin, 209 Pa. Super. 187, 223 A.2d 892 (1966).

[200] Commonwealth ex rel. Ruczynski v. Powers, 421 Pa. 2, 219 A.2d 460 (1966).

[201] Miller v. Miller, 327 Pa. Super. 45, 474 A.2d 1165 (1984); Commonwealth ex rel. Bordlemay v. Bordlemay, 201 Pa. Super. 435, 193 A.2d 845 (1963).

attempted, to the best of his or her capability, to maintain contact with the child will buttress the party's claim.[202]

In *A. O. v. M. O.*, 856 A.2d 1204 (Pa. Super. 2004) the Superior Court held that a mother with primary physical custody did not abandon her role in her daughter's life by deciding to enroll the girl in a boarding school. The court rejected father's contention that because daughter was not living full-time at mother's home, although she did spend weekends there, she should live with him and his family in New York. The trial judge's order granting mother primary physical custody should not be disturbed because mother chose to send the child to a boarding school. The court also gave weight to the facts that the child came home most weekends and in the summer, that mother visited the child during the week and remained active in the child's life. The child's attendance at a boarding school was in her best interests.

Successful efforts by the new custodial parent to frustrate parent–child contacts or to turn the child against the now non-custodial parent will not only detract from the custodial parent's fitness but will damage the custodial parent's custody case.[203] On the other hand, the unexplained failure of the relinquishing parent to remain involved, in any capacity, in the child's life will detract from the relinquishing parent's case.[204]

The failure to aid in the support of the child may also be viewed as an indication of indifference toward the child.[205] If, however, no assis-

---

[202] In re James John M., 333 Pa. Super. 417, 482 A.2d 637 (1984); Commonwealth ex rel. Gorto v. Gorto, 298 Pa. Super. 509, 444 A.2d 1299 (1982); Auman v. Eash, 228 Pa. Super. 242, 323 A.2d 94 (1974); Johnson v. Pinder, 217 Pa. Super. 180, 269 A.2d 511 (1970).

[203] Pamela J.K. v. Roger D.J., 277 Pa. Super. 579, 419 A.2d 1301 (1980); In re Custody of Hernandez, 249 Pa. Super. 274, 376 A.2d 648 (1977); Commonwealth ex rel. Lovell v. Shaw, 202 Pa. Super. 339, 195 A.2d 878 (1963); *see also* 23 Pa.C.S. § 5328(a)(1) & (8).

[204] Commonwealth ex rel. Williams v. Price, 167 Pa. Super. 57, 74 A.2d 668 (1950).

[205] *Id.*; Commonwealth ex rel. Ganster v. McGee, 103 Pa. Super. 12, 157 A. 345 (1931); *see also* In Re V.E., 417 Pa. Super. 68, 611 A.2d 1267 (1992) (Parent whose children have been placed in foster care has affirmative duty to work towards return of children. At minimum, parent whose children have been removed and placed in foster care must show willingness to cooperate with Children and Youth Services (CYS) to obtain rehabilitative services necessary to enable parent to meet duties and obligations inherent in parenthood). Interestingly, new Section 5328(a)(3) provides "the parental

tance is requested by the custodian and the child is well provided for, the effect of failure to support will be tempered.[206] The parent may also be excused if financial difficulties are prevalent throughout the period of non-support.[207]

LOWER COURT CASES

York County

J.W.I. v. H.A.I., C.P. York County, No. 2006-FC-002108-03 (C.C.P. November 17, 2017), *aff'd*, Memorandum Decision, No. 1955 MDA 2017 (Pa. Super. June 28, 2018) (Father chose to delegate his parental role to paternal grandmother. Upon the request of mother, the trial court reduced father's physical custody from shared to partial custody. Mother argued that modification of shared physical custody was warranted because father failed to fully participate in the child's life, and, as such, the child was not living up to her potential. Trial court did not award primary custody to mother because it believed the child would be better off with mother than a babysitter; the basis for the decision was the court's conclusion that father abdicated his parental role. The trial court's order reduced father's shared physical custody to partial custody—alternating weekends, plus an additional weeknight visit each week).

§ 3.4.13. Undermining / Alienation of Parental Relationship with Child

In some child custody cases, the undermining of a parent's relationship with his/her children by the other parent is an important factor. The undermining by one parent of the other parent's relationship with their children has been referred to as "parental alienation," which is a controversial subject in psychological and legal fields. This is because "parental alienation syndrome" (also referred to as PAS) has been debated, analyzed, and criticized in the mental health and legal communities. However, whether or not parental alienation is considered a

---

duties performed by each party on behalf of the child" as an enumerated factor for considering the child's best interest. It is to be seen whether this factor will apply to a party's failure to aid in the support of the child.

[206] In re Custody of Hernandez, 249 Pa. Super. 274, 376 A.2d 648 (1977); Commonwealth ex rel. Thompson v. Altieri, 184 Pa. Super. 431, 135 A.2d 811 (1957).

[207] Johnson v. Pinder, 217 Pa. Super. 180, 269 A.2d 511 (1970).

"syndrome" or not does not negate the fact that a court, in a child custody matter, may find that one parent alienates or undermines the other parent's relationship with the children. Factor 8 of the custody factors (under 23 Pa.C.S. § 5328) provides: "the attempts of a parent to turn the child against the other parent . . . ."[208] Factor 1 provides: "which party is more likely to encourage and permit frequent and continuing contact between the child an another party."[209] In the case of *A.L.B. v. M.D.L.*, the issue of parental alienation and its effect on the child custody order was prominent and resulted in the father losing equal (50/50) shared custody and becoming a partial physical custodian, every other weekend.[210]

LOWER COURT CASES

Berks County

H.L.J. v. R.G.J., Jr., C.P. Berks County, No. 16-16933 (C.C.P. November 27, 2019), *aff'd* Memorandum Decision, No. 2014 MDA 2019 (Pa. Super. July 28, 2020) (The trial court acknowledged that parental alienation is recognized within the field of family therapy; alienation is the family dynamic through which one parent actively discredits the other parent to a child they share. Mother had petitioned the trial court to modify the parties' 2017 custody order so she and the parties' child could attend "intensive reunification therapy" with a therapist in New York. Mother sought to have the therapist qualified as an expert in reunification therapy, specializing in parental alienation. Father objected, arguing that the therapist's methodology was not widely accepted, and, in fact, might be actively opposed by a majority of her peers. The therapist testified that she believed the child would sustain serious psychological damage if intensive reunification therapy were not conducted. Although the ultimate goal was for the child to have a meaningful relationship with both parents, the therapist recommended the rejected parent to have temporary sole custody of the child. The trial court found that the child was suffering from moderate to severe alienation from mother. As a result, the court modified the existing custody order to provide mother with 90 days of sole physical custody of the child, with no contact with father, who previously had primary physical custody of the child. The court reported that it was satisfied that the

---

[208] *See* 23 Pa.C.S. § 5328(a)(8)

[209] *See* 23 Pa.C.S. § 5328(a)(1)

[210] A.L.B. v. M.D.L., 239 A.3d 142 (Pa. Super. 2020) (the trial court reduced father's 50/50 physical custody to every other weekend, because of his severe parental alienation/undermining of mother's relationship with the children. Superior Court affirmed trial court's decision).

therapist utilized a scientific methodology to develop her treatment plan. That scientific methodology was generally accepted in the community of specialists who diagnose and treat parental alienation. The court concluded that the therapist's methodology passed the *Frye* test.).

§ 3.4.14. Race

While the appellate courts of the Commonwealth have had but a few occasions to decide custody disputes involving individuals of different races, increased social tolerance of biracial marriages coupled with recent divorce statistics indicates that satisfaction of any judicial yearning to preside over such cases is not long in the offing.[211] In the cases which have arisen, whether dealing with a child who is the product of a biracial marriage or a situation in which placement of a child in an interracial environment is presented as a custodial alternative, the courts have consistently held that racial considerations are inapplicable in custody proceedings.[212] In *Commonwealth ex rel. Lucas v. Kreischner*,[213] the court stated:

> "In a multiracial society such as ours racial prejudice and tension are inevitable. If . . . children are raised in a happy and stable home, they will be able to cope with prejudice and hopefully learn that people are unique individuals who should be judged as such."[214]

Following the rationale of *Lucas*, the Superior Court in *In re Temos*[215] reversed the trial court's award of custody to the father where the court's decision was based partly on the fact that the mother, who had been the

---

[211] *"Custody Disputes Following the Dissolution of Interracial Marriages: Best Interests of the Child or Judicial Racism?,"* 19 Jour. Fam. Law 97 (1980).

[212] Commonwealth ex rel. Myers v. Myers, 468 Pa. 134, 360 A.2d 587 (1976); Commonwealth ex rel. Lucas v. Kreischner, 450 Pa. 352, 299 A.2d 243 (1973); Milligan v. Davidson, 244 Pa. Super. 255, 367 A.2d 299 (1976); Dates v. Roble, 55 Wash. Co. 169 (1975). See Commonwealth ex rel. Rickert v. Rickert, 223 Pa. Super. 1, 296 A.2d 841 (1972).

[213] 450 Pa. 352, 299 A.2d 243 (1973).

[214] *Id.* at 356, 299 A.2d 246; Commonwealth ex rel. Myers v. Myers, 468 Pa. 134, 360 A.2d 587 (1976).

[215] In re Temos, 304 Pa. Super. 82, 450 A.2d 111 (1982).

child's custodian under a stipulated custody order, had been maintaining a close relationship with a black man. The opinion criticized the trial court's consideration of race stating that in a child custody case ". . . race is not a 'consideration,' 'concern' or 'factor.'"[216]

The court went on to say that although it recognized that the children may, in the future, be subjected to some difficulties because they lived with a black man, "court must never yield to prejudice because it cannot prevent prejudice."[217]

Subsequent to the *Temos* decision, the Pennsylvania Supreme Court was required to determine the effect of race in *In re Davis*,[218] a case in which a black child had been adjudicated dependent and the court's placement choices were between a white couple who had cared for the child in the past and a black couple with whom the child's half brother and sister had been placed. The Court held that it was error (in this case harmless) for the lower court to fail to consider race in deciding the custody question. The opinion distinguished this case from cases in which the courts had found an interracial marriage by a natural parent to be sufficient to warrant a transfer of custody. The Court also discussed at length the disadvantages to which a child of one race placed in an environment of another race would be subject and found "that race should be a factor, but only a factor" in determining the best interests of the child in placement proceedings.[219]

In *Palmore v. Sidote*,[220] the United States Supreme Court determined that a white mother's remarriage to a black man was an improper basis on which to remove the child from the natural mother's custody and return her to the father. The Court looked to the core purpose of the Fourteenth Amendment, the doing away with all government-imposed discrimination and, similar to the language of *Temos*, stated "[the] Constitution cannot control such prejudices but neither can it tolerate them."[221]

---

[216] *Id.* at 99, 450 A.2d 120.

[217] *Id.*

[218] In re Davis, 502 Pa. 110, 465 A.2d 614 (1983).

[219] *Id.* at 133, 465 A.2d 626.

[220] Palmore v. Sidote, 466 U.S. 429, 104 S.Ct. 1879 (1984).

[221] *Id.*, 104 S.Ct. 1882.

Read together, *Temos*, *Davis* and *Palmore* illustrate the difficulties involved in resolving the issue of race in custody disputes. It appears, however, that the United States Supreme Court has somewhat decided the issue by phrasing the question as "whether the reality of private biases and the possible injury they might inflict are permissible considerations for removal of an infant from the custody of its natural mother," and answering that it had little difficulty concluding that they are not.[222] It appears, therefore, that the question of race may not be considered even as "only a factor," as held in *Davis*.

§ 3.4.15. Presumptions, Doctrines, and Policies Generally

The history of child custody decisions is replete with reliance on a variety of presumptions, doctrines, and policies utilized by courts to decide the situs of the best interests of the child, such as the Tender Years Doctrine, separation of siblings, and roots of the tree policy. A growing number of decisions have, however, turned their backs on these simplistic devices and directed the lower court to eschew the use of presumptions, doctrines, and policies in favor of a considered analysis of the particular facts of each case.[223] As one decision noted,

> "a presumption itself contributes no evidence and has no probative quality. It is sometimes said that the presumption will tip the scale when the evidence is balanced. But, in truth, nothing tips the scale but evidence, and a presumption–being a legal rule or legal conclusion–is not evidence . . . In deciding a child custody case, one should avoid the use of a 'presumption,' which tends to focus the analysis on the respective rights of the parties rather than on close scrutiny of all the particular facts relevant to determine what will serve the child's best interest."[224]

---

[222] *Id.*, 104 S.Ct. 1882.

[223] Commonwealth ex rel. Spriggs v. Carson, 470 Pa. 290, 368 A.2d 635 (1977); In re Temos, 304 Pa. Super. 82, 450 A.2d 111 (1982); In re Custody of Hernandez, 249 Pa. Super. 274, 376 A.2d 648 (1977); Tobias v. Tobias, 248 Pa. Super. 168, 374 A.2d 1372 (1977); Commonwealth ex rel. Grillo v. Shuster, 226 Pa. Super. 229, 312 A.2d 58 (1973).

[224] In re Custody of Hernandez, 249 Pa. Super. 274, 284–85, 376 A.2d 648, 653 (1977).

However, in Pennsylvania, under the newly enacted 23 Pa.C.S. § 5327, there is now a codified presumption that exists in cases concerning primary physical custody between a parent and a third party. Under Section 5327(b), in cases involving a parent and a third party, there is a presumption that custody shall be awarded to the parent and the presumption can be rebutted only by clear and convincing evidence.[225] However, under Section 5327, in cases between the parents of a child there are no presumptions and in cases between third parties there are no presumptions.[226]

The doctrines/policies utilized in rendering custody orders are based on psychological or sociological concepts which purport to espouse generally accepted "rules" of child rearing and the workings of the juvenile psyche. In several cases decided prior to the enactment of the new custody statute, the premises upon which the doctrines/policies are based have come under attack as the structure of society has changed or new psychological theories have gained popularity. In virtually all cases, doctrines/policies have been found to be sorely deficient when applied to any but the most clear-cut cases.

The recent Pennsylvania Superior Court decision in the case of *M.J.M. v. M.L.G.*, where the Superior Court found that the Primary Care Taker Doctrine, insofar as it requires positive emphasis on the primary caretaker's status "is no longer viable" in light of the fact that "the parental duties performed by each parent on behalf of the child" is but one of sixteen factors under Section 5328(a) of the custody statute, appears to have sounded the death knell to the few remaining doctrines and policies.[227]

---

[225] 23 Pa.C.S. § 5327(b). *See also* R.L. v. M.A., 209 A.3d 391 (Pa. Super. 2019) (Section 5327 also applies when third party is seeking equal (50/50) physical custody).
[226] 23 Pa.C.S. § 5327(a) & (c).
[227] *See* M.J.M. v. M.L.G., 63 A.3d 331 (Pa. Super. 2013).

§ 3.4.16. Separation of Siblings Policy (Family Unit or Whole Family Doctrine)

Courts of the Commonwealth have long recognized the benefit to a child of growing up in a family atmosphere including siblings from whom the child can learn and develop the skills necessary for successful adult social interaction. As such, the separation of siblings policy has been a consideration since the early days of Pennsylvania custody decisions.[228] The policy holds that unless compelling reasons dictating a contrary result are adduced, siblings should not be separated.[229]

---

[228] Commonwealth v. Addicks, 2 Serg. & Rawle 174 (1815).

[229] In re Davis, 502 Pa. 110, 465 A.2d 614 (1983); Albright v. Commonwealth ex rel. Fetters, 491 Pa. 320, 421 A.2d 157 (1980); Cardamone v. Elshoff, 442 Pa. Super. 263, 659 A.2d 575 (1995) (General rule is that siblings should not be separated without compelling reasons, and this policy is one factor to be considered in determining best interests of child for custody purposes. Trial court's failure to specifically discuss existence of general policy in favor of raising siblings together was not alone reversible error in custody proceeding); Wiskoski v. Wiskoski, 427 Pa. Super. 531, 629 A.2d 996 (1993) (Absent compelling reasons to the contrary, siblings should be raised together whenever possible, in order to provide continuity and stability necessary for young child's development. Awarding custody of child to father was improper, where it would have involved separating child from stepbrothers with whom he had been raised. Father offered no reasons to separate children and trial court failed to consider doctrine of "family unity."); Hockenberry v. Thompson, 428 Pa. Super. 403, 631 A.2d 204 (1993) (Doctrine of family unity precluded granting custody of one of mother's two daughters, where children were raised as sisters, were only 14 months apart in age, and visited father seeking custody together. Absent compelling reasons, "the children should be raised together in one household, for this permits the continuity and stability necessary for a young child's development."); Cyran v. Cyran, 389 Pa. Super. 128, 566 A.2d 878 (1989) ("it has always been a strong policy in our law that in the absence of compelling reasons to the contrary, siblings should be raised together whenever possible"; in defining the phrase "compelling reasons" the court said that the evidence must indicate that it was "necessary" to separate the children, and the evidence was "forceful" in this regard); Pilon v. Pilon, 342 Pa. Super. 52, 492 A.2d 59 (1985); Bresnock v. Bresnock, 346 Pa. Super. 563, 500 A.2d 91 (1985); Haag v. Haag, 336 Pa. Super. 491, 485 A.2d 1189 (1984); Ferencak v. Moore, 300 Pa. Super. 28, 445 A.2d 1282 (1982) and Commonwealth ex rel. Newcomer v. King, 301 Pa. Super. 239, 447 A.2d 630 (1982) (remands partially based on court's failure to adequately consider policy against separation of siblings); In re Custody of Myers, 242 Pa. Super. 225, 363 A.2d 1242 (1976); Commonwealth ex rel. Bowser v. Bowser, 224 Pa. Super. 1, 302

The separation of siblings doctrine, also known as the family unit or whole family doctrine will always succumb to the best interests of each subject child.[230] Similarly, the policy may be outweighed by the strong preference of a child against living with the party in whose favor the doctrine would operate.[231] A child's sibling relationship has been enumerated as a factor to be considered by the court when determining the best interest of the child.[232] The days of the separation of siblings doctrine appear to be numbered as the primary caretaker doctrine was found to be "no longer viable" by the Pennsylvania Superior Court in the case of *M.J.M. v. M.L.G.*[233] A logical conclusion would be that the separation of siblings policy, like the primary caretaker doctrine, is in essence one of sixteen factors contained in Section 5328(a) which are all to be afforded equal weight with the exception of those factors which effect the safety of the child.

While the policy in the Commonwealth is to permit siblings, including half-siblings, to be raised together, it is only one factor for a court to consider, and not a determinant of custody arrangements.[234] It has been found that a trial court correctly determined that it would be in the child's best interest to be separated from her younger half-siblings, because the child felt overly burdened by a responsibility to care for their physical and emotional welfare.[235] Where half-siblings never lived in the same household

---

A.2d 450 (1973); Commonwealth ex rel. Sissel v. Sciulli, 216 Pa. Super. 429, 268 A.2d 165 (1970).

[230] Wiskoski v. Wiskoski, 427 Pa. Super. 531, 629 A.2d 996 (1993) (Factors of preferring that siblings be raised together cannot be elevated automatically above all other factors in custody determination, but it must be weighed in conjunction with other factors); Mahoney v. Mahoney, 354 Pa. Super. 585, 512 A.2d 694 (1986) (the court concluded that the child's best interest would be served by the award of custody to father, although this necessitated child's separation from one half-sibling); Sykora v. Sykora, 259 Pa. Super. 400, 393 A.2d 888 (1978); In re Russo, 237 Pa. Super. 80, 346 A.2d 355 (1975)

[231] In re Russo, 237 Pa. Super. 80, 346 A.2d 355 (1975).

[232] 23 Pa.C.S. § 5328(a)(6).

[233] M.J.M. v. M.L.G., 63 A.3d 331 (Pa. Super. 2013).

[234] Saintz v. Rinker, 902 A.2d 509 (Pa. Super. 2006); Wiskoski v. Wiskoski, 427 Pa. Super. 531, 629 A.2d 996 (1993).

[235] *Id.*

prior to separation, the separation of siblings doctrine was not applied to the older half-sister.[236] Where there was a pre-existing separation of siblings, the separation of siblings doctrine was not applied because the father alienated the older child from the mother and might attempt to do the same with the younger child.[237] A trial court was affirmed by the Superior Court when it separated four minor children where the parties' two sons were thriving at the father's home and the daughters were estranged from the father while living at the mother's home.[238]

The Superior Court held that a trial court erred in denying mother's petition to relocate with her children and in awarding primary physical custody of the children to their respective biological fathers, because the trial court failed to properly weigh the impact of separating the half-siblings from each other, which would result if the children remained in Pennsylvania in the custody of their separate fathers.[239]

In *E.A.L. v. L.J.W.*,[240] the court declared that the policy which favors raising siblings together is only one factor that court must consider in a child custody determination and it is not controlling. In awarding primary custody of two minor children to mother after the children were raised by grandparents, to join half-siblings living with mother, trial court improperly relied too heavily on the policy that favors raising siblings and half-siblings together, to the exclusion of other equally important factors. In *Swope v. Swope*,[241] the Superior Court held that a custody order which awarded mother primary physical custody of the parties' two younger children separate from their older brother, was not in error, where the parties' oldest child, who lived with father, was unemployed and not in school.

As a number of courts have stated:

"the benefits of forcing a child to reside with one of his parents solely for the purpose of keeping the siblings together can be distinctly

---

[236] Johns v. Cioci, 865 A.2d 931 (Pa. Super. 2004).

[237] L. F. F. v. P. R. F., 828 A.2d 1148 (Pa. Super. 2003).

[238] Nomland v. Nomland, 813 A.2d 850 (Pa. Super. 2002).

[239] Ferdinand v. Ferdinand,763 A.2d 820 (Pa. Super. 2000).

[240] E.A.L. v. L.J.W., 443 Pa. Super. 573, 662 A.2d 1109 (1995).

[241] Swope v. Swope, 455 Pa. Super. 587, 689 A.2d 264 (1997).

outweighed by the detrimental effects on that child who prefers not to live with that particular parent."[242]

Numerous courts have noted the stabilizing influence of elder children on younger siblings,[243] and thus the preference of an older child may trigger the policy with respect to more recent offspring and operate to deny the non-preferred party of the custody of any of the children.[244] Conversely, prior to the abrogation of the Tender Years Doctrine, custody of older children might be given to the mother, as the siblings policy was activated subsequent to effective operation of the Tender Years presumption.[245] Along this line, arguments to the effect that the siblings doctrine is inapplicable to an older child who is the sole subject of a custody dispute have been rejected as it has been found that elder siblings may also benefit from interaction with younger family members.[246]

Since the "whole family" concept is the backdrop for the doctrine, the fact that siblings share a half-blood relationship does not dilute the force of the doctrine.[247] The fact that siblings have been raised together and have expressed a desire to live with one another has often been noted and will add support to implementation of the doctrine.[248] On the other hand, a child's wish to live apart from brothers and sisters may or may

---

[242] In re Russo, 237 Pa. Super. 80, 85, 346 A.2d 355, 357–58 (1975).

[243] *E.g.,* Scheeler v. Rudy, 2 D.&C.3d 772 (1977).

[244] Shoup v. Shoup, 257 Pa. Super. 263, 390 A.2d 814 (1978).

[245] Williams v. Williams, 223 Pa. Super. 29, 296 A.2d 870 (1972); *but see* Commonwealth ex rel. Hickey v. Hickey, 213 Pa. Super. 349, 247 A.2d 806 (1968). (Custody of 13-year-old male given to father in accord with preference in spite of award of 3 younger siblings to mother).

[246] Pamela J.K. v. Roger D.J., 277 Pa. Super. 579, 419 A.2d 1301 (1980); Commonwealth ex rel. Steuer v. Steuer, 244 Pa. Super. 302, 368 A.2d 732 (1976); Commonwealth ex rel. Kraus v. Kraus, 185 Pa. Super. 167, 138 A.2d 225 (1958).

[247] In re Davis, 502 Pa. 110, 465 A.2d 614 (1983); Albright v. Commonwealth ex rel. Fetters, 491 Pa. 320, 421 A.2d 157 (1980); Commonwealth ex rel. Oxenreider v. Oxenreider, 290 Pa. Super. 63, 434 A.2d 130 (1981); Pamela J.K. v. Roger D.J., 277 Pa. Super. 579, 419 A.2d 1301 (1980); In re Custody of Myers, 242 Pa. Super. 225, 363 A.2d 1242 (1976).

[248] *See* Albright v. Commonwealth ex rel. Fetters, 491 Pa. 320, 421 A.2d 157 (1980); Commonwealth ex rel. Bowser v. Bowser, 224 Pa. Super. 1, 302 A.2d 450 (1973).

not affect the custody decision depending upon the age of the child and the validity of the reasons in which the preference is grounded.[249]

In spite of the separation of siblings doctrine, a substantial number of orders have split custody in a variety of combinations, each tailored to the circumstances of the particular case. Cases in which the children were separated at an early age and have been thriving in their respective homes for a substantial period appear to present the most likely candidates for orders dividing the children.[250] Also, where custody of the subject child alternates between the parties or there exists an extensive partial custody schedule providing for substantial contacts between the children, the doctrine, with its goals essentially satisfied, appears to have less vitality.[251]

Prior to the enactment of Section 5328, it appeared that in view of the appellate courts' swelling distain for decision by presumption, litigants' decreasing reliance on the doctrine and a shift toward a truer case by case analysis would continue. In fact, one appellate opinion noted that the rationale partially supporting the rejection of the Tender Years Doctrine is equally applicable to the siblings policy, as the paramount concern in custody cases must be the best interests of the child, a determination which should be made without resort to presumption.[252] With the decision of *M.J.M. v. M.L.G.*[253], the separation of siblings doctrine is likely to be watered down as it will be viewed as one of 16 factors comprising an overall best interest analysis.

Absent a specific statutory grant, siblings have no standing to petition for visitation with other siblings, the Pennsylvania Supreme Court ruled in *Ken R. v. Arthur Z.*[254] The court explained that Pennsylvania

---

[249] *See* Tomlinson v. Tomlinson, 248 Pa. Super. 1, 374 A.2d 1386 (1977).

[250] M.D. v. B.D., 336 Pa. Super. 298, 485 A.2d 813 (1984). *E.g.*, Commonwealth ex rel. McKee v. Reitz, 193 Pa. Super. 125, 163 A.2d 908 (1960).

[251] In re Russo, 237 Pa. Super. 80, 346 A.2d 355 (1975).

[252] Sykora v. Sykora, 259 Pa. Super. 400, 393 A.2d 888 (1978). *See* Ellerbe v. Hooks, 490 Pa. 363, 416 A.2d 512 (1980). (Flaherty, J., concurring).

[253] M.J.M. v. M.L.G., 63 A.3d 331 (Pa. Super. 2013).

[254] Ken R. v. Arthur Z., 546 Pa. 49, 682 A.2d 1267 (1996); *see also* D. N. v. V. B., 814 A.2d 750 (Pa. Super. 2002) (Superior Court ruled that an adult half-sister did not have standing to pursue custody of her two half-siblings following the death of their

lawmakers have not seen fit to include siblings in the state statute's "zone of interests." Finding the argument of the child-petitioner in this case that she has a constitutional right to see her two half-sisters to be "wholly inadequate," the court nevertheless expressed sympathy for her position and urged the state legislature to address this matter. At the time of *Ken R. v. Arthur Z*, in order to have standing, a party had to demonstrate a substantial interest in the subject-matter of the litigation that was both direct and immediate. The Supreme Court determined that, although a plaintiff's interest in maintaining a relationship with her siblings was substantial and direct, it was not an immediate interest, and, as such, plaintiff lacked standing to seek visitation. An immediate interest is shown where the interest the party seeks to protect is within the "zone of interests" sought to be protected by the statute or constitutional guarantee in question. The court noted that 23 Pa.C.S. § 5301 (since repealed), which sets forth the Commonwealth's public policy regarding visitation, discusses parents and grandparents, but does not mention siblings.[255] The court therefore concluded that plaintiff's interest did not fall within the zone of interests that section 5301 sought to protect. The court concluded that, in light of Pennsylvania case law and the principles of statutory construction, "we are constrained to find that siblings do not have standing to seek court ordered visitations with their siblings in Pennsylvania."[256] Interestingly, proposed legislation has been introduced that would permit siblings to petition for custody. However, the proposed legislation has not been enacted at this time.

---

mutual father, even though she claimed she was the most significant surviving member of the paternal side of the family to the children. The half-sister did not stand *in loco parentis* to the children, who resided with mother).

[255] It is to be noted that 23 Pa.C.S. § 5321 *et seq.* which replaced 23 Pa.C.S. § 5301 *et seq.* no longer contains the Commonwealth's public policy regarding child custody.

[256] *See also* Frank v. Frank, 833 A.2d 194 (Pa. Super. 2003) (Superior Court refused to grant three teenaged brothers standing to challenge a custody order with claims that their father interfered with their religious freedom. The court held that it is unnecessary for children to intervene in custody cases, as their interests are already well represented in the process by their parents and the court). However, it is to be noted that as of the writing of this book, legislation pertaining to standing for siblings to petition for custody may be introduced.

LOWER COURT CASES

Allegheny County

Hrecznyj v. Roszel, 144 P.L.J. 546 (Allegheny Co. 1996) (Trial court held that it is the Commonwealth's well-articulated policy that siblings, including half-siblings, should be raised together. The court noted that the children's half-sibling had lived with them since his birth, and they did not see him as anything but their brother and expressed fear of loss of their brother/sister relationship. Accordingly, the court held that the children's best interests were served by the maintenance of the long-term and successful primary custodial relationship with father, step-mother and half-brother).

Beaver County

K.P. v. S.P., C.P. Beaver County, No. 13011 of 2010, *aff'd,* Memorandum Decision, No. 1376 WDA 2019 (Pa. Super. February 14, 2020) (Father's hostility and negativity toward mother, as well as his demonstrated disrespect for mother's relationship with her children, created the potential that one child may become alienated from mother and, therefore, constituted a compelling reason to separate the children. The trial court concluded that a policy consideration is to raise siblings together, but compelling interests may warrant a separation of two siblings. The siblings in this case already had different schedules. The children had maintained a good relationship and bond with one another, regardless of their different schedules, their age difference, and their different interests. The court explained that in the majority of cases in which this doctrine has been invoked, the children have been reared together prior to separation or divorce of the parents. In cases where the siblings have not been reared in the same household, the force of the doctrine is less compelling, citing *Johns v. Cioci,* age 65 A.2d 932 (Pa. Super. 2004). The court relied on *L.F.F. v. P.R.F.,* 828 A.2d 1148 (Pa. Super. 2003), as legally and factually analogous. In that case, the Superior Court affirmed the custody order that resulted in sib-lings separation after determining that the record supported the trial court's conclusion that father's severe animosity toward mother and its potential to result in one child's alienation from mother if father was awarded primary physical custody of that child constituted a compelling reason to separate that child from his sibling).

Maker v. May, C. P. Beaver County, No. 11768 of 2004 (C.C.P. 2008) (Absent compelling reasons to the contrary, siblings, including half-brothers and sisters, should be raised together whenever possible. The trial court held that a high priority should be placed on not separating siblings. "Absent compelling reasons to the contrary it is the policy of this Commonwealth that siblings should be raised together whenever possible. *Pilon v. Pilon,* 492 A.2d 59 (Pa. Super. 1985). This factor is not diluted by the fact that the children involved are half-brothers and sisters. *In re Davis,* 465 A.2d 614, 621 (Pa. 1983). While this factor cannot be elevated automatically above all other factors, it must be weighed in conjunction with the others. Good reasons are not necessarily compelling reasons for disrupting the integrity of a family unit. To define compelling reasons, the court observed that evidence must indicate that it was necessary to separate the children, and the evidence was forceful in this regard. Absent these compelling reasons, the children should be raised together in one household, for this permits the continuity and stability for a young child's development.").

Berks County

Carr v. Carr, C.P. Berks County, No. 03-9143 (C.C.P. 2006) (It was in the children's best interests to award custody of the parties' son to father and custody of the parties' daughter to mother because of the extreme sibling rivalry between the two children. Testimony indicated that there was an extreme sibling rivalry between the children, and that the daughter was closely allied with mother. The trial court entered a custody order awarding primary custody of daughter to mother and primary custody of son to father, ignoring the "separation of siblings" doctrine. "On the one hand, the sibling relationship is one of the most important relationships that a child can and should enjoy and learn from in his or her lifetime, but, on the other hand, time apart might be beneficial due to the extreme rivalry between the children." Because the son had attention deficit and hyperactivity disorder, the court awarded father primary custody of the son. The court also noted that the son was at risk of being alienated from his father by mother. The court awarded primary custody of daughter to mother, because daughter was closely allied with mother and because father preferred not to disturb her custody arrangement. The court determined that the greater than normal sibling rivalry between the children warranted time apart).

Leininger v. Leininger, 91 Berks Co. Leg. J. 481 (C.C.P. 1999) (Trial court declared that absent compelling reasons to the contrary, the policy of the law favors the raising of siblings—including half-siblings—together; however, this policy must yield nonetheless to the paramount concern of the best interests of the child. The court acknowledged that it was mindful of the place of the law which, absent compelling reasons to the contrary, favors the raising of siblings together. As only one factor, it is not controlling and must yield to the paramount principle that the best interests of the child is of the Court's greatest concern. It may not be diluted by the fact that the children involved are half-siblings, but it is certainly not automatically elevated above all of the other factors).

Kaag v. Kaag, C.P. Berks Co. No. 96-7194 (C.C.P. 1997) (Held that the custody of two minor siblings was properly split between mother and father, despite the stated policy favoring the raising of siblings together, where the best interests of the children supported the custody split. The court found that although the stated policy of Pennsylvania favored raising siblings together, the policy was not controlling. The court held that the best interests of the children supported the custody split. "Although living apart from his sister may be somewhat upsetting for Patrick, the Court believes that there are many other things to be gained by ordering that each parent have custody of one of the children, including perhaps increased peace at Mother's home.").

Mogel v. Mogel, 87 Berks Co. L. J. 252 (C.C.P. 1995) (A ten-year-old child's stated preference should be considered, especially when the child's statements are made with candor, reasoning, and obvious intelligence. The court also noted that although it cannot be the sole controlling factor in making a custody decision, the preference for raising siblings together is a strong factor. Absent compelling reasons to the contrary, siblings should be raised together whenever possible in order to provide the continuity and stability necessary for a child's development).

Bernstel v. Copenhaver, 85 Berks L. J. 15 (C.C.P. 1992) (The policy of awarding custody so that siblings can be reared together applies to half-siblings as well.).

Bucks County

Warren v. McGrory, 84 Bucks Co. L. Rep. 238 (C.C.P. 2010) (Trial court granted father's petition for shared custody of the parties' 13-year-old son, where father agreed to drop off and pick up the child at school near the home of mother to accommodate additional custody time, a strong bond existed between father and the child, and the child himself indicated a desire for more time with father. Mother objected to shared custody citing the long-standing current arrangement, the negative effect on her other children of less time with the child, and the additional driving time the child would be subjected to. Mother was concerned that the increased time that the child would spend with father would detract from the time he spent with his siblings. In granting father's petition, the trial court noted that in deciding custody, the policy against separation of siblings known as the whole family or family unity doctrine is only one factor, and it is not a controlling factor. The doctrine is more likely to prevail where the children have been reared together prior to separation or divorce of the parents. The court cited with approval *Johns v. Cioci*, 865 A.2d 931, 943 (Pa. Super. 2004) The court also found that mother and father were able to demonstrate sufficient cooperation with each other to allow for a successful shared custody schedule).

Butler County

Valensky v. Valensky, C.P. Butler County, No. FC 94-90850-C (C.C.P. 2000) (Trial court ruled that separation of the parties' two children was not in their best interest and awarded primary physical custody of both children to father; in light of all factors presented in this case, the child's best interests are served by being in the same home with her sibling and in the home with the parent best equipped to address the parenting needs for these children).

Carbon County

D.C.M. v. T.M.M., 12 Carbon L. J. 182 (C.C.P. 1990) (Although siblings should be raised together whenever possible, there are compelling reasons to award primary custody of one of the parties' four children to father. In a close case, the court gives considerable weight to the child's preference. "Of course, we realized that there will be disadvantages resulting from the separation of David from his brother and sisters. David will not spend as much time with his siblings. He therefore, will not be forced to develop the sharing and communicative skills children should acquire to function properly in society. Our order minimizes these detriments by awarding liberal visitation rights to mother. During the time mother has physical custody of David, he will be in the company of his brother and sisters and will learn to share and communicate with his siblings").

Centre County

Hallman v. Steinbeck, C. P. Centre County, No. 2006-2074 (C.C.P. 2008) (One sibling was ordered to remain with grandmother and the other sibling to remain with mother until the end of the school year, since both children were stable and the trial court was reluctant to disturb living arrangements during the school year. A child's desire to be reunited with her sibling and live with their grandmother did not overcome the trial court's determination that the best interests of the child were in remaining with her mother. The court found that the child living with grandmother had done well in school, stated a strong preference for remaining with grandmother, and was provided the best possibility for stability in grandmother's home. As for the younger child living with mother, the court acknowledged the public policy preference for siblings to reside together, but found in the instant case it was better for the younger child to remain with mother until the end of the school year, despite her preference. "The court prefers siblings living together. However, there are rare situations where what is in the best interest of one child is not necessarily in the best interest of the other child. This is such a situation.").

Fulcher v. Rowland, C.P. Centre County, No. 2004-4607 (C.C.P. 2007) (The preference for keeping even half-siblings together can be a determining factor in an award of primary physical custody. Both parents provided loving homes for the child, and both school districts were suitable. Greater weight was given to the child's attachment to the family unit in father's home—her stepmother and stepsister, father and new half-brother. The court also noted that the child was familiar with the children in father's neighborhood, who were to be her classmates in kindergarten. Accordingly, father was awarded primary physical custody, with liberal partial custody to mother).

Columbia County

Norris v. O'Brien, C. P. Columbia County, No. 169 of 1999 (C.C.P. 2001), *aff'd*, 792 A.2d 625 (Pa. Super. 2001) (Where the relevant factors to be considered in custody cases were balanced equally between the parties, it would be in the best interests of the child at issue for the parties to share legal and physical custody, but that her mother's house served as the child's primary residence so as to avoid separating her from her half-sister).

Cumberland County

Commonwealth ex rel. Bear v. Fraker, 26 Cumb. 211 (C.C.P. 1976) (The fact that siblings share a half-blood relationship does not dilute the force of the separation of siblings doctrine).

Delaware County

M.R. v. M.K.W., 91 Del. Co. Rep. 322 (C.C.P. 2004) (Trial court held that although the general rule is that siblings should not be separated without compelling reasons, this policy is but one factor to be considered, together with others, in determining the best interest of the child. The rule must yield to paramount principle that the best interests of the individual child must be the determining factor in custody cases. The best interests of the children in a case must prevail over any abstract policy. Trial court did not err when it separated the two minor children into two separate households. The court found that its custody determination was based upon forceful evidence that a separation of the siblings was necessary in this case).

Fayette County

Livingston v. Thorpe, 64 Fayette Leg. J. 167 (C.C.P. 2001) (It is the well-founded policy that, absent compelling reasons, siblings should be raised together whenever possible. This policy is not diluted by the fact that the children involved are half-brothers and sisters).

Marchezak v. Wesolowsky, 64 Fayette Leg. J. 119 (C.C.P. 2000) (The policy of keeping half-siblings together did not prohibit the court from separating the children and awarding father custody, where the children expressed credible fear of their stepfather. The court noted that its decision would remove the children from the daily contact with their half-sister, but held that the policy to keep siblings together was not controlling and could be rebutted by showing that a different and superior environment was in the children's best interest. "Therefore, the general policy of raising siblings together is only one of the factors necessary for the court to consider when determining the best interests of the child. The best interest of the child is always the paramount principle that will guide a custody determination.").

Indiana County

J.L.W. v. K.A.R., C.P. Indiana County, No. 10161 CD 2012 (C.C.P. August 17, 2016), *aff'd*, Memorandum Decision, No. 1401 WDA 2016 (Pa. Super. March 30, 2017) (The parties shared physical custody until early 2016, when the parties both filed for primary custody of the child. Father wished to enroll the child in his particular elementary school, while mother requested that she be granted primary custody and leave to enroll the child in her elementary school. Following the custody trial, the trial court issued an opinion and order granting mother primary physical custody, with partial custody to father. The trial court reasoned that the child's step-sibling relationships and the extended family available at mother's residence would provide the child with a well-rounded childhood).

M.B. v. S.S., C.P. Indiana County, No. 11468 CD 2002 (C.C.P. 2007) (The policy in Pennsylvania is to allow siblings to be raised together. However, in situations where siblings have lived apart before a separation or divorce, the whole-family doctrine is weaker. Commenting on the separation of siblings doctrine, the court noted that father's case for primary custody was supported by the presence of a younger half-brother in his household. However, the presence of a sibling in father's household did not tip the custody scale in his favor in light of the court's findings that father was likely physically abusive of mother and that he would be less likely to encourage a relationship between his daughter and mother. At the time of the initial hearing in this case, the half-brother was only five months old. Therefore, the whole-family doctrine was less persuasive in this case. "It is well settled that absent compelling reasons to the contrary, the policy in Pennsylvania is to permit siblings, including half-siblings, to be raised together. . . . However, the policy of keeping siblings together is only a consideration and not a controlling factor in the ultimate custody decision. . . . Admittedly, the policy against separation of siblings is nuanced and can best be summarized as thus: While family unity is only one consideration, and not a controlling factor, a court must still find compelling, not just good, reasons to separate siblings. An additional consideration is whether the siblings have been reared together prior to the separation or divorce of the parents. . . . In the majority of cases that have invoked the whole-family doctrine this has been a determinative factor. . . . In this case, the child never lived in the same household with her younger brother, who was born to the father and stepmother following the parents' divorce.").

Lehigh County

Imlay v. Miller, C.P. Lehigh County, No. 2004-FC-0713 (C.C.P. 2011) (Trial court denied father's petition to modify the existing custody order for the parties' children where father's chief motivation seemed to be reduction of his support obligation. Father requested both modification of the custody order and contempt by mother based on the conduct of the parties' 13-year-old daughter in caring for her younger siblings before mother returned home from work and mother's alleged improper monitoring of that conduct. Father alleged that the daughter's behavior corrupted the younger children. Father cited the atmosphere in mother's residence, as well as the children's difficulties in school as reasons for transferring custody of the younger children to him during the school year. The court noted that father lived in a motor home which was insufficient as a residence for the children. Furthermore, father's proposal was not acceptable because it would separate the younger children from their older sister. Finally, the court discussed father's continuing emphasis on the support order he paid for the children and concluded that his primary motivation in requesting a custody modification was so that he could reduce the amount of his court-ordered support).

M.C. v. G.C.N., C. P. Lehigh County, No. 2006-FC-1314 (C.C.P. 2007) (Primary custody of the parties' two remaining children was awarded to mother, despite the fact that three of the children's siblings lived in father's home, because mother's home offered more stability for the children. Maintaining a relationship with siblings was only one factor to be weighed when determining custody, and did not outweigh the stability in mother's home. Since mother had been the primary caretaker for the children for most of their lives, their best interests would be served by continuing primarily in her custody. The court dismissed father's argument that the children should be raised with their half- and step-siblings, as this benefit did not outweigh the stability the children would have in mother's household. "It is true that Pennsylvania has a strong policy that in the absence of compelling reasons to the contrary, siblings should be raised together whenever possible. *Albright v. Commonwealth ex rel. Fetters,* 491 Pa. 320, 421 A.2d 157 (1980). This principle is not diluted by the fact that some children are step-siblings. However, the benefits of having all the children raised in the same household must be weighed against the other evidence. In the instant case, the benefit of having [the children] reside with mother far outweighs the benefit of having all five children in the same household with father. Mother has been a stabilizing factor in these children's lives, providing a consistent parent figure and a secure home environment." Therefore, the court held, it would be disruptive to the two remaining children to grant father primary custody).

Luzerne County

D.L. v. A.G., C.P. Luzerne County, No. 2016-55 (C.C.P. November 3, 2017), *aff'd,* Memorandum Decision, No. 1830 MDA 2017 (Pa. Super. July 11, 2018) (In the past, courts have stated it was the policy of the Commonwealth that, where possible, siblings should be raised together absent compelling reasons to do otherwise, citing *L.F.F. v. P.R.F.,* 828 A.2d 1148, 1152 (Pa. Super. 2003). However, cases such as *L.F.F.* predate the enactment of the current Child Custody Act. Their holdings retain persuasive value, but 23 Pa.C.S. § 5328(a) does not require a court to presume siblings should be raised together; this policy has been assimilated into § 5328(a)(6). Trial court did not abuse its discretion for failing to make this factor dispositive. Because father misstated the law, the trial court did not err when it afforded this factor less weight).

Montgomery County

Schierenbeck v. Schierenbeck, C.P. Montgomery Co., No. 95-22493 (C.C.P. 1997), *aff'd,* 704 A.2d 1128 (Pa. Super. 1997) (Inasmuch as the courts of this Commonwealth recognize that keeping siblings together is but one factor for the court to consider in determining what is in the overall best interest of the children, the trial court determined that the three children's best interests would be best served by living with father during the school year and visiting their half-sister on alternate weekends, for six weeks during the summer and on school holidays. The court afforded mother with more custodial time with the children because of the importance the court placed on the inter-action of the children with their half-sister).

Commonwealth ex rel. Koss v. Koss, 92 Montg. Co. Rep. 362 (C.C.P. 1970) (Child's wish to live apart from brothers and sisters may or may not affect the custody decision depending upon the age of the child and the validity of the reasons in which the prefer-ence is grounded).

Northumberland County

Pfleegor v. Pfleegor, 73 Northumberland Leg J. 1 (C.C.P. 2001) (Trial court held that absent compelling reasons to the contrary, siblings should be raised together whenever possible, in order to provide a continuity and stability necessary for a young child's development, citing *Wiskoski v. Wiskoski*, 427 Pa. Super. 521, 629 A.2d 996 (1993).

Dreese v. Dreese, 70 Northumb. Leg. J. 99 (C.C.P. 1998) (Whenever possible, sib-lings should be raised together, citing *Karner v. McMahon*, 640 A.2d 926 (Pa. Super. 1994).

Seiler v. Seiler, 59 Northumb. Leg. J. 73 (C.C.P. 1987) (In the absence of compelling reasons to the contrary, siblings should be raised together. Custody of the youngest of the parties' three daughters is awarded to the father to be raised with her sisters).

Philadelphia County

Smith v. Phillips, 20 Phila. 255 (C.C.P. 1990) (Although the policy of Pennsylvania family law disfavors the separation of siblings, that preference can be overcome, par-ticularly when the siblings have not established a close bond and have a significant age difference).

Saplansky v. Saplansky, 19 Phila. 29 (C.C.P. 1989) ("It has always been a strong policy in our law that, in the absence of compelling reasons to the contrary, siblings should be raised together whenever possible; to meet the compelling reasons standard, one must demonstrate that it is clearly necessary to separate the siblings.").

Sauer v. Sauer, 14 Phila. Rep. 335 (C.C.P. 1986) (In the absence of compelling reasons to the contrary, siblings should be raised together whenever possible. This prin-ciple applies equally to half-siblings).

Somerset County

Volchko v. Volchko, 59 Somerset Leg. J. 120 (C.C.P. 1991) (The strong policy of the law is that, unless compelling reasons indicate otherwise, siblings should be raised together).

Wyoming County

Pawlukovich v. Peterson, C.P. Wyoming County, No. 99-1247 (C.C.P. 2007) (Trial court ordered the separation of the parties' two siblings where that separation was necessary in order to permit the "therapeutic process" to work better. The court explained that father was entitled to have primary physical-custody of the parties' son because the child, who was suffering serious psychological harm due to the parties' continual conflict, was better able to accept direction from his father and because such placement would help the child lead a less stressful life. The court noted that the ongoing parental disputes had affected the son psychologically. His therapist had diagnosed him with post-traumatic stress disorder, secondary to parental conflict. The court added that normally, it would not consider separating the children, but that separation seemed necessary here in order to permit the therapeutic process to work better).

York County

J.E.C., Jr. v. K.A.S., C.P. York County, No. 2018-FC-001498-03 (C.C.P. August 28, 2019), *aff'd*, Memorandum Decision, No. 1566 MDA 2019 (Pa. Super. April 14, 2020) (Compelling circumstances existed in this case that warranted separating the children. Evidence was presented at the custody trial indicating that mother could not control the parties' middle child. Moreover, the educational, mental/emotional and physical needs of the parties' two youngest children were not being satisfied in mother's care. The decision to separate the three children was supported by the evidence presented at trial and not the result of unreasonableness or partiality, prejudice, bias or ill-will on the part of the trial court).

§ 3.4.17. Tender Years Doctrine

The Tender Years Doctrine, as formerly applied by Pennsylvania courts, held simply that the best interests of children of "tender years" were presumptively served by placing the child in the custody of the natural mother.[257] Children up to the age of approximately 14 years were considered to be of tender years,[258] although as a child approached the upper limits of the category, less weight was given to the doctrine and

---

[257] Carlisle Appeal, 225 Pa. Super. 181, 310 A.2d 280 (1973); Williams v. Williams, 223 Pa. Super. 29, 296 A.2d 870 (1972); Commonwealth ex rel. Hickey v. Hickey, 213 Pa. Super. 349, 247 A.2d 806 (1968).

[258] Williams v. Williams, 223 Pa. Super. 29, 296 A.2d 870 (1972); Commonwealth ex rel. Skurat v. Gearhart, 178 Pa. Super. 245, 115 A.2d 395 (1955).

more weight was placed on the child's preference.[259] Also, the doctrine was thought to be especially applicable where the child was a girl.[260]

While the mother's right to custody was not absolute even in the doctrine's heyday, the presumption carried substantial weight and custody of a young child would be committed to one other than the natural mother only where compelling reasons dictated such a result.[261] Compelling reasons included the parental unfitness of the mother,[262] neglect[263] or abandonment[264] of the child, or unchaste conduct.[265] The presumption was also potentially outweighed by other considerations, appearing alone or, more often, in tandem, such as the strong preference of an older child,[266] or the separation-of-siblings presumption.[267]

The tender years presumption could also be rendered inapplicable or accorded less deference where the mother was employed during the daytime and would not be supplying primary care for the child.[268] Also,

---

[259] In re Russo, 237 Pa. Super. 80, 346, A.2d 355 (1975); Clair Appeal, 219 Pa. Super. 436, 281 A.2d 726 (1971); Commonwealth ex rel. Bender v. Bender, 197 Pa. Super. 397, 178 A.2d 779 (1962).

[260] Commonwealth ex rel. Zeedick v. Zeedick, 213 Pa. Super. 114, 245 A.2d 663 (1968) (Hoffman, J., dissenting).

[261] Carlisle Appeal, 225 Pa. Super. 181, 310 A.2d 280 (1973); Commonwealth ex rel. Baisden v. DeMarco, 215 Pa. Super. 38, 257 A.2d 365 (1969); Commonwealth ex rel. Lovell v. Shaw, 202 Pa. Super. 339, 195 A.2d 878 (1963).

[262] Commonwealth ex rel. Shaak v. Shaak, 171 Pa. Super. 122, 90 A.2d 270 (1952).

[263] Commonwealth ex rel. Rainford v. Cirillo, 222 Pa. Super. 591, 296 A.2d 838 (1972); Commonwealth ex rel. Harry v. Eastridge, 172 Pa. Super. 49, 91 A.2d 910 (1952).

[264] Commonwealth ex rel. Doberstein v. Doberstein, 201 Pa. Super. 102, 192 A.2d 154 (1963).

[265] Commonwealth ex rel. Likovich v. Likovich, 220 Pa. Super. 202, 287 A.2d 156 (1971); Commonwealth ex rel. Kraus v. Kraus, 185 Pa. Super. 167, 138 A.2d 225 (1958); Commonwealth ex rel. Shaak v. Shaak, 171 Pa. Super. 122, 90 A.2d 270 (1952).

[266] Carlisle Appeal, 225 Pa. Super. 181, 310 A.2d 280 (1973); Commonwealth ex rel. Bowser v. Bowser, 224 Pa. Super. 1, 302 A.2d 450 (1973); Commonwealth ex rel. Doberstein v. Doberstein, 201 Pa. Super. 102, 192 A.2d 154 (1963).

[267] Commonwealth ex rel. Doberstein v. Doberstein, 201 Pa. Super. 102, 192 A.2d 154 (1963).

[268] In re Russo, 237 Pa. Super. 80, 346 A.2d 355 (1975); Commonwealth ex rel. Bear v. Fraker, 26 Cumb. 211 (1976).

courts invariably agreed that in all cases the doctrine was subordinate to the best interests and permanent welfare of the child.[269]

In 1975, the tender years presumption was abandoned by a plurality of the Pennsylvania Supreme Court which noted that the doctrine was "offensive to the concept of the equality of the sexes which we have embraced as a constitutional principle within this jurisdiction."[270]

(a) Tender Years Doctrine – Its Evolution

The origin of the tender years doctrine is generally traced to the 1813 holding in *Commonwealth v. Addicks*,[271] in which the Pennsylvania Supreme Court rejected the English common law paternal right to custody in favor of a rule which found that children in their tender minority "stand in need of that kind of assistance that can be afforded by none so well as the mother."[272] Viewing a large majority of post industrial revolution father-breadwinner, mother-homemaker households, the law merely reflected in its rules what appeared to be a sociological exhibition of natural law.[273] Through the force of incessant citation and repetition the doctrine became firmly entrenched as a useful tool in simplifying what might otherwise be a gut-wrenching decision.[274]

For the better part of two centuries the judicial belief in the supremacy of motherhood in the area of child rearing carried such weight that without a demonstration of unfitness on the part of the mother or "compelling reasons," the outcome of a custody contest between a natural mother and anyone else was a foregone conclusion.

---

[269] Commonwealth ex rel. Parikh v. Parikh, 449 Pa. 105, 296 A.2d 625 (1972); Commonwealth ex rel. Bordlemay v. Bordlemay, 201 Pa. Super. 435, 193 A.2d 845 (1963).

[270] Commonwealth ex rel. Spriggs v. Carson, 470 Pa. 290, 300, 368 A.2d 635, 639–40 (1977).

[271] Commonwealth v. Addicks, 5 Binney 519 (Pa. 1813).

[272] *Id.* at 521. *See* Commonwealth ex rel. Hart v. Hart, 14 Phila. 352 (1880); Commonwealth ex rel. Shaak v. Shaak, 171 Pa. Super. 122, 90 A.2d 270 (1952).

[273] Bratt, *Joint Custody,* 67 Ky. L. J. 271, 280–81 (1978–79); Trombetta, *Joint Custody: Recent Research and Overloaded Courtrooms Inspire New Solutions to Custody Disputes,* 19 J. Fam. L. 213, 214–215 (1980–81).

[274] *See* Conway v. Dana, 456 Pa. 536, 318 A.2d 324 (1974).

(b) Tender Years Doctrine – Its Demise

With increasing numbers of women entering the labor force, greater participation by males in the day-to-day rigors of raising children and a resurgence in the cry for the elimination of sex-based discrimination,[275] the foundations of the tender years doctrine steadily eroded. A simultaneous judicial rebellion against decision by presumption in custody actions further dissipated support for the rule.[276]

In 1972, in *Commonwealth ex rel. Parikh v. Parikh*,[277] the doctrine was demoted from its presumptory status to that of a mere "vehicle through which a decision respecting the infant's custodial well-being may be reached where factual considerations do not otherwise dictate a different result."[278] Under *Parikh,* the rule was thus viewed as a procedural aid in the allocation of the burden of proof, interfering less with the thorough analysis of the facts of each case than did the doctrine in its role as presumption.[279] As such, the doctrine would operate in favor of the mother only in circumstances in which the balance of relevant factors was equivocal.[280]

The death knell for the Tender Years Doctrine was sounded in *Commonwealth ex rel. Spriggs v. Carson*,[281] in which a plurality of the Pennsylvania Supreme Court found the doctrine to be at odds with the Equal Rights Amendment to the Pennsylvania Constitution which

---

[275] *See* Bratt, *Joint Custody*, 67 Ky. L. J. 271, 277–79 (1978–79); 48 Fordham L.R. 165, 106 n.7 (1979).

[276] In re Custody of Hernandez, 249 Pa. Super. 274, 376 A.2d 648, 653 (1977); Commonwealth ex rel. Grillo v. Shuster, 226 Pa. Super. 229, 312 A.2d 58 (1973). *See* § 3.4.15.

[277] 449 Pa. 105, 296 A.2d 625 (1972).

[278] *Id.* at 109, 296 A.d 627. *See* Stoyko v. Stoyko, 254 Pa. Super. 78, 385 A.2d 533 (1978).

[279] *See* Commonwealth ex rel. Lee v. Lee, 248 Pa. Super. 155, 374 A.2d 1365 (1977); Bertin & *Klein, Pennsylvania's Developing Child Custody Law, Symposium: Recent Developments in Pennsylvania Family Law,* 25 Vill. L. Rev. 752, 754 (1980).

[280] Commonwealth ex rel. Parikh v. Parikh, 449 Pa. 105, 296 A.2d 625 (1972); Commonwealth ex rel. Veihdeffer v. Veihdeffer, 235 Pa. Super. 447, 344 A.2d 613 (1975); Commonwealth ex rel. Grillo v. Shuster, 226 Pa. Super. 229, 312 A.2d 58 (1973).

[281] Com. ex rel. Spriggs v. Carson, 470 Pa. 290, 368 A.2d 635 (1977).

prohibits gender-based discrimination.[282] The *Spriggs* Court further found the doctrine to be equally offensive to the court's duty to analyze the individual merits of each case and render a best interests determination without resort to artificial legal constructs.

Although lacking the weight of a majority decision, subsequent Superior Court opinions interpreted the *Spriggs* holding as prohibiting consideration of the Tender Years Doctrine as either presumption or procedural rule.[283] Finally, in *Ellerbe v. Hooks*,[284] *a* majority of the Pennsylvania Supreme Court laid the issue to rest by recognizing the abandonment of the doctrine as announced in *Spriggs*.

§ 3.4.18. Costs of Transportation

In a number of custody disputes, the parties reside at a considerable distance from one another, thus creating a substantial travel expense when partial custody rights are granted. While there appear to be no set rules governing the allocation of expenses, in several cases the party moving away and creating the need for extensive travel has been made to bear all, or at least the majority, of the transportation costs.[285]

In the case of *S.S. v. K.F.*, 189 A.3d 1093 (Pa. Super. 2018), a mother requested to relocate to Chester County, Pennsylvania from Bucks County, Pennsylvania. The trial court allowed mother to move to Chester County, but ordered that the children remain in the Pennsbury School District in Bucks County where the mother previously lived but where neither party lived at the time of the trial. As stated by the Superior Court: "[t]he [trial] court therefore allowed Mother to move to Chester County, while purportedly denying a 'relocation,' as the Child Custody

---

[282] *See* Pa. Const., art I, § 28.

[283] *See* Bedio v. Bedio, 268 Pa. Super. 225, 407 A.2d 1331 (1979); Sipe v. Shaffer, 263 Pa. Super. 27, 396 A.2d 1359 (1979); Trefsgar v. Trefsgar, 261 Pa. Super. 1, 395 A.2d 273 (1978); McGowan v. McGowan, 248 Pa. Super. 41, 374 A.2d 1306 (1977).

[284] 490 Pa. 363, 416 A.2d 512 (1980).

[285] Pamela J.K. v. Roger D.J., 277 Pa. Super. 579, 419 A.2d 1301 (1980); McCourt v. Meyers, 268 Pa. Super. 152, 407 A.2d 875 (1979); Commonwealth ex rel. Balla v. Wresky, 165 Pa. Super. 6, 67 A.2d 595 (1949).

Act defines that term."[286] This created a financial burden on the parties, who would have to pay tuition to send their children to the Pennsbury School District. Because neither party requested such relief, and the trial court considered school choice as a custody issue only and made scarce inquiry into the parties' financial situations, the trial court's decision was reversed by the Superior Court. The case was remanded. The Superior Court held: "[o]n remand, unless the parties request otherwise, the court must choose a school that does not financially burden the parties, and it must make its decision by considering both the relocation and custody factors."[287]

In *Wyland v. West Shore School District*,[288] Mr. Wyland and his ex-wife initially both lived in the same school district and the school district provided transportation for the children from both parties' residences to the private school that they attended. When mother moved out of the school district and the new school district began providing transportation for the children from her home to attend the private school, the school district where father resided discontinued providing transportation from his residence on the mornings that he had custody of the children. Father filed a complaint against his school district seeking injunctive relief, arguing that he was a custodial parent and his children resided in the district under the shared custody arrangement. Father argued that under § 1361 of the Public School Code, the district was obligated to continue transporting his children from his home to the private elementary school. The district contended that it had no duty to bus the children because another school district provided transportation to and from mother's residence, which was located in a different school district. The district argued that the district where mother resided was the district of primary residence and had the sole obligation to provide transportation and only one school district was required to provide transportation under the School Code. The district claimed that the Pennsylvania Department of Education (PDE) applied a "single residency rule" for both enrollment and transportation purposes and that children could not have dual residency. The district claimed that PDE's policy was to provide transportation reimbursement

---

[286] S.S. v. K.F., 189 A.3d 1093 (Pa. Super. 2018).
[287] *Id.*
[288] Wyland v. West Shore School District, 52 A.3d 572 (Pa. Cmwlth. 2012).

to only one school district. When students of separated parents lived in two different school districts, PDE designates a district as the district of residence and provides transportation reimbursement to the district in which the child resides. Here, PDE designated mother's district as the district of residence. The trial court granted the preliminary injunction and ordered the district where father resided to resume transportation of the children from father's residence. The district appealed and the Commonwealth Court affirmed the trial court, finding that since the parents had joint and equal custody, the children resided in two different school districts, and the designation of a single school district was not required. Section 1361 of the School Code ensures that if transportation is provided, it is provided to both public and private school students. The court determined that any rule PDE applied to restrict § 1361 was unauthorized.[289]

In *North Allegheny School District v. Gregory P.*,[290] the Commonwealth Court ruled that a school district was not required to provide a special-education student with transportation to both his mother's house and his father's out-of-district house, where mother and father shared joint physical custody and the child lived with each parent on alternating weeks. The court concluded that neither state nor federal law requires that a school district provide transportation to two locations, one of them outside the district, just because the child's parents have chosen a custody arrangement which takes the child outside the district on alternating weeks.

Courts will normally consider the financial ability of each party to share the cost of transportation.[291] Specifically, where a custodial mother moved from Pennsylvania to California, the court found that she must bear the whole obligation of returning the child for one month during the summer.[292] Similarly, a non-custodial mother who had enlisted in the United States Navy was made to bear transportation costs insofar as she

---

[289] *See also* Watts v. Manheim Township School District, 84 A.3d 378 (Pa. Cmwlth. 2014) (school districts to provide transportation to both parents' homes in the district).

[290] N. Atlantic School Dist. v. Gregory P., 687 A.2d 37 (Pa. Cmwlth. 1996).

[291] Pamela J.K. v. Roger D.J., 277 Pa. Super. 579, 419 A.2d 1301 (1980).

[292] Commonwealth ex rel. Balla v. Wreski, 165 Pa. Super. 6, 67 A.2d 595 (1949).

was able to do so.[293] In one case where the custodial mother planned to move to Arizona, the court, in order to encourage visits by the father, imposed the costs of the child's three yearly trips to Pennsylvania on the mother, except that in any calendar year in which the father failed to visit the child in Arizona on at least two occasions, the father would have to reimburse the mother for one-half of the expense.[294]

LOWER COURT CASES

Lycoming County

Bowman v. Cowden, 19 Lyc. 27 (C.C.P. 1992) (Where a parent is required to bear the cost of transporting his children from Iowa to Lycoming County for the purposes of exercising partial custody rights, he is entitled to a reduction in child support to cover the costs of transportation).

§ 3.4.19. Relationship of Duty to Support

The function of the duty to support is solely to ensure that the child has adequate means to develop in a suitable environment. As such, matters of support are independent from the right to have partial custody or supervised physical custody of one's child, and same is not dependent upon fulfillment of the duty to support.[295]

The fact that a parent fails to support a child, without more, will not merit a denial of partial custody,[296] just as the fact that a parent supports a child does not automatically guarantee partial custody.[297] While the support obligation and visitation questions are matters separate and distinct, pursuant to Rule 1915.1(a)(2) the court may issue partial custody orders

---

[293] Pamela J.K. v. Roger D.J., 277 Pa. Super. 579, 419 A.2d 1301 (1980).

[294] McCourt v. Meyers, 268 Pa. Super. 152, 407 A.2d 875 (1980).

[295] Schmidt v. Schmidt, 313 Pa. Super. 83, 459 A.2d 421 (1983); Commonwealth ex rel. Chila v. Chila, 226 Pa. Super. 336, 313 A.2d 339 (1973).

[296] Miller v. Miller, 269 Pa. Super. 83, 409 A.2d 74 (1979); Commonwealth ex rel. Peterson v. Hayes, 252 Pa. Super. 487, 381 A.2d 1311 (1977); Scott v. Scott, 240 Pa. Super. 65, 368 A.2d 288 (1976).

[297] Fernald v. Fernald, 224 Pa. Super. 93, 302 A.2d 470 (1973).

when presiding over support litigation if a claim for partial custody is raised during the course of the support action.

Where partial custody is unjustly denied by the custodian, the supporting non-custodial parent must nonetheless continue payments and may not suspend support pending the restoration of custody privileges.[298] Rather, the non-custodian must petition the court for such orders as are necessary to ensure the unhindered exercise of such rights. In cases of extreme examples of wrongful conduct on the part of the custodian, such as the total concealment of self and child for an extended period of time, the court may suspend the support obligation during the period of misconduct.[299]

LOWER COURT CASES

Lawrence County

Thomas v. Thomas, C.P. Lawrence County, No. 271 of 2009 (C.C.P. 2015) (Trial court found that mother had the legal right to custody of the parties' child, and that it was in the child's best interest for mother to have custody, as father was alienating the child from mother. It would be absurd to conclude that father can act in defiance of a court order granting custody to mother and then use that circumstance to avoid paying the child support that would follow from an award of custody to mother. Father argued that the trial court abused its discretion in awarding child support to mother when mother did not have physical custody of the child and the child had not been in her physical custody for nearly a year. Shortly after a custody order was entered giving mother primary physical custody, the child began running away from mother's home to father's home. Despite the custody order, the child no longer stayed at mother's home. The court found that the child was not staying with mother as a result of father's actions in alienating the child from mother).

Lehigh County

Imlay v. Miller, C.P. Lehigh County, No. 2004-FC-0713 (C.C.P. 2011) (Trial court denied father's petition to modify the existing custody order for the parties' children

---

[298] Commonwealth ex rel. Zercher v. Bankert, 266 Pa. Super. 595, 405 A.2d 1266 (1979); Kramer v. Kelly, 265 Pa. Super. 58, 401 A.2d 799 (1979); Commonwealth ex rel. Chila v. Chila, 226 Pa. Super. 336, 313 A.2d 339 (1973).

[299] Commonwealth ex rel. Chila v. Chila, 226 Pa. Super. 336, 313 A.2d 339 (1973); Commonwealth ex rel. Shaffer v. Shaffer, 90 York 130 (1976), *aff'd per curiam*, 247 Pa. Super. 618, 373 A.2d 1142 (1977).

where father's chief motivation seemed to be reduction of his support obligation. Father requested both modification of the custody order and contempt by mother based on the conduct of the parties' 13-year-old daughter in caring for her younger siblings before mother returned home from work and mother's alleged improper monitoring of that conduct. Father alleged that the daughter's behavior corrupted the younger children. Father cited the atmosphere in mother's residence, as well as the children's difficulties in school as reasons for transferring custody of the younger children to him during the school year. The court noted that father lived in a motor home which was insufficient as a residence for the children. Furthermore, father's proposal was not acceptable because it would separate the younger children from their older sister. Finally, the court discussed father's continuing emphasis on the support order he paid for the children and concluded that his primary motivation in requesting a custody modification was so that he could reduce the amount of his court-ordered support).

§ 3.4.20. Rights of Non-Custodial Parent

While it is no longer possible for the non-custodian to maintain the prior level of contact, the parent retains, until forfeited through improper conduct, the right to be an active participant in the child's life.[300]

During periods of partial custody, a non-custodial parent has parental authority, and restrictions will be imposed on that authority only by consent or upon a clear demonstration that, in the absence of a proposed restriction, partial custody will have a detrimental impact on the child.[301] This right is jealously guarded by the courts, and it is only in the most unusual circumstances that it will be totally severed.[302]

The degree of participation varies from case to case, since it turns on a combination of the fitness, preferences and cooperation of the parties;

---

[300] Pamela J.K. v. Roger D.J., 277 Pa. Super. 579, 419 A.2d 1301 (1980); Fernald v. Fernald, 224 Pa. Super. 93, 302 A.2d 470 (1973).

[301] Zummo v. Zummo, 394 Pa. Super. 30, 574 A.2d 1130 (1990). *See also Sullivan v. Shaw*, 437 Pa. Super. 534, 650 A.2d 882 (1994) ("even when sole legal and physical custody is awarded to one parent, Pennsylvania courts scrupulously protect the non-custodial parent's right to maintain a meaningful parental relationship with his or her child").

[302] Nancy E.M. v. Kenneth D.M., 316 Pa. Super. 351, 462 A.2d 1386 (1983) (court recognized that child would be 18 in a month and thus would no longer be subject to visitation order, but would not deny visitation even for that brief period); Hoffer v. Hoffer, 301 Pa. Super. 289, 447 A.2d 972 (1982); Dena Lynn F. v. Harvey H.F., 278 Pa. Super. 95, 419 A.2d 1374 (1980); Lewis v. Lewis, 271 Pa. Super. 519, 414 A.2d 375 (1979).

the ability of the parent to be physically with the child as restricted by work schedules and geographic limitations;[303] and consideration of the need for as much stability and continuity for the child as possible under the circumstances.[304]

It should also be pointed out that the rights of the non-custodial parent are not affected by the illegitimacy of the child and that once parenthood is established, the rights of both parents are no less than if the child had been born in wedlock.[305]

§ 3.4.21. Child's Refusal to Follow Custody Order

The mere stubborn refusal by a child to participate in custody outings will not be honored, as courts are aware that in many cases the child may simply be reacting to subtle subconscious or overt custodial pressure designed to alienate or undermine the non-custodian.[306] Moreover, where the child staunchly refuses to have contact with the non-custodian, the court may order the custodian to exercise parental authority and deliver the child to the non-custodian.[307] However, where a custody order does not explicitly require one parent to encourage the child to visit with the

---

[303] Smith v. Smith, 307 Pa. Super. 544, 453 A.2d 1020 (1982) (court found that shared custody could be continued in spite of a 120-mile distance between the parties); Pamela J.K. v. Roger D.J., 277 Pa. Super. 579, 419 A.2d 1301 (1980); Scarlett v. Scarlett, 257 Pa. Super. 468, 390 A.2d 1331 (1978).

[304] Pamela J.K. v. Roger D.J., 277 Pa. Super. 579, 419 A.2d 1301 (1980).

[305] Commonwealth ex rel. Peterson v. Hayes, 252 Pa. Super. 487, 381 A.2d 1311 (1977).

[306] In Re Mary Kathryn T., 427 Pa. Super. 515, 629 A.2d 988 (1993) (Child's desire not to visit with parent is not sufficient reason to deny visitation); Nancy E.M. v. Kenneth D.M., 316 Pa. Super. 351, 462 A.2d 1386 (1983) (appellate court found that even though child did not wish to visit with mother and would be turning 18 in a month, visitation should not be denied without proper grounds, even for so short a period of time); In re Stuck, 291 Pa. Super. 61, 435 A.2d 219 (1981) (court expanded visitation in spite of children's opposition); Commonwealth ex rel. Ermel v. Ermel, 259 Pa. Super. 219, 393 A.2d 796 (1978); Comm. ex rel. Lotz v. Lotz, 188 Pa. Super. 241, 146 A.2d 362 (1958); Commonwealth ex rel. Turner v. Strange, 179 Pa. Super. 83, 115 A.2d 885 (1955).

[307] Fernald v. Fernald, 224 Pa. Super. 93, 302 A.2d 470 (1973); Commonwealth ex rel. Lotz v. Lotz, 188 Pa. Super. 241, 146 A.2d 362 (1958).

other, that parent cannot be held in contempt for failing to encourage the child to visit with the other parent.[308]

LOWER COURT CASES
Lancaster County

Dochterman v. Dochterman, C.P. Lancaster County, No. C1-09-07054 (C.C.P. 2015) (Trial court ruled that a parent who fails to exercise periods of partial physical custody and cannot prove a present inability to comply with the court custody order may be found to be in civil contempt of the order, and sanctions may be imposed).

Lebanon County

Boehler v. Boehler, 52 Lebanon L. J. 39, C.P. Lebanon County, No. 2006-20469 (C.C.P. 2014) (The trial court found mother in contempt of court, where mother's conduct and attitude influenced the parties' oldest son's refusal to obey the order granting father partial custody. Father filed a custody modification petition alleging that mother intentionally caused estrangement between him and the parties' three children. Father subsequently filed a petition for contempt, alleging that he had been denied his court-ordered partial custody time with his oldest son because the son refused to comply with the custody order. Father alleged that this intransigence was due to her mother's campaign to estrange him from his son. The court found that mother had a desire to be in complete control of all aspects of custody. When given custody authority, mother exercised it to the exclusion of father. She was also found in contempt of court on multiple occasions for failing to afford father the physical custody time he was permitted to receive by court order. The court observed that mother employed a campaign over many years designed to estrange father from his children. By her words and actions, mother conveyed to the children that father was a violent man who could not be trusted. The court found that the oldest son's oppositional and defiant behavior was the result of the culture of mistrust mother had promoted. The court observed that mother's willful behavior and denial to father of his custody rights made a finding of contempt both necessary and appropriate).

---

[308] K.M.G. v. H.M.W., 171 A.3d 389, (Pa. Super. 2017) (trial court reversed by Superior Court for finding mother in contempt for failing to encourage the child to attend visitation with his father when trial court's prior orders did not include a specific requirement that mother encourage the child to visit with father); Sutliff v. Sutliff, 361 Pa. Super. 194, 522 A.2d 80 (1987) (where custody orders did not specifically or clearly state that mother had to "encourage" her daughter to visit with her father, mother could not be held in contempt for failing to so encourage child).

Philadelphia County

Brady v. Brady, 32 Phila. 14 (C.C.P. 1996) (Trial court found that mother had no affirmative duty to encourage the parties' teenaged sons to visit with father since the custody order did not impose such a duty in writing. The court noted that the order did not impose a further duty on mother to encourage visitation, but merely defined the time father was able to have partial custody. The court opined that to hold mother in contempt based on a petition directed at her but based solely on the children's refusal to visit would be a "grievous injustice" under the circumstances of this case).

§ 3.4.22. Denying Partial Custody

The long established rule holds that a parent may not be denied partial custody unless the parent suffers from such severe mental or moral deficiency so as to constitute a grave threat to the child.[309]

---

[309] Costello v. Costello, 446 Pa. Super. 371, 666 A.2d 1096 (1995) (appropriate standard to apply when presented with issue of parental visitation is whether parent suffers from mental or moral deficiencies that pose great threat to child.); see also In Interest of M.B., 449 Pa. Super. 507, 674 A.2d 702 (1996). (Best interest of child standard applies when determining frequency of parental visitation of child; parental visitation is not usually denied except when grave threat to child can be shown.); Green v. Sneeringer, 431 Pa. Super. 66, 635 A.2d 1074 (1993) (Although best interest of child is always overriding concern, appropriate standard to apply when presented with issue of parental visitation is whether parent suffers from mental or moral deficiencies that pose grave threat to child. Father's conviction for first-degree murder of child's mother was alone evidence of severe mental or moral deficiencies constituting grave threat to child's welfare, and, thus, the premeditated murder justified denial of visitation); In Re Mary Kathyrn T., 427 Pa. Super. 515, 629 A.2d 988 (1993) (Natural parents, even when they have lost custody of their children, should be awarded visitation except in fairly extreme circumstances); In Re Constance W., 351 Pa. Super. 393, 506 A.2d 405 (1986) (Trial court's order forbidding a father to see his child for a year was held to be unreasonable where the record failed to show that the father's "impulsive and somewhat irrational behavior" had any harmful effect upon the child); In re Damon B., 314 Pa. Super. 391, 460 A.2d 1196 (1983); Hughes v. Hughes, 316 Pa. Super. 505, 463 A.2d 478 (1983); Nancy E.M. v. Kenneth D.M., 316 Pa. Super. 351, 462 A.2d 1386 (1983); In re Rhine, 310 Pa. Super. 275, 456 A.2d 608 (1983); Dena Lynn F. v. Harvey H.F., 278 Pa. Super. 95, 419 A.2d 1374 (1980); Lewis v. Lewis, 271 Pa. Super. 519, 414 A.2d 375 (1979); Commonwealth ex rel. Peterson v. Hayes, 252 Pa. Super. 487, 381 A.2d 1311 (1977); *see also* In re B. G., 774 A.2d 757 (Pa. Super. 2001) (trial court, in a dependency case, erred when it issued an order terminating limited supervised visits by the minor's natural parents, where the evidence before the court did not demonstrate

The fact that a parent has ignored a child for extended periods, in one case 11 years, has been held insufficient to warrant an order barring visitation or partial custody.[310] Likewise, the fact that a parent has engaged in marital misconduct or lives with a paramour has been found to fall short of a grave threat to the child.[311]

Where the father shot the mother in the shoulder while she was holding the child, coupled with a pattern of hostile behavior, a sufficient threat was present upon which to base the termination of visitation.[312]

Partial custody privileges sought purely for the purpose of harassing the custodian may be properly denied.[313] A finding of harassment should, however, be made cautiously and only on clear and convincing evidence.[314] Also, many orders granting partial custody bear the caution that such orders are temporary in nature and that contacts which result in adverse effects on the child may at any time be severely curtailed or wholly eliminated.[315] Likewise, denials of partial custody are generally not permanent and may be modified where grounds for denial have dissipated.[316]

---

that the continued visits posed a grave threat to the child. The court explained that in dependency cases, visitation will not be denied where reunification remains the family service goal, unless the visitation poses a "grave threat.").

[310] Nianda v. Nianda, 343 Pa. Super. 298, 494 A.2d 856 (1985) (the Superior Court found no abuse of discretion when the natural mother was awarded 3 weeks summer visitation in her home in California, despite the fact that the mother had failed to exercise visitation rights for almost ten years); Commonwealth ex rel. Brown v. Lane, 90 Pa. Super. 350 (1927). *See* Commonwealth ex rel. Turner v. Strange, 179 Pa. Super. 83, 115 A.2d 885 (1955); Commonwealth ex rel. Boschert v. Cook, 122 Pa. Super. 397, 186 A. 229 (1936).

[311] Commonwealth ex rel. Sorace v. Sorace, 236 Pa. Super. 42, 344 A.2d 553 (1975); Commonwealth ex rel. McNamee v. Jackson, 183 Pa. Super. 522, 132 A.2d 396 (1957).

[312] Hughes v. Hughes, 316 Pa. Super. 505, 463 A.2d 478 (1983).

[313] Miller v. Miller, 269 Pa. Super. 83, 409 A.2d 74 (1979); De Welles v. Dwelle, 214 Pa. Super. 376, 257 A.2d 594 (1969).

[314] Miller v. Miller, 269 Pa. Super. 83, 409 A.2d 74 (1979).

[315] Dena Lynn F. v. Harvey H.F., 278 Pa. Super. 95, 419 A.2d 1374 (1980); Commonwealth ex rel. Peterson v. Hayes, 252 Pa. Super. 487, 381 A.2d 1311 (1977).

[316] In re Damon B., 314 Pa. Super. 391, 460 A.2d 1196 (1983) (court suspended mother's visitation for a six-month period); *see also* Seger v. Seger, 377 Pa. Super. 391, 547 A.2d 424 (1988) (the appropriate way for a custody/visitation order to be modified

LOWER COURT CASES
Allegheny County

Donna S. v. Bernard S., 137 P.L.J. 173 (Allegheny Co. 1989) (Hearsay testimony concerning a minor's statement to her mother and three professionals (therapist, child psychiatrist, and a second therapist when child was two years old) were supportive of opinions of these professionals that there was an extremely high likelihood that the father sexually abused the child and the father should be permitted supervised visitation only. 42 Pa.C.S. Section 5986, which authorizes the use in dependency proceedings of hearsay testimony regarding a child's statements describing acts of sexual contact with a parent, were held applicable to custody proceedings intended to suspend unsupervised visits. Trial court refused to permit Defendant/Father to introduce a polygraph test based upon its inadmissibility because of the unreliability of the tests).

Berks County

Frankenberg v. Frankenberg, 83 Berks L. J. 95 (C.C.P. 1990) (Visitation should be limited or denied only if the parent has been found to possess severe mental or moral deficiencies as to constitute a grave threat to the children's welfare, and here there was no evidence of incidents taking place currently that would warrant restricting or denying father's visitation rights; the court held that the primary consideration in visitation cases is the best interest of the children, and in this case the father does not have any mental or moral deficiencies. Although the mother alleged the father had tried to commit suicide, the court found this could not be used as a basis to restrict visitation. There was no evidence to support that the father ever threatened to harm his children or put them in jeopardy. Father's past conduct must have little bearing in making a present custody order).

Sagl v. Sagl, 82 Berks L. J. 109 (C.C.P. 1989) (A mother's overnight visitation rights will be eliminated where her irregular living arrangements and sleeping patterns create an unstable environment for the children. Continuity and stability are important in the emotional development of young children, and mother's irregular living and sleeping arrangements and fluctuating desire to see her children compel elimination of mother's overnight visitation privileges).

Maciejewski v. Coldren, 82 Berks L. J. 150 (C.C.P. 1989) (There is a strong public policy against limiting the relationship between parent and child, and visitation should be limited or denied only if a parent is found to have severe mental or moral deficiencies constituting a grave threat to the child's welfare; neither the father's past conduct nor the

---

is through a petition for modification. A trial court cannot permanently modify a visitation order without the petition to modify being submitted by one of the parties); Lewis v. Lewis, 271 Pa. Super. 519, 414 A.2d 375 (1979).

disruptive effect of his visitation on the custodial parent's household justify a denial of the father's visitation rights; a father's prior substance abuse problems will not prevent the court from allowing visitation with his child where the problem is under control; the court will refer the parent for drug and alcohol counseling as a precaution).

Cambria County

D.J.B. v. J.L.B., C.P. Cambria County, No. 2005-3380 (C.C.P. May 10, 2017), *aff'd*, Memorandum Decision, No., 842 WDA 2017 (Pa. Super. February 27, 2018) (Mother filed a petition for special relief, requesting that the trial court suspend the parties' child overnight visits with father due to the child's recent exposure to lice at father's residence, and her deteriorating mental health caused by the visits. Trial court temporarily suspended father's overnight custody with his 13-year-old daughter and ordered him to participate in a court-approved counseling program, at his own expense, to address parent–child relationships).

Carbon County

Kuntz v. Allen, 11 Carbon L. J. 82 (C.C.P. 1987) (The fact that a parent has been long absent from a child's life will not, standing alone, bar the parent's right to visit his child. However, where unrebutted psychological testimony indicates that immediate and open visitation of father with his daughter would be harmful to the child because of her hostility, the court will temporarily limit contacts to telephone and mail).

Chester County

Albert v. Keogh, 39 Ches. Co. Rep. 134 (C.C.P. 1991) (A father will be permitted visitation with his daughter pursuant to a program developed by a court-appointed psychologist even though the father had no contact with the child for the first six years of her life; where a father's effort is sincere, visitation will not be denied even though he has never had contact with his daughter).

Dauphin County

Young v. Young, 111 Dauph. 170 (C.C.P. 1991) (Where a father's visitation rights are terminated during pending criminal proceedings for sexual abuse of his children but where the charges are subsequently dropped, the father's petition to vacate the order terminating visitation will be denied since an evaluation of all of the evidence indicates that there was probable abuse).

Zeitlen v. Zeitlen, 107 Dauph. Rep. 31 (C.C.P. 1986) (A father's petition to restore his visitation rights is denied where his mental condition renders him a danger to the welfare of his children. Testimony established that father must take medication daily to curb his illness and that he was not taking medication as prescribed. Father's conduct was erratic, argumentative, and hostile. The denial of any visitation to a father is an unusual order, but will be made if the record shows such severe mental deficiency as to constitute a threat to the welfare of his children).

Fayette County

Lucas v. Lucas, 54 Fayette Leg. J. 11 (C.C.P. 1990) (Sexual abuse by a parent is morally deficient behavior and grounds for denial of visitation rights).

Lucas v. Lucas, 54 Fayette Leg. J. 11 (C.C.P. 1990) (When a custodial parent believes that the non-custodial parent is sexually abusing their children and obtains supporting examinations by medical professionals, a refusal to allow continued visitation does not constitute contempt of a custody order; the non-custodial parent will be limited to supervised visits and required to undergo psychiatric counseling—a custodial parent will not be held in contempt of court for refusing to allow visitation rights to the non-custodial parent when it has been adjudged that the non-custodial parent is a child abuser and is continuing to abuse the child notwithstanding a court order of supervised visitation—the court may order the non-custodial parent to enroll in and attend therapy sessions for the treatment of sexual aggression as a condition precedent of his visitation rights).

Franklin County

Roach v. Faust, 8 Franklin Leg. J. 110 (C.C.P. 1986) (A party seeking to deny visitation rights to a natural parent must show clear and convincing evidence that the parent's presence is a grave threat to the child. The court may, in rare instances, suspend visitation without a showing of severe mental or moral deficiencies in the parent as to constitute a grave threat to the child. Where father is in prison for killing mother, an event that child witnessed, and evidence shows that the visits to father have had adverse psychological effects on 7-year old child, court will suspend visitation).

Lackawanna County

D.B. v. J.B., C.P. Lackawanna County, No. 2015-FC-40549 (C.C.P. May 26, 2017), *aff'd*, Memorandum Decision, No. 1029 MDA 2017 (Pa. Super. December 18, 2017) (It was in the best interest of the minor children for father not to have any contact with them, where father pledged to the facts underlying the allegation of sexually abusing the youngest child, but, when given the opportunity to have supervised visitation with the minor children, he continued to act inappropriately and make the minor children feel uncomfortable. Mother filed a Petition for Emergency Special Relief, along with a Petition to Modify Custody. The trial court granted mother's petition and denied father any contact with the children. Trial court expressed concern regarding father's history of sexual abuse. One child had been a victim of sexual abuse at the hands of father, although father entered a plea to Endangering the Welfare of a Child. The trial court further determined that father had continued to engage in inappropriate behavior with the children, despite having only supervised visitation. The court was highly concerned with the level of inappropriateness with the minor children, even during periods of supervised visitation).

Lebanon County

Geist v. Werner, 26 Lebanon Leg. J. 135 (C.C.P. 1989) (Father of an illegitimate child was denied visitation rights where he has had very little contact with his child, provided support only while under Court order, failed to appear for any preliminary supervised visits permitted by the court, and refused to permit a home study visit).

Lehigh County

Edwards v. Rahab, C.P. Lehigh County, No. 2007-FC-1172 (C.C.P. 2011) (Trial court ruled that mother should have sole legal custody of the parties' daughter and to make all significant decisions in the child's life, where father did not desire a relationship with his daughter and failed to exercise his court-ordered custody rights. The court noted that the child looked forward to her custody times with father, but she was disappointed and upset on the occasions that she knew father was supposed to have custody with her and father did not exercise custody rights. The court noted that providing specified periods for father's exercise of partial physical custody would be a wasted effort because father did not spend the court-ordered time already granted to spend with his daughter. The court declared that mother should no longer be burdened with having to deal with court-ordered custody times for father, which he did not follow. The court noted that father could still have contact with his daughter, but emphasized that the onus was on father to contact mother and agree on visitation. Mother was not obligated to agree to any custodial times for father unless she was satisfied that father would abide by agreements that they reached).

Scotto v. Scotto, 48 Lehigh L. J. 531 (C.C.P. 1998) (Trial court gave preference to well-reasoned wishes of a mature, 16-year old daughter in denying mother's petition for visitation; the child reasonably felt embarrassed and pressured by mother's insistence that the child had been abused by her father. The court granted mother unlimited visitation, but subject to the daughter's agreement as to the time and place of the visits. "In essence, we are acknowledging that there are some family relationships that the court cannot repair. Visitation and counseling by compulsion, in the circumstances that confront us, will have a tendency to cause further deterioration in the long run. We serve the child best by keeping the avenue clear for the mother and child to reunite when each is willing to make changes and take steps toward a healthy relationship that will benefit both.").

Montgomery County

Corbett v. Bonfiglio, C.P. Montgomery County, No 97-10859 (C.C.P. 1998) (Plaintiffs great-grandparents' Petition for Partial Custody/Visitation was dismissed when plaintiffs failed to demonstrate that overnight visitation was in the best interest of the child. The child visits his father every other weekend, and to grant the great-grandparents overnight visitation once a month would leave the child home with his family only one weekend a month). *Goch v. Wurtzel*, 121 Montg. Co. L. Rep. 164 (C.C.P. 1988) (Where stepfather had a hostile relationship with mother and where the child no longer knows stepfather, his request for visitation rights is denied).

Philadelphia County

Taylor et al. v. Connelly, 23 Phila. 471 (C.C.P. 1991) (Father will be awarded partial custody despite allegations of sexual abuse, where there is no evidence of abuse during supervised visitation, when mother fails to present the child for an abuse evaluation and where the child's affirmative responses to sexual abuse questions are the result of mother's poisoning of the child's mind. Courts do not sanction the estrangement of a child from either parent, therefore visitation rights of a non-custodial parent will be guarded carefully. Visitation has been limited or denied only where the parent has been shown to suffer from severe mental or moral deficiencies that constitute a grave threat to the child. Visitation has been granted to parents who have ignored their children for a long time, to parents who have engaged in marital misconduct or who have lived with lovers, and even to parents whose children did not want to see them).

Somerset County

Peterman v. Wellington, 52 Somerset Leg. J. 62 (C.C.P 1993) (Severe deficiencies must be shown by clear and convincing evidence before visitation with a non-custodial parent can be denied. In appropriate circumstances, visitation with an incarcerated parent may properly be denied if the interest of the child so dictates. A general claim of the impropriety of prison visitation without any evidence of a specific adverse effect on the child's physical, intellectual, emotional, and spiritual well-being is not enough to deny visitation to the non-custodial parent).

Peterman v. Wellington, 52 Somerset Leg. J. 62 (C.C.P. 1993) (Pennsylvania law favors visitation with the non-custodial parent; a parent will not be denied the right to see his or her child unless the parent manifests severe mental or moral deficiency that constitutes a real and grave threat to the child's welfare).

York County

In the Interest of: J.P., a Minor, C.P. York County, No. CP-67-DP0000561-2006 (C.C.P. January 10, 2018), *aff'd*, Memorandum Decision, No. 255 MDA 2018 (Pa. Super. August 3, 2018) (Trial court suspended father's unsupervised visitation with his child; father's actions at the unsupervised visits with child caused depression and extreme anxiety and were counterproductive to reunification. The court prohibited father from having contact with the children without the supervision of the children's paternal grandparents. It would not be in the child's best interest or her mental health and well-being for visits to be increased, even for increased supervised visits at this time).

Stambaugh v. Stambaugh, 112 York Leg. Rec. 43 (C.C.P. 1998) (Petitioner, mother's paramour, did not have a right to intervene in a custody matter already pending between the parents. "Petitioner's interest in this purpose is a consequence of his relationship with Mother. Without his connection to Mother, Petitioner would have no expectation of receiving any court ordered right to custody or visitation. Beyond this, however Petitioner's interest in maintaining a relationship with his paramour's children is not an interest sought to be protected by statute. Since Petitioner fails the substantial, direct and immediate test, he lacks standing to pursue visitation of the children. Without standing to pursue visitation, Petitioner cannot utilize Rule 1915.6(b) to intervene in the impending custody action between Mother and Father.").

W.F.C. v. J.R.C., 109 York Leg. Rec. 17 (1994) (In reviewing a case with allegations of sexual abuse, clear and convincing evidence must be shown that such conduct occurred in order to restrict a parent's visitation with his children).

§ 3.4.23. Criminal Background

Under the newly enacted 23 Pa.C.S. § 5329, a trial court must consider each parent and household member's past criminal convictions of the crimes enumerated under Section 5329(a), when a party seeks any form of custody. Section 5329(a) provides that the court shall consider same and determine that the party "does not pose a threat of harm to the child before making any order of custody to that parent." The crimes enumerated under Section 5329(a), include, but are not limited to, corruption of minors, endangering the welfare of children, kidnapping, incest and sexual abuse of children, and driving under the influence of alcohol or controlled substance.[317]

In April 2012, Senate Bill 1167 was passed which amended Subsection 5329(c). Prior to the changes to the statute in April 2012, Subsection (c) titled: "Initial Evaluation" provided that: "The Court shall provide for an evaluation to determine whether: (1) the party or household member who committed an offense under subsection (a) [enumerated offenses] poses a threat to the child; and (2) counseling is necessary for that party or household member."

Prior to the change, Subsection (c) was problematic because it was not clear whether an order could be entered by the court prior to an evaluation

---

[317] 23 Pa.C.S. § 5329(a).

occurring when reading the provision in subsection (a) together with subsection (c). To complicate matters, a question arose as to who conducts the evaluation and what type of an evaluation was required. One side of the argument was that no custody order could be entered if a litigant or household member committed an enumerated offense listed under Section 5329(a) without an evaluation being conducted of that individual by a mental health professional. The other side of the argument was that the trial court was required to make a cursory evaluation and if the court deemed that a more detailed evaluation by a professional was needed the court could order same. The latter interpretation gave the court more discretion and was appealing in situations where a conviction occurred many years ago and was an isolated incident. The change to Subsection (c) remedies the problem. Senate Bill 1167 became effective on June 11, 2012.

Under Senate Bill 1167, Subsection (c) has been rewritten and provides as follows: "At the initial in-person contact with the court, the judge, conference officer or other appointed individual shall perform an initial evaluation to determine whether the party or household member who committed an offense under subsection (a) poses a threat to the child and whether counseling is necessary. The initial evaluation shall not be conducted by a mental health professional. After the initial evaluation, the court may order further evaluation or counseling by a mental health professional if the court determines it is necessary."[318] At this time, it will be up to each county to devise their system regarding the initial evaluation. However, it is clear, by reading the statute, that the case will not be delayed and sent to a mental health professional initially, as the court will perform the initial evaluation.

If the court determines that counseling is necessary, the court shall appoint "a qualified professional specializing in treatment relating to the particular offense to provide counseling to the offending individual."[319] The counseling may include therapy designed to rehabilitate and address issues of physical and sexual abuse and the psychology of the offender,

---

[318] 23 Pa.C.S. § 5329(c); Pa.R.C.P. 1915.3-2(b).
[319] 23 Pa.C.S. § 5329(d)(1); Pa.R.C.P. 1915.3-2(b).

and the effects of abuse on the victim.[320] The court may require subsequent evaluations during or after counseling to determine if further counseling is needed or it may require subsequent evaluations in the event it awards custody to an offending party to determine the continuing best interest of the child, among other things.[321]

The court has the authority to order a party to pay all or a portion of the cost of the evaluation and/or counseling ordered under Section 5329.

Like its predecessor Section 5303(b.2), new Section 5329(b) directs that no court shall award custody, partial custody, or supervised physical custody to a parent who has been convicted of first degree murder of the other parent of the child who is the subject of the order, unless the child is of suitable age and consents to the order.[322]

In the event a party is charged with a crime enumerated under 5329(a), upon the other party learning of this information, under Section 5330 that party may seek a temporary custody order or a modification of an existing order.[323] Section 5330 directs that in such an instance the court shall hold a hearing in an "expeditious manner."[324] The court shall consider whether the party charged of an enumerated offense under Section 5329(a) poses a risk of physical, emotional or psychological harm to the child when evaluating a party's request for a temporary order or modification of an existing order under Section 5330(a).[325] It is to be noted that the statute specifically provides that a party's failure to act under Section 5330 shall not prejudice any party in a custody proceeding.[326]

Pursuant to Rule 1915.3-2, which became effective September 3, 2013, "The petitioner must file and serve with the compliant, or any petition for modification, a verification regarding any criminal or abuse history

---

[320] 23 Pa.C.S. § 5329(d)(2). *See also* the following which was decided under the prior statute regarding counseling: D.R.C. v. J.A.Z., 31 A.3d 677 (Pa. 2011) (Counseling not required for incarcerated prisoners before issuing a custody order).

[321] 23 Pa.C.S. § 5329(e)(1) & (2).

[322] 23 Pa.C.S. § 5329(b).

[323] 23 Pa.C.S. § 5330(a).

[324] *Id.*

[325] 23 Pa.C.S. § 5330(b).

[326] 23 Pa.C.S. § 5330(c).

of the petitioner and anyone living in the petitioner's household."[327] The petitioner should aver in the pleading that he/she has attached the Criminal Record/Abuse History Verification form to the pleading.[328] Further a blank verification form must be attached to the complaint or petition by the petitioner to be served on the respondent.[329] It is important to note that though a respondent is not required to file a responsive pleading under Rule 1915.5, Rule 1915.3-2 requires the respondent to file a verification with the court regarding any criminal or abuse history of the respondent and anyone living in the respondent's household on or before the initial in-person contact with the court, but no later than 30 days after service of the pleading upon the respondent.[330] Further, both parties are required under Rule 1915.3-2 to file and serve updated verifications five days prior to trial.[331]

With the enactment of Section 5329, there was debate whether the court could enter a temporary order on behalf of a party with a criminal history or a party that has a household member with a criminal history pending an evaluation and/or counseling for same. The recently promulgated Rule 1915.3-2(b) settles the debate and authorizes the court to enter such a temporary custody order. Further, questions arose as to whether ARD or other diversionary programs should be considered by the court. The "Note" provided under Rule 1915.3-2(b) states: "The court should not consider ARD or other diversionary programs."

LOWER COURT CASES

Erie County

L.A.B. v. J.P.M., 95 Erie Co. Leg. J. 72 (C.C.P. 2011) (Although mother learned of the paramour's criminal record at the beginning of their relationship, she withheld this information from father. Father objected to mother's request for custody pursuant to § 5329 due to the paramour's criminal record. Father requested an initial criminal conviction evaluation of the paramour pursuant to § 5329 to determine whether he posed a

---

[327] Pa.R.C.P. 1915.3-2(a).
[328] *See* Pa.R.C.P. 1915.15(a).
[329] *Id.*
[330] *Id.*
[331] *Id.*

threat of harm to the child and whether counseling was necessary. After a hearing, the court found that it was in the child's best interest to grant father's requests for primary physical custody and an evaluation of the paramour pursuant to 23 Pa.C.S. § 5329. The court found that the circumstances of the endangering welfare conviction involving a slap to the face of an 11-month old infant leaving bruises, welts and swelling to the child's face are of grave concern given the evidence of paramour's treatment of this father's child. The court found that father's request for a § 5329 evaluation was appropriate and must be granted. The court found that until the results of the evaluation are fully processed and the court determines whether the paramour poses a threat of harm to the child and whether counseling is necessary, the child should not have contact with the paramour. Mother was granted liberal periods of partial physical custody with the child outside the presence of the paramour).

Lehigh County

Klingaman v. Cannon, C.P. Lehigh County, No. 2003-FC-1073 (C.C.P. 2012) (The trial court denied mother's petition to increase her partial custody where mother failed to present testimony regarding her new husband's criminal history. Under the new Custody Act, parties are required to provide evidence regarding the criminal histories of other parties in the household living with the children. Mother's husband recently completed 19 months of confinement at a correctional facility. According to mother, the imprisonment was served for driving under the influence. The court found that it could not guarantee the safety of the children in mother's care, while father was the parent who had provided the daily, appropriate care for the children. The court listed the criminal record of mother's husband and noted that the children's safety was compromised by his DUI convictions and abuse of mother. Mother's husband was ordered to undergo drug and alcohol treatment and drug monitoring, pursuant to 23 Pa.C.S. § 5329. The failure of mother to present husband's testimony prevented the court from determining whether mother's expanded custody would be in the best interest of the children. The court determined that mother must present her husband's full circumstances to the court, including the testimony of husband, at any subsequent hearing wherein she sought to increase her custody rights. The court also expressed concern regarding mother's cigarette smoking. "Mother testified that she smokes one and a half packs of cigarettes a day. The children can no longer be exposed to cigarette smoke. Father has a concern about mother's falling asleep while she is smoking. This is a legitimate concern in view of mother's admitted drowsiness and her admitted smoking of cigarettes around her house.").

§ 3.4.24. Military

Legislation was enacted to protect the custody rights of servicemembers while they are deployed. The statutes regarding same are 51 Pa.C.S. §§ 4109 & 4110. Sections 4109 and 4110 were subsequently amended by Senate Bill 1167 which became effective on June 11, 2012.

The following is Section 4109 in its entirety:

§ 4109. Child custody proceedings during military deployment.

(a) Restriction on change of custody.-If a petition for change of custody of a child of an eligible servicemember is filed with any court in this Commonwealth while the eligible servicemember is deployed in support of a contingency operation, no court may enter an order modifying or amending any previous judgment or order, or issue a new order, that changes the custody arrangement for that child that existed as of the date of the deployment of the eligible servicemember, except that a court may enter a temporary custody order if it is in the best interest of the child.

(a.1) Temporary assignment to family members.-If an eligible servicemember has received notice of deployment in support of a contingency operation, a court may issue a temporary order to an eligible servicemember who has rights to a child under 23 Pa.C.S. § 5323 (relating to award of custody) or former 23 Pa.C.S. Ch. 53 Subch. A (relating to general provisions), including a temporary order to temporarily assign custody rights to family members of the servicemember. In the case of temporary assignment of rights to family members of the servicemember, the following shall apply:

(1) The servicemember may petition the court for a temporary order to temporarily assign custody rights to family members of the servicemember. The servicemember shall be joined in the petition by the family members to whom the servicemember is seeking to assign temporary custody rights. The petition shall include a proposed revised custody schedule for care of the child by the family members. The proposed revised custody schedule may not include custody rights which exceed the rights granted to a servicemember set forth in the order in effect at the time of the filing of the petition to grant temporary custody rights to family members.

(2) The court may issue a temporary order with a revised custody schedule as proposed by the servicemember and the family members or another revised custody schedule as the court deems appropriate, if the court finds that a temporary assignment of custody rights to family members of the servicemember is in the best

interest of the child. In no case shall a temporary order granting custody rights to the family members of a servicemember exceed the custody rights granted to the servicemember set forth in the order in effect at the time of the filing of the petition to assign temporary custody rights to family members.

In the case of any other temporary order issued under this subsection, the court may issue a temporary order if it is in the best interest of the child.

(b) Completion of deployment.-In any temporary custody order entered under subsection (a) or (a.1), a court shall require that, upon the return of the eligible servicemember from deployment in support of a contingency operation, the custody order that was in effect immediately preceding the date of the deployment of the eligible servicemember is reinstated.

(c) Exclusion of military service from determination of child's best interest.-If a petition for the change of custody of the child of an eligible servicemember who was deployed in support of a contingency operation is filed after the end of the deployment, no court may consider the absence of the eligible servicemember by reason of that deployment in determining the best interest of the child.

(d) Failure to appear due to military deployment.-The failure of an eligible servicemember to appear in court due to deployment in support of a contingency operation shall not, in and of itself, be sufficient to justify a modification of a custody [or visitation] order if the reason for the failure to appear is the eligible servicemember's active duty in support of a contingency operation.

(e) Relationship to other laws.-Notwithstanding any other provision of law, the provisions of this section shall be applied with regard to child custody issues related to eligible servicemembers deployed in support of contingency operations.

(f) Definitions.-As used in this section, the following words and phrases shall have the meanings given to them in this subsection:

"Contingency operation." A military operation that:

(1) is designated by the Secretary of Defense as an operation in which members of the armed forces are or may become involved

in military actions, operations or hostilities against an enemy of the United States or against an opposing military force; or

(2) results in the call or order to, or retention on, active duty of members of the uniformed services under 10 U.S.C. § 688 (relating to retired members: authority to order to active duty; duties), 12301(a) (relating to reserve components generally), 12302 (relating to Ready Reserve), 12304 (relating to Selected Reserve and certain Individual Ready Reserve members; order to active duty other than during war or national emergency), 12305 (relating to authority of President to suspend certain laws relating to promotion, retirement, and separation) or 12406 (relating to National Guard in Federal service: call) or any other provision of 10 U.S.C. during a war or during a national emergency declared by the President or Congress.

"Eligible servicemember." A member of the Pennsylvania National Guard or a member of an active or reserve component of the Armed Forces of the United States who is serving on active duty, other than active duty for training, for a period of 30 or more consecutive days, in support of a contingency operation.

"Family members." As defined in 23 Pa.C.S. § 6303 (relating to definitions).

The following is Section 4110 in its entirety:

§ 4110. Expedited or electronic hearing.

(a) Expedited hearing.-Upon motion of an eligible service-memser who has received notice of deployment in support of a contingency operation, the court shall, for good cause shown, hold an expedited hearing in custody matters instituted under section 4109 (relating to child custody proceedings during military deployment) when the military duties of the eligible servicemember have a material effect on the eligible servicemember's ability, or anticipated ability, to appear in person at a regularly scheduled hearing.

(b) Electronic hearing.-Upon motion of an eligible service-member who has received notice of deployment in support of a contingency operation, the court shall, upon reasonable advance notice and for good cause shown, allow the eligible servicemember to present testimony and evidence by electronic means in custody matters instituted under section 4109 when the military duties of the eligible servicemember have a material effect on the eligible servicemember's ability to appear in person at a regularly scheduled hearing.

(c) Definitions.-As used in this section, the following words and phrases shall have the meanings given to them in this subsection unless the context clearly indicates otherwise:

"Contingency operation." As defined in section 4109 (relating to child custody proceedings during military deployment).

"Electronic means." Includes communication by telephone, video conference or the Internet.

"Eligible servicemember." As defined in section 4109 (relating to child custody proceedings during military deployment).

"Matter." As defined in 42 Pa.C.S. § 102 (relating to definitions).

§ 3.4.25. Prisoner Visitation Presumption

Prior to the enactment of the Custody Act in 2011, there was a rebuttable presumption that supervised physical custody with a parent who is incarcerated is not in the best interest of the child pursuant to the Superior Court case of Etter v. Rose.[332] Pursuant to Etter, in considering whether the incarcerated parent has overcome this presumption, "[a]ll relevant factors must be considered, including age of the child, distance and hardship to the child in traveling to the visitation site, the kind of supervision at the visit, identification of the person(s) transporting [her or] him and by what means, the effect on the child physically and emotionally, whether the [parent] has and does exhibit a genuine interest in the child, whether [she or] he maintained reasonable contacts in the past

---

[332] Etter v. Rose, 684 A.2d 1092 (Pa. Super. 1996).; *but see* S.T. v. R.W., 192 A.3d 1155 (Pa. Super. 2018) (trial court erred in making the decision denying incarcerated mother's request for telephone contact with the child because it failed to consider the relevant factors set out in Etter v. Rose that were unique to prison cases pursuant to 23 Pa.C.S. § 5328(a)(16)).

and any other relevant matters impinging on the child's best interests."[333] Since the enactment of the Custody Act in 2011, the rebuttable presumption that supervised physical custody with a parent who is incarcerated is not in the best interest of the child no longer exists.[334] However, the courts are still to consider the Etter factors, which are unique to prison cases, in determining appropriate custody awards.[335] Further, pursuant to 23 Pa.C.S. § 5329(b), "no court shall award custody, partial custody or supervised physical custody to a parent who has been convicted of murder . . . of the other parent of the child who is subject to the order unless the child is of suitable age and consents to the order."[336]

Incarcerated prisoners who petition the court for supervised physical custody are entitled to a hearing, notice of a hearing, and notice of their right to request that they be present at the hearing by means of writ of habeas corpus ad testificandum; courts need not grant the habeas petition and order the prisoner's presence, but courts may not ignore the petition, and the courts must weigh the costs of same against the prisoner's interests in presenting testimony in person.[337]

---

[333] *Id.; see also M.*G. v. L.D., 155 A.3d 1083 (Pa. Super. 2017) (noting the Pennsylvania Supreme Court in D.R.C. v. J.A.Z., 31 A.3d 677 (Pa. 2011), added an 8th factor: the nature of the criminal conduct that culminated in the parent's incarceration, regardless of whether that incarceration is the result of a crime enumerated in section 5329(b)).

[334] S.T. v. R.W., 192 A.3d 1155 (Pa. Super. 2018).

[335] *Id* (the Etter factors are assimilated into the current custody law and are to be addressed under 5328(a)(16)).

[336] 23 Pa.C.S. § 5329(b); *see also Green* v. Sneeringer, 635 A.2d 1074 (Pa. Super. 1993).

[337] Sullivan v. Shaw, 437 Pa. Super. 534, 650 A.2d 882 (1994); *see also* Vanaman v. Cowgill, 363 Pa. Super. 602, 526 A.2d 1226 (1987) (an incarcerated father's right to be present and present evidence at a custody proceeding was violated when an order denying him visitation was entered despite his non-attendance at the hearing; court found that not only notice of a civil hearing is due an imprisoned person, but also specific advisement of his right to attend, and if he wished to attend he could request the court by means of a habeas petition and writ to make arrangements for transportation to attend); *but see* S.T. v. R.W., 192 A.3d 1155 (Pa. Super. 2018) (In the child custody proceeding initiated by the incarcerated mother, the mother suffered a deprivation of her due process rights when she was prevented from fully participating in the hearing and was limited to a pre-hearing written statement because the court's prior procedural guidance, as set out in Sullivan v. Shaw, was outdated in light of technological advancement since that case, and the mother was entitled to be present either by writ of habeas corpus ad

A prisoner's claim for supervised physical custody can be heard without his/her being removed from prison and physically brought to court, and this burden will usually outweigh any risk of erroneously depriving prisoners of their legitimate expectations of custodial time with their children. Rather than physically bringing an inmate to court to present custody claims, the traditional belief was that the more reasonable approach would be to first allow the inmate to file an informal brief with the trial court in which he would offer solutions to the problems of visitation such as transportation, expenses, and frequency.[338] However, with the technological advancement to the ability to communicate and the promulgation of Pa.R.C.P. 1930.3, the informal brief no longer appears to be the more reasonable approach.[339]

Where both parents were incarcerated several hours away from the county in which their children resided and there was psychological evidence that requiring the children to travel to the parents' locations for visits would cause the children extreme stress, the parents should not be transported from state correctional institutions to a county jail in order to visit their children.[340] "If we were to transport these prisoners hundreds of miles to visit their children, we would be setting a precedent for all state prisoners to be transported for the purpose of visiting their families. Such a policy would create chaos in the prison system, not to mention the tremendous expense of time and money in transporting prisoners across the state."[341]

---

testificandum or by electronic communication, Pa.R.C.P. No. 1930.3); *see also* Pa.R.C.P. 1930.3 which provides: "With the approval of the court upon good cause shown, a party or witness may be deposed or testify by telephone, audiovisual or other electronic means at a designated location in all domestic relations matters."

[338] *Id.*; *but see* S.T. v. R.W., 192 A.3d 1155 (Pa. Super. 2018) (prior procedural guidance, as set out in Sullivan v. Shaw, was outdated in light of technological advancement since that case, and the mother was entitled to be present either by writ of habeas corpus ad testificandum or by electronic communication, Pa.R.C.P. No. 1930.3); *see also* Pa.R.C.P. 1930.3 which provides: "With the approval of the court upon good cause shown, a party or witness may be deposed or testify by telephone, audiovisual or other electronic means at a designated location in all domestic relations matters.").

[339] *See* S.T. v. R.W., 192 A.3d 1155 (Pa. Super. 2018).

[340] In re C.J., 729 A.2d 89 (Pa. Super. 1999).

[341] *Id.*

§ 3.4.26. Special Interim Relief

Rule of Civil Procedure 1915.13 empowers the court to grant special interim relief where appropriate, any time after commencement of the action. In a custody proceeding, special relief might include, but is not limited to, the entry of a temporary order of custody, partial custody or visitation; a writ of *ne exeat* directing the parties not to leave the jurisdiction and not to remove the child from the jurisdiction; or appropriate process directing that a child or a party or person having physical custody of a child be brought before the court; and direction that a person post security to appear with the child when directed by the court or to comply with any other court order. This rule supplies the relief formerly available by habeas corpus for production of the child.

In *Mayercheck v. Woods*,[342] a disgruntled father sought the special relief powers of the court to reinstate a custody order that had been suspended for his failure to complete psychological treatment. Father petitioned for a writ of habeas corpus and a writ of prohibition. The Supreme Court rejected the father's contentions and stated that applications of writs are appropriate only where the lower court commits an abuse of its discretion, which did not occur here. The court held that the trial judge properly refused to hear the father's motion for special relief under Pa.R.C.P. 1915.13, finding that "this was not a case of extreme necessity where none of the ordinary remedies at law is applicable or adequate to afford relief." However, subsequent to the trial court's decision, the father completed his therapy, and accordingly the Supreme Court reinstated the petition for special relief and remanded for consistent proceedings.

LOWER COURT CASES

Berks County

Schoen v. Schoen, C.P. Berks County, No. 09-4039 (C.C.P. 2011) (Trial court found that it did not violate mother's constitutionally protected rights by granting father legal authority to have the parties' children vaccinated where immunization was in the children's best interest, and to enroll them in public school where father was better suited

---

[342] Mayercheck v. Woods, 526 Pa. 477, 587 A.2d 696 (1991).

to make decisions regarding the children's education. The parties shared joint legal custody of their two children. Mother had primary physical custody and father had partial custody. Father filed a petition for special relief to allow the children to have routine childhood vaccines and to enroll the children in public school as opposed to their current private school. Mother argued that the children should not be vaccinated and should remain at the private Montessori school they had been attending. The trial court granted father's petition, agreeing with father's expert witness, a board-certified pediatrician, who testified that it was in the best interest of all children to receive all vaccinations recommended by the Center for Disease Control and the American Academy of Pediatrics Physicians. The court also favorably acknowledged the expert's testimony that failing to immunize children could put them at risk of contracting potentially fatal diseases, and that medical research had debunked the existence of any link between childhood vaccinations and autism. The court rejected mother's argument that she opposed to vaccination for religious reasons, noting that mother's objections to vaccinations were based on the supposed autism link instead. The court also agreed with father that attending the public school would be in the children's best interests as opposed to remaining in the private Montessori school. The court granted father the right to determine whether the children would remain in private Montessori school or be enrolled in the local public school. The court noted that the public school district had an excellent academic reputation and was close to the children's home, which was an important benefit to their social development. The court determined that its decision to grant father the unilateral right to decide where the children would go to school was appropriate, given father's superior understanding of the children's educational, developmental and emotional needs).

Lawrence County

Kilhof v. Kilhof, C.P. Lawrence County, No. 10719 of 2011, C.A. (C.C.P. 2011) (The best interest of the children would be served by requiring them to attend private school. At issue in this case was which school district the parties' children should attend. Mother desired the children to attend the public New Castle School District, preferring that the children attend school closer to her residence. Mother also contended that the children would be exposed to a more diverse atmosphere. Since father worked nearby, he would not be prejudiced by the children attending this school district. Father preferred that the children attend school at Holy Redeemer, a private school, which was also located near his residence as well as that of the children's paternal and maternal grandparents. Father was willing to pay for the cost of sending the children to private school, believing that it was in their best interests to have smaller classrooms and more one-on-one contact with teachers. The court noted that when a dispute involves which school district a child should attend, a best interest analysis must include the factors set forth at 23 Pa.C.S. § 5328. The court determined that the best interests of the children here were served by requiring them to attend Holy Redeemer, the private school.).

Musguire v. Pittinger, C.P. Lawrence County, No. 10941 of 2006, C.A. (C.C.P. 2011) (Trial court denied father's Motion for Special Relief seeking to prevent mother from sending their child to private school. Father filed a motion for Special Relief to prevent mother from continuing to enroll the parties' child at the New Castle Christian Academy (NCCA). Father wanted the child to be enrolled in the New Castle Area School District. Mother believed that father's objections to the NCCA began when the Support Orders required him to pay an increasing percentage of the tuition. The trial court denied father's Motion, finding that the child's interests was best served by continuing to allow the child to attend school at the NCCA. The court noted that Pennsylvania courts have held that a court may order a parent to pay for private school tuition if it is a reasonable need, citing *Gibbons v. Kugle*, 908 A.2d 916 (Pa. Super. 2006) and *Pellish v. Gerhart*, 701 A.2d 594 (Pa. Super. 1997). To show a reasonable need, the party seeking to send the child to private school must demonstrate that the child will benefit from such schooling and that the school is consistent with the family's standard of living before the parties' separation. The court concluded that it was in the child's best interest to remain at NCCA, noting that the child had attended NCCA since kindergarten, had made friends at school and felt comfortable there, and was receiving good grades. Father has failed to offer the court any real justification for changing schools).

Lehigh County

Abeln v. Abeln, C.P. Lehigh County, No. 2007-FC-0427 (C.C.P. 2011) (Trial court found that both mother and father should be on an equal footing in providing religious instruction for their child, and therefore the child should be placed in a public school rather than in a Catholic curriculum. Father filed a petition to enroll the parties' son in kindergarten at a Catholic school. Mother wanted the child to enroll in the local public school. Father was raised Roman Catholic, while mother was raised Lutheran. Mother made it clear that she wanted to be part of any decision regarding her son's religious faith and baptism. However, father scheduled and proceeded with the child's baptism without mother's consent or knowledge, even though she shared legal custody of the child at the time. The trial court entered an Order directing that the child be enrolled for kindergarten in the public school. The court explained that a factor in its decision on father's petition was the way father went about the baptism of the child at the parish church which created a taint for mother in educating her son there. The court noted that a second reason for directing that the child be enrolled in public school rather than Catholic school was the fashion in which the parents addressed religion with their son. Both parents tried to teach their respective religious beliefs to their son. Mother was concerned that placing her son in a Catholic school would undermine her attempts to instill her religious values in the child. The court found that mother's concerns were not groundless, Finally, the court found that there was insufficient basis to find that one school was superior to the other. Both schools were academically excellent, and both would provide wonderful educational opportunities for the child. The court concluded that the placement of the child in the public school would serve the child's best interest).

Northumberland County

SK v. TO, C.P. Northumberland County, No. 98-1793 (C.C.P. 2011) (Trial court ruled that it did not err when it limited plaintiff's choices as to the disabled minor's education to enrollment in the Shamokin Area School District and denied plaintiff and the minor child other education options otherwise provided by state and federal law. Mother and father could not agree on the education type the minor child should be receiving. At a hearing on the issue, mother did not present any education platform other than homeschooling for the court to evaluate. While in mother's primary care, the child had been homeschooled. The Shamokin Area School District had concerns about mother's homeschooling portfolio and requested the child to undergo a re-evaluation. The court weighed the pros and cons of each educational platform that the parties presented. The court noted that the Shamokin Area School District had a continuum of services that included programs for special needs students. Due to the fact that the record was replete with the services that mother had provided for the minor child while the child had been in the home school setting coupled with the fact that the educational portfolio lacked evidence of education training and learning, the court found that it was in the best interests of the child to attend a formal school setting).

York County

Staub v. Staub, 121 York Leg. Rec. 42 (C.C.P. 2007) (While traditionally public schools are favored over home schooling when the parents cannot agree, extraordinary circumstances in this case warranted a different result. The children had been home schooled for an extended period of time and were doing extremely well. While the mother had only a high school education, she had sought outside resources to supplement the home education, and father had little involvement in the children's education to date. "We hold that, absent extraordinary circumstances, when two parents sharing legal custody of a child cannot agree whether the child should be home schooled or attend public school, it is usually in the child's best interests to attend public school. We further hold that in this case, the following extraordinary circumstances are present which compel a different result: (1) the children have a significant history of home education; (2) the children are doing extremely well being home educated; (3) despite only a high school education, mother has sought outside resources to supplement the home education; and (4) father has been relatively uninvolved in the children's education to date.").

Chapter 4

STANDING

---

§ 4.1. Generally

§ 4.1. GENERALLY

The enactment of 23 Pa.C.S. §§ 5324 & 5325 set forth the requirements for standing in custody cases.

The following individuals have standing to petition for any form of physical custody or legal custody: (1) A parent of a child;[1] (2) A person standing *in loco parentis* to the child; (3) A grandparent of the child who is not *in loco parentis* if certain factors are met.

Chapter 5 of this book discusses in detail the requirements for a grandparent to have standing to bring a custody action.

Chapter 6 of this book discusses in detail the requirements for a third party to have standing to bring a custody action.

LOWER COURT CASES

Lawrence County

Lee v. Booher, C.P. Lawrence County, No. 10347 of 2013, C.A. (C.C.P. 2013) (Maternal grandmother's preliminary objection raising the issue of plaintiffs' standing to bring the custody matter was untimely; however, the issue of standing cannot be waived and the court accordingly entered a temporary custody order pending a hearing on the issue of standing. The court noted that as a general matter, third parties do not have standing to participate in child custody actions. However, an exception exists which allows a third party to maintain a custody action where the third party stands *in loco parentis* to the child).

---

[1] *See* 1915.3(f) (An unemancipated minor parent may commence, maintain or defend an action for custody of the minor parent's child without the requirement of the appointment of a guardian for the minor parent).

Chapter 5

GRANDPARENTS

§ 5.1.   GRANDPARENTS—GENERALLY

Grandparents are given special treatment in the child custody laws of Pennsylvania. It has been noted that there are "benefits which devolve upon the grandchild from the relationship with his grandparents which he cannot derive from any other relationship."[1] Moreover, in some cases the grandparents filled the role of substitute parents for the child during difficult times in the lives of the child's parents and formed bonds of affection which courts were hesitant to sever, particularly where the relationship had been prolonged, beneficial, and mutual.[2] In addition, except in unusual circumstances, courts have held that a child should not be entirely cut off from one side of his/her ancestry.[3] Like any third party, if a grandparent stands *in loco parentis*, he/she has standing under 23 Pa.C.S. § 5324(2) to bring a custody action.[4] Any other third

---

[1] Commonwealth ex rel. Williams v. Miller, 254 Pa. Super. 227, 233, 385 A.2d 992, 995 (1978), *quoting* Mimkon v. Ford, 66 N.J. 426, 437, 332 A.2d 199, 204 (1975).

[2] Ellerbe v. Hooks, 490 Pa. Super. 363, 416 A.2d 512 (1980); Commonwealth ex rel. Goodman v. Dratch, 192 Pa. Super. 1, 159 A.2d 70 (1960).

[3] Commonwealth ex rel. Williams v. Miller, 254 Pa. Super. 227, 385 A.2d 992 (1978); Commonwealth ex rel. Goodman v. Dratch, 192 Pa. Super. 1, 159 A.2d 70 (1960).

[4] *See* D.G. v. D.B., 91 A.3d 706 (Pa. Super. 2014) (Superior Court found that the periods of co-residence with grandmother, mother and the child were tantamount to

party, except grandparents, who are not *in loco parentis* to the child lack standing to bring a child custody action in the Commonwealth of Pennsylvania.[5] However, grandparents may have standing even if they are not *in loco parentis*.[6] The Pennsylvania Supreme Court also has ruled that a married couple, who raised a child's biological mother under a formal custody agreement with mother's natural father, may seek court-ordered custody with the eight-year-old daughter of the woman they helped raise, even though they were not related by blood or marriage to either the mother or child.[7] This has been known as "in loco grandparentis." Likewise, the Superior Court held that adoptive parents of one of the parents of a child with respect to whom they sought grandparental visitation rights, and who otherwise qualified to seek partial custody/ visitation, had standing to seek custody/visitation under the Grandparent Visitation Act.[8]

---

grandmother's assisting mother and child in a time of need as opposed to grandmother's informal adoption of the child and were not consistent with an intent to assume all of the rights and responsibilities of parenthood and, therefore, she did not stand *in loco parentis* to the child)

[5] *See* Gradwell v. Strausser, 416 Pa. Super. 118, 124, 610 A.2d 999, 1002 (1992) (a third party may maintain an action only where that party stands *in loco parentis*); *see also* 23 Pa.C.S. § 5324. *But see* subsection 4 under 23 Pa.C.S. § 5324 which became effective July 4, 2018, and expands third-party standing in limited circumstances. *See also* Chapter 6 of this book *infra* regarding third parties.

[6] 23 Pa.C.S. §§ 5324 & 5325.

[7] Peters v. Costello, 586 Pa. 102, 891 A.2d 705, 710 (2005). *But see* Hill v. Divecchio, 425 Pa. Super. 355, 625 A.2d 642 (1993) (Unambiguous words of former Grandparents' Visitation Act that state "upon application of parent or grandparent of party" preclude mother's stepfather from asserting cause of action for visitation of stepgrandchild, even if in conjunction with child's natural grandmother); Commonwealth ex rel. Patricia L.F. v. Malbert J.F., 278 Pa. Super. 343, 420 A.2d 572 (1980); Auman v. Eash, 228 Pa. Super. 242, 323 A.2d 94 (1974); Commonwealth ex rel. Kraus v. Kraus, 185 Pa. Super. 167, 138 A.2d 225 (1958).

[8] Little-Stepp v. Cancilla, 896 A.2d 647 (Pa. Super. 2006) (Court relied on Peters v. Costello, 891 A.2d 705 (Pa. Super. 2005), which held that the Act grants standing to non-biological grandparents who stand in loco parentis to one of the parents of the child to whom custody rights are sought, and who otherwise qualify for partial custody/visitation).

§ 5.2. GRANDPARENTS – STANDING FOR ANY FORM OF PHYSICAL CUSTODY OR LEGAL CUSTODY

Under Section 5324(3), a grandparent has standing to bring an action for any form of physical custody or legal custody when the following three criteria are met:

1. The grandparent's relationship with the child began either with the consent of a parent of the child or under an order of court;[9]

2. The grandparent assumed or is willing to assume responsibility for the child; and,

3. One of the following conditions is met:
    a. The child has been determined to be a dependent child under 42 Pa.C.S. § 63;[10] or
    b. The child is substantially at risk due to parental abuse, neglect, drug or alcohol abuse or incapacity[11]; or
    c. The child has for a period of at least 12 consecutive months resided with the grandparent, excluding brief temporary

---

[9] *See* Campbell v. Campbell, 448 Pa. Super. 640, 672 A.2d 835 (1996) (the court held that grandparents had standing to challenge a custody order because they were previously awarded partial physical custody of the minor children and that order was never appealed. Having joint legal custody of the children and partial physical custody, the grandparents had standing to seek primary physical custody. This case was decided under the prior law pertaining to grandparents); *see also* Walkenstein v. Walkenstein, 443 Pa. Super. 683, 663 A.2d 178 (1995) (grandmother had standing to pursue custody action against mother, where grandmother had been granted custody by court order when mother was committed involuntarily to psychiatric hospital and identity of father was unknown. Appropriate standard for adjudication of custody dispute between mother and grandmother required grandmother to carry her burden of proof by clear and convincing evidence).

[10] *See* In The Interest of: C.L.P., a Minor, 126 A.3d 985 (Pa. Super. 2015) (The Custody Act granted standing to grandparents to file for any form of physical or legal custody when their grandchild has been adjudicated dependent, notwithstanding any permanency goal of reunification); M.W. v. S.T. and V.T., 196 A.3d 1065 (Pa. Super. 2018) (trial court did not err in dismissing grandmother's complaint for custody of her grandchildren for lack of standing pursuant to 23 Pa.C.S. § 5324, because, although grandmother had standing when petition was filed, the children were no longer dependent).

[11] *See* G.A.P. v. J.M.W., 194 A.3d 614 (Pa. Super. 2018).

absences of the child from the home, and is removed from the home by the parents, in which case the action must be filed within six months after the removal of the child from the home.

Prior to the enactment of Section 5324, the case law was unclear as to whether the criteria set forth in Section 5324, which previously appeared in Section 5313(b), pertained to standing or the requirements that a grandparent must establish to prevail on the merits of a custody case. Under *R.M. v. Baxter*, 777 A.2d 446 (Pa. 2001),[12] the Pennsylvania Supreme Court determined that grandparents had automatic standing to bring an action for physical and legal custody because the opening line of Section 5313(b) stated as follows: "A grandparent has standing to bring a petition for physical and legal custody of a grandchild."[13] The Pennsylvania Supreme Court in *R.M. v. Baxter* also directed that the other requirements under Section 5313(b), which now appear under Section 5324, were the requirements that a grandparent must establish to prevail on the merits of a custody case. Under the new Section 5324, the ambiguity has now been corrected, as the requirements thereunder pertain to a grandparent's standing to bring an action for any form of physical custody or legal custody in the event they are not *in loco parentis* to the child.

Further, a natural grandparent's right to qualify for standing under 23 Pa.C.S. §§ 5324 & 5325 automatically terminates upon the adoption of the child.[14]

---

[12] In Martinez v. Baxter, 725 A.2d 775 (Pa. Super. 1999), which was affirmed by R.M. v. Baxter ex rel. T.M., 565 Pa. 619, 777 A.2d 446 (2001), the Superior Court held that a grandmother had standing to seek custody of her grandchild, despite the fact that the child had been adjudicated dependent and placed in legal and physical custody of children and youth services.

[13] 23 Pa.C.S. § 5313(b) (repealed).

[14] 23 Pa.C.S. § 5326; E.T.S. v. S.L.H., 54 A.3d 880 (Pa. Super. 2012); *see also* Faust v. Messinger, 345 Pa. Super. 155, 497 A.2d 1351 (1985) (grandmother's entitlement to seek visitation with her grandson was not protected by the due process clause and could be terminated by adoption proceedings where mother was deceased and father had relinquished his parental rights without notice to grandmother and without a hearing); *but see* D.R.L. and D.L. v. K.L.C. and J.C., 216 A.3d 276 (Pa. Super. 2019) (after the parties separated, mother remarried. Thereafter, father died and the mother's husband adopted the child. Mother consented to the paternal grandparents having custodial time, and later their custodial time was contained in a consent order,which included custody

A grandparent seeking physical and/or legal custody of a grandchild who is not *in loco parentis* must plead the facts establishing standing under 23 Pa.C.S. § 5324(3) in paragraph 9 of the complaint.[15]

LOWER COURT CASES

Allegheny County

C.P. and D.P. v. S.C. and C.P., C.P. Allegheny County, No. FD-17-4317-003 (C.C.P. July 18, 2019), *aff'd*, Memorandum Decision, No. 1277 WDA 2019 (Pa. Super. February 19, 2020) (Trial court concluded that paternal grandparents stood *in loco parentis* to the child, and properly determined that paternal grandparents rebutted the presumption that mother should be awarded custody. The court found that paternal grandfather's testimony established that grandparents continuously cared for the child's needs and discharged all parental duties since mother's incarceration in January 2018, and father's subsequent incarceration in July 2018. Accordingly, mother's claim that paternal grandparents lacked standing was meritless. Trial court granted paternal grandparents sole physical and legal custody of the child).

Armstrong County

Mergen v. Mergen, C.P. Armstrong County, No. 2013-0 114–Civil (C.C.P. 2013) (Trial court granted the parents' preliminary objections to paternal grandparents' custody complaint, since grandparents had never acted *in loco parentis* to the child, and the child had not resided with them. Paternal grandparents lived next door and provided care when father was unable to do so. The trial court noted that, while father could not have raised the child without the assistance of paternal grandparents, they had never acted as parents, only as babysitters. Even when the child stayed with them for two months, grandparents were still acting in the role as grandparents, and they never assumed the duties and responsibilities of the child's parents. As a single father, father depended on the grandparents to provide child care for the child during periods of time that father was working or going to school. The living arrangement with grandparents

---

to the grandparents every other weekend, certain holidays, and a week of vacation in the summer. Paternal grandparents petitioned for additional custody and the court provided them with an additional summer vacation week. Grandparents appealed claiming bias of the court and the Superior Court affirmed the trial court's ruling finding no bias. The trial court's decision was also based, in part, on the child's preference and weighing whether granting the paternal grandparents additional custodial time would interfere with the parent–child relationship per 23 Pa.C.S. § 5328(c)(1)).

[15] *See* Pa.R.C.P. 1915.3(e) and 1915.15(a).

was understood to be temporary in nature. At no time had mother or father ever relinquished their places as the child's parents. Since grandparents could not meet either requirement for standing to bring a custody complaint, the preliminary objections of parents were granted and the paternal grandparents' complaint was dismissed).

Jefferson County

L.M. v. D.W. v. L.L.W. and S.J.W., C.P. Jefferson County, No. 1100-2007-CD (C.C.P. May 26, 2017), *aff'd*, Memorandum Decision, No. 959 WDA 2017 (Pa. Super. January 5, 2018) (Trial court Order granted grandparents standing *in loco parentis* pursuant to 23 Pa.C.S. § 5324(2). Grandparents asserted that the child had been in their care seven days every two weeks during her entire life. Essentially, paternal grandparents asserted that they had stood *in loco parentis* to the child since her birth. A parent, through inaction, may acquiesce to the development of an *in loco parentis* relationship. By failing to act while grandparents raised her daughter, mother acted in a manner consistent with her consent to their *in loco parentis* status. Although mother testified that she never gave express permission to grandparents to care for the child, she admitted that while the child was in their care, grandparents attended to the child's daily physical, emotional, and financial needs. For approximately two years the child resided primarily with father in the home of paternal grandparents. The court noted that the grandparents were significantly more than glorified babysitters. Rather, grandparents attended to the child's daily physical, emotional, and financial needs, and they assumed an enduring role that was more significant than a frequent caretaker. Grandparents had shared with mother the parenting responsibility for the entirety of the child's life. The court observed that the record confirmed that grandparents fed, bathed, and entertained the child daily, attended parent–teacher conference, and transported the child to medical appointments and school. Grandparents also assisted the child financially and they consistently had been a stabilizing force in the child's life and ensured her safety. The court concluded that a parent, through inaction, may acquiesce to the development of an in loco parentis relationship. Here, by failing to act while grandparents raised her daughter, mother acted in a manner consistent with her consent to their *in loco parentis* status).

Lawrence County

Winkle v. Winkle, C.P. Lawrence County, No. 11060-2014, C.A. (C.C.P. 2014) (Trial court found that maternal grandparents did not stand *in loco parentis* to the minor child at issue and granted mother's preliminary objections to maternal grandparents' complaint, which was dismissed without prejudice. The court explained that the concept of standing serves to protect an unnecessary intrusion into the "protected domain of the family" by outsiders, even if their intentions are good-natured. Maternal grandparents testified that they cared for the minor child on a daily basis. Other family members in the household also helped care for the minor child. The court concluded that mother, in living with the maternal grandparents, was not trying to abscond from her parental duties, but rather, was relying on the only support system available to her, which given her young age, would otherwise be appropriate).

Higbee v. Curea, C.P. Lawrence County, No. 11099 of 2012, C.A. (C.C.P. 2013) (Trial court granted maternal grandparents' petition to intervene in a custody action where they had established *in loco parentis* status regarding the minor child. The court noted that the phrase "*in loco parentis*" embodies two ideas: (1) the assumption of a parental status, and (2) the discharge of parental duties. While the doctrine of *in loco parentis* establishes a basis for a third-party to have standing in a child custody case, a family's need to protect itself from intruding third parties is also recognized by Pennsylvania courts. Appellate courts have maintained that a third-party may not obtain *in loco parentis* status in opposition to the wishes of the natural parents. Although there exists a presumption that a child's best interests are served by maintaining the family's privacy, such a presumption "must give way where the child has established strong biological bonds with a person who, although not a biological parent, has lived with the child and provides care, nurture, and affection, assuming in the child's eye a stature like that of a parent, citing *J.A.L. v. E.P.H.*, 682 A.2d 1314 (Pa. Super. 1996). Thus, where the child has established a strong relationship with a third party who has lived with the child and provides care, nurture and affection as well as acting in the child's eyes as a parent, a court can grant such a third-party standing. Here, the evidence established that after the child's birth, paternal grandparents were involved in the child's daily life. They frequently visited the child in the hospital, as he had serious health complications. Moreover, the child lived with mother at maternal grandparents' home after being released from the hospital. The court also noted that both mother and father were in high school, so maternal grandparents typically cared for the child while his parents attended school. Therefore, maternal grandparents had provided a significant amount of care, nurture and affection for the child. To the extent possible, maternal grandparents had established a bond with the child, and as such, had established *in loco parentis* status).

Montgomery County

Dettinburn v. Beekley, 147 Montgomery Co. L. Rep. 149 (C.C.P. 2010) (Trial court held that although grandchildren lived with grandparents for a finite period of time, and grandmother performed certain nurturing and childcare duties as a grandparent often does, the grandmother and grandfather did not have standing to seek visitation rights either "*in loco parentis*" or under now repealed 23 Pa.C.S. § 5312 or § 5313, or § 5303 of the Grandparent Visitation Act).

York County

B.S.C., S.P.M. and L.A.M. v. A.R.W., D.J.W. and J.M.W., C.P. York County, No. 2014-FC-001113-03, *aff'd*, Memorandum Decision, No. 115 MDA 2018 (Pa. Super. August 28, 2018) (Maternal grandparents lacked *in loco parentis* standing to pursue custody in this matter, as a third-party cannot place himself or herself *in loco parentis* status in defiance of the parents' wishes. The court acknowledged that maternal grand-parents provided financial support for both mother and the child while mother was residing with them, and that they assisted in caring for the child during mother's periods of visitations. However, the court concluded that their acts were more consistent with the acts of loving grandparents wanting to assist their daughter with their grandchild, rather than showing an intent to assume all of the rights and responsibilities of parenthood, citing *D.G. v. D.B.*, 91 A.3d 706 (Pa. Super. 2014) (refusing to recognize *in loco parentis* status, despite the fact that grandmother financially supported child, provided occasional shelter, meals, laundry, and transportation to and from medical appointments).

§ 5.3. GRANDPARENTS – STANDING FOR PARTIAL PHYSICAL CUSTODY

In addition to grandparents having standing to bring an action for any form of physical custody or legal custody under Section 5324, grandparents also have standing to bring an action for partial physical custody under Section 5325.[16] Section 5325 is a combination of prior Sections 5311, 5312, and 5313(a). However, prior subsection 2 under Section 5325, which mirrored prior Section 5312, has been replaced and became effective July 4, 2018. Under Section 5325, a grandparent and great-grandparent have standing to file an action for partial physical custody under the following situations:

1. where a parent of the child is deceased[17];

2. where the relationship with the child began either with the consent of a parent of the child or under a court order and where the parents of the child:

(i) have commenced a proceeding for custody; and

---

[16] D.G. v. D.B., 91 A.3d 706 (Pa. Super. 2014) (a grandparent qualifying for standing to obtain partial physical custody under Section 5325 does not automatically confer standing to a grandparent later seeking primary physical custody under Section 5324).

[17] *See* J. & S.O. v. C.H., 206 A.3d 1171 (Pa. Super. 2019) (Section 5325 did not violate father's due process rights to raise his child without government interference, Section 5325 did not violate father's equal protection rights).

(ii) do not agree as to whether the grandparents or great grand-parents should have custody under this section;[18] or

3. when the child has, for a period of at least 12 consecutive months, resided with a grandparent or great-grandparent, excluding brief temporary absences of the child from the home, and is removed from the home by the parents, an action must be filed within six months after the removal of the child from the home.

There was prior debate and case law regarding whether now-repealed Section 5312 and prior Section 5325(2) conferred standing on grandparents of children born out of wedlock. By the plain meaning of the words of new § 5325(2), whether the child was born out of wedlock is no longer an issue.[19] The Superior Court has found that a trial court erred in holding that because a custody agreement between a child's estranged parents limited the child's interaction with his paternal grandmother, she did not have standings to seek visitation or partial custody, since the clear language of then 23 Pa.C.S. § 5312 (and the prior version of § 5325) conferred standing

---

[18] In the Pennsylvania Supreme Court case of D.P. v. G.J.P, 146 A.3d 204 (Pa. 2016), the Supreme Court severed the first half of paragraph (2) which previously read: "have been separated for a period of at least six months or" from the remainder of the paragraph of 23 Pa.C.S. § 5325(2) which read: "where the parents of the child have commenced and continued a proceeding to dissolve their marriage," finding the text of the first half to be unconstitutional. Paragraph 2 has since been completely rewritten and became effective July 4, 2018. *See* M.S. v. J.D., 215 A.3d 595 (Pa. Super. 2019) (trial court properly denied a paternal grandmother's petition to intervene in an underlying custody action involving her grandchild in order to seek custody because she lacked standing under 23 Pa.C.S. § 5325(2), as the parents agreed that grandmother should not have custody).

[19] Case law regarding the prior law and its application to children born out of wedlock is as follows: L.A.L. v. V.D., 72 A.3d 690 (Pa. Super. 2013) (Section 5325(2), as did the now-repealed Section 5312, grants standing to grandparents of children born out of wedlock in custody proceedings); Bishop v. Pillar, 399 Pa. Super. 52, 581 A.2d 670 (1990), *aff'd*, 536 Pa. 41, 637 A.2d 976 (1994) ("separated" for six months or more, applied to a child born to couple that had a dating relationship but had neither been married nor maintained a lengthy, strong, or significant relationship before separation); *see also* Helsel v. Puricelli, 927 A.2d 252 (Pa. Super. 2007) (Superior Court held that a grandparent lacked standing to file a complaint for visitation rights because parents, although previously separated, were not separated at the time of filing); Herron v. Seizak, 321 Pa. Super. 466, 468 A.2d 803 (1983).

on the grandmother to pursue partial custody or visitation.[20] Under the new version of § 5325(2), the *Malone* case could have a different meaning, as the agreement between the parties regarding whether the grandparents or great grandparents should have custody is now a factor under the new law.[21]

A natural grandparent's right to qualify for standing under 23 Pa.C.S. §§ 5324 & 5325 automatically terminates upon the adoption of the child.[22]

A grandparent or great-grandparent seeking partial physical custody of a grandchild must plead the facts establishing standing under 23 Pa.C.S. § 5325 in paragraph 9 of the complaint.[23]

LOWER COURT CASES

Berks County

Levengood v. Dematto, C.P. Berks County, No. 11-23597 (C.C.P. 2013) (The trial court dismissed grandparents' petition for partial custody, finding they lacked standing to bring an action, as the grandchild's parents had never married. The trial court interpreted 23 Pa.C.S. § 5325(2) to give standing *only* to those grandparents of grandchildren with married parents). *But see* L.A.L. v. V.D., 72 A.3d 690 (Pa. Super. 2013) (Section 5325(2), as did the now-repealed Section 5312, grants standing to grandparents of children born out of wedlock in custody proceedings).

Bucks County

Connors v. Connors, C.P. Bucks County, No. A06-2012-60110-C-37 (C.C.P. 2012) (The child's paternal grandmother was granted partial physical custody where grandmother had standing to pursue custody and it was in the child's best interest to spend time together. Under 23 Pa.C.S. § 5325, a grandparent may petition for custody rights under certain circumstances, such as when the child's parents have been separated for at least six months. Here, not only have the child's parents been separated for several years, but the biological mother's parental rights had been voluntarily terminated. Citing *Rigler v. Treen*, 660 A.2d 111 (Pa. Super. 1995), the court found that the child had been adopted, but she had been adopted by her paternal grandfather and his current wife. As such, 23 Pa.C.S. § 5326 preserved paternal grandmother's rights to seek partial custody. The court then held

---

[20] *See* Malone v. Stonerook, 843 A.2d 1278 (Pa. Super. 2004).

[21] *See* 23 Pa.C.S. § 5325(2).

[22] 23 Pa.C.S. § 5326; *see also* E.T.S. v. S.L.H., 54 A.3d 880 (Pa. Super. 2012).

[23] *See* Pa.R.C.P. 1915.3(e) and 1915.15(a).

that continued contact with paternal grandmother was in the child's best interests. The child and grandmother had a close relationship, which was extremely important to the child. Grandmother also did not attempt to interfere or usurp the child's relationships with the adoptive parents. Therefore, the court determined that it would be more harmful to the child if she were prevented from having contact with paternal grandmother).

Philadelphia County

F.S. v. B.F., C.P. Philadelphia County, No. OC 1701579, *aff'd*, Memorandum Decision, No. 591 EDA 2019 (Pa. Super. June 24, 2019) (Acknowledged once again Pennsylvania's strong public policy favoring grandparent involvement in a child's life, stating that in some instances a court may overturn even the decision of a fit parent to exclude a grandparent from a grandchild's life, especially where the grandparent's child is deceased and the grandparent relationship is long-standing and significant to the grandchild. The trial court noted that since there were no maternal grandparents, the child had what many children do not have—a loving grandparent who was capable of, and wanted to be part of the child's life and even provide child care when needed by mother. To deny grandfather contact with the child and to deny the child the love of a grandfather because mother "lost trust" in grandfather, or because grandfather expressed an opinion that the six-month-old child would be better with grandfather for two days out of the work week rather than in full-time day care, was both unreasonable and contrary to Pennsylvania law. The court acknowledged Pennsylvania's strong public policy favoring grandparent involvement in a child's life, citing *K.T. v. L.S.,* 118 A.3d 1136 (Pa. Super. 2015).

§ 5.4. GRANDPARENTS – CONSTITUTIONALITY OF STATUTES

In *Troxel v. Granville*, 530 U.S. 57 (2000), the U.S. Supreme Court ruled that a broad Washington state law allowing visitation rights for grandparents and other third parties violated the due process rights of a mother to raise her children as she saw fit. Writing for four members of the court, Justice Sandra Day O'Connor said that the Washington State trial court violated a mother's fundamental right "to make decisions concerning the care, custody and control" of her children when it applied a Washington visitation statute to award grandparents longer visitation time than the mother had agreed upon. O'Connor described the statute as "breathtakingly broad" and said that the trial court failed to give proper weight to the mother's status as a fit custodian of her children and to her having agreed to allow some visitation with the grandparents.

The following is a summary of recent cases addressing the constitutionality of the prior statutes pertaining to grandparent custody rights in Pennsylvania. Though the statutory sections addressed in the following cases have since been repealed, the contents of those statutes are now found in the new statutory sections Pa.C.S. §§ 5324 and 5325. Therefore, the analysis contained in these cases remains relevant.

In *Schmehl v. Wegelin*, 592 Pa. 581, 927 A.2d 183 (2007), a majority of the Pennsylvania Supreme Court held that the section of the Pennsylvania Domestic Relations Code enabling grandparents to seek partial custody or visitation of a grandchild when the child's parents are divorced, engaged in divorce proceedings, or separated for six months or more (repealed Section 5312), does not violate the United States Constitution's equal protection clause, because it is narrowly tailored to recognize the child's and grandparents' interests only in limited circumstances. The classification in the "narrowly tailored" statute here between intact and non-intact families was constitutional in that it served the state's *parens patriae* interest in the well-being of children. The majority found instructive *Hiller v. Fausey*, 904 A.2d 875 (Pa. 2006), in which the Pennsylvania Supreme Court had ruled constitutional now repealed 23 Pa.C.S. § 5311. Section 5311 governed the circumstances in which a grandparent could seek partial custody or visitation when a parent has died. The *Hiller* court concluded that § 5311 was narrowly tailored to serve the interests of those grandparents by requiring trial courts to consider a set of specific factors. In pronouncing § 5311 constitutional, the court in *Hiller* had applied a strict scrutiny standard, identifying the necessary compelling state interest as being the state's "long-standing interest in protecting the health and emotional welfare of children" under its *parens patriae* interest. Acknowledging that *Schmehl* involved a different provision of the Domestic Relations Code and raised equal protection rather than due process concerns, the majority nevertheless determined that "in this context, however, the substantive due process and equal protection inquiries are essentially identical." The majority explained that "in this regard, both inquiries employ a threshold assessment concerning the weight to be ascribed to the parental interest to determine the appropriate level of scrutiny, and both employ a balancing formulation in the application of such scrutiny in which the government's interest is tested, on the one hand, to determine whether it represents an accepted infringement on the parental interest (for purposes of substantive due process), and on the other hand, whether it is sufficient to support a particular classification (for equal protection purposes)." Further noting that both § 5311 and § 5312 were concerned with protecting the health and emotional welfare of children under the state's *parens patriae* interest in circumstances where family continuity is disrupted, the majority also pointed out that *Hiller* was able to withstand the due process challenge only because § 5311 employs a classification scheme restricting its reach to a limited class of grandparents (those whose children have died). As such, the Pennsylvania Supreme Court found the *Hiller* decision to be highly relevant in the *Schmehl* case.

In *Hiller v. Fausey*, 588 Pa. 342, 904 A.2d 875 (2006), the Pennsylvania Supreme Court held that a Pennsylvania law that authorizes the court to award partial custody or visitation to a child's grandparent who is the grandparent or parent of the child's deceased parent is constitutional, and does not violate the Due Process Clause of the United States Constitution as an infringement upon a parent's fundamental rights. Grandparents do not have to prove that being kept away would be harmful to their grandchildren in order to get court-ordered visitation. Now-repealed 23 Pa.C.S. § 5311 did not violate the Due Process Clause as an infringement upon a parent's fundamental rights. The court declared: "We refuse to close our minds to the possibility that in some instances a court may overturn even the decision of a fit parent to exclude a grandparent from a grandchild's life, especially where the grandparent's child is deceased and the grandparent's relationship is long-standing and significant to the grandchild. . . . In the recent past, grandparents have assumed increased roles in their grandchildren's lives, and our cumulative experience demonstrates the many potential benefits of strong inter-generational ties." In *Hiller*, the majority rejected father's assertion that grandparents seeking custody should be required to demonstrate compelling circumstances such as parental unfitness or significant harm to the child resulting from the denial of custody. The court found that a threshold showing of harm to the child was not a prerequisite to such an award. While some other states have required such a finding, "a number of courts have either declined to require third parties to demonstrate harm or have found that grandparents may satisfy the requirement of harm merely by showing that the child will be harmed by the termination of a beneficial relationship with his or her grandparents. . . . Our statute does not require a specific finding of harm, and our precedent militates against requiring grandparents to demonstrate harm as a condition precedent to a grant of visitation or custody." The court found that such a requirement "would set the bar too high." Instead, "We conclude that the stringent requirements of § 5311, as applied in this case, combined with the presumption that parents act in a child's best interest, sufficiently protect the fundamental right of parents without requiring any additional demonstration of unfitness or specific requirement of harm or potential harm."[24]

In the case of *Brown v. Cain*, 351 Pa. Super. 130, 505 A.2d 300 (1986), maternal grandparents were not denied their due process rights to be heard at the pretrial custody conference. The Superior Court held that due process attaches only when a protected liberty interest is affected. Since a pretrial conference before a child custody conference officer only results in a recommendation to the court which will not be binding as a Court order if one of the parties takes a timely exception to the recommendation, no property or liberty interest is affected. The key to due process is that the recommendation from the conference is "in no way binding." A hearing is not required at any particular point in the administrative proceeding so long as a hearing is held before the final order becomes effective.[25]

---

[24] *See* J. & S.O. v. C.H., 206 A.3d 1171 (Pa. Super. 2019) (following Hiller, Superior Court held Section 5325 did not violate father's due process rights to raise his child without government interference, and Section 5325 did not violate father's equal protection rights).

[25] *But see* Hill v. Divecchio, 425 Pa. Super. 355, 625 A.2d 642 (1993) (Unambiguous words of former Grandparents' Visitation Act that state "upon application of parent or grandparent of party" preclude mother's stepfather from asserting cause of action for visitation of step-grandchild, even if in conjunction with child's natural grandmother).

§ 5.5. GRANDPARENTS – CUSTODY –
MERITS OF THE CASE

Even though grandparents are given special treatment regarding standing and the ability to bring a custody action, once the grandparent enters the court after clearing the standing hurdle, they are considered third parties.[26] In Pennsylvania, under the newly enacted 23 Pa.C.S. § 5327, there is now a codified presumption that exists in cases concerning primary physical custody between a parent and a third party. Under Section 5327(b), in cases involving a parent and a third party, there is a presumption that custody shall be awarded to the parent and the presumption can be rebutted only by clear and convincing evidence.[27] The new statute is silent as to whether there is a presumption when a third party is seeking partial physical custody.[28]

When a grandparent brings a custody action against a parent, the court shall consider the factors enumerated under 23 Pa.C.S. § 5328(a) in making a custody determination. If the grandparent is seeking partial physical custody under Section 5325, the grandparent also must satisfy the factors set forth under Section 5328(c).

---

[26] *See* Albright v. Commonwealth ex rel. Fetters, 491 Pa. 320, 421 A.2d 157 (1980); Ellerbe v. Hooks, 490 Pa. 363, 416 A.2d 512 (1980); Burke v. Pope, 374 Pa. Super. 467, 543 A.2d 566 (1988) (caretaker failed to overcome natural mother's prima facie right to custody of children, was not entitled to award of custody based on psychological bonding of children with her, and failed to establish best interests of children entitling her to award of custody; mother was not found to be unfit and had improved her housing situation and was 30 years old while caretaker was 61 years old; the trial court's award of custody to caretaker did not attempt to reunite children with mother. It was error for trial court to make shift of legal custody from nonrelative to mother contingent upon mother demonstrating proof of her ability to adequately maintain and support her children where it had been determined that mother was fit and that a reciprocal loving bond existed between mother and children).

[27] 23 Pa.C.S. § 5327(b); *see also* V.B. and C.B. v. J.E.B and C.C., 55 A.3d 1193 (Pa. Super. 2012); M.J.S. v. B.B. v. B.B., 172 A.3d 651 (Pa. Super. 2018) (presumption in favor of parent over grandparent).

[28] *But see* R.L. v. M.A., 209 A.3d 391 (Pa. Super. 2019) (Section 5327 also applies when third party is seeking equal (50/50) physical custody).

When a grandparent is seeking partial physical custody under Section 5325(1) where a parent of the child is deceased or Section 5325(2) where the parents of the child have commenced and continued a proceeding to dissolve their marriage, the court must also consider: (i) the amount of personal contact between the child and the grandparent prior to the filing of the action; (ii) whether the award interferes with any parent–child relationship; and (iii) whether the award is in the best interest of the child.[29]

When a grandparent is seeking partial physical custody under Section 5325(3) where the child has resided with the grandparent for 12 months consecutively and the grandparent petitions within 6 months after the removal of the child from the home, the court must also consider: (i) whether the award interferes with any parent-child relationship; and (ii) whether the award is in the best interest of the child.[30]

When confronted with the task of choosing between parents and third parties, courts have long maintained that the best interests of the child remain the paramount concern.[31] The case of *Bucci v. Bucci* held that it is

---

[29] 23 Pa.C.S. § 5328(c)(1); *see also* Suroviec v. Mitchell, 347 Pa. Super. 399, 500 A.2d 894 (1985) (it was in the best interest of the children when maternal grandparents were awarded the right to visit grandchildren for five hours on the third Sunday of each month. The Court held this arrangement would not unduly interfere with parent–child relationship between the grandchildren and their father and new wife who had adopted them); Hughes v. Hughes, 316 Pa. Super. 505, 463 A.2d 478 (1983) (court denied grandmother visitation finding that prior contacts between grandmother and grandchild had been minimal and that grandmother's intent in seeking visitation was for benefit of her son, the father, whose visitation request has been denied).

[30] 23 Pa.C.S. § 5328(c)(2).

[31] Albright v. Commonwealth ex rel. Fetters, 491 Pa. 320, 421 A.2d 157 (1980); Ellerbe v. Hooks, 490 Pa. 363, 416 A.2d 512 (1980); In re Snellgrose, 432 Pa. 158, 247 A.2d 596 (1968); Dorsey v. Freeman, 438 Pa. Super. 236, 652 A.2d 352 (1994) (In any custody dispute, whether case involves two natural parents or parent and third party, the court's overriding concern is always to determine what will serve best interests of child; this question may never be subordinated to other considerations, such as fundamental rights and fair play); In Johnson v. Diesinger, 404 Pa. Super. 41, 589 A.2d 1160 (1990), the Superior Court held that partial custody and visitation rights given to the grandmother pursuant to now-repealed 23 Pa.C.S. § 5311 were not in the best interests of the children, for the order would interfere with the parent–child relationship. Moreover, the court held that the lower court created greater rights than the Grandparent Visitation Act was designed to give. The court also noted that the trial court was more

the grandparents who bear the burden of proof in showing that visitation/ partial custody is in the best interest of the child.[32]

In any child custody dispute involving a non-parent, an initial determination must be made as to which parties merit parental status. Natural parents are obviously accorded parental status and the fact that a parent lives with the child's grandparents, who will be caring for the child while the parent works or attends school, does not alter his or her parental standing.[33] Likewise, the desire expressed by a natural parent not seeking custody for him or herself and that the child be placed in the custody of a particular third party will not cause the standard applicable to parents to act in favor of that third party.[34]

In cases decided prior to the enactment of 23 Pa.C.S. §§ 5324, 5325, and 5328, courts have noted that even before the proceeding begins,

---

concerned with the animosity between the father and grandmother and not the well-being of the children. The court emphasized that in any custody proceeding under 23 Pa.C.S. § 5311, the best interest of the child is controlling, and by failing to perform this detailed, child-centered analysis, the trial court committed reversible error. The Superior Court specifically found the frequency of the visits ordered by the trial court given the long distance grandmother must travel with the children (four–five hours each way over a 48-hour period) to be unreasonable. The Superior Court further concluded that given the substantial amount of time the trial court order provided for grandmother with the children, the order was more in line with a shared custody awarded in a divorce action than a partial custody award to a grandparent. The court stressed that the purpose of the Grandparents Act is not to replace a deceased parent with a grandparent as a primary care giver, but rather to continue a healthy relationship with the grandparent if that is in the child's best interest; Commonwealth ex rel. Kraus v. Kraus, 185 Pa. Super. 167, 138 A.2d 225 (1958); Commonwealth ex rel. Shamenek v. Allen, 179 Pa. Super. 169, 116 A.2d 336 (1955).

[32] Bucci v. Bucci, 351 Pa. Super. 457, 506 A.2d 438 (1986); see also Norris v. Tearney, 422 Pa. Super. 246, 619 A.2d 339 (1993).

[33] In Porch v. Porch, 327 Pa. Super. 346, 475 A.2d 831 (1984), the children lived with paternal grandparents and the father resided next door. The court, nevertheless, found that custody would actually rest with the father and that he was merely relying, albeit heavily, on his parents as caretakers. The court, therefore, held that the custody dispute was between the parents, and found the burden of proof to be equal; In re Custody of Scott, 288 Pa. Super. 162, 431 A.2d 338 (1981); McCann v. McCann, 270 Pa. Super. 171, 411 A.2d 234 (1979); Haraschak v. Haraschak, 268 Pa. Super. 173, 407 A.2d 886 (1979).

[34] Palmer v. Tokarek, 279 Pa. Super. 458, 421 A.2d 289 (1980).

"the evidentiary scale is tipped, and tipped hard to the parent's side."[35] It has been explained that the principle of a parent having *a prima facie* right to custody merely instructs the hearing judge that the non-parent bears the burdens of production *and* persuasion and that the non-parent's burden is heavy.[36] Thus, interpretations of the standard which

---

[35] Ellerbe v. Hooks, 490 Pa. 363, 416 A.2d 512 (1980); MacDonald v. Quaglia, 442 Pa. Super. 149, 658 A.2d 1343 (1995) (In cases where custody dispute is between parent and nonparent, evidentiary scales are "tipped hard" in favor of parent); Vicki N. v. Josephine N., 437 Pa. Super. 166, 649 A.2d 709 (1994) (In child custody action between parent or parents and third party, evidentiary scale is tipped hard to parents' side; therefore, judge must first hear all evidence relevant to child's best interest and then decide whether evidence on behalf of third party is weighty enough to bring scale up to even, and down on third party's side); Hockenberry v. Thompson, 428 Pa. Super. 403, 631 A.2d 204 (1993) (A parent's prima facie right to custody will be forfeited only if there are convincing reasons that the child's best interests will be served by an award to a third party. Thus, even before the proceedings start, the evidentiary scale is tipped, and tipped hard, to the parents' side. What the judge must do, therefore, is first, hear all the evidence that is relevant to the child's best interest, and then decide whether the evidence on behalf of the third party is weighty enough to bring the scale up to even, and down on the third party's side); Michael T.L. v. Marilyn J.L., 363 Pa. Super. 42, 525 A.2d 414 (1987); Jones v. Stone, 343 Pa. Super. 416, 495 A.2d 205 (1985); Cady v. Weber, 317 Pa. Super. 481, 464 A.2d 423 (1983); In re Custody of Hernandez, 249 Pa. Super. 274, 376 A.2d 648 (1977); *but see* Rowles v. Rowles, 542 Pa. 443, 668 A.2d 126, (1995); Albright v. Commonwealth ex rel. Fetters, 491 Pa. 320, 421 A.2d 157 (1980) (parenthood only a factor in determining the best interests of the child).

[36] *Id.*; Ellerbe v. Hooks, 490 Pa. 363, 416 A.2d 512 (1980) (To overcome this *prima facie* right, convincing reasons that the best interests of the child will be served by placement with a third party must be presented); Karner v. McMahon, 43 Pa. Super. 290, 640 A.2d 926 (1994) (In seeking custody, nonparent bears burden of persuasion and burden of production, and nonparent's burden is heavy one. Stepfather who had assumed primary parental responsibility for children since 1989 to the present had standing to seek custody of children. Trial court in custody dispute between natural father and stepfather did not abuse its discretion in finding that natural father's *prima facie* right to custody was overcome by convincing reasons that proved that it was in best interest of his children to remain in custody of stepfather; both children considered stepfather to be their real father, and trial court was correct in determining that stepfather would provide a more stable environment for the children; such stability was especially important when both children were still dealing with residual effects of tragic automobile accident; on the other hand, natural father had never had custody of children during the same time period for more than two days, he had divorced for the second time, and had changed jobs several times);

center on the forfeiture of the parental right to custody, as opposed to the interests of the child, or find that parenthood *alone* will defeat the non-parent's claim, are incorrect.[37] Under any of the standards it is not always necessary to prove parental unfitness in order to secure third party custody.[38]

In *Michael T.L. v. Marilyn J.L.*,[39] it was held that the father's objections to the mother's care of four-year-old son did not overcome the prima facie right to custody of natural parents over third parties, and trial court abused its discretion in awarding de facto primary parenting responsibilities to

---

Dorsey v. Freeman, 438 Pa. Super. 236, 652 A.2d 352 (1994) (In custody dispute between parent and nonparent, nonparent bears both burden of persuasion and burden of production concerning evidence; nonparent's evidentiary burden is heavy one, as scales are tipped hard in favor of parent); R.A.R. v. T.M., 434 Pa. Super. 592, 644 A.2d 767 (1994) (compelling circumstances required that maternal grandfather, rather than natural mother, have primary physical custody of child, in light of mother's unwillingness and inability to care for child in his early years and time child spent in grandfather's custody. Specifically, the court found that Mother had been unwilling and unable to care for the child in his early years, and that it would be destructive to remove him from a stable environment where Grandfather has provided him with constant, consistent care.); Snarski v. Krincek, 372 Pa. Super. 58, 538 A.2d 1348 (1988) (in a case involving modification of an existing custody order and dispute between one parent and grandparents, the burden on the grandparents to show why they should have custody of the child is greatly increased over the standard applicable in an initial determination of custody as between two parents); Chapman v. Goodman, 366 Pa. Super. 130, 530 A.2d 926 (1987); In re James John M., 333 Pa. Super. 417, 482 A.2d 637 (1984); Mooreman v. Tingle, 320 Pa. Super. 348, 467 A.2d 359 (1983); Dile v. Dile, 284 Pa. Super. 459, 426 A.2d 137 (1981); In re Custody of Hernandez, 249 Pa. Super. 274, 376 A.2d 648 (1977).

[37] Albright v. Commonwealth ex rel. Fetters, 491 Pa. 320, 421 A.2d 157 (1980).

[38] *E.g.,* Albright v. Commonwealth ex rel. Fetters, 491 Pa. 320, 421 A.2d 157 (1980); Commonwealth ex rel. Bailey v. Sumner, 193 Pa. Super. 79, 163 A.2d 677 (1960); *but see* K. B. II v. C. B. F., 833 A.2d 767 (Pa. Super. 2003) (trial court abused its discretion in removing a child from the custody of his biological mother and placing the child in the custody of his paternal grandparents, without evidence that the mother was unfit or that the child was substantially at risk as the result of abuse, neglect, drug or alcohol abuse or mental illness).

[39] Michael T.L. v. Marilyn J.L., 363 Pa. Super. 42, 525 A.2d 414 (1987); *see also* Hockenberry v. Thompson, 428 Pa. Super. 403, 631 A.2d 204 (1993) (Awarding de facto custody of minor child to paternal grandmother, rather than to mother, was abuse of discretion in light of uncontroverted evidence that father was unwilling and unable to care for child).

third party, child's parental grandmother, as result of court's conditional custody award to father, since record did not indicate that mother's active sex life had any adverse effect on welfare of child, for whom she had maintained primary parenting role. The de facto granting of custody to the parental grandmother was in error where the child was adequately cared for by his mother, with whom he had lived his entire life.

In accordance with the well-established conviction that environmental stability is of vital importance to the child, the length of time which a child has been living continuously with the third party will be considered.[40] For example, in *Ellerbe v. Hooks*,[41] the Pennsylvania Supreme Court refused to disrupt the stable environment of an eleven-year-old girl who, since she was less than two, had been living with her grandmother. A subsequent Superior Court decision held, however, that the fact that grandparents had been providing loving care for a seven-year-old since the time of her birth did not rise to the level of convincing reasons.[42] It should be noted, however, that the mere fact a child has resided with a non-parent, even if for a substantial period of time, will not be sufficient without evidence as to the reasons why the child resided there. To hold otherwise could encourage and enable a third party to defeat a parent by keeping possession of the child and prolonging that status through litigation.[43] In addition, where grandparents are involved, the age of the contesting grandparent has also been considered as relevant to their ability to properly care for the child.[44]

In *Bishop v. Pillar*, the paternal grandparent of a child born out of wedlock was granted visitation with the child over the mother's objection. The

---

[40] Ellerbe v. Hooks, 490 Pa. 363, 416 A.2d 512 (1980); Wrecsics v. Broughton, 285 Pa. Super. 90, 426 A.2d 1155 (1981). *See* §§ 3.4.7 & 3.4.9, *supra*.

[41] 490 Pa. 363, 416 A.2d 512 (1980).

[42] Mooreman v. Tingle, 320 Pa. Super. 348, 467 A.2d 359 (1983) (fact that child lived with grandparents nearly all of his five and one-half years did not rise to level of convincing reasons); Palmer v. Tokarek, 279 Pa. Super. 458, 421 A.2d 289 (1980).

[43] In re James John M., 333 Pa. Super. 417, 482 A.2d 637 (1984).

[44] Commonwealth ex rel. Holschuh v. Holland-Moritz, 448 Pa. 437, 292 A.2d 380 (1972); *see also* In re Davis, 502 Pa. 110, 465 A.2d 614 (1983) (age alone is not determinative, but it can be an important factor); Wrecsics v. Broughton, 285 Pa. Super. 90, 426 A.2d 1155 (1981).

mother appealed, arguing that because there was no legal relationship between the child and the grandparent there was no basis for granting visitation. The Superior Court disagreed and affirmed the trial court. The court found that paternity in this case was not disputed and the fact that the father of the child did not file an acknowledgement of paternity with the Department of Health, pursuant to 23 Pa.C.S. § 8302, did not preclude a grant of visitation to the paternal grandparent. In addition, although father and mother were never married or cohabited, the Superior Court found that the trial court did not err in applying the term "separated" to them and in applying 23 Pa.C.S. § 5312 (now Section 5325(2)) which allows the court to consider partial custody for grandparents when the parents are separated for six months or more. The Superior Court held that in a grandparent partial custody/visitation case, the burden is on the grandparent to establish that it is in the child's best interest to have "some time" with the grandparent. Here, the paternal grandmother demonstrated her love and devotion to grandchild and met her burden of proving that it would be in the child's best interest to spend time with her. In affirming the Superior Court, the Pennsylvania Supreme Court held that the statute providing for visitation rights of grandparents, after parents have been "separated" for six months or more, applied to a child born to couple that had a dating relationship but had neither been married nor maintained a lengthy, strong, or significant relationship before separation.[45] It is to be seen whether *D.P. v. G.J.P*, 146 A.3d 204 (Pa. 2016) will be deemed to have overruled *Bishop*, as the Supreme Court in *D.P.* struck the following language from 23 Pa.C.S. § 5325(2): "have been separated for a period of at least six months or"

---

[45] Bishop v. Pillar, 399 Pa. Super. 52, 581 A.2d 670 (1990), *aff'd*, 536 Pa. 41, 637 A.2d 976 (1994). For an analysis of the Bishop decision, *see* Bertin, Emanuel A., "Grandparents Visitation Rights," 12 *Pennsylvania Family Lawyer* 9 (February 1991); *but see* Rigler v. Treen, 442 Pa. Super. 533, 660 A.2d 111 (1995) (Evidence supported trial court's finding that even minimal visitation by parents of child's biological father, whose parental rights had been terminated and step father subsequently adopted child, was not in child's best interest and would interfere with parent–child relationship); Norris v. Tearney, 422 Pa. Super. 246, 619 A.2d 339 (1993) (Visitation with paternal grandparents was not in child's best interests, notwithstanding love for child and desire to maintain relationship with him, where father's rejection of mother after child's birth had precipitated her hospitalization for severe depression and visitation exacerbated depression to such an extent that she was unable to care for child).

In *Commonwealth ex rel. Davenport v. Montgomery County Children and Youth Services*,[46] a number of factors, including the child's familiarity with the grandparents, the clear superiority of the physical accommodations, instances of ill treatment at the hands of the father and the trial court's finding that the father's "interest in the girl was questionable," combined to support a custody order in favor of the maternal grandparents as against the father.

In *Heddings v. Steele*,[47] evidence in a child custody proceeding warranted an award of custody of children to the paternal grandparents rather than the maternal grandparents, owing to fact that both maternal grandparents were diabetic and overweight, they would be less likely to address and correct one child's weight problem, and the unstructured family arrangement and permissive attitudes of the maternal grandparents would work a severe disservice to the children, while the paternal grandparents' more structured environment would create an atmosphere conducive to health development.

In *Douglas v. Wright*, 801 A.2d 586 (Pa. Super. 2002), in a case where mother died, the Superior Court affirmed the trial court's grant of partial

---

[46] Com. ex rel. v. Davenport, 501 Pa. 472, 462 A.2d 221 (1983); *see also* Vicki N. v. Josephine N., 437 Pa. Super. 166, 649 A.2d 709 (1994) (Trial court did not abuse its discretion in child custody proceeding in awarding custody of child to child's maternal aunt; mother's health was declining owing to cancer, mother had drinking problem, mother and father had violent physical confrontations when they drank too much, aunt had provided child with safe, caring, and stable home since child's birth, and aunt would provide mother with constant access to child); Snarski v. Krincek, 372 Pa. Super. 58, 538 A.2d 1348 (1988) (determination that best interest of child warranted placement of custody with the maternal grandparents rather than with the natural father was supported by evidence that the child had lived for six and one-half of his eight years with the grandparents, that he had been exposed to chaotic conditions while in his father's custody, that he had returned from England where his father was in the military, with his father's second wife, that father was unemployed and living with his parents, and that father had not involved himself with either of his children's lives when the family resided in England. Grandparents were able to show convincing reasons why father's "prima facie" right to custody should be overcome where grandparents were a source of stability for child and father was unable to provide an environment that would serve child's best interest).

[47] Heddings v. Steele, 514 Pa. 569, 526 A.2d 349 (1987).

custody to the maternal grandparents, because the record established that a close and loving relationship existed between the grandparents and the children, and there was no evidence that the grandparents had ever interfered with father's authority over the children. The record developed by the trial court established that a long-term and close relationship existed between the maternal grandparents and the children prior to mother's death and that the children frequently stayed with the grandparents on their farm. The court observed that "maternal grandparents performed many parental duties such as supervising the children on and off the school bus, driving the children to their activities, preparing meals for them, and helping them with homework."

In *Walkenstein v. Walkenstein*, 443 Pa. Super. 683, 663 A.2d 178 (1995), the Superior Court affirmed an order awarding custody to grandparents. The court found no error in the trial court's decision to grant custody to Grandmother. The court noted that the child had attention deficit disorder, and a major change in his home and school situation would not be in his best interest at this time. The court acknowledged that Grandmother's negative attitude toward Mother was a problem, and that Mother had worked very hard to overcome her problems. However, although another court could have decided differently, the trial court's decision in this case was within its discretion.

In *Reefer v. Reefer*, 791 A.2d 372 (Pa. Super. 2002) the Superior Court held that a custody dispute was between father and mother rather than between mother and the paternal grandparents, despite the fact that the children stayed with their paternal grandparents because of father's work schedule. The court found the trial court's ruling inconsistent with its decision in *Porch v. Porch*, 475 A.2d 831 (Pa. Super. 1984). In *Porch*, the court held that the trial court properly treated the custody dispute as one between the mother and father, rather than one between the mother and paternal grandparents, despite the fact that the children actually stayed with their paternal grandparents because of the father's work schedule. The court noted "as in Porch, this is not a case in which Father has surrendered control of Anthony to the paternal grandparents."

In *K. B. II v. C. B. F.*, 833 A.2d 767 (Pa. Super. 2003), the Superior Court ruled that the trial court abused its discretion in removing a child from the custody of his biological mother and placing the child in the custody of his paternal grandparents, without evidence that the mother was unfit or that the child was substantially at risk as the result of abuse, neglect, drug or alcohol abuse or mental illness. The trial court abused its discretion by taking an eight-year-old from his mother, an exotic dancer, and declaring that his grandparents could provide a more stable and nurturing lifestyle. Citing *Charles v. Stehlik*, 744 A.2d 1255 (Pa. 2000), the court noted the Pennsylvania courts' strong preference for the rights of biological parents with respect to a custody challenge by a third-party. The court also cited *Troxel v. Granville*, 530 U.S. 57 (2000), for the proposition that the Due Process Clause of the 14th Amendment pro-tects parents' interests in the care, custody, and control of their children.

LOWER COURT CASES

Adams County

Koontz v. Demaria, C. P. Adams County, No. 08-S-1417 (C.C.P. 2008) (Trial court ruled that non-biological grandparents have the same standing under the Grandparent Visitation Act as biological grandparents, and that the adoptive grandmother here had standing to seek custody. Paternal grandmother's status as adoptive mother of the child's deceased father did not prevent her from seeking visitation under the Grandparent Visita-tion Act. Mother argued that the petitioner's status as an adoptive grandmother, and not the child's biological grandmother, did not allow her standing under the Act. Mother argued that the Grandparent Visitation Act should apply only to biological grandparents and be "narrowly tailored" to those who "enjoyed a relationship with the grandchild before the death of their child." Mother argued that since petitioner had only seen the child a handful of times prior to father's death, the requirements of the standing provision of the Act were not met. Grandmother countered by arguing she held the "same rights as a biological parent and child." She did not allege that she stood in loco parentis to the child, but had automatic rights of standing under § 5311 because the child's father was deceased. The trial court initially declared that whether or not an adoptive grandparent had standing under § 5311 of the Grandparent Visitation Act had not been addressed by an appellate court in Pennsylvania. The court held that there was no difference between the natural and adoptive parents of a deceased parent. The trial judge cited and quoted both *Little-Stepp v. Cancilla*, 896 A.2d 647 (Pa. Super. 2006) and *Peters v. Costello*, 891 A.2d 705 (Pa. 2005), in his decision, noting that the Superior Court granted adoptive grandparents the same standing as biological grandparents in divorce and separation cases. The trial judge also noted that his decision was guided by the Pennsylvania Supreme Court's decision in *Peters*, which provided instruction to define "grandparents" in a broad sense. The court held that this determination ended the inquiry into stand-ing. "It is clear that adoptive parents to one of the parents of the minor child have the same rights as biological grandparents under the Grandparent Visitation Act. Thus, grandmother has standing to bring a partial custody/visitation action under § 5311.").

Smith et ux. v. Moore, 33 Adams Leg. J. 83 (1990) (Trial court denied physical and legal custody to the grandparents because the children's best interests would not be served by an award to a third party. Custody of twin two-year old daughters was awarded to the mother, where she is employed and has a stable residence in the home of her boyfriend's family. The court recognized that parenthood is not a determinative factor, but held that the grandparents did not bear their burden of producing sufficient evidence to overcome the mother's prima facie right to custody).

Allegheny County

A.M. v. N.G. & R.C., Jr., C.P. Allegheny County, No. FD 18-7134-017 (C.C.P. April 30, 2019), *aff'd.*, Memorandum Decision, No. 792 WDA 2019 (Pa. Super. April 2, 2020) (There may be instances in which the facts and circumstances support a finding that a grandparent's claim for visitation is not appropriate. Father's suicide, and the animosity between paternal grandmother, father, and mother prior to (and following) father's death, presented grounds for the trial court's order denying paternal grandmother partial physical custody. Because mother was a fit parent and because she presented credible concerns regarding the children's visitation with paternal grandmother, the trial court determined that it would not be in the best interest of the children for paternal grandmother to have unsupervised partial physical custody. Accordingly, paternal grandmother's visits were properly left to mother's discretion).

Elbert v. Elbert, C. P. Allegheny County, No. FD 03-003363 (C.C.P. 2007) (Child's best interest was served, pursuant to 23 Pa.C.S. § 5312(a) and 23 Pa.C.S. § 5313, which requires balancing of a child's right to "unfettered parent–child relationship" against the preservation of a strong grandparent/grandchild relationship, by granting grandparents four hours of monthly custody and three consecutive overnights each summer. The evidence established that the maternal grandparents interfered with the parent–child relationship. Grandparents' interference included telling the child that mother was a bad mother; not honoring bedtime and other routines; undermining the relationship between mother and father with the child, and calling father a "loser." Evidence indicated that the child experienced stress while with the grandparents and difficulty in custody exchanges. Evidence of positive changes since grandparent time had been limited was introduced. The court noted that when there is interference with the parent–child relationship, the legislation does not require that grandparents be granted any partial custody or visitation. It instead leaves custody determinations regarding grandparents to the discretion of the court. "This determination requires us to balance the value to [the child] of an un-interfered parent–child relationship against the preservation of a strong grandparent–grandchild relationship . . . . We believe that the most appropriate application of 'grandparents' rights' in this case is to award limited custodial time of [the child] to Maternal Grandparents. . . . Weekends are a precious time for working families and it would be unfair and inappropriate to deprive Mother of full weekends with [the child] in order to accommodate additional time for Maternal Grandfather.)"

Beaver County

Noah v. Noah, C.P. Beaver County, No. 10940 of 2006 (C.C.P. 2006) (Trial court held that 23 Pa.C.S. § 5312, which provides visitation rights for grandparents where the parents of the child are separated, does not violate the Equal Protection Clause of the 14th Amendment when applied to a situation where the father—the grandparents' son—is incarcerated and, therefore, unavailable to make decisions about his child. The court explained that 23 Pa.C.S. § 5311 grants grandparents custody rights with their grandchildren where one parent is deceased).

Berks County

Stout v. Weller, C.P. Berks County, No. 05-1589 (C.C.P. 2013) (Continued placement of a child with Tourette's syndrome with maternal grandmother was proper in order to minimize disruption to the child's routine. After testimony from the parties and the guardian *ad litem*, and after review of the psychological evaluations, the trial court determined that grandmother provided the best care and stability for the child, and she was awarded primary custody over both parents. Of all parties involved, grandmother had provided the best oversight, and was instrumental in getting the child's Tourette's syndrome diagnosed and treated. While mother was more nurturing, her history of parenting the child was inconsistent. In addition, father did not have the same level of commitment to the child. Notably, the child could remain in her current school with the friends she felt close to. This factor was important to the child's well-being. The trial court noted that although natural parents are favored in custody decisions, significant to the court's decision here to maintain the status quo and continue the child's placement with grandmother was the child's expressed preference to remain in grandmother's home and to eventually reunite with mother in her home. The court concluded that grandmother and mother were favored on their ability to perform parental duties because they provided a strong level of stability and continuity for the child).

Morganti v. Morganti, 105 Berks Co. L. J. 207 (C.C.P. 2013) (The trial court denied maternal grandparents' petition for custody when it was shown that they had not adequately cared for the child's physical needs and routinely attempted to turn the child against his mother. Here, the bond that mother had with her child, as well as mother's demonstrated ability to care for her child, strongly favored her, whereas mother's parents had clearly attempted to undermine the child's relationship with his mother, had not properly cared for the child, and may have even abused the child. The court found that mother was more likely to encourage and permit continuing contact between the child and maternal grandparents, because maternal grandparents had an "extensive" and "dismal" history of limiting and undermining the child's contact with mother and paternal grandmother. The court emphasized that the degree of conflict between the parties was harmful to the child and that it was mostly attributable to maternal grandparents' conduct. The court awarded mother primary physical and legal custody and granted maternal grandparents five hours per month of partial custody at the discretion of mother).

Krick v. Krick, C. P. Berks County, No. 06-2153 (C.C.P. 2010) (Trial court found that the paternal grandparents did not overcome father's prima facie right to custody and accordingly, father was awarded primary custody. However, because of the paternal grandparents' substantial and long-term relationship with the minor child, it would be inappropriate to eliminate their time with the minor child. The court awarded father primary physical custody of the minor child, with paternal grandparents entitled to shared legal custody and mother entitled to supervised visits every other weekend. The court found that where the custody dispute is between a parent and a third party, the legal standard of proof is different than when between parents, with the evidentiary scale being tipped and tipped hard in favor of the biological parent).

Graff v. Graff, 101 Berks Co. L. J. 1 (C.C.P. 2008) (Trial court held that in light of testimony that mother had prevented grandparents access to the parties' children, as well as the fact that the children had lived with grandparents for three years, the court granted grandparents their own periods of visitation. "As the grandparents were petitioning only for periods of visitation, the fact that they were not the children's care providers is irrelevant. Moreover, the court entered an order permitting the grandparents to intervene in accordance with the stipulation signed by both parties. Here, there was no dispute that mother, father and children had lived with the grandparents in New York from the time the first child was born in August 2002 until August 2005. Thus, the grandparents had standing to seek visitation rights. Moreover, the court inferred from the testimony that the children had always enjoyed a strong relationship with their grandparents that should be encouraged and nurtured. "This court agreed that the grandparents were a positive influence in the children's lives and that their role should continue." The court noted that there was testimony that mother had, on occasion, prevented the grandparents access to the children and that the children had previously lived with grandparents for three years. The court believed it was important to grant grandparents their own periods of visitation).

Weiser v. Wentzel, C.P. Berks County, No. 97-7620 (C.C.P. 1998) (Trial court held that maternal grandparents had standing to bring a custody action, even though they had not acted in loco parentis, where their allegation that their grandchild was in danger due to alcohol and drug abuse satisfied one of the three grounds for standing contained in 23 Pa.C.S. § 5313(b); Section 5313(b) provides that grandparents have standing if they have acted in loco parentis for twelve months, or have assumed responsibility for a child who has been deemed a dependent child, or have deemed it "necessary to assume responsibility for a child who is substantially at risk due to parental abuse, neglect, drug or alcohol abuse or mental illness.").

Nottage-Martin v. Hunt, 86 Berks L. J. 58 (1993) (The grandparent has the burden to show that it would be in the child's best interests to allow visitation). *But see Tubberville v. Tubberville*, 18 Lyc. 119 (1990), holding that step-grandfather, separated from the child's maternal grandmother, does not have standing to bring a custody action under the Grandparents Visitation Act, and any visitation enjoyed by the former step-grandfather must be at the discretion of the natural mother).

Dietrich v. Dietrich, 85 Berks L. J. 51 (1992) (Preliminary objections to grandparent's petition sustained, nothing in the case or statutory law of Pennsylvania legitimizes the intrusion by the courts into family life created by an order directing the parents of a child, both of whom have chosen not to have their child visit a grandparent, to permit such visitation).

Bradford County

Short v. Finogle, C.P. Bradford County, No. 94FC000881 (C.C.P. 1997) (Trial court has refused to follow the Supreme Court's decision in *Rowles v. Rowles*, calling that court's decision "negligible at best," in a non-parent versus parent legal/primary physical custody case. The court stated that it was not bound by that decision because it was not an opinion of a majority of the Court and had no precedential value. Rejecting *Rowles*, the court stated that it was instead bound by the standard articulated in *Ellerbee v. Hooks*, 416 A.2d 512 (Pa. 1980), *i.e.*, that parents have a prima facie right to custody as against third parties. The court stated that: "*Rowles* would be more compelling if empirically the *Ellerbee* standard had proven confusing or unworkable, however, there is no basis to conclude that our trial courts, applying the *Ellerbee* standard, have failed to make decisions in custody disputes between parents and third parties in a manner that is consistent with the best interest of the children involved.").

Carbon County

Highland v. Kresge, 13 Carbon Co. L. J. 283 (C.C.P. 1992) (Court will not award partial custody to grandmother where Court finds detriments to child from hostility between Mother and Grandmother outweighs benefits of relationship with Grandmother. "The quantity and weight of these detriments clearly tip the custodial scales against awarding Grandmother visitation").

Centre County

Colbert v. Payne, C.P. Centre County, No. 2012-3196 (C.C.P. 2012) (Trial court granted grandmother's petition for custody where the child resided with her, mother was unable to care for the child due to substance abuse, and father had been accused of physically abusing the child. Although third parties have a greater burden of proof in pursuing custody, if the best interests of a child are served, and sufficient evidence supports an award, custody can be awarded to a third party. The court noted that grandmother had continued to ensure that the child attended school and noted all the treatment programs initiated by mother. The court noted that grandmother extended herself and worked with paternal grandparents to make sure that the child maintained his relationship with them).

Strong v. Strong, C.P. Centre County, No. 1997-1933 (C.C.P. 2006) (Trial court ruled that custody of children was to be maintained with grandmother and great aunt, with whom the children had been living and who had provided the children with stability. Having the children remain in the custody of grandmother and great aunt, and not the parents, would be in the best interests of the children and would maintain the status quo. The court found that in light of the past turmoil in the children's lives regarding custody, maintenance of stability and status quo was in the best interest of the children. The court relied on testimony from the children's physician and counselor who stated that the grandmother and great aunt provided the stability and continuity the children needed. The court also held that it was in their best interest to remain in their current school rather than disrupt their lives with such a significant change. "In the present matter, although this Court recognizes the preference for biological parents over third parties, this Court determines there are convincing reasons that the children's best interests will be served by maintaining primary physical custody in grandmother and great aunt, with joint legal custody shared among grandmother, father, and mother.").

Clearfield County

Hudzy v. Kline, C.P. Clearfield County, No. 931769 (C.C.P. 1996) (Where the child in question exhibited a marked improvement in her development, emotional outlook and self-confidence after she began living with her maternal grandparents, and her father admitted at the time of the custody hearing that he was not yet in a position to be the custodial parent, the court properly awarded custody of the child to the grandparents. The court explained that while Pennsylvania courts had previously held that parents have a prima facie right to custody of their children, that changed when the state Supreme Court eliminated the presumption in *Rowles v. Rowles*, 668 A.2d 126 (Pa. 1995), and ruled that custody should be determined by the weight of the evidence, weighing parenthood as only a strong factor for consideration).

Clinton County

Wadsworth v. Wadsworth, C.P. Clinton County, No. 1220-95 (C.C.P. 1996) (Where the grandmother had been the child's primary caretaker since infancy with only minimal contact with his natural mother, it would not be in the child's best interest to award primary custody to the child's mother. The court explained that pursuant to *Rowles v. Rowles*, 668 A.2d 126 (Pa. 1995), parents no longer enjoy a prima facie right to custody as against third parties. Rather, courts must now focus on the best interests of the child in deciding custody disputes between parents and third parties. In making this determination, the court must weigh "parenthood as a strong factor for consideration;" however, the ultimate concern of the court should be what affiliation will best serve the child's best interests, including physical, emotional, intellectual, moral, and spiritual well-being. The court determined that the child's best interests would be served by awarding physical and legal custody to the grandmother. The court held that mother was not yet ready to resume the full-time parenting of the child, which she previously gave up many years ago.).

Crawford County

C.S. v. J.B., C.P. Crawford County, No. A.D. 2009-313-S (C.C.P. September 7, 2016), *aff'd,* Memorandum Decision, No. 1534 WDA 2016 (Pa. Super. April 11, 2017) (The trial court awarded joint legal custody of the child at issue to mother and paternal grandmother, and determined that mother and paternal grandmother would share physical custody on a week-on/week-off basis. Mother claimed that a presumption exists with regard to custody matters between parents and third parties, as provided for in 23 Pa.C.S. § 5327(b). Mother also contended that the law presumes parents are fit, and, as such, that their parenting decisions are made in their children's best interest. Thus, mother argued that it was improper for the trial court to analyze the best interest factors listed in 23 Pa.C.S. § 5328. The court noted that the trial court relied heavily on paternal grandparents' performing of parental duties throughout the child's life and its determination that they, rather than mother, were better able to attend to the child's daily needs. The court further found that although mother may not have encouraged frequent contact with paternal grandparents, the grandparents would encourage such contact with mother. The court emphasized that the Commonwealth has not adopted a standard whereby custody is always awarded to a parent as opposed to a third-party, except if there is a showing that the parent is unfit. Rather, the best interest of the child trumps the biological parent's right to custody, citing *Charles v. Stehlik,* 744 A.2d 1255 (Pa. 2000). The court determined that the presumption in § 5327(b) was rebutted by a consideration of the custodial situation during the child's lifetime, including but not limited to, the parents' periods of incarceration, sporadic irresponsibility, and overall lack of stability).

Beach v. Ives, 20 Crawford Leg. J. 242 (C.C.P. 1988) (Where an eight-year-old child had substantially no contact with her father since she was one year old, and the mother of the child died, the best interests of the child require that primary physical custody be awarded to the relative of the deceased mother with whom the child had resided for a period of time, and liberal visitation rights be awarded to the father. Physical custody of an eight-year-old child is awarded to the maternal aunt and uncle where the surviving father has had practically no contact with the child since infancy).

Fulton County

Ramsey v. Maurer, C.P. Fulton County, No. 128 of 1996-C (C.C.P. 1998) (Trial court held that it was in the best interests of the child for custody to be awarded to the child's mother rather than her parental grandmother where, while she had temporary custody of the child, grandmother did not facilitate or encourage contact between mother and child, and where mother had matured and become a stable individual since the court first took jurisdiction over the matter. The court noted that because *Rowles* was a plurality decision, some trial courts have followed its reasoning while others have continued to follow the presumption that custody should be awarded to a parent. The court declared that it would follow *Rowles* and make a determination of what was in the child's best interests. Here, the court concluded that "frequent contact and a good relationship would not be encouraged" if custody were awarded to grandmother. In awarding custody to mother, the court noted that mother had matured to a large degree since her stay at a mental hospital. Also, mother completed her G.E.D. and has held a steady job since her release).

Greene County

Shaffer v. Gaso, 30 The Greene Reports 9 (C.C.P. 2012) (Under the new Custody Act, there is no presumption that a child benefits from extensive contact with grandparents. There being no such presumption or policy, it is incumbent on grandparents to demonstrate that partial custody or visitation with the child is in the child's best interests. Plaintiffs sought partial physical custody as provided by 23 Pa.C.S. § 5325(2), "where the parents of the child have been separated for a period of at least six months." Plaintiff grandmother testified that in the child's early years they provided child care and babysitting for the child and her parents. However, the marriage deteriorated, the parties separated, and plaintiff grandparents did not have much contact with the child in recent years. Moreover, the child felt alienated from grandparents, and wanted no contact with them. The child stated that she did not want to see grandparents. "It is difficult to see how forcing [the child] to spend time with two people she has no desire to see is in her best interest, especially when the mere thought of it seems to cause her such stress. Frankly, it seems to us that plaintiffs are thinking more of their own best interest rather than the child's. . . . We will not force this relationship on a young girl who clearly wants no part of it.").

Indiana County

D.W. and D.W. v. F.T. and J.T., C.P. Indiana County, No. 11815 C.D. 2014 (C.C.P. June 6, 2016), *aff'd*, Memorandum Decision, No. 1007 WDA 2016 (Pa. Super. January 27, 2017) (An award of partial physical custody to grandparents would be contrary to the children's best interests, given that grandparents had expressed little, if any, interest in the children over the last several years, and given that such an award would risk creating additional distress and turmoil in the children's lives. Grandparents sought an Order for partial physical custody of their three grandchildren. Grandparents did not send letters or cards to the children, nor did they attend extracurricular activities. The court further emphasized that grandparents incited conflict with the parents during the rare occasions that they did have contact with the children. Grandparents had only sporadic contact with the children prior to the parents' separation. Following separation, the grandparents visited with the children on four occasions at most. Grandparents made little, if any, other effort to maintain a relationship with the children).

Lancaster County

J.L.S. v. W.S., C.P. Lancaster County, No. CI-12-03067 (C.C.P. 2013) (Trial court awarded grandfather custody of the minor children where grandfather provided financial, emotional and educational support, and there was overwhelming evidence that mother failed to provide a stable home and neglected their care. Mother had a chaotic and erratic history with her two children, where she admitted that she had moved at least eight times, had had multiple relationships, and experienced periods of time where others had cared for the children for months at a time. Grandfather had provided the children with a home when they were abandoned by mother, and had provided financial support, clothing, food and medical treatment. The children developed significant emotional attachments to grandfather and the evidence contradicted mother's assertion that she provided for the children's needs. The trial court first acknowledged that while the presumption of a parent's custody tips the evidentiary scales hard in favor of the parent, it can be overcome by a third party's developing a case for custody with clear and convincing evidence. The court found that grandfather had easily met this burden, and found that it was in the best interests of the children that primary legal and physical custody be placed with grandfather, with partial physical custody with mother).

Gregorio v. Gregorio, C. P. Lancaster County, No. CI-07-04002 (C.C.P. 2007) (Grandparent Visitation Act did not permit great-grandparents automatic standing to seek physical and legal custody unless they stood in loco parentis to the child. The Act distinguished between grandparents and great-grandparents in that great-grandparents were not afforded automatic standing to seek physical and legal custody of great-grandchildren. At issue was whether the great-grandparents, who babysat for their great-granddaughter, had in loco parentis status vis-à-vis the child when at the mother's request they kept her at their house while mother was working, and whether great-grandparents had standing to bring an action for custody pursuant to 23 Pa.C.S. § 5313. "Section 5313(b) clearly specifies only 'grandparents', which we all understand to be the child's parents' parents, while Section 5313(a), which the Legislature clearly intended to cast a wider net for purposes of temporary custody and visitation, specifies both grandparents and great-grandparents. Compared to Section 5313(a), omitting the word great-grandparents in § 5313(b) is a clear indication that in the second section only grandparents are meant. There is no ambiguity present when one compares both sections. This Court will not expand the wording that the Legislature clearly did not wish to be expanded." Plaintiffs did not assert sufficiently specific facts concerning their relationship with the child to show their control of and contributions to her to turn themselves into anything more than great-grandparents who take care of their great-grandchild as a favor to her mother. The court could not find that they stood in loco parentis to the child, and they therefore did not have standing to pursue this action in custody).

Swain v. Vaughn, 74 Lancaster L. Rev. 429 (C.C.P. 1995) (Trial court held that a grandparent may seek visitation or partial custody of children who do not reside with their unmarried parents. The court held that there is a heightened preference for grandparental visitation or partial custody where the natural parents do not live together in the context of a formal marriage. Although the plaintiff was a third party, the court found that she had standing to maintain an action for partial custody and/or visitation of her grandchildren and denied defendant's preliminary objections).

Heiss v. Eckert et al., 72 Lancaster L.R. 504 C.C.P. (1991) (While the Custody and Grandparents Visitation Act does not provide for partial custody by a grandparent, in a case in which the children are residing with unmarried parents, partial custody is to be considered where it is in the best interests of the children; although the parents were not married, but living together, the court found that § 5312 gives a heightened preference toward grandparent visitation where the natural parents of the child are not married. The court held that the Custody and Grandparent Visitation Act does not preclude visitation under other circumstances if visitation is in the best interest of the child).

Novak v. Martin, et al., 71 Lancaster L. Rev. 198 (C.C.P. 1988) (In this custody action by natural father against third party actual custodians of two-year-old child born out of wedlock, wherein it appeared that natural father's past conduct demonstrated very little interest in the child; that the actual custodians had provided a stable, happy home for child; the Court concluded it was in the child's best interest to award primary physical custody to the third party actual custodians. In a custody action, factors that have significant impact on a child's well-being may justify an outcome in favor of a nonparent, even though the parent has not been shown to be unfit).

Lawrence County

Finamore v. Finamore, C. P. Lawrence County, No. 11285 of 2006, C. A. (C.C.P. 2007) (Minor child's grandparents could not obtain custody where there was no evidence that the child had ever been abused or acted in an aggressive, angry manner while with his father. "With regard to a custody challenge by a third party, the Pennsylvania courts have expressed a strong preference for the rights of biological parents," *Charles v. Stehlik*, 560 Pa. 334, 744 A.2d 1255 (2000). While maternal grandparents had an integral and important role in his life, they failed to meet their burden of proving that their grandchild's best interests required that they have primary physical and legal custody. "To the contrary, the natural father's home is appropriate, the father is a licensed practical nurse and capable of caring for the child, there is no evidence that the child has ever been abused in any manner, and there is no evidence that the child acts out in an aggressive, angry manner when he is with the father.").

Lehigh County

Krieg v. Krieg, 46 Lehigh L. J. 598 (C.C.P. 1995). (Maternal grandparents, who had custody of children at the time of the hearing, did not stand in loco parentis, and therefore had no standing to maintain a custody action. Accordingly, a custody order was entered in favor of father, with partial custody/visitation to grandparents).

Luzerne County

Anthony D. and A.D. v. R.D. and J.M., 87 Luzerne Leg. Reg. 31 (C.C.P. 1997) (Held, following *Rowles v. Rowles*, 668 A.2d 126 (Pa. 1995), that in a custody dispute between parents and third parties, such as grandparents, custody is to be determined weighing parenthood as a strong factor for consideration with the ultimate concern being "what affiliation will best serve the child's interests, including physical, emotional, intellectual, moral and spiritual well-being." In this case, the trial court awarded shared legal custody among the child's mother, father and maternal grandparents, with primary physical residence to continue with the grandparents).

Aftewicz v. Aftewicz, 86 Luzerne Leg. Reg. 71 (C.C.P. 1996) (Parents have no prima facie right to custody of children as against third parties, but rather, custody is to be determined by a preponderance of evidence, weighing parenthood as a strong factor for consideration, keeping in mind that the best interest of the child is the goal, with courts considering every fact relevant to the physical, emotional, intellectual, moral and spiritual well-being of the child. The court referred to the decision of the Pennsylvania Supreme Court in *Rowles v. Rowles*, 668 A.2d 126 (Pa. 1995), which eliminated the presumption that a parent has a prima facie right to custody. The court concluded that a continuing relationship by the child with her grandparents, on a one-afternoon-a-month basis, would be in her best interest and beneficial to her emotional and psychological well-being.).

Lycoming County

Pipp v. Pipp, 17 Lycoming Rep. 354 (C.C.P. 1989) (Custody hearing officer did not have authority to award visitation to paternal grandparents because they did not file a petition requesting visitation, they had not indicated an interest in visitation and they had no real contact with the minor).

Monroe County

H.W., I.W., and A.R. v. D.R., C.P. Monroe County, No. 1497 CV 2015 (C.C.P. October 13, 2017), *aff'd*, Memorandum Decision, No. 3712 EDA 2017 (Pa. Super. May 18, 2018) (Trial court concluded that maternal grandparents had presented clear and convincing evidence to overcome the statutory presumption in favor of custody to father, and determined that awarding primary physical custody of the child to maternal grandparents was in the child's best interest. Maternal grandmother testified regarding the child's social and academic progress since living with maternal grandparents. Maternal grandmother took the child to multiple evaluations at the school district and created a full I.E.P. for the child, which included co-teaching, speech and language therapy, and counseling. Maternal grandmother presented evidence from the child's general education teacher, special education teacher, and speech teacher to show that the child had made consistent progress throughout the school year, with school services and support from her maternal grandparents. The trial court found that a majority of the factors, namely 10 total, were in favor of awarding primary custody to maternal grandparents. The trial court did not find any factors to be in favor of father. The court also agreed with the trial court's finding that the child was emotionally closer to the siblings that lived in maternal grandparents' home and that the location of the maternal grandparents' home was favored over the location of father's home. The trial court found other relevant factors to weigh in favor of maternal grandparents).

Montgomery County

S.C. v. A.C. & L.C., C.P. Montgomery County, No. 2007-16468 (C.C.P. July 19, 2016), *aff'd*, Memorandum Decision, No. 2601 EDA 2016 (Pa. Super. May 11, 2017) (Mother lacked the stability necessary to care for her child and to ensure her best interests; accordingly, it entered an order awarding primary physical and sole legal custody of the child to grandparents and awarding partial physical custody to mother. The testimony presented established that mother had a history of instability and erratic behavior. Mother had a history of neglecting the child and placing her in danger, as demonstrated by the fact that mother left the child alone to wander a beach in Puerto Rico. The court noted that mother appeared to have made little progress in terms of remedying these issues. Mother was uncooperative and hostile, and failed to attend her visits with the child consistently).

Perry County

Kocher v. Malone, C.P. Perry County, No. 96-287 C.C.P. 1996) (Trial court held that it was in the best interests of the child to award primary legal and physical custody to the grandparents where, for the two years preceding his mother's death, the child's maternal grandparents took over the primary caregiving duties, and where there was testimony that the relationship between the child and his father was strained due to the father's wife. Citing *Rowles v. Rowles*, 668 A.2d 126 (Pa. 1995), the court stated that the father/son relationship, although a substantial factor, was outweighed by the boy's desire to remain with his maternal grandparents and the boy's need at the present time for psychological counseling, which he received while living with his grandparents).

Philadelphia County

Spada v. Woerle, 29 Phila. 266 (C.C.P. 1994) (Trial court held that it is well-settled that parents of deceased children may obtain reasonable visitation rights to the children of their deceased child whenever such visitation is in the best interest of the child and visitation would not interfere with the parent/child relationship).

York County

J.F.T. v. T.A.B., H.M.B. and C.D.C., C.P. York County, No. 2016-FC-11-03 (C.C.P. July 8, 2016), *aff'd*, Memorandum Decision, No. 1312 MDA 2016 (Pa. Super. March 6, 2017) (Trial court emphasized the well-established legal principle that natural parents have a rebuttable presumption against third parties in custody disputes, 23 Pa.C.S. § 5327(b) (codified the then-existing common-law presumption). Grandmother filed a complaint for custody of the two children. The court awarded mother sole legal custody and primary physical custody of the children, subject to grandmother's rights of partial physical custody. The court found that a majority of the 16 custody factors set forth in 23 Pa.C.S. § 5328(a)(1)-(16) did not weigh in favor of either party, and readily supported a conclusion that both grandmother and mother were fit parties to continue to care for the children. In awarding sole legal and primary physical custody of the children to mother, the trial court essentially concluded that grandmother did not meet her heavy burden of overcoming the statutory presumption in favor of mother. The court found that grandmother failed to meet her burden by clear and convincing evidence).

Knee v. Knee, 113 York Leg. Rec. 41 (C.C.P. 1999) (Trial court found that the fact that grandparents reside with one parent does not deprive them of standing to bring a custody action since there is no requirement in 23 Pa.C.S. § 5313 that the plaintiffs must live apart; however, grandparents are still third parties that bear a heavier burden to convince a court to award custody to them after a hearing on the merits. The Grandparents' Custody and Visitation Act did not require grandparents to live apart from a natural parent in order to be conferred standing, merely that natural parents be separated or divorced).

Metz v. Metz, 113 York Leg. Rec. 52 (C.C.P. 1999) (Grandparents have standing to seek visitation rights even though the parents never married and are not now living together, although they still have a heavier burden of third party to convince the court in a hearing on the merits that they should actually be awarded visitation rights. "Notwithstanding the Supreme Court's division in Bishop, we believe it is the law in this Commonwealth which we must follow unless or until the legislature acts otherwise. . . . In view of the Commonwealth's policy of permitting liberal application of the principles of standing as it applies to grandparents, and based upon the Supreme Court's holding in Bishop we conclude that Grandparents do have standing to seek custody in this matter. We point out, however, that in a hearing on the merits, Grandparents have the 'heavy burden' of a 'third party' to convince a court to award them as opposed to natural parents, rights of custody or visitation.").

Chapter 6

THIRD PARTIES

§ 6.1. THIRD PARTIES – GENERALLY

Generally, custody disputes between a parent and a non-parent third party arise when a child is placed by a parent with a third party who is better able, at that time, to provide for the child. Having become attached to the child or feeling that the parent is unfit to raise the child, the third party refuses to return the child upon request and a custody proceeding ensues.[1] Other situations arise where the custodial parent refuses to permit members of his or her former spouse's family to have contact with the child. Such refusals are commonly spurred by bitterness toward in-laws growing out of the divorce; a reluctance to revive the painful memory of the death of a spouse through the presence of his or her blood relatives; or the desire to raise the child exclusively in the atmosphere of a newly acquired family complete with a new set of in-laws.[2] Until recently, third parties, except grandparents, who are not *in loco parentis* to the child lack standing to bring a child custody action in the Commonwealth of Pennsylvania.[3] However, an amendment to the custody act that became effective July 4, 2018 has opened the door to third parties beyond *in loco parentis* regarding standing.

---

[1] *See* Milligan v. Davidson, 244 Pa. Super. 255, 367 A.2d 299 (1976).

[2] *See* Commonwealth ex rel. Zaffarano v. Genaro, 286 Pa. Super. 436, 429 A.2d 17 (1981). Dullea, *What Are the Visitation Rights of Grandparents in a Divorce?*, N.Y. Times, Dec. 20, 1977 at 40.

[3] *See* 23 Pa.C.S. § 5324; *see also* Gradwell v. Strausser, 416 Pa. Super. 118, 124, 610 A.2d 999, 1002 (1992) (a third party may maintain an action only where that party stands *in loco parentis*).

Subsection 4 has been added to Section 5324 for standing for any form of physical custody or legal custody. Subsection 4 reads as follows, regarding individuals who may file an action for any form of physical custody or legal custody:

Subject to Paragraph (5), an individual who establishes by clear and convincing evidence all of the following:

(I) The individual has assumed or is willing to assume responsibility for the child.

(II) The individual has a sustained, substantial and sincere interest in the welfare of the child. In determining whether the individual meets the requirements of this subparagraph, the court may consider, among other factors, the nature, quality, extent and length of the involvement by the individual in the child's life.

(III) Neither parent has any form of care and control of the child.[4]

(5) Paragraph (4) shall not apply if:

(I) A dependency proceeding involving the child has been initiated or is ongoing; or

(II) There is an order of permanent legal custody under 42 PA.C.S. § 6351(A)(2.1) or (F.1)(3) (relating to disposition of dependent child).[5]

§ 6.2. THIRD PARTY STANDING – *IN LOCO PARENTIS*

In order for a person to have *in loco parentis* standing, that individual must demonstrate the following: (1) the assumption of parental status; (2) the discharge of parental duties; and (3) the consent and knowledge of the parent.[6] However, the application of those three prongs is

---

[4] M.S. v. J.D., 215 A.3d 595 (Pa. Super. 2019) (trial court properly denied a paternal grandmother's petition to intervene in an underlying custody action involving her grandchild in order to seek custody because she lacked standing under 23 Pa.C.S. §§ 5324(4), as grandmother did not establish that she had standing under § 5324(4), as testimony did not prove that mother lacked care and control over the child).

[5] *See* 23 Pa.C.S. § 5324(4) & (5); Pa.R.C.P. 1915.5(a).

[6] *See* M.J.S. v. B.B. v. B.B., 172 A.3d 651 (Pa. Super. 2018).

not necessarily precisely consistent.[7] Other factors previously found to be significant to the determination of *in loco parentis* standing are co-residency, duration of relationship, and whether the biological parent agrees that the third party should play a parenting role.[8] "As each situation is unique, the showing necessary to establish *in loco parentis* status must be flexible and dependent upon the particular facts of each case."[9] As referenced above, *in loco parentis* status cannot be established

---

[7] Peters v. Costello, 586 Pa. 102, 891 A.2d 705, 710 (2005); Argenio v. Fenton, 703 A.2d 1042, 1044 (Pa. Super. 1997); *see also* M.L.S. v. T.H.-S., 195 A.3d 265 (Pa. Super. 2018) (trial court did not err by finding stepfather, a member of the armed forces stationed away from mother and child stood *in loco parentis* to the child under 23 Pa.C.S. § 5324 because he served in place of child's deceased biological father and mother accepted benefits of his childrearing efforts together with any risks associated with that arrangement).

[8] J.A.L. v. E.P.H., 682 A.2d 1314, 1320 (Pa. Super. 1996); *see also* Bupp v. Bupp, 718 A.2d 1278 (Pa. Super. 1998) (mother's former husband and subsequent paramour had standing to seek partial physical custody of the child of which he was not the natural father, where he lived with the child during her first year of life and helped raise her; Superior Court affirmed trial court's determination that Bupp stood *in loco parentis* to child; important factor in determining whether third party has standing is whether third party lived with child and natural parent in a family setting, irrespective of its traditional or nontraditional composition, and developed a relationship with child as a result of the participation and acquiescence of natural parent); *but see* M.L.S. v. T.H.-S., 195 A.3d 265 (Pa. Super. 2018) (trial court did not err by finding stepfather, a member of the armed forces stationed away from mother and child stood *in loco parentis* to the child under 23 Pa.C.S. § 5324 because he served in place of child's deceased biological father and mother accepted benefits of his childrearing efforts together with any risks associated with that arrangement).

[9] *Id.*; *see also* J.F. v. D.B., 897 A.2d 1261, 1274 (Pa. Super. 2006) (*in loco parentis* status cannot be established absent the approval of the child's biological parent); T.B. v. L.R.M., 753 A.2d 873, 884 (Pa. Super. 2000) (where only limited custody rights are sought, the limited nature of the intrusion into the biological family must be considered in deciding standing); Gradwell v. Strausser, 610 A.2d 999 (Pa. Super. 1992) (third party cannot place himself *in loco parentis* in defiance of the parents' wishes and the parent/child relationship); *see also* Argenio v. Fenton, 703 A.2d 1042 (Pa. Super. 1997) (Pennsylvania Superior Court held grandparent who cared for her granddaughter on a daily basis during the child's first year while the child lived in her home did not stand *in loco parentis* to granddaughter).

absent the approval of the child's biological parent.[10] Implied consent by a biological parent is not permissible.[11] The Pennsylvania Supreme Court also has ruled that a married couple, who raised a child's biological mother under a formal custody agreement with mother's natural father, may seek court-ordered custody with the eight-year-old daughter of the woman they helped raise, even though they were not related by blood or marriage to either the mother or child.[12] This has been known as "in loco grandparentis." Likewise, the Superior Court held that adoptive parents of one of the parents of a child with respect to whom they sought grandparental visitation rights, and who otherwise qualified to seek partial custody/visitation, had standing to seek custody/visitation under the Grandparent Visitation Act.[13]

In *J.A.L. v. E.P.H.*,[14] the court found that J.A.L. established *in loco parentis* standing. The parties were former lesbian partners. J.A.L. was present through all of the prenatal and birthing events and maintained a relationship with the child following the birth. After the dissolution of the relationship, J.A.L. sought partial custody of the child the pair had raised together. The court found that J.A.L. had sufficient standing

---

[10] J.F. v. D.B., 897 A.2d 1261, 1274 (Pa. Super. 2006); Gradwell v. Strausser, 610 A.2d 999 (Pa. Super. 1992) (third party cannot place himself *in loco parentis* in defiance of the parents' wishes and the parent/child relationship).

[11] *See* K.W. v. S.L. & M.L., 157 A.3d 498 (Pa. Super. 2017) (Superior Court held implied consent is not permissible under Pennsylvania law).

[12] Peters v. Costello, 586 Pa. 102, 891 A.2d 705, 710 (2005). *But see* Hill v. Divecchio, 425 Pa. Super. 355, 625 A.2d 642 (1993) (Unambiguous awards of Grandparents' Visitation Act that state "upon application of parent or grandparent of party" preclude mother's stepfather from asserting cause of action for visitation of step-grandchild, even if in conjunction with child's natural grandmother); Commonwealth ex rel. Patricia L.F. v. Malbert J.F., 278 Pa. Super. 343, 420 A.2d 572 (1980); Auman v. Eash, 228 Pa. Super. 242, 323 A.2d 94 (1974); Commonwealth ex rel. Kraus v. Kraus, 185 Pa. Super. 167, 138 A.2d 225 (1958).

[13] Little-Stepp v. Cancilla, 896 A.2d 647 (Pa. Super. 2006) (Court relied on Peters v. Costello, 891 A.2d 705 (Pa. Super. 2005), which held that the Act grants standing to non-biological grandparents who stand *in loco parentis* to one of the parents of the child to whom custody rights are sought, and who otherwise qualify for partial custody/visitation).

[14] J.A.L. v. E.P.H., 682 A.2d 1314, 1320 (Pa. Super. 1996).

to bring the suit because the evidence revealed that, in both E.P.H.'s and J.A.L.'s minds, the child was to be a member of their family. The court further stated that the parties' conduct after the child's birth, and before their separation, further supported their intent to create a parent-like relationship between J.A.L. and the child. The fact that E.P.H. was the child's primary caregiver did not diminish the fact that J.A.L. lived with the child for the first ten months of its life, acting as a parenting partner to the child's mother and creating the opportunity for bonding to occur. Here, the former couple maintained an on-and-off relationship for a period of six-and-a-half to eight years, living together for at least one year of the child's life. The daily conduct by both the mother and plaintiff supported the conclusion that both parties encouraged and fostered a special relationship between plaintiff and the child.[15]

More recently, in *A.J.B. v. A.G.B.*,[16] the Superior Court found that the trial court erred in finding that mother's same-sex ex-wife did not have *in loco parentis* status in a custody suit brought by natural father, where mother and ex-wife were married at the time of the child's birth. The Superior Court found relevant cases involving step-parents where it held that former same-sex partners were entitled to *in loco parentis* standing as third parties where they lived with the child and a natural parent in a family setting, whether a traditional family or a nontraditional one, and developed a relationship with the child as a result of the participation and acquiescence of the natural parent, citing the *J.A.L.* case. The court also considered *C.G. v. J.H.*, 172 A.3d 43 (Pa. Super. 2017), wherein the court affirmed the trial court's determination that a former same-sex partner did not stand *in loco parentis*, due to the specific factual circumstances of that case, including a lack of participation in the child's life. The Pennsylvania Supreme Court affirmed the Superior Court in *C.G. v. J.H.*, 193 A.3d 891 (Pa. 2018). In *A.J.B.*, the court explained, the parties demonstrated an intent to jointly raise the child together in a happy marriage. In addition, ex-wife's name was on the child's birth certificate and she was involved in naming of the child. Although known to family

---

[15] *See also* Jones v. Boring Jones, 884 A.2d 915, 2005 PA Super 337 (Pa. Super. 2005) (lesbian partner found to have *in loco parentis* standing).

[16] A.J.B. v. A.G.B., 180 A.3d 1263 (Pa. Super. 2018).

and friends that she was not the child's biological parent, ex-wife held herself out as the child's parent.

In third-party suits for partial custody, the test of standing is a stringent one.[17] Courts have previously held that anyone not a natural parent is to be accorded third party status.[18] The strict requirement for standing has grown out of a respect for the traditionally strong right of parents to raise their children as they see fit.[19] "The right to raise one's children has long been recognized as one of our basic civil rights. Freedom of personal choice in matters of family life, and the concomitant freedom from unwarranted governmental intrusion, is a fundamental liberty interest protected by the Fourteenth Amendment."[20]

A challenge to standing should be raised within the twenty-day time period provided under Rule 1915.5.[21] However, the trial should not be delayed by a standing challenge.[22] At the time of the trial, the trial court may make a determination regarding standing at any time.[23]

A third party lacks standing to seek custody against the natural parents absent statutory authority because a biological parent's *prima facie* right to custody should not be subject to challenge without a clear and convincing showing that the child is not receiving proper parental care.[24]

---

[17] *See* Jackson v. Garland, 424 Pa. Super. 378, 382, 622 A.2d 969, 971 (1993); Weber v. Weber, 362 Pa. Super. 262, 524 A.2d 498 (1987), *appeal dismissed*, 517 Pa. 458, 538 A.2d 494 (1988); Herron v. Seizak, 321 Pa. Super. 466, 469, 468 A.2d 803, 805 (1983).

[18] Ken R. v. Arthur Z., 546 Pa. 49, 682 A.2d 1267 (1996) (In custody-related disputes, "third parties" refers to all persons other than natural parents); Commonwealth ex rel. Patricia L.F. v. Malbert J.F., 278 Pa. Super. 343, 420 A.2d 572 (1980); In re Custody of Hernandez, 249 Pa. Super. 274, 376 A.2d 648 (1977).

[19] Weber v. Weber, 524 A.2d 498 (Pa. Super. 1987).

[20] *Id.*

[21] *See* Kellogg v. Kellogg, 646 A.2d 1246 (Pa. Super. 1994).

[22] *See Id.*

[23] *See Id.*

[24] *See* Cardamone v. Elshoff, 442 Pa. Super. 263, 659 A.2d 575 (1995); Rosado v. Diaz, 425 Pa. Super. 155, 158–60, 624 A.2d 193, 195 (1993); Gradwell v. Strausser, 416 Pa. Super. 118, 123–25, 610 A.2d 999, 1002 (1992); *see also* Helsel v. Blair County

In recognition of this strong parental right, courts have generally found standing in third-party custody cases only where the legislature has specifically authorized the cause of action.[25] In the absence of legislation, courts have been unwilling to intervene, casting the issue as one of interference in family matters by individuals with no legal rights at issue.[26]

After parents refused to let minor daughter visit adult daughter in her residence or at other places outside parents' home because they did not approve of adult daughter's living arrangements, adult daughter sought partial custody of minor daughter. The Superior Court held that the adult daughter lacked standing to bring action for partial custody of minor daughter over objections of parents.[27] The relationship of half-brother to an infant did not establish a legal right to custody of the half-brother,

---

Children & Youth Services, 359 Pa. Super. 487, 519 A.2d 456 (1986). *But see* Rowles v. Rowles, 542 Pa. 443, 668 A.2d 126 (1995). *See also* 23 Pa.C.S. §§ 5327 & 5324.

[25] Jackson, 424 Pa. Super. at 382, 622 A.2d at 971 (holding that maternal aunt lacked standing to seek partial custody of her deceased sister's minor child in the absence of statutory authority); Weber, 362 Pa. Super. at 264, 524 A.2d at 499 (holding that adult sibling lacked standing to seek partial custody of her minor sibling in the absence of statutory authority).

[26] *See* Jackson, 424 Pa. Super. at 971, 622 A.2d at 971. *See also* In re C.F., 436 Pa. Super. 83, 647 A.2d 253 (1994) (trial court could not compel parents to produce minor daughter for visitation with her minor sibling absent statutory authority justifying the interference).

[27] Weber v. Weber, 362 Pa. Super. 262, 524 A.2d 498 (1987). *See also* Ken R. v. Arthur Z., 546 Pa. 49, 682 A.2d 1267 (1996) (Minor child, who had left home of her mother and stepfather, had no standing to sue for visitation privileges as to her half-sisters; legislature gave siblings no statutory authority to interfere with parental decision as to whether or not their children should be exposed to certain people and influences, and child had no right to interfere in absence of statutory authority); In Interest of C.F., 436 Pa. Super. 83, 647 A.2d 253 (1994) (Minor son who had been abandoned by parents and adjudicated dependent filed petition seeking supervised visitation with sister; (1) no statutory basis existed that would mandate court interference with parent's right to undisturbed custody of daughter after son had been adjudicated dependent, and (2) visitation would not be ordered where son had not shown that visitation would be in his best interests and permanent welfare).

who was not a parent and was not acting *in loco parentis*. Thus, half-brother lacked standing to seek custody of an infant.[28]

In *P.T. and K.T. v. M.H.*, 953 A.2d 814 (Pa. Super. 2008), the Superior Court ruled that the trial court properly denied mother's aunt and uncle, who cared for the child at issue for two years, standing to pursue a complaint for custody of the child while dependency proceedings were ongoing. Instead, the aunt and uncle should have sought custody within the contest of the dependency proceedings. The court determined that the issue of appellants' standing to file a custody complaint would not become ripe until the dependency proceedings actually concluded. Instead, appellants should have sought legal custody of the child within the dependency proceedings.[29]

However, in *McDonel v. Sohn*, 762 A.2d 1101 (Pa. Super. 2000), the Superior Court ruled that a child's aunt and uncle may obtain primary custody of a child even though the natural father wanted custody for himself. While acknowledging that father enjoyed a *prima facie* right to custody as against third parties, the court agreed with the trial court that the aunt and uncle had overcome the presumption in favor of father. The court cited the testimony of the psychologist assigned to the case that it would be in the child's best interests for the aunt and uncle to have primary custody. The psychologist had based his recommendation on the relatives' involvement in the child's life since her birth.

---

[28] Helsel v. Blair County Children and Youth Service, 359 Pa. Super. 487, 519 A.2d 456 (1986). *But see* MacDonald v. Quaglia, 442 Pa. Super. 149, 658 A.2d 1343 (1995), where the court held that a finding that cousin had shown a sincere and sustained interest in child, and so had standing to seek visitation, was supported by evidence that cousin and mother were raised in same household, that cousin considered herself to be sister to mother and aunt to child, that cousin had frequent contact with child until four days before mother's death, and that cousin was denied contact with child because maternal grandmother did not want to associate with mother's family.

[29] *See also* Butler v. Illes, 747 A.2d 943 (Pa. Super. 2000) (where the Superior Court held that a maternal aunt who had only limited contact with the child at issue lacked standing as against the child's biological father to seek custody of the child; mere allegations of blood relationship and listing of occasional contacts between maternal aunt and the child were insufficient to support a finding of *in loco parentis* and standing for aunt's custody complaint against father).

In *Vicki N. v. Josephine N.*, the Superior Court held that the child's maternal aunt could be granted *in loco parentis* status in a child custody proceeding where mother abandoned child at the hospital after child's birth for placement in foster care or for adoption. In *Vicki N.*, the mother, who was put on notice of aunt's petitions for custody, chose not to appear in court or otherwise contest petitions until mother filed petition to modify custody, and mother never contested aunt's status *in loco parentis*.[30]

In *Spells v. Spells*,[31] the court found that a stepfather who lives with his spouse and her natural children could assume the status of "*in loco*

---

[30] Vicki N. v. Josephine N., 437 Pa. Super. 166, 649 A.2d 709 (1994); *see also* Cardamone v. Elshoff, 442 Pa. Super. 263, 659 A.2d 575 (1995) (Award of primary physical custody to maternal aunt who stood *in loco parentis* was in child's best interests where mother had changed residences frequently, mother and her husband had separated two or three times, and were both recovering alcoholics and drug addicts. Since residing with aunt, child had missed less school, her grades had improved, her grandmother was at home when child came home from school, and all of child's friends and family were in city where aunt resided while in contrast, mother worked two jobs, including three to four weekends per month, her husband also worked many weekends, and while they worked her brother was placed in the care of husband's 71-year-old mother, and mother and her husband attended meetings several evenings per week to overcome their drug and alcohol addictions); Mollander v. Chiodo, 450 Pa. Super. 247, 675 A.2d 753 (1996) (Plaintiffs, the prospective adoptive parents of a child, maintained their *in loco parentis* status after mother revoked her consent to adoption, and thus had standing to seek custody); Tracey L. v. Mattye F., 446 Pa. Super. 281, 666 A.2d 734 (1995) (child's caretaker, who not only acted *in loco parentis*, but was previously awarded primary custody of child, had standing to challenge order awarding custody to child's biological mother, although caretaker was a third party who had no familial relationship to child); Rasado v. Diaz, 425 Pa. Super. 155, 624 A.2d 193 (1993) (In custody proceeding in which both natural mother and plaintiff who had lived with natural father and had allegedly raised child sought custody, trial court should have taken testimony on question of plaintiff's *in loco parentis* status before summarily dismissing plaintiff's complaint. Plaintiff's living arrangement with natural father of child warranted categorizing her as "third party" and, ordinarily, the appropriate manner for her to obtain custody of child when natural mother also sought custody would be a dependency proceeding. Plaintiff did not need to pursue child custody via dependency proceeding if she was *in loco parentis* with child, and could use complaint in custody to establish best interest of child).

[31] Spells v. Spells, 250 Pa. Super. 168, 378 A.2d 879 (1977); *see also* Kellogg v. Kellogg, 435 Pa. Super. 581, 646 A.2d 1246 (1994) (In a custody action resulting from the murder of children's father by the mother, the court granted primary physical

parentis," since the status involves two concepts—the assumption of a parental status and the discharge of parental duties—the attainment of "*in loco parentis*" is not automatic upon becoming a stepparent. Rather, a stepparent will be required to establish his or her relationship with the child and demonstrate that his or her interest in visitation should be protected. In addition, it has been held that to deny the stepparent the opportunity to demonstrate the existence of the relationship constitutes error.[32]

While some degree of ill-will normally exists between the contesting parties, it has been held that a custodial parent's suspicion or animosity toward a third party is not alone sufficient to support a denial of partial custody/visitation.[33] Where, however, the degree of hostility between the parties is such that the welfare of the child is endangered, partial custody/visitation has been denied.[34] Even where partial custody/visitation

---

custody to the grandmother and partial custody to the father's first wife after finding that she has standing as an individual and representative interest in the welfare of the children. Finding that first wife of man whose second wife had had him murdered had sincere and sustained interest in children of man and second wife and thus had standing in custody action regarding children was supported by evidence that first wife sought to foster healthy relationship between children and her own children from marriage to man, first wife saw children on regular basis, and first wife had shown and continued to show genuine interest in welfare of children).

[32] *Id.*; *see also* Seger v. Seger, 377 Pa. Super. 391, 547 A.2d 424 (1988) (the court held that the absence of a biological relationship between child and adult, who had assumed the role of child's father, would not preclude granting adult custody or visitation, in view of relationship between child and adult, which was such that to abruptly cut off and destroy relationship would be detrimental to child's welfare).

[33] Commonwealth ex rel. Williams v. Miller, 254 Pa. Super. 227, 395 A.2d 992 (1978); *see also* Commonwealth ex rel. Miller v. Miller, 329 Pa. Super. 248, 478 A.2d 451 (1984) (grandparent visitation ordered based on finding that although a degree of animosity existed, it was not irreconcilable and that grandparents had not acted in any way detrimental to the relationship between the parent and child).

[34] Commonwealth ex rel. Zaffarano v. Genaro, 500 Pa. 256, 455 A.2d 1180 (1983) (reversing Superior Court and finding that ill-will between parties would be injurious to the child if grandparent visitation were allowed); Estate of Haertsch, 437 Pa. Super. 187, 649 A.2d 719 (1994) (court, in fashioning order appointing mother as limited permanent guardian of 25-year-old, mildly mentally retarded daughter, was not required to provide for visitation by father against daughter's wishes, where father appeared to have lost affection of daughter because of his intransigence and lack of consideration for her desires to be with her mother and practice her religion and daughter had capacity to

is granted, opinions often include the admonition that if animosities continue and result in harmful effects on the child, the partial custody/visitation order may be revised or visitation rights completely rescinded.[35] Before denying partial custody/visitation entirely, however, the court will normally attempt to place such conditions on the partial custody/visitation so as to defuse the situation.[36] Thus, where the fear of adverse effects arises from the spectre of a forced partial custody/visitation away from the child's accustomed home, the court may specify the place and conditions of the partial custody/visitation so as to alleviate this danger.[37]

Interestingly, the Superior Court has held that an unmarried biological father, whose parental rights as an "unknown father" were terminated to facilitate his child's 2001 adoption by the maternal grandparents, does not have third-party standing to seek partial custody or visitation of the child based on *in loco parentis* status.[38] The court held biological father stood as a third-party to the child, since a parent whose parental rights have been terminated no longer has the custody rights of a parent. The court found that biological father did not stand *in loco parentis* even though it acknowledges that the adoptive parents had allowed biological father to spend unsupervised time with the child on a regular basis, that he had paid for some of the child's activities, and that the child knew he was her father. However, the child never lived with biological father for an extended period of time in a familial setting, and he did not provide food, clothing or shelter for the child, nor did he provide input into the child's educational, spiritual, mental or emotional well-being, and did

---

make informed decision about person with whom she would live and whether she wished to remain in touch with or visit her father); Bucci v. Bucci, 351 Pa. Super. 457, 506 A.2d 438 (1986) (grandparents were awarded a right to visitation even though there was a four-year period during which they did not see or communicate with the grandchild); Commonwealth ex rel. Flannery v. Sharp, 151 Pa. Super. 612, 30 A.2d 810 (1943).

[35] *See, e.g.,* Commonwealth ex rel. Williams v. Miller, 254 Pa. Super. 227, 385 A.2d 992 (1978); Commonwealth ex rel. Goodman v. Dratch, 192 Pa. Super. 1, 159 A.2d 70 (1960).

[36] *See* § 3.3, *supra.*

[37] Commonwealth ex rel. Williams v. Miller, 254 Pa. Super. 227, 385 A.2d 992 (1978); *see also* § 3.3, *supra.*

[38] Morgan v. Weiser, 923 A.2d 1183 (Pa. Super. 2007).

not provide for medical and dental care for the child. The court found that the evidence showed that the periods biological father spent with the child simply "equated time as a babysitter or caretaker." The court also noted that the adoptive parents (maternal grandparents) did not allow plaintiff to assume parental status.[39]

In *In the Interest of G.C.,*[40] the Pennsylvania Supreme Court ruled that foster parents lack standing to seek or contest awards of custody concerning their foster children. Continued placement of a child in foster care is proper where the child's mother has failed to cooperate with the family service plan. Once a child is adjudicated dependent, the issues of custody and continuation of foster care are determined according to the child's best interests.[41]

However, where a child had been declared dependent and placed in foster care, but returned to her parents on temporary basis, the standard for determining whether to return child to foster care was "clear necessity" standard rather than "best interests" of child.[42]

A child who has been adjudicated dependent may not be separated from his or her parents unless evidence is presented revealing that the separation is clearly necessary. After a child has been separated from his or her parents, a different standard applies, namely, custody will be awarded according to the child's best interests.[43]

In *S. A. v. C. G. R.,* 856 A.2d 1248 (Pa. Super. 2004), the Superior Court held that a woman who with her husband participated in the care of a child born to another woman, as a result of a surrogate parenthood arrangement under which she was inseminated with the husband's sperm, stood *in loco parentis* to the child and thus had standing to pursue custody after she and her husband separated. Husband filed preliminary objections contending that wife lacked standing because she was neither the biological mother nor the adoptive parent of the

---

[39] *Id.*

[40] In the Interest of G.C., 558 Pa. 116, 735 A.2d 1226 (1999).

[41] In Interest of Sweeney, 393 Pa. Super. 437, 574 A.2d 690 (1990).

[42] In Interests of S. S., 438 Pa. Super. 62, 651 A.2d 174 (1994).

[43] In Interests of S. S., 438 Pa. Super. 62, 651 A.2d 174 (1994); In Interest of Paul S., 380 Pa. Super. 476, 552 A.2d 288 (1988).

child. He further contended that wife did not stand *in loco parentis* to the child. Wife filed a response claiming that she did indeed have standing in an action over custody of the child based on her relation to the child as his mother by estoppel and *in loco parentis*. The trial court overruled husband's preliminary objections, concluding that wife was the child's "mother by estoppel," and that even if she were not, she stood *in loco parentis* to the child. The Superior Court affirmed the dismissal of husband's preliminary objections, finding that wife had standing to pursue her custody action by virtue of her *in loco parentis* status to the child. However, the court declined to adopt the legal concept of "motherhood by estoppel" advanced by the trial court since it was unnecessary to do so.

In *J. F. v. D. B.*, 897 A.2d 1261 (Pa. Super. 2006), the Superior Court ruled that a third-party gestational carrier, who was not the biological mother of triplets that she delivered and subsequently removed from the hospital against the biological father's wishes, lacked standing to seek custody of the children. The gestational carrier did not have *in loco parentis* status to seek custody of the triplet boys because she was a nonparent third-party who took the children against the father's wishes. The court noted that, under settled Pennsylvania law, persons other than a child's biological or natural parents are third parties for purposes of custody disputes and may not intervene or assume *in loco parentis* status where the natural parent opposes such intervention. The court cited *B.A. v. E.E.*, 741 A.2d 1227 (Pa. 1999), wherein the Supreme Court held that because a child's natural father sought custody himself, prospective adoptive parents could not stand *in loco parentis* despite consent from the child's natural mother. "There is no law in this Commonwealth that accords standing to a surrogate with no biological connection to the child she seeks to take into her custody. Today, on these facts, we decline to grant such a party standing."

Prior to the enactment of 23 Pa.C.S. §§ 5324 & 5325, the ex-wife of a deceased father (whose new wife had him murdered) had standing to pursue custody of her ex-husband's children who he had with his new wife that were in the custody of maternal grandparents (as new wife was serving a sentence of 25 years to life in prison for the murder). The standing issue focused on ex-wife's sustained, substantial and sincere interest in the welfare of the ex-husband's children with whom she developed a relationship through her own children that were born during her marriage with now deceased ex-husband.[44]

Prior to the enactment of 23 Pa.C.S. §§ 5324 & 5325, in the case of *Silfies v. Webster*,[45] the Superior Court held that a married couple who had exercised extensive visitation with a child for over a year, in anticipation of adopting him, had standing to seek custody or visitation following the child's mother's decision not to go forward with the adoption. The court stated that it had previously held that prospective adoptive parents who had stood *in loco parentis* to a child had standing to commence a legal proceeding involving that child. It further noted that in *Mollander v. Chiodo*, 675 A.2d 753 (Pa. Super. 1996), it specifically held that prospective adoptive parents had standing to maintain an action for custody of the subject child.

However, as the adoptive parents supplant the natural parents and the adopted child attains a position equal to that of a natural son or daughter, the adoptive parents should enjoy the benefit of the parental preference.[46] The Superior Court, while instructing the lower court on the proper burden of proof to be applied on remand, found that as "[a] decree of adoption directs 'that the person proposed to be adopted shall have all the rights of a child and heir to the adopting parent . . . and shall be subject to the duties of a child to him . . .' an adoptive parent stands on the same ground as a natural parent with regard to the burden of proof in a custody dispute."[47]

---

[44] *See* Kellogg v. Kellogg, 646 A.2d 1246 (Pa. Super. 1994); *see also* MacDonald v. Quaglia, 658 A.2d 1343 (Pa. Super. 1995) (Court affirmed granting cousin visitation rights in case against maternal grandmother where mother of the child was killed in a car accident and cousin had shown a sustained, substantial, and sincere interest in the welfare of the child).

[45] Silfies v. Webster, 713 A.2d 639 (Pa. Super. 1998).

[46] *See* In re Adoption of Baby Boy (Benjamin), 452 Pa, 149, 305 A.2d 360 (1973); In re Collins' Estate, 393 Pa. 195, 142 A.2d 178 (1958); Rigler v. Treen, 442 Pa. Super. 533, 660 A.2d 111 (1995) (Parents of child's biological father had standing to seek visitation with child despite termination of father's parental rights and adoption of child by stepfather); *but see* 23 Pa.C.S. § 5326.

[47] Commonwealth ex rel. Michael R. and Kristen L.R. v. Robert R.R., 293 Pa. Super. 18, 437 A.2d 969 (1981).

Further, a natural grandparent's right to qualify for standing under 23 Pa.C.S. §§ 5324 & 5325 and an individual's right to quality for standing under Section 5324(1) (*in loco parentis*) automatically terminates upon the adoption of the child.[48]

LOWER COURT CASES
Berks County

Imperial v. Light, 89 Berks Co. L. J. 7 (C.C.P. 1997) (Trial court held that ill-will between the parties can constitute ground to deny grandparent visitation; the court must determine whether the detriment to the child caused by the friction between his or her parent and grandparents will outweigh any benefit to the child which arises from a continuing relationship with his or her grandparents. "It is not the role of the judicial system to repair relationships between adult children and their parents over the objection of one of the parties."); *see also Commonwealth ex rel. Nardo v. O'Bryne*, 83 York 169 (1970); *Posin v. Rothkopf*, 49 Wash. Co. 4 (1968); *Commonwealth ex rel. Goodwin v. Goodwin*, 82 Montg. 187 (1980).

Columbia County

C.L.A. v. P.K. and G.M., C.P. Columbia County, No. 2018-CV-0000348-CU (C.C.P. April 2, 2019), *aff'd.*, Memorandum Decision, No. 632 MDA 2019 (Pa. Super. March 16, 2020) (Partner, who was mother's former same-sex partner, had *in loco parentis* standing as to their child. The court cited to *A.J.B. v. A.G.B.*, 180 A.3d 1263 (Pa. Super. 2018) and *C.G. v. J.H.*, 172 A.3d 43 (Pa. Super. 2017), and determined that partner performed parental duties and participated in medical, religious, speech therapy, and other educational decisions for the child. The trial court credited the time that partner, mother, and the child lived together; their intent to jointly raise the child as a family; the partner's presence for the child's birth; mother's decision to give the child the partner's last name on his birth certificate; partner's payment of expenses for both mother and the child; partner's performance of parental duties; mother's express written intent for partner to take the child as her own; and mother's recordings of the child expressing his parental affection for partner as evidence supporting its determination of *in loco parentis* status for the partner).

Elk County

Donachy v. Thompson, C.P. Elk County, No. 2010-870 (C.C.P. 2011) (Trial court ruled that the plaintiff-boyfriend did not establish that he stood *in loco parentis* to the

---

[48] 23 Pa.C.S. § 5326; E.T.S. v. S.L.H., 54 A.3d 880 (Pa. Super. 2012).

child where the evidence showed that he was only intermittently involved in the child's life and had not assumed parental duties. The child in this case was born to both defendants, the child's natural parents, who were not married. Plaintiff-boyfriend had a relationship with the mother before she became pregnant with the child. After the child's birth in 2005, boyfriend and mother again became romantically involved and lived in each other's residences until 2006. Boyfriend's relationship with mother continued on an intermittent basis for approximately 4 years. The court noted that the child did not know the identity of his natural father. However, father continuously paid child support to mother. After their relationship ended, boyfriend petitioned for custody rights to the child, claiming *in loco parentis* status. Defendants, the natural parents, argued that boyfriend lacked standing to assert a custody complaint. The court dismissed boyfriend's petition, noting that a third-party seeking custody rights to a child must establish that he stands *in loco parentis* to the child. In *loco parentis* status may be established through the assumption of a parental status and the discharge of parental duties. The third party must show evidence of a sustained, substantial and sincere interest in the welfare of the child. The court concluded that boyfriend did not offer clear and convincing evidence of *in loco parentis* status. During the child's infancy, boyfriend interacted with the child and, at times, fed and played with him. But mother did most of the parenting. There was no evidence that boyfriend maintained a material relationship with the child during the periods he was not dating mother. Boyfriend did not present any evidence that he had paid any amount toward the child's living expenses or necessities. The court concluded that while boyfriend cared for the child and was somewhat involved in his activities, he was not involved with essential parenting functions on a day-to-day basis. Parenting in general and *in loco parentis* in particular requires consistent and unyielding involvement with a child's daily life, not sporadic interludes of the pursuit of pleasant pastimes such as trips to the park or bike-riding).

Huntingdon County

Shoup v. Cook, C.P. Huntingdon County, No. 2006-0398 (C.C.P. 2014) (In a dispute involving the custody rights of natural father and stepfather, the trial court held that stepfather should have primary custody during the school year and the parties would have alternating custody during the summer months and other holidays. Mother and father of the parties' 12-year-old child entered into a custody agreement on May 22, 2006. Mother died in 2012. Stepfather filed a praecipe to amend the caption, which substituted stepfather as the defendant in the case, replacing mother. The trial court awarded primary custody with stepfather, citing *Charles v. Stehlik*, 560 Pa. 334, 744 A.2d 1255 (2000) (Supreme Court affirmed primary custody to stepfather, stating that, unlike other states, in Pennsylvania it was not necessary for a party *in loco parentis* to establish that the biological parent was unfit before he or she could obtain primary custody). The court noted that stepfather had been the primary caretaker since mother's death and he had excelled in that role by attending to the medical needs of the child, who had significant medical issues. On the other hand, the natural father could not identify many of the child's physicians and had had limited involvement with the child's education and teachers. Stepfather had been the stabilizing force in the child's life and a change of residential custody would be detrimental. The court also noted that stepfather's fiancée had been a positive influence in the child's life, assisting with child-care and helping the child with his homework).

Jefferson County

L.M. v. D.W. v. L.L.W. and S.J.W., C.P. Jefferson County, No. 1100-2007-CD (C.C.P. May 26, 2017), *aff'd*, Memorandum Decision, No. 959 WDA 2017 (Pa. Super. January 5, 2018) (Trial court Order granted grandparents standing *in loco parentis* pursuant to 23 Pa.C.S. § 5324(2). Grandparents asserted that the child had been in their care seven days every two weeks during her entire life. Essentially, paternal grandparents asserted that they had stood *in loco parentis* to the child since her birth. A parent, through inaction, may acquiesce to the development of an *in loco parentis* relationship. By failing to act while grandparents raised her daughter, mother acted in a manner consistent with her consent to their *in loco parentis* status. Although mother testified that she never gave express permission to grandparents to care for the child, she admitted that while the child was in their care, grandparents attended to the child's daily physical, emotional, and financial needs. For approximately two years the child resided primarily with father in the home of paternal grandparents. The court noted that the grandparents here were significantly more than glorified babysitters. Rather, grandparents attended to the child's daily physical, emotional, and financial needs, and they assumed an enduring role that was more significant than a frequent caretaker. Grandparents had shared with mother the parenting responsibility for the entirety of the child's life. The court observed that the record confirmed that grandparents fed, bathed, and entertained the child daily, attended parent–teacher conferences, and transported the child to medical appointments and school. Grandparents also assisted the child financially and they consistently had been a stabilizing force in the child's life and ensured her safety).

Lawrence County

Whetzel v. Whetzel, C.P. Lawrence County, No. 11491 of 2008, C.A. (C.C.P. September 1, 2016) (Maternal grandfather did not possess *in loco parentis* status in part because mother never voluntarily consented to same. One cannot place himself *in loco parentis* in defiance of the parents' wishes and the parent/child relationship. The trial court explained that although an argument could be made that maternal grandfather had standing to seek primary physical custody because he was granted such custody pursuant to an Order of Court, that Order was entered as a result of the penalty provisions relating to mother's not complying with the relocation statute. Also, the Order was temporary in the respect that it set an expedited hearing, and primary physical custody was regained by mother when the court vacated the Order. The court did not disagree that maternal grandfather had in the past served as primary caretaker of the children and performed parental duties. However, the issue before the court was whether maternal grandfather now had standing to seek primary physical custody based on his *in loco parentis* status. The court again noted that because mother had consistently objected to maternal grandfather's having primary physical custody, maternal grandfather's standing extended only to partial, and not primary, physical custody).

Montgomery County

C.B. v. L.L.D., 152 Montg. Co. L. Rep. 65 (C.C.P. 2014) (Trial court determined that the live-in girlfriend of a child's grandfather did not have standing to file for custody of the child when she did not stand *in loco parentis*. Defendants were mother and father of the child at issue, age 4. Plaintiff testified that while the child lived with her and maternal grandfather, she bought him clothing and toys, and spent a couple of days with him. Plaintiff testified that she placed the child in summer camp, hired a babysitter to pick him up after school, and placed him in day care. Plaintiff also testified that she paid for the child to have health insurance in Pennsylvania. Plaintiff did not live with the child in a natural-parent family setting, and did not develop a relationship with the child as a result of the participation and acquiescence of a natural parent. There was no evidence that mother or father consented to plaintiff's having a parental role in the child's life).

Northampton County

M.W. v. L.W. and W.B., 56 Northampton Co. Rep. 960 (C.C.P. 2011) (Trial court awarded stepfather supervised visitation of his stepdaughter, finding that stepfather had standing to petition for visitation under the doctrine of *in loco parentis*, and stepfather's visitation of stepdaughter served the child's best interest. The court initially noted that in visitation disputes, Pennsylvania courts treat stepparents as unrelated third parties. As such, a stepparent may not petition for visitation with an unrelated child unless he can demonstrate that he has attained *in loco parentis* status. Where a stepparent "seeks not to supplant the natural parent, but only to maintain his relationship with the child through reasonable visitation or partial custody, his or her burden to establish standing is less onerous." The court found that here, stepfather had attained *in loco parentis* status with respect to his stepdaughter, as stepfather testified that he agreed to raise, and actually raised, the stepdaughter as his own child from her birth in 1999 until mother and stepfather separated in 2005. For approximately 2 years thereafter, stepfather was stepdaughter's primary caregiver subject only to mother's weekly periods of partial physical custody. The court rejected the natural father's argument that stepfather failed to attain *in loco parentis* status because father was unaware that stepfather had assumed and discharged parental responsibilities, and that stepfather failed to attain such status because father did not explicitly consent to stepfather's assumption and discharge of parental responsibilities. The court found both arguments unpersuasive, relying on *McDonel v. Sohn*, 762 A.2d 1101, 1106 (Pa. Super. 2000). "Because father failed to object to or otherwise interfere with stepfather's assumption and discharge of parental responsibilities when such assumption and discharge actually occurred, and because father failed to object to or otherwise interfere with the creation of a parent/child relationship between stepfather and [stepdaughter] when such relationship was developing, father may not now claim that stepfather attained *in loco parentis* in defiance of his wishes.").

Beebe v. Peluffo, C. P. Northampton County, No. C-0048-CV-2009-8589 (C.C.P. 2010) (court held that in order to assert a claim for custody or visitation, a third-party, or non-biological parent must first achieve standing pursuant to the theory of *in loco parentis*. In order to establish standing *in loco parentis*, a petitioner, in this case the former paramour of defendant, must demonstrate the assumption of both parental status and the discharge of parental duties with respect to the subject child or children, and the natural parent's agreement with or acquiescence to the same during the relevant period. The former paramour of defendant sought partial physical custody of defendant's natural daughter. The trial court ruled that plaintiff failed to demonstrate a bond with the minor child sufficient to accord him standing to bring the current custody dispute pursuant to the doctrine of *in loco parentis*).

§ 6.3. THIRD PARTY CUSTODY – MERITS OF THE CASE

Once a third party enters the court after clearing the standing hurdle, having been determined *in loco parentis*, the person is not elevated to natural parent status and remains a third party.[49] In Pennsylvania, under 23 Pa.C.S. § 5327, there is now a codified presumption that exists in cases concerning primary physical custody between a parent and a third party. Under Section 5327(b), in cases involving a parent and a third party, there is a presumption that custody shall be awarded to the parent and the presumption can be rebutted only by clear and convincing evidence.[50]

The new statute is silent as to whether there is a presumption when a third party is seeking partial physical custody.[51]

When a third party brings a custody action against a parent, the court shall consider the factors enumerated under 23 Pa.C.S. § 5328 in making a custody determination. When confronted with the task of choosing

---

[49] *See* Kellogg v. Kellogg, 646 A.2d 1246 (Pa. Super. 1994); Jacob v. Shultz-Jacob, 923 A.2d 473 (Pa. Super. 2007).

[50] 23 Pa.C.S. § 5327(b); *see also* V.B. and C.B. v. J.E.B. and C.C., 55 A.3d 1193 (Pa. Super. 2012). M.J.S. v. B.B. v. B.B., 172 A.3d 651 (Pa. Super. 2018).

[51] *But see* R.L. v. M.A., 209 A.3d 391 (Pa. Super. 2019) (Section 5327 also applies when third party is seeking equal (50/50) physical custody).

between parents and third parties, courts have long maintained that the best interests of the child remain the paramount concern.[52]

In any child custody dispute involving a non-parent, an initial determination must be made as to which parties merit parental status. Natural parents are obviously accorded parental status and the fact that a parent lives with the child's grandparents, who will be caring for the child while the parent works or attends school, does not alter his or her parental standing.[53] Likewise, the desire expressed by a natural parent not seeking custody for him or herself, that the child be placed in the custody of

---

[52] Albright v. Commonwealth ex rel. Fetters, 491 Pa. 320, 421 A.2d 157 (1980); Ellerbe v. Hooks, 490 Pa. 363, 416 A.2d 512 (1980); In re Snellgrose, 432 Pa. 158, 247 A.2d 596 (1968); Dorsey v. Freeman, 438 Pa. Super. 236, 652 A.2d 352 (1994) (In any custody dispute, whether case involves two natural parents or parent and third party, court's overriding concern is always to determine what will serve best interests of child; this question may never be subordinated to other considerations, such as fundamental rights and fair play); *see also* MacDonald v. Quaglia, 442 Pa. Super. 149, 658 A.2d 1343 (1995) (In visitation cases, burden on third party is to show only that it is in child's best interest to give some time to third party. Trial court's determination that it was in best interest of child to have visitation with cousin on alternating Saturdays was supported by evidence that cousin and mother were raised in same household, that cousin considered herself to be sister to mother and aunt to child, that cousin had frequent contact with child until four days before mother's death, that cousin spent more time with mother than did maternal grandmother, that cousin was denied contact with child because maternal grandmother did not want to associate with mother's family, and cousin was child's link to his mother and his heritage); In Johnson v. Diesinger, 404 Pa. Super. 41, 589 A.2d 1160 (1990), the Superior Court held that partial custody and visitation rights given to the grandmother pursuant to now-repealed 23 Pa.C.S. § 5311 were not in the best interests of the children, for the order would interfere with the parent–child relationship; Comm. ex rel. Williams v. Miller, 254 Pa. Super. 227, 385 A.2d 992 (1978); Commonwealth ex rel. Kraus v. Kraus, 185 Pa. Super. 167, 138 A.2d 225 (1958); Commonwealth ex rel. Shamenek v. Allen, 179 Pa. Super. 169, 116 A.2d 336 (1955).

[53] In Porch v. Porch, 327 Pa. Super. 346, 475 A.2d 831 (1984), the children lived with the father's grandparents and the father resided next door. The court, nevertheless, found that custody would actually rest with the father and that he was merely relying, albeit heavily, on his parents as caretakers. The court, therefore, held that the custody dispute was between the parents, and found the burden of proof to be equal. In re Custody of Scott, 288 Pa. Super. 162, 431 A.2d 338 (1981); McCann v. McCann, 270 Pa. Super. 171, 411 A.2d 234 (1979); Haraschak v. Haraschak, 268 Pa. Super. 173, 407 A.2d 886 (1979).

a particular third party will not cause the standard applicable to parents to act in favor of that third party.[54]

In a custody dispute between a parent and nonparent, the burden of proof and of persuasion is on the nonparent, and that burden is heavy; however, the hearing court may award custody to the nonparent where the best interests of the child will be clearly served by such decision; the natural parent has a prima facie right to custody of child, but the natural parent's right may be forfeited if convincing reasons appear that the child's best interests will be served by awarding custody to someone else.[55]

In *Albright v. Commonwealth ex rel. Fetters*,[56] the Pennsylvania Supreme Court found that the combination of a stable third party home, a chaotic marital history of the parent, and the separation of siblings doctrine combined to produce convincing reasons supporting a third-party custody order. In *Albright*, in spite of a finding of fitness regarding the natural parent, where the weight of the factors favoring third-party

---

[54] Palmer v. Tokarek, 279 Pa. Super. 458, 421 A.2d 289 (1980).

[55] E.A.L. v. L.J.W., 443 Pa. Super. 573, 662 A.2d 1109 (1995); *see also* B.A. v. E.E. ex rel. C.E., 559 Pa. 545, 741 A.2d 1227 (1999); Argenio v. Fenton, 703 A.2d 1042 (Pa. Super. 1997); J.A.L. v. E.P.H., A.2d 1314 (Pa. Super. 1996); *but see* Rowles v. Rowles 542 Pa. 443, 668 A.2d 126 (1995).

[56] 491 Pa. 320, 421 A.2d 157 (1980); In re David L.C., 376 Pa. Super. 615, 546 A.2d 694 (1988) (award of child custody to child's 64-year-old-great-grandmother was proper. Great-grandmother had been providing child with homelife bounded by stability, care, and natural love, and court could properly place greater weight on bonding, which had already taken place between child and great-grandmother, where natural mother wanted custody so that she could place the child immediately in a closed adoption situation. Although the court will not ordinarily outweigh the natural parent's interest in the custody of his or her child owing to psychological bonding between the child and a third party, the trial court felt the prospect of a closed adoption with termination of all ties with blood relatives militated towards allowing the child to remain with his great-grandmother with whom he had established strong psychological bonding. The Superior Court affirmed, and held that although a third party must carry a heavy burden in custody proceeding to prove that he can best provide for child, it is not necessary to show that the natural parent is unfit, since factors other than fitness of the natural parent must also be weighed).

custody were sufficient to overcome the prevailing standard, the child was placed with the third party.[57]

In *Charles v. Stehlik*, 744 A.2d 1255 (Pa. 2000), the Pennsylvania Supreme Court held that it was in the best interests of the child at issue to award custody to his stepfather rather than his biological father following the death of mother, where the child had lived with stepfather since he was an infant and where uprooting the child would likely cause severe psychological trauma. Acknowledging that the biological father would normally be given custody, the court stressed its continued adherence to the belief that the best interest of the child can justify a non-parent custody award, even though the biological parent has not been shown to be unfit.

In *Jones v. Boring Jones*, 884 A.2d 915 (Pa. Super. 2005), the Superior Court, using a best interest of the child analysis, ruled that the non-biological parent of a lesbian couple was entitled to primary physical custody of twins born to her partner during the parties' relationship. The court found that the nonbiological parent's evidence that it was in the children's best interest to live with her tipped the scale that had weighed in favor of biological mother's *prima facie* right to custody. The court declared: "Once it is established that someone who is not the biological parent is *in loco parentis*, that person does not need to establish that the biological parent is unfit, but instead must establish by clear and convincing evidence that it is in the best interest of the children to maintain that relationship or be with that person." The court cited as authority *Ellerbe v. Hooks*, 416 A.2d 512 (Pa. 1980), and *Charles v. Stehlik*, 744 A.2d 1255 (Pa. 2000). Here, "while the scale was tipped in favor of the mother, the partner produced clear and convincing reasons to even the scale then tip it on her side." The court explained that the partner did not establish that the mother was unfit, and was not required to do so, but did clearly and convincingly establish that the children would be better off with her as the primary custodian and that the children's relationship with both parties would be better fostered if she had custody.

---

[57] *E.g.*, Albright v. Commonwealth ex rel. Fetters, 491 Pa. 320, 421 A.2d 157 (1980); Ellerbe v. Hooks, 490 Pa. 363, 416 A.2d 512 (1980).

In *McDonel v. Sohn*, 762 A.2d 1101 (Pa. Super. 2000), the Superior Court ruled that a child's aunt and uncle may obtain primary custody of a child even though the natural father wanted custody for himself. While acknowledging that father enjoyed a *prima facie* right to custody as against third parties, the court agreed with the trial court that the aunt and uncle had overcome the presumption in favor of father. The court cited the testimony of the psychologist assigned to the case that it would be in the child's best interests for the aunt and uncle to have primary custody. The psychologist had based his recommendation on the relatives' involvement in the child's life since her birth.

LOWER COURT CASES
Adams County

Smith v. Haar, C.P. Adams County, No. 11-S-1162 (C.C.P. 2012) (Trial court held that an adoptive mother's paramour had no standing to seek custody, even if he had established *in loco parentis* status before the adoption. Section 5326 of the new Child Custody Act terminates the right to seek custody of any party to a child when a child has been adopted by anyone other than a stepparent, grandparent or great-grandparent. Section 5326 extinguished the custody standing of adoptive mother's paramour, where he relied on his *in loco parentis* status prior to the adoption. Paramour filed a complaint for custody, alleging *in loco parentis* standing, seeking shared physical and legal custody of the children. Adoptive mother filed preliminary objections, alleging that plaintiff did not have standing to file the custody action under the new Custody Act, 23 Pa.C.S. § 5326. Mother argued that under § 5326, the paramour's rights to seek physical or legal custody based on *in loco parentis* were automatically terminated after adoption. Paramour argued that he still could assert common-law *in loco parentis* standing since it was not repealed by the Custody Act. Paramour believed that § 5326 applied only to grandparents and that his *in loco parentis* status established prior to the adoption was sufficient to confer standing. The trial court found that paramour did not have standing to pursue custody of the children adopted by mother. Paramour's assertion of his right to pursue custody of the two children under the common law doctrine of *in loco parentis* could not circumvent the adoption provisions of the new Custody Act. "The effect of 23 Pa.C.S. § 5326 to terminate rights of third parties at the time of adoption cannot be circumvented by espousing the common-law doctrine of *in loco parentis*." Upon adoption, § 5326 terminates any custody rights that had been granted under § 5324 prior to the adoption of the child by an individual other than a stepparent, grandparent or great-grandparent).

Naill v. Naill, 31 Adams Leg. J. 137 (C.C.P. 1989) (Although parenthood is an important consideration in the best interests of a child, it is not determinative and other factors that have a significant impact on the well-being of a child can justify a finding in favor of the non-parent, even though the parent has not been shown to be unfit; thus, despite the father's incarceration, custody of children is awarded to their stepmother where the best interests of the children would not be served by awarding custody to the mother).

Berks County

Hine v. Wells, 102 Berks Co. L. J. 130 (C.C.P. 2010) (In a custody dispute between mother and foster parents, the trial court recognized that the best interest of the child governed, but also that there was an extra burden on the foster parents, as they were not the natural parents of the child. Even before the proceedings started, the evidentiary scale is tipped hard to the biological parents' side. The court noted that where the custody dispute is between a biological parent and a third party, the burden of proof is not evenly balanced. In such instances, the parents have a prima facie right to custody, which will be forfeited only if convincing reasons appear that the child's best interests will be served by an award to the third party. Thus, the court held, even before the proceedings start, the evidentiary scale is tipped, and tipped hard, to the biological parents' side, citing *Jones v. Jones*, 884 A.2d 915, 917 (Pa. Super. 2005)).

Chambers v. Chambers, 97 Berks Co. L. J. 225 (C.C.P. 2005) (Where the child's adult brother had *in loco parentis* status and where it was in the child's best interests for him to live with his adult brother rather than with his father, the adult brother was entitled to sole legal and primary physical custody of the child. Brother's stable home and regular contact with the child supported an award of custody to him, where father's contact with the child had been irregular for the past seven years, and he was not able to provide as much stability. The court observed that the brother and the child at issue had a very good relationship, and the brother had been a constant in the child's life for many years. The child was thriving in school, and his continuation in the same school district was a factor the court found to be critical in this case. In addition, the child expressed a desire to continue living with his older brother. Thus, the court found that third parties can be awarded custody over a parent if they can provide the more stable home that meets the child's best interests).

Moyer v. Smith, 85 Berks L. J. 241 (C.C.P. 1993) (Absent a prima facie right to custody, a third party lacks standing to seek custody of a child as against the natural parents. Plaintiffs, half-brother and sister to a minor child, may amend the petition for custody/ visitation of the child to establish standing based upon abuse of the child or the contention that they have stood *in loco parentis* to the child). *Miller v. Kehl*, 84 Berks L. J. 127 (1992) (Trial court held that the child's great aunt and uncle overcame the parent's prima facie right to custody by showing that the child's interests would best be served by awarding custody to them. The court based its conclusion on the fact the parents had previously relinquished primary physical custody to the aunt and uncle, and since then had made no convincing attempts to retrieve the child. Also, the aunt and uncle had been the primary care givers since birth and best able to provide a stable environment).

Carbon County

Eckhart v. Gibbon, C.P. Carbon County, No. 97-1767 (C.C.P. 1997) (Plaintiff's petition for child custody was dismissed by the court for lack of standing, because plaintiff was a third party and failed to allege sufficient facts to establish that he stood *in loco parentis* to the minor children. The court concluded that plaintiff's petition failed to establish the necessary *in loco parentis* relationship because he merely alleged that the children had lived with him for several years and that he was the only parent to which the children related. Those were insufficient facts to support plaintiff's challenge to the custody of the natural parents, the court said. The petition contained allegations that plaintiff had *in loco parentis* status, which would have given him standing to seek custody as a third party. The court noted that "in the area of child custody, principles of standing have been applied with particular scrupulousness because they serve not only to protect the interest of the court system by assuring that actions are litigated by appropriate parties, but also to prevent intrusion into the protected domain of the family by those who are merely strangers, however well-meaning.").

D.C.M. v. T.M.M., 12 Carbon L. J. 182 (C.C.P. 1990) (A court will make no distinction between natural and adoptive parent in analysis of what is in the child's best interest. Both stand equally before the court and each bears the affirmative burden of proving that an award of custody to him or her would be in the best interest of the child).

Centre County

Greenland v. Smith, C. P. Centre County, No. 2005-3568 (C.C.P. 2006) (Trial court held that the maternal aunt and uncle of the children at issue had standing to seek custody where the children had been under their care since their father's death. The court observed that "Pennsylvania courts generally find standing in third-party visitation and custody cases only where the Legislature specifically authorizes the cause of action or where the party stands *in loco parentis* to the child." The court acknowledged that the third parties that have been accorded standing to pursue primary custody have typically had actual custody at the time the action was brought. "However, standing determinations ultimately turn on which is in the best interest of the child. The Pennsylvania Superior Court has recognized that even though the requirement of in loco parentis status for third parties seeking child custody rights is often stated as though it were a rigid rule, 'it is important to view the standard in light of the purpose of standing principles generally: to ensure that actions are brought only by those with a genuine, substantial interest. When so viewed, it is apparent that the showing necessary to establish *in loco parentis* status must in fact be flexible and dependent upon the particular facts of the case.'" The court noted that here, plaintiff and defendant lived together with the children for a period of time prior to marriage, during which time defendant took on household and parenting responsibilities associated with the usual caretaking of children. Moreover, the parties lived together as a family for one and one-half years, and the children established a relationship with defendant when they were very young. "An important factor in determining whether a third party has standing is whether the third party lived with the child and the natural parent in a family setting, irrespective of its traditional or non-traditional composition, and developed a relationship with the child as a result of the participation and acquiescence of the natural parent.").

Clearfield County

Clark v. Boal, C.P. Clearfield Co., No. 95-862-CD (C.C.P. 1997) (Trial court held that, despite evidence that the mother was unstable and exhibited poor judgment, custody of the child was awarded, under the presumption favoring the mother's right to custody, to the mother instead of third-party plaintiffs. Instead of following the plurality decision in *Rowles v. Rowles*, 668 A.2d 126 (Pa. 1995), in which the state Supreme Court had abandoned a natural parent's presumed right to custody against third parties, the court applied the standard set forth in *Ellerbe v. Hooks*, 416 A.2d 512 (Pa. 1980). The court stated that *Rowles*, which held that parents should not automatically have the upper hand in custody cases, was not the law in Pennsylvania. However, relying on the *Ellerbe* presumption granting the mother as a natural parent a prima facie right to custody of her own child, it returned custody to the mother based on evidence that she met minimal DPW standards, while granting partial custody right to plaintiffs).

Lawrence County

Schmidt v. Brown and Rosta, C.P. Lawrence County, No. 11700 of 2009, C.A. (C.C.P. 2011) (Trial court awarded legal and primary physical custody of the minor child to a third party (neighbors) subject to the natural parents' partial custody, because the natural parents were unable to provide a stable, supportive environment. The Schmidts (neighbors) frequently babysat Reilly (age 10) and her siblings, and they became especially attached to Reilly, as her parents would leave her with the Schmidts for extended visits when they felt the same was necessary. In 2005, mother moved to Arizona and from that point until 2008, Reilly moved back and forth from her mother's residence in Arizona to the Schmidts' residence. In 2008, Reilly and her older sister permanently moved in with the Schmidts. Father lived in Lawrence County but did not have primary custody of any of his children. In 2009, the Schmidts filed a complaint for custody of Reilly, stating that Reilly had moved 14 times in three years, and lacked a stable, supportive environment. The Schmidts were granted temporary physical custody of Reilly pending a custody conciliation conference taking place. In December 2009, pursuant to a temporary custody order, the Schmidts were granted sole legal and primary physical custody of Reilly, subject to the partial custody rights of mother and father. A custody trial was held on May 3, 2011. The trial court awarded legal custody and primary physical custody of Reilly to the Schmidts, subject to the partial custody rights of father and mother. The court initially acknowledged that when a custody dispute is between a natural parent and a third party, the burden of proof "is heavily placed on the third party who wishes to overcome the natural parent's prima facie right to custody." The paramount concern is the best interest of the child. Here, the court found that Reilly suffered "an indescribable trauma" upon being abruptly and permanently separated from her mother in 2008. Although it was mother and father's choice to leave Reilly with the Schmidts based on their belief that it was in her best interest, they now had to face the "consequences which naturally result from such action." The court looked to the Schmidts with "profound admiration and awe" and found that they cared for Reilly as if she were their own and "never asked for anything in return." The court believed that awarding mother primary custody would be a "repetition of the emotional disturbance Reilly unfortunately suffered three years ago.").

Lehigh County

Keels v. Brockington, C.P. Lehigh County, No. 97-FC-24 (C.C.P. 1997) (Trial court ruled that plaintiff had standing to seek custody of the child at issue as against the child's aunts, where plaintiff has shown interest in the welfare of the child both before and after the death of the child's mother and where the child has expressed a preference for plaintiff. The court denied the defendant's motion to dismiss and awarded custody to plaintiff, the family friend. The court held that a party seeking to establish standing in a custody dispute between parties must demonstrate by clear and convincing evidence that he or she has shown a "sustained, substantial and sincere interest in the welfare of the child," relying on *Kellog v. Kellog*, 646 A.2d 1246 (Pa. Super. 1994). The court determined that plaintiff made the requisite showing in that she has had an ongoing relationship with the child since the child and her mother had lived with plaintiff).

Luzerne County

In Re S.P. and A.P., 87 Luzerne Leg. Rep. 62 (C.C.P. 1997) (Trial court declared that a third party, seeking to establish standing in a custody case against another third party, is required to prove by clear and convincing evidence that he or she has shown sustained, substantial and sincere interest in the welfare of the child. The children, aged eight, had been removed from their parents' custody and placed in permanent foster care. In allowing intervention, the court referred to *Kellogg v. Kellogg*, 646 A.2d 1246 (Pa. Super. 1994), in which opposing third parties sought to establish standing in a custody action. The court in *Kellogg* held that the third party is required to prove by clear and convincing evidence that he or she has shown sustained, substantial and sincere interest in the welfare of the child. The court ruled that the aunt and uncle's sustained, substantial and sincere interest in the children, as brought out by their testimony, was sufficient to award them standing).

Monroe County

Farnon v. Peters, C. P. Monroe County, No. 9772 Civil 2005 (C.C.P. 2006) (Trial court held that the children's paternal aunt had standing to seek custody of the children where the aunt had lived with and helped raise the children for several years.

The court denied mother's preliminary objections, concluding that the aunt met the legal requirements of standing to seek court-ordered contact with the children. A third party may have standing in custody proceedings if he or she has shown a prima facie right to custody. This right may be established if the party has stood *in loco parentis* to the child by assuming a parental status and discharging parental duties. An important factor is whether the third-party has lived with the child and the natural parent in a family setting, irrespective of its traditional and nontraditional composition, and developed a relationship with the child as a result of the participation and acquiescence of the natural parent. In addition, where only limited custody rights are sought, the limited nature of the intrusion into the biological family must be considered in deciding whether standing has been made out. Here, the evidence indicated that the aunt had lived with both children for several years and had cared for them on a daily basis. She had also assisted grandmother with the responsibility of raising them. The court noted that mother was a teenager when she gave birth to both children and that both the aunt and the grandmother provided significant assistance in caring for the children. "Once this close bond is created with the mother's approval between an aunt and her nieces, the law recognizes the right of the aunt to assert a request for custodial rights.").

Buzzard v. Griffin, C.P. Monroe County, No. 235 DR 2000 (C.C.P. 2000) (Trial court found that although the defendant was not the biological or adoptive mother of plaintiff's children, she did have *in loco parentis* standing to pursue custody where she lived with the children and their father in a family setting and developed a relationship with the children, with father's approval. The court noted that the *in loco parentis* basis for standing recognizes "that the need to guard the family from intrusions by third parties and to protect the rights of the natural parent must be tempered by the paramount need to protect the child's best interest. Thus, while it is presumed that a child's best interest is served by maintaining the family's privacy and autonomy, that presumption must give way where the child has established strong psychological bonds with a person who, although not a biological parent, has lived with the child and has provided care, and nurture, and affection, assuming in the child's eye a stature like that of a parent. Where such a relationship is shown, our courts recognize that the child's best interest requires that the third party be granted standing so as to have the opportunity to litigate fully the issue of whether that relationship should be maintained even over a natural parent's objections.").

Parton v. Parton, 36 D.&C. 4th 241 (Monroe Co. 1996) (Trial court held that where stepfather lived with and cared for his stepsons for over five years, he attained *in loco parentis* status, and thus had standing to sue for partial physical custody. In support of its decision, the court noted that stepfather had lived with and cared for the boys for over five years, and had provided them with financial and emotional support. The court remarked that stepfather was one of the most stable influences in the boys' lives. The court noted that the law is constantly changing in this area, referring to the recent case of *Rowles v. Rowles*, 668 A.2d 126 (Pa. 1995), which ruled that natural parents do not necessarily have a prima facie right to their children—third parties can fight for custody as well. Citing several cases including *Gradwell v. Strausser*, 416 Pa. Super. 118, 610 A.2d 999 (1992), the court said that if a third party can establish *in loco parentis* status, he or she would have standing to fight for custody).

Northumberland County

Dreese v. Dreese, 70 Northumberland Leg. J. 99 (C.C.P. 1998) (Trial court awarded father custody of his minor son following mother's death, despite mother's expressed desire that the child reside with her second husband, because the son's best interests would be served by awarding father custody. The court noted that the fact that a child has not lived with a parent for a considerable length of time will not alone defeat that parent's right to custody. The court also determined that it was not bound by mother's expressed desire that her son reside with her second husband, despite the fact that son expressed the same desire. The court reasoned that son's desire to remain with mother's second husband constituted an attempt to comply with his mother's wishes).

Warren County

T.J.M. v. N.H.M., C.P. Warren County, No. A.D. 204 of 2018 (C.C.P. November 27, 2018), *aff'd*, Memorandum Decision, No. 57 WDA 2019 (Pa. Super. July 15, 2019) (Trial court awarded father and maternal aunt shared legal custody of father's child with mother. The court awarded maternal aunt primary physical custody during the school year and father partial physical custody every other weekend. The trial court addressed the burden of proof required, given that maternal aunt is a third party, and each of the custody factors pursuant to 23 Pa.C.S. § 5328(a) on the record at the close of the hearing. Maternal aunt, as a third-party, had met her burden of proof for an award of primary physical custody. The court noted that the child had gone months without seeing his father for whatever reason, and had been cared for exclusively by maternal aunt. To completely disrupt the stability and consistency in the child's life was determined, by clear and convincing evidence, not to be in the child's best interest).

York County

Lamka v. Lamka, 112 York Leg. Rec. 168 (C.C.P. 1999) (Stepmother does have standing to intervene in order to substantiate her alleged *in loco parentis* status despite the fact that she is an unrelated third party and the parents had reached an agreement regarding their custody rights. "The Court cannot deny Stepmother the opportunity to substantiate her alleged *in loco parentis* status despite the fact that she is an unrelated third party to a custody action. Whether one achieves the status of *in loco parentis* is a factual determination within the trial court's realm and as such, "the hearing court must permit a step-parent to establish what his relationship is and to demonstrate that his interest in visitation is permitted." *Spells v. Spells*, 250 Pa. Super. 168, 378 A.2d 879 (1977). We believe we must permit Stepmother the opportunity to present evidence as to her relationship with the child to resolve the threshold question of her standing to intervene in this matter.").

T. A. v. J. L. and B. B., 111 York Leg. Rec. 184 (C.C.P. 1998) (Where petitioner had no parental relationship with the children, he did not have such an interest to be granted standing to pursue partial custody and therefore lacked standing to bring the action. Relying on *Ken R. on Behalf of C.R. v. Arthur Z.*, 546 Pa. 49, 53, 682 A.2d 1267, 1270 (1996), the court held that: "Petitioner does not have an immediate interest in this custody case because his interest in maintaining a relationship with these children does not fall within the zone of interests protected by the legislature. Since Petitioner does not have an immediate interest in this case, he is without standing to pursue partial custody or visitation of the children.").

Chapter 7

BURDEN OF PROOF

§ 7.1. Generally

§ 7.1. GENERALLY

For the purpose of allocating the burden of proving in whose custody the best interests of the child will be served, custody cases may be divided into four categories; those between the natural parents; those between a parent or parents and a third party; those between a third party and a third party; and those involving parents and the state.[1]

In custody disputes between parents, the parents are viewed as having an equal interest in the child's welfare and thus the evidentiary scale is evenly balanced at the outset.[2] The concept that the parents of a child begin a custody dispute on an equal footing has been alternately stated as both parents having the burden of proof by a preponderance of the evidence,[3] and neither party having the burden of proof.[4] Regardless of the phraseology employed, it is clear that there are no presumptions in favor of either parent and the court must make its determination based solely on the particular facts and circumstances of each case. It is the function of the court to act as an arbiter, to hear and assess all relevant

---

[1] In re Custody of Hernandez, 249 Pa. Super. 274, 376 A.2d 648 (1977).

[2] 23 Pa.C.S. § 5327(a); best interest of child for custody purposes when two parents are involved is evaluated on scale initially weighed equally as to each parent; when scale is tipped in favor of one of the parents, the other must come forward with evidence to reverse balance. Sawko v. Sawko, 425 Pa. Super. 450, 625 A.2d 692 (1993); In re Custody of White, 270 Pa. Super. 165, 411 A.2d 231 (1979); Lewis v. Lewis, 267 Pa. Super. 235, 406 A.2d 375 (1979); In re Custody of Hernandez, 249 Pa. Super. 274, 376 A.2d 648 (1977).

[3] In re Temos, 304 Pa. Super. 82, 450 A.2d 111 (1982).

[4] Beichner v. Beichner, 294 Pa. Super. 36, 439 A.2d 737 (1982); Commonwealth ex rel. Oxenreider v. Oxenreider, 290 Pa. Super. 63, 434 A.2d 130 (1981); In re Custody of Hernandez, 249 Pa. Super. 274, 376 A.2d 648 (1977).

evidence and make an award to the party who demonstrates by a preponderance of the evidence that the best interests of the child lie in a grant of custody to that party.[5]

In disputes between a parent[s] and a third party, "there shall be a presumption that custody shall be awarded to the parent. The presumption in favor of the parent may be rebutted by clear and convincing evidence."[6] The third party's burden is considerably weightier than that of the parent.[7] The judicial belief that the continuity of the blood relationship is almost presumptively in the child's best interest, as well as society's, best interest,[8] and the recognition of the protection extended to the "biological" family by the United States Constitution,[9] contributes to the vitality of the stated rule that parents are vested with a *prima facie* right to custody.[10] Furthermore, this right will be forfeited only if "convincing reasons" dictate that the best interests of the child will be served by an award of custody to a third party.[11] Thus, the third party, will bear both the burden of production and the burden of persuasion.[12]

In custody disputes between a third party against another third party, the burden of proof is allocated equally and the party who presents a preponderance of evidence demonstrating that the best interests of the child are served by an award of custody in their favor will prevail.[13] This is true even where one party is related to the child and no distinctions,

---

[5] In re Custody of Hernandez, 249 Pa. Super. 274, 376 A.2d 648 (1977).

[6] 23 Pa.C.S. § 5327(b). *See also* R.L. v. M.A., 209 A.3d 391 (Pa. Super. 2019) (Section 5327 also applies when third party is seeking equal (50/50) physical custody).

[7] For a discussion of non-parent custody claims, *see* Chapter 6, *supra. See also* R.L. v. M.A., 209 A.3d 391 (Pa. Super. 2019).

[8] Ellerbe v. Hooks, 490 Pa. 363, 416 A.2d 512 (1980).

[9] *Id. See* Moore v. City of East Cleveland, 431 U.S. 494 (1977); Stanley v. Illinois, 405 U.S. 645 (1972); May v. Anderson, 345 U.S. 528 (1953).

[10] Ellerbe v. Hooks. 490 Pa. 363, 416 A.2d 512 (1980).

[11] *Id.*; Commonwealth ex rel. Witherspoon v. Witherspoon, 252 Pa. Super. 589, 384 A.2d 936 (1978); In re Custody of Hernandez, 249 Pa. Super. 274, 376 A.2d 648 (1977); Commonwealth ex rel. Kraus v. Kraus, 185 Pa. Super. 167, 138 A.2d 225 (1958).

[12] Ellerbe v. Hooks, 490 Pa. 363, 416 A.2d 512 (1980); In re Custody of Hernandez, 249 Pa. Super. 274, 376 A.2d 648 (1977).

[13] 23 Pa.C.S. § 5327(c); In re Spencer, 305 Pa. Super. 434, 451 A.2d 725 (1982).

for the purpose of the burden of proof, are made between related and non-related parties.[14]

By statutory mandate expressing legislative preference toward the family as the institution best suited for child rearing,[15] the state, as the moving party, bears the heaviest burden. Consequently, the state must make a showing of "clear necessity" in order to deprive the natural parents of custody.[16]

LOWER COURT CASES

Berks County

Salazar v. Gabriel, C. P. Berks County, No. 03-6532 (C.C.P. 2003) (Trial court refused to stay father's custody proceedings under the Soldiers' and Sailors' Civil Relief Act of 1940. The court denied aunt's motion for a stay of proceedings, and directed that counsel be appointed to protect mother's interest while serving in the military. "Clearly, given the absence of Mother while she is serving our nation in the Armed Forces stationed in Iraq, and the fact that the children have not been with a parent since January 2003, an inquiry into the status of the children, their safety, and what temporary custodial arrangement would be in their best interest is required.")

Bernstel v. Copenhaver, 85 Berks L. J. 15 (C.C.P. 1992) (A parent's *prima facie* right to custody is forfeited only if convincing reasons appear that the child's best interest will be served by awarding custody to a non-parent, as in custody disputes, courts favor natural parents over third parties).

---

[14] *Id.*

[15] *See* Juvenile Act, 42 Pa.C.S. § 6301 *et seq.*; Child Protective Services Law, 11 P.S. § 2201 *et seq.*; In re Custody of Hernandez, 249 Pa. Super. 274, 376 A.2d 648 (1977).

[16] In re Custody of Hernandez, 249 Pa. Super. 274, 376 A.2d 648 (1977); *see also* In re Clouse, 244 Pa. Super. 396, 368 A.2d 780 (1976).

Chapter 8

RELOCATION

§ 8.1. RELOCATION – PRESENTLY

With the enactment of the Custody Act in 2011, Section 5337 governs relocation actions. Section 5337 applies to any proposed relocation regardless of whether it is intrastate or interstate as long as it "significantly impairs the ability of a nonrelocating party to exercise custodial rights."[1]

Pursuant to the statute, no relocation shall occur unless every individual with custody rights to the child or children consents to same[2] or the court approves the proposed relocation.[3]

Under the statute and rules of civil procedure, there are strict notice provisions.[4] The parent proposing to relocate, "shall" notify all persons who have custody rights to the child[ren] by certified mail, return receipt requested.[5] This notice shall be given no later than the 60th day before the date of the proposed move or the 10th day after the date that the party proposing to move knows of the relocation, if that person did not know or could not have reasonably known of the proposed relocation in time to comply with the 60-day notice requirement, and it is not reasonably possible to postpone the date of the proposed relocation to comply with

---

[1] 23 Pa.C.S. §§ 5322 & 5337(a).

[2] 23 Pa.C.S. § 5337(b)(1).

[3] 23 Pa.C.S. § 5337(b)(2).

[4] *See* 23 Pa.C.S. § 5337(c); Pa.R.C.P. 1915.17. However, if notice provisions are not adhered to by the parent intending to relocate and the other party does not raise the issue at trial, the issue is deemed waived on appeal. *See* E.D. v. M.P., 33 A.3d 73 (Pa. Super. 2011).

[5] *See* 23 Pa.C.S. § 5337(c)(1)&(2); Pa.R.C.P. 1915.17(a).

the 60-day notice requirement.[6] The fact that a party serves a relocation notice on the other parent and files a petition for relocation requesting a hearing does not amount to that party tacitly conceding that the proposed move is a "relocation" under the custody statute warranting an analysis under Section 5337.[7] In situations where neither party is seeking to relocate and only the child or children would be moving a significant distance if custody is shifted from one parent to the other, the case is not considered a relocation case for purposes of triggering the notice provisions under Section 5337.[8]

Pursuant to Section 5337(c)(3), the notice shall contain the following:

1. The address of the intended new residence.

2. The mailing address, if not the same as the address of the intended new residence.

3. Names and ages of the individuals in the new residence, including individuals who intend to live in the new residence.

4. The home telephone number of the intended new residence, if available.

5. The name of the new school district and school.

6. The date of the proposed relocation.

7. The reasons for the proposed relocation.

8. A proposal for a revised custody schedule.

9. Any other information which the party proposing the relocation deems appropriate.

10. A counter-affidavit as provided under subsection (d)(1) which can be used to object to the proposed relocation and the modification of a custody order.

---

[6] *See* 23 Pa.C.S. § 5337(c)(2)(i) & (ii)(A) & (B).

[7] *See* C.M.K. v. K.E.M., 43 A.3d 417 (Pa. Super. 2012); *but see* J.M. v. K.W., 164 A.3d 1260 (Pa. Super. 2017).

[8] *See* D.K. v. S.P.K., 102 A.3d 467 (Pa. Super. 2014).

11. A warning to the nonrelocating party that if the nonrelocating party does not file with the court an objection to the proposed relocation within 30 days after receipt of the notice, that party shall be foreclosed from objecting to the relocation.[9]

A party entitled to receive notice under the relocation section must, within 30 days of receiving the notice, serve the counter-affidavit similar to that provided in Section 5337(d)(1) on the party proposing the relocation or modification of the custody order by certified mail, return receipt requested, addressee only or pursuant to Pa.R.C.P. 1930.4 if he/she objects to the proposed relocation and/or the modification of the custody order.[10] If there is an existing child custody case, the party objecting shall also file the counter-affidavit with the court.[11] Under Rule 1915.17(c), if "no objection to a proposed change of a child's residence is timely served after notice, the proposing party may change the residence of the child and such shall not be considered a 'relocation' under statute or rule."[12] The party proposing the relocation may also seek an order of court even if he or she does not receive a counter-affidavit from the other party after properly serving the other party with his/her notice. In such an instance, the party proposing the relocation shall file: (1) a complaint for custody and petition to confirm relocation when no custody case exists, or (2) a petition to confirm relocation when there is an existing custody case and (3) a proposed order including the information set forth at 23 Pa.C.S. § 5337(c)(3).[13] The party seeking to relocate shall also file an affidavit stating that he/she provided proper notice of the proposed relocation and that no objection was filed, along with proof that the notice was given by copy of the signed return receipt with the person's signature on same and the full notice given.[14]

---

[9] Pursuant to 23 Pa.C.S. § 5337(c)(4), if any of the information required in the notice is not known by the party seeking to move at the time the notice is sent, that party shall promptly notify all interested individuals upon learning of the information.

[10] See 23 Pa.C.S. § 5337(d)(1); Pa.R.C.P. 1915.17(b).

[11] See Pa.R.C.P. 1915.17(b).

[12] Pa.R.C.P. 1915.17(c).

[13] Pa.R.C.P. 1915.17(e).

[14] See 23 Pa.C.S. § 5337(e)(1) & (2)

If an objection is received by the party proposing to relocate, the party seeking to relocate shall file with the court the following: (1) a complaint for custody or petition for modification; (2) a copy of the notice of proposed relocation served on the non-relocating party; (3) a copy of the counter-affidavit indicating an objection to the relocation; and (4) a request for a hearing.[15] Pursuant to the recently promulgated rules of civil procedure pertaining to child custody, relocation cases shall follow an expedited procedure, and there shall be no requirement of mediation or parenting education prior to an expedited hearing before a judge.[16]

If a notice is properly served and the party opposing relocation properly serves an objection to the relocation but the party proposing to relocate does not follow the procedure under Rule 1915.17(f), the non-relocating party shall file the following with the court: (1) a complaint for custody or petition to modify; (2) a counter-affidavit as set forth under 23 Pa.C.S. § 5337(d)(1), and (3) a request for a hearing.[17]

If notice is not provided and the non-relocating party seeks a court order preventing the relocation, the non-relocating party shall file with the court the following: (1) a complaint for custody or petition for modification; (2) a statement of objection to relocation; and (3) a request for hearing.[18] Further, the court may consider the failure to provide the notice as a factor in making a decision regarding relocation or modification and a basis for ordering the return of the child to the nonrelocating party if the relocation already occurred without reasonable notice.[19] The court may also order reasonable expenses and counsel fees incurred by the party objecting to a relocation if proper notice was not given along with finding the relocating party in contempt and imposing sanctions.[20] Section 5337(k) provides that a party's failure to provide notice is subject to mitigation if the court determines that it was caused by abuse.[21]

---

[15] Pa.R.C.P. 1915.17(f); 23 Pa.C.S. § 5337(e)(3) & (4).

[16] Pa.R.C.P. 1915.17(d); *see also* 23 Pa.C.S. § 5337(d)(1) & (g)(1).

[17] Pa.R.C.P. 1915.17(g).

[18] Pa.R.C.P. 1915.17(h).

[19] *See* 23 Pa.C.S. § 5337(j).

[20] *Id.*

[21] *See* 23 Pa.C.S. § 5337(k).

Prior to the enactment of the custody statute in 2011, child relocation was analyzed by applying the factors set forth in the seminal case of *Gruber v. Gruber*, 583 A.2d 434 (Pa. Super. 1990) and its progeny within the overall best-interest-of-the-child analysis. The new statute provides at least 10 factors under Section 5337(h) to be considered by the court in granting or denying a relocation request.[22] The best interest of the child is contained in these factors. Further, the *"Gruber* factors" are also contained in the list. The following are the factors that the court shall consider:[23]

1. The nature, quality, extent of involvement and duration of the child's relationship with the party proposing to relocate and with the nonrelocating party, siblings and other significant persons in the child's life.

2. The age, developmental stage, needs of the child and the likely impact the relocation will have on the child's physical, educational and emotional development, taking into consideration any special needs of the child.

3. The feasibility of preserving the relationship between the nonrelocating party and the child through suitable custody arrangements, considering the logistics and financial circumstances of the parties.

4. The child's preference, taking into consideration the age and maturity of the child.

---

[22] It is reversible error if the court does not analyze all of the relocation factors, and the court shall reference the factors and provide explanations for its conclusion on the record or in its decision pursuant to Section § 5823(d). *See* E.D. v. M.P., 33 A.3d 73 (Pa. Super. 2011); *see also* A.V. v. S.T., 87 A.3d 818 (Pa. Super. 2014) (The trial court erred when it granted a mother's petition to relocate with the parties' minor children to New Jersey because it also modified the prior physical custody agreement, but it failed to consider statutory factors under 23 Pa.C.S. § 5328(a) in addition to those it considered with respect to relocation under 23 Pa.C.S. § 5337); D.K. v. S.P.K., 102 A.3d 467 (Pa. Super. 2014)) (Trial court shall consider the factors under 23 Pa.C.S. § 5337 in addition to those listed under Section 5328(a) even in situations where neither party is seeking to relocate but a change in custody would result in moving the child a significant distance).

[23] 23 Pa.C.S. § 5337(h) provides that the court should give "weighted consideration to those factors which affect the safety of the child."

5. Whether there is an established pattern of conduct of either party to promote or thwart the relationship of the child and the other party.

6. Whether the relocation will enhance the general quality of life for the party seeking the relocation, including, but not limited to, financial or emotional benefit or educational opportunity.

7. Whether the relocation will enhance the general quality of life for the child, including, but not limited to, financial or emotional benefit or educational opportunity.

8. The reasons and motivation of each party for seeking or opposing the relocation.[24]

9. The present and past abuse committed by a party or member of the party's household and whether there is a continued risk of harm to the child or an abused party.

10. Any other factor affecting the best interest of the child.

The court shall hold an expedited full hearing on the proposed relocation after a timely objection is filed and before the relocation occurs.[25] The court may also on its own motion hold an expedited full hearing before the relocation occurs.[26] However, if the court finds that exigent circumstances exist, the court may permit the relocation pending an expedited full hearing.[27] If the court grants a relocation, it shall modify any existing custody order or establish a new order.[28] The court shall also specify the method by which future modifications can be made if desired by either party.[29]

---

[24] *See also* S.J.S. v. M.J.S., 76 A.3d 541 (Pa. Super. 2013) (trial court denied mother's proposed relocation, in part, because her motives for moving were driven by her romance with a boyfriend and not by the children's best interests).

[25] *See* 23 Pa.C.S. § 5337(g)(1); *see also* Pa.R.C.P. 1915.17(d).

[26] *See* 23 Pa.C.S. § 5337(g)(2).

[27] *See* 23 Pa.C.S. § 5337(g)(3).

[28] *See* 23 Pa.C.S. § 5337(g)(4).

[29] *See* 23 Pa.C.S. § 5337(f).

In the event a party relocates prior to the expedited full hearing, the court "shall not confer any presumption in favor of the relocation."[30] Adopting an inference that the prior relocation is in the child's best interest would require the party opposing the relocation to bear the burden of rebutting the inference contrary to Section 5337(i) that provides the party proposing to relocate bears the burden of establishing that the relocation is in the best interest of the child.[31] In following Section 5337(l) by not conferring a presumption in favor of the relocation, the court may not disregard evidence and facts related to the period after a relocation that occurred prior to the hearing.[32] The Superior Court has ruled that doing so would result in a presumption against relocation and would be contrary to considering all factors under Sections 5328(a) and 5337(h).[33] The trial court is to impose the same allocation of burdens set forth in the custody statute regardless of whether a relocation occurred prior to the hearing when considering the best interest of the child.[34] If a party relocates after an objection is made, but prior to a relocation hearing, the relocating parent may be found in contempt.[35]

The party seeking relocation has the burden of establishing that the proposed relocation is in the best interest of the child as shown under the factors in Section 5337(h).[36] As was provided in *Gruber* and its progeny, Section 5337(i)(2) provides that each party has the burden to prove the integrity of his/her motives for proposing the relocation or objecting to same.

---

[30] *See* 23 Pa.C.S. § 5337(l); *see also,* E.D. v. M.P., 33 A.3d 73 (Pa. Super. 2011).

[31] *See* B.K.M. v. J.A.M., 50 A.3d 168 (Pa. Super. 2012); *see also* S.J.S. v. M.J.S., 76 A.3d 541 (Pa. Super. 2013).

[32] *Id.*

[33] *Id.*

[34] *Id.*

[35] *See* J.M. v. K.W., 164 A.3d 1260 (Pa. Super. 2017) (Father filed a petition for special relief and contempt after mother moved and the court found mother in contempt).

[36] *See* 23 Pa.C.S. § 5337(i)(1); C.M.K. v. K.E.M., 43 A.3d 417 (Pa. Super. 2012) (mother failed to meet her burden of proving that relocation was in child's best interest, as trial court determined that the proposed move would have significantly impaired father's custodial rights where father regularly exercised periods of partial physical custody and was actively involved in child's life, school activities and extracurricular activities); *see also* S.J.S. v. M.J.S., 76 A.3d 541 (Pa. Super. 2013).

The trial court shall address all of the relevant custody and relocation factors when rendering its decision.[37] Failure to do so may result in a remand on appeal. In the case of *A.M.S. v. M.R.C.*,[38] while the trial court addressed the relocation factors, it did not always identify the factors specifically and did not consider the history of drug or alcohol abuse and the mental and physical condition of the members of the relocating party's household, which were important, as the relocating party proposed to live with her sister and her sister's family after the relocation. Without such an analysis, the Superior Court remanded the case as it found that it could not conclude that the trial court considered all of the relevant factors. The Superior Court in the *A.M.S.* case also held that its ruling in the case of *C.B. v. J.B. and M.B. and T.B.*, 65 A.3d 946 (Pa. Super. 2013), applies to relocation cases prospectively. The *C.B.* decision requires trial courts to set forth the reasons for its decision at or near the time it issues its decision in a custody proceeding.

A trial court did not abuse its discretion by denying a mother's petition to relocate the parties' two daughters seven and one-half hours from Erie to Buckingham, Pennsylvania, because the children were doing well in school and their activities, had a strong bond with their father and extended family, mother's employment prospects in the new area were not clear, and mother's motives for moving were not driven by the children's best interests but by her romance with a boyfriend.[39] The court found that mother's desire to relocate for a better life for the children and improving her financial

---

[37] *See* A.M.S. v. M.R.C., 70 A.3d 830 (Pa. Super. 2013); *see also* S.J.S. v. M.J.S., 76 A.3d 541 (Pa. Super. 2013) (proper for court to analyze both custody factors and relocation factors when no prior custody order exists); A.V. v. S.T., 87 A.3d 818 (Pa. Super. 2014) (The trial court erred when it granted a mother's petition to relocate with the parties' minor children to New Jersey because it also modified the prior physical custody agreement, but it failed to consider statutory factors under 23 Pa.C.S. § 5328(a) in addition to those it considered with respect to relocation under 23 Pa.C.S. § 5337); D.K. v. S.P.K., 102 A.3d 467 (Pa. Super. 2014) (Trial court shall consider the factors under 23 Pa.C.S. § 5337 in addition to those listed under Section 5328(a) even in situations where neither party is seeking to relocate but a change in custody would result in moving the child a significant distance).

[38] *Id.*

[39] S.J.S. v. M.J.S., 76 A.3d 541 (Pa. Super. 2013).

difficulties cannot be at the expense of the children's relationship with father.[40] When a parent desires to relocate to be with a significant other, the trial court may consider the impact on the children should the parent's romance fail.[41] The Superior Court reversed a trial court's granting of a mother's petition to relocate, when the mother's proposed relocation would enhance her general quality of life but was not in the child's best interest.[42]

In relocation cases, one parent may desire to move to a different school district. When parties cannot resolve a dispute over which school to send their children, the court may decide based on the best interests of the children.[43] "If the court is addressing a request to modify custody in conjunction with the choice of school, the court's choice of school may factor into the court's custody decision. . . . The court's choice of school may in fact require it to modify the parties' physical custody award, in particular "when the parties live far apart, making it impractical for one parent to transport the child to school."[44] "Continuity in an educational environment is an important, but not controlling, factor to be considered by the court in making a school or custody decision, and over-emphasis on this factor may constitute an abuse of discretion."[45]

In the case of *S.S. v. K.F.*, 189 A.3d 1093 (Pa. Super. 2018), a mother requested to relocate to Chester County, Pennsylvania from Bucks County, Pennsylvania. The trial court allowed mother to move to Chester County,

---

[40] *Id.*

[41] *Id.*

[42] *See* D.K.D. v. A.L.C., 141 A.3d 566 (Pa. Super. 2016) (Trial court initially denied mother's relocation request and then reversed itself after subsequent hearing on Mother's reconsideration motion where she presented new evidence regarding, inter alia, accepting a new job. Superior Court reversed trial court finding custodial parent seeking to relocate had burden of establishing relocation was in child's best interest. Though mother demonstrated that a move to Florida would enhance her general quality of life, mother failed to prove the relocation was in child's best interest under the ten relocation factors. Interestingly, on remand, Superior Court directed trial court to fashion a custody order with father as primary physical custodian, though Mother previously had primary physical custody of the child).

[43] *See* S.W.D. v. S.A.R., 96 A.3d 396, 403-04 (Pa. Super. 2014).

[44] S.S. v. K.F., 189 A.3d 1093 (Pa. Super. 2018) (*citing* S.W.D. v. S.A.R., 96 A.3d 396, 403-04 (Pa. Super. 2014)).

[45] *Id.* (*citing* Fox v. Garzilli, 875 A.2d 1104, 1110 (Pa. Super. 2005)).

but ordered that the children remain in the Pennsbury School District in Bucks County where the mother previously lived but where neither party lived at the time of the trial. As stated by the Superior Court: "[t]he [trial] court therefore allowed Mother to move to Chester County, while purportedly denying a 'relocation,' as the Child Custody Act defines that term."[46] This created a financial burden on the parties who would have to pay tuition to send their children to the Pennsbury School District. Because neither party requested such relief and the trial court considered school choice as a custody issue only and made scarce inquiry into the parties' financial situations, the trial court's decision was reversed by the Supe-rior Court. The case was remanded. The Superior Court held: "[o]n remand, unless the parties request otherwise, the court must choose a school that does not financially burden the parties, and it must make its decision by considering both the relocation and custody factors."[47]

If relocation is granted and a shared physical custody schedule can continue, the question may arise as to the transportation of the children by the school district. In *Wyland v. West Shore School District*,[48] Mr. Wyland and his ex-wife initially both lived in the same school district and the school district provided transportation for the children from both parties' residences to the private school that they attended. When mother moved out of the school district and the new school district began providing transportation for the children from her home to attend the private school, the school district where father resided discontinued providing transportation from his residence on the mornings that he had custody of the children. Father filed a complaint against his school district seeking injunctive relief, arguing that he was a custodial parent and his children resided in the district under the shared custody arrangement. Father argued that under § 1361 of the Public School Code, the district was obligated to continue transporting his children from his home to the private elementary school. The district contended that it had no duty to bus the children because another school district provided transportation to and from mother's residence, which was located in a different school district. The district argued that the district where mother resided was the district of primary residence and had

---

[46] S.S. v. K.F., 189 A.3d 1093 (Pa. Super. 2018).
[47] *Id.*
[48] Wyland v. West Shore School District, 52 A.3d 572 (Pa. Cmwlth. 2012).

the sole obligation to provide transportation and only one school district was required to provide transportation under the School Code. The district claimed that the Pennsylvania Department of Education (PDE) applied a "single residency rule" for both enrollment and transportation purposes and that children could not have dual residency. The district claimed that PDE's policy was to provide transportation reimbursement to only one school district. When students of separated parents lived in two different school districts, PDE designates a district as the district of residence and provides transportation reimbursement to the district in which the child resides. Here, PDE designated mother's district as the district of residence. The trial court granted the preliminary injunction and ordered the district where father resided to resume transportation of the children from father's residence. The district appealed and the Commonwealth Court affirmed the trial court, finding that since the parents had joint and equal custody, the children resided in two different school districts, and the designation of a single school district was not required. Section 1361 of the School Code ensures that if transportation is provided, it is provided to both public and private school students. The court determined that any rule PDE applied to restrict § 1361 was unauthorized.[49]

LOWER COURT CASES

Adams County

Y.L.P. v. R.R.P., C.P. Adams County, No. 15-S-821 (C.C.P. June 30, 2017), *aff'd*, Memorandum Decision, No. 1189 MDA 2017 (Pa. Super. December 4, 2017) (Father resided in Cumberland County, Penn-sylvania, and mother resided in Adams County, Pennsylvania. Mother filed her Notice of Proposed Relo-cation to Netcong, New Jersey, because she desired to live with her significant other, with whom she had one child, and was expecting another. Mother was a stay-at-home parent and intended to remain so when she moved to New Jersey. Trial court, after considering all of the relocation factors, any of which fa-vored both parents, found that the best interest of the children would be served by granting mother's proposed relocation, as she was the more available parent and the children had a sibling in her home, with whom they were bonded. The court acknowledged that father's time would be substantially impacted by moth-er's relocation. The court noted that if relocation was granted, it would be impossible

---

[49] *See also* Watts v. Manheim Township School District, 84 A.3d 378 (Pa. Cmwlth. 2014) (school districts are to provide transportation to both parent's homes in the district).

to maintain an equally shared physical custody schedule. However, the court found that, while an equal physical custody schedule was impossible to maintain if mother relocated, father's relationship with the children could be maintained and preserved through ample, regularly scheduled custodial time. A schedule of significant partial physical custody was provided for father, including most of the summer months, alternating weekends during the school year, and extended weekends).

Allegheny County

M.A. v. M.G., C.P. Allegheny County, No. FD 13-001728-006 (C.C.P. August 5, 2019), *aff'd*, Memorandum Decision, No. 1228 WDA 2019 (Pa. Super. March 16, 2020) (Trial court denied mother's petition to relocate from Pittsburgh, Pennsylvania, to Hartford, Connecticut, with the parties children, because mother failed to prove that it was in the best interest of the children to completely uproot them from an environment in which they were doing well just for a higher-paying position. The court noted that mother was able to find suitable employment in Pittsburgh, just at a somewhat lower salary. The trial court considered the issues suggested by mother, including the children's relationship with mother and the monetary benefits of relocating. The trial court found that they did not outweigh the benefits to the children remaining in Pittsburgh).

M.C.-F. v. V.M., C.P. Allegheny County, No. FD 05-007279005, *aff'd*, Memorandum Decision, No. 270 WDA 2018 (Pa. Super. November 21, 2018) (Trial court denied mother's request to relocate with the child to Antioch, Tennessee, with stepfather and mother's two children born of her marriage to stepfather. The trial court also ruled that should mother elect to remain in Allegheny County with the child, mother and father would share physical custody of the child, according to a week-on/week off schedule. Should mother elect to relocate to Tennessee without the child, father would be granted primary physical custody of the child, and mother would be granted partial physical custody of the child every summer. Where mother filed her notice of Proposed Relocation less than three weeks prior to her planned move, and mother was on actual, timely notice of father's objection to the Proposed Relocation, given the imminence of the proposed move at that time, strict adherence to procedural formalisms of the filing of the Counter-Affidavit would have unnecessarily delayed the court's review of the matter).

A.P. v. S.P., C.P. Allegheny County, No. FD-14-006270-008 (C.C.P. November 1, 2017), *aff'd*, Memorandum Decision, No. 1792 WDA 2017 (Pa. Super. July 24, 2018) (Mother met her burden of proving that a move to Montréal, Canada from Allegheny County, Pennsylvania, would be in the children's best interest, and that their lives would be enhanced by the move; the court listed each of the relocation factors set forth in 23 Pa.C.S. § 5337(h), as well as each of the custody factors enumerated in § 5328(a), and provided a clear and thorough explanation of how the court decided each factor. During the school year, father was provided with one long weekend a month in Allegheny County and custody time should he travel to Montréal. Father was given summer and substantial quality time. Mother's career was virtually stalled in Pittsburgh,

Allegheny County. In order to progress, she needed to relocate. She chose to relocate to Montréal, where her long-term boyfriend was stationed. Part of mother's choice to move to Montréal was to be closer to him and the trial court was not blind to that, nor did mother try to hide it. The trial court did not find, as father claimed, that being near her boyfriend was mother's principal reason for requesting relocation. To the contrary, the trial court found mother to be a pragmatic and ambitious person who would not request this move if it did not also enhance her career and benefit her family financially. Mother's move brought not just career enhancement for mother, but also a significant increase in salary, a housing stipend and private school tuition for the children. These increased benefits would have both a direct and indirect positive effect on the children, and would also ensure that mother had the funds for the children's monthly transportation to see father).

Kercher v. Kercher, 160 P.L.J. 507 (Allegheny County 2012) (The trial court denied mother's request to relocate from the marital residence in Allegheny County to a residence in New Castle. The trial court found that father enjoyed significantly more time with the children prior to mother's unilateral choice to move. The court found that father was more actively engaged with the children then was mother. He was heavily involved in the children's day-to-day care, including medical, educational, recreational, cultural, and religious issues. The children had strong relationships with the paternal grandparents, who resided in the Pittsburgh area. The children's school in Allegheny County was more suitable to the children in that it was smaller and more intimate than the school in which mother had placed them in New Castle during the separation. The court determined that father would offer the children more stability and continuity and would facilitate a more protective environment for the children. The court rejected mother's argument that a move back from New Castle to Allegheny County would disrupt the children's lives, noting that mother did not show such concern when she unilaterally moved them from Allegheny County to New Castle in the first place. The court also found that mother had no compelling reason to stay in New Castle, as her employment was in Pittsburgh).

Dix v. Dix, 159 p.l.j. 280 (Allegheny County 2011) (Trial court decided a relocation issue under new custody act, even though mother's petition for relocation was filed prior to the enactment of the new custody act. Mother requested that she be permitted to relocate to Virginia with the child in order to remarry. The trial court granted mother's request for relocation. The trial court determined that there were advantages to mother's move as she was planning to remarry and her new husband was employed in Virginia. He already had established a strong relationship with the child and would have sufficient income to support mother and the child. No improper motives were detected and the proposed custody arrangement for the child would actually double the amount of father's overnight custody and provided for extensive summer custody. In addition to the relocation factors, the court examined what would serve the child's best interests and determined that mother had been the primary caretaker of the child, coordinating its medical care. The timing for relocation was not greatly disruptive as the child had not yet begun school. Mother had also never thwarted father's custody time).

Lucero v. Lucero, 159 P.L.J. 461 (Allegheny County, 2011) (Trial court granted mother's request to relocate with the parties' children to Clarkston, Michigan, after considering the factors set forth in the new custody relocation statute. Mother sought to relocate with the parties' children to Michigan due to her plans to remarry and move to Michigan where her fiancé was employed. Father was viewed as being historically deceptive with mother, not being significantly involved with the children, not being involved in the children's educational ventures and extracurricular activities, and having questionable motives regarding his attempts to prevent the relocation. Father was viewed as focusing more on one of the children rather than on both and having behaved in ways that questioned his devotion to the children. Father traveled considerably for his employment and the children would have to be supervised by nannies if they were to live with father rather than relocate with mother. In analyzing the facts under the new custody relocation statute, the court found that the children were thriving with mother, developed a bond with their future stepfather, and there was no reason to believe that they would not continue to excel in school once a relocation was effectuated. The move would have no negative impact on the children. The relationship between father and the children would be adequately preserved. Mother had never thwarted father's custody in the past. Father's motives, however, were viewed with skepticism considering his history of deceiving mother and his history of attempting to exercise control over her).

Armstrong County

A.M.P. v. D.M.P., C.P. Armstrong County, No. 2014-1232-Civil (C.C.P. January 6, 2020), *aff'd*, Memorandum Decision, No. 182 WDA 2020 (Pa. Super. August 27, 2020) (Trial court modified a custody award, as mother and father were clearly on notice that custody would be at issue during a relocation/custody trial. Pursuant to the parties' July 2015 Consent Order, the parties shared legal custody of their child and mother had primary physical custody. Mother provided father with a Notice of Proposed Relocation from Armstrong County, Pennsylvania to Tallmadge, Ohio, which stated that the reason for relocation was that mother's fiancé resided in Ohio and they planned to marry upon her relocation. Father filed a Counter-Affidavit objecting to the proposed relocation. The trial court denied mother's request to relocate and awarded father primary physical custody of the child. The court cited with approval *C.A.J. v. D.S.M.*, 136 A.3d 504, 509 (Pa. Super. 2016) (concluding that if the parties had notice that custody would be at issue, the court is permitted to modify custody without a pending petition for modification) and *S.W.D. v. S.A.R.*, 96 A.3d 396, 405-06 (Pa. Super. 2014) (indicating that if notice of a proceeding adequately advises a party that custody will be at issue, a court may entertain the request to permanently modify a custody order after hearing in that proceeding).

Wright v. Wright, C.P. Armstrong County, No. 2010-1637-Civil (C.C.P. 2011) (Mother was not in contempt of a custody order when she moved to another county 20 miles away, since the relocation did not impair father's custody rights. The parties were the parents of two minor children. The parties were subject to a custody consent order that called for shared physical and legal custody, with mother being the primary custodian. Father alleged that mother moved without requesting permission to relocate as required by law and enrolled one of the children in school in that county without consulting father. Father noted that, instead of being 4 miles away, the children were now 30 miles away. Father filed a motion for contempt and sought counsel fees. Mother testified that she previously notified father of her intention to move and that he had no objection at that time. Mother noted that father's custody with the children had not changed, except for one night, and that she continued to transport the children to father's residence. The court analyzed the motion under 23 Pa.C.S. § 5322(a) to address the question of whether mother had relocated. The court found that not only were father's custody rights not substantially impaired, they had not been impaired at all. Thus, mother's move did not constitute a relocation and mother was not required to follow the statutory procedure for relocation custody cases. While the court did not condone mother's unilateral actions, it could not find that she was in contempt of the current custody order, as she did discuss the move with father and did not frustrate his custody rights. A party cannot be in contempt of a custody order upon relocating if the non-custodial parent's custody rights are not impaired).

Berks County

Witman v. Strickler, C.P. Berks County, No. 06-10752 (C.C.P. August 8, 2018) (Mother demonstrated that a proposed move to Missouri to take advantage of an opportunity to own a working cattle farm was in her minor child's best interest. However, mother failed to demonstrate that it was necessary to move immediately. Mother argued that the move represented a wonderful opportunity for her family and would enhance the family's quality of life. The trial court granted mother's petition to relocate but delayed the move until the end of the school year. The court considered the factors for relocation set forth in 23 Pa.C.S. § 5337(h). The court noted that on balance, there was the potential for financial and educational benefits, through the experience of working with horses, and would be positive for the minor child emotionally because of her great desire to become a horse trainer. The court granted the relocation request, citing the cattle farm's owners, generous offer, but ruled that the relocation should not take place until the end of the child's current school year).

DuHaime v. Sarau, C.P. Berks County, No. 16-5834 (C.C.P. August 8, 2016) (Trial court allowed mother to relocate to Florida, since father had consented to a valid, if informal, agreement. The informal agreement was examined to determine whether father had consented to the relocation. Under 23 Pa.C.S. § 5337(b), a relocation is permitted to occur when "every individual who has custody rights to the child consents to the proposed relocation." The court found that relocation would be permissible based on the agreement of the parties. An analysis of the relocation factors was therefore unnecessary. The court found that the best interests of the children would be served by granting mother primary physical custody during the school year, with father to have custody during the summer months).

Nagle v. Korotkikh, C.P. Berks County, No. 11-5007 (C.C.P. 2016) (Trial court denied mother's petition for an expedited hearing to permit her to relocate to the state of Wisconsin. Mother failed to consider that the minor child had a substantial relationship with father and his family, and those relationships should continue to be nurtured. The proposed relocation would affect the degree and quality of the relationship, due to a change in the frequency of interaction. Mother had problems with the humidity in the Pennsylvania region, sometimes resulting in her having difficulty in breathing. Father objected to the proposed relocation, believing this would adversely affect his custodial time with the minor child, and would also affect the paternal grandparents, with whom the minor child had a close relationship. Father admitted that he does not see the minor child on weekdays during the school year due to his work schedule, even though mother has offered to provide him with additional visitation. However, father had developed a routine for his weekends with the minor child, where he spent time with the minor child and took the minor child to see one or both of the grandparents' homes).

Thompson v. Stoudt, 105 Berks Co. L. J. 19, No. 11-22373 (C.C.P. 2012) (Trial court denied mother's request to relocate, finding that the best interests of the children would be adversely affected and the children would not receive any substantial benefits, and outweighed the benefits mother would receive through the relocation. After considering the factors set forth in 23 Pa.C.S. § 5337, as well as the best interests of the child, the trial court denied mother's petition to relocate. The court determined that mother had a better relationship with the children then did father, but that father did have a positive bond with the children. The court noted that because father had custody every other week, the relocation would substantially change his interaction with the children. Father's visitation would be limited to weekends, because he testified that traveling to Carbon County during the week would not be feasible. The court was particularly concerned that the relocation would decrease the amount of time that the parties' son could spend with father and his paternal grandfather, with whom he had a good relationship. The court also noted that while the move would benefit mother by allowing her to live with her paramour, it did not offer any enhanced opportunities for the children. Rather, the move would disrupt the stability that the children currently enjoyed. "The disturbance in the lives of the children, particularly how it affects the interaction between father and children, and secondarily, changing school districts and lifestyle, outweighs the benefits that mother would receive from the move.").

Erb v. Palmer, 104 Berks Co. L. J. 385 (C.C.P. 2012) (Mother's relocation to West Virginia would adversely interfere with father's relationship with the child, especially considering the distance and the financial burden required to maintain father's relationship with the child through regular visitation. The court granted mother primary physical custody conditioned upon her residing within a reasonable distance of father's residence in Berks County. Mother's new residence in West Virginia was approximately 7 hours from father's residence. The court noted that the most important factor was the nature, quality and extent of involvement and duration of the child's relationship with both parties. This factor weighed heavily in father's favor in opposing the relocation. Although mother was the stay-at-home primary caretaker of the child, father had a close and loving relationship with his son and was involved in the child's recreational activities. The court believed that mother's relocation to West Virginia would adversely interfere with father's relationship with the child. Commuting between West Virginia and Pennsylvania to exchange custody would cause a financial hardship on both parties which would ultimately affect father's relationship with his son, and would deplete scarce financial resources that would otherwise be available for the benefit of the child. The court was also disturbed that mother's abrupt move to West Virginia clearly disrupted father's close bond and relationship with his son. Moreover, mother moved to West Virginia without any job prospects and continued to be unemployed).

Miller v. Lee, C.P. Berks County, No. 09-12926 (C.C.P. 2012) (The trial court denied mother's request to relocate to Alabama with the parties' child where husband's new employment position did not benefit the family's financial position to a degree that would warrant disrupting the child's relationship with father. Father objected to the proposed relocation because he would lose the frequent interaction that he currently enjoyed with his daughter. At the hearing, mother advised the court that if her petition was denied, she intended to remain at her current residence in Berks County, Pennsylvania. Mother's proposed custody modification would provide father with an equivalent number of visitation days. However, the court determined that this did not mean the relocation would not have a negative impact on the child's relationship with her father. The court noted that the visitation would occur mainly during the summer months, which would eliminate any opportunity for father to become involved in the child's education and prevented them from engaging in certain activities they enjoyed, such as hunting and fishing. Father's financial condition would also prohibit him from traveling frequently to Alabama. The court found that the increase in stepfather's salary was substantial but not overwhelming. The court also found it significant that stepfather chose to transfer to Alabama and his employer did not pressure him or threaten to fire him if he did not. While mother presented compelling reasons for the relocation, the court determined that those reasons were not substantial enough to diminish the relationship between father and daughter).

Blair County

C.B.J. v. A.L.S., C.P. Blair County, No. 2016-GN-3494, *aff'd*, Memorandum Decision, No. 1466 WDA 2018 (Pa. Super. March 29, 2019) (The trial court granted the request of mother to relocate with the parties' daughter (age 15) and son (age 12) from Tyrone, Pennsylvania, to Arlington, Texas. The children were very close to their mother, who had been the primary caretaker, and they both expressed a desire to relocate and an optimism that the relocation would be a good opportunity for them. The children had a closer emotional relationship with mother than with father. The court found that neither parent was actively failing to support or attempting to thwart the relationship of the children with the other parent).

Bucks County

Zukley v. Zukley, 84 Bucks Co. L. Rep. 182 (C.C.P. 2010) (Trial court held that in considering a petition for relocation, the court must consider the availability of realistic visitation arrangements that will adequately foster an ongoing relationship between the child and the noncustodial parent. After separation, each parent sought primary custody of the children and mother also sought permission to relocate out-of-state to Maryland. Father objected to the move because he contended he should have primary custody. The trial court granted mother sole legal custody and primary physical custody of the children and permission to relocate to Maryland. The court found that father's behavior was not in the best interest of the children, including such conduct as having his son committed to a mental health facility without cause and repeatedly claiming that the son had autism when in fact he did not. In addition, mother had been the children's primary caretaker prior to separation. Mother had no family support system in her current location and a strong family support system and a job offer in her proposed place of relocation. The court found that father's opposition to relocation did not come out of a concern for his children; rather, his opposition was motivated by a desire to prevail over mother. Finally, the court found that mother's desire to relocate was not intended to prevent father from seeing his children; in fact, mother proposed a schedule of visitation that clearly indicated that she was willing to cooperate with visitation).

Centre County

Noss v. Merrill, C.P. Centre County, No. 2015-4607 (C.C.P. 2016) (Trial court found that the factors for relocation did not outweigh the disruption it would cause the children, and mother's petition for relocation was denied. The parties had shared custody with a schedule that gave father primary custody during the school year, visiting with mother every weekend, and in the summer, mother had primary custody during the week with father having most weekends. Mother filed a proposed relocation to York County, approximately 1½ hours from the children's home in Centre County).

Barr v. Barr, C.P. Centre County, No. 2009-3033 (C.C.P. 2012) (Trial court allowed mother to relocate with the parties' two children to Hawaii, where the move would benefit the children because mother's emotional and financial situation would be improved and the children's relationship with their father, who lived in Washington State, would not be impacted.

Crawford County

Tedesco v. Tedesco, 30 Crawford Co. Leg. J. 9 (C.C.P. 2012) (The trial court ruled that moving a child from Meadville, Crawford County, to Edinboro, Erie County, where the parents live 21.4 miles apart, was not a "relocation" as the term is defined in 23 Pa.C.S. § 5322, since it does not "significantly impair" the rights of the non-custodial parent, so the analysis required for relocation does not apply. Father argued that mother had relocated the child to Edinboro, Erie County, without following the proper relocation procedure set forth in § 5337. Father was concerned about the child traveling with his mother from Edinboro to Meadville, Crawford County, father's residence, during the winter months. Father was also concerned that he would lose what he referred to as the "pulse" of the child, and he would not know as well what was going on with the child on a day-to-day basis. Mother argued that she was willing to provide all transportation to allow father to have the same amount of time with the child, and that the only effect of mother living in Edinboro was that there may be some minimal loss of time on Thursdays for father. The court held that pursuant to *C.M.K. v. K.E.M.*, 43 A.3d 417 (Pa. Super. 2012), the court is free to consider first whether a "relocation" has even occurred. Under the facts in this case, the court concluded that no relocation had occurred. The court explained that mother was willing to provide all transportation to allow father to have almost the same amount of time with the child. As for keeping a handle on the "pulse" of the child, the court agreed with mother that this could be done by daily telephone contact. The court acknowledged that it may be a bit more of an inconvenience for father to attend school events in Edinboro and keep track of those events, but it could not conclude that that taken alone, or everything taken together, significantly impaired the ability of father to exercise his custodial rights).

Tedesco v. Tedesco, 29 Crawford County Leg. J. 291 (C.C.P. 2011) (Trial court held that moving a child 20 miles away, across the county line and into another school district, constitutes "relocation" under 23 Pa.C.S. § 5322(a), since it "significantly impairs" the custodial rights of the other parent, so the parent who proposes the move must begin proceedings with a Notice of Relocation under 23 Pa.C.S. § 5337(c) and (d). Plaintiff-father filed a Petition for Contempt presenting an issue under the current custody relocation provisions, 23 Pa.C.S. § 5337, not specifically addressed by the statute. Defendant-wife argued that her move 20 miles away into another school district did not "significantly" impair the plaintiff's ability to exercise his custodial rights. Therefore, she argued, she could make the move without any relocation proceeding. The trial court acknowledged that the current relocation statute, 23 Pa.C.S. § 5337(d), does not provide any particular guidance as to what a non-relocating party does if that party believes what has occurred is a relocation and the other party does not. The court stated that since the statute did not really address this issue, the court, with its equitable powers, must fashion a remedy).

Cumberland County

E.R. v. C.G., C.P. Cumberland County, No. 062786, *aff'd* Memorandum Decision, No. 2 MDA 2019 (Pa. Super. July 5, 2019) (Trial court granted the petition filed by mother, a physician-specialist, to allow mother to relocate to St. Maarten Island with the parties' youngest child so that mother could accept employment at the American University of the Caribbean School of Medicine (AUC). The child stated that it was her preference to move to St. Maarten with mother. The child also testified that CIA would be a better school for her than the schools in Pennsylvania because it would prepare her for travel or living outside of the United States. Mother also testified that father's relationship with the child was non-existent. The child testified that she is very close with mother, and that she had lived with mother for her entire life. The child stated that she was afraid of father because of his bad temper. The trial court entered an Order granting mother's Petition for Relocation and continuing the existing custody order awarding shared legal custody to the parties, primary physical custody of the child to mother, and partial physical custody to father. The court noted that the evidence at the hearing showed that the relocation would not affect any relationship between father and the child, since any arguable relationship between them was already fraught with difficulties caused by the interaction between them over the years, and not solely attributable to mother, as father argued).

E.S.C. v. D.L.C., C.P. Cumberland County, No. 2013-1927 Civil (C.C.P. 2013) (Trial court granted mother interim custody, where it had previously denied her primary custody if she relocated, and mother subsequently abandoned her plans to relocate. The trial court awarded primary physical custody to father, but indicated that it would revisit its order if mother abandoned her plans to move to California. The court believed that the relocation of the children to California would not be in their best interests. After the entry of this order, mother decided to remain in Pennsylvania and sought modification of the existing order. After examining the custody factors enumerated in 23 Pa.C.S. § 5328(a), the court then determined that mother was the parent who was much more involved with the care of the children and their day-to-day lives. While the court still believed that mother's plan to move to California was motivated solely by her own self-interest, it concluded that her decision to abandon the plan when it meant the loss of her children showed that she was able to put their needs before her own. The court reasoned that the best interests of the children were served by maintaining the status quo, particularly in an environment where they had thrived. The court noted that it is hardly unusual for the issue of physical custody to be affected by the abandonment of a parent's plan to relocate).

H.C.L. v. R.V.L., 61 Cumberland Law J. 283 (C.C.P. 2012) (Husband argued that there were no suitable alternative custody arrangements available to preserve father's relationship with his children if mother relocated to Washington when he presently had six overnights out of every 14 days and other periods of custody totaling a minimum of 150 to 160 overnights a year (over 40% of the calendar year), and the relocation would reduce his weekly contact to custody approximately 72 days per year. The trial court acknowledged that the relocation would result in the detriment of diminished contact with father. However, the court concluded that the best interests of these closely bonded children was dependent upon their continued primary residence in a common household, with each other and with their mother, and that a denial of relocation would thwart those interests, with irreparable harm to the children).

J.E.F. v. K.J.F., 125 Dauphin Co. Rep. 196 (C.C.P. 2013) (Because the evidence did not indicate that mother's move from Harrisburg to Hamburg, Berks County, would significantly impair father's ability to exercise his custodial rights, mother's proposed move was not a "relocation" under the definition in the new custody statute. The court noted that the children would not be changing schools or physicians. Father failed to present evidence that the children's move would break the continuity and frequency of his involvement with them, particularly with regard to school-related activities. The court rejected father's assertion that the relocation would cause the children to spend an inordinate amount of time traveling. Father failed to make any connection between the children's travel time and his loss of custodial rights).

Price v. Porter, 125 Dauph. Co. Rep. 78 (C.C.P. 2012) (Trial court permitted mother to relocate to Arkansas with the parties' child in order to pursue a three-year, out-of-state doctoral program leading to a Ph.D. in Criminal Justice. The program included free tuition, stipend, three-year (rather than four-year) completion and health insurance. Father opposed the relocation because he believed it would completely devastate the child by removing him from the child's life and because the child would have no family in Arkansas. Father's family was in Dauphin County, and his mother and brother were involved in the child's life. After reviewing the factors for relocation set forth at 23 Pa.C.S. § 5337, as well as the factors to consider when awarding custody set forth at 23 Pa.C.S. § 5328, the trial court granted the relocation, but under the condition that mother return to central Pennsylvania after she has obtained her doctoral degree, or three years passes, whichever shall occur first, to the extent that she is able to move back to the area. Mother was directed to use her best efforts to locate employment and return to the Central Pennsylvania area by May 15, 2015. The court found that mother's increased education would enhance the child's quality of life, and viewed mother's relocation as "temporary." The court noted that the relocation to Arkansas was a short-term, three-year move. The court found that mother had no motive other than her education in deciding to move to Arkansas. The three-year as opposed to four-year doctoral program, combined with the very lucrative package, covering full tuition, stipend and health insurance, could not be duplicated by other schools).

Dauphin County

M.B.F. v. E.T.F., C.P. Dauphin County, No. 2018-CV-1060-CU, *aff'd*, *M.B.F. v. E.T.F.*, Memorandum Decision, No. 294 MDA 2019 (Pa. Super. July 5, 2019) (The trial court found that relocation would enhance mother's quality of life, and, in turn, the child's quality of life, based on the increased financial income quite predictable for a physician who completed a fellowship as opposed to a mere residency. After the parties divorced in 2015, mother subsequently married stepfather, who was in a plastic surgery residency at a local hospital. The trial court entered an order granting mother permission to relocate to Wisconsin. The court also issued a separate custody order/parenting plan, which addressed physical custody arrangements for the child for the year in question, corresponding to stepfather's one-year fellowship in Wisconsin. The trial court concluded that while father was an active parent, mother was even more active and thus was the primary parent. The court agreed with the trial court that relocation would not cause as great an impact on the child as it would if he were older, when his social network undoubtedly will broaden and his bonds with other children will become much deeper. The court also noted that the child would benefit from relocation because the local school in Wisconsin offered a pre-K program while her current school district in Dauphin County did not).

Delaware County

S.D.H. v. A.H., No. 2016-7725 (C.C.P. July 5, 2017), *aff'd,* Memorandum Decision, No. 2426 EDA 2017 (Pa. Super. March 12, 2018) (The trial court issued an order awarding joint legal custody to father and mother, primary physical custody to mother, partial physical custody to father, and permitting mother to relocate from Glen Mills, Delaware County, Pennsylvania, to Honey Brook, Chester County, Pennsylvania, with the parties' children. With respect to the relocation factors, the trial court specifically found that 23 Pa.C.S. § 5337(h)(2), the likely impact of relocation on the child, and § 5337(h)(6) and (h)(7), prospective improvements to the quality of life of mother and children, respectively, favored relocation, and that the remaining factors would not negatively impact the children's relationship with father. The trial court rejected father's suggestion that the physical home in Glen Mills was superior to the physical home provided by mother, such that the move could not be sanctioned. The trial court declared: "That is simply nonsense. To suggest that the bigger house and the nicer neighborhood wins is not the law. The emotional well-being of the children, along with their physical health and maintenance trumps the nicer home. In this case that warrants allowing the move with mother." The court found that mother had valid reasons to move with the children to Honey Brook and limiting father's time with the children was not the motivation. The court also credited mother' evidence that her move to Honey Brook was one of necessity due to what the court perceived as genuine concern with father's reaction to her leaving, and that mother had little financial, emotional, or family support other than a friend in Honey Brook, and that mother moved to the only place she would have some support).

McShane v. McShane, C.P. Delaware County, No. C.P.-23-CV-014826-2000 (C.C.P. 2015) (Trial court held that the estrangement of the minor child from father, as a direct result of mother's actions in repeatedly excluding father from all major decisions affecting the child despite their joint legal custody, had undoubtedly harmed the minor child, father and the minor child's relationship, and their ability to communicate. The trial court granted father primary physical custody in California and mother partial physical custody).

C.C. v. R.W.W., C.P. Delaware County, No. 2014-001370 (C.C.P. 2015) (The trial court issued a custody order requiring mother to return to Delaware County after improperly relocating to Florida with the parties' minor child without court approval. The trial court issued a final custody order which denied mother's relocation to Florida, noting that mother failed to comply with 23 Pa.C.S. § 5337(c) where she had not filed a Notice of Relocation, a Petition to Relocate or the appropriate Affidavit of Consent from father. Mother was required to return to Delaware County within 60 days of the date of the final order. The court took issue with mother's unilateral move to Florida, without court approval, without the approval of father, and without providing any evidence that she had tried and was unsuccessful in finding a residence or a job in Pennsylvania or Delaware, where mother had lived and where her fiancé was also living at the time they moved to Florida. The court heard credible testimony that father saw the minor child every other weekend until just before mother moved to Florida without consent. In addition, the court noted that mother failed to consider that the cost and expenses associated with the minor child's transportation to and from Florida which would render it nearly impossible for father to spend a significant amount of quality time with the minor child if mother remained residing in Florida).

Erie County

Moffett v. Moffett, 98 Erie Co. L.J. 66, C.P. Erie County, No. 12358-2013 (C.C.P. 2015) (The trial court awarded primary physical custody to mother and permitted her relocation to Nevada, where mother had a career opportunity in Nevada and other relatives were located there; the relocation would be in the best interest of the child).

J.S. v. S.M., 94 Erie Co. Leg. J. 91 (C.C.P. 2011) (Trial court reiterated that a party proposing a relocation has the burden of establishing that the relocation will serve the best interest of the child as shown under the relocation factors at 23 Pa.C.S. § 5337(h). Each party has the burden of establishing the integrity of that party's motives in either seeking the relocation or seeking to prevent the relocation, under 23 Pa.C.S. § 5337(i)(2). The court found that it was in the child's best interest here to deny the relocation request, finding that the child's needs for stability and continuity in his education, family life and community life required the child to remain in Erie, Pennsylvania and not North Carolina. Mother wanted to live with the child and the mother's fiancé. Mother had been in a long-distance relationship which was not firmly established. The outcome of that relationship, and mother's appointment prospects were uncertain. The court also noted that mother failed to establish the proposed move was in the child's best interest or would enhance the general quality of the child's life. Mother's financial security in North Carolina would hinge on the employment of the fiancé, who owed no duty of support to the mother or the child. "The child's ties to Erie are too strong, and the mother's situation in North Carolina is too tenuous, for the court to grant the mother's relocation request.").

Lackawanna County

M.G. v. B.N., C.P. Lackawanna County, No. 2015-FC-41365 (C.C.P. October 31, 2017), *aff'd*, Memorandum Decision, No. 1728 MDA 2017 (Pa. Super. June 27, 2018) (Trial court granted mother's petition for relocation, permitting her to move from Lackawanna County, Pennsylvania to Phillipsburg, New Jersey. The trial court also modi-fied the parties' custody arrangement. The court initially recognized the bonds the child had with both parties and their extended families in Lackawanna County. Nevertheless, the trial court found the first custody factor weighed in favor of permitting mother's relocation because the relocation would not interfere with the child's relationships with father or the parties' extended families. The court found that the parties' revised custody arrangement ensured that the child was present during Thursday dinners father had with his extended family and permitted the child to be present for one-half of the Sunday dinners father had with his immediate family. In addition, the trial court found that maternal grandmother traveled to New Jersey between two and four times per month and would be available to assist mother in caring for the child in New Jersey).

Lancaster County

R.M. v. S.M.F., C.P. Lancaster County, No. CI-13-03345 (C.C.P. August 11, 2016) (Mother failed to prove that the children's situation would be improved by her relocation to Texas and that psychological distancing of the children from their father would only increase, based on mother's demonstrated resistance and willful contempt for the court-ordered custody order. Father had been an active parent in the children's lives. He spent time with them on two nights during each workweek and had them in his care every other weekend. The court noted that father opposed mother's relocation request because if the children were permitted to relocate to Texas, father's relationship with the children would wither and disappear. The court observed that mother would exert no effort for father to have time with the children if she moved to Texas. Moreover, father could not afford the extra transportation costs associated with transporting two young children and an accompanying adult between Texas and Pennsylvania several times per year. The court cited with approval the Superior Court's recent decision in *D.K.D. v. A.L.C.,* 141 A.3d 566 (Pa. Super. 2016), wherein the court reversed the trial court's approval of a parent's relocation request (which the trial court had initially approved, but then had denied upon reconsideration). The key element in the Superior Court's analysis was the feasibility of preserving the child's relationship with the child's father (the non-relocation parent) and militated against allowing mother to relocate out-of-state with the parties' children. This key element was consistent with the court's analysis and determinations in this case).

Bhalala v. Fellenbaum, C.P. Lancaster County, No. CI-10-02282 (C.C.P. July 27, 2016) (Father provided no supporting evidence to prove that he or the child would reap any measurable benefit if the court approved his relocation from East Earl, Pennsylvania to Downingtown, Pennsylvania. Father's decision to relocate was a direct response to mother's returing to the child's life and father's desire to eliminate mother's and maternal grandparents' role in the child's life).

Lawrence County

Malinchak v. Peterson, C.P. Lawrence County, No. 10709 of 2012, C.A. (C.C.P. 2015) (The trial court ruled that any benefit to mother's relocation to Texas would be outweighed by the detriment to the child's relationship with her father; accordingly, the court denied mother's petition to relocate. Mother stated that her desire to relocate was primarily based upon a job opportunity provided to her new husband by her mother-in-law).

D'Amico v. Mills, C.P. Lawrence County, No. 11683 2008, C.A. (C.C.P. 2012) (Trial court granted father's petition to relocate with the children to Florida, where doing so would give the children the benefit of relationships with extended family members and would allow father to offer them a better quality of life. The court also determined that father's reasons to relocate were genuine and not to thwart mother's relationships with the children. Father desired to provide a stronger support system for his youngest daughters. Father had sustained an injury and had been unable to work since 2009 and relied heavily on his parents for financial support. Father intended to enroll in school in Florida and seek employment in a different profession. Living in Florida would also mean that the children would be closer to their maternal grandparents in Atlanta).

Tanner v. Tanner, C.P. Lawrence Co., No. 10290 of 2008, C.A. (C.C.P. 2011) (Trial court granted mother's petition to relocate, where: (1) mother wished to move in with fiancé; (2) the distance of the move was only 21 miles and would therefore not impair father's partial custody; (3) the parties could share the burden of transporting the children; and (4) the children were mature enough to adapt to a new environment. Father opposed the petition because he was concerned about how the children would react to a new school and that the children would lose the benefit of the extra-curricular activities and relationships they had established, and that the extra distance he had to travel to exercise his visitation rights would make his contact with the children more difficult. The distance from father's employment to mother's residence at the time the petition was filed was 13.6 miles. After the relocation, the distance would be 33.3 miles. The court observed that mother wished to relocate to improve her living situation, as she felt her current residence was not in a safe neighborhood for the children, and mother was to be married shortly and wished to reside with her fiancé. Mother investigated the school district where the children would be enrolled and found it appropriate for the children. The court found father enthusiastic and supportive and did not believe that an additional 10 or 20 miles should interfere with his active role in the lives of his children).

Prioletti v. Prioletti, C.P. Lawrence County, No. 10398 of 2006, C.A. (C.C.P. 2011) (Trial court acknowledged that the relocation of the parties' minor children with mother was in the children's best interest, but chose to stay the actual relocation until mother was able to find a suitable residence and appropriate school for the children, as well as to provide proper notice to father and the court. After the parties' divorce, mother remarried to a member of the United States Army, who was relocated to Hayden, Idaho. Mother petitioned for relocation, seeking to relocate with the parties' three children to Idaho. Mother stated that she wished to continue to function as an intact family and believed that her children would adapt easily to the move. She testified that she was the primary caregiver and that her new husband provided and cared for the children more than their father. Mother also contended that father had never consistently visited the children after the divorce, and had been absent from his children's lives because of drugs and alcohol. Father objected to the relocation. After examining the factors set forth in 23 Pa.C.S. § 5337(h), the relocation statute, the court found that mother's request to relocate was genuine and not intended to hinder father's relationship with the children. Mother proposed reasonable alternatives for father to communicate with the children during the school year and planned to have the children return to Pennsylvania in the summer. Mother intended to find an appropriate residence and a good school district *after* she relocated. The court rejected father's contention that omitting these facts from her petition for relocation rendered mother's petition invalid. The court interpreted § 5337(c)(4) to mean that a petition to relocate cannot be rendered invalid merely because specific factors were missing from the petition and notice. The court can consider these missing factors as relevant to its determination of whether to grant or deny a petition to relocate).

Lebanon County

Sims-Lewis v. Lewis, 49 Lebanon Co. Leg. J. 163 (C.C.P. 2012) (The trial court, based on an analysis of the relocation factors, found that mother's proposed relocation should be denied since mother failed to establish that the relocation served the best interest of the child. Mother failed to establish that the child's physical, educational and emotional development was substantially enhanced by the relocation, that the impact on the child's physical and emotional development would be severe if mother was permitted to relocate, and that the feasibility of preserving the relationship between child and father through suitable custody arrangements was very slim. The court was not convinced that relocation would benefit the child considering her family, friends, school, etc. were located in Lebanon, Pennsylvania. Among the court's further findings was that mother's primary motivation for seeking relocation was to reside with her boyfriend rather than economic advancement. The court found that father did not have any motivation for opposing the relocation other than the fact that he wanted to maintain a relationship with the child. The court encouraged father to build on his existing relationship with the child by finding a suitable residence of his own so that he could exercise overnight visitation with the child, and with the child having a separate room in his residence. In the event father failed to obtain a suitable residence for overnight visitation, the court provided in its Order that mother could petition the court again to revisit the issue of relocation).

Musselwhite v. Kessler, C.P. Lebanon County, No. 2010-20137 (C.C.P. 2011) (Trial court ruled that father was permitted to relocate with his three-year old daughter so that Father could attend graduate school in California, as he had consistently provided for the child's needs, would reap an economic advantage from the move and made a substantial effort to keep the child in touch with mother and her extended family. The parties had never been married and father was about to graduate from Lebanon Valley College. Father had been accepted in a chemistry doctorate program at the University of California at Berkeley. Both parties were presently employed part-time and resided with their parents. The child had resided with both parties and her maternal grandparents at the grandparents' residence. The child currently resided with father and her paternal grandparents at the grandparents' residence. The trial court applied each of the 10 factors set forth in the new custody statute dealing with relocation, 23 Pa.C.S. § 5337(i), and granted father's Petition to Relocate. The court found that father met his burden that the relocation was in the best interest of the child. "Father's education can open many doors for both him and the child and can provide him a substantial economic benefit which will, in turn, benefit the child. If father chooses to seek a professorship, college will be more affordable for the child. Moreover, the child will be exposed to diverse cultures and ideas in a setting conducive to learning." The court determined that father was essentially the sole provider and had a very close bond with the child whereas mother chose to leave father and child, and for periods of time, only communicated with the child on an intermittent basis without providing a reason and noted that it was clear that she was not able to properly provide a stable home at this point in her life. The court was concerned about the child being away from both sets of grandparents, but believed that father would keep his promise to provide close communication by phone and through video conferencing).

Lehigh County

Garcia v. Berrios, C.P. Lehigh County, No. 2004-FC-1074 (C.C.P. 2013) (Mother's desire to relocate to North Carolina to live with her husband was not a sufficient basis to grant a petition for relocation where the child had strong ties to her extended family, and the benefit to the child had not been proven. Relocation may not be granted if a parent cannot show that the benefits of relocation outweigh its drawbacks. While mother and stepfather provided a good home for the child, and the court understood that mother wanted to live with her husband, the court could not find that mother had met her burden of proof that relocation was in the child's best interest. The court noted that father had always exercised his custody rights and that the child was close to her extended family on both sides. The court found that an important part of the child's life was her relationship with her relatives, particularly her grandparents, who lived in or near Lehigh County. A relocation to North Carolina would disrupt her living among her extended family network in this area which was crucial to the child's happiness. The court also noted that mother failed to present evidence that the education available to the child in North Carolina was superior to her current schooling or that mother would be better off in either her studies or employment if she relocated).

D.R. v. Y.B., C.P. Lehigh County, No. 2008-FC-0042 (C.C.P. 2012) (Trial court denied mother's petition to relocate from Lehigh County to Delaware County where the proposed move was not prompted by financial need and father's mid-week custody with children would be abolished; spending less time with father would cause the children to suffer. Although the quality of a parent's life may be enhanced from a financial standpoint, maintaining the children's regular contact with the non-custodial parent may defeat a petition for relocation. Mother sought to move closer to new husband's place of employment, which was an hour away from their current home, and proposed

eliminating father's alternate week overnight visitation with the children. Mother testified that the move would allow her family greater income so that she could decrease her
work hours. The court found that the children had been thriving under the existing
custody arrangement and the children did not want to see their time with their father
decreased. Father spent a considerable amount of time with the children, with two visits
during the week and on alternating weekends. The relocation would also make it harder
for the children to continue their relationships with the extended family members. The
court noted that the proposed move by mother would result in a two-hour, 100-mile
round-trip commute for either father or the children, which would make regular weekly
visits during the school year difficult. The court found that while the move would certainly enhance mother's new family, any benefit to the children was outweighed by the
diminished regular contact they enjoyed with father. Since the move was not prompted
by any economic hardship suffered by mother, the court declined to advance the financial well-being of mother and her new husband to the detriment of the relationship of
father and the children).

Contrucci v. Casner, C.P. Lehigh County, No. 2011-FC-0801 (C.C.P. 2012) (Trial
court denied mother's petition to relocate to Florida, after finding that mother did not
establish that the move would greatly improve the quality of life for herself or the
parties' child, even though the relocation would have enabled her to live rent-free
with her parents. Mother intended to attend college and look for work in Florida. The
maternal grandparents and other family members also lived in Florida. The court
noted that father was an active parent, and his involvement in the child's life was
important to the child. The court believed that a move to Florida by mother with the
child would necessarily lessen father's steady involvement to the child's detriment.
The court noted that until mother decided that she wanted to move to Florida, she and
father had the understanding that they would be actively and regularly involved in
their son's life. Thus, there were no suitable custody arrangements with a move to
Florida to preserve the close relationship that both parents had with the child. The
court concluded that mother did not demonstrate that the quality of life for herself or
the child would be enhanced by the proposed relocation to Florida. The court ruled
that it would be in the child's best interests for mother to retain primary custody in
Pennsylvania with extensive partial custody for father. The court found that because
of the parties' many positive attributes as parents, it was appropriate that they continue to be joint legal custodians).

McKean County

A.S. v. R.G., C.P. McKean County, No. 165 C.D. 2017 (C.C.P. May 8, 2019), *aff'd.*,
Memorandum Decision, No. 857 WDA 2019 (Pa. Super. November 15, 2019) (Where
neither parent was relocating but the child could be moving a significant distance, the
trial court's consideration of the relocation factors, in addition to the custody factors,
was appropriate. The court reiterated that in a custody case where neither parent is
relocating, but the children stand to move a significant distance, trial courts should still

consider the relevant relocation factors of § 5337(h) in their § 5328(a) best interests custody analysis, citing *D.K. v. S.P.K.*, 102 A.3d 467, 478 (Pa. Super. 2014). The court noted that in the current circumstances, where neither parent was relocating but the child could be moving a significant distance, the trial court's consideration of the relocation factors in addition to the custody factors was appropriate. It is permissible for the trial court to consider the relative wealth of the parties to determine whether either party is unable to provide adequately for the child, citing *Roadcap v. Roadcap*, 778 A.2d 687 (Pa. Super. 2001). The court noted that where the income of one party is so inadequate that it precludes raising the child in a decent manner, then the parties' financial situations are relevant. The comparative finances of the parties was only one of a multitude of factors considered by the trial court).

Mercer County

D.A. v. A.A., C.P. Mercer County, No. 2017-1001, *aff'd*, Memorandum Decision, No. 1571 WDA 2018 (Pa. Super. June 19, 2019) (While the trial court ruled that relocation to Florida would enhance father's general quality of life because of his employment opportunity and extended family who live in Florida, that relocation would not enhance the children's general quality of life. Rather, the court concluded that the children would suffer greatly emotionally being separated from their mother. The court awarded mother primary physical custody and father partial physical custody for two months during the summer, and it directed that the parties alternate physical custody on holidays. The trial court delineated each of the 10 relocation factors and provided an analysis under each factor in its opinion that accompanied the order. The court noted that the children, during their *in camera* interviews, "unequivocally and without hesitation" stated that they wished to live with mother. The trial court accordingly afforded considerable weight to the children's uniform preference to live with mother, citing 23 Pa.C.S. § 5337(h)(4).

Monroe County

F.F. v. R.A.L., C.P. Monroe County, No. 139 DR 2015, 9167 CV 2017 (C.C.P. February 27, 2019), *aff'd*, Memorandum Decision, No. 961 EDA 2019 (Pa. Super. November 1, 2019) (Trial court denied mother's request to relocate from Monroe County to Montgomery County, awarding both parties shared legal custody, awarded mother primary physical custody contingent upon her return to Monroe County, and denied father's petition for contempt. Mother's relocation imposed an obligation on father to travel from Monroe County to Montgomery County in order to obtain custody of the child. Given the substantial distance involved, and father's inability to transport himself to exchanges, it was apparent that this obligation impaired father's ability to significantly exercise custodial rights. Mother was requesting that the court impair father's ability to exercise custodial rights going forward by imposing a significant transportation obligation on him. The primary reason for mother's relocation to Montgomery County was that she wanted to live with her paramour, who had obtained a job in that area).

Song v. Valderrama, C.P. Monroe County, No. 1836 CV 2019 (C.C.P. August 5, 2019) (Trial court permitted mother to relocate from Monroe County, Pennsylvania to Orlando, Florida with the parties' minor child, because the move would improve the child's general quality of life. Although the court acknowledged that the move would affect father's contact with his son, evidence revealed that the move to Florida would improve the child's general quality of life. The court stated that it was impressed with mother's concern for the child's health issue and that the relocation could resolve some of them. The court also noted that mother was financially providing for the child and that father was not providing child support. The court ordered mother to bear the full cost of the child's transportation until the summer of 2020, when the parties were ordered to share equally in the transportation costs for their child).

Humphrey v. Humphrey, C.P. Monroe County, No. 3047 CV 2014 (C.C.P. December 6, 2017) (Mother's proposed relocation with two of the parties' minor children from Pennsylvania to Delaware was not in the best interests of the children. Father objected to mother's motion to relocate to Delaware with the parties' two children. Father argued that the proposed move to Delaware would negatively affect his relationship with the children. Father stated he experienced difficulty in arranging to see the children because mother did not respond to text messages. The trial court denied mother's request to relocate to Delaware with the children. The court held in-camera hearings with all three of the parties' minor children. The children all expressed a preference to live in a stable environment where they had the support of family members, friends and teachers. The court recognized that, although mother's increased professional and financial prospects would benefit the children, it agreed with father that relocating the younger children to Delaware would have a significant negative impact on their close relationships with father and their siblings. The court believed that the best interests of the minor children would be served by remaining in the East Stroudsburg area where they can benefit from the presence of both parents, siblings, and extended family, while continuing to participate in school and extracurricular activities in which they currently participated. Both children had a strong involvement in their community and had done very well in school. The court emphasized that it considered the relocation factors set forth in 23 Pa.C.S. § 5337(h) and that relocation would substantially disrupt the educational and emotional development of the children).

Quartararo v. Williams, C.P. Monroe County, No. 8850 CV 2012 (C.C.P. March 6, 2017) (The trial court, after considering factors set forth in 23 Pa.C.S. § 5328(a) and the factors set forth in 23 Pa.C.S. § 5337(h), granted mother's request for relocation. The court recognized that mother relocated due to a change in her employment. Mother believed that her life would improve because her new job was better financially. The court observed that mother now worked more stable hours, which provided the special needs child with additional stability in his education and family life. The court found it clear that mother would benefit financially from the move and new position, which would allow for a more regular schedule to spend quality time with the child. The court also considered the relatively insignificant 40-mile distance between Emmaus and Monroe County, as well as father's admission that mother's relocation was not of a significant geographic distance. The exchange of custody would not be dramatically affected. The court noted that father had been consistently involved in the child's life and would remain in a close relationship with the child in spite of the move to Emmaus).

Carson v. Barletta, C.P. Monroe County, No. 1186 CV 2016 (C.C.P. August 1, 2016) *aff'd*, Memorandum Decision, No. 3115 EDA 2016 (Pa. Super. April 5, 2017) (Mother's proposed relocation with the children, with a grant of primary physical custody, was in the best interests of the children due to father's problems controlling anger and substance abuse and mother's better capacity to provide care and support for the children. Mother testified that she would work full-time and that her new job was at a higher hourly rate. Mother believed that the move would improve the general quality of the children's lives. The new school offered three- and four-year-old children with developmental delays a preschool program, which would benefit the children).

Deiana v. Rarick, C.P. Monroe County, No. 484 DR 2008 (C.C.P. 2013) (Trial court denied mother's request to relocate with the children from Monroe County to Dennis, Massachusetts, where she failed to present any evidence that the move was necessary for employment or affordable housing, and the distance from father's residence was too far to maintain a regular visitation schedule. The trial court concluded that although there was no evidence mother had an ulterior motive for seeking permission to relocate with the children, there was no compelling reason to disrupt the children's lives with a move that was not substantially designed to improve their quality of life. The court held that the first factor, considering the party more likely to encourage and permit frequent and continuing contact between the children and the other parent, slightly favored mother. During mother's sole physical custody of the children, she encouraged the children's visits and contacts with father. However, the court noted that mother, who remarried and had additional children, had no ties to Dennis, Massachusetts, where she proposed moving with the children. Mother simply developed an interest in the area after vacationing there several years ago. The court noted that a vacation is significantly different from living in the area year-round. The court determined that mother was not required to relocate for employment or better educational opportunities for the children and her proposed living arrangements involved temporary housing with a friend. The court was not confident that mother had thoroughly thought out the relocation of her family to Dennis, Massachusetts. The only connection with that area was a mutual friend of mother and her husband. The court explained that continuity and stability in the children's lives dictated against uprooting them from their home where they had immediate and extended family and a solid relationship with their father).

Lento v. Lento, C.P. Monroe County, No. 7425 CV 2012 (C.C.P. 2013) (Trial court denied mother's petition for relocation from Monroe County to Barnegat, New Jersey, where she failed to establish the move was necessary because of employment, affordable housing or other factors and where the children had strong bonds with their father and four siblings. Mother argued that the move was necessary because she was unable to find employment in the area of her current home, housing was less expensive, and there were enhanced educational opportunities for the children. Father opposed the relocation, claiming the children's relationship with him and the children's siblings would suffer. Father argued that he had always been a part of the children's lives, and although he works full-time, he had helped raise the children when he was home).

Sorrentino v. Sorrentino, C.P. Monroe County, No. 1195 DR 2008 (C.C.P. 2013) (Trial court denied mother's petition for relocation, finding that mother's proposal to relocate the children to Florida would not substantially improve their quality of life. Mother filed a petition seeking leave to relocate with her children to Florida, where she contended she would have a lower cost-of-living and be able to obtain a job as a certified nursing assistant. Father opposed the petition, arguing that he already had difficulty visiting the children and in light of his financial difficulties, it would be impossible for him to see them if they were relocated to Florida. The trial court denied mother's petition to relocate, finding that the move would not be in the best interest of the children because it would not substantially improve their quality of life. The court observed that mother's proposal was not "thoroughly researched." She did not have a home in Florida yet, had not secured employment there, did not present a realistic daycare plan and failed to recognize the expense of securing a suitable home in a state over 1000 miles away).

Montgomery County

A.D.D. v. A.L.B., 155 Montg. Co. L. Rep. 69 (C.C.P. April 17, 2017) (Trial court held that a court is not required to consider relocation factors when modifying custody of a child if neither of the parents is relocating, even if it means modifying the main residence of the child. The court granted father primary physical custody during the school year, when the child would be in first grade. Father was not relocating and mother was remaining in Lancaster County. As neither mother nor father was relocating, there was no change of circumstances on this issue for the court to assess. Since only the percentage of time that the child would be spending with each parent was changing, the relocation provisions of 23 Pa.C.S. § 5337, were not triggered, and the notice was not required under § 5337(c)).

S.W. v. S.W., 154 Montgomery Co. L. Rep. 57 (C.C.P. September 21, 2016) (In custody relocation cases, a trial court should seek to sacrifice the noncustodial parent's interests as little as possible "in the face of the competing and often compelling interest" of a custodial parent who seeks a better life in another geographical location. The court found that mother failed to meet her burden that relocation in this case would enhance the quality of life for the children, or that it would be in their best interests. The court found that, based on the testimony at the hearings, mother's specific employment opportunity did not outweigh the children's need for stability and continuity in their lives, nor did it outweigh the importance of father maintaining an active role in the children's lives. There was testimony offered that mother wanted to move to Maryland to start a new life farther away. The court observed that the testimony at the hearings, and in the child interviews demonstrated to the court, that father shared a close, warm, and positive relationship with the children and had done so since their births. Although father testified that he travels 75% of the time for his job, he followed the custody arrangement currently in place, and he also testified that if the children were to remain in Pennsylvania, he would be able to make adjustments to his work schedule to allow him to care for the children and to be available for them. The burden is on the relocating parent to establish a significant improvement in the quality of life for that parent and child. Here, the court found that mother had not done so).

J.G. v. J.G., C.P. Montgomery County, No. 2012-18650 (C.C.P. October 18, 2016), *aff'd.,* Memorandum Decision, No. 3743 EDA 2016 (Pa. Super. May 22, 2017) (The trial court denied mother's request to relocate to Florida with the parties' nine-year-old child because the child's loss from being separated from father and father's extended family would outweigh any benefit gained by mother in relocating. The court found credible the testimony and opinion of the custody evaluator, who was appointed by agreement of the parties. The court admitted into evidence the evaluator's thorough and comprehensive custody evaluation report. The custody evaluator stated that he did not recommend that the child relocate to Florida, noting that the benefits derived by mother as a result of the move would have to be weighed against the losses incurred by the child by being displaced from father and father's extended family. The evaluator noted that the child would continue to derive benefit from being exposed to father, particularly as he grew older).

Northampton County

B.I.D. v. A.M., C.P. Northampton County, No. C-48-2015-5404 (C.C.P. October 17, 2016), *aff'd,* Memorandum Decision, No. 3591 EDA 2016 (Pa. Super. September 1, 2017) (The relocation factors supported denying mother's Notice of Proposed Relocation. Father's consistent and significant role in the child's life strongly outweighed mother's reasons for relocation. Although mother pointed to ostensibly legitimate reasons for relocation, these reasons did not support granting mother's request to relocate. The court emphasized that the evidence reflected that mother's proposed relocation would impose significant burdens on father and would substantially interfere with his ability to continue his relationship with the child. If mother were permitted to move to North Carolina, father would have to travel up to 11 hours to see the child and, as a result, would not have as much time to spend with the child. Moreover, the court found, despite testifying about her optimistic goals for improvements in her life, mother failed to establish that the quality of life for her or the child would be improved in North Carolina. Mother did not have a job arranged in North Carolina. Mother stated that she intended to earn a paralegal degree but was not enrolled in any program, and her statements regarding support from family in North Carolina were vague and unsubstantiated. Thus, the court found no error or abuse of discretion on the part of the trial court in denying mother's petition for relocation. Accordingly, the trial court was not required to perform an analysis of the 16 custody factors as set forth at 23 Pa.C.S. § 5328).

D.P.L. v. V.I.R., C.P. Northampton County, No. C-48-CV-2016-05812 (C.C.P. December 21, 2016), *aff'd*, Memorandum Decision, No. 207 EDA 2017 (Pa. Super. August 17, 2017) (Mother filed a petition for relocation, seeking to relocate with the children to Smyrna, Delaware, to reside in the home owned by her new husband. The trip from Bethlehem to Smyrna took approximately 2½ hours by automobile. Father objected to the proposed relocation. Mother explained that the relocation would allow her to spend more time with her children and be more involved in their education, social life, and physical activities. She testified that the school system was comparable to the school district that the children currently attended. Ultimately, mother desired to move to Delaware so that she and the children could be closer to her new husband. Both children stated their preference to relocate to Delaware and acknowledged their extreme animosity toward father. The trial court entered an order denying mother's petition to relocate to Delaware. The trial court considered the 10 relocation factors enumerated in § 5337(h) and found that § 5337(h) (1), (2), (3), and (5) favored father to varying degrees, and that, while § 5337(h)(6) and (7) militated in favor of mother, those considerations were insufficient to warrant a relocation).

F.G. v. S.K., C.P. Northampton County, No. C-48-CV-2013-1898 (C.C.P. 2013) (Trial court denied mother's petition to relocate where the court was skeptical that the type of appointment she had obtained in Milwaukee was not available closer to father's residence. Also, mother's failure to provide reasonable notice of the proposed relocation to father was a factor in the court's determination regarding the relocation. The court expressed serious concerns about the reasons behind mother's proposed relocation. Mother planned to uproot the child from the location in which she had lived most of her life and where father and much of the child's extended family resided, primarily because mother found a job in the Milwaukee as a landlord's administrative assistant. The court did not consider the proposed relocation to be well conceived or necessary for the well-being of the child and/or mother. In addition, mother failed to meet her burden of proving that the proposed relocation would serve the best interest of the child. The child had excelled academically in Bethlehem and had many friends there. Further, father and much of the child's extended family resided locally or in the New York City area).

Philadelphia County

A.M.A. v. O.H.F., C.P. Philadelphia County, No. DR #0C 1412022 (C.C.P. August 23, 2018), *aff'd.*, Memorandum Decision, No. 2695 EDA 2018 (Pa. Super. July 15, 2019) (23 Pa.C.S. § 5337(j) makes consideration of father's failure to provide reasonable notice to mother regarding his relocation optional. The statute indicates that the trial court "may" consider the failure to provide reasonable notice for various purposes, not that the court "shall" or "must" consider it. Even if the language of the statute were mandatory, it was clear that the trial court did consider this issue. The court noted that while father may not have complied with the technical requirements of § 5337(c), in that he alerted mother of his move less than a week in advance, the court found that mother received reasonable notice nonetheless).

Susquehanna County

M.W. v. A.R., C.P. Susquehanna County, No. 2017-979, *aff'd,* Memorandum Decision, No. 22 MDA 2018 (Pa. Super. November 9, 2018) (Mother issued a notice of proposed relocation from Thompson, Pennsylvania to Florida with the parties' two minor children. Father filed a counter-affidavit objecting to relocation. The trial court denied mother's petition to relocate and granted father primary physical custody, and granted mother partial physical custody of the children if mother remained in Florida. Contrary to mother's argument based on the primary caretaker doctrine, the law no longer requires the trial court to give emphasis to a parent's status as the primary caregiver, citing *M.J.M. v. M.L.G.,* 63 A.3d 331 (Pa. Super. 2013) (the primary caretaker doctrine, insofar as it required positive emphasis on the primary caretaker's status, is no longer viable.). The court also concluded that relocation would impose a substantial burden on the children's relationship with father and the paternal grandparents under the first relocation factor).

S.M. v. R.J., C.P. Susquehanna County, No. 2016-397 (C.C.P. October 3, 2019*), aff'd,* Memorandum Decision, No. 1802 MDA 2016 (Pa. Super. April 21, 2017) (The trial court considered all of the factors required by 23 Pa.C.S. § 5337(h) and concluded that mother's relocation with the child should be denied. The court found that in a relocation case, as in any custody case, the paramount concern remains the child's, not the parent's, best interest. The court declared: "It is beyond the belief of this court that any parent would petition to relocate their children if said relocation would not contribute to the personal happiness and emotional well-being of the petitioning parent. If these particular benefits to the relocating parent were to carry such weight alone, few relocation petitions would demand much attention and time by the court, few would be denied, and the best interest of the children would take a backseat to the best interests of the relocating parent in virtually every case.").

Westmoreland County

M.P. v. J.M.R., 93 Westmoreland L. J. 151 (C.C.P. 2011) (Trial court ruled that where mother failed to submit objective, credible facts at trial which would support the alleged benefits of relocation of the children, including specific information about where the children will live, the school they will attend, and how mother will financially support the children, the petition for relocation must be denied. Mother did not present any testimony of school officials with regard to the details of the child's enrollment in the new school; there was no evidence regarding class-size, the academic curriculum, or the current academic needs of the child, and how those would be met in the proposed new school. Moreover, mother failed to provide credible evidence with regard to her current family income and expenses. The court noted that mother's failure to submit a plan of substitute visitation during the trial on her petition for relocation demonstrated her failure to recognize the implications of her proposed relocation of the children, and thus, in light of the requirements of the custody statute, the court denied the petition for relocation, and instead granted mother partial physical custody during the children's summer vacation and time off school. Finally, the court observed that mother had not sent the required notice by certified mail, as required by 23 Pa.C.S. § 5337(c). Sending an e-mail notification did not satisfy the statute's requirement that notice be sent by certified mail, return receipt requested).

York County

T.A. v. J.D., P/K/A/ J.G., C.P. York County, No. 2018-FC-183-03, *aff'd*, Memorandum Decision, No. 296 MDA 2020 (Pa. Super. July 27, 2020) (The language in 23 Pa.C.S. §5337 is mandatory; it provides no exception for a claim that a party entitled to notice was "aware of" or had "agreed to" the relocation. Discussing 23 Pa.C.S. § 5337(c), which addresses the notice the party proposing relocation must provide to the non-relocating party, the court found that mother did not file a notice of relocation before she moved. Thus, the court held, mother complied with neither the form nor the time requirement for notice of relocation as set forth in § 5337(c). Since mother did not provide notice, father was not provided with a Counter-Affidavit for objection to the proposed relocation).

§ 8.2. RELOCATION—HISTORICALLY

Many Pennsylvania cases have addressed the issue of Relocation prior to the enactment of the custody statute in 2011. It is important to understand the historical background and the cases leading up to the sweeping enactment of the custody statute. In *Reibstein v. Reibstein*,[50] the court found that the mother's and child's relocation from within a few blocks of the father, into another, but adjoining county, was not adverse to the best interests of the child, nor did it reflect unfavorably on the mother's stability or parental fitness, and the court thus refused to enjoin the move. However, in *Pappert v. Pappert*,[51] the trial court refused to permit the custodial parent to relocate out of state with the children, stating that such a move was not in the best interests of the minor children. The mother remarried, to a Maine State Policeman who was a heavy-drinking philanderer, whom she had seen just twice prior to the marriage, and whom she married prior to introducing her new husband to the children. New father was of very poor character. Mother

---

[50] Reibstein v. Reibstein, 322 Pa. Super. 629, 470 A.2d 1017 (1984).
[51] Pappert v. Pappert, 137 P.L.J. 201 (C.C.P. 1989).

and natural father were subject to a custody order that provided for substantial time for the children to be in the care of natural father. Upon mother's remarriage, she desired to move with the children to Maine to be with new husband. Trial court held that the mother was free to move to Maine, but without the children, who were to remain in Allegheny County, with or without mother. If mother moved to Maine, custody of the children would be with the father. In support of its decision, the trial court emphasized:

i. The major role father played in the children's lives;

ii. The extended family support system available to father;

iii. The benefit of keeping the children in their familiar community and maintaining continuity and stability in their lives;

iv The impulsive decision on the part of the mother to marry and move to Maine;

v. The instability and undesirability of the mother's new husband; and

vi. The harm from children's removal from his familiar locale, setting, and family outweighs harm from change of custodial relationship.

Trial court declared that the standard in custody cases is not what is in the best interest and welfare of the parents, but what is in the best interest and welfare of the children. First and foremost, continuity and stability are important elements in a young child's development. The children's move to Maine with mother would severely limit father's contact in favor of living with a man with whom it would be a "mistake" to reside.

In *Lozinak v. Lozinak*,[52] the Superior Court affirmed the trial court's refusal to permit mother to take the parties' eight-year-old daughter to Iowa, a state to which mother had no prior connections except for being the place where her new husband's employment and relatives were located. Mother was granted primary physical custody upon the condition that she remain in Pennsylvania, with primary physical custody to

---

[52] Lozniak v. Lozniak, 390 Pa. Super. 597, 569 A.2d 353 (1990).

be placed with father if mother decided to move. The appellate court held that the order of the trial court was a proper resolution of the best interests of the child in light of the equally strong parenting skills of both parents, the child's significant relationships with teachers, classmates, friends and relations in Pennsylvania and equivalent economic levels of both parents. The court noted that there was no economic, educational, religious, health, or emotional compulsion justifying the relocation of the daughter to Iowa. The court found that mother's intended removal of the minor child was inspired mainly by her desire to frustrate and ultimately defeat father's partial custody. The court concluded that mother's actions would remove the minor child from the only source of permanency that her young life had, that is, her attachment to her blood relatives on both sides of her family, whom she sees frequently, as well as her friends, school, and home. Mother was given 30 days to decide to live in Iowa or Pennsylvania. If she moved, custody would change.

In *Clapper v. Clapper,*[53] the Pennsylvania Superior Court affirmed the trial court's denial of a mother's petition to relocate to Connecticut, since it was not in the best interests of the parties' children. Both parents maintained a good relationship with the children and mother wished to relocate for motives of self-improvement.

Where remaining in Pennsylvania would be no less disruptive to the child's life than moving out of state, the Superior Court held that the mother was permitted to take the parties' child with her upon relocation to England.[54] The parties, who are both British subjects, had moved to the United States with their one-year-old child but then separated two years later. Although both parties filed for custody, they managed to agree upon a joint custody schedule for one year. The disruption in this arrangement occurred when Mother accepted a new job that required her to return to England to live. The trial court found that both parties had families in England, that neither intended to remain in the United States permanently, and that they wanted the child raised according to British customs. Further, the Court found that, although both parties were fit,

---

[53] Clapper v. Clapper, 396 Pa. Super. 49, 578 A.2d 17 (1990).

[54] Bernard v. Green, 412 Pa. Super. 201, 602 A.2d 1380 (March 27, 1990 as a memorandum and filed as an opinion on February 6, 1992).

Mother had made more arrangements for the child's care and education in England and such was most conducive to the child's stability. Father's plans, by contrast, were described as speculative and uncertain.

Prior to the decision of the Superior Court in *Gruber v. Gruber,*[55] the sole standard by which "relocation" questions were resolved was the "best interest of the child," a standard that the court recognized offered little guidance and allowed for inconsistent and irrational results. *See Clapper, supra,* and *Lozinak, supra.* In *Gruber,* the mother appealed from an order denying her permission to move out of state to Illinois with the parties' children and conditioning her continued retention of primary physical and legal custody of the children on remaining in Pennsylvania. The appellate court reversed the trial court and formulated a test for deciding relocation issues. The standard the court formulated was based on the observation that in determining the best interests of the child, the main focus must be on the primary custodial family. The court emphasized that the interests of the custodial parent and the quality of life for the custodial parent are inextricably bound with the interests of the child for whom he or she is responsible. Where a custodial parent seeks to relocate to another state, the task of the court is to sacrifice the non-custodial parent's interest as little as possible in the face of competing and often compelling interests of the custodial parent who seeks a better life in another geographical location. The court recognized several *important interests that must be accommodated* in relocation cases including:

(1) The custodial parent's desire to exercise autonomy over basic decisions that will directly affect his or her life and that of the children;

(2) a child's strong interest in maintaining and developing a meaningful relationship with the non-custodial parent;

(3) the interest of the non-custodial parent in sharing in the love and rearing of his or her children;

---

[55] Gruber v. Gruber, 400 Pa. Super. 174, 583 A.2d 434 (1990).

(4) the state's interest in protecting the best interests of the children;

(5) sacrificing the non-custodial parent's interest as little as possible; and

(6) custodial parent's interest in seeking a better life in another geographical location.

In order to accommodate these interests and decide whether the custodial parent and children should be permitted to relocate at a geographical distance from the non-custodial parent, what became known as the "*Gruber* factors" were established to determine under what circumstances a parent who has primary custody may relocate outside the jurisdiction. The *Gruber* factors are as follows:

(1) the potential advantages of the move and the likelihood that the move will substantially improve the quality of life for the custodial parent and the children and is not the result of a momentary whim on the part of the custodial parent;

(2) the integrity of the motives of both the custodial parent and the non-custodial parent in either seeking the move or opposing it must be established;

(3) the availability of alternative, realistic substitute visitation or partial custody arrangements must be explored, which will adequately foster an ongoing relationship between the child and the non-custodial parent. (*Note:* the mere necessity of shifting visitation will not defeat a move that offers real advantage to custodial parent and children).

Gruber also allocated the *burdens of proof* as follows: Initial burden is on the party seeking the move to establish that it is likely to significantly improve the quality of life for the parent and children; each party then has the burden to establish the integrity of his or her motives; and, finally, the court must consider the feasibility of reasonable alternative visitation to insure a continuing, meaningful relationship with the non-custodial parent.

The court then applied the then–newly-articulated standard to the facts of the case before it. Mother had three young children and was seeking permission to relocate with them to Illinois. Trial court concluded that mother ought to have primary physical custody but that she would lose it if she moved out of the jurisdiction. Mother's intended move was motivated by a desire to live with her brother who had offered to support her both financially and emotionally. She testified and had a physician testify that she suffered stress and depression in Pennsylvania where she was surrounded by former in-laws and where she had no family or friends. She and her former husband had frequent confrontations, often in front of the children. She was unemployed and had little prospect for self-support given the youth of her children. Based on these and similar considerations, the Superior Court held that mother had met her burden of demonstrating that the move would substantially improve the quality of life for the children and herself. The record also established the integrity of the motives of each parent. Finally, substitute visitation is available. Father testified that he has an annual leave of thirty days from his job, and that his parents can help with child care in the event he has partial custody of the children when he has to work. Although father may prefer the current visitation schedule, this factor does not outweigh the advantages of the move for the mother and the children.

Thus, mother was entitled to relocate to Illinois and still retain primary custody of children; mother's ability to be an effective parent to her children was seriously undermined by the difficulty and unhappiness of her life in Pennsylvania, the move to Illinois was likely to substantially promote the well-being of mother and make her a better parent, there was no evidence that mother had an illegitimate motive in seeking the move or that father had such a motive in resisting the move, and there was no overly burdensome impediment to a revised, realistic visitation schedule that adequately could foster a continuing relationship between father and children. When the custodial parent seeks to relocate at a geographical distance to secure a substantial advantage for the custodial parent and children, and the non-custodial parent challenges the move, the move will not be disallowed simply because visitation cannot continue in the existing pattern.

In *Lee v. Fontaine*,[56] the Superior Court affirmed a trial court's custody modification order that authorized the custodial mother to move with the parties' four minor children to Washington State. On appeal, father contended that the decision in *Gruber* altered the best interests standard in custody relocation cases to a more specified three-prong test. The Superior Court affirmed the trial court's decision that the relocation of the custodial parent with her children was in the children's best interest. As the trial court properly noted, the advantages of the move far outweigh the disadvantages. The Superior Court aligned itself with *Gruber*, but stressed that the best interest standard set forth in now repealed 23 Pa.C.S. § 5301 *et seq.* controls the issue of relocation, and any "judicially determined precondition may amplify, but do not alter, the best interest standard."

In *Plowman v. Plowman*,[57] the Superior Court held that due process requires that the evidentiary hearing applying the *Gruber* analysis must be conducted *before* the child is relocated outside the jurisdiction, or within a reasonable time thereafter.

In *Lambert v. Lambert*,[58] the Superior Court again emphasized that the ultimate objective in resolving relocation cases is the best interest of the children. The court remanded the case to the trial court for a hearing to inquire into the reasons for mother's move and the benefit it would offer her and children. Because the best interests are allied with the custodial parent's quality of life, the court also appropriately examined the factors set forth in the *Gruber* decision.

In *Kaneski v. Kaneski*,[59] the Superior Court affirmed the trial court's decision denying the father's request to modify the existing custody order and permitting the mother to relocate. Applying the *Gruber* analysis, the Court concluded the move was in the best interests of the children. Discussing the first prong, the Court pointed out that the benefit to the children does not have to be a direct one.

---

[56] Lee v. Fontaine, 406 Pa. Super. 487, 594 A.2d 724 (1991). *See also* Betters v. Betters, 49 Beaver Co. Leg. J. 27 (C.C.P. 1992) (While the factors in Gruber v. Gruber must be considered, the factors do not replace the overriding concern of the best interests of the children).

[57] Plowman v. Plowman, 409 Pa. Super. 143, 597 A.2d 701 (1991).

[58] Lambert v. Lambert, 409 Pa. Super. 552, 598 A.2d 561 (1991).

[59] Kaneski v. Kaneski, 604 A.2d 1075 (Pa. Super. 1992).

It was initially thought that *Gruber* would provide a checklist for custody relocation cases. However, as noted in *Lee, Plowman, Lambert* and *Kaneski,* the factors set forth in *Gruber* are significant but not the only factors to be considered by a court in determining the best interests of the children. A full analysis of all the factors that come into play in the assessment of the best interests of the children is necessary. As established in *Plowman*, a full and detailed evidentiary hearing tailored to the circumstances of the case is essential to the resolution of a relocation issue. Numerous articles have discussed the relocation issues in a custody case.[60]

In *White v. White,*[61] the court held that it was in an eight-year-old child's best interests to refuse mother's request to relocate from Pennsylvania to California, despite the fact that it would be beneficial for child to spend time with mother's family in California; mother had not secured employment in California, father and son enjoyed a meaningful relationship, father's motive in opposing relocation was not retaliatory or spiteful, and it was the opinion of a court-appointed psychologist that mother had not thought out the move and had too-little concern for any disruptive effect the move would have on the child, who had spent a large portion of his life with father and his family. Thus, the trial court properly exercised its discretion in finding that it was in child's best interests to deny mother's relocation petition in ordering that if mother chose to relocate, temporary custody of child would be granted to father with suitable partial custody arrangements made for mother pending outcome of custody proceeding and, if mother did not relocate, temporary custody order was to remain in effect, and in ordering that both mother and father attend counseling for parenting skills.

In *Vineski v. Vineski,*[62] the court held that mother's desire to relocate to an area with a better economy, her need to find a warmer climate owing to her arthritis, and her wish to find a small town similar to the one she was leaving, were all adequately supported by the record and were reasonable desires for relocation. The Superior Court held that upon application of

---

[60] *See, e.g.,* Wilder, "Relocation Hearings Relocated," 12 Pennsylvania Family Lawyer No. 6 (December 1991); Pollock, "*Judicial Intervention Revisited on Parental Relocation Cases after Gruber,*" 12 Pennsylvania Family Lawyer No. 5 (November 1991).

[61] White v. White, 437 Pa. Super. 446, 650 A.2d 110 (1994).

[62] Vineseki v. Vineski, 450 Pa. Super. 183, 675 A.2d 722 (1996).

the factors set forth in *Gruber v. Gruber*, it could not be said that the trial court committed a gross abuse of discretion in concluding the wife's reasons for relocation were reasonable.

In *Zalenko v. White*,[63] the Superior Court held that where the trial court found all three prongs of *Gruber v. Gruber* to have been satisfied, it erred in denying mother's relocation petition on the ground that the relocation would not benefit the child individually. Citing its decision in *Kaneski v. Kaneski*, 604 A.2d 1075 (Pa. Super. 1992), the court held that the trial court committed an error of law in concluding that, although mother would benefit substantially from the move, her child would not. The court explained that a child's best interests will be indirectly but genuinely served when an anticipated move is likely to substantially enhance the quality of life of the custodial parent. The court found that "indirect benefits flow to the children" of the custodial parent benefiting from a proposed move. The court concluded that the trial court committed an error of law in concluding that, although mother would benefit substantially from the move, the child would not. Because the court found that the remaining prongs of the *Gruber* test were satisfied, the trial court erred in denying the petition for relocation.

When all factors are equal, a trial court may not order custody forfeited by the relocating parent solely due to the relocation, the court declared in *Gancas v. Schultz*.[64] When both parents are equally able to raise their child, the court must consider the availability of realistic substitute visitation arrangements that will foster an ongoing relationship between the child and the non-relocating parent. The Superior Court held that the trial court erred when it concluded that mother's request to relocate the daughter to New Jersey mandated an order of primary physical custody to the father simply because mother's move would upset the existing custody and visitation arrangements.

In *Baldwin v. Baldwin*,[65] the Superior Court ruled that the trial court properly denied a custodial mother's request to relocate to South Carolina

---

[63] Zalenko v. White, 701 A.2d 227 (Pa. Super. 1997).
[64] Gancas v. Schultz, 453 Pa. Super. 324, 683 A.2d 1207 (1996).
[65] Baldwin v. Baldwin, 710 A.2d 610 (Pa. Super. 1998).

with her daughter to accept new employment, where, after losing employment, mother did not seek alternative employment in Pennsylvania; the majority of the children's relatives lived in Pennsylvania; and mother could not be relied upon to maintain the child's relationship with father. The court noted that an inquiry into the custodial parent's motives in relocating was proper under *Gruber*.

In *Clapper v. Harvey*,[66] the Superior Court held that a non-custodial mother's petition to modify custody so as to permit the child to live with her in Florida should be judged under the same test as a custodial parent's petition to relocate with a child, *i.e.*, the factors set forth in *Gruber v. Gruber*. The court agreed with the mother that a proper "best interests of the child" analysis in a case where the petitioning parent seeks to relocate the child to another jurisdiction includes consideration of the factors outlined in *Gruber v. Gruber*, 583 A.2d 434 (Pa. Super. 1990).

In *Beers v. Beers*,[67] a split three-judge Superior Court panel ruled that *Gruber* could apply to intrastate relocations.

A unanimous Superior Court panel in *Perrott v. Perrott*[68] (*per curiam*) reversed an Allegheny County trial court's May 2, 1997 denial of a custodial mother's request for leave to relocate her children to suburban Philadelphia, and remanded. The custodial mother sought leave in order to allow her to accept a major job promotion within her rapidly consolidating health services company. *Perrott* represents the first authoritative and unanimous precedent to approve intrastate and cross-state relocation issues since the non-precedential, split-panel decision (majority, concurrence, and dissent) in *Beers v. Beers*, 710 A.2d 1206 (Pa. Super. March 30, 1998) (affirming denial of leave to relocate intrastate).

In *Mealy v. Arnold*,[69] the Superior Court found that the trial court had misapplied the *Gruber* standard when it refused to consider non-economic benefits that would accrue to mother upon relocation.

---

[66] Clapper v. Harvey, 716 A.2d 1271 (Pa. Super. 1998).

[67] Beers v. Beers, 710 A.2d 1206, (Pa. Super. March 30, 1998).

[68] Perrott v. Perrott, 713 A.2d 666 (Pa. Super. 1998) (per curiam).

[69] Mealy v. Arnold, 733 A.2d 652 (Pa. Super. 1999).

In *Thomas v. Thomas,*[70] the Superior Court held that in relocation cases where the parties have equal shared physical custody of their children, the *Gruber* factors apply and should be considered as part of an overall "best interest of the child" analysis; accordingly, the *Gruber* analysis applied to cases involving parents with joint custody. In analyzing the first prong of *Gruber*, the Superior Court noted, where there is shared physical custody, "both [family units] must be scrutinized similarly in the examination of the competing custodial environments. . . ."

In *Anderson v. McVay,*[71] the Superior Court held that mother was not required under the *Gruber* test to show that her proposed relocation would have direct and tangible benefits for her two children, and thus she satisfied the first prong of the test by demonstrating that her relocation would improve the quality of her life, which would indirectly benefit the children.

In *McAlister v. McAlister,*[72] the Superior Court again ruled that where parents had joint custody of their two children, and where mother wished to relocate with the children out-of-state, the trial court erred in failing to analyze the *Gruber* factors in the context of two competing custodial environments pursuant to the Superior Court's recent holding in *Thomas v. Thomas.*

A custodial mother's move with her children to another area in the same county does not trigger application of the *Gruber* analysis, the Superior Court declared in *Zoccole v. Zoccole.*[73]

In *Hurley v. Hurley,*[74] the Superior Court held that prior to an initial custody order, both parties share the burden of proof and persuasion; in deciding whether to allow mother's relocation out-of-state, and the trial

---

[70] Thomas v. Thomas, 739 A.2d 206 (Pa. Super. 1999).

[71] Anderson v. McVay, 743 A.2d 1472 (Pa. Super. 1999).

[72] McAlister v. McAlister, 747 A.2d 390 (Pa. Super. 2000).

[73] Zoccole v. Zoccole, 751 A.2d 248 (Pa. Super. 2000).

[74] Hurley v. Hurley, 754 A.2d 1283 (Pa. Super. 2000).

court should have considered the *Gruber* factors as part of an overall best interest analysis without placing a burden of proof on either party.

In *Maurer v. Maurer,*[75] the Superior Court found that the lower court properly denied mother's petition to relocate to Florida with the parties' minor children, where she established that the only improvement from the move was an increased economic status, but offered no evidence regarding how the move would affect the children's social develop-ment or future education and offered only insignificant evidence of an alternative visitation plan. The court noted that in all instances where a custodial parent seeks to relocate and the non-custodial parent opposes the move, the burden is on the custodial parent to establish a significant improvement in the quality of life for that parent and child.

Mother's proposed move to California in order to pursue a new busi-ness venture with her new husband was not in the best interests of her children, the Superior Court declared in *Meyer-Liedtke v. Liedtke,*[76] where the move did not appear to be necessary and would greatly disrupt the stability and continuity of her children's lives.

In *Richards v. Hepfer,*[77] the Superior Court held that the trial court properly granted the paternal grandmother primary custody, where she had cared for the child for nearly all of her life without support from mother or father and was adequately able to provide for the child's best interest; moreover, the *Gruber* relocation analysis applied to a custody case where paternal grandmother was the primary custodian and mother was the opposing party.

In *Ferdinand v. Ferdinand,*[78] the Superior Court held that the trial court should have considered, in deciding whether to allow a mother to move out-of-state with her two children from different marriages, the importance of keeping the siblings together.

---

[75] Maurer v. Maurer, 758 A.2d 711 (Pa. Super. 2000).
[76] Meyer-Liedtke v. Liedtke, 762 A.2d 1111 (Pa. Super. 2000).
[77] Richards v. Hepfer, 764 A.2d 623 (Pa. Super. 2000).
[78] Ferdinand v. Ferdinand, 763 A.2d 820 (Pa. Super. 2000).

In *Boyer v. Schake,*[79] the Superior Court held that the trial court erred in applying *Gruber* to mother's relocation request, when it ignored mother's evidence of economic benefit and in concluding that the increased travel time that father would need for visitation was unacceptable. The trial court relied on *Mauer v. Mauer,* 758 A.2d 711 (Pa. Super. 2000), in concluding that "an economic benefit is insufficient in itself to satisfy the first *Gruber* factor."

In Burkholder v. Burkholder,[80] the Superior Court found that mother met her burden of proof with respect to her petition to retain custody of her children following a move to Florida, where the evidence showed that the move substantially improved the quality of life for her and her children and that the move was for the sole purpose of improving their quality of life. The record supports a finding that Mother's move to Florida was not just a momentary whim and has resulted in substantial improvement in the quality of her life and the lives of the children.

In *Graham v. Graham,*[81] the Superior Court ruled that the trial court abused its discretion by granting mother's petition to relocate to Florida, because the record did not support the trial court's determination that the potential advantages of the move would improve substantially the quality of life for mother and child and that the move was not part of a momentary whim by mother. The court noted that the only reason mother proffered for the proposed move was to be with her boyfriend, whom she had no plans to marry.

In *Tripathi v. Tripathi,*[82] the Superior Court found that because father was a non-custodial parent, this case was only marginally a case in which the *Gruber* formula is or should be applicable, and the *Gruber* factors had "only superficial application to the circumstances of this case, which is better determined pursuant to the traditional concepts applicable to custody cases and the best interest of the child."

---

[79] Boyer v. Schake, 799 A.2d 124 (Pa. Super. 2002).
[80] Burkholder v. Burkholder, 790 A.2d 1053 (Pa. Super. 2002).
[81] Graham v. Graham, 794 A.2d 912 (Pa. Super. 2002).
[82] Tripathi v. Tripathi, 787 A.2d 436 (Pa. Super. 2001).

In *Bednarek v. Velázquez*,[83] the Superior Court held that the trial court properly conducted a *Gruber* analysis in a case involving mother's proposed relocation within Pennsylvania, since the determination whether to apply the *Gruber* analysis in cases involving an intrastate move should be left to the discretion of the trial court.

In *Dranko v. Dranko*,[84] the Superior Court ruled that in considering mother's petition for relocation, the trial court did not err in refusing to consider mother's alternative visitation schedule after it determined that relocation would not substantially improve the quality of the children's lives. The court found that the benefit to mother in remarrying was outweighed by the children's stability and close ties to family in Allegheny County.

In *Marshall v. Marshall*,[85] the Superior Court ruled that the trial court erred in treating mother as the primary custodial family unit while considering her relocation request, because the order providing mother with primary physical custody was only an interim order intended to provide for the parties' rights pending resolution of the mother's relocation request and a full custody hearing. The trial court should have scrutinized both homes without preference, particularly when father had also petitioned for primary custody.

In *Arnold v. Arnold*,[86] the Superior Court found that the trial court properly considered the *Gruber* factors in approving mother's proposed relocation with her children to Canada, and the trial court was not required to consider any additional factors because the move was to a foreign country rather than interstate. After applying the *Gruber* factors, the trial court concluded that the move to Canada was in the best interests of the children and was based on sound economic reasons that would benefit the family.

In *Geiger v. Yeager*,[87] the Superior Court ruled that the trial court properly concluded that mother's proposed relocation to North Carolina

---

[83] Bednarek v. Velázquez, 830 A.2d 1267 (Pa. Super. 2003).
[84] Dranko v. Dranko, 824 A.2d 1215 (Pa. Super. 2003).
[85] Marshall v. Marshall, 814 A.2d 1226 (Pa. Super. 2002).
[86] Arnold v. Arnold, 847 A.2d 674 (Pa. Super. 2004).
[87] Geiger v. Yeager, 846 A.2d 691 (Pa. Super. 2004).

was advantageous under *Gruber v. Gruber*, because mother had already secured a job from an employer that would help to advance her education. A custodial parent's quality of life is inextricably linked to the best interests of a child.

In *Kirkendall v. Kirkendall*,[88] the Superior Court held that even though mother had been primary caretaker for most of the child's life, mother's decision to relocate to California and father's present role as primary caretaker balanced out mother's earlier role. Moreover, because the order awarding primary custody had not been entered prior to mother's relocation request, the trial court did not err in applying the *Gruber* factors in determining custody. The trial court further decided the *Gruber* factors did not support the child's relocation. While the move to California would improve mother's economic and non-economic welfare, those factors did not overcome the benefits to the child from remaining in Pennsylvania.

In *Landis v. Landis*,[89] the Superior Court held that the trial court erred in relying exclusively on the minor child's need to bond with both parents in denying mother's petition to relocate. The trial court granted mother sole legal custody and a continuation of shared physical custody between mother and father, but denied mother's request to relocate.

In *Goldfarb v. Goldfarb*,[90] the Superior Court ruled that the trial court erred in failing to allow mother to return to Israel with the parties' children. It was "manifestly unreasonable" for a trial court to predicate its custody award to an Israeli mother on her remaining in the United States. Economic and social benefits available to mother on her return to Israel were a greater benefit to the children than remaining in the United States to be close to the father. The trial court initially entered a shared custody order but later granted mother primary physical custody predicated on her continued residence in the United States. The trial court said that mother's relocation to Israel would result in the transfer of primary custody to father.

---

[88] Kirkendall v. Kirkendall, 844 A.2d 1261 (Pa. Super. 2004).
[89] Landis v. Landis, 869 A.2d 1003 (Pa. Super. 2005).
[90] Goldfarb v. Goldfarb, 861 A.2d 340 (Pa. Super. 2004).

In *Johns v. Cioci,*[91] the Superior Court affirmed the trial court's denial of mother's petition for relocation; however, the court reversed the trial court's order granting primary physical custody to father and remanded for further proceedings. The court upheld the trial court's determination that mother had not met her burden of proof as to any of the factors set forth in *Gruber v. Gruber.*[92]

In *Billhime v. Billhime,*[93] the Superior Court ruled that the trial court erred by failing to fully consider the economic and non-economic benefits of mother's proposed relocation. Mother filed an emergency petition for custody requesting permission to relocate with the minor children to Florida. Mother testified she wished to return to Orlando, Florida to benefit from the love, support, and encouragement of her extensive family, many friends from childhood, and her church community, now that she and father were separated. The trial court denied mother's petition to relocate to Florida. Mother appealed and the Superior Court agreed with mother and reversed and remanded, determining that the trial court incorrectly applied the factors of the leading case on parental relocation, *Gruber v. Gruber.*[94]

In *Fuehrer v. Fuehrer,*[95] the Superior Court ruled that the trial court erred in granting mother's petition to relocate with the children to the Netherlands, as it was based on mother's romantic whim, rather than the best interests of mother and children as a whole.

The trial court properly denied mother's relocation request where moving to California would only marginally improve her family's financial circumstances and would take the child away from father and a specialized education plan, the Superior Court held in *Ketterer v. Seifert.*[96]

In *Collins v. Collins,*[97] the Superior Court held that where no custody order existed, the trial court erred by focusing on mother's request for relocation before deciding which parent should receive primary custody.

---

[91] Johns v. Cioci, 865 A.2d 931 (Pa. Super. 2004).
[92] Gruber v. Gruber, 583 A.2d 434 (Pa. Super. 1990).
[93] Billhime v. Billhime, 869 A.2d 1031 (Pa. Super. 2005).
[94] Gruber v. Gruber, 583 A.2d 434 (Pa. Super. 1990).
[95] Fuehrer v. Fuehrer, 906 A.2d 1198 (Pa. Super. 2006).
[96] Ketterer v. Seifert, 902 A.2d 533 (Pa. Super. 2006).
[97] Collins v. Collins, 897 A.2d 466 (Pa. Super. 2006).

In *Speck v. Spadafore*,[98] the Superior Court ruled that mother's desire to cohabit with the man she planned to marry did not provide enough of a reason to grant her petition to relocate, where there was no substantial evidence of any distinct benefits to the child.

The trial court did not abuse its discretion when it denied mother's petition to relocate with the parties' child and in refusing to accept a court-appointed custody evaluator's recommendation that the petition be granted, the Superior Court held in *Masser v. Miller*.[99] The court noted that it is in the court's discretion whether to apply the *Gruber* test to intrastate relocations. Because the trial court chose to apply it to the instant case, the Superior Court also applied the test. The proposed relocation was within Pennsylvania, and amounted to only 45 minutes to one-hour travel time away from Appellant's current abode." The court also agreed with the trial court that mother did not meet her burden under *Gruber*.

In *Hogrelius v. Martin*,[100] the Superior Court affirmed the trial court's decision to grant grandmother's Motion to Relocate with the parties' minor child to Virginia. The evidence supported the trial court's decision that mother's proposed relocation, with a larger home and better school district, was in the best interests of the parties' minor child. Although an alternative custody schedule arranged after a parent relocates necessarily reduces the frequency of the other parent's interaction with the child, relocation should not be denied for that reason alone.

In *Klos v. Klos*,[101] the Superior Court held that the application of the *Gruber* analysis is not mechanically applied when the absent parent had already moved out of state and when the best interests of the children are of primary concern. The court found that the best interests of the children were superior to any *Gruber* analysis in determining whether father in Florida should be awarded custody of the parties' children. The court noted that this case consisted of an unusual departure from either the traditional *Gruber v. Gruber*[102] analysis or the "equal-footing" analysis

---

[98] Speck v. Spadafore, 895 A.2d 606 (Pa. Super. 2006).

[99] Masser v. Miller, 913 A.2d 912 (Pa. Super. 2006).

[100] Hogrelius v. Martin, 950 A.2d 345 (Pa. Super. 2008).

[101] Klos v. Klos, 934 A.2d 724 (Pa. Super. 2007).

[102] Gruber v. Gruber, 583 A.2d 434 (Pa. Super. 1990).

set forth in *Collins v. Collins*.[103] The father was awarded primary custody when mother, the primary caretaker, was shown to be emotionally and physically abusive to the children.

In *R.M.G. v. F.M.G.*,[104] the Superior Court ruled that, while the trial court improperly engaged in a *Ferdinand* sibling analysis and a *Gruber* relocation analysis when neither was warranted, the court did not err or abuse its discretion in increasing mother's physical custody where it was in the best interest of the children. A material change in circumstances is not a prerequisite to modification. The parties reached an agreement whereby father would retain primary physical custody of the children and mother would permit father to relocate with the children to Altoona in so that father could reside with his girlfriend. Subsequently, mother petitioned to modify the parties' agreement. The trial court issued an order by which the parties continued to share physical and legal custody of the children. However, the trial court's order increased mother's period of physical custody, as well as father's responsibility for transportation costs. Father appealed, arguing that mother had not proven a change of circumstances. Father asserted that the trial court erred and abused its discretion by granting modification of an existing custody order in the absence of a substantial change in circumstances, citing *Gianvito v. Gianvito*.[105] The Superior Court affirmed. However, although it found no abuse of discretion on the part of the trial court, the Superior Court disagreed with the legal analysis undertaken by the trial court in conjunction with its factual findings. Specifically, the court determined that the trial court placed undue weight on *Ferdinand v. Ferdinand*[106] and improperly applied the *Gruber* test in its analysis. Unlike *Ferdinand*, where the trial court ordered separation of half-siblings who had resided together with their mother, the case here involved two siblings who were already residing apart from their two half-siblings as a result of the consent order agreed to by mother and father. Moreover, unlike *Gruber*, where the court considered factors to be weighed in conjunction with a parent's request to relocate with children, the court here was faced with a situation where

---

[103] Collins v. Collins, 897 A.2d 466 (Pa. Super. 2006).
[104] R.M.G. v. F.M.G., 986 A.2d 1234 (Pa. Super. 2009).
[105] Gianvito v. Gianvito, 975 A.2d 1164 (Pa. Super. 2009).
[106] Ferdinand v. Ferdinand, 763 A.2d 820 (Pa. Super. 2000).

mother had already agreed to father's relocation with the children. Under the circumstances, neither *Ferdinand* nor *Gruber* were applicable.

Nevertheless, the Superior Court recognized that it could affirm a trial court's ruling on any basis. The court declared: "However, there has been no 'substantial change' required in Pennsylvania since 1988 when our Supreme Court specifically pronounced that no substantial changed circumstance was required to modify a custody order under the statutory provisions of the Custody and Grandparents' Visitation Act," citing *Karis v. Karis*.[107]

In *Durning v. Balent/Kurdilla*,[108] the mother, who lived in Alaska and had primary physical custody of the child, developed renal failure and was unable to care for the child. The maternal grandmother traveled to Alaska and brought the child to her home in Pennsylvania. Without permission, the father, who lived in Pennsylvania, took the child. Father then filed a petition to modify the existing Pennsylvania custody order, seeking to obtain primary physical custody of the child. Thereafter, the mother travelled to Pennsylvania to resume custody of the child and the father refused. Following a custody conciliation conference, Father was awarded primary physical custody of the child. Mother sought primary custody of the child and wished to relocate from Alaska to North Carolina where her husband was being re-stationed. The trial court issued its order providing the parties with shared physical custody on a week-on / week-off basis. Mother appealed. The appellate court noted that had the mother not become ill, the child would have remained with her in Alaska until her husband was re-stationed in North Carolina. The trial court ignored that the mother was the primary caregiver until she became ill as well as a number of factors that weighed against father having increased custody. The trial court's decision to order shared physical custody of the child on a week-on/week-off basis was unreasonable as the mother was moving to North Carolina, and the record supported the mother's position that she was not living with her mother in Pennsylvania and only came to Pennsylvania to regain custody of the child. The trial court abused its discretion in failing to maintain primary physical custody of the child with the mother based on her historical

---

[107] Karis v. Karis, 518 Pa. 601, 544 A.2d 1328 (1988).
[108] Durning v. Balent/Kurdilla, 19 A.3d 1125 (Pa. Super. 2011).

role as caregiver and the potential dangers of the disruption of established patterns. The trial court erred in finding that the mother did not satisfy the *Gruber* factors. The trial court's order was vacated and the matter was remanded for the entry of an order that the mother was to retain primary physical custody and relocate with the child to North Carolina.

Though this case was decided after the effective date of the new custody statute, because the action was filed prior to the effective date, the court analyzed the case under the law that existed prior to the enactment of the new law.

Chapter 9

CHILD PREFERENCE / CHILD TESTIMONY / *IN CAMERA* INTERVIEW OF CHILD

---

§ 9.1. Child Preference

§ 9.2. Child Testimony/*In Camera* Interview of Child

---

§ 9.1. CHILD PREFERENCE

In applying the "best interests of the child" standard, the welfare of the child is the central focus and paramount factor in any custody action.[1] Assuming the child is age appropriate, it is the responsibility of the trial judge to adduce the child's preference in every case.[2]

As the age of the child is important, there are cases that hold that the older the child, the greater the weight attached to the preferences.[3] While there is no fixed age below which a child's wishes will be totally disregarded by the court, the refusal by the court to conduct an interview with children aged five and six has been held not to be an abuse of discretion.[4] Further, it has been held that a ten-year-old was probably

---

[1] *See* § 1.1., *supra.*

[2] 23 Pa.C.S. § 5328(7).

[3] In re Davis, 502 Pa. 110, 465 A.2d 614 (1983) (little weight given to preference of six-year-old); In re Temos, 304 Pa. Super. 82, 450 A.2d 111 (1982) (preference of children ages 6 and 7½ discounted); Williams v. Williams, 223 Pa. Super. 29, 296 A.2d 870 (1972); Palmer v. Tokarek, 279 Pa. Super. 458, 421 A.2d 289, 294 (1980); Kozlowski v. Kozlowski, 362 Pa. Super. 516, 524 A.2d 995 (1987) (Preferences of children involved in custody modification proceeding could be considered by trial court, since the children involved were 16 and 14 years of age);

[4] In re Davis, 502 Pa. 110, 465 A.2d 614 (1983) (court did not err in refusing to interview six-year-old on the record even where court gave some weight to the expressed preference of the child); Commonwealth ex rel. Michael R. v. Robert R.R., 314 Pa. Super. 335, 460 A.2d 1167 (1983) (court refused to establish a *per se* rule that failure to interview a child is error where record is comprehensive and opinion thorough); In re Custody of Pearce, 310 Pa. Super. 254, 456 A.2d 597 (1983) (strong

quite close to the youngest age at which a child's preference should be accorded great weight in determining custody.[5]

It is essential to note, however, that the chronological age of a child is not conclusive as to the weight to be assigned to the preference. Careful examination of the maturity, honesty and intelligence of the child is crucial to the proper balancing of the preference element.[6]

This method of analysis has enabled courts to attach great weight to the preference of a "normal, bright, 10-year-old who does quite well in school"[7] as well as that of a "serious, truthful and concerned 9-year-old,"[8]

---

preference of four-year-old coupled with maintenance of status quo was decisive); Sipe v. Shaffer, 263 Pa. Super. 27, 396 A.2d 1359 (1979) (refusal by court to interview five- and six-year-old held proper).

[5] Commonwealth ex rel. Bowser v. Bowser, 224 Pa. Super. 1, 302 A.2d 450 (1973).

[6] McMillen v. McMillen, 529 Pa. 198, 602 A.2d 845 (1992) (the Supreme Court held that the eleven-year-old child's preference was not controlling but was an important factor to be considered in determining the best interests of the child. Such preference must be based on good reasons, and the child's maturity and intelligence must be considered. The trial court must determine what weight to give a child's testimony as to his preference.); Commonwealth ex rel. Holschuh v. Holland-Moritz, 448 Pa. 437, 292 A.2d 380 (1972); Myers v. DiDomenico, 441 Pa. Super. 341, 657 A.2d 956 (1995) (While express wishes of child are not controlling in a custody decision, those wishes do constitute an important factor that must be carefully considered in determining the child's best interests. In considering the wishes of a child in a custody decision, court must take into account the child's maturity and intelligence and whether the child's preference is based on good reasons); E.A.L. v. L.J.W., 443 Pa. Super. 573, 662 A.2d 1109 (1995) (the Superior Court ruled that in awarding primary custody of minor children to mother after children were raised by the grandparents, the trial court improperly failed to consider the rational preferences of the children, ages 12 and 10 at the time of hearing, to stay with grandparents); Mahoney v. Mahoney, 354 Pa. Super. 585, 512 A.2d 694 (1986) (trial judge gave weight to the fact that child was an intelligent ten-year-old boy who repeatedly indicated his preference to live with his father in California rather than his mother in Pennsylvania); *see also* Sipe v. Shaffer, 263 Pa. Super. 27, 396 A.2d 1359 (1959); Martincheck v. Martincheck, 262 Pa. Super. 346, 396 A.2d 788 (1979); Shoup v. Shoup, 257 Pa. Super. 263, 390 A.2d 814 (1978).

[7] Commonwealth ex rel. Bowser v. Bowser, 224 Pa. Super. 1, 302 A.2d 450 (1973). *See also* Stoyko v. Stoyko, 254 Pa. Super. 78, 385 A.2d 533 (1978) (strong preference of ten-year-old given weight).

[8] In re Russo, 237 Pa. Super. 80, 346 A.2d 355, 357 (1975).

while according little weight to the preference of a "slow and perhaps retarded" 12-year-old,[9] without sacrifice of consistency.

It was held that a trial court acted unreasonably and abused its discretion in failing to honor a preference of a 12-year-old girl based on good reasons.[10] On the other hand, a trial court was affirmed in discounting a child's preference that was coerced.[11] As the function of the preference analysis is to ascertain the desire of the child, it is essential that the preference arise of the child's own volition rather than as a product of the overt or more often times, subtle persuasion of parents or siblings.[12] Moreover, a discovery by the court of such underlying motivation will result in the virtual dismissal of the preference as a factor in the custody decision.[13]

---

[9] Commonwealth ex rel. Hickey v. Hickey, 213 Pa. Super. 349, 247 A.2d 806 (1968);

[10] Johns v. Cioci, 865 A.2d 931 (Pa. Super. 2004) (the Superior Court concluded that the trial court erred by failing to give sufficient weight to the child's preference to live with mother. At age 12, the child was old enough for the trial court to honor her preference. Moreover, the child recited two reasons for her preference—that she liked living with mother and liked her school. "Our case law has ample precedent in which the custody preference of 11 or 12-year-old children was honored. The child in the present case is an intelligent and articulate 12-year-old girl, who is academically gifted and excels in school. In essentially dismissing her testimony because of her youth or because it was deemed not as based on good or consistent reason, the trial court acted unreasonably and abused its discretion.").

[11] Saintz v. Rinker, 902 A.2d 509 (Pa. Super. 2006) (the Superior Court ruled that the trial court properly transferred primary physical custody of a child from mother to father, despite the child's statement during an *in camera* interview that she wished to remain with mother. The court believed that the child's comment was motivated by fear of mother's reaction; thus, a child's stated preference to stay with mother did not control a custody decision, when the trial court properly believed that mother psychologically manipulated the child. The court agreed with the trial court that the child's "response that she wanted to live with her mother was coerced by her knowledge that her mother would have access to her responses." The trial court found the child's indication that she wanted to live with mother incredible. Instead, the trial court properly credited the child's spontaneous comments made to her counselor and to a court-appointed psychologist that she wished to live with father but was afraid to communicate her desires to mother).

[12] In re Leskovich, 253 Pa. Super. 349, 385 A.2d 373 (1978).

[13] Witmayer v. Witmayer, 320 Pa. Super. 372, 467 A.2d 371 (1983); Pamela J.K. v. Roger D.J., 277 Pa. Super. 579, 419 A.2d 1301 (1980); In re Leskovich, 253 Pa. Super. 349, 385 A.2d 373 (1978).

Judges are aware of the tendency of young children to frequently change their minds, particularly in response to parental pressure or promise of material benefits.[14] Thus, courts will not consider the preference, even of an older child, unless it is accompanied by sound, relevant and persuasive reasons.[15] "A court must not simply accept a child's statement of preference, instead the court must critically examine the reasons underlying the child's statement, for a too-ready acceptance of the statement would be in effect an abdication by the court of its responsibility to decide for itself what will be in the child's best interest."[16]

The adamance or indifference with which the preference is expressed constitutes still another variable which should be considered by the court. Although even the most vehement preference may be outweighed by invocation of the best interests doctrine, numerous cases illustrate

---

[14] McCourt v. Meyers, 268 Pa. Super. 152, 407 A.2d 875 (1979); In re Leskovich, 253 Pa. Super. 349, 385 A.2d 373 (1978); Bender v. Bender, 197 Pa. Super. 397, 178 A.2d 779 (1972).

[15] Commonwealth ex rel. Holschuh v. Holland-Moritz, 448 Pa. 437, 292 A.2d 380 (1972); Ellingsen v. Magsamen, 337 Pa. Super. 14, 486 A.2d 456 (1984) (preference based on location of father's home found to lack sufficient basis); Grieb v. Driben, 312 Pa. Super. 375, 458 A.2d 1007 (1983) (court remanded for a full hearing based on the fact that the trial court had given the unsupported preference of a sixteen-year-old child controlling weight); K.L.H. v. G.D.H., 318 Pa. Super. 330, 464 A.2d 1368 (1983) (preference of eleven- and thirteen-year-olds not controlling as basis for preference not convincing); In re Liberto, 291 Pa. Super. 26, 435 A.2d 201 (1981); Parks v. Parks, 284 Pa. Super. 400, 426 A.2d 108 (1981); Shoup v. Shoup, 257 Pa. Super. 263, 390 A.2d 814 (1978); Tomlinson v. Tomlinson, 248 Pa. Super. 196, 374 A.2d 1386 (1977). *See also* Altus-Baumhor v. Baumhor, 407 Pa. Super. 276, 595 A.2d 1147 (1991).

[16] Hooks v. Ellerbe, 257 Pa. Super. 219, 390 A.2d 791, 795 (1978), *rev'd on other grounds*, Ellerbe v. Hooks, 490 Pa. 63, 416 A.2d 512 (1980); King v. King, 889 A.2d 630 (Pa. Super. 2005) (the Superior Court held that the trial court did not abuse its discretion by awarding primary physical custody of the parties' 12-year-old daughter to father despite testimony from the child that she desired to be with mother and testimony from a custody evaluator that custody should remain with mother). Unlike other cases, in which children have expressed a desire based on the hatred directed toward one parent, (*see* Watters v. Watters, 757 A.2d 966 (Pa. Super. 2000)), or where the children based their preference in an attempt to avoid an environment replete with foul language, inappropriate sexual activity, smoking, drinking, and the threat of physical harm, . . . [the children's] reasons are less than compelling. As set forth in Watters the reasons for the child's choice must comport with what is in the best interest of the children.

that a preference voiced in emphatic terms will be significantly more persuasive than a preference bearing overtones of ambivalence.[17]

A bare preference, or one accompanied by invalid reasons, will be accorded little or no weight.[18] Courts scrutinize all reasons offered, and courts may disregard preferences based on promises of ponies, private telephones, or separate bedrooms.[19] Thus, where both parties are capable of adequately supporting the child, proffered reasons which are tainted by visions of material advantages to be provided by one party appear to be subject to particular scrutiny.[20] Consistent with this line of reasoning, courts have discounted a preference based solely on a custodial setting with a "more open" atmosphere, which the court found to be substantially based on a move to a new house complete with "her own bedroom and with other material advantages."[21] Similarly, preferences which are "location-based" rather than "party-oriented" have been carefully analyzed by the courts[22] as in the case of the preferences of young children

---

[17] Commonwealth ex rel. E.H.T. v. R.E.T., 285 Pa. Super. 444, 427 A.2d 1370 (1981); L.D. v. B.D., 291 Pa. Super. 589, 436 A.2d 657 (1981) (little weight given to vacillating preference of 5-year-old); see also In re Custody of Pearce, 310 Pa. Super. 254, 456 A.2d 597 (1983) (strong preference of four-year-old coupled with maintenance of status quo was decisive); McCourt v. Meyers, 268 Pa. Super. 152, 407 A.2d 875 (1979); Stoyko v. Stoyko, 254 Pa. Super. 78, 385 A.2d 533 (1978); In re Russo, 237 Pa. Super. 80, 346 A.2d 355 (1975); Commonwealth ex rel. McDonald v. McDonald, 183 Pa. Super. 411, 132 A.2d 710 (1957).

[18] Tomlinson v. Tomlinson, 248 Pa. Super. 196, 374 A.2d 1386 (1977).

[19] Tomlinson v. Tomlinson, 248 Pa. Super. 196, 374 A.2d 1386, 1389 (1977).

[20] Swope v. Swope, 455 Pa. Super. 587, 689 A.2d 264 (1997) (father argued that the trial court erred in disregarding the children's expressed preference to live with him. The Superior Court found that the trial court had considered the children's preference, but determined that because it was largely based on father's leniency, it should not have been afforded controlling weight. While the preference of a child in a custody case is a factor to be carefully considered, here the preference lacked a sufficient basis to be accorded controlling weight); Tomlinson v. Tomlinson, 248 Pa. Super. 196, 374 A.2d 1386, 1389 (1977).

[21] Tomlinson v. Tomlinson, 248 Pa. Super. 196, 374 A.2d 1386, 1389 (1977); but see Shoup v. Shoup, 257 Pa. Super. 263, 390 A.2d 814 (1978) (court impressed with validity of reasons in spite of allegations of material advantage); Clair Appeal, 219 Pa. Super. 436, 281 A.2d 726 (1971).

[22] Trefsgar v. Trefsgar, 261 Pa. Super. 1, 395 A.2d 273 (1978).

solely concerning familiarity with the neighborhood and the consequent proximity of friends[23] or a preference based on the fact that there were more friends and there was "more to do" at a proposed custodial abode.[24]

Reasons supporting a given preference which courts have generally found persuasive tend to be linked with the love, care, or affection a child will receive in one custodial setting contrasted with the absence thereof, or reports of mistreatment at the alternative location.[25] Courts have credited explanations indicating that the child was subjected to an immoral atmosphere,[26] inadequate nutrition or health care,[27] obscene language, or excessive drinking by a parent or newly acquired spouse thereof[28] or that the child would get more love with the preferred party.[29]

The Pennsylvania Supreme Court has held that where the households of both parents were equally suitable, the child's preference could not but tip the evidentiary scale in favor of that parent.[30]

---

[23] Baisden v. Demarco, 215 Pa. Super. 38, 257 A.2d 365 (1969). *But see* Clair Appeal, 219 Pa. Super. 436, 281 A.2d 726 (1971) (13- and 14-year-old children had built up strong friendships).

[24] Trefsgar v. Trefsgar, 261 Pa. Super. 1, 395 A.2d 273 (1978).

[25] Brooks v. Brooks, 319 Pa. Super. 268, 466 A.2d 152 (1983) (court found that children's belief that their father would take care of them, help them with school work and take them places, to be sound reasons); Melzer v. Witsberger, 299 Pa. Super. 153, 445 A.2d 499 (1982) (court considered preference based on better schools at father's house, harassment by older sibling at mother's home, and more attention devoted by father); Wrecsics v. Broughton, 285 Pa. Super. 90, 426 A.2d 1155 (1981); Commonwealth ex rel. Murphy v. Walters, 258 Pa. Super. 418, 392 A.2d 863 (1978); Shoup v. Shoup, 257 Pa. Super. 263, 390 A.2d 814 (1978); In re Russo, 237 Pa. Super. 80, 346 A.2d 355 (1975); Commonwealth ex rel. Bowser v. Bowser, 224 Pa. Super. 1, 302, A.2d 450 (1973).

[26] In re Snellgrose, 432 Pa. 158, 247 A.2d 596 (1980); In re Children of Bro, 33 Som. 39 (1973).

[27] Commonwealth ex rel. Murphy v. Walters, 258 Pa. Super. 418, 392 A.2d 863 (1978).

[28] Commonwealth ex rel. Bowser v. Bowser, 224 Pa. Super. 1, 302 A.2d 450 (1973).

[29] Wrecsics v. Broughton, 285 Pa. Super. 90, 426 A.2d 1155 (1981); Commonwealth ex rel. Murphy v. Walters, 258 Pa. Super. 418, 392 A.2d 863 (1978).

[30] McMillen v. McMillen, 529 Pa. 198, 602 A.2d 845 (1992) (Pennsylvania Supreme Court reversed appellate court and reinstated trial court's decision awarding general custody to father. Since parties' divorce in 1981, father sought modification of custody order granting primary physical custody to mother. During trial court hearing, ten-year-old child testified that he would prefer to live with father and step-mother because he

Where both parents are equally loving and capable parents, and the children were ages, 16, 14, 12, and 10, it was an abuse of discretion for the trial court not to interview the children and elicit their preferences.[31]

A child's preference to not be separated from his/her siblings has also been given weight by the courts.[32]

A child's preference, although not controlling, is a factor to be carefully considered, so long as it is based on good reasons.[33] The weight

---

did not get along with mother or step-father. His testimony also revealed that step-father threatened him, and mother was ambivalent to these threats. The court found that these were sufficient reasons to afford the child's preference significant weight. Superior Court vacated lower court order and held the record did not demonstrate any reason to change custody because child's best interests were not served by changing custody based on child's preference. Supreme Court reversed and held that trial court did not abuse its discretion by giving weight to child's preference for it was properly considered along with child's maturity and intelligence and tipped the scales in favor of an award of custody to father); *see also* Myers v. DiDomenico, 441 Pa. Super. 341, 657 A.2d 956 (1995) (court held that since mother's and father's respective households constitute equally suitable environments within which the children can be properly raised, then the children's preference to live with Father could not help but tip the evidentiary scale in favor of Father. Maturity, intelligence, and the ability of children to express their preferences are all factors to be carefully considered by a court when deciding child custody).

[31] Bovard v. Baker, 775 A.2d 835 (Pa. Super. 2001) (mother claimed that trial court erred in failing to interview or receive testimony from her four children, Superior Court reversed and remanded case for evidentiary hearing to consider the express preferences of the children, with due regard for each child's reasons, level of maturity, and intelligence).

[32] Bowser v. Bowser, 224 Pa. Super. 1, 302 A.2d 450 (1973).

[33] Cardamone v. Elshoff, 442 Pa. Super. 263, 659 A.2d 575 (1995) (While express wishes of child are not controlling in custody decisions, such wishes do constitute an important factor that must be carefully considered in determining child's best interests); Snarski v. Krinick, 372 Pa. Super. 58, 538 A.2d 1348 (1988) (trial court did not err in according some weight to the express preference of an eight-year-old child to remain in the custody of his maternal grandparents rather than in the custody of father, where the child indicated his preference was due not only to the toys that his grandparents gave him, but also to unpleasant incidents that had occurred during the time that he lived with his father); Bresnock v. Bresnock, 346 Pa. Super. 563, 500 A.2d 91 (1985) (preference of a child to remain in the custody of her grandparents is a factor which should be considered but is not controlling); McCourt v. Meyers, 258 Pa. Super. 152,

which may be assigned to a preference varies from almost no weight accorded;[34] to some weight given, such that the preference tips the balance when all other considerations are equal;[35] to according such weight to the preference that it outweighs other factors which support a decision contrary to the preference.[36]

In all custody cases, the question of the proper weight to be attached to a child's preference is committed to the sound discretion of the trial judge and will not be disturbed on appeal except where abuse of discretion is found.[37] Notwithstanding the broad discretion of the trial court, a proper balancing of the preference should rely heavily upon examination of the child's age, including an intelligence-maturity evaluation; the reasons offered for the preference; and the origins of the preference.[38]

The importance of the inclusion of the child's preference in custody litigation is threefold. First, the preference, while constituting only one

---

407 A.2d 875 (1979); Shoup v. Shoup, 257 Pa. Super. 263, 390 A.2d 814 (1978); Commonwealth ex rel. Murphy v. Walters, 258 Pa. Super. 418, 392 A.2d 863 (1978); Tobias v. Tobias, 248 Pa. Super. 168, 374 A.2d 1372 (1977).

[34] Pamela J.K. v. Roger D.J., 277 Pa. Super. 579, 419 A.2d 1301 (1980).

[35] Carlisle Appeal, 225 Pa. Super. 181, 310 A.2d 280 (1973); Commonwealth ex rel. Bowser v. Bowser, 224 Pa. Super. 1, 302 A.2d 450 (1973); *see also* Bovard v. Baker, 775 A.2d 835 (Pa. Super. 2001).

[36] In re Russo, 237 Pa. Super. 80, 346 A.2d 355 (1975); *see* Carlisle Appeal, 225 Pa. Super. 181, 310 A.2d 280 (1973).

[37] Boylan v. Boylan, 395 Pa. Super. 280, 577 A.2d 218 (1990) (trial court did not err in considering children's preference before ruling that primary custody of children should be with mother; each child had given specific reasons for remaining with mother and trial court stated it was impressed by children's candor, reasoning, and obvious intelligence; appellate court noted that the trial court accorded considerable weight to the children's preference to remain with their mother); Haller v. Haller, 377 Pa. Super. 330, 547 A.2d 393 (1988) (although the children expressed a preference for remaining with their father, the weight to be given their preference is to be determined by the trial judge. "[I]t is the responsibility of the trial judge to weigh that preference according to the age, intelligence, and maturity of the child." Note that the children were 7 and 5 years of age at the time of trial); Commonwealth ex rel. Grimes v. Grimes, 281 Pa. Super. 484, 422 A.2d 572 (1980); *see also* King v. King, 889 A.2d 630 (Pa. Super. 2005) (trial court did not abuse its discretion by awarding custody contrary to child's preference).

[38] B.C.S. v. J.A.S., 994 A.2d 600 (Pa. Super. 2010).

of the many factors to be considered by the court, may serve as a tie-breaker in circumstances where the custody arguments of the opposing parties are evenly balanced. In such cases, where a preference toward one custodial setting is offered and properly supported by a child of sufficient age and maturity, the probability is that a child's best interests will be consistent with his or her stated preference.[39] In addition, even in cases where custody is not awarded to the preferred party, the preference may be highly relevant on the issue of reasonable partial custody.[40]

Second, the function of the preference is to provide the court with a full and complete record.[41] Thus, rendering a custody decision while failing to consult the child, particularly an older child, about his or her preference as to where and under whose control the formative years of his or her life will be spent, constitutes a glaring omission and may dictate a remand by the appellate courts.

Third, eliciting the child's preference has its origin in the psychological well-being of the child. The Pennsylvania Superior Court succinctly summarized this rationale stating:

> "when a child of the age of the boy here involved (12) is emphatic in his preference, we must seriously consider the emotional effect upon him were he compelled to follow a course which he detests and fears. No desires are as strong nor fears as great as the desires and fears of youth. A twelve-year-old boy is an individual and reacts as one. His lack of control over his own destiny can be frustrating to the degree that it becomes emotionally disturbing and permanently harmful."[42]

---

[39] Carlisle Appeal, 225 Pa. Super. 181, 310 A.2d 280, 282, fn. 4 (1973).

[40] Strapple v. Strapple, 263 Pa. Super. 187, 397 A.2d 809 (1979).

[41] Moore v. Moore, 634 A.2d 163 (Pa. 1993).

[42] Commonwealth ex rel. Bowser v. Bowser, 224 Pa. Super. 1, 302 A.2d 710, 713 (1957). *See* Watters v. Watters, 757 A.2d 966 (Pa. Super. 2000) (Superior Court credited son's outspoken animosity toward mother as a reason for awarding primary custody to father, even though mother was a perfectly fit parent and retained custody of his sister. "Where, as here, the child's mental state is threatened by his current custody situation, and his stability is largely dependant upon the presence of one parent rather than the other, the child belongs where his emotional equilibrium may be maintained if not actually improved.").

LOWER COURT CASES

Adams County

Naill v. Naill, 31 Adams Leg. J. 137 (C.C.P. 1989) (Although not controlling, a child's express preference to remain with a particular custodian is a factor to consider).

Berks County

Milbrandt v. Karow, C.P. Berks County, No. 97-08118 (C.C.P. 2008) (Where a high-school–aged child expressed depression and unease with mother and happiness and security with father, primary custody was properly left with father. The child testified that she was depressed and sad during visits with her mother, but safe and happy with father. She flourished academically and socially in father's environment. "Based upon the strong and well-defined issues of the minor child, and given her age and maturity with regard to the decision-making process as it pertains to her relationship with mother, this Court sees no reason to disrupt the current custody with father.").

Goodling v. Goodling, C.P. Berks County, No. 96-2802 (C.C.P. 1998) (Trial court held that the children's preference should be controlling in a custody action where the children were mature and expressed their preference for one of two proposed custody schedules in an articulate and reasonable manner. The court explained that the children both wanted the same schedule, they provided legitimate reasons for their preferences, and such preferences were sound and justified. The court further found that the children are intelligent, mature individuals who are closer to adulthood than childhood.).

Klahold v. Klahold, 36 D.&C. 4th 469 (Berks Co. 1996) (Trial court held that no change of primary physical custody was warranted where mother had always been the primary caretaker and had done a good job, where the child had a strong preference for remaining with mother, and where the recommendation of the custody evaluation was not to change primary custody. While acknowledging that a child's wishes are not control-ling, the court emphasized that it had to consider these wishes as an important factor in determining the child's best interests, citing *In Re Custody of Pearce*, 456 A.2d 597 (Pa. Super. 1983). Here, the child told the court that she wanted to live with mother and visit father less often. Citing the child's best interests as the prevailing standard in all custody disputes, the court accorded great weight to the findings and recommendations of the psychologist who had performed the custody evaluation. A hearing judge must consider uncontradicted expert testimony, the court stated, referring to *Murphy v. Hatala*, 504 A.2d 917 (Pa. Super. 1986). The recommendation that there be no change in primary physical custody, the court noted, was consistent with both the child's stated preference and the court's independent assessment that there was no basis for such a change.).

Mogel v. Mogel, 87 Berks Co. L. J. 252 (C.C.P. 1995) (A ten-year-old child's stated preference should be considered, especially when the child's statements are made with candor, reasoning, and obvious intelligence. The court also noted that although it cannot be the sole controlling factor in making a custody decision, the preference for raising siblings together is a strong factor. Absent compelling reasons to the contrary, siblings should be raised together whenever possible in order to provide the continuity and stability necessary for a child's development.).

Myers v. Myers, 85 Berks L. J. 27 (C.C.P. 1992) (A minor child's expressed preference to remain with a particular custodian is clearly a factor that should be considered, but it is not controlling. The weight to be accorded the child's preference is to be determined by the trial court; court did not find child's preference controlling where child, age 6, gave no reasons for his preference).

Carbon County

Michael B. v. Kimberly R., 15 Carbon Co. L. J. 187 (C.C.P. 1999) (While not controlling, the children's preferences carry great weight, since they were able to articulate them rationally and with conviction. The court found that this conviction, in combination with the loving relationship the children had with foster parents and mother's unexplained absences, warranted a custody award to foster parents).

Chester County

Fairfield v. Fairfield, 49 Chester Co. L. Rep. 286 (C.C.P. 2001) (Trial court held that although mother had been the primary custodian of her two minor children for all but one year of their lives, she failed to show why she should regain custody she gave up as a result of her move to Iowa; the children's preference for living with mother because of her more relaxed style of parenting was not a compelling reason to change custody. "While we have considered the children's stated desire to move to Iowa we do not believe their choice is based on sound reasoning and therefore is not binding on us").

Cumberland County

A.J.S. v. M.L.S., C.P. Cumberland County, No. 2010-2689 Civil (C.C.P. 2016) (Trial court held that the attempts of a parent to turn the children against the other parent weighed in favor of awarding father primary physical custody. While the teenage children had voiced a preference for living primarily with mother and having very little contact with father, the court found that this preference was not well reasoned and was based mostly upon mother's actions (consciously and subconsciously) to alienate the children from their father).

Kennedy v. Hartzell, 37 Cumberland L. J. 146 (C.C.P. 1986) (Although a child's custodial preference may be entitled to consideration, the law does not allow children to determine their own custodial arrangements contrary to their best interests and welfare. Where a satisfactory joint physical and legal custody arrangement exists whereby a 13-year-old boy lives with his father during the summer school vacation period and his mother during the school year and attends her school district, where both parents are equally fit or nearly so, where the mother is a stronger influence on keeping the child in school and doing well, and where a change in residency would impose maternal duties upon the child's sister and a consequent deterioration of their relationship, the prior arrangement and order will not be changed, notwithstanding the child's preference to remain with his father during the school year).

Commonwealth ex rel. Bear v. Fraker, 26 Cumberland L. J. 211 (C.C.P. 1976) (Preference of eight-year-old should be considered but need not be given great weight).

Dauphin County

Wingate v. Wingate, 112 Dauph. 62 (C.C.P. 1992) (The court has a responsibility to weigh a child's preference according to his age, intelligence, and maturity of the child. A child at age five is far too young to accord weight to his preference. A second child, although 10 years old, is not of an age, intelligence, or maturity for the Court to accord his preference controlling weight).

Delaware County

McShane v. McShane, C.P. Delaware County, No. C.P.-23-CV-014826-2000 (C.C.P. 2015) (Mother had consistently thwarted the relationship between father and the child by not allowing father to have his full visitation with the child, as well as providing the child with court documents that had undoubtedly negatively shaped and influenced the way in which the child viewed father. Court held that father should have primary custody of the child and child should relocate to California to live with father).

Grambo v. Hood, 44 Del. L. J. 63 (C.C.P. 1992) (Recognizing that the best interest of the child is the foundation of any custody proceeding, the court held that this interest was best served by awarding custody to the father who could provide a more stable environment. Although preference of the child should not be given undue weight, the court concluded the child's desire to stay with her father reflected this stability and must be considered).

C.S. & M.S. v. C.B. & E.S., 43 Del. L. J. 290 (C.C.P. 1991) (On remand from the Superior Court, the trial court held that the child's best interest would best be served by changing a prior order granting custody to the grandparents to awarding custody to the mother. In the original proceeding, the appellate court found the child (age thirteen) to be very immature and consequently dismissed her preference to reside with her mother. The Court also believed the mother was unable to provide a positive environment because of her sexual preference. However, the current testimony of the child (at age fifteen) expressing a desire to live with her mother revealed a much more mature individual. The Court heavily weighed this preference and also the fact that the mother had married and the husband was a positive male role model for the child. Thus, in the current proceeding, the Court concluded the mother's ability to provide a stable environment and the child's preference warranted that custody be awarded to the mother).

Houck v. Roegner, 75 Del. Co. Rep. 354 (C.C.P. 1988) (A child of less than eleven years of age does not have the experience or maturity to decide his own custody, but his wishes are an important factor to be considered).

Lawrence County

Moon v. Moon, C. P. Lawrence County, No. 10474 of 1997, C.A. (C.C.P. 2000) (Trial court found that where mother had been the primary caretaker of the parties' two children and there was no evidence suggesting that she was unfit to continue in this role, the youngest child's desire to live with father because he was more lenient was not a compelling reason to transfer custody. Thus, where both parents are deemed to be equally fit, custody should not be transferred from the parent who has been the primary caretaker of the children. "Here, Mother continues to provide a stable home life for the children. The environment that the children live in is highly structured and emphasizes the moral, religious and educational development of the children. The only negative factor that the Court sees in the mother is her continued and unrelenting failure to encourage a relationship between the children and the father. . . . The law requires the Court to leave Naomi with her primary physical custodian and in the residence where she has always lived with her sister unless compelling reasons are advanced to do otherwise. The Court finds that all the reasons advanced, being otherwise premised upon Naomi's desire to lead a less restrictive and more liberal lifestyle, do not amount to compelling reasons to change the status quo at this stage in her life.").

Lehigh County

Carew v. Rivera, C.P. Lehigh County, No. 2009-FC-0230 (C.C.P. 2011) (Trial court determined that the child's preference to reside with mother was outweighed by father's consistent and capable parenting and mother's history of instability. The child, age 11, expressed a preference to live with mother and her three half-siblings. After considering the factors set forth at 23 Pa.C.S. § 5328(a), the trial court concluded that the child's best interests would be served if father retained primary physical custody. Mother was denied primary custody due to her history of abandonment and her failure to consistently communicate with father regarding important issues related to the child. The court held that though the child expressed a preference to live with mother, other factors supported an award of custody to father, particularly, father's consistent, capable parenting as opposed to mother's unpredictability. The trial court must weigh all factors and consider the best interest of the child based on the totality of the circumstances. The court noted that in making its decision, it was aware of the admirable policy of the law to keep siblings together).

Montgomery County

Silbermann v. Silbermann, C.P. Montgomery County, No. 95-03460 (C.C.P. 1996) (The weight to be given a child's testimony as to his or her preference is best determined by the judge before whom the child appears, citing *Lombardo v. Lombardo*, 527 A.2d

525 [Pa. 1987]. Here, the court explained that it considered the preferences of the children when making its custody decision, but found that the preferences were not based on good reasons, and, therefore, could not outweigh the fact that the mother had been the primary caretaker of the children since their births).

Philadelphia County

Smith v. Phillips, 20 Phila. 255 (C.C.P. 1990) (Although the express wishes of a child are not controlling in custody matters, they do constitute an important factor that must be considered in determining the child's best interest; the weight to be accorded such preference is to be determined by the trial court; in assessing the weight to be accorded the child's preference, his or her intelligence and maturity is to be considered, with increased weight being accorded said preference as the child becomes mature; a child's stated preference may be sufficient to support a conclusion that a change of custody is warranted).

Carr v. Carr, 17 Phila. 581 (C.C.P. 1988) (The court, in a custody matter, may consider the following factors in arriving at its decision: 1) where the child's friends live; 2) whether or not the non-custodial parent failed to consistently exercise his visitation rights prior to the filing of the custody petition; 3) that the non-custodial parent entertains almost every weekend and is a heavy drinker; and 4) that the non-custodial parent resides with his or her paramour).

Somerset County

Gramann v. Cole, 51 Somerset Leg. J. 213 (C.C.P. 1992) (A child's preference, although not controlling, is a factor to be considered so long as it is based upon good reasons; in assessing the weight to be accorded the child's preference, the child's maturity and intelligence are to be considered with increased weight being accorded the preference as the child grows older; where no reason, or a very inadequate reason for the preference is given for the child's choice, courts have given no weight thereto).

In re Children of Bro, 33 Somerset Leg. J. 39 (C.C.P. 1973) (The weight which may be assigned to a child's preference may be accorded such weight that it outweighs other factors which support a decision contrary to the preference).

§ 9.2. CHILD TESTIMONY/*IN CAMERA* INTERVIEW OF CHILD

At some point in each custody action, except those involving very young children,[43] the trial judge will in most instances conduct an

---

[43] *E.g.*, Sipe v. Shaffer, 263 Pa. Super. 27, 396 A.2d 1359 (1979).

interview with the child, out of the presence of the contesting parties. The interview has numerous purposes, the initial function being the discovery of the child's preference, if one exists, toward one litigant or the other.[44] A second intention served through the interview is the confirmation of facts or incidents concerning the proposed custodians which may be relevant as bearing on the character or credibility of the contestants.[45] Thus, where the testimony of the parties conflicts as to certain incidents, the *in camera* interview may bring to light the actual circumstances surrounding the disputed testimony. In addition, the *in camera* interview is necessary to fulfill the trial court's duty to produce a comprehensive record so as to enable the appellate court to properly discharge its reviewing function on appeal.[46] However, the trial court has discretion as to whether it will interview the child/children.[47]

The Pennsylvania Supreme Court Rules of Civil Procedure governing custody were promulgated on November 8, 1982, and became effective on January 1, 1983, applicable to all actions pending at that time. Rule 1915.11(b) addresses the *in camera* interview of the child, and appears at the end of this book.

Rule 1915.11(b)[48] provides as follows:

> The court may interview a child, whether or not the child is the subject of the action, in open court or in chambers. The interview shall be conducted in the presence of the attorneys and, if permitted by the court, the parties. The attorneys shall have the right to

---

[44] *See* § 9.1, *supra.*

[45] Commonwealth ex rel. Bowser v. Bowser, 224 Pa. Super. 1, 302 A.2d 450 (1973.)

[46] *See* Chapter 17, *infra.*

[47] T.D. v. E.D., 194 A.3d 1119 (Pa. Super. 2018) (trial court's decision not to interview 8-year-old child on the single issue of whether child should travel by air as an unaccompanied minor affirmed). Examples of other cases where court did not require child testimony: Staub v. Dolm, 960 A.2d 848 (Pa. Super. 2008) (deciding between public and home schooling); Fox v. Garzilli, 875 A.2d 1104 (Pa. Super. 2005) (ordering that the children attend school in the mother's school district); Dolan v. Dolan, 548 A.2d 632 (Pa. Super. 1988) (deciding between public and private school).

[48] Effective July 1, 2016, Rule 1915.11 was revised by changing the word "interrogate" to "interview" regarding the court's interaction with a child in custody cases.

interview the child under the supervision of the court. The interview shall be part of the record.

By reviewing the clear meaning and words in Rule 1915.11(b), the trial court does not have the discretion of whether the attorneys should be present during the interrogation/interview and whether the interrogation/interview should be on the record, as the Rule uses the word "shall" with regard to same.[49]

Preservation of a record of the *in-camera* interview is clearly the foremost procedural requirement directed by the holdings.[50] On appeal, in most cases where the trial judge fails to cause the interview to be recorded and transcribed and where it is evident that the custody decision rested in whole or in part on the testimony of the child, the appellate court will be ill-equipped to perform its reviewing function and will remand for expansion of the record.[51] In addition, the requirement of a transcript is a right serving the interests of the subject child and may not be ignored by the court or waived by a litigant either through stipulation

---

[49] Ottolini v. Barrett, 954 A.2d 610 (Pa. Super. 2008) (trial court erred when it chose to interview children without counsel present and not on the record; Superior Court reversed trial court); A. O. v. M. O., 856 A.2d 1204 (Pa. Super. 2004) (father argued that trial court erred because attorneys were not permitted to directly question child. Superior Court found trial court did not err when trial judge, when questioning the child, allowed parties to be present but asked all of the questions posed to her by counsel. "It is discretionary with the judge exactly how to elicit truthful information from a child." The judge, in his opinion, stated: "The Court believed that such an approach was the best way to make [Child] feel comfortable and, in turn, provide candid answers. And so, by allowing the attorneys to ask the Child questions through the Court, the requirements of Pa. R.C.P. 1915.11(b) were met."); In Sutliff v. Sutliff, 361 Pa. Super. 194, 522 A.2d 80 (1987), it was held that the trial court, in a visitation and custody proceeding, violated the civil procedure rule at a hearing by refusing right of mother's counsel to interrogate the child under court supervision; Gerald G., Jr. v. Theresa G., 284 Pa. Super. 498, 426 A.2d 157 (1981); Gunter v. Gunter, 240 Pa. Super. 382, 361 A.2d 307 (1976).

[50] In re Snellgrose, 432 Pa. 158, 247 A.2d 596 (1968); Commonwealth ex rel. Scott v. Rider, 248 Pa. Super. 383, 375 A.2d 149 (1977); Gunter v. Gunter, 240 Pa. Super. 382, 361 A.2d 307 (1976).

[51] Commonwealth ex rel. Scott v. Rider, 248 Pa. Super. 383, 375 A.2d 149 (1977); Gunter v. Gunter, 240 Pa. Super. 382, 361 A.2d 307 (1976); Commonwealth ex rel. Grillo v. Shuster, 226 Pa. Super. 229, 312 A.2d 58 (1973).

or failure to request transcription.[52] However, the Superior Court, in distinguishing *Gunter v. Gunter*, affirmed the lower court in its award of custody, despite the lower court's failure to transcribe its interview with the children, but summarized the interview on the record.[53]

LOWER COURT CASES

Bucks County

McLaughlan v. Ermert, C.P. Bucks County, No. AO 6-2001-62559-C-37 (C.C.P. 2011) (Trial court rejected father's request that the court interview the parties' children outside the presence of either party, since doing so would have been in violation of Pa.R.Civ.P. 1915.11(b). The court indicated that since only one of the parties was represented, the court would hear from the children in open court. Father argued that the court committed an error of law and abuse of discretion by failing to interview the children *in camera*. The court ruled that it did not err as a matter of law or abuse its discretion in failing to interview the parties' children *in camera* where such an

---

[52] Gunter v. Gunter, 240 Pa. Super. 382, 361 A.2d 307 (1976).

[53] N.H.M. v. P.O.T., 947 A.2d 1268 (Pa. Super. 2008), the Superior Court ruled that the trial court properly awarded primary custody of the parties' minor children to father because of the minor son's sexual abuse in mother's home, even though the trial court did not transcribe its interviews with the parties' children. The court rejected mother's argument that the record was insufficient to support the trial court's conclusion that inappropriate sexual conduct had occurred between her son and the paramour's son, because the trial court did not transcribe its interview of the parties' children. The court acknowledged that it had held in Gunter v. Gunter, 361 A.2d 307 (Pa. Super. 1976), that the record was insufficient to determine the child's best interests in the parties' custody case because the trial court did not transcribe its interview with the child. However, the court determined that the instant case was distinguishable because, unlike in Gunter, the record contained sufficient evidence to support the trial court's conclusion that the children's best interests would be served by transferring primary custody to father. The court noted that the trial court summarized the interview on the record, and noted that inappropriate sexual contact occurred between the two children which caused the plaintiff's son emotional harm. The court also cited testimony from father that his son had revealed 30 sexual incidents between him and the paramour's son over a two-year period and that the paramour's son had threatened him with a pocket knife, testimony from the paternal grandmother regarding similar revelations from the child, and testimony from mother and the paramour that they were aware of "sexual exploration" between the two children. A therapist who had treated the family also testified regarding the son's emotional issues.

interview would have violated Rule 1915.11(b). The court ruled that it declined to interview the children *in camera*, since mother was unrepresented at the hearing. The court allowed father to call the children to testify in open court before both parties, but father declined this offer. The court held that it never prevented the interrogation of the children. Rather, the court made it clear that if father wanted to have the children questioned, the court would permit it in open court. Also, the court gave father the opportunity to present the testimony of the children, but father decided not to do so).

Schuylkill County

M.D. v. A.D., C.P. Schuylkill County, No. S-1551-2011, *aff'd*, Memorandum Decision, No. 592 MDA 2018 (Pa. Super. September 12, 2018) (Pa.R.Civ.P. 1915.11(b), governing interviews of children at custody hearings, provides in part, "the court *may* interview a child, whether or not the child is a subject of the action, in open court or in chambers;" the Rule does not mandate that trial court's interview children who are the subjects of a custody matter. In deciding not to interview the oldest child, the trial court stated, "we'll take her preference for what it's worth in... [the expert's] report, wherein she stated she wanted to spend more time with mother." The trial court stated on the record in open court that it would consider the oldest child's preference stated to the expert to spend more time with mother).

Chapter 10

EVIDENCE

---

§ 10.1. EVIDENCE – PRIVILEGE

In a custody dispute, the court must have the benefit of all available information concerning the parties and the child prior to its rendering of a best interests determination.[1] In affirmation of this policy, appellate courts are quick to remand if the judge does not fulfill his/her responsibility of developing a full and complete record. It is at this point where

---

[1] It is the trial court's duty to "ensure that as full and complete a record as possible is created when a decision as important as the welfare of a child is at issue." Moore v. Moore, 634 A.2d 163 (Pa. 1993).

the development of the complete record and the policies protecting the confidential nature of certain relationships collide.

Statutes designating various types of testimony as privileged are enacted for purposes wholly foreign and, in most cases, in conflict with the truth-seeking function of the adversary system. When attorneys, psychiatrists, psychologists, or clergy perform their duties, public policy deems it essential that individuals be permitted to speak without reservation so that the particular professional is able to render his or her services with full knowledge of the surrounding circumstances. Were it to become common knowledge that the professional was readily subject to subpoena and in a position to reveal the layperson's most intimate thoughts, actions, secrets or fantasies, public confidence and trust in the professions would diminish and would-be patients might be reluctant to seek counseling, diagnosis, or treatment.[2] Further, it is important for the practitioner to remember that discovery is not as of right in custody cases and leave of court is required.[3]

§ 10.1.1. Evidence – Privilege – Physicians

Physicians are afforded a testimonial privilege under the physician–patient privilege statute. The legislation provides that no physician may, in a civil matter, disclose any information acquired in attending the patient in a professional capacity if such information tends to blacken the character of the patient.[4]

Though the statute is called: "Physicians not to disclose information," and the text of the statute pertains to "information" acquired by the physician, the protections of the statute have been limited to "communications" from the patient to the physician and, therefore, any information garnered from physical examination or observation does not fall within the scope

---

[2] *See* Statutory authority and In re "B", 482 Pa. 471, 394 A.2d 419 (1978) (constitutional right of privacy).

[3] *See* Pa.R.C.P. 1930.5.

[4] 42 Pa.C.S. § 5929; Commonwealth ex rel. Romanowicz v. Romanowicz, 213 Pa. Super. 382, 248 A.2d 238 (1968).

of the statute.[5] In addition, a plurality of the Pennsylvania Supreme Court added the further prerequisite that the records or testimony sought must actually contain the communications of the patient in order to be privileged.[6] Thus, the opinions and conclusions of the physician, although based directly on the communications, but not including the patient's words, will not be protected.

The provision prohibiting the physician's testimony without the consent of the patient makes it clear that the privilege is vested in the patient and that the physician has no independent right to refuse to give testimony.[7] With regard to the "blackening the character" provision, a requirement which narrows the privilege considerably, it has been stated that outside knowledge of the fact that an individual has undergone psychiatric treatment does not rise to the threshold level and is consequently not privileged.[8] This holding occurred at a time when a psychiatrist came under the narrow privilege pertaining to a physician.[9] Presently, a psychiatrist and psychologist have a statutory privilege together which is on the same basis as the attorney–client privilege.[10]

The physician–patient privilege and the policy of presenting all relevant information to the custody judge have clashed on but a few reported occasions, the first in which psychiatric testimony was admitted after a finding that the disputed information fell short of the statutory requirements for protection of physicians.[11] In *Romanowicz v. Romanowicz*,[12] however, the Superior Court held proper the exclusion of all testimony as to a party's psychiatric examination without reference to either the communications or the blackening prerequisites.

---

[5] In re "B", 482 Pa. 471, 394 A.2d 419 (1978); In re Phillips' Estate, 295 Pa. 349, 145 A. 437 (1929).

[6] In re "B", 482 Pa. 471, 394 A.2d 419 (1978).

[7] *See* 42 Pa.C.S. § 5929; Commonwealth ex rel. Romanowicz v. Romanowicz, 213 Pa. Super. 382, 248 A.2d 238 (1968).

[8] In re "B", 482 Pa. 471, 394 A.2d 419 (1978).

[9] *Id.*

[10] 42 Pa.C.S. § 5944.

[11] Commonwealth ex rel. Beemer v. Beemer, 9 Leb. 26 (1962).

[12] 213 Pa. Super. 382, 248 A.2d 238 (1968).

In the Pennsylvania Supreme Court case of *In re "B"*, 482 Pa. 471, 394 A.2d 419 (1978), a plurality of the court narrowly interpreted the language of the statute and found that the psychiatric records of the mother of a juvenile delinquent did not meet the requirements of the legislation.[13] Although not a custody case, the strict construction will undoubtedly be relied upon by custody litigants seeking the testimony of physicians.

§ 10.1.2. Evidence – Privilege – Psychiatrists and Psychologists

The privilege accorded the psychiatrist/psychologist–patient relationship is solely a creature of statutory origin.[14] The statute prohibits the examination of any licensed psychiatrist/psychologist as to any information acquired in the course of professional services rendered on behalf of a client.[15] In granting the privilege, the Legislature expressly provided that the protection of the confidentiality of the relationship shall be on the same basis as that between attorney and client and that it may be waived only upon written consent of the client.[16]

Where a psychologist is appointed by the court, upon agreement of the parties, for the purpose of assisting the court in a custody determination, a party cannot later assert the psychologist/client privilege in order to keep the testimony and report out of evidence as the privilege, provided under 42 Pa.C.S. § 5944, applies to information obtained in the course of the rendering of professional services and not to information acquired as a result of a court-ordered evaluation. Even in the event that the court were to find the statutory privilege applicable, the law requires that the privilege yield where the psychologist's testimony is both material and necessary to the resolution of issues at hand.[17]

---

[13] In re "B", 482 Pa. 471, 394 A.2d 419 (1978) (Note: At the time of the decision, psychiatrists came under the privilege pertaining to physicians).

[14] 42 Pa.C.S. § 5944.

[15] 42 Pa.C.S. § 5944; *see also* M.M. v. L.M., 55 A.3d 1167 (Pa. Super. 2012) (Pursuant to § 5944, opinions, observations, and diagnoses by psychiatrists and psychologists are discoverable but not the patient's communications to the psychiatrist or psychologist without written consent of the patient).

[16] *Id.*

[17] Fox v. Anderson-Fox, 120 Montg. Co. L. Rep. 163 (1987).

A licensed psychologist is properly precluded from testifying concerning the child's development and sexual-abuse history where the information was obtained from the parent who had already testified to these factors. Since the psychologist received her information from the mother, her testimony would be only a reiteration of mother's testimony, which was already before the court.[18] Moreover, a psychologist's testimony as to her opinion of the truth of the accusations is impermissible under *Commonwealth v. Seese.*[19]

In the case of *Gates v. Gates*, 967 A.2d 1024 (Pa. Super. 2009), the Superior Court determined that mental health records were not protected by Section 5944 since the requested records contained no actual communications. However, the mental health records were protected under the Mental Health Procedures Act, which is discussed in section 10.1.3., *infra*, of this book immediately following this section.

LOWER COURT CASES

York County

Kunkel v. Kunkel, 116 York Leg. Rec. 129 (C.C.P. 2003) (Trial court, in considering a request for medical and psychological records in connection with a custody proceeding for which privilege was asserted, held that: (1) a parent involved in custody litigation waives his or her privilege concerning medical and psychological information, but absent a compelling reason the information is limited to the observations, conclusions, diagnoses, and prognoses of the treating professional; and (2) the children's privilege must yield to the inquiry of a party to develop a complete record so that the observations, diagnoses, and prognoses of their counselor are similarly available; but (3) the records of a non-party, such as a new spouse, are privileged absent a compelling reason why they should be made available).

§ 10.1.3. Evidence – Privilege – Mental Health Procedures Act – 50 P.S. § 711(a)

The case of *Gates v. Gates*, 967 A.2d 1024 (Pa. Super. 2009), protected in-patient mental health services records under the Mental Health

---

[18] M.C. v. R.W., 398 Pa. Super. 183, 580 A.2d 1124 (1990).
[19] Commonwealth v. Seese, 512 Pa. 439, 517 A.2d 920 (1986).

Procedures Act,[20] after finding the statutory privilege for a psychiatrist under 42 Pa.C.S. § 5944 insufficient to protect said records.[21] The patient's constitutional right to privacy, likewise, applied to protect said records.

The pertinent facts in *Gates* are as follows:

In *Gates v. Gates*, the Superior Court ruled that a trial court could not compel mother to disclose her mental health care records in a custody proceeding, as such records were protected by the Mental Health Procedures Act ("MHPA"). The court held that it could not emphasize too strongly the importance of confidentiality in mental health treatment.

Father learned that mother had received "inpatient mental health services" at a hospital for a two-week period. Father then filed a petition for special relief, seeking an order directing mother to release her mental health records. The trial court entered an order directing mother to execute a consent to release her mental health records to father. It specifically directed her to release her treatment summaries, hospital admission and discharge summaries, reason for hospitalization, current medications, and treatment plans.

Mother refused to consent to the release of the records, alleging that the records were privileged pursuant to the statutory privileges in the Judicial Code, 42 Pa.C.S. § 5944, and the Mental Health Procedures Act, 50 P.S. § 711(a). Mother acknowledged that the trial court had the authority to order her to submit to a mental health evaluation pursuant to Pa.R.Civ.P. 1915.8, but still would not consent to the release of her records.

Father contended that because the instant case involved a custody matter where the trial court must consider the children's best interest, the MHPA privilege did not apply. The trial court entered an order holding mother in contempt, suspending her custodial rights altogether and awarded father counsel fees of $625.

---

[20] 50 P.S. § 711(a).
[21] *See also*, M.M. v. L.M., 55 A.3d 1167 (Pa. Super. 2012).

The Superior Court reversed the trial court's order directing mother to release her mental health records to father and the court. It also vacated the order holding mother in contempt, determining that she was justified in refusing to disclose her mental health records to avoid irreparable harm had the documents been released pending the outcome of her appeal. The court ruled that the trial court violated mother's right to privacy by ordering her to sign releases making her mental health records available. The court initially determined that the records were not protected by a confidential communication privilege pursuant to 42 Pa.C.S. § 5944, since the requested records contained no actual communications. Therefore, to the extent the records ordered to be released did not contain communications mother made to her psychiatrist, the records were not protected under 42 Pa.C.S. § 5944. However, the court held that the MHPA contained a broad provision that applied to all records concerning mother's mental health treatment, and therefore the MHPA offered broader protection than the privilege set forth in the Judicial Code. Because the MHPA protects all mental health treatment records, this provision would preclude the release of the records.

The Superior Court also concluded that the MHPA is equally applicable in a custody dispute as it is in a civil matter. The court noted that this was particularly the case where there were less intrusive alternatives to evaluate how a party's mental health affected the child's best interest. The court provided examples of such less intrusive means, such as using mother's testimony at a custody hearing concerning the circumstances of her hospitalization, or requesting that the court direct the party to submit to a psychological evaluation pursuant to Pa.R.Civ.P. 1915.8. The court noted that simply because the trial court has the authority to direct a party to submit to a mental health evaluation does not mean that the court has the power to direct her to release all of her mental health treatment records.

The Superior Court also found that mother was justified in her refusal to release the records because she would have been "irreparably harmed," if she had followed the trial court's order. The court cited *Zane v. Friends Hospital*, 836 A.2d 25 (Pa. 2003), in which the Pennsylvania Supreme Court overturned a contempt of court ruling and allowed a hospital's refusal to release medical records "because the prior holding was clearly erroneous and would create a manifest injustice if followed." The court declared: "Similar to the defendants in Zane, if mother had complied with the trial court's order to release her mental health records before we had an opportunity to resolve the issue of confidentiality, she would have suffered irretrievable injustice if we had determined the privilege applied."

LOWER COURT CASES

Allegheny County

A.J.D. v. E.K., C.P. Allegheny County, No. FD-008406-017 (C.C.P. August 15, 2019), *aff'd.*, Memorandum Decision, No. 1402 WDA 2019 (Pa. Super. March 27, 2020) (Trial court was justified in ordering mother to obtain an independent evaluation to better inform the trial court on the current status of mother's mental health. *Citing* Gates v. Gates, 967 A.2d 1024 (Pa. Super. 2009), the court reiterated that court-ordered mental health evaluations are the preferred method of determining whether a party's mental health problems would affect their child's best interest. Thus, the trial court did not err in ordering an updated psychological evaluation, pursuant to Pa.R.Civ.P. 1915.8, to specifically address mother's current mental health status as it related to her parenting and care of the parties' child. The court highlighted that since the court-ordered psychological evaluation was the least intrusive means to determine how a parent's mental health condition would affect a child's best interest, it was the preferred method).

Carbon County

Leskin v. Christman, 17 Carbon Co. Leg. J. 184 (C.C.P. 2006) (Trial court held that the statutory psychotherapist–patient privilege and the confidentiality provisions of the Mental Health Procedures Act prohibited father from obtaining access to mother's mental health records in a child-custody dispute. Potential evidence of a parent's mental health or emotional condition, while relevant to a child custody dispute, may not be compelled when protected from disclosure by either the psychotherapist–patient privilege, 42 Pa.C.S. § 5944, or the confidentiality provision of the Mental Health Procedures Act, 60 P.S. § 7111. "Although worded as a testimonial privilege, this statute, as interpreted by our appellate courts, shields from disclosure all confidential communications made and information given by a patient to a psychiatrist or licensed psychologist, or their agent, for purposes of obtaining or facilitating treatment." The court further noted that where the privilege applies, the privileged material may not be subjected to even an *in camera* review by the court. Here, father failed to show that disclosure of the materials requested would not violate the privilege. The court rejected father's argument that the best interest and proper placement of the child should overcome the privilege. "To do what Father requests, to balance the merits of a statutory privilege against a party's claimed need for disclosure, presupposes that the court may unilaterally substitute its judgment for the presumptively valid judgment of the Legislature and that to do so, on an ad hoc basis, is preferable to a rule of uniform application. . . . When a privilege is properly invoked, unless the purpose of the privilege would be frustrated by its enforcement or extraordinary circumstance exists, the privilege and the public policy underlying the privilege must not be unpredictably discarded." Accordingly, the court concluded "to the extent the records requested contain confidential communications made by the Mother to her psychiatrist, or made any reference to such communications, they are privileged.").

§ 10.1.4. Evidence – Privilege – Attorneys

The common law attorney–client privilege, as codified, prohibits an attorney from testifying as to confidential communications made to him or her by the client unless the privilege is waived by the client.[22] The statute also bans compelled testimony by the client as to such communications.[23] In the recent Pennsylvania Supreme Court case of *AIG v. Gillard*,[24] the Pennsylvania Supreme Court held that "the attorney–client privilege operates in a two-way fashion to protect confidential client-to-attorney or attorney-to-client communications made for the purpose of obtaining or providing professional legal advice."[25] This differs from the previous standard of the privilege operating in a "one-way" fashion pertaining to the communications from the client to the attorney.

As is true of other testimonial privileges, attorney–client confidentiality is unconcerned with the suppression of evidence which may be of great significance to the custody determination. Rather, the privilege serves the policy of fostering a trusting relationship and open dialogue between attorney and client.[26]

---

[22] 42 Pa.C.S. § 5928.
[23] *Id.*
[24] AIG v. Gillard, 11 A.3d 44 (Pa. 2011).
[25] *Id.*
[26] In re Estate of Kofsky, 487 Pa. 473, 409 A.2d 1358 (1979); Lebeau v. Lebeau, 72 D.&C.2d 589 (1975).

§ 10.1.5. Evidence – Privilege – Marriage Counselors

In general, communications to marriage counselors are not privileged and are subject to discovery in custody suits. Section 5948, however, renders communications of a confidential character to a qualified professional privileged and inadmissible in divorce matters and custody matters unless the party concerned waives this privilege.[27] Marriage counselors are included in the statute's definition of "qualified professional."

Since many of the counseling sessions take place with both spouses present, the privilege will, in those cases, be waived.[28] Also, as parties to custody suits place their mental and emotional states at issue, the privilege should either be deemed to have been waived or at least construed very narrowly in order to permit access to information which may be crucial to the best-interests determination.[29]

§ 10.1.6. Evidence – Privilege – Clergy

The statute granting a testimonial privilege to members of the clergy provides that "no clergyman, priest, rabbi or minister of the gospel of any regularly established church shall be compelled or allowed to reveal any information acquired secretly and in confidence while in the course of his duties."[30] The provision expressly excludes self-ordained ministers or religious organizations in which members other than the leaders are deemed ministers.[31] The statute also provides for waiver with the consent of the communicant.[32]

In a Superior Court opinion, a case was remanded to the lower court because, *inter alia*, it was not clear on the record that the information sought to be introduced was acquired "secretly and in confidence" and as such the

---

[27] 42 Pa.C.S. Pa.C.S. § 5948.

[28] Loutzenhiser v. Doddo, 436 Pa. 512, 260 A.2d 745 (1970).

[29] *See* Bertin & Klein, *Pennsylvania's Developing Child Custody Law, Symposium: Recent Developments in Pennsylvania Family Law,* 25 Vill. L. Rev. 752, 767 (1980); *but see* Gates v. Gates, 967 A.2d 1024 (Pa. Super. 2009).

[30] 42 Pa.C.S. § 5943. *See* McGrogan Will, 26 D.&C.2d 37 (1961).

[31] 42 Pa.C.S. § 5943.

[32] *Id.*

trial court's refusal to permit the testimony of the clergyman was error.[33] In the same opinion the court also noted that the introduction of the testimony of a clergyman could present problems with respect to the witness's qualifications to present opinions as either a lay or expert witness.[34]

§ 10.1.7. Evidence – Miscellaneous Statutory Privileges

- **35 P.S. § 7608** – Confidentiality of HIV-Related Information
- **35 P.S. § 10225.306** – Older Adult Protective Services Act
- **71 P.S. § 1610.108** – Drug and Alcohol Abuse – Confidentiality of Records
- **42 Pa.C.S. § 6352.1** – Juvenile Treatment Records
- **42 Pa.C.S. § 5944** – Confidential Communications to Psychiatrists or Licensed Psychologists
- **42 Pa.C.S. § 5929** – Physicians Not to Disclose Information
- **23 Pa.C.S. § 6340** – Release of Information in Confidential Child Protective Service Reports
- **23 Pa.C.S. § 6116** – Communications to Domestic Violence Counselors
- **42 Pa.C.S. § 5945.1** – Confidential Communications to Sexual Assault Counselors
- **42 Pa.C.S. § 5942** – Confidential Communications to School Personnel
- **42 Pa.C.S. § 5949** – Confidential Mediation Communications and Documents

[33] Commonwealth ex rel. M.B., J.B. & S.B. v. L.D.B., 295 Pa. Super. 1, 440 A.2d 1192 (1982).
[34] Id.

§ 10.2.   EVIDENCE – CONSTITUTIONAL RIGHT OF PRIVACY

In a juvenile delinquency proceeding, a plurality of the Pennsylvania Supreme Court held in *In re "B"*[35] that the psychotherapist–patient relationship was protected by the right of privacy in the Constitutions of the United States and the Commonwealth of Pennsylvania.

In *In re "B,"* a psychiatrist was cited for contempt for his refusal to release the psychiatric records of the mother of a juvenile who had been adjudicated delinquent. The opinion began by discussing, then dismissing, the appellant's claim that the records were protected by Pennsylvania's narrow physician–patient privilege statute. The court went on to find, however, that the psychotherapist–patient relationship has deeper roots than the privilege statute and held that the contempt citation was unwarranted since the records were shielded by the constitutional right to privacy.

The holding of *In re "B"*[36] was adopted in the area of child custody in the case of *Commonwealth ex rel. Gorto v. Gorto.*[37] In *Gorto*, the appellant argued on review that the psychiatric records of the mother had been "blanked out" between one hearing and the other. The Superior Court found that the issue was moot due to the constitutional shield of privacy established by *In re "B."* Quoting extensively from that decision, the court concluded by noting that the mother in this case had undergone a court-ordered examination which gave the court a clear picture of her current psychiatric make-up, and that to delve into her past psychiatric records is an impermissible invasion of privacy.

An interesting case involving one's right to privacy has been reported in a case involving a tape-recorded phone conversation. In *Larrison v. Larrison*, 750 A.2d 895 (Pa. Super. 2000), the Superior Court ruled that the trial court in a custody dispute did not err by admitting into evidence a tape-recorded phone conversation between the subject children's mother and their father's sister, in which the mother directed a string of hostile and

---

[35] In re "B", 482 Pa. 471, 394 A.2d 419 (1978).

[36] In re "B", 482 Pa. 471, 394 A.2d 419 (1978).

[37] Commonwealth ex rel Gorto v. Gorto, 298 Pa. Super. 509, 444 A.2d 1299 (1982).

obscene comments at her and the father. In Pennsylvania, a tape-recording of a telephone conversation is not admissible in a court proceeding unless both parties to the conversation consented to the recording. Because mother placed the call to her sister-in-law's residence in New York, and the sister-in-law made the recording when mother called her, the court was required to determine which state's wiretap law governed the admissibility of the recording. The court reasoned that in this case New York possessed the greater interest in allowing its citizens to record phone calls lawfully with only the consent of the sender or the receiver. While Pennsylvania has an interest in protecting its citizens from having their phone calls recorded without proper consent, Pennsylvania courts have no power to control activities occurring within another state, the court said.

§ 10.3.   EVIDENCE – BEST EVIDENCE

§ 10.3.1. Best Evidence – Reports of Doctors, Investigators and Social Workers

While the opinions of experts in the area of family and child dynamics are welcome by the courts, written reports are excluded from the record, and trial courts are forbidden to rely on the contents of such reports unless the author of the report is subjected to examination and cross-examination.[38] It should be noted, however, that the exclusion is not based on the evidentiary rules which limit the introduction of such reports in other areas of civil practice. Rather, the prohibition finds its origin in the need to form a sufficiently complete record so as to enable the appellate court to properly execute its reviewing functions.[39] As cross-examination of witnesses is deemed vital to the comprehensiveness of the record, custody decisions have found that written reports are inadequate for this purpose. The author

---

[38] Coble v. Coble, 323 Pa. Super. 445, 470 A.2d 1002 (1984); Hall v. Luick, 314 Pa. Super. 460, 461 A.2d 248 (1983); Dunsmore v. Dunsmore, 309 Pa. Super. 503, 455 A.2d 723 (1983); Commonwealth ex rel. Michael R. v. Robert R.R., 314 Pa. Super. 335, 460 A.2d 1167 (1983); Palmer v. Tokarek, 279 Pa. Super. 458, 421 A.2d 289 (1980); Kessler v. Gregory, 271 Pa. Super. 121, 412 A.2d 605 (1979).

[39] English v. English, 322 Pa. Super. 234, 469 A.2d 270 (1983); Kessler v. Gregory, 271 Pa. Super. 121, 412 A.2d 605 (1979). *But see* Commonwealth ex rel. Robinson v. Robinson, 505 Pa. 226, 478 A.2d 800 (1984) (appellate court cannot raise issue *sua sponte*).

of the report must therefore be present to testify.[40] It was held that it was error for a lower court to admit a home-study report without affording the parties an opportunity to cross-examine the preparer as to its contents, including an opportunity to cross-examine anyone quoted in such reports where the quoted facts are relied upon for any conclusion.[41]

School records may qualify as business records for the purpose of the hearsay exception.[42] However, report cards do not constitute official records.[43]

In a custody proceeding, the transcript of testimony taken at a child custody conference before a master is inadmissible under 42 Pa.C.S. § 5934, since it is not a proceeding of record and a judge is to decide to whom an award of custody is to be made, even though the witnesses who testified at the conference were allegedly unavailable at the time of the trial *de novo*. The trial judge could not be precluded from the right to hear all evidence first-hand.[44]

In several cases, the rule has not been strictly adhered to and it has been held that where a report was introduced as a "joint exhibit" with both parties and counsel present, with the author present, and no objection to admission offered, it was not error for the court to consider the report.[45] The Pennsylvania Supreme Court held that it was error for the Superior Court to raise *sua sponte* the issue of the failure of the author of a report to testify when none of the parties objected at trial or raised

---

[40] Palmer v. Tokarek, 279 Pa. Super. 458, 421 A.2d 289 (1980); Jones v. Floyd, 276 Pa. Super. 76, 419 A.2d 102 (1980); Wood v. Tucker, 231 Pa. Super. 461, 332 A.2d 191 (1974); *see also* Pa.R.C.P. 1915.8(b).

[41] Sandra L.H. v. Joseph M.H., 298 Pa. Super. 409, 444 A.2d 1241 (1982); *see also* In Re Baby Boy S., 420 Pa. Super. 37, 615 A.2d 1355 (1992) (Results of home study conducted by probation officer were not germane in proceeding to terminate mother's parental rights, where mother no longer resided in home scrutinized by probation officer; therefore, trial court properly restricted cross-examination of witness regarding those results).

[42] Schwarcz v. Schwarcz, 378 Pa. Super. 170, 548 A.2d 556 (1988); Phillippi v. School District of Springfield Twp., 28 Pa. Commonwealth Ct. 185, 367 A.2d 1133 (1977).

[43] *See* Schwarcz, *supra*; 42 Pa.C.S. §§ 6014 and 6108(c).

[44] Ashford v. Ashford, 395 Pa. Super. 125, 576 A.2d 1076 (1990).

[45] Sipe v. Shaffer, 263 Pa. Super. 27, 396 A.2d 1359 (1979). *See* K.L.H. v. G.D.H., 318 Pa. Super. 330, 464 A.2d 1368 (1983) (no error where trial court stated that it would rely only on certain portions of the report which were not objected to by the appellant).

the matter on appeal.[46] Furthermore, where a report is admitted and considered by the court but the court's decision is sufficiently supported by independent evidence, remand is not mandated and consideration of the report may be treated as harmless error.[47] On the other hand, where a party is denied access to an *ex parte* report, a denial of due process will be found and remand required.[48]

LOWER COURT CASES

York County

Lloyd v. Lloyd, C.P. York County, No. 2004 FC1280-Y03 (C.C.P. 2005) (Trial court held that mother was entitled to obtain the report of an expert whom the father had intended to call as a witness at trial, despite father's subsequent decision not to introduce the expert's testimony or report at trial. The court noted that the parties' dispute was governed by Pa.R.Civ.P. 4003.5 and 9. Rule 4003.5(3) states, "A party may not discover facts known or opinions held by an expert who has been retained or specially employed by another party in anticipation of litigation or preparation for trial and who is not expected to be called as a witness at trial, except a medical expert as provided in Rule 4010(b) or except on order of court as to any other expert upon a showing of exceptional circumstances." Here, father's pretrial memorandum indicated his intent to call the custody evaluator as an expert at trial. "He placed mother on notice of that intention, and mother relied on that in foregoing her own expert." The court concluded that "an expert, whether hired by a particular party or appointed by the court in custody litigation, is an expert subject to Rule 4010, and as such, materials including a detailed written report of the examiner setting out the examiner's findings, including results of all tests made, diagnoses and conclusions are discoverable by a party as provided in that rule." The court added that "this conclusion is reached regardless of the status of the expert as a witness at trial.").

---

[46] Commonwealth ex rel. Robinson v. Robinson, 505 Pa. 226, 478 A.2d 800 (1984).

[47] Mooreman v. Tingle, 320 Pa. Super. 348, 467 A.2d 359 (1983); Sandra L.H. v. Joseph M.H., 298 Pa. Super. 409, 444 A.2d 1241 (1982); Carlisle Appeal, 225 Pa. Super. 181, 310 A.2d 280 (1973).

[48] Moran v. Moran, 417 Pa. Super. 549, 612 A.2d 1075 (1992) (Communication in form of letters sent by mother to Court, father's counsel, and conciliator were not *ex parte* communications and could be considered by trial court on issue of custody where all relevant parties were notified of the communications); Wood v. Tucker, 231 Pa. Super. 461, 332 A.2d 191 (1974); *see also* Ottolini v. Barrett, 954 A.2d 610 (Pa. Super. 2008).

§ 10.3.2. Best Evidence – Author's Required Testimony and Cross-Examination

The requirement that an author of a report be present at the hearing to testify as to the findings of his or her investigation and be subject to cross-examination is a function of each litigant's due process right to in-court presentation of evidence.[49] As one court stated:

> in almost every setting where important decisions turn on questions of fact, due process requires an opportunity to confront and cross-examine adverse witnesses.[50]

Rule 1915.8(b) provides that if the report or any information from the evaluator is provided to the court, the evaluator shall be subject to cross-examination by all counsel and any unrepresented party without regard as to who obtains or pays for the evaluation. Thus, where a party requests and is denied an opportunity to cross-examine the author of a report, a remand is ordinarily required.[51]

---

[49] Cyran v. Cyran, 389 Pa. Super. 128, 566 A.2d 878 (1989) (expert's reports may not be used in any manner in custody case unless either the author testifies and is subject to cross-examination or both parties consent; a child custody litigant has a due process right to in-court examination of the author of reports adverse to the litigant; when a litigant is unlawfully deprived of the right to cross-examination the author of such reports, and the court relies on them, then reversal of the hearing court's decision is mandated). *Note*: For an analysis of the Cyran decision, *see* Bertin, Emanuel A., "Trial Court Reversed for Failure to Apply Important Child Custody Procedures," 11 *Pennsylvania Family Lawyer* 134 (March, 1990); Coble v. Coble, 323 Pa. Super. 445, 470 A.2d 1002 (1984); Hall v. Luick, 314 Pa. Super. 460, 461 A.2d 248 (1983); Shaffer v. Gaal, 312 Pa. Super. 399, 458 A.2d 1021 (1983); Palmer v. Tokarek, 279 Pa. Super. 458, 421 A.2d 289 (1980); Wood v. Tucker, 231 Pa. Super. 461, 332 A.2d 191 (1974).

[50] Wood v. Tucker, 231 Pa. Super. 461, 463, 332 A.2d 191, 192 (1974).

[51] Ottolini v. Barrett, 954 A.2d 610 (Pa. Super. 2008) (Rule 1915.8(b) provides that if the report or any information from the evaluator is provided to the court, the evaluator shall be subject to cross-examination by all counsel and any unrepresented party without regard to who obtains or pays for the evaluation); Schwarcz v. Schwarcz, 378 Pa. Super. 170, 548 A.2d 556 (1988) (trial court followed inappropriate procedures in child custody proceeding by admitting updated school records into evidence over objection of father without any testimony by custodian or other qualified witness being presented by party offering exhibits, but such error did not require reversal of custody

Where pertinent evidence concerning the child's best interest lies outside of the state, § 5412 of the Uniform Child Custody Jurisdiction and Enforcement Act provides that courts of the Commonwealth may request the courts of other states to have evaluations made and the certified copies of the evaluations be forwarded to the court presiding over a pending proceeding.[52]

§ 10.3.3. Best Evidence – Waiver

Courts have held on a number of occasions that the concept of waiver does not apply in child custody proceedings.[53] Thus, a party's failure to timely object to a lack of access to written reports, or to the failure of the court to transcribe an *in camera* interview will not be construed as a waiver.[54]

A Pennsylvania Supreme Court decision has held that where issues are not raised on appeal, they are waived, and that it was error for the Superior Court to raise them *sua sponte*.[55] The Court noted that abrogation of the waiver doctrine promotes "interminable and vexatious litigation" which hinders achievement of a just result. The issue of whether an issue not raised at trial is waived on appeal was not presented to the Court. A Superior Court decision held that where a party fails to object at trial to the introduction of a report, without the author's testimony, his complaint will not be heard on appeal.[56]

---

determination as custody determination was supportable even without resort to two updated school records); Rummel v. Rummel, 263 Pa. Super. 97, 397 A.2d 13 (1979).

[52] 23 Pa.C.S. § 5412.

[53] Palmer v. Tokarek, 279 Pa. Super. 458, 421 A.2d 289 (1980); *see* Sipe v. Shaffer, 263 Pa. Super. 27, 396 A.2d 1359 (1979).

[54] Palmer v. Tokarek, 279 Pa. Super. 458, 421 A.2d 289 (1980); Gunter v. Gunter, 240 Pa. Super. 382, 361 A.2d 307 (1976).

[55] Commonwealth ex rel. Robinson v. Robinson, 505 Pa. 226, 478 A.2d 800 (1984); Schwarcz v. Schwarcz, 378 Pa. Super. 170, 548 A.2d 556 (1988) (we do not believe, however, that interminable and vexatious litigation, which abrogation of the waiver doctrine would promote, is any better a method for achieving a just result in a child custody case than it would be in any other type of proceeding before the courts).

[56] Ellingsen v. Magsamen, 337 Pa. Super. 14, 486 A.2d 456 (1984); *see also* Schwarcz v. Schwarcz, 378 Pa. Super. 170, 548 A.2d 556 (1988) (failure of father to

Likewise, the failure of a party to file exceptions to the inclusion of temporary supervision by a child services agency in a custody order does not extinguish the party's right to challenge the order on appeal.[57]

§ 10.4.   EVIDENCE – *RES JUDICATA*

Sections 5406 and 5445(f), which, in essence, codify Pennsylvania's case law on the subject and provide that a properly issued custody decree is conclusive as to all issues of law and fact decided, and are binding on all parties properly served or notified or who have submitted to the jurisdiction of the court and, who had an opportunity to be heard, except to the extent the determination has been modified.[58] In order to have such effect, the decree must have been rendered in accordance with the jurisdictional requirements of the UCCJEA.[59]

§ 10.5.   EVIDENCE – ACCESS TO RECORDS

23 Pa.C.S. § 5336 provides the parent/s of the subject child who have sole or shared legal custody with access to the child's medical, school, dental or religious records as well as the address of the child and the other parent. The Act does, however, provide exceptions to release of certain information regarding the address of a victim of abuse, confidential information from an abuse counselor or shelter, information protected under Chapter 67 (relating to domestic and sexual violence victim address confidentiality), and information independently protected from disclosure by the child's right to confidentiality under the Mental Health Procedures Act or other statute.[60]

---

object to admission into evidence in a child custody proceeding of alleged hearsay waived any arguments pertaining to the alleged hearsay statements).

[57] In re Custody of Frank, 283 Pa. Super. 229, 423 A.2d 1229 (1980).

[58] 23 Pa.C.S. §§ 5406 & 5445(f). Hamm v. Hamm, 431 Pa. Super. 283, 636 A.2d 652 (1992) (Denial, pending custody conference, of mother's petition to transfer child custody case to Nebraska did not constitute previous favorable decision to father so as to invoke doctrine of *res judicata* upon mother's subsequent petition to transfer, where denial appeared temporary).

[59] *Id.*

[60] 23 Pa.C.S. § 5336(b).

In addition to the specific protections with regard to access to information, the court may, in its discretion and upon a statement on the record of its grounds, deny access to any or all parts of the information described in the Act.[61]

§ 10.6.   EVIDENCE – HEARSAY

The hearsay rule and the exceptions thereto apply to statements of children repeated in court by their parents or third parties.[62] However, if hearsay is not objected to, the hearsay will be admitted under the doctrine of waiver.[63]

The hearsay issue exists in termination of parental rights cases as well.[64]

---

[61] 23 Pa.C.S. § 5336(c).

[62] Fox v. Garzilli, 875 A.2d 1104, 1110 (Pa. Super. 2005).

[63] Schwarcz v. Schwarcz, 378 Pa. Super. 170, 548 A.2d 556 (1988) (father in custody proceeding was not prejudiced by trial court's reliance on child's statements, as reflected by mother, that father had disciplined child inappropriately, as mother testified that she discussed episode with father and that during discussion father admitted he had disciplined child in manner described so as to corroborate any hearsay testimony. Trial court properly admitted testimony of mother regarding recommendation by teachers, as related to mother by school official, for limited purpose of knowing what mother did in response to recommendations so as to allow trial court to properly assess mother's response); Heddings v. Steele, 344 Pa. Super. 399, 496 A.2d 1166 (1985) (the court held that decedent's statements concerning numerous incidents of incest and sexual abuse by her father were both relevant and material in case in which decedent's father sought custody of decedent's minor children. These statements were admissible under exception for declaration made against social interest).

[64] In re M.T., R.T., & H.T., (Appeal of L.T.), 414 Pa. Super. 372, 607 A.2d 271 (1992) (holding the trial court committed harmless error by admitting hearsay statements by the children; the statements had no impact upon the question of whether the conditions for termination of parental rights had been met; also, there was other properly admitted evidence introduced at the hearing that provided substantially similar testimony, therefore the error in admitting the hearsay statements was harmless); In re Baby H., 401 Pa. Super. 530, 585 A.2d 1054 (1991) (statement by mother denying that the putative father was the father of her child was admissible in a proceeding to terminate the father's parental rights; the statement was admitted to show it had been made and considered by father in requesting a paternity test, rather than show the truth of the mother's statement).

LOWER COURT CASES

Philadelphia County

Jones v. Holloway, C.P. Philadelphia County, Case I.D. 94-06066 (C.C.P. 2000), vacated and remanded, 769 A.2d 1215 (Pa. Super. 2000) (Trial court properly permitted a psychologist and counselor to read their notes into evidence regarding what occurred during family counseling sessions, despite the existence of a hearsay objection. The court's family counselor testified that during a joint counseling session, father became hostile, and that the session was terminated due to father's refusal to discontinue his unacceptable behavior. Father argued that the court erred in permitting hearsay evidence. The psychologist and counselor who counseled the parties were present at trial and read their notes into evidence. The counselor testified from his notes that father became hostile during a counseling session and started finger-pointing and casting blame on mother, at which point the child started crying. "The hearsay rule, particularly where it involves what a child of tender years says and does, is very liberally construed." The court reasoned that testimony that might have been excluded in another type of case is often permitted in custody cases, since every effort is made to provide a solution that meets the best interest of the child. In addition, the court noted that reading reports into evidence is a permitted procedure under Pa. R. Evid. 803.1(1), since the psychologist and counselor were present, qualified and available for cross-examination).

§ 10.7. EVIDENCE—ADMISSIBILITY OF ELECTRONIC COMMUNICATIONS

The introduction of electronic communications in custody trials is becoming commonplace. This is an area of the law that is ever evolving. In the trial court case of *Light v. Esbenshade*,[65] the Lebanon County trial court, in a custody dispute, noted, in part, that because Pennsylvania law regarding the authenticity of E-communications was still evolving, it would take this opportunity to offer an opinion to explain why it would admit some exhibits and exclude others. The court ruled that circumstantial evidence could be used to establish the authenticity of disputed text messages and e-mails, even without testimony from an Internet or cellular service provider. In disputing the father's allegations that the mother refused to allow the father to see their child during certain weekends and that mother precluded telephone contact between himself and the child, the

---

[65] Light v. Esbenshade, C.P. Lebanon County, No. 2009-20401 (C.C.P. 2013).

mother relied on text messages allegedly sent by the father, some of which indicated that he did not want to continue having custody of the child and that he wanted to sign over his parental rights in return for the mother's withdrawal of her child support complaint. The father communicated with the mother via text messages from seven different phone numbers.

The father denied that he ever offered to give up his parental rights in return for the termination of his child-support obligation. The father objected to the authenticity of the texts and e-mails. Father testified that none of his cell phones were password-protected. He hypothesized that others could have taken the telephones and sent the offending text messages. The father also argued that the mother could have fabricated the text messages. Based upon these factors, the father argued that none of the proffered e-communications should be admitted without technical testimony from his Internet or cell phone provider.

In overruling a number of the father's objections, the trial judge admitted some of e-communications into evidence. The court conducted extensive legal research regarding the admissibility of electronic communications and social media. The court noted that there is not unanimity among the appellate courts relating to the authenticity of e-communications.[66] Regardless, the court was nevertheless able to glean several important common themes from all of the cases it reviewed: (1) authentication required a fact-specific analysis, there was no one-size-fits-all rule that either guarantees or precludes admissibility of e-communications; (2) direct evidence from an Internet or cell phone provider is not required. While such evidence is relevant, no case has required that a provider's technician be present to verify when, how and by whom a message was sent; (3) circumstantial evidence is

---

[66] *See* Hood-Ohara v. Willis, 873 A.2d 757 (Pa. Super. 2005) (a PFA case where emails were excluded as hearsay and had authenticity problems where proposed author denied writing the emails); In re F.P., 878 A.2d 91 (Pa. Super. 2005) (in juvenile delinquency case transcripts of instant messages admitted into evidence affirmed by Superior Court); Comm. v. Koch, 39 A.3d 996 (Pa. Super. 2011), *aff'd by* 106 A.3d 705 (Pa. 2014) (in criminal case regarding drug investigation text messages were admitted into evidence, as electronic writings can be authenticated by contents in the same way that a communication by postal mail can be authenticated. Circumstantial evidence may suffice where the circumstances support a finding that the writing is genuine).

critical to determining authenticity. In the case of e-communications, the contents of the actual messages are vital to determine whether they were actually sent and/or seen by the objecting party; (4) the bar of authenticity is neither high nor difficult to hurdle. The proponents' burden to prove authenticity is "slight".

The court concluded: "Even though the law of evidence as relates to e-communications is still evolving, we are confident that Pennsylvania's use of circumstantial evidence to establish authenticity will persevere. To be sure, the form of the circumstantial evidence has changed and will continue to change with the advent of new technology. However, we are confident that the legal precept that authenticity can be based upon circumstantial evidence will remain ingrained within Pennsylvania law."

Chapter 11

EXPERTS

§ 11.1. Generally

§ 11.1.   GENERALLY

In custody cases, one or both parties may retain a psychiatric/psycho-logical expert who will interview the child and the parties and report the findings to the court. In many instances, however, a court-appointed psy-chiatric/psychological expert will also be employed to evaluate the child and the parties.[1] Rule of Civil Procedure 1915.8 provides a procedure for court appointed mental or physical examination of the child as well as a cross reference to Rule 1915.18 which provides a sample order that should be substantially in the same form as the order entered by the court in appointing the examination.

The value of expert psychological testimony in child custody disputes has been debated with opponents arguing that the predictive value of such testimony regarding the best interests of the child is at best min-imal.[2] It is further argued that reliance on such expert testimony will result in delegating the decision to the expert.

---

[1] Commonwealth ex rel. Lettie H.W. v. Paul T.W., 281 Pa. Super. 262, 422 A.2d 159 (1980); Commonwealth ex rel. Weber v. Weber, 272 Pa. Super. 88, 414 A.2d 682 (1979) (where mother was mentally unstable and father had a drinking problem, Superior Court remanded case for development of the record and a psychological evaluation of both parties); In re Clouse, 244 Pa. Super. 404, 368 A.2d 780 (1976).

[2] Okpaku, *Psychology: Impediment or Aid in Child Custody Cases,* 29 Rutg. L. Rev. 11 17, 1136–53 (1976); Moorman v. Tingle, 467 A.2d 359 (Pa. Super. 1983) (Superior Court in upholding the trial court's decision, determined that is was clearly within the judge's purview to determine what of the testimony he considered credible. He was also not required to accept as true the dire predictions of the psychologist); *See* Com-monwealth ex rel. Hickey v. Hickey, 213 Pa. Super. 349, 247 A.2d 806 (1968).

At the opposite end, proponents of psychological examinations emphatically stress the need for such input, noting that expert testimony provides the court with a full and complete record and provides the court with insights, impressions, and opinions useful to the court for the determination of the best interest.[3] As one court aptly stated: "the significance of the child's statements is not in their accuracy but in how they reveal the psychological impact of the [party's] behavior on the child."[4]

In some instances, it may be reversible error for a judge not to solicit or consider competent expert testimony to assist the judge in a custody case.[5] The debate will continue concerning the proper fit of experts in child custody cases.[6]

The court in *Rupp v. Rupp,*[7] included the failure to conduct psychiatric testing among its reasons for remanding even though no testimony was received to indicate that the child was anything but well adjusted. Any sweeping interpretation of the psychological examination directive of *Rupp* is, however, somewhat limited by the court's expressed concern over the possible effects of the mother's meretricious relationships on

---

[3] Gunter v. Gunter, 240 Pa. Super. 382, 361 A.2d 307 (1976) (Superior Court remanded with instructions to the lower court to supplement the incomplete record. Among the deficiencies cited was the fact that no psychiatric examination of the child had been conducted in spite of the parent's reports that the child was seemingly disturbed.).

[4] Tobias v. Tobias, 248 Pa. Super. 168, 173–74, 374 A.2d 1372, 1375 (1977) (*quoting and affirming lower court*). See Levy, Alan M., *The Meaning of the Child's Preference in Child Custody Determination,* 8 J. Psych. & L. 221 (Sum. 1980).

[5] See K.W.B. v. E.A.B., 698 A.2d 609 (Pa. Super. 1997); E.A.L. v. L.J.W., 662 A.2d 1109 (Pa. Super. 1995); Commonwealth ex rel. Weber v. Weber, 272 Pa. Super. 88, 414 A.2d 682 (1979); *but see* T.M. v. H.M., 210 A.3d 283 (Pa. Super. 2019) (Trial court declining to order full custody evaluation under Pa.R.C.P. 1915.8(a) was not an abuse of discretion because the trial court aptly determined that a full custody evaluation was not necessary in light of all the information elicited at the full custody trial. Further, trial court emphasized that the doctor indicated that a full custody evaluation might result in increasing the already rampant animosity between the parties).

[6] See Bertin, Michael E., *Finding the Fit, The Continuing Controversy Over Custody Evaluations in Child Custody Cases,* Phila. Lawyer Magazine, Vol. 68, No. 4 (Winter 2006).

[7] Rupp v. Rupp, 268 Pa. Super. 467, 408 A.2d 883 (1979); *see also* Gunter v. Gunter, 240 Pa. Super. 382, 361 A.2d 307 (1976).

the child's well-being, an area which the trial court had failed to explore.[8] Thus, while it is clear that psychological examination of the child is frequently employed by trial courts, and may be ordered on remand, the lack of such testimony will not, in and of itself, support a remand in the face of an otherwise complete record.[9]

A trial court, in custody disputes, has discretion to accept or refuse expert testimony.[10] There was no prejudice, bias, or ill will where the trial judge accepted the expert testimony of the court-appointed expert over mother's own expert psychologist, as the Superior Court deferred to the trial court's determination with regard to the credibility and the weight of the evidence.[11] On the other hand, the Superior Court has held that so long as the trial court's conclusions are founded in the record, the lower court was not obligated to accept the conclusions of the experts.[12] A trial court's exclusion of expert testimony from a psychologist was not an

---

[8] *Id.*

[9] Lewis v. Lewis, 271 Pa. Super. 519, 414 A.2d 375 (1979).

[10] M.A.T. v. G.S.T., 989 A.2d 11 (Pa. Super. 2010); *see also* In re Donna W., 325 Pa. Super. 39, 472 A.2d 635 (1984) ("One of the greatest mistakes we can make is to regard as simple what is complex. If psychiatrists and psychologists knew how to achieve a child's best interests, deciding child custody cases would be comparable to diagnosing and treating a known medical condition. But psychiatrists and psychologists don't know—as the record of their disagreements in this case demonstrates. They can help by enriching the court's understanding of the complexities of how children develop, and the court may sometimes gain assurance from their counsel. But never may a court escape its responsibilities by accepting as law the dictates of one school of thought over those of another school.").

[11] S. M. v. J. M., 811 A.2d 621 (Pa. Super. 2002).

[12] Nomland v. Nomland, 813 A.2d 850 (Pa. Super. 2002); *see also* Jacob v. Shultz-Jacob, 923 A.2d 473 (Pa. Super. 2007); Hanson v. Hanson, 878 A.2d 127 (Pa. Super. 2005) (the Superior Court held that the trial court did not abuse its discretion in awarding primary physical custody to father, even though a custody evaluator predicted that father would manifest psychological problems due to his past abuse and depression. The court found support for the trial court's findings that father did not pose a danger and was a suitable parent. "Despite [the custody evaluator's] evaluation, the court evidently concluded that father is psychologically capable of caring for his children. Such a finding is supported by father's testimony that he is not a danger to himself, that he sought treatment, and that he has maintained a stable life for five years. Moreover, we find ample support that father is a suitable parent, despite the actual or potential psychological problems noted by [the evaluator]."); *but see* M.A.T. v. G.S.T., 989 A.2d 11

abuse of discretion where the psychologist had not seen or evaluated the children and was to be called to render an opinion on the necessity of an evaluation prior to relocation.[13] A trial court's refusal to admit an expert report was not an error when the expert testified and the opposing party was offered an opportunity to recall the expert after the report was not admitted.[14] The Superior Court has held that a trial court did not err in allowing mother to present a report and testimony of a custody evaluator who had been initially hired by father but later rejected as an expert.[15] A party who hires an expert custody evaluator but chooses not to use the expert's report cannot bar the report from discovery.[16]

(Pa. Super. 2010) (Superior Court found that trial court abused its discretion by totally discounting uncontradicted expert testimony).

[13] B. K. v. J. K., 823 A.2d 987 (Pa. Super. 2003) (the Superior Court ruled that where father sought to relocate with two of the parties' minor children, the trial court did not abuse its discretion by refusing to allow a psychologist to testify regarding the general benefits of a psychological evaluation in relocation proceedings. The court observed that the psychologist had not seen or evaluated the children involved in the custody dispute, and was prepared to offer only general testimony about the benefits of having children undergo a psychological evaluation before they are allowed to relocate. Since the trial court extensively interviewed the children, it was in the best position to determine whether the children exhibited any psychological factors that required further assessment prior to a decision on relocation, the court determined. Accordingly, the trial court's exclusion of testimony from the psychologist was not an abuse of discretion); *but see* E.A.L. v. L.J.W., 443 Pa. Super. 573, 662 A.2d 1109 (1995) (the court held that in awarding primary custody of minor children to mother after children were raised by grandparents, the trial court improperly failed to take competent expert testimony to determine effect of transfer of custody on children; expert testimony was required for trial court to be fully informed of factor for determination.).

[14] *See* Jacob v. Shultz-Jacob, 923 A.2d 473 (Pa. Super. 2007).

[15] Lloyd v. Lloyd, 889 A.2d 1246 (Pa. Super. 2005) (Superior Court stated: "Our analysis is direct and simple. Hire an expert custody evaluator and such opinion evidence will be made known to the court. To do otherwise would be a disservice to the child or children. This is not to say such evidence will be automatically accepted by the fact finder. It is to say, knowing such evidence exists and to shield such from disclosure presents a less than full and complete record. We literally can conceive of no circumstance where non-disclosure benefits the child").

[16] *Id. See also* M.O. v. F.W., 42 A.3d 1068 (Pa. Super. 2012) (trial court was upheld in entering prior custody evaluation report into evidence though expert did not testify when it was found that father was not denied due process by the report's admission because, *inter alia*, witnesses testified about conclusions in the report, father referenced

In *A.J.B. v. M.P.B.*, 945 A.2d 744 (Pa. Super. 2008), the Superior Court explained that the trial court erred when it allowed an expert witness to testify about the cumulative effect of pornographic images on the human brain and then impute that general testimony to the father in a custody case. Despite the trial court's error in allowing such testimony, the Superior Court affirmed the trial court and found that error by the trial court was harmless, as the trial court had independent evidence of father's impaired judgment, and that he could not supplant his own needs and interest for the sake of the child. The father's failure to abide by the earlier custody orders, and decisions he made in caring for the child, showed that he had a lack of judgment which could prove detrimental to the child. Father admitted he was a habitual and constant viewer of pornography. Mother alleged that father was addicted to pornography, and sought to introduce an expert witness to testify about the social effects of pornography and the probability of harm to the child if the court awarded father extended, overnight custody. The Superior Court found that the record did not support the qualification of the expert, who was not a physician, psychiatrist, or psychologist, as an expert relating to the physical effect of extended use of pornography on the brain, and did not support her competence to testify that such use impaired the user's ability to distinguish between reality and pornographic fantasy, as she had no scientific and psychological expertise as to the impact pornography would have on father's relationship with his child.

An expert may be appointed *sua sponte* and, if so, pursuant to Pa.R.C.P. 1915.8(b), the expert is subject to cross examination.[17]

LOWER COURT CASES

Berks County

H.L.J. v. R.G.J., Jr., C.P. Berks County, No. 16-16933 (C.C.P. November 27, 2019), *aff'd* Memorandum Decision, No. 2014 MDA 2019 (Pa. Super. July 28, 2020) (The trial court acknowledged that parental alienation is recognized within the field of

---

the report in his testimony, father hired another expert to rebut the report, and father and mother hired the expert previously to conduct the evaluation).

[17] Ottolini v. Barrett, 954 A.2d 610 (Pa. Super. 2008).

family therapy; alienation is the family dynamic through which one parent actively discredits the other parent to a child they share. Mother had petitioned the trial court to modify the parties' 2017 custody order so she and the parties' child could attend "intensive reunification therapy" with a therapist in New York. Mother sought to have the therapist qualified as an expert in reunification therapy, specializing in parental alienation. Father objected, arguing that the therapist's methodology was not widely accepted, and, in fact, might be actively opposed by a majority of her peers. The therapist testified that she believed the child would sustain serious psychological damage if intensive reunification therapy were not conducted. Although the ultimate goal was for the child to have a meaningful relationship with both parents, the therapist recommended the rejected parent to have temporary sole custody of the child. The trial court found that the child was suffering from moderate to severe alienation from mother. As a result, the court modified the existing custody order to provide mother with 90 days of sole physical custody of the child, with no contact with father, who previously had primary physical custody of the child. The court reported that it was satisfied that the therapist utilized a scientific methodology to develop her treatment plan. That scientific methodology was generally accepted in the community of specialists who diagnose and treat parental alienation. The court concluded that the therapist's methodology passed the *Frye* test.).

Ehling v. DeMatto, 92 Berks Co. Leg. J. 33 (C.C.P. 1999) (Trial court held that it was not bound by the custody recommendation of its appointed expert. "While this Court shares Dr. Sternlieb's view that the parties are each devoted to the children, it cannot join his recommendation of shared physical custody. Due consideration to a court appointed evaluator's opinion must not be confused with blind obedience. The trial court is not obligated to delegate its decision-making responsibility to the expert.").

Shepard v. Shepard, 83 Berks L. J. 25 (C.C.P. 1991) (Trial court awarded primary physical custody to the father despite the expert testimony against such a decision; the court held that although it is obligated to consider the experts' testimony, it is not obligated to delegate to the expert the responsibility of making the decision).

Bucks County

Sexton v. Haug, C.P. Bucks County, No. AO6-03-61759-C-28 (C.C.P. 2005) (Trial court refused to give weight to a custody evaluation report in deciding to grant equal custody to the parents of four children. The court hesitated to dramatically reduce either parent's custody because the testimony showed that the children had benefited so well from the parenting of both mother and father. Continuation of this custody arrangement would best serve the children's best interests. The court said it correctly discounted a report by custody evaluators recommending that mother receive primary custody because those recommendations were based at least in part on factual determinations that the record did not support and credibility determinations that differed from the court's own determinations. Citing *Johns v. Cioci*, 865 A.2d 931 (Pa. Super. 2004), the court stressed that issues of the weight and credibility of evidence are within the sole discretion of the trial court).

Delaware County

A. J. S. v. C. R. B., 91 Delaware Co. Rep. 355 (C.C.P. 2004) (A court is under no obligation to accept an expert's recommendation when the court has found substantial and independent reasons on the record indicating that such finding would not be in the child's best interest. The findings of the expert must merely be considered, but need not be afforded controlling weight, as the ultimate decision in a custody matter is what is truly in the best interests of the child, taking into account all relevant factors. "The trier of fact is not bound by the testimony or report of any expert witness, *i.e.*, custody evaluator, and is under no obligation to accept the conclusions of such an expert witness. . . . When an expert opinion is uncontradicted or unqualified, a child custody court abuses its fact-finding discretion if it totally discounts expert evaluation. . . . However, to say that a court cannot discount uncontradicted evidence is merely to rephrase the requirement [to say] that a child custody court's conclusion has competent evidence to support it. . . . So long as the trial court's conclusions are founded in the record, the lower court is not obligated to accept the conclusions of the experts.").

Commonwealth ex rel. Richards v. Richards, 57 Del. Co. 164 (C.C.P. 1969) (Where the mental health of one of the parties is at issue, the court may order a psychiatric examination of one or all of the parties by an independent, court-appointed expert).

Lawrence County

Pounds v. Blair, C.P. Lawrence County, No. 10711 of 2010, C.A. (C.C.P. 2011) (Trial court overruled the intervenors' objections to the qualifications of a psychologist appointed by the court to assess plaintiff-father in a child custody matter, where the psychologist had significant experience treating sex offenders, although he did not have a certificate in such services. The intervenors objected to the psychologist's qualifications. The trial court overruled the intervenors' objection, finding that the psychologist was a qualified professional. The court noted that in *Ramer v. Ramer*, 914 A.2d 894 (Pa. Super. 2006), the Superior Court clarified the meaning of a "qualified professional." The court there held that a qualified professional must be able to assess whether the parent poses a threat of harm to a child after considering the parent's mental health status as well as the crimes committed and the underlying nature of the offenses. Here, the psychologist testified that he had a doctorate degree in psychology and a master's degree in social work and had prior experience counseling sex offenders. The psychologist also described his counseling methods in detail. The court determined that the psychologist's "overwhelming experience" in treating individuals convicted of sex crimes rendered him qualified to counsel plaintiff. The court did not find it significant that the psychologist did not have a certificate of training in this area. The court did not interpret § 5329 and the *Ramer* case as standing for the proposition that a certificate was necessary).

Lehigh County

Mittl v. Mittl, 53 Lehigh L. J. 920 (C.C.P. 2010) (Trial court denied mother's petition for a custody evaluation, without prejudice, finding that the decision to order an evaluation is left to the responsible exercise of discretion by the trial judge).

Montgomery County

A.A. v. B.B., 142 Montgomery Co. L. Rep. 329 (C.C.P. 2005) (Trial court denied father's petition to terminate the child psychologist's involvement in this matter because father failed to demonstrate that her removal would be in the child's best interest. Father, whose visitation with his child was to be supervised by a child psychologist, filed a petition with the court to remove the psychologist from the case and appoint a different mental health professional to supervise visitation. The court held that defendant/father's complaints were not sufficient for the court to conclude that there had been any inappropriate action on the part of the psychologist that would justify her removal from this case, there was no detriment to the child in keeping the psychologist involved in the case, and the continuity of having the psychologist remain in the case was in the child's best interest).

Northumberland County

Price v. Price, 75 Northumberland Leg. J. 278 (C.C.P. 2003) (Trial court held that the credibility of expert witnesses will be discounted where the expert did not observe interaction between the child and his natural mother and where his concern about suicide was conclusory).

Dreese v. Dreese, 70 Northumberland Leg. J. 99 (C.C.P. 1998) (Trial court is not bound by the psychologist's recommendations).

Philadelphia County

Sauer v. Sauer, 14 Phila. Rep. 335 (C.C.P. 1986) (Trial court has the discretion to accept or refuse expert testimony).

Chapter 12

COURT-ORDERED COUNSELING

§ 12.1. IN GENERAL

The authority for court-ordered counseling has its roots in the judicial responsibility to preserve existing familial relationships.[1] The statutory authority for the court to order counseling is located in 23 Pa.C.S. § 5333. This duty is also recognized in the Divorce Code which mandates, in "uncontested" cases, a counseling order when requested by one of the parties.[2]

The decision to use or refrain from court-ordered counseling should rest within the sound discretion of the trial judge who must assess the benefits and detriments and order counseling only when appropriate. Under Section 5329, after the initial evaluation of a party or household member is conducted by the court to determine whether the party or household member who committed an offense under subsection Section 5329(a) poses a threat to the child and whether counseling is necessary, the court may order further evaluation or counseling by a mental health professional if the court determines it is necessary.[3]

The court may also grant temporary custody to either or both parents in the event a party has been charged with a criminal offense enumerated under Section 5329.[4] The procedure for the granting of temporary custody is set out in Rule 1915.13.

---

[1] Lewis v. Lewis, 271 Pa. Super. 519, 414 A.2d 375 (1979).

[2] 23 Pa.C.S. § 3302.

[3] 23 Pa.C.S. § 5329(c); Pa.R.C.P. 1915.3-2(b).

[4] *See* 23 Pa.C.S. § 5330. In Ramer v. Ramer, 914 A.2d 894 (Pa. Super. 2006), the Superior Court ruled that the trial court erred in failing to order a qualified professional to provide counseling to father before awarding him physical custody of the parties'

LOWER COURT CASES
Allegheny County

S.B. v. S.S., C.P. Allegheny County, No. FD-008183-10 (C.C.P. March 16, 2017), *aff'd*, Memorandum Decision, No. 561 WDA 2017 (Pa. Super. December 18, 2017) (It was clearly within the court's authority to order counseling that is necessary to effectuate a custody order. Pursuant to 23 Pa.C.S. § 5333, the court may, as part of a custody order, require the parties to attend counseling sessions. In addition, in a custody case, the court should solicit competent expert testimony to assist it in determining the effect of transfer of custody onto a child. The court explained that this is necessary in order for the court to be fully informed on this aspect of the case, citing *E.A.L. v. L.J.W.*, 662 A.2d 1109 (Pa. Super. 1995). Trial court found that not only had mother alienated the child from father, she also alienated him from his extended family and isolated him from his lifelong home, his friends, and his community. The court found that Family Bridges was the best option for achieving reunification of the child with his father and extended family. The court noted that although the Aftercare Professional was not actually providing counseling, he was providing services necessary to restore mother's custodial rights with the child).

Lycoming County

E.M. v. R.M., C.P. Lycoming County, No. 00-20, 433 (C.C.P. 2011) (Trial court granted grandmother's request to suspend family counseling between mother, grandmother and the child at issue. This was a custody dispute between the mother and grandmother for the custody of a 16-year-old child. The matter involved a request by grandmother, on behalf of the child, to suspend family counseling. The request was opposed by mother. Grandmother had primary physical and shared legal custody of the child. The court had previously ordered family counseling. The child's family therapist recommended cessation of family counseling because of the effect it has had on the child. The child encountered difficulty when confronted with counseling that involved her mother. After hearing testimony from several of the family counselors, the trial court decided to grant grandmother's request for suspension of family counseling).

---

minor children, where father was previously convicted for indecent assault and indecent exposure. The court determined that the trial court did not satisfy the requirements of now-repealed 23 Pa.C.S. § 5303(b) and (c). Section 5303 required the trial court to consider the criminal conduct of a parent convicted of a statutorily enumerated offense before entering a custody or visitation order. Father had pleaded guilty to crimes enumerated in § 5303(b), including indecent assault and indecent exposure. The clinical psychologist who evaluated father was not a qualified professional under the statute because he had no specialized training in evaluating sex offenders, and the one-time evaluation of father could not be considered counseling.

Chapter 13

COUNSEL FOR CHILD/*GUARDIAN AD LITEM*

§ 13.1. Counsel for Child
§ 13.2. Guardian *Ad Litem*

§ 13.1. COUNSEL FOR CHILD

Pursuant to 23 Pa.C.S. § 5335(a) and Pa.R.C.P. 1915.11(a), the court may appoint counsel to represent the child in a custody action on its own motion, or the motion of a party, if the court determines that the appointment of counsel will help in resolving the issues in the custody case.[1] The appointment decision is in the discretion of the trial judge.[2] Appointment of independent counsel may come into play when the contest becomes so caustic that the children's interests are totally submerged.[3] In these instances, "trial courts are sufficiently astute to appreciate the situation when it arises and act accordingly."[4] However, counsel for the child

---

[1] 23 Pa.C.S. § 5335(a); Pa.R.C.P. 1915.11(a).

[2] Lewis v. Lewis, 271 Pa. Super. 519, 414 A.2d 375 (1979); Smith v. Smith, 246 Pa. Super. 607, 371 A.2d 998 (1977). *See, e.g.*, Palmer v. Tokarek, 279 Pa. Super. 458, 421 A.2d 289 (1980); *but see* Commonwealth ex rel. Robinson v. Robinson, 505 Pa. 226, 478 A.2d 800 (1984) (Zappala, J. dissenting) (arguing that independent counsel should be appointed in every case so as to facilitate the requirement that a full record be developed through the presentation of evidence on behalf of the child rather than relying on the testimony presented by the advocates and thus relieving the need for incessant remands with instructions to the trial court to more fully develop the record).

[3] Mooreman v. Tingle, 320 Pa. Super. 348, 467 A.2d 359 (1983) (counsel not appointed for child as parties focused on best interests of child in spite of animosity between them); Lewis v. Lewis, 267 Pa. Super. 235, 406 A.2d 781 (1979). *Contra*, Watson, *The Children of Armageddon: Problems of Custody Following Divorce*, 21 Syracuse L.R. 55, 66 (1969); J. GOLDSTEIN, A. FREUD & A. SOLNIT, BEYOND THE BEST INTERESTS OF THE CHILD (1973). For a discussion of arguments pro and con, *see* Brosky & Alford, *Sharpening Solomon's Sword: Current Considerations in Child Custody Cases*, 81 Dick. L.R. 683, 693–95 (1976–77).

[4] Lewis v. Lewis, 271 Pa. Super. 519, 414 A.2d 375 (1979).

should not be appointed in custody cases between parents without the existence of extraordinary circumstances.[5] The court may order a party or parties to pay all or part of the cost of the child's counsel.[6] The counsel for the child shall not be subject to examination and shall represent the legal interests of the child and zealously represent the child as any other client in an attorney–client relationship.[7] If the child's counsel testifies in court, he/she shall be subject to examination.[8]

It should be noted, however, that this is limited to custody disputes and that independent counsel may be more desirable or even required by statute in other types of actions.[9]

Once counsel for a child is appointed, the question arises as to the proper approach to be taken in representing the child. Prior to the enactment of Section 5335 and promulgation of the revisions to Rule 1915.11(a), the Pennsylvania Supreme Court in *In re Davis*,[10] made it clear that counsel must perform his or her own investigation of the facts and form an opinion as to the best interests of the child. The Court was quick to caution further that counsel does a disservice to the child/client if the child's preference is not presented to the court along with whatever reasonable support exists for that viewpoint. With the promulgation of Rule 1915.11-2 and the revision to Rule 1915.11(a), it is clear that a counsel for the child is the child's attorney and advocates for the child's position and the child's legal interests and a guardian *ad litem* represents a child's best interests. Rule 1915.11(a) specifically states: "Counsel for the child shall not perform the role of a guardian *ad litem* or best interest attorney." Rule 1915.11-2 specifically states: "The guardian *ad litem* shall not act as the child's counsel or represent the child's legal interests."[11] Prior to the promulgation of Rule 1915.11-2 and the revision of Rule 1915.11(a) which became effective on September 3, 2013, the roles of a counsel for

---

[5] C.W. v. K.A.W., 774 A.2d 745 (Pa. Super. 2001).
[6] 23 Pa.C.S. § 5335(d); Pa.R.C.P. 1915.11(a).
[7] 23 Pa.C.S. § 5335(a) & (c); Pa.R.C.P. 1915.11(a).
[8] 23 Pa.C.S. § 5335(c).
[9] *Id.*; Smith v. Smith, 246 Pa. Super. 607, 371 A.2d 998 (1977); 42 Pa.C.S. § 6337.
[10] 502 Pa. 110, 465 A.2d 614 (1983).
[11] *See also* M.G. v. L.D., 155 A.3d 1083 (Pa. Super. 2017).

the child and a guardian *ad litem* where blurred. The role of the guardian *ad litem* is discussed in more detail in Section 13.2 of this book.

§ 13.2.   GUARDIAN *AD LITEM*

Pursuant to 23 Pa.C.S. § 5334(a) which became effective in 2011, the court may appoint a guardian *ad litem* to represent the child in a custody action on its own motion or on the motion of a party. The court also has the power to assess the cost of same upon either or both parties or otherwise as provided by law.[12] Pa.R.C.P. 1915.11-2(a), which became effective on September 3, 2013, states that a guardian *ad litem* shall be a licensed attorney or licensed mental health professional. Further, in the official Note under Rule 1915.11-2, and in Rule 1915.25 it states: "23 Pa.C.S. § 5334 is suspended insofar as it (1) requires that a guardian ad litem be an attorney . . . ." Rule 1915.11-2(a) also provides that the guardian *ad litem* represents the child's best interest and shall not act as the child's counsel or represent the child's legal interests.[13] The official Note under Rule 1915.11-2 and Rule 1915.25 further state that Section 5334 is suspended insofar as it "permits the guardian ad litem to represent both the best interests and legal interests of the child."[14] Prior to the promulgation of Rule 1915.11-2, a guardian *ad litem* had to be an attorney and represented the legal interest and best interest of the child.[15]

The guardian *ad litem* is no longer permitted to examine and cross-examine witnesses and present witnesses and evidence on behalf of the child.[16] The guardian *ad litem* shall be subject to cross-examination if called to testify by either party or the court.[17] In a written report to

---

[12] 23 Pa.C.S. § 5334(a); *see also* S.C.B. v. J.S.B., 218 A.3d 905 (Pa. Super. 2019) (Superior Court held that the trial court erred in ordering mother to pay her share of the GAL fees without holding a hearing, since the amount of the fees remained disputed).

[13] Pa.R.C.P. 1915.11-2(a); *see also* M.G. v. L.D., 155 A.3d 1083 (Pa. Super. 2017).

[14] Pa.R.C.P. 1915.11-2, Note; Pa.R.C.P. 1915.25.

[15] 23 Pa.C.S. § 5334(a) &(b).

[16] Pa.R.C.P. 1915.11-2, Note; Pa.R.C.P. 1915.25.

[17] Pa.R.C.P. 1915.11-2. 23 Pa.C.S. § 5334 is suspended insofar as it prohibits the guardian *ad litem from testifying. See Note to* Pa.R.C.P. 1915.11-2.

the court, the guardian *ad litem* shall make specific recommendations regarding the child's best interest "including any services necessary to address the child's needs and safety."[18] The guardian *ad litem's* report shall be filed of record and provided to each party and the court no later than 20 days prior to trial.[19] The parties are also permitted to file written comments to the guardian *ad litem's* report, which shall also be part of the record, pursuant to Section 5334.[20] The guardian *ad litem* must also participate in all proceedings, be prepared to testify, conduct investigations, and interview potential witnesses, including the child's parents.[21]

The guardian *ad litem* shall also advise the court as to the child's wishes.[22]

Under Section 5334, if there are substantial allegations of abuse of the child, the court shall appoint a guardian *ad litem* for the child, if counsel for the child is not appointed under Section 5335 or if the court is satisfied that only with the appointment will the relevant information be presented.[23] The court is required to make a finding that the appointment is necessary to assist the court in determining the best interests of the child.[24]

Prior to the enactment of 23 Pa.C.S. § 5334, the Pennsylvania Superior Court had opined that the appointment of a guardian *ad litem* is not proper absent extraordinary circumstances and if appointed cannot be a delegation of judicial responsibility to the guardian *ad litem*.[25] The facts of the Superior Court case and two lower court cases following the Superior Court case are set forth below:

In *C.W. v. K.A.W.*, 774 A.2d 745 (Pa. Super. 2001), the Superior Court wrote: "We note that a guardian *ad litem* is not normally appointed in custody cases involving natural parents. A guardian *ad litem* is a person

---

[18] 23 Pa.C.S. § 5334(b)(6).
[19] Pa.R.C.P. 1915.11-2(c).
[20] 23 Pa.C.S. § 5334(b)(6).
[21] 23 Pa.C.S. § 5334(b); Pa.R.C.P. 1915.11-2(c).
[22] 23 Pa.C.S. § 5334(b)(8).
[23] 23 Pa.C.S. § 5334(c).
[24] Pa.R.C.P. 1915.11-2(a).
[25] C.W. v. K.A.W., 774 A.2d 745 (Pa. Super. 2001).

appointed by the court to represent a minor child's interest in particular litigation before the court. The appointment of a guardian *ad litem* is generally reserved for those actions where the trial court deems it necessary because the child's interest may be adversely affected, *e.g.*, adoptions. However, in custody cases involving natural parents, despite the bitterness of each party towards each other, both parties are focused on the best interests of the child. Moreover, in a custody case, the trial court is obliged to ascertain the child's best interest. Since both parties and the trial court are focused on the child's best interests, it appears that the appointment of a guardian *ad litem* would not be proper absent extraordinary circumstances, and we note that bitterness between the parties does not rise to the level of extraordinary circumstances needed for appointment of a guardian *ad litem*.

In *C.W.*, Mother alleged that prior to becoming pregnant Father did not want a child due to his lifestyle and work environment but said that if they had one that it would be Mother's sole responsibility to raise, and where after the child's birth the Mother alleged that the father became overprotective of the child and micromanaged the child's life in a smothering manner, but Father claimed that the Mother practically abandoned the child after birth. Mother then contended that father should have *no* contact with the child because she believed that father had sexually abused the child. For that reason, mother failed and refused to produce the child pursuant to the court's custody order, and she completely thwarted father's right to legal and partial physical custody of the child. Because of these facts, the court declared that extraordinary circumstances requiring the appointment of a guardian *ad litem* existed. "In short, we do not believe Mother is acting in the best interest of the child in totally depriving the child of any contact with her Father. Under the circumstances, we believe the appointment of a guardian *ad litem* is necessary to ensure that the child's interest is not adversely affected."

The Superior Court in *C.W.* reversed a physical custody award in favor of the Mother, finding that the court's reliance upon the guardian *ad litem* for evidentiary rulings and recommendations constituted reversible error. The Superior Court ruled that the trial court abused its discretion by delegating its judicial powers to the guardian *ad litem*. The superior court stated that the purpose of a guardian *ad litem* is to represent a child's best interests when no one else will, not to sway the court. "We recognize that the trial court states that the guardian *ad litem*'s recommendations were only advisory and were treated as such. However, even assuming this was true, there is, at minimum, an appearance of impropriety."

In *Goldfarb v. Goldfarb,* 141 Mont. Co. L. Rep. 305 (C.C.P. 2004), *reversed in part and remanded,* 861 A.2d 340 (Pa. Super. 2004), the trial court refused to appoint a guardian *ad litem* in a custody case in which the natural parents are the parties arguing for custody. Despite evidence of bitterness between the parties, the bitterness was not such to rise to the level of extraordinary circumstances which would justify a guardian *ad litem.* "It is not customary to appoint a guardian *ad litem* in a custody case in which the natural parents are the parties arguing for custody. . . . It is the role of the court to appoint a guardian *ad litem* in order to protect a minor child's interest in an action before the court. However, in a custody case, absent extreme circumstances, it is the role of the court to ascertain the best interest of the child, and therefore the role of protecting the children's interests is assumed by the court. . . . While it is clear from Mother's petition that there is bitterness between the parties and difficulty with communicating with one another, 'bitterness between the parties ordinarily does not rise to the level of extraordinary circumstances needed for an appointment of a guardian *ad litem.* The Court, therefore, believes that the granting of Mother's request for the appointment of a guardian *ad litem* was neither necessary nor proper in the present case.'"

LOWER COURT CASES

Allegheny County

G.R.R. v. C.L.R., C.P. Allegheny County, No. FD 18-008000-005 (C.C.P. November 18, 2019), *aff'd,* Memorandum Decision, No. 1844 WDA 2019 (Pa. Super. August 13, 2020) (The appointment of a GAL in a custody matter is not mandatory, pursuant to Pa.R.Civ.P. 1915.11-2. Citing *M.B.S. v. W.E.,* 232 A.3d 922 (Pa. Super. 2020), the court found that it was not necessary to appoint a GAL because it was presented with an intelligent, verbal child who had no apparent difficulty communicating with the court, with a thorough psychological evaluation, and with competent counsel presenting relevant information).

Montgomery County

Goldfarb v. Goldfarb, 141 Mont. Co. L. Rep. 305 (C.C.P. 2004), *reversed in part and remanded,* 861 A.2d 340 (Pa. Super. 2004) (Trial court refused to appoint a guardian *ad litem* in a custody case in which the natural parents are the parties arguing for custody. Despite evidence of bitterness between the parties, the bitterness was not such to rise to the level of extraordinary circumstances which would justify a guardian *ad litem.* "It is not customary to appoint a guardian *ad litem* in a custody case in which the natural parents are the parties arguing for custody. . . . It is the role of the court to appoint a guardian *ad litem* in order to protect a minor child's interest in an action before the court. However, in a custody case, absent extreme circumstances, it is the role of the court to ascertain the best interest of the child, and therefore the role of protecting the children's interests is assumed by the court. . . . While it is clear from Mother's petition that there is bitterness between the parties and difficulty with communicating with one another, 'bitterness between the parties ordinarily does not rise to the level of extraordinary circumstances needed for an appointment of a guardian *ad litem.* The Court, therefore, believes that the granting of Mother's request for the appointment of a guardian *ad litem* was neither necessary nor proper in the present case.'").

Librett v. Marran, 141 Mont. Co. L. Rep. 33 (C.C.P. 2003), *appeal quashed,* 854 A.2d 1278 (Pa. Super. 2004) (Trial court held that the appointment of a guardian *ad litem* was appropriate in this child custody case involving natural parents due to the extraordinary circumstances surrounding the case. "Our exhaustive research finds no case law prohibiting the appointment of a guardian *ad litem* in a custody case involving natural parents. In fact, we were able to find only a single case addressing the appointment of a guardian *ad litem* in such a situation, and that case addresses the issue in a footnote".).

Chapter 14

ENFORCEMENT

§ 14.1. Enforcement—Contempt Proceedings
§ 14.2. Enforcement—Criminal Sanctions
§ 14.3. Enforcement—Counsel/Attorney Fees

§ 14.1. ENFORCEMENT – CONTEMPT PROCEEDINGS

23 Pa.C.S. § 5323(g) provides penalties for noncompliance with an order of custody, including imprisonment for a period not to exceed six months, a fine not to exceed $500, probation for a period not to exceed six months, nonrenewal, suspension or denial of operating privileges, and counsel fees and costs. Orders committing a person to jail shall specify the condition which, when fulfilled, will result in the release of the individual.[1] Counsel fees and costs were not previously listed as a punishment under the prior contempt section 4346, which has since been replaced by Section 5323(g).[2]

The courts of the Commonwealth are empowered to enforce their lawful custody orders through the issuance of contempt citations.[3] Although an adjudication of contempt may be either civil or criminal depending

---

[1] *See* 23 Pa.C.S. § 5323(g), and Pa.R.C.P. 1915.12(e).

[2] *See also* Hopkins v. Byes, 954 A.2d 654 (Pa. Super. 2008) and Holler v. Smith, 928 A.2d 330 (Pa. Super. 2007) (attorneys fees awarded in custody contempt action).

[3] Brocker v. Brocker, 429 Pa. 513, 241 A.2d 336 (1968); Commonwealth ex rel. Beghian v. Beghian, 408 Pa. 408, 184 A.2d 270 (1962); Rosenburg v. Rosenburg, 350 Pa. Super. 268, 504 A.2d 350 (1986) (visitation orders are to be enforced by contempt proceedings and not by an automatic termination of custody); *but see* V.C. v. L.P., 179 A.3d 95 (Pa. Super. 2018) (contempt order issued by PA trial court vacated by PA Superior Court when New York court had exclusive, continuing jurisdiction); *see also* S.G. v. J.M.G.,186 A.3d 995 (Pa. Super. 2018) (Superior Court reversed trial court's finding that an expert child custody evaluator had no standing to bring a contempt action and requesting the court to enforce its order directing mother to pay a portion of his fees).

upon the dominant purpose of the citation,[4] all but a few such decrees in custody and related cases are civil. Where the custody citation issues in order to vindicate the dignity and authority of the court, and to protect the interests of the general public, it is criminal.[5] If the court is attempting to coerce a party to act or refrain therefrom, or to compensate a complainant for losses sustained, the citation is civil.[6]

---

[4] In re B, 482 Pa. 471, 394 A.2d 419 (1978); Goodman v. Goodman, 383 Pa. Super. 374, 556 A.2d 1379 (1989) (civil and criminal contempt are distinguished on the basis that "dominant purpose of the judicial response to contumacious behavior" rather than the basis of the conduct of the contemnor, because the same conduct can give rise to either type of contempt. If the dominant purpose of the court is to prospectively coerce the contemnor with an order of court, the adjudication is civil. However, if the dominant purpose is to punish the contemnor for disobedience of the court's order or some other contemptuous act, the adjudication is criminal); Fatemi v. Fatemi, 371 Pa. Super. 101, 537 A.2d 840 (1988) (distinction between civil and criminal contempt is not determined by any particular act; rather it is determined by the dominant purpose of the judicial response to contumacious behavior. If the dominant purpose of court in imposing contempt is to prospectively coerce the contemnor to comply with an order of the court, the contempt is civil. If dominant purpose of court is to punish the contemnor for disobedience of the court's order, the adjudication of contempt is criminal); Cahalin v. Goodwin, 280 Pa. Super. 228, 421 A.2d 696 (1980).

[5] In re "B," 482 Pa. 471, 394 A.2d 419 (1978); Commonwealth v. Charlett, 481 Pa. 22, 391 A.2d 1296 (1978).

[6] In re "B," 482 Pa. 471, 394 A.2d 419 (1978); Hopkins v. Byes, 954 A.2d 654 (Pa. Super. 2008) (Superior Court ruled that trial court did not err in ordering mother to pay father's attorney fees of $500 as a sanction related to his petition for contempt of the parties' custody order, without first ascertaining mother's ability to pay); Holler v. Smith, 928 A.2d 330 (Pa. Super. 2007) (Superior Court upheld an award of counsel fees as a sanction for dilatory, vexatious and obdurate behavior, without a discussion relative to the contemnor's ability to pay); Lambert v. Lambert, 409 Pa. Super. 552, 598 A.2d 561 (1991) (holding that violation of a custody order is a significant basis for contempt proceedings, but not enough to be the sole basis of an award of custody); Fatemi v. Fatemi, 371 Pa. Super. 101, 537 A.2d 840 (1988) (trial court did not abuse its discretion in imposing *lis pendens* upon custodial parent's home after custodial parent refused to comply with custody order pursuant to divorce decree, had moved residence, had made himself unavailable to court, and had disregarded court's order to appear at show-cause hearing); Sutliff v. Sutliff, 361 Pa. Super. 194, 522 A.2d 80 (1987) (contempt order fining mother for failure to encourage her child to visit with her father in accordance with custody orders was civil and not criminal, as the purpose was to protect best interests of child and benefit father, not to vindicate authority of court. Custody orders did not specifically or clearly state that mother had to "encourage" her daughter

The penalty for either civil or criminal contempt may be imprisonment, a fine, or both. In the case of civil contempt, the contemnor must, at any time, be able to purge him or herself of the contempt by compliance.[7] On the other hand, a criminal contempt citation carries a determinate sentence, or a fixed fine, which the contemnor is powerless to avoid.[8]

The procedure which must be employed before a civil citation may issue is well settled and involves a five-step process which consists of: 1) a rule to show cause why attachment should issue; 2) an answer and hearing; 3) a rule absolute; 4) a hearing on the contempt citation; and 5) an adjudication of contempt.[9] This procedure has, however, been somewhat streamlined by Pennsylvania Rule of Civil Procedure 1915.12, containing a form for the notice and order to appear.

In *Flannery v. Iberti*, 763 A.2d 927 (Pa. Super. 2000), the Superior Court held that despite mother's repeated failure to comply with court custody orders, father's petition for civil contempt against mother was properly denied, where the concerns raised in the contempt petition were addressed by the modification of the underlying custody order. The court acknowledged that mother consumed alcohol in violation of her probation and custody order, tested positive for cocaine and failed to provide advanced notice of new child-care providers. However, because the trial court had vacated the custody orders that mother had violated, mother would have no way of purging herself of contempt, the court noted. Rather than promote additional litigation, the trial court sought to remove the chief source of trouble by limiting mother's unsupervised contact with the child and awarded primary legal and physical custody to father.

In *Harcar v. Harcar*, 982 A.2d 1230 (Pa. Super. 2009), the Superior Court held that a trial court abused its discretion when it failed to

---

to visit with her father, and thus the mother could not be held in contempt for failing to so encourage child).

[7] Simmons v. Simmons, 232 Pa. Super. 168, 335 A.2d 764 (1975).

[8] In re Matorano, 464 Pa. 66, 346 A.2d 22 (1975).

[9] Commonwealth ex rel. Magaziner v. Magaziner, 434 Pa. 1, 253 A.2d 263 (1969); Cahalin v. Goodman, 280 Pa. Super. 228, 421 A.2d 696 (1980); Crislip v. Harshman, 243 Pa. Super. 349, 365 A.2d 1260 (1976).

impose sanctions upon a mother when the trial court found that she was in contempt of its orders by not returning her child to Pennsylvania after retaining the child in Turkey and initiating a custody action there. The Superior Court rejected the trial judge's reasons for not imposing any sanctions—that the child had now lived in Turkey for almost 2 years and the Pennsylvania father was on an overseas sabbatical. The Superior Court held that by refusing to punish mother, the trial judge was permitting her to engage in disobedience of the custody orders. "This is precisely the type of behavior which this Court in *Goodman v. Goodman*, 556 A.2d 1379 (Pa. Super. 1989) stated that we will not condone." *Goodman* involved a mother who violated a Pennsylvania custody order by taking her child to Germany, where she had initiated a custody proceeding prior to the child's arrival, and bench warrants were issued after mother refused to comply with the Pennsylvania trial court's order to return the child to the United States.[10]

Generally, a trial court may not modify a custody order on a non-temporary basis without having before it a formal petition to modify filed by one of the parties.[11] However, the trial court is not prevented, under appropriate circumstances, to alter a custody order when it is in the best interest of the child to do so.[12] This issue most often presents itself when a contempt petition is before the court and the court changes custody at the conclusion of the proceeding. The primary concern is whether a litigant is deprived of his/her right to due process by not receiving proper notice that custody could be changed. Therefore, in cases where a contempt petition is before the court without a claim to modify custody, it has been found to be improper for a court to change custody at the conclusion of the hearing.[13] However, it has been held that a separate

---

[10] *See also* N.A.M. v. M.P.W., 168 A.3d 256 (Pa. Super. 2017) (Superior Court found that trial court abused its discretion by failing to impose any sanctions on mother despite her flagrant and ongoing contempt of court orders that had been continuing for 10 years; the Superior Court found that the order appealed was a collateral order and was appealable as of right and remanded the case for imposition of sanctions).

[11] Choplosky v. Choplosky, 400 Pa. Super. 590, 584 A.2d 340 (1990).

[12] *Id.*

[13] G.A. v. D.L., 72 A.3d 264 (Pa. Super. 2013) (trial court erred when it modified the parties' custody order by reinstating the prior custody order where only a petition for contempt was before the court and no mention of modification was raised in the

petition to modify is not necessary where the petitioner in a contempt proceeding sought a change in custody in his petition for contempt, as the respondent would then have notice that custody could be modified at the proceeding.[14]

Service of a contempt petition on a represented party's attorney is proper service regardless of whether the attorney notifies his/her client, and could result in a finding of contempt against the represented party *in absentia* if the party does not attend the contempt hearing.[15]

LOWER COURT CASES

Allegheny County

H.P.T. v. R.A.R., C.P. Allegheny County, No. FD 08-7200-001 (C.C.P. February 5, 2020) *aff'd*, Memorandum Decision, No. 226 WDA 2020 (Pa. Super. August 18, 2020) (The trial court found mother in contempt for withholding custody from father after

---

contempt petition); P.H.D. v. R.R.D., 56 A.3d 702 (Pa. Super. 2012) (improper to modify custody where no petition to modify custody was before the court); Everett v. Parker, 889 A.2d 578 (Pa. Super. 2005) (the Superior Court held that transfer of custody cannot be ordered unless both parties receive notice that transfer of custody will be an issue at a hearing. The trial court did not have authority to find mother in contempt of a custody order and then transfer custody to father where mother did not receive adequate notice of the contempt hearing or that custody was to be an issue at that hearing); Langendorfer v. Spearman, 797 A.2d 303 (Pa. Super. 2002); Choplosky v. Choplosky, 400 Pa. Super. 590, 584 A.2d 340 (1990); Seger v. Seger, 377 Pa. Super. 391, 547 A.2d 424 (1988) (following a hearing on a petition for contempt, trial court lacked authority to modify custody/visitation order absent filing of petition for modification by any party to order); Steele v. Steele, 376 Pa. Super. 174, 545 A.2d 376 (1988) (appropriate manner to bring about change in custody/visitation order is by petition for modification).

[14] Guadagnino v. Montie, 435 Pa. Super. 603, 646 A.2d 1257 (1994) (trial court did not abuse its discretion in modifying the custody order at a contempt hearing when petition sought change of custody in his contempt petition. There was adequate notice that the custody order would be challenged, and it was not necessary to remand case for reinstatement of the original custody order so that another hearing can be held on the petition for modification of custody, as "such action would result in a waste of judicial resources."); *but see* Langendorfer v. Spearman, 797 A.2d 303 (Pa. Super. 2002) (discussed *infra* in the body of this chapter of this book).

[15] G.A. v. D.L., 72 A.3d 264 (Pa. Super. 2013).

their then 11-year-old child told mother he was afraid of father when father attempted to discipline him. The trial court heard evidence of a recorded telephone conversation between father and child in which mother was whispering instructions to the child, and ultimate-ly found the child's testimony to be coached by mother and not credible. The trial court ordered mother to pay father's counsel fees and provide father with 21 days of make-up physical custody. The court noted that the Superior Court had rejected a similar argument in *Luminella v. Marcocci*, 814 A.2d 711 (Pa. Super. 2002), when a mother, who withheld custody from her children's father in viola-tion of an existing custody order, argued that she should not be held in contempt because she feared for her children's safety. A parent "is not permitted to ignore the order and unilaterally institute measures she feels appropriate instead of the order.").

J.R. v. L.T., C.P. Allegheny County, No. FD 07-003697 (C.C.P. August 26, 2016), *aff'd*, Memorandum Decision, No. 1394 WDA 2016 (Pa. Super. October 26, 2017) (Trial court found that father's claims of contempt where either lacking in merit, de minimis in view of the contempt standard, or overly vague. The trial court dismissed father's petition, finding that there was no contempt. The court determined that the alleged actions, even if true, did not rise to the level of contempt. Mother's failure to register the child's summer camp on Our Family Wizard did not constitute willful non-compliance and did not present father from exercising his custodial rights. Moreover, it did not have the effect of keeping father in the dark, as the child told his father of the camp during one of their nightly phone calls. The court noted that Pa.R.Civ.P. 1915.12 allows for a hearing on a petition for contempt, but does not mandate one. Here, the court held, no hearing was needed because the alleged misconduct of mother did not rise to the level of contempt).

Rehak v. Thompson, C.P. Allegheny County, No. FD-07-003697-004 (C.C.P. December 2, 2016) (Mother was not in contempt of court for *de minimis* custody order violations for her failure to log the child's summer camp activity on a shared calendar and her occa-sional failure to have the child ready at the exact time scheduled for custody exchanges or telephone calls. The court found that the alleged actions, even if true, did not rise to the level of contempt. The court found that mother's failure to register the child's summer camp on Our Family Wizard did not constitute willful noncompliance. It did not prevent father from exercising his custodial rights. It did not even have the effect of keeping father in the dark, as the child readily told his father about the camp during one of their nightly telephone calls. Similarly, the court found father's vague allegations of occasional tardiness in terms of telephone calls and custody exchanges were not indicative of even a colorable claim of contempt. The court declared: "Despite father's persistent insistence, this Court refuses to construe the Domestic Relations Code in the medieval sense.").

Bucks County

Corbus v. Corbus, 83 Bucks Co. L. Rep. 311 (C.C.P. 2010) (Trial court, after finding father in contempt of a custody order requiring him to provide transportation to moth-er's family to visit the parties' children, ordered father to place money in escrow to provide the required transportation. The court held that a financial obligation imposed on a party specifically to remedy that party's contempt of a custody order is not a support obligation).

Cornagie v. Cornagie, 83 Bucks Co. L. Rep. 139 (C.C.P. 2009) (Trial court found that continued failure by the custodial parent to give appropriate notice of a substantial deviation to an ordered visitation schedule will result in a finding of contempt).

Columbia County

M.C. v. T.B., C.P. Columbia County, No. 2013-CV-545 (C.C.P. August 9, 2017), *aff'd*, Memorandum Decision, No. 1386 MDA 2017 (Pa. Super. February 14, 2018) (Father's failure to allow maternal grand-mother and mother to exercise their partial physical custody pursuant to the existing custody order was volitional and done with wrongful intent. The trial court found father in contempt of the outstanding custody order and fined him $500. The court also directed that father be incarcerated for a period of not less than 60 days, and that father could purge this sentence by making a proper and mutually agreed-upon arrangement for makeup visitation time).

Elk County

M.J.C. v. B.L.B., C.P. Elk County, No. 2015-359 (C.C.P. March 27, 2017), aff'd, Memorandum Decision, No. 642 WDA 2017 (Pa. Super. March 6, 2018) (Father filed a petition for civil contempt, alleging that mother was in violation of the custody order for failure to proceed in moving forward with unsupervised visitation. The court found that mother had refused to permit unsupervised visits despite father's completion of all of the prerequisites outlined in the custody order. The trial court held that mother was in civil contempt of court. The court imposed a six-month term of incarceration as a sanction for mother's contempt of the prior custody order. Father produced documenta-tion to mother evidencing the completion of his obligations under the custody order. Nevertheless, mother refused unsupervised visitation, and stated that visits were to continue to be supervised. All of the requisite elements of civil contempt present in the instant matter. The court found that mother's actions were volitional and done with wrongful intent. Her refusal was not by accident, happenstance, or circumstances beyond her control. The order clearly provided for automatic progression to unsupervised visitation and provided mother with a reasonable and expeditious remedy if she had any issues with that progression. The court found that mother consciously disregarded the custody order in violation of both its letter and spirit, which violation was volitional and intentional).

Fayette County

Lucas v. Lucas, 54 Fayette Leg. J. 11 (C.C.P. 1990) (Held that a custodial parent will not be held in contempt of court for refusing to allow visitation rights to the non-custodial parent when it has been adjudged that the non-custodial parent is a child abuser and is continuing to abuse the children notwithstanding a court order of supervised visitation).

Lancaster County

Dochterman v. Dochterman, C.P. Lancaster County, No. C1-09-07054 (C.C.P. 2015) (Trial court ruled that a parent who fails to exercise periods of partial physical custody and cannot prove a present inability to comply with the court custody order may be found to be in civil contempt of the order, and sanctions may be imposed).

Lawrence County

Forsyth v. Forsyth, C.P. Lawrence Co., No. 11768 2006, C.A. (C.C.P. 2011) (Trial court held mother in contempt for failing to abide by previous custody orders when she failed to have the children ready and available for scheduled visitations with father).

Lebanon County

Karl v. Karl, 35 Lebanon Co. Leg. J. 44, No. 87-20167 (C.C.P. 1997) (Trial court declared that, in dealing with contempt matters, the court must focus on three specific elements: (1) Was a valid Court Order in existence; (2) Did defendant know of the Order; and (3) Did defendant disobey the Order. If the court finds that these three elements have been established, and that the defendant had the ability to comply with the Order, sanctions can be imposed. The court noted father's history of failing to attend hearings or comply with orders. The court ordered that father was to pay the expenses mother incurred as a direct result of his contempt. These included her expense of $800.00 for airfare, her lodging, car rental and other expenses for returning to Lebanon County for the contempt hearing. The court also ordered father to contribute to the mother's attorney's fees associated with the contempt proceeding in the amount of $1,000.00).

Montgomery County

J.P.H. v. S.M.R.H., No. 2013-07094 (C.C.P. June 3, 2016), *aff'd*, Memorandum Decision, No. 2067 EDA 2016 (Pa. Super. March 31, 2017) (Pursuant to an agreed order, the parties shared legal custody of their children. They shared physical custody of their two sons, and mother had primary physical custody of the parties' daughter. Father subsequently filed a petition for contempt, alleging that mother had unilaterally enrolled their daughter at South Elementary in the Perkiomen Valley School District, a different school, in violation of the parties' agreement. The court held a hearing on the contempt petition, noting that since the parents shared legal custody of the children, neither parent could change their schooling unilaterally. The trial court did not hold that the parents could not change the children's schools, but that they could not do so *unilaterally*, stating that the children would remain in their current schools absent written agreement signed by both parties that was specific that they attend another school. The trial court directed mother to pay father's attorney's fees in the amount of $7,171.25).

§ 14.2. ENFORCEMENT – CRIMINAL SANCTIONS

One of the sanctions available for non-compliance with a custody order is a citation for criminal contempt. While virtually all citations in custody actions are civil and, designed to coerce the contemnor into compliance, where the party's conduct is so contumelious so as to require vindication of judicial authority, the court is not without power to issue, after proper procedures, a criminal contempt citation.[16]

While the parents of subject children have been exempted from punishment under certain kidnapping laws,[17] several statutes provide penalties for parental child snatchers.[18] On the state level, one who knowingly or recklessly entices a minor away from its lawful custodian without privilege to do so shall be guilty of a felony of the third degree, felony of the

---

[16] *See* Barrett v. Barrett, 476 Pa. 253, 368 A.2d 616 (1977); Ingebrethsen v. Ingebrethsen, 443 Pa. Super. 256, 661 A.2d 403 (1995) (Mother, who was held in contempt for failing to deliver child to father as required by order establishing custody and visitation, was subject to criminal contempt as she did not have opportunity to purge herself of contempt findings and, consequently, was entitled to the essential procedural safeguards that attend criminal proceedings generally, including right to bail, right to be notified of accusations against her and reasonable time to prepare defense, assistance of counsel and right, upon demand, to jury); Fatemi v. Fatemi, 371 Pa. Super. 101, 537 A.2d 840 (1988) (custodial parent was required to obtain permission of trial court before changing his residence and moving with children to his native Iran and was in violation of custody order. Custody order, which forbade either party from doing anything to undermine the relationship of the children with either parent, gave sufficient notice that a change of residence without the court's permission would constitute a willful violation and support a contempt finding. The court entered orders imposing a $25,000 fine, contempt jail time, *lis pendens* on custodial parent's home, and change of custody from father to mother); Kozlowski v. Kozlowski, 362 Pa. Super. 516, 524 A.2d 995 (1987) (evidence of record supported finding of contempt against mother for failing to comply with court orders granting father visitation privileges); Bruzzi v. Bruzzi, 332 Pa. Super. 346, 481 A.2d 648 (1984) (father was held to be in indirect contempt for taking and failing to return his children for a period of one week in violation of custody order allowing him partial custody during the weekend. The court found, however, that the court's sanction of imprisonment was not statutorily authorized and that a fine was the only permissible punishment for the contempt).

[17] *See, e.g.,* 18 U.S.C. § 1201.

[18] 18 U.S.C. § 1204.

second degree, or misdemeanor of the second degree depending on the circumstances enumerated under 18 Pa.C.S. § 2904(c).[19]

The fact that the accused is a parent, guardian, or lawful custodian, is a defense, provided that the party is not acting contrary to an order of court.[20] An additional defense exists if the actor believed his action was necessary to protect the child from danger to the child's welfare.[21] A parent removing a child over 14 years old at its own behest and without enticement or intent to commit a criminal offense will likewise be a defense.[22]

Where the actor is not a parent and acts with knowledge that his conduct would cause serious alarm for the safety of the child, or acts in reckless disregard of such, the offense will be graded a felony of the second degree carrying a maximum penalty of ten years imprisonment, a $25,000.00 fine, or both.[23]

The statute also provides for a second degree misdemeanor offense where:

> "the actor acted with good cause for a period of time not in excess of 24 hours; and

> (i) the victim child is the subject of a valid order of custody issued by a court of this Commonwealth;

> (ii) the actor has been given either partial custody or visitation rights under said order; and

---

[19] 18 Pa.C.S. § 2904. *See also* Commonwealth v. Ortiz, 197 A.3d 256 (Pa. 2018) (a majority of the Pennsylvania Supreme Court found that a finding that a biological parent committed the crime of interfering with a custody order under 18 Pa.C.S. § 2904(a) and (c) cannot also serve as an underlying felony for a charge and conviction for kidnapping a minor under 18 Pa.C.S. § 2901(a.1)(2)).

[20] 18 Pa.C.S. § 2904(b)(3).

[21] 18 Pa.C.S. § 2904(b)(1). *See also* Commonwealth v. H.D., 217 A.3d 880 (Pa. Super. 2019) (a judgment of sentence was reversed for interfering with custody of a child, 18 Pa.C.S. § 2904, since the trial court erred by instructing the jury that it needed to determine if defendant reasonably believed the child's welfare was in imminent danger. The statute does not require a belief of defendant that the child is in danger to be reasonable).

[22] 18 Pa.C.S. § 2904(b)(2).

[23] 18 Pa.C.S. §§ 1101, 1103, 2904(c)(1).

(iii) the actor is a resident of this Commonwealth and does not remove the child from the Commonwealth."[24]

A misdemeanor of the second degree carries a maximum penalty of a $5,000.00 fine, two years of imprisonment, or both.[25]

A child-snatching parent might also be subject to charges under the Commonwealth's general kidnapping statute,[26] although the purposes of that Act, the grading of the crime, and the enactment of the interference with custody provisions discussed above, render that possibility highly improbable.[27]

On the Federal level, the Parental Kidnapping Prevention Act (PKPA) also provides sanctions for child snatchers.[28] The PKPA provides, in pertinent part, that the Fugitive Felon Act[29] shall be applicable to parental kidnappings involving interstate or international flight. That Act provides for fines of up to $5,000.00 and/or imprisonment for up to five years.[30]

The sanctions of the Act are, however, activated only in states in which state law gives the abductions felony status.

LOWER COURT CASES

Berks County

Hollis v. Hollis, 31 D.&C. 4th 346 (Berks Co. 1996) (Mother was held in contempt for failure to cooperate with father where, in order to use part of her previously awarded compensatory time, mother unilaterally decided to retain physical custody of the child during certain periods of time which would otherwise have been father's. The court

---

[24] 18 Pa.C.S. § 2904(c)(2).

[25] 18 Pa.C.S. §§ 1101, 1104.

[26] 18 Pa.C.S. § 2901. *See also* Commonwealth v. Ortiz, 197 A.3d 256 (Pa. 2018) (a majority of the Pennsylvania Supreme Court found that a finding that a biological parent committed the crime of interfering with a custody order under 18 Pa.C.S. § 2904(a) and (c) cannot also serve as an underlying felony for a charge and conviction for kidnapping a minor under 18 Pa.C.S. § 2901(a.1)(2)).

[27] *See* Commonwealth v. Chubb, 3 D.&C. 3d 676 (1977).

[28] 28 U.S.C. § 1738A.

[29] 18 U.S.C. § 1073.

[30] *Id.*

found that when mother ignored father's wishes and unilaterally decided to deviate from the custody schedule, she violated the custody order because her compensatory time could not be used at her sole discretion. The court stated that if the parties could not agree about periods of compensatory time, they had to resort to court intervention because neither party was in a position superior to the other. Here, mother chose to ignore father's wishes and acted unilaterally in not following the custody schedule).

Lebanon County

Spinglorn v. Spinglorn, 25 Lebanon Leg. J. 128 (C.C.P. 1988) (Trial court held father in contempt of custody order for failing to assume custody during the periods detailed in the order. The father does not have a right to "not exercise his right" for partial custody, as the interests of the child are paramount. The court held that, while it could not force the defendant to be a concerned, loving father, it could order him to fulfill his parental obligation to visit his son in accordance with a prior custody order by holding him in contempt. In reaching this conclusion, the court observed that it had not heard any evidence to indicate any hardship that prevents the defendant from compliance, and that it was in the child's best interests to develop a relationship with his father, the defendant).

Montgomery County

DiFilippo v. DiFilippo, C.P. Montgomery County, No. 87-09710 (C.C.P. 1995) (Custody of the child should be transferred to the father after the mother was adjudicated in contempt of the visitation provisions of the court's prior custody orders. The court concluded that where a litigant is given adequate notice that a custody order will be challenged in the course of a contempt hearing, and where the trial judge is adequately familiar with the history of the case, the trial court may transfer custody at the conclusion of the contempt hearing when it is in the best interests of the child, citing *Guadagnino v. Montie*, 645 A.2d 1257 (Pa. Super. 1994)).

§ 14.3.   ENFORCEMENT – COUNSEL/ATTORNEY FEES

In *M.C. v. R.W.*,[31] the Pennsylvania Superior Court noted that counsel fees can be assessed in cases where a party's actions in conducting custody litigation are arbitrary, vexatious, or in bad faith, pursuant to 42 Pa.C.S. § 2503(6).[32]

---

[31] M.C. v. R.W., 398 Pa. Super. 183, 580 A.2d 1124 (1990).

[32] *See also* 23 Pa.C.S. § 5339; Chen v. Saindi, 100 A.3d 587 (Pa. Super. 2014) (trial court's order of counsel fees for repetitive filings reversed by Superior Court).

In *Holler v. Smith*, 928 A.2d 330 (Pa. Super. 2007), the Superior Court found that the trial court properly entered an order awarding attorney fees to the child's father as a result of mother's vexatious conduct. The attorney fees award need not be filed within 30 days of the disposition of child custody. Mother and maternal grandparents argued that the trial court lacked jurisdiction to award attorney fees where father's petition was filed more than 30 days after entry of final judgment. They asserted that the trial court's order of January 14, 2005, constituted a final order such that any appeal or modifications sought, such as an award of attorney fees, had to be filed within 30 days of that order pursuant to 42 Pa.C.S. § 5505 and *Freidenbloom v. Weyant*, 814 A.2d 1253 (Pa. Super. 2003), holding that an order may be modified or rescinded within 30 days under 42 Pa.C.S. § 5505 such that a petition for attorney fees may be considered. In *Freidenbloom*, the court determined a petition filed more than 30 days after the final judgment was untimely. Because a child custody order is by nature open to change at any time, the standard limitations on petitions for attorney fees do not apply. "Custody matters are a special creature." The court referred to *Kassam v. Kassam*, 811 A.2d 1023 (Pa. Super. 2002), in which the court held "child custody orders are temporary in nature and always subject to change if new circumstances affect the welfare of a child." Unlike other actions that have a clear beginning, middle and end, custody orders may be repeatedly modified. The court also noted that the statute relied upon to award attorney fees, 42 Pa.C.S. § 2503(7), does not contain a provision indicating when such an action may be deemed untimely.

In *Goodman v. Goodman*,[33] the court, under a combination of 42 Pa.C.S. §§ 1726 and 2503 and 42 Pa.C.S. § 5356 (costs, travel costs, and fees) of the former Uniform Child Custody Jurisdiction Act, awarded father $16,000 in fees and costs in the context of a contempt and international abduction-enforcement matter.

A defendant convicted of interference with custody of children could properly be required to make restitution for her former husband's trip expenses and private investigator fees that were incurred as a direct result of the defendant's abduction of the children, since such expenses

---

[33] Goodman v. Goodman, 383 Pa. Super. 374, 556 A.2d 1379 (1989).

would not have been incurred "but for" defendant's crime. In *Commonwealth v. Harner*,[34] a unanimous state Supreme Court has ruled that parents who violate custody orders by abducting their children can be forced to pay restitution to the custodial parent. The Supreme Court found that although the state's criminal code "does not authorize restitution upon conviction of tampering with custody rights," trial courts can use the sentencing code to grant restitution. "Such sentences are encouraged and give the trial court the flexibility to determine all the direct and indirect damages caused by a defendant and then permit the court to order restitution so that the defendant will understand the egregiousness of his conduct, be deterred from repeating this conduct, and be encouraged to live in a responsible way." "It is, however, the lower court's obligation to determine what loss or damage has been caused, and what amount of restitution appellant can afford to pay, and how it should be paid."[35]

LOWER COURT CASES

Allegheny County

M.G. v. S.J., C.P. Allegheny County, No. FD-07-009307-004 (C.C.P. July 20, 2017), *aff'd*, Memorandum Decision, No. 1122 WDA 2017 (Pa. Super. March 16, 2018) (Father filed a petition alleging that mother was in contempt of the final custody order. Father alleged that (1) mother traveled with the parties' child outside of Allegheny County for longer than 24 hours without advising father, in violation of their custody order, and (2) mother enrolled the child in summer programs without first consulting father, in violation of the custody order. Mother countered that father was attempting to annoy and harass her and she requested counsel fees. The court entered a custody order that denied father's petition for contempt and awarded mother $600 in counsel fees. The court explained that it denied father's petition for contempt because the allegations therein pertained to previous custody orders, hearings and appeals, all of which had been dealt with before. Father's contempt petition consisted entirely of claims that were either previously litigated, de minimis, or utterly devoid of merit. Accordingly, the court found that it was within the trial court's discretion to conclude that the imposition of counsel fees was appropriate).

---

[34] Commonwealth v. Harner, 402 Pa. Super. 472, 587 A.2d 347 (1991), *aff'd*, 533 Pa. 14, 617 A.2d 702 (1992).

[35] *Id.*

M.M.-R. v. J.R.R., No. 08-008935-016 (C.C.P. November 9, 2017), *aff'd*, Memorandum Decision, No. 1835 WDA 2017 (Pa. Super. June 4, 2018) (Father took custody of the child, stating that he would return the child to mother's care later that evening. However, when mother attempted to retrieve the child, father insisted that the child did not feel safe with her and would spend the night at his home. Mother subsequently filed a petition for special relief in which she averred that she had no contact with the child since the father took the child and refused to return the child to her care. The court found that father used the child's refusal to return to mother's care as an excuse to violate the prior custody orders. The court entered an order directing that father return the child to mother. The court found father in contempt of the physical custody provisions of its prior orders, sanctioned him $20,000 in counsel fees payable at $300 per month, and denied his request for modification of custody. The court also awarded mother five weeks of custody make-up time with the child. The court found that its sanction against father was not excessive, based on his employment. The court ordered father to pay mother's counsel fees in monthly $300 increments, which allowed father to pay off the balance slowly over the course of approximately 5 1/2 years).

Clarke v. Clarke, C.P. Allegheny County. (C.C.P. 1983) (Judge Strassburger found a custodian in contempt of the travel arrangements portion of a partial custody order and awarded $500 in fees. The court there equated "contumacious conduct" with "obdurate or vexatious" conduct).

Bucks County

Smith v. Young, 84 Bucks Co. L. Rep. 550 (C.C.P. 2011) (An award of counsel fees can be considered counterproductive in a protracted custody matter as it may allow the parties to continue the derisive environment in which the subject child is living. Father argued, among other things, that the trial court erred in not addressing attorney's fees in light of the burdensome number of petitions filed by grandmother in this father/grandmother visitation dispute. The court declared: "In light of this litigiousness, this court did not fail to address ... father's request for attorney's fees but exercised its discretion when reasoning that the imposition of punitive measures would only protract the instant matter further and be counterproductive in providing a child with a necessary stable environment free of the divisiveness embodied in this unfortunate custody dispute. Therefore, father's concerns regarding . . . attorney's fees are unfounded.").

Carbon County

Skrimcovsky v. Michalik, 13 Carb. Co. L. J. 113 (C.C.P. 1991) (Award of attorney's fees is proper where allegations of sexual abuse by mother are vexatious and used for sole purpose of disrupting father's relationship with child; such an award is proper pursuant to 42 Pa.C.S. § 2503(6), which allows the assessment of attorney's fees where a party's action in conducting litigation is arbitrary, vexatious or in bad faith).

Lycoming County

M.D.G. v. M.C.M. and P.R.G. and D.S.G., C.P. Lycoming County, No. 16-21, 649 (C.C.P. April 20, 2017), *aff'd,* Memorandum Decision, No. 1699 MDA 2017 (Pa. Super. April 4, 2018) (Trial court order granted a Petition for Civil Contempt for Disobedience of Custody Order, and ordered mother to pay reasonable counsel fees in the amount of $1000 to grandparents and to father, and to provide make-up custody time to grandparents and father. The court found mother in contempt and ordered that the weekly visits with father and bi-weekly visits with grandparents resumed and that grandparents have make-up custody time. Mother had not allowed father or grandparents to see the child for more than 10 weeks and failed to answer any phone call or text messages for six weeks. Grandparents were to have physical custody of the child every other weekend. Grandmother and father drove to mother's home, but mother had relocated. Father testified that he had no contact with his son for 16 weeks. The court found that the record supported a finding of contempt because grandparents credibly testified that mother affirmatively and repeatedly refused to comply with her obligations under the court's custody order. The trial court noted that mother had a history of intentionally withholding custody and concealing her whereabouts and contact information from the other parties and from the court. The court rejected the contention that mother withheld custody time because of the advice of counsel, noting that there was nothing in the record that lawfully gave mother the right to withhold custody).

Montgomery County

J.P.H. v. S.M.R.H., No. 2013-07094 (C.C.P. June 3, 2016), *aff'd,* Memorandum Decision, No. 2067 EDA 2016 (Pa. Super. March 31, 2017) (Pursuant to an agreed order, the parties shared legal custody of their children. They shared physical custody of their two sons, and mother had primary physical custody of the parties' daughter. Father subsequently filed a petition for contempt, alleging that mother had unilaterally enrolled their daughter at South Elementary in the Perkiomen Valley School District, a different school, in violation of the parties' agreement. The court held a hearing on the contempt petition, noting that since the parents shared legal custody of the children, neither parent could change their schooling unilaterally. The trial court did not hold that the parents could not change the children's schools, but that they could not do so *unilaterally,* stating that the children would remain in their current schools absent written agreement signed by both parties that was specific that they attend another school. The trial court directed mother to pay father's attorney's fees in the amount of $7,171.25).

V.E.B. v. A.L.W., 133 Montgomery Co. L. Rep. 229 (C.C.P. 2016) (Trial court found mother proved that father had willfully violated the terms of the Agreed Custody Order, therefore, the trial court ordered father to pay counsel fees in the amount of $1,100 plus a fine in the amount of $1,000 for a total of $2,100. Father conceded that he willfully violated the duties he voluntarily assumed pursuant to the Agreed Custody Order. In spite of that concession, father argued that mother was required to prove his ability to pay $2,100 before sanctions could be entered against him. The trial court disagreed and held that mother did not have an absolute duty to prove father's ability to pay the sanctions imposed. The court noted that that argument was rejected in *Hopkins v. Byes*, 954 A.2d 654 (Pa. Super. 2008)).

Chapter 15

MODIFICATION OF COURT ORDER

---

§ 15.1. Generally
§ 15.2. Counsel Fees—Repetitive Filings

---

§ 15.1. GENERALLY

Custody orders are temporary in nature and are thus subject to modification upon petition.[1] 23 Pa.C.S. § 5338(a) provides: "Upon petition, a
court may modify a custody order to serve the best interest of the child."
Section 5338(b) provides that Section 5338 applies to any custody order
entered by a court of the Commonwealth of Pennsylvania or any other
state subject to the jurisdictional requirements set forth in the Uniform
Child Custody Jurisdiction and Enforcement Act. Section 5338 is a codification of the Pennsylvania Supreme Court ruling in the case of *Karis
v. Karis* which held that a change in circumstances was not necessary in
order to modify a custody order.[2]

---

[1] 23 Pa.C.S. § 5338(a); Holler v. Smith, 928 A.2d 330 (Pa. Super. 2007); Kassam
v. Kassam, 811 A.2d 1023 (Pa. Super. 2002); Dile v. Dile, 284 Pa. Super. 459, 426
A.2d 137 (1981); Miller v. Miller, 269 Pa. Super. 83, 409 A.2d 74 (1979); Scarlett
v. Scarlett, 257 Pa. Super. 468, 390 A.2d 1331 (1978); Commonwealth ex rel. Peterson
v. Hayes, 252 Pa. Super. 487, 381 A.2d 1311 (1977).
[2] Karis v. Karis, 518 Pa. 601, 544 A.2d 1328 (1988); *see also* Sawko v. Sawko, 425
Pa. Super. 450, 625 A.2d 692 (1993) (In determining child custody issue, trial court
may inquire into best interest of child regardless of whether substantial change in circumstances has been shown); Altus-Baumhor v. Baumhor, 407 Pa. Super. 276, 595
A.2d 1147 (1991) (holding that the court may inquire into the best interest of the child
irrespective of whether a substantial change in circumstances has been demonstrated);
McMillen v. McMillen, 529 Pa. 198, 602 A.2d 845 (1991); McMillen v. McMillen, 529
Pa. 198, 602 A.2d 845 (1991); Belan v. Belan, 399 Pa. Super. 458, 582 A.2d 684
(1990); Bishop v. Pillar, 399 Pa. Super. 52, 581 A.2d 670 (1990); S.H. v. B.L.H., 392
Pa. Super. 137, 572 A.2d 730 (1990); Martin v. Martin, 386 Pa. Super. 328, 562 A.2d
1389 (1989), *allocatur denied*, 524 Pa. 629, 574 A.2d 70 (1990); Jaindl v. Myers, 520
Pa. 147, 553 A.2d 407 (1989).

In the seminal case of *Karis*, the Pennsylvania Supreme Court held that a custody order may be modified from partial to shared custody despite the absence of any substantial change in circumstances. It felt that the best interests of the child may override the need for a finding of "substantial" change and, therefore, reversed the Superior Court, which held that as a matter of law, the party contesting the partial custody order must establish a substantial change in circumstances before the trial court may consider the petition. Although there had been no change of circumstances in the year and one-half since the prior order had been entered, the trial court made an inquiry into the best interests of the child and modified the order. The Supreme Court held that the Custody and Grandparents' Visitation Act mandated a reversal of the decision and reinstatement of the trial court order. "Consequently, we hold that a petition for modification of a partial custody to a shared custody order requires the court to inquire into the best interests of the child regardless of whether a 'substantial' change in circumstances has been shown." For a detailed analysis of the *Karis* decision see: Bertin, E., *Pennsylvania Family Lawyer*, Volume IX, No. 5, November-December, 1988, pp. 45–46; Widman, J., and "Substantial Change in Situation Unnecessary in Custody Switch," *Pennsylvania Law Journal-Reporter*, Vol. XI, No. 35, September 12, 1988.

It should be noted that where no court order has been obtained, and custody has been determined by agreement of the parties, the best interests standard will be the sole criterion and there never was a changed circumstances requirement.[3] Moreover, it has been held that even where the agreement of the parties is adopted by the court and incorporated into an order, that a subsequent hearing should not be treated as a modification hearing.[4]

---

[3] Artzt v. Artzt, 383 Pa. Super. 23, 566 A.2d 409 (1989) (a contract pertaining to the custody of a minor child is always subject to being set aside or modified in the best interest of the child. It is not necessary that a court find a change of circumstances to do so); *see* Haraschak v. Haraschak, 268 Pa. Super. 173, 407 A.2d 886 (1979).

[4] Nemeth v. Nemeth, 289 Pa. Super. 334, 433 A.2d 94 (1981); *see also* Moran v. Moran, 417 Pa. Super. 549, 612 A.2d 1075 (1992) (Court-appointed conciliator's proposed order encompassing parents' "agreement" regarding custody arrangement was not a final order, and therefore, trial court committed reversible error by not

Courts have repeatedly noted that custody orders, unlike most judicial decrees, are by nature subject to reevaluation and modification.[5] The modification of a custody order is initiated with a petition to modify. It is the court's responsibility to fully discuss the possible effect on a child of a change in custody.[6]

In *Jackson v. Beck*,[7] the Superior Court ruled that an award of shared physical custody did not require equal division of the child's time between both parents. Shared physical custody required a division of the child's time between parents that would best serve the child, not her parents. Father's petition to modify a joint-custody award from 60–40 in favor of mother to a 50–50 split was denied because the court found that father's petition was motivated by father's own interests rather than the best interests of the child. Father failed to demonstrate that the custody arrangement he proposed would further the best interest of the child. Rather, the evidence revealed that the modifications were designed to serve father's own interests and motivations, specifically his desire for joint custody on an equal basis. "It is axiomatic that the potential harm that may result from the disruption of established patterns of care and emotional bonds underscores the need for continuity, stability, and finality imparted to custody arrangements. Thus, we repeatedly

---

granting a hearing after receiving letters from mother and infant's doctor indicating that proposed custody arrangement would adversely affect infant by interfering with her breast-feeding schedule; conciliators do not issue orders, but rather summarize and propose orders).

[5] *See* footnote 1 of this section, *supra*; In the Interest of A.E., 722 A.2d 213 (Pa. Super. 1998) (trial court erred when it transferred custody from mother to father after conducting an informal shelter care hearing, because a shelter care proceeding without a determination of dependency is not a substitute for a custody proceeding. The trial court had allowed the father to misuse a dependency proceeding as a means of gaining custody. The court noted that Justin S. recognized only a court's authority to transfer custody without a dependency determination where the court conducted full hearings and the evidence supported a dependency determination).

[6] *See* R.S. v. T.T., 113 A.3d 1254 (Pa. Super. 2015) (*quoting* E.A.L. v. L.J.W., 662 A.2d 1109 (Pa. Super. 1995)); *see also* E.B. v. D.B., 209 A.3d 451 (Pa. Super. 2019) (Superior Court concluded that the trial court abused its discretion by modifying custody and the interim order prematurely and without sufficient explanation or justification as to why modification was in the child's best interest).

[7] Jackson v. Beck, 858 A.2d 1250 (Pa. Super. 2004).

have emphasized that a party requesting modification must prove that the alteration of an existing custody arrangement is in the child's best interest. . . . The proposed modifications are calculated to achieve a mathematically precise division of the child's time and appear to stem from father's belief that splitting this child down the middle is the fairest means to resolve an impasse, a resolution we find unacceptable."

In *Jordan v. Jackson*,[8] the Superior Court held that because the trial court considered the best interests of the child, and not just mother's rehabilitation, it properly modified the existing custody order to award mother primary physical custody over that of paternal grandparents. The paramount concern in a child custody case is the best interest of the child, based upon a consideration of all factors that legitimately affect the child's physical, intellectual, moral, and spiritual well-being. In the case of a custody challenge by a third party, however, this analysis is "weighted." The court explained that in custody contests between a parent and a third party such as a grandparent, the third party bears the burden of proof and persuasion that convincing reasons exist such that an award of custody to the third-party is in the child's best interest. Grandparents failed to overcome the presumption in favor of mother by providing convincing reasons why awarding custody to them would serve the child's best interests.

In *Walkenstein v. Walkenstein*,[9] the Superior Court affirmed an order awarding custody to grandparents. The court found no error in the trial court's decision to grant custody to Grandmother. The court noted that the child had attention deficit disorder, and a major change in his home and school situation would not be in his best interest at this time. The court acknowledged that Grandmother's negative attitude toward Mother was a problem, and that Mother had worked very hard to overcome her problems. However, although another court could have decided differently, the trial court's decision in this case was within its discretion.

Generally, a trial court may not modify a custody order on a non-temporary basis without having before it a formal petition to modify filed

---

[8] Jordan v. Jackson, 876 A.2d 443 (Pa. Super. 2005).
[9] 443 Pa. Super. 683, 663 A.2d 178 (1995).

by one of the parties.[10] However, the trial court is not prevented, under appropriate circumstances, to alter a custody order when it is in the best interest of the child to do so.[11] This issue most often presents itself when a contempt petition is before the court and the court changes custody at the conclusion of the proceeding. The primary concern is whether a litigant is deprived of his/her right to due process by not receiving proper notice that custody could be changed. Therefore, in cases where a contempt petition is before the court without a claim to modify custody, it has been found to be improper for a court to change custody at the conclusion of the hearing.[12] However, it has been held that a separate petition to modify is not necessary where the petitioner in a contempt proceeding sought a change in custody in his petition for contempt, as the respondent would then have notice that custody could be modified at the proceeding.[13]

---

[10] Choplosky v. Choplosky, 400 Pa. Super. 590, 584 A.2d 340 (1990).

[11] *Id.; see also* E.B. v. D.B., 209 A.3d 451 (Pa. Super. 2019) (Superior Court concluded that the trial court abused its discretion by modifying custody and the interim order prematurely and without sufficient explanation or justification as to why modification was in the child's best interest).

[12] G.A. v. D.L., 72 A.3d 264 (Pa. Super. 2013) (trial court erred when it modified the parties' custody order by reinstating the prior custody order where only a petition for contempt was before the court and no mention of modification was raised in the contempt petition); P.H.D. v. R.R.D., 56 A.3d 702 (Pa. Super. 2012) (improper for a court to *sua sponte* modify custody where no petition to modify custody was before the court); Everett v. Parker, 889 A.2d 578 (Pa. Super. 2005) (the Superior Court held that transfer of custody cannot be ordered unless both parties receive notice that transfer of custody will be an issue at a hearing. The trial court did not have authority to find mother in contempt of a custody order and then transfer custody to father where mother did not receive adequate notice of the contempt hearing or that custody was to be an issue at that hearing); Langendorfer v. Spearman, 797 A.2d 303 (Pa. Super. 2002); Choplosky v. Choplosky, 400 Pa. Super. 590, 584 A.2d 340 (1990); Seger v. Seger, 377 Pa. Super. 391, 547 A.2d 424 (1988) (following a hearing on a petition for contempt, trial court lacked authority to modify custody/visitation order absent filing of petition for modification by any party to order); Steele v. Steele, 376 Pa. Super. 174, 545 A.2d 376 (1988)) (appropriate manner to bring about change in custody/visitation order is by petition for modification).

[13] C.A.J. v. D.S.M., 136 A.3d 504 (Pa. Super. 2016) (trial court can modify a child custody order on a contempt petition, though a petition to modify custody is not before the court, if the petition before the court expressly states that the litigant is seeking custody, or seeking review of custody, or that custody will be an issue before the court); Guadagnino v. Montie, 435 Pa. Super. 603, 646 A.2d 1257 (1994) (trial court did not abuse its discretion in modifying the custody order at a contempt hearing when

In *P.H.D v. R.R.D.*,[14] a contempt petition was before the trial court and the trial court dismissed the contempt petition but "clarified" the existing order which modified the order by forbidding the father from appearing at places where the children would be reasonably expected to be. The Superior Court held that the trial court cannot *sua sponte* modify a custody order when a petition to modify is not before the court. The Superior Court stressed that the father's due process rights were violated by the trial court when it modified the order. Further, the Superior Court analyzed whether the "clarification" was tantamount to a modification. The Superior Court looked to the Uniform Child Custody Jurisdiction and Enforcement Act ("UCCJEA") that defines modification as: "[a] child custody determination that changes, replaces, supersedes or is otherwise made after a previous determination concerning the same child, whether or not it is made by the court that made the previous determination." The Superior Court found that the trial court's order containing the "clarification" "unquestionably imposed new and severe restrictions on Father, and therefore modified the earlier custody orders."

In, *G.A. v. D.L.*,[15] the trial court erred when it modified the parties' custody order by reinstating the prior custody order where only a petition for contempt was before the court and no mention of modification was raised in the contempt petition. The Superior Court relied on *P.H.D v. R.R.D.*, 56 A.3d 702 (Pa. Super. 2012) in making its decision.

In *Choplosky v. Choplosky*,[16] the Superior Court held that a trial court may not act to modify a custody order on a non-temporary basis without having before it a formal petition to modify filed by one of the parties. In *Choplosky*, the parties were before the trial court on father's petition to hold mother in contempt for failing to seek his assent before the children

---

petitioner sought change of custody in his contempt petition. There was adequate notice that the custody order would be challenged, and it was not necessary to remand case for reinstatement of the original custody order so that another hearing can be held on the petition for modification of custody, as "such action would result in a waste of judicial resources."); *but see* Langendorfer v. Spearman, 797 A.2d 303 (Pa. Super. 2002) (discussed *infra* in this chapter of this book).

[14] P.H.D v. R.R.D., 56 A.3d 702 (Pa. Super. 2012).

[15] G.A. v. D.L., 72 A.3d 264 (Pa. Super. 2013).

[16] Choplosky v. Choplosky, 400 Pa. Super. 590, 584 A.2d 340 (1990).

were given non-emergency medical treatment. At the conclusion of the hearing, the trial court entered an order modifying custody and granting sole legal custody to the mother. The Superior Court reversed, finding that while the trial court may have had authority to temporarily modify custody as an aspect of special relief, it could not permanently do so without a petition to modify and adequate notice to the parties. A trial court is without authority to permanently modify custody based on a contempt petition alone without a petition to modify before it. While efforts to modify custody orders can be entertained at any time, courts must not allow the parties to forego general notice requirements.[17]

In *Langendorfer v. Spearman*,[18] the Superior Court ruled that the trial court committed a "clear abuse of discretion" during contempt proceedings against father when it permanently modified custody and awarded mother full custody despite the fact that a formal petition to modify custody had not been filed by either party and the contempt petition did not request a change in custody.[19] Pursuant to *Choplosky v. Choplosky*, 584 A.2d 340 (Pa. Super. 1990), and *Rosenberg v. Rosenberg*, 504 A.2d 350 (Pa. Super. 1986), the trial court could not permanently modify a custody order when no petition for modification had been filed. *Langendorfer* appears distinguishable from *C.A.J. v. D.S.M.*[20] and *Guadagnino v. Montie*[21] (discussed *infra*) as there was notice that custody would be at issue in the contempt petition filed in *C.A.J.* and *Guadagnino*.

---

[17] *See also* E.B. v. D.B., 209 A.3d 451 (Pa. Super. 2019) (Superior Court concluded that the trial court abused its discretion by modifying custody and the interim order prematurely and without sufficient explanation or justification as to why modification was in the child's best interest).

[18] Langendorfer v. Spearman, 797 A.2d 303 (Pa. Super. 2002).

[19] *See also* J.M. v. K.W., 164 A.3d 1260 (Pa. Super. 2017) (trial court abused its discretion in changing custody of the child as a contempt sanction because there was no express notice that custody would be at issue at a hearing).

[20] C.A.J. v. D.S.M., 136 A.3d 504 (Pa. Super. 2016) (trial court can modify a child custody order on a contempt petition, though a petition to modify custody is not before the court, if the petition before the court expressly states that the litigant is seeking custody, or seeking review of custody, or that custody will be an issue before the court).

[21] Guadagnino v. Montie, 435 Pa. Super. 603, 646 A.2d 1257 (1994).

In *Guadagnino v. Montie*,[22] it was held that a court presiding over father's petition for contempt could also transfer custody of child to father, where it was made clear, both in father's petition and during contempt hearing, that father was also requesting primary custody, where the court was familiar, from having presided over prior custody disputes between same parties, with the parties' past history, present circumstances, and abilities to care for the child, and where the court made the change because it was in the best interest of the child, rather than as sanction for contempt. Trial court did not abuse its discretion by finding mother in contempt of the custody order and transferring custody to father based on evidence that mother continually opposed father's right of access to the child, that she telephoned father with a frequency that bordered on harassment, that she was confrontational with father in front of the child, that she refused to transfer child to father at times and places appointed, and that on one occasion when she was supposed to transfer the child to father, she went instead to the police station and claimed that father was attempting to kidnap the child.

Other reasons for modification petitions may be found in an altered work schedule which conflicts with the standing order;[23] a geographic move which may necessitate fewer but more extended blocks of partial custody;[24] the elimination of a negative condition influencing the initial order;[25] or a finding that visits by certain parties are having an adverse effect on the child.[26]

It has also been held that where one party so obstructs the custody rights of the other to the extent that the best interests of the child are no

---

[22] *Id.*

[23] Scarlett v. Scarlett, 257 Pa. Super. 468, 390 A.2d 1331 (1978).

[24] Smith v. Smith, 307 Pa. Super. 544, 453 A.2d 1020 (1982); Maron v. Maron, 78 Del. Rep. 14 (1990) (father's weekend and holiday visitation schedule will be modified to accommodate father's travel time from his out-of-state residence to pick up the child and to better serve the best interests of the child, and mother and father may make mutually agreeable modifications).

[25] Dile v. Dile, 284 Pa. Super. 459, 426 A.2d 137 (1981).

[26] Commonwealth ex rel. Peterson v. Hayes, 252 Pa. Super. 487, 381 A.2d 1311 (1977); Commonwealth ex rel. Goodwin v. Goodwin, 82 Montg. 328 (1963).

longer served, modification of the prior order and even a change of custody may be warranted.[27]

On appeal from a decision regarding modification of a visitation order, the appellate court will apply the same standard of review utilized on appeal from a custody order.[28]

A trial court did not abuse its discretion when it consolidated proceedings on mother's and father's petitions to modify custody in a divorce action with father's petition to hold mother in contempt for allegedly intentionally violating terms of existing order of shared legal and physical custody; all petitions addressed the custody order, its implementation, and possible violations.[29]

The question of consolidation is one that must necessarily be left to the discretion of the trial judge and where the issues are the same and they arise out of the same transaction or occurrence.[30] When the decision to consolidate does not tend to place the objecting party at a disadvantage, or give an undue advantage to his adversary, the action of the court in ordering cases to be tried together will not be reversed.[31]

LOWER COURT CASES

Berks County

Morris v. Morris, C.P. Berks County, No. 08-15427 (C.C.P. 2014) (Trial court modified its previous custody order and reduced father's visitation with the parties' minor child during the school week, where the child's disrupted schedule required traveling to and from each parent's home during the week, and this disruption contributed to his difficulties at school. Father filed a petition to modify the existing custody order, seeking additional weekly visitation. Mother believed that the child's issues at school resulted from the existing custody schedule, which resulted in the child's spending one night at mother's home, then the next night at father's home, and so on. The trial court

---

[27] Hartman v. Hartman, 328 Pa. Super. 154, 476 A.2d 938 (1984); Pamela J.K. v. Roger D.J., 227 Pa. Super. 579, 419 A.2d 1301 (1980).

[28] Bury v. Bury, 312 Pa. Super. 393, 458 A.2d 1017 (1983).

[29] Hill v. Hill, 422 Pa. Super. 533, 619 A.2d 1086 (1993).

[30] Pa.R.C.P. 213.

[31] *Id.*

modified the existing custody schedule and held that the shared custody schedule be adjusted to eliminate overnight visits with father on weekdays during the school year. The court agreed with mother's contention that the child's constant moving back and forth from one household to the other was a substantial contributor to the child's problems at school. The court agreed that the schedule should be modified to eliminate weekday visitation with father during the school year).

Scarano v. Scarano, C.P. Berks County, No. 08-291 (C.C.P. 2013) (Trial court denied father's petition to modify custody where testimony indicated that father was more passively involved with the child, and the child required more interaction due to her Asperger's Syndrome. The special needs of a child may limit contact with a non-custodial parent if such limitation is deemed to be in the child's best interest. While father had a positive involvement with the child's education, he had not pursued any involvement with any professionals regarding the child's diagnoses or treatment. He had not discussed his reservations about the child's diagnoses with any professionals and appeared to take interest in the child's treatment only when he wanted to be sure that she could cope with being in his upcoming wedding. The court noted that mother might be slightly overprotective, but had expended great energy learning about the child's condition and educated herself on how to deal with issues on a daily basis. Mother had been the leader in tending to the child's medical, educational, social, and physical needs. On the other hand, father had denied the existence of the child's conditions until only recently, and the court was still not convinced that he had truly accepted the diagnoses. The court performed the analysis required under 23 Pa.C.S. § 5328, and found mother to be the more nurturing parent who was aware of and actively attempted to meet all of the child's needs. The court believed that a change to father's home would be disruptive to the routine and stability and would not be beneficial to the child. While father was clearly unhappy with the amount of time he currently was able to spend with the child, the court ruled that the child's best interests and her particular needs required that she have a minimum of change and that she needed the focused help of at least one of her parents. Since mother had been performing that role since the child's birth, the court found that the child's needs were met if she continued in this role).

Clearfield County

L.M.S. v. M.S.S., C.P. Clearfield County, No. 2013-1234 C.D. (C.C.P. April 24, 2017), *aff'd in part, rev'd in part*, Memorandum Decision, No. 744 WDA 2017 (Pa. Super. January 5, 2018) (The parties operated under a shared custody agreement until mother filed a Petition to Modify Custody in anticipation of the child's starting kindergarten the following school year. The trial court granted mother's petition and awarded her primary physical custody of the child. Father was awarded partial physical custody every other weekend and at other such times as the parties agreed. The court placed particular emphasis on the fact that the child would soon be starting kindergarten, and that it would be in his best interest that he has the same routine on a daily basis as he moved into another phase of his life. Both parties agreed that the child's time could no longer be split equally between the parties once the child became enrolled in school. Given the fact that the parties agreed that a continued joint physical custody arrangement was not feasible, the Superior Court, on appeal, did not discern any abuse of discretion or error of law in the trial court's awarding mother primary physical custody and shared legal custody of the child).

Cumberland County

A.J.S. v. M.L.S., C.P. Cumberland County, No. 2010-2689 Civil (C.C.P. January 19, 2016) (Trial court held that the attempts of a parent to turn the children against the other parent weighed in favor of awarding father primary physical custody, as the court must consider that issue under 23 Pa.C.S. § 5328(a)(8). It was in the best interest of the children for father to receive primary physical custody during the school year when he could best help them focus on academic success, and for mother to receive primary physical custody of the children during the summer months when she could best help them focus on social development).

Layton v. Layton, C. P. Cumberland County, No. 04-4217 (C.C.P. 2009) (Trial court held that a child's transfer to a new school based on mother's move to a new school district was not a basis to modify custody. Transfer to a new school district was not viewed as a change in circumstances sufficient to warrant modification of a custody order. An existing trial court order had granted mother primary physical custody but gave father partial physical custody six out of every 14 days. When mother remarried, she moved approximately 6 miles away from the child's current school district. Father filed a petition seeking equal shared custody so that the child could maintain enrollment in her current school. Father did not want the child to change from her previous elementary school where she had done well, was involved in numerous activities, and where she had a lot of friends. The trial court denied father's petition and amended the parties' custody order to grant mother's request to allow the parties' daughter to change schools).

Lawrence County

Jones v. Lyles, C.P. Lawrence County, No. 10417 of 2010 (C.C.P. 2014) (Trial court granted plaintiff's motion to dismiss defendant's petition for modification of a custody order because the court was unable to comply with the time constraints of Pa.R.Civ.P. 1915.4(c). Defendant filed a petition for modification of a custody order. Plaintiff subsequently moved to dismiss the petition pursuant to Pa.R.Civ.P. 1915.4(c), which provides that trials and hearings shall be scheduled to be heard on consecutive days whenever possible but if not on consecutive days, then "the trial or hearing shall be concluded not later than 45 days from commencement." The court cited with approval *J.M. v. S.T.*, 885 WDA 2011 (Pa. Super. 2012), which considered Rule 1915.4(b) and concluded that it did not give a trial court discretion in continuing custody trials and maintaining its docket and that custody trials had to be strictly scheduled within the limits set forth in the rule. The court noted that although Rule 1915.4(b) was modified after *J.M.* to give the court more discretion in scheduling and continuing custody cases, Rule 1915.4(c) had not been so modified. Therefore, because it had been unable to complete the trial in this matter within 45 days due to uncontested continuances requested by the parties, the court held that it had to comply with the time limits in Rule 1915.4(c) and dismissed defendant's petition. The court noted that the case established precedent for the court to scrutinize future requests for continuances in all custody cases and implement stronger standards, despite legitimate requests from counsel).

Shearer v. Davis, C.P. Lawrence County, No. 10677 of 2013 (C.C.P. April 2, 2014) (Trial court granted father's petition for modification of custody and provided him with primary physical custody of the children during the school year. The court noted that both parties were capable of adequately providing for the children and that both parties demonstrated good parenting skills. However, the court found that the child custody factors in 23 Pa.C.S. § 5328(a) weighed slightly in father's favor. Testimony showed that father provided a more structured life and that he placed more emphasis on education. Father taught the children letters and numbers, but the children would forget what they had learned because mother had not continued the lessons. The court noted that a strong factor in favor of father was his work schedule as opposed to mother's work schedule. Father's schedule allowed him to spend more time with the children on school days when they returned home from school. However, wife's work schedule from 2 PM to 10 PM indicated that she would not be home after school or have much time to spend with the children during the week. The court noted that providing primary physical custody to father during the school year would institute more stability to the children, as they would be able to return directly home after school because father's fiancé would be at home to provide child care until father returned home from work. Also, father's mother lived close by and was available to assist in child care as needed).

Finamore v. Finamore, C.P. Lawrence County, No. 11285 of 2006 (C.C.P. 2009) (Trial court, citing *Karis v. Karis*, 544 A.2d 1328 (Pa. 1988), ruled that a court no longer required a change in circumstances to review a custody order. The court must inquire into the best interest of the child regardless of whether a "substantial" change in circumstances has been shown).

Lehigh County

A.D.W. v. F.W., Jr., C.P. Lehigh County, No. 2014-FC-0538 (C.C.P. September 29, 2016), *aff'd*, Memorandum Decision, No. 2792 EDA 2016 (Pa. Super. May 4, 2017) (The trial court found that so long as the parties had notice that custody would be at issue, the trial court was permitted to modify custody without a pending petition for modification, citing *C.A.J. v. D.S.M.*, 136 A.3d 504, 509 (Pa. Super. 2016). The court denied mother's petition to relocate and modified the parties' custody arrangement such that mother no longer had primary physical custody. Rather, the parties shared physical custody equally. The court noted that mother's counsel acquiesced to a potential custody modification by not objecting to the court's observation that the parties' custody arrangements were open to modification).

Lopinto v. Lopinto, C.P. Lehigh County, No. 2009-FC-1246 (C.C.P. 2012) (The trial court awarded mother sole legal and physical custody of the parties' children where the court had serious concerns about father's use of drugs, the fact that he had not participated in the custody proceedings, and the lack of attention to the children's needs on crucial issues in their lives. The trial court entered a custody order in which the parties shared legal and physical custody of their children. Mother filed a petition for modification of custody, arguing that circumstances had changed since the entry of that order. Father did not appear for the hearing or for the conference conducted prior to the hearing. Mother testified that father was irresponsible, a regular user of marijuana and was abusive to her in the past. The court had granted a protection from abuse order in the past. Mother also testified that father ignored the children, and associated with undesirable people. The trial court gave weighted consideration to the factors set forth in 23 Pa.C.S. § 5328(a), and granted mother's petition for modification. The court determined that it would have been preferable for father to participate at the hearing, because all of the facts were not completely presented. However, the court determined that it was necessary that mother be made sole legal and physical custodian. Father was granted regular contact but only as approved by mother and if she was assured that the children would be safe and the circumstances were appropriate).

Montgomery County

A.D.D. v. A.L.B., 155 Montg. Co. L. Rep. 69 (C.C.P. April 17, 2017) (Trial court held that a court is not required to consider relocation factors when modifying custody of a child if neither of the parents is relocating, even if it means modifying the main residence of the child. The court granted father primary physical custody during the school year, when the child would be in first grade. Father was not relocating and mother was remaining in Lancaster County. As neither mother nor father was relocating, there was no change of circumstances on this issue for the court to assess. Since only the percentage of time that the child would be spending with each parent was changing, the relocation provisions of 23 Pa.C.S. § 5337 were not triggered and the notice was not required under § 5337(c)).

DiFilippo v. DiFilippo, C.P. Montgomery County, No. 87-09710 (C.C.P. 1995) (Custody of the child should be transferred to the father after the mother was adjudicated in contempt of the visitation provisions of the court's prior custody orders. The court concluded that where a litigant is given adequate notice that a custody order will be challenged in the course of a contempt hearing, and where the trial judge is adequately familiar with the history of the case, the trial court may transfer custody at the conclusion of the contempt hearing when it is in the best interests of the child, citing *Guadagnino v. Montie*, 645 A.2d 1257 (Pa. Super. 1994)).

Venango County

A.B. v. L.M.H., C.P. Venango County, No. Civ. 473-2011, *aff'd,* Memorandum Decision, No. 484 WDA 2018 (Pa. Super. December 14, 2018) (The trial court awarded mother and father shared legal and physical custody of the parties' 10-year-old daughter. The trial court awarded father primary physical custody during the school year, and mother partial custody two out of three weekends during the school year. Mother filed a Petition for Modification requesting primary physical custody of the child during the school year. The trial court appointed counsel for the child. The trial court then denied mother's modification petition. The trial court stated that while it took testimony from the child, she very significantly did not wish to express any preference as to living primarily with either party, and indicated she had a very good relationship with both parents. The child testified that she likes the activities she does with father and the activities she does with mother. The court noted that mother's implication at the hearing that father's occasional glass of wine, in light of his history of alcoholism and DUI offenses, impacted his ability to care for the child was unsubstantiated. Mother offered no testimony regarding the effect or significance of father's occasional glass of wine).

§ 15.2. COUNSEL FEES—REPETITIVE FILINGS

Under 23 Pa.C.S. § 5339: "a court may award reasonable interim or final counsel fees, costs and expenses to a party if the court finds that the conduct of another party was obdurate, vexatious, repetitive or in bad faith." It is the belief of many that repetitive litigation is not in the best interests of the child. Because of this, the enactment of Section 5339 in 2011 was well received. The Pennsylvania Superior Court addressed the application of Section 5339 for the first time in the case of *Chen v. Saidi.*[32]

In the *Chen* case, the father filed seven petitions over seven years. The trial court awarded counsel fees because of Father's repetitive filings.

---

[32] Chen v. Saindi, 100 A.3d 587 (Pa. Super. 2014); *see also,* A.L.-S. v. B.S., 117 A.3d 338 (Pa. Super. 2015) (Superior Court's reversal of trial court consistent with the *Chen* case); Lowe v. Lowe, 110 A.3d 211 (Pa. Super. 2015) (under Pa.R.Civ.P. 1023.1, 1023.3, and 1023.4, (1) a court may sua sponte impose sanctions against a party only if it first directs that party to show cause why sanctions are not merited; and (2) in the absence of any motion for sanctions, a court that imposes sanctions on its own initiative may impose a penalty to be paid into court or directives of a nonmonetary nature, and may not award payment to the other party).

However, the Superior Court reversed the trial court because it found that "each petition sought distinct relief pertaining to a variety of legitimate issues that typically arise in a custody matter." The Superior Court further held that it could not be found that each petition was without relative merit. Lastly, the Superior Court stated that there was no indication that any of the filings affected the child's best interest. Therefore, based on the *Chen* case, the practitioner should be mindful that the fact that a litigant files many petitions in a case does not in and of itself warrant the awarding of counsel fees. It is important to note that the Superior Court in *Chen* highlighted that one of the father's petitions was resolved by agreement and another was granted in part. For guidance, the Superior Court also looked to 42 Pa.C.S.§ 2503 which allows for an award of counsel fees.

LOWER COURT CASES

Bucks County

G.A. v. J.S., C.P. Bucks County, No. A06-06-61075-C-32 (C.C.P. March 24, 2016), *aff'd*, Memorandum Decision, No. 860 EDA 2016 (Pa. Super. November 3, 2016) (Father's conduct was obdurate, vexatious and repetitive, and his petitions sought to merely rehash and reargue issues decided years before. Father's attempts at obstruction and his dilatory conduct were both well-established and not contradicted, and an award of fees to mother's counsel was therefore entirely appropriate).

Lehigh County

S.P. v. B.S., C.P. Lehigh County, No. 2015-FC-1443, *aff'd*, Memorandum Decision, No. 1204 EDA 2018 (Pa. Super. January 16, 2019) (Mother's filing multiple Petitions for Special Relief regarding the children's passport matter was repetitive. However, although repetition alone may be grounds for imposition of counsel fees, the court concluded that the circumstances here did not warrant an award. After balancing mother's repetitive filings regarding the passports against father's *pro se* repetitive voluminous single-spaced filings regarding possession of the marital residence, mortgage payments, and other various issues, despite his being represented by counsel, that the circumstances in this matter did not warrant an award of counsel fees. The court found that although mother engaged in conduct that had not served to move the parties' case forward in an orderly and expeditious manner, the same could be said for father. Accordingly, the court rejected father's request for counsel fees).

Chapter 16

JURISDICTION

§ 16.1. UNIFORM CHILD JURISDICTION AND ENFORCEMENT ACT (UCCJEA)—GENERALLY

Prior to 1977, the status of child custody jurisdiction law in Pennsylvania, and many areas of the country, was often described as chaotic. In that year, estimates placed the number of parent-initiated child abductions between 25,000 and 100,000 per year.[1] In spite of such alarming

---

[1] 23 Pa.C.S. § 5338(a); Holler v. Smith, 928 A.2d 330 (Pa. Super. 2007); Kassam v. Kassam, 811 A.2d 1023 (Pa. Super. 2002); Dile v. Dile, 284 Pa. Super. 459, 426 A.2d

figures the laws in most states provided virtually no recourse for persons from whom children had been taken. In fact, the willingness of the courts to ignore the custody determinations of sister states and counties in favor of their own views actually encouraged "grab, run, and file" tactics by parents wary of the expense, or unsatisfied with the results, of pursuing proper legal channels.

With the passage in 1977 of the Uniform Child Custody Jurisdiction Act[2] (UCCJA) and its intrastate counterpart, the Commonwealth Child Custody Jurisdiction Act[3] (CCCJA), the following year, Pennsylvania took a quantum leap toward stemming the child-snatching tide. The UCCJA, however, still did not resolve many issues surrounding multiple states exercising jurisdiction of a custody matter. In 2004, Pennsylvania passed the Uniform Child Custody Jurisdiction and Enforcement Act[4] (UCCJEA). Many of the states have also adopted the UCCJEA. The UCCJEA has refined some of the jurisdictional problems that remained under the UCCJA.

The crux of the UCCJEA lies in the restrictions it imposes on courts prior to the assumption of jurisdiction over a custody dispute. The rationale supporting the limitation of jurisdiction approach posits that as long as parents feel that courts are available to hear the merits of their cases, parents will not hesitate to pack up their children and proceed from jurisdiction to jurisdiction until a sympathetic ear can be found. Once it becomes general knowledge that it is no longer possible, except under specified circumstances, to bring the details of one's plight before the bench, the impetus for interstate flight dissipates.[5] However, parents who are willing to flee with the children and live in

---

137 (1981); Miller v. Miller, 269 Pa. Super. 83, 409 A.2d 74 (1979); Scarlett v. Scarlett, 257 Pa. Super. 468, 390 A.2d 1331 (1978); Commonwealth ex rel. Peterson v. Hayes, 252 Pa. Super. 487, 381 A.2d 1311 (1977).

[2] Uniform Child Custody Jurisdiction Act, P.L. 29, No. 1977-20 (codified at 42 Pa.C.S. §§ 5341–66) (1981).

[3] Commonwealth Child Custody Jurisdiction Act, P.L. 108, No. 1978-47 (codified at 42 Pa.C.S. § 5364) (1981).

[4] 23 Pa.C.S. §§ 5401–5482.

[5] See Reed v. High, 254 Pa. Super. 367, 385 A.2d 1384 (1978) (Spaeth, J., concurring).

secrecy in defiance of an outstanding court order will not be deterred by the UCCJEA.

Section 5402 contains the definitions used in the Act, and Pa.R.C.P. 1915.1 sets forth the definitions used in the procedural rules.

§ 16.1.1. UCCJEA – Basis of Jurisdiction

There are primarily 3 scenarios where jurisdictional issues arise in custody litigation: (1) when custody litigation is first initiated; (2) when a party seeks to modify an existing custody order; or (3) when an emergency arises. These three scenarios will be addressed in turn below.

§ 16.1.1.1. UCCJEA – Initial Child Custody Jurisdiction

23 Pa.C.S. § 5421 provides when a court in Pennsylvania has jurisdiction to make an initial child custody determination. Section 5421 provides four scenarios where Pennsylvania has jurisdiction to make an initial child custody determination.

First, Pennsylvania has jurisdiction to make an initial child custody determination only if Pennsylvania is the home state of the child on the date of the commencement of the proceeding or was the home state of the child within six months before the commencement of the proceeding and the child is absent from Pennsylvania but a parent or a person acting as a parent continues to live in Pennsylvania.[6]

Second, Pennsylvania has jurisdiction to make an initial child custody determination only if a court of another state does not have jurisdiction under the first scenario or a court of the home state of the child has declined to exercise jurisdiction on the ground that Pennsylvania is the more appropriate forum under Section 5427 (Inconvenient Forum) or Section 5428 (Jurisdiction Declined by Reason of Conduct) and: (i) the child and the child's parents, or the child and at least one parent or a person acting as a parent, have a significant connection with Pennsylvania other than mere physical presence; and (ii) substantial evidence is

---

[6] 23 Pa.C.S. § 5421(a)(1). *See also* 23 Pa.C.S. § 5402 for the definition of a "person acting as a parent" and R.M. v. J.S., 20 A.3d 496 (Pa. Super. 2011) for an analysis of same.

available in Pennsylvania concerning the child's care, protection, training and personal relationships.[7]

Third, Pennsylvania has jurisdiction to make an initial child custody determination only if all courts having jurisdiction under the first two scenarios have declined to exercise jurisdiction on the ground that a court of Pennsylvania is the more appropriate forum to determine the custody of the child under Section 5427 (Inconvenient Forum) or Section 5428 (Jurisdiction Declined by Reason of Conduct).[8]

Fourth, Pennsylvania has jurisdiction to make an initial child custody determination only if no court of any other state would have jurisdiction under the criteria specified in Sections 5421(a)(1)–(3).[9]

"Home state" is defined as the state in which the child lived with parents or persons acting as parents, for at least six consecutive months immediately preceding the commencement of the custody proceeding action; where the child is younger than six months old, "home state" means the state in which the child lived from birth with parents or persons acting as parents.[10]

As stated above, Section 5421(a)(1) grants initial jurisdiction to a competent court if (1) the Commonwealth is the home state at the time of the commencement of the proceeding or (2) the Commonwealth had been the home state of the child within six months of the commencement of the proceeding, and the child is absent from the state, and a parent or person acting as a parent continues to reside within the Commonwealth.[11] Thus, where one parent takes the child from Pennsylvania and moves to another state, the home state jurisdiction continues for six months so as to give the remaining parent a reasonable opportunity to

---

[7] 23 Pa.C.S. § 5421(a)(2). *See also* 23 Pa.C.S. § 5402 for the definition of a "person acting as a parent" and R.M. v. J.S., 20 A.3d 496 (Pa. Super. 2011) for an analysis of same.

[8] 23 Pa.C.S. § 5421(a)(3); *see also* Earl R.D. v. Linda H.S., 297 Pa. Super. 78, 443 A.2d 307 (1982) (court found that it had jurisdiction since North Carolina would not, under its own statutory provisions, have jurisdiction, but declined to exercise jurisdiction finding Vermont, the child's new home state, to be a more convenient forum).

[9] 23 Pa.C.S. § 5421(a)(4).

[10] 23 Pa.C.S. § 5402.

[11] 23 Pa.C.S. § 5421(a)(1).

file for custody in Pennsylvania, before the Commonwealth loses its home state jurisdiction base.[12] Translated, this means that a state may not claim home state jurisdiction unless the child has been located within the state for a continuous period of at least six months. Once the six-month period is established, the state will continue to be the home state for as long as the child remains within the state. Argument has been raised as to whether Section 5402 and Section 5421 are in conflict with one another regarding the six-month rule for home state jurisdiction. Section 5402 defines "home state" as the state where the Child lived for "six consecutive months **immediately** before the commencement of a child custody proceeding." (Emphasis added). Section 5421(a)(1) reflects that Pennsylvania has home state jurisdiction over a custody matter if it was the child's home state "within six months before the commencement of the proceeding." The debate is whether there can be a break between the six-month period and the filing. Recently, the Pennsylvania Superior Court addressed this issue and stated: "we conclude, based upon the stated legislative purpose of prioritizing home state jurisdiction and the history behind the UCCJEA, it was the intent of the General Assembly that there be a six month window for a state to establish home state jurisdiction in circumstances where a child is no longer in Pennsylvania at the time the custody action commences."[13] Therefore, if a child is absent at the time of filing but has otherwise resided in the state for at least six months prior thereto, home state status will not be lost. As such, once qualified as

---

[12] Boudwin v. Boudwin, 419 Pa. Super. 570, 615 A.2d 786 (1992) (Virginia was child's "home state," for purposes of jurisdiction determination under Uniform Child Custody Jurisdiction Act (UCCJA), where child lived with his mother in Virginia for one year at which time he went to live with his father in Pennsylvania but returned less than one month later to Virginia at which time mother filed custody action); Zellat v. Zellat, 351 Pa. Super. 623, 506 A.2d 946 (1986); Beese v. Calehuff, 356 Pa. Super. 137, 514 A.2d 182 (1986) (Pennsylvania lacked jurisdiction to hear custody case when wife removed child from Florida, child's home state jurisdiction, without the husband's permission); Rohrer v. Rohrer, 345 Pa. Super. 469, 498 A.2d 919 (1985); Adriance v. Adriance, 329 Pa. Super. 168, 478 A.2d 16 (1984); M.D. v. B.D., 336 Pa. Super. 298, 485 A.2d 813 (1984); Friedenberger v. Friedenberger, 355 Pa. Super. 622, 485 A.2d 68 (1984); see Bertin, *Child Custody-Child Snatching, A Guide to the General Practitioner,* 52 Pa. Bar Q. 54 (Jan. 1981); In re D.L.S. and J.L.S., 278 Pa. Super. 446, 420 A.2d 625 (1980).

[13] R.M. v. J.S., 20 A.3d 496 (Pa. Super. 2011).

the "home state", a state retains home state jurisdiction for a six-month period commencing on the date the child leaves the state.

The rationale for extending the filing period for six months is further buttressed by the fact that no other state will qualify as a home state prior to the expiration of the six-month period following the child's departure from the Commonwealth. It is only logical to look first to the state in which the child has spent his or her last significant block of time for the most current and reliable information as to the child's best interests.

Traditionally, it was believed that if the parent remaining fails to file in Pennsylvania within six months after the absconding parent has left the state with the child, home state jurisdiction in Pennsylvania is lost and the remaining parent must find other jurisdictional bases on which to proceed in Pennsylvania or pursue the removing parent and file suit in the jurisdiction where he or she has settled. However, with the enactment of 23 Pa.C.S. § 5337 (pertaining to relocation), it appears that additional safeguards are in place when a parent seeks to relocate with a child.

In the case of a child less than six months old, the state in which the child has lived since birth will be the home state.[14] If such child has lived in more than one state, courts will presumably look to the alternate provisions to determine proper jurisdiction. If there is no home state for the child, then the court will analyze which state has the maximum minimum contacts.[15] Also, temporary absences, such as visits out of the state, will not affect the calculation of the six-month period.[16] A trial court should hold a hearing to determine whether an absence from the home state is temporary or permanent.[17]

In *Bouzos-Reilly v. Reilly*,[18] the child lived in New York for 88 days after he was born. When the child was 3 months old, Mother moved with

---

[14] 23 Pa.C.S. § 5402.

[15] R.M. v. J.S., 20 A.3d 496 (Pa. Super. 2011) (*citing* Dincer v. Dincer, 549 Pa. 309, 319, 701 A.2d 210, 215 (1997)); Bouzos-Reilly v. Reilly, 2009 PA Super 165, 980 A.2d 643 (2009).

[16] 23 Pa.C.S. § 5402.

[17] R.M. v. J.S., 20 A.3d 496 (Pa. Super. 2011); Bouzos-Reilly v. Reilly, 2009 PA Super 165, 980 A.2d 643 (2009); *see also* M.E.V. v. R.D.V., 57 A.3d 126 (Pa. Super. 2012).

[18] Bouzos-Reilly v. Reilly, 980 A.2d 643 (Pa. Super. 2009).

the child to Pittsburgh to reside with her family. After approximately 3 months, Mother filed a complaint for custody in Pennsylvania. Father filed a motion to dismiss Mother's action in Pennsylvania, claiming that Pennsylvania lacked jurisdiction and that New York was the Child's home state because Mother's move to Pittsburgh was temporary. Approximately 2 weeks after Father filed his motion to dismiss, a New York judge scheduled a telephone conference "that involved limited argument by the parties' counsel and the PA trial court judge." The Pennsylvania judge then granted Father's motion to dismiss the custody action. Mother appealed. The Pennsylvania judge was reversed and the case was remanded for a full hearing to determine whether Mother's move to Pennsylvania was "indefinite" or "temporary." The Superior Court stated that: "[s]ince the motion to dismiss was filed in Pennsylvania, it is the obligation of the Pennsylvania court to make its own determination as to whether the move was temporary after hearing relevant witnesses." The Superior Court stressed that the Pennsylvania court could not dismiss the action and make the jurisdiction determination without a full hearing. Further, the Superior Court stated: "[i]f it is determined that the move [by Mother] was not temporary, then there is no home state. In that case, there must be a determination under 23 Pa.C.S. § 5421(a)(2) as to which state is the more appropriate forum based on where there are the most significant connections."

In *M.E. V. v. R.D.V.*,[19] the mother had relocated to Pennsylvania from New Jersey temporarily and did not reside in Pennsylvania permanently for the requisite six-month period when the father filed an action in New Jersey. The mother subsequently filed an action in Pennsylvania. The Pennsylvania trial court denied the father's preliminary objections and determined that Pennsylvania was the home state of the children. The Superior Court reversed the trial court and determined that Pennsylvania did not have jurisdiction to determine if it had jurisdiction over the custody matter, as New Jersey was the proper state to make the determination. A child custody proceeding, as defined by the statute, was commenced in New Jersey prior to the child custody proceeding being commenced in Pennsylvania regardless of the fact that no custody proceedings were scheduled or pending in New Jersey, and neither party contended that an initial child custody

---

[19] M.E.V. v. R.D.V., 57 A.3d 126 (Pa. Super. 2012).

determination had been made in the matter which was the trial court's reasoning for deciding that an action was not commenced in New Jersey. The Superior Court found that it was "incumbent upon the trial court to stay the Pennsylvania proceeding, contact the New Jersey courts in accordance with 23 Pa.C.S. § 5410, regarding communication between courts, who would then have the opportunity to exercise or decline jurisdiction." The Superior Court determined that failure to follow this procedure was an abuse of discretion, and therefore the court reversed the trial court's order as it lacked jurisdiction to enter same. The Superior Court also found that the trial court abused its discretion in determining that Pennsylvania was the children's home state for purposes of making an initial custody determination under 23 Pa.C.S. § 5421. The testimony of the mother (quoted in the opinion) reflected that the mother moved to Pennsylvania temporarily until two months prior to her filing an action in Pennsylvania when she informed the father that she did not intend to return to New Jersey. Therefore, the children's home state was New Jersey.

It is also important to note that an agreement of the parties to confer jurisdiction on a court that would not otherwise have jurisdiction under the UCCJEA is ineffective.[20]

LOWER COURT CASES

Carbon County

Fink v. Fink, C.P. Carbon County, No. 11-0477 (C.C.P. 2011) (Trial court held that it did not have jurisdiction over the parties' custody proceedings where it could not be considered the children's home state, even though the parties had significant contacts with the county. When more than one court could have jurisdiction over a custody matter, the court which can be determined to be the home jurisdiction of the children has controlling jurisdiction. The parties' son had lived in Northampton County with his paternal grandfather for the six months immediately preceding the custody proceedings. Daughter had lived in Northampton County until September 2010, then moved to Lehigh County, and then to Carbon County. The court transferred the matter to Northampton County. Under the Uniform Child Custody Jurisdiction and Enforcement Act (UCCJEA), 23 Pa.C.S. § 5421, a court has jurisdiction to make an initial custody determination if it is the home state of the child or was the home state within six months

---

[20] *See* S.K.C. v. J.L.C., 94 A.3d 402 (Pa. Super. 2014) (court analyzed comments to 23 Pa.C.S. § 5421).

prior to commencement of the proceedings or if a court of another state does not have or declines jurisdiction and the parent and child have significant connections with the state. Section 5421 defines "home state" as the state in which the child lived with a parent or a person acting as a parent for at least six consecutive months immediately prior to commencement of the proceedings, 23 Pa.C.S. § 5421(a)(1), and *R.M. v. J.S.*, 20 A.3d 496, 503-504 (Pa. Super. 2011). The court noted that daughter had lived in three different counties in the six months prior to the proceedings. However, because she had lived in Northampton County within the six months leading to the proceedings and for at least six months before October 2010, the court determined that Northampton County had jurisdiction. Northampton County also had jurisdiction over the matter regarding son because he had lived in that county for at least six consecutive months before the proceedings began. Accordingly, the court determined that, although Carbon County had a jurisdictional claim based on significant contacts among the parties, the custody complaint should have been filed in Northampton County).

Berks County

Dotson v. Stroud, C.P. Berks County, No. 17-3656 (C.C.P. August 14, 2017 (Trial court declined to exercise jurisdiction over a custody dispute when, although the children were born in Pennsylvania, the family relocated to North Carolina with the intent to reside there, and then one parent returned to Pennsylvania, with the intent to remain there for the foreseeable future. North Carolina, where the children received significant medical care, was the more appropriate forum. The court determined that under the circumstances of this case, Pennsylvania was an inconvenient forum, and that the case should be heard in North Carolina. While father's North Carolina residency was short, the parties chose to move to North Carolina together. Of paramount importance in the determination of the custody issues in this case was the children's health concerns. The children required certain medical care, and mother had in place the necessary pediatric and physical therapy in North Carolina. To the extent evidence would be required from healthcare professionals, North Carolina would provide a more convenient forum. Accordingly, the court declined to exercise jurisdiction in Pennsylvania, and concluded that North Carolina was the more appropriate forum in this case).

§ 16.1.1.2. UCCJEA – Jurisdiction When Modifying Child Custody Order

When modifying a custody order, pursuant to the UCCJEA, the proper state to file the petition is the state where the order was issued unless none of the parties and the child no longer reside in that state.[21]

---

[21] *See* 23 Pa.C.S. §§ 5422 & 5423. *See also* V.C. v. L.P., 179 A.3d 95 (Pa. Super. 2018) (mother filed a modification and contempt action in PA where she and the child lived against grandmother, though grandmother resided in New York—the state that issued the

Once before the court, the court may determine that jurisdiction should no longer be in the state pursuant to § 5422 (Exclusive, continuing jurisdiction), § 5423 (Jurisdiction to modify determination), and § 5427 (Inconvenient forum). If none of the parties and the child remain in the state that issued the custody order, the petition should be brought in the child's home state.[22] It is important to note that jurisdiction attaches when a petition is filed (also referred to as the "snapshot date.")[23] Therefore, regardless of whether jurisdiction was proper when the initial custody order was entered, jurisdiction should be re-analyzed again at the time of the subsequent filings, as continuing jurisdiction ceases when the child, the parents, and all persons acting as parents physically leave the state to live elsewhere prior to the filing of a petition to modify.[24] It is also important to note that if the parties and child

---

order; Pennsylvania Super Court vacated order by Pennsylvania trial court finding grandmother in contempt, since New York did not relinquish exclusive, continuing jurisdiction); B.L. v. T.B. and F.L., 152 A.3d 1014 (Pa. Super. 2016) (Superior Court affirmed lower court's dismissal of case, under the exclusive continuing jurisdiction section of the UCCJEA, because the order was entered in Texas, and the parents remained in Texas, Texas is the appropriate jurisdiction to hear modification actions of the order); A.L.-S. v. B.S., 117 A.3d 338 (Pa. Super. 2015) (Superior Court reversed trial court's dismissal of modification action as Ohio no longer had exclusive, continuing jurisdiction pursuant to UCCJEA as the parties and children no longer lived in Ohio and Pennsylvania met the home state criteria for jurisdiction); T.A.M. v. S.L.M., 104 A.3d 30 (Pa. Super. 2014) (Superior Court reversed trial court's erroneous dismissal of action where trial court found Pennsylvania lacked jurisdiction to modify Tennessee order because Tennessee court did not relinquish jurisdiction. As the parties and the child no longer resided in Tennessee, Pennsylvania may find that the parties and child no longer reside in Tennessee and decide the case if Pennsylvania is the home state); B.J.D. v. D.L.C., 19 A.3d 1081 (Pa. Super. 2011) (trial court lacked subject matter jurisdiction to enter custody order transferring case to Oklahoma where neither the parties nor the child resided in Pennsylvania and no longer had connections with Pennsylvania, and had no intention to return; pursuant to 23 Pa.C.S. § 5422, Pennsylvania no longer had exclusive, continuing jurisdiction over the child custody matter).

[22] See 23 Pa.C.S. §§ 5421, 5422 & 5423.

[23] See 23 Pa.C.S. § 5422 & the Uniform Law Comment thereto. See also T.D. v. M.H., 219 A.3d 1190 (Pa. Super. 2019) ("snapshot date" is the date that the pending action was commenced (the date the complaint for custody/petition to modify was filed), not the date that the petition to transfer jurisdiction pursuant to Section 5422 was filed).

[24] Id.

leave the state and exclusive, continuing jurisdiction ceases, exclusive and continuing jurisdiction is not re-established if a party returns to the state. In such an instance, the proper jurisdiction will be the state that qualifies under Section 5421 (regarding initial jurisdiction).[25]

Therefore, when seeking to modify a custody order, the primary applicable sections of the UCCJEA are § 5422 (Exclusive, continuing jurisdiction), § 5423 (Jurisdiction to modify determination), and § 5427 (Inconvenient forum). Sections 5422 and 5423 should be read together.

Section 5422 (Exclusive, continuing jurisdiction) provides, in pertinent part:

[A] court of this Commonwealth which has made a child custody determination consistent with section 5421 (relating to initial child custody jurisdiction) or 5423 (relating to jurisdiction to modify determination) has exclusive, continuing jurisdiction over the determination until:

(1) a court of the Commonwealth determines that neither the child, nor the child and one parent, nor the child and a person acting as a parent have a significant connection with this Commonwealth and that substantial evidence is no longer available in the Commonwealth concerning the child's care, protection, training and personal relationships; or

(2) a court of this Commonwealth or a court of another state determines that the child, the child's parents and any person acting as a parent do not presently reside in the Commonwealth.

Section 5423 (Jurisdiction to modify determination), provides as follows:

Except as otherwise provided in section 5424 (relating to temporary emergency jurisdiction), a court of this Commonwealth may not modify a child custody determination made by a court of another state unless a court of this Commonwealth has jurisdiction to make an initial determination under section 5421 (a)(1) or (2) (relating to initial child custody jurisdiction) and:

---

[25] *Id.*

(1) the court of the other state determines it no longer has exclusive, continuing jurisdiction under section 5422 (relating to exclusive, continuing jurisdiction) or that a court of this Commonwealth would be a more convenient forum under section 5427 (relating to inconvenient forum); or

(2) a court of this Commonwealth or a court of the other state determines that the child, the child's parents and any person acting as a parent do not presently reside in the other state.

Section 5427 (Inconvenient Forum) provides as follows:

(a) GENERAL RULE.—A court of this Commonwealth which has jurisdiction under this chapter to make a child custody determination may decline to exercise its jurisdiction at any time if it determines that it is an inconvenient forum under the circumstances and that a court of another state is a more appropriate forum. The issue of inconvenient forum may be raised upon motion of a party, the court's own motion or request of another court.

(b) FACTORS.—Before determining whether it is an inconvenient forum, a court of this Commonwealth shall consider whether it is appropriate for a court of another state to exercise jurisdiction. For this purpose, the court shall allow the parties to submit information and shall consider all relevant factors,[26] including:

(1) whether domestic violence has occurred and is likely to continue in the future and which state could best protect the parties and the child;

(2) the length of time the child has resided outside this Commonwealth;

(3) the distance between the court in this Commonwealth and the court in the state that would assume jurisdiction;

(4) the relative financial circumstances of the parties;

---

[26] *See* J.C. v. K.C., 179 A.3d 1124 (Pa. Super. 2018) (trial court reversed for not having the parties submit information relevant to the enumerated factors to determine an inconvenient forum).

(5) any agreement of the parties as to which state should assume jurisdiction;[27]

(6) the nature and location of the evidence required to resolve the pending litigation, including testimony of the child;

(7) the ability of the court of each state to decide the issue expeditiously and the procedures necessary to present the evidence; and

(8) the familiarity of the court of each state with the facts and issues in the pending litigation.

(c) STAY.—If a court of this Commonwealth determines that it is an inconvenient forum and that a court of another state is a more appropriate forum, it shall stay the proceedings upon condition that a child custody proceeding be promptly commenced in another designated state and may impose any other condition the court considers just and proper.

(d) JURISDICTION DECLINED.—A court of this Commonwealth may decline to exercise its jurisdiction under this chapter if a child custody determination is incidental to an action for divorce or another proceeding while still retaining jurisdiction over the divorce or other proceeding.

A quick review of these factors readily reveals the section's purpose as an attempt to assure, through a considered balancing of the relevant concerns, that the court which hears the merits is in the best position to do so and, to that end, encourages restraint in the exercise of jurisdiction by the less appropriate forum.[28] It should also be noted that the provisions

---

[27] *See* S.K.C. v. J.L.C., 94 A.3d 402 (Pa. Super. 2014) (A forum selection clause may not be considered for purposes of determining subject matter jurisdiction under 23 Pa.C.S. § 5422).

[28] The following cases were decided under the now-repealed UCCJA: Merman v. Merman, 412 Pa. Super. 247, 603 A.2d 201 (1992) (although Pennsylvania is the home state for purposes of determining custody under the Uniform Child Custody Jurisdiction Act, 23 Pa.C.S. § 5341 *et seq.,* it need not exercise jurisdiction where another state constitutes a more appropriate and convenient forum; in certain circumstances a trial court may determine that the home state is not the most appropriate forum. One state

dealing with inconvenient forum apply to both initial determinations and modification petitions.[29]

The following four cases are important cases to review regarding exclusive continuing jurisdiction and inconvenient forum under the UCCJEA.

---

may defer its valid jurisdiction to another forum under 23 Pa.C.S. § 5348(e). The Uniform Child Custody Jurisdiction Act at 23 Pa.C.S. § 5348(c) enumerates some of the factors that a trial court can consider in deciding whether to defer jurisdiction to another forum); Simpkins v. Disney, 416 Pa. Super. 243, 610 A.2d 1062 (1992) (Pennsylvania may not assert jurisdiction in a custody dispute under the Uniform Child Custody Jurisdiction Act, 23 Pa.C.S. § 5341 *et seq.*, where the child has been living with his mother in Maryland, negating home state jurisdiction and where a custody proceeding is pending in Maryland; where a child is moved to Maryland shortly after Pennsylvania custody proceedings are filed and where the other parent files proceedings in Maryland, the Pennsylvania court has jurisdiction as the child's "home state" under the Uniform Child Custody Jurisdiction Act, 23 Pa.C.S. §§ 5343, 5344, but will decline to exercise jurisdiction and the proceedings will be stayed since the child has established closer connections with Maryland and since relevant evidence concerning the child's care and relationships is more readily available in Maryland. Even if Pennsylvania has significant contacts jurisdiction over a child custody case, it could not exercise that jurisdiction in light of pending Maryland action); In re: Adoption of K.S., 399 Pa. Super. 29, 581 A.2d 659 (1990) (jurisdiction in a custody/visitation matter is properly declined based on *forum non conveniens* and the matter transferred to the state of Delaware under the Uniform Child Custody Jurisdiction Act, 42 Pa.C.S. § 5341 *et seq.*, where Delaware is the home state of the child and is also the home state of the natural parents and of the persons with whom the child has been living since birth); for an analysis of the K.S. decision, *see* Bertin, Emanuel A., "*Forum Non Conveniens* Analyzed in Adoption/Custody Proceedings," 12 *Pennsylvania Family Lawyer* 10 (February 1991); Joselit v. Joselit, 375 Pa. Super. 203, 544 A.2d 59 (1988) (Pennsylvania court was more appropriate forum to decide child custody in divorce proceeding than was New York court, where only connection child had with New York was his temporary hospitalization and recuperation in that state. Child was born in Pennsylvania and lived his entire life in Pennsylvania, child's parents lived in Pennsylvania until their separation, child was residing with father who continued to be domiciled in Pennsylvania, and Pennsylvania was state of marital domicile. Fact that child's grandparents lived in New York, that child was temporarily hospitalized in New York, and that child's mother received psychiatric treatment in New York did not make the New York court more appropriate forum).

[29] 23 Pa.C.S. § 5427(a).

The first case is the case of *Billhime v. Billhime*, 952 A.2d 1174 (Pa. Super. 2008). People may remember the case name of *"Billhime"* from the 2005 relocation case involving the same parties where the trial court of Montour County, Pennsylvania, denied Mother's petition to relocate to Florida, and the Superior Court reversed the trial court's decision (*see Billhime*, 869 A.2d 1031 (Pa. Super. 2005)). Since Mother moved with the children to Florida in 2005, there had been a number of petitions filed and modifications of the custody order in Pennsylvania with Mother remaining the primary physical custodian of the parties' children in Florida. On June 8, 2006, Father filed a petition to modify custody seeking primary custody of the children in Pennsylvania. On February 28, 2007, Mother responded by filing a motion requesting that the trial court relinquish jurisdiction to Florida. The trial court denied Mother's motion claiming that under the UCCJEA the court retains exclusive continuing jurisdiction (§ 5422) since Father remained a resident of Pennsylvania. However, the Superior Court reversed the trial court and remanded the case with the instruction that if the trial court determines that it lacks jurisdiction to make an initial custody determination pursuant to Section 5421 (regarding whether the court has jurisdiction to make an initial determination—which this trial court will no longer have) Mother's motion to relinquish jurisdiction should be granted. The Superior Court focused on the fact that the information relating to the children's welfare and the children's significant contacts are in Florida (such as schools, family, friends, doctors, and extracurricular activities) and the children visited Pennsylvania only several times per year. This case is a good example of the UCCJEA solving some of the past problems of the UCCJA. Under the UCCJA, people filed petitions to modify in multiple states. As stated above, under the UCCJEA, the issuing state is the correct state to file modification petitions or motions to transfer if one of the parents remains in the issuing state. However, this case demonstrates that if there are no longer significant contacts in the issuing state, jurisdiction could be lost.

In the second case, *A.D. v. M.A.B.*, 989 A.2d 32 (Pa. Super. 2010), a child custody order was entered in Pennsylvania and the father remained in Pennsylvania. The father petitioned the court to modify the custody order. The Philadelphia County judge transferred the case to Michigan for a number of reasons, mainly inconvenient forum. The father claimed, *inter alia*, that the court erred in transferring jurisdiction from Pennsylvania to

Michigan because the parties' agreement contained a "forum selection clause." The language in the clause stated: "Father may petition for visitation in the future. . . . In the event that Father does wish to petition to see [Child] in the future . . . he may do so in Philadelphia. . . ." The Superior Court disagreed that the clause in the agreement was a "forum selection clause" and was instead "permissive" language. The Superior Court further indicated that even if the language in the agreement was a "forum selection clause" it would not be determinative of where the case should be heard. The court held that under Section 5427 (inconvenient forum), there are 8 factors to consider. Factor 5 pertains to whether there is any agreement of the parties as to which state should assume jurisdiction. The court stressed that Factor 5 is only one of eight factors to be considered, and when weighing all the factors, Pennsylvania was an inconvenient forum and Michigan was overwhelmingly more appropriate.

In the third case, *Rennie v. Rosenthol*, 995 A.2d 1217 (Pa. Super. 2010), the Superior Court held in that under the plain meaning of Section 5422(a)(1) of the UCCJEA, a court that makes an initial custody determination retains exclusive, continuing jurisdiction until neither the child nor the child and one parent or a person acting as a parent have a significant connection with Pennsylvania **and** substantial evidence concerning the child's care, protection, training, and personal relationships is no longer available here. The use of the term "and" requires that exclusive jurisdiction continues in Pennsylvania until **both** a significant connection to Pennsylvania and the requisite substantial evidence are lacking. Mother and father were living in Pennsylvania when they adopted a child. Subsequently, mother and father separated and mother moved to Minnesota. The trial court entered an extensive custody agreement that modified the existing custody order. Father filed a petition seeking modification of this order, requesting a transfer of primary custody to him and Pennsylvania along with a petition for contempt. Mother filed a Motion to Relinquish Jurisdiction to Minnesota, based on 23 Pa.C.S. § 5422(a)(1) of the UCCJEA. The trial court found mother in contempt and ruled that it would retain jurisdiction over the custody modification proceeding. Mother appealed and asserted that the trial court abused its discretion when it refused to relinquish jurisdiction, arguing that she and the child did not have a significant connection to Pennsylvania because they had lived in another state for six years. Mother asserted that she lived in

Pennsylvania for only a short period of time and that the child's connections to Pennsylvania were minimal. The Superior Court affirmed,
holding that Pennsylvania will retain jurisdiction as long as a significant
connection with Pennsylvania exists and substantial evidence concerning
the child's care, protection, training, and personal relationship is present.
The court rejected mother's allegation that because she did not have a
connection to Pennsylvania, there was no significant connection with that
state. The court noted that a "significant connection" will be found where
one parent resides and exercises parenting time in the state and maintains a meaningful relationship with the child. The UCCJEA does not
specify that courts must determine that the parent with primary custody
of a child has a significant connection with the state to retain jurisdiction. Here, the evidence established that father lived in the Philadelphia
area and that he and the child had a significant connection to Pennsylvania. The child spent time with grandparents in Pennsylvania and visited
other family and friends in the state. She had a strong relationship with
father, grandparents and her stepsisters. The court found that the child
and her father had a significant connection to Pennsylvania. "Because
we have concluded that there is a significant connection to Pennsylvania,
mother has failed to satisfy the requirements of § 5422(a)(1). Indeed, it
is unnecessary to consider whether there is substantial evidence available in Pennsylvania concerning the child's care, protection, training, and
personal relationships as both prongs under § 5422(a)(1) must be lacking
in order to relinquish jurisdiction." This case differs from *Billhime* and
A.D., in that it requires both prongs under Section 5422 to be met.[30]

The fourth case, *BTW on behalf of TL v. PJL*, 956 A.2d 1014 (Pa. Super.
2008), is a protection from abuse case. However, because there was a

---

[30] *See also* S.K.C. v. J.L.C., 94 A.3d 402 (Pa. Super. 2014); J.S. v. R.S.S., 231 A.3d
942 (Pa. Super. 2020) (the Superior Court held that under the Uniform Child Custody
Jurisdiction and Enforcement Act, Pennsylvania retains exclusive continuing jurisdiction even though the parent (father) and child relocated to a foreign nation, where
mother's failure to exercise custody was partly due to deceptive behavior of father in
taking the child to that country. The trial court entered an order which awarded sole
legal and primary physical custody of the child to mother. The order awarded supervised partial physical custody to father "at mutually convenient times which the parties
are able to coordinate.").

cross-over with custody in the case and the jurisdictional issue thereunder was decided under the UCCJEA, this case will be addressed. In this case, maternal grandmother had partial custody of the child and step-mother had primary physical custody of the child pursuant to a Pennsylvania custody order. Maternal grandmother is a Pennsylvania resident and step-mother is a resident of Maryland. Maternal grandmother filed a protection from abuse action in Pennsylvania against step-mother for striking the child multiple times for not cleaning up her room. The petition also alleged that step-mother and father would drink and take drugs and then drive the child. A protection from abuse order was entered and custody was transferred to maternal grandmother. Step-mother appealed and raised two issues: (1) the court did not have jurisdiction as the subject matter was not related to a custody issue and the alleged harm occurred outside of Pennsylvania; (2) there was insufficient evidence to warrant an entry of a protection from abuse order. Under the UCCJEA (§ 5422), the issuing state of a custody order retains exclusive continuing jurisdiction. Because the protection from abuse petition placed step-mother's custody of the child at issue, the Superior Court looked to 23 Pa.C.S. § 5402 which defines "child custody proceeding[s]." Under the definition, "protection from domestic violence" is listed. Therefore, the Superior Court affirmed the trial court's order and found that jurisdiction was appropriate. The Superior Court also found that there was sufficient evidence to warrant the entry of the protection from abuse order precluding contact between step-mother and child for 3 years. (*see* the opinion for details of the abuse). Some argue that the reasoning in this case contradicts the reasoning in *Billhime*.

It should be recognized that when a prior order has been entered, a court may have lost its jurisdiction to modify the order but may retain the power to enforce it.[31]

In *Shaw v. Shaw*,[32] the Superior Court ruled that the Pennsylvania courts did not lose jurisdiction to enforce a four-year-old custody order

---

[31] Commonwealth ex rel. Taylor v. Taylor, 332 Pa. Super. 67, 480 A.2d 1188 (1984).

[32] Shaw v. Shaw, 719 A.2d 359 (Pa. Super. 1998). ("[T]here is a great difference between modification jurisdiction, which involves holding an evidentiary hearing on the best interests of the child in order to determine custody, and enforcement jurisdiction, which is limited to determining whether the prior custody order can be enforced, *i.e.*, whether the decree was valid when entered and never modified") (*quoting* Com. ex

where the children had relocated to Ohio years prior to the enforcement action; the trial court did not lose the ability to enforce the order where there had been no modification by any other court. The court noted that under *Commonwealth ex rel. Taylor v. Taylor*, 480 A.2d 1188 (Pa. Super. 1984), a trial court could properly hold a party in contempt even though it no longer had jurisdiction to modify the underlying custody decree. So long as a custody decree has not been modified by an order issued by another forum, it is enforceable by the original forum. Because mother frustrated father's right to partial custody by concealing the whereabouts of the children, the trial court did not err in finding that she had violated the provisions of the custody orders. As such, the court affirmed the grant of father's contempt petition.

LOWER COURT CASES

Allegheny County

W.P.L. v. A.S.L., C.P. Allegheny County, No. FD 08-1745-005 (C.C.P. August 18, 2016), *aff'd*, Memorandum Decision, No. 1280 WDA 2016 (Pa. Super. April 11, 2017) (Jurisdiction in Pennsylvania is defeated only where a significant connection with Pennsylvania no longer exists and substantial evidence relating to the child's care, protection, training, and personal relationships is no longer available within the Commonwealth. Thus, a significant connection and substantial evidence must *both* be absent from the Commonwealth for jurisdiction to be relinquished. Mother asked the Pennsylvania court to relinquish jurisdiction in favor of the courts of her new residence in California. It was evident that father exercised parenting time with the child in Pennsylvania during the child's scheduled visitation. As such, the child had a significant connection with this Commonwealth. Because the court concluded that there was a significant connection to Pennsylvania, mother failed to satisfy the requirements of 23 Pa.C.S. § 5422(a)(1).

Lee v. Lee, 140 P.L.J. 193 (Allegheny County 1992) (Trial court found that in a custody jurisdictional dispute where Mother lived in England with the children and Father lived in Pennsylvania, both England and Pennsylvania had jurisdiction under the Uniform Child Custody Jurisdiction Act (UCCJA), 23 Pa.C.S. § 5341 *et seq.,* but that Pennsylvania should decline jurisdiction in favor of England on the basis of *forum non*

---

rel. Taylor v. Taylor, 332 Pa. Super. 67, 72, 480 A.2d 1188, 1190 (1984)). A lower court may hold a party in contempt even though it no longer has jurisdiction to modify the underlying custody decree. Goodman v. Goodman, 383 Pa. Super. 374, 394, 556 A.2d 1379, 1389 (1989)).

conveniens. The parties had separated and Mother returned to England with the minor children. Both parties commenced legal actions regarding the children—Mother in England, Father in Pennsylvania. Father invoked the Convention on the Civil Aspects of International Child Abduction ("Hague Convention"), 42 U.S.C. § 11601, to require the return of the children to Pennsylvania. After much litigation on both sides of the Atlantic, the trial court declined jurisdiction on the basis of *forum non conveniens*).

Adams County

White v. Farley, 33 Adams L. J. 11 (C.C.P. 1990) (Trial court declined to assume jurisdiction on the basis that Pennsylvania had never been the home state of the child, Pennsylvania has no substantial connections to the child, and Pennsylvania was an inconvenient forum; thus, a Pennsylvania court will not exercise jurisdiction in an interstate custody dispute under the Uniform Child Custody Jurisdiction Act, 42 Pa.C.S. § 5341 *et seq.,* where the child's home state is Maryland and where the best interests of the child do not warrant assertion of jurisdiction. Even if the court had jurisdiction, it would decline to exercise it under 42 Pa.C.S. § 5348, since Maryland is the more convenient forum).

Berks County

DeAngelis v. DeAngelis, 103 Berks Co. L. J. 299 (C.C.P. August 1, 2011) (Trial court ruled that Pennsylvania retained jurisdiction over a custody action because the child involved had a significant connection to Pennsylvania, despite having lived in Maryland for the last four years. Even if the majority of information about the child's care existed in another jurisdiction, the trial court can maintain jurisdiction over its originally issued custody order if the child maintains significant contacts within the court's jurisdiction and a parent remains in the issuing state. After the parties separated, mother relocated with the child from Pennsylvania to Maryland in 2006. Father continued to reside in Pennsylvania. The court awarded mother primary physical custody and granted father visitation rights. Father later filed a petition to modify the custody order and sought primary custody. Mother alleged that Pennsylvania no longer had jurisdiction over the matter under the Uniform Child Custody Jurisdiction and Enforcement Act, 23 Pa.C.S. § 5422. The Pennsylvania trial court denied mother's petition, finding that mother failed to meet the two-prong test set forth in 23 Pa.C.S. § 5422(a)(1). In order to challenge jurisdiction, mother must prove that "neither the child, nor the child and one parent" have a "significant connection" with the state *and* secondly, that "substantial evidence is no longer available" in the state regarding the child's "care, protection, training and personal relationships." The court determined that mother must establish *both* prongs to prove that the Pennsylvania court no longer retained exclusive jurisdiction over this custody matter, citing *Rennie v. Rosenthal*, 995 A.2d 1217 (Pa. Super. 2010). The court found that while the child's investment in Pennsylvania was "not as extensive" as it was in Maryland, the child had enough of an important and meaningful connection with Pennsylvania for that court to retain jurisdiction. The court agreed with father that both he and the child maintained a significant connection with

Pennsylvania. The minor child had resided in Pennsylvania for several years before moving to Maryland and spent his visitation time, including weekends, holidays, vacations and extensive stays over the summer, with father in Pennsylvania).

Carbon County

Fink v. Fink, 18 Carbon Co. L. J. 550 (C.C.P. 2011) (Under the UCCJEA, home jurisdiction has exclusive priority over, and is not merely preferable to, other forms of jurisdiction. The UCCJEA expressly provides that jurisdiction based on "significant contacts" can be exercised only if another county does not have "home county" jurisdiction, or if such jurisdiction exists, the home county has declined to exercise its jurisdiction. The court agreed with father that as between different states, 23 Pa.C.S. § 5421 defines subject matter jurisdiction, that is "the competency of a given court to determine controversies of a particular class or kind to which the case presented for its consideration belongs." The real question, however, was whether in its intrastate application, as provided for in 23 Pa.C.S. § 5471, the allocation of jurisdiction between and among the courts of this Commonwealth is one of subject matter jurisdiction or one of venue. "This issue, to our knowledge, has not been directly addressed by the courts." After considering several cases, including *Wagner v. Wagner*, 887 A.2d 282, 288 (Pa. Super. 2005) (Pennsylvania courts will not assume jurisdiction under "significant connections" test unless it appears that no other state may assume jurisdiction under the "home state" test, or if such jurisdiction exists, the home county has declined to exercise its jurisdiction), the court determined that since neither of these two scenarios applied, it was without jurisdiction to issue a custody decree. Accordingly, the matter was transferred to Northampton County for appropriate proceedings).

Centre County

Keiski v. Fritz, C. P. Centre County, No. 2009-2374 (C.C.P. 2009) (Trial court declined jurisdiction even though Pennsylvania was the home state, since Minnesota had been the site of all previous custody litigation. The court denied mother's emergency motion and declined to assume jurisdiction. The court ruled that the fact that Pennsylvania was the home state under the Uniform Child Custody Jurisdiction Act did not prevent a court from determining that jurisdiction was better held by the trial court in Minnesota. The fact that Minnesota was no longer the home state under the UCCJA did not mean that jurisdiction rested exclusively in Pennsylvania, particularly since the Minnesota order did not specifically relinquish jurisdiction and provided Minnesota contact numbers for mediation service for the parties).

Delaware County

McGrapham v. Saienni, 33 D.&C. 4th 444 (Del. Co. 1996) (Trial court held that despite the existence of a prior consent order regarding custody and visitation in the state of Delaware, a Pennsylvania trial court properly exercised jurisdiction over mother's complaint to confirm custody of her son, where the son had significant contacts with Pennsylvania and it was in his best interests for the court to exercise jurisdiction. The court found that because the child is doing well with the mother in Pennsylvania, Pennsylvania should have jurisdiction. While the Court conceded that Pennsylvania was not the home state, it relied on 23 Pa.C.S. § 5349(b), in finding that the best interests of the child warranted assumption of jurisdiction. Mother's allegation of unsafe conditions and the child's own testimony of his desire not to return because of those conditions convinced the court to hear the case. The court cited with approval *Baines v. Williams*, 635 A.2d 1077 (Pa. Super. 1993), where the court ruled that in order for a trial court to exercise jurisdiction, the interest of the child must be reviewed and jurisdiction should not be declined if required in the best interest of the child. Further, because the child had been living in Pennsylvania, significant contacts existed here with regard to the child's present and future care, protection, training and personal relationships. With regard to the Delaware custody order, the court noted that neither mother nor father had lived in that state for a period of years).

Lawrence County

Lynch v. Lynch, C.P. Lawrence County, No. 10467 of 2014, C.A. (C.C.P. 2015) (Trial court held that the parties no longer had significant contacts to the county of jurisdiction over this custody matter pursuant to their agreement, and it was now an inconvenient forum. Mother filed a petition for transfer of custody on grounds of inconvenient forum, citing the parties' current connections to Allegheny County. Mother argued that for the past 13 months both parties had primarily been living in Allegheny County).

Elsbury v. Elsbury, C.P. Lawrence County, No. 11153 of 2007, C.A. (C.C.P. 2011) (Trial court transferred the parties' custody case to Florida where father had relocated with the children three years prior and the children no longer had significant contact with Pennsylvania. After father was awarded partial visitation rights, he petitioned for special relief claiming that mother's ongoing mental health issues severely impacted her ability to care for the children. The court granted father temporary physical custody. Father later petitioned to relocate with the children to Florida so that he could accept a career opportunity with the United States Air Force. The court granted the petition and awarded mother partial visitation rights. Mother later petitioned to modify the custody order, but father petitioned to relinquish jurisdiction in the Pennsylvania court and transfer the matter to Florida. The court granted father's petition to transfer and ordered the case to be transferred to the appropriate Florida court. The court noted that the issue of jurisdiction in custody proceedings is controlled by the Uniform Child Custody Jurisdiction and Enforcement Act, 23 Pa.C.S. § 5401, *et seq.* Section 5422 of the Act provides that, if a court determines that there is no longer significant contact with the Commonwealth and the children or with the children and one parent, the court does not have the authority to make custody determinations. A court must also consider, under § 5422(a)(1), whether there is still substantial evidence in the Commonwealth regarding the child's care, protection, training and personal relationships. Here, father testified that he and the children had resided in Florida since 2008, that he had found employment and established a residence for the children there and that the children went to school in Florida and received their primary medical care there. Alternatively, mother testified that the children traveled to Pennsylvania twice a year for extended visits, that all of the children's family resided in Pennsylvania (except their father), and that prior to the relocation, the children had lived only in the New Castle, Pennsylvania area. Citing *Kriebel v. Kriebel*, 812 A.2d 579 (Pa. 2002), the court found mother's evidence insufficient to retain jurisdiction in Pennsylvania. "For almost 3 years, the children have lived continuously in Florida, with the exception of their semi-annual visits to Pennsylvania. They are enrolled in school in Florida, receive on-going care from physicians and psychiatrists in Florida, and are involved in other activities in Florida. Furthermore, all of the necessary information regarding the children's schooling, treatment, and general lifestyle is located in Florida and not readily available to this Court.").

Gregg v. McDonald, C. P. Lawrence County, No. 11161 of 2006, C.A. (C.C.P., 2007) (A Pennsylvania court lacked jurisdiction to hear this child-custody case where the child had relocated with mother to Indiana. Pennsylvania was no longer the child's home state under the Uniform Child Custody Jurisdiction and Enforcement Act. The court cited § 5422(a)(1) of the UCCJEA, regarding significant connections with Pennsylvania. The court found that the child lacked sufficient contacts in Pennsylvania for jurisdiction to be retained. The child had moved with mother to Indiana more than one year ago, long enough to be enrolled in school there. The child's occasional visits to Pennsylvania to be with father were not sufficient to confer jurisdiction. The court rejected father's arguments that the child attends school and church in Lawrence County and is seen by a counselor there. The court noted that father enrolled the child in school over mother's objections, after refusing to return the child to her).

Lycoming County

LA v. AD, C.P. Lycoming County, No. 14-20, 695 (C.C.P. 2014) (The court considered the effect of a forum-selection clause entered into by the parties. The parties had agreed to North Carolina remaining as the forum. At the time, it was intended that neither party would reside in North Carolina. The court cited with approval the recent Superior Court decision in *S.K.C. v. J.L.C.*, 94 A.3d 402 (Pa. Super. 2014), which held that "two parents may not agree, via a forum selection clause, to litigate their child custody dispute in a court that lacks subject matter jurisdiction under the UCCJEA." Since neither parent nor the child resided in North Carolina, the North Carolina Court lacked subject matter jurisdiction which could not be retained through the use of the forum selection clause. The court concluded that it had jurisdiction to modify the North Carolina Court order, as Pennsylvania was the child's home state and none of the parties resided in North Carolina).

Somerset County

Holt v. Holt, 50 Somerset L. J. 191 (C.C.P. 1992) (Under traditional *forum non conveniens* analysis, courts are to consider factors such as the relative ease of access to the sources of proof, availability of compulsory process for attendance of unwilling witnesses, the cost of obtaining the attendance of willing witnesses, the possible need for a view of the premises, and all other practical problems to make trial expeditious and inexpensive).

§ 16.1.1.3. UCCJEA – Temporary Emergency Jurisdiction

Temporary emergency jurisdiction is applicable where the child has either been abandoned, subjected to, or threatened with abuse or mistreatment.[33] The physical presence of the child within the Commonwealth is required for jurisdiction under this provision.[34]

In the event there is no existing custody order that is entitled to be enforced and a custody action has not been commenced in a court having jurisdiction over the action at the time of the emergency, a child custody determination under Section 5424 (Temporary emergency jurisdiction) shall remain in effect until a custody order is obtained from a court of a state having jurisdiction over the matter.[35] However, if no action is thereafter commenced, the emergency order becomes final if the order so provides and that state will become the home state of the child.[36]

In the event there is an existing custody order that is entitled to be enforced or a custody action has been commenced in a court having jurisdiction over the action at the time of the emergency, a child custody determination under the Section 5424 (Temporary emergency jurisdiction) shall specify a period that the court considers adequate to the person seeking the emergency order to obtain an order from the state having proper jurisdiction and the temporary emergency order will remain in effect until a custody order is obtained from the court of the state that has jurisdiction within the period specified in the order or the period expires.[37] Further, pursuant to Section 5424(d) of the UCCJEA, in an emergency situation, the court of Pennsylvania shall communicate with

---

[33] 23 Pa.C.S. § 5424; *but see* In re C.P., 354 Pa. Super. 107, 511 A.2d 210 (1986) (the now-repealed UCCJA did not give Pennsylvania jurisdiction over a non-resident father's request that a runaway juvenile be returned to him where there was no prior custody determination, neglect was never established, and no emergency conditions existed which might have permitted review of custody).

[34] *Id.*

[35] 23 Pa.C.S. § 5424(b).

[36] *Id.*

[37] 23 Pa.C.S. § 5424(c).

the court where the existing order was issued or the action has been commenced.

It is hoped that courts will utilize this section in keeping with the Act's purposes of avoiding jurisdictional competition and assuring that the court rendering the custody decision is the court with the closest connection to the child. Courts should, therefore, be wary and assume emergency jurisdiction only when clearly warranted. As the Uniform Law Comment to the section states, this "extraordinary jurisdiction is reserved for extraordinary circumstances."[38] Furthermore, even when the situation satisfies the section's intent, a court assuming emergency jurisdiction should issue only such orders as are necessary for the immediate protection of the child and leave the long-term custody determination to the court most qualified under the other jurisdictional provisions.

LOWER COURT CASES

Berks County

Reitnour v. Reitnour, 83 Berks L. J. 17 (C.C.P. 1990) (Applying the jurisdictional elements of the Uniform Child Custody Jurisdiction Act, the court would not have jurisdiction over a custody action involving the plaintiff and defendant because Pennsylvania is not the home state of the children involved and there is no "substantial connection" with Pennsylvania providing the basis for the court to accept jurisdiction to serve the best interest of the children. Pennsylvania courts will not assert jurisdiction over child custody disputes where the children have not lived in Pennsylvania since 1980 and have their substantial social, family, and educational ties in New York state).

Padua v. Padua, 82 Berks L. J. 388 (C.C.P. 1990) (The generally recognized manner of determining where a custody action will be litigated is the home state of the child, and the Uniform Child Custody Jurisdiction Act (UCCJA), which has been adopted by Pennsylvania as well as the other possible forums for this case, defines home state as the state in which the child lived immediately preceding the time involved with his parents, a parent, a person acting as parent, or in an institution for at least six consecutive months. Where the child has not lived with a parent or person acting as a parent for six months before filing of a custody petition and where the father is in the Air Force and in the process of being transferred so that he has no home available, Pennsylvania may assert emergency jurisdiction where the mother and child have been living in the state for two months).

---

[38] Uniform Law Comment to 23 Pa.C.S. § 5424.

Carbon County

Burghardt v. Burghardt, 14 Carbon Co. L. J. 326 (C.C.P. 1996) (Where Alabama was the home state of mother and children for the past ten months, the children's teachers and therapists were in Alabama, and both parties had retained counsel in Alabama to litigate pending custody issues, Alabama was the proper venue for resolving the parties' custody dispute. The court declared that the transfer of the case to Alabama was consistent with the purposes of the Uniform Child Custody Act, and not a reward to a recalcitrant litigant attempting to avoid the jurisdiction of the local court.).

Bollinger v. Bollinger, 12 Carbon L. J. 229 (C.C.P. 1990) (A Pennsylvania court has jurisdiction over a child custody action despite a prior Florida action where all parties have significant Pennsylvania contacts, where substantial evidence concerning the child's care, protection, training, and personal relationships are in Pennsylvania, and where the child is moved to Florida solely to establish jurisdiction there).

Clearfield County

Brady v. Brady, 25 D.&C. 3d 196 (Clearfield County 1982) (The six-month rule applies where there is a question between two or more courts of Common Pleas in Pennsylvania).

Clinton County

Bowes v. Bowes, C.P. Clinton County, No. 697-92 (C.C.P. 1996) (A Pennsylvania court had jurisdiction over a child custody hearing because the Commonwealth had more substantial contacts with the child than did her home state of Florida, and because evidence of alleged child abuse was located within the Commonwealth. The court noted that Pennsylvania courts have jurisdiction when it is the best interest of the child for the court to assume jurisdiction because (1) the child and at least one of the contestants seeking custody have a "significant connection" with Pennsylvania and (2) "substantial evidence is available concerning the child's present or future care, protection, training and personal relationships." Here, Florida's connections with the child were less substantial than her connections with Pennsylvania. There was substantial evidence that the child had been abused and might continue to be abused to hold that she needed protection and that it was in her best interest for the court to assume jurisdiction over the matter).

Delaware County

McGragham v. Saienni, 33 D.&C. 4th 444 (Delaware County 1996) (Trial court held that despite the existence of a prior consent order regarding custody and visitation in the state of Delaware, a Pennsylvania trial court properly exercised jurisdiction over mother's complaint to confirm custody of her son, where the son had significant contacts with Pennsylvania and it was in his best interests for the court to exercise jurisdiction. The court found that because the child is doing well with the mother in Pennsylvania, Pennsylvania should have jurisdiction. While the court conceded that Pennsylvania was not the home state, it relied on 23 Pa.C.S. § 5349(b), in finding that the best interests of the child warranted assumption of jurisdiction. Mother's allegation of unsafe conditions and the child's own testimony of his desire not to return because of those conditions convinced the court to hear the case. The court cited with approval *Baines v. Williams*, 635 A.2d 1077 (Pa. Super. 1993), where the court ruled that in order for a trial court to exercise jurisdiction, the interest of the child must be reviewed and jurisdiction should not be declined if required in the best interest of the child. Further, because the child had been living in Pennsylvania, significant contacts existed here with regard to the child's present and future care, protection, training and personal relationships. With regard to the Delaware custody order, the court noted that neither mother nor father had lived in that state for a period of years).

Sims v. Jefferson, 83 Del. Co. Rep. 72 (C.C.P. 1995) (Where the child in question has lived in Maryland in the custody of his father for the last two years, the Pennsylvania court did not have subject matter jurisdiction over the mother's complaint for custody of the child, because it did not qualify as the child's home state under 23 Pa.C.S. § 5344. Section 5344 requires that: (1) the Commonwealth be the home state of the child within six months before commencement of the proceeding, or had been the home state within six months before a parent (or person acting as parent) continues to live here and the child is absent because of his/her removal or retention by a person claiming custody and, (2) it is the best interest of the child that a court of the Commonwealth assume jurisdiction because, (a) the child and at least one contestant have significant connection here and, (b) there is substantial evidence available here concerning the care, protection, training, and relationships of the child.).

Jefferson County

Fritzsche v. Fritzsche, C.P. Jefferson County, Number 763-2006 CD (C.C.P. 2006) (Trial court declined to exercise temporary emergency jurisdiction where there was no evidence that the child was in immediate danger of suffering harm. Mother requested that the Pennsylvania courts exercise temporary emergency jurisdiction pursuant to 23 Pa.C.S. § 5424. That provision allows Pennsylvania courts to exercise temporary emergency jurisdiction if a child has been abandoned or it is necessary in an emergency to protect the child because she, her sibling, or her parent is subject to or threatened with mistreatment or abuse. At issue was whether this case should be returned to Maryland for disposition on the question of the custody of the parties' minor child. The trial court dismissed mother's Pennsylvania custody complaint and directed the prothonotary to transfer the record to the Maryland courts. After reviewing pertinent parts of the UCCJEA and the PKPA, the court determined that Maryland clearly had jurisdiction over the matter of the child's custody).

Lawrence County

Weingartner v. Weingartner, 40 D.&C. 4th 564 (Lawrence Co. 1995) (Where the child in question had resided with father in one county for the two years immediately preceding the filing of a custody action, and the child had gone to school, church, and Sunday school in that county, the child had substantial contacts with that county so that jurisdiction in that county was appropriate. The court found that the son's attendance at school church and Sunday school classes in Lawrence County were sufficient to constitute "significant contacts" with the county, and outweighed the less significant contacts he had with Beaver County, specifically his mother's, sister's, and maternal grandmother's residency there, and the fact that Beaver County was where the original custody "decree" had been entered into).

Montgomery County

Jacobson v. Glassmire, C.P. Montgomery County, No. 86-09509 (C.C.P. 1997) (Trial court held that the New Jersey courts had jurisdiction over a custody matter involving a child who lived in New Jersey and who visited Pennsylvania only to see his father. Pennsylvania was not the home state of the child, the court noted, and his only contacts with Pennsylvania were his visits with his father).

Ferguson-Berman v. Berman, 121 Montg. Co. L. Rep. 291 (C.C.P. 1988) (The two bases of jurisdiction under the Uniform Child Custody Jurisdiction Act are "home state" jurisdiction and "significant contacts" jurisdiction. While Pennsylvania courts have generally given favor to home state jurisdiction over that based on significant contacts, this preference will not apply in all instances. Neither Pennsylvania nor Ohio is the "home state" where the minor child lives with her mother in Ohio whenever in school and visits her father at all other times except for two weeks in the summer, as such periods are more than temporary absences and constitute the father's portion of shared physical custody. Though the minor child resides with her mother in Ohio for most of the year and attends school there, Pennsylvania is not an inconvenient forum or one without "significant contacts" where most of the minor's extended family resides in Pennsylvania, previous agreements as to custody were entered into in this state, the mother never took steps to record the Pennsylvania orders in Ohio, and where she failed to ask that Ohio assume jurisdiction until after the father had filed his petition to modify custody).

Westmoreland County

Anthony v. Anthony, 71 Westmoreland L. J. 131 (1989) (Pennsylvania courts may exercise jurisdiction over a child custody petition even though the mother moved to Pennsylvania only days before filing the petition where her family is from Pennsylvania and where she moved to get her life in order and after the father was convicted of child molesting and was incarcerated in North Carolina; mother's relocation to Pennsylvania from North Carolina, although less than one month before her filing of a custody petition in Westmoreland County, established a significant connection between the Commonwealth and the mother and child in that the mother returned to her family and began a job, and the child, as of the time of hearing, had begun treatment with a pediatrician and a psychologist; the primacy of home state jurisdiction can be outweighed where a non-home state is the site of connections to the child and at least one parent which are more substantial than those of the home state).

York County

Kessler v. Kessler, 112 York Leg. Rec. 173 (C.C.P. 1999) (Lower court may hold a party in contempt even though it no longer has jurisdiction to modify the underlying custody decree. The court declared: There is a difference between "modification" jurisdiction and "enforcement" jurisdiction).

§ 16.1.2. UCCJEA – Simultaneous Proceedings

Where a proceeding concerning the custody of the child is pending in another state exercising jurisdiction in substantial conformity with the UCCJEA, § 5426(a) prohibits the courts of the Commonwealth from exercising jurisdiction in the matter except as provided under the temporary emergency jurisdiction Section 5424.[39] If, however, the court of the other state has stayed its proceeding because Pennsylvania is the more appropriate forum, or for other reasons, courts of the Commonwealth may exercise jurisdiction.[40] Also, where a Pennsylvania court determines that on the basis of the facts involved that an action has already been commenced in another state having jurisdiction, the Pennsylvania court shall stay the proceedings and communicate with the other court.[41] Thereafter, if the court having appropriate jurisdiction does not determine that Pennsylvania is the more convenient forum, the Pennsylvania court shall dismiss the proceeding before it.[42]

---

[39] 23 Pa.C.S. § 5426(a); Carpenter v. Carpenter, 326 Pa. Super. 570, 474 A.2d 1124 (1984) (Pennsylvania court was notified of pending action in Massachusetts, communicated with that court, was advised that court would continue to exercise *parens patriae* jurisdiction, and on that basis stayed the Pennsylvania action).

[40] *Id.*

[41] *See* C.L. v. Z.M.F.H., 18 A.3d 1175 (Pa. Super. 2011).

[42] 23 Pa.C.S. § 5426(b); Levinson v. Levinson, 354 Pa. Super. 407, 512 A.2d 14 (1986) (the lower court properly stayed a determination of the jurisdictional issue in Pennsylvania since a proceeding was pending in Minnesota); In re D.L.S. and J.L.S., 278 Pa. Super. 446, 420 A.2d 625 (1980). *But see* In the Interest of Deborah Mobley, 356 Pa. Super. 1,

If a modification proceeding is before the court, the court shall determine whether there is a pending action to enforce the order in another state.[43] If there is another action pending in another state to enforce the order, the Pennsylvania court may stay the proceeding pending the entry of the enforcement order, enjoin the parties from continuing with the enforcement proceeding, or continue with the modification action.[44]

In order to facilitate the discovery and resolution of multiple suit conflicts, the Act includes procedures designed to bring to light information regarding simultaneous suits, as well as promote communication and cooperation between courts, so that the more appropriate forum may be expeditiously determined.[45]

In the case of *C.L. v. Z.M.F.H.*,[46] simultaneous proceedings existed in the Oglala Sioux Tribal Court and the Commonwealth of Pennsylvania. In *C.L.*, there was no home state, no state with exclusive, continuing jurisdiction, and more than one state with significant connections. Pursuant to 23 Pa.C.S. § 5426, a court of this Commonwealth is prohibited from exercising jurisdiction if a proceeding has been commenced in a court of another state having jurisdiction. Pursuant to 23 Pa.C.S. § 5404 (b) and (c), a court of Pennsylvania shall treat a tribe as if it were a state of the United States and the orders from tribal courts shall be recognized and enforced if made by a tribe under factual circumstances in substantial conformity with the jurisdictional standards of the UCCJEA. In *C.L.*, the Pennsylvania Superior Court found that the trial court properly concluded that there were simultaneous proceedings in the Tribal Court and the trial court, as at the time father commenced his custody action in the trial court in Pennsylvania, mother had already commenced a custody action in the Tribal Court. After the mother filed a petition in Pennsylvania under the UCCJEA to enforce the tribal court's order, the trial court had a phone conference with the tribal

---

514 A.2d 111 (1986) (under now repealed UCCJA, change of jurisdiction from Pennsylvania to South Carolina was proper when (1) the child is a resident of another state while under protective supervision in Pennsylvania (2) the state in which the child has become a resident agrees to accept jurisdiction and continue protective supervision.

[43] 23 Pa.C.S. § 5426(c).

[44] *Id.*

[45] 23 Pa.C.S. §§ 5426(b) & 5429.

[46] C.L. v. Z.M.F.H., 18 A.3d 1175 (Pa. Super. 2011).

court and ruled that the tribal court had jurisdiction over the custody dispute pursuant to 23 Pa.C.S. § 5426 since the Tribal Court action was filed first.

LOWER COURT CASES
Berks County

Childers v. Childers, 34 D.&C. 4th 511 (Berks Co. 1996) (Jurisdiction of a custody dispute was declined because all the evidence indicated that the father consented to the child moving to Florida, the mother was not trying to deprive the father of contact with the child and the parties clearly did not have sufficient contacts with Pennsylvania. Under the Uniform Child Custody Jurisdiction Act, Florida could assume jurisdiction if evidence regarding the child's well-being and the most contacts were there. Since father consented to mother's move to Florida (with the child), there was no proof that mother tried to deprive father of visitation, and mother had made good faith efforts to maintain contact between father and child and had established a life in Florida, the court determined that Florida had the necessary contacts and information regarding the child and, accordingly, transferred jurisdiction).

Delaware County

Pucard v. Carver, 77 Del. Co. Rep. 502 (C.C.P. 1990) (A court in California, rather than Pennsylvania, properly exercises jurisdiction over a custody matter under the Uniform Child Custody Jurisdiction Act, 42 Pa.C.S. § 5341 *et seq.*, where the home state of the child is in California, a custody proceeding has been pending in California for a number of years and the child has substantial contacts with California).

Lawrence County

Speer v. Brunswick, 36 D.&C. 4th 131 (Lawrence Co. 1997) (Trial court held that where a child lived in Pennsylvania only for the first two weeks of his life, Pennsylvania was not the child's home state nor did the child have significant contacts with Pennsylvania, and thus the court lacked jurisdiction over the instant custody dispute; it would be in a child's best interest to hold custody proceedings in Ohio, where the child lived nearly all his life, instead of Pennsylvania, where he lived with his maternal grandmother for only two weeks).

§ 16.1.3. UCCJEA – Conduct of the Petitioner

Section 5428 of the UCCJEA provides that except for situations of temporary emergency custody, the court shall decline to exercise its jurisdiction if the person seeking to invoke jurisdiction has engaged in unjustifiable conduct. However, Section 5428 provides three exceptions where the court may exercise jurisdiction in such a situation: (1) the parents and all persons acting as parents have acquiesced in the exercise of jurisdiction; (2) a court of the state otherwise having jurisdiction determines that Pennsylvania is a more appropriate forum; or (3) no court of any other state would have jurisdiction under the criteria provided under Sections 5421–5423.[47] The trial court should hold a hearing to determine if it should decline jurisdiction on the basis of whether the person seeking to invoke jurisdiction engaged in unjustifiable conduct pursuant to 23 Pa.C.S. § 5428 when same is alleged.[48]

The court also has the ability to fashion an appropriate remedy to ensure the safety of the child and prevent the unjustifiable conduct from reoccurring if the court declines to exercise jurisdiction pursuant to Section 5428(a).[49] The court may also stay the proceeding until an action is brought in the court having jurisdiction over the matter.[50] In addition to dismissing or staying the action, the court may assess necessary and reasonable costs against the party seeking to invoke jurisdiction.[51] Necessary and reasonable costs include: attorney's fees, communication expenses, investigative fees, expenses for witnesses, and travel expenses.[52]

LOWER COURT CASES

Adams County

White v. Farley, 33 Adams L. J. 11 (C.C.P. 1990) (Trial court declined to assume jurisdiction on the basis that Pennsylvania had never been the home state of the child, Pennsylvania has no substantial connections to the child, and Pennsylvania was an inconvenient forum; thus, a Pennsylvania court will not exercise jurisdiction in an interstate custody dispute under the Uniform Child Custody Jurisdiction Act, 42 Pa.C.S. § 5341 *et seq.*, where the child's home state is Maryland and where the best interests of the child do not warrant assertion of jurisdiction. Even if the court had jurisdiction, it would decline to exercise it under 42 Pa.C.S. § 5348, since Maryland is the more convenient forum).

---

[47] 23 Pa.C.S. § 5428(a).
[48] R.M. v. J.S., 20 A.3d 496 (Pa. Super. 2011).
[49] 23 Pa.C.S. § 5428(b).
[50] *Id.*
[51] 23 Pa.C.S. § 5428(c).
[52] *Id.*

Allegheny County

Lee v. Lee, 140 P.L.J. 193 (Allegheny County, 1992) (Trial court found that in a custody jurisdictional dispute where Mother lived in England with the children and Father lived in Pennsylvania, both England and Pennsylvania had jurisdiction under the Uniform Child Custody Jurisdiction Act (UCCJA), 23 Pa.C.S. § 5341 *et seq.*, but that Pennsylvania should decline jurisdiction in favor of England on the basis of *forum non conveniens*. The parties had separated and Mother returned to England with the minor children. Both parties commenced legal actions regarding the children—Mother in England, Father in Pennsylvania. Father invoked the Convention on the Civil Aspects of International Child Abduction ("Hague Convention"), 42 U.S.C. § 11601, to require the return of the children to Pennsylvania. After much litigation on both sides of the Atlantic, the trial court declined jurisdiction on the basis of *forum non conveniens*).

Berks County

Lynch v. Lynch, 83 Berks L. J. 107 (C.C.P. 1990) (Preliminary objection based on a procedurally defective pleading alleging lack of jurisdiction filed by the opposing party will be denied where no prejudice results since the importance of custody issues requires resolution on the merits).

Carbon County

Burghardt v. Burghardt, 14 Carbon Co. L. J. 326 (C.C.P. 1996) (Where Alabama was the home state of mother and children for the past ten months, the children's teachers and therapists were in Alabama, and both parties had retained counsel in Alabama to litigate pending custody issues, Alabama was the proper venue for resolving the parties' custody dispute. The court declared that the transfer of the case to Alabama was consistent with the purposes of the Uniform Child Custody Act, and not a reward to a recalcitrant litigant attempting to avoid the jurisdiction of the local court).

Cumberland County

Krusen v. Krusen, 45 Cumberland L. J. 337 (C.C.P. 1996) (Pennsylvania maintained jurisdiction over a petition to modify a custody order, where a Pennsylvania court issued the original custody order, Pennsylvania's initial exercise of jurisdiction was proper, the parties has sufficient contacts with Pennsylvania, and where Pennsylvania was not an overly inconvenient forum. With regard to the UCCJA, the court found that continued jurisdiction was still proper in Pennsylvania based on 1) the family's residence in Pennsylvania prior to the initial custody order; 2) the father's continued residence in Pennsylvania; and 3) the continued presence of the child in Pennsylvania for substantial periods of time on a regular basis. In addition, the court was not persuaded that Pennsylvania was so inconvenient for the parties that it warranted transferring jurisdiction to North Dakota, where mother currently resides).

Delaware County

McGrapham v. Saienni, 33 D.&C. 4th 444 (Del. Co. 1996) (Trial court held that despite the existence of a prior consent order regarding custody and visitation in the state of Delaware, a Pennsylvania trial court properly exercised jurisdiction over mother's complaint to confirm custody of her son, where the son had significant contacts with Pennsylvania and it was in his best interests for the court to exercise jurisdiction. The court found that because the child is doing well with the mother in Pennsylvania, Pennsylvania should have jurisdiction. While the Court conceded that Pennsylvania was not the home state, it relied on 23 Pa.C.S. § 5349(b), in finding that the best interests of the child warranted assumption of jurisdiction. Mother's allegation of unsafe conditions and the child's own testimony of his desire not to return because of those conditions convinced the court to hear the case. The court cited with approval. *Baines v. Williams*, 635 A.2d 1077 (Pa. Super. 1993), where the court ruled that in order for a trial court to exercise jurisdiction, the interest of the child must be reviewed and jurisdiction should not be declined if required in the best interest of the child. Further, because the child had been living in Pennsylvania, significant contacts existed here with regard to the child's present and future care, protection, training and personal relationships. With regard to the Delaware custody order, the court noted that neither mother nor father had lived in that state for a period of years).

Montgomery County

Gibbons v. Gibbons, 126 Montg. L. Rep. 312 (C.C.P. 1991) (Jurisdiction will be relinquished in favor of pending Louisiana custody proceedings where the children and their mother have resided near relatives in Louisiana for more than one year, where substantial evidence regarding their welfare is in Louisiana and where the children have been abducted into Pennsylvania; a court that has jurisdiction under this Act to make an initial or modification decree may decline to exercise its jurisdiction any time before making a decree if it finds that it is an inconvenient forum to make a custody determination under the circumstances of the case and that a court of another state is a more appropriate forum).

Gibbons v. Gibbons, 126 Montg. L.R. 312 (C.C.P. 1991) (If the petitioner for an initial decree has wrongfully taken the child from another state or has engaged in conduct intending to benefit his position in a custody hearing, the court may decline to exercise jurisdiction if it is just and proper under the circumstances).

Somerset County

Holt v. Holt, 50 Somerset L. J. 191 (C.C.P. 1992) (Under traditional *forum non conveniens* analysis, courts are to consider factors such as the relative ease of access to the sources of proof, availability of compulsory process for attendance of unwilling witnesses, the cost of obtaining the attendance of willing witnesses, the possible need for a view of the premises, and all other practical problems to make the trial expeditious and inexpensive).

Holt v. Holt, 50 Somerset L. J. 191 (C.C.P. 1992) (Although Mother and Father might at one point agree on a forum to hear their custody disputes, such an agreement should not govern forever, especially where both parties and the child have moved away from the agreed-upon forum for a significant period of time and where essentially all significant contact with the original forum has ceased; in such a case, the interest of the child and the purposes stated by the prefatory provisions of the UCCJA must override the parties' agreement).

§16.1.4. UCCJEA – Registration and Enforcement of Custody Decree

Pursuant to Sections 5445 and 5443 a custody order of a court of another state may be registered in Pennsylvania and enforced in this state. The order shall be enforced in Pennsylvania if the issuing state exercised jurisdiction in substantial conformity with the UCCJEA and the determination has not been modified.[53] Section 5445 provides the procedural steps to be taken by the party seeking to register the order and the steps to be taken by the court in registering the order.[54]

§16.1.5. UCCJEA – *Res Judicata* Effect of Custody Determination

The question of the *res judicata* effect of custody determinations is handled by Sections 5406 and 5445(f) which, in essence, codify Pennsylvania's case law on the subject and provide that a properly issued custody decree is conclusive as to all issues of law and fact decided, and is binding on all parties properly served or notified or who have submitted to the jurisdiction of the court and, who had an opportunity to be heard, except to the extent the determination has been modified.[55] In

---

[53] 23 Pa.C.S. § 5443; *see* Adriance v. Adriance, 329 Pa. Super. 168, 478 A.2d 16 (1984) (Pennsylvania court refused to enforce Nevada decree, because Nevada court assumed jurisdiction under provisions not substantially similar to those of the then-UCCJA).

[54] *See* 23 Pa.C.S. § 5445 in Appendix A(4) of this book.

[55] 23 Pa.C.S. §§ 5406 & 5445(f); Hamm v. Hamm, 431 Pa. Super. 283, 636 A.2d 652 (1992) (temporary denial, pending custody conference, of mother's petition to transfer child custody case to Nebraska did not constitute previous favorable decision to father so as to invoke doctrine of *res judicata* upon mother's subsequent petition to transfer.).

order to have such effect, the decree must have been rendered in accordance with the jurisdictional requirements of the UCCJEA.[56]

§ 16.1.6. UCCJEA – Additional Procedures

The numerous other sections of the UCCJEA largely spell out the procedures intended to facilitate the attainment of the purposes of the Act. The sections provide, *inter alia*, for notice and opportunity to be heard for all parties, parents whose parental rights have not been terminated, and anyone having physical custody of the child.[57] Further, so as to provide the broadest spectrum of information to assist the courts in determining the most appropriate forum, as well as deciding the best interests of the child, the Act includes provisions encouraging communication and cooperation between the courts of the various states;[58] giving authority for orders and requests for orders mandating the appearance of persons within the jurisdiction at proceedings outside of the state and vice versa;[59] permitting the courts of the Commonwealth to request the courts of other states to hold hearings, conduct studies and forward the results to the Commonwealth;[60] and providing for the requesting,[61] filing[62] and preservation of documents[63] generated in this and other states, which may have a bearing on the custody determination.

§ 16.1.7. UCCJEA – Intrastate Application

Section 5471 provides that the provisions of the UCCJEA pertaining to the courts of different states shall also allocate jurisdiction and functions between and among the courts of the common pleas of Pennsylvania, *i.e.*, intrastate.[64]

---

[56] *Id.*
[57] *Id.* at § 5408.
[58] *Id.* at §§ 5426, 5427, 5429.
[59] *Id.* at § 5412.
[60] *Id.*
[61] *Id.* at § 5412.
[62] *Id.* at §§ 5443, 5445.
[63] *Id.* at § 5412.
[64] *See* J.K. v. W.L.K., 102 A.3d 511 (Pa. Super. 2014) (When both parents and child moved from the issuing county (Chester County) to another county (Montgomery

LOWER COURT CASES
Lawrence County

Lynch v. Lynch, C.P. Lawrence County, No. 10467 of 2014, C.A. (C.C.P. 2015) (Trial court held that the parties no longer had significant contacts to the county of jurisdiction over this custody matter pursuant to their agreement, and it was now an inconvenient forum. Mother filed a petition for transfer of custody on grounds of inconvenient forum, citing the parties' current connections to Allegheny County. Mother argued that for the past 13 months both parties had primarily been living in Allegheny County).

Lycoming County

J.P. v. M.U., C.P. Lycoming County, No. 03-20, 45 (C.C.P. 2011) (Mother's request for a change of venue from Lycoming County to York County was denied, even though mother had resided with the child in York County for three years, since Lycoming County had entered the original custody order, father continued to live there and the child had meaningful contacts within Lycoming County. Even though a child may reside in another county, the county issuing the current custody order maintains jurisdiction and can modify the order if the child and one parent maintain contacts within the county and it is not an inconvenient forum.).

§ 16.1.8. UCCJEA – International Application

Section 5405 provides that the policies of the UCCJEA are extended into the international area, and that custody decrees of the appropriate authorities of other nations will be enforced in the same manner as are decrees from other states.[65]

County), the issuing county loses exclusive continuing venue over the matter).

[65] 23 Pa.C.S. § 5405; *see also* B.A.B. v. J.J.B., 166 A.3d 395 (Pa. Super. 2017); Goodman v. Goodman, 383 Pa. Super. 374, 556 A.2d 1379 (1989) (the provisions of UCCJA relating to the recognition and enforcement of custody decrees apply to custody decrees of foreign countries involving legal institutions similar in nature to our institutions rendered by appropriate authorities of other nations as long as reasonable safeguards of due process are met); Black v. Black, 441 Pa. Super. 358, 657 A.2d 964 (1995) (Canada would have jurisdiction as "home state" of child to modify Arizona custody decree, and thus Pennsylvania court did not have jurisdiction under subdivision of the Uniform Child Custody Jurisdiction Act (UCCJA) applicable when no other state would have jurisdiction or another state has declined to exercise jurisdiction on ground that the Commonwealth is the more appropriate forum, even though Canadian court had previously determined that Arizona was appropriate forum for adjudicating initial custody dispute, where father never contested jurisdiction of

In *Dincer v. Dincer*,[66] the Pennsylvania Supreme Court ruled that Pennsylvania lacked jurisdiction over the parties' custody dispute, where the parties' children were born and raised in Belgium and had lived in Pennsylvania for only two weeks prior to the commencement of proceedings, and where the children's only other contact with Pennsylvania was their yearly visits to their maternal grandparents. Pennsylvania was not the children's home state, given that they were present in the state for only two weeks before mother filed for custody, and that their yearly visits to their grandparents' home were not enough to establish a significant connection between the children and the Commonwealth. The home state is the preferred basis for the jurisdiction pursuant to the then-UCCJA (and now the UCCJEA). UCCJA/UCCJEA defines the "home state" as "the state in which the child immediately preceding the time involved lived with his parents, a parent or a person acting as parent, for at least six consecutive months." In this case, the children were in Montgomery County for only two weeks before Mrs. Dincer filed the custody action and, therefore, had no significant connection to the Commonwealth.

A woman's wrongful removal of her child from his home in the United States to Switzerland defeats her petition for his return after he was "spirited" back to the United States by his father, the district court held in *Von Wussow-Rowan v. Rowan*.[67] The district court noted that while the Hague Convention makes it wrongful to remove a child from his place of habitual residence, "[I]t is by no means clear . . . that it is wrong

---

Arizona court, which awarded mother sole custody and permitted her to return to Canada to permanently reside with the child, and mother could not be accused of abducting child or forum shopping since she complied with Canadian court order and award of custody by Arizona court, and Canada was now child's home state); Hovav v. Hovav, 312 Pa. Super. 305, 458 A.2d 972 (1983) (Pennsylvania court declined jurisdiction where valid Israeli custody order entered after hearing, with notice and opportunity to be heard, conducted under principles substantially similar to those guiding Pennsylvania courts, and no party had significant contacts to Pennsylvania); Hattoum v. Hattoum, 295 Pa. Super. 169, 441 A.2d 403 (1982) (court found that significant contacts with Pennsylvania were established where father lived in state and children visited for four months per year).

[66] Dincer v. Dincer, 549 Pa. 309, 701 A.2d 210 (1997).

[67] Von Wussow-Rowan v. Rowan, No. 98-3641 (E.D. Pa. August 6, 1998).

for a parent to use self-help in returning the child to his place of usual residence."

LOWER COURT CASES
Erie County

Szymczyk v. Wilton, 72 Erie Leg. J. 223 (C.C.P. 1989) (A Canadian custody decree is enforceable and petitioner's custody complaint is dismissed since the child's residence in Canada for virtually all of his life eliminates any significant contacts with Pennsylvania and since the child will not be endangered if returned to Canada. Under the Uniform Child Custody Jurisdiction Act, an Erie County, Pennsylvania, court cannot assume jurisdiction over a custody matter ongoing in a Canadian court where it is not the "home" jurisdiction, there are not significant contacts with this court, and there is no evidence of an emergency whereby the child may suffer physical or emotional harm).

Montgomery County

Dincer v. Dincer, C.P. Montgomery County, No. 94-24367 (C.C.P. 1998) (Held that the trial court did not err when it granted father's petition to enforce a Belgian custody order, because the Pennsylvania Supreme Court had previously ruled that Pennsylvania did not have jurisdiction under the Uniform Child Custody Jurisdiction Act, and the doctrine of *res judicata* and the law of the case barred mother from relitigating the issue of jurisdiction. Because the Supreme Court conclusively determined that the trial court had correctly ruled that Pennsylvania was not the "home state" of the children for UCCJA purposes, the issue of jurisdiction was *res judicata*, the court concluded).

§ 16.2. JURISDICTION – PARENTAL KIDNAPPING PREVENTION ACT (PKPA)

In December of 1980, in response to a growing number of interstate custody disputes and child snatchings, the Parental Kidnapping Prevention Act (PKPA) became law.[68] The PKPA attempts to discourage parental kidnappings with a three-pronged approach centering on the recognition and enforcement of the custody decrees of the several states;

---

[68] Parental Kidnapping Prevention Act, P.L. 96-611, 94 Stat. 3573 (1980); 18 U.S.C. § 1073; 28 U.S.C. § 1738A; 42 U.S.C. § 663.

Federal assistance in locating missing parents; and the application of the Fugitive Felon Act to parental abductions.[69]

Completely reversing prior case law which refused to require that full faith and credit be given to the custody decrees of other states, Title 28, § 1738A, of the United States Code, essentially adopts the jurisdictional criteria of the then-Uniform Child Custody Jurisdiction Act (and now the Uniform Child Custody Jurisdiction and Enforcement Act) and mandates that the courts of each state:

> "shall enforce according to its terms and shall not modify except as provided in . . . this section, any child custody determination made consistently with the provisions of this section by a court of another state."[70]

The section also provides for the continuing jurisdiction of the issuing court as well as notice and opportunity to be heard for contestants, parents, and persons with physical custody of the child.[71]

In *Barndt v. Barndt*,[72] the Superior Court addressed the reach of the UCCJA and the interplay of it and the federal Parental Kidnapping Prevention Act (PKPA), and held that Pennsylvania courts are precluded by the PKPA from modifying a North Dakota custody order where the North Dakota court had jurisdiction to issue the original decree and maintained exclusive continuing jurisdiction over the matter. In *Barndt*, the father petitioned for modification of a North Dakota custody decree, granting primary physical custody to the mother. Following the parties' divorce in 1983, the mother and children continued to reside in North Dakota, the marital domicile. Two years after the parties' divorce, the father moved to his parents' home in Pennsylvania. In June of 1986, the children came to Pennsylvania for an extended visit, which had been arranged and agreed upon by the parties. In March of 1987, the father refused to return the children as agreed, and petitioned for modification

---

[69] *Id.*

[70] Parental Kidnapping Prevention Act of 1980, P.L. No. 96-61 1, § 8, 94 Stat. 3569 (1980); 28 U.S.C. § 1738A.

[71] *Id.*

[72] Barndt v. Barndt, 397 Pa. Super. 321, 580 A.2d 320 (1990). *See also* In Re Adoption of K.S., 399 Pa. Super. 29, 581 A.2d 659 (1990).

of custody in the Pennsylvania courts. The trial court granted custody to the father. Subsequent to the change in custody, mother appealed to the North Dakota courts. North Dakota declined to take action. Judge Kelly concluded that even if Pennsylvania had subject matter jurisdiction, the federal Parental Kidnapping Prevention Act (PKPA) barred jurisdiction under the facts of this case. Consequently, the custody order was vacated and jurisdiction relinquished to the courts of North Dakota. Although "Home State Jurisdiction" was but one of the five (5) bases upon which a Pennsylvania court can find jurisdiction under the then-existing UCCJA, 23 Pa.C.S. § 5344, the PKPA gives priority to home state jurisdiction. If the foreign custody decree satisfies the jurisdictional requirements of both the PKPA and the issuing state's own version of the UCCJA when entered, then the foreign state has exclusive, continuing jurisdiction over any interstate custody dispute. The court also emphasized that in cases of conflict between the UCCJA and the PKPA, federal law controls in proceedings to modify a custody decree from a sister state. Since North Dakota continued to have jurisdiction under its own law and remained the residence of mother, North Dakota had exclusive continuing jurisdiction over all modifications and changes to its order. Any modification sought by father, the court held, must be brought in North Dakota courts. Under the UCCJEA, the problem that occurred in *Barndt* would most likely have not occurred, since under the UCCJEA, the appropriate state to file the modification would have been North Dakota and if Father desired to transfer the action to Pennsylvania, he would have had to make such an attempt in the North Dakota court.

The PKPA also encourages courts to afford priority to custody determinations and to award fees and expenses against parties wrongfully removing a child from the custody of the lawful custodian or retaining the child after a visitation or partial custody period or where appropriate.[73]

The second segment of the PKPA involves the use of the Federal Parent Locator Service, formerly available only in child support cases, to provide information as to the whereabouts of absconded parents.[74] However, before a parent may utilize the service his or her state must have

---

[73] 28 U.S.C. § 1738A.
[74] 42 U.S.C. § 663.

entered into an agreement with the Federal government which provides that upon application of an "authorized person" such as a court, or an attorney having the authority to enforce custody determinations, the service will be available for the purpose of: 1) enforcing any Federal or State law in connection with a parental abduction, or 2) enforcing any child custody determination.[75]

The final provision of the PKPA states that it was the intent of the Congress to make the Fugitive Felon Act[76] applicable to cases involving interstate or international flight to avoid prosecution.[77] As such, the facilities of the Federal Bureau of Investigation and the Justice Department are available to apprehend parental abductors.

LOWER COURT CASES

Allegheny County

Erickson v. Kannenberg, 140 P.L.J. 334 (Allegheny County 1992) (The parties divorced in Minnesota in 1986. Custody of their two minor children was dealt with by a stipulated judgment and decree, giving Mother primary physical custody of the children and Father substantial partial custody. In 1987, Mother wanted to relocate from Minnesota to Ohio and the parties amicably entered into a stipulation to that effect resulting in an Order to Amend Judgment and Decree and, subsequently, an Amended Judgment and Decree in Minnesota. It was the last custody determination entered in the case. In 1989, Mother moved with the children to Pennsylvania and the children continued to spend "substantial periods of time in Minnesota when Father enjoyed partial custody." In April, 1991, Mother presented a Petition for Modification of Custody Order to the Pennsylvania court. Father filed preliminary objections asserting that Pennsylvania lacked jurisdiction or, in the alternative, should decline jurisdiction and that Minnesota was a more convenient forum. The trial court sustained father's preliminary objections and declined to accept jurisdiction over the custody dispute. Mother's appeal asserts that the trial court erred in refusing to exercise jurisdiction contrary to the Uniform Child Custody Jurisdiction Act, (UCCJA), 23 Pa.C.S. § 5341 *et seq.* The trial court, *sua sponte*, felt it was barred from exercising jurisdiction by the Parental Kidnapping Prevention Act, 28 U.S.C. § 1738A, which provides in essence that a court shall not exercise jurisdiction in a custody

---

[75] *Id.*

[76] 18 U.S.C. § 1073.

[77] Parental Kidnapping Prevention Act of 1980, P.L. No. 96-611, § 10 (1980); 18 U.S.C. § 1073.

proceeding where a court of another state: (1) has previously entered a custody order; (2) had jurisdiction consistent with its own law and the PKPA when it entered that order; (3) continues to have jurisdiction under its own law; and (4) is the residence of either the child at issue or any contestant. The court acknowledged that it had jurisdiction under the UCCJA but was prohibited from exercising such jurisdiction owing to the Federal PKPA).

Lee v. Lee, 140 P.L.J. 193 (Allegheny County, 1992) (Held that the Parental Kidnapping Prevention act (P.K.P.A.), 28 U.S.C. § 1738A(b)(a), does not apply in the national arena since it is applicable only to custody determinations made by a "state").

§ 16.3. JURISDICTION – THE HAGUE CONVENTION

§ 16.3.1. Jurisdiction – The Hague Convention – Generally

The Hague Convention on the Civil Aspects of International Child Abduction[78] is a treaty that enables children under the age of 16 to be recovered after the child has been taken or "wrongfully removed or retained" from the country of their "habitual residence."[79]

In the case of *Didon v. Castillo*, the Circuit Court outlined a two-pronged analytical test that courts should use when determining a child's habitual residence country. The first prong is the living test. Under the living test, the court determines whether the child or children have multiple residence countries. If the children are determined to have multiple residence countries, the court then moves to the second test which is the fact-intensive inquiry. Under the fact-intensive inquiry, the court considers the child's contacts with and experience in his/her surroundings and focuses on whether the child developed a certain routine and acquired a sense of environmental normalcy by forming meaningful connections with the people and places the child encountered in a country prior to the removal/retention date. The first test determines whether there is a residence country, and the second, fact-intensive inquiry test determines which residence is the habitual residence.[80]

---

[78] *See* Appendix D of this book for reprint of The Hague Convention.

[79] *See* Article 12. *See also* Didon v. Castillo, 2016 US App. Lexis 17467 (3d. Cir. 2016) (Circuit Court held that the Hague Convention intended only for there to be one habitual residence of a child, and the child cannot have concurrent habitual residence countries).

[80] *See* Didon v. Castillo, 2016 US App. Lexis 17467 (3d. Cir. 2016).

Pursuant to the Hague Convention, if the child has been removed and/ or retained from the country of their habitual residence for less than one year, the child shall be returned.[81] In situations where the child has been retained for over a year, the judicial or administrative authority shall order the return of the child unless it is demonstrated that the child is now settled in his/her new environment.[82]

§ 16.3.2. Jurisdiction – The Hague Convention – Analysis by the State Department

ANALYSIS OF HAGUE CONVENTION

(PREPARED BY STATE DEPARTMENT)

Legal Analysis of the Hague Convention on the Civil Aspects of International Child Abduction[83]

Introduction

The Hague Convention on the Civil Aspects of International Child Abduction consists of six chapters containing forty-five articles. While not formally incorporated into the Convention, a model form was prepared when the Convention was adopted by the Hague Conference on Private International Law and was recommended for use in making application for the return of wrongfully removed or retained children. A copy of that form is annexed to this Legal Analysis. (The form to be used for the return of children from the United States may seek additional information.)

Table of Contents

To facilitate understanding of the convention by the Senate and the use and interpretation of the Convention by parents, judges, lawyers and public and private agency personnel, the articles are analyzed and discussed in the following categories:

I. Children Protected by the Convention (Preamble, Article 1)
  A. Age (Articles 4, 36, 18, 29, 34, 13)
  B. Residence (Article 4)
  C. Timing/cases covered (Article 35)

---

[81] *Id.*

[82] *Id.*; *see also* Lozano v. Montoya Alvarez, 134 S. Ct. 1224, 188 L. Ed. 2d 200 (2014) (1-year period cannot be extended by equitable tolling when child was concealed and parent did not locate child until after the 1-year period).

[83] *See* Federal Register Document 86-6495, March 25, 1986.

D. Effect of custody order concerning the child
   1. Existing custody orders (Articles 17, 3)
   2. Pre-decree removals or retentions (Article 3)

II. Conduct Actionable Under the Convention
A. International "child abduction" not criminal: Hague Convention distinguished from extradition treaties (Article 12)
   B. "Wrongful removal or retention" (Articles 1, 3, 5(a))
      1. Holders of rights protected by the Convention (*i.e.*, with respect to whom the removal or retention is wrongful)
         (a) "Person, institution or other body" (Article 3(a), (b))
         (b) "Jointly or alone" (Article 3(a), (b))
      2. Defined
         (a) Breach of "custody rights" (Articles 3(a), 5(a))
         (b) "Custody rights" determined by law of child's habitual residence (Articles 3(a), 31, 32, 33)
         (c) Sources of "Custody rights" (Article 3, last paragraph)
            i. Operation of law (Articles 3, 15)
            ii. Judicial or administrative decision (Article 3)
            iii. Agreement having legal effect (Article 3)
         (d) "Actually exercised" (Articles 3(b), 5, 8(c), 13)

III. Judicial Proceedings for Return of the Child
   A. Right to seek return (Articles 29, 12, 34, 8)
   B. Legal advice and costs (Articles 25, 26, 42)
   C. Pleading requirements (Articles 8, 24)
   D. Admissibility of evidence (Articles 30, 23)
   E. Judicial promptitude/status report (Article 11)
   F. Judicial notice (Article 14)
   G. Court determination of "wrongfulness" (Articles 15.3, 11, 12, 14)
   H. Constraints upon courts in requested states in making substantive custody decisions (Article 16)
   I. Duty to return not absolute
      1. Temporal qualifications
         (a) Article 4
         (b) Article 35
         (c) Article 12
      2. Article 13 limitations on return obligation
         (a) Legislative history (Articles 13, 20)
         (b) Non-exercise of custody rights (Articles 13(a), 3(b))
         (c) Grave risk of harm/intolerable situation (Article 13(b))
         (d) Child's preference (Article 13)
         (e) Role of social studies
      3. Article 20
      4. Custody order no defense to return (Article 17)

   J. Return of the child (Article 12)
      1. Return order not on custody merits (Article 19)
      2. Costs, fees and expenses shifted to abductor (Article 26)

IV. Central Authority (Articles 1, 10, 21)
  A. Establishment of Central Authority (Article 6)
  B. Duties (Article 7)
  C. Other Tasks (Articles 8, 9, 10, 11, 15, 21, 26, 27, 28)
    1. Processing applications (Articles 8, 9, 27, 28)
    2. Assistance in connection with judicial proceedings
      (a) Request for status report (Article 11)
      (b) Social studies/background reports (Article 13)
      (c) Determination of "wrongfulness" (Article 15)
      (d) Costs (Article 26), reservation (Articles 42, 22)

V. Access Rights—Article 21
  A. Remedies for breach (Articles 21, 12)
  B. Defined (Article 5(b))
  C. Procedure for obtaining relief (Articles 21, 8, 7)
  D. Alternative remedies (Articles 18, 29, 34)

VI. Miscellaneous and Final Clauses
  A. Article 36
  B. Articles 37 and 38
  C. Articles 42, 43 and 44
  D. Articles 39 and 40
  E. Article 41
  F. Article 45

Annexes

Recommended Return Application Form

Bibliography

Guide to Terminology Used in the Legal Analysis

"Abduction" as used in the Convention title is not intended in a criminal sense. That term is shorthand for the phrase "wrongful removal or retention" which appears throughout the text, beginning with the preambular language and Article 1. Generally speaking, "wrongful removal" refers to the taking of a child from the person who was actually exercising custody of the child. "Wrongful retention" refers to the act of keeping the child without the consent of the person who was actually exercising custody. The archetype of this conduct is the refusal by the noncustodial parent to return a child at the end of an authorized visitation period. "Wrongful retention" is not intended by this Convention to cover refusal by the custodial parent to permit visitation by the other parent. Such obstruction of visitation may be redressed in accordance with Article 21.

The term "abductor" as used in this analysis refers to the person alleged to have wrongfully removed or retained a child. This person is also referred to as the "alleged wrongdoer" or the "respondent."

The term "person" as used in this analysis includes the person, institution or other body who (or which) actually exercised custody prior to the abduction and is seeking the child's return. The "person" seeking the child's return is also referred to as "applicant" and "petitioner."

The terms "court" and "judicial authority" are used throughout the analysis to mean both judicial and administrative bodies empowered to make decisions on petitions made pursuant to this Convention. "Judicial decree" and "court order" likewise includes decisions made by courts or administrative bodies.

"Country of origin" and "requesting country" refer to the child's country ("State") of habitual residence prior to the wrongful removal or retention. "Country addressed" refers to the country ("State") where the child is located or the country to which the child is believed to have been taken. It is in that country that a judicial or administrative proceeding for return would be brought.

"Access rights" correspond to "visitation rights."

References to the "reporter" are to Elisa Perez-Vera, the official Hague Conference reporter for the Convention. Her explanatory report is recognized by the Conference as the official history and commentary on the Convention and is a source of background on the meaning of the provisions of the Convention available to all States becoming parties to it. It is referred to herein as the "Perez-Vera Report." The Perez-Vera Report appears in *Actes et documents de la Quatorzieme Session (1980), Volume III, Child Abduction*, edited by the Permanent Bureau of the Hague Conference on Private International Law, The Hague, Netherlands. (The volume may be ordered from the Netherlands Government Printing and Publishing Office, 1 Christoffel Plantijnstraat, Postbox 20014, 2500 EA The Hague, Netherlands.)

I. Children Protected by the Convention

A fundamental purpose of the Hague Convention is to protect children from wrongful international removals or retentions by persons bent on obtaining their physical and/or legal custody. Children who are wrongfully moved from country to country are deprived of the stable relationships which the Convention is designed promptly to restore. Contracting States are obliged by Article 2 to take all appropriate measures to implement the objectives of the Convention as set forth in Article 1: (1) To secure the prompt return of children wrongfully removed to or retained in any Contracting State; and (2) to ensure that rights of custody and of access under the law of one Contracting State are effectively respected in other Contracting States. While these objectives are universal in their appeal, the Convention does not cover all children who might be victims of wrongful takings or retentions. A threshold inquiry, therefore, is whether the child who has been abducted or retained is subject to the Convention's provisions. Only if the child falls within the scope of the Convention will the administrative and judicial mechanisms of the Convention apply.

A. Age

The Convention applies only to children under the age of sixteen (16). Even if a child is under sixteen at the time of the wrongful removal or retention as well as when the Convention is invoked, the Convention ceases to apply when the child reaches sixteen. Article 4.

Absent action by governments to expand coverage of the Convention to children aged sixteen and above pursuant to Article 36, the Convention itself is unavailable as the legal vehicle for securing return of a child sixteen or older. However, it does not bar return of such child by other means.

Articles 18, 29 and 34 make clear that the Convention is a nonexclusive remedy in cases of international child abduction. Article 18 provides that the Convention does not limit the power of a judicial authority to order return of a child at any time, presumably under other laws, procedures or comity, irrespective of the child's age. Article 29 permits the person who claims a breach of custody or access rights as defined by Articles 3 and 21, to bypass the Convention completely by invoking any applicable laws or procedures to secure the child's return. Likewise, Article 34 provides that the Convention shall not restrict the application of any law in the State addressed for purposes of obtaining the child's return or for organizing visitation rights. Assuming such laws are not restricted to children under sixteen, a child sixteen or over may be returned pursuant to their provisions.

B. Residence

In order for the Convention to apply the child must have been "habitually resident in a Contracting State immediately before any breach of custody or access rights." Article 4. In practical terms, the Convention may be invoked only where the child was habitually resident in a Contracting State and taken to or retained in another Contracting State. Accordingly, child abduction and retention cases are actionable under the Convention if they are international in nature (as opposed to interstate), and provided the Convention has entered into force for both countries involved. *See* discussion of Article 38, VI.B, infra.

To illustrate, take the case of a child abducted to California from his home in New York. The Convention could not be invoked to secure the return of such child. This is true even if one of the child's parents is an American citizen and the other a foreign national. The Uniform Child Custody Jurisdiction Act (UCCJA) and/or the Parental Kidnapping Prevention Act (PKPA), domestic state and federal law, respectively, would govern the return of the child in question. If the same child were removed from New York to Canada, application under the Convention could be made to secure the child's return provided the Convention had entered into force both for the United States and the Canadian province to which the child was taken. An alternative remedy might also lie under other Canadian law. If the child had been removed from Canada and taken to the United States, the aggrieved custodial parent in Canada could seek to secure the child's return by petitioning for enforcement of a Canadian custody order pursuant to the UCCJA, or by invoking the Convention, or both.

C. Timing/Cases Covered

Article 35 states that the Convention shall apply as between Contracting States only to wrongful removals or retentions occurring after its entry into force in those States. Following a strict interpretation of that Article, the Convention will not apply to a child who is wrongfully shifted from one Contracting State to another if the wrongful removal or retention occurred before the Convention's entry into force in those States. However, under a liberal interpretation Article 35 could be construed to cover wrongful removal or retention cases which began before the Convention took effect but which continued and were ongoing after its entry into force.

D. Effect of Custody Order Concerning the Child
1. Existing Custody Orders

Children who otherwise fall within the scope of the Convention are not automatically removed from its protections by virtue of a judicial decision awarding custody to the alleged wrongdoer. This is true whether the decision as to custody was made, or is entitled to recognition, in the State to which the child has been taken. Under Article 17 that State cannot refuse to return a child solely on the basis of a court order awarding custody to the alleged wrongdoer made by one of its own courts or by the courts of another country. This provision is intended to ensure, *inter alia,* that the Convention takes precedence over decrees made in favor of abductors before the court had notice of the wrongful removal or retention.

Thus, under Article 17 the person who wrongfully removes or retains the child in a Contracting State cannot insulate the child from the Convention's return provisions merely by obtaining a custody order in the country of new residence, or by seeking there to enforce another country's order. Nor may the alleged wrongdoer rely upon a stale decree awarding him or her custody, the provisions of which have been derogated from subsequently by agreement or acquiescence of the parties, to prevent child's return under the Convention. Article 3.

It should be noted that Article 17 does permit a court to take into account the reasons underlying an existing custody decree where it applies the Convention.

2. Pre-Decree Removals *or Retentions*

Children who are wrongfully removed or retained prior to the entry of a custody order are protected by the Convention. There need not be a custody order in effect in order to invoke the Convention's return provisions. Accordingly, under the Convention a child will be ordered returned to the person with whom he or she was habitually resident in pre-decree abduction cases as well as in cases involving violations of existing custody orders.

Application of the Convention to pre-decree cases comes to grips with the reality that many children are abducted or retained long before custody actions have been initiated. In this manner a child is not prejudiced by the legal inaction of his or her physical custodian, who may not have anticipated the abduction, and the abductor is denied any legal advantage since the child is subject to the return provisions of the Convention.

The Convention's treatment of pre-decree abduction cases is distinguishable from the Council of Europe's Convention on Recognition and Enforcement of Decisions Relating to the Custody of Children, adopted in Strasbourg, France in November 1979 ("Strasbourg Convention"), and from domestic law in the United States, specifically the UCCJA and the PKPA, all of which provide for enforcement of custody decrees. Although the UCCJA and PKPA permit enforcement of a decree obtained by a parent in the home state after the child has been removed from that state, in the absence of such decree the enforcement provisions of those laws are inoperative. In contrast to the restoration of the *legal* status quo ante brought about by application of the UCCJA, the PKPA, and the Strasbourg Convention, the Hague Convention seeks restoration of the *factual* status quo ante and is not contingent on the existence of a custody decree. The Convention is premised upon the notion that the child should be promptly restored to his or her country of habitual residence so that a court there can examine the merits of the custody dispute and award custody in the child's best interest.

Pre-decree abductions are discussed in greater detail in the section dealing with actionable conduct. *See* II.B(2)(c)(i).

II. Conduct Actionable Under the Convention
A. "International Child Abduction" Not Criminal: Hague Convention Distinguished *From Extradition Treaties*

Despite the use of the term "abduction" in its title, the Hague Convention is not an extradition treaty. The conduct made actionable by the Convention—the wrongful removal or retention of children—is wrongful not in a criminal sense but in a civil sense.

The Hague Convention establishes civil procedures to secure the return of so-called "abducted" children. Article 12. In this manner the Hague Convention seeks to satisfy the overriding concern of the aggrieved parent. The Convention is not concerned with the question of whether the person found to have wrongfully removed or retained the child returns to the child's country of habitual residence once the child has been returned pursuant to the Convention. This is in contrast to the criminal extradition process which is designed to secure the return of the fugitive wrong-doer. Indeed, when the fugitive-parent is extradited for trial or to observe a criminal sentence, there is no guarantee that the abducted child will also be returned.

While it is uncertain whether criminal extradition treaties will be routinely invoked in international custody cases between countries for which the Hague Convention is in force, nothing in the Convention bars their application or use.

B. Wrongful Removal *or Retention*

The Convention's first stated objective is to secure the prompt return of children who are wrongfully removed from or retained in any Contracting State. Article 1(a). (The second stated objective, i.e., to ensure that rights of custody and of access under the law of one Contracting State are effectively exercised in other Contracting States (Article 1(B)), is discussed under the head "Access Rights," V., infra.) The removal or retention must be wrongful within the meaning of Article 3, as further clarified by Article 5(a), in order to trigger the return procedures established by the Convention. Article 3 provides that the removal or retention of a child is to be considered wrongful where:

(a) it is in breach of custody rights attributed to a person, an institution or another body, either jointly or alone, under the law of the State in which the child was habitually resident immediately before the removal or retention; and (b) at the time of the removal or retention those rights were actually exercised, either jointly or alone, or would have been so exercised but for the removal or retention.

This Article is a cornerstone of the Convention. It is analyzed by examining two questions:

1. Who holds rights protected by the Convention (or, with respect to whom is the removal or retention deemed to be wrongful?); and

2. What are the factual and legal elements of a wrongful removal or retention?

1. Holders of Rights Protected by the Convention

(a) "Person, institution or other body." While the child is the ultimate beneficiary of the Convention's judicial and administrative machinery, the child's role under the convention is passive. In contrast, it is up to the "person, institution or other body" (hereinafter referred to simply as "the person") who "actually exercised" custody of the child prior to the abduction, or who would have exercised custody but for the abduction, to invoke the Convention to secure the child's return. Article 3(a), (b). It is this person who holds the rights protected by the Convention and who has the right to seek relief pursuant to its terms.

Since the vast majority of abduction cases arises in the context of divorce or separation, the person envisioned by Article 3(a) most often will be the child's parent. The typical scenario would involve one parent taking a child from one Contracting State to another Contracting State over objections of the parent with whom the child had been living.

However, there may be situations in which a person other than a biological parent has actually been exercising custody of the child and is therefore eligible to seek the child's return pursuant to the Convention. An example would be a grandparent who has had physical custody of a child following the death of the parent with whom the child had been residing. If the child is subsequently removed from the custody of the grandparent by the surviving parent, the aggrieved grandparent could invoke the Convention to secure the child's return. In another situation, the child may be in the care of foster parents. If custody rights exercised by the foster parents are breached, for instance, by abduction of the child by its biological parent, the foster parents could invoke the Convention to secure the child's return.

In the two foregoing examples (not intended to be exhaustive) a family relationship existed between the victim-child and the person who had the right to seek the child's return. However, institutions such as public or private child care agencies also may have custody rights the breach of which would be remediable under the Convention. If a natural parent relinquishes parental rights to a child and the child is subsequently placed in the care of an adoption agency, that agency may invoke the Convention to recover the child if the child is abducted by its parent(s).

(b) *"Jointly or alone."* Article 3(a) and (b) recognize that custody rights may be held either jointly or alone. Two persons, typically mother and father, can exercise joint custody, either by court order following a custody adjudication, or by operation of law prior to the entry of a decree. The Convention does not distinguish between these two situations, as the commentary of the Convention reporter indicates:

Now, from the Convention's standpoint, the removal of a child by one of the joint holders without the consent of the other, is wrongful, and this wrongfulness derives in this particular case, not from some action in breach of a particular law, but from the fact that such action has disregarded the rights of the other parent which are also protected by law, and has interfered with their normal exercise. The convention's true nature is revealed most clearly in these situations: it is not concerned with establishing the person to whom custody of the child will belong at some point in the future, nor with the situations in which it may prove necessary to modify a decision awarding joint custody on the basis of facts which have subsequently changed. It seeks, more simply, to prevent a later decision on the matter being influenced by a change of circumstances brought about through unilateral action by one of the parties. Perez-Vera Report, paragraph 71 at 447–448.

Article 3(a) ensures the application of the convention to pre-decree abductions, since it protects the rights of a parent who was exercising custody of the child jointly with the abductor at the time of the abduction, before the issuance of a custody decree.

2. "Wrongful Removal or Retention" Defined

The obligation to return an abducted child to the person entitled to custody arises only if the removal or the retention is wrongful within the meaning of the Convention. To be considered wrongful, certain factual and legal elements must be present.

(a) *Breach of "custody rights."* The removal or retention must be in breach of "custody rights," defined in Article 5(a) as "rights relating to the care of the person of the child, and, in particular, the right to determine the the child's place of residence."

Accordingly, a parent who sends his or her child to live with a caretaker has not relinquished custody rights but rather has exercised them within the meaning of the Convention. Likewise, a parent hospitalized for a protracted period who places the child with grandparents or other relatives for the duration of the illness has effectively exercised custody.

(b) *"Custody rights" determined by law of child's habitual residence.* In addition to including the right to determine the child's residence (Article 5(a)), the term "custody rights" covers a collection of rights which take on more specific meaning by reference to the law of the country in which the child was habitually resident immediately before the removal or retention. Article 3(a). Nothing in the Convention limits this "law" to the internal law of the State of the child's habitual residence. Consequently, it could include the laws of another State if the choice of law rules in the State of habitual residence so indicate.

If a country has more than one territorial unit, the habitual residence refers to the particular territorial unit in which the child was resident, and the applicable laws are those in effect in that territorial unit. Article 31. In the United States, the law in force in the state in which a child was habitually resident (as possibly preempted by federal legislation enacted in connection with U.S. ratification of the Convention) would be applicable for the determination as to whether a removal or retention is wrongful.

Articles 32 and 33 also control, respectively, how and whether the Convention applies in States with more than one legal system. Perez-Vera Report, paragraphs 141 and 142 at 470.

(c) *Sources of "custody rights."* Although the Convention does not exhaustively list all possible sources from which custody rights may derive, it does identify three sources. According to the final paragraph of Article 3, custody rights may arise: (1) by operation of law; (2) by reason of a judicial or administrative decision; or (3) by reason of an agreement having legal effect under the law of that State.

i. *Custody rights arising by operation of law.* Custody rights which arise by operation of law in the State of habitual residence are protected; they need not be conferred by court order to fall within the scope of the Convention. Article 3. Thus, a person whose child is abducted prior to the entry of a custody order is not required to obtain a custody order in the State of the child's habitual residence as a prerequisite to invoking the Convention's return provisions.

In the United States, as a general proposition both parents have equal rights of custody of their children prior to the issuance of a court order allocating rights between them. If one parent interferes with the other's equal rights by unilaterally removing or retaining the child abroad without consent of the other parent, such interference could constitute wrongful conduct within the meaning of the Convention. (See excerpts from Perez-Vera Report quoted at II.B.1(b), *supra*.) Thus, a parent left in the United States after a pre-decree abduction could seek return of a child from a Contracting State abroad pursuant to the Convention. In cases involving children wrongfully brought to or retained in the United States from a Contracting State abroad prior to the entry of a decree, in the absence of an agreement between the parties the question of wrongfulness would be resolved by looking to the law of the child's country of habitual residence.

Although a custody decree is not needed to invoke the Convention, there are two situations in which the aggrieved parent may nevertheless benefit by securing a custody order, assuming the courts can hear swiftly a petition for custody. First, to the extent that an award of custody to the left-behind parent (or other person) is based in part upon an express finding by the court that the child's removal or retention was wrongful within the meaning of Article 3, the applicant anticipates a possible request by the judicial authority applying the Convention, pursuant to Article 15, for a court determination of wrongfulness. This may accelerate disposition of a return petition under the Convention. Second, a person outside the United States who obtains a custody decree from a foreign court subsequent to the child's abduction, after notice and opportunity to be heard have been accorded to the absconding parent, may be able to invoke either the Convention or the UCCJA, or both, to secure the child's return from the United States. The UCCJA may be preferable inasmuch as its enforcement provisions are not subject to the exceptions contained in the Convention.

ii. *Custody rights arising by reason of judicial or administrative decision.* Custody rights embodied in judicial or administrative decisions fall within the Convention's scope. While custody determinations in the United States are made by State courts, in some Contracting States, notably the Scandinavian countries, administrative bodies are empowered to decide matters relating to child custody including the allocation of custody and visitation rights. Hence the reference to "administrative decisions" in Article 3.

The language used in this part of the Convention can be misleading. Even when custody rights are conferred by court decree, technically speaking the Convention does not mandate recognition and enforcement of that decree. Instead, it seeks only to restore the factual custody arrangements that existed prior to the wrongful removal or retention (which incidentally in many cases will be the same as those specified by court order).

Finally, the court order need not have been made by a court in the State of the child's habitual residence. It could be on originating from a third country. As the reporter points out, when custody rights were exercised in the State of the child's habitual residence on the basis of a foreign decree, the Convention does not require that the decree have been formally recognized. Perez-Vera Report, paragraph 69 at 447.

iii. *Custody rights arising by reason of agreement having legal effect.* Parties who enter into a private agreement concerning a child's custody have recourse under the Convention if those custody rights are breached. Article 3. The only limitation is that the agreement have legal effect under the law of the child's habitual residence.

Comments of the United States with respect to language contained in an earlier draft of the Convention (*i.e.*, that the agreement "have the force of law") shed some light on the meaning of the expression "an agreement having legal effect." In the U.S. view, the provision should be interpreted expansively to cover more than only those agreements that have been incorporated in or referred to in a custody judgment. *Actes et documents de la Quatorzieme Session, (1980) Volume III. Child Abduction,* Comments of Governments at 240. The reporter's observations affirm a broad interpretation of this provision:

As regards the definition of an agreement which has "legal effect" in terms of a particular law, it seems that there must be included within it any sort of agreement which is not prohibited by such a law and which may provide a basis for presenting a legal claim to the competent authorities. Perez-Vera Report, paragraph 70 at 447.

(d) *"Actually exercised."* The most predictable fact pattern under the Convention will involve the abduction of a child directly from the parent who was actually exercising physical custody at the time of the abduction.

To invoke the Convention, the holder of custody rights must allege that he or she actually exercised those rights at the time of the breach or would have exercised them but for the breach.

Article 3(b). Under Article 5, custody rights are defined to include the right to determine the child's place of residence. Thus, if a child is abducted from the physical custody of the person in whose care the child has been entrusted by the custodial parent who was "actually exercising" custody, it is the parent who placed the child who may make application under the Convention for the child's return.

Very little is required of the applicant in support of the allegation that custody rights have actually been or would have been exercised. The applicant need only provide some preliminary evidence that he or she actually exercised custody of the child, for instance, took physical care of the child. Perez-Vera Report, paragraph 73 at 448. The Report points out the informal nature of the pleading and proof requirements; Article 8(c) merely requires a statement in the application to the Central Authority as to "the grounds on which the applicant's claim for return of the child is based." *Id.*

In the scheme of the Convention it is presumed that the person who has custody actually exercised it. Article 13 places on the alleged abductor the burden of proving the nonexercise of custody rights by the applicant as an exception to the return obligation. Here, again, the reporter's comments are insightful:

Thus, we may conclude that the Convention, taken as a whole, is built upon the tacit presumption that the person who has care of the child actually exercises custody over it. This idea has to be overcome by discharging the burden of proof which has shifted, as is normal with any presumption (*i.e.* discharged by the "abductor" if he wishes to prevent the return of the child.) Perez-Vera Report paragraph 73 at 449.

III. Judicial Proceedings for Return of the Child

A. Right to Seek Return

When a person's custody rights have been breached by the wrongful removal or retention of the child by another, he or she can seek return of the child pursuant to the Convention. This right of return is the core of the Convention. The Convention establishes two means by which the child may be returned. One is through direct application by the aggrieved person to a court in the Contracting State to which the child has been taken or in which the child is being kept. Articles 12, 29. The other is through application to the Central Authority to be established by every Contracting State. Article 8. These remedies are not mutually exclusive; the aggrieved person may invoke either or both of them. Moreover, the aggrieved person may also pursue remedies outside the Convention. Articles 18, 29 and 34. This part of the report describes the Convention's judicial remedy in detail. The administrative remedy is discussed in IV, infra.

Articles 12 and 29 authorize any person who claims a breach of custody rights within the meaning of Article 3 to apply for the child's return directly to the judicial authorities of the Contracting State where the child is located.

A petition for return pursuant to the Convention may be filed any time after the child has been removed or retained up until the child reaches sixteen. While the window of time for filing may be wide in a particular case without threat of technically losing rights under the Convention, there are numerous reasons to commence a return proceeding promptly if the likelihood of a voluntary return is remote. The two most crucial reasons are to preclude adjudication of custody on the merits in a country other than the child's habitual residence (see discussion of Article 16, *infra*) and to maximize the chances for the child's return by reducing the alleged abductor's opportunity to establish the child is settled in a new environment (see discussion of Article 12, *infra*).

478

A petition for return would be made directly to the appropriate court in the Contracting State where the child is located. If the return proceedings are commenced less than one year from the date of the wrongful removal or retention, Article 12 requires the court to order the return of the child forthwith. If the return proceedings are commenced a year or more after the alleged wrongful removal or retention, the court remains obligated by Article 12 to order the child returned unless it is demonstrated that the child is settled in its new environment.

Under Article 29 a person is not precluded from seeking judicially-ordered return of a child pursuant to laws and procedures other than the Convention. Indeed, Articles 18 and 34 make clear that nothing in the Convention limits the power of a court to return a child at any time by applying other laws and procedures conducive to that end.

Accordingly, a parent seeking return of a child from the United States could petition for return pursuant to the Convention, or in the alternative or additionally, for enforcement of a foreign court order pursuant to the UCCJA. For instance, an English father could petition courts in New York either for return of his child under the Convention and/or for recognition and enforcement of his British custody decree pursuant to the UCCJA. If he prevailed in either situations, the respective court could order the child returned to him in England. The father in this illustration may find the UCCJA remedy swifter than invoking the Convention for the child's return because it is not subject to the exceptions set forth in the Convention, discussed at III.I., *infra*.

B. Legal Advice and Costs

Article 25 provides for the extension of legal aid and advice to foreign applicants on the same basis and subject only to the same eligibility requirements as for nationals of the country in which that aid is sought.

Article 26 prohibits Central Authorities from charging applicants for the cost and expenses of the proceedings or, where applicable, those arising from the participation of legal counsel or advisers. This provision will be of no help to an applicant, however, if the Contracting State in question has made a reservation in accordance with Articles 26 and 42 declaring that it shall not be bound to assume any costs resulting from the participation of legal counsel or advisers or from court proceedings, except insofar as those costs may be covered by its system of legal aid and advice.

It is expected that the United States will enter a reservation in accordance with Articles 26 and 42. This will place at least the initial burden of paying for counsel and legal proceedings on the applicant rather than on the federal government. Because the reservation is nonreciprocal, use of it will not automatically operate to deny applicants from the United States free legal services and judicial proceedings in other Contracting States. However, if the Contracting State in which the child is located has itself made use of the reservation in question, the U.S. applicant will not be eligible for cost-free legal representation and court proceedings. For more information on costs, including the possibility that the petitioner's costs may be levied on the abductor if the child is ordered returned, see II.J 2 and IV.C(d) of this analysis.

C. Pleading Requirements

The Convention does not expressly set forth pleading requirements that must be satisfied by an applicant who commences a judicial return proceeding. In contrast, Article 8 sets forth the basis requirements for an application placed before a Central Authority (discussed IV.C(1), infra) for the return of the child. Since the objective is identical—the child's return—whether relief is sought through the courts or through intercession of the Central Authority, it follows that a court should be provided with at least as much information as a Central Authority is to be provided in a return application filed in compliance with Article 8. To ensure that all necessary information is provided, the applicant may wish to append to the petition to the court a completed copy of the recommended model form for return of a child (see annex A to this analysis).

In addition to providing the information set forth in Article 8, the petition for return should allege that the child was wrongfully removed or retained by the defendant in violation of custody rights that were actually being exercised by the petitioner. The petition should state the source of the custody rights, the date of the wrongful conduct, and the child's age at that time. In the prayer for relief, the petitioner should request the child's return and an order for payment by the abducting or retaining parent of all fees and expenses incurred to secure the child's return.

Any return petition filed in a court in the United States pursuant to the Convention must be in English. Any person in the United States who seeks return of a child from a foreign court must likewise follow the requirements of the foreign state regarding translation of legal documents. See Perez-Vera Report, paragraph 132 at page 467.

D. Admissibility of Evidence

Under Article 30, any application submitted to the Central Authority or petition submitted to the judicial authorities of a Contracting State, and any documents or information appended thereto, are admissible in the courts of the State. Moreover, under Article 23, no legalization or similar formalities may be required. However, authentication of private documents may be required. According to the official report, "any requirement of the internal law of the authorities in question that copies or private documents be authenticated remains outside the scope of this provision." Perez-Vera Report, paragraph 131 at page 467.

E. Judicial Promptitude/Status Report

Once an application for return has been filed, the court is required by Article 11 "to act expeditiously in proceedings for the return of children." To keep matters on the fast track, Article 11 gives the applicant or the Central Authority of the requested State the right to request a statement from the court of the reasons for delay if a decision on the application has not been made within six weeks from the commencement of the proceedings.

F. Judicial Notice

In ascertaining whether there has been a wrongful removal or retention of a child within the meaning of Article 3, Article 14 empowers the court of the requested State to take notice directly of the law and decisions in the State of the child's habitual residence. Standard procedures for the proof of foreign law and for recognition of foreign decisions would not need to be followed and compliance with such procedures is not to be required.

G. Court Determination of "Wrongfulness"

Prior to ordering a child returned pursuant to Article 12, Article 15 permits the court to request the applicant to obtain from the authorities of the child's State of habitual residence a decision or other determination that the alleged removal of retention was wrongful within the meaning of

Article 3. Article 15 does not specify which "authorities" may render such a determination. It therefore could include agencies of government (e.g., state attorneys general) and courts. Central Authorities shall assist applicants to obtain such a decision or determination. This request may only be made where such a decision or determination is obtainable in that State.

This latter point is particularly important because in some countries the absence of the defendant-abductor and child from the forum makes it legally impossible to proceed with an action for custody brought by the left-behind parent. If an adjudication in such an action were a prerequisite to obtaining a determination of wrongfulness, it would be impossible for the petitioner to comply with an Article 15 request. For this reason a request for a decision or determination on wrongfulness can not be made in such circumstances consistent with the limitation in Article 15. Even if local law permits an adjudication of custody in the absence of the child and defendant (*i.e.,* postabduction) or would otherwise allow a petitioner to obtain a determination of wrongfulness, the provisions of Article 15 will probably not be resorted to routinely. That is so because doing so would convert the purpose of the Convention from seeking to restore the *factual* status quo prior to an abduction to emphasizing substantive legal relationships.

A further consideration in deciding whether to request an applicant to comply with Article 15 is the length of time it will take to obtain the required determination. In countries where such a determination can be made only by a court, if judicial dockets are seriously backlogged, compliance with an Article 15 order could significantly prolong disposition of the return petition, which in turn would extend the time that the child is kept in a state of legal and emotional limbo. If "wrongfulness" can be established some other way, for instance by taking judicial notice of the law of the child's habitual residence as permitted by Article 14, the objective of Article 15 can be satisfied without further prejudice to the child's welfare or undue delay of the return proceeding. This would also be consistent with the Convention's desire for expeditious judicial proceedings as evidenced by Article 11.

In the United States, a left-behind parent or other claimant can petition for custody after the child has been removed from the forum. The right of action is conferred by the UCCJA, which in many states also directs courts to hear such petitions expeditiously. The result of such proceeding is a temporary or permanent custody determination allocating custody and visitation rights, or joint custody rights, between the parties. However, a custody determination on the merits that makes no reference to the Convention may not by itself satisfy an Article 15 request by a foreign court for a determination as the wrongfulness of the conduct within the meaning of Article 3. Therefore, to ensure compliance with a possible Article 15 request the parent in the United States would be well-advised to request an explicit finding as to the wrongfulness of the alleged removal or retention within the meaning of Article 3 in addition in seeking custody.

H. Constraints Upon Courts in Requested States in Making Substantive Custody Decisions.

Article 16 bars a court in the country to which the child has been taken or in which the child has been retained from considering the merits of custody claims once it has received notice of the removal or retention of the child. The constraints continue either until it is determined that the child is not to be returned under the Convention, or it becomes evident that an application under the Convention will not be forthcoming within a reasonable time following receipt of the notice.

A court may get notice of a wrongful removal or retention in some manner other than the filing of a petition for return, for instance by communication from a Central Authority, from the aggrieved party (either directly or through counsel), or from a court in a Contracting State which has stayed or dismissed return proceedings upon removal of the child from that State.

No matter how notice may be given, once the tribunal has received notice, a formal application for the child's return pursuant to the Convention will normally be filed promptly to avoid a decision on the merits from being made. If circumstances warrant a delay in filing a return petition, for instance pending the outcome of private negotiations for the child's return or interventions toward that end by the Central Authority, or pending determination of the location of the child and alleged abductor, the aggrieved party may nevertheless wish to notify the court as to the reason(s) for the delay so that inaction is not viewed as a failure to proceed under the Convention.

I. Duty to Return Not Absolute

The judicial duty to order return of a wrongfully removed or retained child is not absolute. Temporal qualifications on this duty are set forth in Articles 12, 4 and 35. Additionally, Articles 13 and 20 set forth grounds upon which return may be denied.

1. Temporal Qualifications

Articles 4, 35 and 12 place time limitations on the return obligation.

(a) *Article 4.* Pursuant to Article 4, the Convention ceases to apply once the child reaches age sixteen. This is true regardless of when return proceedings were commenced and irrespective of their status at the time of the child's sixteenth birthday. *See* I.A., *supra.*

(b) *Article 35.* Article 35 limits application of the Convention to wrongful removals or retentions occurring after its entry into force between the two relevant Contracting States. But *see* I.C., *supra.*

(c) *Article 12.* Under Article 12, the court is not obligated to return a child when return proceedings pursuant to the Convention are commenced a year or more after the alleged removal or retention *and* it is demonstrated that the child is settled in its new environment. The reporter indicates that "(T)he provision does not state how this fact is to be proved, but it would seem logical to regard such a task as falling upon the abductor or upon the person who opposes the return of the child . . ." Perez-Vera Report, paragraph 109 at page 459.

If the Convention is to succeed in deterring abductions, the alleged abductor must not be accorded preferential treatment by courts in his or her country of origin, which, in the absence of the Convention, might be prone to favor "home forum" litigants. To this end, nothing less than substantial evidence of the child's significant connections to the new country is intended to suffice to meet the respondent's burden of proof. Moreover, any claims made by the person resisting the child's return will be considered in light of evidence presented by the applicant concerning the child's contacts with and ties to his or her State of habitual residence. The reason for the passage of time, which may have made it possible for the child to form ties to the new country, is also relevant to the ultimate disposition of the return petition. If the alleged wrongdoer concealed the child's whereabouts from the custodian necessitating a long search for the child and thereby delayed the commencement of a return proceeding by the applicant, it is highly questionable whether the respondent should be permitted to benefit from such conduct absent strong countervailing considerations.

2. Article 13 Limitations on the Return Obligation

(a) Legislative history. In drafting Articles 13 and 20, the representatives of countries participating in negotiations on the Convention were aware that any exceptions had to be drawn very narrowly lest their application undermine the express purposes of the Convention—to effect the prompt return of abducted children. Further, it was generally believed that courts would understand and fulfill the objectives of the Convention by narrowly interpreting the exceptions and allowing their use only in clearly meritorious cases, and only when the person opposing return had met the burden of proof. Importantly, a finding that one or more of the exceptions provided by Articles 13 and 20 are applicable does not make refusal of a return order mandatory. The courts retain the discretion to order the child returned even if they consider that one or more of the exceptions applies. Finally, the wording of each exception represents a compromise to accommodate the different legal systems and tenets of family law in effect in the countries negotiating the Convention, the basic purpose in each case being to provide for an exception that is narrowly construed.

(b) *Non-exercise of custody rights.* Under Article 13(a), the judicial authority may deny an application for the return of a child if the person having the care of the child was not actually exercising the custody rights at the time of the removal or retention, or had consented to or acquiesced in the removal or retention. This exception derives from Article 3(b) which makes the Convention applicable to the breach of custody rights that were actually exercised at the time of the removal or retention, or which would have been exercised but for the removal or retention.

The person opposing return has the burden of proving that custody rights were not actually exercised at the time of the removal or retention, or that the applicant had consented to or acquiesced in the removal or retention. The reporter points out that proof that custody was not actually exercised does not form an exception to the duty to return if the dispossessed guardian was unable to exercise his rights precisely because of the action of the abductor. Perez-Vera Report, paragraph 115 at page 461.

The applicant seeking return need only allege that he or she was actually exercising custody rights conferred by the law of the country in which the child was habitually resident immediately before the removal or retention. The statement would normally include a recitation of the circumstances under which physical custody had been exercised, *i.e.,* whether by the holder of these rights, or by a third person on behalf of the actual holder of the custody rights. The applicant would append copies of any relevant legal documents or court orders to the return application. *See* III.C., *supra*, and Article 8.

(c) *Grave risk of harm/intolerable situation.* Under Article 13(b), a court in its discretion need not order a child returned if there is a grave risk that return would expose the child to physical harm or otherwise place the child in an intolerable situation.

This provision was not intended to be used by defendants as a vehicle to litigate (or relitigate) the child's best interests. Only evidence directly establishing the existence of a grave risk that would expose the child to physical or emotional harm or otherwise place the child in an intolerable situation is material to the court's determination. The person opposing the child's return must show that the risk to the child is grave, not merely serious.

A review of deliberations on the Convention reveals that "intolerable situation" was not intended to encompass return to a home where money is in short supply, or where educational or other opportunities are more limited than in the requested State. An example of an "intolerable situation" is one in which a custodial parent sexually abuses the child. If the other parent removes or retains the child to safeguard it against further victimization, and the abusive parent then petitions for the child's return under the Convention, the court may deny the petition. Such action would protect the child from being returned to an "intolerable situation" and subjected to a grave risk of psychological harm.

(d) *Child's preference.* The third, unlettered paragraph of Article 13 permits the court to decline to order the child returned if the child objects to being returned and has attained an age and degree of maturity at which it is appropriate to take account of the child's views. As with the other Article 13 exceptions to the return obligation, the application of this exception is not mandatory. This discretionary aspect of Article 13 is especially important because of the potential for brainwashing of the child by the alleged abductor. A child's objection to being returned may be accorded little if any weight if the court believes that the child's preference is the product of the abductor parent's undue influence over the child.

(e) *Role of social studies.* The final paragraph of Article 13 requires the court, in considering a respondent's assertion that the child should not be returned, to take into account information relating to the child's social background provided by the Central Authority or other competent authority in the child's State of habitual residence. This provision was the dual purpose of ensuring that the court has a balanced record upon which to determine whether the child is to be returned, and preventing that abductor from obtaining an unfair advantage through his or her own forum selection with resulting ready access to evidence of the child's living conditions in that forum.

3. Article 20

Article 20 limits the return obligation of Article 12. It states: "The return of the child under the provisions of Article 12 may be refused if this would not be permitted by the fundamental principles of the requested State relating to the protection of human rights and fundamental freedoms."

The best explanation for this unique formulation is that the Convention might never have been adopted without it. The negotiating countries were divided on the inclusion of a public policy exception in the Convention. Those favoring a public policy exception believed that under some extreme circumstances not covered by the exceptions of Article 13 a court should be excused from returning a child to the country of habitual residence. In contrast, opponents of a public policy exception felt that such an exception could be interpreted so broadly as to undermine the fabric of the entire Convention.

A public policy clause was nevertheless adopted at one point by a margin of one vote. That clause provided: "Contracting States may reserve the right not to return the child when such return would be manifestly incompatible with the fundamental principles of the law relating to the family and children in the State addressed." To prevent imminent collapse of the negotiating process engendered by the adoption of this clause, there was a swift and determined move to devise a different provision that could be invoked on the rare occasion that return of a child would utterly shock the conscience of the court or offend all notions of due process.

The resulting language of Article 20 has no known precedent in other international agreements to serve as a guide in its interpretation. However, it should be emphasized that this exception, like the others, was intended to be restrictively interpreted and applied, and is not to be used, for example, as a vehicle for litigating custody on the merits or for passing judgment on the political system of the country from which the child was removed. Two characterizations of the effect to be given Article 20 are recited below for illumination.

The following explanation of Article 20 is excerpted from paragraph 118 of the Perez-Vera Report at pages 461–2:

It is significant that the possibility, acknowledged in *Article 20,* that the child may not be returned when its return 'would not be permitted by the fundamental principles of the requested State relating to the protection of human rights and fundamental freedoms' has been placed in the last article of the chapter: it was thus intended to emphasize the always clearly exceptional nature of this provision's application. As for the substance of this provision, two comments only are required. Firstly, even if its literal meaning is strongly reminiscent of the terminology used in international texts concerning the protection of human rights, this particular rule is not directed at developments which have occurred on the international level, but is concerned only with the principles accepted by the law of the requested State, either through general international law and treaty law, or through internal legislation. Consequently, so as to be able to refuse to return a child on the basis of this article, it will be necessary to show that the fundamental principles of the requested State concerning the subject-matter of the Convention do not permit it; it will not be sufficient to show merely that its return would be incompatible, even manifestly incompatible, with these principles. Secondly, such principles must not be invoked any more frequently, nor must their invocation be more readily admissible than they would be in their application to purely internal matters. Otherwise, the provision would be discriminatory in itself, and opposed to one of the most widely recognized fundamental principles in internal laws. A study of the case law of different countries shows that the application by ordinary judges of the laws on human rights and fundamental freedoms is undertaken with a care which one must expect to see maintained in the international situations which the Convention has in view.

A.E. Anton, Chairman of the Commission on the Hague Conference on Private International Law that drafted the Convention, explained Article 20 in his article, "The Hague Convention on International Child Abduction," 30 I.C.L.Q. 537, 551–2 (July, 1981), as follows:

Its acceptance may in part have been due to the fact that it states a rule which many States would have been bound to apply in any event, for example, by reason of the terms of their constitutions. The reference in this provision to "the fundamental principles of the requested State" make it clear that the reference is not one to international conventions or declarations concerned with the protection of human rights and fundamental freedoms which have been ratified or accepted by Contracting States. It is rather to the fundamental provisions of the law of the requested State in such matters . . . If the United Kingdom decides to ratify the Hague Convention, it will, of course, be for the implementing legislation or the courts to specify what provisions of United Kingdom law come within the scope of Article 20. The Article, however, is merely permissive and it is to be hoped that States will exercise restraint in availing themselves of it.

4. Custody Order No Defense to Return

See I.D.1, supra, for discussion of Article 17.

J. Return of the Child

Assuming the court has determined that the removal or retention of the child was wrongful within the meaning of the Convention and that no exceptions to the return obligation have been satisfactorily established by the respondent, Article 12 provides that "the authority concerned shall order the return of the child forthwith." The Convention does not technically require that the child be returned to his or her State of habitual residence, although in the classic abduction case this will occur. If the petitioner has moved from the child's state or habitual residence the child will be returned to the petitioner, not the State of habitual residence.

1. Return Order Not on Custody Merits

Under Article 19, a decision under the Convention concerning the return of the child shall not be taken to be a determination on the merits of any custody issue. It follows that once the factual status quo ante has been restored, litigation concerning custody or visitation issues could proceed. Typically this will occur in the child's State of habitual residence.

2. Costs, Fees, and Expenses Shifted to Abductor

In connection with the return order, Article 26 permits the court to direct the person who removed or retained the child to pay necessary expenses incurred by or on behalf of the applicant to secure the child's return, including expenses, costs incurred or payments made for locating the child, costs of legal representation of the applicant, and those of returning the child. The purposes underlying Article 26 are to restore the applicant to the financial position he or she would have been in had there been no removal or retention, as well as to deter such conduct from happening in the first place. This fee shifting provision has counterparts in the UCCJA (sections 7(g), 8(c), 15(d)) and the PKPA (28 U.S.C. 1738A note).

IV. Central Authority

In addition to creating a judicial remedy for cases of wrongful removal and retention, the Convention requires each Contracting State to establish a Central Authority (hereinafter "CA") with the broad mandate of assisting applicants to secure the return of their children or the effective exercise of their visitation rights. Articles 1, 10, 21. The CA is expressly directed by Article 10 to take all appropriate measures to obtain the voluntary return of children. The role of the CA with respect to visitation rights is discussed in V., *infra*.

A. Establishment of Central Authority

Article 6 requires each Contracting State to designate a Central Authority to discharge the duties enumerated in Articles 7, 9, 10, 11, 15, 21, 26, 27, and 28.

In France, the Central Authority is located within the Ministry of Justice. Switzerland has designated its Federal Justice Office as CA, and Canada has designated its Department of Justice. However, each Canadian province and territory in which the Convention has come into force has directed its Attorney General to serve as local CA for cases involving that jurisdiction.

In the United States it is very unlikely that the volume of cases will warrant the establishment of a new agency or office to fulfill Convention responsibilities. Rather, the duties of the CA will be carried out by an existing agency of the federal government with experience in dealing with authorities of other countries.

The Department of State's Office of Citizens Consular Services (CCS) within its Bureau of Consular Affairs will most likely serve as CA under the Hague Convention. CCS presently assists parents here and abroad with child custody-related problems within the framework of existing laws and procedures. The Convention should systematize and expedite CCS handling of requests from abroad for assistance in securing the return of children wrongfully abducted to or retained in the United States, and will provide additional tools with which CCS can help parents in the United States who are seeking return of their children from abroad.

The establishment of an interagency coordinating body is envisioned to assist the State Department in executing its functions as CA. This body is to include representatives of the departments of State, Justice, and Health and Human Services.

In addition to the mandatory establishment of a CA in the national government, Contracting States are free to appoint similar entities in political subdivisions throughout the country. Rather than mandating the establishment of a CA in every state, it is expected that state governments in the United States will be requested on a case-by-case basis to render specified assistance, consistent with the Convention, aimed at resolving international custody and visitation disputes with regard to children located within their jurisdiction.

B. Duties

Article 7 enumerates the majority of the tasks to be carried out either directly by the CA or through an intermediary. The CA is to take "all appropriate measures" to execute these responsibilities. Although they are free to do so, the Convention does not obligate Contracting States to amend their internal laws to discharge Convention tasks more efficaciously. See Perez-Vera Report, paragraph 63 at page 444.

The following paragraphs of subsections of Article 7 of the convention are couched in terms of the tasks and functions of the United States CA. The corresponding tasks and functions of the CA's in other States party to the Convention will be carried out somewhat differently in the context of each country's legal system.

Article 7(a). When the CA in the United States is asked to locate a child abducted from a foreign contracting State to this country, it would utilize all existing tools for determining the whereabouts of missing persons. Federal resources available for locating missing persons include the FBI-operated National Crime Information Center (NCIC) computer (pursuant to Pub. L. No. 97-292, the Missing Children Act), the Federal Parent Locator Service or Motor Vehicle Bureau and the Internal Revenue Service, Attorney General and Secretary of Education may be requested to conduct field and/or record searches. Also at the state level, public or private welfare agencies can be called upon to verify discreetly any address information about the abductor that may be discovered.

Article 7(b). To prevent further harm to the child, the CA would normally call upon the state welfare agency to take whatever protective measures are appropriate and available consistent with that state's child abuse and neglect laws. The CA, either directly or with the help of state authorities, may seek a written agreement from the abductor (and possibly from the applicant as well) not to remove the child from the jurisdiction pending procedures aimed at return of the child. Bonds or other forms of security may be required.

Article 7(c). The CA, either directly or through local public or private mediators, attorneys, social workers, or other professionals, would attempt to develop an agreement for the child's voluntary return and/or resolution of other outstanding issues. The obligation of the CA to take or cause to be taken all appropriate measures to obtain the voluntary return of the child is so fundamental a purpose of this Convention that it is restated in Article 10. However, overtures to secure the voluntary return of a child may not be advisable if advance awareness by the abductor that the Convention has been invoked is likely to prompt further flight and concealment of the child. If the CA and state authorities are successful in facilitating a voluntary agreement between the parties, the applicant would have no need to invoke or pursue the Convention's judicial remedy.

Article 7(d). The CA in the United States would rely upon court personnel or social service agencies in the child's state of habitual residence to compile information on the child's social background for the use of courts considering exceptions to a return petition in another country in which an abducted or retained child is located. *See* Article 13.

Article 7(e). The CA in the United States would call upon U.S. state authorities to prepare (or have prepared) general statements about the law of the state of the child's habitual residence for purposes of application of the Convention in the country where the child is located, *i.e.,* to determine whether a removal or retention was wrongful.

Article 7(f) and (g). In the United States the federal CA will not act as legal advocated for the applicant. Rather, in concert with state authorities and interested family law attorneys, the CA through state or local bodies, will assist the applicant in identifying competent private legal counsel or, if eligible, in securing representation by a Legal Aid or Legal Services lawyer. In some states, however, the Attorney General or local District Attorney may be empowered under the state law to intervene on behalf of the applicant-parent to secure the child's return.

In some foreign Contracting States, the CA may act as the legal representative of the applicant for all purposes under the Convention.

Article 28 permits the CA to require written authorization empowering it to act on behalf of the applicant, or to designate a representative to act in such capacity.

Article 7(h). Travel arrangements for the return of a child from the United States would be made by the CA or by state authorities closest to the case in cooperation with the petitioner and/or interested foreign authorities. If it is necessary to provide short-term care for the child pending his or her return, the CA presumably will arrange for the temporary placement of the child in the care of the person designated for that purpose by the applicant, or, failing that, request local authorities to appoint a guardian, foster parent, etc. The costs of transporting the child are borne by the applicant unless the court, pursuant to Article 26, orders the wrongdoer to pay.

Article 7(i). The CA will monitor all cases in which its assistance has been sought. It will maintain files on the procedures followed in each case and the ultimate disposition thereof. Complete records will aid in determining how frequently the Convention is invoked and how well it is working.

C. Other Tasks
1. **Processing** Applications

Article 8 sets forth the required contents of a return application submitted to a CA, all of which are incorporated into the model form recommended for use when seeking a child's return pursuant to the Convention (see Annex A of this analysis). Article 8 further provides that an application for assistance in securing the return of a child may be submitted to a CA in either the country of the child's habitual residence or in any other Contracting State. If a CA receives an application with respect to a child whom it believes to be located in another Contracting State, pursuant to

Article 9 it is to transmit the application directly to the appropriate CA and inform the requesting CA or applicant of the transmittal.

It is likely that an applicant who knows the child's whereabouts can expedite the return process by electing to file a return application with the CA in the country in which the child is located. The applicant who pursues this course of action may also choose to file a duplicate copy of the application for information purposes with the CA in his or her own country. Of course, the applicant may prefer to apply directly to the CA in his or her own country even when the abductor's location is known, and rely upon the CA to transfer documents and communicate with the foreign CA on his or her behalf. An applicant who does not know the whereabouts of the child will most likely file the return application with the CA in the child's State of habitual residence.

Under Article 27, a CA may reject an application if "it is manifest that the requirements of the Convention are not fulfilled or that the application is otherwise not well founded." The CA must promptly inform the CA in the requesting State, or the applicant directly, of its reasons for such rejection. Consistent with the spirit of the Convention and in the absence of any prohibition on doing so, the applicant should be allowed to correct the defects and refile the application.

Under Article 28, a CA may require the applicant to furnish a written authorization empowering it to act on behalf of the applicant, or designating a representative so to act.

2. Assistance in Connection with Judicial Proceedings

(a) Request for status report. When an action has been commenced in court for the return of a child and no decision has been reached by the end of six weeks, Article 11 authorizes the applicant or the CA of the requested State to ask the judge for a statement of the reasons for the delay. The CA in the country where the child is located may make such a request on its own initiative, or upon request of the CA of another Contracting State. Replies received by the CA in the requested State are to be transmitted to the CA in the requesting State or directly to the applicant, depending upon who initiated the request.

(b) *Social studies/background reports.* Information relating to the child's social background collected by the CA in the child's state of habitual residence pursuant to Article 7(d) may be submitted for consideration by the court in connection with a judicial return proceeding. Under the last paragraph of Article 13, the court must consider home studies and other social background reports provided by the CA or other competent authorities in the child's State of habitual residence.

(c) *Determination of "wrongfulness."* If a court requests an applicant to obtain a determination from the authorities of the child's State of habitual residence that the removal or retention was wrongful, Central Authorities are to assist applicants, so far as practicable, to obtain such a determination. Article 15.

(d) *Costs.* Under Article 26, each CA bears its own costs in applying the Convention. The actual operating expenses under the Convention will vary from one Contracting State to the next depending upon the volume of incoming and outgoing requests and the number and nature of the procedures available under internal law to carry out specified Convention tasks.

Subject to limited exceptions noted in the next paragraph, the Central Authority and other public services are prohibited from imposing any charges in relation to applications submitted under the Convention. Neither the applicant nor the CA in the requesting State may be required to pay for the services rendered directly or indirectly by the CA of the requested State.

The exceptions relate to transportation and legal expenses to secure the child's return. With respect to transportation, the CA in the requested State is under no obligation to pay for the child's return. The applicant can therefore be required to pay the costs of transporting the child. With respect to legal expenses, if the requested State enters a reservation in accordance with Articles 26 and 42, the applicant can be required to pay all costs and expenses of the legal proceedings, and those arising from the participation of legal counsel or advisers. However, see III.J 2 of this analysis discussing the possibility that the court ordering the child's return will levy these and other costs upon the abductor. Even if the reservation under Articles 26 and 42 is entered, under Article 22 no security, bond or deposit can be required to guarantee the payment of costs and expenses of the judicial or administrative proceedings falling within the Convention.

Under the last paragraph of Article 26 the CA may be able to recover some of its expenses from the person who engaged in the wrongful conduct. For instance, a court that orders a child returned may also order the person who removed or retained the child to pay the expenses incurred by or on behalf of the petitioner, including costs of court proceedings and legal fees of the petitioner. Likewise, a court that issues an order concerning visitation may direct the person who prevented the exercise of visitation rights to pay necessary expenses incurred by or on behalf of the petitioner. In such cases, the petitioner could recover his or her expenses, and the CA could recover its outlays on behalf of the petitioner, including costs associated with, or payments made for, locating the child and the legal representation of the petitioner.

V. Access Rights—Article 21

A. Remedies for Breach

Up to this point this analysis has focused on judicial and administrative remedies for the removal or retention of children in breach of custody rights. "Access rights," which are synonymous with "visitation rights," are also protected by the Convention, but to a lesser extent than custody rights. While the Convention preamble and Article 1(b) articulate the Convention objective of ensuring that rights of access under the law of one state are respected in other Contracting States, the remedies for breach of access rights are those enunciated in Article 21 and do not include the return remedy provided by Article 12.

B. Defined

Article 5(b) defines "access rights" as including "the right to take a child for a limited period of time to a place other than the child's habitual residence."

A parent who takes a child from the country of its habitual residence to another country party to the Convention for a summer visit pursuant to either a tacit agreement between the parents or a court order is thus exercising his or her access rights. Should that parent fail to return the child at the end of the agreed upon visitation period, the retention would be wrongful and could give rise to a petition for return under Article 12. If, on the other hand, a custodial parent resists permitting the child to travel abroad to visit the noncustodial parent, perhaps out of fear that the child will not be returned at the end of the visit, this interference with access rights does not constitute a wrongful retention within the meaning of Article 3 of the Convention. The parent whose access rights have been infringed is not entitled under the Convention to the child's "return," but may request the Central Authority to assist in securing the exercise of his or her access rights pursuant to Article 21.

Article 21 may also be invoked as a precautionary measure by a custodial parent who antici-pates a problem in getting the child back at the end of a visit abroad. That parent may apply to the CA of the country where the child is to visit the noncustodial parent for steps to ensure the return of the child at the end of the visit—for example, through appropriate imposition of a per-formance bond or other security.

C. Procedure for Obtaining Relief

Procedurally Article 21 authorizes a person complaining of, or seeking to prevent, a breach of access rights to apply to the CA of a Contracting State in the same way as a person seek-ing return of the child. The application would contain the information described in Article 8, except that information provided under paragraph (c) would be the grounds upon which the claim is made for assistance in organizing or securing the effective exercise of rights of access.

Once the CA receives such application, it is to take all appropriate measures pursuant to Article 7 to promote the peaceful enjoyment of access rights and the fulfillment of any conditions to which the exercise of those rights is subject. This includes initiating or facilitating the institu-tion of proceedings, either directly or through intermediaries, to organize or protect access rights and to secure respect for conditions to which these rights are subject.

If legal proceedings are instituted in the Contracting State in which the noncustodial parent resides, Article 21 may not be used by the noncustodial parent to evade the jurisdiction of the courts of the child's habitual residence, which retain authority to define and/or condition the exercise of visitation rights. A parent who has a child abroad for a visit is not to be allowed to exploit the presence of the child as a means for securing from the CA (or court) in that country more liberal visitation rights than those set forth in a court order agreed upon in advance of the visit. Such result would be tantamount to sanctioning forum-shopping contrary to the intent of the Convention. Any such application should be denied and the parent directed back to the appro-priate authorities in the State of the child's habitual residence for consideration of the desired modification. Pending any such modification, once the lawful visitation period has expired, the custodial parent would have the right to seek the child's return under Article 3.

The Perez-Vera Report gives some limited guidance as to how CA's are to cooperate to secure the exercise of access rights:

> . . . it would be advisable that the child's name not appear on the passport of the holder of the right to access, whilst in 'transfrontier' access cases it would be sensible for the holder of the access rights to give an undertaking to the Central Authority of the child's habitual residence to return the child on a particular date and to indicate also the places where he intends to stay with the child. A copy of such an undertaking would then be sent to the Central Authority of the habitual residence of the holder of the access rights, as well as to the Central Authority of the State in which he has stated his intention of staying with the child. This would enable the authorities to know the whereabouts of the child at any time and to set in motion proceedings for bringing about its return, as soon as the stated time-limit has expired. Of course, none of the measures could by itself ensure that access rights are exercised properly, but in any event we believe that this Report can go no further: the specific measures which the Central Authorities concerned are able to take

will depend on the circumstances of each case and on the capacity to act enjoyed by each Central Authority. Perez-Vera Report, paragraph 128 at page 466.

D. Alternative Remedies

In addition to or in lieu of invoking Article 21 to resolve visitation-related problems, under Articles 18, 29 and 34 an aggrieved parent whose access rights have been violated may bypass the CA and the Convention and apply directly to the judicial authorities of a Contracting State for relief under other applicable laws.

In at least one case it is foreseeable that a parent abroad will opt in favor of local U.S. law instead of the Convention. A noncustodial parent abroad whose visitation rights are being thwarted by the custodial parent resident in the United States could invoke the UCCJA to seek enforcement of an existing foreign court order conferring visitation rights. Pursuant to section 23 of the UCCJA, a state court in the United States could order the custodial parent to comply with the prescribed visitation period by sending the child to the parent outside the United States. This remedy is potentially broader and more meaningful than the Convention remedy, since the latter does not include the right of return when a custodial parent obstructs the noncustodial parent's visitation rights, *i.e.,* by refusing to allow the other parent to exercise those rights. It is possible that a parent in the United States seeking to exercise access rights with regard to a child habitually resident abroad may similarly find greater relief under foreign law than under the Convention.

VI. Miscellaneous and Final Clauses

A. Article 36

Article 36 permits Contracting States to limit the restrictions to which a child's return may be subject under the Convention, i.e., expand the return obligation or cases to which the Convention will apply. For instance, two or more countries may agree to extend coverage of the Convention to children beyond their sixteenth birthdays, thus expanding upon Article 4. Or, countries may agree to apply the Convention retroactively to wrongful removal and retention cases arising prior to its entry into force for those countries. Such agreement would remove any ambiguity concerning the scope of Article 35. The Department of State is not proposing that the United States make use of this Article.

B. Articles 37 and 38

Chapter VI of the Hague Convention consists of nine final clauses concerned with procedural aspects of the treaty, most of which are self-explanatory. Article 37 provides that states which were members of the Hague Conference on Private International Law at the time of the Fourteenth Session (October 1980) may sign and become parties to the Convention by ratification, acceptance or approval. Significantly, under Article 38 the Convention is open to accession by non-member States, but enters into force only between those States and member Contracting States which specifically accept their accession to the Convention. Article 38.

C. Articles 43 and 44

In Article 43 the Convention provides that it enters into force on the first day of the third calendar month after the third country has deposited its instrument of ratification, acceptance, approval or accession. For countries that become parties to the Convention subsequently, the Convention enters into force on the first day of the third calendar month following the deposit of the instrument of ratification. Pursuant to Article 43, the Convention entered into force on December 1, 1983 among France, Portugal and five provinces of Canada, and on January 1, 1984 for Switzerland. As of January 1, 1986 it is in force for all provinces and territories of Canada with the exception of Alberta, the Northwest Territories, Prince Edward Island and Saskatchewan.

The Convention enters into force in ratifying countries subject to such declarations or reservations pursuant to Articles 39, 40, 24 and 26 (third paragraph) as may be made by each ratifying country in accordance with Article 42.

The Convention remains in force for five years from the date it first entered into force (*i.e.,* December 1, 1983), and is renewed tacitly every five years absent denunciations notified in accordance with Article 44.

D. Articles 39 and 40

Article 39 authorizes a Contracting State to declare that the Convention extends to some or all of the territories for the conduct of whose international relations it is responsible.

Under Article 40, countries with two or more territorial units having different systems of law relative to custody and visitation rights may declare that the Convention extends to all or some of them. This federal state clause was included at the request of Canada to take account of Canada's special constitutional situation. The Department of State is not proposing that the United States make use of this provision. Thus, if the United States ratifies the Convention, it would come into force throughout the United States as the supreme law of the land in every state and other jurisdiction.

E. Article 41

Article 41 is another provision inserted at the request of one country, and is best understood by reciting the reporter's explanatory comments:

Finally a word should be said on Article 41, since it contains a wholly novel provision in Hague Conventions. It also appears in the other Conventions adopted at the Fourteenth Session, *i.e., the Convention on International Access to Justice,* at the express request of the Australian delegation.

This article seeks to make it clear that ratification of the Convention by a State will carry no implication as to the internal distribution of executive, judicial and legislative powers in that State.

This may seem self-evident, and this is the point which the head of the Canadian delegation made during the debates of the Fourth Commission where it was decided to insert such a provision in both Conventions (see P.v. No. 4 of the Plenary Session). The Canadian delegation, openly expressing the opinion of a large number of delegations, regarded the insertion of this article in the two Conventions as unnecessary. Nevertheless, Article 41 was adopted, largely to satisfy the Australian delegation, for which the absence of such a provision would apparently have created insuperable constitutional difficulties. Perez-Vera Report, paragraph 149 at page 472.

F. Article 45

Article 45 vests the Ministry of Foreign Affairs of the Kingdom of the Netherlands, as depository for the Convention, with the responsibility to notify Hague Conference member States and other States party to the Convention of all actions material to the operation of the Convention.

Annex A

The following model form was recommended by the Fourteenth Session of the Hague Conference on Private International Law (1980) for use in making applications pursuant to the 1980 Hague Convention on the Civil Aspects of International Child Abduction for the return of wrongfully removed or retained children. The version of the form to be used for requesting the return of such children from the United States will probably seek additional information, in particular to help authorities in the United States in efforts to find a child whose whereabouts are not known to the applicant.

Request for Return

Hague Convention of 25 October 1980 on the Civil Aspects of International Child Abduction.

Requesting Central Authority or Applicant

Requested Authority

Concerns the following child: _____ who will attain the age of 16 on _____, 19_____.

Note.—The following particulars should be completed insofar as possible.
I—Identity of the Child and its Parents
1 Child
Name and first names ....
Date and place of birth ....
Passport or identity card no., if any...
Description and photo, if possible (see annexes) ....
2 parents
2.1 Mother:
Name and first names ....
Date and place of birth ....
Nationality..
Occupation ....
Habitual residence...
Passport or identity card no., if any...
2.2 Father:
Name and first names ....
Date and place of birth ....
Nationality..
Occupation ....
Habitual residence...
Passport or identity card no., if any...

2.3 Date and Place of Marriage...

II—Requesting Individual or Institution (who actually exercised custody before the removal or retention) ....

3 Name and first names ....

Nationality of individual applicant...

Occupation of individual applicant ....

Address..

Passport or identity card no., if any...

Relation to the child ....

Name and address of legal adviser, if any...

III—Place Where the Child Is Thought to Be

4.1 Information concerning the person alleged to have removed or retained the child

Name and first names ....

Date and place of birth, if known..

Nationality, if known..

Occupation ....

Last known address ....

Passport or identity card no., if any...

Description and photo, if possible (see annexes) ....

4.2 Address of the child..

4.3 Other persons who might be able to supply additional information relating to the whereabouts of the child ....

IV—Time, Place, Date and Circumstances of the Wrongful Removal or Retention

V—Factual or Legal Grounds Justifying the Request ....

VI—Civil Proceedings in Progress ....

VII—Child Is to Be Returned to:

a. Name and first names ....

Date and place of birth ....

Address..

Telephone number ....

b. Proposed arrangements for return of the child..

VIII—Other Remarks

IX—List of Documents Attached*

Date ....

Place ....

Signature and/or stamp of the requesting Central Authority or applicant.................

ANNEX B—BIBLIOGRAPHY

Vinion, L. When Custody Conflicts Cross The Border. A Primer on International Disputes Over Children. 15 Family Advocate 30 (Spring, 1993).

Explanatory Report by E. Perez-Vera, Hague Conference on Private International Law, Actes et documents de la Quatorzieme session, vol. III, 1980, p. 426.

Anton, A.E.—The Hague Convention on International Child Abduction; 30 Int'l & Comp. L.Q. (1981), p. 537.

Bodenheimer, B.—The Hague Convention on International Child Abduction; XIV Fam. L.Q. (1980), p. 99.

Chatin, L.—Les conflicts relatifs a la garde des enfantes et àu droit de visite en droit international prive; Travaux du Comite Francais de droit international prive, Seance du 12 mai 1982, Publication du Ministere de la Justice.

Crouch, R.E.—Effective Measures Against International Child Snatching; 131 New L. J. (1981), p. 592.

Deschenaux, D.—La Convention de La Haye sur les aspects civils de l'enlevement international d'enfants, du 25 octobre 1980; XXXVII Schweizerisches Jahrbuch fur internationales Recht (1981), p. 119.

Dyer, A.—International child abduction by parents; 168 Recueil des Cours de l'Academie de droit international de La Haye (1980), p. 231.

Eekelaar, J.M.—The Hague Convention on the Civil Aspects of International Child Abduction; Explanatory Documentation prepared for Commonwealth Jurisdictions, Commonwealth Secretariat, 1981.

Farquhar, K.B.—The Hague Convention on International Child Abduction Comes to Canada; 4 Can. J. Fam. L. (1983), p. 5.

Frank, R.J.—American and International Responses to International Child Abductions, 16 N.Y.U.J. Int'l L. & Pol. (Winter 1984), p. 415.

Hoff, P., Schulman, J. and Volenik, A.—Interstate Child Custody Disputes and Parental Kidnapping: Policy, Practice and Law. Legal Services Corporation—American Bar Association. 1982.

Huesstege, R.—Internationale Kindesentfuehrungen und Landesverfassungsrecht; IPRax (1982), p. 95—Der Uniform Child Custody Jurisdiction Act—Rechtsvergleichende Betrachtungen zu Internationalen Kindesentfuehrengen, Verlag fur Standesamtswesen, Frankfurt am Main, 1982.

Morgenstern, B.R.—The Hague Convention on the Civil Aspects of International Child Abduction: The Need for Ratification; 10 N.C.J. Int'l L. & Com. Reg. (1985), p. 463.

Reymond, P.H.—Convention de La Hague et Convention de Strasbourg. Aspects comparatifs des conventions concernant l'enlevement d'un enfant par l'un de ses parents; Revue de droit suisse 1981, p. 329.

Schulman, J.—cf. Hoff, P.

Vink, E.L.M.—Enkele civielrichtelijke aspecten van de internationale ontvoeringen van kinderen door een van de ouders; Leiden, mai 1981.

Volenik, A.—cf. Hoff, P.

Westbrook, G.R.—Law and Treaty

Responses to International Child Abductions; 20 Va. J. Int'l L. (1980), p. 669

§ 16.3.3. Jurisdiction – The Hague Convention – Cases

The following are cases that apply to The Hague Convention:

In *Lozano v. Montoya Alvarez*,[84] the United States Supreme Court unanimously affirmed the Second Circuit and held that the 1-year period where the court shall order the return of the child forthwith cannot be extended by equitable tolling when child was concealed and parent did not locate child until after the 1-year period. In *Lozano*, the mother left the United Kingdom with the child and settled in New York. Sixteen months later the father located the child in New York and filed a Petition for Return of Child pursuant to the Hague Convention. Finding that the petition was filed more than one year after the child was removed from the U.K., the court denied the petition on the basis that the child was now settled in New York. The court also held that the 1-year period could not be extended by equitable tolling. The Second Circuit affirmed and the United States Supreme Court affirmed the decision. According to the Supreme Court, "without a presumption of equitable tolling, the Convention does not support extending the 1-year period during concealment. Article 12 explicitly provides for the period to commence on 'the date of the wrongful removal or retention' and makes no provision for an extension."

In *Chafin v. Chafin*,[85] the United States Supreme Court unanimously held that a father's appeal of a District Court order allowing his child's mother to take the child to Scotland was not moot simply because the child was no longer in the United States. Petitioner-Father was a U.S. citizen and a sergeant in the U.S. Army. Respondent-Mother was a United Kingdom citizen. The parties married and had a daughter born in Germany with dual United States and United Kingdom citizenship. The mother and child moved to Scotland when the father was deployed to Afghanistan and established residency there, but moved to Alabama when father was transferred there. Shortly after the move to Alabama, the couple divorced. Mother obtained an order from the District Court under the Hague Convention allowing her to move the child back to Scotland, establishing it as the child's "habitual residence." Father appealed the District Court's

---

[84] Lozano v. Montoya Alvarez, 134 S. Ct. 1224, 188 2. Ed. 2d 200 (2014).
[85] Chafin v. Chafin, 568 U. S. __, 133 S. Ct. 1017; 185 L. Ed. 2d 1 (Feb. 19, 2013).

order to the U.S. Court of Appeals for the Eleventh Circuit, which dismissed the appeal as moot because the child and her mother had already moved to Scotland.

The Supreme Court ruled that the case was not moot, and vacated the Eleventh Circuit Court's decision. The Court found that Father continued to contend that his daughter's country of habitual residence was the United States, and could argue his case under the exceptions to the Hague Convention command. Justice Roberts, speaking for the Court, stated that even though Scotland may ignore a re-return order, U.S. courts would still retain jurisdiction, and a valid controversy would still exist as to where the parties' daughter would be raised. Enforcement of the order may be uncertain, but it would not typically render the case moot. "Mr. Chafin's claim for re-return—under the convention itself or according to general equitable principles—cannot be dismissed as so implausible that it is insufficient to preserve jurisdiction, and his prospects of success are therefore not pertinent to the mootness inquiry."

In *Abbott v. Abbott*,[86] the United States Supreme Court ruled that an order prohibiting the removal of a child from a country without the non-custodial parent's consent is enforceable under the Hague Convention. Father's *ne exeat* right to consent before mother could remove the child from Chile, granted by the Chilean Family Court, was a "right of custody," so that father could seek a return remedy after mother's removal without his consent, under the Hague Convention. The Chilean court granted father direct and regular visitation rights, which automatically gave him joint right to decide his child's country of residence, under Chilean law, the Convention defined "right of custody" to include the right to determine the child's place of residence, and, although the father's right was inchoate, it would have been exercised but for the child's removal by mother. After the Abbotts, a married couple, moved to Chile and separated, the Chilean courts granted respondent wife daily care and control of their 15-year-old minor son, while awarding petitioner husband visitation rights. Husband also had a *ne exeat* right to consent before wife could take the child out of the country under the Chile Minors Law. When wife brought the child to Texas without permission from husband

---

[86] Abbott v. Abbott, 560 U.S. 1, 130 S.Ct. 1983, 176 L.Ed. 2d 789 (U.S. 2010).

or the Chilean Family Court, husband filed suit in the Federal District Court moving to enforce the *ne exeat* order and seeking an order requiring his son's return to Chile under the Hague Convention. The United States District Court for the Western District of Texas denied father's request, and the Fifth Circuit affirmed. Federal courts have disagreed on whether the *ne exeat* clause conferred a right of custody or a lesser right of access under the Hague Convention. In this case, the United States Court of Appeals for the Fifth Circuit ruled it was only a right of access. A majority of the United States Supreme Court reversed and remanded, finding that a parent has a right of custody under the Hague Convention by reason of that parent's *ne exeat* right. Justice Anthony Kennedy, writing for the majority, said that the *ne exeat* clause in the Chilean court order conferred a "right of custody" on the noncustodial father within the meaning of the Hague Convention. Because the clause conferred a right of custody, father was entitled to file a petition to return the child to Chile. The majority relied upon the Hague Convention's purpose to deter child abductions as well as the "broad acceptance" of this interpretation in international caselaw. The court noted that wife mistakenly claimed that a *ne exeat* right cannot qualify as a right of custody because the Hague Convention requires that any such rights be capable of exercise. When one parent removes a child without seeking the *ne exeat* holder's consent, it is an instance where the right would have been exercised but for the removal or retention. The court concluded that the Fifth Circuit's conclusion that a breach of a *ne exeat* right does not give rise to a return remedy would render the Hague Convention meaningless in many cases where it is most needed.

In *Foster v. Foster*, 654 F. Supp. 2d 348 (E.D. Pa. 2009), Western Pennsylvania District Court found that mother failed to meet the high burden of demonstrating the likelihood of a grave risk of harm to the parties' child and granted father's Petition for Return of a Minor Child to Canada pursuant to the Hague Convention. When the child was eight years old, mother took him to a shelter for abused women. Mother and the child subsequently moved to her parents' home in Ohio. Father then petitioned for the child's return to Canada pursuant to the Hague Convention. In order to succeed in a petition seeking return of a child, a petitioner must demonstrate by a preponderance of the evidence in a wrongful removal or retention occurred. For a removal to be wrongful, a petitioner must establish that: (a) the respondent removed or retained the child from the child's nation of habitual residence, and (b) under the law of the child's nation of habitual residence, the petitioner was exercising parental custody rights over the child at the time of removal or retention, or that he would have exercised said rights but for the removal or retention.

Mother acknowledged that father had established the elements of a wrongful removal under Article 3 of the Hague Convention. However, she raised the "grave risk of harm" defense set forth in Article 13(b), claiming, that along with abusing her, the father had disciplined the child by spanking him with a wooden spoon until red marks appeared, mistreated him, and called him names when he did not exhibit athletic ability. Under Article 13(b), a court is not bound to order the return of the child if there is a grave risk that his or her return would expose the child to physical or psychological harm or otherwise place the child in an intolerable situation. This exception is to be construed narrowly and requires proof by clear and convincing evidence. *In Re: Application of Ariel Adan*, 437 F.3d 381, 390 (3rd Cir. 2006).

The District Court found that spankings, name-calling, and physical discipline inflicted on the child by his father did not support mother's claim that he will be subjected to a grave risk of harm if father's Hague Convention petition for his return to Canada was granted. Following federal case law, the court found that the "regrettable" incidents were "isolated and sporadic," and that mother had not shown that Canadian authorities were unable to provide adequate protection for the child. *McManus v. McManus*, 354 F.Supp.2d 62, 69-70 (D. Mass. 2005). Although the trial judge found father to be domineering, excessively demanding and impatient, and his parenting skills left much to be desired, the court concluded that, nevertheless, mother had failed to demonstrate by the clear and convincing standard that the child would be subject to a grave risk of physical harm if returned to Canada. Father's actions toward the child were more akin to the "isolated and sporadic abuse" noted in *McManus*. While regrettable, they were insufficient to establish a grave risk of harm to the child when compared to the pervasive, severe, and dangerous behavior described in *Van De Sande v. Van De Sande*, 431 F.3d 567 (7th Cir. 2005). "Indeed, the evidence of abuse here falls short even of that described in *Simcox v. Simcox*, 511 F.3d 594 (6th Cir. 2007), a case which the Sixth Circuit categorized as 'admittedly a close question.'" The Sixth Circuit noted that the more difficult question is at precisely what level the risk to the child is grave, not merely serious.

The court explained that if a respondent is able to produce clear and convincing evidence of a grave risk of harm to the child, she must then demonstrate that the courts in the country of habitual residence, for whatever reason, may be incapable or unwilling to give the child adequate protection. Here, mother failed to demonstrate by clear and convincing evidence that the child would face a grave risk of psychological harm if ordered to return to Canada. Mother's witness, an expert in the field of clinical and forensic psychology who had performed a clinical interview of the child, stated that he was reluctant to predict grave psychological harm with any degree of psychological certainty. The expert explained that his ability to do so would have been greater if the child had been subjected to more serious physical or psychological abuse. The witness also implied that his concerns regarding harm to the child might be less acute if mother were to accompany the child's return to Canada. Finally, the court found that no evidence has been produced, as required by *In Re: Application of Ariel Adan*, 437 F.3d 381 (3rd Cir. 2006), that the Canadian judiciary or other authorities were incapable or unwilling to give the child adequate protection. *Foster v. Foster*, W.D. Pa., ___ F.Supp.2d ___, C.A. No. 09-93 Erie (W.D. Pa. 2009).

In *Clarke v. Clarke*, Civil Action No. 08-690 (E.D. Pa. 2008), a federal District Court ruled that mother, who extended her children's nine-week visit to Pennsylvania to almost 7 months and then refused to return them to the family's home in Australia, cannot have the benefit of such delay in arguing that the children had become acclimatized to Pennsylvania and thus should remain there. The court granted father's Hague Convention petition for the children's return, finding that the parties did not share a parental intent to shift the children's habitual residence to the United States. The court determined that Australia was the children's habitual residence and that mother's failure to return them there "makes this a wrongful retention case." A petitioner cannot claim that the removal or retention of a child is "wrongful" unless the child to whom the petition relates is habitually residing in a State signatory to the Convention and has been removed to or retained in a different State. In rejecting mother's claim that the children's habitual residence had shifted to the United

States, the court applied the standard set out in *Feder v. Evans-Feder*, 63 F.3d 217 (3rd Cir. 1995), which consists of an analysis of the child's circumstances in his or her habitual residence and the parents' present shared intentions regarding their child's presence there. *Feder* described the child's habitual residence as the place where he or she has been physically present for an amount of time sufficient for acclimatization and which has a "degree of settled purpose" from the child's perspective. "This standard focuses on the parent's shared intentions, the period of time sufficient for acclimatization and the child's degree of settled purpose." The court found that, here, the parties did not share a parental intent as to the children's habitual residence being Pennsylvania. The court observed that the parties never discussed mother's decision to retain the children in the United States, and father never consented to her permanent retention of the children. The court explained that mother could not take advantage of the almost seven-month period during which she led father to believe that the family was returning to Australia to claim that the children had become "acclimatized." The court noted that "it would be fundamentally unfair to allow [mother] to retain the children in the United States, without the father's consent and then claim in court that the children have grown accustomed to their new surroundings. It is precisely this type of behavior that undermines the purpose of the Hague Convention." The court also determined that the children did not have a "settled purpose" to reside in the United States. The court found that they came to the United States on a vacation, that their lives had been unsettled during their time there, and that they "do not have a routine or sense of environmental normalcy in the United States and many of their possessions remained in Australia." The court also found that there was no support in the evidence that the children acclimatized themselves enough in Pennsylvania to call it home. The court also rejected mother's contention that the children would face a grave risk of harm if returned to Australia, noting that Australian authorities had fully investigated mother's report that father sexually abused their son and did not find any evidence supporting it.

In *Yang v. Tsui*, 499 F.3d 259 (3rd Cir. 2007), the Third Circuit held that a federal trial court did not err in ordering a wrongfully retained child's return to her mother in Canada, even though the child had expressed a desire to remain with her father in the United States. Addressing the

Hague Child Abduction Convention's "wishes of the child" defense for the first time, the court acknowledged that the child has now spent half her life with her father and half-siblings in the United States, but pointed out that her attachment to them and to her life in the United States was the result of father's misconduct. The court found that the "wishes of the child" exception did not prevent the return of the child to her mother in Canada. Additionally, the court agreed with the District Court that this was not an appropriate case in which to apply the exception. The attachments the child had to Pittsburgh and her family there, father's wife and marital children, were created because of father's wrongful retention. The three weeks that she resided with him but was not wrongfully retained by him, when mother was hospitalized, is not the period in which she grew attached to her family and life in Pittsburgh. "Rather, it was the passage of time during the years of wrongful retention and litigation of this case that created her desire to remain in Pittsburgh. . . . If the District Court applied the exception in this case, it would encourage parents to wrongfully retain a child for as long as possible. . . . A lengthy wrongful retention could enable the child to become more comfortable in his or her new surroundings, which may create a desire to remain in his or her new home." The application of the exception in this case would reward father for violating mother's custody rights, and defeat the purpose of the Convention. Even if the record supported a finding that father had met his burden of proving the applicability of the exception, the District Court could not be said to have abused its discretion in refusing to apply it. Rather, it construed the exception narrowly in order to effectuate the purpose of the Convention.

In *Karkkainen v. Kovalchuk*, 445 F.3rd 280 (3rd Cir. 2006), the Third Circuit ruled that the District Court properly held that the parties' 11-year-old daughter was a habitual resident of the United States, where the evidence showed that the child had acclimatized to the United States and that there was a degree of settled purpose, from the child's perspective, to remain in the United States prior to father's retention of the child in the United States. Citing *Feder v. Evans-Feder*, 63 F.3d 217 (3rd Cir. 1995), the court explained that the threshold question requires a determination of the child's habitual residence immediately before the alleged wrongful retention. "We have stated that a child's habitual residence is the place where he or she has been physically present for an amount of time sufficient for acclimatization and which has a degree of settled purpose from the child's perspective. Simply put, this inquiry considers whether a child has made a country her home before the date of her removal or retention." The court determined that here there was evidence that the child had acclimatized herself to the United States during the summer of 2003, prior to the date of retention, and essentially chose to abandon Finland as her principal residence. The court noted that the child was highly intelligent and was enrolled in American classes and engaged in sports activities, and that she had formed meaningful connections with people and places in the United States in the summer of 2003. "Though the relatively short period of time Maria was present in the United States makes it a close question, we hold that Maria was acclimatized to the United States on the date of her retention and that her conduct demonstrated a degree of settled purpose to remain here." The court concluded: "We are mindful that we should avoid setting the bar for acclimatization too low lest (sic) we create an incentive for a parent to remove or retain a child in the hope that the child will quickly acclimatize and not be returned." The court decided that in the "unique circumstances of this case, [the child's] experiences in the United States prior to her retention crossed the line that demarcates acclimatization and indicate a degree of settled purpose of her perspective."

In *In Re: Application of Adan*, 437 F.3d 381 (3rd Cir. 2006), the Third Circuit held that Argentina was the child's country of habitual residence, for purposes of the Hague Convention, even though she was born in the United States, where she moved to Argentina with her mother and father when she was three months old, she lived in Argentina until her mother removed her to the United States, her parents were both from Argentina, and her father was an Argentine citizen. The Hague Convention does not allow the state in which a child has been wrongfully taken to decide who should have custody, and thus a determination by the host country that a party has custody rights in the country of origin for purposes of determining whether removal was wrongful has no bearing on the merits of a subsequent custody determination in the country of origin once the child is returned.

In *Yang v. Tsui*, 416 F.3d 199 (3rd Cir. 2005), the Third Circuit Court of Appeals ruled that because this case did not satisfy the requirements for *Younger* abstention, the District Court erred in abstaining from consideration of plaintiff's petition seeking return of her child under the Convention on the Civil Aspects of International Child Abduction and the International Child Abduction Remedies Act. This case presented an issue of first impression, namely, whether a District Court should abstain from a Hague Convention petition when a state court custody proceeding is pending. After examining other Circuits' application of *Younger* abstention principles to Hague cases, the court emphasized that the Convention's implementing legislation, the International Child Abduction Remedies Act, 42 U.S.C. § 11601, expressly provides for concurrent federal and state court jurisdiction, and found that where the Convention had not been raised in pending state court custody litigation, abstention was inappropriate.

As to *Younger* abstention, three requirements must be met before it is appropriate: (1) there must be an ongoing state judicial proceeding, implicating important state interest, to which a federal plaintiff is a party and with which the federal proceeding will interfere; (2) the State proceedings must implicate important state interests; and (3) the State proceedings afford an adequate opportunity to raise the claims. The Hague Convention requires that any state court custody litigation be stayed pending the outcome of Hague Convention litigation. The purpose of the Hague Convention is to provide for a reasoned determination of where jurisdiction is appropriate, the court noted. "Therefore, it is consistent with this purpose that it is the custody determination, not the Hague Convention Petition, that should be held in abeyance if proceedings are going forward in both state and federal courts." The court concluded that the District Court erred in permitting the state court custody proceedings to go forward. *Yang* had not raised the Hague Convention in state court. A federal proceeding would not have interfered with state court proceedings. "It would make the Hague Convention and ICARA meaningless if a federal court abstained in a Hague Convention Petition because child custody was being disputed in state court," the court determined, adding that "if the District Court's analysis were to be accepted, ICARA would be a hollow statute."

In *Baxter v. Baxter*, 423 F.3d 363 (3rd Cir. 2005), the Third Circuit Court of Appeals ruled that forcing the return of a child unlawfully retained in the United States by mother, to Australia, the place of the child's habitual residence and residence of the father, would not expose the child to a risk of physical or psychological harm or otherwise place the child in an intolerable situation. Thus, the grave-risk exception of the Hague Convention on the Civil Aspects of International Child Abduction did not apply. The court ruled that the District Court did not give proper consideration to father's claim that mother wrongfully retained their child in the United States under the Hague Convention by terminating its analysis after holding that father consented to the child's removal from Australia at the time of his departure. The child's habitual residence prior to the contested retention was Australia, and the District Court never addressed father's claim that the child was wrongfully retained in the United States. The court found that father did not consent to mother's permanent retention of the child in the United States or acquiesce to a current arrangement where the child lived in the United States with mother and her new boyfriend, after his consent to allow the child to travel with mother from his home in Australia to grandmother's home in the United States.

In *Whiting v. Krassner*, 391 F.3d 540 (3rd Cir. 2004) the United States Court of Appeals for the Third Circuit held that Canada was a one-year-old child's "habitual residence" immediately before father removed the child to the United States, as required to support mother's Hague Convention claim against the father, even though the child had been in Canada only two months and the couple's shared intent was for a limited stay for the child in Canada. The couple's written child-custody agreement preceding mother's and child's relocation from the United States to Canada showed a degree of settled purpose by spelling out that the child would reside in a specified location in Canada for a two-year period and then would return to the United States no later than the specified date upon fulfillment of certain conditions. The Third Circuit held that the fact that mother and her daughter were to return to the United States, subject to certain conditions, did not in any way diminish the parties' settled intention that they were to remain in Canada for at least two years. "Our review of the case law concerning the definition of 'habitual residence' under the Hague Convention leaves us convinced that the framework we established in Feder and further cemented in Delvoye continues to provide the best guidance for determining a child's habitual residency. In Feder, we stated that 'a child's habitual residence is the place where he or she has been physically present for an amount of time sufficient for acclimatization and which has a degree of settled purpose from the child's perspective.' We went on to modify this requirement both in Feder, itself, and later in Delvoye when the situation involves a very young child. In these circumstances, we recognized that the shared intent of the parents in determining the residence of their children was of paramount importance. . . . Today, we further attempt to clarify the definition of habitual residence when the child involved is very young. In such a case, acclimatization is not nearly as important as the settled purpose and shared intent of the child's parents in choosing a particular habitual residence. . . . It is clear that when [father] removed [the child] from Canada and took her to the United States, his acts were disruptive of an agreed-upon intention."

In *Delvoye v. Lee*, 329 F.3d 330 (3d Cir. 2003), the Third Circuit held that the District Court properly denied father's petition for the return of his child to Belgium under the Hague Child Abduction Convention. The court agreed with the finding that father, who had residences in New York and Belgium, had failed to prove that Belgium, where the child was born two months before he was taken by his mother to New York, was the child's country of habitual residence. A child born in a country that is not his or her mother's habitual residence but merely where she is temporarily present may have no habitual residence until he or she has lived in a country on a more stable footing. Accordingly, the court concluded, father had failed to establish his son's habitual residence in Belgium, and thus the child could not have been wrongfully removed from such a habitual residence by his mother.

In *Egervary v. Rooney*, No. 96-3039 (E.D. Pa. 2000), the District Court held that two attorneys who, while representing a Hungarian mother seeking to gain custody of her child, participated in the execution of an *ex parte* federal court order for seizure of the child from his father in Pennsylvania, were acting as federal agents for purposes of establishing their liability for violation of the father's due process rights. The court explained that *Bivens v. Six Unknown Agents of the Federal Bureau of Narcotics*, 403 U.S. 388 (1971), recognizes a cause of action in tort against "federal agents" acting "under color of authority" for damages arising out of the agents' "unconstitutional conduct."

In *Egervary v. Rooney*, 80 F. Supp. 2d 491 (E.D. Pa. 2000), an attorney who arranged for the return of the child to his mother in Hungary after he was taken from there by his American father may be liable to the father for violating his due process rights. After reviewing the relevant case law, the court determined that Egervary had been entitled to, and denied, a prompt, state-initiated post-deprivation hearing to ratify the removal of his son. "Even when an imminent threat of harm justifies removing the child from their parent's custody without prior process, there must be a prompt, state-initiated post-deprivation hearing to ratify the removal."

In *Bromley v. Bromley*,[87] the U.S. District Court held that a father who moved to England following his United States divorce must look to state law rather than the Hague Convention on the Civil Aspects of International Child Abduction to enforce the divorce decree's access/visitation provisions. The court ruled that it lacked jurisdiction over the grievances brought by father, explaining that the Convention does not provide a remedy in such situations. The court ruled that it did not have the authority to enforce the rights of access of father under the Convention, absent a "wrongful" removal of a child. The court acknowledged that no federal court has yet addressed the right to access to children under the Convention, as contrasted with ordering the return of children. The federal court determined that it could not address the father's visitation/access rights because there is no remedy under the Convention for obstacles to access rights absent a "wrongful" removal. The court explained that Article 21 of the Convention simply states that the promotion of effective rights of access may be effectuated by application to the "Central Authorities," but does not provide the courts with independent authority to remedy such a situation. The court pointed out that the Convention's silence as to any remedy for access rights is in sharp contrast to Article 12, which clearly provides power to judicial authorities to order the return of a child "wrongfully" removed. "We believe, therefore, that the plain language of the Convention does not provide federal courts with jurisdiction over access rights." Noting that case law makes clear that the Convention cannot be invoked without a breach of custody rights, the court found that in the United Kingdom, Article 21 has been described as toothless because it does not confer jurisdiction to determine matters relating to access. Moreover, it added, many commentators have criticized this failure to provide a remedy concerning the access rights of parents. The

---

[87] Bromley v. Bromley, No. 98-MC-0180 (E.D. Pa. December 15, 1998).

court held, therefore, that since the mother already has legal custody of the children and has neither "wrongfully" removed nor retained them from the country of their habitual residence, there is no cause of action under the Convention. Also stressing the general refusal of federal courts to hear child custody matters, the court advised the father that the proper jurisdiction for his action is a state court that has full authority to enforce and modify the parties' original Texas divorce decree.

In *Burns v. Burns*, No. 96-6268 (E.D. Pa. 1996), a Pennsylvania District Court held that a state court's denial of a mother's petition for relief under the Hague Convention, submitted in the father's divorce action, barred her subsequent, independent petition for relief under the Convention in the federal courts. Noting that in the divorce action the mother had specifically sought special relief under the Hague Convention based on her claim that the father was wrongfully retaining the children in this country, the court found that the state appellate court had rejected her arguments under the Convention. The district court thus refused to allow her a "second bite at the apple" in federal court, suggesting that she appeal the appellate court's decision. The federal court held that it must accord full faith and credit to the state court's decision under 42 U.S.C. § 11603(g). Therefore, the court concluded that because the state court had already ruled on her Hague Convention claim, it must dismiss the present action.

In *Feder v. Evans-Feder*,[88] the United States Court of Appeals for the Third Circuit ruled where a child lived with his parents in Australia for six months before returning to the United States with his mother and being "wrongfully retained" here, Australia was the "habitual residence" of the child within the meaning of the Hague Child Abduction Convention. The court remanded the case for a determination of whether an exception existed to the Hague Convention's general rule that a child's return is mandatory where he or she has been wrongfully retained by a parent.

In *Axford v. Axford*, the Eastern District of Pennsylvania ruled that father, who was awarded joint custody of his son by an English court, must return the child to his ex-wife pursuant to the Hague Convention,

---

[88] Feder v. Evans-Feder, 63 F.3d 217 (3rd Cir. 1995).

where father brought the child to the United States in violation of both the mother's custody rights and a court order barring the child's unilateral removal from the United Kingdom. Petitioner-wife, a citizen of the United Kingdom and resident of England, and her ex-husband shared custody of their son, who had autism. When the parents divorced, the English court entered a joint custody order that barred either parent's removal of the child from the United Kingdom without the consent of the other parent or the court. Mother discovered that father and his current wife had taken the child to the United States without the consent of petitioner or the English court. Mother located them in Pennsylvania and filed a petition under the Hague Convention on the Civil Aspects of International Child Abduction for the child's return to England. Pending an evidentiary hearing on that petition, mother filed an expedited *ex parte* motion for expedited service of the petition and for the surrender of the passports of father and the child. Petitioner-mother testified by telephone from England. The Eastern District court entered an order requiring father to surrender his and the child's passports to the United States Marshal's Service to prevent them from fleeing the jurisdiction. The court noted that such relief was appropriate under the Hague Convention to prevent the child's further removal and concealment while mother's petition was adjudicated. After the evidentiary hearing, the District Court ordered that the child be returned to mother and that father pay mother's attorney fees. The court found that at the time of his removal by father, the child had lived in England since birth and that it thus was his habitual residence. Neither mother nor the English court consented to father's removal of the child and father acted in violation of mother's custody rights. The court further found that mother was clearly exercising her custody rights at the time of the child's removal and noted that the record showed that up until that time mother had "regularly asserted her joint custody rights." The court was thus required to order the child's return to England unless father could establish one of the Hague Convention's affirmative defenses.

The court found that father's only arguable defense, the "grave risk" defense, was not appropriate here. Under the Hague Convention, a wrongful removal may nonetheless be justified if respondent can produce clear and convincing evidence that "there is a grave risk that his or her return would expose the child to physical or psychological harm or otherwise place the child in an intolerable situation." Such a defense or "narrowly drawn" exception applies to situations in which the child faces a real risk of physical, sexual or psychological abuse upon return. A respondent must also demonstrate that the court in the country of the child's habitual residence may be incapable or unwilling to adequately protect the child. The court noted that mother presented the examining psychologist's report and testimony, in which he opined that the child would not be at risk if returned to her care. Also, the child had expressed no fear of either the mother or her partner and that father's allegations of abuse were raised and dismissed in the English court.

With regard to mother's request for attorneys' fees, the court declared: "Pursuant to 42 U.S.C. § 11607(b)(3), because this Court granted the Petition, it shall order the respondent to pay necessary expenses incurred by or on behalf of the petitioner, including court costs, legal fees, foster home or other care during the course of the proceedings in the action, and transportation costs related to the return of the child, unless the respondent establishes that such order would be clearly inappropriate." The court noted that the "lodestar approach" is the appropriate method for determining the amount of reasonable attorneys' fees. Under this approach, a court must multiply the number of hours reasonably expended by a reasonable hourly rate. A court determines a reasonable hourly rate by assessing the prevailing party's attorney's experience and skill compared with the market rates in the relevant community for lawyers of reasonably comparable skill, experience, and reputation. The court found that counsel's hourly rate of $150 per hour was reasonable, and approved attorneys' fees in the amount of $9,660. Mother was also entitled to transportation costs related to returning her child to England and hotel expenses incurred in connection with this matter. *Axford v. Axford*, No. 09-2914 (E.D. Pa. 2009).

LOWER COURT CASES

Lehigh County

Gjondla v. Gjondla, 47 Lehigh L. J. 8 (C.C.P. 1996) (Trial court found mother's retention of the minor child to be wrongful and contrary to the custody rights of the father where the minor child resided, for the first five months of her life, in joint custody of her parents in Lehigh County, Pennsylvania; the parties jointly agreed to take a vacation to Poland for two weeks; and the mother declared that she did not want to return to the United States and that she would not allow the minor child to return to this country with the father. The court found that the retention of the child in Poland by mother was a violation of the Hague Convention, which was ratified by the United States in 1988. The court, pursuant to Article 15 of the Convention, determined that the habitual residence of the child was Lehigh County, Pennsylvania and that the child's retention in Poland by mother was wrongful within the meaning of Article 3 of the Convention and a breach of the custody rights of her father. The court ordered the return of the child to Lehigh County, pursuant to Article 18 of the Convention, after which a final hearing on custody would be held).

Chapter 17

APPEALS

---

§ 17.1. Appeal From Custody Order
§ 17.2. Appellate Review of Custody Order

§ 17.1. APPEAL FROM CUSTODY ORDER

Appeals of child custody orders follow the Children's Fast Track. This differs from the appeal process of non-child custody orders. Pursuant to Pa.R.A.P. 1925(a)(2)(i): "the concise statement of errors complained of on appeal shall be filed and served with the notice of appeal required by Rule 905."[1] However, the Pennsylvania Superior Court has declined to extend the bright-line waiver rule the Supreme Court adopted in *Commonwealth v. Castillo*, 888 A.2d 775 (Pa. 2005), to deem an appellant's issues waived in a Children's Fast Track case for failing to comply with the amended rule of filing the concise statement of errors complained of on appeal concurrently with the notice of appeal.[2] However, if a court (trial court or Superior Court) issues an order to file a Rule 1925(b) statement, and the appellant files the 1925(b) statement after the court ordered deadline, any claims on appeal will be deemed waived.[3]

"In civil cases, Rule 1925(b) implicates the notice procedure set in Pa.R.C.P. 236, which involves the following steps: (1) the court must

---

[1] Pa.R.A.P. 1925(a)(2)(i).

[2] J.P. v. S.P., 991 A.2d 904 (Pa. Super. 2010); J.M.R. v. J.M., 1 A.3d 902 (Pa. Super. 2010); In Re: K.T.E.L., 983 A.2d 745 (Pa. Super. 2009).

[3] *Id.*; *see also* Giles v. Douglass, 747 A.2d 1236 (Pa. Super. 2000) (Superior Court refused to review father's appeal of the grant of primary physical custody to mother; where father did not submit a Pa.R.A.P. 1925(b) statement of matters complained of on appeal which held that he failed to preserve any appellate issues); S.S. v. T.J., 212 A.3d 1026 (Pa. Super. 2019) (Superior Court held that father's *pro se* appeal of the denial of his petition to modify custody failed because his Pa.R.A.P. 1925(b) statement was not sufficiently coherent to allow the trial court to understand the specific allegations of error).

order the Rule 1925(b) Statement; (2) the order must be filed with the prothonotary; (3) upon receipt of an order from a judge, the prothonotary must immediately docket the order and record in the docket the date it was made; and (4) the prothonotary must furnish a copy of the order to each party or attorney and must record in the docket the giving of a notice. If any one of these procedural steps is missing, the appellant's failure to comply with Rule 1925(b) will not result in waiver of the issues raised."[4]

Further, it is important to remember that pursuant to Pennsylvania Rule of Civil Procedure 205.1, the controlling date to determine "timeliness" is the date that the trial court receives the Rule 1925(b) Statement and not the date it was mailed.[5] Pursuant to Rule 205.1: "A paper sent by mail shall not be deemed filed until received by the appropriate officer."[6]

In custody appeals, upon receipt of the notice of appeal and the concise statement of errors complained of on appeal, the trial judge has 30 days to file of record at least a brief opinion of the reasons for the order or the rulings or for the errors complained of if the reasons for the order do not already appear of record.[7] The brief opinion may, but need not refer to the transcript of the hearing.[8] As a reminder, in every case, including cases where there may be no appeal, 23 Pa.C.S. § 5323(d) provides that the court shall delineate the reasons for its decision on the record in open court or in a written opinion or order.[9] Further, an order of custody must be entered as a separate written order, or as a separate section of a written opinion and not only in a transcript.[10] If the custody decision is entered

---

[4] J.P. v. S.P., 991 A.2d 904 (Pa. Super. 2010) (*citing* Forest Highlands Community Ass'n v. Hammer, 879 A.2d 223, 227 (Pa. Super. 2005)).

[5] *See* J.P. v. S.P., 991 A.2d 904 (Pa. Super. 2010).

[6] Pa.R.C.P. 205.1.

[7] Pa.R.A.P. 1925(a)(2)(ii).

[8] *Id.*

[9] 23 Pa.C.S. § 5323(d); Pa.R.C.P. 1915.10.

[10] *See* R.L.P. v. R.F.M., 110 A.3d 201 (Pa. Super. 2015).

as a separate section of an opinion, it must be designated as such by the use of the heading titled "Order."[11]

A notice of appeal from a custody order may be filed with the clerk of the lower court at any time within 30 days of the entry of the initial custody order.[12] Cross-appeals may be filed within 14 days of the date on which the first notice of appeal was filed.[13] Failure to appeal a custody order within the allotted period finalizes the order as to the parties to the action as of the time of the entry of the order.[14]

An extension of time for taking appeal can be permitted only in those cases where there has been fraud or some breakdown in the court's operation. Where an appeal was not taken from termination of parental rights because three weeks after the entry of the decree parents' attorney's mother had a massive heart attack that required him to be at her side for the next two weeks, during which the parents called to direct their attorney to take appeal, the parents' petition to File Notice of Appeal *nunc pro tunc* was denied. Appellants' attorney's absence from his office for two weeks without making special arrangements to ensure fulfillment of his professional obligations was not adequate reason to disregard the strict time periods for taking appeals.[15]

A court lacks the authority to vacate a custody order beyond the 30-day appeal period. Under Pa.R.C.P. 1915.10(b) motions for post-trial relief may not be filed to an order of custody.[16]

---

[11] *Id.*

[12] Pa.R.A.P. 902, 903(a); *see also* R.L.P. v. R.F.M., 110 A.3d 201 (Pa. Super. 2015) (Superior Court provided reminder that pursuant to Pa.R.A.P. 905(a)(5) "a notice of appeal filed after the announcement of a determination but before the entry of an appealable order shall be treated as filed after such entry and on the day thereof.").

[13] Pa.R.A.P. 903(b).

[14] A request for a stay pending appeal of a modified custody order will be denied where the appeal period has expired. Hunter v. McGraw, 32 Adams Leg. J. 119 (1990); Commonwealth ex rel. Swanson v. Barry, 199 Pa. Super. 244, 184 A.2d 370 (1962).

[15] In re Interest of C.K., 369 Pa. Super. 445, 535 A.2d 634 (1987).

[16] Moore v. Moore, 393 Pa. Super. 256, 574 A.2d 105 (1990).

Upon appeal, it becomes the burden of the moving party to demonstrate that the order of the lower court is erroneous, based on mistake of law[17] or premised on an abuse of discretion.[18]

It should also be noted that, as in other forms of litigation, where an appeal is taken from a custody order, the lower court loses jurisdiction over the subject matter of the case until the appellate court rules subject to the exceptions stated in Pa.R.A.P. 1701(b).[19] Likewise, the filing of a motion for reconsideration does not toll the appeal period. [20] The trial court must expressly grant reconsideration to toll the appeal period.[21]

Pa.R.A.P. 1701(b)(3) allows a trial court to entertain a petition for reconsideration after an appeal is taken as long as the petition is timely filed. Timely grant of reconsideration by the trial court renders an already filed notice of appeal inoperative—the time for appeal begins to run anew when the trial court renders a decision after reconsideration. However, the denial of a motion/petition for reconsideration does not restart the clock for the 30-day window to appeal, as such a denial is not final or otherwise appealable.[22] Therefore, to be safe, the filing of an appeal along with the motion for reconsideration is the best method as reiterated by the J.P. decision.[23] But note the discussion in *Moore v. Moore*,[24] which appears to suggest that a petition for reconsideration cannot be entertained by the trial court even if timely filed, thereby placing custody cases outside the operation of Pa.R.A.P. 1701(b)(3).

---

[17] Trefsgar v. Trefsgar, 261 Pa. Super. 1, 395 A.2d 273 (1978); Commonwealth ex rel. O'Hey v. McCurdy, 199 Pa. Super. 22, 184 A.2d 290, (1962); Commonwealth ex rel. Hough v. Hough, 173 Pa. Super. 484, 116 A.2d 274 (1955).

[18] In re Custody of Neal, 260 Pa. Super. 1, 393 A.2d 1057 (1978); Tobias v. Tobias, 248 Pa. Super. 168, 374 A.2d 1372 (1977).

[19] Bartle v. Bartle, 304 Pa. Super. 348, 450 A.2d 715 (1982).

[20] Valentine v. Wroten, 397 Pa. Super. 526, 580 A.2d 757 (1990).

[21] *Id. See also* JP v. JS, 214 A.3d 1284 (Pa. Super. 2019) (the Superior Court in J.P. suggests that the trial court should also vacate the order in addition to granting the reconsideration petition).

[22] *See* J.P. v. J.S., 214 A.3d 1284 (Pa. Super. 2019).

[23] *Id.*

[24] Moore v. Moore, 393 Pa. Super. 256, 574 A.2d 105 (1990).

In *Valentine v. Wroten*,[25] the Superior Court held that an order denying reconsideration is not appealable. The court quashed an appeal from an order denying reconsideration of an order that denied a request for temporary custody of minor children in a protection from abuse action. The appeal was not filed within thirty days of the original order, and the trial court did not expressly grant reconsideration within the thirty-day appeal period. Consequently, the majority concluded that the appeal was untimely. The trial court's granting of a rule to show cause did not operate to toll the thirty-day appeal period. The trial court must expressly grant reconsideration to toll the appeal period.

A child custody order will be considered a "final order" and appealable only if it is both entered after the court has completed its hearings on the merits and intended by the court to constitute a complete resolution of custody claims pending between parties.[26] However, an order granting third-party *in loco parentis* status for standing in a custody proceeding has been found to be immediately appealable since a parent has a fundamental right to be free of custody litigation involving third parties and would incur a substantial financial burden as a result of litigation and lost time with the child during the appeal process.[27]

In *Kreig v. Kreig*, 743 A.2d 509 (Pa. Super. 1999), the Superior Court ruled that the trial court's denial of father's pre-trial motion to recuse a judge from further child custody proceedings was not a final order from

---

[25] Valentine v. Wroten, 397 Pa. Super. 526, 580 A.2d 757 (1990).

[26] G.B. v. M.M.B., 448 Pa. Super. 133, 670 A.2d 714 (1996) (Trial court's interim order, during marital dissolution and custody proceedings, for partial custody of sons by father was not final appealable order, where order was entered before trial court had completed hearing on merits, where order was not intended to constitute a complete resolution of the parties' dispute regarding partial custody, and where the order was designed to stabilize the parties' relationship during pendency of custody litigation): L.J.C. v. A.W., 160 A.3d 201 (Pa. Super. 2017) (order ruling that grandfather lacked standing to seek primary physical custody was nonappealable where it did not completely resolve custody claims because grandfather could still seek expanded partial physical custody at a pending merits hearing); *see also* K.M.G. v. H.M.W., 171 A.3d 839 (Pa. Super. 2017) (at a contempt proceeding, because the contempt order disposed of all pending claims in the custody action, the contempt order falls within the scope of a final order as defined by Pa.R.A.P. 341).

[27] *See* K.W. v. S.L. & M.L., 157 A.3d 498 (Pa. Super. 2017).

which the father could appeal. The court also noted the father's motion to recuse did not fit within any of the parameters of Rules 311 and 313, which allow appeals as of right from certain interlocutory orders and collateral orders, and therefore, it was not an interlocutory or collateral order that was immediately appealable.

In *Kohut v. Blough*, 860 A.2d 1044 (Pa. Super. 2004) the Superior Court ruled that unless a trial court certifies, or a benefiting party agrees, denials of petitions to transfer venue are interlocutory and unappealable. Here, because the party benefiting from the trial court's denial of a motion to transfer venue in a child custody matter did not file a timely election for the order to be deemed final, the court did not have jurisdiction to hear the case. Pa.R.A.P. 311(b)(1) provides that an appeal from an order denying the transfer of venue is appealable as of right if "the plaintiff, petitioner or other party benefiting from the order files of record, within 10 days after the entry of the order an election that the order shall be deemed final." Here, mother, as the party who benefited from the order, did not file a timely election to have the order deemed final. Therefore, the court determined it did not have jurisdiction to hear this appeal.

An order granting the biological father intervenor status in a pending child custody action was interlocutory and unreviewable, because the order was not intended to constitute a complete resolution of the custody action and did not qualify as a collateral order.[28]

Contempt orders are appealable only after the imposition of sanctions.[29] Further, if a contempt order disposes of all pending claims in the

---

[28] Beltran v. Piersody, 748 A.2d 715 (Pa. Super. 2000), *but see* K.C. and V.C. v. L.A., 128 A.3d 774 (Pa. 2015) (Supreme Court reversed Superior Court's quashing of appeal by third parties in a custody action where trial court denied their petition for intervention asserting standing under 23 Pa.C.S. § 5324 (*in loco parentis*); trial court denied intervention petition based on foster care relationship of third parties not giving rise to *in loco parentis* status for purposes of custody; Superior Court quashed appeal as denial of intervention petition not being a final order; in reversing the Superior Court and remanding the case, the Supreme Court found that the order in question was appealable as a collateral order under Pa.R.A.P 313, as the order met the 3-pronged test under Rule 313(b)).

[29] *See* K.M.G. v. H.M.W., 171 A.3d 839 (Pa. Super. 2017) (*citing* Genovese v. Genovese, 623, 550 A.2d 1021 (Pa. Super. 1988)) (though trial court stated it was not

custody action, the contempt order can fall within the scope of a final appealable order as defined by Pa.R.A.P. 341.[30]

The Superior Court has quashed an appeal when the appellant/mother was appealing an order of contempt after she allegedly abducted the child. As of the time of her appeal she continued to defy the trial court's order by failing to present the child to father for his period of partial custody. The court issued a warrant for mother's arrest and she remained a fugitive at the time of the appeal. In quashing mother's appeal, the Superior Court stated: "While quashing the appeal may not accomplish enforcement of the trial court's order, it will assuredly not grace this appeal with validity."[31]

In *Basham v. Basham*,[32] the Superior Court held that the trial court erred in denying father's petition for contempt of custody without a hearing; where a petition alleges refusal to comply with a court order, and the trial court denies the petition, the denial order is appealable. The court declared: "The court below has not advised this court of its reasons for summarily dismissing Appellant's petition. Rather, the trial judge has opined that his order is not final and therefore is not appealable. That determination is, however, contrary to established case law. Where a petition alleges refusal to comply with a court order, and the trial court denies the petition, the denial order is appealable."

In *In re: L.M.*, 923 A.2d 505 (Pa. Super. 2007), the Superior Court ruled that where the trial court docket did not indicate that mother had received notices of relevant court orders in a termination-of-rights case, neither her appeal nor her Rule 1925(b) statement was untimely. The court found that the docket indicated that the termination order was

---

imposing any sanctions, ordering mother to engage in family counseling with father because family counseling was never previously ordered and could be conducted only at financial cost to Mother constituted a sanction); *but see* N.A.M. v. M.P.W., 168 A.3d 256 (Pa. Super. 2017) (Superior Court found that trial court abused its discretion by failing to impose any sanctions on mother despite her flagrant and ongoing contempt of court orders that had been continuing for 10 years; the Superior Court found that the order appealed was a collateral order and was appealable as of right and remanded the case for imposition of sanctions).

[30] *Id.*

[31] Librett v. Marran, 854 A.2d 1278 (Pa. Super. 2004).

[32] Basham v. Basham, 713 A.2d 673 (Pa. Super. 1998).

entered, but did not show that notice of the entry of the order was given to mother. Failure to provide notice violated Pa. R.Civ.P. 236. Accordingly, the court declined to find mother's appellate issues waived. Therefore, the 30-day period was not triggered and mother's appeal was not untimely. However, the court found that no bond existed between mother and L.M., and concluded that there was no evidence to suggest that severing the ties between mother and L.M. would be harmful to the child. "Our careful review of the record reveals considerable unchallenged evidence that little if any bond existed between Mother and L.M. . . . There was absolutely no evidence that severing the ties between Mother and L.M. would have a negative effect on the child. Rather, unrefuted testimony indicated that L.M. was strongly bonded to her foster mother and was thriving in her foster home."

In *In the Interest of J.S.C.*, 851 A.2d 189 (Pa. Super. 2004), the Superior Court ruled that the Monroe County CYS did not have a right to appeal an order directing visitation between a child in its custody and her mother who was incarcerated. The trial court's order compelling visitation between a dependent child and her mother was not final and appealable. The order was also not appealable under the collateral order doctrine. The collateral order doctrine exists as an exception to the finality rule and permits immediate appeal as of right from an otherwise interlocutory order where an appellant demonstrates that the order appealed from meets the following elements: (1) it is separable from and collateral to the main cause of action; (2) the right involved is too important to be denied review; and (3) the question presented is such that if review is postponed until final judgment in the case, the claimed right will be irreparably lost. Here, CYS did not show that it possessed a right that was too important to be denied review and that would be lost if review were postponed until final judgment.

In *In re J.S.*, 795 A.2d 985 (Pa. Super. 2001), the Superior Court ruled that the trial court's order was interlocutory and therefore not appealable, since the order did not change the placement goal or direct a change in custody. The court noted that, generally, a change of placement goal is appealable. However, here the order was not final because it did not dispose of all claims and all parties, it was not expressly defined as a final order by statute, and it was not entered as a final order under Pa.R.A.P. 341(c). "The order does not fall under any of the categories of interlocutory appeals as of right under Pa. R.A.P. 311, is not an interlocutory appeal by permission under Pa. R.A.P. 312, and is not a collateral order under Pa. R.A.P. 313 in part because the order is not separable from and collateral to the main cause of action." Rather, the order was interlocutory and unappealable because it did not change the placement goal or order a change in custody.

In *In Re: S.W.*, 781 A.2d 1247 (Pa. Super. 2001), the Superior Court held that where the parents of three minor children exhausted their appellate rights after their parental rights were terminated, they could not challenge the effectiveness of counsel since such a claim may not be raised through a collateral attack by post-decree petition and/or appeal after normal appeals have been exhausted. The court found that the parents had exhausted their appellate rights. The record indicated that the parents first complained of ineffective assistance of counsel only after their petition for allowance of appeal was denied. Citing *In Re: T. M. F.*, 573 A.2d 1035 (Pa. Super. 1990), the court noted that "any determination as to ineffectiveness of counsel must be raised expeditiously in the context of the original appeal, as a collateral attack by post-decree petition and/or appeal, after normal appeals have been exhausted, is not permissible."

In *M.B.S. v. W.E.*, 232 A.3d 922 (Pa. Super. 2020), the Superior Court ruled that since the child at issue would turn 18 in before any potential remand, and the Child Custody Act did not provide an exception for a child who was 18 and still in high school, the court had no jurisdiction and mother's claims challenging the trial court's grant of legal custody to father were moot. In other words, the trial court would not be able to proceed on remand before it lost subject matter jurisdiction. The court also noted that the child's educational status had no bearing upon the child's parents' ability to exercise legal or physical custody over him pursuant to the Child Custody Act.

LOWER COURT CASES

Berks County

Ludwig v. Stepien, C.P. Berks County, No. 04-16445 (C.C.P. 2006) (Mother waived the issues she wished to raise on appeal by failing to serve a copy of her Rule 1925(b) statement on the trial judge. Moreover, mother's appeal was interlocutory and, thus, unappealable because the orders at issue did not dispose of all claims relating to the custody of the parties' minor children. Because mother failed to comply with the rule's requirement that she serve the trial judge with a copy of her concise statement of matters complained of on appeal, mother waived the issues she wished to raise on appeal).

§ 17.2.   APPELLATE REVIEW OF CUSTODY ORDER

Consideration of appellate review of a custody order necessarily involves an analysis of the relative functions and duties of the courts at both the trial and appellate levels. The primary responsibility of the trial court is that of fact-finding. It thus devolves upon the trial judge to ascertain every available fact which may have a bearing on the best interests of the child, and ensure that a full and complete record is created when a decision as important as the welfare of a child is at issue.[33] Where the parties themselves do not present sufficient testimony, it becomes the duty of the trial judge to make such orders and conduct such investigations as required to supplement the parties' presentations.[34] This will enable the appellate court to properly discharge its reviewing function.

The Supreme Court in *Moore v. Moore*, 535 Pa. 18, 634 A.2d 163 (1993), *citing McMillen v. McMillen*, 529 Pa. 198, 202, 602 A.2d 845, 847 (1992), articulated the proper standard of review in a custody case:

The scope of review of an appellate court reviewing a child custody order is of the broadest type; the appellate court is not bound by the deductions or inferences made by the trial court from its findings of fact, nor must the reviewing court accept a finding that has no competent evidence to support it. However, this broad scope of review does not vest in the reviewing Court the duty or the privilege of making its own independent determination. Thus an appellate court is empowered to determine

---

[33] Moore v. Moore, 634 A.2d 163 (Pa. 1993); Swope v. Swope, 689 A.2d 264 (Pa. Super. 1997); Zummo v. Zummo, 574 A.2d. 1130 (Pa. Super. 1990); Costello v. Costello, 446 Pa. Super. 371, 666 A.2d 1096 (1995).

[34] Parks v. Parks, 284 Pa. Super. 400, 426 A.2d 108 (1981); Lewis v. Lewis, 267 Pa. Super. 235, 406 A.2d 781 (1979); Commonwealth ex rel. Cox v. Cox, 255 Pa. Super. 508, 388 A.2d 1082 (1978).

whether the trial court's incontrovertible factual findings support its factual conclusions, but it may not interfere with those conclusions unless they are unreasonable in view of the trial court's factual findings; and thus, represent a gross abuse of discretion.[35]

There is no distinction between a "gross abuse of discretion," and an "abuse of discretion." The standard of review is "whether the trial court's conclusions are unreasonable as shown by the evidence of record."[36]

In *Commonwealth ex rel. Robinson v. Robinson*,[37] the Pennsylvania Supreme Court reversed the Superior Court based on the appellate court's intrusion into the domain of the fact-finder. The Court stated that unless there exists a "gross abuse of discretion" in the fact-finding process, both the facts found and the factual conclusions flowing therefrom are not to be disturbed by the appellate court. Quoting from *Commonwealth ex rel. Spriggs v. Carson*,[38] the Court indicated that at

---

[35] Moore v. Moore, 634 A.2d at 168 (internal citations omitted). By footnote, the Supreme Court in Moore pointed out that, although "the McMillen Court used the phrase 'scope of review' it is obvious that they were clearly defining the 'standard of review'. The 'scope of review' refers to the jurisdiction of the Court to review properly preserved issues, while the 'standard of review' sets forth the guidelines within which the properly preserved issues be considered and decided." *Id.*, 634 A.2d at 168; Commonwealth ex rel. Pierce v. Pierce, 493 Pa. 292, 426 A.2d 555 (1981); Commonwealth ex rel. Myers v. Myers, 468 Pa. 134, 360 A.2d 587 (1976); Garrity v. Garrity, 268 Pa. Super. 217, 407 A.2d 1323 (1979).

[36] Moore v. Moore, 634 A.2d at 168 n.4.

[37] Com. v. Robinson v. Robinson, 505 Pa. 226, 478 A.2d 800 (1984).

[38] 470 Pa. 290, 368 A.2d 635 (1977); *see also* McMillen v. McMillen, 529 Pa. 198, 602 A.2d 845 (1992) (an appellate court is empowered to determine whether the trial court's incontrovertible factual findings support its factual conclusions, but it may not interfere with those conclusions unless they are unreasonable in view of the trial court's factual findings, and thus, represent a gross abuse of discretion); Karis v. Karis, 518 Pa. 601, 544 A.2d 1328 (1988) (an appellate court is empowered to determine whether the trial court's incontrovertible factual findings support the trial court's legal conclusions, but may not interfere with those conclusions unless they are unreasonable in light of the trial court's factual findings); Lombardo v. Lombardo, 515 Pa. 139, 527 A.2d 525 (1987); Cardamone v. Elshoff, 442 Pa. Super. 263, 659 A.2d 575 (1995) (Scope of review of appellate court reviewing in child custody order is of the broadest type; appellate court is not bound by deductions or inferences made by trial court from its findings of fact, nor must reviewing court accept finding that has no competent evidence to support it, but reviewing court does not have the duty or privilege to make its

least the trial court's factual findings and factual conclusions would be subject to a gross abuse of discretion standard of review. This approach was extensively propounded in a Superior Court case, *In Re Donna W.,*[39] decided prior to *Robinson*. In *In Re Donna W.,* the court went to great lengths to explain the interplay of the abuse of discretion standard for factual findings and the independent review of the legal conclusions drawn therefrom, and to stress that the two are not mutually exclusive. In so doing, the court offered a four-stage analysis in which the appellate court first examines the procedural aspects of the record and determines whether sufficient testimony has been taken and the court has filed a complete and comprehensive opinion. Next, the court looks at the trial court's findings of fact to determine whether they are supported by the record. Assuming all is in order, the court would scrutinize the trial court's conclusions to ascertain that no errors of law have been committed. Finally, the court will then determine what proper inferences and deductions should be drawn from the facts as found by the trial court.

In *Ellingsen v. Magsamen,*[40] the court found that a gross abuse of discretion standard is to be applied to all phases of the trial court's decision.

In order to ensure that the best interests of the child are being served, the court must conduct a comprehensive review of the case.[41] This review consists of an examination of the record and a judgment on its completeness; a careful scrutiny of the trial court's opinion to determine whether

---

own independent determination); Kaneski v. Kaneski, 413 Pa. Super. 173, 604 A.2d 1075 (1992) (an appellate court may review the factual findings of the trial court to determine if they are factually supported, but may not interfere with these conclusions unless they are unreasonable and thus constitute a gross abuse of discretion); Johnson v. Diesinger, 404 Pa. Super. 41, 589 A.2d 1160 (1991) (on appeal the court may determine whether the trial court's factual findings support its conclusion, but it cannot disturb these conclusions unless unsupported by the evidence); Barron v. Barron, 406 Pa. Super. 401, 594 A.2d 682 (1991); Andrews v. Andrews, 411 Pa. Super. 286, 601 A.2d 352 (1991).

[39] 325 Pa. Super. 39, 472 A.2d 635 (1984).

[40] Ellingsen v. Magsamen, 337 Pa. Super. 14, 486 A.2d 456 (1984).

[41] Mahoney v. Mahoney, 354 Pa. Super. 585, 512 A.2d 694 (1986); Murphey v. Hatala, 350 Pa. Super. 433, 504 A.2d 917 (1986); Parks v. Parks, 284 Pa. Super. 400, 426 A.2d 108 (1981); In re Custody of Myers, 242 Pa. Super. 225, 363 A.2d 1242 (1976).

the opinion thoroughly analyzes the testimony; and a careful review of the merits and an independent judgment as to the best interests of the child based on that review. Although the scope of appellate review is broad, courts of review are bound by the lower court's findings of fact supported by the record, since it is the trial judge who sees the witnesses, hears their testimony, and is therefore better able to make an assessment of their credibility.[42] Incursion into the fact-finding province by the Superior Court has been cause for reversal on appeal to the Pennsylvania Supreme Court.[43]

At the conclusion of its review, the appellate court may either affirm, remand, or reverse the decision of the lower court. Affirmance of a custody order will occur in one of two situations, the first being where all relevant factors have been presented in testimony and the judge has filed a comprehensive opinion demonstrating an accurate understanding of the facts and applicable principles of law.[44] In such cases, the appellate

---

[42] Commonwealth ex rel. Spriggs v. Carson, 470 Pa. 290, 368 A.2d 635 (1977); Norris v. Tearney, 422 Pa. Super. 246, 619 A.2d 339 (1993) ("In reviewing a custody order, we are not bound by findings of fact made by the trial court which are unsupported in the record, nor are we bound by the court's inferences drawn from the facts. However, on issues of credibility and weight of the evidence, we defer to the findings of the trial judge, who has had the opportunity to observe the proceedings and the demeanor of the witnesses. Only where we find that the custody order is manifestly unreasonable as shown by the evidence of record . . . will an appellate court interfere with the trial court's determination"); Altus-Baumhor v. Baumhor, 407 Pa. Super. 276, 595 A.2d 1147 (1991); Artzt v. Artzt, 383 Pa. Super. 23, 566 A.2d 409 (1989); Nancy E.M. v. Kenneth D.M., 316 Pa. Super. 351, 462 A.2d 1386 (1983); Parks v. Parks, 284 Pa. Super. 400, 426 A.2d 108 (1981); In re Clouse, 244 Pa. Super. 404, 368 A.2d 780 (1976); Clair Appeal, 219 Pa. Super. 436, 281 A.2d 726 (1971); Commonwealth ex rel. Doberstein v. Doberstein, 201 Pa. Super. 102, 192 A.2d 154 (1963).

[43] Commonwealth ex rel. Davenport v. Montgomery County Children and Youth Services, 501 Pa. 472, 462 A.2d 221 (1983); Commonwealth ex rel. Spriggs v. Carson, 470 Pa. 290, 368 A.2d 635 (1977).

[44] Harner v. Harner, 330 Pa. Super. 343, 479 A.2d 583 (1984); see Wrecsics v. Broughton, 285 Pa. Super. 90, 426 A.2d 1155 (1981); McCourt v. Meyers, 268 Pa. Super. 152, 407 A.2d 875 (1979); In re Custody of Neal, 260 Pa. Super. 151, 393 A.2d 1057 (1978).

court must defer to the judgment of the trial court unless an abuse of discretion is present.[45]

Credibility determinations made by the trial court are accorded great deference, for it is the trial court which witnesses the demeanor of the parties and sees and hears the evidence first-hand. Therefore, unless a gross abuse of discretion is shown, appellate courts will not interfere with orders awarding custody. The appellant has the burden to establish such an abuse in order to prevail.[46]

A second type of case suitable for affirmation consists of a slightly deficient trial record, a not so comprehensive opinion, or both. In spite of such shortcomings, the appellate court may feel that enough evidence has been presented and the trial court's opinion is sufficiently enlightening to enable it to formulate an independent decision which, in such cases, is in agreement with that of the lower court.[47]

Reversal of a custody order generally occurs when the trial court has either based its decision on a mistake of fact or has erroneously applied

---

[45] Wiskoski v. Wiskoski, 427 Pa. Super. 531, 629 A.2d 996 (1993) (Trial court displayed improper bias against mother in custody proceeding; trial court concluded mother exaggerated based on her unsophistication and determined her to be incredible based on her testimony that she had overcome her abuse of alcohol); Haller v. Haller, 377 Pa. Super. 330, 547 A.2d 393 (1988) (in reviewing custody matters, appellate court is empowered to determine whether trial court's incontrovertible factual findings support trial court's conclusions, but may not interfere with those conclusions unless they are unreasonable in light of trial court's factual findings and, thus, represent gross abuse of discretion. Burden of proving that trial court's custody decree is manifestly erroneous or constitutes gross abuse of discretion rests on appellant, and absent such proof, appellate court must affirm decision of trial judge, who has singular advantage of observing demeanor of parties and hearing testimony of witnesses); Murphey v. Hatala, 350 Pa. Super. 433, 504 A.2d 917 (1986) (the trial court abused its discretion when it failed to accept the expert testimony as persuasive); Tobias v. Tobias, 248 Pa. Super. 168, 374 A.2d 1372 (1977).

[46] Stolarik v. Novak, 401 Pa. Super. 171, 584 A.2d 1034 (1991); Artzt v. Artzt, 383 Pa. Super. 23, 566 A.2d 409 (1989); Mumma v. Mumma, 380 Pa. Super. 18, 550 A.2d 1341 (1988).

[47] Nancy E.M. v. Kenneth D.M., 316 Pa. Super. 351, 462 A.2d 1386 (1983); Commonwealth ex rel. Husack v. Husack, 273 Pa. Super. 192, 417 A.2d 233 (1979); Sweeney v. Sweeney, 241 Pa. Super. 235, 361 A.2d 302 (1976).

or relied on a statement of law.[48] Outright reversal will, however, be ordered only where the facts on the record are sufficiently clear to allow the appellate court to make its own determination of the best interests of the child.[49] Reversal may also occur when the reviewing court disagrees with the weight accorded certain factors or finds fault with the inferences or conclusions drawn by the trial court.[50]

---

[48] In re Custody of Hernandez, 249 Pa. Super. 274, 376 A.2d 648 (1977).

[49] McAnallen v. McAnallen, 300 Pa. Super. 406, 446 A.2d 918 (1982); *see also* Johnson v. Diesinger, 404 Pa. Super. 41, 589 A.2d 1160 (1991) (in a custody proceeding it is reversible error not to take into consideration the best interest of the children); Parks v. Parks, 284 Pa. Super. 400, 426 A.2d 108 (1981); Jon M.W. v. Brenda K., 279 Pa. Super. 50, 420 A.2d 738 (1980); Pamela J.K. v. Roger D.J., 277 Pa. Super. 579, 419 A.2d 1301 (1980); In re Custody of Hernandez, 249 Pa. Super. 274, 376 A.2d 648 (1977).

[50] C.B. v. J.B. and M.B. and T.B., 65 A.3d 946 (Pa. Super. 2013) (New custody Act requires that the trial court address each factor in Section 5328 before deadline by which litigant must file notice of appeal and preferably by time custody order issued or shortly thereafter); A.M.S. v. M.R.C., 70 A.3d 830 (Pa. Super. 2013) (Reasoning in C.B. v. J.B. and M.B. and T.B., 65 A.3d 946 (Pa. Super. 2013) applies to relocation decisions as well); A.V. v. S.T., 87 A.3d 818 (Pa. Super. 2014) (The trial court erred when it granted a mother's petition to relocate with the parties' minor children to New Jersey because it also modified the prior physical custody agreement, but it failed to consider statutory factors under 23 Pa.C.S. § 5328(a) in addition to those it considered with respect to relocation under 23 Pa.C.S. § 5337); *see also* M.O. v. J.T.R., 85 A.3d 1058 (Pa. Super. 2014) (court need not address all 16 factors under § 5328 when deciding discrete and narrow issues ancillary to materially unchallenged custody arrangement); S.W.D. v. S.A.R., 96 A.3d 396 (Pa. Super. 2014) (deciding a legal custody dispute such as the selection of a school that does not affect the form of the custody arrangement does not require an analysis of all of the 16 custody factors under Section 5328(a) as it is considered an ancillary issue); V.B. and C.B. v. J.E.B. and C.C., 55 A.3d 1193 (Pa. Super. 2012) (when trial court abused its descretion and the record is sufficiently developed the appellate court may substitute its judgment for that of the trial court and decide the case on the merits. Superior court reversed trial court, reversed custody award to grandparents and awarded father custody and remanded case for trial court to fashion custody schedule); M.P. v. M.P., 54 A.3d 950 (Pa. Super. 2012) (trial court order denying mother with sole legal custody permission to travel to Ecuador with child reversed by Superior Court); Smith v. Smith, 307 Pa. Super. 544, 453 A.2d 1020 (1982) (reversed trial court's modification on joint custody arrangement and order of sole custody, finding that trial court placed undue emphasis on fact that parties would be living 120 miles from each other); Robert H.H. v. May L.H., 293 Pa. Super. 431, 439 A.2d 187 (1982); L.D. v. B.D., 291 Pa. Super. 589, 436 A.2d 657 (1981);

Circumstances commonly prompting reversal include reliance on the defunct Tender Years Doctrine;[51] the failure to accord proper weight to a specific factor such as the time spent in the uninterrupted custody of one of the parties[52] or the preference of the child;[53] or the failure to properly apply an accepted policy or doctrine.[54] One trial court also triggered reversal by improperly characterizing a dispute as one between a parent and a non-parent and consequently applying an incorrect burden of proof.[55]

The third alternative, remand, is the most prevalent order entered by the appellate courts. The large majority of remands fall into one of three categories. Where the trial judge fails in his or her responsibility to fully and properly develop the record of testimony, the appellate court may remand for additional hearings.[56] Deficiencies cited in this respect frequently consist of failure to obtain disinterested testimony as to the parties' homes and/or parenting abilities;[57] failure to elicit testimony from newly acquired spouses or individuals with whom a party resides;[58] failure to obtain psy-

---

Commonwealth ex rel. Pierce v. Pierce, 493 Pa. 292, 426 A.2d 555 (1981); Haraschak v. Haraschak, 268 Pa. Super. 173, 407 A.2d 886 (1979); Trefsgar v. Trefsgar, 261 Pa. Super. 1, 395 A.2d 273 (1978).

[51] Miller v. Miller, 327 Pa. Super. 45, 474 A.2d 1165 (1984); Haraschak v. Haraschak, 268 Pa. Super. 173, 407 A.2d 886 (1979); Bedio v. Bedio, 268 Pa. Super. 225, 407 A.2d 1331 (1979); McGowan v. McGowan, 248 Pa. Super. 41, 374 A.2d 1306 (1977).

[52] Haraschak v. Haraschak, 268 Pa. Super. 173, 407 A.2d 886 (1979).

[53] Commonwealth ex rel. Pierce v. Pierce, 493 Pa. 292, 426 A.2d 555 (1981); Commonwealth ex rel. Bowser v. Bowser, 224 Pa. Super. 1, 302 A.2d 450 (1973).

[54] Commonwealth ex rel. Steuer v. Steuer, 244 Pa. Super. 302, 368 A.2d 732 (1976).

[55] Haraschak v. Haraschak, 268 Pa. Super. 173, 407 A.2d 886 (1979).

[56] Bowers v. Widrig, 318 Pa. Super. 198, 464 A.2d 1299 (1983); Beichner v. Beichner, 294 Pa. Super. 36, 439 A.2d 737 (1982); Kozlowski v. Kozlowski, 362 Pa. Super. 516, 524 A.2d 1995 (1987); Kessler v. Gregory, 271 Pa. Super. 121, 412 A.2d 605 (1979); Lewis v. Lewis, 267 Pa. Super. 235, 406 A.2d 781 (1979); Valentino v. Valentino, 259 Pa. Super. 395, 393 A.2d 885 (1978).

[57] Bowers v. Widrig, 318 Pa. Super. 198, 464 A.2d 1299 (1983); V.B. v. M.L.T.B., 321 Pa. Super. 36, 467 A.2d 880 (1983); J.F.G. v. K.A.G., 278 Pa. Super. 25, 419 A.2d 1337 (1980).

[58] In re Custody of J.S.S., 298 Pa. Super. 428, 444 A.2d 1251 (1982); J.F.G. v. K.A.G., 278 Pa. Super. 25, 419 A.2d 1337 (1980); Lewis v. Lewis, 267 Pa. Super. 235, 406 A.2d 781 (1979); Valentino v. Valentino, 259 Pa. Super. 395, 393 A.2d 885 (1978).

chiatric evidence where the mental state of one of the parties has been placed at issue;[59] or the failure to ascertain the child's preference or utilizing improper procedures in so doing.[60] Remand may also be required in cases in which the court admits into evidence the reports of experts without the testimony of the author of the report, thus depriving a party of the opportunity to cross-examine the witness, as well as depriving the appellate court of a complete record on which to base its decision.[61]

A second type of remand is ordered where the trial judge, having heard ample testimony, fails to comprehensively analyze the information. In such cases, the sufficiency of the record will enable the appellate court to reach a decision in spite of the trial opinion's inadequacies.[62] In other instances, however, the testimony may be such that without a clear, thorough opinion from the trier of fact who has observed the presentation of the evidence, the appellate court is ill-equipped to render a best-interests determination.[63] It is in this latter circumstance that the reviewing court will order a remand for a comprehensive opinion, pointing out precisely which aspects of the initial opinion it finds defective.[64] Similarly, where it is clear that the trial judge has errantly relied on a misstatement of law or fact or has improperly weighed a factor, the appellate court may remand with directions to file a supplemental opinion rectifying the error.[65]

---

[59] Commonwealth ex rel. Newcomer v. King, 301 Pa. Super. 239, 447 A.2d 630 (1982); Rupp v. Rupp, 268 Pa. Super. 467, 408 A.2d 883 (1979); Gunter v. Gunter, 240 Pa. Super. 382, 361 A.2d 307 (1976).

[60] Commonwealth ex rel. Lee v. Lee, 248 Pa. Super. 155, 374 A.2d 1365 (1977).

[61] Ottolini v. Barrett, 954 A.2d 610 (Pa. Super. 2008); Coble v. Coble, 323 Pa. Super. 445, 470 A.2d 1002 (1984); Hall v. Luick, 314 Pa. Super. 460, 461 A.2d 248 (1983); English v. English, 322 Pa. Super. 234, 469 A.2d 270 (1983). *But see* Commonwealth ex rel. Robinson v. Robinson, 505 Pa. 226, 234, 478 A.2d 800 (1984) (Supreme Court found that where reports are admitted without the testimony of the author, there are no objections, and the matter is not raised on appeal by either party, the issue should not be raised *sua sponte* by the Superior Court).

[62] *See* § 17.2, n. 42 & 44.

[63] Strapple v. Strapple, 263 Pa. Super. 187, 397 A.2d 809 (1979); Commonwealth ex rel. Forrester v. Forrester, 25 8 Pa. Super. 397, 392 A.2d 852 (1978).

[64] Strapple v. Strapple, 263 Pa. Super. 187, 397 A.2d 809 (1979).

[65] Commonwealth ex rel. C.A.F. v. M.R.F., 281 Pa. Super. 258, 422 A.2d 157 (1980); Garrity v. Garrity, 268 Pa. Super. 217, 407 A.2d 1323 (1979); Commonwealth

Flaws requiring remand for a comprehensive opinion generally include failure to comment on the credibility of the witnesses;[66] failure to analyze the parties' parenting abilities or capacity to financially provide for the child;[67] failure to analyze the effects of certain factors on the child;[68] or the failure to investigate the work schedules, party availability or babysitting arrangements of one or both parties.[69] Remand may also be ordered where the court fails to provide for appropriate custody by the non-custodial party.[70]

Many cases requiring only a more thorough opinion have, however, been lingering about the judicial system for substantial periods of time. In such cases the Superior Court, while ordering only a comprehensive opinion, will often note that the testimony on the record may be somewhat stale and that the trial judge, in his or her discretion, may wish to conduct additional hearings to update the record.[71] A rehearing

---

ex rel. Schall v. Schall, 251 Pa. Super. 262, 380 A.2d 478 (1977); Commonwealth ex rel. Ulmer v. Ulmer, 231 Pa. Super. 144, 331 A.2d 665 (1974).

[66] Cady v. Weber, 317 Pa. Super. 481, 464 A.2d 423 (1983); Commonwealth ex rel. Newcomer v. King, 301 Pa. Super. 239, 447 A.2d 630 (1982); In re Custody of White, 270 Pa. Super. 165, 411 A.2d 231 (1979); Kimmey v. Kimmey, 269 Pa. Super. 346, 409 A.2d 1178 (1979).

[67] Commonwealth ex rel. Forrester v. Forrester, 258 Pa. Super. 397, 392 A.2d 852 (1978).

[68] Rupp v. Rupp, 268 Pa. Super. 467, 408 A.2d 883 (1979).

[69] Commonwealth ex rel. Lettie H.W. v. Paul T.W., 281 Pa. Super. 262, 422 A.2d 159 (1980); Garrity v. Garrity, 268 Pa. Super. 217, 407 A.2d 1323 (1979).

[70] In re Axling, 498 Pa. Super. 225, 445 A.2d 1193 (1982); Strapple v. Strapple, 263 Pa. Super. 187, 397 A.2d 809 (1979); Sweeney v. Sweeney, 241 Pa. Super. 235, 361 A.2d 302 (1976).

[71] Alfred v. Braxton, 442 Pa. Super. 381, 659 A.2d 1040 (1995) (Custody decision remanded where trial court did not prepare a comprehensive opinion explaining the basis for its decision. The court said, "a trial court opinion must reveal to the appellate court that the lower court conducted a thorough analysis of the record. We are unable to glean any reasons, let alone specific ones, for the trial court's decision." The court remanded the matter reluctantly, noting that it had no alternative where the trial court offered no guidance as to the credibility of the witnesses and made no comment on the relative suitability of the parents); Warren v. Rickabaugh, 410 Pa. Super. 431, 600 A.2d 218 (1991) (on appeal, an appellate court cannot review a decision of the trial court where the lower court did not explain its reasoning in the record. Superior Court could not review trial court's order that travel expenses of children pursuant to

to effect a current re-evaluation of the situation was, however, ordered in a case in which the final hearing on the merits had occurred over two years prior to the date of the Superior Court's opinion.[72]

The fact that the trial judge is no longer sitting has, in some cases, been a partial catalyst in the appellate court's opting to make an independent decision rather than remand. This may occur when the trial record and opinion are sufficiently complete so as to allow for a responsible discharge of the reviewing function, but still leave room for improvement.[73] Thus, on the rationale that to put the child through a fresh battery of litigation is at odds with the best interests of the child, the court will render rather than remand.

It must be noted that a trial court opinion with some findings of fact and discussion of credibility is a *sine qua non* to such a decision as the appellate court is in no position to make such judgments based solely on the cold record.[74]

Unlike findings of fact, appellate courts are not bound by the inferences and conclusions of the trial court.[75] As such, all inferences and conclusions must be based on competent evidence lest the court's decisions

---

custody order be divided between parents, where trial court did not place its rationale on the record, thus requiring remand); Artzt v. Artzt, 383 Pa. Super. 23, 566 A.2d 409 (1989) (effective appellate review in custody disputes requires that the hearing court file a "complete and comprehensive opinion" that contains an exhaustive analysis of the record and specific reasons for the court's ultimate decision by findings of fact and conclusions of law. A remand was dictated by the failure to file an opinion); Parks v. Parks, 284 Pa. Super. 400, 426 A.2d 108 (1981); Garrity v. Garrity, 268 Pa. Super. 217, 407 A.2d 1323 (1979); Valentino v. Valentino, 259 Pa. Super. 395, 393 A.2d 885 (1978); Commonwealth ex rel. Forrester v. Forrester, 258 Pa. Super. 397, 392 A.2d 852 (1978); Commonwealth ex rel. Ulmer v. Ulmer, 231 Pa. Super. 144, 331 A.2d 665 (1974).

[72] Commonwealth ex rel. Lettie H.W. v. Paul T.W., 281 Pa. Super. 262, 422 A.2d 159 (1980).

[73] Parks v. Parks, 284 Pa. Super. 400, 426 A.2d 108 (1981); Commonwealth ex rel. Husack v. Husack, 273 Pa. Super. 192, 417 A.2d 233 (1979); Tomlinson v. Tomlinson, 248 Pa. Super. 196, 374 A.2d 1386 (1977).

[74] Delbaugh v. Delbaugh, 337 Pa. Super. 587, 487 A.2d 417 (1985).

[75] Commonwealth ex rel. Pierce v. Pierce, 493 Pa. 292, 426 A.2d 555 (1981); Commonwealth ex rel. Spriggs v. Carson, 470 Pa. 290, 368 A.2d 635 (1977).

become highly vulnerable to reversal or remand.[76] Appellate courts will, however, give substantial weight to these inferences and conclusions, when adequately accounted for, under the same rationale supporting the conclusiveness of the trial court's findings of fact.[77]

A third type of remand will be ordered where the record is too incomplete to allow for an independent judgment by the reviewing court and where the trial court's opinion is inadequate. In such cases, an order directing additional hearings and a complete and comprehensive opinion will issue.[78]

A proceeding in which the trial court ordered that a minor be placed in the continued custody of her parents will be remanded where the court did not give counsel for the minor and the children and youth services agency an opportunity to present their case and did not perform a comprehensive and searching inquiry in determining the minor's best interests. *In re Donna H*,[79] Donna had been placed in CYS foster care for 12 months because of drug and alcohol abuse by her mother. The mother completed therapy and regained custody of Donna. However, in January, 1991, the police stopped Donna's mother for DUI and found Donna, 20 months old, unrestrained in the back seat. CYS had argued that this incident placed Donna at risk of serious harm from her mother and that she should, therefore, be placed in CYS foster care. The Superior Court held that the trial court did not give counsel for CYS and Donna the opportunity to present their case as to meet their burden of clear and convincing evidence that Donna was at risk. The trial judge should have received evidence from all interested parties.

---

[76] Jon M.W. v. Brenda K., 279 Pa. Super. 50, 420 A.2d 738 (1980); Tomlinson v. Tomlinson, 248 Pa. Super. 196, 374 A.2d 1386 (1977); Commonwealth ex rel. Steuer v. Steuer, 244 Pa. Super. 302, 368 A.2d 732 (1976).

[77] In re Clouse, 244 Pa. Super, 404, 368 A.2d 780 (1976); Clair Appeal, 219 Pa. Super. 436, 281 A.2d 726 (1971); Commonwealth ex rel. Dinsmore v. Dinsmore, 198 Pa. Super. 480, 182 A.2d 66 (1962).

[78] Summers v. Summers, 273 Pa. Super, 285, 417 A.2d 651 (1979); Commonwealth ex rel. Weber v. Weber, 272 Pa. Super. 88, 414 A.2d 682 (1979); Rupp v. Rupp, 268 Pa. Super. 467, 408 A.2d 883 (1979).

[79] 412 Pa. Super. 205, 602 A.2d 1382 (1992). *See also* Altus-Baumhor v. Baumhor, 407 Pa. Super. 276, 595 A.2d 1147 (1991).

LOWER COURT CASES

Montgomery County

Schulman v. Schulman, 129 Montg. Co. L.R. 370 (C.C.P. 1993) (In reviewing the custody order, the appellate court defers to the findings of the trial court on issues of credibility and weight of the evidence, as the trial judge has the opportunity to observe the proceedings and the demeanor of the witnesses).

Chapter 18

TERMINATION OF PARENTAL RIGHTS

§ 18.1. Generally

§ 18.1. GENERALLY

Where a party is seeking not only custody of the child but also an involuntary termination of parental rights, abandonment must be demonstrated.[1] Abandonment of a child consists of conduct on the part of the parent which indicates a settled purpose to evade all parental obligations and relinquish all claims to the child, which conduct must persist for a period of at least six months.[2]

As an allegation of abandonment involves an inquiry into the intent of the parent, it may be refuted with testimony similar to that used to explain the relinquishment of custody.[3] Furthermore, courts are sensitive to the finality and great emotional impact on parent and child of a termination of parental rights and are thus unwilling to reach such a finding unless clearly warranted by the record.[4]

---

[1] In re Adoption of Sarver, 444 Pa. 507, 281 A.2d 890 (1971); Auman v. Eash, 228 Pa. Super. 242, 323 A.2d 94 (1974).

[2] In re Adoption of Sarver, 444 Pa. 507, 281 A.2d 890 (1971); In re Adoption of Austin, 426 Pa. 441, 233 A.2d 526 (1967); Hunter Adoption Case, 421 Pa. 287, 218 A.2d 764 (1966).

[3] See In re Adoption of R.W.B., 485 Pa. 168, 401 A.2d 347 (1979); In re Adoption of F., 475 Pa. 197, 380 A.2d 311 (1977); In re Adoption of M.T.T., 467 Pa. 88, 354 A.2d 564 (1976); In re Adoption of Farabelli, 460 Pa. 423, 333 A.2d 846 (1975).

[4] In re Adoption of F., 475 Pa. 197, 380 A.2d 311 (1977); In re Adoption of Sarver, 444 Pa. 507, 281 A.2d 890 (1971); see also In re B.G., 774 A.2d 757 (Pa. Super. 2001) (trial court, in a dependency case, erred when it issued an order terminating limited supervised visits by the minor's natural parents, where the evidence before the court did not demonstrate that the continued visits posed a grave threat to the child. The court explained that in dependency cases, visitation will not be denied where reunification remains the family service goal, unless the visitation poses a "grave threat."); In re

The grounds for involuntary termination of parental rights are set forth at 23 Pa.C.S. § 2511, which provides:

§ 2511. *Grounds for involuntary termination*

(a) *General rule.*—The rights of a parent in regard to a child may be terminated after a petition filed on any of the following grounds:

(1) The parent by conduct continuing for a period of at least six months immediately preceding the filing of the petition either has evidenced a settled purpose of relinquishing parental claim to a child or has refused or failed to perform parental duties.

(2) The repeated and continued incapacity, abuse, neglect or refusal of the parent has caused the child to be without essential parental care, control or subsistence necessary for his physical or mental well-being and the conditions and causes of the incapacity, abuse, neglect or refusal cannot or will not be remedied by the parent.

(3) The parent is the presumptive but not the natural father of the child.

(4) The child is in the custody of an agency, having been found under such circumstances that the identity or whereabouts of the parent is unknown and cannot be ascertained by diligent search and the parent does not claim the child within three months after the child is found.

(5) The child has been removed from the care of the parent by the court or under a voluntary agreement with an agency for a period of at least six months, the conditions which led to the removal or placement of the child continue to exist, the parent cannot or will not remedy those conditions within a reasonable period of time, the services or assistance reasonably available to the parent are not likely to remedy the conditions which led to the removal or placement of the child within a reasonable period of time and termination

---

Mary Kathryn T., 629 A.2d 988 (Pa. Super. 1993) (denial of partial custody will be ordered only upon showing of clear and convincing evidence that partial custody poses a grave threat to child).

of the parental rights would best serve the needs and welfare of the child.

(6) In the case of a newborn child, the parent knows or has reason to know of the child's birth, does not reside with the child, has not married the child's other parent, has failed for a period of four months immediately preceding the filing of the petition to make reasonable efforts to maintain substantial and continuing contact with the child and has failed during the same four-month period to provide substantial financial support for the child.

(7) The parent is the father of a child conceived as a result of a rape or incest.

(8) The child has been removed from the care of the parent by the court or under a voluntary agreement with an agency, 12 months or more have elapsed from the date of removal or placement, the conditions which led to the removal or placement of the child continue to exist and termination of parental rights would best serve the needs and welfare of the child.

(b) *Other considerations.*—The court in terminating the rights of a parent shall give primary consideration to the developmental, physical and emotional needs and welfare of the child. The rights of a parent shall not be terminated solely on the basis of environmental factors such as inadequate housing, furnishings, income, clothing and medical care if found to be beyond the control of the parent. With respect to any petition filed pursuant to subsection (a) (1), (6) or (8), the court shall not consider any efforts by the parent to remedy the conditions described therein which are first initiated subsequent to the giving of notice of the filing of the petition.

(c) *Right to file personal and medical history information.*—At the time the decree of termination is transmitted to the parent whose rights have been terminated, the court shall advise the parent, in writing, of his or her continuing right to place and update personal and medical history information, whether or not the medical condition is in existence or discoverable at the time of adoption, on file with the court and with the Department of Public Welfare pursuant to section 2905(d) (relating to impounding of proceedings and access to records).

Herein follows an extensive summary of case law pertaining to termination of parental rights.

In the Interest of: T.M.W., 232 A.3d 937 (Pa. Super. 2020) (An order granting a petition for involuntary termination of parental rights and a change of placement goal to adoption was vacated by the Superior Court when the parent faithfully attended every supervised semiweekly visit with the child, was cooperative with DHS services and believed she was receiving appropriate mental health treatment. Accordingly, the court concluded that the trial court erred in changing the goal from reunification to adoption where the evidence simply did not support a change, citing *In Re: A.K.,* 936 A.2d 528 (Pa. Super. 2007).

In Re: Adoption of M.C.F., 230 A.3d 1217 (Pa. Super. 2020) (The remedy in a termination of parental rights case should be the same as in a criminal case—the court must deny the petition to withdraw and remand for counsel to file an advocate's brief. The *Anders* principles have been extended to cases involving the termination of parental rights; however, courts have yet to address the remedy when a non-frivolous issue has been discovered. Although the court found that father's counsel had substantially complied with the technical requirements for withdrawal, the court concluded that counsel had overlooked a potentially meritorious issue—specifically, whether mother had demonstrated that her termination petitions were cognizable because there were anticipated valid adoptions, as mother and fiancée had not yet married at the time mother filed her petitions. The court determined that this issue was not so lacking in merit that counsel should be permitted to withdraw. The court explained that while ultimately, father may not be entitled to any relief, the court could not say that the appeal was wholly frivolous, i.e., without any basis in law or fact).

In the Interest of: D.N.G., a Minor, 230 A.3d 361 (Pa. Super. 2020) (Trial court erred in terminating mother's parental rights where her child was provided ineffective assistance of counsel and where the child expressed opposition to the adoption which was supported by the child's GAL. The child was deprived of his statutory right to counsel to advance his legal interest. The court agreed with mother that appointed counsel did not satisfy the mandate of 23 Pa.C.S. §2313(a), and provided inadequate representation because he neglected to advocate for his client's legal interest. Counsel merely advised the trial court of the child's stated preference but failed to present evidence or testimony or legal argument in support of the child's opposition to adoption and desire to return to mother's care. Counsel failed to join mother in presenting permanent legal custody as an option in lieu of the adoption, or join with the GAL in opposing termination of mother's parental rights. The court noted that while legal representation in this context necessarily involves talking to the child client and reporting the child's preferences to the court, it is in no way limited to those two actions. To the contrary, the court held, pursuant to the majority of justices in *In Re: Adoption of L.B.M.,* 161 A.3d 172, 180 (Pa. 2017), the attorney was required to advocate on behalf of the child and provide zealous client-directed representation of the son's legal interests. Here, counsel did not represent the child's legal interests in advising the court of his client's preference. He did not ask any questions relative to his client's desire to preserve mother's parental rights, and declined to present any legal argument in his client's favor).

In the Interest of: J.R.R., a Minor, 229 A.3d 8 (Pa. Super. 2020) (Trial court erred in involuntarily terminating father's parental rights when it found a bond between parent and child but failed to make findings as to the emotional impact involuntary termination would have on the child. The court recognized that severing close parental ties is usually extremely painful. As such, the court declared that it must consider whether a natural parental bond existed between the child and parent, and whether termination would destroy an existing, necessary and beneficial relationship, citing *In Re: E.M.,* 620 A.2d 481 (Pa. 1993) (order terminating parental rights of the mother reversed by the Supreme Court where the evidence supported termination under §2511(a), but the trial court did not fully explore the emotional needs of the children under §2511(b)). The court noted that the trial court emphasized that it was very impressed with, and greatly commended, the efforts of natural father and the very important bond he had developed with his son under difficult circumstances).

In the Interest of: D.R.-W, 227 A.3d 905 (Pa. Super. 2020) (Father's parental rights were properly terminated where father maintained minimal contact with his children, who had a stronger bond with their foster family, and where the parent's substance abuse and failure to comply with the case plan objectives demonstrated his inability to parent or to remedy the circumstances necessitating the children's placement. The court held that the record supported the trial court's decision to involuntarily terminate father's parental rights pursuant to 23 Pa.C.S. §2511(a)(2). The court noted that DHS was required to obtain emergency custody after father abandoned the children with their maternal grandmother and disappeared. Father later tested positive for opiates and failed to comply with substance abuse assessments, and was incarcerated for a parole violation).

In Re: Adoption of K.M.G., 219 A.3d 662 (Pa. Super. 2019) (Majority of the Superior Court concluded that it lacked authority to consider, *sua sponte*, whether a conflict existed between a child's legal interest and the child's best interest in the context of a contested termination of parental rights proceeding. In *In Re: Adoption of T.M.L.M.*, 184 A.3d 585 (Pa. Super. 2018) the Superior Court had held that it was obligated in every involuntary termination matter to *sua sponte* make an independent determination of whether a GAL had a conflict of interest. The majority now overruled *T.M.L.M.*, ruling instead that it only had the authority and the obligation to *sua sponte* raise the issue of whether the trial court appointed any counsel for a child in an involuntary termination proceeding. The court held that it did not have the authority to review *sua sponte* whether a conflict existed between counsel's representation and the child's stated preference in an involuntary termination of parental rights proceeding. The majority then ruled that it had no authority or obligation to delve into the quality of the representation when it was appointed by the trial court. The court noted that the trial court provided the parties with the opportunity to raise the GAL's conflict of interest and that no party took that opportunity. The majority also noted that the trial court's order appointing the GAL found that the GAL could adequately represent the children's best interest and legal interests without conflict. The majority held that it had no authority or obligation to *sua sponte* review for conflict of interest due to other protections, including a GAL's professional responsibility to notify the court of a conflict of interest and the standing of any party participating in the proceedings to raise a potential conflict of interest to the trial court).

In Re: Involuntary Termination of Parental Rights, J.R.E., a Minor, 218 A.3d 920 (Pa. Super. 2019) (Trial court erred in terminating mother's parental rights because it made no effort to examine mother's explanation for her conduct and did not properly weigh father's lack of cooperation and reasonable accommodation in mother's efforts to maintain contact with the child at issue. Although the record established that mother had no contact with the child during the relevant statutory period, and very little contact for a lengthy period prior to that timeframe, it was equally clear that the lack of contact and support was due, in substantial part, to a lack of cooperation and reasonable accommodation on the part of father, the custodial parent. In addition, the court found that in the circumstances of this case in which the child believed his stepmother was his biological mother, permanently severing mother's bond to perpetuate a relationship built on a misrepresentation, did not clearly serve the long-term well-being and emotional interests of the child. The court held that in the absence of an individualized assessment of the explanations offered by mother who faced permanent severance of her parental conduct to the child, there could be no reasoned determination that the circumstances of this case clearly called for involuntary termination).

In Re: Q.R.D., 214 A.3d 233 (Pa. Super. 2019) (Superior Court affirmed the trial court's decree involuntarily terminating father's parental rights, as the record supported the trial court's finding that the child's preferred outcome was not ascertainable at the time of the hearing, there was no conflict between the child's best interests and legal interests, representation by the child's attorney satisfied the requirements of 23 Pa.C.S. § 2313(a), and stepfather provided clear and convincing evidence to support the termination. The child's attorney credibly testified that the child was immature and did not understand legal proceedings, remember who his father was or have a preferred outcome. The court found that the trial court's appointment of the attorney in the prior action, who represented the child's best interests at the hearing, satisfied § 2313(a)'s mandate that the trial court appoint counsel to represent the child. The court found that legal precedent provided that if the child was incapable of expressing a preferred outcome, there could be no conflict between the child's legal interest and his or her best interest. The court also declared that since father refused or failed to perform parental duties for more than six months prior to the filing of the petition in order to preserve the parent–child relationship, stepfather met his burden under 23 Pa.C.S. § 2511(a)(1). While mother was less than cooperative in enabling father to visit the child, father made no reasonable efforts to overcome her lack of cooperation or maintain contact with his child).

In Re: B.J.Z., 207 A.3d 914 (Pa. Super. 2019) (Superior Court rejected father's argument that the trial court erred in a termination of parental rights case, by allowing statements made by the two oldest children into evidence by way of statements to the court made by the children's legal-interests attorney. Relying on *In Re: Adoption of L.B.M.*, 161 A.3d 172 (Pa. 2017), the court held that it is permissible for the legal-interest counsel to advise the court regarding the children's wishes, to the extent that those wishes could be ascertained. Testimony as to what a child tells other people is admissible in order to establish that child's mental state at the time he or she made the comment, citing *In Re: Child M.*, 681 A.2d 793, 800 (Pa. Super. 1996). Mental health professionals, caseworkers, and the foster parents could testify about their direct observations of the child's conduct).

In Re: C.M.K., a Minor, 203 A.3d 258 (Pa. Super. 2019) (Superior Court ruled that the trial court erred when it denied CYF's petition to involuntarily terminate father's parental rights where the full record revealed father's ongoing drug use and inconsistent attendance at court-ordered drug and family therapy sessions, including those with his children, which indicated a neglect to remedy the causes of his parental incapacity. The court found that the record showed that father was not in compliance with court-ordered alcohol, drug and behavioral treatment, noting that father tested positive for cocaine, had his visits changed to supervised, and failed to appear for multiple drug screenings and family therapy appointments. The court noted that father admitted that he had committed acts of domestic violence against mother, acknowledged the extent of her injuries, and acknowledged that both of their children had likely witnessed the violence).

In Re: K.R., 200 A.3d 969 (Pa. Super. 2018) (A majority of the Superior Court found that CYF met its burden of proving by clear and convincing evidence that mother's parental rights had to be terminated under 23 Pa.C.S. § 2511(a)(8). The majority noted that the court did appoint a GAL who appeared for the children at the termination hearing, the GAL stated that the children expressed their wish to be adopted by their foster family and agreed that CYF met its burden to terminate parental rights. The majority found that the Orphans' Court did not err by not appointing counsel for the children's legal interests because the children were able to express their preferences to the GAL, the GAL expressed those preferences as well as the children's best interests to the Orphans' Court, there was no conflict in those positions and the children's legal interests were adequately represented).

In Re: Adoption of: N.N.H., 197 A.3d 777 (Pa. Super. 2018) Mother's petition to involuntarily terminate father's parental rights was properly denied where mother failed to demonstrate that father's conduct warranted termination; a single threat of violence was insufficient to warrant the drastic step of termination. For the prior six months father had diligently pursued custody rights to exercise his parental duties. Mother acknowledged that she obstructed father's efforts to contact the child due to mother's and father's domestic violence history. But mother also acknowledged that father had regularly written and called the child until mother changed her cell phone number and began refusing his e-mail. Although the court acknowledged that father apparently threatened mother during a conversation with the child, it held that the strife between mother and father, although extremely concerning, was not a basis to permanently sever the parent–child relationship).

In Re: Adoption of: K.C., a Minor, 199 A.3d 470 (Pa. Super. 2018) (Superior Court rejected mother's argument that the evidence was insufficient to meet the requirements of 23 Pa.C.S. § 2511(a)(1) because mother did not know that failing to perform parental duties for six months could lead to a termination of her parental rights; mother's claimed unawareness was irrelevant. The Superior Court affirmed the decree of the trial court granting paternal grandparents' Petition for Termination of Mother's Parental Rights. The court found that mother's claimed unawareness was irrelevant, as her alleged lack of knowledge of the law did not eliminate her obligation to perform parental duties, or undermine the conclusion that she failed to discharge her duties during the relevant six month period. The court rejected mother's argument that the trial court should have granted her request for drug testing of paternal grandparents. No evidence suggested an ongoing drug or alcohol problem, and the failure to order testing based on a single, remote occurrence did not undermine the court's conclusion that termination was in the child's best interest).

In Re: J.T.M., a Minor, 193 A.3d 403 (Pa. Super. 2018) (Trial court did not abuse its discretion in involuntarily terminating father's parental rights, because incarcerated father made no effort to resist the obstacles that limited his ability to maintain a relationship with the child, sending only one letter in six months to the child, the child had not seen father in several years, the child did not want to be placed in father's care, and no conflict existed that warranted the appointment of separate legal counsel for the child. When the best interests and legal interests align and the attorney represents the child's articulated legal interest, and what the attorney views as the best interest, no conflict exists warranting appointment of separate legal counsel for the child).

In Re: J.T.M., a Minor, 193 A.3d 403 (Pa. Super. 2018) (Trial court did not abuse its discretion in involuntarily terminating father's parental rights, because incarcerated father made no effort to resist the obstacles that limited his ability to maintain a relationship with the child, sending only one letter in six months to the child, the child had not seen father in several years, the child did not want to be placed in father's care, and no conflict existed that warranted the appointment of separate legal counsel for the child. Child's legal interests and best interests were aligned throughout the termination proceedings. During the hearing, the child informed the court he did not want to be placed in father's care, and that he hoped to live in a foster home and be adopted. The child's GAL argued on behalf of the child during the hearing and supported the termination of father's parental rights. The attorney GAL represented the child's articulated legal interest, and what the GAL viewed as the child's best interest. The court noted that no conflict existed that would warrant the appointment of separate legal counsel for the child. When the best interests and legal interests align, and the attorney represents the child's articulated legal interest, and what the attorney views as the best interest, no conflict exists warranting appointment of separate legal counsel for the child.).

In *In Re: Adoption of J.N.M., a Minor*, 177 A.3d 937 (Pa. Super. 2018) (Trial court did not err in terminating mother's parental rights where mother and her two children had an undisputed bond, but the bond was unhealthy given mother's mental health problems, continued drug use and ongoing criminal problems. Despite a strong parent–child bond, reunification was not viable since the mother was serving a sentence after being convicted of several offenses since the birth of a child, and failed to address her mental health issues or conditions necessitating placement.

The children had been removed from mother's care for almost 3 years and had been exposed to deplorable conditions in mother's home, as well as domestic violence. Despite the passage of three years, mother failed to remedy the conditions leading to removal of the children. More-over, mother had been sentenced to incarceration until at least 2019, at a minimum. Mother failed to complete any treatment programs and still struggled with her mental health and remaining sober, and her visitation with the children was inconsistent. Accordingly, the court held that the trial court did not err in terminating mother's parental rights pursuant to § 2511(a)(8). The court noted that the trial court acknowledged the children's strong bond with mother, but found that termination best served the children's needs due to the unhealthy nature of the relationship. The court found that, despite the strong bond and some negative impact to the children by terminating mother's parental rights, there was no indication that the children would suffer extreme emotional consequences if the relationship with mother was severed).

In the Interest of: M.R.F., III, 182 A.3d 1050 (Pa. Super. 2018) (Foster parents of a four-year-old child had no standing to intervene in a dependency proceeding where the goal of reunification with mother was never changed and mother never consented to her child's permanent placement with foster parents. The court explained that, whether an individual has standing to participate in dependency proceedings is a question of law. Under the Juvenile Act, party status in dependency proceedings it is limited to three classes of persons: the parents of the juvenile whose dependency is at issue; the legal custodian of the juvenile; or the person whose care and control of the juvenile is it in question. The court found that foster parents here did not fit within any of the classes of individuals with standing in a dependency action. Rather, the court held, they were foster parents to the child and that status did not change at any time in the proceedings. Generally, foster parents do not have standing to participate in dependency proceedings, citing 42 Pa.C.S. § 6336.1. Foster parents, pre-adoptive parents or relatives providing care are entitled only to notice of the hearing and the right to submit a report regarding the child's adjustment, progress and condition. Foster parents were not a party to the dependency proceedings. They were neither the parents nor legal custodians of the child and they were not the people whose care and control was in question. Therefore, foster parents did not have standing to participate in the depend-ency proceedings as a party possessing the rights to counsel, to argue their own interests, to introduce evidence, and/or to cross-examine witnesses, pursuant to 42 Pa.C.S. § 6336.1(a), § 6337, and § 6338. The court also relied upon In Re: J.F., 27 A.3d 10 17 (Pa. Super. 2011) (since foster parent lacked standing, she did not have rights of a party, *i.e.*, the right to counsel, call witnesses, and conduct cross-examination).

In the Interest of: N.M., a Minor, 186 A.3d 998 (Pa. Super. 2018) (Orders denying kinship care and involuntarily terminating paren-tal rights were reversed where the parents complied with service plan goals and where there was no recorded evidence to find that kinship care would place the child at risk. The orders were motivated by the trial court's desire to have parents admit to child abuse rather than the proper purpose of maintaining family unity. Trial court abused its discretion in denying parents' request to have the child transferred to kinship care, holding that the trial court's grave concerns with N.M.'s safety in kin-ship care were unsupported by the record. The court noted that paternal grandmother was willing and able to care for the child, and that E.M. had thrived in her care upon his initial placement. The court held that to deny kinship care based on the unsupported speculation that parents would abuse visitation rights and visit paternal grandmother's home without agency supervision was overreaching. The court concluded that the trial court's repeated refusal to consider approved kinship care, in light of the fact that it also found parents fully compliant with their treatment goals, and where DHS supported kinship placement with paternal grand-mother, was an abuse of discretion and was not supported by the record).

In Re: K.J.H., 180 A.3d 411 (Pa. Super. 2018) (Superior Court held that the trial court erred in violating 23 Pa.C.S. § 2313(a) by failing to appoint counsel for minor children in a parental rights termination pro-ceeding. The court declared that, before it reached the issues presented by paternal grandparents, it would address sua sponte the Or-phans' Court's failure to appoint counsel for the child. A majority of the Supe-rior Court held that the trial court was statutorily obligated to appoint counsel pursuant to 23 Pa.C.S. § 2313(a), and that the failure to do so was a structural error. The court also relied on In re Adoption of G.K.T., 75 A.3d 521, 526 (Pa. Super. 2013), and In Re: Adop-tion of N.A.G.,

471 A.2d 871 (Pa. Super. 1984) (holding that 23 Pa.C.S. § 2313(a) creates a statutory right for a child to have counsel appointed who actively advances his or her needs and welfare and owes loyalty exclusively to him or her). The majority further noted that, because mother was contesting the petition, the trial court was also mandated to appoint her counsel, and thus the child's minority and lack of counsel meant that he was unable to raise this issue by himself. Accordingly, the majority ruled that the trial court erred in not appointing counsel for the child, vacated the order denying paternal grandparents' termination petition, and remanded for further proceedings).

In Re: Adoption of: T.M.L.M., a Minor, 184 A.3d 585 (Pa. Super. 2018) (Minor child in this case involving the potential involuntary termination of mother's parental rights was deprived of his right to counsel where the assigned counsel expressed concern only for the child's best interests but did not address the child's preferred outcome. The child was deprived of his statutory right to counsel, pursuant to 23 Pa.C.S. § 2313(a)).

The court addressed *sua sponte* whether the attorney appointed to represent the child satisfied the requirements of 23 Pa.C.S. § 2313(a), which provides that a child has a statutory right to counsel in contested, involuntary termination proceedings. The court noted that it must raise the failure to appoint statutorily required counsel for children *sua sponte*, as children are unable to raise the issue on their own behalf due to their minority, citing *In Re: K.J.H.*, 180 A.3d 411 (Pa. Super. 2018). The court noted that the Pennsylvania Supreme Court recently decided *In Re Adoption of L.B.M.*, 161 A.3d 172 (Pa. 2017), in which a majority of the justices opined that a child's dependency guardian *ad litem* may serve as his counsel, so long as the guardian *ad litem*'s dual role in representing a child's legal interests and his best interest does not create a conflict of interest. A child's legal interests are distinct from his best interests, and the child's legal interests are synonymous with his preferred outcome, while the child's best interests must be determined by the court. The court explained that like adult clients, effective representation of a child requires, at a bare minimum, attempting to ascertain the client's position and advocating in a manner designed to effectuate that position. The court concluded that, where a court appoints an attorney, ostensibly as counsel, but the attorney never attempts to ascertain the client's position directly and advocates solely for the child's best interest, the child has been impermissibly deprived of his statutory right to counsel serving his legal interests, citing *L.B.M.* The court concluded, that, based upon its review of the record, it had no basis to conclude that the attorney effectively represented the child's legal interests in this matter. Accordingly, the court held that the child was deprived of his statutory right to counsel. The court declared that, upon remand, the court shall appoint separate coun-sel for the child to represent his legal interests).

In *In Re: Adoption of L.B.M., a Minor*, 161 A.3d 172 (Pa. 2017), the Pennsylvania Supreme Court ruled that the trial court erred in failing to appoint independent legal counsel for children in involuntary termination of parental rights proceedings after determining that appointed Guardian ad litem's representation would best represent the children's interest. The plain language of § 2313(a) explicitly mandated the appointment of independent counsel who could advocate for the children's legal interest, as opposed to a Guardian ad litem (GAL) who advocated for the children's best interest. The trial court denied mother's motion for the appointment of legal counsel for the children pursuant to 23 Pa.C.S. § 2313(a), and concluded that the GAL's representation would best serve the children's interest. In support of its decision to deny mother's motion, the trial court relied upon *In Re: K.M.,* 53 A.3d 781 (Pa. Super. 2012), in which the Superior Court held that § 2313(a) did not require appointment of an attorney when a GAL, who was an attorney, had been appointed. A majority of the Supreme Court reversed and remanded the case.

In *In the Matter of the Adoption of: M.A.B.,* 166 A.3d 434 (Pa. Super. 2017), the Superior Court held that the trial court erred in denying a petition to terminate mother and father's parental rights to two special needs children based on a "reasonable probability" that the causes and conditions which led to their placement could be remedied and reunification achieved.

In *In Re: Adoption of C.A.S., a Minor,* 166 A.3d 353 (Pa. Super. 2017), the Superior Court ruled that the trial court erred in failing to grant a continuance and in finding that father waived his right to counsel in a hearing to involuntarily terminate his parental rights. Here, father received six documents, including a blank *in forma pauperis* statement. The court found that since father could have easily been misled by the conflicting and inaccurate instructions, the trial court erred in finding that he waived his right to counsel and failing to grant a continuance. The court emphasized that trial courts must ensure that parents are advised of the right to counsel and are provided with clear instructions on how to petition for counsel.

In *In Re: D.L.B., Minor Child*, 166 A.3d 322 (Pa. Super. 2017), the Superior Court ruled that there was ample evidence to justify the trial court's termination of father's parental rights under 23 Pa.C.S. § 2511(a)(2) because the child was in a pre-adoptive foster home for all of her life, father never had custody of the child, and had virtually no contact or involvement in the child's life.

In *In the Interest of D.F., a Minor*, 165 A.3d 960 (Pa. Super. 2017), the Superior Court ruled that the trial court properly terminated mother's parental rights when the child was adjudicated dependent shortly after birth, and had strongly bonded with foster/pre-adoptive mother. Mother's mental health and drug and alcohol problems interfered with her ability to care for the child, she had not utilized all available resources to deal with her problems and failed to do what was necessary to establish a parent–child relationship.

In *In Re: Adoption of: A.C., a Minor*, 162 A.3d 1123 (Pa. Super. 2017), the Superior Court held that the trial court properly refused to terminate father's parental rights because CYS failed to show that grounds for termination existed under 23 Pa.C.S. § 2511(a)(1) or (a)(2). Father maintained contact and visitation with the child throughout his incarceration and regularly visited the child after his release. The mere existence of pending charges, without more, is unlikely to meet the "clear and convincing" standard set forth in § 2511.

In *In the Interest of: H.K., a Minor*, 161 A.3d 331 (Pa. Super. 2017), the Superior Court held that the trial court was not required to consider whether CYF undertook reasonable efforts to locate father and his family in deciding to terminate father's parental rights.

In *In the Interest of: A.N.P., a Minor*, 155 A.3d 55 (Pa. Super. 2017), the Superior Court ruled that the trial court violated mother's due process rights as well as the Adoption and Juvenile Acts by precluding her from being heard in a petition to terminate her parental rights, where the trial judge excused mother from the hearing without informing her that she would not be permitted reentry to the court proceedings, and then refused to allow mother's counsel to present evidence in the form of mother's testimony. The court found that when the trial court indicated that mother was excused from the hearing when she felt ill, the trial court did not and could not have properly placed any constraints on her return to the proceedings.

In *In The Interest of: J.J.L., A Minor,* 150 A.3d 475 (Pa. Super. 2016), the Superior Court found that the trial court properly involuntarily terminated mother's rights to her child because, contrary to mother's assertion, the ADA was not applicable to a proceeding regarding the termination of parental rights under the Adoption Act. The court noted that in a dispositional review, the focus of the court was on the child's best interest.

In *In Re: S.S.W.,* 125 A.3d 413 (Pa. Super. 2015) the Superior Court affirmed the denial of a petition for involuntary termination of parental rights of father, where father made an emotional turnaround and obtained psychiatric and spiritual counseling, job training, and steady responsible work. Mother and stepfather's children had been in sole custody of mother since January 4, 2013. Father had not attempted contact with mother or the children since that time. Mother and stepfather filed a petition seeking termination of father's parental rights pursuant to 23 Pa.C.S. § 2511(a)(1) and (b). The Orphans' Court noted that father had participated in two months of counseling for which a certificate of completion was provided to the Somerset County probation officer. The Orphans' Court found father had undergone a reversal in his mental outlook through having secured a new job, job training and steady responsible work. The Orphans' Court found that mother and stepfather failed to prove by clear and convincing evidence that termination of father's parental rights was appropriate under § 2511(a)(1), and entered an order to that effect. Mother and stepfather appealed, and Superior Court affirmed the lower court.

In *In Re: A.R., a Minor,* 125 A.3d 420 (Pa. Super. 2015) the Superior Court held that the denial of a continuance of a termination hearing was not an abuse of discretion when father appeared without counsel despite having proper notice of the hearing and the right to counsel, and prior instructions regarding how to obtain an attorney if he could not afford one.

Father appeared at the termination hearing unrepresented, and requested a continuance to allow him time to obtain counsel. The trial court determined that father had proper notice of the hearing and sufficient time to obtain counsel prior to the hearing. Thus, the court denied father's request for a continuance, and father proceeded with the hearing *pro se*.

In *In Re: Adoption of G.L.L., a Minor*, 124 A.3d 344 (Pa. Super. 2015), the Superior Court found that the trial court properly denied the CYF petition to involuntarily terminate mother's parental rights, because there was a demonstrated bond between mother and child and the negative impact of keeping the child in foster care was outweighed by the permanent damage he would sustain from the termination of mother's parental rights. The court agreed with the trial court that termination would not serve the needs and welfare of the child pursuant to 23 Pa.C.S. § 2511(b).

In *Adoption of: C.J.P., a Minor*, 114 A.3d 1046 (Pa. Super. 2015) the Superior Court ruled that the trial court did not err in granting CYS' Petition to Terminate Mother's Parental Rights; the trial court was not permitted to consider mother's remedial actions taken to address her mental health issues and housing problems after CYS filed a petition to involuntarily terminate her parental rights. The trial court terminated mother's parental rights pursuant to 23 Pa.C.S. §§ 2511(a)(1), (2), (5), (8) and (b), finding that mother's parental rights should be terminated due to her unwillingness and/or inability to address her mental health issues. The court also emphasized mother's lack of stable housing, presentment and hostility toward others and refusal to cooperate with CYS. Mother claimed that she was trying to comply with CYS "little-by-little" but that she could not do everything that had been asked of her.

In *In Re: Adoption of: C.D.R.*, 111 A.3d 1212 (Pa. Super. 2015), the Superior Court held that the trial court properly involuntarily terminated mother's parental rights where mother's repeated incarceration, inconsistent participation in CYS services, and apparent abandonment of CYS reunification efforts demonstrated an inability to remedy her incapacity to parent.

In *In The Interest of: T.A.C.*, 110 A.3d 1028 (Pa. Super. 2015), the Superior Court ruled that the trial court did not err in terminating mother's parental rights where mother had not sufficiently treated her mental health conditions. The fact that mother's significant mental health issues still existed supported the trial court's conclusion that her parental rights should be terminated.

In *In Re: K.H.B.*, 107 A.3d 175 (Pa. Super. 2014), the Superior Court found that the trial court erred in determining that CYF failed to meet its burden of proof that terminating mother's and father's parental rights met the needs and welfare of the child pursuant to 23 Pa.C.S. § 2511(b) and in requiring adoptive aunt to sign a post-adoption contact agreement. The trial court found that CYF met its burden of proof that grounds for termination existed against mother and father pursuant to 23 Pa.C.S. § 2511(a)(5), but did not meet its burden of proof that termination met the needs and welfare of the child pursuant to § 2511(b).

In *In Re: M.M., a Minor*, 106 A.3d 114 (Pa. Super. 2014), the Superior Court affirmed the trial court's ruling that mother failed to provide her children with a safe environment and that the termination of mother's parental rights was in the children's best interest. Although the children had a bond with mother, the bond was not necessarily meaningful or healthy. The court noted that it was evident from the record that the trial court emphasized the childrens' safety and did not focus on mother's incarceration.

In *In The Interest of: X.J., a Minor*, 105 A.3d 1 (Pa. Super. November 20, 2014), the Superior Court vacated a decree involuntarily terminating mother's parental rights where mother, who was statutorily entitled to representation during termination proceedings, was unrepresented by counsel during the termination proceedings and was not provided with notice of a right to counsel. The court noted that the Adoption Act required that a court appoint counsel for indigent client, and noted that *In Re: J.T.*, 983 A.2d 771, 774 (Pa. Super. 2009) provided that an indigent parent in a termination of parental rights case had a constitutional right to counsel. The court further held that a parent in termination proceedings was also entitled to be advised of his or her right to counsel during the proceedings, citing *In Re: Adoption of R.I.*, 312 A.2d 601, 603 (Pa. 1973). The court found that mother was represented by counsel solely in the dependency proceedings. However, mother was neither advised of her right to counsel in the termination proceedings, nor afforded legal representation at any time in the termination proceedings in Orphans' Court.

In *In The Interest of: M.T.*, 101 A.3d 1163 (Pa. Super. 2014), the Superior Court held that involuntary termination of parental rights was in the best interest of the children, and was supported by clear and convincing evidence, and the record supported the change of placement goal from reunification to adoption.

In *In Re: T.S.M., a Minor*, 71 A.3d 251 (Pa. 2013), the Pennsylvania Supreme Court discussed how trial courts should weigh the existence of "pathological" emotional bonds between parents and children and concluded that trial courts must determine whether the trauma caused by breaking those bonds are outweighed by the benefit of moving the children to a permanent home. The family at issue had been involved with the Allegheny County Office of Children, Youth, & Family Services (CYF) for nearly a decade and each child had between six and 13 foster placements. As a result, the children had been denied necessary permanency and most were experiencing significant psychological and behavioral problems.

In *In Re: Adoption of G.K.T.*, 75 A.3d 521 (Pa. Super. 2013), the Superior Court found that the Orphans' Court erred by failing to appoint counsel for the infant child at issue and in overruling father's preliminary objections challenging improper venue. The Orphans' Court had granted the petition of the adoptive couple to involuntarily terminate father's parental rights to his infant son and issued a decree of adoption.

In *In The Matter of: J.F.M.*, 71 A.3d 989 (Pa. Super. 2013), the Superior Court found that the trial court properly ruled that termination of mother's parental rights was in the child's best interests and would serve her well-being by allowing her to be with her foster family, with whom she had bonded. Mother argued that she substantially complied with all her family-service plan objectives except for one, demonstrating appropriate parenting skills.

In *In the Matter of the Involuntary Termination of Parental Rights to E.M.I.*, 57 A.3d 1278 (Pa. Super. 2012), the lower court denied mother's petition for the involuntary termination of parental rights of father, where mother intended to terminate father's parental rights to their minor child in order to proceed with the intended adoption of the child by her same-sex partner. Mother offered insufficient evidence that the proposed adoption of the child by her same-sex partner would serve the child's best interest.

In *In The Interest of: K.M., a Minor,* 53 A.3d 781 (Pa. Super. 2012), the Superior Court affirmed the Orphans' Court's decision to terminate mother's parental rights to her minor child pursuant to the Adoption Act, and agreed that the appointed guardian *ad litem,* an attorney, could also serve as the child's legal counsel. The child, age 3, had been in placement since birth. Mother, age 17, was ordered to complete parenting classes, drug and alcohol treatment, mental health services and to maintain safe and stable housing. After her initial compliance, mother failed to abide by the rules established by the Luzerne County CYS and neglected the child's medical conditions. CYS filed a petition to involuntarily terminate mother's parental rights under 23 Pa.C.S. § 2511(a) (2), (5) and (8) and § 2511(b). Counsel was appointed and, following three days of testimony, the Orphans' Court terminated mother's parental rights. Mother appealed, challenging the Orphans' Court's decision denying her motion to appoint counsel on the child's behalf during the contested termination proceedings pursuant to 23 Pa.C.S. § 2313(a). Mother claimed that the appointment of counsel was mandatory under § 2313(a) and that a guardian *ad litem* could not play a dual role as both legal counsel for the child and guardian *ad litem.* Mother argued that innate differences existed between the two roles that precluded one attorney from serving a child in both capacities. The Superior Court disagreed, finding that the appointed guardian *ad litem* could also serve as the child's legal counsel.

In *In Re: Adoption of S.P.,* 47 A.3d 817 (Pa. 2012), the Pennsylvania Supreme Court concluded that the Superior Court erred in reversing the trial court's decision to terminate father's parental rights where father had been incarcerated since prior to the child's birth and never provided the child with essential parental care. Initially, the trial court found that father had been incarcerated since prior to the child's birth, did not have a relationship with her, had never been able to provide for the child and had not sent any prison earnings to the child. The trial court also explained that the child's special needs required a caregiver who could provide constant attention and father did not have that ability. Accordingly, the trial court concluded that father's parental rights should be terminated. On appeal, the Superior Court reversed in an *en banc* 5-4 decision based on evidence of father's efforts to establish and maintain a relationship with the child and his efforts to prepare himself to assume parental responsibilities and entry into the workforce. The Superior Court ruled that incarceration alone was not a sufficient reason to terminate father's parental rights and found that CYS failed to meet its burden of proving grounds for termination under 23 Pa.C.S. § 2511(a)(2). The Supreme Court granted allocatur and found that the trial court did not err in finding that terminating father's rights would serve the best interests of the child under § 2511(b), considering that she did not have a relationship with father and he could not provide for her and her special needs.

In *In Re: R.I.S. and A.I.S.,* 36 A.3d 567 (Pa. 2011), a majority of the Pennsylvania Supreme Court reiterated the principle that a parent's incarceration, standing alone, cannot constitute proper grounds for the termination of his or her parental rights. CYS filed petitions to terminate mother and father's parental rights and to change the goal from reunification to adoption. The trial court entered orders denying the goal change petitions and the involuntary termination petitions with respect to father. The court concluded that CYS had not proven any of the statutory bases for the involuntary termination of father's rights, and characterized the CYS position as seeking termination based solely on the existence and length of father's sentence of incarceration. The Superior Court reversed, but did so in a very divided ruling by a three-judge panel. The single judge who authored the Memorandum Opinion in which neither of her colleagues joined stated that "incarceration alone cannot constitute grounds for termination," but nonetheless concluded that "father's incarceration was evidence of his parental incapacity".

Upon review of the facts presented at trial, a Supreme Court majority reversed the Superior Court and concluded that there was competent evidence to support the trial court's denial of the petition for involuntary termination as to father. The court declared: "We state emphatically that this court has never adopted or countenanced a view that incarceration alone is *per se* evidence of parental incapacity or that it represents appropriate and sufficient grounds for the involuntary termination of parental rights. Indeed, the law in Pennsylvania is quite the opposite, and we reiterate the definitive principle that when a parent uses the opportunities that are available in prison to make sincere efforts to maintain a place of importance in the lives of his or her children, incarceration alone will not serve as grounds for the involuntary termination of his or her parental rights."

The court noted that in *In Re B.N.M.,* 856 A.2d 847 (Pa. Super. 2004), the court stated, "Where a parent is incarcerated, the fact of incarceration does not, in itself, provide grounds for the termination of parental rights." Because it was evident that the conditions at the time of the child's removal no longer existed, the trial court erred as a matter of law when it held that the child welfare agency had met its burden of proof as to the second element under § 2511(a)(8). "Rather, the question is whether under subsection (a)(8) the conditions at the time of placement still exists. It is evident that they do not. Consequently, we conclude that the court erred as a matter of law when it held that the Agency had met its burden of proof as to the second element required under subsection (a)(8)."

In *In Re: Adoption of K.J.,* 936 A.2d 1128 (Pa. Super. 2007), the Superior Court held that a mother whose parental rights were terminated while she was in prison for the murder of one of her children was not entitled to a delay in that termination while she appealed the murder conviction. The trial court did not err in finding that mother was unable to remedy the conditions that led to termination due to her incarceration, despite her efforts to maintain contact with the children. The children's best interests were served by termination, where mother was serving a prison sentence for murdering their sibling and would not be freed before the children's majority. While parental incarceration is not sufficient grounds for termination, it is not an excuse for failing to live up to parental responsibilities either. The court acknowledged that in the case of an incarcerated parent, the fact of incarceration alone does not provide sufficient grounds for the termination of parental rights. Likewise, a parent's incarceration does not preclude termination of parental rights if the incarcerated parent fails to utilize given resources and to take affirmative steps to support a parent–child relationship. As such, a parent's responsibilities are not tolled during incarceration. Furthermore, mother had no real bond with the children, having seen none of them in three years and having had nothing to do with the youngest child at all. The court concluded that the children should not be kept waiting in foster care in the vain hope that mother will serve less than her minimum sentence in prison. Accordingly, the court held that the trial court had clear and convincing proof that termination of mother's parental rights would serve the best interests of the children.

In *In Re: Adoption of W.J.R.,* 952 A.2d 680 (Pa. Super. 2008), the Superior Court held that the trial court properly terminated father's parental rights where his continued periods of incarceration caused the child to be without parental care and evidenced an unwillingness to remedy the conditions that first led to the child's placement. The court noted the trial court's findings that father's continued periods of incarceration and refusal to comply with drug treatment and family service plan goals caused the child to be continuously without parental care. Further, the fact that father pleaded guilty to drug and firearms charges after the trial court initially dismissed the termination petition showed that father was not willing or able to remedy the conditions that led to the child's placement in the first place. The court found that the trial court properly reasoned that father's continued incarceration and resulting unavailability to parent the child, along with father's refusal to comply with drug treatment and other FSP goals, demonstrated incapacity, abuse, neglect, or refusal which caused the child to be without essential parental care.

Where mother had been unable to form a parental relationship with her child at any time, even before her incarceration, the Superior Court held in *In Re: Adoption of C.L.G.,* 956 A.2d 999 (Pa. Super. 2008), that it was not necessary to inquire into the steps taken to maintain that relationship during the parent's incarceration. While an inquiry into the steps taken to maintain the parent–child relationship during a parent's incarceration is required before terminating parental rights, where there was no such relationship before incarceration, termination could be proper. Here, mother had been unable to form a parental relationship at any time with the child, even before her incarceration, and where there was no relationship, it was not necessary to inquire into the steps taken to maintain that relationship. The court relied on *In Re: Z.S.W.,* 946 A.2d 726, 732 (Pa. Super. 2008), which held that a child's life simply cannot be put on hold in the hope that a parent will summon the ability to handle the responsibilities of parenting. It would not be in the best interest of the child to leave her in a state of "proverbial limbo in anticipation of a scenario that is speculative at best." While it appeared that mother had managed to remain drug-free in the confines of incarceration, whether she could maintain that status among the external pressures of the outside world remained to be proven. Although mother exhibited substantial progress in meeting the objectives set for her, her inability to provide a proper home for the child continued to exist, and the court found that the trial court appropriately concluded that the conditions which led to the removal or placement of the child continued to exist.

In *In Re: Adoption of L.B.J.,* 24 A.3d 862 (Pa. 2011), a majority of the Supreme Court ruled that the trial court erred in terminating the parental rights of a biological mother to her child and in finding that no bond existed between mother and child. The court vacated the Order of the Superior Court and remanded for an immediate evidentiary hearing. The Superior Court had affirmed the termination of mother's parental rights, despite the fact that father and stepmother were now separated and intended to divorce. The Superior Court held that the obstacles placed in mother's path by father, the court, and CYS were not sufficient to overcome the evidence presented by father that mother had abandoned the child for the statutory period of six months.

In *In Re: C.T. and G.T.F.,* 944 A.2d 779 (Pa. Super. 2008), the Superior Court ruled that the trial court properly terminated father's parental rights where the Department of Human Services established clear and convincing evidence of the statutory grounds for termination and where a review of the evidence indicated that the alleged parental bond between father and the children did not exist. The trial court observed that father had had no contact with the children for the first 10 months of their commitment to DHS and that father's supervised visitation with them once his whereabouts was ascertained was limited to 20 or fewer occasions by the time of the termination hearing. Father attempted no contact with the children outside of those supervised visits. "The mere fact that Father participated in supervised visits with his children at a McDonald's restaurant every other week for some time period does not demonstrate the existence of a parental bond, particularly where, as here, no additional contact was even attempted between those visits. Moreover . . . the absence of a true bond between Father and the children contrasted sharply with the testimony regarding their strong relationship with the family with whom they have resided and where they are thriving in a nurturing environment. Unfortunately for

Father, his unsubstantiated declaration in his brief that there exists a 'strong bond between Father and children' simply cannot suffice as evidence of such."

In *In Re: I.G.,* 939 A.2d 950 (Pa. Super. 2007), the Superior Court found that the trial court erred in finding that no bond existed between incarcerated father and his children, and that termination of his parental rights would have no effect on the children. Termination of parental rights must be based on evidence of a parent's conduct warranting termination and the impact of termination on the needs and welfare of the children. The trial court's determination that no bond existed between father and his children was not supported in the record. The court found that the evidence suggested that there may in fact be a bond between father and children, as father maintained regular weekly contact with the children by telephone from prison. Contrary to the trial court's findings, the court held that father had tried to assume parental responsibility since mother's abandonment, and had not shown a settled purpose to relinquish his rights. Moreover, there was no testimony regarding the likely effect on the children of permanently severing any bond that might exist. Accordingly, the trial court's conclusion that termination would have no effect on the children, without evidence of such, could not stand.

In *In Re: Involuntary Termination of Parental Rights to E.A.P.,* 944 A.2d 79 (Pa. Super. 2008), the Superior Court ruled that mother's parental rights were properly terminated where (1) mother has been repeatedly incarcerated for most of the child's life; (2) despite mother's participation in various prison programs, her sex offender status has prevented her from fostering a continued and close relationship with the child; and (3) there was no bond between mother and the child. The court acknowledged that although incarceration will certainly affect a parent's capability of performing parental duties, and may render a parent incapable of performing parental duties under the above statute, incarceration alone is not sufficient to support termination under the statute. Likewise, a parent's incarceration does not preclude termination of parental rights if the incarcerated parent fails to utilize given resources and to take affirmative steps to support a parent–child relationship. Nor does it toll parental responsibilities. Imprisonment is but one factor the trial court must consider in analyzing a parent's performance. While incarcerated, a parent is expected to utilize whatever resources are available to him while in prison in order to foster a continuing close relationship with his children. However, the court noted, where disruption of the family already has occurred, with no reasonable prospect of reuniting it, the policy of restraint is much less powerful. Grounds for termination are not limited to affirmative misconduct, but may include acts of incapacity to perform parental duties. A parent desiring parental rights must exert himself or herself to take and maintain a place of importance in the child's life.

In *In The Interest of: B.L.J., Jr.*, 938 A.2d 1068 (Pa. Super. 2007), the Superior Court held that the prospective adoptive parents had *in loco parentis* status to petition to terminate mother's parental rights, where mother abandoned the child to live with grandmother, and grandmother pursued the prospective adoptive parents as suitable replacement custodians before her death. Prospective adoptive parents could pursue a termination petition after the custodian's death, since they had been awarded temporary legal custody prior to the custodian's death and were entitled to have a court determine their rights. The court explained that under 23 Pa.C.S. § 2512, a petition for the involuntary termination of parental rights may be brought by an individual standing *in loco parentis* to the child.

In *In Re: P.S.S.C. and P.D.S.C.*, 32 A.3d 1281 (Pa. Super. 2011), the Superior Court ruled that the record supported father's contention that his language barrier and lack of counsel made it impossible for him to understand and act upon his parental rights and responsibilities regarding the termination process, which were all communicated in English. Because of this language impediment, there was insufficient evidence on the record to support termination of father's parental rights under 23 Pa.C.S. § 2511(a). Father testified that all of the paperwork sent to him from the Lebanon County CYS was written completely in English and that he was unable to understand them. Father also testified that he was under the impression that he could not have any contact with the children, including speaking with them over the telephone. The Superior Court reversed, finding that it was not clear from the record that father evidenced a settled purpose to relinquish his parental rights or was unable, unwilling or incapable of performing his parental duties based on his inability to understand the English language.

In *In The Interest of: M.S.K.*, 936 A.2d 103 (Pa. Super. 2007), the Superior Court ruled that an attorney's negligence in failing to file an appeal was not a sufficient basis to allow father, whose parental rights were terminated, to file an appeal *nunc pro tunc*. *Nunc pro tunc* appeals will be allowed only upon a showing of extraordinary circumstances involving fraud or some breakdown in the trial court's operation through a default of its officers. The Superior Court declined to overrule an earlier decision in *In Re: Adoption of W.R.*, 823 A.2d 1013 (Pa. Super. 2003), wherein it was held that an appeal *nunc pro tunc* could be allowed only after the showing of extraordinary circumstances involving fraud or some breakdown in the trial court's operation through a default of its officers. Here, father's first attorney was negligent in failing to file a timely appeal. The court was not persuaded that the parental rights involved prompted a distinction in allowing the appeal, since the Pennsylvania Supreme Court had already held that an attorney's negligence for failure to file an appeal did not warrant *nunc pro tunc* relief, citing *Criss v. Wise*, 781 A.2d 1156 (Pa. 2001). "Regardless of whether our Supreme Court in *Criss* intended its holding to be applied to termination of parental rights cases, as we have already stated, we are bound to apply the holding set forth in *In Re: Adoption of W.R.*, that an attorney's negligence for failure to file an appeal does not warrant *nunc pro tunc* relief."

In *In the Matter of: A.K. and L.K.*, 936 A.2d 528 (Pa. Super. 2007), the Superior Court affirmed the trial court's decision to change the placement goal for an incarcerated father's children from reunification to adoption, as this was in the best interests of the children. The court rejected father's argument that the trial court erred in changing the placement goal to adoption without considering the bonds between father and the children. Father argued that the trial court considered only the bond between the children and their foster parents, and did not hear evidence as to the bond between the children and father. The court disagreed. "After considering this evidence relative to bonding, the trial court determined that the children's bond to their foster parents was of greater import than any bond that they might still have with father. The evidence strongly supports the trial court's determination, and thus we will not disturb it."

In *In The Matter of: S.B.*, 943 A.2d 973 (Pa. Super. 2008), the Superior Court ruled that the trial court properly changed the parties' family goal from "return home" to adoption, despite the parents' compliance with permanency plans, because the adoption placement would permit the minor child to have the sense of permanency she deserved. The court explained that the child's safety and emotional stability controlled the analysis, even in light of the parent's substantial compliance. The trial court's decision to change the goal to adoption would permit the child to have the sense of permanency she deserved. "We see no evidence of an improper legal standard or an abuse of discretion in the court's decision. Here, the court conducted a thorough review of the case, heard expert witnesses, considered permanent legal custody as an option, but concluded that adoption best suited the safety and protection, physical, mental and moral welfare of [the child]. Therefore, we decline to second-guess the court's decision."

In *In the Matter of T.D., a Minor*, 949 A.2d 910 (Pa. Super. 2008), the Superior Court ruled that the trial court properly determined that termination of parental rights was in the child's best interest despite the fact that an emotional bond existed between the 12-year-old child and his parents and the child desired reunification. The court agreed that clear and convincing evidence supported the trial court's determination that termination of parental rights was warranted under 23 Pa.C.S. § 2511(a) (1) and (2). The record established that both parents had failed to perform parental duties for at least six months preceding the filing of the January 11, 2007, petition for termination. Despite CYS's best efforts to reunify the child with his parents, the parents failed to take the required steps toward assuming full parental responsibilities. Mother had not demonstrated sobriety to CYS, or completed mental health evaluations, drug and alcohol evaluations, and parenting classes. Likewise, father had not completed an acceptable drug and alcohol evaluation. Also, father did not file an acceptable mental health evaluation until after CYS changed the goal to termination. The court distinguished this case from others where the desires of older children against termination were honored. In this case, even though the child had reached the age where his consent was required for adoption, he had the possibility of adoptive homes and he was still young enough where adoption could have a significant impact on his well-being.

In *In the Interest of: B.C.,* 36 A.3d 601 (Pa. Super. 2012), a majority of the Superior Court found that the trial court's termination of father's parental rights based on 23 Pa.C.S. § 2511(a)(5) and (a)(8) was proper. The trial court granted the petition and terminated father's parental rights. Father appealed, arguing that the CYS Family Safety Plan created a financial hardship on him. The court noted that father's claims were waived for failing to raise any of his appellate issues at the termination hearing. The court explained that a Rule 1925(b) statement cannot be used to raise a claim for the first time on appeal. Nevertheless, the court proceeded to address the trial court's termination order. The majority then explained that the termination of parental rights is a bifurcated process. The initial focus is on the conduct of the parent. If the trial court determines that the parent's conduct warrants termination under § 2511(a), it must engage in an analysis of the best interest of the child under § 2511(b), taking into primary consideration the developmental, physical, and emotional needs of the child. Although CYS filed its petition based on § 2511(a)(8), the trial court cited § 2511(a)(5) as the relevant statutory provision. The court noted that it could affirm a termination order based on any subsection of § 2511(a) on appeal, citing *In Re: B.L.W.,* 843 A.2d 380, 384 (Pa. Super. 2004). The court found termination based on § 2511(a)(5) was proper. The child was removed from the care of father far beyond the six-month period prescribed by § 2511(a)(5). Moreover, there were aggravated circumstances because father had been convicted of statutory sexual assault of a child. The court found the record was replete with instances of father's failure to remedy the parental deficiencies that led to the child's removal. The court concluded that father either could not or would not remedy the conditions that led to the child's removal. The record also showed father's apathy relative to his FSP goals, including his failure to attend many of the hearings pertaining to the child's dependency.

In *In Re: N.A.M.,* 33 A.3d 95 (Pa. Super. 2011), the Superior Court affirmed the involuntary termination of mother's parental rights to her four children pursuant to 23 Pa.C.S. § 2511(a)(2) and (b). The trial court granted DHS's petition to terminate mother's parental rights to all four children pursuant to 23 Pa.C.S. § 2511(a)(1), (2), (5) and (8). Mother appealed, claiming that the Orphans' Court erred in finding that DHS established the statutory grounds to terminate parental rights pursuant to § 2511(a) and (b). Mother argued that the Orphans' Court ignored the evidence she presented to show her love for the children and her compliance with the family service plan goals and objectives. She also argued that DHS could not establish that terminating her parental rights was in the best interest of the children when a formal bonding evaluation was not performed. The Superior Court affirmed the Orphans' Court's decision to terminate mother's parental rights pursuant to § 2511(a)(2) and (b). The court found that mother was only minimally compliant with her family service plan objectives. She never requested mental health services, she exhibited "disturbing behavior" during her visitations with the children, showed poor parenting abilities, had anger management problems, as well as ongoing substance abuse and mental health issues. The court then addressed whether the involuntary termination of parental rights would best serve the needs and welfare of the children under § 2511(b). The court acknowledged that a parent's emotional bond with her children is a major aspect of the best interest analysis, but it is only one of the many factors to be considered. The court rejected mother's assertions and found that the Orphans' Court performed an adequate needs and welfare analysis and properly determined that terminating mother's parental rights was in the children's best interest.

In *In Re: C.W.U., Jr., a Minor,* 33 A.3d 1 (Pa. Super. 2011), the Superior Court could find no competent evidence to support the trial court's decision that termination of father's parental rights was not in the child's best interest. The trial court abused its discretion in refusing to terminate father's parental rights and inappropriately treated the termination petition regarding mother and father as inextricably intertwined. The GAL and CYF argued that the trial court erred in finding that the evidence did not support the termination of each parent's rights. CYF also argued that the trial court improperly based its decision with respect to father on the fact that it did not terminate mother's parental rights. The Superior Court affirmed the decree denying the termination of mother's parental rights, but reversed the decree denying the termination of father's parental rights. The court noted that under 23 Pa.C.S. § 2511(b), a court must determine if termination of parental rights would be in the best interest of the child by considering, among other things, the nature and status of the parent–child bond. Here, the court explained, the trial court conceded that it refused to terminate father's parental rights because it did not wish to leave the child without a father and because it was not terminating mother's parental rights and treated the termination petitions as "inextricably intertwined." The trial court also gave much weight to the fact that there was no pre-adoptive father. Thus, the court found there was no competent evidence to support the trial court's decision that termination of father's parental rights was not in the child's best interests.

In *In Re: Adoption of M.R.B.*, 25 A.3d 1247 (Pa. Super. 2011), the Superior Court ruled that the trial court erred in failing to find that the child placement agency proved by clear and convincing evidence the statutory grounds for terminating father's parental rights pursuant to 23 Pa.C.S. § 2511(a)(6). BCS filed a petition to voluntarily terminate father's parental rights pursuant to 23 Pa.C.S. § 2511(a)(6) and (b). The trial court denied BCS's petition to terminate father's parental rights and found that BCS did not prove the statutory grounds for termination of parental rights under § 2511(a)(6). BCS appealed, arguing that the trial court erred in failing to terminate father's parental rights when it required BCS to prove the birth father's "purpose and intent" to forgo his parental rights. The Superior Court agreed, and reversed and remanded. The court found that clear and convincing evidence established that father failed to make reasonable efforts to contact his child or provide financial support during the four-month period immediately preceding the filing of the petition. Indeed, father did nothing within the applicable four-month period. The court found that the trial court "conflated" aspects of § 2511(a)(6), which applies specifically to parental rights over newborn children, with § 2511(a)(1), which applies to all children generally. "Unlike the statutory grounds for terminating parental rights pursuant to § 2511(a)(6), subsection (a)(1) requires the moving party to demonstrate that the parent has evidenced a settled purpose of relinquishing his or her parental claim to the child." Thus, the trial court erred in granting the "purpose and intent" elements into that subsection in this case. The court also rejected father's argument that a PFA Order imposed on him prevented him from making reasonable efforts to maintain substantial and continuing contact with the child or to provide substantial financial support.

In *In Re: Adoption of G.R.L.*, 26 A.3d 1124 (Pa. Super. 2011), the Superior Court rejected the parents' claim that the Office of Children and Youth failed to meet the requirements of the Kinship Care Program at 62 P.S. § 1303. Moreover, the termination hearing was not the proper stage to inquire into the best adoptive alternatives for the children, and it would be premature to resolve at the termination hearing grandfather's expressed desire to adopt the children.

In *In Re: K.Z.S.*, 946 A.2d 753 (Pa. Super. 2008), the Superior Court found sufficient evidence to support the trial court's decision to terminate mother's parental rights to the child pursuant to 23 Pa.C.S. § 2511. A court may terminate parental rights under § 2511(a)(1) where the parent demonstrates a settled purpose to relinquish parental claim to a child or fails to perform parental duties for at least the six months prior to the filing of the termination petition. The court must examine the individual circumstances of each case and consider all explanations offered by the parent facing a termination of his parental rights to determine if the evidence, in light of the totality of the circumstances, clearly warrants the involuntary termination.

In *In re: C.P.*, 901 A.2d 516 122 (Pa. Super. 2006), the Superior Court held that the trial court erred in terminating mother's parental rights without assessing the impact termination would have on the child's relationship with mother. The court noted that a party seeking termination of parental rights must prove that parental conduct meets one of the enumerated grounds for termination provided under 23 Pa.C.S. § 2511(a) and that termination promotes the emotional needs and welfare of the child, as required by § 2511(b). The court recognized that the complete and irrevocable termination of parental rights is one of the most serious and severe steps a court can take, carrying with it great emotional impact for the parent and child. The court determined that the trial court failed to explain why termination would be in the child's best interest under § 2511(b) and failed to make any reference to the impact termination would have on the child's relationship with mother. Thus, the trial court rendered only a "cursory" conclusion without supporting evidence.

In *In re: B.,N.M.*, 856 A.2d 847 (Pa. Super. 2004) the Superior Court found that where father failed to contact his child within six months of mother's filing of the termination petition and failed to act reasonably to enforce his rights, the statutory requirements for the involuntary termination of his parental rights were satisfied. The court noted that although father had revived his efforts to contact mother and the child after he first received a request for voluntary termination of his parental rights, he had ceased such efforts for at least eight months prior to the filing of the petition for involuntary termination "Father knew that Mother would not facilitate contact with Child, but chose not to utilize resources available to him in prison, or personal contacts outside of prison, for help to establish visitation with or legal custody of Child. Thus, for seven years of Child's life, from 1994 until 2002, Father allowed himself to remain uninformed as to what legal options were available to him as a non-custodial parent. . . . Father took no part in any decision-making during Child's life, relying on Mother to determine whether he would be part of Child's life." The court found that father, therefore, failed to act reasonably to enforce his rights and failed to contact the child within the six months of the termination petition. "Where a parent is incarcerated, the fact of incarceration does not, in itself, provide grounds for the termination of parental rights. However, a parent's responsibilities are not tolled during incarceration. The focus is on whether the parent utilized resources available while in prison to maintain a relationship with his or her child. An incarcerated parent is expected to utilize all available resources to foster a continuing close relationship with his or her children. A parent cannot protect his parental rights by merely stating that he does not wish to have his rights terminated."

In *In re: R. L. T. M.,* 860 A.2d 190 (Pa. Super. 2004) the Superior Court ruled that the trial court did not abuse its discretion by denying a petition to terminate mother's parental rights, despite mother's failure to perform parental duties or comply with family services plan, where a psychologist testified that terminating the child's bond with mother would not be in his best interests. Although factual grounds for termination of parental rights existed, the bond between mother and child was such that termination would not serve the needs and welfare of the child. The expert who conducted the assessment of the child acknowledged the problems in the parental relationship, but nonetheless said the child viewed mother as his parent and, because of his moderate mental retardation, would not likely understand a termination of mother's parental rights, thus exacerbating his feelings of loss. The expert also viewed as significant the fact that the child had lived with mother for nine years, and that there were positive aspects to their relationship. The court said that CYS' focus on mother's failure to perform her parental duties and meet the goals of the family service plan was misplaced and did nothing to affect the evidence of bonding between mother and child.

In *In Re: J.F.,* 862 A.2d 1258 (Pa. Super. 2004) the Superior Court held that in deciding whether to consent to a voluntary termination of parental rights, a child protective agency must adhere to a standard of reasonableness in withholding or giving its consent. Moreover, the trial court must independently review the agency's decision. An agency's refusal to consent to a petition to voluntarily relinquish parental rights was subject to the court's review as to reasonableness of refusal. Parents filed a petition to voluntarily relinquish their parental rights. Pursuant to 23 Pa.C.S. § 2501 *et seq.,* CYS' consent was required. CYS refused to consent to voluntary termination at that time. The trial court denied parents' petition, ruling that CYS had not consented to the petition and that a standard of reasonableness did not apply to CYS' decision. Parents appealed, arguing that CYS' decision to withhold consent to a parent's voluntary relinquishment of his or her rights is subject to a standard of reasonableness and to judicial review. Finding that this was an issue of first impression, the Superior Court relied upon *In Re: Adoption of Hess,* 608 A.2d 10 (Pa. 1992). In *Hess,* the Supreme Court held that an agency's consent to adoption of a minor in its custody, which is required pursuant to 23 Pa.C.S. § 2711(a)(5), must be reasonable. "We find no rational or policy ground not to extend the holding of *Hess* to voluntary relinquishment of parental rights." Consequently, the court held that an agency shall be held to a standard of reasonableness in its refusal to consent to a petition for voluntary relinquishment.

In *In re: Adoption of J.E.F.,* 587 Pa. 650, 902 A.2d 402 (Pa. 2006), the Supreme Court held that the state agency's refusal to consent to a petition for adoption of a child in its custody does not deprive a person who otherwise has a stake in the litigation standing to pursue such interest. Nothing in the Adoption Act precludes any party from filing a petition for adoption, including a custodial agency's failure to grant consent to a petitioning party. The court also held that the termination of a parent's rights as to his or her child does not operate to sever the child's relationship with other relatives. The court found that *In re Adoption of Hess,* 608 A.2d 10 (Pa. 1992), which recognized that grandparents may intervene in adoption proceedings after parental rights have been terminated, logically supports a holding that the aunt and uncle here had standing to seek to adopt the children and to participate in the adoption proceedings below. The court emphasized that its conclusion that the aunt and uncle had standing did not mean that they would, or should, be permitted to proceed. "We merely hold that custodial agency's refusal to consent to their petition to adopt does not, by itself, operate to deprive appellees of standing to participate." It is up to the trial court to consider whether it is in the children's best interests to dispense with § 2711's consent requirement.

In *In Re: K.C.*, 903 A.2d 12 (Pa. Super. 2006), the Superior Court held that the trial court properly allowed a teenaged child to remain in foster care placement, despite the fact that father successfully satisfied the goals of the original family service plan for reunification, because the child provided mature and reasonable explanations for not wishing to return to father's home. In a case of first impression, the court emphasized that the child, an intelligent, mature, teenaged girl, testified she did not wish to return to father's home and that she was angry with father because of his former drug use and parenting style. The court approved of the trial court's decision not to force a relationship with father on the child where father's own actions had prevented the formation of a strong bond. When a child is adjudicated dependent, the best interest of the child dictates the terms of placement. "When a child is adjudicated dependent, the child's proper placement turns on what is in the child's best interest, not on what the parent wants or which goals the parent has achieved." The expressed wishes of the child are one factor for the court to consider in the best-interest analysis. Moreover, the child's wishes must be based upon good reasons, and the child's maturity and intelligence must be taken into account. Here, given the child's age, maturity and intelligence, and the facts of the case, the court determined that the trial court did not abuse its discretion in approving continued foster care placement and ordering a goal change, despite father's satisfaction of the initial family service plan goals.

In *In re: M.B.*, 869 A.2d 542 (Pa. Super. 2005) the Superior Court held that the trial court did not abuse its discretion in entering a protective order denying mother direct access to confidential court documents after discovering that mother's witness possessed a copy of such documents. The order promoted the best interest of the child. "There is a compelling interest in protecting minor children's privacy rights and the protection of a minor child's privacy is a key aspect of the Juvenile Act. This Court has held that Pennsylvania's Juvenile Act demonstrates our Legislature's compelling interest in safeguarding children involved in juvenile proceedings. Additionally, the confidentiality of documents prepared in the course of proceedings under the Juvenile Act is protected from dissemination. Only persons having a legitimate interest in the proceedings may also have access to the information, but only with prior approval of the court." Further, the court determined that the confidentiality orders did not deny mother due process rights because mother had access to the documents through her attorney as well as the ability to question witnesses with regard to the documents.

In *In re: S.M.B.,* 856 A.2d 1235 (Pa. Super. 2004) the Superior Court held that mother's refusal to comply with the programs designed to assist her and her children has left the children without proper medical care, a stable home, or a drug-free environment. Additionally, the record clearly and convincingly demonstrated that mother was unwilling or unable to put herself in a position to provide the necessary care and protection her children needed and deserved. The court concluded that it agreed with the trial court's conclusion that the needs and welfare of the children demanded that they be afforded a nurturing environment where their special needs and developmental delays could be addressed and the children could flourish. Therefore, the court found that terminating mother's parental rights, and allowing the children to be adopted, would be in accordance with § 2511(b).

In *In re: S. H.,* 879 A.2d 802 (Pa. Super. 2005) the Superior Court found that the trial judge did not abuse her discretion by failing to recuse herself from a hearing on the termination of mother's parental rights, even though she had sentenced mother on a prior criminal conviction and presided over the child's dependency hearing. The court rejected mother's argument that because the judge sentenced her in a prior criminal matter and presided over the child's dependency hearings, the judge cannot preside impartially over the termination proceedings. "Regardless of which trial judge sentenced mother, the fact of mother's incarceration on the drug charges would have been known at the termination proceedings." Further, the trial judge's "involvement with Child's goal change and dependency hearings is appropriate in termination proceedings."

There may be no termination of parental rights absent a showing by clear and convincing evidence that a parent's rights should be terminated.[5] In *Adoption of M.A.R.,*[6] the Superior Court affirmed the trial court's decision terminating the parental rights of the mother. The court found that the elements for termination under 23 Pa.C.S. § 2511(a)(5) were established by clear and convincing evidence: the mother, a prior intravenous drug user, refused to undergo a full drug evaluation or treatment program, she

---

[5] In re Adoption of M.A.R., 405 Pa. Super. 131, 591 A.2d 1133 (1991). *See also* In Re: D.J.S., 737 A.2d 283 (Pa. Super. 1999) (The involuntary termination of an incarcerated father's parental rights was justified where the father failed to perform his parental duties for a period of six months prior to the filing of the petition for termination and where the father's post-petition efforts did not evidence a serious intention to recultivate a relationship with his child or to undertake a parental role); In Re Adoption of Dale A., 453 Pa. Super. 106, 683 A.2d 297 (1997) (Where the evidence clearly showed that father failed to perform parental duties for more than six months, and that his own inaction, rather than his long incarceration, prevented him from being involved in his sons' lives, father's parental rights were properly terminated. Father's incarceration did not prevent him from being a father; his own inaction did, the court said. Moreover, a parent's responsibilities are not tolled during incarceration, the court explained. Here, father's contact with his children was sporadic and did not cause him to maintain a place of importance in the children's lives); T.J.B. v. E.C., 438 Pa. Super. 529, 652 A.2d 936 (1995) (Terminating parental rights of natural parent to his child carries with it a constitutional significance because of the importance of the rights involved and consequently, "clear and convincing evidence" is necessary to prove the statutory grounds necessary to terminate parental rights and, in this context, "clear and convincing evidence" means testimony that is so clear, direct, weighty, and convincing as to enable trier of fact to come to clear conviction, without hesitancy, of the truth of the precise facts in issue); In re Bowman, 436 Pa. Super. 10, 647 A.2d 217 (1994) (Party seeking to terminate parental rights bears the burden of proving by clear and convincing evidence the statutory grounds for doing so); In re E.M., 533 Pa. 114, 620 A.2d 481 (1993) (In proceeding to involuntarily terminate parental rights, burden of proof is upon party seeking termination to establish by clear and convincing evidence existence of grounds for doing so. Fact that there is parental incapacity does not in itself require that parental rights be terminated; rather, termination must be decreed only where it serves needs and welfare of children); In Re Baby Boy S., 420 Pa. Super. 37, 615 A.2d 1355 (1992) (Application of clear and convincing standard, as opposed to beyond a reasonable doubt standard, was appropriate when determining whether to terminate mother's parental rights, even though mother suffered from mental handicap); In re E.S.M., 424 Pa. Super. 296, 622 A.2d 388 (1993).

[6] In re Adoption of M.A.R., 405 Pa. Super. 131, 591 A.2d 1133 (1991).

continued to maintain a living arrangement with the child's natural father (a convicted drug offender), she refused to attend to the special needs of her child, and failed to take advantage of services offered to her by CYS. The court held that the mother demonstrated a gross inability to care for her child with severe medical problems (caused by her drug use during pregnancy), and the child's well-being warranted termination.

Though mother had failed to perform her parental duties for over four years, termination of her parental rights was improper where there was no evidence of the effect of termination on her children, the Supreme Court held in *In the Matter of the Adoption of Charles E.D.M., II.*[7] The court determined that it was not clear that termination would serve the best interest of the children. The court referred to *In Re Bowman*, 666 A.2d 274 (Pa. 1995), which held that termination of parental rights should serve the best interest of the children. Because the record lacked competent evidence that termination of April D's parental rights would serve the needs and welfare of the children, the court found that the trial court erred in terminating those rights.

---

[7] In the Matter of the Adoption of Charles E.D.M., II., 550 Pa. 595, 708 A.2d 88 (1998). *See also* In re: Involuntary Termination of C.W.S.M., 839 A.2d 410 (Pa. Super. 2003) (trial court erred in granting a petition to involuntarily terminate father's parental rights, where it failed to consider the emotional bond between father and children and the effect of termination on the children; majority referred to Matter of Adoption of Charles E.D.M., II, 708 A.2d 88 (Pa. 1998) noting "our Supreme Court has held that where there is a lack of evidence as to the effect termination of parental rights will have on the child, there is not competent evidence to allow the trial court to make a proper determination under Section 2511(b)."); In Re: Adoption of A.P. and A.P., 920 A.2d 1269 (Pa. Super. 2007) (Trial court did not abuse its discretion in re-opening the record for a bonding assessment regarding the impact of the involuntary termination of parental rights of two children. The court found that the trial court's actions were consistent with In re: T.F., 847 A.2d 738 (Pa. Super. 2004), which had reversed a trial court decision to grant a termination petition and remanded the case to the trial court to develop evidence regarding the impact of the termination of parental rights on the children); In re: T.F., 847 A.2d 738 (Pa. Super. 2004) (trial court erred in failing to adequately assess the effect that termination of mother's parental rights would have on the emotional needs and welfare of her children before ordering termination. Even though mother had not remedied her drug addiction, nor had she visited her children in foster care, the matter was remanded for consideration of the needs and welfare of the children in relation to termination of mother's parental rights).

In *In Re Adoption of Godzak*,[8] the Superior Court held that although father failed to perform any parental duties with regard to his daughter for a period in excess of six months, the trial court erred in terminating his parental rights where the record was devoid of any evidence of the effect that the termination would have on the child. The Superior Court concluded that the trial court had not undertaken the analysis required by section 2511(b). Rather, the only rationale provided by the court for its decision was that the daughter was now a member of a complete family that provides physical, emotional, and spiritual support. The record was devoid of any evidence concerning the effect termination of father's parental rights would have on daughter. Because no evidence was presented at the initial hearing about what effect the termination would have on the child, the trial court was unable to assess her needs and welfare if father's rights were terminated. Without such evidence, the trial court erred in terminating father's parental rights.

In *In re: S.G.*, 922 A.2d 943 (Pa. Super. 2007), the Superior Court held that because mother's mental health issues were an impediment to her ability to function and parent, changing the placement goal for her two minor children to adoption was warranted. The court stated that it was in the children's best interest to change the placement goal to adoption so they could grow up in stable home environments, given that mother's past counseling had been unsuccessful and her future mental health improvement was speculative. Testimony established that mother suffered from post-traumatic stress disorder, generalized anxiety disorder, attention deficit disorder, amnestic disorder, intermittent explosive disorder and depression not otherwise specified. While mother cited testimony showing she had made some small progress in therapy, the court noted that such progress must be weighed against mother's limited understanding of her circumstances and her inability to fully avail herself of counseling services. The court also observed that mother's arguments focused almost entirely on her conduct and did not take into account undisputed evidence of the children's substantial improvement in school and social activities since their removal from mother's home.

---

[8] In Re: Adoption of Godzak, 719 A.2d 365 (Pa. Super. 1998).

In *In re: K.C.F.*, 928 A.2d 1046 (Pa. Super. 2007), the Superior Court upheld the trial court's ruling that a mother's claim that her three dependent children were unlikely to be adopted was insufficient reason for rejecting the CYA's petition to terminate her parental rights to the children. The court rejected mother's claim that the children would not be adopted because of their age. Mother contended that the trial court failed to consider the fact that the children were not in pre-adoptive homes. The court noted that mother offered only a bald allegation that her children's ages would prevent them from being adopted. The court noted that the termination statute does not require children to be placed in a pre-adoptive home as a precondition to termination of parental rights. The court also rejected mother's claim that the CYA's expert witness, a psychologist who conducted more than 20 custody evaluations, was not qualified to testify about the bonds between mother and the children. However, the court remanded the case to allow the parties to offer testimony on the parental bond between mother and the children, and the impact the termination order would have on the children.

In *In re Adoption of R.J.S.*, 901 A.2d 502 (Pa. Super. 2006), the Superior Court held that the trial court erred in refusing to terminate mother's parental rights for failure to meet statutory requirements and in failing to assess the emotional bond between mother and the children. The court found that the trial court erred in concluding that mother's conduct did not satisfy the statutory requirements for termination under § 2511(a)(8), because mother was making progress toward remedying the problems that existed. Section 2511(a)(8) requires a showing that the child has been removed from the care of the parent for at least 12 months, that the conditions that led to removal still exist and that termination would serve the needs and welfare of the child. The court concluded that the parties presented almost no direct relevant evidence regarding the emotional bond between mother and the children. The presence or absence of a bond was not directly addressed in any way by the testimony of any witness for either party. More importantly, there was absolutely no testimony concerning the likely effect on the children of permanently severing any bond that might exist. The court remanded the case for a presentation of evidence regarding the possibility of such a bond and the effect that termination would have on that bond, if one existed.

The Superior Court ruled in *In the Matter of B.L.W.*[9] that county child-protective agencies could not seek termination of parental rights in a case where the agency failed to follow through on a rehabilitation plan for a mother who was unable to protect her daughter from sexual abuse. The agency failed to prove that mother's parental rights should have been terminated when it was unable to provide the services mother required in order to care for the child and did not undertake reasonable efforts to obtain services from any other agency. "The troubling part of this case . . . is the fact that while CYS set goals for Mother to meet so that she could be reunited with her daughter, these parameters were unobtainable, at least in part, due to CYS' own inaction or refusal/inability to act." While the agency's obligation is not boundless, it must put forth a "good-faith effort" to make available services needed to make reunification possible.

The purpose of involuntary termination provisions is not to punish an ineffective or negligent parent, but rather to dispense with the need for parental consent to an adoption when, by choice or neglect, the parent has failed to meet the continuing needs of the child.[10]

The best-interests balancing analysis has no place in determining whether the statutory requisites for termination of parental rights have been met. In terminating both parents' parental rights, the trial court correctly followed the "totality of the circumstances" standard rather than the "best interests" standard in determining that parents had repeatedly demonstrated that they could not provide for even minimal needs of their children, one of whom was retarded and the other of whom suffered from emotional problems.[11]

---

[9] In the Matter of B.L.W., 843 A.2d 380 (Pa. Super. 2004).

[10] In re B.E., 474 Pa. 139, 377 A.2d 153 (1977).

[11] In Interest of Coast, 385 Pa. Super. 450, 561 A.2d 762 (1989). *See also* In Re E.S.M., 424 Pa. Super. 296, 622 A.2d 388 (1993) (Court considering whether to involuntarily terminate parental rights must examine individual circumstances of care and any explanation offered by parent to determine if evidence, in light of totality of circumstances, clearly warrants involuntary termination of parental rights); In Re Baby Boy S., 420 Pa. Super. 37, 615 A.2d 1355 (1992) (While grounds for termination of parental rights and best interests of child are separate considerations in termination proceeding, termination hearings need not be bifurcated, and evidence need not be separated into the equivalent of liability and damages assessments).

The Superior Court in *In re M.T., R.T. & H.T.*,[12] affirmed the termination of the parental rights of both parents based on their ongoing neglect and inability to care for their three developmentally impaired children. The court found the children were dangerously unsanitary, physically neglected and subjected to uninhabitable living conditions, and in addition the court noted the evidence of physical and possible sexual abuse. The Superior Court held that the elements of 23 Pa.C.S. § 2511(a)(5) were met: (1) the parents by conduct continuing for a period of more than six months had evinced a settled purpose of relinquishing their parental claim to the children or have refused or failed to perform parental duties; (2) the continued existence of the conditions that led to the children's removal; (3) the parents would not or could not remedy the situation; (4) services available were not likely to remedy the situation; and (5) termination best served the needs of the children. The court stressed that the parents' lack of motivation and uncooperative attitude to see that the basic needs of the children were met made it doubtful that she would be able to provide the specialized care and instruction the three children will need as they develop.

However, in *Baby Boy H,*[13] the Superior Court affirmed the dismissal of a petition to terminate the parental rights of the father. Pursuant to

---

[12] In re M.T., R.T., and H.T., 414 Pa. Super. 372, 607 A.2d 271 (1992); In Re Baby Boy S., 420 Pa. Super. 37, 615 A.2d 1355 (1992) (Evidence supported trial court's decision to terminate mother's parental rights, where psychological evaluations indicated that mother's borderline intellectual function and her emotional immaturity and instability were irremediable, mother's husband appeared little better equipped to deal with child than mother, mother had moved to another state, and mother, other than on one occasion, made no attempt to see child and to send him gifts or cards for over three years.).

[13] Baby Boy H., 401 Pa. Super. 530, 585 A.2d 1054 (1991). *See also* In Re Adoption of Atencio, 539 Pa. 161, 650 A.2d 1064 (1994) (Competent evidence supported trial court's denial of mother's petition to involuntarily terminate father's parental rights and, thus, Superior Court erred in finding abuse of discretion merely because record also supported contrary conclusion; while there was period in excess of six months where father did not perform any parental duties regarding child, and record revealed no post-abandonment contact between father and his son, father set forth number of reasons explaining his lack of contact with his son, including fact that father lived in California, and including mother's alleged attempts to keep child from having any type of relationship with father. Failure to pay child support is not, standing alone, adequate ground for terminating parental rights); In re: Adoption of L.D.S., 445 Pa. Super. 393,

23 Pa.C.S. § 2511(a)(1), the foster parents had argued the father has exhibited conduct for a period of six months which evinced a settled purpose of relinquishing his parental claims by abandoning the child. Recognizing that all factors be considered where the father failed to perform his parental duties, the Superior Court held competent evidence supports the finding that the obstructive factors of the mother prevented the father from seeing the baby despite his efforts of reasonable firmness to overcome these factors. The father testified that his work schedule made visitations difficult, that he had fought for custody, and continuously resisted the termination of his parental rights. As a result, the court found the foster parents did not show by clear and convincing evidence that termination of parental rights was in the child's best interest.

In *In the Interest of R.Z.T.*,[14] a decree of termination of a father's parental rights was vacated by the Superior Court because the trial court did not enter a *decree nisi* after the termination proceeding. The court cited *In re Adoption of Hamilton*, 362 Pa. Super. 249, 523 A.2d 1176 (1987), in which the Superior Court vacated a decree terminating parental rights because no *decree nisi* or post-trial motions were entered.

In the case of *In Re: J.J.F.*,[15] the Superior Court held that the trial court erred in failing to issue a *decree nisi* after terminating father's parental rights. *In the Interest of R.Z.T.* and the many cases cited therein make it abundantly clear that in equity matters such as involuntary termination of parental rights, Pennsylvania Rule of Civil Procedure 1517 requires the trial court to enter of record a statement of the issues, findings of fact, discussion of the issue(s) of law, its conclusion, and a *decree nisi*. Pa.R.C.P. 1517. This, in turn, allows a party to file a motion for post-trial relief within ten days. Pa.R.C.P. 227.1. The purpose for the procedure is straightforward: it "allows the court an opportunity to correct any errors that it may have made prior to the entry of the final decree . . .").

---

665 A.2d 840 (1995) (where in an eight-month period, defendant visited her child at the youth service on only two occasions, and twice called the agency, the trial court properly concluded that defendant failed to perform her parental duties for six months, and termination of the defendant's parental rights was warranted.).

[14] In the Interest of: R.Z.T., 707 A.2d 1156 (Pa. Super. 1998).

[15] In Re: J.J.F. 729 A.2d 79 (Pa. Super. 1999).

The Pennsylvania Supreme Court in *In Re Adoption of N.M.B.*[16] ruled that a trial court did not have subject matter jurisdiction to hear mother's petition to terminate parental rights, where father was a resident of Texas and where, under Texas law, the Texas courts retained exclusive continuing jurisdiction over father's right to visitation and access to the child set forth in a prior Texas decree. Finding that the termination of the father's rights would be a modification of the prior decree regarding his rights of access to the child, the court reasoned that Texas retained continuing exclusive modification jurisdiction. In making this determination, the court applied Pennsylvania's Uniform Child Custody Jurisdiction Act, the federal Parental Kidnapping Prevention Act and Texas law. The court stated that the UCCJA allows Pennsylvania to modify the Texas order only where Pennsylvania is the child's home state and it appears that "the court which rendered the decree does not now have jurisdiction."

In *In Re: F.B.*, 927 A.2d 268 (Pa. Super. 2007), the Superior Court ruled that the trial court erred in granting grandparents' petition to intervene in dependency proceedings based upon its finding that the grandparents stood *in loco parentis* to the child. *In loco parentis* status cannot be considered in determining whether a child has a parent for purposes of determining dependency. The court determined that the question of whether grandparents had achieved *in loco parentis* status was irrelevant to the court's granting of grandparents' petition to intervene in the dependency proceedings and as to its determination of dependency. Pursuant to *In the Interest of L.C.*, 900 A.2d 378 (Pa. Super. 2006), only three classes of persons have party status in dependency proceedings: the parents of the child whose dependency status is at issue; the legal custodian of the child whose dependency is at issue; or the person whose care or control of the child is in question. In the instant case, grandparents did not fit within any of these categories, and thus did not have standing. "They are not entitled to party status which would entitle them the right to participate, to be heard on his or her own behalf, to introduce evidence, and/or to cross-examine witnesses." The court also observed that in *In Re: Davis*, 432 A.2d 600 (Pa. Super. 1981), and *In Re: C.B.*, 861 A.2d 287 (Pa. Super.

---

[16] In Re Adoption of N.M.B., 564 Pa. 117, 764 A.2d 1042 (2000).

2004), the court stated that "the doctrine of *in loco parentis* would *not* be used to determine whether a person was a parent, legal guardian, or legal custodian for purposes of determining whether a child was a dependent child. . . . *Davis* stands for the sound proposition that the doctrine of *in loco parentis* should not be employed when determining whether a child has a parent for purposes of determining whether a child is dependent and thus, whether agency involvement should be initiated." However, the court explained, grandparents had a right to notice of dependency hearings and a right to be heard. The court also stressed that its decision was based only on the trial court's improper consideration of *in loco parentis* status and had no effect on grandparents' petition for custody.

In *In re: C.M.S.*, 884 A.2d 1284 (Pa. Super. 2005), the Superior Court held that a child's prospective adoptive parents stood *in loco parentis* to the child where they cared for her since she was several days old. Adoption was in the child's best interest where mother consented to the adoption and father did not, but father made no effort to bond with the child for the first year of the child's life. The court determined that the prospective adoptive parents in this case had standing to file a petition to terminate the parental rights of the child's biological father, who had not asserted those rights during the first year of the child's life. The court noted that the Adoption Act specifies who may bring a petition to terminate parental rights: "The individual having custody or standing *in loco parentis* to the child and who has filed a report of intention to adopt." 23 Pa.C.S. § 2512(a)(3).

In *In re: Interest of H.S.W.C.B.*,[17] the Supreme Court found that a trial court's order denying petitions to change a family goal from reunification to adoption and to terminate parental rights was final, and, therefore, appealable. The court reasoned that maintaining the *status quo* without any appellate review of a trial court's orders in dependency or termination proceedings could put the needs and welfare of the child at risk. Moreover, pursuant to Pa.R.Civ.P. 1915.10, all orders dealing with custody or visitation, with the exception of enforcement

---

[17] In re: Interest of H.S.W.C.B, 575 Pa. 473, 836 A.2d 908 (Pa. 2003).

or contempt proceedings, are final when entered. The court adopted the holding in *In re: A.L.D.*, 797 A.2d 326 (Pa. Super. 2002), that all decrees in termination of parental rights cases are considered final, appealable orders. "An order granting or denying a status change, as well as an order terminating or preserving parental rights, shall be deemed final when entered."

A pre-existing reunification goal does not bar a social service agency from involuntarily terminating the parental rights of a mother whose two children had both been in foster care for more than one year, the Superior Court held in *In re: M. G. & J. G.*[18] The court held that a goal change from reunification to adoption is not a necessary prerequisite to the initiation of involuntary termination proceedings. "It is precisely because these children, under their natural mother's stewardship had been, and are being, denied the right to develop into competent adulthood that we readily affirmed the order in this case."

In *In re: Adoption of S.E.G.*, 587 Pa. 568, 901 A.2d 1017 (Pa. 2006), the Supreme Court held that a family service plan goal change from reunification to adoption need not be formally changed before any petition for termination can be filed.

The trial court in *In re P.A.B.*[19] terminated parental rights of mentally retarded parents of three children, two with developmental disabilities

---

[18] In re: M. G. & J. G., Minors, 855 A.2d 68 (Pa. Super. 2004). *See also* In re: N.W., 859 A.2d 501 (Pa. Super. 2004).

[19] In re P.A.B., 391 Pa. Super. 79, 570 A.2d 522 (1990). *See also* In Re E.M., 533 Pa. 114, 620 A.2d 481 (1993) (Where there has not been adequate consideration of emotional needs of children, termination of parental rights cannot be sustained. Although there was evidence that mentally retarded mother had been unable to provide proper care for her children, her parental rights could not be involuntarily terminated in absence of consideration of important element relating to needs and welfare of children: to wit, emotional bond between mother and children); In re: B.L.W., 843 A.2d 380 (Pa. Super. 2004) (trial court properly terminated mother's parental rights pursuant to 23 Pa.C.S. § 2511(a)(2) because mother, who was mildly mentally retarded, was unable to protect her children from sexual abuse. "There are many cases where in the inability of the parent to provide children with the necessary care, control and subsistence necessary for their physical or mental well-being cannot or will not be remedied. Clearly, in the instant case, despite mother's stated desire to raise her child, her

and one with a heart disease requiring medication—during children's placement in foster care, parents had met visitation schedule and participated in all classes required by CYS—on appeal, Superior Court reversed termination and held that the status of mental incapacity is not alone sufficient to terminate parental rights, even though the first four elements of 23 Pa.C.S. § 2511(a)(5) were met: (1) removal from parental care for 6-month period, (2) continued existence of condition that led to removal, (3) parents cannot or will not remedy condition within reasonable period, (4) services available are not likely to remedy situation, the trial court must still consider the needs and welfare of the children before ordering termination—parents in the instant case had maintained strong parental bond with children despite separation and as such, termination would be detrimental to children's needs and welfare—court noted that there were no planned or potential adoptions in sight for the children which would replace the bond with their parents.

In re E.S.M.,[20] the court held that involuntary termination of father's parental rights, based on failure to perform parental duties, was in child's

---

incapacity cannot be remedied."); In re: A.R.M.F., 837 A.2d 1231 (Pa. Super. 2003) (clear and convincing evidence supported the trial court's termination of the rights of mentally retarded parents under the Adoption Act. CYS met its burden under § 2511(a) (2). That section requires that three elements be satisfied: (1) repeated and continued incapacity, abuse, neglect or refusal; (2) such incapacity, abuse, neglect or refusal has caused the child to be without essential parental care, control or subsistence necessary for his physical or mental well being; and (3) the causes of such deficiencies cannot or will not be remedied).

[20] In re E.S.M., 424 Pa. Super. 296, 622 A.2d 388 (1993). *See also* In Re: Adoption of J. D. S., a Minor, 763 A.2d 867 (Pa. Super. 2000) (the involuntary termination of a divorced father's parental rights, so as to free his child for adoption by the mother's new husband, must be vacated where the mother's marriage is no longer intact. The court vacated the order terminating father's parental rights and dismissed the petition for adoption, finding that the separation of mother and husband prevented the termination of the natural father's parental rights. The court ruled that mother's second husband lacked the requisite standing to file a petition for involuntary termination of father's parental rights because he no longer resided with the child or the child's mother, and the evidence strongly suggested that the second marriage would end in divorce. The court acknowledged that father had little or no contact with the child in the past three years. Nevertheless, the court determined that in the absence of an intact marital relationship between mother and her second husband, the requisite statutory basis for terminating

best interest where child lived with persons interested in adopting child for three and one-half years and since child was three weeks old, child's needs were provided for; child's mother desired adoption; father would have difficult time financially supporting child, his paramour, and two other children; and father did not have high school diploma and was on probation.

In re: Adoption of A.C.H.,[21] the Superior Court found that the trial court's failure to consider a parent–child bond or the needs and welfare of the child in connection with a termination of parental rights petition was reversible error, despite the fact that the child had been in foster care for years and mother lacked emotional, mental, and financial stability. The court agreed that CYF established by clear and convincing evidence that mother was currently incapable of adequately parenting the child due to her continued unstable lifestyle. However, the court observed that section 2511(a)(5) and (b) requires that before terminating the parent–child relationship, the court is required to consider the best interests of the child.

In *Adoption of B.J.R.*[22] evidence supported involuntary termination of mother's parental rights with respect to 12-year-old son who was an educable mentally retarded child; evidence supported determinations that mother was unable to remedy within reasonable period of time conditions that led to son's removal from her home, that there was only a "loose" bond between mother and son, and that son's needs and welfare would best be served by termination of parental rights, even disregarding allegations that son was sexually abused by mother's paramour—absence of indication that prospective adoptive family had been found for child did not preclude involuntary termination of parental rights to child where such termination was otherwise warranted.[23]

---

father's rights and adoption by mother's second husband did not exist. Remarking that no gain to the child or society would be achieved by terminating the father's rights to permit adoption by a stepfather who no longer resided with the mother, the court asserted that the "policy consideration for permitting a stepparent adoption is defeated by the separation and contemplation of divorce.").

[21] In re: Adoption of A.C.H., 803 A.2d 224 (Pa. Super. 2002).

[22] Adoption of B.J.R., 397 Pa. Super. 11, 579 A.2d 906 (1990).

[23] *See also In re: Adoption of J.F,* 392 Pa. Super. 39, 572 A.2d 223 (1990) (petition to terminate parental rights of natural mother filed by father and his wife—statute

In *In re: G.D.G.,*[24] clear and convincing evidence supported trial court's decision to terminate the parental rights of mentally retarded mother, despite claim that she had improved based on characterization of actions by child psychiatrist observing her as "problematic"—her interactions with 12-year-old daughter continued to be discordant, disruptive, and anxiety-producing and mother continued to avoid joint activity with daughter—in contrast to *In re: P.A.B. supra,* no parental bond had been established between parent and child—child had been in foster care 11 years and was uncomfortable in the presence of mother, who showed no inclination to establish relationship with child—termination was not based on mother's incapacity, but failure to perform affirmative parental duties.

The Superior Court in *In re E.M.*[25] affirmed the trial court's decision terminating the mother's parental rights. The court found that the mentally retarded mother could not adequately care for her children and pursuant to 23 Pa.C.S. § 2511(a)(b) the needs and welfare of the children were adequately safeguarded through termination.

In *In re Adoption of Faith M. and Victoria M.,*[26] father's parental rights were properly terminated when he failed to visit, communicate or provide support for his children.

In *In re: J.W.,*[27] the Superior Court affirmed a decree terminating parental rights of mother who suffered from schizophrenia and failed to avail herself of available mental health services—trial court did not abuse its discretion in terminating parental rights of mother where record sustains trial court's conclusion that the mother has neither the

---

permitting individual having custody of child to petition for termination refers to legal custody, not physical custody, and as such, wife was not proper party to action—however, mother was not prejudiced since father was also petitioner—in addition wife's participation satisfied requirement that adoption be contemplated in action by one parent to terminate other's parental rights—evidence established that mother failed to perform her parental responsibilities for at least six months, supporting termination of her parental rights; evidence indicated that mother did not take reasonable action to see her child, which she could have done had she so desired).

[24] In re G.D.G., 392 Pa. Super. 575, 573 A.2d 612 (1990).
[25] In re E.M., 401 Pa. Super. 129, 584 A.2d 1014 (1990).
[26] In re Adoption of Faith M. and Victoria M., 509 Pa. 238, 501 A.2d 1105 (1985).
[27] In re J.W., 396 Pa. Super. 379, 578 A.2d 952 (1990).

capacity nor inclination to take the remedial steps required to meet the minimum parental skills necessary to care for the four children, either now or in the foreseeable future. Although the mother expressed her intent to perform her parental role, this intent did not result in action until shortly before the termination hearing when the mother, on advice of counsel, scheduled an appointment with the Mental Health Services—parent's avowed intent to cooperate in remediation program at the eleventh hour, after a long period of uncooperativeness as to the utilization of necessary and available services, may properly be rejected as untimely and/or insincere, in a proceeding of petition to terminate parental rights.

Where it was clear that a biological mother had not been successful in her remedial and rehabilitative efforts over the long period of time in which her son had been in foster placement, the mother's parental rights were properly terminated, the Superior Court held in *In Re Lilley.*[28] "What the mother attempts to preserve is her sense of worth by holding on to the illusion of motherhood. In doing so, she would deny her child, in name only, the right to be totally assimilated into the only family he has known. The price he would pay is too high to satisfy her need. Sometimes the greatest act of love a parent can express is to let the child go. Such is the case here."

In *In Re: J. T. and R. T.,*[29] the Superior Court found that a mother's parental rights were properly terminated because she did not obtain suitable housing and did not improve her parenting ability during the period her children were placed in foster care and because the evidence showed that the children's needs and welfare were best served in foster care. The court acknowledged that mother made significant efforts to correct the sanitary problems that led to the children's placement. Nevertheless, the court found that mother did not obtain suitable housing and showed no improvement in her parenting ability throughout the period of placement. Further, mother failed to follow up with counseling from the agency to assist with her mental health problems. Mother also acknowledged that she would be unable to manage the children without weekly home visits

---

[28] In The Interest of: Carl Lilley, 719 A.2d 327 (Pa. Super. 1998).
[29] In Re: J. T. and R. T., 817 A.2d 505 (Pa. Super. 2003).

from the county agency and intensive involvement from other related agencies.

In *In re: Adoption of M.E.P.,*[30] the Superior Court found that mother's parental rights were properly terminated where mother was incapable of learning parenting skills, even with hands-on help, showed little interest in her baby's development, and would never be able to live on her own. Mother's intellectual disability and her inability to leave her own mother's household made training in parental skills impossible and prevented her from bonding with her child, thus prompting termination of parental rights.

In *In Re: J.D.W.M.,*[31] the Superior Court found that the trial court properly terminated mother's parental rights where she had consistently refused to comply with a family service plan and evidenced lack of commitment to reuniting with her children. The mother's argument that health and emotional issues prevented her compliance did not excuse her actions. "We find mother's actions and attitude fully demonstrate her unwillingness and/or inability to care for the children. The record is devoid of any evidence that even suggests mother is capable of providing the children with a safe and healthy environment in which to live. To the contrary, it is clear mother has failed entirely to perform parental duties and there is no evidence appellant will ever change in this respect." The children were doing well in the care of a loving foster parent and termination of mother's parental rights provided the children with the best chance for healthy and happy lives. "A child's life, happiness and vitality simply cannot be put on hold until the parent finds it convenient to perform parental duties."

In *In re: J. A. S.,*[32] the Superior Court held that parents' rights to a child would be terminated when intensive assistance from a county agency was not enough to overcome their mental disabilities and allow them to adequately care for the child. The court reviewed the testimony of social workers as to their efforts to counsel the parents as to the appropriate activities and methods for caring for the child. The court found

---

[30] In re: Adoption of M.E.P., 825 A.2d 1266 (Pa. Super. 2003).
[31] In Re: J.D.W.M., 810 A.2d 688 (Pa. Super. 2002).
[32] In Re: J. A. S., Jr., A Minor, 820 A.2d 774 (Pa. Super. 2003).

that the evidence established that the parents failed to progress toward established goals, despite the intensive in-home programs and therapies they received. The court noted that despite support, extensive in-home services, assistance and abundant time to remedy the problems which necessitated the child's removal from the parents' custody, neither parent was able to meet the irreducible minimum requirements of care for the child.

In *In re: Coast,*[33] the Superior Court affirmed a final decree terminating the parental rights of the alcoholic parents and denying them visitation of their retarded and emotionally unstable children. The court's inquiry is not to balance the prospective adoptive home or foster home versus the parents' home, but rather the court is to inquire whether the parents are capable of performing the parental duties required of them by society. If the parents cannot fulfill these duties, only then must they relinquish the rights of the parents. Section 2511(a)(1)–(5) sets forth grounds for termination of parental rights. Section 2511(b) provides that in the termination of parental rights, the court shall give primary consideration to the "needs and welfare of the children." Therefore, once the statutory requirements for involuntary termination have been met, the court may consider the children's best interest to determine whether or not to terminate parental rights, however, the "needs and welfare of the child" is not a basis upon which to terminate the parental rights.

In *In The Matter of Adoption of C.A.E.,*[34] termination of parental rights was supported by competent evidence indicating that prematurely born child was in a precarious physical state and needed constant care and attention and that mother, who had only sporadically visited child during his 14 months in hospital, had shown little interest in the child and was incapable of caring for him.

The Superior Court held in *In re: Adoption of T.B.B.*[35] that the trial court did not err in terminating mother's parental rights where the trauma mother previously inflicted upon her two minor sons was so severe that it could not be remedied. Evidence established that the children had been

---

[33] In re Coast, 385 Pa. Super. 450, 561 A.2d 762 (1989).
[34] In Matter of Adoption of C.A.E., 516 Pa. 419, 532 A.2d 802 (1987).
[35] In re: Adoption of T.B.B., 835 A.2d 387 (Pa. Super. 2003).

removed from mother's care for almost five years, *i.e.*, 4½ years longer than required by 23 Pa.C.S. § 2511(a)(5). Moreover, "no evidence demonstrates that the conditions which necessitated removal of the boys have been or can be remedied because the prior trauma the boys suffered at the hand of Mother was so severe. The reason for the extended separation of Mother from the boys is the result of Mother's prior actions."

In *In re Angry*[36] termination of parental rights was sufficiently supported by evidence of parents' history of mental illness, though neither parent had ever had custody of child, where both parents were unable to establish living arrangements for themselves, attempts at assistance were thwarted by problematic and threatening behavior of both parents, and it was unlikely that the situation would improve.

In *In Re: C.P. and B.P.*,[37] the Superior Court held that where medical experts testified that father physically and emotionally abused his children, causing them to suffer from depression and post-traumatic stress disorder, and where mother failed to protect the children from father, the trial court properly adjudicated a minor child as dependent. The court observed that a finding of dependency under 42 Pa.C.S. § 6302 must be predicated on evidence of conduct by the parent that places the health, safety or welfare of the child at risk. The evidence before the trial court clearly and convincingly established that the children were dependent under the standards set forth in the Juvenile Act.

The Pennsylvania Supreme Court held, in *Baby Boy A v. Catholic Social Services*,[38] that a father's failure to do anything to find out more

---

[36] In re Angry, 361 Pa. Super. 180, 522 A.2d 73 (1987).

[37] In Re: C. P. and B.P., 836 A.2d 984 (Pa. Super. 2003).

[38] Baby Boy A. v. Catholic Soc. Serv., 512 Pa. 517, 517 A.2d 1244 (1986). *See also* In the Interest of C. S., 761 A.2d 1197 (Pa. Super. 2000) (an incarcerated father's parental rights were involuntarily terminated where his failure to maintain contact with his son reflected a refusal to perform parental duties for at least six months prior to the filing of the termination petition. The court relied on evidence indicating that father had phoned the child only once and written him approximately six times during his 3-year stay in foster care); In Re Adoption of C.A.W. and A.A.W., 453 Pa. Super. 277, 683 A.2d 911 (1996) (father's parental rights were properly terminated where father was in prison and would not be eligible for parole for 28 years, and the crimes for which he had twice been incarcerated involved the sexual abuse of minors); In Re E.S.M., 424

about his child or to have any communication with the child during the 15 months that the father was in prison following his first knowledge of the existence of his child established abandonment as a matter of law, for the purpose of termination of parental rights, even though the father was illiterate.

In Re: Adoption of J. M. M.,[39] the Superior Court held that while father's incarceration was not by itself grounds for the termination of his parental rights, father's failure to see his child in over two years and his failure to otherwise maintain a parent–child relationship constituted a failure to perform his parental duties justifying the termination of his parental rights. Although father presented evidence that he participated in the prison's rehabilitative and education services, the trial court found that father had not seen his daughter in over two years and that his only effort to create or maintain a parent–child relationship consisted of sending daughter two cards. The court held that this was not sufficient to preserve his rights. The court noted that § 2511 does not require that the parent demonstrate both a settled purpose of relinquishing parental claim to a child *and* refusal or failure to perform parental duties. Accordingly, parental rights may be terminated pursuant to this section if the parent either demonstrates a settled purpose of relinquishing parental claim to a child *or* fails to perform parental duties. The court stated that "given father's failure to perform parental duties and given that he has been unable to remain out of jail for any

---

Pa. Super. 296, 622 A.2d 388 (1993) (Involuntary termination of father's parental rights, on ground of failure to perform parental duties, was mandated where father did not personally contact persons attempting to adopt child or their attorney until almost nine months after child's birth despite having means to do so, father did not respond to initial adoption papers until more than six months after receiving them and then only after additional inquiries from persons seeking adoption); In Re V.E., 417 Pa. Super. 68, 611 A.2d 1267 (1992) (Parental rights may be forfeited where incarcerated parent does not exercise reasonable firmness in declining to yield to obstacles to maintaining close relationship with children. Father's rights in his children were properly terminated where, following removal of children from home based on father's physical and sexual abuse and father's subsequent incarceration, father failed to have any communication with children and did not even contact Children and Youth Sevices (CYS) to obtain children's address or telephone number).

[39] In the Matter of the Adoption of J. M. M., 782 A.2d 1024 (Pa. Super. 2001).

period of time, we agree with the trial court in terminating his parental rights." Accordingly, the termination was supported by clear and convincing evidence in the record.

In *In re: G.P.–R.,*[40] the Superior Court ruled that father's rights to his child were properly terminated, where father was incarcerated at the time of the child's birth and sent only a few letters to the child upon his release. The court determined that the trial court's termination of father's parental rights was supported by its findings that father had no contact with the child and made no attempt to perform his parental duties. "In the instant case, Father was entitled to and received his procedural due process rights, having had the opportunity to attend various hearings, present evidence, and cross-examine the Agency's witnesses in connection with both petitions. He was also represented by an attorney." The court properly weighed father's credibility and found that he had not offered any legal excuse for failing to maintain contact with the child upon his release from prison.

In *In re: J. L. C.,*[41] the Superior Court ruled that father's parental rights were properly terminated where he failed to maintain any connection with his children during the time period in which he was incarcerated. The court agreed with the trial court finding that father did not attempt to maintain a connection with the children while in jail. The court noted that although "the mere fact that a parent is in jail is not grounds to terminate parental rights, . . . the mere fact that a parent is in jail does not mean that he can forego trying to maintain a bond with his children." Under Pennsylvania law, an incarcerated parent is expected to utilize whatever resources are available to him to foster a continuing close relationship with his children. "It is clear from the limited involvement Father had with the children that he did not bond with the children in the way a parent should bond with his or her children. It is not enough that both boys know their father, enjoy being with him, and love their dad. That is not bonding. . . . Being a parent means assuming responsibility so that a real bond develops, not just having a casual relationship with one's children. . . . While Father spent a good deal of time stating what he

---

[40] In re: G.P.–R., 851 A.2d 967 (Pa. Super. 2004).
[41] In re: J. L. C. and J. R. C., 837 A.2d 1247 (Pa. Super. 2003).

planned to do in the future, his actions to date carry more weight than his promises for the future. . . . It is appropriate to rely on past behavior rather than future promises."

In *In re: J.N.F.*, 887 A.2d 775 (Pa. Super. 2005), the court held that the trial court did not have a duty to ensure an incarcerated parent's participation in a termination hearing. The termination petition clearly informed the parent of his obligation to notify the court if he desired to challenge the termination. The trial court is required to appoint counsel and make arrangements for a parent's testimony at a termination hearing only after the parent has notified the court of his/her objection to the termination by established court procedure. The burden is on the parent who objects to a termination to properly advise the trial court of an objection to a petition and the need for appointed counsel. Here, the trial court did not err in terminating father's parental rights in his absence when father failed to properly notify the court of his need for appointed counsel or his desire to contest the petition. The court noted that 23 Pa.C.S. § 2313(A.1) states that a trial court shall appoint counsel during termination proceedings "upon petition of the parent." Here, the termination petition clearly communicated to father his option to obtain counsel under this provision. Because father did not petition the court for appointment of an attorney, the court was under no obligation to provide one for him.

In *In re: Adoption of J.J.*,[42] an involuntary termination of a father's parental rights owing to his inability to remedy conditions that led to

---

[42] In re: Adoption of J.J., 511 Pa. 590, 515 A.2d 883 (1986). *See also* In Re: K.C.W., 689 A.2d 294 (Pa. Super. 1997) (reversed a trial court's order that terminated a mother's parental rights for failure to remove herself from the children's abusive father); The Interest of: JOV and JAV, 454 Pa. Super. 630, 686 A.2d 421 (1996) (held that where parents were unable to explain how their minor child was injured on several occasions, the trial court properly placed the child in the care and custody of a county youth services agency. The court cited with approval In Re Jeffrey S., 628 A.2d 439 (Pa. Super. 1993)); In re Adoption of Baby Boy J, 354 Pa. Super. 575, 512 A.2d 689 (1986) (father's parental rights were terminated when the court found that he was totally disinterested in the rearing and development of his child); In the Matter of K.L.P., 354 Pa. Super. 241, 511 A.2d 852 (1986) (mother's failure to attend appointments and review hearings concerning her child, and failure to maintain any contact with child after August 29,

his son being placed in the care of a children's services agency was supported by evidence that the son had been in the custody of Children and Youth Services virtually from birth, that the father had never had custody of or provided support for the son, and that the father was uncooperative with the agency in efforts to assist him in establishing a relationship with the child and planning for the child's future. The termination was due to repeated and continued incapacity, abuse, neglect, or refusal, which caused the child to be without essential parental care and that could not or would not be remedied. Evidence was supported by testimony of a social worker that the father never requested visits with the son until after he received the notice of termination proceedings, and that visits between father and son were devoid of any appropriate interaction between him and the child.

In *In re: A.R.,*[43] the Superior Court found that mother and father's parental rights were properly terminated where more than 12 months had elapsed since their children were removed, and, during that time, they failed to remedy the conditions that led to the removal of the children. The court rejected father's argument that the two older children should have been asked their preference concerning adoption, stating that "as Father is well aware, this is not a custody matter where older children are given the opportunity to express their preferences. The state, as *parens patriae*, has a duty to care for its more dependent citizens, especially young people who are without the requisite parental supervision. . . . In proceedings such as these, the children do not decide what is best for them."

In *In re: C.M.S.,*[44] the Superior Court found that father demonstrated a settled intent to relinquish his parental rights where he failed to perform

---

1983, constituted clear and convincing evidence that supported the involuntary termination of mother's parental rights); In re T.L.G. and D.A.G., 351 Pa. Super. 256, 505 A.2d 628 (1986) (termination of father's parental rights on grounds that he had refused and failed to perform his parental duties for a period of at least 6 months was not supported by sufficient evidence; especially when mother as custodial parent refused to give father her telephone number or address); In the Interest of: Q.J.R., 444 Pa. Super. 460, 664 A.2d 164 (1995) (where the mother had failed to feed, clothe, and care for her children, and police could not locate the mother at the time the child was removed from the home, the trial court properly terminated the mother's parental rights).

[43] In re: A.R., 837 A.2d 560 (Pa. Super. 2003).
[44] In re: C.M.S., 832 A.2d 457 (Pa. Super. 2003).

any parental duties for a period exceeding six months prior to the filing of the termination petition and failed to exercise reasonable firmness in attempting to overcome obstacles placed in his path by mother and the adoption intermediary. The court found that father made no effort and did not exert "reasonable firmness" in attempting to find the child in the interim months. Although father had been deceived, he took no legal action to force the disclosure of the child's location, but merely sat and waited for the arrival of adoption papers. Father did voice his opposition to the adoption prior to the birth, but under Pennsylvania law, the court declared, "a parent cannot protect his parental rights by merely stating that he does not wish to have his parental rights terminated." The court noted that under § 2511(a)(6), a "parent is required to exert a sincere and genuine effort to maintain a parent–child relationship; the parent must use all available resources to preserve the parental relationship and must exercise 'reasonable firmness' in resisting obstacles placed in the path of maintaining the parent–child relationship." Here, father did not maintain any contact with the child and therefore failed to perform any parental duties for a period exceeding six months prior to the filing of the petition.

As an allegation of abandonment involves an inquiry into the intent of the parent, it may be refuted with testimony similar to that used to explain the relinquishment of custody.[45]

Furthermore, courts are sensitive to the finality and great emotional impact on parent and child of a termination of parental rights and are thus unwilling to reach such a finding unless clearly warranted by the record. *See also* the following: *In re Bownan*, 542 Pa. 268, 666 A.2d 274 (1995) (Supreme Court affirmed a Superior Court's decision to halt the termination of a military serviceman's parental rights to his two children, even though father rarely had contact with the children and often missed visits); *Adoption of M.S.*, 445 Pa. Super. 177, 664 A.2d 1370, (1995) (trial court properly refused to terminate parental rights on grounds of relinquishment or abandonment where the child's custodians placed obstacles in the mother's path); *T.J.B. v. E.C.*, 438 Pa. Super. 529, 652 A.2d 936 (1995) (Natural father's actions during the four months prior to the filing

---

[45] Matter of Adoption of Mullen, 321 Pa. Super. 496, 468 A.2d 1098 (1983); In re Santelia, 318 Pa. Super. 413, 465 A.2d 21 (1983).

of prospective adoptive parents' petition to involuntarily terminate his parental rights to newborn child constituted reasonable efforts to maintain continuing and substantial contacts with child so as to preclude the granting of the petition); *In Re E.S.M.*, 424 Pa. Super. 296, 622 A.2d 388 (1993) (Parents who fail to meet their parental obligations for six-month period do not automatically forfeit their parental rights; six-month requirement in involuntary termination rights statute should not be mechanically applied); *In re Adoption of Kristy D. Hamilton*, 379 Pa. Super. 274, 549 A.2d 1291 (1988) (parents who fail to have contact with child or to meet their obligations to a child for six months do not automatically forfeit their parental rights); *In re Adoption of Stunkard*, 380 Pa. Super. 107, 551 A.2d 253 (1988) (petition by licensed adoption agency/intermediary (Golden Cradle) to terminate parental rights of unwed father. Mother gave new baby to adoption agency immediately after leaving the hospital. Mother voluntarily relinquished her rights one and one-half months after birth. Father filed a petition for custody 3 1/2 months after birth. Adoption agency filed a petition to terminate father's rights four months after birth. For two years minor child resided with pre-adoptive parents whose identity and location were held in confidence by the adoption agency. Father was therefore unable to perform parental duties. One month prior to the filing of this petition, the agency was aware of the father's desire to claim his daughter and fought to prevent him from having any contact with her. Superior Court affirmed trial court's refusal to terminate parental rights, and held that the unwed father's failure to inquire about his daughter since placement with the pre-adoptive parents does not constitute failure to perform parental duties for a period in excess of six months so as to permit termination of parental rights); *In Interest of C.W.*, 360 Pa. Super. 136, 519 A.2d 1030 (1987) (termination of parental rights of a mother was improper, where the mother had, since initial removal of her child, entered into an apparently stable marriage with a man who could provide a healthy atmosphere for the minor child, and had assumed responsibility for raising stepchildren as well as another child of her own, and was by all accounts a very capable and devoted parent. Parental rights may be terminated only when it appears that a parent cannot or will not remedy conditions which gave rise to the parent's incapacity).

In *In re Adoption of S. M.*, 816 A.2d 1117 (Pa. Super. 2003), the Superior Court held that the trial court improperly terminated father's parental rights where the evidence did not clearly and convincingly establish that termination was in the best interest of the child. "While father has not always been an exemplary model of paternal duty and care, neither has he been, we conclude, so clearly deficient in those attributes as to justify the Commonwealth's irrevocable severance of the legal and natural parent/child bond. . . ."

In 1982 the United States Supreme Court, recognizing the gravity of termination of parental rights, held that the due process clause of the Fourteenth Amendment requires that the standard of proof in involuntary termination proceedings be one of "clear and convincing evidence."[46] This has been followed in numerous Pennsylvania decisions. For example, *see* the following: *In Re E.M.*, 533 Pa. 114, 620 A.2d 481 (1993). In cases where there has been an involuntary termination of parental rights by the Orphans' Court, the scope of appellate review is limited to the determination of whether the decree of termination is supported by competent evidence); *In Re Baby Boy S.*, 420 Pa. Super. 37, 615 A.2d 1355 (1992) (Superior Court's scope of review of termination of parental rights is limited to determining whether decree is reinforced by competent proof; trial judge's action in deciding case, its findings of fact, and its resolution of evidentiary conflicts are to be accepted unless they are unsupported by record or reveal abuse of discretion or error of law); *In Re V.E.*, 417 Pa. Super. 68, 611 A.2d 1267 (1992) (On appeal from order terminating parental rights, Superior Court's scope of review is limited to determining whether decree of termination is supported by competent evidence); *In re Baby Boy H.*, 401 Pa. Super. 530, 585 A.2d 1054 (1991) (holding the standard of review in involuntary termination of parental rights is limited to the determination of whether competent evidence supports the trial court's decision. The evidence must be so clear and convincing that where termination is warranted it can be reached without hesitation). *See also In re Adoption of M.A.R.*, 405 Pa. Super. 131, 591 A.2d 1133 (1991) (there may be no termination of parental rights absent a showing by clear and convincing evidence that the parent's rights should be terminated); *In re: Adoption of B.J.R.*, 397 Pa. Super. 11, 579 A.2d 906 (1990) (a Superior Court panel affirmed a decree terminating

---

[46] Santosky v. Kramer, 455 U.S. 745 (1982).

the parental rights of a mother of limited intellectual ability and whose child is mentally retarded—termination pursuant to 23 Pa.C.S. § 2511(a) (5): mother's inability to rehabilitate herself—competent evidence supported the trial court's conclusion that the natural mother could not and would unlikely remedy, within a reasonable time, the conditions that led to placement of her mentally retarded child—although the mother exerted effort in her attempt to become a better parent, she was unable to internalize the parenting skills taught to her—court distinguished *In re: P.A.B., supra,* strength of parent/child bond—although Children and Youth Services had no prospective adoptive parents for the child, this fact did not prevent the court from involuntarily terminating parental rights where termination is otherwise warranted); *Matter of J.P.,* 393 Pa. Super. 1, 573 A.2d 1057 (1990) (following adjudication of dependency, child may not be separated from parents unless evidence presented establishes that separation is required by clear necessity—trial court properly found child to be dependent and properly placed child with foster parents—attorney's allegedly ineffective failure to present testimony and medical records of child's physician to rebut allegations of sexual abuse and to adequately cross-examine rebuttal witness played no part in finding of dependency and did not entitle mother to new trial); *In the Interest of A.P.,* 692 A.2d 240 (Pa. Super. 1997). (Father's Fourteenth Amendment rights were not violated by a tele-conferencing termination proceeding, when father had appointed counsel present at the hearing, had previously met with the attorney and had the opportunity to confer privately with counsel during the hearing); *In Interest of Feidler,* 392 Pa. Super. 524, 573 A.2d 587 (1990) (children will be returned to their natural parents with agency services to be provided since a separation of minor children from their natural parents will not be permitted unless there is clear and convincing evidence that every reasonable effort has been made to keep the family together—and convincing evidence did not establish that parents intentionally violated court order requiring family to participate in drug and alcohol abuse evaluation and treatment by failing to attend two scheduled meetings with social services agency psychologist such that removal of children from home was justified; meetings were not part of court order, which dealt with specific treatment center; moreover, failure to attend one meeting was excused and missing second meeting did not represent violation of order); *Adoption of T.M.F.,* 392 Pa. Super. 598, 573 A.2d 1035 (1990) (allegation of ineffectiveness of counsel in representing parent in termination of parental rights proceeding is reviewed on the total record with the determination to be made as to whether the parties received a fair hearing, whether the proof supports the decree by a standard of clear and convincing evidence, and whether any failure of attorney stewardship was the cause of a decree of termination—a mere assertion of ineffectiveness of counsel will not be the basis for remand or rehearing of parental rights termination proceeding even if the court were to find ineffectiveness of counsel representing parents in termination of parental rights proceeding; the decree of termination will stand if result would unlikely have been different despite a more perfect stewardship); *Quick v. Quick*, 384 Pa. Super. 412, 559 A.2d 42 (1989) (for the court to terminate the parental rights of the parent, there must be clear and convincing evidence of the reasons as required in 23 Pa.C.S. § 2511(a)(1)–(5). In the within case, the retarded and emotionally disturbed children were sexually abused by appellant/mother's husband and other adults while in the care of appellant/mother); *Baby Boy A. v. Catholic Social Services*, 512 Pa. 517, 517 A.2d 1244 (1986) (state and federal constitutions require clear and convincing evidence that the statutory elements for termination of parental rights exist before termination is possible); *In re Adoption of A.N.D.*, 360 Pa. Super. 157, 520 A.2d 31 (1986) (evidence that natural mother attempted to give up the child on several occasions, that her parenting skills were lacking when she was in charge of the child, that she did not show affection or adequately assume the role of caretaker, and that she did not take part in planning to achieve even minimum stability as to child care, housing and employment during the six months between time she gave up child to a couple seeking adoption and hearing, was sufficient to support the trial court's finding that the couple met their burden of showing, under the standards of clear and convincing evidence, that the mother lacked current capacity to parent and refused to take care of child, for their action to terminate mother's parental rights); *In the Matter of Adoption of Codyus Apollo Ellengsen*, 348 Pa. Super. 169, 501 A.2d 1123 (1985) (termination of mother's parental rights for repeated and continued incapacity was not justified in the absence of evidence that the mother could not be able to remedy the causes of her incapacity); *In the Matter of the Adoption of A.K.M. and S.M.C.*, 350 Pa. Super. 581, 504 A.2d 1303 (1986) (no clear and convincing evidence was established that mother's deficiencies could not be remedied in a proceeding to terminate mother's parental rights). *But see Appeal of G.T.W. and S.W.*, 348 Pa.

Super. 333, 502 A.2d 235 (1985) (trial court concluded that six-month period of treatment failed to improve parents' mental condition enough to permit them to avoid termination of parental rights); *In Interest of C.W.*, 360 Pa. Super. 136, 519 A.2d 1030 (1987) (termination of parental rights could not be based upon hearsay testimony; although a psychiatrist testified that the child had difficulty sleeping and had emotional trauma, the psychiatrist's information was given to her by the person who had custody of the child); *In Matter of Adoption of S.B.B.*, 372 Pa. Super. 456, 539 A.2d 883 (1988), (it was held that there is no provision in the Adoption Act case law that mandates the presence of the parents whose rights are subject to a termination petition. Grant or denial of continuance is within the discretion of the trial court. Appellant/Parents were denied a continuance of York County Children and Youth Services petition to terminate parental rights. Request for continuance was based upon the father's incarceration for third-degree murder of his 6-week-old son and mother's inability to arrange transportation to the hearing).

An action to involuntarily terminate parental rights is commenced by filing a petition with the Orphans' Court and serving the notice as prescribed by 23 Pa.C.S. § 2513. Preliminary objections are not applicable in matters involving involuntary termination of parental rights.[47] Persons whose parental rights have been terminated must be allowed to appeal even if they cannot afford to pay court fees.[48]

In *In Re: J.E., a Minor and E.E., a Minor,*[49] the Superior Court affirmed the trial court's decision to terminate the parental rights of the natural

---

[47] *See* In re: K.B. (Minor), 763 A.2d 436 (Pa. Super. 2000) (trial court properly conducted a hearing and terminated the parents' rights in their absence, when affidavits showed the parents had been personally served with notice of the hearing nearly three weeks before the hearing was scheduled. The court held that where the parents failed to comply with the plan, resulting in custodial termination and alleged that service of the termination hearing was ineffective, the hand delivery of the same by a competent adult was sufficient notice. Since proper service took place and the parents chose not to attend the termination hearing, the decree was properly entered and was therefore affirmed).

[48] M.L.B. v. S.L.J., 65 U.S. Law Week 4035, No. 95-853 (December 16, 1996).

[49] In Re: J.E., a Minor and E.E., a Minor, 745 A.2d 1250 (Pa. Super. 2000). *See also* In re L.S.G., 767 A.2d 587 (Pa. Super. 2001) (sufficient evidence existed to support the trial court's termination of mother's parental rights to her two minor children, where

parents, where the evidence established that the parents repeatedly failed to complete the parenting classes and therapy provided to them and the minor children expressed the desire for permanency and stability in their lives. The court noted that 23 Pa.C.S. § 2511 sets forth the grounds that must be established in order to involuntarily terminate parental rights. The court explained that under § 2511(a)(5), parental rights may be terminated when a child has been removed from the home and the parents cannot or will not remedy the conditions which led to the removal of the child from the home. "If a parent fails to cooperate or appears incapable of benefiting from the reasonable efforts supplied over a realistic period of time, CYS has fulfilled its mandate and upon proof of satisfaction of the reasonable good-faith effort, the termination petition may be granted."

In *In The Matter of the Adoption of: A. J. B.,*[50] the Superior Court held that an Orphans' Court judge was correct in applying a reasonableness standard with respect to a child welfare agency's refusal to consent to a mother's voluntary termination of her parental rights. The court noted that its research revealed no Pennsylvania case law involving a situation in which an agency files a petition to involuntarily terminate a parent's parental rights, but then refuses to consent to a petition to voluntarily relinquish parental rights filed by that same parent. The court determined that the trial court reasonably relied on the ruling in *In re Adoption of Hess,* 608 A.2d 10 (Pa. 1992) in deciding this case, and affirmed, refusing

---

mother failed to take parenting classes, missed supervised visitations and generally demonstrated that she was incapable of parenting her children. The court noted that mother was unwilling or unable to accept the responsibilities that come with being a parent. The court also observed that she failed to make the children a priority in her life and did not take advantage of the parenting training and education that CYF's intervention afforded her. The children, who were now four and five years old, could not "wait in limbo for their mother to grow up."); In re: N.C., N.E.C., 763 A.2d 913 (Pa. Super. 2000) (Superior Court found that the parental rights of mother and father were properly terminated where they failed to develop adequate parenting skills despite receiving services from a variety of social agencies for over six years. "Although it is unfortunate that Appellants' inability to provide adequate care for their children stems at least in part from inherent deficiencies, the law is clear that parents who are incapable of performing parental duties are no less unfit than parents who refuse to perform them.").

[50] In The Matter of the Adoption of: A. J. B., 797 A.2d 264 (Pa. Super. 2002).

to dismiss mother's voluntary relinquishment petition. The court noted that if OCY was successful in the involuntary termination proceeding, it could use that as a possible aggravating circumstance in any future cases involving mother. "The result of a finding of aggravated circumstances in future proceedings would allow OCY and the Orphans' Court to 'decline to make reasonable efforts to reunite the family and the agency would be relieved of the burden of providing services to the mother.' We find this position by OCY to be clearly self-serving, and believe that it fails to consider the best interests of A. J. B., . . . Where a parent believes that he or she cannot provide adequate care for a child, or where a parent has abused or neglected or is likely to abuse or neglect a child, it would be imprudent for this court to place impediments in the way of the voluntary relinquishment of parental rights to a child who previously has been adjudicated dependent."

In The Interest of A. L. D., Jr., a Minor,[51] the Superior Court ruled that the Orphans' Court erred when it postponed the termination of a mother's parental rights to attempt reunification; the role of an Orphans' Court in a termination of parental rights proceeding is to decide whether the youth services agency has met its burden of proof. The authority to determine the propriety of a placement goal lies with the juvenile court, not the Orphans' Court. "As a general matter, the adjudication of dependency and the propriety of the placement goal lies within the auspices of the Juvenile Court Division of the Court of Common Pleas, not with the Orphans' Court Division. Thus, in the context of dependency, it is the Juvenile Court that can reconsider its order and change the service plan goal back to reunification, not the Orphans' Court." Therefore, the Orphans' Court exceeded its jurisdiction when it directed further efforts at reunification and in postponing termination of mother's parental rights. "With regard to the court's directive for further efforts at reunification, we conclude that the court exceeded its jurisdiction."

In Re: In The Interest of B. L. L.,[52] the Superior Court ruled that the trial court did not err in failing to grant a continuance to a hearing on a

---

[51] In The Interest of A. L. D., Jr., a Minor, 797 A.2d 326 (Pa. Super. 2002).
[52] In Re: In the Interest of B. L. L., 787 A.2d 1007 (Pa. Super. 2001).

petition to terminate mother's parental rights in order to permit her child to testify, because there is no legal authority requiring or permitting the child's testimony to be considered in reviewing a termination petition. Moreover, in the only Pennsylvania case addressing the issue, *In Re: Child M.,* 681 A.2d 793 (Pa. Super. 1996), the Superior Court specifically refused to create such a requirement.

In *In re Adoption of A. M. B.,*[53] the Superior Court held that the trial court did not err in denying mother's voluntary petition to terminate her parental rights because granting mother's petition would have run counter to the policy considerations underlying the Adoption and State Families Act of 1997. "In summation, once the agency in an involuntary termination proceeding establishes that the elements of abuse, abandonment and/or neglect have been proven by clear and convincing evidence, the child has not been reunited by reasonable efforts and time, and/or aggravated circumstances of a previous effort with the family establish sufficient bases for termination, the agency will prevail. . . . Where the reasonable effort requirements have been fulfilled and permanent placement is deemed necessary, voluntary relinquishment is redundant and a finding of involuntary termination having to do with parental fitness, rather than the best interest of the child, is a consistent and viable finding under both federal and Pennsylvania statutes."

In *In The Interest of L.C.,* 900 A.2d 378 (Pa. Super. 2006), the Superior Court held that grandmother did not have standing to appear as a party in her grandchild's dependency proceedings, even though she would have had standing in a custody litigation. Possible standing in a custody litigation did not confer standing on a non-parent in dependency proceedings, which is determined by the Juvenile Act.

In *In The Interest of: M.J.S.,* 903 A.2d 1 (Pa. Super. 2006), the Superior Court found that the biological father was equitably estopped from asserting paternity after the termination of his parental rights and the entry of an adoption decree, because father failed to assert paternity for the first years of the child's life and knew that someone else had been named as the child's father. Father's failure to act after the entry of the

---

[53] In the Matter of the Adoption of A.M.B., 812 A.2d 659 (Pa. Super. 2002).

adoption decree, and after his knowledge of court procedure was demonstrated, prompted dismissal of his petition to vacate the adoption decree filed three years after the adoption.

In *In re G.T.*, 897 A.2d 1197 (Pa. Super. 2006), the Superior Court held that father's parental rights were properly terminated despite the unavailability of significant portions of the hearing transcript, as father did not attempt to re-create the record, as required by Pa.R.A.P. 1923. Under this rule, an appellant may provide a substitute for an unavailable transcript by preparing "a statement of the evidence or proceedings from the best available means, including his recollection." Here, however, father made no attempt to take advantage of this opportunity under Rule 1923, despite the fact that he was represented by counsel and was aware that the transcript was missing. The court also noted that the evidence that appeared in the record supported the goal change and termination of father's parental rights. The trial court had noted that father missed visitations with his children, did not comply with court-ordered random drug screens, did not comply with his reunification plan and did not establish a loving bond with the children despite the fact that he saw them frequently.

In *In Re: Adoption of J.M.*, 991 A.2d 321 (Pa. Super. 2010), the Superior Court found that the trial court erred in failing to terminate father's parental rights based on his promise to establish a relationship with the child in the future. Whether or not the needs and welfare of a child are met by parental termination must be based on current circumstances at the time of the hearing, not on future promises.

In *In Re: Z.P., a Minor Child*, 994 A.2d 1108 (Pa. Super. 2010), the Superior Court held that clear and convincing evidence demonstrated grounds to terminate father's parental rights under 23 Pa.C.S. § 2511(a) and (b), where the child had already been in foster care for two years, father's ability to care for the child and remain available to the child was entirely speculative and would take significant additional time to establish, father had identified no viable kinship care options, and immediate permanency would best serve the child's needs and welfare. The court found that absolutely no bond existed between the child and parent, and that father's recent efforts to straighten out his life did not require that the child be put in harm's way or indefinitely postpone adoption.

LOWER COURT CASES

Allegheny County

In re Doe Children, 136 P.L.J. 339 (Allegheny Co. 1988) (A major purpose of the law providing for the termination of parental rights is to provide stability for children who have been removed from their natural families for lengthy periods of time. In evaluating whether the conditions that led to the removal and placement continue to exist, no violation of due process exists on the ground that, during the pendency proceedings, the court issued no formal findings of fact or conclusions of law as to what conditions led to the removal or placement of the children because counsel for the mother could have requested that these proceedings be transcribed at the time of the dependency hearing; mother's counsel raised no questions prior to trial concerning the reasons for the removal and placement; the mother had a criminal conviction for endangering the welfare of her children and all parties addressed the only issue, which was whether the mother now had the ability to protect and care for her children).

Berks County

In re C.L.M., 98 Berks Co. L. J. 293 (C.C.P. 2006) (Trial court held that mother was not entitled to maintain her parental rights to a special-needs child because she failed to perform parental duties, neglected the child, and did not recognize the problems of caring for the child's unique needs. The court explained that 23 Pa.C.S. § 2511(a) governs the termination of parental rights. This section provides that termination may be based on a finding that a "parent by conduct continuing for a period of at least six months immediately preceding the filing of the petition either has evidenced a settled purpose of relinquishing parental claim to a child or has refused or failed to perform parental duties." The court also looks at whether the "repeated and continued incapacity, abuse, neglect or refusal of the parent has caused the child to be without essential parental care." Here, the court found that the parents had continued to use drugs and alcohol and had failed to take the time to learn how to deal with a special-needs child. Moreover, the parents had not seen the child for at least a year and a half. Father has been incarcerated for much of the child's life. The court also noted that the child has made a positive adjustment to her new home, where she was considered part of the family and received the medical services to meet her needs. Taking into account the parents' behavior and C.M.'s status in her current home, the court concluded it was in the child's best interest to terminate parental rights and allow the process of adoption to go forward).

In re J.C.F., 90 Berks Co. Leg. J. 13 (C.C.P. 1998) (Trial court found that the involuntary termination of father's parental rights was not warranted where father repeatedly raised his objection to the child being given up for adoption and made continued efforts to maintain contact with the child. Petitioners failed to satisfy the criteria of 23 Pa.C.S. § 2511(a)(1) because father had not evinced a settled purpose to relinquish his parental rights for a period of six months. Rather, father opposed adoption and stated that he wanted custody of J.C.F. Moreover, the court held, father's failure to visit J.C.F. was due to his inability to obtain leave from the Army and lack of cooperation from those involved with J.C.F.'s adoption. Petitioners likewise failed to demonstrate that father's parental rights should be terminated pursuant to 23 Pa.C.S. § 2511 (a)(6) because father did make reasonable efforts to maintain substantial and continuing contacts with J.C.F.).

In re J.L.M., 82 Berks Co. L. J. 341 (C.C.P. 1989) (A mentally impaired mother's parental rights were terminated when she failed to cooperate with a county to obtain necessary rehabilitation services to enable her to fulfill her parental duties and responsibilities. Mother refused to correct any of the conditions that led to the minor's placement. There was no indication that she would rectify the problems within a reasonable period of time).

Bucks County

In re Strickler, 53 Bucks L. Rep. 191 (C.C.P. 1988) (Where the absence of communication with the child results from the deliberate conduct of the opposing parent, it cannot be used as the basis for termination of parental rights).

Carbon County

In re: Lisa M, 12 Carbon L. J. 83 (C.C.P. 1989) (Trial court terminated a father's parental rights for failure to perform parental duties where he had no contact with the child for more than 10 years. The court felt that the support payments made over a long period of time were insufficient to fulfill parental duties under 23 Pa.C.S. § 2511(a)(1)).

In re Deamm, 11 Carbon L.R. 305 (C.C.P. 1988) (Pursuant to Adoption Act, parental rights may be terminated if the parent's conduct indicates a failure to perform parental duties for at least six months and if the needs and welfare of the child are best served by termination. The father's parental rights were terminated where the father had only minimal contact with the child despite residing only a short distance away, did not pay required support, offered no plausible reasons for his conduct, and where the needs and the welfare of the child favor termination of the rights).

Chester County

Adoption of N.L.R., a Minor, 48 Chester Co. Rep. 8 (C.C.P. 1999) (Trial court terminated father's parental rights and allowed for his daughter's adoption, where father, who visited his daughter only twice in over nine years, failed to perform his parental duties for a period far in excess of the statutory six-month period. In reaching its decision, the court relied in part on the Supreme Court decision, *Matter of Adoption of David C.,* 387 A.2d 804 (Pa. 1978), in which the court, presented with facts similar to those in the instant case, ordered the termination of a father's parental rights. Although the father claimed he did not visit with his son because he did not know how to communicate with him, the justices rebuked the father for resolving his "perceived problem by eliminating all efforts at communication," rather than by confronting it. The same reasoning applied in the instant case).

Fayette County

In re Adoption of Malone, 51 Fayette Leg. J. 41 (C.C.P. 1987) (An action to involuntarily terminate parental rights is commenced by filing a petition with the Orphans' Court and serving the notice as prescribed by 23 Pa.C.S. § 2513. Preliminary objections are not applicable in matters involving involuntary termination of parental rights).

Franklin County

In re: Adoption of B.M.N., C.P. Franklin Co., No. A.D. 2005-1 (C.C.P. 2005) (Trial court held that mother's sporadic contact with the child, even if it was caused by mother's significant physical and emotional problems, did not excuse her failure to attempt to have contact with the child and justified the termination of her parental rights. The maintenance of a parent–child relationship cannot be postponed until a more convenient time for a parent, regardless of the parent's physical or psychological problems. While mother had significant health and psychological problems of her own, the court found that she was not so incapacitated as to exert a reasonable firmness in continuing her relationship. The court declared: "A parent cannot yield to every problem she encounters, but must make every effort to overcome difficult circumstances in order to maintain the parent–child relationship. A parent must show reasonable firmness in trying to exercise her duties and to assert her claim through an authentic effort to communicate and maintain her association with the child. A parent cannot postpone her duties or claims until a more convenient time or set of circumstances. . . . The evidence is clear and convincing that mother has continually disappointed the child, taking that relationship for granted and allowing it to dwindle under the assumption that it could be resurrected once her own circumstances improved. However, parental duties and claims cannot simply be postponed until a more convenient time and it is unfair to ignore a child's need for parental attention and stability.").

Lebanon County

In re Adoption of Root, 26 Lebanon Leg. J. 98 (C.C.P. 1988) (Where the father's efforts to maintain contact with the child were thwarted by the mother, his parental rights were not terminated).

Lycoming County

In Re: Adoption of ZA, C.P. Lycoming County, No. 6331 (C.C.P. 2013) (Father's rights could not be terminated when mother did not advise father of the child's new phone number and made contact with the child impossible. Father's parental rights could not be terminated where mother closed off the only avenue of contact, even if father did not make the strongest possible attempts to locate the child. While the court noted that father could have spoken to mother at any of the four support hearings during this time, it found father's testimony credible that mother would not acknowledge him at the hearings. While the court could not find that father made an exhaustive effort to maintain contact with the child, it did not agree that mother met her burden in showing that father evidenced a settled purpose of relinquishing his parental claim to the child. Father did not know where mother lived, and their custody exchanges had always been at a half-way point. The court explained that while a parent has an affirmative duty to be part of a child's life, mother cannot put up roadblocks and then asked the court to terminate the rights of father based on his lack of content).

Northumberland County

In Re: N.T. and C.T., 84 Northumberland Leg. J. 1 (C.C.P. 2012) (When a parent does not express or relinquish any legal rights to a third party, but instead turns to them in aid in the raising of her children, that does not confer standing under "*in loco parentis,*" and the court will not open the floodgates to this theory because then teachers, babysitters, and siblings may all be entitled to legal standing. Grandparents argued that the trial court erred by denying them standing when the facts of record demonstrated that grandparents stood *in loco parentis* to the children at the time of removal and their care and control was in question by CYS. Grandparents contended that a person who stands *in loco parentis* to a child at the time of removal and whose care and control of the child is in question has standing to be considered a party in a dependency action. Grandparents argued that they established *in loco parentis* standing through testimony that they assumed parental status and discharged parental duties. The trial court disagreed, noting that the law affords great fortitude to the rights of natural parents over their children. "In today's society, it is axiomatic that children are not constantly in the care of their natural parents, but instead others who temporarily fill those roles. On a daily basis, children attend daycare/school, are babysat by grandparents, or are even taken care of by an older sibling. To then assume that the parental duties and rights become vested in these actors instead of a parent is incomprehensible. Rather, these services act as a crutch that parents lean upon to stay afloat throughout life's endeavors and hardships." The court further declared: "If the trial court is to accept the [grandparents'] logic and confer standing to them as a party, the liberty of mother's legal parental rights diminishes. To merely reside or perform some parental role with the minors in question does not give latitude to intervene with legal action. Opening this door presumes that teachers, babysitters, and siblings are all entitled to legal standing.").

Pike County

In re Adoption of CJ-MW, 40 D.&C.4th 1 (Pike County 1999) (A mother who has no desire to raise her own child cannot voluntarily terminate her parental rights in order to allow the grandmother to adopt the child. Because the mother lived in the same house as the grandmother and child, it would be too confusing for the child if the grandmother adopted him. "We do not attempt to contradict that role reversals may be a reality for this family where a biological mother acts more as a sibling and a biological grandmother acts more as a mother; such relationships certainly would not be the first of their kind. However, an attempt to create a legal fiction in these relationships is inappropriate. Regardless of whether there is an adoption, the role the grandmother now serves can continue, especially now that she has legal custody. This court believes that it is, to say the least, confusing for a child to grow up in a household where its mother is known as its sister, its grandmother is known as its mother, and its father does not exist").

Chapter 19

PARENTING COORDINATION

§ 19.1. Historically
§ 19.2. The Revival of Parenting Coordination
§ 19.3. Form Order Appointing Parenting Coordinator
§ 19.4. Form of Summary and Recommendation of Parenting Coordinator

§ 19.1. HISTORICALLY

The area of parenting coordination was gaining popularity in the courts across the Commonwealth of Pennsylvania until May 23, 2013, when Pa.R.C.P. 1915.11-1 became effective and eliminated the use of parenting coordination. Pursuant to Rule 1915.11, any order appointing a parenting coordinator was deemed vacated as of May 23, 2013.

A parenting coordinator was an individual who was appointed in custody cases to assist in enforcing and executing a custody order on issues subordinate to "major" custody issues such as legal custody or changing primary physical custody. The Association of Family and Conciliation Courts (AFCC) explained that "The Parenting Coordinator role is most frequently reserved for those high-conflict parents who have demonstrated their longer-term inability or unwillingness to make parenting decisions on their own, to comply with parenting agreements and orders, to reduce their child-related conflicts, and to protect their children from the impact of that conflict."[1] The seminal case regarding parenting coordination was the case of *Yates v. Yates*, 963 A.2d 535 (Pa. Super. 2008).

In *Yates*, the Superior Court found that the trial court did not delegate its judicial authority to a parenting coordinator appointed to assist the parties in executing a custody order. The court directed the coordinator to resolve only ancillary custody issues. The trial court granted shared legal custody of the parties' child to father and mother,

---

[1] Yates v. Yates, C. P. Bucks County, No. A06-02-63378-C (C.C.P. 2008).

607

awarded father primary physical custody, and appointed a parenting coordinator to help the parties implement the custody order. Father appealed, arguing, *inter alia*, that the trial court erred in appointing a parenting coordinator.

The Superior Court affirmed the trial court's order in part and vacated in part. The court noted that a court may appoint a parenting coordinator in especially contentious custody cases with high-conflict parents who have trouble making parenting decisions on their own. The court rejected father's argument that the trial court delegated its decision-making authority to the parenting coordinator, concluding that the trial court had properly resolved all of the major custody issues in its custody order. The court rejected father's assertion that the appointment of the parenting coordinator was tantamount to an improper delegation of judicial decision-making authority. The court found that limited delegation of judicial authority is permissible to address ancillary custody matters that do not touch upon the core issues of legal, physical or shared custody. The trial court empowered the parenting coordinator to resolve only ancillary disputes, such as determining temporary variances in the custody schedule, exchanging information and communication, and coordinating the child's recreational and extracurricular activities.

The *Yates* court held that the Supreme Court permited the limited delegation of judicial authority to address ancillary custody matters under similar circumstances where the decisions did not determine core issues regarding legal, physical, or shared custody.[2] However, an order appointing a parenting coordinator had to provide the trial court with the ability to review the parenting coordinator's decisions *de novo*.[3] This was all superseded by the promulgation of Rule 1915.11-1 in 2013. However, that all changed on August 9, 2018, as discussed in Section 19.2 of this book.

---

[2] Yates v. Yates, 963 A.2d 535 (Pa. Super. 2008), *but see* Pa.R.C.P. 1915.11-1 (only judges may make decisions in child custody cases)

[3] *Id.*; *see also* A.H. v. C.M., 58 A.3d 823 (Pa. Super. 2012) (Trial court erred in not providing *de novo* review of parenting coordinator's decision in accordance with the *Yates* decision).

LOWER COURT CASES

Delaware County

Aborlleile v. Chilutti, 97 Delaware Co Rep. 1 (C.C.P. 2009) (Trial court ruled that it had the authority to unilaterally appoint a parenting coordinator when it was in the best interest of the child to do so. The parties to this child custody action had a history of conflict for nearly 10 years. The list of disagreements by the parents about the child was voluminous. The parties demonstrated hostility and a lack of respect for each other during the protracted hearings. The custody evaluator, who was agreed to by the parties, recommended the appointment of a parenting coordinator).

§ 19.2. THE REVIVAL OF PARENTING COORDINATION

On August 9, 2018, the Pennsylvania Supreme Court ordered the revision of Rule 1915.11-1 reinstating parenting coordination effective March 1, 2019, and promulgated new Rule 1915.22 which provides the form order appointing a parenting coordinator and Rule 1915.23 which provides the form of the Summary and Recommendation of the parenting coordinator. Below is Rule 1915.11-1. See Sections 19.3. and 19.4. of this book for the forms provided under Rules 1915.22, and 1915.23.

The following is Rule 1915.11-1, which is the new parenting coordination rule (Note that the beginning of the Rule reflects the portion that is being replaced):

[Rule 1915.11-1. Elimination of Parenting Coordination. Only judges may make decisions in child custody cases. Masters and hearing officers may make recommendations to the court. Courts shall not appoint any other individual to make decisions or recommendations or alter a custody order in child custody cases. Any order appointing a parenting coordinator shall be deemed vacated on the date this rule becomes effective. Local rules and administrative orders authorizing the appointment of parenting coordinators also shall be deemed vacated on the date this rule becomes effective.]

---The text below replaces the current rule ---

Rule 1915.11-1. Parenting Coordination. If a judicial district implements a parenting coordination program, the court shall maintain a roster of qualified individuals to serve as parenting coordinators and establish the hourly rate at which parenting coordinators shall be compensated. The parenting coordinator shall attempt to resolve issues arising out of the custody order by facilitating an agreement between the parties and, if unable to reach an agreement, recommend a resolution to the court.

(a) Appointment of a Parenting Coordinator.

    (1) After a final custody order has been entered, a judge may appoint a parenting coordinator to resolve parenting issues in cases involving repeated or intractable conflict between the parties affecting implementation of the final custody order. A parenting coordinator should not be appointed in every case. The appointment may be made on the motion of a party or the court's motion.

    (2) Unless the parties consent and appropriate safety measures are in place to protect the participants, including the parenting coordinator and other third parties, a parenting coordinator shall not be appointed if:

        (i) the parties to the custody action have a protection from abuse order in effect;

        (ii) the court makes a finding that a party has been the victim of domestic violence perpetrated by a party to the custody action, either during the pendency of the custody action or within 36 months preceding the filing of the custody action; or

        (iii) the court makes a finding that a party to the custody action has been the victim of a personal injury crime, as defined in 23 Pa.C.S. § 3103, which was perpetrated by a party to the custody action.

        (iv) If a party objects to the appointment of a parenting coordinator based on an allegation that the party has been the victim of domestic violence perpetrated by a party to the custody action, the court shall have a hearing on the issue and may consider abuse occurring beyond the 36 months provided in subdivision (a)(2)(ii).

    (3) The appointment of a parenting coordinator shall be for a specified period, which shall not exceed 12 months. A party may petition the court for an extension of the appointment

or the court in its discretion may extend the appointment for an additional period.

(4) the parenting coordinator seeks to withdraw from service in a case, the parenting coordinator shall petition the court and provide a copy of the petition to the parties or the parties' attorneys.

(5) The parenting coordinator shall set forth in a separate written agreement with the parties:

    (i)   the amount of any retainer;

    (ii)   the hourly rate to be charged;

    (iii) the process for invoices and payment for services;

    (iv) information on the parenting coordination process; and

    (v)   provide a signed copy of the agreement to the parties before initiating any services.

Note: The parenting coordinator shall include in the parties' written agreement the hourly rate established by the judicial district.

(b) Qualifications of the Parenting Coordinator.

(1) A parenting coordinator shall be licensed to practice in the Commonwealth of Pennsylvania as either an attorney or a mental health professional with a master's degree or higher. At a minimum, the parenting coordinator shall have:

    (i)   practiced family law for five years or have five years of professional post-degree experience in psychiatry, psychology, counseling, family therapy, or other comparable behavioral or social science field; and

    (ii)   specialized training by a provider approved or certified by the American Psychological Association, Pennsylvania Psychological Association, American Bar Association, Pennsylvania Bar Association, Pennsylvania Bar Institute, or American Academy of Matrimonial Lawyers. The training shall include:

    (A) five hours in the parenting coordination process;

    (B) ten hours of family mediation;

    (C) five hours of training in domestic violence; and

    (D) in each two-year period after the initial appointment, ten continuing education credits on any topic related to parenting coordination with a minimum of two hours on domestic violence.

    (2) An attorney or a mental health professional seeking an appointment as a parenting coordinator:

        (i)   shall sign an affidavit attesting that he or she has met the qualifications outlined in (b)(1);

        (ii)   shall submit the affidavit to the president judge or administrative judge of the judicial district where the parenting coordinator is seeking appointment; and

        (iii) after submission of the initial affidavit, a parenting coordinator shall submit a new affidavit every two years attesting that he or she continues to meet the qualifications for a parenting coordinator outlined in (b)(1).

(c)   Appointment Order. The parenting coordinator's authority as delineated in subdivision (d) shall be included in the order appointing the parenting coordinator, which shall be substantially in the form set forth in Pa.R.C.P. No. 1915.22.

(d)   Scope of Authority of the Parenting Coordinator. The parenting coordinator shall have the authority to recommend resolutions to the court on issues related to the custody order if the parties are unable to reach an agreement.

    (1) To implement the custody order and resolve related parenting issues about which the parties cannot agree, the parenting coordinator is authorized to recommend resolutions to the court about issues that include, but are not limited to:

        (i)   places and conditions for custodial transitions between households;

        (ii)   temporary variation from the custodial schedule for a special event or particular circumstance;

        (iii) school issues, apart from school selection;

        (iv) the child(ren)'s participation in recreation, enrichment, and extracurricular activities, including travel;

        (v)   child-care arrangements;

        (vi) clothing, equipment, toys, and personal possessions of the child(ren);

        (vii) information exchanges (e.g., school, health, social) between the parties and communication with or about the child(ren);

(viii) coordination of existing or court-ordered services for the child(ren) (e.g., psychological testing, alcohol or drug monitoring/testing, psychotherapy, anger management);

(ix) behavioral management of the child(ren); and

(x)   other related custody issues that the parties mutually have agreed in writing to submit to the parenting coordinator, which are not excluded in subdivision (d)(2).

(2) The following issues are excluded from the parenting coordinator's scope of authority:

(i)   a change in legal custody as set forth in the custody order;

(ii) a change in primary physical custody as set forth in the custody order;

(iii) except as set forth in subdivision (d)(1)(ii), a change in the court-ordered custody schedule that reduces or expands the child(ren)'s time with a party;

(iv) a change in the residence (relocation) of the child(ren);

(v)   determination of financial issues, other than allocation of the parenting coordinator's fees as set forth in subdivision (g)(1);

(vi) major decisions affecting the health, education, or religion of the child(ren); and

(vii) other issues limited by the appointing judge.

(3) Unless the parties consent, the parenting coordinator shall not contact collateral sources or speak with the child(ren) and to effectuate this provision, the parties shall execute releases, as necessary, authorizing the parenting coordinator to communicate with the appropriate individuals. Any communication with the collateral sources or child(ren) shall be limited to the issue(s) currently before the parenting coordinator.

(e) Communications. No Testimony.

(1) Communication between the parties or the parties' attorneys and the parenting coordinator is not confidential.

(2) A party or a party's attorney may communicate in writing with the parenting coordinator, but shall contemporaneously

send a copy of the written communication to the other party or the other party's attorney. Documents, recordings, or other material that one party gives to the parenting coordinator shall be promptly made available to the other party or the other party's attorney for inspection and copying.

(3) The parties and their attorneys may receive, but not initiate, oral *ex parte* communication with the parenting coordinator. A parenting coordinator may initiate oral communication with a party or party's attorney, but shall promptly advise the other party or the other party's attorney of the communication.

(4) Communication between the parenting coordinator and the court shall be in writing and copies of the written communication shall be sent contemporaneously to the parties or the parties' attorneys.

(5) A party cannot compel the testimony of a parenting coordinator without an order of court.

(f) Recommendations. Objecting to the Recommendation. Judicial Review. Record Hearing.

(1) The parenting coordinator shall provide to the parties notice and an opportunity to be heard on the issues.

(2) The parenting coordinator's recommendation shall be in writing on the Summary and Recommendation of the Parenting Coordinator form set forth in Pa.R.C.P. No. 1915.23 and sent to the court for review within two days after hearing from the parties on the issues. The parenting coordinator shall serve a copy of the Summary and Recommendation on the parties or the parties' attorneys.

(3) A party objecting to the recommendation shall file a petition for a record hearing before the court within five days of service of the Summary and Recommendation of the Parenting Coordinator form. The petition must specifically state the issues to be reviewed and include a demand for a record hearing. A copy of the recommendation shall be attached to the petition. In accordance with Pa.R.C.P. No. 440, the objecting party shall serve the petition on the other party or the other party's attorney and the parenting coordinator.

(4) If the parties do not file an objection within five days of service of the parenting coordinator's recommendation, the court shall:

(i)   approve the recommendation;

(ii)   approve the recommendation in part and conduct a record hearing on issues not approved;

(iii) remand the recommendation to the parenting coordinator for more specific information; or

(iv)   not approve the recommendation and conduct a record hearing on the issues.

(5) As soon as practical, the court shall conduct a record hearing on the issues specifically set forth in the petition. The court shall render a decision within the time set forth in Pa.R.C.P. No. 1915.4(d).

(6) If a party makes a timely objection, the recommendation shall become an interim order of court pending further disposition by the court.

(g) Fees.

(1) The appointing judge shall allocate between the parties the fees of the parenting coordinator. The parenting coordinator may reallocate the fees, subject to the approval of the court, if one party has caused a disproportionate need for the services of the parenting coordinator.

(2) To limit the financial burden on the parties, a parenting coordinator should meet with the parties only upon a request of a party to resolve an issue about which the parties disagree.

(3) Waiver of fees or reduced fees. Judicial districts implementing a parenting coordination program shall effectuate a policy or program by local rule so that indigent or low-income parties may participate in the parenting coordination program at a reduced fee or no fee.

§ 19.3.   FORM ORDER APPOINTING PARENTING COORDINATOR

The following is Rule 1915.22 which provides the form order for appointing a parenting coordinator:

Rule 1915.22. Form of Order Appointing Parenting Coordinator. The order appointing a parenting coordinator pursuant to Pa.R.C.P. No. 1915.11-1 shall be in substantially the following form:

(Caption)

ORDER OF COURT

AND NOW, this _____ day of _____ , 20__, it is hereby ordered as follows:

1. APPOINTMENT AND TERM:

Pursuant to Pa.R.C.P. No. 1915.11-1,_____ is appointed as the parties' parenting coordinator for a term of _____ months (not exceeding 12 months).

Legal counsel for _____ , or either party, if unrepresented, shall provide copies of all orders, pleadings and custody evaluations in this case to the parenting coordinator within ten (10) days of the date of this order.

2. ROLE OF THE PARENTING COORDINATOR:

(a)   The parenting coordinator shall attempt to resolve issues arising out of the custody order by facilitating an agreement between the parties and, if unable to reach an agreement, recommend a resolution to the court.

(b)   The parenting coordinator shall not function as the attorney, advocate, counselor, or psychotherapist for the parties, the parties' child(ren), or family. However, the parenting coordinator is permitted and encouraged to facilitate communication and agreement between the parties when conflicts arise and shall always act in a manner conducive to the best interests of the child(ren).

3. PARENTING COORDINATOR'S SCOPE OF AUTHORITY:

To implement the custodial arrangement set forth in the custody order and resolve related parenting issues about which the parties cannot agree, the parenting coordinator is authorized to recommend resolutions to the court about issues that include, but are not limited to:

(a) places and conditions for transitions between households;

(b) temporary variation from the schedule for a special event or particular circumstance;

(c) school issues, apart from school selection;

(d) the child(ren)'s participation in recreation, enrichment, and extracurricular activities, including travel;

(e) child-care arrangements;

(f) clothing, equipment, toys, and personal possessions of the child(ren);

(g) information exchanges (e.g., school, health, social) and communication with or about the child(ren);

(h) coordination of existing or court-ordered services for the child(ren) (e.g., psychological testing, alcohol or drug monitoring/testing, psychotherapy, anger management);

(i) behavioral management of the child(ren); and

(j) other related custody issues that the parties mutually have agreed in writing to submit to the parenting coordinator, which are not excluded in Paragraph 4.

4. EXCLUSIONS FROM PARENTING COORDINATOR'S AUTHORITY:

(a) The following specific issues are excluded from the parenting coordinator's scope of authority:

(1) a change in legal custody as set forth in the custody order;

(2) a change in primary physical custody set forth in the custody order;

(3) other than as set forth in Paragraph 3(b), a change in the court-ordered custody schedule that reduces or expands the child(ren)'s time with a party;

(4) a change in the residence (relocation) of the child(ren);

(5) determination of financial issues, other than allocation of the parenting coordinator's fees as set forth in Pa.R.C.P 1915.11-1(g)(1);

(6) major decisions affecting the health, education, or religion of the child(ren); and

(7) Other:_____

(b) Unless the parties consent, the parenting coordinator shall not contact collateral sources or speak with the child(ren). The parties shall execute releases, as necessary, authorizing the parenting coordinator to communicate with the appropriate individuals. Any communication with the collateral sources or child(ren) shall be limited to the issue(s) currently before the parenting coordinator.

5. COMMUNICATIONS:

(a) The parenting coordinator shall determine the protocol of all communications, interviews, and sessions, including who shall attend the sessions (including the children), and whether the sessions will be conducted in person or by other means. The protocols should include measures addressing the safety of all participants.

(b) Communication between the parties or their attorneys and the parenting coordinator is not confidential.

(c) The parties and their attorneys shall have the right to receive, but not initiate, oral ex parte communication with the parenting coordinator. The parenting coordinator shall promptly advise the other party or the other party's attorney of the communication. A party or a party's attorney may communicate in writing with the parenting coordinator, but shall contemporaneously send a copy of the written communication to the other party or the other party's attorney. Documents, recordings, or other material that one party gives to the parenting coordinator must be promptly made available to the other party or the other party's attorney for inspection and copying.

(d) Communication between the parenting coordinator and the court shall be in writing and copies of the written communication shall be sent contemporaneously to the parties or the parties' attorneys.

(e) A party cannot compel the testimony of a parenting coordinator without an order of court.

6. PARENTING COORDINATION PROCESS:

(a) The parenting coordinator shall provide to the parties notice and an opportunity to be heard on the issues.

(b) The parenting coordinator's recommendation shall be in writing on the Summary and Recommendation of the Parenting Coordinator form set forth in Pa.R.C.P. No. 1915.23 and sent to the court for review within two days after hearing from the parties on the issues. The parenting coordinator shall serve a copy of the Summary and Recommendation on the parties or the parties' attorneys.

(c) A party objecting to the recommendation shall file a petition for a record hearing before the court within five days of service of the Summary and Recommendation of the Parenting Coordinator form. The petition must specifically state the issues to be reviewed and include a demand for a record hearing. A copy of the recommendation shall be attached to the petition. In accordance with Pa.R.C.P. No. 440, the objecting party shall serve the petition upon the other party or the party's attorney and the parenting coordinator.

7. RECORD HEARING:

(a) If the parties do not file an objection within five days of service of the parenting coordinator's recommendation, the court shall:

(1) approve the recommendation;

(2) approve the recommendation in part and conduct a record hearing on issues not approved;

(3) remand the recommendation to the parenting coordinator for more specific information; or

(4) not approve the recommendation and conduct a record hearing on the issues.

(b) As soon as practical, the court shall conduct a record hearing on the issues specifically set forth in the petition. The court shall render a decision within the time set forth in Pa.R.C.P. No. 1915.4(d).

(c) If a party makes a timely objection, the recommendation shall become an interim order of court pending further disposition by the court.

8. ALLOCATION OF FEES:

(a) The parties will share the obligation to pay the fees of the parenting coordinator as follows: ___% Mother, ___% Father, ___% Third party. Fees may be reallocated by the court or the parenting coordinator if a party has disproportionately caused the need for the services of the parenting coordinator.

(b) The judicial district's established hourly rate for parenting coordinators shall be set forth in a separate written agreement entered into between the parties and the parenting coordinator.

(c) The parties will pay a joint retainer to the parenting coordinator in the percentages set forth above in an amount to be set forth in a separate agreement between the parties and the parenting coordinator. After each session, or at least once monthly, the parenting coordinator shall provide the parties with an invoice of charges incurred. The retainer may be replenished as services are rendered. Funds remaining at the conclusion of the parenting coordinator's appointment shall be returned to the parties.

9. TERMINATION/WITHDRAWAL OF PARENTING COORDINATOR:

(a) The parties may not terminate the parenting coordinator's services without court approval.

(b) A party seeking the termination of the parenting coordinator's services shall serve the other party or the party's attorney and parenting coordinator with a copy of the petition for termination.

(c) If the parenting coordinator seeks to withdraw from service in a case, the parenting coordinator shall petition the court and provide a copy of the petition to the parties or the parties' attorneys.

10. APPEAL:

If there is an appeal of the underlying custody order or this order, then this order shall be stayed during the pendency of the appeal.

BY THE COURT:

J.

§ 19.4. FORM OF SUMMARY AND RECOMMENDATION OF PARENTING COORDINATOR

The following is Rule 1915.23 which provides the form of the Summary and Recommendation of the parenting coordinator:

Rule 1915.23. Form of the Summary and Recommendation of the Parenting Coordinator.

The recommendation of the parenting coordinator shall be in writing and shall be in substantially the following form:

(Caption)

SUMMARY AND RECOMMENDATION
OF THE PARENTING COORDINATOR

The undersigned, the duly appointed parenting coordinator in the above-captioned matter, pursuant to the Order of Court dated _____, 20__, after submission of the issue described below and after providing the parties with an opportunity to heard on the issue, the parenting coordinator sets forth the following:

SUMMARY OF THE ISSUE(S)

1. Description of the issue(s):

_____

_____

2. The respective parties' position on the issue(s):

_____

_____

_____

_____

RECOMMENDATION

_____

_____

_____

_____

_____

_____

Within five days of the date set forth below, a party may object to this recommendation by filing a petition with the court and requesting a record hearing before the judge as set forth in Pa.R.C.P. No. 1915.11-1(f)(3).

The undersigned parenting coordinator certifies that this Summary and Recommendation of the Parenting Coordinator has been served on the court and the parties or the parties' attorneys on the date set forth below

_____   _____

Date   Parenting Coordinator

ORDER OF COURT

JUDICIAL REVIEW OF PARENTING
COORDINATOR'S RECOMMENDATION

☐ The Recommendation is approved.

☐ The Recommendation is approved in part. The issue(s) not approved by the court is/are:

_____

_____

and a record hearing is scheduled for_____, 20___ at_____ a.m./p.m. before the undersigned.

☐ The Recommendation is remanded to the parenting coordinator for additional information on the following issue(s): _____

_____

☐ The Recommendation is not approved and a record hearing on the issue(s) is scheduled for _____, 20___ at a.m./p.m. before the undersigned.

By the Court:

_____

J.

Chapter 20

DISCOVERY

§ 20.1. Generally

§ 20.1. GENERALLY

Discovery is not as of right in custody cases and leave of court is required.[4] The court may enter an order quashing a subpoena, notice to attend or notice to produce and enter a protective order precluding the service of further discovery in custody actions without authorization of discovery.[5] *See* Chapters 3, 4, 6, 10, and 11 of this book for a more detailed analysis of evidence and experts.

LOWER COURT CASES

Franklin County

Harris v. Varner, 23 Franklin Co. Leg. J. 134 (C.C.P. 2005) (trial court held that Pa.R.Civ.P. 1930.5 and Pa.R.Civ.P. 1915.5 bar discovery in custody cases without first seeking permission from the court. However, Pa.R.Civ.P. 1930.5(a) and Pa.R.Civ.P. 1915.5(c) allow the court to consider a special order for limited discovery in custody cases. The issue before the court was whether the court should grant plaintiff's Motion to Quash a Subpoena which defendant's counsel served upon the Fulton County Domestic Relations Office. The subpoena ordered the Fulton County Domestic Relations Office to produce "a copy of entire Domestic Relations file in re the above referenced matter." In support of her argument that defendant's subpoena should be quashed, plaintiff referred to Pa.R.Civ.P. 1930.5(a) governing domestic relations generally and 1915.5(c) governing custody matters specifically. Defendant argued that the issuance of a subpoena under the circumstances was not discovery.

The court declared: "It is abundantly clear, based both on the placement of the rules for subpoenas in the chapter on Depositions and Discovery, and upon the explanatory comment, that the Rules of Civil Procedure in Pennsylvania include subpoenas

---

[4] *See* Pa.R.C.P. 1915.5(c) & 1930.5(a).
[5] *See* Pa.R.C.P. 234.4 & 4012.

as a form of discovery. Accordingly, the fair and logical answer to the Defendant's first posed issue is that the subpoena in question—seeking production of documents from a non-party—does violate the Pennsylvania Rules of Civil Procedure 1930.5(a) and 1915.5(c) because it was obtained without first applying to the Court for a special Order. . . . the Rules of Civil Procedure relating to Domestic Relations matters generally and to custody matters in particular envision potential abuses in Domestic Relations matters; and those rules therefore forbid discovery unless a cogent case can be made to the Court for a special order allowing necessary and focused discovery.").

Northampton County

Davis v. Peppers, 52 Northampton Co. Rep. 172 (C.C.P. 2011) (Trial court held that there was nothing in the 2011 amendments to the custody statutes that would indicate a departure from the general rule that discovery should not be permitted in custody cases. Plaintiff in a custody action filed a motion to permit discovery. As the basis for the motion, plaintiff asserted that discovery was necessitated by the 2011 amendments to the statutes governing custody matters. Plaintiff argued that discovery would aid the court in making a custody determination pursuant to the statutory factors set out at 23 Pa.C.S. § 5328. The trial court denied the request upon a finding that there was nothing about the statutory changes necessitating a departure from the general rule that discovery should not be permitted in custody cases. The court noted that the current custody statute, enacted on January 24, 2011, is essentially a codification of prior case law. There is nothing about the statute itself that necessitates discovery. There was no compelling reason or exigency suggesting that discovery was necessary to the disposition of the instant case).

APPENDICES

APPENDIX A. State Statutes

    Appendix A(1): Title 23, Part VI, Ch. 51. General Provisions

    Appendix A(2): Title 23, Part VI, Ch. 53. Child Custody

    Appendix A(3): Title 23, Part VI, Ch. 53. Custody (*Repealed*)

    Appendix A(4): Title 23, Part VI, Ch. 54. UCCJEA

    Appendix A(5): Title 23, Part VI, Ch. 55. Liability for Tortious Acts of Children

    Appendix A(6): Title 23, Part VI, Ch. 56. Standby Guardianship Act

    Appendix A(7): Title 42, Ch. 74. Collaborative Law Process

    Appendix A(8): Title 51, Military Affairs

APPENDIX B. Federal Statutes

    Appendix B(1): 28 U. S. C. § 1738A. Full Faith and Credit Given to Child Custody Determinations (PKPA).

    Appendix B(2): 42 U. S. C. § 663. Use of Federal Parent Locator Service in Connection With Enforcement or Determination of a Child Custody in Cases of Parental Kidnapping of a Child.

    Appendix B(3): 18 U. S. C. § 1073. Flight to Avoid Prosecution or Giving Testimony

    Appendix B(4): 18 U. S. C. § 1204. International Parental Kidnapping.

APPENDIX C. Pennsylvania Rules of Civil Procedure (Pa. R. C. P.)— Custody

APPENDIX D. Convention on the Civil Aspects of International Child Abduction (Hague Convention)

APPENDIX E. FORMS

    FORM 1. Notice to Defend

    FORM 2. Custody Complaint

    FORM 3. Petition to Modify Custody

    FORM 4. Petition for Contempt

    FORM 5. Petition for Writ *Ne Exeat*

    FORM 6. Petition for Mental Examination

    FORM 7. Petition for Home Study

    FORM 8. Notice of Intent to Relocate

    FORM 9. Counter-Affidavit Regarding Relocation

    FORM 10. Statement of Objection to Relocation

APPENDIX A

STATE STATUTES

TITLE 23

PART VI: CHILDREN AND MINORS

Chapter

Enactment. Part VI was added October 30, 1985, P. L. 264, No. 66, effective in 90 days.

Cross References. Part VI is referred to in section 5948 of Title 42 (Judiciary and Judicial Procedure).

(Amended Through September 30, 2020)

APPENDIX A(1)

CHAPTER 51: GENERAL PROVISIONS
Sec.

Enactment. Chapter 51 was added December 19, 1990, P. L. 1240, No. 206, effective in 90 days.

§ 5101.   Attainment of full age.

(a) Age for entering into contracts.—Any individual 18 years of age and older shall have the right to enter into binding and legally enforceable contracts and the defense of minority shall not be available to such individuals.

(b) Age for suing and being sued.—Except where otherwise provided or prescribed by law, an individual 18 years of age and older shall be deemed an adult and may sue and be sued as such.

§ 5102.   Children declared to be legitimate.

(a) General rule.—All children shall be legitimate irrespective of the marital status of their parents, and, in every case where children are born out of wedlock, they shall enjoy all the rights and privileges as if they had been born during the wedlock of their parents except as otherwise provided in Title 20 (relating to decedents, estates and fiduciaries).

(b) Determination of paternity.—For purposes of prescribing benefits to children born out of wedlock by, from and through the father, paternity shall be determined by any one of the following ways:

(1)   If the parents of a child born out of wedlock have married each other.

(2)   If, during the lifetime of the child, it is determined by clear and convincing evidence that the father openly holds out the child to be his and either receives the child into his home or provides support for the child.

(3)   If there is clear and convincing evidence that the man was the father of the child, which may include a prior court determination of paternity.

§ 5103.   Acknowledgment and claim of paternity.

(a) Acknowledgment of paternity.—The father of a child born to an unmarried woman may file with the Department of Public Welfare, on forms prescribed by the department, an acknowledgment of paternity of the child which shall include the consent of the mother of the child, supported by her witnessed statement subject to 18 Pa. C. S. § 4904 (relating to unsworn falsification to authorities). In such case, the father shall have all the rights and duties as to the child which he would have had if he had been married to the mother at the time of the birth of the child, and the child shall have all the rights and duties as to the father which the child would have had if the father had been married to the mother at the time of birth. The hospital or other person accepting an acknowledgment of paternity shall provide written and oral notice, which may be through the use of video or audio equipment, to the birth mother and birth father of the alternatives to, the legal consequences of and the rights and respon-sibilities that arise from, signing the acknowledgement.

(b) Claim of paternity.—If the mother of the child fails or refuses to join in the acknowledgment of paternity provided for in subsection (a), the Department of Public Welfare shall index it as a claim of paternity. The filing and indexing of a claim of paternity shall not confer upon the putative father any rights as to the child except that the putative father shall be entitled to notice of any proceeding brought to terminate any parental rights as to the child.

(c) Duty of hospital or birthing center.—Upon the birth of a child to an unmarried woman, an agent of the hospital or birthing center where the birth occurred shall:

(1)   Provide the newborn's birth parents with an opportunity to com-plete an acknowledgment of paternity. The completed, signed and witnessed acknowledgement shall be sent to the Department of Public Welfare. A copy shall be given to each of the birth par-ents. This acknowledgement shall contain:

    (i)   A signed, witnessed statement subject to 18 Pa. C. S. § 4904 (relating to unsworn falsification to authorities) by the birth mother consenting to the acknowledgment of paternity.

    (ii)   A signed, witnessed statement subject to 18 Pa. C. S. § 4904 by the birth father acknowledging his paternity.

    (iii)   A written explanation of the parental duties and parental rights which arise from signing such a statement.

    (iv)   The Social Security numbers and addresses of both birth parents.

(2)   Provide written information, furnished by the department to the birth mother and birth father, which explains the benefits of

having the child's paternity established, the availability of paternity establishment services and the availability of child support enforcement agencies.

(d) Conclusive evidence.—Notwithstanding any other provision of law, an acknowledgment of paternity shall constitute conclusive evidence of paternity without further judicial ratification in any action to establish support. The court shall give full faith and credit to an acknowledgment of paternity signed in another state according to its procedures.

(e) Transfer.—The Department of Health shall transfer to the Department of Public Welfare all acknowledgments or claims of paternity filed with the Department of Health under prior statutes.

(f) Certifications.—The Department of Public Welfare shall provide necessary certifications under Part III (relating to adoption) as to whether any acknowledgment or claim of paternity has been filed in regard to any child who is a prospective adoptive child.

(g) Recission.—

(1) Notwithstanding any other provision of law, a signed voluntary, witnessed acknowledgement of paternity subject to 18 Pa. C. S. § 4904 shall be considered a legal finding of paternity, subject to the right of any signatory to rescind the acknowledgment within the earlier of the following:

    (i)   sixty days; or

    (ii) the date of an administrative or judicial proceeding relating to the child, including, but not limited to, a domestic relations section conference, or a proceeding to establish a support order in which the signatory is a party.

(2) After the expiration of the 60 days, an acknowledgment of paternity may be challenged in court only on the basis of fraud, duress or material mistake of fact, which must be established by the challenger through clear and convincing evidence. An order for support shall not be suspended during the period of challenge except for good cause shown.

(h) Penalties for noncompliance.—The department may impose a civil penalty of not to exceed $500 per day upon a hospital or birthing center which is not in compliance with the provisions of this section. A penalty under this subsection is subject to 2 Pa. C. S. Ch. 5 Subch. A (relating to practice and procedures of Commonwealth agencies) and Ch. 7 Subch. A (relating to judicial review of Commonwealth agency action).

(i) Status of father.—The name of the father shall be included on the record of birth of the child of unmarried parents only if one of the following applies:

(1) The father and mother have signed a voluntary acknowledgement of paternity.

(2) A court or administrative agency of competent jurisdiction has issued an adjudication of paternity.

§ 5104.   Blood tests to determine paternity.

(a) Short title of section.—This section shall be known and may be cited as the Uniform Act on Blood Tests to Determine Paternity.

(b) Scope of section.—

(1) Civil matters.—This section shall apply to all civil matters.

(2) Criminal proceedings.—This section shall apply to all criminal proceedings subject to the following limitations and provisions:

   (i)   An order for the tests shall be made only upon application of a party or on the initiative of the court.

   (ii) The compensation of the experts shall be paid by the party requesting the blood test or by the county, as the court shall direct.

   (iii) The court may direct a verdict of acquittal upon the conclusions of all the experts under subsection (f). Otherwise, the case shall be submitted for determination upon all the evidence.

(iv)   The refusal of a defendant to submit to the tests may not be used in evidence against the defendant.

(c) Authority for test.—In any matter subject to this section in which paternity, parentage or identity of a child is a relevant fact, the court, upon its own initiative or upon suggestion made by or on behalf of any person whose blood is involved, may or, upon motion of any party to the action made at a time so as not to delay the proceedings unduly, shall order the mother, child and alleged father to submit to blood tests. If any party refuses to submit to the tests, the court may resolve the question of paternity, parentage or identity of a child against the party or enforce its order if the rights of others and the interests of justice so require.

(d) Selection of experts.—The tests shall be made by experts qualified as examiners of blood types, who shall be appointed by the court. The experts shall be called by the court as witnesses to testify to their findings and shall be subject to cross-examination by the parties. Any party or person at whose suggestion the tests have been ordered may demand that other experts qualified as examiners of blood types perform independent tests under order of court, the results of which may be offered in evidence. The number and qualifications of experts shall be determined by the court.

(e) Compensation of experts.—The compensation of each expert witness appointed by the court shall be fixed at a reasonable amount. It shall be paid as the court shall order. Subject to general rules, the court may order that it be paid by the parties in such proportions and at such times as it shall prescribe or that the proportion of any party be paid by the county and that, after payment by the parties or the county, or both, all or part or none of it be taxed as costs in the action. Subject to general rules, the fee of an expert witness called by a party but not appointed by the court shall be paid by the party calling him, but shall not be taxed as costs in the action.

(f) Effect of test results.—If the court finds that the conclusions of all the experts as disclosed by the evidence based upon the tests are that the alleged father is not the father of the child, the question of paternity, parentage or identity of a child shall be resolved accordingly. If the experts disagree in their findings or conclusions, the question shall be submitted upon all the evidence.

(g) Effect on presumption of legitimacy.—The presumption of legitimacy of a child born during wedlock is overcome if the court finds that the conclusions of all the experts as disclosed by the evidence based upon the tests show that the husband is not the father of the child.

§ 5105. Fingerprinting of children.

Notwithstanding the provisions of 54 Pa. C. S. § 702(b) (relating to change by order of court), a child who is 12 years of age or younger shall not be required to submit a set of fingerprints for the purpose of a name change under 54 Pa. C. S. Ch. 7 (relating to judicial change of name).

1998 Amendment. Act 127, § 9 added this section.

CHAPTER 52: UNIFORM CHILD ABDUCTION PREVENTION

Enactment. Chapter 52 was added January 22, 2014, P.L.8, No.5, effective in 90 days.

§ 5201. Scope of chapter.

This chapter relates to uniform child abduction prevention.

633

§ 5202. Definitions.

The following words and phrases when used in this chapter shall have the meanings given to them in this section unless the context clearly indicates otherwise:

"Abduction." The wrongful removal or wrongful retention of a child.

"Child." An unemancipated individual who is under 18 years of age.

"Child custody determination." Any judgment, decree or other order of a court providing for the legal custody, physical custody or visitation with respect to a child. The term includes a permanent, temporary, initial and modification order.

"Child custody proceeding." A proceeding in which legal custody, physical custody or visitation with respect to a child is at issue. The term includes a proceeding for divorce, dissolution of marriage, separation, neglect, abuse, dependency, guardianship, paternity, termination of parental rights or protection from domestic violence.

"Court." An entity authorized under the law of a state to establish, enforce or modify a child custody determination.

"Petition." A motion or its equivalent.

"Record." Information that is inscribed on a tangible medium or that is stored in an electronic or other medium and is retrievable in perceivable form.

"State." A state of the United States, the District of Columbia, Puerto Rico, the Virgin Islands or any territory or insular possession subject to the jurisdiction of the United States. The term includes a federally recognized Indian tribe or nation.

"Travel document." Records relating to a travel itinerary, including travel tickets, passes, reservations for transportation or accommodations. The term does not include a passport or visa.

"Wrongful removal." The taking of a child that breaches rights of custody or visitation given or recognized under the laws of this Commonwealth.

"Wrongful retention." The keeping or concealing of a child that breaches rights of custody or visitation given or recognized under the laws of this Commonwealth.

§ 5203. Cooperation and communication among courts.

Sections 5410 (relating to communication between courts), 5411 (relating to taking testimony in another state) and 5412 (relating to cooperation between courts; preservation of records) apply to cooperation and communication among courts in proceedings under this chapter.

§ 5204. Actions for abduction prevention measures.

(a) Court.—A court on its own motion may order abduction prevention measures in a child custody proceeding if the court finds that the evidence establishes a credible risk of abduction of the child.

(b) Party.—A party to a child custody determination or another individual or entity having a right under the laws of this Commonwealth or any other state to seek a child custody determination for the child may file a petition seeking abduction prevention measures to protect the child under this chapter.

(c) Prosecutors or public officials.—A prosecutor or public authority designated under section 5455 (relating to role of prosecutor or public official) may seek a warrant to take physical custody of a child under section 5209 (relating to warrant to take physical custody of child) or other appropriate prevention measures.

§ 5205. Jurisdiction.

(a) General rule.—A petition under this chapter may be filed only in a court that has jurisdiction to make a child custody determination with respect to the child at issue under Chapter 54 (relating to uniform child custody jurisdiction and enforcement).

(b) Emergency jurisdiction.—A court of this Commonwealth has temporary emergency jurisdiction under section 5424 (relating to temporary emergency jurisdiction) if the court finds a credible risk of abduction.

§ 5206. Contents of petition.

A petition under this chapter must be verified and include a copy of any existing child custody determination, if available. The petition must specify the risk factors for abduction, including the relevant factors described under section 5207 (relating to factors to determine risk of abduction). Subject to section 5429(e) (relating to information to be submitted to court), if reasonably ascertainable, the petition must contain:

(1) the name, date of birth and gender of the child;

(2) the customary address and current physical location of the child;

(3) the identity, customary address and current physical location of the respondent;

(4) a statement of whether a prior action to prevent abduction or domestic violence has been filed by a party or other individual or entity having custody of the child and the date, location and disposition of the action;

(5) a statement of whether a party to the proceeding has been arrested for a crime related to domestic violence, stalking or child abuse or neglect and the date, location and disposition of the case; and

(6) any other information required to be submitted to the court for a child custody determination under section 5429.

§ 5207. Factors to determine risk of abduction.

(a) **Evidence supporting risk.**—In determining whether there is a credible risk of abduction of a child, the court shall consider any evidence that the petitioner or respondent:

(1) has previously abducted or attempted to abduct the child;

(2) has threatened to abduct the child;

(3) has recently engaged in activities that may indicate a planned abduction, including:

   (i) abandoning employment;

   (ii) selling a primary residence;

(iii)   terminating a lease;

(iv)   closing bank or other financial management accounts, liquidating assets, hiding or destroying financial documents or conducting any unusual financial activities;

(v)   applying for a passport or visa or obtaining travel documents for the respondent, a family member or the child; or

(vi)   seeking to obtain the child's birth certificate or school or medical records;

(4)   as engaged in domestic violence, stalking or child abuse or neglect;

(5)   has refused to follow a child custody determination;

(6)   lacks strong familial, financial, emotional or cultural ties to this Commonwealth or the United States;

(7)   has strong familial, financial, emotional or cultural ties to another state or country;

(8)   is likely to take the child to a country that:

(i)   is not a party to the Hague Convention on the Civil Aspects of International Child Abduction and does not provide for the extradition of an abducting parent or for the return of an abducted child;

(ii)   is a party to the Hague Convention on the Civil Aspects of International Child Abduction but:

(A)   the Hague Convention on the Civil Aspects of International Child Abduction is not in force between the United States and that country;

(B)   according to the most recent compliance report issued by the United States Department of State, is noncompliant; or

(C)   lacks legal mechanisms for immediately and effectively enforcing a return order under the Hague Convention on the Civil Aspects of International Child Abduction;

(iii)   poses a risk that the child's physical or emotional health or safety would be endangered in the country because of

637

specific circumstances relating to the child or because of human rights violations committed against children;

(iv)   has laws or practices that would:

(A)   enable the respondent, without due cause, to prevent the petitioner from contacting the child;

(B)   restrict the petitioner from freely traveling to or exiting from the country because of the petitioner's gender, nationality, marital status or religion; or

(C)   restrict the child's ability legally to leave the country after the child reaches the age of majority because of a child's gender, nationality or religion;

(v)   is included by the United States Department of State on a current list of state sponsors of terrorism;

(vi)   does not have an official United States diplomatic presence in the country; or

(vii)   is engaged in active military action or war, including a civil war, to which the child may be exposed;

(9)   is undergoing a change in immigration or citizenship status that would adversely affect the respondent's ability to remain in the United States legally;

(10)   has had an application for United States citizenship denied;

(11)   has forged or presented misleading or false evidence on government forms or supporting documents to obtain or attempt to obtain a passport, a visa, travel documents, a Social Security card, a driver's license or other government-issued identification card or has made a misrepresentation to the United States Government;

(12)   has used multiple names to attempt to mislead or defraud; or

(13)   has engaged in any other conduct the court considers relevant to the risk of abduction.

(b) Good faith.—In the hearing on a petition under this chapter, the court shall consider any evidence that the respondent believed in good faith that the respondent's conduct was necessary to avoid imminent harm to the child or respondent and any other evidence that may be relevant to whether the respondent may be permitted to remove or retain the child.

Cross References. Section 5207 is referred to in section 5206 of this title.

§ 5208.   Provisions and measures to prevent abduction.

(a) Contents of discretionary orders.—If a petition is filed under this chapter, the court may enter an order that must include:

(1)   the basis for the court's exercise of jurisdiction;

(2)   the manner in which notice and opportunity to be heard were given to the persons entitled to notice of the proceeding;

(3)   a detailed description of each party's custody and visitation rights and residential arrangements for the child;

(4)   a provision stating that a violation of the order may subject the party in violation to civil and criminal penalties; and

(5)   identification of the child's country of habitual residence at the time of the issuance of the order.

(b) Abduction prevention orders.—

(1)   If, at a hearing on a petition under this chapter or on the court's own motion, the court after reviewing the evidence finds a credible risk of abduction of the child, the court shall enter an abduction prevention order.

(2)   The order must include the provisions required by subsection (a) and measures and conditions, including those in subsections (c), (d) and (e), that are reasonably calculated to prevent abduction of the child, giving due consideration to the custody and visitation rights of the parties.

(3)   The court shall consider:

    (i)   the age of the child;

    (ii)   the potential harm to the child from an abduction;

    (iii)   the legal and practical difficulties of returning the child to the jurisdiction if abducted; and

    (iv)   the reasons for the potential abduction, including evidence of domestic violence, stalking or child abuse or neglect.

(c) **Restrictions.**—An abduction prevention order may include one or more of the following:

(1)   an imposition of travel restrictions that require that a party traveling with the child outside a designated geographical area provide the other party with the following:

    (i)   the travel itinerary of the child;

    (ii)   a list of physical addresses and telephone numbers at which the child can be reached at specified times; and

    (iii)   copies of all travel documents;

(2)   a prohibition of the respondent directly or indirectly:

    (i)   removing the child from this Commonwealth, the United States or another geographic area without permission of the court or the petitioner's written consent;

    (ii)   removing or retaining the child in violation of a child custody determination;

    (iii)   removing the child from school or a child-care or similar facility; or

    (iv)   approaching the child at any location other than a site designated for supervised visitation;

(3)   a requirement that a party register the order in another state as a prerequisite to allowing the child to travel to that state;

(4)   with regard to the child's passport:

(i)   a direction that the petitioner place the child's name in the United States Department of State's Child Passport Issuance Alert Program;

(ii)   a requirement that the respondent surrender to the court or the petitioner's attorney any United States or foreign passport issued in the child's name, including a passport issued in the name of both the parent and the child; and

(iii)   a prohibition upon the respondent from applying on behalf of the child for a new or replacement passport or visa;

(5)   as a prerequisite to exercising custody or visitation, a requirement that the respondent provide:

(i)   to the United States Department of State Office of Children's Issues and the relevant foreign consulate or embassy, an authenticated copy of the order detailing passport and travel restrictions for the child;

(ii)   to the court:

     (A)   proof that the respondent has provided the information in subparagraph (i); and

     (B)   an acknowledgment in a record from the relevant foreign consulate or embassy that no passport application has been made or passport issued on behalf of the child;

(iii)   to the petitioner, proof of registration with the United States Embassy or other United States diplomatic presence in the destination country and with the Central Authority for the Hague Convention on the Civil Aspects of International Child Abduction, if that convention is in effect between the United States and the destination country, unless one of the parties objects; and

(iv)   a written waiver under 5 U.S.C. § 552a (relating to records maintained on individuals), with respect to any document, application or other information pertaining to the child authorizing its disclosure to the court and the petitioner; and

(6)   upon the petitioner's request, a requirement that the respondent obtain an order from the relevant foreign country containing

terms identical to the child custody determination issued in the United States.

(d) Conditions on custody and visitation.—In an abduction prevention order, the court may impose conditions on the exercise of custody or visitation that:

(1) limit visitation or require that visitation with the child by the respondent be supervised until the court finds that supervision is no longer necessary and order the respondent to pay the costs of supervision;

(2) require the respondent to post a bond or provide other security in an amount sufficient to serve as a financial deterrent to abduction, the proceeds of which may be used to pay for the reasonable expenses of recovery of the child, including reasonable attorney fees and costs if there is an abduction; and

(3) require the respondent to obtain education on the potentially harmful effects to the child from abduction.

(e) Prevention of imminent abduction.—To prevent imminent abduction of a child, a court may:

(1) issue a warrant to take physical custody of the child under section 5209 (relating to warrant to take physical custody of child) or the laws of this Commonwealth other than this chapter;

(2) direct the use of law enforcement to take any action reasonably necessary to locate the child, obtain return of the child or enforce a custody determination under this chapter or the laws of this Commonwealth other than this chapter; or

(3) grant any other relief allowed under the laws of this Commonwealth other than this chapter.

(f) Cumulative remedies.—The remedies provided in this chapter are cumulative and do not affect the availability of other remedies to prevent abduction.

§ 5209. Warrant to take physical custody of child.

(a) Ex parte.—If a petition under this chapter contains allegations and the court finds that there is a credible risk that the child is imminently likely to be wrongfully removed, the court may issue an ex parte warrant to take physical custody of the child.

(b) Hearing.—The respondent on a petition under subsection (a) must be afforded an opportunity to be heard at the earliest possible time after the ex parte warrant is executed, but not later than the next judicial day unless a hearing on that date is impossible. In that event, the court shall hold the hearing on the first judicial day possible.

(c) Requirements.—An ex parte warrant under subsection (a) to take physical custody of a child must:

(1) Recite the facts upon which a determination of a credible risk of imminent wrongful removal of the child is based.

(2) Direct law enforcement officers to take physical custody of the child immediately.

(3) State the date and time for the hearing on the petition.

(4) Provide for the safe interim placement of the child pending further order of the court.

(d) Search of databases.—If feasible, before issuing a warrant and before determining the placement of the child after the warrant is executed, the court may order a search of the relevant databases of the National Crime Information Center system and similar state databases to determine if either the petitioner or respondent has a history of domestic violence, stalking or child abuse or neglect.

(e) Service.—The petition and warrant must be served on the respondent when or immediately after the child is taken into physical custody.

(f) Enforcement.—

(1) A warrant to take physical custody of a child, issued by this Commonwealth or another state, is enforceable throughout this Commonwealth.

(2) If the court finds that a less intrusive remedy will not be effective, it may authorize law enforcement officers to enter private property to take physical custody of the child. If required by exigent circumstances, the court may authorize law enforcement officers to make a forcible entry at any hour.

(g) **Fees and costs.**—If the court finds, after a hearing, that a petitioner sought an ex parte warrant under subsection (a) for the purpose of harassment or in bad faith, the court may award the respondent reasonable attorney fees, costs and expenses.

(h) **Other relief.**—This chapter does not affect the availability of relief allowed under the laws of this Commonwealth other than this chapter.

Cross References. Section 5209 is referred to in sections 5204, 5208 of this title.

§ 5210. Duration of abduction prevention order.

An abduction prevention order remains in effect until the earliest of:

(1) the time stated in the order;

(2) the emancipation of the child;

(3) the child's attaining 18 years of age; or

(4) the time the order is modified, revoked, vacated or superseded by a court with jurisdiction under sections 5421 (relating to initial child custody jurisdiction), 5422 (relating to exclusive, continuing jurisdiction) and 5423 (relating to jurisdiction to modify determination) and applicable laws of this Commonwealth.

§ 5211. Uniformity of application and construction.

In applying and construing this chapter, consideration must be given to the need to promote uniformity of the law with respect to its subject matter among states that enact it.

§ 5212. Relation to Electronic Signatures in Global and National Commerce Act.

To the extent permitted by section 102 of the Electronic Signatures in Global and National Commerce Act (Public Law 106-229, 15 U.S.C. § 7002), this chapter may supersede provisions of that act.

APPENDIX A(2)

CHAPTER 53: CHILD CUSTODY

Enactment. Chapter 53 was added Nov. 23, 2010, P. L. ____, effective in 60 days [Jan. 24, 2011].

§ 5321. Scope of chapter.

This chapter applies to disputes relating to child custody matters.

§ 5322. Definitions.

(a) **This chapter.**—The following words and phrases when used in this chapter shall have the meanings given to them in this subsection unless the context clearly indicates otherwise:

"Abuse." As defined in section 6102 (relating to definitions).

"Adult." An individual 18 years of age or older.

"Agency." Any organization, society, institution, court facility or other entity which provides for the care of a child. The term does not include a county children and youth social service agency.

"Child." An unemancipated individual under 18 years of age.

"Legal custody." The right to make major decisions on behalf of the child, including, but not limited to, medical, religious and educational decisions.

"Parental duties." Includes meeting the physical, emotional and social needs of the child.

"Partial physical custody." The right to assume physical custody of the child for less than a majority of the time.

"Physical custody." The actual physical possession and control of a child.

"Primary physical custody." The right to assume physical custody of the child for the majority of time.

"Relocation." A change in a residence of the child which significantly impairs the ability of a nonrelocating party to exercise custodial rights.

"Shared legal custody." The right of more than one individual to legal custody of the child.

"Shared physical custody." The right of more than one individual to assume physical custody of the child, each having significant periods of physical custodial time with the child.

"Sole legal custody." The right of one individual to exclusive legal custody of the child.

"Sole physical custody." The right of one individual to exclusive physical custody of the child.

"Supervised physical custody." Custodial time during which an agency or an adult designated by the court or agreed upon by the parties monitors the interaction between the child and the individual with those rights.

(b) Other law.—in a statutory provision other than in this chapter, when the term "visitation" is used in reference to child custody, the term may be construed to mean:

(1) partial physical custody;

(2) shared physical custody; or

(3) supervised physical custody.

JT. ST. GOVT. COMM. COMMENT-2010

It is intended that shared legal custody includes consultation on major decisions and reasonable consent of the parties.

§ 5323.   Award of custody.

(a) Types of award.—After considering the factors set forth in section 5328 (relating to factors to consider when awarding custody), the court may award any of the following types of custody if it is in the best interest of the child:

(1) Shared physical custody.

(2) Primary physical custody.

(3) Partial physical custody.

(4) Sole physical custody.

(5) Supervised physical custody.

(6) Shared legal custody.

(7) Sole legal custody.

(b) Interim award.—The court may issue an interim award of custody to a party who has standing under section 5324 (relating to standing for any form of physical custody or legal custody) or 5325 (relating to standing for partial physical custody and supervised physical custody), in the manner prescribed by the Pennsylvania Rules of Civil Procedure governing special relief in custody matters.

(c) Notice.—Any custody order shall include notice of a party's obligations under section 5337 (relating to relocation).

(d) Reasons for award.—The court shall delineate the reasons for its decision on the record in open court or in a written opinion or order.

(e) Safety conditions.—After considering the factors under section 5328(a)(2), if the court finds that there is an ongoing risk of harm to the child or an abused party and awards any form of custody to a party who committed the abuse or who has a household member who committed the abuse, the court shall include in the custody order safety conditions designed to protect the child or the abused party.

(f) Enforcement.—In awarding custody, the court shall specify the terms and conditions of the award in sufficient detail to enable a party to enforce the court order through law enforcement authorities.

(g) Contempt for noncompliance with any custody order.—

(1)   A party who willfully fails to comply with any custody order may, as prescribed by general rule, be adjudged in contempt. Contempt shall be punishable by any one or more of the following:

(i)   Imprisonment for a period of not more than six months.

(ii)   A fine of not more than $500.

(iii)   Probation for a period of not more than six months.

(iv)   An order for nonrenewal, suspension or denial of operating privilege under section 4355 (relating to denial or suspension of licenses).

(v)   Counsel fees and costs.

(2)   An order committing an individual to jail under this section shall specify the condition which, when fulfilled, will result in the release of that individual.

(h) Parties in same residence.—Parties living separate and apart in the same residence may seek relief under this chapter, but any custody order made under such a circumstance shall be effective only upon:

(1) one party physically vacating the residence; or

(2) an order awarding one party exclusive possession of the residence.

JT. ST. GOVT. COMM. COMMENT-2010

Under subsection (a), the court should address both physical and legal custody in any award of custody. Subsection (b) provides for an interim award of special relief in accordance with the Pennsylvania Rule of Civil Procedure No. 1915.13. The explicit sanction of counsel fees and costs in subsection (g)(1)(v) is consistent with 23 Pa.C.S. §§ 3502(e)(7) regarding the sanction for failure to comply with an equitable distribution order and 3703(7) regarding payment of arrearages for alimony and alimony *pendente lite.* Subsection (h) removes a long-standing obstacle to a party who otherwise has standing to commence a custody action.

§ 5324. Standing for any form of physical custody or legal custody.

The following individuals may file an action under this chapter for any form of physical custody or legal custody:

(1) A parent of the child.

(2) A person who stands in loco parentis to the child.

(3) A grandparent of the child who is not in loco parentis to the child:

　(i) whose relationship with the child began either with the consent of a parent of the child or under a court order;

　(ii) who assumes or is willing to assume responsibility for the child; and

　(iii) when one of the following conditions is met:

　　(A) the child has been determined to be a dependent child under 42 Pa.C.S. Ch. 63 (relating to juvenile matters);

　　(B) the child is substantially at risk due to parental abuse, neglect, drug or alcohol abuse or incapacity; or

      (C) the child has, for a period of at least 12 consecutive months, resided with the grandparent, excluding brief temporary absences of the child from the home, and is removed from the home by the parents, in which case the action must be filed within six months after the removal of the child from the home.

(4)   Subject to paragraph (5), an individual who establishes by clear and convincing evidence all of the following:

      (i)   The individual has assumed or is willing to assume responsibility for the child.

      (ii)   The individual has a sustained, substantial and sincere interest in the welfare of the child. In determining whether the individual meets the requirements of this subparagraph, the court may consider, among other factors, the nature, quality, extent and length of the involvement by the individual in the child's life.

      (iii) Neither parent has any form of care and control of the child.

(5)   Paragraph (4) shall not apply if:

      (i)   a dependency proceeding involving the child has been initiated or is ongoing; or

      (ii)   there is an order of permanent legal custody under 42 Pa.C.S. § 6351(a)(2.1) or (f.1)(3) (relating to disposition of dependent child).

(May 4, 2018, P.L.112, No.21, eff. 60 days).

Note: The addition of 23 Pa. C.S. Sect. 5324(4) and (5) shall apply to all custody proceedings irrespective of whether the proceeding was commenced before, on or after the effective date of this section.

2018 Amendment. Act 21 added pars. (4) and (5). Section 3 of Act 21 provided that the addition of pars. (4) and (5) shall apply to all custody proceedings irrespective of whether the proceeding was commenced before, on or after the effective date of section 3.

Cross References. Section 5324 is referred to in sections 5323, 5325, 5326 of this title.

§ 5325. Standing for partial physical custody and supervised physical custody.

In addition to situations set forth in section 5324 (relating to standing for any form of physical custody or legal custody), grandparents and great-grandparents may file an action under this chapter for partial physical custody or supervised physical custody in the following situations:

(1) where the parent of the child is deceased, a parent or grandparent of the deceased parent may file an action under this section;

(2) where the relationship with the child began either with the consent of a parent of the child or under a court order and where the parents of the child:

   (i)   have commenced a proceeding for custody; and

   (ii) do not agree as to whether the grandparents or great-grandparents should have custody under this section; or

(3) when the child has, for a period of at least 12 consecutive months, resided with the grandparent or great-grandparent, excluding brief temporary absences of the child from the home, and is removed from the home by the parents, an action must be filed within six months after the removal of the child from the home.

(May 4, 2018, P.L.112, No.21, eff. 60 days)

2018 Amendment. Act 21 amended par. (2).

Cross References. Section 5325 is referred to in sections 5323, 5326, 5328 of this title.

JT. ST. GOVT. COMM. COMMENT-2010

See § 5328(c).

§ 5326. Effect of adoption.

Any rights to seek physical custody or legal custody rights and any custody rights that have been granted under section 5324 (relating to standing for any form of physical custody or legal custody) or 5325 (relating to standing for partial physical custody and supervised physical custody) to a grandparent or great-grandparent prior to the adoption of the child by an individual other than a stepparent, grandparent or great-grandparent shall be automatically terminated upon such adoption.

§ 5327. Presumption in cases concerning primary physical custody.

(a) Between parents.—In any action regarding the custody of the child between the parents of the child, there shall be no presumption that custody should be awarded to a particular parent.

(b) Between a parent and third party.—In any action regarding the custody of the child between a parent of the child and a nonparent, there shall be a presumption that custody shall be awarded to the parent. The presumption in favor of the parent may be rebutted by clear and convincing evidence.

(c) Between third parties.—In any action regarding the custody of the child between a nonparent and another nonparent, there shall be no presumption that custody should be awarded to a particular party.

§ 5328. Factors to consider when awarding custody.

(a) Factors.—In ordering any form of custody, the court shall determine the best interest of the child by considering all relevant factors, giving weighted consideration to those factors which affect the safety of the child, including the following:

(1) Which party is more likely to encourage and permit frequent and continuing contact between the child and another party.

(2) The present and past abuse committed by a party or member of the party's household, whether there is a continued risk of harm to the child or an abused party and which party can better provide adequate physical safeguards and supervision of the child.

(2.1) The information set forth in section 5329.1(a) (relating to consideration of child abuse and involvement with protective services).

(3) The parental duties performed by each party on behalf of the child.

(4) The need for stability and continuity in the child's education, family life and community life.

(5) The availability of extended family.

(6) The child's sibling relationships.

(7) The well-reasoned preference of the child, based on the child's maturity and judgment.

(8) The attempts of a parent to turn the child against the other parent, except in cases of domestic violence where reasonable safety measures are necessary to protect the child from harm.

(9) Which party is more likely to maintain a loving, stable, consistent and nurturing relationship with the child adequate for the child's emotional needs.

(10) Which party is more likely to attend to the daily physical, emotional, developmental, educational and special needs of the child.

(11) The proximity of the residences of the parties.

(12) Each party's availability to care for the child or ability to make appropriate child-care arrangements.

(13) The level of conflict between the parties and the willingness and ability of the parties to cooperate with one another. A party's effort to protect a child from abuse by another party is not evidence of unwillingness or inability to cooperate with that party.

(14) The history of drug or alcohol abuse of a party or member of a party's household.

(15) The mental and physical condition of a party or member of a party's household.

(16) Any other relevant factor.

(b) Gender neutral.—In making a determination under subsection (a), no party shall receive preference based upon gender in any award granted under this chapter.

(c) Grandparents and great-grandparents.—

(1) In ordering partial physical custody or supervised physical custody to a party who has standing under section 5325(1) or (2) (relating to standing for partial physical custody and supervised physical custody), the court shall consider the following:

    (i)   the amount of personal contact between the child and the party prior to the filing of the action;

    (ii)   whether the award interferes with any parent-child relationship; and

    (iii)   whether the award is in the best interest of the child.

(2)   In ordering partial physical custody or supervised physical custody to a parent's parent or grandparent who has standing under section 5325(3), the court shall consider whether the award:

    (i)   interferes with any parent-child relationship; and

    (ii)   is in the best interest of the child.

(Dec. 18, 2013, P.L.1167, No.107, eff. Jan. 1, 2014)

2013 Amendment. Act 107 added subsec. (a)(2.1). See section 6 of Act 107 in the appendix to this title for special provisions relating to applicability.

Cross References. Section 5328 is referred to in sections 5323, 6340 of this title; section 6307 of Title 42 (Judiciary and Judicial Procedure).

JT. ST. GOVT. COMM. COMMENT-2010

The factors under subsection (a) are not listed in order of preference. Subsection (a)(6) is intended to include full-blood siblings, half-blood siblings, step-siblings and adoptive siblings.

§ 5329.   Consideration of criminal conviction.

(a) Offenses.—Where a party seeks any form of custody, the court shall consider whether that party or member of that party's household has been convicted of or has pleaded guilty or no contest to any of the offenses in this section or an offense in another jurisdiction substantially equivalent to any of the offenses in this section. The court shall consider such conduct and determine that the party does not pose a threat of harm to the child before making any order of custody to that party when considering the following offenses:

- 18 Pa.C.S. Ch. 25 (relating to criminal homicide).

- 18 Pa.C.S. § 2702 (relating to aggravated assault).

- 18 Pa.C.S. § 2706 (relating to terroristic threats).

- 18 Pa.C.S. § 2709.1 (relating to stalking).

- 18 Pa.C.S. § 2901 (relating to kidnapping).

- 18 Pa.C.S. § 2902 (relating to unlawful restraint).

- 18 Pa.C.S. § 2903 (relating to false imprisonment).

- 18 Pa.C.S. § 2910 (relating to luring a child into a motor vehicle or structure).

- 18 Pa.C.S. § 3121 (relating to rape).

- 18 Pa.C.S. § 3122.1 (relating to statutory sexual assault).

- 18 Pa.C.S. § 3123 (relating to involuntary deviate sexual intercourse).

- 18 Pa.C.S. § 3124.1 (relating to sexual assault).

- 18 Pa.C.S. § 3125 (relating to aggravated indecent assault).

- 18 Pa.C.S. § 3126 (relating to indecent assault).

- 18 Pa.C.S. § 3127 (relating to indecent exposure).

- 18 Pa.C.S. § 3129 (relating to sexual intercourse with animal).

- 18 Pa.C.S. § 3130 (relating to conduct relating to sex offenders).

- 18 Pa.C.S. § 3301 (relating to arson and related offenses).

- 18 Pa.C.S. § 4302 (relating to incest).

- 18 Pa.C.S. § 4303 (relating to concealing death of child).

- 18 Pa.C.S. § 4304 (relating to endangering welfare of children).

- 18 Pa.C.S. § 4305 (relating to dealing in infant children).

- 18 Pa.C.S. § 5902(b) (relating to prostitution and related offenses).

- 18 Pa.C.S. § 5903(c) or (d) (relating to obscene and other sexual materials and performances).

- 18 Pa.C.S. § 6301 (relating to corruption of minors).

- 18 Pa.C.S. § 6312 (relating to sexual abuse of children).

- 18 Pa.C.S. § 6318 (relating to unlawful contact with minor).

- 18 Pa.C.S. § 6320 (relating to sexual exploitation of children).

- Section 6114 (relating to contempt for violation of order or agreement).

- The former 75 Pa.C.S. § 3731 (relating to driving under influence of alcohol or controlled substance).

- 75 Pa.C.S. Ch. 38 (relating to driving after imbibing alcohol or utilizing drugs).

Section 13(a)(1) of the act of April 14, 1972 (P.L.233, No.64), known as The Controlled Substance, Drug, Device and Cosmetic Act, to the extent that it prohibits the manufacture, sale or delivery, holding, offering for sale or possession of any controlled substance or other drug or device.

(b) Parent convicted of murder—No court shall award custody, partial custody or supervised physical custody to a parent who has been convicted of murder under 18 Pa.C.S. § 2502(a) (relating to murder) of the other parent of the child who is the subject of the order unless the child is of suitable age and consents to the order.

(b.1) Parent convicted of certain sexual offenses.—

(1) Notwithstanding any provision of this chapter to the contrary and subject to paragraph (2), if a parent who is a victim of any of the offenses set forth in this paragraph objects, no court shall award any type of custody set forth in section 5323 (relating to award of custody) to the other parent of a child conceived as a result of any of the following offenses for which the other parent has been convicted:

- 18 Pa.C.S. § 3121.

- 18 Pa.C.S. § 3122.1.

- 18 Pa.C.S. § 3124.1, where the offense involved sexual intercourse.

- 18 Pa.C.S. § 3124.2 (relating to institutional sexual assault), where the offense involved sexual intercourse.

- 18 Pa.C.S. § 4302.

(2) A court may award any type of custody set forth in section 5323 to a parent who has been convicted of an offense under paragraph (1) if:

    (i) the parent who is a victim had an opportunity to address the court;

    (ii) the child is of suitable age and consents to the custody order; and

    (iii) the court determines the award is in the best interest of the child.

(3) Paternity of the child shall be established by voluntary acknowledgment of paternity or blood, genetic or other paternity testing acceptable to the court. The cost of the testing shall be borne by the parent who was convicted of the offense.

(c) Initial evaluation.—At the initial in-person contact with the court, the judge, conference officer or other appointed individual shall perform an initial evaluation to determine whether the party or household member who committed an offense under subsection (a) poses a threat to the child and whether counseling is necessary. The initial evaluation shall not be conducted by a mental health professional. After the initial evaluation, the court may order further evaluation or counseling by a mental health professional if the court determines it is necessary.

(d) Counseling.—

(1) Where the court determines under subsection (c) that counseling is necessary, it shall appoint a qualified professional specializing in treatment relating to the particular offense to provide counseling to the offending individual.

(2) Counseling may include a program of treatment or individual therapy designed to rehabilitate the offending individual which addresses, but is not limited to, issues regarding physical and sexual abuse, the psychology of the offender and the effects of the offense on the victim.

(e) Subsequent evaluation.—

(1) At any time during or subsequent to the counseling under subsection (d), the court may require another evaluation to determine whether further counseling is necessary.

(2) If the court awards custody to a party who committed an offense under subsection (a) or who shares a household with an individual who committed an offense under subsection (a), the court may require subsequent evaluations on the rehabilitation of the offending individual and the well-being of the child subsequent to the order. If, upon review of a subsequent evaluation, the court determines that the offending individual poses a threat of physical, emotional or psychological harm to the child, the court may schedule a hearing to modify the custody order.

(f) Costs—The court may order a party to pay all or part of the costs of the counseling and evaluations under this section.

(Apr. 12, 2012, P.L.241, No.32, eff. 60 days; Oct. 1, 2015, P.L.172, No.40, eff. 60 days; May 4, 2018, P.L.112, No.21, eff. 60 days)

2018 Amendment. Act 21 amended subsec. (a) intro. par.

2015 Amendment. Act 40 added subsec. (b.1). Section 3 of Act 40 provided that subsec. (b.1) shall apply to any action regarding custody of a child under Chapter 43 or 53 that is filed on or after the effective date of section 3.

2012 Amendment. Act 32 amended subsec. (c).

Cross References. Section 5329 is referred to in section 5330 of this title; section 1904 of Title 42 (Judiciary and Judicial Procedure).

§ 5330.   Consideration of criminal charge.

(a) Expedited hearing.—A party who has obtained information under 42 Pa. C. S. § 1904 (relating to availability of criminal charge information in child custody proceedings) or otherwise about a charge filed against the other party for an offense listed under section 5329(a) (relating to consideration of criminal conviction) may move for a temporary custody order or modification of an existing custody order. The court shall hold the hearing under this subsection in an expeditious manner.

(b) Risk of harm.—In evaluating any request under subsection (a), the court shall consider whether the party who is or has been charged with an offense set forth in section 5329(a) poses a risk of physical, emotional or psychological harm to the child.

(c) **No prejudice.**—Failure to either apply for information under 42 Pa. C. S. § 1904 or act under this section shall not prejudice any party in a custody proceeding.

§ 5331.   Parenting plan.

(a) **Purpose.**—In a contested custody proceeding, the court may require the parties to submit parenting plans for the care and custody of the child to aid the court in resolving the custody dispute. A parenting plan and the position of a party as set forth in that parenting plan shall not be admissible as evidence by another party.

(b) **Contents.**—A parenting plan shall include the following:

(1)   The schedule for personal care and control of the child, including parenting time, holidays and vacations.

(2)   The education and religious involvement, if any, of the child.

(3)   The health care of the child.

(4)   Child-care arrangements.

(5)   Transportation arrangements.

(6)   A procedure by which proposed changes, disputes and alleged breaches of the custody order may be adjudicated or otherwise resolved through mediation, arbitration or other means.

(7)   Any matter specified by the court.

(8)   Any other matter that serves the best interest of the child.

(c) **Form.**—If the court orders the parties to propose a parenting plan, it shall be submitted to the court in substantially the following form:

CAPTION

PARENTING PLAN

This parenting plan involves the following child/children:

Child's Name   Age   Where does this child live?

1 . . . .

2 . . . .

3 . . . .

If you have children not addressed by this parenting plan, name here:

Child's Name . . . . .Age
Where does this child live? . . . .

1 . . . .

2 . . . .

3 . . . .

Legal Custody (who makes decisions about certain things):

Circle one

Diet . . . . .Both parties decide together / Plaintiff / Defendant

Religion . . . . Both parties decide together / Plaintiff / Defendant

Medical Care . . . . Both parties decide together / Plaintiff / Defendant

Mental Health Care . . . .Both parties decide together / Plaintiff / Defendant

Discipline . . . . Both parents decide together / Plaintiff / Defendant

Choice of School . . . . Both parents decide together / Plaintiff / Defendant

Choice of Study . . . . . . .Both parents decide together / Plaintiff / Defendant

School Activities . . Both parents decide together / Plaintiff / Defendant

Sports Activities . . . Both parents decide together / Plaintiff / Defendant

Additional items. . . Both parents decide together / Plaintiff / Defendant

Explain what process you will use to make decisions?

(For example, the parent confronted with or anticipating the choice will call the other parent when the choice presents itself, and the other parent must agree or disagree within 24 hours of any deadline)

. . . .

Physical Custody (where the child/children live)

The child's/children's residence is with . . . .

Describe which days and which times of the day the child/children will be with each person:

Sunday Monday Tuesday Wednesday Thursday Friday Saturday

. . . .

Describe where and when the child/children will be dropped off and/or picked up (day and time of day)?

Drop-Off

Where. . . . .

When . . . .

Pick-Up

Where. . . . .

When . . . .

If one of you doesn't show up, how long will the other wait?. . . . .
. . . .

If there are any extraordinary costs (taxi, train, airplane, etc.), who will pay for which costs?

. . . .
. . . .

HOLIDAYS

Where will the child/children stay?

HOLIDAY	YEAR A	YEAR B	EVERY YEAR
Martin Luther King Day	. . . .	. . . .	. . . .
President's Day	. . . .	. . . .	. . . .
Easter	. . . .	. . . .	. . . .
Memorial Day	. . . .	. . . .	. . . .
Fourth of July	. . . .	. . . .	. . . .
Labor Day	. . . .	. . . .	. . . .
Yom Kippur	. . . .	. . . .	. . . .
Rosh Hashanah	. . . .	. . . .	. . . .
Thanksgiving	. . . .	. . . .	. . . .
Vacation after Thanksgiving	. . . .	. . . .	. . . .
Christmas Vacation	. . . .	. . . .	. . . .
Kwanzaa	. . . .	. . . .	. . . .
New Year's Eve/Day	. . . .	. . . .	. . . .
Spring Vacation	. . . .	. . . .	. . . .
Easter Sunday	. . . .	. . . .	. . . .
Child's Birthday	. . . .	. . . .	. . . .
Mother's Day	. . . .	. . . .	. . . .
Father's Day	. . . .	. . . .	. . . .
Other	. . . .	. . . .	. . . .
Other	. . . .	. . . .	. . . .
Other	. . . .	. . . .	. . . .
Summer Vacation Plans	. . . .	. . . .	. . . .

Special Activities or School Activities

Will both of you attend?

Child's Name	Activity	If not, which of you will attend?
. . . .	. . . .	. . . .
. . . .	. . . .	. . . .
. . . .	. . . .	. . . .

Temporary changes to this parenting schedule

From time to time, one of you might want or need to rearrange the parenting time schedule due to work, family or other events. You can attempt to agree on these changes. If you cannot agree, the parent receiving the request will make the final decision.

The parent asking for the change will ask . . . . . . in person . . . . by letter/mail. . . . . by phone

No later than

. . . . 12 hours. . . . . 24 hours. . . . 1 week. . . . . 1 month

The parent being asked for a change will reply. . . . in person. . . . . by letter/mail. . . . . by phone

No later than

. . . . . 12 hours . . . . 24 hours . . . . 1 week . . . . 1 month

May parents contact one another? . . . .

When the child/children is/are with one of you, how may they contact the other parent? . . . .

When and how may . . . . contact the child?

. . . .

In the event that proposed changes, disputes or alleged breaches of this parenting plan and custody order are necessary or desired, the parties agree that such changes will be addressed by the following method (specify method of arbitration, mediation, court action, etc.):

. . . .

The following matter or matters as specified by the court:

. . . .

Other (Anything else you want to agree on)

. . . .

    Date . . . .
                                         Signature of Mother

    Date . . . .
                                         Signature of Father

    Date . . . .
                                         Signature of Witness

JT. ST. GOVT. COMM. COMMENT-2010

Subsection (b)(3) is intended to cover such issues as who will take the child to the doctor and how to ensure that the child receives proper medication.

§ 5332.   Informational programs.

(a) Attendance.—The court may direct the parties to attend informational programs concerning parental duties.

(b) Process not delayed.—Subsequent proceedings and the entry of any order or decree shall not be delayed because of the lack of participation in any informational program by one of the parties.

(c) Costs.—The court may order a party to pay all or part of the costs of the informational programs under this section.

§ 5333.   Counseling as part of order.

(a) Attendance.—The court may, as part of a custody order, require the parties to attend counseling sessions.

(b) Abuse.—In situations involving abuse, the court may order individual counseling for the abuser but may not order the parties to attend joint counseling.

(c) Verification.—Each party's participation in the counseling sessions shall be verified by the counselor.

(d) Costs.—The court may order a party to pay all or part of the costs of the counseling sessions under this section.

§ 5334. Guardian ad litem for child.

(a) Appointment.—The court may on its own motion or the motion of a party appoint a guardian ad litem to represent the child in the action. The court may assess the cost upon the parties or any of them or as otherwise provided by law. The guardian ad litem must be an attorney at law.

(b) Powers and duties.—The guardian ad litem shall be charged with representation of the legal interests and the best interests of the child during the proceedings and shall do all of the following:

(1) If appropriate to the child's age and maturity, meet with the child as soon as possible following the appointment, and on a regular basis thereafter.

(2) On a timely basis, be given access to relevant court records, reports of examination of the parents or other custodian of the child and medical, psychological and school records.

(3) Participate in all proceedings.

(4) Conduct such further investigation necessary to ascertain relevant facts for presentation to the court.

(5) Interview potential witnesses, including the child's parents and caretakers, if any. The guardian ad litem may examine and cross-examine witnesses and present witnesses and evidence necessary to protect the best interests of the child.

(6) Make specific recommendations in a written report to the court relating to the best interests of the child, including any services necessary to address the child's needs and safety. The court

shall make the written report part of the record so that it may be reviewed by the parties. The parties may file with the court written comments regarding the contents of the report. The comments filed by the parties shall also become part of the record.

(7) Explain the proceedings to the child to the extent appropriate given the child's age, mental condition and emotional condition.

(8) Advise the court of the child's wishes to the extent that they can be ascertained and present to the court whatever evidence exists to support the child's wishes. When appropriate because of the age or mental and emotional condition of the child, determine to the fullest extent possible the wishes of the child and communicate this information to the court. A difference between the child's wishes under this paragraph and the recommendations under paragraph (6) shall not be considered a conflict of interest for the guardian ad litem.

(c) Abuse.—If substantial allegations of abuse of the child are made, the court shall appoint a guardian ad litem for the child if:

(1) counsel for the child is not appointed under section 5335 (relating to counsel for child); or

(2) the court is satisfied that the relevant information will be presented to the court only with such appointment.

(d) Evidence subject to examination.—A guardian ad litem may not testify except as authorized by Rule 3.7 of the Rules of Professional Conduct, but may make legal argument based on relevant evidence that shall be subject to examination by the parties.

(e) Costs.—The court may order a party to pay all or part of the costs of appointing a guardian ad litem under this section.

§ 5335. Counsel for child.

(a) Appointment.—The court may appoint counsel to represent the child if the court determines that the appointment will assist in resolving the issues in the custody proceeding. If a child has legal counsel and a guardian ad litem, counsel shall represent the legal interests of the child and the guardian ad litem shall represent the best interests of the child.

(b) Abuse.—Substantial allegations of abuse of the child constitute a reasonable basis for appointing counsel for the child.

(c) Not subject to examination.—Counsel appointed by the court for the child shall not be subject to examination unless such counsel testifies in the matter.

(d) Costs.—The court may order a party to pay all or part of the costs of appointing counsel for the child under this section.

§ 5336. Access to records and information.

(a) General rule.—Except as provided in subsections (b) and (c):

(1) A party granted sole or shared legal custody under section 5323 (relating to award of custody) shall be provided access to:

    (i) the medical, dental, religious and school records of the child;

    (ii) the address of the child and any other party; and

    (iii) any other information that the court deems necessary or proper.

(2) Access to any records and information pertaining to the child may not be denied solely based upon a parent's physical custody schedule.

(3) Upon request, a parent, party or entity possessing any information set forth in paragraph (1) shall provide it to any party granted sole or shared legal custody.

(b) Nondisclosure of confidential information.—The court shall not order the disclosure of any of the following information to any parent or party granted custody:

(1) The address of a victim of abuse.

(2) Confidential information from an abuse counselor or shelter.

(3) Information protected under Chapter 67 (relating to domestic and sexual violence victim address confidentiality).

(4) Information independently protected from disclosure by the child's right to confidentiality under the act of July 9, 1976 (P.L. 817, No.143), known as the Mental Health Procedures Act, or any other statute.

(c) **Other information.**—The court may determine not to release information set forth in subsection (a), in which case it shall state the reason for its denial on the record.

§ 5337.   Relocation.

(a) **Applicability.**—This section applies to any proposed relocation.

(b) **General rule.**—No relocation shall occur unless:

(1) every individual who has custody rights to the child consents to the proposed relocation; or

(2) the court approves the proposed relocation.

(c) **Notice.**—

(1) The party proposing the relocation shall notify every other individual who has custody rights to the child.

(2) Notice, sent by certified mail, return receipt requested, shall be given no later than:

(i) the 60th day before the date of the proposed relocation; or

(ii) the tenth day after the date that the individual knows of the relocation, if:

(A) the individual did not know and could not reasonably have known of the relocation in sufficient time to comply with the 60-day notice; and

(B) it is not reasonably possible to delay the date of relocation so as to comply with the 60-day notice.

(3) Except as provided by section 5336 (relating to access to records and information), the following information, if available, must be included with the notice of the proposed relocation:

 (i) The address of the intended new residence.

 (ii) The mailing address, if not the same as the address of the intended new residence.

 (iii) Names and ages of the individuals in the new residence, including individuals who intend to live in the new residence.

 (iv) The home telephone number of the intended new residence, if available.

 (v) The name of the new school district and school.

 (vi) The date of the proposed relocation.

 (vii) The reasons for the proposed relocation.

 (viii) A proposal for a revised custody schedule.

 (ix) Any other information which the party proposing the relocation deems appropriate.

 (x) A counter-affidavit as provided under subsection (d)(1) which can be used to object to the proposed relocation and the modification of a custody order.

 (xi) A warning to the nonrelocating party that if the nonrelocating party does not file with the court an objection to the proposed relocation within 30 days after receipt of the notice, that party shall be foreclosed from objecting to the relocation.

(4) If any of the information set forth in paragraph (3) is not known when the notice is sent but is later made known to the party proposing the relocation, then that party shall promptly inform every individual who received notice under this subsection.

(d) Objection to proposed relocation.—

(1) A party entitled to receive notice may file with the court an objection to the proposed relocation and seek a temporary or permanent order to prevent the relocation. The nonrelocating

party shall have the opportunity to indicate whether he objects to relocation or not, and whether he objects to modification of the custody order or not. If the party objects to either relocation or modification of the custody order, a hearing shall be held as provided in subsection (g)(1). The objection shall be made by completing and returning to the court a counter-affidavit, which shall be verified subject to penalties under 18 Pa. C. S. § 4904 (relating to unsworn falsification to authorities), in substantially the following form:

COUNTER-AFFIDAVIT REGARDING RELOCATION

This proposal of relocation involves the following child/children:

Child's Name	Age	Currently residing at:

. . . .

Child's Name	Age	Currently residing at:

. . . .

Child's Name	Age	Currently residing at:

. . . .

I have received a notice of proposed relocation and

1. . . . . I do not object to the relocation and I do not object to the modification of the custody order consistent with the proposal for revised custody schedule as attached to the notice.

2. . . . . I do not object to the relocation, but I do object to modification of the custody order, and I request that a hearing be scheduled:

     a. . . . . Prior to allowing (name of child/children) to relocate.

     b. . . . . After the child/children relocate.

3. . . . . I do object to the relocation and I do object to the modification of the custody order, and I further request that a hearing be held on both matters prior to the relocation taking place.

. . . .

I understand that in addition to checking (2) or (3) above, I must also file this notice with the court in writing and serve it on the other party by certified mail, return receipt requested. If I fail to do so within 30 days of my receipt of the proposed relocation notice, I shall be foreclosed from objecting to the relocation.

. . . .

I verify that the statements made in this counter-affidavit are true and correct. I understand that false statements herein are made subject to the penalties of 18 Pa. C. S. § 4904 (relating to unsworn falsification to authorities).

Date:

. . . .

(2) An objection made under this subsection shall be filed with the court within 30 days of receipt of the proposed relocation notice, and served on the other party by certified mail, return receipt requested.

(3) If notice of the proposed relocation has been properly given and no objection to the proposed relocation has been filed in court, then it shall be presumed that the nonrelocating party has consented to the proposed relocation.

(4) If a party who has been given proper notice does not file with the court an objection to the relocation within 30 days after receipt of the notice but later petitions the court for review of the custodial arrangements, the court shall not accept testimony challenging the relocation.

(e) **Confirmation of relocation.**—If no objection to the proposed relocation is filed under subsection (d), the party proposing the relocation shall file the following with the court prior to the relocation:

(1) an affidavit stating that the party provided notice to every individual entitled to notice, the time to file an objection to the proposed relocation has passed and no individual entitled to receive notice has filed an objection to the proposed relocation;

(2) Proof that proper notice was given in the form of a return receipt with the signature of the addressee and the full notice that was sent to the addressee.

(3) a petition to confirm the relocation and modify any existing custody order; and

(4) a proposed order containing the information set forth in subsection (c)(3).

(f) Modification of custody order.—If a counter-affidavit regarding relocation is filed with the court which indicates the nonrelocating party both has no objection to the proposed relocation and no objection to the modification of the custody order consistent with the proposal for revised custody schedule, the court may modify the existing custody order by approving the proposal for revised custody schedule submitted under section 5337(c)(viii), and shall specify the method by which its future modification can be made if desired by either party. If a counter-affidavit regarding relocation is filed with the court which indicates the nonrelocating party objects either to the proposed relocation or to the modification of the custody order consistent with the proposal for revised custody schedule, the court shall modify the existing custody order only after holding a hearing to establish the terms and conditions of the order pursuant to the relocation indicating the rights, if any, of the nonrelocating parties.

(g) Hearing.—

(1) Except as set forth in paragraph (3), the court shall hold an expedited full hearing on the proposed relocation after a timely objection has been filed and before the relocation occurs.

(2) Except as set forth in paragraph (3), the court may, on its own motion, hold an expedited full hearing on the proposed relocation before the relocation occurs.

(3) Notwithstanding paragraphs (1) and (2), if the court finds that exigent circumstances exist, the court may approve the relocation pending an expedited full hearing.

(4) If the court approves the proposed relocation, it shall:

(i) modify any existing custody order; or

(ii) establish the terms and conditions of a custody order.

(h) Relocation factors.—In determining whether to grant a proposed relocation, the court shall consider the following factors, giving weighted consideration to those factors which affect the safety of the child:

(1) The nature, quality, extent of involvement and duration of the child's relationship with the party proposing to relocate and with the nonrelocating party, siblings and other significant persons in the child's life.

(2) The age, developmental stage, needs of the child and the likely impact the relocation will have on the child's physical, educational and emotional development, taking into consideration any special needs of the child.

(3) The feasibility of preserving the relationship between the nonrelocating party and the child through suitable custody arrangements, considering the logistics and financial circumstances of the parties.

(4) The child's preference, taking into consideration the age and maturity of the child.

(5) Whether there is an established pattern of conduct of either party to promote or thwart the relationship of the child and the other party.

(6) Whether the relocation will enhance the general quality of life for the party seeking the relocation, including, but not limited to, financial or emotional benefit or educational opportunity.

(7) Whether the relocation will enhance the general quality of life for the child, including, but not limited to, financial or emotional benefit or educational opportunity.

(8) The reasons and motivation of each party for seeking or opposing the relocation.

(9) The present and past abuse committed by a party or member of the party's household and whether there is a continued risk of harm to the child or an abused party.

(10) Any other factor affecting the best interest of the child.

(i) Burden of proof.—

(1) The party proposing the relocation has the burden of establishing that the relocation will serve the best interest of the child as shown under the factors set forth in subsection (h).

(2) Each party has the burden of establishing the integrity of that party's motives in either seeking the relocation or seeking to prevent the relocation.

(j) Failure to provide reasonable notice.—The court may consider a failure to provide reasonable notice of a proposed relocation as:

(1) a factor in making a determination regarding the relocation;

(2) a factor in determining whether custody rights should be modified;

(3) a basis for ordering the return of the child to the nonrelocating party if the relocation has occurred without reasonable notice;

(4) sufficient cause to order the party proposing the relocation to pay reasonable expenses and counsel fees incurred by the party objecting to the relocation; and

(5) a ground for contempt and the imposition of sanctions against the party proposing the relocation.

(k) Mitigation.—Any consideration of a failure to provide reasonable notice under subsection (i) shall be subject to mitigation if the court determines that such failure was caused in whole, or in part, by abuse.

(l) Effect of relocation prior to hearing.—If a party relocates with the child prior to a full expedited hearing, the court shall not confer any presumption in favor of the relocation.

JT. ST. GOVT. COMM. COMMENT-2010

Subsection (c) is not intended to abrogate the expedited hearing process set forth in *Plowman v. Plowman,* 409 Pa. Super. 143, 597 A.2d 701 (1991).

Rule 1930.4 of the Pennsylvania Rules of Civil Procedure governs the service of original process in domestic relations matters.

It is intended that if a party chooses to file under subsection (e), then the party must file all four items listed.

§ 5338.   Modification of existing order.

(a) Best interest of the child.—Upon petition, a court may modify a custody order to serve the best interest of the child.

(b) Applicability.— Except as provided in 51 Pa.C.S. § 4109 (relating to child custody proceedings during military deployment), this section shall apply to any custody order entered by a court of this Common-wealth or any other state subject to the jurisdictional requirements set forth in Chapter 54 (relating to uniform child custody jurisdiction and enforcement).

JT. ST. GOVT. COMM. COMMENT-2010

Subsection (a) codifies the standard used in *Karis v. Karis,* 518 Pa. 601, 544 A.2d 1328 (1988), where the Supreme Court held that "a petition for modification of a partial custody to shared custody order requires the court to inquire into the best interest of the child regardless of whether a 'substantial' change of circumstances has been shown." 518 Pa. at 607-8.

§ 5339.   Award of counsel fees, costs and expenses.

Under this chapter, a court may award reasonable interim or final counsel fees, costs and expenses to a party if the court finds that the conduct of another party was obdurate, vexatious, repetitive or in bad faith.

§ 5340.   Court-appointed child custody health care
or behavioral health practitioners.

No party to a child custody matter in which the court has appointed a licensed health care or behavioral health practitioner to assist the court by conducting an examination or evaluation of the parties involved or making a recommendation concerning a child custody agreement or order may be permitted to file a complaint against the practitioner with the practitioner's State licensing board prior to the final agreement or order being issued and for 60 days thereafter. As used in this section, "licensed health care or behavioral health practitioner" means a person who is licensed, certified, accredited or otherwise regulated by the Commonwealth to provide health care or behavioral health services.

APPENDIX A(3)

CHAPTER 53: CUSTODY (Repealed)
Subchapter
> A. General Provisions [Repealed]
> B. Child Custody Jurisdiction [Repealed]

SUBCHAPTER A: GENERAL PROVISIONS [REPEALED]

Note: Subchapter A of Chapter 53 was repealed by Act 2010-112, enacted Nov. 23, 2010, effective in 60 days (January 24, 2011). A proceeding under the former provisions of 23 Pa. C. S. Chapter 53, which was commenced before the effective date of this act shall be governed by the law in effect at the time the proceeding was initiated. Therefore, these repealed sections are included here.

§ 5301.   Declaration of policy. [Repealed]

The General Assembly declares that it is the public policy of this Commonwealth, when in the best interest of the child, to assure a reasonable and continuing contact of the child with both parents after a separation or dissolution of the marriage and the sharing of the rights and responsibilities of child rearing by both parents and continuing contact of the child or children with grandparents when a parent is deceased, divorced or separated.

§ 5302.   Definitions. [Repealed]

The following words and phrases when used in this subchapter shall have the meanings given to them in this section unless the context clearly indicates otherwise:

- "Child." Any unemancipated person under 18 years of age.

- "Legal custody." The legal right to make major decisions affecting the best interest of a minor child, including, but not limited to, medical, religious and educational decisions.

- "Partial custody." The right to take possession of a child away from the custodial parent for a certain period of time.

- "Physical custody." The actual physical possession and control of a child.

- "Shared custody." An order awarding shared legal or shared physical custody, or both, of a child in such a way as to assure the child of frequent and continuing contact with and physical access to both parents.

- "Visitation." The right to visit a child. The term does not include the right to remove a child from the custodial parent's control.

§ 5303.   Award of custody, partial custody or visitation. [Repealed]

(a) General rule.—

(1) In making an order for custody or partial custody, the court shall consider the preference of the child as well as any other factor

which legitimately impacts the child's physical, intellectual and emotional well-being.

(2) *In making an order for custody, partial custody or visitation to either parent, the court shall consider, among other factors, which parent is more likely to encourage, permit and allow frequent and continuing contact and physical access between the noncustodial parent and the child.*

(3) *The court shall consider each parent and adult household member's present and past violent or abusive conduct which may include, but is not limited to, abusive conduct as defined under the act of October 7, 1976 (P. L. 1090, No. 218), known as the Protection From Abuse Act.*

(b) Consideration of criminal conviction.—If a parent has been convicted of or has pleaded guilty or no contest to an offense as set forth below, the court shall consider such criminal conduct and shall determine that the parent does not pose a threat of harm to the child before making an order of custody, partial custody or visitation to that parent:

(1) *18 Pa. C. S. Ch. 25 (relating to criminal homicide);*

(2) *18 Pa. C. S. § 2901 (relating to kidnapping);*

(3) *18 Pa. C. S. § 2902 (relating to unlawful restraint);*

(4) *18 Pa. C. S. § 3121 (relating to rape);*

(5) *18 Pa. C. S. § 3122.1 (relating to statutory sexual assault);*

(6) *18 Pa. C. S. § 3123 (relating to involuntary deviate sexual intercourse);*

(7) *18 Pa. C. S. § 3124.1 (relating to sexual assault);*

(8) *18 Pa. C. S. § 3125 (relating to aggravated indecent assault);*

(9) *18 Pa. C. S. § 3126 (relating to indecent assault);*

(10) *18 Pa. C. S. § 3127 (relating to indecent exposure);*

(11) *18 Pa. C. S. § 4302 (relating to incest);*

(12) *18 Pa. C. S. § 4304 (relating to endangering welfare of children);*

(13) 18 Pa. C. S. § 5902(b) (relating to prostitution and related offenses); or

(14) 18 Pa. C. S. § 6312 (relating to sexual abuse of children).

(b.1) Consideration of criminal charge.—

(1) A parent who has obtained information under 42 Pa. C. S. § 1904 (relating to availability of criminal charge information in child custody proceedings) of the charge filed against the other parent for an offense listed in paragraph (2) may move for a temporary custody order or to modify an existing custody, partial custody or visitation order. The temporary custody or modification hearing shall be scheduled expeditiously.

(2) In evaluating any request for temporary custody or modification of a custody, partial custody or visitation order, the court shall consider whether the parent who is or has been charged with an offense listed below poses a risk of harm to the child:

   (i)   18 Pa. C. S. Ch. 25;

   (ii)   18 Pa. C. S. § 2702 (relating to aggravated assault);

   (iii)   18 Pa. C. S. § 2706 (relating to terroristic threats);

   (iv)   18 Pa. C. S. § 2709.1 (relating to stalking);

   (v)   18 Pa. C. S. § 2901;

   (vi)   18 Pa. C. S. § 2902;

   (vii)   18 Pa. C. S. § 2903; (relating to false imprisonment);

   (viii)   18 Pa. C. S. § 3121;

   (ix)   18 Pa. C. S. § 3122.1;

   (x)   18 Pa. C. S. § 3123;

   (xi)   18 Pa. C. S. § 3124.1;

   (xii)   8 Pa. C. S. § 3125;

   (xiii)   18 Pa. C. S. § 3126;

   (xiv)   18 Pa. C. S. § 3127;

    (xv)   18 Pa. C. S. § 3301 (relating to arson and related offenses);

    (xvi)   18 Pa. C. S. § 4302;

    (xvii)   18 Pa. C. S. § 4304;

    (xviii)   18 Pa. C. S. § 6312; and

    (xix)   23 Pa. C. S. § 6114 (relating to contempt for violation of order or agreement).

  (3)   Failure to apply for information under 42 Pa. C. S. § 1904 or to act under this subsection shall not prejudice any parent in a custody or visitation proceeding.

  (b.2) Parent convicted of murder.—*No court shall award custody, partial custody or visitation to a parent who has been convicted of murder under 18 Pa. C. S. § 2502(a) (relating to murder of the first degree) of the other parent of the child who is the subject of the order, unless the child is of suitable age and consents to the order.*

  (c) Counseling.—*In making a determination to award custody, partial custody or visitation pursuant to subsection (b), the court shall appoint a qualified professional to provide counseling to an offending parent described in subsection (b) and shall take testimony from that professional regarding the provision of such counseling prior to issuing any order of custody, partial custody or visitation. Counseling, required in accordance with this subsection, shall include a program of treatment or individual therapy designed to rehabilitate a parent which addresses, but is not limited to, issues regarding physical and sexual abuse, domestic violence, the psychology of the offender and the effects of abuse on the victim. If the court awards custody, partial custody or visitation to an offending parent described in subsection (b), the court may require subsequent periodic counseling and reports on the rehabilitation of the offending parent and the well-being of the child following an order relating to custody, partial custody or visitation. If, upon review of a subsequent report or reports, the court determines that the offending parent poses a threat of harm to the child, the court may schedule a hearing and modify the order of custody or visitation to protect the well-being of the child.*

  (d) Sole custody.—*The court shall award sole custody when it is in the best interest of the child.*

§ 5304. *Award of shared custody. [Repealed]*

An order for shared custody may be awarded by the court when it is in the best interest of the child:

(1) upon application of one or both parents;

(2) when the parties have agreed to an award of shared custody; or

(3) in the discretion of the court.

§ 5305. *Counseling. [Repealed]*

(a) General rule.—The court may require the parents to attend counseling sessions and may consider the recommendations of the counselors prior to awarding sole or shared custody. These counseling sessions may include, but shall not be limited to, discussions of the responsibilities and decision making arrangements involved in both sole and shared custody and the suitability of each arrangement to the capabilities of each parent or both parents.

(b) Temporary custody.—The court may temporarily award custody to either parent or both parents pending resolution of any counseling.

(c) Report.—The court may require the counselor to submit a report if the court desires and within such reasonable time as the court determines.

§ 5306. *Plan for implementation of custody order. [Repealed]*

The court, in its discretion, may require the parents to submit to the court a plan for the implementation of any custody order made under this subchapter. Upon the request of either parent or the court, the domestic relations section of the court or other party or agency approved by the court shall assist in the formulation and implementation of the plan.

§ 5307. *Denial of custody under agreement or plan. [Repealed]*

When the court declines to enter an order awarding custody either as agreed to by the parents or under the plan developed by the parents, the court shall state its reasons for denial on the record.

§ 5308.   Removal of party or child from jurisdiction. [Repealed]

If either party intends to or does remove himself or the child from this Commonwealth after a custody order has been made, the court, on its own motion or upon motion of either party, may review the existing custody order.

§ 5309.   Access to records and information. [Repealed]

(a) General rule.—Except as provided in subsections (b) and (c), each parent shall be provided access to all the medical, dental, religious or school records of the child, the residence address of the child and of the other parent and any other information that the court deems necessary.

(b) Court determination not to release information.—The court, in its discretion, may determine not to release any part or parts of the information in this section but in doing so must state its reason for denial on the record.

(c) Nondisclosure of confidential information.—The court shall not order that the address of a shelter for battered spouses and their dependent children or otherwise confidential information of a domestic violence counselor be disclosed to the defendant or his counsel or any party to the proceedings.

§ 5310.   Modification of existing custody orders. [Repealed]

Except as provided in 51 Pa. C. S. § 4109 (relating to child custody proceedings during military deployment), any order for the custody of the child of a marriage entered by a court in this Commonwealth or any state may, subject to the jurisdictional requirements set forth in Chapter 54 (relating to uniform child custody jurisdiction and enforcement), be modified at any time to an order of shared custody in accordance with this subchapter.

§ 5311.   When parent deceased. [Repealed]

If a parent of an unmarried child is deceased, the parents or grandparents of the deceased parent may be granted reasonable partial custody *or visitation rights, or both, to the unmarried child by the court upon a finding that partial custody or visitation rights, or both, would be in the best interest of the child and would not interfere with the parent-child relationship. The court shall consider the amount of personal contact between the parents or grandparents of the deceased parent and the child prior to the application.*

§ 5312.   *When parents' marriage is dissolved or parents are separated. [Repealed]*

In all proceedings for dissolution, subsequent to the commencement of the proceeding and continuing thereafter or when parents have been separated for six months or more, the court may, upon application of the parent or grandparent of a party, grant reasonable partial custody or visitation rights, or both, to the unmarried child if it finds that visitation rights or partial custody, or both, would be in the best interest of the child and would not interfere with the parent-child relationship. The court shall consider the amount of personal contact between the parents or grandparents of the party and the child prior to the application.

§ 5313.   *When grandparents may petition. [Repealed]*

(a) Partial custody and visitation.—If an unmarried child has resided with his grandparents or great-grandparents for a period of 12 months or more and is subsequently removed from the home by his parents, the grandparents or great-grandparents may petition the court for an order granting them reasonable partial custody or visitation rights, or both, to the child. The court shall grant the petition if it finds that visitation rights would be in the best interest of the child and would not interfere with the parent-child relationship.

(b) Physical and legal custody.—A grandparent has standing to bring a petition for physical and legal custody of a grandchild. If it is in the best interest of the child not to be in the custody of either parent and if it is in the best interest of the child to be in the custody of the grandparent, the court may award physical and legal custody to the grandparent. This subsection applies to a grandparent:

(1)   who has genuine care and concern for the child;

(2) whose relationship with the child began with the consent of a parent of the child or pursuant to an order of court; and

(3) who for 12 months has assumed the role and responsibilities of the child's parent, providing for the physical, emotional and social needs of the child, or who assumes the responsibility for a child who has been determined to be a dependent child pursuant to 42 Pa. C. S. Ch. 63 (relating to juvenile matters) or who assumes or deems it necessary to assume responsibility for a child who is substantially at risk due to parental abuse, neglect, drug or alcohol abuse or mental illness. The court may issue a temporary order pursuant to this section.

§ 5314. Exception for adopted children. [Repealed]

Sections 5311 (relating to when parent deceased), 5312 (relating to when parents' marriage is dissolved or parents are separated) and 5313 (relating to when child has resided with grandparents) shall not apply if the child has been adopted by a person other than a stepparent or grandparent. Any visitation rights granted pursuant to this section prior to the adoption of the child shall be automatically terminated upon such adoption.

§ 5315. Court-appointed child custody health care or behavioral health practitioners. [Repealed]

No party to a child custody matter in which the court has appointed a licensed health care or behavioral health practitioner to assist the court by conducting an examination or evaluation of the parties involved or making a recommendation concerning a child custody agreement or order may be permitted to file a complaint against the practitioner with the practitioner's State licensing board prior to the final agreement or order being issued and for 60 days thereafter. As used in this section, "licensed health care or behavioral health practitioner" means a person who is licensed, certified, accredited or otherwise regulated by the Commonwealth to provide health care or behavioral health services.

SUBCHAPTER B

CHILD CUSTODY JURISDICTION (UCCJA)

Note: Subchapter B of Chapter 53 (the UCCJA) was repealed by Act 2004–39, enacted June 15, 2004, effective in 60 days. A proceeding under 23 Pa. C. S. Ch. 53 which was commenced before the effective date of this act [August 15, 2004] is governed by the law in effect at the time the proceeding was initiated.

APPENDIX A(4)

CHAPTER 54: UNIFORM CHILD CUSTODY JURISDICTION AND ENFORCEMENT (UCCJEA)

Subchapter

Enactment. Chapter 54 was added June 15, 2004, P. L.236, No.39, effective in 60 days.

SUBCHAPTER A

General Provisions

Sec.

§ 5401. Short title of chapter.

This chapter shall be known and may be cited as the Uniform Child Custody Jurisdiction and Enforcement Act.

§ 5402.   Definitions.

The following words and phrases when used in this chapter shall have the meanings given to them in this section unless the context clearly indicates otherwise:

- "Abandoned." Left without provision for reasonable and necessary care or supervision.

- "Child." An individual who has not attained 18 years of age.

- "Child custody determination." A judgment, decree or other order of a court providing for legal custody, physical custody or visitation with respect to a child. The term includes a permanent, temporary, initial and modification order. The term does not include an order relating to child support or other monetary obligation of an individual.

- "Child custody proceeding." A proceeding in which legal custody, physical custody or visitation with respect to a child is an issue. The term includes a proceeding for divorce, separation, neglect, abuse, dependency, guardianship, paternity, termination of parental rights and protection from domestic violence, in which the issue may appear. The term does not include a proceeding involving juvenile delinquency, contractual emancipation or enforcement under Subchapter C (relating to enforcement).

- "Commencement." The filing of the first pleading in a proceeding.

- "Court." An entity authorized under the law of a state to establish, enforce or modify a child custody determination.

- "Home state." The state in which a child lived with a parent or a person acting as a parent for at least six consecutive months immediately before the commencement of a child custody proceeding. In the case of a child six months of age or younger, the term means the state in which the child lived from birth with any of the persons mentioned. A period of temporary absence of any of the mentioned persons is part of the period.

- "Initial determination." The first child custody determination concerning a particular child.

- "Issuing court." The court that makes a child custody determination for which enforcement is sought under this chapter.

- "Modification." A child custody determination that changes, replaces, supersedes or is otherwise made after a previous determination concerning the same child, whether or not it is made by the court that made the previous determination.

- "Person." An individual, corporation, business trust, estate, trust, partnership, limited liability company, association, joint venture, government or governmental subdivision, agency or instrumentality, public corporation or any other legal or commercial entity.

- "Person acting as a parent." A person, other than a parent, who:

  (1) has physical custody of the child or has had physical custody for a period of six consecutive months, including any temporary absence, within one year immediately before the commencement of a child custody proceeding; and

  (2) has been awarded legal custody by a court or claims a right to legal custody under the laws of this Commonwealth.

- "Physical custody." The physical care and supervision of a child.

- "State." A state of the United States, the District of Columbia, Puerto Rico, the United States Virgin Islands or any territory or insular possession subject to the jurisdiction of the United States.

- "Tribe." A Native American tribe or band, or Alaskan Native village, which is recognized by Federal law or formally acknowledged by a state.

- "Warrant." An order issued by a court authorizing law enforcement officers to take physical custody of a child.

§ 5403. Proceedings governed by other law.

This chapter does not govern an adoption proceeding or a proceeding pertaining to the authorization of emergency medical care for a child.

§ 5404. Application to Native American tribes.

(a) **Primacy of Indian Child Welfare Act.**—A child custody proceeding that pertains to a Native American child as defined in the Indian Child Welfare Act of 1978 (Public Law 95-608, 25 U. S. C. § 1901 et seq.) is not subject to this chapter to the extent that it is governed by the Indian Child Welfare Act of 1978.

(b) **Tribe treated as state.**—A court of this Commonwealth shall treat a tribe as if it were a state of the United States for the purpose of applying Subchapter B (relating to jurisdiction) and this subchapter.

(c) **Tribal custody determinations.**—A child custody determination made by a tribe under factual circumstances in substantial conformity with the jurisdictional standards of this chapter must be recognized and enforced under Subchapter C (relating to enforcement).

§ 5405. International application of chapter.

(a) **Foreign country treated as state.**—A court of this Commonwealth shall treat a foreign country as if it were a state of the United States for the purpose of applying Subchapter B (relating to jurisdiction) and this subchapter.

(b) **Foreign custody determinations.**—Except as otherwise provided in subsection (c), a child custody determination made in a foreign country under factual circumstances in substantial conformity with the jurisdictional standards of this chapter must be recognized and enforced under Subchapter C (relating to enforcement).

(c) **Violation of human rights.**—A court of this Commonwealth need not apply this chapter if the child custody law of a foreign country violates fundamental principles of human rights.

§ 5406. Effect of child custody determination.

A child custody determination made by a court of this Commonwealth that had jurisdiction under this chapter binds all persons who have been served in accordance with the laws of this Commonwealth or notified in accordance with section 5408 (relating to notice to persons outside

Commonwealth) or who have submitted to the jurisdiction of the court and who have been given an opportunity to be heard. As to those persons, the determination is conclusive as to all decided issues of law and fact except to the extent the determination is modified.

§ 5407.   Priority.

If a question of existence or exercise of jurisdiction under this chapter is raised in a child custody proceeding, the question, upon request of a party, must be given priority on the calendar and handled expeditiously.

§ 5408.   Notice to persons outside Commonwealth.

(a) General rule.—Notice required for the exercise of jurisdiction when a person is outside this Commonwealth may be given in a manner prescribed by the laws of this Commonwealth for service of process or by the law of the state in which the service is made. Notice must be given in a manner reasonably calculated to give actual notice but may be by publication if other means are not effective.

(b) Proof of service.—Proof of service may be made in the manner prescribed by the laws of this Commonwealth or by the law of the state in which the service is made.

(c) Submission to jurisdiction.—Notice is not required for the exercise of jurisdiction with respect to a person who submits to the jurisdiction of the court.

§ 5409.   Appearance and limited immunity.

(a) General rule.—A party to a child custody proceeding, including a modification proceeding or a petitioner or respondent in a proceeding to enforce or register a child custody determination, is not subject to personal jurisdiction in this Commonwealth for another proceeding or purpose solely by reason of having participated or of having been physically present for the purpose of participating in the proceeding.

(b) Service.—A person who is subject to personal jurisdiction in this Commonwealth on a basis other than physical presence is not immune from service of process in this Commonwealth. A party present in this Commonwealth who is subject to the jurisdiction of another state is not immune from service of process allowable under the laws of that state.

(c) Acts committed while in this Commonwealth.—The immunity granted by subsection (a) does not extend to civil litigation based on acts unrelated to the participation in a proceeding under this chapter committed by an individual while present in this Commonwealth.

§ 5410.   Communication between courts.

(a) General rule.—A court of this Commonwealth may communicate with a court in another state concerning a proceeding arising under this chapter.

(b) Participation of parties.—The court may allow the parties to participate in the communication. If the parties are not able to participate in the communication, they must be given the opportunity to present facts and legal arguments before a decision on jurisdiction is made.

(c) Matters of cooperation between courts.—Communication between courts on schedules, calendars, court records and similar matters may occur without informing the parties. A record need not be made of the communication.

(d) Record.—Except as otherwise provided in subsection (c), a record must be made of a communication under this section. The parties must be informed promptly of the communication and granted access to the record.

(e) Definition.—As used in this section, the term "record" means information that is inscribed on a tangible medium or that is stored in an electronic or other medium and is retrievable in perceivable form.

§ 5411.   Taking testimony in another state.

(a) General rule.—In addition to other procedures available to a party, a party to a child custody proceeding may offer testimony of witnesses who are located in another state, including testimony of the parties and the child, by deposition or other means allowable in this Commonwealth for testimony taken in another state. The court on its own motion may order that the testimony of a person be taken in another state and may prescribe the manner in which and the terms upon which the testimony is taken.

(b) Means and location.—A court of this Commonwealth may permit an individual residing in another state to be deposed or to testify by telephone, audiovisual means or other electronic means before a designated court or at another location in that state. A court of this Commonwealth shall cooperate with courts of other states in designating an appropriate location for the deposition or testimony.

(c) Transmission of documentary evidence.—Documentary evidence transmitted from another state to a court of this Commonwealth by technological means that do not produce an original writing may not be excluded from evidence on an objection based on the means of transmission.

§ 5412. Cooperation between courts; preservation of records.

(a) Assistance of another state.—A court of this Commonwealth may request the appropriate court of another state to:

(1) hold an evidentiary hearing;

(2) order a person to produce or give evidence pursuant to procedures of that state;

(3) order that an evaluation be made with respect to the custody of a child involved in a pending proceeding;

(4) forward to the court of this Commonwealth a certified copy of the transcript of the record of the hearing, the evidence otherwise presented and any evaluation prepared in compliance with the request; and

(5) order a party to a child custody proceeding or any person having physical custody of the child to appear in the proceeding with or without the child.

(b) Assistance to another state.—Upon request of a court of another state, a court of this Commonwealth may hold a hearing, enter an order or forward transcripts, evidence and evaluations described in subsection (a).

(c) Expenses.—Travel and other necessary and reasonable expenses incurred under subsections (a) and (b) may be assessed against the parties according to the laws of this Commonwealth.

(d) Preservation of records.—A court of this Commonwealth shall preserve the pleadings, orders, decrees, records of hearings, evaluations and other pertinent records with respect to a child custody proceeding until the child attains 18 years of age. Upon appropriate request by a court or law enforcement official of another state, the court shall forward a certified copy of those records.

SUBCHAPTER B

Jurisdiction

§ 5421. Initial child custody jurisdiction.

(a) General rule.—Except as otherwise provided in section 5424 (relating to temporary emergency jurisdiction), a court of this Commonwealth has jurisdiction to make an initial child custody determination only if:

(1) this Commonwealth is the home state of the child on the date of the commencement of the proceeding, or was the home state of the child within six months before the commencement of the proceeding and the child is absent from this Commonwealth but a parent or person acting as a parent continues to live in this Commonwealth;

(2) a court of another state does not have jurisdiction under paragraph (1), or a court of the home state of the child has declined to exercise jurisdiction on the ground that this Commonwealth is the more appropriate forum under section 5427 (relating to inconvenient forum) or 5428 (relating to jurisdiction declined by reason of conduct), and:

    (i) the child and the child's parents, or the child and at least one parent or a person acting as a parent, have a significant connection with this Commonwealth other than mere physical presence; and

    (ii) substantial evidence is available in this Commonwealth concerning the child's care, protection, training and personal relationships;

(3) all courts having jurisdiction under paragraph (1) or (2) have declined to exercise jurisdiction on the ground that a court of this Commonwealth is the more appropriate forum to determine the custody of the child under section 5427 or 5428; or

(4) no court of any other state would have jurisdiction under the criteria specified in paragraph (1), (2) or (3).

(b) Exclusive jurisdictional basis.—Subsection (a) is the exclusive jurisdictional basis for making a child custody determination by a court of this Commonwealth.

(c) Physical presence and personal jurisdiction unnecessary.— Physical presence of or personal jurisdiction over a party or a child is not necessary or sufficient to make a child custody determination.

§ 5422. Exclusive, continuing jurisdiction.

(a) **General rule.**—Except as otherwise provided in section 5424 (relating to temporary emergency jurisdiction), a court of this Commonwealth which has made a child custody determination consistent with section 5421 (relating to initial child custody jurisdiction) or section 5423 (relating to jurisdiction to modify determination) has exclusive, continuing jurisdiction over the determination until:

(1) a court of this Commonwealth determines that neither the child, nor the child and one parent, nor the child and a person acting as a parent have a significant connection with this Commonwealth and that substantial evidence is no longer available in this Commonwealth concerning the child's care, protection, training and personal relationships; or

(2) a court of this Commonwealth or a court of another state determines that the child, the child's parents and any person acting as a parent do not presently reside in this Commonwealth.

(b) **Modification where court does not have exclusive, continuing jurisdiction.**—A court of this Commonwealth which has made a child custody determination and does not have exclusive, continuing jurisdiction under this section may modify that determination only if it has jurisdiction to make an initial determination under section 5421.

§ 5423. Jurisdiction to modify determination.

Except as otherwise provided in section 5424 (relating to temporary emergency jurisdiction), a court of this Commonwealth may not modify a child custody determination made by a court of another state unless a court of this Commonwealth has jurisdiction to make an initial determination under section 5421 (a)(1) or (2) (relating to initial child custody jurisdiction) and:

(1) the court of the other state determines it no longer has exclusive, continuing jurisdiction under section 5422 (relating to exclusive, continuing jurisdiction) or that a court of this Commonwealth would be a more convenient forum under section 5427 (relating to inconvenient forum); or

(2) a court of this Commonwealth or a court of the other state determines that the child, the child's parents and any person acting as a parent do not presently reside in the other state.

§ 5424. Temporary emergency jurisdiction.

(a) **General rule.**—A court of this Commonwealth has temporary emergency jurisdiction if the child is present in this Commonwealth and the child has been abandoned or it is necessary in an emergency to protect the child because the child or a sibling or parent of the child is subjected to or threatened with mistreatment or abuse.

(b) **No previous custody determination or proceeding.**—If there is no previous child custody determination that is entitled to be enforced under this chapter and a child custody proceeding has not been commenced in a court of a state having jurisdiction under sections 5421 (relating to initial child custody jurisdiction) through 5423 (relating to jurisdiction to modify determination), a child custody determination made under this section remains in effect until an order is obtained from a court of a state having jurisdiction under sections 5421 through 5423. If a child custody proceeding has not been or is not commenced in a court of a state having jurisdiction under sections 5421 through 5423, a child custody determination made under this section becomes a final determination if it so provides and this Commonwealth becomes the home state of the child.

(c) **Previous custody determination or proceeding.**—If there is a previous child custody determination that is entitled to be enforced under this chapter or a child custody proceeding has been commenced in a court of a state having jurisdiction under sections 5421 through 5423, any order issued by a court of this Commonwealth under this section must specify in the order a period that the court considers adequate to allow the person seeking an order to obtain an order from the state having jurisdiction under sections 5421 through 5423. The order issued in this Commonwealth remains in effect until an order is obtained from the other state within the period specified or the period expires.

(d) **Mandatory communication between courts.**—A court of this Commonwealth which has been asked to make a child custody determination under this section, upon being informed that a child custody proceeding has been commenced in or a child custody determination has been made by a court of a state having jurisdiction under sections 5421 through 5423, shall immediately communicate with the other court. A court of this Commonwealth which is exercising jurisdiction pursuant to sections 5421 through 5423, upon being informed that a child custody proceeding has been commenced in or a child custody determination has been made by a court of another state under a statute similar to this section, shall immediately communicate with the court of that state to resolve the emergency, protect the safety of the parties and the child and determine a period for the duration of the temporary order.

§ 5425. Notice; opportunity to be heard; joinder.

(a) **General rule.**—Before a child custody determination is made under this chapter, notice and an opportunity to be heard in accordance with the standards of section 5408 (relating to notice to persons outside Commonwealth) must be given to all persons entitled to notice under the laws of this Commonwealth as in child custody proceedings between residents of this Commonwealth, any parent whose parental rights have not been previously terminated and any person having physical custody of the child.

(b) **Lack of notice or opportunity to be heard.**—This chapter does not govern the enforceability of a child custody determination made without notice or any opportunity to be heard.

(c) **Joinder and intervention.**—The obligation to join a party and the right to intervene as a party in a child custody proceeding under this chapter are governed by the laws of this Commonwealth as in child custody proceedings between residents of this Commonwealth.

§ 5426. Simultaneous proceedings.

(a) **General rule.**—Except as otherwise provided in section 5424 (relating to temporary emergency jurisdiction), a court of this Commonwealth may not exercise its jurisdiction under this subchapter if, at the time of the commencement of the proceeding, a proceeding concerning the custody of the child has been commenced in a court of another state having jurisdiction substantially in conformity with this chapter, unless the proceeding has been terminated or is stayed by the court of the other state because a court of this Commonwealth is a more convenient forum under section 5427 (relating to inconvenient forum).

(b) **Stay; communication with other court.**—Except as otherwise provided in section 5424, a court of this Commonwealth, before hearing a child custody proceeding, shall examine the court documents and other information supplied by the parties pursuant to section 5429 (relating to information to be submitted to court). If the court determines that a child custody proceeding has been commenced in a court in another state having jurisdiction substantially in accordance with this chapter, the court of this Commonwealth shall stay its proceeding and communicate with the court of the other state. If the court of the state having jurisdiction substantially in accordance with this chapter does not determine that the court of this Commonwealth is a more appropriate forum, the court of this Commonwealth shall dismiss the proceeding.

(c) **Modification.**—In a proceeding to modify a child custody determination, a court of this Commonwealth shall determine whether a proceeding to enforce the determination has been commenced in another state. If a proceeding to enforce a child custody determination has been commenced in another state, the court may:

(1) stay the proceeding for modification pending the entry of an order of a court of the other state enforcing, staying, denying or dismissing the proceeding for enforcement;

(2) enjoin the parties from continuing with the proceeding for enforcement; or

(3) proceed with the modification under conditions it considers appropriate.

§ 5427. Inconvenient forum.

(a) **General rule.**—A court of this Commonwealth which has jurisdiction under this chapter to make a child custody determination may decline to exercise its jurisdiction at any time if it determines that it is an inconvenient forum under the circumstances and that a court of another state is a more appropriate forum. The issue of inconvenient forum may be raised upon motion of a party, the court's own motion or request of another court.

(b) Factors.—Before determining whether it is an inconvenient forum, a court of this Commonwealth shall consider whether it is appropriate for a court of another state to exercise jurisdiction. For this purpose, the court shall allow the parties to submit information and shall consider all relevant factors, including:

(1) whether domestic violence has occurred and is likely to continue in the future and which state could best protect the parties and the child;

(2) the length of time the child has resided outside this Commonwealth;

(3) the distance between the court in this Commonwealth and the court in the state that would assume jurisdiction;

(4) the relative financial circumstances of the parties;

(5) any agreement of the parties as to which state should assume jurisdiction;

(6) the nature and location of the evidence required to resolve the pending litigation, including testimony of the child;

(7) the ability of the court of each state to decide the issue expeditiously and the procedures necessary to present the evidence; and

(8) the familiarity of the court of each state with the facts and issues in the pending litigation.

(c) Stay.—If a court of this Commonwealth determines that it is an inconvenient forum and that a court of another state is a more appropriate forum, it shall stay the proceedings upon condition that a child custody proceeding be promptly commenced in another designated state and may impose any other condition the court considers just and proper.

(d) Jurisdiction declined.—A court of this Commonwealth may decline to exercise its jurisdiction under this chapter if a child custody determination is incidental to an action for divorce or another proceeding while still retaining jurisdiction over the divorce or other proceeding.

§ 5428. Jurisdiction declined by reason of conduct.

(a) **General rule.**—Except as otherwise provided in section 5424 (relating to temporary emergency jurisdiction) or by other laws of this Commonwealth, if a court of this Commonwealth has jurisdiction under this chapter because a person seeking to invoke its jurisdiction has engaged in unjustifiable conduct, the court shall decline to exercise its jurisdiction unless:

(1) the parents and all persons acting as parents have acquiesced in the exercise of jurisdiction;

(2) a court of the state otherwise having jurisdiction under sections 5421 (relating to initial child custody jurisdiction) through 5423 (relating to jurisdiction to modify determination) determines that this Commonwealth is a more appropriate forum under section 5427 (relating to inconvenient forum); or

(3) no court of any other state would have jurisdiction under the criteria specified in sections 5421 through 5423.

(b) **Jurisdiction declined; remedy.**—If a court of this Commonwealth declines to exercise its jurisdiction pursuant to subsection (a), it may fashion an appropriate remedy to ensure the safety of the child and prevent a repetition of the unjustifiable conduct, including staying the proceeding until a child custody proceeding is commenced in a court having jurisdiction under sections 5421 through 5423.

(c) **Jurisdiction declined, expenses.**—If a court dismisses a petition or stays a proceeding because it declines to exercise its jurisdiction pursuant to subsection (a), it shall assess against the party seeking to invoke its jurisdiction necessary and reasonable expenses, including costs, communication expenses, attorney fees, investigative fees, expenses for witnesses, travel expenses and child care during the course of the proceedings unless the party from whom fees are sought establishes that the assessment would be clearly inappropriate. The court may not assess fees, costs or expenses against this Commonwealth unless authorized by law other than this chapter.

§ 5429. Information to be submitted to court.

(a) **General rule.**—Subject to the rules set forth in Chapter 53 (relating to child custody) providing for the confidentiality of procedures, addresses and other identifying information in a child custody proceeding, each party in its first pleading or in an attached affidavit shall give information, if reasonably ascertainable, under oath as to the child's present address or whereabouts, the places where the child has lived during the last five years and the names and present addresses of the persons with whom the child has lived during that period. The pleading or affidavit must state whether the party:

(1) has participated as a party or witness or in any other capacity in any other proceeding concerning the custody of or visitation with the child and, if so, identify the court, the case number and the date of the child custody determination, if any;

(2) knows of any proceeding that could affect the current proceeding, including proceedings for enforcement and proceedings relating to domestic violence, protective orders, termination of parental rights and adoptions, and, if so, identify the court, the case number and the nature of the proceeding; and

(3) knows the names and addresses of any person not a party to the proceeding who has physical custody of the child or claims rights of legal custody or physical custody of or visitation with the child and, if so, the names and addresses of those persons.

(b) **Stay.**—If the information required by subsection (a) is not furnished, the court, upon motion of a party or its own motion, may stay the proceeding until the information is furnished.

(c) **Additional information.**—If the declaration as to any of the items described in subsection (a)(1) through (3) is in the affirmative, the declarant shall give additional information under oath as required by the court. The court may examine the parties under oath as to details of the information furnished and other matters pertinent to the court's jurisdiction and the disposition of the case.

(d) Duty to disclose other proceedings.—Each party has a continuing duty to inform the court of any proceeding in this Commonwealth or any other state that could affect the current proceeding.

(e) Identifying information.—If a party alleges in an affidavit or a pleading under oath that the health, safety or liberty of a party or child would be jeopardized by disclosure of identifying information, the information must be sealed and may not be disclosed to the other party or the public unless the court orders the disclosure to be made after a hearing in which the court takes into consideration the health, safety or liberty of the party or child and determines that the disclosure is in the interest of justice.

§ 5430. Appearance of parties and child.

(a) General rule.—In a child custody proceeding in this Commonwealth, the court may order a party to the proceeding who is in this Commonwealth to appear before the court in person with or without the child. The court may order any person who is in this Commonwealth and who has physical custody or control of the child to appear in person with the child.

(b) Party outside this Commonwealth.—If a party to a child custody proceeding whose presence is desired by the court is outside this Commonwealth, the court may order that a notice given pursuant to section 5408 (relating to notice to persons outside Commonwealth) include a statement directing the party to appear in person with or without the child and informing the party that failure to appear may result in a decision adverse to the party.

(c) Personal safety.—The court may enter any orders necessary to ensure the safety of the child and of any person ordered to appear under this section.

(d) Expenses.—If a party to a child custody proceeding who is outside this Commonwealth is directed to appear under subsection (b) or desires to appear personally before the court with or without the child, the court may require another party to pay reasonable and necessary travel and other expenses of the party so appearing and of the child.

SUBCHAPTER C

Enforcement

§ 5441.   Definitions.

The following words and phrases when used in this subchapter shall have the meanings given to them in this section unless the context clearly indicates otherwise:

- "Petitioner." A person who seeks enforcement of an order for return of a child under the Hague Convention on the Civil Aspects of International Child Abduction or enforcement of a child custody determination.

- "Respondent." A person against whom a proceeding has been commenced for enforcement of an order for return of a child under the Hague Convention on the Civil Aspects of International Child Abduction or enforcement of a child custody determination.

§ 5442.   Enforcement under Hague Convention.

Under this subchapter a court of this Commonwealth may enforce an order for the return of the child made under the Hague Convention on the Civil Aspects of International Child Abduction as if it were a child custody determination.

§ 5443.   Duty to enforce.

(a) General rule.—A court of this Commonwealth shall recognize and enforce a child custody determination of a court of another state if the latter court exercised jurisdiction in substantial conformity with this chapter or the determination was made under factual circumstances meeting the jurisdictional standards of this chapter and the determination has not been modified in accordance with this chapter.

(b) Remedies.—A court of this Commonwealth may utilize any remedy available under other laws of this Commonwealth to enforce a child custody determination made by a court of another state. The remedies provided in this subchapter are cumulative and do not affect the availability of other remedies to enforce a child custody determination.

§ 5444.   Temporary visitation.

(a) General rule.—A court of this Commonwealth which does not have jurisdiction to modify a child custody determination may issue a temporary order enforcing:

(1)   a visitation schedule made by a court of another state; or

(2)   the visitation provisions of a child custody determination of another state that does not provide for a specific visitation schedule.

(b) Time to obtain permanent change in visitation.—If a court of this Commonwealth makes an order under subsection (a)(2), it shall specify in the order a period that it considers adequate to allow the petitioner to obtain an order from a court having jurisdiction under the criteria specified in Subchapter B (relating to jurisdiction). The order remains in effect until an order is obtained from the other court or the period expires.

§ 5445. Registration of child custody determination.

(a) **General rule.**—A child custody determination issued by a court of another state may be registered in this Commonwealth, with or without a simultaneous request for enforcement, by sending to the appropriate court in this Commonwealth:

(1) a letter or other document requesting registration;

(2) two copies, including one certified copy, of the determination sought to be registered and a statement under penalty of perjury that to the best of the knowledge and belief of the person seeking registration the order has not been modified; and

(3) except as otherwise provided in section 5429 (relating to information to be submitted to court), the name and address of the person seeking registration and any parent or person acting as a parent who has been awarded custody or visitation in the child custody determination sought to be registered.

(b) **Duties of registering court.**—On receipt of the documents required by subsection (a), the registering court shall:

(1) cause the determination to be filed as a foreign judgment, together with one copy of any accompanying documents and information, regardless of their form; and

(2) serve notice upon the persons named pursuant to subsection (a)(3) and provide them with an opportunity to contest the registration in accordance with this section.

(c) **Notice.**—The notice required by subsection (b)(2) must state that:

(1) a registered determination is enforceable as of the date of the registration in the same manner as a determination issued by a court of this Commonwealth;

(2) a hearing to contest the validity of the registered determination must be requested within 20 days after service of notice; and

(3) failure to contest the registration will result in confirmation of the child custody determination and preclude further contest of that determination with respect to any matter that could have been asserted.

(d) Contest over validity of registered order.—A person seeking to contest the validity of a registered order must request a hearing within 20 days after service of the notice. At that hearing, the court shall confirm the registered order unless the person contesting registration establishes that:

(1) the issuing court did not have jurisdiction under Subchapter B (relating to jurisdiction);

(2) the child custody determination sought to be registered has been vacated, stayed or modified by a court having jurisdiction to do so under Subchapter B; or

(3) the person contesting registration was entitled to notice, but notice was not given in accordance with the standards of section 5408 (relating to notice to persons outside Commonwealth), in the proceedings before the court that issued the order for which registration is sought.

(e) Failure to contest.—If a timely request for a hearing to contest the validity of the registration is not made, the registration is confirmed as a matter of law and the person requesting registration and all persons served must be notified of the confirmation.

(f) Res judicata.—Confirmation of a registered order, whether by operation of law or after notice and hearing, precludes further contest of the order with respect to any matter that could have been asserted at the time of registration.

§ 5446. Enforcement of registered determination.

(a) General rule.—A court of this Commonwealth may grant any relief normally available under the laws of this Commonwealth to enforce a registered child custody determination made by a court of another state.

(b) **Modification.**—A court of this Commonwealth shall recognize and enforce, but may not modify, except in accordance with Subchapter B (relating to jurisdiction), a registered child custody determination of a court of another state.

§ 5447. Simultaneous proceedings.

If a proceeding for enforcement under this subchapter is commenced in a court of this Commonwealth and the court determines that a proceeding to modify the determination is pending in a court of another state having jurisdiction to modify the determination under Subchapter B (relating to jurisdiction), the enforcing court shall immediately communicate with the modifying court. The proceeding for enforcement continues unless the enforcing court, after consultation with the modifying court, stays or dismisses the proceeding.

§ 5448. Expedited enforcement of child custody determination.

(a) **Verification.**—A petition under this subchapter must be verified. Certified copies of all orders sought to be enforced and of any order confirming registration must be attached to the petition. A copy of a certified copy of an order may be attached instead of the original.

(b) **Petition.**—A petition for enforcement of a child custody determination must state:

(1) whether the court that issued the determination identified the jurisdictional basis it relied upon in exercising jurisdiction and, if so, what the basis was;

(2) whether the determination for which enforcement is sought has been vacated, stayed or modified by a court whose decision must be enforced under this chapter and, if so, identify the court, the case number and the nature of the proceeding;

(3) whether any proceeding has been commenced that could affect the current proceeding, including proceedings relating to domestic violence, protective orders, termination of parental rights and adoptions and, if so, identify the court, the case number and the nature of the proceeding;

(4)   the present physical address of the child and the respondent, if known;

(5)   whether relief in addition to the immediate physical custody of the child and attorney fees is sought, including a request for assistance from law enforcement officials and, if so, the relief sought; and

(6)   if the child custody determination has been registered and confirmed under section 5445 (relating to registration of child custody determination), the date and place of registration.

(c) Hearing.—Upon the filing of a petition, the court shall issue an order directing the respondent to appear in person with or without the child at a hearing and may enter any order necessary to ensure the safety of the parties and the child. The hearing must be held on the next judicial day after service of the order unless that date is impossible. In that event, the court shall hold the hearing on the first judicial day possible. The court may extend the date of hearing at the request of the petitioner.

(d) Contest over validity of custody determination.—An order issued under subsection (c) must state the time and place of the hearing and advise the respondent that at the hearing the court will order that the petitioner may take immediate physical custody of the child and the payment of fees, costs and expenses under section 5452 (relating to costs, fees and expenses) and may schedule a hearing to determine whether further relief is appropriate unless the respondent appears and establishes that:

(1)   the child custody determination has not been registered and confirmed under section 5445 and that:

(i)   the issuing court did not have jurisdiction under Subchapter B (relating to jurisdiction);

(ii)   the child custody determination for which enforcement is sought has been vacated, stayed or modified by a court having jurisdiction to do so under Subchapter B; or

(iii) the respondent was entitled to notice, but notice was not given in accordance with the standards of section 5408 (relating to notice to persons outside Commonwealth), in the proceedings before the court that issued the order for which enforcement is sought; or

(2) the child custody determination for which enforcement is sought was registered and confirmed under section 5444 (relating to temporary visitation), but has been vacated, stayed or modified by a court of a state having jurisdiction to do so under Subchapter B.

§ 5449. Service of petition and order.

Except as otherwise provided in section 5451 (relating to warrant to take physical custody of child), the petition and order must be served by any method authorized by the laws of this Commonwealth upon respondent and any person who has physical custody of the child.

§ 5450. Hearing and order.

(a) **General rule.**—Unless the court issues a temporary emergency order pursuant to section 5424 (relating to temporary emergency jurisdiction), upon a finding that a petitioner is entitled to immediate physical custody of the child, the court shall order that the petitioner may take immediate physical custody of the child unless the respondent establishes that:

(1) the child custody determination has not been registered and confirmed under section 5445 (relating to registration of child custody determination) and that:

(i) the issuing court did not have jurisdiction under Subchapter B (relating to jurisdiction);

(ii) the child custody determination for which enforcement is sought has been vacated, stayed or modified by a court of a state having jurisdiction to do so under Subchapter B; or

(iii) the respondent was entitled to notice, but notice was not given in accordance with the standards of section 5408 (relating to notice to persons outside Commonwealth), in the proceedings before the court that issued the order for which enforcement is sought; or

(2) the child custody determination for which enforcement is sought was registered and confirmed under section 5445 but has been vacated, stayed or modified by a court of a state having jurisdiction to do so under Subchapter B.

(b) Costs, fees and expenses.—The court shall award the costs, fees and expenses authorized under section 5452 (relating to costs, fees and expenses) and may grant additional relief, including a request for the assistance of law enforcement officials, and set a further hearing to determine whether additional relief is appropriate.

(c) Refusal to testify.—If a party called to testify refuses to answer on the ground that the testimony may be self-incriminating, the court may draw an adverse inference from the refusal.

(d) Spousal privilege unavailable.—A privilege against disclosure of communications between spouses and a defense of immunity based on the relationship of husband and wife or parent and child may not be invoked in a proceeding under this subchapter.

§ 5451.   Warrant to take physical custody of child.

(a) General rule.—Upon the filing of a petition seeking enforcement of a child custody determination, the petitioner may file a verified application for the issuance of a warrant to take physical custody of the child if the child is immediately likely to suffer serious physical harm or be removed from this Commonwealth.

(b) Petition.—If the court, upon the testimony of the petitioner or other witness, finds that the child is imminently likely to suffer serious physical harm or be removed from this Commonwealth, it may issue a warrant to take physical custody of the child. The petition must be heard on the next judicial day after the warrant is executed unless that date is impossible. In that event, the court shall hold the hearing on the first judicial day possible. The application for the warrant must include the statements required by section 5448(b) (relating to expedited enforcement of child custody determination).

(c) Warrant.—A warrant to take physical custody of a child must:

(1)   recite the facts upon which a conclusion of imminent serious physical harm or removal from the jurisdiction is based;

(2)   direct law enforcement officers to take physical custody of the child immediately; and

(3)   provide for the placement of the child pending final relief.

(d) Time of service.—The respondent must be served with the petition, warrant and order immediately after the child is taken into physical custody.

(e) Enforcement.—A warrant to take physical custody of a child is enforceable throughout this Commonwealth. If the court finds on the basis of the testimony of the petitioner or other witness that a less intrusive remedy is not effective, it may authorize law enforcement officers to enter private property to take physical custody of the child. If required by exigent circumstances of the case, the court may authorize law enforcement officers to make a forcible entry at any hour.

(f) Appearance of child.—The court may impose conditions upon placement of a child to ensure the appearance of the child and the child's custodian.

§ 5452.   Costs, fees and expenses.

(a) General rule.—The court shall award the prevailing party, including a state, necessary and reasonable expenses incurred by or on behalf of the party, including costs, communication expenses, attorney fees, investigative fees, expenses for witnesses, travel expenses and child care during the course of the proceedings, unless the party from whom fees or expenses are sought establishes that the award would be clearly inappropriate.

(b) Assessment against a state.—The court may not assess fees, costs or expenses against a state unless authorized by law other than this chapter.

§ 5453. Recognition and enforcement.

A court of this Commonwealth shall accord full faith and credit to an order issued by another state and consistent with this chapter which enforces a child custody determination by a court of another state unless the order has been vacated, stayed or modified by a court having jurisdiction to do so under Subchapter B (relating to jurisdiction).

§ 5454. Appeals.

An appeal may be taken from a final order in a proceeding under this subchapter in accordance with expedited appellate procedures in other civil cases. Unless the court enters a temporary emergency order under section 5424 (relating to temporary emergency jurisdiction), the enforcing court may not stay an order enforcing a child custody determination pending appeal.

§ 5455. Role of prosecutor or public official.

(a) General rule.—In a case arising under this chapter or involving the Hague Convention on the Civil Aspects of International Child Abduction, the prosecutor or other appropriate public official may take any lawful action, including resort to a proceeding under this subchapter or any other available civil proceeding to locate a child, obtain the return of a child or enforce a child custody determination if there is:

(1) an existing child custody determination;

(2) a request to do so from a court in a pending child custody proceeding;

(3) a reasonable belief that a criminal statute has been violated; or

(4) a reasonable belief that the child has been wrongfully removed or retained in violation of the Hague Convention on the Civil Aspects of International Child Abduction.

(b) Authority.—A prosecutor or appropriate public official acting under this section acts on behalf of the court and may not represent any party.

§ 5456. Role of law enforcement.

At the request of a prosecutor or other appropriate public official acting under section 5455 (relating to role of prosecutor or public official), a law enforcement officer may take any lawful action reasonably necessary to locate a child or a party and assist a prosecutor or appropriate public official with responsibilities under section 5455.

§ 5457. Costs and expenses.

If the respondent is not the prevailing party, the court may assess against the respondent all direct expenses and costs incurred by the prosecutor or other appropriate public official and law enforcement officers under section 5455 (relating to role of prosecutor or public official) or 5456 (relating to role of law enforcement).

SUBCHAPTER D

Intrastate Application

§ 5471. Intrastate application.

The provisions of this chapter allocating jurisdiction and functions between and among courts of different states shall also allocate jurisdiction and functions between and among the courts of common pleas of this Commonwealth.

SUBCHAPTER E

Miscellaneous Provisions

§ 5481. Application and construction.

In applying and construing this chapter, consideration must be given to the need to promote uniformity of the law with respect to its subject matter among states that enact it.

§ 5482. Severability.

If any provision of this chapter or its application to any person or circumstance is held invalid, the invalidity does not affect other provisions or applications of this chapter which can be given effect without the invalid provision or application, and to this end the provisions of this chapter are severable.

APPENDIX A(5)

CHAPTER 55: LIABILITY FOR TORTIOUS ACTS OF CHILDREN

Sec.
5501. Definitions.
5502. Liability of parents.
5503. Establishing liability in criminal or juvenile proceedings.
5504. Establishing liability in civil proceedings.
5505. Monetary limits of liability.
5506. Double recovery for same injury prohibited.
5507. Indemnity or contribution from child prohibited.
5508. Liability of parent not having custody or control of child.
5509. Other liability of parent or child unaffected.

Enactment. Chapter 55 was added December 19, 1990, P. L. 1240, No. 206, effective in 90 days.

§ 5501. Definitions.

The following words and phrases when used in this chapter shall have the meanings given to them in this section unless the context clearly indicates otherwise:

- "Child." An individual under 18 years of age.

- "Injury." Includes injury to the person and theft, destruction or loss of property.

- "Parent." Includes natural or adoptive parents.

- "Person." Includes government units and Federal agencies.

- "Tortious act." A willful tortious act resulting in injury.

§ 5502. Liability of parents.

Any parent whose child is found liable or is adjudged guilty by a court of competent jurisdiction of a tortious act shall be liable to the person who suffers the injury to the extent set forth in this chapter.

§ 5503.   Establishing liability in criminal or juvenile proceedings.

(a) General rule.—In any criminal proceeding against a child and in any proceeding against a child under 42 Pa. C. S. Ch. 63 (relating to juvenile matters), the court shall ascertain the amount sufficient to fully reimburse any person who has suffered injury because of the tortious act of the child and direct the parents to make payment in the amount not to exceed the limitations set forth in section 5505 (relating to monetary limits of liability).

(b) Noncompliance with direction of court.—If the parents fail to comply with the direction of the court, the amount may be recovered in a civil action against the parents or either of them.

§ 5504.   Establishing liability in civil proceedings.

(a) Petition.—If a judgment has been rendered against the child in a civil action for injury because of the tortious act of the child and the judgment has not been satisfied within a period of 30 days, the injured person may petition the court for a rule to show cause why judgment should not be entered against the parent.

(b) Answer and trial.—The parent may file an answer to the petition, and, if there is any dispute as to unlitigated facts, the case shall be set down for trial.

(c) Judgment.—If there is no dispute as to the unlitigated facts, the court shall authorize the entry of a judgment against the parent. In no case shall the judgment against the parent exceed the limitations set forth in section 5505 (relating to monetary limits of liability).

(d) Action against parent.—Notwithstanding any provision to the contrary, a victim of a willful, tortious act of a child may initiate a civil action directly against the parent or parents of the child who committed the tortious act for the purpose of receiving compensation for the injuries suffered, not to exceed the limitations set forth in section 5505.

§ 5505.   Monetary limits of liability.

(a) General rule.—Liability of the parents under this chapter shall be limited to:

(1)   The sum of $1,000 for injuries suffered by any one person as a result of one tortious act or continuous series of tortious acts.

(2)   The sum of $2,500 regardless of the number of persons who suffer injury as a result of one tortious act or continuous series of tortious acts.

(b) Proceedings where loss exceeds liability.—In the event that actual loss as ascertained by the court or the judgment against the child exeeds $2,500, the parents shall be discharged from further liability by the payment of $2,500 into court. The court shall cause all aggrieved parties to submit itemized statements of loss in writing and shall make distribution proportionately, whether the claims be for injuries to the person or for theft, destruction or loss of property. The court may take testimony to assist it in making proper distribution and may appoint a master to accomplish this purpose. All costs and fees incurred in these proceedings shall be paid from the $2,500 paid into court.

(c) Joint acts by children of same parent.—The limitations on liability set forth in subsections (a) and (b) shall be applicable when two or more children of the same parent engage jointly in the commission of one tortious act or series of tortious acts.

§ 5506.   Double recovery for same injury prohibited.

In no case shall there be a double recovery for one injury. Any judgment against a child resulting from a tortious act for which a parent makes payment under this chapter shall be reduced by the amount paid by the parent.

§ 5507.   Indemnity or contribution from child prohibited.

The parent shall have no right of indemnity or contribution against the child.

§ 5508. Liability of parent not having custody or control of child.

(a) **General rule.**—No liability may be imposed upon a parent under this chapter if, at the time of commission of the tortious act, the parent has neither custody of the child nor is entitled to custody of the child or if the child is institutionalized or emancipated.

(b) **Exception.**—No parent is absolved of liability due to the desertion of the child by the parent.

§ 5509. Other liability of parent or child unaffected.

The liability imposed upon parents by this chapter shall not limit the common-law liability of parents for damages caused by a child and shall be separate and apart from any liability which may be imposed upon the child.

APPENDIX A(6)

CHAPTER 56: STANDBY GUARDIANSHIP ACT
Subchapter
    A. Preliminary Provisions
    B. General Provisions

Enactment. Chapter 56 was added November 24, 1998, P. L. 811, No. 103, effective in 60 days.

The General Assembly finds and declares as follows:

(1)   Existing law does not provide adequately for the needs of a parent who is terminally ill, or who is periodically incapable of caring for the needs of a minor due to the parent's incapacity or debilitation resulting from illness, and who desires to make long-term plans for the future of a minor without terminating or limiting in any way the parent's legal rights.

(2)   It is the intent of the General Assembly to create an expeditious procedure which will enable a parent who is terminally ill or periodically incapable or debilitated to make long-term plans for a minor without terminating or limiting in any manner parental rights.

SUBCHAPTER A

PRELIMINARY PROVISIONS

Sec.
5601. Short title of chapter.
5602. Definitions.
5603. Scope.

§ 5601.   Short title of chapter.

This chapter shall be known and may be cited as the Standby Guardianship Act.

§ 5602. Definitions.

The following words and phrases when used in this chapter shall have the meanings given to them in this section unless the context clearly indicates otherwise:

- "Alternate."A person with all the rights, responsibilities and qualifications of a standby guardian who shall become a standby guardian only in the event that the currently designated standby guardian is unable or refuses to fulfill his obligation.

- "Attending physician."A physician who has primary responsibility for the treatment and care of the designator. If physicians share responsibility, another physician is acting on the attending physician's behalf or no physician has primary responsibility, any physician who is familiar with the designator's medical condition may act as an attending physician under this chapter.

- "Coguardian." A person who, along with a parent, shares physical or legal custody, or both, of a child.

- "Consent." A written authorization signed by the designator in the presence of two witnesses, who shall also sign the writing. The witnesses must be 18 years of age or older and not named in the designation.

- "Court." Family Court Division or domestic relations section of a court of common pleas, unless otherwise provided by local rules of court.

- "Debilitation." A person's chronic and substantial inability, as a result of a physically incapacitating disease or injury, to care for a dependent minor.

- "Designation." A written document naming the standby guardian. A parent, a legal custodian or a legal guardian may designate an alternate standby guardian in the same writing.

- "Designator." A parent, a legal custodian or a legal guardian who appoints a standby guardian.

- "Determination of debilitation." A written finding made by an attending physician which states that the designator suffers from a

721

physically incapacitating disease or injury. No identification of the illness in question is required.

- "Determination of incapacity." A written finding made by an attending physician which states the nature, extent and probable duration of the designator's mental or organic incapacity.

- "Incapacity." A chronic and substantial inability, resulting from a mental or organic impairment, to understand the nature and consequences of decisions concerning the care of the designator's dependent minor and a consequent inability to care for the minor.

- "Standby guardian." A person named by a designator to assume the duties of coguardian or guardian of a minor and whose authority becomes effective upon the incapacity, debilitation and consent, or death of the minor's parent.

- "Triggering event." A specified occurrence stated in the designation which empowers a standby guardian to assume the powers, duties and responsibilities of guardian or coguardian.

§ 5603. Scope.

The provisions of Chapter 53 (relating to custody) and 20 Pa. C. S. Ch. 25 (relating to wills) shall apply to standby guardians, coguardians, guardians and any alternates unless otherwise specified in this chapter. Nothing in this chapter shall be construed to deprive any parent, custodial or noncustodial, of legal parental rights. Nothing in this chapter shall be construed to relieve any parent, custodial or noncustodial, of a duty to support a child under the provision of 23 Pa. C. S. Ch. 43 (relating to support matters generally).

SUBCHAPTER B

GENERAL PROVISIONS

§ 5611. Designation.

(a) **General rule.**—A custodial parent, a legal custodian or legal guardian may designate a standby guardian by means of a written designation unless the minor has another parent or adoptive parent:

(1) whose parental rights have not been terminated or relinquished;

(2) whose whereabouts are known; and

(3) who is willing and able to make and carry out the day-to-day child-care decisions concerning the minor.

(b) **Exception where other parent consents.**—Notwithstanding subsection (a), a parent, legal custodian or local guardian may designate a standby guardian with the consent of the other parent.

(c) **Contents.**—

(1) A designation of a standby guardianship shall identify the custodial parent, legal custodian or legal guardian making the designation, the minor or minors, any other parent, the standby guardian and the triggering event or events upon which a named standby guardian shall become a coguardian or guardian. If desired, different standby guardians may be designated for different triggering events. The designation shall also include the signed consent of the standby guardian, and the signed consent of any other parent or an indication why the other parent's consent is not necessary.

(2) The designation shall be signed by the designating parent, legal custodian or legal guardian in the presence of two witnesses, who are 18 years of age or older and not otherwise named in the designation, who shall also sign the designation. If the parent, legal custodian or legal guardian is physically unable to sign the designation, the parent, legal custodian or legal guardian may direct another person not named in the designation to sign on the parent's, legal custodian's or the legal guardian's behalf in the presence of the parent, legal custodian or legal guardian and the witnesses.

(3) A parent, legal custodian or legal guardian may also, but need not, designate an alternate to in the designation.

(4) A designation may, but need not, be in the following form:

I (insert name of designator) do hereby appoint (insert name, address and telephone number or standby guardian) as the standby guardian of (insert name(s) of minor(s)) to take effect upon the occurrence of the following triggering event or events (insert specific triggering events.)

I hereby revoke all former wills and codicils to the extent that there is a conflict between those formerly executed documents and this, my duly executed standby guardian designation.

I am the (insert designator's relationship to minor(s)) of (insert name(s) of minor(s)).

(Insert name(s) of minor(s)'s other parent(s)) is the father/mother of (insert name(s) or minor(s)).

His/her address is:

(Check all that apply):

_____   He/she died on (insert date of death). _____ His/her parental rights were terminated or relinquished on (insert date of termination or relinquishment).

_____   His/her whereabouts are unknown. I understand that all living parents whose rights have not been terminated must be given notice of this designation pursuant to the Pennsylvania Rules of Civil Procedure or a petition to approve this designation may not be granted by the court.

_____   He/she is unwilling and unable to make and carry out day-to-day child-care decisions concerning the minor.

_____   He/she consents to this designation and has signed this form below.

By this designation I am granting (insert name and standby guardian) the authority to act for 60 days following the occurrence of the triggering event as a coguardian with me, or in the event of my death, as guardian of my minor child(ren).

Optional: I hereby nominate (insert name, address, and telephone number of alternate standby guardian) as the alternate standby guardian to a assume the duties of the standby guardian named above in the event the standby guardian is unable or refuses to act as a standby guardian.

If I have indicated more than one triggering event, it is my intent that the triggering event which occurs first shall take precedence. If I have indicated "my death" as the triggering event, it is my intent that the person named in the designation to be standby guardian for my minor child(ren) in the event of my death shall be appointed as guardian of my minor child(ren) when I die.

It is my intention to retain full parental rights to the extent consistent with my condition and to retain the authority to revoke the standby guardianship if I so choose.

This designation is made after careful reflection, while I am of sound mind.

(Date)   (Designator's signature)

(Witness's signature)   (Witness's signature)

(Number and street)   (Number and street)

(City, State and Zip Code) (City, State and Zip Code) (IF APPLICABLE): I (insert name of other parent) hereby consent to this designation.

(Date)   (Signature of other parent)

(Address of other parent)

I, (insert name of standby guardian) hereby accept my nomination as standby guardian of (insert minor(s) name(s)), I understand that my rights and responsibilities toward the minor child(ren) named above will become effective upon the occurrence of the above-stated triggering event or events. I further understand that in order to continue caring for the child(ren), I must file a petition with the court within 60 days of the occurrence of the triggering event.

(Date)   (Signature of standby parent)

§ 5612.   Petition for approval of a designation.

(a) **General rule.**—A petition for court approval of a designation under this chapter may be made at any time by filing with the court a copy of the designation. If the triggering event has not occurred on or before the time of filing, only the designator may file the petition. If the triggering event has occurred on or before the time of filing, the standby guardian named in the designation may file the petition and the petition shall also contain one of the following:

(1)   A determination of the designator's incapacity.

(2)   A determination of the designator's debilitation and the designator's signed and dated consent.

(3)   A copy of the designator's death certificate.

(b) **Notice.**—

(1)   The petitioner shall notify any person named in the designation within ten days of the filing of the petition and of any hearing thereon.

(2)   If the petition alleges that a nondesignating parent cannot be located, that parent shall be notified in accordance with the notice provisions of the Pennsylvania Rules of Civil Procedure in Custody Matters. No notice is necessary to a parent whose parental rights have previously been terminated or relinquished.

(c) **Jurisdiction.**—For purposes of determining jurisdiction under this chapter, the provisions of Chapter 54 (relating to uniform child custody jurisdiction and enforcement) shall apply.

(d) **Presumptions.**—In a proceeding for judicial appointment of a standby guardian, a designation shall constitute a rebuttable presumption that the designated standby guardian is capable of serving as coguardian or guardian. When the designator is the sole surviving parent, when the parental rights of any noncustodial parent have been terminated or relinquished or when all parties consent to the designation, there shall be a rebuttable presumption that entry of the approval order is in the best interest of the child. In any case, if the court finds entry of the approval

727

order to be in the best interest of the child, the court shall enter an order approving the designation petition.

(e) Approval without hearing.—Approval of the designation without a hearing is permitted when the designator is the sole surviving parent, when the parental rights of any noncustodial parent have been terminated or relinquished or when all parties consent to entry of the approval order.

(f) Hearing.—In the event a hearing is required, it shall be conducted in accordance with the proceedings set forth in Chapters 53 (relating to custody) and 54.

(g) Court appearance.—The designator need not appear in court if the designator is medically unable to appear.

§ 5613. Authority of standby guardian.

(a) General rule.—The standby guardian shall have authority to act as coguardian or guardian upon the occurrence of the triggering event. The commencement of the standby guardian's authority to act as coguardian pursuant to: a determination of incapacity; a determination of debilitation and consent; or, the receipt of consent alone, shall not itself divest the designator of any parental rights, but shall confer upon the standby guardian concurrent or shared custody of the child. The commencement of the standby guardian's authority to act as guardian pursuant to the death of the designator shall not confer upon the standby guardian more than physical and legal custody of the child as defined in Ch. 53 (relating to custody). A coguardian shall assure frequent and continuing contact with and physical access to the child and shall further assure the involvement of the parent, to include, to the greatest extent possible, in the decision making on behalf of the child.

(b) Effect of filing.—The designator may file a petition for approval of a designation with the court at any time. If the petition is approved by the court before the occurrence of the triggering event, the standby guardian's authority will commence automatically upon the occurrence of the triggering event. No further petition or confirmation is necessary. If a designation has been made, but the petition for approval of the designation has not been filed and a triggering event had occurred, the standby guardian shall have temporary legal authority to act as a coguardian or guardian of the minor without the direction of the court for a period of 60 days. The standby guardian shall, within that period, file a petition for approval in accordance with section 5612 (relating to petition for approval of a designation). If no petition is filed within the specified 60 days, the standby guardian shall lose all authority to act as coguardian or guardian. If a petition is filed but the court does not act upon it within the 60-day period, the temporary legal authority to act as coguardian shall continue until the court orders otherwise.

(c) **Parental rights.**—The commencement of a coguardian's or guardian's authority under this subchapter may not, itself, divest a parent or legal guardian of any parental or guardianship rights.

(d) **Restored capacity.**—If a licensed physician determines that the designator has regained capacity, the coguardian's authority which commenced pursuant to the occurrence of a triggering event shall become inactive and the coguardian shall return to having no authority. Failure of a coguardian to comply with this provision and to immediately return the minor to the designator's care shall entitle the designator to an emergency hearing in a court of competent jurisdiction.

§ 5614. Revocation.

(a) **Prepetition.**—Prior to a petition being filed under section 5612 (relating to petition for approval of a designation) the designator may revoke a standby guardianship by simple destruction of the designation and notification of the revocation to the standby guardian.

(b) **Postpetition.**—After a petition has been filed, the designator may revoke a standby guardianship by:

(1)   executing a written revocation;

(2)   filing the revocation with the court; and

(3)   notifying the persons named in the designation of the revocation in writing.

(c) Unwritten revocation.—Regardless of whether a petition has been filed, an unwritten revocation may be considered by the court if it can be proven by clear and convincing evidence.

§ 5615. Conflicting documents.

If a parent has appointed a testamentary guardian of the person or estate of a minor by will under 20 Pa. C. S. § 2519 (relating to testamentary guardian) and there is a conflict between that will and a duly executed written standby guardian designation, the document latest in date of execution shall prevail.

§ 5616. Bond.

In no event shall a standby guardian be required to post bond prior to the occurrence of the triggering event. The court may require a bond if the standby guardian is designated the coguardian or guardian of the estate of a minor but will not require a bond for the coguardianship or guardianship of the person of a minor.

APPENDIX A(7)

Title 42.   Judiciary and Judicial Procedure.

42 Pa C. S. Sec. 7401–7411

CHAPTER 74: COLLABORATIVE LAW PROCESS

§ 7401.   Short title and scope of chapter.

(a) Short title.—This chapter shall be known and may be cited as the Collaborative Law Act.

(b) Scope.—This chapter shall apply to a collaborative law process between family members and arising from a participation agreement that meets the requirements of section 7405 (relating to collaborative law participation agreement).

§ 7402.   Definitions.

The following words and phrases when used in this chapter shall have the meanings given to them in this section unless the context clearly indicates otherwise:

"Collaborative communication." A statement or question that concerns the collaborative law process or a collaborative matter and that occurs after the parties sign a collaborative law participation agreement but before the collaborative law process is concluded. The term does not include a written settlement agreement that is signed by all parties to the agreement.

"Collaborative law process." A procedure to resolve a claim, transaction, dispute or issue without intervention by a tribunal, in which procedure all parties sign a collaborative law participation agreement, all parties are represented by counsel and counsel is disqualified from representing the parties in a proceeding before a tribunal.

"Collaborative matter." A dispute, transaction, claim or issue for resolution that is described in a participation agreement concerning any of the following:

(1) Marriage, divorce and annulment.

(2) Property distribution, usage and ownership.

(3) Child custody, visitation and parenting time.

(4) Parentage.

(5) Alimony, alimony pendente lite, spousal support and child support.

(6) Prenuptial, marital and postnuptial agreements.

(7) Adoption.

(8) Termination of parental rights.

(9) A matter arising under 20 Pa.C.S. (relating to decedents, estates and fiduciaries).

(10) A matter arising under 15 Pa.C.S. Pt. II (relating to corporations).

"Family members." All of the following:

(1) Spouses and former spouses.

(2) Parents and children, including individuals acting in loco parentis.

(3) Individuals currently or formerly cohabiting.

(4) Other individuals related by consanguinity or affinity.

"Nonparty participant." A person other than a party or a party's attorney that participates in the collaborative law process. The term may include, but is not limited to, support persons, mental health professionals, financial neutrals and potential parties.

"Party." A person that signs a collaborative law participation agreement and whose consent is necessary to resolve a collaborative matter.

"Person." An individual, corporation, business trust, estate, trust, partnership, limited liability company, association, joint venture, public corporation, government or governmental subdivision, agency or instrumentality or any other legal or commercial entity.

"Proceeding." A judicial, administrative, arbitral or other adjudicative process before a tribunal.

"Related matter." A matter involving the same parties, dispute, transaction, claim or issue as a collaborative matter.

"Tribunal." A court, arbitrator, administrative agency or other body acting in an adjudicative capacity that has jurisdiction to render a binding decision directly affecting a party's interests in a matter.

§ 7403.   Beginning the collaborative law process.

(a) Voluntariness.—Participation in a collaborative law process is voluntary and may not be compelled by a tribunal. A party may terminate the collaborative law process at any time with or without cause.

(b) Commencement.—A collaborative law process shall begin when the parties sign a collaborative law participation agreement. Parties to a proceeding pending before a tribunal may enter into a collaborative law process to resolve a matter related to the proceeding.

§ 7404.   Assessment and review.

(a) General assessment.—Before entering into a collaborative law participation agreement, a prospective party shall:

(1) Assess factors the prospective party's attorney reasonably believes relate to whether the collaborative law process is appropriate for the matter and for the parties, including a prospective party or nonparty participant's history, if any, of violent or threatening behavior.

(2) Review information that the attorney reasonably believes is sufficient for the prospective party to make an informed decision about the material benefits and risks of a collaborative law process, as compared with other alternatives.

(b) Threatening or violent behavior.—

(1) Before a prospective party signs a collaborative law participation agreement, an attorney shall inquire whether the prospective party has a history of threatening or violent behavior toward any party or nonparty participant who will be part of the collaborative law process.

(2) If an attorney learns or reasonably believes, before commencing or at any point in the collaborative law process, that a party or prospective party has engaged in or has a history of threatening or violent behavior toward any other party or nonparty participant, the attorney may not begin or continue the collaborative law process unless the party or prospective party:

(i) Requests beginning or continuing the collaborative law process.

(ii) Indicates that the safety of all parties to the collaborative law process can be protected adequately during the collaborative law process.

(c) Private cause of action.—An attorney's failure to protect a party under this section shall not give rise to a private cause of action against the attorney.

§ 7405.   Collaborative law participation agreement.

(a) Requirements.—A collaborative law participation agreement must:

(1) Be in writing.

(2) Be signed by the parties.

    (3) State the parties' intention to resolve a collaborative matter through a collaborative law process.

    (4) Describe the nature and scope of the collaborative matter.

    (5) Identify the attorney who represents each party in the collaborative law process.

    (6) Include a statement that the representation of each attorney is limited to the collaborative law process and that the attorneys are disqualified from representing any party or nonparty participant in a proceeding related to a collaborative matter, consistent with this chapter.

(b) Optional provisions.—Parties may include in a collaborative law participation agreement additional provisions not inconsistent with this chapter or other applicable law, including, but not limited to:

    (1) An agreement concerning confidentiality of collaborative communications.

    (2) An agreement that part or all of the collaborative law process will not be privileged in a proceeding.

    (3) The scope of voluntary disclosure.

    (4) The role of nonparty participants.

    (5) The retention and role of nonparty experts.

    (6) The manner and duration of a collaborative law process under sections 7403 (relating to beginning the collaborative law process) and 7406 (relating to concluding the collaborative law process).

(c) Nonconforming agreements.—This chapter shall apply to an agreement that does not meet the requirements of subsection (a) if:

    (1) The agreement indicates an intent to enter into a collaborative law participation agreement.

    (2) The agreement is signed by all parties.

(3) A tribunal determines that the parties intended to and reasonably believed that they were entering into a collaborative law agreement subject to the requirements of this chapter.

§ 7406. Concluding the collaborative law process.

(a) General rule.—A collaborative law process shall be concluded by:

(1) Resolution of the collaborative matter, as evidenced by a signed record.

(2) Resolution of a part of the collaborative matter and agreement by all parties that the remaining parts of the collaborative matter will not be resolved in the collaborative law process, as evidenced by a signed record.

(3) Termination under subsection (b).

(4) A method specified in the collaborative law participation agreement.

(b) Termination.—A collaborative law process shall be terminated when:

(1) A party gives written notice to all parties that the collaborative law process is terminated.

(2) A party begins or resumes a pending proceeding before a tribunal related to a collaborative matter without the agreement of all parties.

(3) Except as provided in subsection (c), a party discharges the party's attorney or the attorney withdraws from further representation of a party. An attorney who is discharged or withdraws shall give prompt written notice to all parties and nonparty participants.

(c) Continuation.—Notwithstanding the discharge or withdrawal of a collaborative attorney, a collaborative law process shall continue if, not later than 30 days after the date that the notice under subsection (b)(3) is sent, the unrepresented party engages a successor attorney and the participation agreement is amended to identify the successor attorney.

§ 7407.   Disqualification of collaborative attorney.

(a) Rule.—

(1) Except as provided in subsection (b), an attorney who represents a party in a collaborative law process and any law firm or government agency with which the attorney is associated shall be disqualified from representing any party or nonparty participant in a proceeding related to the collaborative matter.

(2) Requesting the approval of a settlement agreement by a tribunal shall be considered part of the collaborative law process and not a related proceeding.

(b) Exception.—Disqualification under subsection (a) shall not operate to prevent a collaborative attorney from seeking or defending an emergency order to protect the health, safety or welfare of a party or a family member.

§ 7408.   Disclosure of information.

During the collaborative law process, parties shall provide timely, full, candid and informal disclosure of information related to the collaborative matter without formal discovery, and shall update promptly previously disclosed information that has materially changed.

§ 7409.   Confidentiality.

A collaborative law communication shall be confidential to the extent provided by the laws of this Commonwealth or as specified in the collaborative law participation agreement.

§ 7410.   Privilege.

(a) General rule.—Except as otherwise provided in this section, a collaborative communication is privileged, may not be compelled through discovery and shall not be admissible as evidence in an action or proceeding. Evidence that is otherwise admissible and subject to discovery shall not become inadmissible or protected from discovery solely because of its disclosure or use in a collaborative law process.

(b) Waiver.—

(1) A party may waive a privilege belonging to the party only if all parties waive the privilege and, in the case of a communication by a nonparty participant, only if the nonparty participant and all parties waive the privilege.

(2) If a party discloses a privileged collaborative communication that prejudices another party, the disclosing party waives the right to assert a privilege under this section to the extent necessary for the party prejudiced to respond to the disclosure or representation.

(c) Nonapplicability.—Privilege under subsection (a) shall not apply to:

(1) A communication that is not subject to the privilege by agreement of the parties according to the terms of a participation agreement.

(2) A communication that is made during a session of a collaborative law process that is open, or required by law to be open, to the public.

(3) A communication sought, obtained or used to:

  (i) threaten or plan to inflict bodily injury, commit or attempt to commit a crime; or

  (ii) conceal ongoing criminal activity.

(d) Exceptions.—The following exceptions apply to the privilege under subsection (a):

(1) A communication sought or offered to prove or disprove facts relating to a claim or complaint of professional misconduct or malpractice or a fee dispute.

(2) A communication sought or offered to prove facts relating to the abuse, neglect, abandonment or exploitation of a child or abuse of an adult.

(3) A communication sought or offered in a criminal proceeding or in an action to enforce, void, set aside or modify a settlement agreement where a tribunal or court of competent jurisdiction finds

that the evidence is not otherwise available and the need for the evidence substantially outweighs the interest in protecting the privilege.

(e) Limitation.—

(1) If a collaborative communication is subject to an exception under subsection (d), only the part of the collaborative communication necessary for the application of the exception may be disclosed or admitted.

(2) Disclosure or admission of evidence under subsection (d) does not make the evidence or any other collaborative communication discoverable or admissible for any other purpose.

(f) Construction.—This section shall not be construed to affect the scope of another applicable privilege under State law or rule of court.

§ 7411.   Professional responsibility.

This chapter shall not affect the professional responsibility obligations and standards applicable to an attorney or other person professionally licensed or certified under State law.

(June 28, 2018, P.L. 381, No. 55, effective in 60 days).

APPENDIX A(8)

Title 51.   Military Affairs.

Part II. Pennsylvania National Guard, Pennsylvania Guard And Militia

Subpart D. Rights and Immunities

51 Pa. C. S. Sec. 4109

§ 4109.   Child custody proceedings during military deployment.

(a) Restriction on change of custody.—If a petition for change of custody of a child of an eligible servicemember is filed with any court in this Commonwealth while the eligible servicemember is deployed in support of a contingency operation, no court may enter an order modifying or amending any previous judgment or order, or issue a new order, that changes the custody arrangement for that child that existed as of the date of the deployment of the eligible servicemember, except that a court may enter a temporary custody order if it is in the best interest of the child.

(a.1) Temporary assignment to family members.-If an eligible servicemember has received notice of deployment in support of a contingency operation, a court may issue a temporary order to an eligible servicemember who has rights to a child under 23 Pa.C.S. § 5323 (relating to award of custody) or former 23 Pa.C.S. Ch. 53 Subch. A (relating to general provisions), including a temporary order to temporarily assign custody rights to family members of the servicemember. In the case of temporary assignment of rights to family members of the servicemember, the following shall apply:

(1) The servicemember may petition the court for a temporary order to temporarily assign custody rights to family members of the servicemember. The servicemember shall be joined in the petition by the family members to whom the servicemember is seeking to assign temporary custody rights. The petition shall include a proposed revised custody schedule for care of the child by the family members. The proposed revised custody schedule may not include custody rights which exceed the rights granted to a servicemember

740

set forth in the order in effect at the time of the filing of the petition to grant temporary custody rights to family members.

(2) The court may issue a temporary order with a revised custody schedule as proposed by the servicemember and the family members or another revised custody schedule as the court deems appropriate, if the court finds that a temporary assignment of custody rights to family members of the servicemember is in the best interest of the child. In no case shall a temporary order granting custody rights to the family members of a servicemember exceed the custody rights granted to the servicemember set forth in the order in effect at the time of the filing of the petition to assign temporary custody rights to family members.

In the case of any other temporary order issued under this subsection, the court may issue a temporary order if it is in the best interest of the child.

(b) **Completion of deployment.**—In any temporary custody order entered under subsection (a) or (a.1), a court shall require that, upon the return of the eligible servicemember from deployment in support of a contingency operation, the custody order that was in effect immediately preceding the date of the deployment of the eligible servicemember is reinstated.

(c) **Exclusion of military service from determination of child's best interest.**—If a petition for the change of custody of the child of an eligible servicemember who was deployed in support of a contingency operation is filed after the end of the deployment, no court may consider the absence of the eligible servicemember by reason of that deployment in determining the best interest of the child.

(d) **Failure to appear due to military deployment.**—The failure of an eligible servicemember to appear in court due to deployment in support of a contingency operation shall not, in and of itself, be sufficient to justify a modification of a custody order if the reason for the failure to appear is the eligible servicemember's active duty in support of a contingency operation.

(e) Relationship to other laws.—Notwithstanding any other provision of law, the provisions of this section shall be applied with regard to child custody issues related to eligible servicemembers deployed in support of contingency operations.

(f) Definitions.—As used in this section, the following words and phrases shall have the meanings given to them in this subsection:

"Contingency operation." A military operation that:

(1) is designated by the Secretary of Defense as an operation in which members of the armed forces are or may become involved in military actions, operations or hostilities against an enemy of the United States or against an opposing military force; or

(2) results in the call or order to, or retention on, active duty of members of the uniformed services under 10 U. S. C. § 688 (relating to retired members: authority to order to active duty; duties), 12301(a) (relating to reserve components generally), 12302 (relating to Ready Reserve), 2304 (relating to Selected Reserve and certain Individual Ready Reserve members; order to active duty other than during war or national emergency), 12305 (relating to authority of President to suspend certain laws relating to promotion, retirement, and separation) or 12406 (relating to National Guard in Federal service: call) or any other provision of 10 U. S. C. during a war or during a national emergency declared by the President or Congress.

"Eligible servicemember." A member of the Pennsylvania National Guard or a member of an active or reserve component of the Armed Forces of the United States who is serving on active duty, other than active duty for training, for a period of 30 or more consecutive days, in support of a contingency operation.

"Family members." As defined in 23 Pa.C.S. § 6303 (relating to definitions).

§ 4110. Expedited or electronic hearing.

(a) Expedited hearing.-Upon motion of an eligible servicemember who has received notice of deployment in support of a contingency operation, the court shall, for good cause shown, hold an expedited hearing in custody matters instituted under section 4109 (relating to child custody proceedings during military deployment) when the military duties of the eligible servicemember have a material effect on the eligible servicemember's ability, or anticipated ability, to appear in person at a regularly scheduled hearing.

(b) Electronic hearing.-Upon motion of an eligible servicemember who has received notice of deployment in support of a contingency operation, the court shall, upon reasonable advance notice and for good cause shown, allow the eligible servicemember to present testimony and evidence by electronic means in custody matters instituted under section 4109 when the military duties of the eligible servicemember have a material effect on the eligible servicemember's ability to appear in person at a regularly scheduled hearing.

(c) Definitions.-As used in this section, the following words and phrases shall have the meanings given to them in this subsection unless the context clearly indicates otherwise:

"Contingency operation." As defined in section 4109 (relating to child custody proceedings during military deployment).

"Electronic means." Includes communication by telephone, video conference or the Internet.

"Eligible servicemember." As defined in section 4109 (relating to child custody proceedings during military deployment).

"Matter." As defined in 42 Pa.C.S. § 102 (relating to definitions).

APPENDIX B

FEDERAL STATUTES

APPENDIX B(1)

(PKPA)

28 U.S.C. § 1738A. Full Faith and Credit Given to Child Custody Determinations, (PKPA).

(a) The appropriate authorities of every State shall enforce according to its terms, and shall not modify except as provided in subsections (f), (g), and (h) of this section, any custody determination or visitation determination made consistently with the provisions of this section by a court of another State.

(b) As used in this section, the term—

(1) "child" means a person under the age of eighteen;

(2) "contestant" means a person, including a parent or grandparent, who claims a right to custody or visitation of a child;

(3) "custody determination" means a judgment, decree, or other order of a court providing for the custody of a child, and includes permanent and temporary orders, and initial orders and modifications;

(4) "home State" means the State in which, immediately preceding the time involved, the child lived with his parents, a parent, or a person acting as parent, for at least six consecutive months, and in the case of a child less than six months old, the State in which the child lived from birth with any of such persons. Periods of temporary absence of any such persons are counted as part of the six-month or other period;

(5) "modification" and "modify" refer to a custody or visitation determination which modifies, replaces, supersedes, otherwise is made subsequent to, a prior custody or visitation determination

745

concerning the same child, whether made by the same court or not;

(6) "person acting as a parent" means a person, other than a parent, who has physical custody of a child and who has either been awarded custody by a court or claims a right to custody;

(7) "physical custody" means actual possession and control of a child;

(8) "State" means a State of the United States, the District of Columbia, the Commonwealth of Puerto Rico, or a territory or possession of the United States; and

(9) "visitation determination" means a judgment, decree, or other order of a court providing for the visitation of a child and includes permanent and temporary orders and initial orders and modifications.

(c) A child custody or visitation determination made by a court of a State is consistent with the provisions of this section only if—

(1) such court has jurisdiction under the law of such State; and

(2) one of the following conditions is met:

(A) such State (i) is the home State of the child on the date of the commencement of the proceeding, or (ii) had been the child's home State within six months before the date of the commencement of the proceeding and the child is absent from such State because of his removal or retention by a contestant or for other reasons, and a contestant continues to live in such State;

(B) (i) it appears that no other State would have jurisdiction under subparagraph (A), and

(ii) it is in the best interest of the child that a court of such State assume jurisdiction because

(I) the child and his parents, or the child and at least one contestant, have a significant connection with such State other than mere physical presence in such State, and

    (II)   there is available in such State substantial evidence concerning the child's present or future care, protection, training, and personal relationships;

(C)   the child is physically present in such State and

    (i)   the child has been abandoned, or

    (ii)   it is necessary in an emergency to protect the child because the child, a sibling, or parent of the child has been subjected to or threatened with mistreatment or abuse;

(D)   (i)it appears that no other State would have jurisdiction under subparagraph (A), (B), (C), or (E), or another State has declined to exercise jurisdiction on the ground that the State whose jurisdiction is in issue is the more appropriate forum to determine the custody or visitation of the child, and (ii) it is in the best interest of the child that such court assume jurisdiction; or

(E)   the court has continuing jurisdiction pursuant to subsection (d) of this section.

(d) The jurisdiction of a court of a State which has made a child custody or visitation determination consistently with the provisions of this section continues as long as the requirement of subsection (c)(1) of this section continues to be met and such state remains the residence of the child or of any contestant.

(e) Before a child custody or visitation determination is made, reasonable notice and opportunity to be heard shall be given to the contestants, any parent whose parental rights have not been previously terminated and any person who has physical custody of a child.

(f) A court of a State may modify a determination of the custody of the same child made by a court of another State, if—

(1)   it has jurisdiction to make such a child custody determination; and

747

(2) the court of the other State no longer has jurisdiction, or it has declined to exercise such jurisdiction to modify such determination.

(g) A court of a State shall not exercise jurisdiction in any proceeding for a custody or visitation determination commenced during the pendency of a proceeding in a court of another State where such court of that other State is exercising jurisdiction consistently with the provisions of this section to make a custody determination.

(h) A court of a State may not modify a visitation determination made by a court of another State unless the court of the other State no longer had jurisdiction to modify such determination or has declined to exercise jurisdiction to modify such determination.

APPENDIX B(2)

42 U.S.C. § 663. Use of Federal Parent Locator Service in Connection With Enforcement or Determination of a Child Custody in Cases of Parental Kidnapping of a Child.

(a) Agreements with States for use of Federal Parent Locator Service

The Secretary shall enter into an agreement with every State under which the services of the Federal Parent Locator Service established under section 653 of this title shall be made available to each State of the purpose of determining the whereabouts of any parent or child when such information is to be used to locate such parent or child for the purpose of—

(1) enforcing any State or Federal law with respect to the unlawful taking or restraint or a child; or

(2) making or enforcing a child custody or visitation determination.

(b) Requests from authorized persons for information

An agreement entered into under subsection (a) of this section shall provide that the State agency described in section 654 of this title will, under procedures prescribed by the Secretary in regulations, receive and transmit to the Secretary requests from authorized persons for information as to (or useful in determining) the whereabouts of any parent or child when such information is to be used to locate such parent or child for the purpose of—

(1) enforcing any State or Federal law with respect to the unlawful taking or restraint of a child; or

(2) making or enforcing a child custody or visitation determination.

(c) Information which may be disclosed

Information authorized to be provided by the Secretary under subsection (a), (b), (e), or (f) of this section shall be subject to the same conditions with respect to disclosure as information authorized to be provided under section 653 of this title, and a request for information by the Secretary under this section shall be considered to be a request for information under section 653 of this title which is authorized to be provided under such section. Only information as to the most recent address and place of employment of any parent or child shall be provided under this section.

(d) "Custody determination" and "authorized person" defined

For purposes of this section—

(1) the term "custody or visitation determination" means a judgment, decree or other order of a court providing for the custody or visitation of a child, and includes permanent and temporary orders, and initial orders and modification;

(2) the term "authorized person" means—

(A) any agent or attorney of any State having an agreement under this section, who has the duty or authority under the law of such State to enforce a child custody or visitation determination;

(B) any court having jurisdiction to make or enforce such a child custody or visitation determination, or any agent of such court; and

(C) any agent or attorney of the United States, or of a State having an agreement under this section, who has the duty or authority to investigate, enforce, or bring a prosecution with respect to the unlawful taking or restraint of a child.

(e) Agreements on use of Federal Parent Locator Service with United States Central Authority under Convention on the Civil Aspects of International Child Abduction

The Secretary shall enter into an agreement with the Central Authority designated by the President in accordance with section 11606 of this title, under which the services of the Federal?Parent Locator Service established under section 653 of this title shall be made available to such Central Authority upon its request for the purpose of locating any parent or child on behalf of an applicant to such Central Authority within the meaning of section 11602(1) of this title. The Federal Parent Locator Service shall charge no fees for services requested pursuant to this subsection.

(f) Agreement to assist in locating missing children under Parent Locator Service

The Secretary shall enter into an agreement with the Attorney General of the United States, under which the services of the Federal Parent Locator Service established under section 653 of this title shall be made available to the Office of Juvenile Justice and Delinquency Prevention upon its request to locate any parent or child on behalf of such Office for the purpose of—

(1) enforcing any State or Federal law with respect to the unlawful taking or restraint of a child, or

(2) making or enforcing a child custody or visitation determination.

The Federal Parent Locator Service shall charge no fees for services requested pursuant to this subsection.

APPENDIX B(3)

18 U.S.C. § 1073. Flight to Avoid Prosecution or Giving Testimony.

Whoever moves or travels in interstate or foreign commerce with intent either (1) to avoid prosecution, or custody or confinement after conviction, under the laws of the place from which he flees, for a crime, or an attempt to commit a crime, punishable by death or which is a felony under the laws of the place from which the fugitive flees, or (2) to avoid giving testimony in any criminal proceedings in such place in which the commission of an offense punishable by death or which is a felony under the laws of such place, is charged, or (3) to avoid service of, or contempt proceedings for alleged disobedience of, lawful process requiring attendance and the giving of testimony or the production of documentary evidence before an agency of a State empowered by the law of such State to conduct investigations of alleged criminal activities, shall be fined under this title or imprisoned not more than five years, or both. For the purposes of clause (3) of this paragraph, the term "State" includes a State of the United States, the District of Columbia, and any commonwealth, territory, or possession of the United States.

Violations of this section may be prosecuted only in the Federal judicial district in which the original crime was alleged to have been committed, or in which the person was held in custody or confinement, or in which an avoidance of service of process or a contempt referred to in clause (3) of the first paragraph of this section is alleged to have been committed, and only upon formal approval in writing by the Attorney General, the Deputy Attorney General, the Associate Attorney General, or an Assistant Attorney General of the United States, which function of approving prosecutions may not be delegated.

APPENDIX B(4)

18 U.S.C. § 1204. International Parental Kidnapping

(a) Whoever removes a child from the United States, or attempts to do so, or retains a child (who has been in the United States) outside the United States with intent to obstruct the lawful exercise of parental rights shall be fined under this title or imprisoned not more than 3 years, or both.

(b) As used in this section-

(1)   the term "child" means a person who has not attained the age of 16 years; and

(2)   the term "parental rights", with respect to a child, means the right to physical custody of the child-

    (A)   whether joint or sole (and includes visiting rights); and

    (B)   whether arising by operation of law, court order, or legally binding agreement of the parties.

(c) It shall be an affirmative defense under this section that-

(1)   the defendant acted within the provisions of a valid court order granting the defendant legal custody or visitation rights and that order was obtained pursuant to the Uniform Child Custody Jurisdiction Act or the Uniform Child Custody Jurisdiction and Enforcement Act and was in effect at the time of the offense;

(2)   the defendant was fleeing an incidence or pattern of domestic violence; or

(3)   the defendant had physical custody of the child pursuant to a court order granting legal custody or visitation rights and failed to return the child as a result of circumstances beyond the defendant's control, and the defendant notified or made reasonable attempts to notify the other parent or lawful custodian of the child of such circumstances within 24 hours after the visitation period had expired and returned the child as soon as possible.

(d) This section does not detract from The Hague Convention on the Civil Aspects of International Parental Child Abduction, done at The Hague on October 25, 1980.

APPENDIX C

PENNSYLVANIA RULES OF CIVIL PROCEDURE (PA.R.C.P.)—CUSTODY (AMENDED THROUGH SEPTEMBER 30, 2020) RULES 1915.1–1915.25

ACTIONS FOR CUSTODY, PARTIAL CUSTODY AND VISITATION OF MINOR CHILDREN

Explanatory Comment—1981
Introduction

In an era of legislative and judicial activism, the law of custody has not remained untouched. In the procedural context, the legislature has enacted the Uniform Child Custody Jurisdiction Act and has extended, in general, its provisions to intrastate proceedings. At the same time, "the Pennsylvania Superior Court, in its continuing redefinition and refinement of the adversarial and judicial functions essential to child-custody disputes, has drawn up a catalog of criteria whose imposition removes that area of law from the realm of caprice." (Hon. Lawrence W. Kaplan, "The Child Advocate in Custody Litigation," as published in The Changing Direction of Child Custody Litigation: The Modern Approach, PBI publication No. 1980-140, p. 86.)

It is in furtherance of the legislative and judicial objective of the appropriate and prompt disposition of custody disputes that these rules governing the custody, partial custody and visitation of minor children are promulgated.

Effective Date

Order of the Supreme Court, Eastern District, June 25, 1982, extended the effective date of Rules 1915.1 to 1915.25 to January 1, 1983.

RULE 1915.1.   SCOPE. DEFINITIONS

(a) These rules govern the practice and procedure in all actions for legal and physical custody of minor children, including habeas corpus proceedings and claims for custody asserted in an action of divorce.

(b) As used in this chapter, unless the context of a rule indicates otherwise, the following terms shall have the following meanings:

"action," all proceedings for legal and physical custody and proceedings for modification of prior orders of any court;

"child," an unemancipated individual under 18 years of age;

"conference officer," an individual who presides over an office conference pursuant to Pa.R.C.P. No. 1915.4-2(a) or the initial non-record proceeding under Pa.R.C.P. No. 1915.4-3(a). For purposes of these rules, a conciliator is synonymous with a conference officer;

"custody," the legal right to keep, control, guard, care for, and preserve a child and includes the terms "legal custody," "physical custody," and "shared custody;"

"hearing officer," a lawyer who conducts a record hearing on partial custody cases pursuant to Pa.R.C.P. No. 1915.4-2(b);

"home county," the county in which the child lived with either or both parents, a person acting as a parent, or in an institution for at least six consecutive months immediately preceding the filing of the action, and in the case of a child less than six months old, the county in which the child lived from birth with any of the persons mentioned. A period of temporary absence of the child from the physical custody of the parent, institution, or person acting as parent shall not affect the six-month or other period;

"in loco parentis," a person who puts himself or herself in the situation of a lawful parent by assuming the obligations incident to the parental relationship without going through the formality of a legal adoption. The status of in loco parentis embodies two ideas:

(1) the assumption of a parental status; and

(2) the discharge of parental duties;

"legal custody," the right to make major decisions on behalf of the child, including, but not limited to, medical, religious, and educational decisions;

"mediator," an individual qualified under Pa.R.C.P. No. 1940.4 and who assists custody litigants independently from the procedures set forth in Pa.R.C.P. Nos. 1915.1-1915.25 by engaging the litigants in the alternative dispute principles in Pa.R.C.P. No. 1940.2 to resolve custody matters in whole or in part;

"mediation," the confidential process by which a neutral mediator assists the parties in attempting to reach a mutually acceptable agreement on issues arising in a custody action. Mediation is not a court proceeding; rather, it is an independent, non-record proceeding in lieu of court involvement for the purpose of assisting the parties to address the child's best interest. An agreement reached by the parties must be based on the voluntary decisions of the parties and not the decision of the mediator. The agreement may resolve all or only some of the disputed issues. The parties are required to mediate in good faith, but are not compelled to reach an agreement. While mediation is an alternative means of conflict resolution, it is not a substitute for the benefit of legal advice. The participants in mediation shall be limited to the parties to the custody action, primarily the child's parents and persons acting as parents. Except as provided in Pa.R.C.P. No. 1940.5(c), nonparties, including children, grandparents, and the parties' attorneys, shall not participate in the mediation.

"non-record proceeding," the initial office conference set forth in Pa.R.C.P. No. 1915.4-3. Mediation, as outlined in Pa.R.C.P. No. 1940.1-1940.9, shall not be construed as a non-record proceeding;

"partial physical custody," the right to assume physical custody of the child for less than a majority of the time;

"person acting as a parent," a person other than a parent, including an institution, who has physical custody of a child and who has either been awarded custody by a court or claims a right to custody. See also the definition of in loco parentis;

"physical custody," the actual physical possession and control of a child;

"primary physical custody," the right to assume physical custody of the child for the majority of time;

"relocation," a change in a residence of the child that significantly impairs the ability of a non-relocating party to exercise custodial rights;

"shared legal custody," the right of more than one individual to legal custody of the child;

"shared physical custody," the right of more than one individual to assume physical custody of the child, each having significant periods of physical custodial time with the child;

"sole legal custody," the right of one individual to exclusive legal custody of the child;

"sole physical custody," the right of one individual to exclusive physical custody of the child; and

"supervised physical custody," custodial time during which an agency or an adult designated by the court or agreed upon by the parties monitors the interaction between the child and the individual with those rights.

Adopted Dec. 10, 1981, effective July 1, 1982; effective date extended to Jan. 1, 1983 by order of June 25, 1982. Readopted and amended Nov. 8, 1982, effective Jan. 1, 1983; March 30, 1994, effective July 1, 1994; Nov. 19, 2008, imd. effective; Aug. 1, 2013, effective Sept. 3, 2013; Feb. 8, 2018, effective April 1, 2018.

RULE 1915.2.   VENUE.

(a) An action may be brought in any county

   (1)

   (i)   which is the home county of the child at the time of commencement of the proceeding, or

   (ii)   which had been the child's home county within six months before commencement of the proceeding and the child is absent from the county but a parent or person acting as parent continues to live in the county; or

(2) when the court of another county does not have venue under subdivision (1), and the child and the child's parents, or the child and at least one parent or a person acting as a parent, have a significant connection with the county other than mere physical presence and there is available within the county substantial evidence concerning the child's, protection, training and personal relationships; or

(3) when all counties in which venue is proper pursuant to subdivisions (1) and (2) have found that the court before which the action is pending is the more appropriate forum to determine the custody of the child; or

(4) when it appears that venue would not be proper in any other county under prerequisites substantially in accordance with paragraph (1), (2) or (3); or

(5) when the child is present in the county and has been abandoned or it is necessary in an emergency to protect the child because the child or a sibling or parent of the child is subjected to or threatened with mistreatment or abuse.

(b) Physical presence of the child or a party, while desirable, is not necessary or sufficient to make a child custody determination except as provided in subdivision (a)(5) above.

(c) The court at any time may transfer an action to the appropriate court of any other county where the action could originally have been brought or could be brought if it determines that it is an inconvenient forum under the circumstances and the court of another county is the more appropriate forum. It shall be the duty of the prothonotary of the court in which the action is pending to forward to the prothonotary of the county to which the action is transferred certified copies of the docket entries, process, pleadings and other papers filed in the action. The costs and fees of the petition for transfer and the removal of the record shall be paid by the petitioner in the first instance to be taxable as costs in the case.

Adopted Dec. 10, 1981, effective July 1, 1982; effective date extended to Jan. 1, 1983 by order of June 25, 1982. Readopted Nov. 8, 1982, effective Jan. 1, 1983 and applied to pending actions; amended March 30, 1994, effective July 1, 1994; amended Nov. 19, 2008, eff. immediately.

Official Note:

Under the Uniform Child Custody Jurisdiction and Enforcement Act, 23 Pa.C.S. § 5401 et seq., the court may decline to exercise its jurisdiction in a particular action despite the action having been brought in a county of proper venue. Section 5426 of the act, relating to simultaneous proceedings in other courts, provides for the mandatory refusal by the court to exercise its jurisdiction in an action. Section 5427 of the act, relating to inconvenient forum, and § 5428 of the act, relating to jurisdiction declined by reason of conduct, provide for the discretionary refusal by the court to exercise its jurisdiction.

Explanatory Comment—2008

Subdivision (a) of Rule 1915.2 incorporates the categories of jurisdiction for initial custody determinations and temporary emergency proceedings in the Uniform Child Custody Jurisdiction and Enforcement Act at 23 Pa.C.S.A. §§ 5421 and 5424 as the venue provisions for these rules, restating them in rule form without change in substance. Subdivision (a) follows the policy of § 5471 of the Uniform Child Custody Jurisdiction and Enforcement Act, which provides that the provisions of the act "allocating jurisdiction and functions between and among courts of different states shall also allocate jurisdiction and functions between and among courts of common pleas of this Commonwealth."

Subdivision (b), relating to the effect of the physical presence of the child or a party within a county, § 5421(c) without substantial change.

Subdivision (c) follows the inconvenient forum provisions or 23 Pa.C.S.A. § 5427.

RULE 1915.3. COMMENCEMENT OF ACTION. COMPLAINT. ORDER

(a) Except as provided in subdivision (c), the plaintiff shall commence a custody action by filing a verified complaint substantially in the form provided by Pa.R.C.P. No. 1915.15(a).

Note: See Pa.R.C.P. No. 1930.1(b). This rule may require attorneys or unrepresented parties to file confidential documents and documents containing confidential information that are subject to the *Case Records Public Access Policy of the Unified Judicial System of Pennsylvania.*

(b) An order shall be attached to the complaint or petition for modification directing the defendant to appear at a time and place specified. The order shall be substantially in the form provided by Pa.R.C.P. No. 1915.15(c).

Note: See Uniform Child Custody Jurisdiction and Enforcement Act, 23 Pa.C.S. § 5430(d), relating to costs and expenses for appearance of parties and child, and 23 Pa.C.S. § 5471, relating to intrastate application of the Uniform Child Custody Jurisdiction and Enforcement Act.

(c) A custody claim that is joined with a divorce action shall be asserted in the divorce complaint or a subsequent petition, which shall be substantially in the form provided by Pa.R.C.P. No. 1915.15(a).

Note: See Pa.R.C.P. No. 1920.13(b)(claims that are joined in a divorce action shall be raised in a complaint or a subsequent petition).

(d) If the child's mother is not married and the child has no legal or presumptive father, a putative father initiating a custody action shall file a paternity claim pursuant to 23 Pa.C.S. § 5103 and attach a copy to the custody complaint.

Note: If a putative father is uncertain of paternity, the correct procedure is to commence a civil action for paternity pursuant to the procedures set forth at Pa.R.C.P. No. 1930.6.

(e) Pleading Facts Establishing Standing.

(1) An individual seeking physical or legal custody of a child, who is *in loco parentis* to the child, shall plead facts establishing standing under 23 Pa.C.S. § 5324(2) in Paragraph 9(a) of the complaint in Pa.R.C.P. No. 1915.15(a).

(2) A grandparent seeking physical or legal custody of a grandchild, who is not *in loco parentis* to the child, shall plead facts establishing standing under 23 Pa.C.S. § 5324(3) in Paragraph 9(b) of the complaint in Pa.R.C.P. No. 1915.15(a).

(3) An individual seeking physical or legal custody of a child, who is not *in loco parentis* to the child, shall plead facts establishing

standing under 23 Pa.C.S. § 5324(4) and (5) in Paragraph 9(c) of the complaint in Pa.R.C.P. No. 1915.15(a).

(4) A grandparent or great-grandparent seeking partial physical custody or supervised physical custody of a grandchild or great-grandchild shall plead facts establishing standing under 23 Pa.C.S. § 5325 in Paragraph 9(d) of the complaint in Pa.R.C.P. No. 1915.15(a).

(f) An unemancipated minor parent may commence, maintain, or defend a custody action of the minor parent's child without the requirement of the appointment of a guardian for the minor parent.

Adopted Dec. 10, 1981, effective July 1, 1982; effective date extended to Jan. 1, 1983 by order of June 25, 1982. Readopted Nov. 8, 1982, effective Jan. 1, 1983. Amended Oct. 30, 2001, imd. effective; Oct. 31, 2002, imd. effective; Nov. 19, 2008, imd. effective; Aug. 1, 2013, effective Sept. 3, 2013; July 20, 2015, effective Sept. 1, 2015; Jan. 5, 2018, effective Jan. 6, 2018; June 1, 2018, effective July 1, 2018; July 27, 2020, effective Oct. 1, 2020.

Explanatory Comment—2020

Act of May 4, 2018, P.L. 112, No. 21, amended 23 Pa.C.S. § 5324 by adding a new class of third-party standing for individuals seeking custody of a child whose parents do not have care and control of the child. The individual seeking custody may or may not be related to the child. Subject to Section 5324(5), the newly added standing provision requires that: (1) the individual has assumed or is willing to assume responsibility for the child; (2) the individual has a sustained, substantial, and sincere interest in the child's welfare; and (3) the child's parents do not have care and control of the child. A plaintiff proceeding under Section 5324(4) shall satisfy the requirements of that provision by clear and convincing evidence. Additionally, if a juvenile dependency proceeding has been initiated, or is ongoing, or there is an order for permanent legal custody, Section 5324(5) provides that an individual cannot assert standing under Section 5324(4).

Consistent with the Act 21 of 2018 statutory changes, subdivision (e) has been revised to include a third party seeking custody of a child under 23 Pa.C.S. § 5324(4). The subdivision has been reorganized to sequentially follow the statutory provisions in 23 Pa.C.S. §§ 5324(2)-(4) and 5325. Similarly, the Complaint for Custody Paragraph 9 in Pa.R.C.P. No. 1915.15(a) has been reorganized to sequentially follow the statutory provisions and rules sequence, as well. See Pa.R.C.P. No. 1915.15(a).

RULE 1915.3-1.   WITHDRAWAL OF PLEADING. DISCONTINUANCE OF ACTION

Rule 1915.3. Commencement of Action. Complaint. Order

(a) Withdrawal of Pleading. A custody pleading cannot be withdrawn after the issuance of a scheduling order or notice of conference regarding claims made in the pleading except

   (1) by leave of court after notice to the non-moving party, or
   (2) by written agreement of the parties.

(b) Discontinuance of a Custody Action.

   (1) A custody action may be discontinued by praecipe only upon a verified statement by the moving party that the complaint has not been served.
   (2) A custody action cannot be discontinued after the complaint has been served except

      (A) by leave of court after notice to the non-moving party, or

      (B) by written agreement of the parties.

Adopted June 25, 2013, effective July 25, 2013.

RULE 1915.3-2. CRIMINAL RECORD OR ABUSE HISTORY

(a) Criminal Record or Abuse History Verification. A party must file and serve with the complaint, any petition for modification, any counterclaim, any petition for contempt or any count for custody in a divorce complaint or counterclaim a verification regarding any criminal record or abuse history of that party and anyone living in that party's household. The verification shall be substantially in the form set forth in subdivision (c) below. The party must attach

a blank verification form to a complaint, counterclaim or petition served upon the other party. Although the party served need not file a responsive pleading pursuant to Rule 1915.5, he or she must file with the court a verification regarding his or her own criminal record or abuse history and that of anyone living in his or her household on or before the initial in-person contact with the court (including, but not limited to, a conference with a conference officer or judge or conciliation, depending upon the procedure in the judicial district) but not later than 30 days after service of the complaint or petition. A party's failure to file a Criminal Record or Abuse History Verification may result in sanctions against that party. Both parties shall file and serve updated verifications five days prior to trial.

(b) Initial Evaluation. At the initial in-person contact with the court, the judge, conference officer, conciliator or other appointed individual shall perform an initial evaluation to determine whether the existence of a criminal or abuse history of either party or a party's household member poses a threat to the child and whether counseling is necessary. The initial evaluation required by 23 Pa.C.S. § 5329(c) shall not be conducted by a mental health professional. After the initial evaluation, the court may order further evaluation or counseling by a mental health professional if the court determines it is necessary. Consistent with the best interests of the child, the court may enter a temporary custody order on behalf of a party with a criminal history or a party with a household member who has a criminal history, pending the party's or household member's evaluation and/or counseling.

Official Note:

The court shall consider evidence of criminal record or abusive history presented by the parties. There is no obligation for the court to conduct an independent investigation of the criminal record or abusive history of either party or members of their household. The court should not consider ARD or other diversionary programs. When determining whether a party or household member requires further evaluation or counseling, or whether a party or household member poses a threat to a child, the court should give consideration to the severity of the offense, the age of the offense, whether the victim of the offense was a child or family member and whether the offense involved violence.

(c) Verification. The verification regarding criminal or abuse history shall be substantially in the following form:

(Caption)

CRIMINAL RECORD / ABUSE HISTORY VERIFICATION

I _____, hereby swear or affirm, subject to penalties of law including 18 Pa.C.S. § 4904 relating to unsworn falsification to authorities that:

1. Unless indicated by my checking the box next to a crime below, neither I nor any other member of my household have been convicted or pled guilty or pled no contest or was adjudicated delinquent where the record is publicly available pursuant to the Juvenile Act, 42 Pa.C.S. § 6307 to any of the following crimes in Pennsylvania or a substantially equivalent crime in any other jurisdiction, including pending charges:

Check all that apply	Crime	Self	Other household member	Date of conviction, guilty plea, no contest plea or pending charges	Sentence
☐	18 Pa.C.S. Ch. 25 (relating to criminal homicide)	☐	☐	_____	_____
☐	18 Pa.C.S. § 2702 (relating to aggravated assault)	☐	☐	_____	_____
☐	18 Pa.C.S. § 2706 (relating to terroristic threats)	☐	☐	_____	_____
☐	18 Pa.C.S. § 2709.1 (relating to stalking)	☐	☐	_____	_____
☐	18 Pa.C.S. § 2901 (relating to kidnapping)	☐	☐	_____	_____

Check all that apply	Crime	Self	Other household member	Date of conviction, guilty plea, no contest plea or pending charges	Sentence
☐	18 Pa.C.S. § 2902 (relating to unlawful restraint)	☐	☐	_____	_____
☐	18 Pa.C.S. § 2903 (relating to false imprisonment)	☐	☐	_____	_____
☐	18 Pa.C.S. § 2910 (relating to luring a child into a motor vehicle or structure)	☐	☐	_____	_____
☐	18 Pa.C.S. § 3121 (relating to rape)	☐	☐	_____	_____
☐	18 Pa.C.S. § 3122.1 (relating to statutory sexual assault)	☐	☐	_____	_____
☐	18 Pa.C.S. § 3123 (relating to involuntary deviate sexual intercourse)	☐	☐	_____	_____
☐	18 Pa.C.S. § 3124.1 (relating to sexual assault)	☐	☐	_____	_____
☐	18 Pa.C.S. § 3125 (relating to aggravated indecent assault)	☐	☐	_____	_____
☐	18 Pa.C.S. § 3126 (relating to indecent assault)	☐	☐	_____	_____
☐	18 Pa.C.S. § 3127 (relating to indecent exposure)	☐	☐	_____	_____
☐	18 Pa.C.S. § 3129 (relating to sexual intercourse with animal)	☐	☐	_____	_____

Check all that apply	Crime	Self	Other household member	Date of conviction, guilty plea, no contest plea or pending charges	Sentence
☐	18 Pa.C.S. § 3130 (relating to conduct relating to sex offenders)	☐	☐	_____	_____
☐	18 Pa.C.S. § 3301 (relating to arson and related offenses)	☐	☐	_____	_____
☐	18 Pa.C.S. § 4302 (relating to incest)	☐	☐	_____	_____
☐	18 Pa.C.S. § 4303 (relating to concealing death of child)	☐	☐	_____	_____
☐	18 Pa.C.S. § 4304 (relating to endangering welfare of children)	☐	☐	_____	_____
☐	18 Pa.C.S. § 4305 (relating to dealing in infant children)	☐	☐	_____	_____
☐	18 Pa.C.S. § 5902(b) (relating to prostitution and related offenses)	☐	☐	_____	_____
☐	18 Pa.C.S. § 5903(c) or (d) (relating to obscene and other sexual materials and performances)	☐	☐	_____	_____
☐	18 Pa.C.S. § 6301 (relating to corruption of minors)	☐	☐	_____	_____
☐	18 Pa.C.S. § 6312 (relating to sexual abuse of children)	☐	☐	_____	_____

Check all that apply	Crime	Self	Other household member	Date of conviction, guilty plea, no contest plea or pending charges	Sentence
☐	18 Pa.C.S. § 6318 (relating to unlawful contact with minor)	☐	☐	_____	_____
☐	18 Pa.C.S. § 6320 (relating to sexual exploitation of children)	☐	☐	_____	_____
☐	23 Pa.C.S. § 6114 (relating to contempt for violation of protection order or agreement)	☐	☐	_____	_____
☐	Driving under the influence of drugs or alcohol	☐	☐	_____	_____
☐	Manufacture, sale, delivery, holding, offering for sale or possession of any controlled substance or other drug or device	☐	☐	_____	_____

2. Unless indicated by my checking the box next to an item below, neither I nor any other member of my household have a history of violent or abusive conduct, or involvement with a Children & Youth agency, including the following:

Check all that apply	Self	Other household member	Date
☐	A finding of abuse by a Children & Youth Agency or similar agency in Pennsylvania or similar statute in another jurisdiction	☐	_____

Check all that apply	Self	Other household member	Date
☐	Abusive conduct as defined under the Protection from Abuse Act in Pennsylvania or similar statute in another jurisdiction	☐	_____
☐	Involvement with a Children & Youth Agency or similar agency in Pennsylvania or another jurisdiction. Where?:	☐	_____
☐	Other:	☐	_____

3. Please list any evaluation, counseling or other treatment received following conviction or finding of abuse:

_____

_____

4. If any conviction above applies to a household member, not a party, state that person's name, date of birth and relationship to the child.

_____

_____

5. If you are aware that the other party or members of the other party's household has or have a criminal/abuse history, please explain:

_____

_____

I verify that the information above is true and correct to the best of my knowledge, information or belief. I understand that false

statements herein are made subject to the penalties of 18 Pa.C.S. § 4904 relating to unsworn falsification to authorities.

_____

Signature

_____

Printed Name

Adopted Aug. 1, 2013, effective Sept. 3, 2013. Amended May 14, 2014, effective June 13, 2014; July 20, 2015, effective Sept. 1, 2015.

RULE 1915.4.   PROMPT DISPOSITION OF CUSTODY CASES

(a) Initial Contact With the Court. Depending upon the procedure in the judicial district, the parties' initial in-person contact with the court (including, but not limited to a conference with a conference officer pursuant to Rule 1915.4-2, a conference with a judge, conciliation, mediation and/or class/seminar) shall be scheduled to occur not later than 45 days from the filing of a complaint or petition.

(b) Listing Trials Before the Court. Depending upon the procedure in the judicial district, within 180 days of the filing of the complaint either the court shall automatically enter an order scheduling a trial before a judge or a party shall file a praecipe, motion or request for trial, except as otherwise provided in this subdivision. If it is not the practice of the court to automatically schedule trials and neither party files a praecipe, motion or request for trial within 180 days of filing of the pleading, the court shall, sua sponte or on motion of a party, dismiss the matter unless a party has been granted an extension for good cause shown, or the court finds that dismissal is not in the best interests of the child. The extension shall not exceed 60 days beyond the 180 day limit. A further reasonable extension may be granted by the court upon agreement of the parties or when the court finds, on the record, compelling circumstances for a further reasonable extension. If an extension is granted and, thereafter, neither party files a praecipe, motion or request for trial within the time period allowed by the extension, the court shall, sua sponte or on the motion of a party, dismiss the matter unless the court finds that dismissal is not in the best interests of the child. A motion to dismiss, pursuant to this rule, shall be filed and served upon the opposing party. The opposing party shall have 20 days from the date of service to file an objection. If no objection is filed, the court shall dismiss the case. Prior to a sua sponte dismissal, the court shall notify the parties of an intent to dismiss the case unless an objection is filed within 20 days of the date of the notice.

(c) Trial. Trials before a judge shall commence within 90 days of the date the scheduling order is entered. Trials and hearings shall be scheduled to be heard on consecutive days whenever possible but, if not on consecutive days, then the trial or hearing shall be concluded not later than 45 days from commencement.

(d) Prompt Decisions. The judge's decision shall be entered and filed within 15 days of the date upon which the trial is concluded unless, within that time, the court extends the date for such decision by order entered of record showing good cause for the extension. In no event shall an extension delay the entry of the court's decision more than 45 days after the conclusion of trial.

(e) Emergency or Special Relief. Nothing in this rule shall preclude a party from seeking, nor a court from ordering, emergency or interim special relief at any time after the commencement of the action.

Official Note:

For service of original process in custody, partial custody and visitation matters, see Rule 1930.4.

Rescinded June 20, 1985 effective Jan. 1, 1986. Note amended Oct. 2, 1995, effective Jan. 1, 1996. Replaced by new rule; Adopted Nov. 30, 2000, effective March 1, 2001; Amended June 25, 2013, effective July 25, 2013.

Explanatory Comment—2000

A new rule requiring prompt custody trials was recommended by a special committee established by the Pennsylvania Superior Court. That committee concluded that the interests of children who are the subjects of custody litigation would best be served by a requirement that the litigation be concluded within specific time frames.

RULE 1915.4-1. ALTERNATIVE HEARING
PROCEDURES FOR PARTIAL CUSTODY ACTIONS.

(a) A custody action shall proceed as prescribed by Pa.R.C.P. No. 1915.4–3 unless the court, by local rule, adopts the alternative hearing procedure authorized by Pa.R.C.P. No. 1915.4–2 pursuant to which an action for partial custody may be heard by a hearing officer, except as provided in subdivision (b).

(b) Promptly after the parties' initial contact with the court as set forth in Pa.R.C.P. No. 1915.4(a), a party may move the court for a hearing before a judge, rather than a hearing officer, in an action for partial custody where:

(1) there are complex questions of law, fact or both; or
(2) the parties certify to the court that there are serious allegations affecting the child's welfare.

(c) The president judge or the administrative judge of the family division of each county shall certify that custody proceedings generally are conducted in accordance with either Pa.R.C.P. No. 1915.4–2 or Pa.R.C.P. No. 1915.4–3. The certification shall be filed with the Domestic Relations Procedural Rules Committee of the Supreme Court of Pennsylvania and shall be substantially in the following form:

I hereby certify that _____ County conducts its custody proceedings in accordance with Pa.R.C.P. No. ___.

_____

(President Judge)

_____

(Administrative Judge)

Note:

For a complete list of the Alternative Hearing Procedures for each county: http://www.pacourts.us/courts/supreme–court/committees/rules–committees/domestic–relations–procedural–rules–committee.

Explanatory Comment

These rules provide an optional procedure for using hearing officers in partial custody cases. The procedure is similar to the one provided for support cases in Pa.R.C.P. No. 1910.12: a conference, record hearing before a hearing officer and argument on exceptions before a judge. The terms "conference officer" and "hearing officer" have the same meaning here as in the support rules.

It is important to note that use of the procedure prescribed in Pa.R.C.P. Nos. 1915.4–1 and 1915.4–2 is optional rather than mandatory. Counties which prefer to have all partial custody cases heard by a judge may continue to do so.

These procedures are not intended to replace or prohibit the use of any form of mediation or conciliation. On the contrary, they are intended to be used in cases which are not resolved through the use of less adversarial means.

The intent of the 2007 amendments to Pa.R.C.P. Nos. 1915.4–1 and 1915.4–2, and Pa.R.C.P. No. 1915–4.3, was to clarify the procedures in record and non-record custody proceedings. When the first proceeding is non-record, no exceptions are required and a request for a de novo hearing may be made.

In lieu of continuing the practice of including in the Note a 67–county list identifying the hearing procedure selected by the local county court, the list can now be found on the Domestic Relations Procedural Rules Committee website.

Adopted July 15, 1994, effective Jan. 1, 1995. Amended Nov. 30, 2000, effective March 1, 2001; Oct. 30, 2007, imd. effective; April 8, 2008, imd. effective; Aug. 1, 2013, effective Sept. 3, 2013; October 14, 2016, effective December 1, 2016.

RULE 1915.4-2.   PARTIAL CUSTODY. OFFICE CONFERENCE. HEARING RECORD. EXCEPTIONS. ORDER

(a) Office Conference.

(1) The office conference shall be conducted by a conference officer.

(2) If the respondent fails to appear at the conference before the conference officer as directed by the court, the conference may proceed without the respondent.

(3) The conference officer may make a recommendation to the parties relating to partial custody or supervised physical custody of the child or children. If an agreement for partial custody or supervised physical custody is reached at the conference, the conference officer shall prepare a written order in conformity with the agreement for signature by the parties and submission to the court together with the officer's recommendation for approval or disapproval. The court may enter an order in accordance with the agreement without hearing the parties.

(4) At the conclusion of the conference, if an agreement relating to partial custody or supervised physical custody has not been reached, the parties shall be given notice of the date, time and place of a hearing before a hearing officer, which may be the same day, but in no event shall be more than forty-five days from the date of the conference.

(b) Hearing.

(1) The hearing shall be conducted by a hearing officer who must be a lawyer, and a record shall be made of the testimony. A hearing officer who is a lawyer employed by, or under contract with, a judicial district or appointed by the court shall not practice family law before a conference officer, hearing officer, permanent or standing master, or judge of the same judicial district.

(2) The hearing officer shall receive evidence and hear argument. The hearing officer may recommend to the court that the parties and/or the subject child or children submit to examination and evaluation by experts pursuant to Rule 1915.8.

(3) Within ten days of the conclusion of the hearing, the hearing officer shall file with the court and serve upon all parties a report containing a recommendation with respect to the entry of an order of partial custody or supervised physical custody. The report may be in narrative form stating the reasons for the recommendation and shall include a proposed order, including a specific schedule for partial custody or supervised physical custody.

(4) Within twenty days after the date the hearing officer's report is mailed or received by the parties, whichever occurs first, any party may file exceptions to the report or any part thereof, to rulings on objections to evidence, to statements or findings of fact, to conclusions of law, or to any other matters occurring during the hearing. Each exception shall set forth a separate objection precisely and without discussion. Matters not covered by exceptions are deemed waived unless, prior to entry of the final order, leave is granted to file exceptions raising those matters. If exceptions are filed, any other party may file exceptions within twenty days of the date of service of the original exceptions.

(5) If no exceptions are filed within the twenty-day period, the court shall review the report and, if approved, enter a final order.

(6) If exceptions are filed, the court shall hear argument on the exceptions within forty-five days of the date the last party files exceptions, and enter an appropriate final order within fifteen days of argument. No motion for Post-Trial Relief may be filed to the final order.

Adopted July 15, 1994, effective Jan. 1, 1995. Amended Nov. 30, 2000, effective March 1, 2001; Aug. 8, 2006, imd. effective; Oct. 30, 2007, imd. effective; Aug. 1, 2013, effective Sept. 3, 2013; March 4, 2015, effective April 3, 2015.

Explanatory Comment—2006

The time for filing exceptions has been expanded from ten to twenty days. The purpose of this amendment is to provide ample opportunity for litigants and counsel to receive notice of the entry of the order, to assure Commonwealth-wide consistency in calculation of time for filing and to conform to applicable general civil procedural rules.

RULE 1915.4-3.   NON-RECORD PROCEEDINGS. TRIAL

(a) Non-Record Proceedings. In judicial districts utilizing an initial non-record proceeding, *i.e.*, office conference, if an agreement is not finalized by the conclusion of the proceeding, the conference officer shall promptly notify the court that the matter should be listed for

trial. A lawyer employed by, or under contract with, a judicial district or appointed by the court to serve as a conference officer to preside over a non-record proceeding shall not practice family law before a conference officer, hearing officer, permanent or standing master, or judge of the same judicial district.

(b) Trial. The trial before the court shall be de novo. The court shall hear the case and render a decision within the time periods set forth in Pa.R.C.P. No. 1915.4.

Adopted Oct. 30, 2007, imd. effective. Amended Aug. 1, 2013, effective Sept. 3, 2013; March 4, 2015, effective April 3, 2015; Feb. 8, 2018, effective April 1, 2018.

Explanatory Comment—2018

The amendment to this rule, in conjunction with the amendment to Pa.R.C.P. No. 1915.1, standardizes terminology used in the custody process and identifies court personnel by title and in some cases qualifications. Of note, the term "mediator," which had been included in the rule, has been omitted and is specifically defined in Pa.R.C.P. No. 1915.1.

As in the support rules, custody conference officers preside over conferences and hearing officers preside over hearings. Regardless of the individual's title, presiding over a conference or a hearing triggers the family law attorney practice preclusion in this rule and in Pa.R.C.P. No. 1915.4-2(b) in the case of a hearing officer. Mediators, as defined in Pa.R.C.P. No. 1915.1 and as qualified in Pa.R.C.P. No. 1940.4, do not preside over custody conferences or hearings; rather, mediators engage custody litigants in alternative dispute resolution methods pursuant to Chapter 1940 of the Rules of Civil Procedure and, as such, the preclusion from practicing family law in the same judicial district in which an attorney/mediator is appointed is inapplicable.

RULE 1915.4-4. PRE-TRIAL PROCEDURES

A pre-trial conference in an initial custody or modification proceeding shall be scheduled before a judge at the request of a party or sua sponte by the court and the procedure shall be as set forth in this rule. If a party wishes to request a pre-trial conference, the praecipe set forth in sub-division (g) shall be filed. The scheduling of a pre-trial conference shall not stay any previously scheduled proceeding unless otherwise ordered by the court.

(a) The praecipe may be filed at any time after a custody conciliation or conference with a conference officer unless a pre-trial conference has already been scheduled or held. The pre-trial conference may be sched-uled at any time, but must be scheduled at least 30 days prior to trial.

(b) Not later than five days prior to the pre-trial conference, each party shall file a pre-trial statement with the prothonotary's office and serve a copy upon the court and the other party or counsel of record. The pre-trial statement shall include the following matters, together with any additional information required by special order of the court:

   (1) the name and address of each expert whom the party intends to call at trial as a witness;
   (2) the name and address of each witness the party intends to call at trial and the relationship of that witness to the party. Inclusion of a witness on the pre-trial statement constitutes an affirmation that the party's counsel or the self-represented party has communicated with the witness about the substance of the witness's testimony prior to the filing of the pretrial statement; and
   (3) a proposed order setting forth the custody schedule requested by the party.

In addition to the above items included in the pre-trial statement, any reports of experts and other proposed exhibits shall be included as part of the pre-trial statement served upon the other party or opposing counsel, but not included with the pre-trial statement served upon the court.

Note: See Pa.R.C.P. No. 1930.1(b). This rule may require attorneys or unrepresented parties to file confidential documents and documents containing confidential information that are subject to the Case Records *Public Access Policy of the Unified Judicial System of Pennsylvania.*

(c) If a party fails to file a pre-trial statement or otherwise comply with the requirements of subdivision (b), the court may make an appropriate order under Pa.R.C.P. No. 4019(c)(2) and (4) governing sanctions.

(d) Unless otherwise ordered by the court, the parties may amend their pre-trial statements at any time, but not later than seven days before trial.

(e) At the pre-trial conference, the following shall be considered:

(1) issues for resolution by the court;
(2) unresolved discovery matters;
(3) any agreements of the parties;
(4) issues relating to expert witnesses;
(5) settlement and/or mediation of the case;
(6) such other matters as may aid in the disposition of the case; and
(7) if a trial date has not been scheduled, it shall be scheduled at the pre-trial conference.

(f) The court shall enter an order following the pre-trial conference detailing the agreements made by the parties as to any of the matters considered, limiting the issues for trial to those not disposed of by agreement and setting forth the schedule for further action in the case. Such order shall control the subsequent course of the action unless modified at trial to prevent manifest injustice.

(g) The praecipe for pre-trial conference shall be substantially in the following form:

(Caption)

PRAECIPE FOR PRE-TRIAL CONFERENCE

To the Prothonotary:

Please schedule a pre-trial conference in the above-captioned custody matter pursuant to Pa.R.C.P. No. 1915.4-4.

The parties' initial in-person contact with the court (conference with a conference officer or judge, conciliation or mediation) occurred on _____.

PLAINTIFF/DEFENDANT/ATTORNEY
FOR PLAINTIFF/DEFENDANT

Adopted June 25, 2013, effective July 25, 2013. Amended October 28, 2015, effective January 1, 2016; Jan. 5, 2018, effective Jan. 6, 2018; June 1, 2018, effective July 1, 2018.

Explanatory Comment

In 2013, the Domestic Relations Procedural Rules Committee (the "Committee") recognized there was a wide disparity in pre-trial procedures in custody cases among the various judicial districts. By adopting this rule, the Supreme Court established uniform state-wide pre-trial procedures in custody cases. With an eye toward re-ducing custody litigation, the rule encourages early preparation and court involvement for purposes of expedited resolutions. The rule was based upon the pretrial procedures in divorce cases as set forth in Pa.R.C.P. No. 1920.33(b). The rule does not affect, however, the First Judicial District's practice of conducting a pre-trial conference upon the filing of a motion for a protracted or semi-protracted trial.

In 2015, the Committee expressed concern the rule as previously adopted by the Supreme Court allowed for an interpretation contrary to the intent of the rule. The Committee proposed and the Court adopted an amendment to the rule to clarify the rule's mandate as it relates to witnesses. As a goal of any pre-trial conference is to settle the case, in whole or in part, the Committee believed a best practice in reaching that goal is having a thorough knowledge of the case, including the substance of anticipated witness testimony. As amended, the rule plainly states that counsel or a self-represented party is required to discuss with the witness their testimony prior to including the witness on the pre-trial statement.

Unlike Pa.R.C.P. No. 1920.33(b), the rule does not require inclusion of a summary of the witness's testimony in the pre-trial statement; but rather, an affirmation by counsel or self-represented party that there was actual communication with each witness about the witness's testimony. With the additional information from witnesses, counsel, self-represented parties and the trial court can better engage in more fruitful settlement discussions at the pre-trial conference.

RULE 1915.5. QUESTION OF JURISDICTION, VENUE, OR STANDING. COUNTERCLAIM. DISCOVERY. NO RESPONSIVE PLEADING BY DEFENDANT REQUIRED

(a) Question of Jurisdiction, Venue, or Standing.

(1) A party shall raise jurisdiction of the person or venue by preliminary objection.

(2) A party may raise standing by preliminary objection or at a custody hearing or trial.

(3) The court may raise standing sua sponte.

(4) In a third-party plaintiff custody action in which standing has not been resolved by preliminary objection, the court shall address the third-party plaintiff's standing and include its standing decision in a written opinion or order.

Note: The court may raise at any time a question of (1) jurisdiction over the subject matter of the action or (2) the exercise of its jurisdiction pursuant to Section 5426 of the Uniform Child Custody Jurisdiction and Enforcement Act, relating to simultaneous proceedings in other courts, Section 5427, relating to inconvenient forum, and Section 5428, relating to jurisdiction declined by reason of conduct. The Uniform Child Custody Jurisdiction and Enforcement Act, 23 Pa.C.S. § 5407, provides that, upon request of a party, an action in which a question of the existence or exercise of jurisdiction is raised shall be given calendar priority and handled expeditiously.

(b) A party may file a counterclaim asserting the right of physical or legal custody within 20 days of service of the complaint upon that party or at the time of hearing, whichever first occurs. The claim shall be in the same form as a complaint as required by Pa.R.C.P. No. 1915.3.

(c) There shall be no discovery unless authorized by special order of court.

Note: The rule relating to discovery in domestic relations matters generally is Pa.R.C.P. No. 1930.5.

(d) Except as set forth in subdivisions (a) and (b), a responsive pleading shall not be required. If a party files a responsive pleading, it shall not delay a hearing or trial.

Adopted Dec. 10, 1981, effective July 1, 1982; effective date extended to Jan. 1, 1983 by order of June 25, 1982. Readopted Nov. 8, 1982, effective Jan. 1, 1983. Amended March 30, 1994, effective July 1, 1994; May 5, 1997, effective July 1, 1997; Nov. 19, 2008, imd. effective; Aug. 1, 2013, effective Sept. 3, 2013; July 7, 2014, effective August 6, 2014; July 27, 2020, effective Oct. 1, 2020.

Explanatory Comment—1994

Under subdivision (a), the defendant may but is not required to plead to the complaint. All averments may be disputed by the defendant at the custody hearing. An attorney who wishes to file another pleading may do so. However, the action is not to be delayed to permit its filing.

Explanatory Comment—2020

Act of May 4, 2018, P.L. 112, No. 21, amended 23 Pa.C.S. § 5324 by adding a new class of third-party standing for individuals seeking custody of a child whose parents do not have care and control of the child. Subject to the limitations in 23 Pa.C.S. § 5324(5), the newly added standing provision requires that: (1) the individual has assumed or is willing to assume responsibility for the child; (2) the individual has a sustained, substantial, and sincere interest in the child's welfare; and (3) the child's parents do not have care and control of the child. A plaintiff proceeding under Section 5324(4) shall satisfy the requirements of that provision by clear and convincing evidence.

Typically, when a third party is seeking custody of a child, the child's parents can raise the issue of the third party's standing to pursue custody. However, Section 5324(4) permits a party to seek custody of a child only when the child's parents do not have care and control of the child. If the parents' lack of care and control also results in their non-participation in the custody litigation, the third party's standing may go unchallenged. Subdivision (a) has been amended by including two new subdivisions to address this circumstance. Subdivision (a)(3) permits the court to raise standing *sua sponte* and, if third-party standing is not resolved by preliminary objection, the court shall address the standing issue in its written opinion or order as required by subdivision (a)(4).

RULE 1915.6.   JOINDER OF PARTIES

(a)(1) If the court learns from the pleadings or any other source that a parent whose parental rights have not been previously terminated or a person who has physical custody of the child is not a party to the action, it shall order that the person be joined as a party. Such person shall be served with a copy of all prior pleadings and notice of the joinder substantially in the form prescribed by Rule 1915.16(a).

(2) The person joined must file any objection to the order of joinder within twenty days after notice of the order.

(3) The person joined may file a counterclaim asserting a right to physical or legal custody in the form required for a complaint by Rule 1915.3. A copy of the counterclaim shall be served upon all other parties to the action as provided by Rule 440.

(b) If the court learns from the pleadings or any other source that any other person who claims to have custodial rights with respect to the child is not a party to the action, it shall order that notice be given to that person of the pendency of the action and of the right to intervene therein. The notice shall be substantially in the form prescribed by Rule 1915.16(b).

Adopted Dec. 10, 1981, effective July 1, 1982; effective date extended to Jan. 1, 1983 by order of June 25, 1982. Readopted Nov. 8, 1982, effective Jan. 1, 1983; amended March 30, 1994, effective July 1, 1994; Nov. 19, 2008, imd. effective; Aug. 1, 2013, effective Sept. 3, 2013.

Explanatory Comment—1994

The position taken by the rules is that a person in physical custody of the child and a parent whose parental rights have not been terminated are necessary parties to a custody determination. While it may be desirable to have other persons who claim custody rights as parties to the action, their joinder is not a prerequisite to a custody determination.

RULE 1915.7.   CONSENT ORDER

If the parties have an agreement regarding custody and request that the court enter a consent order incorporating the agreement's terms:

(a) the parties shall submit to the court a proposed custody order bearing the parties' written consent; or

(b) the parties may state the agreement on the record, provided that:

(1) within ten days of placing the agreement on the record, the parties comply with subdivision (a); or

(2) the court memorializes the oral agreement from the record into a written custody order.

Note: See **Pa.R.C.P. No. 1930.1(b). This rule may require attorneys or unrepresented parties to file confidential documents and documents containing confidential information that are subject to the *Case Records Public Access Policy of the Unified Judicial System of Pennsylvania.***

See **Pa.R.C.P. No. 1915.10(b) regarding written custody order requirements.**

Adopted Dec. 10, 1981, effective July 1, 1982; effective date extended to Jan. 1, 1983 by order of June 25, 1982. Readopted and amended Nov. 8, 1982, effective Jan. 1, 1983. Amended Aug. 1, 2013, effective Sept. 3, 2013; Jan. 5, 2018, effective Jan. 6, 2018; June 1, 2018, effective July 1, 2018; June 3, 2019, effective Oct. 1, 2019.

Explanatory Comment—1981

As in other types of litigation, determination of an action through agreement of the parties is a desirable goal. However, the power of the parties to enter into an agreement is not absolute. In Com. ex rel. Veihdeffer v. Veihdeffer, 235 Pa.Super. 447, 344 A.2d 613, 614 (1975), the Superior Court stated:

It is well settled that an agreement between the parties as to custody is not controlling but should be given weight taking into consideration all the circumstances. . . . A child cannot be made the subject of a contract with the same force and effect as if it were a mere chattel has long been established law.

If the parties seek to have their agreement incorporated into a consent order, Rule 1915.7 provides two methods of presenting the agreement to the court. The first is by noting the agreement on the record. The second is by submitting to the court a proposed order bearing the written consent of the parties. Whichever method is used, however, the parties must be present before the court unless the court directs otherwise. The child affected by the order need be present only if the court so directs.

Explanatory Comment—2019

The Rule has been amended to ensure that when a custody agreement is orally placed on the record that a written custody order prepared by the parties memorializing the parties' agreement is timely submitted to the court or the court memorializes the oral agreement into a written custody order. The amendment avoids the untenable circumstance that the only written record of the parties' oral agreement is a transcription of what had been placed on the record. Transcription agreements are often cumbersome and difficult to discern as to the custody terms and provisions, which makes enforcement difficult. This amendment is consistent with the holding in *R.L.P. v. R.F.M.*, 110 A.3d 201 (Pa. Super. 2015).

RULE 1915.8.   PHYSICAL AND MENTAL EXAMINATION OF PERSONS.

(a) The court may order the child(ren) and/or any party to submit to and fully participate in an evaluation by an appropriate expert or experts. The order, which shall be substantially in the form set forth in Rule 1915.18, may be made upon the court's own motion, upon the motion of a party with reasonable notice to the person to be examined, or by agreement of the parties. The order shall specify the place, manner, conditions and scope of the examination and the person or persons by whom it shall be made and to whom distributed. In entering an

order directing an evaluation pursuant to this rule, the court shall consider all appropriate factors including the following, if applicable:

(1) the allocation of the costs, including insurance coverage, if any, attendant to the undertaking of the evaluation and preparation of the resultant report and court testimony of any appointed expert;

(2) the execution of appropriate authorizations and/or consents to facilitate the examination;

(3) any deadlines imposed regarding the completion of the examination and payment of costs;

(4) the production of any report and of underlying data to counsel and/or any unrepresented party upon the completion of the examination; and

(5) any additional safeguards that are deemed appropriate as a result of the alleged presence of domestic violence and/or child abuse.

(b) Unless otherwise directed by the court, the expert shall deliver to the court, to the attorneys of record for the parties, to any unrepresented party, and to the guardian ad litem and/or counsel for the child, if any, copies of any reports arising from the evaluation setting out the findings, results of all tests made, diagnosis and conclusions. No reports shall be filed of record or considered evidence unless and until admitted by the court. Any report which is prepared at the request of a party, with or without a court order, and which a party intends to introduce at trial, must be delivered to the court and the other party at least thirty days before trial. If the report or any information from the evaluator is provided to the court, the evaluator shall be subject to cross-examination by all counsel and any unrepresented party without regard to who obtains or pays for the evaluation.

(c) If a party refuses to obey an order of court made under subdivision (a) of this rule, the court may make an order refusing to allow the disobedient party to support or oppose designated claims or defenses, prohibiting the party from introducing in evidence designated documents, things or testimony, prohibiting the party from introducing evidence of physical or mental condition, or making such other order as is just. The willful failure or refusal of a party to comply with an order entered pursuant to this rule may also give rise to a finding of contempt and the imposition of such sanctions as may be deemed appropriate by the court, including, but not limited to, an adverse inference against the non-complying party.

(d) A petition for contempt alleging failure to comply with an order entered pursuant to subdivision (a) of this rule shall be treated in an expedited manner.

Explanatory Comment—2007

This rule addresses the process for any number of expert evaluations a court may order in a custody case, including, but not limited to, physical, mental health, custody and/or drug and alcohol evaluations, and/or home studies. Since the initial promulgation of this rule in 1981, the frequency of utilizing professionals as expert witnesses in child custody litigation has increased considerably. In appropriate cases, evaluations have served as a means to provide the court with a full and complete record and to facilitate settlement of the litigation.

The proposed revisions to Rule 1915.8 are intended to afford the trial court and the parties a more flexible and case-sensitive means of determining the scope and parameters of a physical and/or mental examination, including deadlines, costs, underlying data, and access. In many instances, the previous sixty-day deadline was impractical and ignored. While some cases demanded that the evaluation be completed in less than 60 days, others demanded far more time than that. The revisions to this rule also specifically permit the trial court to draw an adverse inference from one party's failure to comply with an order pursuant to this rule.

The provisions of this Rule 1915.8 amended May 16, 1994, effective July 1, 1994; amended May 23, 2007, effective August 1, 2007; amended August 2, 2010, effective immediately.

RULE 1915.9.   NO DEFAULT JUDGMENT.

No judgment may be entered by default or on the pleadings.

Adopted Dec. 10, 1981, effective July 1, 1982; effective date extended to Jan. 1, 1983 by order of June 25, 1982. Readopted Nov. 8, 1982, effective Jan. 1, 1983 and applied to pending actions.

Explanatory Comment—1981

An order of custody, partial custody or visitation may be obtained in several ways. If the parties reach an agreement, they may seek a consent order pursuant to Rule 1915.7. If they do not reach an agreement and contest the right to the relief sought, the court will enter an order after a hearing pursuant to Rule 1915.10.

Rule 1915.9 governs two additional situations. The first is where there is no appearance by the defendant. In such a case, there is both no consent with respect to the relief sought but also no contest. The rule provides that there shall be no judgment entered by default.

The second is where the parties seek judgment as a matter of law, i.e., on the pleadings. While any action will probably involve questions of law, the determination of the best interest of a child is never a purely legal determination. Rather, a multitude of factual determinations is required. Thus the rule provides that there shall be no judgment entered on the pleadings.

RULE 1915.10.   DECISION. ORDER

(a) The court may make the decision before the testimony has been transcribed. The court shall state the reasons for its decision on the record in open court or in a written opinion or order.

Note: See **23 Pa.C.S. § 5323(d).**

(b) The court shall enter a custody order as a separate written order or in a separate section of a written opinion.

(1) The court's order shall state sufficiently specific terms to enforce the order.

(2) If the court has made a finding that a party or child is at risk of harm, the court's order shall include safety provisions for the endangered party's or child's protection.

(c) A custody order shall include a notice outlining the parties' obligations under 23 Pa.C.S. § 5337, regarding a party's intention to relocate with a minor child.

Note: See **23 Pa.C.S. § 5323(c) and Pa.R.C.P. No. 1915.17.**

(d) A party may not file a motion for post-trial relief to an order of legal or physical custody.

Adopted Dec. 10, 1981, effective July 1, 1982; effective date extended to Jan. 1, 1983 by order of June 25, 1982. Readopted and amended Nov. 8, 1982, effective Jan. 1, 1983. Amended Oct. 19, 1983, effective Jan. 1, 1984; Nov. 7, 1988, effective Jan. 1, 1989; Aug. 1, 2013, effective Sept. 3, 2013; June 3, 2019, effective October 1, 2019.

Explanatory Comment—2013

The custody statute, at 23 Pa.C.S. § 5323(d), requires the court to delineate the reasons for its decision on the record in open court or in a written opinion or order. Subdivision (b) further defines and reinforces the requirements found in 23 Pa.C.S. § 5323(e). Examples of safety provisions include, but are not limited to: supervised physical custody, supervised or neutral custody exchange location, neutral party presence at custody exchange, telephone or computer-facilitated contact with the child, no direct contact between the parties, third-party contact for cancellations, third-party transportation and designating secure, neutral location for a child's passport. The statute, at 23 Pa.C.S. § 5323, requires that any custody order must include notice of a party's obligations when there is a proposed relocation under 23 Pa.C.S. § 5337. Rule 1915.17 also addresses relocation.

Explanatory Comment—2019

Subdivision (b) further defines and reinforces the requirements in 23 Pa.C.S. § 5323(e). Examples of safety provisions include, but are not limited to, supervised physical custody, a supervised or neutral custody exchange location, a neutral third-party present at custody exchanges, telephone or computer-facilitated contact with the child, no direct contact between the parties, third-party contact for cancellations, third-party transportation, and designating a secure, neutral location as respository for a child's passport.

Additionally, subdivision (b) requires a court to enter a custody order as a separate written order or in a separate section of a written opinion. The subdivision also addresses the practice of orally entering a custody order on the record without formalizing the custody order in writing. In such circumstances, the parties' only documentation of the custody order is a transcription of the oral record. In *R.L.P. v. R.F.M.*, 110 A.3d 201 (Pa. Super. 2015), the Superior Court held that "in order to be sufficiently specific to be enforced, an order of custody must be entered as a separate written order, or as a separate section of a written opinion." *Id. at 206.* Despite the Superior Court's decision, the practice of placing custody orders on the record without subsequently entering a written order has continued, which has been problematic for enforcement and understanding of the agreement's or order's terms.

RULE 1915.11.   APPOINTMENT OF ATTORNEY FOR CHILD. INTERVIEW OF CHILD. ATTENDANCE OF CHILD AT HEARING OR CONFERENCE

(a) The court may on its own motion, or the motion of a party, appoint an attorney to represent the child in the action. Counsel for the child shall represent the child's legal interests and zealously represent the child as any other client in an attorney-client relationship. Counsel for the child shall not perform the role of a guardian *ad litem* or best interests attorney. The court may assess the cost of the child's attorney upon the parties in such proportions as the court deems appropriate or as otherwise provided by law. The order appointing an attorney to represent the child shall be in substantially the form set forth in Pa.R.C.P. No. 1915.19.

(b) The court may interview a child, whether or not the child is the subject of the action, in open court or in chambers. The interview shall be conducted in the presence of the attorneys and, if permitted by the court, the parties. The attorneys shall have the right to interview the child under the supervision of the court. The interview shall be part of the record.

(c) Unless otherwise directed by the court, the child who is the subject of the action shall not be required to attend a hearing before the court or a conference.

Note:

A party may bring a child to a conference or hearing but, in the absence of an order of court, is not required to do so.

Adopted Dec. 10, 1981, effective July 1, 1982; effective date extended to Jan. 1, 1983 by order of June 25, 1982. Readopted Nov. 8, 1982, effective Jan. 1, 1983. Amended April 29, 1991, effective July 1, 1991; Aug. 1, 2013, effective Sept. 3, 2013; May 18, 2016, effective July 1, 2016.

Explanatory Comment—1991

Rule 1915.15(b) provides a form of order to appear at a conference or hearing in an action for custody, partial custody or visitation of minor children. Prior to its recent amendment, the form required that one or more children who are the subject of the action attend the hearing or conference.

However, the presence of a child in court is not always necessary or desirable. The experience may be traumatic and disruptive. Consequently, the child should not be required to attend a hearing or conference in every case. When the presence of a child is required and the custodial party does not voluntarily bring the child, the court may issue an order for the child's attendance.

Subdivision (c) has been added to Rule 1915.11 to provide that, in the absence of an order of court, a child who is the subject of the action need not be brought to a conference or a hearing before the court. The form of order to appear provided by Rule 1915.15(b) has been revised to implement this policy.

RULE 1915.11-1.   ELIMINATION OF PARENTING COORDINATION

Only judges may make decisions in child custody cases. Masters and hearing officers may make recommendations to the court. Courts shall not appoint any other individual to make decisions or recommendations or alter a custody order in child custody cases. Any order appointing a parenting coordinator shall be deemed vacated on the date this rule becomes effective. Local rules and

administrative orders authorizing the appointment of parenting coordinators also shall be deemed vacated on the date this rule becomes effective.

Adopted April 23, 2013, effective May 23, 2013.

Note: The current RULE 1915.11-1 is effective until March 1, 2019, when new RULE 1915.11-1 becomes effective.

RULE 1915.11-1. PARENTING COORDINATION

If a judicial district implements a parenting coordination program, the court shall maintain a roster of qualified individuals to serve as parenting coordinators and establish the hourly rate at which parenting coordinators shall be compensated. The parenting coordinator shall attempt to resolve issues arising out of the custody order by facilitating an agreement between the parties and, if unable to reach an agreement, recommend a resolution to the court.

(a) *Appointment of a Parenting Coordinator.*

(1) After a final custody order has been entered, a judge may appoint a parenting coordinator to resolve parenting issues in cases involving repeated or intractable conflict between the parties affecting implementation of the final custody order. A parenting coordinator should not be appointed in every case. The appointment may be made on the motion of a party or the court's motion.

(2) Unless the parties consent and appropriate safety measures are in place to protect the participants, including the parenting coordinator and other third parties, a parenting coordinator shall not be appointed if:

(i) the parties to the custody action have a protection from abuse order in effect;
(ii) the court makes a finding that a party has been the victim of domestic violence perpetrated by a party to the custody action, either during the pendency of the custody action or within 36 months preceding the filing of the custody action; or

(iii) the court makes a finding that a party to the custody action has been the victim of a personal injury crime, as defined in 23 Pa.C.S. § 3103, which was perpetrated by a party to the custody action.

(iv) If a party objects to the appointment of a parenting coordinator based on an allegation that the party has been the victim of domestic violence perpetrated by a party to the custody action, the court shall have a hearing on the issue and may consider abuse occurring beyond the 36 months provided in subdivision (a)(2)(ii).

(3) The appointment of a parenting coordinator shall be for a specified period, which shall not exceed 12 months. A party may petition the court for an extension of the appointment or the court in its discretion may extend the appointment for an additional period.

(4) If the parenting coordinator seeks to withdraw from service in a case, the parenting coordinator shall petition the court and provide a copy of the petition to the parties or the parties' attorneys.

(5) The parenting coordinator shall set forth in a separate written agreement with the parties:

(i) the amount of any retainer;

(ii) the hourly rate to be charged;

(iii) the process for invoices and payment for services;

(iv) information on the parenting coordination process; and

(v) provide a signed copy of the agreement to the parties before initiating any services.

(b) *Qualifications of the Parenting Coordinator.*

(1) A parenting coordinator shall be licensed to practice in the Commonwealth of Pennsylvania as either an attorney or a mental health professional with a master's degree or higher. At a minimum, the parenting coordinator shall have:

(i) practiced family law for five years or have five years of professional post-degree experience in psychiatry, psychology, counseling, family therapy, or other comparable behavioral or social science field; and

(ii) specialized training by a provider approved or certified by the American Psychological Association, Pennsylvania Psychological Association, American Bar Association, Pennsylvania Bar Association, Pennsylvania Bar Institute, or American Academy of Matrimonial Lawyers. The training shall include:

(A) five hours in the parenting coordination process;
(B) ten hours of family mediation;
(C) five hours of training in domestic violence; and

(D) in each two-year period after the initial appointment, ten continuing education credits on any topic related to parenting coordination with a minimum of two hours on domestic violence.

(2) An attorney or a mental health professional seeking an appointment as a parenting coordinator:

(i) shall sign an affidavit attesting that he or she has met the qualifications outlined in (b)(1);
(ii) shall submit the affidavit to the president judge or administrative judge of the judicial district where the parenting coordinator is seeking appointment; and
(iii) after submission of the initial affidavit, a parenting coordinator shall submit a new affidavit every two years attesting that he or she continues to meet the qualifications for a parenting coordinator outlined in (b)(1).

(c) *Appointment Order.* The parenting coordinator's authority as delineated in subdivision (d) shall be included in the order appointing the parenting coordinator, which shall be substantially in the form set forth in Pa.R.C.P. No. 1915.22.

(d) *Scope of Authority of the Parenting Coordinator.* The parenting coordinator shall have the authority to recommend resolutions to the court on issues related to the custody order if the parties are unable to reach an agreement.

(1) To implement the custody order and resolve related parenting issues about which the parties cannot agree, the parenting coordinator is authorized to recommend resolutions to the court about issues that include, but are not limited to:

(i) places and conditions for custodial transitions between households;

(ii) temporary variation from the custodial schedule for a special event or particular circumstance;

(iii) school issues, apart from school selection;

(iv) the child(ren)'s participation in recreation, enrichment, and extracurricular activities, including travel;

(v) child-care arrangements;

(vi) clothing, equipment, toys, and personal possessions of the child(ren);

(vii) information exchanges (e.g., school, health, social) between the parties and communication with or about the child(ren);

(viii) coordination of existing or court-ordered services for the child(ren) (e.g., psychological testing, alcohol or drug monitoring/testing, psychotherapy, anger management);

(ix) behavioral management of the child(ren); and

(x) other related custody issues that the parties mutually have agreed in writing to submit to the parenting coordinator, which are not excluded in subdivision (d)(2).

(2) The following issues are excluded from the parenting coordinator's scope of authority:

(i) a change in legal custody as set forth in the custody order;

(ii) a change in primary physical custody as set forth in the custody order;

(iii) except as set forth in subdivision (d)(1)(ii), a change in the court-ordered custody schedule that reduces or expands the child(ren)'s time with a party;

(iv) a change in the residence (relocation) of the child(ren);

(v) determination of financial issues, other than allocation of the parenting coordinator's fees as set forth in subdivision (g)(1);

(vi) major decisions affecting the health, education, or religion of the child(ren); and

(vii) other issues limited by the appointing judge.

(3) Unless the parties consent, the parenting coordinator shall not contact collateral sources or speak with the child(ren) and to effectuate this provision, the parties shall execute releases, as necessary, authorizing the parenting coordinator to communicate with the

appropriate individuals. Any communication with the collateral sources or child(ren) shall be limited to the issue(s) currently before the parenting coordinator.

(e) *Communications*. No Testimony.

(1) Communication between the parties or the parties' attorneys and the parenting coordinator is not confidential.

(2) A party or a party's attorney may communicate in writing with the parenting coordinator, but shall contemporaneously send a copy of the written communication to the other party or the other party's attorney. Documents, recordings, or other material that one party gives to the parenting coordinator shall be promptly made available to the other party or the other party's attorney for inspection and copying.

(3) The parties and their attorneys may receive, but not initiate, oral ex parte communication with the parenting coordinator. A parenting coordinator may initiate oral communication with a party or party's attorney, but shall promptly advise the other party or the other party's attorney of the communication.

(4) Communication between the parenting coordinator and the court shall be in writing and copies of the written communication shall be sent contemporaneously to the parties or the parties' attorneys.

(5) A party cannot compel the testimony of a parenting coordinator without an order of court.

(f) *Recommendations*. Objecting to the Recommendation. Judicial Review. Record Hearing.

(1) The parenting coordinator shall provide to the parties notice and an opportunity to be heard on the issues.

(2) The parenting coordinator's recommendation shall be in writing on the Summary and Recommendation of the Parenting Coordinator form set forth in Pa.R.C.P. No. 1915.23 and sent to the court for review within two days after hearing from the parties on the issues. The parenting coordinator shall serve a copy of the Summary and Recommendation on the parties or the parties' attorneys.

(3) A party objecting to the recommendation shall file a petition for a record hearing before the court within five days of service of the Summary and Recommendation of the Parenting Coordinator form. The petition must specifically state the issues to be reviewed and include a demand for a record hearing. A copy of the recommendation shall be attached to the petition. In accordance with Pa.R.C.P. No. 440, the objecting party shall serve the petition on the other party or the other party's attorney and the parenting coordinator.

(4) If the parties do not file an objection within five days of service of the parenting coordinator's recommendation, the court shall:

(i) approve the recommendation;

(ii) approve the recommendation in part and conduct a record hearing on issues not approved;

(iii) remand the recommendation to the parenting coordinator for more specific information; or

(iv) not approve the recommendation and conduct a record hearing on the issues.

(5) As soon as practical, the court shall conduct a record hearing on the issues specifically set forth in the petition. The court shall render a decision within the time set forth in Pa.R.C.P. No. 1915.4(d).

(6) If a party makes a timely objection, the recommendation shall become an interim order of court pending further disposition by the court.

(g) *Fees.*

(1) The appointing judge shall allocate between the parties the fees of the parenting coordinator. The parenting coordinator may reallocate the fees, subject to the approval of the court, if one party has caused a disproportionate need for the services of the parenting coordinator.

(2) To limit the financial burden on the parties, a parenting coordinator should meet with the parties only upon a request of a party to resolve an issue about which the parties disagree.

(3) Waiver of fees or reduced fees. Judicial districts implementing a parenting coordination program shall effectuate a policy or program by local rule so that indigent or low-income parties may participate in the parenting coordination program at a reduced fee or no fee.

Adopted August 9, 2018, effective March 1, 2019.

RULE 1915.11-2. APPOINTMENT OF GUARDIAN AD LITEM

(a) The court may, on its own motion or the motion of a party, appoint a guardian ad litem to represent the best interests of the child in a custody action. The guardian ad litem shall be a licensed attorney or licensed mental health professional. The guardian ad litem shall not act as the child's counsel or represent the child's legal interests. Prior to appointing a guardian ad litem, the court shall make a finding that the appointment is necessary to assist the court in determining the best interests of the child.

(b) The court may order either or both parties to pay all or part of the costs of appointing a guardian ad litem.

(c) The guardian ad litem shall file of record and provide copies of any reports prepared by the guardian ad litem to each party and the court not later than 20 days prior to trial. The admissibility of the report shall be determined at the hearing. Prior to disclosure to the parties of confidential information prohibited by 23 Pa.C.S. § 5336, the court shall make a determination of whether the information may be disclosed. The guardian ad litem shall attend all proceedings and be prepared to testify. The guardian ad litem shall be subject to cross-examination if called to testify by either party or the court.

(d) The order appointing a guardian ad litem shall be in substantially the form set forth in Rule 1915.21.

Official Note:

23 Pa.C.S. § 5334 is suspended insofar as it (1) requires that a guardian ad litem be an attorney, (2) permits the guardian ad litem to represent both the best interests and legal interests of the child, (3) provides the

guardian ad litem the right to examine, cross-examine, present witnesses and present evidence on behalf of the child, and (4) prohibits the guardian ad litem from testifying.

Adopted Aug. 1, 2013, effective Sept. 3, 2013.

RULE 1915.12. CIVIL CONTEMPT FOR DISOBEDIENCE OF CUSTODY ORDER. PETITION. FORM OF PETITION. SERVICE. ORDER

(a) A petition for civil contempt shall begin with a notice and order to appear in substantially the following form:

NOTICE AND ORDER TO APPEAR

Legal proceedings have been brought against you alleging you have willfully disobeyed an order of court for custody.

If you wish to defend against the claim set forth in the following pages, you may but are not required to file in writing with the court your defenses or objections.

Whether or not you file in writing with the court your defenses or objections, you must appear in person in court on _____ (Day and Date), at _____.M. (Time), in Courtroom _____, _____ (Address).

IF YOU DO NOT APPEAR IN PERSON, THE COURT MAY ISSUE A WARRANT FOR YOUR ARREST.

If the court finds that you have willfully failed to comply with its order, you may be found to be in contempt of court and committed to jail, fined or both.

YOU SHOULD TAKE THIS PAPER TO YOUR LAWYER AT ONCE. IF YOU DO NOT HAVE A LAWYER, GO TO OR TELEPHONE THE OFFICE SET FORTH BELOW. THIS OFFICE CAN PROVIDE YOU WITH INFORMATION ABOUT HIRING A LAWYER.

IF YOU CANNOT AFFORD TO HIRE A LAWYER, THIS OFFICE MAY BE ABLE TO PROVIDE YOU WITH INFORMATION ABOUT AGENCIES THAT MAY OFFER LEGAL SERVICES TO ELIGIBLE PERSONS AT A REDUCED FEE OR NO FEE.

_____

(Name)

_____

(Address)

_____

(Telephone Number)

                                BY THE COURT:

                                _____
                                                          J.

Date: _____

  (b) The petition shall allege the facts which constitute willful failure to comply with the custody order, a copy of which shall be attached to the petition.

  (c) The petition shall be in substantially the following form:

                          (Caption)

              **PETITION FOR CIVIL CONTEMPT FOR
              DISOBEDIENCE OF CUSTODY ORDER**

The Petition of _____, respectfully represents:

1. That on _____, Judge _____ entered an Order awarding (Petitioner) (Respondent) (shared legal custody) (sole legal custody) (partial physical custody) (primary physical custody) (shared physical custody) (sole physical custody) (supervised physical custody) of the minor child(ren)

(NAME(S) OF CHILD(REN))

A true and correct copy of the order is attached to this petition.

2. Respondent has willfully failed to abide by the order in that

3. Petitioner has attached the Criminal Record/Abuse History Verification form required pursuant to Pa.R.C.P. No. 1915.3-2.

WHEREFORE, Petitioner requests that Respondent be held in contempt of court.

_____

(Attorney for Petitioner) (Petitioner)

I verify that the statements made in this petition are true and correct. I understand that false statements herein are made subject to the penalties of 18 Pa.C.S. § 4904 relating to unsworn falsification to authorities.

_____   _____

Date   Petitioner

(d) The petition shall be served upon the respondent by personal service or regular mail. No answer to the petition shall be required. If service is by mail, the hearing on the petition shall not be held sooner than seven days after mailing of the petition unless the court for cause shown orders an earlier hearing. If the respondent fails to appear, the court shall continue the hearing and may order personal service by the sheriff or constable, or alternative service as accepted by the court, of the petition and notice of a new hearing date, or the court may issue a bench warrant for production of the respondent in court and not for imprisonment.

(e) After hearing, an order committing a respondent to jail for contempt of a custody order shall specify the condition which must be fulfilled to obtain release of the respondent.

Official Note:

See the Uniform Child Custody Jurisdiction and Enforcement Act, 23 Pa.C.S. §§ 5443 and 5445, relating to registration and enforcement of custody decrees of another state, and 23 Pa.C.S. § 5471, relating to intrastate application of the Uniform Child Custody Jurisdiction and Enforcement Act.

Adopted Dec. 10, 1981, effective July 1, 1982. Effective date extended to Jan. 1, 1983 by order of June 25, 1982. Readopted and amended Nov. 8, 1982, effective Jan. 1, 1983. Amended Dec. 2, 1994, effective March 1, 1995; March 18, 2004, effective June 16, 2004; Nov. 19, 2008, imd. effective; Aug. 1, 2013, effective Sept. 3, 2013; July 20, 2015, effective September 1, 2015.

RULE 1915.13.   SPECIAL RELIEF

At any time after commencement of the action, the court may on application or its own motion grant appropriate interim or special relief. The relief may include, but is not limited to, the award of temporary legal or physical custody; the issuance of appropriate process directing that a child or a party or person having physical custody of a child be brought before the court; and a direction that a person post security to appear with the child when directed by the court or to comply with any order of the court.

Official Note:

This rule supplies relief formerly available by habeas corpus for production of the child.

Adopted Dec. 10, 1981, effective July 1, 1982; effective date extended to Jan. 1, 1983 by order of June 25, 1982. Readopted Nov. 8, 1982, effective Jan. 1, 1983. Amended Aug. 1, 2013, effective Sept. 3, 2013.

Explanatory Comment—1981

Rule 1915.13 contains a broad provision empowering the court to provide special relief where appropriate. In a custody proceeding, such special relief might include relief in the nature of a writ of ne exeat, directing the parties not to leave the jurisdiction and not to remove the child from the jurisdiction.

The rule catalogs several types of relief which might be granted, including the entry of a temporary order of custody, partial custody or visitation. The rule specifically provides that the power of the court to grant special relief shall not be limited to the types of relief cataloged.

RULE 1915.14.   DISOBEDIENCE OF ORDER. ARREST. CONTEMPT

If a person disobeys an order of court other than a custody order, the court may issue a bench warrant for the arrest of the person and if the disobedience is willful may, after hearing, adjudge the person to be in contempt.

Official Note:

For disobedience of a custody order, see Rule 1915.12.

Adopted Dec. 10, 1981, effective July 1, 1982; effective date extended to Jan. 1, 1983 by order of June 25, 1982. Readopted Nov. 8, 1982, effective Jan. 1, 1983. Amended Aug. 1, 2013, effective Sept. 3, 2013.

RULE 1915.15.   FORM OF COMPLAINT. CAPTION. ORDER. PETITION TO MODIFY A CUSTODY ORDER

(a) The complaint in an action for custody shall be substantially in the following form:

(Caption)

COMPLAINT FOR (CUSTODY)

1. The plaintiff is ,_____

residing at _____
　　　　　　　(Street)　　　　(City)　　(Zip Code)　(County)

2. The defendant is ,_____

residing at _____
　　　　　　　(Street)　　　　(City)　　(Zip Code)　(County)

3. Plaintiff seeks (shared legal custody) (sole legal custody) (partial physical custody) (primary physical custody) (shared physical custody) (sole physical custody) (supervised physical custody) of the following child(ren):

Name	Present Residence	Age

The child (was)(was not) born out of wedlock.

The child is presently in the custody of_____**, (Name) who resides at** _____
　　　　　　　　(Street)　　　　　　(City)　　　　(State)

During the past five years, the child has resided with the following persons and at the following addresses:

(List All Persons)	(List All Addresses)	(Dates)

A parent of the child is _____, currently residing at
_____.

This parent is (married) (divorced) (single).

A parent of the child is _____, currently residing at
_____.

This parent is (married) (divorced) (single).

4. Plaintiff's relationship to the child is that of _____.

Plaintiff currently resides with the following persons:

Name	Relationship

5. Defendant's relationship to the child is that of _____.

Defendant currently resides with the following persons:

Name	Relationship

6. Plaintiff (has) (has not) participated as a party or witness, or in another capacity, in other litigation concerning the custody of the child in this or another court. The court, term and number, and its relationship to this action is:

_____

_____

Plaintiff (has) (has no) information of a custody proceeding concerning the child pending in a court of this Commonwealth or any other state. The court, term and number, and its relationship to this action is: _____

Plaintiff (knows) (does not know) of a person not a party to the proceedings who has physical custody of the child or claims to have custodial rights with respect to the child. The name and address of such person is: _____

7. The child's best interest and permanent welfare will be served by granting the relief requested because (set forth facts showing that the granting of the relief requested will be in the child's best interest and permanent welfare:

_____

_____

8. Each parent whose parental rights to the child have not been terminated and the person who has physical custody of the child have been named as parties to this action. All other persons, named below, who are known to have or claim a right to custody of the child will be given notice of the pendency of this action and the right to intervene:

Name	Address	Basis of Claim

9.(a) If the plaintiff is seeking physical or legal custody of a child and is *in loco parentis* to the child, the plaintiff shall plead facts establishing standing under 23 Pa.C.S. § 5324(2).

_____

_____

_____

   (b) If the plaintiff is a grandparent seeking physical or legal custody of a grandchild and is not *in loco parentis* to the child, the plaintiff shall plead facts establishing standing under 23 Pa.C.S. § 5324(3).

_____

_____

(c) If the plaintiff is seeking physical or legal custody of a child and is not *in loco parentis* to the child, the plaintiff shall plead facts establishing standing pursuant to 23 Pa.C.S. § 5324(4) and (5).

_____

_____

(d) If the plaintiff is a grandparent or great-grandparent seeking partial physical custody or supervised physical custody of a grandchild or great-grandchild, the plaintiff shall plead facts establishing standing under 23 Pa.C.S. § 5325.

_____

_____

10. Plaintiff has attached the Criminal Record/Abuse History Verification form required pursuant to Pa.R.C.P. No. 1915.3-2.

Wherefore, plaintiff requests the court to grant (shared legal custody) (sole legal custody) (partial physical custody) (primary physical custody) (shared physical custody) (sole physical custody) (supervised physical custody) of the child.

_____
Attorney for Plaintiff

I verify that the statements made in this Complaint are true and correct. I understand that false statements herein are made subject to the penalties of 18 Pa.C.S. § 4904 relating to unsworn falsification to authorities.

_____
Plaintiff

Note: The form of complaint is appropriate if there is one plaintiff and one defendant and the custody of one child is sought or the custody of several children is sought and the information required by Paragraphs 3 to 7 is identical for all of the children. If there are more than two parties, the complaint should be appropriately adapted to accommodate them. If the custody of several children is sought and the information required is not identical for all of the children, the complaint should contain a separate paragraph for each child.

See Pa.R.C.P. No. 1930.1(b). This rule may require attorneys or unrepresented parties to file confidential documents and documents containing confidential information that are subject to the *Case Records Public Access Policy of the Unified Judicial System of Pennsylvania.*

(b) A petition to modify a custody order shall be substantially in the following form:

(Caption)

PETITION FOR MODIFICATION OF A CUSTODY ORDER

1. Petitioner is _____ and resides at _____ .

2. Respondent is _____ and resides at _____ .

3. Petitioner respectfully represents that on _____, 20 ___ an Order of Court was entered for (shared legal custody) (sole legal custody) (partial physical custody) (primary physical custody) (shared physical custody) (sole physical custody) (supervised physical custody). A true and correct copy of the Order is attached.

4. This Order should be modified because: _____

_____

_____

_____ .

5. Petitioner has attached the Criminal Record/Abuse History Verification form required pursuant to Pa.R.C.P. No. 1915.3-2.

WHEREFORE, Petitioner requests that the Court modify the existing Order because it will be in the best interest of the child(ren).

_____

(Attorney for Petitioner) (Petitioner)

I verify that the statements made in this petition are true and correct. I understand that false statements herein are made subject to the penalties of 18 Pa.C.S. § 4904 relating to unsworn falsification to authorities.

_____   _____
        Date   Petitioner

Note: See **Pa.R.C.P. No. 1930.1(b).** This rule may require attorneys or unrepresented parties to file confidential documents and documents containing confidential information that are subject to the *Case Records Public Access Policy of the Unified Judicial System of Pennsylvania*.

(c) The order to be attached at the front of the complaint or petition for modification shall be substantially in the following form:

(Caption)

ORDER OF COURT

You, _____, (defendant) (respondent), have been sued in court to (OBTAIN)(MODIFY) (shared legal custody) (sole legal custody) (partial physical custody) (primary physical custody) (shared physical custody) (sole physical custody) (supervised physical custody) of the child(ren):

You are ordered to appear in person at _____(Address),

on _____(Day and Date), at _____(Time), ____.M., for

[ ] a conciliation or mediation conference.

[ ] a pretrial conference.

[ ] a hearing before the court.

If you fail to appear as provided by this order, an order for custody may be entered against you or the court may issue a warrant for your arrest.

You must file with the court a verification regarding any criminal record or abuse history regarding you and anyone living in your household on or before the initial in-person contact with the court

809

(including, but not limited to, a conference with a conference officer or judge or conciliation) but not later than 30 days after service of the complaint or petition.

No party may make a change in the residence of any child which significantly impairs the ability of the other party to exercise custodial rights without first complying with all of the applicable provisions of 23 Pa.C.S. § 5337 and Pa.R.C.P. No. 1915.17 regarding relocation.

YOU SHOULD TAKE THIS PAPER TO YOUR LAWYER AT ONCE. IF YOU DO NOT HAVE A LAWYER, GO TO OR TELEPHONE THE OFFICE SET FORTH BELOW. THIS OFFICE CAN PROVIDE YOU WITH INFORMATION ABOUT HIRING A LAWYER. IF YOU CANNOT AFFORD TO HIRE A LAWYER, THIS OFFICE MAY BE ABLE TO PROVIDE YOU WITH INFORMATION ABOUT AGENCIES THAT MAY OFFER LEGAL SERVICES TO ELIGIBLE PERSONS AT A REDUCED FEE OR NO FEE.

_____ (Name)

_____ (Address)

_____ (Telephone)

AMERICANS WITH DISABILITIES ACT OF 1990

The Court of Common Pleas of _____ County is required by law to comply with the Americans with Disabilities Act of 1990. For information about accessible facilities and reasonable accommodations available to disabled individuals having business before the court, please contact our office. All arrangements must be made at least 72 hours prior to any hearing or business before the court. You must attend the scheduled conference or hearing.

BY THE COURT:

Date:_____   _____

J.

Adopted Dec. 10, 1981, effective July 1, 1982; effective date extended to Jan. 1, 1983 by order of June 25, 1982. Readopted and amended Nov. 8, 1982, effective Jan. 1, 1983. Amended April 29, 1991, effective July 1, 1991; Dec. 2, 1994, effective March 1, 1995; March 2, 2000, imd. effective; March 18, 2004, effective June 16, 2004; Nov. 19, 2008, imd. effective; Aug. 1, 2013, effective Sept. 3, 2013; July 20, 2015, effective September 1, 2015; May 18, 2016, effective July 1, 2016; Jan. 5, 2018, effective Jan. 6, 2018; June 1, 2018, effective July 1, 2018; July 27, 2020, effective Oct. 1, 2020.

EXPLANATORY COMMENT—2008

In an effort to promote uniformity of practice throughout the Commonwealth, several forms are included in the rules. Two aspects of these forms are worthy of mention. First, much of the information which must be set forth in the complaint is required by the Uniform Child Custody Jurisdiction and Enforcement Act, 23 Pa.C.S.A. § 5429. Second, the complaint is verified by use of a statement that it is subject to the penalties of the Crimes Code relating to unsworn falsification to authorities. A notary public is not needed.

EXPLANATORY COMMENT—2020

Act of May 4, 2018, P.L. 112, No. 21, amended 23 Pa.C.S. § 5324 by adding a new class of third-party standing for individuals seeking custody of a child whose parents do not have care and control of the child. The individual seeking custody may or may not be related to the child. Subject to the limitations in 23 Pa.C.S. § 5324(5), the newly added standing provision requires that: (1) the individual has assumed or is willing to assume responsibility for the child; (2) the individual has a sustained, substantial, and sincere interest in the child's welfare; and (3) the child's parents do not have care and control of the child. A plaintiff proceeding under Section 5324(4) shall satisfy the requirements of that provision by clear and convincing evidence. Additionally, if a juvenile dependency proceeding has been initiated, or is ongoing, or if there is an order for permanent legal custody, Section 5324(5) provides that an individual cannot assert standing under Section 5324(4).

Consistent with the Act's statutory change, the Complaint for Custody Paragraph 9 has been revised to include a third party seeking custody of a child under 23 Pa.C.S. § 5324(4) and has been reorganized to sequentially follow the statutory provisions in 23 Pa.C.S. §§ 5324(2)-(4) and 5325. Similarly, Pa.R.C.P. No. 1915.3(e) has been reorganized to sequentially follow the statutory provision sequence. See Pa.R.C.P. No. 1915.3(e).

RULE 1915.16.   FORM OF ORDER AND NOTICE. JOINDER. INTERVENTION

(a) The order and notice joining a party in an action under Rule 1915.6(a) shall be substantially in the following form:

(Caption)

ORDER AND NOTICE

A complaint has been filed in the Court of Common Pleas of _____ County concerning custody of the following child(ren): _____.

The Court has learned you may have a legal interest in custody of the child(ren) named.

A hearing will be held in Courtroom _____ of the Court of Common Pleas, _____ (Address), on _____ (Day and Date), at _____ (Time), ____.M. If you wish to protect any legal interest you may have or wish to present evidence to the Court on those matters, you should appear at the place and time and on the date above.

If you have the child(ren) in your possession or control, you must appear and bring them to the Courthouse with you.

If you wish to claim a right of custody, you may file a counterclaim.

If you fail to appear as provided by this order or to bring the child(ren), an order for custody may be entered against you or the Court may issue a warrant for your arrest.

YOU SHOULD TAKE THIS PAPER TO YOUR LAWYER AT ONCE. IF YOU DO NOT HAVE A LAWYER, GO TO OR TELEPHONE THE OFFICE SET FORTH BELOW. THIS OFFICE CAN PRO-VIDE YOU WITH INFORMATION ABOUT HIRING A LAWYER.

IF YOU CANNOT AFFORD TO HIRE A LAWYER, THIS OFFICE MAY BE ABLE TO PROVIDE YOU WITH INFORMATION ABOUT AGENCIES THAT MAY OFFER LEGAL SERVICES TO ELIGIBLE PERSONS AT A REDUCED FEE OR NO FEE.

_____ (Name)

_____ (Address)

_____ (Telephone)

AMERICANS WITH DISABILITIES ACT OF 1990

The Court of Common Pleas of _____ County is required by law to comply with the Americans with Disabilities Act of 1990. For information about accessible facilities and reasonable accommodations available to disabled individuals having business before the court, please contact our office. All arrangements must be made at least 72 hours prior to any hearing or business before the court.

BY THE COURT:

Date:_____   _____

                                                                          J.

(a) The order for notice of the pendency of the action and the right to intervene required by Rule 1915.6(b) shall be substantially in the following form:

(Caption)

ORDER AND NOTICE

A complaint has been filed in the Court of Common Pleas of _____ County concerning custody of the following child(ren): _____.

The Court has learned you claim custodial rights with respect to the child(ren) named.

A hearing will be held in courtroom _____ of the Court of Common Pleas, _____ (Address), on _____ (Day and Date), at _____ (Time), ____.M. If you wish to assert your claim to custodial rights with respect to the child(ren) or wish to present evidence to the Court on those matters, you should petition the Court, on or before the above date, for leave to intervene in the proceedings.

YOU SHOULD TAKE THIS PAPER TO YOUR LAWYER AT ONCE. IF YOU DO NOT HAVE A LAWYER, GO TO OR TELE-PHONE THE OFFICE SET FORTH BELOW. THIS OFFICE CAN PROVIDE YOU WITH INFORMATION ABOUT HIRING A LAW-YER. IF YOU CANNOT AFFORD TO HIRE A LAWYER, THIS OFFICE MAY BE ABLE TO PROVIDE YOU WITH INFORMA-TION ABOUT AGENCIES THAT MAY OFFER LEGAL SERVICES TO ELIGIBLE PERSONS AT A REDUCED FEE OR NO FEE.

_____ (Name)

_____ (Address)

_____ (Telephone)

AMERICANS WITH DISABILITIES ACT OF 1990

The Court of Common Pleas of _____ County is required by law to comply with the Americans with Disabilities Act of 1990. For information about accessible facilities and reasonable accommodations available to disabled individuals having business before the court, please contact our office. All arrangements must be made at least 72 hours prior to any hearing or business before the court.

BY THE COURT:

Date:_____   _____
                                                                                                            J.

Adopted Dec. 10, 1981, effective July 1, 1982; effective date extended to Jan. 1, 1983 by order of June 25, 1982. Readopted Nov. 8, 1982, effective Jan. 1, 1983. Amended Dec. 2, 1994, effective March 1, 1995; March 18, 2004, effective June 16, 2004; Aug. 1, 2013, effective Sept. 3, 2013.

RULE 1915.17.   RELOCATION. NOTICE AND COUNTER-AFFIDAVIT

(a) A party proposing to change the residence of a child which significantly impairs the ability of a non-relocating party to exercise custodial rights must notify every other person who has custodial rights to the child and provide a counter-affidavit by which a person may agree or object. The form of the notice and counter-affidavit are set forth in subdivisions (i) and (j) below. The notice shall be sent by certified mail, return receipt requested, addressee only or pursuant to Pa.R.C.P No. 1930.4, no later than the sixtieth day before the date of the proposed change of residence or other time frame set forth in 23 Pa.C.S. § 5337(c)(2).

(b) If the other party objects to the proposed change in the child's residence, that party must serve the counter-affidavit on the party proposing the change by certified mail, return receipt requested, addressee only, or pursuant to Pa.R.C.P. No. 1930.4 within 30 days of receipt of the notice required in subdivision (a) above. If there is an existing child custody case, the objecting party also shall file the counter-affidavit with the court.

(c) If no objection to a proposed change of a child's residence is timely served after notice, the proposing party may change the residence of the child and such shall not be considered a "relocation" under statute or rule.

(d) The procedure in any relocation case shall be expedited. There shall be no requirement for parenting education or mediation prior to an expedited hearing before a judge.

(e) If the party proposing the relocation seeks an order of court, has served a notice of proposed relocation as required by 23 Pa.C.S. § 5337, has not received notice of objection to the move and seeks confirmation of relocation, the party proposing the relocation shall file:

(1) a complaint for custody and petition to confirm relocation, when no custody case exists, or

(2) a petition to confirm relocation when there is an existing custody case and

(3) a proposed order including the information set forth at 23 Pa.C.S. § 5337(c)(3).

(f) If the party proposing the relocation has received notice of objection to the proposed move after serving a notice of proposed relocation as required by 23 Pa.C.S. § 5337 et seq., the party proposing relocation shall file:

(1) a complaint for custody or petition for modification, as applicable;

(2) a copy of the notice of proposed relocation served on the non-relocating party;

(3) a copy of the counter-affidavit indicating objection to relocation; and

(4) a request for a hearing.

(g) If the non-relocating party has been served with a notice of proposed relocation and the party proposing relocation has not complied with subdivision (f) above, the non-relocating party may file:

(1) a complaint for custody or petition for modification, as applicable;

(2) a counter-affidavit as set forth in 23 Pa.C.S. § 5337(d)(1), and

(3) a request for a hearing.

(h) If a non-relocating party has not been served with a notice of proposed relocation and seeks an order of court preventing relocation, the non-relocating party shall file:

(1) a complaint for custody or petition for modification, as applicable;

(2) a statement of objection to relocation; and

(3) a request for a hearing.

(i) The notice of proposed relocation shall be substantially in the following form:

(Caption)

NOTICE OF PROPOSED RELOCATION

You,_____, are hereby notified that_____
(party proposing relocation) _____ proposes to relocate with the following minor child(ren):_____
_____.

Address of the proposed new residence:

_____

☐ *Check here if the address is confidential pursuant to 23 Pa.C.S.
§ 5336(b).*

Mailing address of intended new residence (if not the same as above)

_____

☐ *Check here if the address is confidential pursuant to 23 Pa.C.S.
§ 5336(b).*

Names and ages of the individuals who intend to reside at the new
residence:

Name	Age
_____	_____
_____	_____
_____	_____

☐ *Check here if the information is confidential pursuant to 23 Pa.C.S.
§ 5336(b) or (c).*

Home telephone number of the new residence:

☐ *Check here if the information is confidential pursuant to 23 Pa.C.S.
§ 5336(b) or (c).*

Name of the new school district and school the child(ren) will attend after relocation:

_____

☐ *Check here if the information is confidential pursuant to 23 Pa.C.S. § 5336(b) or (c).*

Date of the proposed relocation:

☐ *Check here if the information is confidential pursuant to 23 Pa.C.S. § 5336(b) or (c).*

Reasons for the proposed relocation:

_____

_____

_____

☐ *Check here if the information is confidential pursuant to 23 Pa.C.S. § 5336(b) or (c).*

Proposed modification of custody schedule following relocation:

_____

_____

_____

_____

Other information:

_____

YOU SHOULD TAKE THIS PAPER TO YOUR LAWYER AT ONCE. IF YOU DO NOT HAVE A LAWYER, GO TO OR TELE-PHONE THE OFFICE SET FORTH BELOW. THIS OFFICE CAN PROVIDE YOU WITH INFORMATION ABOUT HIRING A LAWYER.

IF YOU CANNOT AFFORD TO HIRE A LAWYER, THIS OFFICE MAY BE ABLE TO PROVIDE YOU WITH INFORMATION

ABOUT AGENCIES THAT MAY OFFER LEGAL SERVICES TO ELIGIBLE PERSONS AT A REDUCED FEE OR NO FEE.

_____

_____

_____

Note: See **Pa.R.C.P. No. 1930.1(b).** This rule may require attorneys or unrepresented parties to file confidential documents and documents containing confidential information that are subject to the Case Records Public Access Policy of the Unified Judicial System of Pennsylvania.

(j) The counter-affidavit that must be served with the relocation notice shall be substantially in the following form as set forth in 23 Pa.C.S.§ 5337(d):

(Caption)

COUNTER-AFFIDAVIT REGARDING RELOCATION

This proposal of relocation involves the following child/children:

Child's Name	Age	Currently residing at:
Child's Name	Age	Currently residing at:
Child's Name	Age	Currently residing at:

I have received a notice of proposed relocation and (*check all that apply*):

1. ☐ I do not object to the relocation

2. ☐ I do not object to the modification of the custody order consistent with the proposal for modification set forth in the notice.

3. ☐ I do not object to the relocation, but I do object to modification of the custody order.

4. ☐ I plan to request that a hearing be scheduled by filing a request for hearing with the court:

a. ☐ Prior to allowing (name of child/children) to relocate.

b. ☐ After the child/children relocate.

5. ☐ I do object to the relocation

6. ☐ I do object to the modification of the custody order.

I understand that in addition to objecting to the relocation or modification of the custody order above, I must also serve this counter-affidavit on the other party by certified mail, return receipt requested, addressee only, or pursuant to Pa.R.C.P. No. 1930.4, and, if there is an existing custody case, I must file this counter-affidavit with the court. If I fail to do so within 30 days of my receipt of the proposed relocation notice, I understand that I will not be able to object to the relocation at a later time.

I verify that the statements made in this counter-affidavit are true and correct. I understand that false statements herein are made subject to the penalties of 18 Pa.C.S. § 4904 (relating to unsworn falsification to authorities).

_____

(Date)   **(Signature)**

Note: See Pa.R.C.P. No. 1930.1(b). This rule may require attorneys or unrepresented parties to file confidential documents and documents containing confidential information that are subject to the Case Records Public Access Policy of the Unified Judicial System of Pennsylvania.

Adopted Aug. 1, 2013, effective Sept. 3, 2013. Amended July 20, 2015, effective September 1, 2015; Jan. 5, 2018, effective Jan. 6, 2018; June 1, 2018, effective July 1, 2018.

RULE 1915.18.   FORM OF ORDER DIRECTING
EXPERT EXAMINATION AND REPORT.

The order of court directing expert evaluation in a custody matter pursuant to Rule 1915.8 shall be in substantially the following form:

(Caption)

ORDER OF COURT

AND NOW, this _____ day of _____, 20__, it is hereby ORDERED, that:

1. The evaluator [ ] shall be _____ or [ ] will be selected by the parties.

2. The evaluator shall conduct a
   [ ]   Physical Evaluation
   [ ]   Psychological Evaluation
   [ ]   Custody Evaluation
   [ ]   Drug and/or Alcohol Evaluation
   [ ]   Home Study
   [ ]   Other (Specify)   _____

3. The evaluator [ ] shall [ ] shall not make specific recommendations for legal and physical custody. If the evaluator makes specific recommendations, the evaluator shall state the specific reasons for the recommendations.

4. The parties shall participate fully with the evaluator on a timely basis, including retaining the evaluator upon appropriate terms, scheduling appointments, paying promptly, participating in all sessions and in appropriate testing recommended by the evaluator and executing any reasonable consents relating to themselves and their children.

[ ] 5. If the evaluation is a medical necessity, the service may be covered by insurance. If so, both parties shall promptly cooperate to maximize the use of available insurance coverage, if any, and to notify the other party of the result. The [ ] plaintiff [ ] defendant shall submit the costs to his or her insurance first. The cost of the unreimbursed portion of the evaluation shall preliminarily

be allocated between the parties with the plaintiff paying ___ % and the defendant paying ___ % with-out prejudice to the ultimate apportionment of such costs by subsequent agreement of the parties or order of court.

[ ] 6. The cost of the evaluation shall be borne by the county, subject to reimbursement by _____.

7. The cost for the evaluator's time for depositions and/or testimony for hearing shall be [ ] allocated ____ % to the plaintiff and ____ % to the defendant or [ ] paid by the party seeking the testimony.

[ ] 8. The evaluator may consult with and/or interview any person the evaluator reasonably believes can provide relevant information, including other experts and/or fact witnesses.

[ ] 9. The evaluator may utilize the services of another qualified professional (e.g. to perform additional services) without court approval.

[ ] 10. Subject to the applicable rules of evidence, the evaluator's file (including notes, exhibits, correspondence, test interpretations and, to the extent it is not a violation of copyright law or applicable professional rules, raw test data) shall promptly be made available to counsel for the parties.

[ ] 11. Provided that the parties cooperate on a timely basis, the evaluator shall deliver his or her report to counsel for the parties, any unrepresented party, the guardian ad litem and/or counsel for the child, if any, and to the court at least ___ days prior to the first day of trial. The report shall not be filed of record.

[ ] 12. Prior to and/or subsequent to the submission of the evaluator's written report, counsel for the parties shall not be permitted to communicate with the evaluator as to substantive issues, without the consent or direct participation of counsel for the other party.

13. If the report or any information from the evaluator is provided to the court, the evaluator shall be subject to cross examination by all counsel and any unrepresented party regardless of who obtains or pays for the services of the evaluator.

14. The evaluator shall be provided with a copy of this order.

15. The evaluator's report shall not be inappropriately disseminated.

[ ] 16. Other provisions:_____

FAILURE TO COMPLY WITH THE TERMS OF THIS ORDER MAY RESULT IN FINES, IMPRISONMENT OR OTHER SANCTIONS.

BY THE COURT:

_____
                                                    J.

Adopted May 16, 1994, effective July 1, 1994. Amended May 23, 2007, effective Aug. 1, 2007; Aug. 2, 2010, imd. effective; Jan. 5, 2018, effective Jan. 6, 2018.

RULE 1915.19.   FORM OF ORDER APPOINTING COUNSEL FOR THE CHILD

The order appointing an attorney to represent a child in a child custody action pursuant to Rule 1915.11 shall be in substantially the following form:

(Caption)

ORDER OF COURT

AND NOW, THIS _____day of _____, 20__, it is hereby ordered as follows:

Pursuant to Pa.R.C.P. No. 1915.11, is appointed as attorney for the minor child _____(D.O.B. _____) in connection with the civil proceedings related to the custody of the minor child.

Counsel for the child shall zealously represent the legal interests of the child as any other client in an attorney-client relationship and shall not act as the child's guardian ad litem or best interests attorney. The child's attorney shall not be called to testify and communications between the child's attorney and the child shall be privileged, consistent with the attorney-client relationship.

It is ordered and decreed that all relevant schools, police departments, hospitals and social service agencies including home and school agencies who have records, reports and/or information pertaining to the child relevant to the custody of the child, shall allow the child's attorney access to all files and records in its possession, custody or control and shall cooperate in responding to all relevant inquires. These files/records may include but are not limited to medical, psychological or psychiatric charts including evaluations and progress notes and records, X-rays, photographs, tests, test evaluations, intake and discharge summaries, police records, and school records including report cards, educational assessments and educational plans, relevant to this custody dispute and/or relevant to any special needs or requirements of the child. The child's attorney shall have the right to copy any part of the files and records maintained in connection with the child.

It is further ordered and decreed that the child's attorney shall be permitted to see and speak with the child, and family, medical and/or social service providers connected with this case, and take all steps appropriate to and consistent with this order.

The fees for the child's attorney shall be paid as follows:

This appointment shall terminate upon the entry of a final order resolving the petition pending as of the date of this order or as provided in subsequent order of court.

BY THE COURT:

_____

J.

Adopted Aug. 1, 2013, effective Sept. 3, 2013.

RULE 1915.21.   FORM OF ORDER APPOINTING GUARDIAN AD LITEM

The order appointing a guardian ad litem in a child custody action pursuant to Rule 1915.11-2 shall be in substantially the following form:

(Caption)

ORDER OF COURT

AND NOW, THIS _____ day of _____, 20__, it is hereby ordered as follows:

Pursuant to Pa.R.C.P. No. 1915.11-2, _____ is appointed as guardian ad litem for the minor child _____(D.O.B. _____) in connection with the civil proceedings related to the custody of the minor child.

The child's guardian ad litem shall represent the best interests of the child. The guardian ad litem shall not act as the child's attorney or represent the child's legal interests.

It is ordered and decreed that all relevant schools, police departments, hospitals and social service agencies including home and school agencies who have records, reports and/or information pertaining to the child relevant to the custody of the child, shall allow the guardian ad litem access to all files and records in its possession, custody or control and shall cooperate in responding to all relevant inquires. These files/records may include but are not limited to medical, psychological or psychiatric charts including evaluations and progress notes and records, X-rays, photographs, tests, test evaluations, intake and discharge summaries, police records, and school records including report cards, educational assessments and educational plans, relevant to this custody dispute and/or relevant to any special needs or requirements of the child. The guardian ad litem shall have the right to copy any part of the files and records maintained in connection with the child.

It is further ordered and decreed that the guardian ad litem shall be permitted to see and speak with the child, and family, medical and/or social service providers connected with this case, and take all steps appropriate to and consonant with this order.

The guardian ad litem shall provide copies of any reports prepared by the guardian ad litem to each party, or to their counsel, and to the court not later than 20 days prior to trial. The guardian ad litem shall attend all proceedings and be prepared to testify. The guardian ad litem shall be subject to cross-examination if called to testify by either party or the court.

The fees for the guardian ad litem shall be paid as follows:

_____

This appointment shall terminate upon the entry of a final order resolving the petition pending as of the date of this order or as provided in subsequent order of court.

BY THE COURT:

_____

J.

Adopted Aug. 1, 2013, effective Sept. 3, 2013.

RULE 1915.22.   FORM OF ORDER APPOINTING PARENTING COORDINATOR

The order appointing a parenting coordinator pursuant to Pa.R.C.P. No. 1915.11-1 shall be in substantially the following form:

(Caption)

ORDER OF COURT

AND NOW, this_____ day of _____, 20 ___, it is hereby ordered as follows:

1. APPOINTMENT AND TERM:

Pursuant to Pa.R.C.P. No. 1915.11-1, _____is appointed as the parties' parenting coordinator for a term of months (not exceeding 12 months).

Legal counsel for ,or either party, if unrepresented, shall provide copies of all orders, pleadings and custody evaluations in this case to the parenting coordinator within ten (10) days of the date of this order.

2. ROLE OF THE PARENTING COORDINATOR:

(a) The parenting coordinator shall attempt to resolve issues arising out of the custody order by facilitating an agreement between the parties and, if unable to reach an agreement, recommend a resolution to the court.

(b) The parenting coordinator shall not function as the attorney, advocate, counselor, or psychotherapist for the parties, the parties' child(ren), or family. However, the parenting coordinator is permitted and encouraged to facilitate communication and agreement between the parties when conflicts arise and shall always act in a manner conducive to the best interests of the child(ren).

3. PARENTING COORDINATOR'S SCOPE OF AUTHORITY:

To implement the custodial arrangement set forth in the custody order and resolve related parenting issues about which the parties cannot agree, the parenting coordinator is authorized to recommend resolutions to the court about issues that include, but are not limited to:

(a) places and conditions for transitions between households;

(b) temporary variation from the schedule for a special event or particular circumstance;

(c) school issues, apart from school selection;

(d) the child(ren)'s participation in recreation, enrichment, and extracurricular activities, including travel;

(e) child-care arrangements;

(f) clothing, equipment, toys, and personal possessions of the child(ren);

(g) information exchanges (e.g., school, health, social) and communication with or about the child(ren);

(h) coordination of existing or court-ordered services for the child(ren) (e.g., psychological testing, alcohol or drug monitoring/testing, psychotherapy, anger management);

(i) behavioral management of the child(ren); and

(j) other related custody issues that the parties mutually have agreed in writing to submit to the parenting coordinator, which are not excluded in Paragraph 4.

4. EXCLUSIONS FROM PARENTING COORDINATOR'S AUTHORITY:

(a) The following specific issues are excluded from the parenting coordinator's scope of authority:

(1) a change in legal custody as set forth in the custody order;

(2) a change in primary physical custody set forth in the custody order;

(3) other than as set forth in Paragraph 3(b), a change in the courtordered custody schedule that reduces or expands the child(ren)'s time with a party;

(4) a change in the residence (relocation) of the child(ren);

(5) determination of financial issues, other than allocation of the parenting coordinator's fees as set forth in Pa.R.C.P. 1915.11-1(g) (1);

(6) major decisions affecting the health, education, or religion of the child(ren); and

(7) Other:_____

(b) Unless the parties consent, the parenting coordinator shall not contact collateral sources or speak with the child(ren). The parties shall execute releases, as necessary, authorizing the parenting coordinator to communicate with the appropriate individuals. Any communication with the collateral sources or child(ren) shall be limited to the issue(s) currently before the parenting coordinator.

5. COMMUNICATIONS:

(a) The parenting coordinator shall determine the protocol of all communications, interviews, and sessions, including who shall attend the sessions (including the children), and whether the sessions will be conducted in person or by other means. The protocols should include measures addressing the safety of all participants.

(b) Communication between the parties or their attorneys and the parenting coordinator is not confidential.

(c) The parties and their attorneys shall have the right to receive, but not initiate, oral ex parte communication with the parenting coordinator. The parenting coordinator shall promptly advise the other party or the other party's attorney of the communication. A party or a party's attorney may communicate in writing with the parenting coordinator, but shall contemporaneously send a copy of the written communication to the other party or the other party's attorney. Documents, recordings, or other material that one party gives to the parenting coordinator must be promptly made available to the other party or the other party's attorney for inspection and copying.

(d) Communication between the parenting coordinator and the court shall be in writing and copies of the written communication shall be sent contemporaneously to the parties or the parties' attorneys.

(e) A party cannot compel the testimony of a parenting coordinator without an order of court.

6. PARENTING COORDINATION PROCESS:

(a) The parenting coordinator shall provide to the parties notice and an opportunity to be heard on the issues.

(b) The parenting coordinator's recommendation shall be in writing on the Summary and Recommendation of the Parenting Coordinator form set forth in Pa.R.C.P. No. 1915.23 and sent to the court for review within two days after hearing from the parties on the issues. The parenting coordinator shall serve a copy of the Summary and Recommendation on the parties or the parties' attorneys.

(c) A party objecting to the recommendation shall file a petition for a record hearing before the court within five days of service of the Summary and Recommendation of the Parenting Coordinator form. The petition must specifically state the issues to be reviewed and include a demand for a record hearing. A copy of the recommendation shall be attached to the petition. In accordance with Pa.R.C.P. No. 440, the objecting party shall serve the petition upon the other party or the party's attorney and the parenting coordinator.

7. RECORD HEARING:

(a) If the parties do not file an objection within five days of service of the parenting coordinator's recommendation, the court shall:

(1) approve the recommendation;

(2) approve the recommendation in part and conduct a record hearing on issues not approved;

(3) remand the recommendation to the parenting coordinator for more specific information; or

(4) not approve the recommendation and conduct a record hearing on the issues.

(b) As soon as practical, the court shall conduct a record hearing on the issues specifically set forth in the petition. The court shall render a decision within the time set forth in Pa.R.C.P. No. 1915.4(d).

(c) If a party makes a timely objection, the recommendation shall become an interim order of court pending further disposition by the court.

8. ALLOCATION OF FEES:

(a) The parties will share the obligation to pay the fees of the parenting coordinator as follows: __% Mother, __% Father, __% Third party. Fees may be reallocated by the court or the parenting coordinator if a party has disproportionately caused the need for the services of the parenting coordinator.

(b) The judicial district's established hourly rate for parenting coordinators shall be set forth in a separate written agreement entered into between the parties and the parenting coordinator.

(c) The parties will pay a joint retainer to the parenting coordinator in the percentages set forth above in an amount to be set forth in a separate agreement between the parties and the parenting coordinator. After each session, or at least once monthly, the parenting coordinator shall provide the parties with an invoice of charges incurred. The retainer may be replenished as services are rendered. Funds remaining at the conclusion of the parenting coordinator's appointment shall be returned to the parties.

9. TERMINATION/WITHDRAWAL OF PARENTING COORDINATOR:

(a) The parties may not terminate the parenting coordinator's services without court approval.

(b) A party seeking the termination of the parenting coordinator's services shall serve the other party or the party's attorney and parenting coordinator with a copy of the petition for termination.

(c) If the parenting coordinator seeks to withdraw from service in a case, the parenting coordinator shall petition the court and provide a copy of the petition to the parties or the parties' attorneys.

10. APPEAL:

If there is an appeal of the underlying custody order or this order, then this order shall be stayed during the pendency of the appeal.

BY THE COURT:

_____

J.

Adopted August 9, 2018, effective March 1, 2019.

RULE 1915.23. FORM OF THE SUMMARY AND RECOMMENDATION OF THE PARENTING COORDINATOR

The recommendation of the parenting coordinator shall be in writing and shall be in substantially the following form:

(Caption)

SUMMARY AND RECOMMENDATION |OF THE PARENTING COORDINATOR

The undersigned, the duly appointed parenting coordinator in the above-captioned matter, pursuant to the Order of Court dated _____, 20__, after submission of the issue described below and after provid-ing the parties with an opportunity to heard on the issue, the parenting coordinator sets forth the following:

SUMMARY OF THE ISSUE(S)

1. Description of the issue(s):

_____

_____

_____

2. The respective parties' position on the issue(s):

_____

_____

_____

RECOMMENDATION

_____

_____

_____

Within five days of the date set forth below, a party may object to this recommendation by filing a petition with the court and requesting a record hearing before the judge as set forth in Pa.R.C.P. No. 1915.11-1(f)(3).

The undersigned parenting coordinator certifies that this Summary and Recommendation of the Parenting Coordinator has been served on the court and the parties or the parties' attorneys on the date set forth below

_____

_____

_____   _____

Date   Parenting Coordinator

ORDER OF COURT

JUDICIAL REVIEW OF PARENTING
COORDINATOR'S RECOMMENDATION

[ ] The Recommendation is approved.

[ ] The Recommendation is approved in part. The issue(s) not approved by the court is/are: _____

_____

and a record hearing is scheduled for _____, 20__ at _____ a.m./ p.m. before the undersigned.

[ ] The Recommendation is remanded to the parenting coordinator for additional information on the following issue(s): _____

_____

[ ] The Recommendation is not approved and a record hearing on the issue(s) is scheduled for _____, 20__ at _____ a.m./p.m. before the undersigned.

BY THE COURT:

Date:_____   _____

                                                                  J.

Adopted August 9, 2018, effective March 1, 2019.

RULE 1915.24.   ACTS OF ASSEMBLY NOT SUSPENDED.

The following Acts or parts of Acts of Assembly shall not be deemed suspended or affected:

(1) Chapter 63 of the Judicial Code, 42 Pa.C.S. § 6301 et seq., known as the Juvenile Act;

(2) Section 5341 et seq. of the Domestic Relations Code, 23 Pa.C.S. § 5341 et seq., known as the Uniform Child Custody Jurisdiction Act, except to the extent suspended by Rule 1915.25 governing Suspension of Acts of Assembly;

(3) The Act of December 19, 1990, No. 206, 23 Pa.C.S. § 6301 et seq., known as the Child Protective Services Law;

(4) The Act of October 7, 1976, No. 218, as amended, 23 Pa.C.S. § 6101 et seq., known as the Protection from Abuse Act; and

(5) Chapter 53, Subchapter A of Title 23 of the Consolidated Statutes, 23 Pa.C.S. § 5301 et seq., setting forth general custody provisions.

Adopted Dec. 10, 1981, effective July 1, 1982; effective date extended to Jan. 1, 1983 by Order of June 25, 1982. Readopted and amended Nov. 8, 1982, effective Jan. 1, 1983 and applied to pending actions; amended Nov. 7, 1988, effective Jan. 1, 1989, amended March 30, 1994, effective July 1, 1994.

RULE 1915.25.   SUSPENSION OF ACTS OF ASSEMBLY

Section 5351 of the Domestic Relations Code, 23 Pa.C.S. § 5351, of the Uniform Child Custody Jurisdiction Act, relating to additional parties, is suspended insofar as it provides for the joinder of a person not a party who claims to have custody or visitation rights with respect to the child.

Official Note:

Rule 1915.6(b) provides that a person not a party who claims to have custody or visitation rights with respect to the child shall be given notice of the pendency of the proceedings and of the right to intervene.

23 Pa.C.S. § 5334 is suspended insofar as it (1) requires that a guardian ad litem be an attorney, (2) permits the guardian ad litem to represent both the best interests and legal interests of the child, (3) provides the guardian ad litem the right to examine, cross-examine, present witnesses and present evidence on behalf of the child, and (4) prohibits the guardian ad litem from testifying.

Adopted Dec. 10, 1981, effective July 1, 1982; effective date extended to Jan. 1, 1983 by order of June 25, 1982. Readopted Nov. 8, 1982, effective Jan. 1, 1983. Amended March 30, 1994, effective July 1, 1994; Aug. 1, 2013, effective Sept. 3, 2013.

RULES RELATING TO DOMESTIC RELATIONS MATTERS
GENERALLY
RULES 1930.1–1931
(AMENDED THROUGH SEPTEMBER 30, 2020)

RULE

> 1930.1. Form of Pleadings. Form of Caption.
>
> 1930.2. No Post-Trial Practice. Motions for Reconsideration.
>
> 1930.3. Testimony by Electronic Means.
>
> 1930.4. Service of Original Process in Domestic Relations Matters.
>
> 1930.5. Discovery in Domestic Relations Matters.
>
> 1930.6. Paternity Actions.
>
> 1930.7. Status Conference.
>
> 1930.8. Self-Represented Party
>
> 1930.9. Family Court Forms
>
> 1931. Family Court Rules

RULE 1915.30.1. FORM OF CAPTION.
CONFIDENTIAL INFORMATION AND CONFIDENTIAL
DOCUMENTS. CERTIFICATION.

(a) The form of the caption in all domestic relations matters shall be substantially in the following form:

In the Court of Common Pleas of _____ County, Pennsylvania

A. Litigant,	)	
Plaintiff	)	
vs.	)	**No. (Docket Number)**
B. Litigant,	)	
Defendant	)	

(Title of Pleading)

Note: **As domestic relations matters are no longer quasi-criminal, the phrase "Commonwealth ex rel." shall not be used in the caption of any domestic relations matter.**

(b) Unless public access is otherwise constrained by applicable authority, any attorney, or any party if unrepresented, who files a document pursuant to these rules with the prothonotary's office shall comply with the requirements of Sections 7.0 and 8.0 of the Case Records *Public Access Policy of the Unified Judicial System of Pennsylvania* (Policy) including a certification of compliance with the Policy and, as necessary, a Confidential Information Form, unless otherwise specified by rule or order of court, or a Confidential Document Form in accordance with the Policy.

Note: Applicable authority includes but is not limited to statute, procedural rule, or court order. The Case Records Public Access Policy of the Unified Judicial System of Pennsylvania (Policy) can be found on the website of the Supreme Court of Pennsylvania at http://www.pacourts.us/public-records. Sections 7.0(D) and 8.0(D) of the Policy provide that the certification shall be in substantially the following form:

I certify that this filing complies with the provisions of the Case Records Public Access Policy of the Unified Judicial System of Pennsylvania that require filing confidential information and documents differently than non-confidential information and documents.

The Confidential Information Form and the Confidential Doc-ument Form can be found at http://www.pacourts.us/public-records. In lieu of the Confidential Information Form, Section 7.0(C) of the Policy provides for a court to adopt a rule or order permitting the filing of a document in two versions, a "Redacted Version" and an "Unredacted Version."

Adopted Dec. 2, 1994, effective March 1, 1995. Amended Jan. 5, 2018, effective Jan. 6, 2018; June 1, 2018, effective July 1, 2018.

RULE 1930.2.   NO POST-TRIAL PRACTICE.
MOTIONS FOR RECONSIDERATION.

(a) There shall be no motions for post-trial relief in any domestic relations matter, including Protection of Victims of Sexual Violence or Intimidation matters.

Note:

Pa.R.C.P. No. 1957.

(b) A party aggrieved by the decision of the court may file a motion for reconsideration in accordance with Pa.R.A.P 1701(b)(3). If the court does not grant the motion for reconsideration within the time permitted, the time for filing a notice of appeal will run as if the motion for reconsideration had never been presented to the court.

Note:

Pennsylvania Rule of Appellate Procedure 903 states that the Notice of Appeal shall be filed within 30 days after the entry of the order from which the appeal is taken, except as otherwise set forth in that rule.

(c) The court shall render its reconsidered decision within 120 days of the date the motion for reconsideration is granted, except as set forth in subdivision (e). If the court's decision is not rendered within 120 days, the motion shall be deemed denied.

(d) If the court does not enter a reconsidered decision within 120 days, the time for filing a notice of appeal will begin to run anew from the date of entry of the reconsidered decision or from the 121st day after the motion for reconsideration was granted.

(e) If the court grants the motion for reconsideration and files its order within the 30–day appeal period, the court may issue an order during the applicable 120–day period directing that additional testimony be taken. If the court issues an order for additional testimony, the reconsidered decision need not be rendered within 120 days, and the time for filing a notice of appeal will run from the date the reconsidered decision is rendered.

[Adopted March 30, 1994, effective July 1, 1994; amended October 6, 2016, effective January 1, 2017.]

Explanatory Comment—1994

All post-trial practice in domestic relations cases is abolished by this rule. In order to allow the trial court to take a second look at a case before it is appealed to the Superior Court, the rule allows a request for reconsideration to be filed in accordance with Appellate Rule 1701(b)

(3). The aim of these rules is to ensure that domestic cases are moved as quickly as possible toward a final resolution, and thus the requirement of Appellate Rule 1701 that the motion for reconsideration be filed and granted within the third day appeal period is adopted here. If the motion for reconsideration is granted, the time for filing the notice of appeal is tolled. However, if it is not granted, there is no extension of the appeal period, so that the matter proceeds without delay.

If the court grants the motion for reconsideration, it has 120 days in which to enter a reconsidered decision. The appeal period begins to run anew upon the entry of the reconsidered decision, or on the 121st day if the decision is not entered within the 120 day period. The time limit does not apply where the court determines that it is necessary to take additional testimony. In that event, the time for filing a notice of appeal begins to run anew when the reconsidered decision is entered.

RULE 1930.3.   TESTIMONY BY ELECTRONIC MEANS.

With the approval of the court upon good cause shown, a party or witness may be deposed or testify by telephone, audiovisual or other electronic means at a designated location in all domestic relations matters.

Adopted Dec. 8, 1994, effective July 1, 1995. Amended May 31, 2000, effective July 1, 2000.

Explanatory Comment—2000

This rule is amended to implement 23 Pa.C.S. § 4342(j) which sets forth the various electronic methods that may be used to take testimony in an action for support. It also extends these methods to all domestic relations matters.

RULE 1930.4.   SERVICE OF ORIGINAL PROCESS IN DOMESTIC RELATIONS MATTERS.

(a) *Persons Who May Serve*. Original process in all domestic relations matters, including Protection of Victims of Sexual Violence or Intimidation matters, may be served by the sheriff or a competent adult:

(1) by handing a copy to the defendant;

(2) by handing a copy:

(i) at the residence of the defendant to an adult member of the family with whom the defendant resides; but if no adult member of the family is found, then to an adult person in charge of such residence;

(ii) at the residence of the defendant to the clerk or manager of the hotel, inn, apartment house, boarding house or other place of lodging at which the defendant resides;

(iii) at any office or usual place of business of the defendant to the defendant's agent or to the person for the time being in charge; or

(3) pursuant to special order of court.

Note:

Pa.R.C.P. No. 76 for the definition of "competent adult." Original process served on an incarcerated person in a domestic relations action must also include notice of any hearing in such action and specific notice of the incarcerated individual's right to apply to the court for a writ of to enable him or her to participate in the hearing. The writ is available if an incarcerated individual wishes to testify as provided by statute or rule, or if the incarcerated individual's testimony is sought by another. , 526 A.2d 1226 (Pa. Super. 1987). *See* 23 Pa.C.S. § 4342(j) and Pa.R.C.P. No. 1930.3. In determining whether a writ of should be issued, a court must weigh the factors set forth in , 554 A.2d 563 (Pa. Super. 1989).

(b) *Service in Protection From Abuse and Protection of Victims of Sexual Violence or Intimidation Matters*. If personal service cannot be completed within 48 hours after a Protection From Abuse or a Protection of Victims of Sexual Violence or Intimidation petition is filed, the court may authorize alternative service by special order as set forth in subdivision (a)(3), including, but not limited to, service by mail pursuant to subdivision (c) of this rule.

(c) *Service by Mail*.

(1) Except in Protection from Abuse and Protection of Victims of Sexual Violence or Intimidation matters, original process in all domestic relations matters may be served by mailing the original process, a notice or order to appear, if required, and other orders

or documents, as necessary, to the defendant's last known address by both regular and certified mail.

(i) Delivery of the certified mail shall be restricted to the addressee only and a return receipt shall be requested.

(ii) If the certified mail is refused by the defendant, but the regular mail is not returned within 15 days, service may be deemed complete.

(iii) If the mail is returned with notation by the postal authorities that it was unclaimed, service shall be made by another means pursuant to these rules.

(2) In Protection from Abuse and Protection of Victims of Sexual Violence or Intimidation matters, original process may be served by mail pursuant to this rule, if authorized by the court under subdivision (a)(3).

Note:

Nothing in this rule is intended to preclude a judicial district from utilizing the United States Postal Service's return receipt electronic option, or any similar service that electronically provides a return receipt, when using certified mail, return receipt requested.

(d) *Acceptance of Service.* In lieu of service pursuant to this rule, the defendant or the defendant's authorized agent may accept service of original process as set forth in Pa.R.C.P. No. 402(b).

(e) *Service Within the Commonwealth.* Original process shall be served on a defendant located within the Commonwealth within 30 days of the filing of the original process.

(f) *Service Outside of the Commonwealth.* Original process shall be served on a defendant located outside the Commonwealth within 90 days of the filing of the original process:

(1) by any means authorized by this rule;
(2) in the manner provided by the law of the jurisdiction in which defendant will be served;
(3) in the manner provided by treaty; or
(4) as directed by the foreign authority in response to a letter rogatory or request.

In Protection from Abuse matters, a defendant outside of the Commonwealth must be personally served with original process Service may be made either in accordance with subdivisions (a) and (b) governing personal service or as provided for by the law in the jurisdiction where the defendant resides or is located. If personal service cannot be completed within 48 hours after the filing of the original process, service outside of the Commonwealth may be made by other means authorized by this rule.

Note:

Sections 5323 and 5329(2) of the Judicial Code, 42 Pa.C.S. §§ 5323 and 5329(2), provide additional alternative procedures for service outside the Commonwealth. For Protection from Abuse matters, personal service outside of the Commonwealth must be attempted first before service can be made by certified and regular mail or by other means prescribed in subsection (f) for out-of-state service.

(g) *Reinstatement of Original Process.* If service is not made as required by subdivision (e) or (f), the prothonotary shall reinstate the original process upon praecipe accompanied by the original process, or praecipe indicating that the original process has been lost or destroyed accompanied by a substituted original process.

(1) Original process may be reinstated at any time and any number of times. A new party defendant may be named in a reinstated original process.

(2) Reinstated original process shall be served as required by subdivision (e) or (f).

(h) *Proof of Service.*

(1) Proof of service shall state:

(i) the date and time of service;

(ii) the place of service;

(iii) the manner in which service was made;

(iv) the identity of the person served; and

(v) other facts necessary for the court to determine whether proper service has been made.

(2) *Original Process Served.*

(i) *Personal Service Pursuant to Subdivision (a).*

(A) The person serving the original process shall complete a proof of service.

(B) If a person other than a sheriff serves the original process, the proof of service shall be by an affidavit.

(C) The proof of service shall be filed in the appropriate filing office within 10 days of the date of service.

(ii) *Service by Mail Pursuant to Subdivision (c).*

(A) Proof of service by mail shall be by an affidavit that includes the certified mail return receipt signed by the defendant except as set forth in (B).

(B) If the defendant has refused to accept the certified mail, the proof of service shall include the returned envelope with the notation that the defendant refused to accept delivery and an affidavit stating that the regular mail was not returned within 15 days after mailing.

(C) The proof of service shall be filed in the appropriate filing office within 10 days of the date the defendant signed the certified mail return receipt or after the passage of time set forth in subdivision (c)(1)(ii).

(iii) *Acceptance of Service Pursuant to Subdivision (d).*

(A) If the defendant or the defendant's authorized agent accepts service of the original process as set forth in subdivision (d), the defendant or the defendant's authorized agent shall sign an Acceptance of Service.

(B) The Acceptance of Service shall be filed in the appropriate filing office within 10 days of accepting service.

Official Note: See Pa.R.C.P. No. 402(b) for the prescribed form document.

(3) *Original Process Not Served.*

(i) If the defendant cannot be served within the time allowed in subdivision (e) or (f), the person attempting service shall complete a proof of no service promptly.

(ii) If a person other than a sheriff attempts service of the original process, the proof of no service shall be by an affidavit stating with particularity the efforts made to effect service.

(iii) The proof of no service shall be filed in the appropriate filing office within 10 days of the expiration of time allowed for service in subdivision (e) or (f).

Official Note: See Pa.R.C.P. No. 1910.4(a). The Domestic Relations Section is the filing office for child support, spousal support and alimony pendente lite cases.

See Pennsylvania Rule of Professional Conduct 7.3(b)(4). The timing of an attorney's solicitation of a prospective client in actions governed by the Family Court Rules, see Pa.R.C.P. No. 1931(a), and actions pursuant to the Protection of Victims of Sexual Violence or Intimidation Act, see 42 Pa.C.S. §§ 62A03—62A20, is restricted until proof of service appears on the docket.

(i) *Appearance at Hearing or Conference.* A party appearing for the hearing or conference will be deemed to have been served.

Adopted Oct. 2, 1995, effective Jan. 1, 1996. Amended March 9, 1998, effective July 1, 1998; May 14, 1999, effective July 1, 1999; Oct. 11, 2002, imd. effective; Aug. 8, 2006, imd. effective; March 4, 2014, effective April 3, 2014; March 4, 2015, effective April 3, 2015; October 6, 2016, effective January 1, 2017; September 12, 2018, effective September 28, 2018.

Explanatory Comment—1995

This new rule replaces the numerous rules which previously governed service of process in domestic relations matters.

RULE 1930.5.   DISCOVERY IN DOMESTIC RELATIONS MATTERS.

(a) There shall be no discovery in a simple support, custody, Protection from Abuse, or Protection of Victims of Sexual Violence or Intimidation proceedings unless authorized by order of court.

(b) Discovery shall be available without leave of court in accordance with Pa.R.C.P. Nos. 4001-4025 in alimony, equitable distribution, counsel fee and expense, and complex support proceedings.

Adopted May 5, 1997, effective July 1, 1997; amended March 9, 1998, effective July 1, 1998, March 2, 2000, effective immediately; June 5, 2001, effective immediately; October 6, 2016, effective January 1, 2017.

Explanatory Comment—1997

Whether a support case is complex is to be determined by motion before the court for a separate listing pursuant to Rules 1910.11(j)(1) and 1910.12(c)(1). It is not necessary, however, to have a case listed separately on grounds of complexity of factual or legal issues in order to engage in discovery. If discovery is needed in a support case which does not require a separate listing, the court should grant leave to engage in it.

Explanatory Comment—2000

Subdivision (b) has been amended to clarify that the adjective "complex" applies only to a support proceeding.

RULE 1930.6.   PATERNITY ACTIONS. SCOPE. VENUE. COMMENCEMENT OF ACTION.

(a) This rule shall govern the procedure by which a putative father may initiate a civil action to establish paternity and seek genetic testing. Such an action shall not be permitted if an order already has been entered as to the paternity, custody, or support of the child, or if a support or custody action to which the putative father is a party is pending.

(b) An action may be brought only in the county in which the defendant or the child(ren) reside.

(c) An action shall be commenced by filing a verified complaint to establish paternity and for genetic testing substantially in the form set forth in subdivision (1). The complaint shall have as its first page the Notice of Hearing and Order set forth in subdivision (2).

Note: See **Pa.R.C.P. No. 1930.1(b)**. This rule may require attorneys or unrepresented parties to file confidential documents and documents containing confidential information that are subject to the Case Records *Public Access Policy of the Unified Judicial System of Pennsylvania.*

(1) The complaint filed in a civil action to establish paternity shall be substantially in the following form:

(Caption)

COMPLAINT TO ESTABLISH PATERNITY AND FOR GENETIC TESTING

Plaintiff, _____ requests genetic testing to establish paternity pursuant to 23 Pa. C.S. § 4343 and in support of that request states that:

1. Plaintiff is an adult individual who resides at _____

_____

_____

2. Defendant is an adult individual who resides at _____

_____

_____

3. Defendant is the natural mother and Plaintiff believes that he may be the natural father of the following child(ren):

Child's Name   Date of Birth

_____   _____

_____   _____

4. The above-named children reside at the following address with the following individuals:

Address   Person(s) Living with Child   Relationship to Child

_____

_____

5. Defendant was/was not married at the time the child(ren) was/ were conceived or born.

6. Defendant is/is not now married. If married, spouse's name: _____

_____

7. There is/is not a custody, support or other action involving the paternity of the above-named child(ren) now pending in any jurisdiction. Identify any such actions by caption and docket number

_____

8. There has/has not been a determination by any court as to the paternity of the child(ren) in any prior support, custody, divorce or any other action. If so, identify the action by caption and docket number _____

9. Plaintiff agrees to pay all costs associated with genetic testing directly to the testing facility in accordance with the procedures established by that facility.

Wherefore, Plaintiff requests that the court order Defendant to submit to genetic testing and to make the child(ren) available for genetic testing.

I verify that the statements made in this complaint are true and correct to the best of my knowledge, information and belief. I understand that false statements herein are made subject to the penalties of 18 Pa. C.S. § 4904 relating to unsworn falsification to authorities.

_____
Petitioner

(2) The Notice of Hearing and Order required by this rule shall be substantially in the following form:

(Caption)

NOTICE OF HEARING AND ORDER

YOU HAVE BEEN SUED IN COURT. If you wish to defend against the claims set forth in the following papers, you must appear at the hearing scheduled below. If you fail to do so, the case may proceed against you and a final order may be entered against you granting the relief requested by the plaintiff.

Plaintiff and Defendant are directed to appear on the _____ day of _____, 20__ at __.m. in courtroom _____ for a hearing on Plaintiff's request for genetic testing. If you fail to appear as ordered, the court may enter an order in your absence requiring you and your child(ren) to submit to genetic tests.

YOU SHOULD TAKE THIS PAPER TO YOUR LAWYER AT ONCE. IF YOU DO NOT HAVE A LAWYER, GO TO OR TELEPHONE THE OFFICE SET FORTH BELOW. THIS OFFICE CAN PROVIDE YOU WITH INFORMATION ABOUT HIRING A LAWYER. IF YOU CANNOT AFFORD TO HIRE A LAWYER, THIS OFFICE MAY BE ABLE TO PROVIDE YOU WITH INFORMATION ABOUT AGENCIES THAT MAY OFFER LEGAL SERVICES TO ELIGIBLE PERSONS AT A REDUCED FEE OR NO FEE.

(name)

_____

(address)

_____

(telephone number)

_____

AMERICANS WITH DISABILITIES ACT OF 1990

The Court of Common Pleas of _____ County is required by law to comply with the Americans with Disabilities Act of 1990. For infor-mation about accessible facilities and reasonable accommodations available to disabled individuals having business before the court, please contact our office. All arrangements must be made at least 72 hours prior to any hearing or business before the court. You must attend the scheduled conference or hearing.

(d) Service. Service of original process and proof of service in a civil action to establish paternity shall be in accordance with Rule 1930.4.

(e) Hearing and Order. At the hearing, the judge will determine whether or not the plaintiff is legally entitled to genetic testing and, if so, will issue an order directing the defendant and the child(ren) to submit to genetic testing, the cost of which shall be borne by the plaintiff.

Adopted June 15, 2001, imd. effective. Amended June 24, 2002, imd. effective; March 18, 2004, effective June 16, 2004; Jan. 5, 2018, effective Jan. 6, 2018; June 1, 2018, effective July 1, 2018.

EXPLANATORY COMMENT—2001

Where the paternity of a child born out-of-wedlock is disputed, 23 Pa.C.S. § 4343 provides that the court shall make the determination of paternity in a civil action without a jury. That statutory provision also states, "A putative father may not be prohibited from initiating a civil action to establish paternity." Rule 1930.6 governs the procedures by which a putative father may initiate a civil action to establish paternity outside the context of a support or custody proceeding.

RULE 1930.7.   STATUS CONFERENCE.

At any time in the proceedings, the court, the court's designee or the master, sua sponte or upon application of any party, may hold a status conference, in person or by any other means permitted by these rules, with counsel or with counsel and the parties in order to review the case status and expedite the litigation.

Adopted August 18, 2006, effective immediately.

RULE 1930.8.   SELF-REPRESENTED PARTY

(a) A party representing himself or herself shall enter a written appearance which shall state an address, which need not be his or her home address, where the party agrees that pleadings and other legal papers may be served, and a telephone number through which the party may be contacted. The entry of appearance may include a facsimile number as provided by Pa.R.C.P. No. 1012.

(b) A self-represented party is under a continuing obligation to provide current contact information to the court, to other self-represented parties, and to attorneys of record.

(c) When a party has an attorney of record, the party may assert his or her self-representation by:

(1) Filing a written entry of appearance and directing the prothonotary/court clerk to remove the name of his or her counsel of record with contemporaneous notice to said counsel, or

(2) Filing an entry of appearance with the withdrawal of appearance signed by his or her attorney of record.

(d) The self-represented party shall provide a copy of the entry of appearance to all self-represented parties and attorneys of record.

(e) The assertion of self-representation shall not delay any stage of the proceeding.

(f) The entry of appearance of a self-represented party shall be substantially in the following form:

[CAPTION]

ENTRY OF APPEARANCE OF SELF-REPRESENTED PARTY PURSUANT TO Pa.R.C.P. No. 1930.8

I, _____, Plaintiff or Defendant (circle one), represent myself in the within action.

REMOVAL OR WITHDRAWAL OF COUNSEL OF RECORD (If Applicable)

___ Remove _____, Esq., as my attorney of record.

___ Withdraw my appearance for the filing party.

          Esq. (Print name)   ID#

          SIGNATURE   DATE:

I understand that I am under a continuing obligation to provide current contact information to the court, to other self-represented parties, and to attorneys of record.

All pleadings and legal papers can be served on me at the address listed below, which may or may not be my home address pursuant to Rule 1930.8:

Print Name

Signature   Telephone number

Address   FAX

City, State, Zip Code   Date

THE PARTY FILING THIS ENTRY OF APPEARANCE MUST PROVIDE NOTICE BY SENDING A COPY TO ALL PARTIES AND ATTORNEYS, INCLUDING THE ATTORNEY REMOVED FROM THE CASE.

Official Note:

This form cannot be used when filing for support through the Department of Public Welfare Bureau of Child Support Enforcement's E-Services program. An entry of appearance form is available on the E-Services site for individuals filing through that program.

Adopted June 5, 2013, effective July 5, 2013. Amended March 4, 2015, effective April 3, 2015.

Explanatory Comment—2013

Withdrawal of appearance by counsel of record without the entry of appearance by a self-represented party is governed by Pa.R.C.P. No. 1012. Service of original process in domestic relations matters is governed by Pa.R.C.P. No. 1930.4. Service of legal papers other than original process is governed by Pa.R.C.P. No. 440.

RULE 1930.9. FAMILY COURT FORMS

Forms adopted by the Supreme Court of Pennsylvania and included in the Pennsylvania Rules of Civil Procedure relating to the practice and procedure of domestic relations matters shall be accepted for filing in all jurisdictions. Some of these forms may be maintained for public access at a website designated by the Supreme Court of Pennsylvania.

Note: Pa.R.C.P. No. 205.2 provides: "No pleading or other legal paper that complies with the Pennsylvania Rules of Civil Procedure shall be refused for filing by the prothonotary based on a requirement of a local rule of civil procedure or judicial administration . . ."

Adopted June 16, 2014, effective July 16, 2014.

RULE 1931. FAMILY COURT RULES.

(a)   **Actions Governed by These Rules:**

    (1) Divorce, Annulment, Dissolution of Marriage.

        (i) Equitable Distribution.

        (ii) Alimony/Alimony Pendente Lite.

        (iii) Counsel Fees, Costs and Expenses.

    (2) Child Custody.

        (i) Legal Custody.

        (ii) Physical Custody.

        (iii) Partial Custody/Visitation.

    (3) Support.

        (i) Child Support.

        (ii) Spousal Support.

        (iii) Modification and Enforcement.

    (4) Paternity.

    (5) Protection From Abuse.

(b)   Commencement of Action.

(1) Unified Family Court Docketing. All actions under these Family Court Rules which involve identical parties shall be entered on the court's docket under the same primary case number. Additional letters or numbers may be added parenthetically to specify the type of action, judge assigned or other identifying information.

(2) Custody Agreements. If, at a support proceeding, it appears that resolution of custody issues will facilitate compliance with the child support order, the conference officer, hearing officer or master may provide the parties with a form custody complaint and form custody agreement, along with information as to where to file the completed documents, the filing fee and how to contact the lawyers referral service. The support conference officer, hearing officer or master shall not participate in custody negotiations, preparation of the forms or provide legal advice.

(c)   Consolidation of Family Court Matters.

(1) General Rule. Two or more actions under these Family Court Rules involving the same parties and common questions of law and/or fact shall be consolidated for hearing or trial unless the court determines that it is inappropriate or impractical to do so.

(2) Trial Continuity. Trials before a judge or hearings before a master shall be scheduled to be heard on consecutive days or within a ten (10) day period. If not completed within the time allotted, the trial or hearing shall be concluded within ninety (90) days of the date of the commencement of the trial or hearing, unless a shorter time frame is required by statute or another procedural rule.

(3) Prompt Decisions.

(i) Except as provided in subdivision (ii) below, in any matter brought under these Family Court Rules, a decision by a conference officer, master or judge shall be entered, filed and served upon counsel for the parties, or any party not represented by counsel, not later than thirty (30) days after the conference, hearing or trial concludes, unless a shorter time frame is required by statute or another procedural rule.

(ii) The time for entering and filing a decision may be extended if, within thirty (30) days of the conclusion of the conference, hearing or trial, the court extends the date for such decision by order entered of record showing good cause for the extension. In no event shall an extension delay entry of the decision more than sixty (60) days after the conclusion of the conference, hearing or trial.

(d)   **Continuing Education for Family Court Personnel.**

(1) **Program Development.** Courses of instruction that include, at a minimum, the following topics shall be developed or approved by the Administrative Office of Pennsylvania Courts (AOPC):

(i) The substantive law and procedural aspects of the areas of law governed by these Family Court Rules;

(ii) Domestic violence;

(iii) Child development;

(iv) Family dynamics;

(v) Addictions and treatments;

(vi) Asset valuation;

(vii) Community resources.

(2) **Initial Training.** Within one (1) year of assignment to cases governed by these Family Court Rules, each master, hearing officer, conciliator, mediator and other court personnel designated by the president or administrative judge of each judicial district shall successfully complete the coursework developed or approved by the AOPC.

(3) **Continuing Education.** Each master, hearing officer, conciliator, mediator and other court personnel designated

by the president or administrative judge who is assigned to cases governed by these Family Court Rules shall successfully complete six (6) hours of continuing education developed or approved by the AOPC each calendar year following the calendar year in which the initial training was completed.

(4) Compliance. The AOPC shall monitor compliance with the educational requirements of this rule.

Explanatory Comment 2002

This new rule is suspended in all judicial districts except the First (Philadelphia), Fifth (Allegheny County), Twenty-third (Berks County) and Forty-fifth (Lackawanna County) Judicial Districts until further order of the Supreme Court of Pennsylvania.

(December 17, 2002, effective immediately in the First, Fifth, Twenty-Third and Forty-Fifth Judicial Districts).

RULES RELATING TO VOLUNTARY MEDIATION IN CUSTODY ACTIONS (AMENDED THROUGH SEPTEMBER 30, 2020)

RULE

EXPLANATORY COMMENT

Introduction

In recent years, the use of mediation as a means for alternative dispute resolution of custody and visitation cases has received widespread attention from legislators, judges, attorneys, and mental health professionals. As two noted mediation experts observed: "[c]ourts are ill-equipped to mandate particular visitation schedules and custodial arrangements, the wisdom of which depend on the situations of the parents and children rather than on legal rules." Nancy G. Rogers & Craig A. McEwen, Mediation Law Policy Practice 230 (1989). Many share this frustration with the adversarial system and a growing body of research suggests that mediation may be the more satisfactory and desirable means of conflict resolution in these cases. Mediation offers more flexibility both in terms of the subject matter that may be discussed during mediation and the range of solutions available to the parties. Effective mediation also assists the parties in shaping their own framework for future discussion and resolution of conflicts that arise following separation and divorce.

In 1996, the Pennsylvania legislature amended the Divorce Code, Act No. 20-1996, § 2, codified at 23 Pa.C.S. §§ 3901–3904, to encourage local courts to establish voluntary mediation programs for divorce and custody cases. The following Rules of Civil Procedure are intended to govern custody cases only. They set forth the procedures for referring cases to mediation, minimum mediator qualifications, the duties of the mediator, the procedures for terminating mediation as well as sanctions for noncompliance with these rules. These are all areas in which statewide uniformity of practice and procedure is essential to successful mediation in Pennsylvania. These rules are flexibly designed to encourage the establishment of mediation programs.

Pursuant to 23 Pa.C.S. § 3903, the Supreme Court is directed to monitor and evaluate the overall effectiveness of mediation programs statewide. At present, the Domestic Relations Procedural Rules Committee is working on the development of uniform statewide reporting requirements and evaluation forms. Reporting is necessary to assess the overall effectiveness of mediation as an alternative to litigation and it will eventually be required. The current lack of reporting requirements, however, should not be a cause for delay in the establishment of mediation programs or the implementation of statewide mediation rules.

These rules do not address confidentiality and privilege in the context of mediation. Those issues are governed by 42 Pa.C.S. § 5949, and the Committee concluded that to address them further in the rules would confuse rather than clarify any legal issues arising from the statutory language.

RULE 1940.1.   APPLICABILITY OF RULES TO MEDIATION.

The rules in this chapter shall apply to all court-established custody mediation programs and to any court-ordered mediation of individual custody cases.

Explanatory Comment—1999

23 Pa.C.S. § 3901 authorizes a court to establish a mediation program for both divorce and custody cases. At the present time, these rules apply only to court-connected mediation of custody cases because most, if not all, court-connected mediation programs that have been established for domestic relations, are limited to mediation of custody disputes. If, in the

future, these programs expand to include mediation of divorce issues, these rules will be revised accordingly.

These rules do not apply to private mediation, which may be agreed to by the parties and conducted independent of the custody proceeding. They do apply, however, whenever the court refers a custody case for mediation, regardless of whether the referral is made to a formal program established and operated by the court or to a less formal arrangement between courts and mediators such as a court-approved list of mediators or, in the absence of such a list, to individual mediators appointed by the court to mediate particular cases.

RULE 1940.2.   DEFINITIONS.

As used in this Chapter, the following terms shall have the following meanings:

"Mediation," the confidential process by which a neutral mediator assists the parties in attempting to reach a mutually acceptable agreement on issues arising in a custody action. Mediation is not a court proceeding; rather, it is an independent, non-record proceeding in lieu of court involvement for the purpose of assisting the parties to address the child's best interest. An agreement reached by the parties must be based on the voluntary decisions of the parties and not the decision of the mediator. The agreement may resolve all or only some of the disputed issues. The parties are required to mediate in good faith but are not compelled to reach an agreement. While mediation is an alternative means of conflict resolution, it is not a substitute for the benefit of legal advice. The participants in mediation shall be limited to the parties to the custody action, primarily the child's parents and persons acting as parents. Except as provided in Pa.R.C.P. No. 1940.5(c), nonparties, including children, grandparents, and the parties' attorneys, shall not participate in the mediation.

Note: See Pa.R.C.P. No. 1915.1 for the definition of a person acting as a parent.

"Memorandum of Understanding," the written document prepared by a mediator that contains and summarizes the resolution

857

reached by the parties during mediation. A Memorandum of Understanding is primarily for the benefit of the parties and is not legally binding on either party.

"Orientation Session," the initial process of educating the parties on the mediation process so that they can make an informed choice about continued participation in mediation. This process may be mandated by the court and may be structured to include either group or individual sessions. An orientation session may also include an educational program for parents and children on the process of divorce and separation and the benefits of mediation in resolving custody disputes.

Adopted Oct. 28, 1999, imd. effective. Amended Feb. 8, 2018, effective April 1, 2018.

EXPLANATORY COMMENT—1999

The definitions of "orientation session" and "mediation" follow the legislative distinction between the initial orientation session, which the court may order the parties to attend, and actual mediation of the issues in dispute by the parties, which may be ordered only upon the parties' agreement. See 23 Pa.C.S. § 3901(b). The purpose of the orientation session is to educate the parties on the availability of mediation, the advantages and disadvantages of mediation, and the process of mediation so that the parties can make an informed decision about whether they wish to proceed further with mediation.

The definition of mediation set forth in this rule is not intended to restrict, expand or otherwise modify the statutory definition of mediation in 42 Pa.C.S. § 5949(c) relating to confidentiality. The statutory provision defines mediation for the purpose of determining when confidentiality and privilege attach to communications made or documents submitted during a mediation session.

RULE 1940.3.   ORDER FOR ORIENTATION SESSION AND MEDIATION. SELECTION OF MEDIATOR.

(a) Except as provided in (b), the court may order the parties to attend an orientation session at any time upon motion by a party, stipulation of the parties, or the court's own initiative.

(b) The court may not order an orientation session if a party or a child of either party is or has been the subject of domestic violence or child abuse either during the pendency of the action or within 24 months preceding the filing of the action.

Official Note:

See also Rule 1940.6(a)(4) requiring termination of mediation when the mediator finds that the proceeding is "inappropriate" for mediation. The mediator has a continuing ethical obligation, consistent with Rule 1940.4(b), during the mediation to screen for abuse and to terminate the mediation in the event he or she determines that the abuse renders the case unsuitable for mediation.

(c) Following the orientation session and with the consent of the parties, the court may refer the parties to mediation. The mediation may address any issues agreed to by the parties unless limited by court order.

Explanatory Comment—1999

Rule 1940.3 describes the circumstances under which a case may be referred to mediation. Consistent with 23 Pa.C.S. § 3901(c)(2), it prohibits the referral of any case involving past or present domestic violence or abuse because of the substantial imbalance of negotiating power that exists between the parties. The parties themselves, however, may always agree to mediation. Although each court may devise its own procedures for screening these cases, screening must occur prior to referral of a case to the orientation session.

RULE 1940.4.   MINIMUM QUALIFICATIONS OF THE MEDIATOR.

(a) A mediator must have at least the following qualifications:

(1) a bachelor's degree and practical experience in law, psychiatry, psychology, counseling, family therapy or any comparable behavioral or social science field;

(2) successful completion of basic training in domestic and family violence or child abuse and a divorce and custody mediation program approved by the Association for Conflict Resolution, American Bar Association, American Academy of Matrimonial Lawyers or Administrative Office of Pennsylvania Courts;

(3) mediation professional liability insurance; and

(4) additional mediation training consisting of a minimum of 4 mediated cases totaling 10 hours under the supervision of a mediator who has complied with subdivisions (1) through (3) above and is approved by the court to supervise other mediators.

(b) The mediator shall comply with the ethical standards of the mediator profession as well as those of his or her primary profession and complete at least 20 hours of continuing education every two years in topics related to family mediation.

(c) A post-graduate student enrolled in a state or federally accredited educational institution in the disciplines of law, psychiatry, psychology, counseling, family therapy or any comparable behavioral or social science field may mediate with direct and actual supervision by a qualified mediator.

Explanatory Comment—1999

Mediator qualifications are a key component of any successful mediation program. This rule sets forth the minimum qualifications that a mediator must have in order to participate in court-connected mediation. Local courts may impose additional, more stringent qualifications.

In addition to a bachelor's degree and practical experience, a mediator must have basic training in a program approved by one of the organizations listed in subdivision (a)(2). While these are the organizations which have been recommended by mediators and other training professionals, the Domestic Relations Procedural Rules Committee and the Administrative Office of Pennsylvania Courts may, from time to time, propose to the Court that additional organizations be added to this list. Subdivision (a)(3) of the rule requires the mediator to have his or her own professional liability insurance. Prior to mediating independently, subdivision (a)(4) of the rule requires that the mediator co-mediate at least four cases under the supervision of a court-connected mediator.

RULE 1940.5.   DUTIES OF THE MEDIATOR.
ROLE OF THE MEDIATOR.

(a) As part of the orientation session, the mediator must inform the parties in writing of the following:

(1) the costs of mediation;

Note: **Pa.R.C.P. No. 240** sets forth the procedures for obtaining leave to proceed *in forma pauperis* when the parties do not have the financial resources to pay the costs of litigation. This rule applies to court-connected mediation services as well, so that parties without sufficient resources may file a petition seeking a waiver or reduction of the costs of mediation.

(2) the process of mediation;

(3) that the mediator does not represent either or both of the parties;

(4) the nature and extent of any relationships with the parties and any personal, financial, or other interests that could result in a bias or conflict of interest;

(5) that mediation is not a substitute for the benefit of independent legal advice; and

(6) that the parties should obtain legal assistance for drafting any agreement or for reviewing any agreement drafted by the other party.

(b) When mediating a custody dispute, the mediator shall ensure that the parties consider fully the best interests of the child or children.

(c) With the consent of the parties, the mediator may meet with the parties' children or invite other persons to participate in the mediation.

(d) The role of the mediator is to assist the parties in identifying the issues, reducing misunderstandings, clarifying priorities, exploring areas of compromise, and finding points of agreement.

Adopted Oct. 28, 1999, imd. effective. Amended Feb. 8, 2018, effective April 1, 2018.

EXPLANATORY COMMENT—1999

Rule 1940.5 sets forth the mediator's responsibilities to the parties. Subdivision (c) permits the participation of third persons with the consent of both parties. Such persons would include attorneys, other family members, mental health professionals or any other person who may be of assistance in resolving the disputed issues.

RULE 1940.6.   TERMINATION OF MEDIATION.

(a) Mediation shall terminate upon the earliest of the following circumstances to occur:

(1) a determination by the mediator that the parties are unable to reach a resolution regarding all of the issues subject to mediation;

(2) a determination by the mediator that the parties have reached a resolution regarding all of the issues subject to mediation;

(3) a determination by the mediator that the parties have reached a partial resolution and that further mediation will not resolve the remaining issues subject to mediation; or

(4) a determination by the mediator that the proceedings are inappropriate for mediation.

(b) If the parties reach a complete or partial resolution, the mediator shall, within 14 days, prepare and transmit to the parties a Memorandum of Understanding. At the request of a party, the mediator shall also transmit a copy of the Memorandum of Understanding to the party's counsel.

(c) If no resolution is reached during mediation, the mediator shall, within 14 days, report this in writing to the court, without further explanation.

Explanatory Comment—1999

This rule sets forth the circumstances for termination of mediation. Subdivision (a)(4) reflects the mediator's continuing ethical obligation, consistent with Rule 1940.4(b), to screen for domestic violence, substance abuse and any other factors, which make the case unsuitable for mediation.

Subdivision (b) requires the mediator to prepare a Memorandum of Understanding, as that term is defined in Rule 1940.2.

Reducing the parties' resolution to a binding and enforceable agreement is accomplished either by the parties' attorneys or, if not represented, the parties themselves, but in no event is the mediator responsible for drafting the parties' agreement. Court approval of the final agreement is not necessary for the purpose of enforcing it to the same extent as a court order.

RULE 1940.7.   MEDIATOR COMPENSATION

Mediators shall be compensated for their services at a rate to be established by each court.

Explanatory Comment—1999

Mediator compensation is necessary to establish and maintain a quality mediation program. Presently, however, the absence of a statewide office for alternative dispute resolution means that each court must develop and secure its own funds for the mediation program. Because the availability of such funds varies significantly from court to court, each court may establish its own rate and method of compensation at this time, provided that the fees are structured so that all parties are assured equal access to mediation services. As Pennsylvania moves in the direction of a unified judicial system, a statewide fee schedule setting forth uniform fee standards may eventually be established for mediation compensation.

RULE 1940.8.   SANCTIONS.

On its own motion or a party's motion, the court may impose sanctions against any party or attorney who fails to comply or causes a party not to comply with these mediation rules. Sanctions may include an award of mediation costs and attorney fees, including those reasonably incurred in pursuing the sanctions.

Note: To the extent court orders are employed to direct parties regarding mediation, contempt proceedings may also be instituted to enforce these orders.

RULE 1940.9.   EXISTING MEDIATION PROGRAMS.

These rules shall not affect any existing mediation program established in any judicial district pursuant to local rule prior to October 29, 1999. However, any changes or amendments to any existing program shall be consistent with these rules.

Adopted October 27, 2000, effective immediately.

Explanatory Comment—2000

This new rule is consistent with 23 Pa. C.S. § 3904.

RULE 1953.   COMMENCEMENT OF ACTION.

(a) Except as provided in subdivision (b), an action shall be commenced by filing with the prothonotary a petition alleging the need for protection from the defendant with respect to sexual violence or intimidation. The petition shall be identical in content to the form set forth in Pa.R.C.P. No. 1959(b) and shall have the Notice of Hearing and Order set forth in Pa.R.C.P. No. 1959(a) as the first page(s).

(b) If an emergency order has been entered pursuant to 42 Pa.C.S. § 62A09, an action shall be commenced by filing with the prothonotary the certified emergency order and any documentation in support.

(c) Any fees associated with this action shall not be charged to the plaintiff.

Note: See **Pa.R.C.P. No. 1930.1(b). This rule may require attorneys or unrepresented parties to file confidential documents and documents containing confidential information that are subject to the Case Records** *Public Access Policy of the Unified Judicial System of Pennsylvania.*

Adopted June 29, 2015, effective July 1, 2015. Amended Jan. 5, 2018, effective Jan. 6, 2018; June 1, 2018, effective July 1, 2018.

RULE 1959.   FORMS FOR USE IN PROTECTION OF VICTIMS OF SEXUAL VIOLENCE OR INTIMIDATION ACTIONS. NOTICE AND HEARING. PETITION. TEMPORARY PROTECTION ORDER. FINAL PROTECTION ORDER.

(a) The Notice of Hearing and Order required by Pa.R.C.P. No. 1953 shall be identical in content to the following form:

(Caption)

NOTICE OF HEARING AND ORDER

YOU HAVE BEEN SUED IN COURT. If you wish to defend against the claims set forth in the following papers, you must appear at the hearing scheduled herein. If you fail to appear, the case may proceed against you and a FINAL order may be entered against you granting the relief requested in the petition.

A hearing on the matter is scheduled for the _____ day of _____, 20 ___ at _____ _.m. in Courtroom _____ at _____ Courthouse, _____, Pennsylvania.

If a temporary protection order has been entered, you MUST obey the order until it is modified or terminated by the court after notice and a hearing. If you disobey that order, the police or sheriff may arrest you. A violation of this order may subject you to a charge of indirect criminal contempt. A violation may also subject you to prosecution and criminal penalties under the Pennsylvania Crimes Code. Under 18 U.S.C. § 2265, an order entered by the court may be enforceable in all fifty (50) States, the District of Columbia, Tribal Lands, U.S. Territories and the Commonwealth of Puerto Rico. If you travel outside of the state and intentionally violate this order, you may be subject to federal criminal proceedings under the Violence Against Women Act, 18 U.S.C. § 2262.

YOU SHOULD TAKE THIS PAPER TO YOUR LAWYER IMMEDIATELY. YOU HAVE THE RIGHT TO HAVE A LAWYER REPRESENT YOU AT THE HEARING. THE COURT WILL NOT, HOWEVER, APPOINT A LAWYER FOR YOU. IF YOU DO NOT HAVE A LAWYER, GO TO OR CALL THE OFFICE SET FORTH BELOW. THIS OFFICE CAN PROVIDE YOU WITH

INFORMATION ABOUT HIRING A LAWYER. IF YOU CANNOT AFFORD TO HIRE A LAWYER, THIS OFFICE MAY BE ABLE TO PROVIDE YOU WITH INFORMATION ABOUT AGENCIES THAT MAY OFFER LEGAL SERVICES TO ELIGIBLE PERSONS AT A REDUCED FEE OR NO FEE. IF YOU CANNOT FIND A LAWYER, YOU MAY HAVE TO PROCEED WITHOUT ONE.

County Lawyer Referral Service
(insert Street Address)
(insert City, State, and ZIP)
(insert Phone Number)

AMERICANS WITH DISABILITIES ACT OF 1990

The Court of Common Pleas of _____ County is required by law to comply with the Americans with Disabilities Act of 1990. For information about accessible facilities and reasonable accommodations available to disabled individuals having business before the court, please contact our office. All arrangements must be made at least 72 hours prior to any hearing or business before the court. You must attend the scheduled conference or hearing.

BY THE COURT:

Date:_____   _____

Judge

(b) The petition in an action filed pursuant to the Act shall be identical in content to the following form:

(Caption)

PETITION FOR PROTECTION OF VICTIMS OF

☐   SEXUAL VIOLENCE

☐   SEXUAL VIOLENCE AGAINST A MINOR CHILD

☐   INTIMIDATION

1. Plaintiff:

_____

First   Middle   Last Name

Plaintiff's Address:

_____

_____

☐   Plaintiff's address is confidential pursuant to 42 Pa.C.S.
    § 62A11.

Plaintiff's Date of Birth: _____

I am filing this petition on behalf of ☐ myself or ☐ another person.

If you checked "myself," please answer all questions referring to yourself as "Plaintiff." If you checked "another person," please answer all questions referring to that person as "Plaintiff," and provide your name and address below.

Name:_____

Address:_____

If you checked "another person," indicate your relationship to the plaintiff: _____

2. Defendant:

DEFENDANT IDENTIFIERS

First	Middle	Last Name	DOB	HEIGHT
SEX	WEIGHT	RACE	EYES	HAIR

SSN _____

DRIVERS LICENSE #	EXP DATE	STATE

Defendant's Address:

_____

_____

3. Name(s) of other designated person(s) under 42 Pa.C.S. § 62A07(b)(1):

_____

_____

_____

4. Is there a relationship between Plaintiff and Defendant? _____.
If yes, what is the relationship?

_____

_____

_____

5. Have Plaintiff and Defendant been involved in any other legal proceedings? If so, state when and where the case was filed and the court docket number, if known:

_____

_____

_____

6. Has Defendant been involved in any criminal proceedings?

_____

_____

_____

If you answered Yes, is Defendant currently on probation or parole?

_____

7. (a) The facts of the most recent incident of sexual violence are as follows:

_____

_____

Approximate Date: _____

Approximate Time: _____

Place: _____

Describe in detail what happened, including any physical or sexual abuse, threats, injury, incidents of stalking, medical treatment sought, and/or calls to law enforcement (attach additional sheets of paper if necessary):

_____

_____

_____

(b) The facts of the most recent incident of intimidation are as follows:

_____

_____

Approximate Date: _____

Approximate Time: _____

Place: _____

Describe in detail what happened, including medical treatment sought, and/or calls to law enforcement (attach additional sheets of paper if necessary):

_____

_____

_____

8. If Defendant has committed prior acts of sexual violence or intimidation against Plaintiff, describe these prior incidents, and indicate approximately when such acts occurred (attach additional sheets of paper if necessary):

_____

_____

_____

9. Identify the sheriff, police department, or other law enforcement agency in the area in which Plaintiff lives that should be provided with a copy of the protection order:

_____

_____

_____

10. Is Plaintiff in immediate and present danger from Defendant? If so, please describe:

_____

_____

_____

FOR THE REASONS SET FORTH ABOVE, I REQUEST THAT THE COURT ENTER A TEMPORARY ORDER AND, AFTER A HEARING, A FINAL ORDER THAT WOULD INCLUDE ALL OF THE FOLLOWING RELIEF (CHECK ALL FORMS OF RELIEF REQUESTED):

☐ **A. Restrain Defendant from having any contact with the victim, including, but not limited to, entering the victim's residence, place of employment, business, or school.**

☐ **B. Prohibit indirect contact through third parties.**

☐ **C. Prohibit direct or indirect contact with other designated persons.**

☐ **D. Order Defendant to pay the fees of this action.**

☐ **E. Order the following additional relief, not listed above:**

_____

_____

_____

_____

☐ **F. Grant such other relief as the court deems appropriate, including, but not limited to, issuing an order under 42 Pa.C.S. § 62A11(b) related to the non-disclosure of the victim's address, telephone number, whereabouts or other demographic information.**

☐ **G. Order the police, sheriff or other law enforcement agency to serve the Defendant with a copy of this petition, any order issued, and the order for the hearing. Plaintiff will inform the designated authority of any addresses, other than Defendant's residence, where Defendant can be served.**

VERIFICATION

I verify that the statements made in this petition are true and correct to the best of my knowledge. I understand that false statements herein are made subject to the penalties of 18 Pa.C.S. § 4904, relating to unsworn falsification to authorities.

_____

Signature   Date

Note: See Pa.R.C.P. No. 1930.1(b). This rule may require attorneys or unrepresented parties to file confidential documents and documents containing confidential information that are subject to the Case Records *Public Access Policy of the Unified Judicial System of Pennsylvania.*

(c) The Temporary Order of Court, or any continued, amended or modified Temporary Order of Court, entered pursuant to the Act shall be identical in content to the following form:

(Caption)

TEMPORARY ORDER FOR PROTECTION
OF VICTIMS OF

• SEXUAL VIOLENCE

• SEXUAL VIOLENCE AGAINST A MINOR CHILD

• INTIMIDATION

1. Plaintiff:

_____

First   Middle   Last Name

Plaintiff's Address:

_____

_____

☐ Plaintiff's address is confidential pursuant to 42 Pa.C.S. § 62A11.

Defendant:

DEFENDANT IDENTIFIERS

First	Middle	Last Name	DOB	HEIGHT

SEX	WEIGHT	RACE	EYES	HAIR

SSN _____

DRIVERS LICENSE #	EXP DATE	STATE

Defendant's Address:

_____

_____

AND NOW, this _____ day of _____, 20 ___, upon consideration of the attached Petition for Protection of Victims of Sexual Violence or Intimidation, the court hereby enters the following Temporary Order:

☐ Plaintiff's request for a Temporary Protection Order is denied.

☐ Plaintiff's request for a Temporary Protection Order is granted.

1. The following person is protected under this order:

_____

2. Defendant is:

☐ A. Restrained from having any contact with the victim, including, but not limited to, entering the victim's residence, place of employment, business, or school.

☐ B. Prohibited from indirect contact with the victim through third parties.

☐ C. Prohibited from direct or indirect contact with the following designated persons:

_____

☐ 3. Additional relief, including, but not limited to, issuing an order under 42 Pa.C.S. § 62A11(b) related to the non-disclosure of the victim's address, telephone number, whereabouts or other demographic information:

_____

_____

_____

_____

☐ 4. A certified copy of this order shall be provided to the sheriff or police department where Plaintiff resides and any other agency specified (insert name of agency):

_____

☐ 5. THIS ORDER SUPERSEDES ANY PRIOR PROTECTION OF VICTIMS OF SEXUAL VIOLENCE OR INTIMIDATION ORDER OBTAINED BY THE SAME PLAINTIFF AGAINST THE SAME DEFENDANT.

☐ 6. THIS ORDER APPLIES IMMEDIATELY TO THE DEFENDANT AND SHALL REMAIN IN EFFECT UNTIL _____ (insert expiration date) OR UNTIL OTHERWISE MODIFIED OR TERMINATED BY THIS COURT AFTER NOTICE AND A HEARING.

NOTICE TO THE DEFENDANT

Defendant is hereby notified that violation of this order may result in arrest for indirect criminal contempt. Under 18 U.S.C. § 2265, an order entered by the court may be enforceable in all fifty (50) States, the District of Columbia, Tribal Lands, U.S. Territories and the Commonwealth of Puerto Rico. If you travel outside of the state and intentionally violate this order, you may be subject to federal criminal proceedings under the Violence Against Women Act, 18 U.S.C. § 2262. Consent of Plaintiff shall not invalidate this order, which can only be changed or modified through the filing of appropriate court papers for that purpose. 42 Pa.C.S. § 62A17. Defendant is further notified that violation of this order may subject him/her to prosecution and criminal penalties under the Pennsylvania Crimes Code.

873

NOTICE TO SHERIFF, POLICE AND
LAW ENFORCEMENT OFFICIALS

The police department and sheriff who have jurisdiction over Plaintiff's residence, the location where a violation of this order occurs, or where Defendant may be located, shall enforce this order. The court shall have jurisdiction over any indirect criminal contempt proceeding, either in the county where the violation occurred or where this protective order was entered. An arrest for violation of paragraphs 2 and 3 of this order may be without warrant, based solely on probable cause, whether or not the violation is committed in the presence of the police or any sheriff. 42 Pa.C.S. § 62A12.

When Defendant is placed under arrest for violation of the order, Defendant shall be taken to the appropriate authority or authorities before whom Defendant is to be arraigned. A "Complaint for Indirect Criminal Contempt" shall then be completed and signed by the police officer, sheriff or Plaintiff. Plaintiff's presence and signature are not required to file the complaint.

If sufficient grounds for violation of this order are alleged: (1) Defendant shall be arraigned; (2) bond set, if appropriate; and (3) both parties shall be given notice of the date of the hearing.

BY THE COURT:

Date:_____   _____

                                                                    Judge

(d) The form of the Affidavit of Service in a proceeding under the Act shall be substantially in the following form:

(Caption)

AFFIDAVIT OF SERVICE

I,

_____

, the undersigned, hereby state that I served a copy of the Notice of Hearing and Order, Petition and Temporary Order in the above-captioned action upon Defendant by handing the papers to _____

at the following address _____
on the _____ day of _____, 20 ___, at approximately _____ o'clock _.m.

I verify that the statements made in this Affidavit are true and correct. I understand that false statements herein are made subject to the penalties of 18 Pa.C.S. § 4904, relating to unsworn falsification to authorities.

_____
(Signature)

_____
(Title)

_____
(Address)

_____
(Date)

THIS FORM MUST BE COMPLETED AND SIGNED BY THE PERSON WHO SERVES THE DEFENDANT WITH THE NOTICE OF HEARING AND ORDER, PETITION AND TEMPORARY ORDER. IT MUST BE FILED WITH THE PROTHONOTARY OR BROUGHT TO THE COURT ON THE HEARING DATE.

(e) The Final Order of Court, or any amended, modified or extended Final Order of Court, entered pursuant to the Act shall be identical in content to the following form:

(Caption)

FINAL ORDER FOR PROTECTION OF VICTIMS OF

• SEXUAL VIOLENCE

• SEXUAL VIOLENCE AGAINST A MINOR CHILD

• INTIMIDATION

Plaintiff:

_____
First   Middle   Last Name

Plaintiff's Address:

_____

_____

☐   Plaintiff's address is confidential pursuant to 42 Pa.C.S. § 62A11.

Defendant:

DEFENDANT IDENTIFIERS

_____

| First | Middle | Last Name | DOB | HEIGHT |

_____

| SEX | WEIGHT | RACE | EYES | HAIR |

SSN _____

_____

| DRIVERS LICENSE # | EXP DATE | STATE |

The court hereby finds that it has jurisdiction over the parties and the subject matter and that Defendant has been provided with reasonable notice and opportunity to be heard.

Defendant was served in accordance with Pa.R.C.P. No. 1954(a) and provided notice of the time, date and location of the hearing scheduled in this matter.

☐ AND NOW, this _____ day of _____, 20 ___, upon consideration of the attached Petition for Protection of Victims of Sexual Violence or Intimidation, the court hereby enters the following Final Order:

Order Effective Date: _____ Order Expiration Date:_____

It is ORDERED, ADJUDGED AND DECREED as follows:

This order is entered (check one) ☐ by agreement; ☐ by agreement without an admission; ☐ after a hearing and decision by the court; ☐ after a hearing at which Defendant was not present, despite proper service being made; ☐ by default. Without regard as to how the order was entered, this is a final order of court subject to full enforcement pursuant to the Protection of Victims of Sexual Violence or Intimidation Act.

☐ Plaintiff's request for a final protection order is denied.

OR

☐ Plaintiff's request for a final protection order is granted.

1. The following person is protected under this order:

_____

2. Defendant is:

☐ A. Restrained from having any contact with the victim, including, but not limited to, entering the victim's residence, place of employment, business or school.

☐ B. Prohibited from indirect contact with the victim through third parties.

☐ C. Prohibited from direct or indirect contact with the following designated persons:

_____

☐ D. Ordered to pay the fees of this action.

☐ 3. Additional relief, including, but not limited to, issuing an order under 42 Pa.C.S. § 62A11(b) related to the non-disclosure of the victim's address, telephone number, whereabouts or other demographic information:

_____

_____

_____

☐ 4. Because this order followed a contested proceeding, or a hearing at which Defendant was not present, despite being served with a copy of the petition, temporary order and notice of the date, time and place of the hearing, Defendant is ordered to pay an additional $100 surcharge to the court, which shall be distributed in the manner set forth in 42 Pa.C.S. § 62A05(c.1).

☐ **5. THIS ORDER SUPERSEDES ANY PRIOR PROTECTION OF VICTIMS OF SEXUAL VIOLENCE OR INTIMIDATION ORDER OBTAINED BY THE SAME PLAINTIFF AGAINST THE SAME DEFENDANT.**

NOTICE TO THE DEFENDANT

Defendant is hereby notified that violation of this order may result in arrest for indirect criminal contempt. Under 18 U.S.C. § 2265, an order entered by the court may be enforceable in all fifty (50) States, the District of Columbia, Tribal Lands, U.S. Territories and the Commonwealth of Puerto Rico. If you travel outside of the state and intentionally violate this order, you may be subject to federal criminal proceedings under the Violence Against Women Act, 18 U.S.C. § 2262. Consent of Plaintiff shall not invalidate this order, which can only be changed or modified through the filing of appropriate court papers for that purpose. 42 Pa.C.S. § 62A17. Defendant is further notified that violation of this order may subject him/her to prosecution and criminal penalties under the Pennsylvania Crimes Code.

NOTICE TO SHERIFF, POLICE AND LAW ENFORCEMENT OFFICIALS

The police department and sheriff who have jurisdiction over Plaintiff's residence, the location where a violation of this order occurs, or where Defendant may be located, shall enforce this order. The court shall have jurisdiction over any indirect criminal contempt proceeding, either in the county where the violation occurred or where this protective order was entered. An arrest for violation of paragraphs 2 and 3 of this order may be without warrant, based solely on probable cause, whether or not the violation is committed in the presence of the police or any sheriff. 42 Pa.C.S. § 62A12.

When Defendant is placed under arrest for violation of the order, Defendant shall be taken to the appropriate authority or authorities before whom Defendant is to be arraigned. A "Complaint for Indirect Criminal Contempt" shall then be completed and signed by the police officer, sheriff or Plaintiff. Plaintiff's presence and signature are not required to file the complaint.

If sufficient grounds for violation of this order are alleged: (1) Defendant shall be arraigned; (2) bond set, if appropriate; and (3) both parties shall be given notice of the date of the hearing.

BY THE COURT:

Date:_____   _____
                                                    Judge

If a Final Order of Court is entered pursuant to the consent of the plaintiff and the defendant, both shall sign the order along with their counsel, if any:

_____

(Plaintiff's Signature)

_____

(Defendant's Signature)

_____

(Plaintiff's attorney's signature)

_____

(Defendant's attorney's signature)

Note: **Pa.R.C.P. No. 1959(a), (b), (c), and (e) utilize the phrase "shall be identical in content" in reference to the form documents provided under those subparagraphs, which include the Notice of Hearing, the Petition for Protection of Victims of Sexual Violence or Intimidation, the Temporary Order, and the Final Order. In using "shall be identical in content" rather than the more usual phrase "shall be substantially in the following form," the intent of the rule is to ensure only the relevant information and relief authorized under the Act is incorporated into any third-party generated form document while allowing for stylistic differences as to format and layout.**

Adopted June 29, 2015, effective July 1, 2015. Amended Oct. 27, 2016, effective in 60 days (Dec. 27, 2016); Jan. 5, 2018, effective Jan. 6, 2018; June 1, 2018, effective July 1, 2018.

APPENDIX D

CONVENTION ON THE CIVIL ASPECTS OF INTERNATIONAL CHILD ABDUCTION (HAGUE CONVENTION)

The Convention on the Civil Aspects of International Child Abduction, done at The Hague on October 25, 1980, establishes legal rights and procedures for the prompt return of children who have been wrongfully removed or retained, as well as for securing the exercise of visitation rights. Children who are wrongfully removed or retained within the meaning of the Convention are to be promptly returned unless one of the narrow exceptions set forth in the Convention applies. The Convention provides a sound treaty framework to help resolve the problem of international abduction and retention of children and will deter such wrongful removals and retentions.

The States signatory to the present Convention,

Firmly convinced that the interests of children are of paramount importance in matters relating to their custody,

Desiring to protect children internationally from the harmful effects of their wrongful removal or retention and to establish procedures to ensure their prompt return to the State of their habitual residence, as well as to secure protection for rights of access,

Have resolved to conclude a Convention to this effect, and have agreed upon the following provisions—

CHAPTER 1
SCOPE OF THE CONVENTION

Article 1

The objects of the present Convention are—

a. to secure the prompt return of children wrongfully removed to or retained in any contracting State; and

b. to ensure that rights of custody and of access under the law of one Contracting State are effectively respected in the other Contracting States.

Article 2

Contracting States shall take all appropriate measures to secure within their territories the implementation of the objects of the Convention. For this purpose they shall use the most expeditious procedures available.

Article 3

The removal or the retention of a child is to be considered wrongful where—

a. it is in breach of rights of custody attributed to a person, an institution or other body, either jointly or alone, under the law of the State in which the child was habitually resident immediately before the removal or retention; and

b. at the time of removal or retention those rights were actually exercised, either jointly or alone, or would have been so exercised but for the removal or retention.

The rights of custody mentioned in sub-paragraph (a) above, may arise in particular by operation of law or by reason of a judicial or administrative decision, or by reason of an agreement having legal effect under the law of that State.

Article 4

The Convention shall apply to any child who was habitually resident in a Contracting State immediately before any breach of custody or access rights. The Convention shall cease to apply when the child attains the age of 16 years.

Article 5

For the purposes of this Convention—

a. 'rights of custody' shall include rights relating to the care of the person of the child and, in particular, the right to determine the child's place of residence;

b. 'rights of access' shall include the right to take a child for a limited period of time to a place other than the child's habitual residence.

CHAPTER II

CENTRAL AUTHORITIES

Article 6

A Contracting State shall designate a Central Authority to discharge the duties which are imposed by the Convention upon such authorities.

Federal States, States with more than one system of law or States having autonomous territorial organizations shall be free to appoint more than one Central Authority and to specify the territorial extent of their powers. Where a State has appointed more than one Central Authority, it shall designate the Central Authority to which applications may be addressed for transmission to the appropriate Central Authority within that State.

Article 7

Central Authorities shall co-operate with each other and promote co-operation amongst the competent authorities in their respective States to secure the prompt return of children and to achieve the other object's of this Convention.

In particular, either directly or through any intermediary, they shall take all appropriate measures—

a. to discover the whereabouts of a child who has been wrongfully removed or retained;

b. to prevent further harm to the child or prejudice to interested parties by taking or causing to be taken provisional measures;

c. to secure the voluntary return of the child or to bring about an amicable resolution of the issues;

d. to exchange, where desirable, information relating to the social background of the child;

e. to provide information of a general character as to the law of their State in connection with the application of the Convention;

f. to initiate or facilitate the institution of judicial or administrative proceedings with a view to obtaining the return of the child and, in a proper case, to make arrangements for organizing or securing the effective exercise of rights of access;

g. where the circumstances so require, to provide or facilitate the provisions of legal aid and advice, including the participation of legal counsel and advisers;

h. to provide such administrative arrangements as may be necessary and appropriate to secure the safe return of the child;

i. to keep each other informed with respect to the operation of this Convention and, as far as possible, to eliminate any obstacles to its application.

CHAPTER III

RETURN OF CHILDREN

Article 8

Any person, institution or other body claiming that a child has been removed or retained in breach of custody rights may apply either to the Central Authority of the child's habitual residence or to the Central

Authority of any other Contracting State for assistance in securing the return of the child.

The application shall contain—

a. information concerning the identity of the applicant, of the child and of the person alleged to have removed or retained the child;

b. where available, the date of birth of the child;

c. the grounds on which the applicant's claim for return of the child is based;

d. all available information relating to the whereabouts of the child and the identity of the person with whom the child is presumed to be.

The application may be accompanied or supplemented by—

e. an authenticated copy of any relevant decision or agreement;

f. a certificate or an affidavit emanating from a Central Authority, or other competent authority of the State of the child's habitual residence, or from a qualified person, concerning the relevant law of that State;

g. any other relevant document.

Article 9

If the Central Authority which receives an application referred to in Article 8 has reason to believe that the child is in another Contracting State, it shall directly and without delay transmit the application to the Central Authority of that Contracting State and inform the requesting central authority, or the applicant, as the case may be.

Article 10

The Central Authority of the State where the child is shall take or cause to be taken all appropriate measures in order to obtain the voluntary return of the child.

Article 11

The judicial or administrative authorities of Contract States shall act expeditiously in proceedings for the return of children.

If the judicial or administrative authority concerned has not reached a decision within six weeks from the date of commencement of the proceedings, the applicant or the Central Authority of the requested State, on its own initiative or if asked by the Central Authority of the requesting State, shall have the right to request a statement of the reasons for the delay. If a reply is received by the Central Authority of the requested State, that Authority shall transmit the reply to the Central Authority of the requesting State, or to the applicant, as the case may be.

Article 12

Where a child has been wrongfully removed or retained in Terms of Article 3 and, at the date of the commencement of the proceedings before the judicial or administrative authority of the Contracting State where the child is, a period of less than one year has elapsed from the date of the wrongful removal or retention, the authority concerned shall order the return of the child forthwith.

The judicial or administrative authority, even where the proceedings have been commenced after the expiration of the period of one year referred to in the preceding paragraph, shall also order the return of the child, unless it is demonstrated that the child is now settled in its new environment.

Where the judicial or administrative authority in the requested State has reason to believe that the child has been taken to another State, it may stay the proceedings or dismiss the application for the return of the child.

Article 13

Notwithstanding the provisions of the preceding Article, the judicial or administrative authority of the requested State is not bound to order the return of the child if the person, institution or other body which opposes its return establishes that—

a. the person, institution or other body having the care of the person of the child was not actually exercising the custody rights at the time of removal or retention, or had consented to or subsequently acquiesced in the removal or retention; or

b. there is a grave risk that his or her return would expose the child to physical or psychological harm or otherwise place the child in an intolerable situation.

The judicial or administrative authority may also refuse to order the return of the child if it finds that the child objects to being returned and has attained an age and degree of maturity at which it is appropriate to take account of its views.

In considering the circumstances referred to in this Article, the judicial and administrative authorities shall take into account the information relating to the social background of the child provided by the Central Authority or other competent authority of the child's habitual residence.

Article 14

In ascertaining whether there has been a wrongful removal or retention within the meaning of Article 3, the judicial or administrative authorities of the requested State may take notice directly of the law of, and of judicial or administrative decisions, formally recognized or not in the State of the habitual residence of the child, without recourse to the specific procedures for the proof of that law or for the recognition of foreign decisions which would otherwise be applicable.

Article 15

The judicial or administrative authorities of a Contracting State may, prior to the making of an order for the return of the child, request that the applicant obtain from the authorities of the State of the habitual residence of the child a decision or other determination that the removal or retention was wrongful within the meaning of Article 3 of the Convention, where such a decision of determination may be obtained in that State. The Central Authorities of the Contracting States shall so far as practicable assist applicants to obtain such a decision or determination.

Article 16

After receiving notice of a wrongful removal or retention of a child in the sense of Article 3, the judicial or administrative authorities of the Contracting State to which the child has been removed or in which it has been retained shall not decide on the merits of rights of custody until it has been determined that the child is not to be returned under this Convention or unless an application under this Convention is not lodged within a reasonable time following receipt of the notice.

Article 17

The sole fact that a decision relating to custody has been given in or is entitled to recognition in the requested State shall not be a ground for refusing to return a child under this Convention, but the judicial or administrative authorities of the requested State may take account of the reasons for that decision in applying this Convention.

Article 18

The provisions of this Chapter do not limit the power of a judicial or administrative authority to order the return of the child at any time.

Article 19

A decision under this Convention concerning the return of the child shall not be taken to be a determination on the merits of any custody issue.

Article 20

The return of the child under the provisions of Article 12 may be refused if this would be permitted by the fundamental principles of the requested State relating to the protection of human rights and fundamental freedoms.

CHAPTER IV

RIGHTS OF ACCESS

Article 21

An application to make arrangements for organizing or, securing the effective exercise of rights of access may be presented to the Central Authorities of the Contracting States in the same way as an application for the return of a child.

The Central Authorities are bound by the obligations of co-operation which are set forth in Article 7 to promote the peaceful enjoyment of access rights and the fulfillment of any conditions to which the exercise of those rights may be subject. The Central Authorities shall take steps to remove, as far as possible, all obstacles to the exercise of such rights.

The Central Authorities, either directly or through intermediaries, may initiate or assist in the institution of proceedings with a view to organizing or protecting these rights and securing respect for the conditions to which the exercise of these rights may be subject.

CHAPTER V

GENERAL PROVISIONS

Article 22

No security, bond or deposit, however described, shall be required to guarantee the payment of costs and expenses in the judicial or administrative proceedings falling within the scope of this Convention.

Article 23

No legalization or similar formality may be required in the context of this Convention.

Article 24

Any application, communication or other document sent to the Central Authority of the requested State shall be in the original language, and shall be accompanied by a translation into the official language or one of the official languages of the requested State or, where that is not feasible, a translation into French or English.

However, a Contracting State may, by making a reservation in accordance with Article 42, object to the use of either French or English, but not both, in any application, communication or other document sent to its Central Authority.

Article 25

Nationals of the Contracting States and persons who are habitually resident within those States shall be entitled in matters concerned with the application of this Convention to legal aid and advice in any other Contracting State on the same conditions as if they themselves were nationals of and habitually resident in that State.

Article 26

Each Central Authority shall bear its own costs in applying this Convention.

Central Authorities and other public services of Contracting States shall not impose any charges in relation to applications submitted under this Convention. In particular, they may not require any payment from the applicant towards the costs and expenses of the proceedings or, where applicable, those arising from the participation of legal counsel or advisers. However, they may require the payment of the expenses incurred or to be incurred in implementing the return of the child.

However, a Contracting State may, by making a reservation in accordance with Article 42, declare that it shall not be bound to assume any costs referred to in the preceding paragraph resulting from the participation of legal counsel or advisers or from court proceedings, except insofar as those costs may be covered by its system of legal aid and advice.

Upon ordering the return of a child or issuing an order concerning rights of access under this Convention, the judicial or administrative authorities may, where appropriate, direct the person who removed or retained the child, or who prevented the exercise or rights of access, to pay necessary expenses incurred by or on behalf of the applicant, including travel expenses, any costs incurred or payments made for locating the child, the costs of legal representation of the applicant, and those of returning the child.

Article 27

When it is manifest that the requirements of this Convention are not fulfilled or that the application is otherwise not well founded, a Central Authority is not bound to accept the application. In that case, the Central Authority shall forthwith inform the applicant or the Central Authority through which the application was submitted, as the case may be, of its reasons.

Article 28

A Central Authority may require that the application be accompanied by a written authorization empowering it to act on behalf of the applicant, or to designate a representative so to act.

Article 29

This Convention shall not preclude any person, institution or body who claims that there has been a breach of custody or access rights within the meaning of Article 3 or 21 from applying directly to the judicial or administrative authorities of a Contracting State, whether or not under the provisions of this Convention.

Article 30

Any application submitted to the Central Authorities or directly to the judicial or administrative authorities of a Contracting State in accordance with the terms of this Convention, together with documents and any other information appended thereto or provided by a Central Authority, shall be admissible in the courts or administrative authorities of the Contracting States.

Article 31

In relation to a State which in matters of custody of children has two or more systems of law applicable in different territorial units—

a. any reference to habitual residence in that State shall be construed as referring to habitual residence in a territorial unit of that State;

b. any reference to the law of the State of habitual residence shall be construed as referring to the law of the territorial unit in that State where the child habitually resides.

Article 32

In relation to a State which in matters of custody of children has two or more systems of law applicable to different categories of persons, any reference to the law of that State shall be construed as referring to the legal system specified by the law of that State.

Article 33

A State within which different territorial units have their own rules of law in respect of custody of children shall not be bound to apply this Convention where a State with a unified system of law would not be bound to do so.

Article 34

This Convention shall take priority in matters within its scope over the Convention of 5 October 1961 concerning the powers of authorities and the law applicable in respect of the protection of minors, as between Parties to both Conventions. Otherwise the present Convention shall not restrict the application of an international instrument in force between the State of origin and the State addressed or other law of the State addressed for the purposes of obtaining the return of a child who has been wrongfully removed or retained or of organizing access rights.

Article 35

This Convention shall apply as between Contracting States only to wrongful removals or retentions occurring after its entry into force in those States.

Where a declaration has been made under Article 39 or 40, the reference in the preceding paragraph to a Contracting State shall be taken to refer to the territorial unit or units in relation to which this Convention applies.

Article 36

Nothing in this convention shall prevent two or more Contracting States, in order to limit the restrictions to which the return of the child may be subject, from agreeing among themselves to derogate from any provisions of this Convention which may imply such a restriction.

CHAPTER VI

FINAL CLAUSES

Article 37

The Convention shall be open for signature by the States which were Members of the Hague Conference on Private International Law at the time of its Fourteenth Session.

It shall be ratified, accepted or approved and the instruments of ratification, acceptance or approval shall be deposited with the Ministry of Foreign Affairs of the Kingdom of the Netherlands.

Article 38

Any other State may accede to the Convention.

The instrument of accession shall be deposited with the Ministry of Foreign Affairs of the Kingdom of the Netherlands.

The Convention shall enter into force for a State acceding to it on the first day of the third calendar month after the deposit of its instrument of accession.

The accession will have effect only as regards the relations between the acceding State and such Contracting States as will have declared their acceptance of the accession. Such a declaration will also have to be made by any Member State ratifying, accepting or approving the Convention after an accession. Such declaration shall be deposited at the Ministry of

Foreign Affairs of the Kingdom of the Netherlands; this Ministry shall forward through diplomatic channels, a certified copy to each of the Contracting States.

The Convention will enter into force as between the acceding State and the State that has declared its acceptance of the accession on the first day of the third calendar month after the deposit of the declaration of acceptance.

Article 39

Any State may, at the time of signature, ratification, acceptance, approval or accession, declare that the Convention shall extend to all the territories for the international relations of which it is responsible, or to one or more of them. Such a declaration shall take effect at the time the Convention enters into force for that State.

Such declaration, as well as any subsequent extension, shall be notified to the Ministry of Foreign Affairs of the Kingdom of the Netherlands.

Article 40

If a Contracting State has two or more territorial units in which different systems of law are applicable in relation to matters dealt with in this Convention, it may at the time of signature, ratification, acceptance, approval or accession declare that this Convention shall extend to all its territorial units or only to one or more of them and may modify this declaration by submitting another declaration at any time.

Any such declaration shall be notified to the Ministry of Foreign Affairs of the Kingdom of the Netherlands and shall state expressly the territorial units to which the Convention applies.

Article 41

Where a Contracting state has a system of government under which executive, judicial and legislative powers are distributed between central and other authorities within that State, its signature or ratification, acceptance or approval of, or accession to this Convention, or its making of any declaration in terms of Article 40 shall carry no implication as to the internal distribution of powers within that State.

Article 42

Any State may, not later than the time of ratification, acceptance, approval or accession, or at the time of making a declaration in terms of Article 39 or 40, make one or both of the reservations provided for in Article 24 and Article 26, third paragraph. No other reservation shall be permitted.

Any State may at any time withdraw a reservation it has made. The withdrawal shall be notified to the Ministry of Foreign Affairs of the Kingdom of the Netherlands.

The reservation shall cease to have effect on the first day of the third calendar month after the notification referred to in the preceding paragraph.

Article 43

The Convention shall enter into force on the first day of the third calendar month after the deposit of the third instrument of ratification, acceptance, approval or accession referred to in Articles 37 and 38.

Thereafter the Convention shall enter into force—

1. for each State ratifying, accepting, approving or acceding to it subsequently, on the first day of the third calendar month after the deposit of its instrument of ratification, acceptance, approval or accession;

2. for any territory or territorial unit to which the Convention has been extended in conformity with Article 39 or 40, on the first day of the third calendar month after the notification referred to in that Article.

Article 44

The Convention shall remain in force for five years from the date of its entry into force in accordance with the first paragraph of Article 43 even for States which subsequently have ratified, accepted, approved it or acceded to it. If there has been no denunciation, it shall be renewed tacitly every five years.

Any denunciation shall be notified to the Ministry of Foreign Affairs of the Kingdom of the Netherlands at least six months before the expiry of the five year period. It may be limited to certain of the territories or territorial units to which the Convention applies. The denunciation shall have effect only as regards the State which has notified it. The Convention shall remain in force for the other Contracting States.

Article 45

The Ministry of Foreign Affairs of the Kingdom of the Netherlands shall notify the States Members of the Conference, and the States which have acceded in accordance with Article 38, of the following:

1. the signatures and ratifications, acceptances and approvals referred to in Article 37;

2. the accessions referred to in Article 38;

3. the date on which the Convention enters into force in accordance with Article 43;

4. the extensions referred to in Article 39;

5. the declarations referred to in Articles 38 and 40;

6. the reservations referred to in Article 24 and Article 26, third paragraph, and the withdrawals referred to in Article 42;

7. the denunciations referred to in Article 44.

In witness whereof the undersigned, being duly authorized thereto, have signed this Convention.

Done at The Hague, on the 25th day of October 1980 in the English and French languages, both texts being equally authentic, in a single copy which shall be deposited in the archives of the Government of the Kingdom of the Netherlands, and of which a certified copy shall be sent, through diplomatic channels, to each of the States Members of the Hague Conference on Private International Law at the date of its Fourteenth Session.

Other provisions:

Signatories to the Hague Convention on the Civil Aspects of International Child Abduction, done at the Hague October 25, 1980. The following nations are signatories to the Hague convention on the Civil Aspects of International Child Abduction, done at the Hague October 25, 1980 and entered into force for the United States July 1, 1988:

Argentina	Italy
Australia	Luxembourg
Austria	Macedonia, the former Yugoslav
Belgium	Republic of
Bosnia and Herzegovina	Netherlands
Canada	Norway
China	Portugal
Croatia	Serbia and Montenegro
Czech Republic	Slovak Republic
Denmark	Spain
Finland	Sweden
France	Switzerland
Germany	Turkey
Greece	United Kingdom
Ireland	United States
Israel	Venezuela

The convention applies in the following States or territories as a result of accession (the date given is the date of entry into force for the acceding State). Article 38 of the Convention provides in part: "The accession will have effect only as regards the relations between the acceding State and such Contracting States as will have declared their acceptance of the accession. Such a declaration will also have to be made by any Member State ratifying, accepting or approving the Convention after an accession."

Bahamas, Jan. 1, 1994

Belarus, April 1, 1998

Belize, Sept. 1, 1989

Brazil, Jan. 1, 2000

Bulgaria, Aug. 1, 2003

Burkina Faso, Aug. 1, 1992

Chile, May 1, 1994

Colombia, March 1, 1996

Costa Rica, Feb. 1, 1999

Cyprus, Feb. 1, 1995

Dominican Republic, Nov. 1, 2004

Ecuador, April 1, 1992

El Salvador, May 1, 2001

Estonia, July 1, 2001

Fiji, June 1, 1999

Georgia, Oct. 1, 1997

Guatemala, May 1, 2002

Honduras, March 1, 1994

Hungary, July 1, 1986

Iceland, Nov. 1, 1996

Japan, April 1, 2014

Latvia, Feb. 1, 2002

Lithuania, Sept. 1, 2002

Malta, Jan. 1, 2000

Mauritius, June 1, 1993

Mexico, Sept. 1, 1991

Moldova, Republic of, July 1, 1998

Monaco, Feb. 1, 1993

Morocco, Dec. 1, 2012

New Zealand, Aug. 1, 1991

Nicaragua, March 1, 2001

Panama, May 1, 1994

Paraguay, Aug. 1, 1998

Peru, Aug. 1, 2001

Poland, Nov. 1, 1992

Romania, Feb, 1, 1993

Saint Kitts and Nevis, Aug. 1, 1994

Singapore, May 1, 2012

Slovenia, June 1, 1994

South Africa, Oct. 1, 1997

Sri Lanka, Dec. 1, 2001

Thailand, April 1, 2016

Trinidad and Tobago, August 1, 2013

Turkmenistan, March 1, 1998

Uruguay, Feb. 1, 2000

Uzbekistan, Aug. 1, 1999

Zimbabwe, July 1, 1995

For additional information regarding ratifications, dates when the Convention entered into force for the parties, territorial application, etc., see http://www.hcch. net/index_en.php?act=conventions.text&cid=24, and http://travel.state.gov/abduction/resources/congressreport/congress-report_1487.html

APPENDIX E

FORMS

NOTE: PLEASE BE SURE TO CHECK WITH EACH COUNTY TO DETERMINE WHETHER ANY COUNTY-SPECIFIC FORMS SUCH AS COVER SHEETS OR NOTICES TO DEFEND ARE REQUIRED TO BE USED WHEN FILING A PLEADING IN THAT COUNTY

Form 1. Notice to Defend
Form 2. Custody Complaint
Form 3. Petition to Modify Custody
Form 4. Petition for Contempt
Form 5. Petition for Writ *Ne Exeat*
Form 6. Petition for Mental Examination
Form 7. Petition for Home Study
Form 8. Notice of Intent to Relocate
Form 9. Counter-Affidavit Regarding Relocation
Form 10. Statement of Objection to Relocation

FORM 1

NOTICE TO DEFEND

IN THE COURT OF COMMON PLEAS OF _____
CIVIL ACTION - LAW

_____ :

_____ (Plaintiff)   :   NO. _____

                      :

    VS.   :

                      :

_____ (Defendant)   :   IN CUSTODY

_____ :

<u>ORDER OF COURT / NOTICE TO DEFEND</u>

You have been sued in court to obtain/modify custody, partial custody of the child/ren:_____.

You are ordered to appear in person at _____ on _____ at ____, __.M., for :

_____ a conciliation or mediation conference.

_____ a pretrial conference.

_____ a hearing before the court.

If you fail to appear as provided by this order, an order for custody, or partial custody may be entered against you or the court may issue a warrant for your arrest.

YOU SHOULD TAKE THIS PAPER TO YOUR LAWYER AT ONCE. IF YOU DO NOT HAVE A LAWYER, GO TO OR TELEPHONE THE OFFICE SET FORTH BELOW TO FIND OUT WHERE YOU CAN GET LEGAL HELP. THIS OFFICE CAN PROVIDE YOU WITH INFORMATION ABOUT HIRING A LAWYER. IF YOU CANNOT AFFORD TO HIRE A LAWYER, THIS OFFICE

MAY BE ABLE TO PROVIDE YOU WITH INFORMATION ABOUT AGENCIES THAT MAY OFFER LEGAL SERVICES TO ELIGIBLE PERSONS AT A REDUCED FEE OR NO FEE.

(LAWYER REFERENCE SERVICE)

_____

(name)

_____

(address)

_____

(phone number)

AMERICANS WITH DISABILITIES ACT OF 1990

The Court of Common Pleas of _____ County is required by law to comply with the Americans with Disabilities Act of 1990. For information about accessible facilities and reasonable accommodations available to disabled individuals having business with the court, please contact our office. Arrangements must be made at least 72 hours prior to any hearing/business with the court. You must attend the scheduled conference or hearing.

END OF FORM

FORM 2

CUSTODY COMPLAINT

IN THE COURT OF COMMON PLEAS OF _____
CIVIL ACTION - LAW

_____ :

_____ (Plaintiff)   :   NO. _____

                         :

     VS.   :

                         :

_____ (Defendant)   :   IN CUSTODY

_____ :

<u>COMPLAINT FOR CUSTODY</u>

1.   Plaintiff is _____ (hereinafter referred to as "Mother/Father"), an adult individual residing at _____ _____.

2.   Defendant is _____ (hereinafter referred to as "Father/Mother"), an adult individual residing at _____ _____.

3.   Mother/Father seeks (primary physical custody) (partial physical custody) (supervised physical custody) and (sole legal) (shared legal custody) of the following child/ren:

NAME   AGE   SEX   D.O.B. RESIDENCE

The child/ren was / was not born out of wedlock.

The child/ren is presently in the primary custody of _____ who resides at _____.

For the past five years, the child/ren has resided with the following persons and at the following addresses:

Dates   With Whom   Addresses

The Mother of the child/ren is _____, currently residing at _____.

The Father of the child/ren is _____, currently
residing at _____.

4.   The relationship of Plaintiff to the children is that of
_____. The Plaintiff currently resides with the fol-
lowing persons: _____.

5.   The relationship of the Defendant to the children is that of
_____. The Defendant currently resides with the
following persons: _____.

6.   Plaintiff has/has not participated as a party or witness, or in
another capacity, in other litigation concerning the custody of the child
in this or another court. The court, term and number, and its relationship
to this action is: _____.

Plaintiff has/has no information of a custody proceeding concerning the child/ren pending in a court of this Commonwealth or any
other jurisdiction.

Plaintiff does/does not know of a person not a party to the proceedings who has physical custody of the child/ren or claims to have
custody rights with respect to the child/ren. The name and address of
such person is: _____.

7.   The best interest and permanent welfare of the child/ren will be
served by granting the relief requested because _____.

8.   Each parent whose parental rights to the child/ren have not been
terminated and the person who has physical custody of the child/ren have
been named as parties to this action. All other persons, named below,
who are known to have or claim a right to custody of the child/ren will
be given notice of the pendency of this action and the right to intervene:
_____.

9.   (a) [If the plaintiff is seeking physical or legal custody of a child
and is *in loco parentis* to the child, the plaintiff shall plead facts establishing standing under 23 Pa.C.S. § 5324(2)].

(b) [If the plaintiff is a grandparent seeking physical or legal custody of a grandchild and is not *in loco parentis* to the child, the plaintiff shall plead facts establishing standing under 23 Pa.C.S. § 5324(3)].

(c) [If the plaintiff is seeking physical or legal custody of a child and is not *in loco parentis* to the child, the plaintiff shall plead facts establishing standing pursuant to 23 Pa.C.S. § 5324(4) and (5)].

(d) [If the plaintiff is a grandparent or great-grandparent seeking partial physical custody or supervised physical custody of a grandchild or great-grandchild, the plaintiff shall plead facts establishing standing under 23 Pa.C.S. § 5325].

10. I have attached the Criminal Record/Abuse History Verification form required pursuant to Pa.R.C.P. 1915.3-2.

WHEREFORE, Plaintiff respectfully requests that this Honorable Court grant him/her sole/shared legal and primary/partial/supervised physical custody of the child/ren.

Respectfully submitted,

_____ Attorney for Plaintiff

VERIFICATION

I,_____, verify that the statements made in the foregoing pleading are true and correct to the best of my knowledge, information and belief. I understand that false statements herein are made subject to the penalties of 18 Pa. C.S. Section 4904, relating to unsworn falsification to authorities.

_____

Dated: _____

END OF FORM

FORM 3
PETITION TO MODIFY CUSTODY

IN THE COURT OF COMMON PLEAS OF _____
CIVIL ACTION - LAW

_____   :

_____ (Plaintiff)   :   NO. _____

                                     :

VS.   :

                                     :

_____ (Defendant)   :   IN CUSTODY

                                     :

_____   :

PETITION TO MODIFY CUSTODY

1.   Petitioner is _____ (hereinafter referred to as "Mother/Father"), the plaintiff/defendant in the above-captioned custody action, who resides at _____.

2.   Respondent is _____ (hereinafter referred to as "Father/Mother"), the plaintiff/defendant in the above-captioned custody action, who resides at _____.

3.   The parties are the parents of the following minor child/ren: _____.

4.   The child/ren was / was not born out of wedlock.

5.   On _____, this Honorable Court entered an order providing: _____. A true and correct copy of the order is made a part hereof and attached hereto as Exhibit "A."

6.   The order should be modified because: _____.

7.   Petitioner has attached the Criminal Record/Abuse History Verification form required pursuant to Pa.R.C.P. No. 1915.3-2.

WHEREFORE, Petitioner respectfully requests that this Honorable Court modify the existing custody order as follows _____ because it will be in the best interest of the child/ren.

Respectfully submitted,

_____-

Attorney for Plaintiff

VERIFICATION

I,_____, verify that the statements made in the foregoing pleading are true and correct to the best of my knowledge, information and belief. I understand that false statements herein are made subject to the penalties of 18 Pa. C.S. Section 4904, relating to unsworn falsification to authorities.

_____

Dated: _____

END OF FORM

FORM 4

PETITION FOR CONTEMPT

IN THE COURT OF COMMON PLEAS OF _____
CIVIL ACTION - LAW

_____ :		
_____ (Plaintiff) :	NO. _____	
:		
VS. :		
:		
_____ (Defendant) :	IN CUSTODY	
_____ :		

<u>RULE</u>

AND NOW, this _____ day of _____, 20__, upon consideration of Petitioner's Petition for Contempt, a Rule is granted on the Respondent to show cause why such requested relief should not be granted.

Rule returnable the _____ day of _____, 20__ at ____, __.m., Court Room ___, of the _____ County Courthouse, _____, PA.

BY THE COURT:

_____

J.

IN THE COURT OF COMMON PLEAS OF _____
CIVIL ACTION - LAW

_____ :

_____ (Plaintiff)   :   NO. _____

                   :

     VS.   :

                   :

_____ (Defendant)   :   IN CUSTODY

_____ :

<u>ORDER</u>

AND NOW, the _____ day of _____, 20__, upon consideration of Petition for Contempt filed by Petitioner, _____, and after a hearing thereon, it is hereby ORDERED and DECREED that:

1.   Respondent is found in civil contempt of this Honorable Court's Order of _____;

2.   [additional relief sought];

3.   Respondent shall pay Petitioner's attorney's fees, costs and expenses incurred in connection with the filing, preparation and disposition of her/his Petition for Contempt in the amount of $_____ by certified or cashier's/bank check made payable to _____ within _____ days of the date of this Order or suffer sanctions.

BY THE COURT:

_____

                                       J.

IN THE COURT OF COMMON PLEAS OF _____
CIVIL ACTION - LAW

_____ :

_____ (Plaintiff) : NO. _____

  :

VS. :

  :

_____ (Defendant) : IN CUSTODY

_____ :

<u>PETITION FOR CONTEMPT</u>

Petitioner, _____, by and through her/his attorneys, _____ files the instant Petition for Contempt and in support thereof, avers the following:

1.   Petitioner is _____, plaintiff in the above-captioned matter.

2.   Respondent is _____, defendant in the above-captioned matter.

3.   The parties are the parents of _____ minor child/ren: _____.

4.   On _____, this Honorable Court entered a custody order providing, inter alia, _____. A true and correct copy of the order is incorporated herein and attached hereto as Exhibit "A."

5.   [insert facts relating to violations of the order].

6.   _____ has willfully and intentionally disobeyed this Honorable Court's _____ order.

7.   _____ believes that _____ will continue to violate the Court's order, unless this Court enters an order of contempt against him/her.

8. _____ has incurred, and will continue to incur, counsel fees, costs and expenses because of _____'s failure and refusal to abide by the terms of the custody order.

9. _____ has incurred attorney's fees, costs and expenses attendant to the preparation and filing of this Petition for Contempt and will incur additional fees attendant to any hearing thereon.

10. _____ avers that for all of the foregoing reasons, this Court should enter an order finding _____ in contempt of this Honorable Court's order.

WHEREFORE, _____ respectfully requests that this Honorable Court enter an order:

1. Finding _____ in civil contempt of this Honorable Court's order of _____;

2. [additional relief sought];

3. Directing _____ to pay _____'s attorney's fees, costs and expenses incurred in connection with the filing, preparation and disposition of this Petition in the amount of $_____ by certified or cashier's/bank check made payable to _____ within _____ days of the date of the order resulting from this petition or suffer sanctions; and

4. Granting such other relief that the court deems appropriate in child/ren's best interest.

Respectfully submitted,

_____-
Attorney for Petitioner

VERIFICATION

I, _____, verify that the statements made in the attached pleading are true and correct. I understand that false statements herein are made subject to the penalties of 18 Pa. C.S. § 4904 relating to unsworn falsification to authorities.

_____

Dated: _____

END OF FORM

FORM 5

PETITION FOR WRIT *NE EXEAT*

IN THE COURT OF COMMON PLEAS OF _____

CIVIL ACTION - LAW

_____   :

_____ (Plaintiff)   :   NO. _____

       :

     VS.   :

       :

_____ (Defendant)   :   IN CUSTODY

_____   :

RULE

AND NOW, this _____ day of _____, 20__ upon consideration of _____'s Petition for Writ Ne Exeat, Respondent is ordered to show cause why, if any, such requested relief should not be granted.

RULE RETURNABLE on the _____ day of _____, 20___ at _____ __.M. in Court Room _____, _____, PA.

BY THE COURT:

_____

                                      J.

IN THE COURT OF COMMON PLEAS OF _____
CIVIL ACTION - LAW

_____ :

_____ (Plaintiff)   :   NO. _____

                                    :

    VS.   :

                                    :

_____ (Defendant)   :   IN CUSTODY

_____ :

ORDER

AND NOW, this _____ day of _____, 20__, upon consideration of the attached Petition filed on behalf of _____, a Writ *Ne Exeat* is hereby issued against _____.

It is further ORDERED and DECREED that _____ will not remove the parties' child, _____, from the _____County region without either a written agreement between the parties or an order of this court allowing same, after hearing on said issue.

BY THE COURT:

_____
                                              J.

IN THE COURT OF COMMON PLEAS OF _____
CIVIL ACTION - LAW

_____ :

_____ (Plaintiff)   :   NO. _____

                       :

     VS.   :

                       :

_____ (Defendant)   :   IN CUSTODY

_____ :

PETITION FOR WRIT NE EXEAT UNDER Pa.R.C.P. 1915.13

Petitioner, by and through *her/his* attorneys, _____, files this Petition for Writ *Ne Exeat*, and in support thereof, avers the following:

1. Petitioner is _____ ("Father/Mother"), defendant/plaintiff in the above-captioned custody action.

2. Respondent is _____ ("Mother/Father"), plaintiff/defendant in the above captioned custody action.

3. The parties are the parents of their child/ren, _____.

4. On _____, this Honorable Court entered a custody order providing, *inter alia*, _____. A true and correct copy of the order is incorporated herein and attached hereto as Exhibit "A."

5. _____ believes and, therefore, avers that _____ may leave the jurisdiction with the parties' child/ren and may not return.

6. _____ does not consent to _____ removing the parties' child/ren from the jurisdiction.

7. _____ believes and, therefore, avers that without this Honorable Court issuing a Writ *Ne Exeat* against _____ restraining her/him from removing the parties' child/ren from the jurisdiction, _____

will remove the child from the jurisdiction without _____'s consent and may not return with the child/ren.

WHEREFORE, petitioner, _____, respectfully requests this Honorable Court to issue a Writ *Ne Exeat* against respondent.

Respectfully submitted,

By: _____

Attorney for Petitioner

VERIFICATION

I,_____, verify that the statements made in the foregoing pleading are true and correct to the best of my knowledge, information and belief. I understand that false statements herein are made subject to the penalties of 18 Pa. C.S. Section 4904, relating to unsworn falsification to authorities.

_____

Dated: _____

END OF FORM

FORM 6

PETITION FOR MENTAL EXAMINATION

IN THE COURT OF COMMON PLEAS OF _____

CIVIL ACTION - LAW

_____ :

_____ (Plaintiff) : NO. _____

:

VS. :

:

_____ (Defendant) : IN CUSTODY

_____ :

RULE

AND NOW, this _____ day of _____, 20__, upon consideration of Plaintiff's Petition for Mental Examination Pursuant to Rule 1915.8, a Rule is granted on the Respondent to show cause why such requested relief should not be granted.

Rule returnable the _____ day of _____, 20__ at ____, __.m., Court Room ___, of _____ County Courthouse, _____, Pennsylvania.

BY THE COURT:

_____

J.

IN THE COURT OF COMMON PLEAS OF _____
CIVIL ACTION - LAW

_____ :

_____ (Plaintiff)   :   NO. _____

                        :

     VS.   :

                        :

_____ (Defendant)   :   IN CUSTODY

_____ :

ORDER

AND NOW, this _____ day of _____, 20__, it is hereby ORDERED, that:

[Use order provided in Pa.R.C.P. 1915.18]

BY THE COURT:

_____
                                    J.

IN THE COURT OF COMMON PLEAS OF _____
CIVIL ACTION - LAW

_____   :

_____ (Plaintiff)   :   NO. _____

                                   :

      VS.   :

                                   :

_____ (Defendant)   :   IN CUSTODY

_____   :

PETITION FOR MENTAL EXAMINATION PURSUANT TO RULE 1915.8

Defendant/Plaintiff, by and through his/her attorneys, _____, files this Petition for Mental Examination Pursuant to Rule 1915.8 and avers as follows:

1. Petitioner is _____, plaintiff/defendant in the above-captioned custody action.

2. Respondent is _____, plaintiff/defendant in the above-captioned custody action.

3.   Father and Mother are the parents of the following minor child/ren: _____.

4.   This Honorable Court entered a custody order providing, *inter alia,* _____.

5.   _____ has displayed behavior that causes concern. For example:

    a.   _____

    b.   _____

    c.   _____

6.   Based on _____'s statements, behavior and conduct, Mother/Father is greatly concerned about _____'s mental health and well-being, and the effects that this may have on the child/ren.

7.   Mother/Father believes that it is essential that this Honorable Court appoint a psychiatrist/psychologist to perform a mental examination of _____ in accordance with Rule 1915.8 and to issue a written report thereafter. Father/Mother will be fully cooperative in participating with interviews with the expert to provide information and eyewitness observations.

WHEREFORE, Petitioner, _____, respectfully requests that this Honorable Court enter an order:

A.   Directing that a Mental Examination of _____, by a psychiatrist/psychologist, be conducted with the cost being split evenly between the parties.

B.   After conducting the Mental Examination of _____, pursuant to Rule 1915.8, the psychiatrist/psychologist shall issue a written report setting out the findings, results of all tests made, diagnosis and conclusions and deliver it to the parties and the court; and

C.   Such other relief that this Honorable Court deems appropriate in the child's best interest, upon the court's review of the expert's report.

Respectfully submitted,

By: _____

Attorney for Petitioner

VERIFICATION

I,_____, verify that the statements made in the foregoing pleading are true and correct to the best of my knowledge, information and belief. I understand that false statements herein are made subject to the penalties of 18 Pa. C.S. Section 4904, relating to unsworn falsification to authorities.

_____

Dated: _____

END OF FORM

FORM 7
PETITION FOR HOME STUDY

IN THE COURT OF COMMON PLEAS OF _____
CIVIL ACTION - LAW

_____ :

_____ (Plaintiff)   :   NO. _____

                         :

      VS.   :

                         :

_____ (Defendant)   :   IN CUSTODY

_____ :

R U L E

AND NOW, this _____ day of _____, 20__, upon consideration of the foregoing Petition of _____, the Court grants a Rule upon the Respondent in the above-captioned matter to show cause why the Petition for Home Study should not be granted.

RULE RETURNABLE on the ____ day of _____, 20__ at _____.M. in Court Room ____, of the _____ County Courthouse, _____, PA.

BY THE COURT:

_____

                                    J.

IN THE COURT OF COMMON PLEAS OF _____
CIVIL ACTION - LAW

_____ :

_____ (Plaintiff)   :   NO. _____

                                    :

      VS.   :

                                      :

_____ (Defendant)   :   IN CUSTODY

_____ :

ORDER

AND NOW, this _____ day of _____, 20__, upon consideration of Petitioner's Petition for Home Study, it is hereby ORDERED AND DECREED that said Petition is GRANTED and a home study of _____'s home will be conducted, with the costs to be paid by _____.

                                    BY THE COURT:

                                  _____

                                                  J.

IN THE COURT OF COMMON PLEAS OF _____
CIVIL ACTION - LAW

_____ :

_____ (Plaintiff)   :   NO. _____

                           :

   VS.   :

                           :

_____ (Defendant)   :   IN CUSTODY

_____ :

PETITION FOR HOME STUDY

1. Petitioner herein is Defendant, _____ ("Mother").

2. Respondent herein is Plaintiff, _____ ("Father").

3. The parties are the parents of the following minor child/ren: _____.

4. On _____, the parties attended a custody conference.

5. At the _____ custody conference, the parties could not agree to a home study being conducted of _____'s residence.

6. _____ believes and therefore avers that it is in the best interest of the child/ren that a home study be conducted of _____'s residence because of its poor condition and dangerous location.

WHEREFORE, Petitioner respectfully requests this Honorable Court order a home study be conducted of _____'s residence, with the costs to be paid by _____.

Respectfully submitted,

_____
Attorney for Petitioner

<u>VERIFICATION</u>

I, _____, verify that the statements made in the foregoing pleading are true and correct to the best of my knowledge, information and belief. I understand that false statements herein are made subject to the penalties of 18 Pa. C.S. Section 4904, relating to unsworn falsification to authorities.

_____

Dated: _____

END OF FORM

FORM 8
NOTICE OF INTENT TO RELOCATE

IN THE COURT OF COMMON PLEAS OF _____
CIVIL ACTION - LAW

_____ :

_____ (Plaintiff)   :   NO. _____

                            :

     VS.   :

                            :

_____ (Defendant)   :   IN CUSTODY

_____ :

NOTICE OF INTENT TO RELOCATE

You, _____, are hereby notified that _____
(party proposing relocation) _____ proposes to relocate with the
following minor child(ren):

Child's Name   Age   Currently residing at:

Child's Name   Age   Currently residing at:

Child's Name   Age   Currently residing at:

To object to the proposed relocation, you must complete the attached
counter-affidavit and serve it on the other party by certified mail, return
receipt requested, addressee only, or pursuant to Pa.R.C.P. No. 1930.4
within 30 days of receipt of this notice.

If there is an existing child custody case, you also must file the counter-
affidavit with the court. If you do not object to the proposed relocation

within 30 days, the party proposing relocation has the right to relocate and may petition the court to approve the proposed relocation and to modify any effective custody orders or agreements.

FAILURE TO OBJECT WITHIN 30 DAYS WILL PREVENT YOU FROM OBJECTING TO THE RELOCATION ABSENT EXIGENT CIRCUMSTANCES.

1.   Address of intended new residence:

2.   The mailing address, if not the same as the address of the intended new residence:

3.   Names and ages of the individuals in the new residence, including individuals who intend to live in the new residence:

4.   The home telephone number of the intended new residence, if available:

5.   The name of the new school district and school the child(ren) will attend after relocation:

6.   The date of the proposed relocation:

7.   The reasons for the proposed relocation:

8.   Proposed modification of custody schedule following relocation:

9.   Any other information which the party proposing the relocation deems appropriate:

10. A counter-affidavit as provided under 23 Pa.C.S. § 5337(d)(1) which can be used to object to the proposed relocation and the modification of custody is attached hereto.

YOU SHOULD TAKE THIS PAPER TO YOUR LAWYER AT ONCE. IF YOU DO NOT HAVE A LAWYER, GO TO OR TELEPHONE THE OFFICE SET FORTH BELOW. THIS OFFICE CAN PROVIDE YOU WITH INFORMATION ABOUT HIRING A LAWYER.

IF YOU CANNOT AFFORD TO HIRE A LAWYER, THIS OFFICE MAY BE ABLE TO PROVIDE YOU WITH INFORMATION ABOUT AGENCIES THAT MAY OFFICE LEGAL SERVICES TO ELIGIBLE PERSONS AT A REDUCED FEE OR NO FEE.

_____

_____

_____

Date:_____   _____

PARTY

END OF FORM

FORM 9

COUNTER-AFFIDAVIT REGARDING RELOCATION

IN THE COURT OF COMMON PLEAS OF _____
CIVIL ACTION - LAW

_____ :

_____ (Plaintiff) : NO. _____

:

VS. :

:

_____ (Defendant) : IN CUSTODY

_____ :

COUNTER-AFFIDAVIT REGARDING RELOCATION

This proposal of relocation involves the following child/children:

Child's Name   Age   Currently residing at:

Child's Name   Age   Currently residing at:

Child's Name   Age   Currently residing at:

I have received a notice of proposed relocation and

1. _____ I do not object to the relocation.

2. _____ I do not object to the modification of the custody order consistent with the proposed modification set forth in the notice.

3. _____ I do not object to the relocation, but I do object to modification of the custody order.

4. _____ I plan to request that a hearing be scheduled by filing a request for hearing with the court:

    a._____ Prior to allowing (name of child/children) to relocate.

930

b._____ After the child/children relocate.

5. _____ I do object to the relocation.

6. _____ I do object to the modification of the custody order.

I understand that in addition to objecting to the relocation or modification of the custody order above, I must also serve this counter-affidavit on the other party by certified mail, return receipt requested, addressee only, or pursuant to Pa.R.C.P. No. 1930.4, and, if there is an existing custody case, I must file this counter-affidavit with the court. If I fail to do so within 30 days of my receipt of the proposed relocation notice, I understand that I will not be able to object to the relocation at a later time.

I verify that the statements made in this counter-affidavit are true and correct. I understand that false statements herein are made subject to the penalties of 18 Pa.C.S. § 4904 (relating to unsworn falsification to authorities).

Date:_____   _____

PARTY

END OF FORM

FORM 10

STATEMENT OF OBJECTION TO RELOCATION

(Pursuant to Pa.R.C.P. 1915.17(h), this form shall be filed with either a complaint for custody or petition for modification along with a request for hearing when seeking to prevent a relocation where no notice has been served)

IN THE COURT OF COMMON PLEAS OF _____
CIVIL ACTION - LAW

_____ :

_____ (Plaintiff)   :   NO. _____

                                            :

VS.   :

                                            :

_____ (Defendant)   :   IN CUSTODY

_____ :

STATEMENT OF OBJECTION TO RELOCATION

Petitioner, by and through her/his attorneys, _____, files this Statement of Objection to Relocation in accordance with Pa.R.C.P. 1915.17(h), and in support thereof, avers the following:

1.   Petitioner is _____ ("Father/Mother"), defendant/plaintiff in the above-captioned custody action.

2.   Respondent is _____ ("Mother/Father"), plaintiff/defendant in the above captioned custody action.

3.   The parties are the parents of their child/ren, _____.

4.   On _____, this Honorable Court entered a custody order providing, *inter alia*, _____. A true and correct copy of the order is incorporated herein and attached hereto as Exhibit "A."

5. _____ believes and, therefore, avers that _____ may relocate with the parties' child/ren.

6. _____ has not been served with a notice of proposed relocation.

7. _____ does not consent to _____ relocating with the parties' child/ren.

8. _____ objects to _____ relocating with the parties' children for the following reasons:_____.

9. Pursuant to Pa.R.C.P. 1915.17(h), _____ is filing a complaint for custody/petition for modification and a request for a hearing simultaneously with this Statement of Objection to Relocation.

WHEREFORE, petitioner, _____, respectfully requests this Honorable Court to schedule a hearing on petitioner's objection to relocation.

Respectfully submitted,

_____

Attorney for Petitioner

<u>VERIFICATION</u>

I, _____, verify that the statements made in the foregoing pleading are true and correct to the best of my knowledge, information and belief. I understand that false statements herein are made subject to the penalties of 18 Pa. C.S. Section 4904, relating to unsworn falsification to authorities.

_____

Dated: _____

END OF FORM

TABLE OF CASES

A

D

E

F

G

H

I

J

K

L

M

TABLE OF CASES

N

O

P

Q

R

S

T

W

Y

TABLE OF STATUTES

U.S.C.

TABLE OF RULES

INDEX

References are to the Pennsylvania Custody Statutes, Custody Court Rules, Federal Custody Statutes and Text Sections. Where no title to a statutory section is given, assume 23 Pa.C.S.